Criminal Justice in Action 9e

Criminal Justice in Action 9e

Larry K. Gaines

California State University, San Bernardino

Roger LeRoy Miller

Institute for University Studies, Arlington, Texas

CENGAGE
Learning·

Australia • Brazil • Japan • Singapore • United Kingdom • United States

CENGAGE
Learning

Criminal Justice in Action
9th Edition
Larry K. Gaines
Roger LeRoy Miller

VP for Social Science and Qualitative Business: Erin Joyner

Product Director: Marta Lee-Perriard

Sr. Product Manager: Carolyn Henderson Meier

Associate Content Developer: Jessica Alderman

Product Assistant: Valerie Kraus

Marketing Manager: Kara Kindstrom

Marketing Director: Jennifer Levanduski

Marketing Coordinator: Erica Low

Production Director: Brenda Ginty

Sr. Content Project Manager: Ann Borman

Sr. Content Digitization Project Manager: Jackie Hermesmeyer

Manufacturing Planner: Judy Inouye

Sr. Inventory Analyst: Jessica Sayers

Sr. IP Director: Julie Geagan-Chavez

IP Analyst: Jen Nonenmacher

IP Project Manager: Betsy Hathaway

Art Director: Andrei Pasternak

Interior and Cover Designer: Jeanne Calabrese

Cover Image: Jim Richardson/Getty Images

Design Elements: rifle cross-hairs: Brankica /ShutterStock.com; abstract blue and gray background (all features): 13Imagery/ShutterStock .com; A Question of Ethics, goddess of justice statue: Hans-Joerg Nisch/ShutterStock.com; Discretion in Action, barbed wire: somchai rakin/ShutterStock.com; CJ & Technology: ShutterStock.com; Comparative Criminal Justice, Myth vs Reality: saicle/ShutterStock.com; Landmark Cases: kentoh/ShutterStock.com; CJ in Action: iStockPhoto.com/Macie J Noskowski

For product information and technology assistance, contact us at **Cengage Learning Customer & Sales Support, 1-800-354-9706**

For permission to use material from this text or product, submit all requests online at **www.cengage.com/permissions** Further permissions questions can be emailed to **permissionrequest@cengage.com**

Library of Congress Control Number: 2015949177

Student Edition ISBN: 978-1-305-63375-9

Looseleaf Edition ISBN: 978-1-305-66403-6

Cengage Learning
20 Channel Center Street
Boston, MA 02210
USA

Cengage Learning is a leading provider of customized learning solutions with employees residing in nearly 40 different countries and sales in more than 125 countries around the world. Find your local representative at **www.cengage.com**

Cengage Learning products are represented in Canada by Nelson Education, Ltd.

To learn more about Cengage Learning Solutions, visit **www.cengage.com**

Purchase any of our products at your local college store or at our preferred online store **www.cengagebrain.com**

Printed in the United States of America
Print Number: 01   Print Year: 2015

Contents in Brief

Contents

PART TWO : THE POLICE AND LAW ENFORCEMENT

Special Features

Comparative Criminal Justice

Careers in CJ

A Question of Ethics

Landmark Cases

Preface

Continuing a tradition established by its eight predecessors, the Ninth Edition of *Criminal Justice in Action* provides students with all the facts, analyses, and real-life examples they will need to be successful in this course. Relying on the help and advice of the many criminal justice professors who have adopted this best-selling textbook over the years, we are confident that we have established an invaluable introduction to the field.

Pushed by the constantly changing, constantly challenging world of crime and justice, however, we feel that we have upped the ante for ourselves and for those who study and teach this book. In this edition, we offer the criminal justice system not simply as a subject to be learned and taught, but as a crucial American institution to be critiqued and held to the highest moral and ethical standards.

Ethics, Discretion, and Public Policy

Criminal Justice in Action provides students not only with the tools to understand how the criminal justice system *does* work, but also the opportunity to express their opinions on how the criminal justice system *should* work. This opportunity presents itself primarily in three components new to the Ninth Edition:

- **Ethics Challenges.** Each chapter contains three of these short challenges, placed at the end of a section. Besides reinforcing an important concept from that section, the challenges allow students to explore their own values in the context of the criminal justice system. Subjects covered include the use of deception during police interrogations (Chapter 7), for-profit bail (Chapter 9), and the ability of juvenile suspects to understand their *Miranda* rights (Chapter 15).

- **CJ Policy—Your Take.** This chapter-specific margin feature engages students by asking them to critique a hot-button criminal justice policy issue. Examples include Oregon's Death with Dignity Act (Chapter 1), state "stand-your-ground" self-defense laws (Chapter 4), and the disenfranchisement of ex-convicts (Chapter 13).

- **Discretion in Action.** A remodeled version of the popular You Be the _____, this feature asks students to step into the shoes of a criminal justice professional

or other CJ participant and make a difficult decision. As revised, the feature emphasizes the pivotal role that discretion plays in the criminal justice system, a subject that we have expanded upon over the past several editions of *Criminal Justice in Action*.

This expanded coverage of ethics, policy, and discretion allows us to present a *panoramic* view of important criminal justice issues. Chapter 6, for example, opens with a description of the extent to which the nation's local law enforcement agencies are using body-worn cameras to record the actions of police officers. Throughout the chapter, the issue is revisited as we discuss policies that limit a police officer's discretion regarding the operation of body-worn cameras, how such cameras may influence a police officer's ethical decision making, the role of the cameras in ensuring police accountability, and the legal ramifications of use-of-force evidence gathered by this new technology.

Careers in Criminal Justice

We are well aware that many students using this text are interested in a criminal justice career. Consequently, as in previous editions, each chapter of *Criminal Justice in Action, Ninth Edition,* includes a Careers in CJ feature in which a criminal justice practitioner presents a personal account of his or her profession.

Furthermore, it is evident that social media are crucial to the twenty-first-century job search. Accordingly, each Career in CJ feature includes a **Social Media Career Tip** to help students succeed in today's difficult labor market. These tips will help students use Web sites such as Facebook and LinkedIn to find potential employers, network, and present themselves as viable candidates for employment.

Further Changes to the Ninth Edition

Each chapter in the Ninth Edition begins with a new "ripped from the headlines" vignette that introduces the themes to be covered in the pages that follow. Furthermore, the text continues to reflect the ever-changing nature of our topic, with with hundreds of new references to **research involving crime and criminal behavior** and **real-life examples describing actual crimes.** The Ninth Edition also includes dozens of **new features and figures,** as well as **discussions of every relevant United States Supreme Court decision** that has been handed down since the previous edition.

Three other extensive changes to the Ninth Edition involve topics crucial to the American criminal justice system:

- **Mental Illness.** Starting with an overview of the subject in Chapter 1, we have significantly increased our coverage of the **challenges facing the criminal justice systems involving the mentally ill.** Seven chapters of *Criminal Justice in Action* now include in-depth discussions of this subject, covering a variety of issues such as the link between mental illness and offending and victimization, and the impact of mentally ill inmates on American prisons and jails.

- **Public Trust in Law Enforcement.** A series of high-profile incidents in which law enforcement agents have either injured or killed unarmed civilians has led to **increased public scrutiny of police use of force.** We examine this controversial topic from the point of view of community members who feel they are unfairly targeted by police violence, and from the point of view of police officers who feel they are placed in a "no win" situation when it comes to use-of-force law and practice.

- **Privacy versus Security.** Chapter 16 of the Ninth Edition includes a new section that covers the **controversies surrounding the federal government's efforts to balance civil liberties and homeland security.** The section focuses on **complex issues of mass surveillance and privacy in the age of terrorism,** and discusses how far we, the people, should allow the government to stretch the Fourth Amendment when it comes to collecting our personal data.

Concentrated Critical Thinking

As with previous editions, the Ninth Edition of *Criminal Justice in Action* focuses on developing critical thinking. Almost every feature and photo caption in the textbook includes a critical thinking question, and students are provided with five additional such questions at the end of each chapter. Chapter-opening vignettes are followed by three critical analysis questions, which relate back to the

vignette and introduce themes important to the upcoming chapter. Other critical-thinking tools in *Criminal Justice in Action, Ninth Edition,* include:

- **Learning Objectives.** At the beginning of each chapter, students are introduced to up to ten learning objectives (LOs) for that chapter. For example, in Chapter 10, "The Criminal Trial," Learning Objective 2 (LO2) asks students to "Explain what 'taking the Fifth' really means." The area of text that furnishes the information is marked with a square LO2 graphic, and, finally, the correct answer is found in the chapter-ending materials. This continuous active learning will greatly expand students' understanding of dozens of crucial criminal justice topics.

- **CJ in Action Features.** Each of the chapter-ending CJ in Action features introduces students to a controversial topic from the chapter and provides them with "for" and "against" arguments related to that topic. Then, using information and knowledge gained from the chapter, the student is asked to write a short essay giving her or his opinion on the controversy. These features not only help students improve their writing and critical-thinking skills, but they also act as a review for the material in the chapter. Topics covered in these chapter-ending features include gun control, racial profiling, and police officers in schools.

Chapter-by-Chapter Organization of the Text

This edition's sixteen chapters blend the principles of criminal justice with current research and high-interest examples of what is happening in the world of crime and crime prevention right now. What follows is a summary of each chapter, along with a description of some of the revisions to the Ninth Edition.

Part 1: The Criminal Justice System

Chapter 1 provides an introduction to the criminal justice system's three major institutions: law enforcement, the courts, and corrections. The chapter also answers conceptual questions such as "what is crime?" and "what are the values of the American criminal justice system?"

- Students are introduced to an "un-American" set of criminal justice values in a **new** Comparative Criminal Justice feature ("No Hate Allowed") describing a Swedish law that criminalizes hate speech.

- The chapter closes with a **new discussion of the disproportionate number of inmates suffering from mental illness** in our prisons and jails. This discussion serves as an introduction to the topic of criminal justice and the mentally ill, which will be revisited throughout the textbook.

Chapter 2 focuses on criminology, giving students insight into why crime occurs before shifting their attention toward how society goes about fighting it. The chapter addresses the most widely accepted and influential criminological hypotheses, including choice theories, trait theories, sociological theories, social process theories, and social conflict theories.

- The three **new** Ethics Challenges in this chapter ask students to give their views on the punishment of women suffering from postpartum depression who harm their children, the sale of violent video games to minors, and the treatment of drug addicts by providing them with free heroin.

- A **new discussion on the nation's changing legal and moral treatment of marijuana** includes a comparison of legalization and decriminalization laws in various states and an explanation of how the federal government has reacted to these trends.

Chapter 3 furnishes students with an understanding of two areas fundamental to criminal justice: (1) the practical definitions of crime, such as the difference between felonies and misdemeanors and different degrees of criminal conduct, and (2) the various modes of measuring crime, including the FBI's Uniform Crime Reports and the U.S. Department of Justice's National Crime Victimization Survey.

- A **new** chapter-opening vignette ("Video Evidence") utilizes the controversial case of former professional football player Ray Rice to explore the often fraught relationship between victims of domestic violence and the criminal justice system.

- An **expanded** focus on the crime of sexual assault and its victims includes a **new** discussion of the ramifications of the federal government's decision to change the official definition of rape and a **new** Discretion in Action feature ("'Yes' Means 'Yes'") explores legislative efforts to reduce sexual assault on college campuses.

Chapter 4 lays the foundation of criminal law. It addresses constitutional law, statutory law, and other sources of American criminal law before shifting its focus to the legal framework that allows the criminal justice system to determine and punish criminal guilt.

- What happens when technology moves faster than criminal law? A **new** CJ & Technology feature ("Revenge Porn") addresses this issue in the context of a particularly unpleasant form of online misbehavior.

- A **new** Question of Ethics feature ("Due Justice?") explains the debate surrounding the federal government's decision to kill a U.S. citizen in Yemen without following the procedure of criminal law.

Part 2: The Police and Law Enforcement

Chapter 5 acts as an introduction to law enforcement in the United States today. This chapter offers a detailed description of the country's numerous local, state, and federal law enforcement agencies and examines the responsibilities and duties that come with a career in law enforcement.

- An **updated** section on diversity in law enforcement includes a **new** discussion of **recruiting efforts to increase the number of women and members of minority groups** in American police forces.

- A **new** CJ Policy—Your Take margin feature asks students to consider the interaction between criminal law and immigration law: should the federal government focus its energies on removing *all* undocumented immigrants from this country, or only those who have committed serious crimes?

Chapter 6 puts students on the streets and gives them a gritty look at the many challenges of being a law enforcement officer. It starts with a discussion of the importance of discretion in law enforcement and then moves on to policing strategies and issues in modern policing, such as use of force, corruption, and the "thin blue line."

- Throughout the chapter, the emergent issue of **police accountability** is given panoramic coverage, including a **new** chapter-opening vignette ("The Camera's Eye") on body-worn cameras for law enforcement officers, an **updated** discussion on how police use of force has impacted relations with minority communities across the country, and a **new** chapter-ending CJ in Action feature ("Militarizing Local Police") that focuses on the public outcry over aggressive policing tactics.

- A **new** Landmark Cases feature ("*Maryland v. King*") summarizes the United States Supreme Court's recent ruling regarding state laws that allow the collection of DNA samples from those who have been arrested for, but not convicted of, committing a crime.

Chapter 7 examines the sometimes uneasy relationship between law enforcement and the U.S. Constitution by explaining the rules of being a police officer. Particular emphasis is placed on the Fourth, Fifth, and Sixth Amendments, giving students an understanding of crucial concepts such as probable cause, reasonableness, and custodial interrogation.

- A **new** section on **cell phones and the Fourth Amendment** features discussions of the legality of law enforcement efforts to track these devices and the Supreme Court's recent decision that police officers need a warrant to search the content of a suspect's cell phone.

- A **new** section discusses the role that police interrogation tactics may play in the **troubling phenomenon of false confessions.**

Part 3: Criminal Courts

Chapter 8 takes a big-picture approach in describing the American court system, giving students an overview of the basic principles of our judicial system, the state and federal court systems, and the role of judges in the criminal justice system.

- The court system's ability to live up to societal expectations of truth and justice, a running theme of the third part of this textbook, is explored in the chapter's **new** Discretion in Action feature ("Eyewitness Identification"), which places students in the shoes of a judge who must decide whether it is fair to uphold a conviction based entirely on a single eyewitness identification. In making her or his decision, the student must consider the **extent to which this practice has led to wrongful convictions** in the United States.

- A **new** CJ Policy—Your Take margin feature explores the question of whether politicians should make a concerted effort to appoint more women and members of minority groups as judges.

Chapter 9 provides students with a rundown of pretrial procedures and highlights the role that these procedures play in America's adversary system. Thus, pretrial procedures such as establishing bail and plea bargaining are presented as part of the larger "battle" between the prosecution and the defense.

- To help students understand how a suspect is formally accused of committing a crime, a **new** chapter-opening vignette ("Trading Paint") explains why NASCAR driver Tony Stewart avoided manslaughter charges despite causing the death of fellow racer Kevin Ward, Jr.

- An **updated** discussion on the operation of grand juries uses the example of the St. Louis County (Missouri) grand jury that failed to indict police officer Darren Wilson for the shooting death of unarmed suspect Michael Brown. The discussion also includes a **new** CJ Policy—Your Take margin feature on the topic of grand jury secrecy.

Chapter 10 puts the student in the courtroom and gives her or him a strong understanding of the steps of the criminal trial. The chapter also attempts to answer the fascinating but ultimately frustrating question, "Are criminal trials in this country fair?"

- Three **new** figures use excerpts from actual court records to give students a first-hand understanding of three crucial aspects of the criminal trial: jury selection, the opening statement, and the art of the cross-examination.

- An **updated** discussion of the most common causes of wrongful convictions emphasizes on steps taken by prosecutors and judges to reverse this troubling trend.

Chapter 11 links the many different punishment options for those who have been convicted of a crime with the theoretical justifications for those punishments. The chapter also examines punishment in the policy context, weighing the public's desire for ever-harsher criminal sanctions against the consequences of such governmental strategies.

- The subject of mandatory minimum sentencing arises several times in this chapter. First, a **new** chapter-opening vignette ("A Long Time Gone") introduces the growing national concern caused by such sentences for nonviolent offenders. Then, a **new** discussion of efforts to **repeal state mandatory minimum sentencing laws** shows how these laws have fallen into some disrepute.

- An **updated** overview of the declining use of the death penalty in the United States includes **new** discussions of problems surrounding lethal injection drugs and the Supreme Court's recent decision concerning capital punishment of the mentally ill.

Part 4: Corrections

Chapter 12 makes an important point, and one that is often overlooked in the larger discussion of the American corrections system: not all of those who are punished need to be placed behind bars. This chapter explores the community corrections options, from probation to parole to intermediate sanctions such as intensive supervision and home confinement.

- A **new** chapter-opening vignette ("Family Ties") compares two possible sentencing options—prison or probation—for a young women who killed her cousin while driving drunk.

- Recognizing trends of innovative thinking among corrections officials, we include an **updated** discussion of **risk assessment tools** and **"swift and certain" punishments** designed to keep probationers from recidivating.

Chapter 13 focuses on prisons and jails. Record-high rates of incarceration have pushed these institutions to the forefront of the criminal justice system, and this chapter explores the various issues—such as overcrowding and the emergence of private prisons—that have resulted from the prison population boom.

- Continuing our focus on mentally ill offenders and the criminal justice system, we include an **updated** discussion on the **challenges facing jail administrators** because of **high rates of mental illness among inmates.**

- Three **new** Ethics Challenges ask students to comment on ethical issues surrounding low wages for inmate employment, health care in private prisons, and the practice of charging pretrial detainees for their meals behind bars.

Chapter 14 is another example of our efforts to get students "into the action" of the criminal justice system, this time putting them in the uncomfortable position of being behind bars. It also answers the question, "What happens when the inmate is released back into society?"

- A **new** CJ & Technology feature ("Contraband Cell Phones") focuses on the difficulties facing prison administrators when it comes to keeping cell phones out of the hands of inmates and the consequences of cell phone use behind bars.

- A **new** section entitled **"What Works in Reentry"** describes strategies developed by corrections officials to **help ex-convicts succeed following release from prison,** including reentry courts and various laws designed to aid offenders in the difficult task of finding post-incarceration employment.

Part 5: Special Issues

Chapter 15 examines the juvenile justice system, giving students a comprehensive description of the path taken by delinquents from first contact with police to trial and punishment. The chapter contains a strong criminological component as well, scrutinizing the various theories of why certain juveniles turn to delinquency and what steps society can take to stop them from doing so before it is "too late."

- Tracking the consequences of two recent Supreme Court decisions restricting life-without-parole sentences for juvenile offenders, a **new** chapter-opening vignette ("Life Lessened") features the first Florida inmate to have his sentence reduced because of the Court's rulings and a **new** CJ Policy—Your Take margin feature asks students their opinions on the continuing use of lengthy sentences for young, violent offenders.

- A **new** Discretion in Action feature ("Juvenile Drunk Driving") asks students to decide whether a seventeen-year-old who commits vehicular homicide should be charged as a juvenile or as an adult.

Chapter 16 concludes the text by taking an expanded look at three crucial criminal justice topics: (1) privacy in the age of terrorism, (2) cyber crime, and (3) white-collar crime.

- Starting with a discussion of four decades worth of crucial antiterrorism legislation, a **new** section entitled **"Security vs. Liberty"** gives students a comprehensive look at the current state of civil liberties in the context of homeland security. The section includes discussions of the constitutionality of governmental mass surveillance techniques and the use of Internet speech to ensnare potential "known wolf" domestic terrorists.

- A **new** Question of Ethics feature ("Buyer Beware") examines whether practices by employees at auto companies such as General Motors and Toyota that lead to the deaths of drivers should be considered white-collar crimes and punished accordingly.

Special Features

Supplementing the main text of *Criminal Justice in Action, Ninth Edition,* are more than one hundred eye-catching, instructive, and penetrating special features. These features, described below with examples, have been designed to enhance the student's understanding of a particular criminal justice issue.

Careers in CJ: As stated before, many students reading this book are planning a career in criminal justice. We have provided them with an insight into some of these careers by offering first-person accounts of what it is like to work as a criminal justice professional. Each Career in CJ feature also includes a **Social Media Career Tip** to help students succeed in today's competitive labor market for criminal justice professionals.

- In Chapter 15, Carl McCullough, a former professional football player, provides an inside look at his duties as a resident youth worker at a juvenile detention center in Hennepin County, Minnesota.

Mastering Concepts: Some criminal justice topics require additional explanation before they become crystal clear in the minds of students. This feature helps students to master many of the essential concepts in the textbook.

- In Chapter 7, this feature helps students understand the legal differences between a police stop and a police arrest.

Discretion in Action: This **revised** feature puts students in the position of a criminal justice actor in a hypothetical case or situation that is based on a real-life event. The facts of the case or situation are presented with alternative possible outcomes, and the student is asked to take the part of the criminal justice professional or lay participant and make a decision. Students can then consult Appendix B at the end of the text to learn what actually happened in the offered scenario.

- "Murder or Manslaughter?" (Chapter 4), a **new** feature, requires students to play the role of prosecutor and charge a defendant who killed his girlfriend under murky circumstances with first degree murder, second degree murder, or involuntary manslaughter.

CJ & Technology: Advances in technology are constantly transforming the face of criminal justice. In these features, which appear in nearly every chapter, students learn of one such emergent technology and are asked to critically evaluate its effects.

- This **new** feature in Chapter 7 describes how law enforcement officers are using through-the-wall sensors to determine the movements of suspects, and the constitutional ramifications of their ability to do so.

Comparative Criminal Justice: The world offers a dizzying array of different criminal customs and codes, many of which are in stark contrast to those accepted in the United States. This feature provides dramatic and sometimes perplexing examples of foreign criminal justice practices in order to give students a better understanding of our domestic ways.

- "The Great Firewall of China" (Chapter 16), an **updated** feature, describes China's recent efforts to limit and control the use of the Internet through criminal laws to an extent that is unimaginable to most Americans.

A Question of Ethics: Ethical dilemmas occur in every profession, but the challenges facing criminal justice professionals often have repercussions beyond their own lives and careers. In this feature, students are asked to place themselves in the shoes of police officers, prosecutors, defense attorneys, and other criminal justice actors facing ethical dilemmas: Will they do the right thing?

- In "The 'Dirty Harry' Problem" (Chapter 6), a police detective is trying to save the life of a young girl who has been buried alive with only enough oxygen to survive for a few hours. Is he justified in torturing the one person—the kidnapper—who knows where the girl is buried?

Landmark Cases: Rulings by the United States Supreme Court have shaped every area of the criminal justice system. In this feature, students learn about and analyze the most influential of these cases.

- In Chapter 14's "*Brown v. Plata*" (2011), the Supreme Court ordered California corrections officials to reduce the state's prison population after deciding that overcrowding was denying inmates satisfactory levels of health care.

Myth vs Reality: Nothing endures like a good myth. In this feature, we try to dispel some of the more enduring myths in the criminal justice system while at the same time asking students to think critically about their consequences.

- "Are Too Many Criminals Found Not Guilty by Reason of Insanity?" (Chapter 4) dispels the notion that criminal justice is "soft" because it lets scores of "crazy" defendants go free due to insanity.

Extensive Study Aids

Criminal Justice in Action, Ninth Edition, includes a number of pedagogical devices designed to complete the student's active learning experience. These devices include the following:

- Concise **chapter outlines** appear at the beginning of each chapter. The outlines give students an idea of what

to expect in the pages ahead, as well as a quick source of review when needed.

- Dozens of **key terms** and a **running glossary** focus students' attention on major concepts and help them master the vocabulary of criminal justice. The chosen terms are boldfaced in the text, allowing students to notice their importance without breaking the flow of reading. On the same page that a key term is highlighted, a margin note provides a succinct definition of the term. For further reference, a glossary at the end of the text provides a full list of all the key terms and their definitions. This edition includes **nearly twenty** new key terms.

- Each chapter has at least six **figures,** which include graphs, charts, and other forms of colorful art that reinforce a point made in the text. This edition includes twenty new figures.

- Hundreds of **photographs** add to the overall readability and design of the text. Each photo has a caption, and most of these captions include a critical-thinking question dealing with the topic at hand. This edition includes nearly one hundred new photos.

- At the end of each chapter, students will find five **Questions for Critical Analysis.** These questions will help the student assess his or her understanding of the just-completed chapter, as well as develop critical-thinking skills.

Acknowledgments

Throughout the creation of the nine editions of this text, we have been aided by hundreds of experts in various criminal justice fields and by professors throughout the country, as well as by numerous students who have used the text. We sincerely thank all who participated on the revision of *Criminal Justice in Action.* We believe that the Ninth Edition is even more responsive to the needs of today's criminal justice instructors and students alike because we have taken into account the constructive comments and criticisms of our reviewers and the helpful suggestions of our survey respondents.

We continue to appreciate the extensive research efforts of Shawn G. Miller and the additional legal assistance of William Eric Hollowell. Product Manager Carolyn Henderson-Meier supplied crucial guidance to the project through her suggestions and recommendations. At the production end, we once again feel fortunate to have enjoyed the services of our content project manager, Ann Borman, who oversaw virtually all aspects of this book. Additionally, we wish to thank the designer of this new edition, Jeanne Calabrese, who has created what we believe to be the most dazzling and student-friendly design of any text in the field. We are also thankful for the services of all those at Lachina who worked on the Ninth Edition, particularly Molly Montanaro. The eagle eyes of Sue Bradley and Beverly Peavler, who shared the duties of copyediting and proofreading, were invaluable.

A special word of thanks must also go to those responsible for creating the MindTap that accompanies *Criminal Justice in Action,* including content developer Jessica Alderman. We are also grateful to Jessica for ensuring the timely publication of supplements, along with content development services manager Joshua Taylor. A final thanks to all of the great people in marketing who helped to get the word out about the book, including marketing manager Kara Kindstrom, who has been tireless in her attention to this project.

Any criminal justice text has to be considered a work in progress. We know that there are improvements that we can make. Therefore, write us with any suggestions that you may have.

L. K. G.

R. L. M.

Dedication

This book is dedicated to my good friend and colleague, Lawrence Walsh, of the Lexington, Kentucky, Police Department. When I was a rookie, he taught me about policing. When I became a researcher, he taught me about the practical applications of knowledge. He is truly an inspiring professional in our field.

L.K.G.

To Bill Hayes,

Thanks for your lasting friendship.

R.L.M.

Criminal Justice Today

Chapter Outline		Corresponding Learning Objectives
What Is Crime?	**1**	Describe the two most common models of how society determines which acts are criminal.
	2	Define *crime*.
The Purpose of the Criminal Justice System	**3**	Explain two main purposes of the criminal justice system.
The Structure of the Criminal Justice System	**4**	Outline the three levels of law enforcement.
	5	List the essential elements of the corrections system.
Discretion and Ethics	**6**	Explain the difference between the formal and informal criminal justice processes.
	7	Define ethics, and describe the role that it plays in discretionary decision making.
Criminal Justice Today	**8**	Contrast the crime control and due process models.
	9	Explain the defining aspects of a terrorist act, and identify one common misperception concerning domestic terrorism.
	10	List the major issues in criminal justice today.

To target your study and review, look for these numbered Learning Objective icons throughout the chapter.

deadly force in Ferguson

the way Dorian Johnson tells it, he and his friend Michael Brown were walking down the middle of a street in Ferguson, Missouri, on the afternoon of August 14, 2014, when white police officer Darren Wilson pulled up beside them. From inside his police vehicle, according to Johnson, Wilson ordered the pair to "get the 'F' on the sidewalk" and then, unprovoked, grabbed Brown around the neck and shot the eighteen-year-old African American. After a brief attempt to escape, Brown stopped, raised his hands, and faced the police officer, who by now was also on foot. Wilson proceeded to shoot Brown several times in the chest, killing him, in Johnson's words, "like an animal."

Appearing before a grand jury, Wilson gave a markedly different version of the events that led to Brown's death. The police officer testified that he stopped Brown and Johnson because they fit the description of two suspects who had just stolen cigarillos from a nearby convenience store. In Wilson's telling, an altercation followed during which Brown punched him numerous times in the face and tried to grab his service weapon. Brown then fled the scene, with Wilson in pursuit on foot. After a short chase, Brown turned and charged Wilson, who felt he had no choice but to shoot the other man in self-defense.

On November 24, 2014, a grand jury determined that Wilson would not face criminal charges for killing Brown. Although the jurors heard testimony from dozens of eyewitnesses and had access to physical evidence supporting Wilson's account of the incident, the decision sparked demonstrations—some violent—nationwide. "The system failed us again," said one protester, expressing the outrage felt by many African Americans over what they perceive as a pattern of unchecked police brutality against young black men. Countering allegations of racial bias in the Wilson case, one criminal justice expert said, "It's really pretty straightforward—a police officer can use deadly force when it's necessary to prevent bodily injury or death."

▲ On November 26, 2014, Los Angeles police officers cordon off protesters following a Missouri grand jury's decision not to charge Ferguson police officer Darren Wilson in the shooting death of Michael Brown.

Photo by Mintaha Neslihan Eroglu/Anadolu Agency/Getty Images

1. What might be some of the reasons that law enforcement officers have the authority to use deadly force to protect themselves or others from injury or death?

2. If one accepts Officer Darren Wilson's version of the incident, do you feel that he was justified in shooting Michael Brown? Why or why not? What additional information might you need to make your decision?

3. In Wilson's account of the confrontation, what steps could he have taken to avoid killing Brown? Should he have taken those steps? Explain your answer.

What Is Crime?

Many observers—and not just those who took to the streets—were shocked that Darren Wilson was able to escape *any* criminal punishment for his role in the death of Michael Brown. In fact, American law enforcement agents commit about four hundred "justifiable homicides" each year.[1] To determine whether Wilson's killing of Brown was justified, and therefore not a potential crime, the grand jury relied on Missouri's "use of force" law. This law states that a law enforcement agent may use "deadly force" against a suspect if the suspect is resisting a lawful arrest or "may otherwise endanger life or inflict serious physical injury unless arrested without delay."[2]

Because Brown's actions could reasonably be seen as posing a threat of injury to Wilson, the police officer's response was, according to Professor David Klinger of the University of Missouri at St. Louis, "awful but lawful."[3] As this dramatic example shows, a *crime* is not simply an act that seems dishonest or dangerous or taboo, even if that act involves the death of a human being. A **crime** is a wrong against society that is *proclaimed by law* and that, if committed under specific circumstances, is punishable by the criminal justice system.

Determining Criminal Behavior

One problem with the definition of crime just provided is that it obscures the complex nature of societies. A society is not static—it evolves and changes, and its concept of criminality evolves and changes as well. Furthermore, different communities can have different ideas of what constitutes a crime. Missouri's "use of force" statute is particularly favorable for law enforcement agents. If the scenario described in the opening of this chapter had taken place in a different state, Darren Wilson might have been charged with criminal wrongdoing.

International examples can be even more striking. In 2014, six Iranians (three men and three women) were arrested for posting a YouTube video of themselves dancing to Pharrell Williams's hit song "Happy" on a Tehran rooftop. It is highly unlikely that American courts, bound by American traditions of freedom of speech and expression, would allow any police action against an individual for making a "vulgar" video that "hurt public chastity." (See the feature *Comparative Criminal Justice—No Hate Allowed* to learn about another foreign custom that runs counter to our legal traditions.)

To more fully understand the concept of crime, it will help to examine the two most common models of how society "decides" which acts are criminal: the consensus model and the conflict model.

LEARNING OBJECTIVE **1** Describe the two most common models of how society determines which acts are criminal.

The Consensus Model The term *consensus* refers to general agreement among the majority of any particular group. Thus, the **consensus model** rests on the assumption that as people gather together to form a society, its members will naturally come to a basic agreement with regard to shared norms and values. Those individuals whose actions deviate from the established norms and values are considered to pose a threat to the well-being of society as a whole and must be sanctioned (punished). The society passes laws to control and prevent unacceptable behavior, thereby setting the boundaries for acceptable behavior within the group.[4]

The consensus model, to a certain extent, assumes that a diverse group of people can have similar **morals.** In other words, they share an ideal of what is "right" and "wrong." Consequently, as public attitudes toward morality change, so do laws. In seventeenth-century America, a person found guilty of *adultery* (having sexual relations with

Crime An act that violates criminal law and is punishable by criminal sanctions.

Consensus Model A criminal justice model in which the majority of citizens in a society share the same values and beliefs. Criminal acts are acts that conflict with these values and beliefs and that are deemed harmful to society.

Morals Principles of right and wrong behavior, as practiced by individuals or by society.

Comparative Criminal Justice

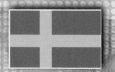

No Hate Allowed

After reading an online article about sexual violence against women in Egypt, Swedish politician Michael Hess felt compelled to offer his opinion on the subject. "When are you journalists going to realize that it is deeply ingrained in Islamic culture to rape and mistreat those women who do not abide by the teachings of Islam?" Hess wrote. He then claimed that higher-than-normal rates of sexual assault in certain areas of Sweden were caused by the presence of Islamic immigrants.

In the United States, with its long tradition of freedom of expression, such comments would not be subject to punishment. In Sweden, however, criminal law prohibits any speech that threatens or expresses disrespect for groups or individuals based on ethnicity, race, nationality, creed, or sexual orientation. Consequently, Hess was convicted of "hate speech" and fined about $5,000.

Swedish law protects a citizen's right to make "hateful" statements in private. Such speech only becomes a crime when it is expressed publicly or, as in Hess's case, on the Internet. In recent years, Swedish courts have fined a woman $560 for yelling "Death to Jews" in a crowd and sentenced an artist to six months behind bars for exhibiting a poster that showed three African men with nooses around their necks.

For Critical Analysis

Besides Sweden, Western democracies such as Canada, Britain, Denmark, and Germany have criminal laws that punish hate speech. Do you think that the United States should criminalize public speech that "threatens" or "disrespects" members of minority groups? What would be some of the consequences—both intended and unintended—of such a law?

Conflict Model A criminal justice model in which the content of criminal law is determined by the groups that hold economic, political, and social power in a community.

someone other than one's spouse) could expect to be publicly whipped, branded, or even executed. Furthermore, a century ago, one could walk into a pharmacy and purchase heroin. Today, social attitudes have shifted to consider adultery a personal issue, beyond the reach of the state, and to consider the sale of heroin a criminal act.

The Conflict Model Some people reject the consensus model on the ground that moral attitudes are not constant or even consistent. In large, democratic societies such as the United States, different groups of citizens have widely varying opinions on controversial issues of morality and criminality such as abortion, the war on drugs, immigration, and assisted suicide. These groups and their elected representatives are constantly coming into conflict with one another. According to the **conflict model,** then, the most politically powerful segments of society—based on class, income, age, and race—have the most influence on criminal laws and are therefore able to impose their values on the rest of the community.

Consequently, what is deemed criminal activity is determined by whichever group happens to be holding power at any given time. Because certain groups do not have access to political power, their interests are not served by the criminal justice system. In the wake of Darren Wilson's fatal shooting of Michael Brown discussed earlier, many observers saw the grand jury's decision as further evidence of a national power structure that systematically protects police officers who kill young black men. In one poll conducted after Brown's death, 57 percent of African Americans said that Wilson's actions were unjustified, compared to 18 percent of the survey's white respondents.[5]

An Integrated Definition of Crime

Considering both the consensus and conflict models, we can construct a definition of crime that will be useful throughout this textbook. For our purposes, crime is an action or activity that is:

Define *crime.*
LEARNING
OBJECTIVE

1. Punishable under criminal law, as determined by the majority or, in some instances, by a powerful minority.
2. Considered an *offense against society as a whole* and prosecuted by public officials, not by victims and their relatives or friends.
3. Punishable by sanctions based on laws that bring about the loss of personal freedom or life.

At this point, it is important to understand the difference between crime and **deviance,** or behavior that does not conform to the norms of a given community or society. Deviance is a subjective concept. For example, some segments of society may think that smoking marijuana or killing animals for clothing and food is deviant behavior. Deviant acts become crimes only when society as a whole, through its legislatures, determines that those acts should be punished—as is the situation today in the United States with using certain drugs but not with eating meat. Furthermore, not all crimes are considered particularly deviant—little social disapprobation is attached to those who fail to follow the letter of parking laws. In essence, criminal law reflects those acts that we, as a society, agree are so unacceptable that steps must be taken to prevent them from occurring.

▲ E-cigarettes, such as the one shown in this photo, deliver the drug nicotine to users without some of the tobacco-related health risks of traditional cigarettes. Nicotine is, however, highly addictive. **Why might e-cigarette use be considered deviant behavior by minors, but not by adults?** Joe Raedle/Getty Images

Types of Crime

The manner in which crimes are classified depends on their seriousness. Federal, state, and local legislation has provided for the classification and punishment of hundreds of thousands of different criminal acts, ranging from jaywalking to first degree murder. For general purposes, we can group criminal behavior into six categories: violent crime, property crime, public order crime, white-collar crime, organized crime, and high-tech crime.

Violent Crime Crimes against persons, or *violent crimes,* have come to dominate our perspectives on crime. There are four major categories of violent crime:

- **Murder,** or the unlawful killing of a human being.
- **Sexual assault,** or *rape,* which refers to coerced actions of a sexual nature against an unwilling participant.
- **Assault** and **battery,** two separate acts that cover situations in which one person physically attacks another (battery) or, through threats, intentionally leads another to believe that he or she will be physically harmed (assault).
- **Robbery,** or the taking of funds, personal property, or any other article of value from a person by means of force or fear.

As you will see in Chapter 4, these violent crimes are further classified by *degree,* depending on the circumstances surrounding the criminal act. These circumstances include the intent of the person committing the crime, whether a weapon was used, and (in cases other than murder) the level of pain and suffering experienced by the victim.

Deviance Behavior that is considered to go against the norms established by society.

Murder The unlawful killing of one human being by another.

Sexual Assault Forced or coerced sexual intercourse (or other sexual acts).

Assault A threat or an attempt to do violence to another person that causes that person to fear immediate physical harm.

Battery The act of physically contacting another person with the intent to do harm, even if the resulting injury is insubstantial.

Robbery The act of taking property from another person through force, threat of force, or intimidation.

Careers in CJ

FASTFACTS

Youth intervention specialist/ gang investigator Job description:

- Conducts assessments and refers at-risk youth to appropriate activities, programs, or agencies.
- Serves as a liaison between the police department, schools, other agencies, and the community regarding gang and other youth-related matters.

What kind of training is required?

- A bachelor's degree in counseling, criminal justice, or other social science-related field. Bilingual (English/ Spanish) skills are desired.

Annual salary range?

- $50,000–$60,000

Courtesy F. W. Gill

F. W. Gill
Gang Investigator

The problem, for most of these kids, is that nobody cares. Their parents don't, or can't, get involved in their children's lives. (How many times have I heard parents deny that their son or daughter is a gang banger, even though it's obvious?) Teachers are in the business of teaching and don't, or can't, take the time to get to know their most troubled students. So, when I'm dealing with gang members, the first thing I do is listen. I don't lecture them, I don't tell them that they are throwing away their lives. I just listen. You'd be amazed how effective this can be—these kids, who look so tough on the outside, just want an adult to care.

Not that there is any magic formula for convincing a gang member to go straight. It is very difficult to get someone to change his or her lifestyle. If they don't want to change—really want to change—then nothing I can say or do is going to make much of a difference. Unfortunately, there are many lost causes. I've even had a couple of cases in which a juvenile was afraid to leave the gang because his father was a gang member, and he insisted that the boy stay in the gang. I have had some success in convincing gang members to turn their lives around by joining the military. The military provides discipline and a new outlook on life, things that these kids badly need. The way I look at it, in some cases, war is the best shot these kids have at saving their own lives.

> **SOCIAL MEDIA CAREER TIP** When you are posting on Facebook, assume that your post will be published in your local newspaper and read by a potential employer. So, if you think the post might reflect poorly on you as a potential employee, keep it offline.

Property Crime The most common form of criminal activity is *property crime,* or those crimes in which the goal of the offender is some form of economic gain or the damaging of property. There are three major forms of property crime:

1. Pocket picking, shoplifting, and the stealing of any property without the use of force are covered by laws against **larceny,** also known as theft.
2. **Burglary** refers to the unlawful entry of a structure with the intention of committing a serious crime such as theft.
3. *Motor vehicle theft* describes the theft or attempted theft of a motor vehicle. Motor vehicles include any vehicle commonly used for transportation, such as a motorcycle or motor scooter, but not farm equipment or water craft.

Arson is also a property crime. It involves the willful and malicious burning of a home, automobile, commercial building, or any other construction.

Public Order Crime The concept of **public order crimes** is linked to the consensus model discussed earlier. Historically, societies have always outlawed activities that are considered contrary to public values and morals. Today, the most common public order crimes include public drunkenness, prostitution, gambling, and illicit drug use. These crimes are sometimes referred to as *victimless crimes* because they often harm

Larceny The act of taking property from another person without the use of force with the intent of keeping that property.

Burglary The act of breaking into or entering a structure (such as a home or office) without permission for the purpose of committing a felony.

Public Order Crime Behavior that has been labeled criminal because it is contrary to shared social values, customs, and norms.

only the offender. As you will see throughout this textbook, however, that term is rather misleading. Public order crimes may create an environment that gives rise to property and violent crimes.

White-Collar Crime Nonviolent crimes committed by business entities or individuals to gain a personal or business advantage.

Organized Crime Illegal acts carried out by illegal organizations engaged in the market for illegal goods or services, such as illicit drugs or firearms.

White-Collar Crime

Business-related crimes are popularly referred to as **white-collar crimes.** The term *white-collar crime* is broadly used to describe an illegal act or series of acts committed by an individual or business entity using some nonviolent means to obtain a personal or business advantage. As you will see in Chapter 16, when we consider the topic in much greater detail, certain property crimes fall into this category when committed in a business context. Although the extent of this criminal activity is difficult to determine with any certainty, the Association of Certified Fraud Examiners estimates that white-collar crime costs businesses worldwide as much as $3.7 trillion a year.[6]

Organized Crime

White-collar crime involves the use of legal business facilities and employees to commit illegal acts. For example, a bank teller can't embezzle unless he or she is first hired as a legal employee of the bank. In contrast, **organized crime** describes illegal acts by illegal organizations, usually geared toward satisfying the public's demand for unlawful goods and services. Organized crime broadly implies a conspiratorial and illegal relationship among any number of persons engaged in unlawful acts. More specifically, groups engaged in organized crime employ criminal tactics such as violence, corruption, and intimidation for economic gain.

The hierarchical structure of organized crime operations often mirrors that of legitimate businesses, and, like any corporation, these groups attempt to capture a sufficient percentage of any given market to make a profit. For organized crime, the traditional preferred markets are gambling, prostitution, illegal narcotics, and loan sharking (lending funds at higher-than-legal interest rates), along with more recent ventures into counterfeiting and credit-card scams.

High-Tech Crime

The newest variation on crime is directly related to the increased presence of computers in everyday life. The Internet, with approximately 2.9 billion users worldwide, is the site of numerous *cyber crimes,* such as selling pornographic materials, soliciting minors, and defrauding consumers through bogus financial investments. The dependence of businesses on computer operations has left corporations vulnerable to sabotage, fraud, and embezzlement. Both corporations and individuals are susceptible to the theft of private information via the Internet—annually, nearly 100 million personal records are stolen through online data breaches.[7]

The issue of cyber security will become even more important in the near future as tiny computers wirelessly connected to the Internet are placed in cars, kitchen appliances, and other objects of everyday use. Figure 1.1 describes several of the most common cyber crimes, and we will address this particular criminal activity in much greater detail in Chapter 16.

EthicsChallenge

Earlier in this section, we used the example of killing animals for clothing and food as behavior that, although deviant to some, is generally accepted by the majority. What is a widespread activity that, although considered "normal" in modern American society, goes against your personal values or morals? What is the likelihood that this activity eventually will become illegal in the United States? ■

FIGURE 1.1 Types of Cyber Crime

Cyber Crimes against Persons and Property

- *Cyber Fraud:* Any misrepresentation knowingly made over the Internet with the intention of deceiving another person.
- *Identity Theft:* The appropriation of identity information, such as a person's name, driver's license, or Social Security number, to illegally access the victim's financial resources.
- *Cyberstalking:* Use of the Internet, e-mail, or any other form of electronic communication to attempt to contact and/or intimidate another person.

Cyber Crimes in the Business World

- *Hacking:* The act of employing one computer to gain illegal access to the information stored on another computer.
- *Malware Production:* The creation of programs harmful to computers, such as worms, Trojan horses, and viruses.
- *Intellectual Property Theft:* The illegal appropriation of property that results from intellectual creative processes, such as films, video games, and software, without compensating its owners.

Cyber Crimes against the Community

- *Online Child Pornography:* The illegal selling, posting, and distributing of material depicting children engaged in sexually explicit conduct.
- *Online Gambling:* The use of the Internet to conduct gambling operations that would be illegal if carried out in the "real" world.

The Purpose of the Criminal Justice System

Defining which actions are to be labeled "crimes" is only the first step in safeguarding society from criminal behavior. Institutions must be created to apprehend alleged wrongdoers, to determine whether these persons have indeed committed crimes, and to punish those who are found guilty according to society's wishes. These institutions combine to form the **criminal justice system.** As we begin our examination of the American criminal justice system in this introductory chapter, it is important to have an idea of its purpose.

LEARNING

Explain two main purposes of the criminal justice system. **3**

OBJECTIVE

Maintaining Justice

As its name implies, the explicit goal of the criminal justice system is to provide *justice* to all members of society. Because **justice** is a difficult concept to define, this goal can be challenging, if not impossible, to meet. Broadly stated, justice means that all individuals are equal before the law and that they are free from arbitrary arrest or seizure as defined by the law. In other words, the idea of justice is linked with the idea of fairness. Above all, we want our laws and the means by which they are carried out to be fair.

Justice and fairness are subjective terms, which is to say that people may have different concepts of what is just and fair. If a woman who has been beaten by her husband retaliates by killing him, what is her just punishment? Reasonable persons could disagree, with some thinking that the homicide was justified and that she should be treated leniently. Others might insist that she should not have taken the law into her own hands. Police officers, judges, prosecutors, prison administrators, and other employees of the criminal justice system must decide what is "fair." Sometimes, their course of action is obvious, but often, as we shall see, it is not.

Criminal Justice System The interlocking network of law enforcement agencies, courts, and corrections institutions designed to enforce criminal laws and protect society from criminal behavior.

Justice The quality of fairness that must exist in the processes designed to determine whether individuals are guilty of criminal wrongdoing.

Protecting Society

Within the broad mandate of "maintaining justice," Megan Kurlychek of the University at Albany, New York, has identified four specific goals of our criminal justice system:

1. To protect society from potential future crimes of the most dangerous or "risky" offenders.
2. To determine when an offense has been committed and provide the appropriate punishment for that offense.
3. To rehabilitate those offenders who have been punished so that it is safe to return them to the community.
4. To support crime victims and, to the extent possible, return them to their pre-crime status.[8]

Again, though these goals may seem straightforward, they are fraught with difficulty. Take the example of Anthony Elonis, from eastern Pennsylvania, who became distraught after he lost his job and his wife left him. Elonis took his frustration onto Facebook, where he wrote rap lyrics promising the "most heinous school shooting ever imagined" and telling his wife, "I'm not going to rest until your body is a mess, soaked in blood and dying from all the little cuts."[9] Elonis was convicted of using interstate communications to threaten harm, and sentenced to forty-four months behind bars. Using a process we will discuss in Chapter 10, Elonis appealed his conviction, claiming that his words were merely an expression of grief and depression, and that he never intended to harm anyone. Elonis compared himself to well-known rap artists such as Eminem who routinely use violent imagery in their lyrics.

In 2014, Elonis's appeal reached the United States Supreme Court, which had to answer several crucial questions regarding the case. When is the act of making threats using the Internet a crime? How much freedom should individuals such as Elonis have to express themselves in cyber space? How should we protect potential victims such as Elonis's wife, for whom such online threats can be psychologically damaging? As will be shown repeatedly throughout this textbook, cases and questions without easy answers reveal a great deal about the workings of the American criminal justice system. (See this chapter's *CJ Policy—Your Take* feature to consider another controversial crime issue: physician-assisted suicide.)

The Structure of the Criminal Justice System

Society places the burden of maintaining justice and protecting our communities on those who work for the three main institutions of the criminal justice system: law enforcement, the courts, and corrections. In this section, we take an introductory look at these institutions and their role in the criminal justice system as a whole.

The Importance of Federalism

To understand the structure of the criminal justice system, you must understand the concept of **federalism,** which means that government powers are shared by the national (federal) government and the states. The framers of the U.S. Constitution, fearful of tyranny and a too-powerful central government, chose the system of federalism as a compromise.

Federalism A form of government in which a written constitution provides for a division of powers between a central government and several regional governments.

The appeal of federalism was that it established a strong national government capable of handling large-scale problems while allowing for state powers and local traditions. For example, we just noted that physician-assisted suicide, though banned in most of the country, is legal in Oregon. It is also legal in Montana, New Mexico, Vermont, and Washington. About a decade ago, the federal government challenged the decision made by voters in Oregon and Washington to allow the practice. The United States Supreme Court sided with the states, ruling that the principle of federalism supported their freedom to differ from the majority viewpoint in this instance.[10]

The Constitution gave the national government certain express powers, such as the power to coin money, raise an army, and regulate interstate commerce. All other powers were left to the states, including police power, which allows the states to enact whatever laws are necessary to protect the health, morals, safety, and welfare of their citizens. As the American criminal justice system has evolved, the ideals of federalism have ebbed somewhat. Specifically, the powers of the national government have expanded significantly. In the early 1900s, only about one hundred specific activities were illegal under federal criminal law. Today, there are more than 4,500 federal criminal statutes, meaning that Americans are increasingly likely to come in contact with the federal criminal justice system.[11]

Law Enforcement The ideals of federalism can be clearly seen in the local, state, and federal levels of law enforcement. Though agencies from the different levels cooperate if the need arises, they have their own organizational structures and tend to operate independently of one another. We briefly introduce each level of law enforcement here and cover them in more detail in Chapters 5, 6, and 7.

Outline the three levels of law enforcement.

LEARNING **4** OBJECTIVE

Local Law Enforcement On the local level, the duties of law enforcement agencies are split between counties and municipalities. The chief law enforcement officer of most counties is the county sheriff. The sheriff is usually an elected post, with a two- or four-year term. In some areas, where city and county governments have merged, there is a county police force, headed by a chief of police. As Figure 1.2 shows, the bulk of all police officers in the United States are employed on a local level. The majority of these work in departments that consist of fewer than 10 officers, though a large city such as New York may have a police force of about 34,500.

FIGURE 1.2 Local, State, and Federal Employees in Our Criminal Justice System

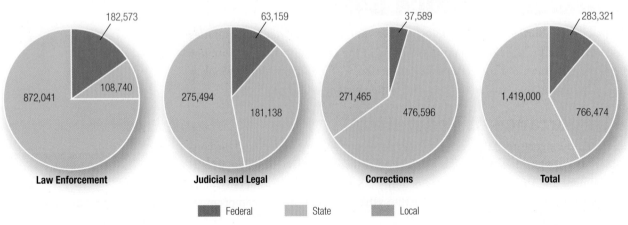

Law Enforcement	Judicial and Legal	Corrections	Total
182,573	63,159	37,589	283,321
108,740	181,138	476,596	766,474
872,041	275,494	271,465	1,419,000

■ Federal   ■ State   ■ Local

Source: Bureau of Justice Statistics, *Justice Expenditure and Employment in the United States, 2010* (Washington, D.C.: U.S. Department of Justice, July 2013), Table 2.

Local police are responsible for the "nuts and bolts" of law enforcement work. They investigate most crimes and attempt to deter crime through patrol activities. They apprehend criminals and participate in trial proceedings, if necessary. Local police are also charged with "keeping the peace," a broad set of duties that includes crowd and traffic control and the resolution of minor conflicts between citizens. In many areas, local police have the added obligation of providing social services such as dealing with domestic violence and child abuse.

State Law Enforcement Hawaii is the only state that does not have a state law enforcement agency. Generally, there are two types of state law enforcement agencies, those designated simply as "state police" and those designated as "highway patrols." State highway patrols concern themselves mainly with infractions on public highways and freeways. Other state law enforcers include fire marshals, who investigate suspicious fires and educate the public on fire prevention; and fish, game, and watercraft wardens, who police a state's natural resources and often oversee its firearms laws. Some states also have alcoholic beverage control officers, as well as agents who investigate welfare and food stamp fraud.

Federal Law Enforcement The enactment of new national anti-terrorism, gun, drug, and violent crime laws over the past forty years has led to an expansion in the size and scope of the federal government's participation in the criminal justice system. The Department of Homeland Security, which we will examine in detail in Chapter 5, combines the police powers of twenty-four federal agencies to protect the United States from terrorist attacks. Other federal agencies with police powers include the Federal Bureau of Investigation (FBI), the Drug Enforcement Administration (DEA), the U.S. Secret Service, and the Bureau of Alcohol, Tobacco, Firearms and Explosives (ATF). In fact, almost every federal agency, including the postal and forest services, has some kind of police power.

Federal law enforcement agencies operate throughout the United States, and often work in cooperation with their local and state counterparts. There can be tension between the different branches of law enforcement, however, when state criminal law and federal criminal law are incompatible. For example, even though states such as Alaska, Colorado, Oregon, and Washington have legalized the sale and possession of small amounts of marijuana, the drug is still illegal under federal law. Consequently, federal officers are authorized to make marijuana arrests in those states, regardless of any changes to the states' criminal codes.

The Courts The United States has a *dual court system,* which means that we have two independent judicial systems, one at the federal level and one at the state level. In practice, this translates into fifty-two different court systems: one federal court system and fifty different state court systems, plus that of the District of Columbia. In general, those defendants charged with violating federal criminal law will face trial in federal court, while those defendants charged with violating state law will appear in state court.

The *criminal court* and its work group—the judge, prosecutors, and defense attorneys—are charged with the weighty responsibility of determining the innocence or guilt of criminal suspects. We will cover these important participants, their roles in the criminal trial, and the court system as a whole in Chapters 8, 9, 10, and 11.

Corrections Once the court system convicts and sentences an offender, she or he is delegated to the corrections system. (Those convicted in a state court will be under the control of that state's corrections system, and those convicted of a federal crime will find themselves under the control of the federal corrections system.) Depending on the seriousness of the crime and their individual needs, offenders are placed on probation, incarcerated, or transferred to community-based correctional facilities.

- *Probation,* the most common correctional treatment, allows the offender to return to the community and remain under the supervision of an agent of the court known as a probation officer. While on probation, the offender must follow certain rules of conduct. When probationers fail to follow these rules, they may be incarcerated.
- If the offender's sentence includes a period of *incarceration,* he or she will be remanded to a correctional facility for a certain amount of time. *Jails* hold those convicted of minor crimes with relatively short sentences, as well as those awaiting trial or involved in certain court proceedings. *Prisons* house those convicted of more serious crimes with longer sentences. Generally speaking, counties and municipalities administer jails, while prisons are the domain of federal and state governments.
- *Community-based corrections* have increased in popularity as jails and prisons have been plagued with problems of funding and overcrowding. Community-based correctional facilities include halfway houses, residential centers, and work-release centers. They operate on the assumption that all convicts do not need, and are not benefited by, incarceration in jail or prison.

The majority of those inmates released from incarceration are not finished with the corrections system. The most frequent type of release from a jail or prison is *parole,* in which an inmate, after serving part of his or her sentence in a correctional facility, is allowed to serve the rest of the term in the community. Like someone on probation, a parolee must conform to certain conditions of freedom, with the same consequences if these conditions are not followed. Issues of probation, incarceration, community-based corrections, and parole will be covered in Chapters 12, 13, and 14.

▼ On any given day, America's jails hold approximately 730,000 inmates, including these residents of the Orange County jail in Santa Ana, California. **What are the basic differences between jails and prisons?** Lucy Nicholson/Reuters/Landov

The Criminal Justice Process

In its 1967 report, the President's Commission on Law Enforcement and Administration of Justice asserted that the criminal justice system

> is not a hodgepodge of random actions. It is rather a continuum—an orderly progression of events—some of which, like arrest and trial, are highly visible and some of which, though of great importance, occur out of public view.[12]

The commission's assertion that the criminal justice system is a "continuum" is one that many observers would challenge.[13] Some liken the criminal justice system to a sports team, which is the sum of an indeterminable number of decisions, relationships, conflicts, and adjustments.[14] Such a volatile mix is not what we generally associate with a "system." For most, the word **system** indicates a certain degree of order and discipline. That we refer to our law enforcement agencies, courts, and correctional facilities as part of a "system" may reflect our hopes rather than reality. Still, it will be helpful to familiarize yourself with the basic steps of the *criminal justice process,* or the procedures through which the criminal justice system meets the expectations of society. These basic steps are provided in Figure 1.3.

System A set of interacting parts that, when functioning properly, achieve a desired result.

FIGURE 1.3 The Criminal Justice Process

This diagram provides a simplified overview of the basic steps of the criminal justice process, from criminal act to release from incarceration. Next to each step, you will find the chapter of this textbook in which the event is covered.

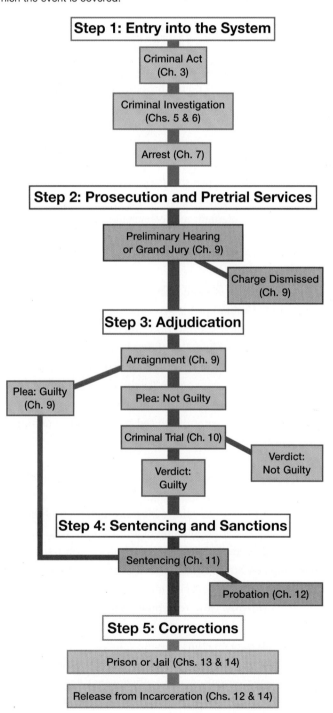

Step 1: Entry into the System
- Criminal Act (Ch. 3)
- Criminal Investigation (Chs. 5 & 6)
- Arrest (Ch. 7)

Step 2: Prosecution and Pretrial Services
- Preliminary Hearing or Grand Jury (Ch. 9)
- Charge Dismissed (Ch. 9)

Step 3: Adjudication
- Arraignment (Ch. 9)
- Plea: Guilty (Ch. 9)
- Plea: Not Guilty
- Criminal Trial (Ch. 10)
- Verdict: Guilty
- Verdict: Not Guilty

Step 4: Sentencing and Sanctions
- Sentencing (Ch. 11)
- Probation (Ch. 12)

Step 5: Corrections
- Prison or Jail (Chs. 13 & 14)
- Release from Incarceration (Chs. 12 & 14)

In his classic study of the criminal justice system, Herbert Packer, a professor at Stanford University, compared the ideal criminal justice process to an assembly line "down which moves an endless stream of cases, never stopping."[15] In Packer's image of assembly-line justice, each step of the **formal criminal justice process** involves a series of "routinized operations" with the end goal of getting the criminal defendant from point A (his or her arrest by law enforcement) to point B (the criminal trial) to point C (if guilty, her or his punishment).[16] As Packer himself was wont to point out, the daily operations of criminal justice rarely operate so smoothly. In this textbook, the criminal justice process will be examined as the end product of many different decisions made by many different criminal justice professionals in law enforcement, the courts, and corrections.

Discretion and Ethics

Practically, the formal criminal justice process suffers from a serious drawback: it is unrealistic. Law enforcement agencies do not have the staff or funds to investigate *every* crime, so they must decide where to direct their limited resources. Increasing caseloads and a limited amount of time in which to dispose of them constrict many of our nation's courts. Overcrowding in prisons and jails affects both law enforcement agencies and the courts—there is simply not enough room for all convicts.

The criminal justice system relies on *discretion* to alleviate these pressures. By **discretion,** we mean the authority to choose between and among alternative courses of action, based on individual judgment and conscience. Collectively, the discretionary decisions made by criminal justice professionals are said to produce an **informal criminal justice process** that does not operate within the rigid confines of formal rules and laws.

Explain the difference LEARNING between the formal and **6** informal criminal justice processes. OBJECTIVE

Informal Decision Making

By its nature, the informal criminal justice system relies on the discretion of individuals to offset the rigidity of criminal statutes and procedural rules. For example, even if a prosecutor believes that a suspect is guilty, she or he may decide not to bring charges against the suspect if the case is weak or the police erred during the investigative process. In many instances, prosecutors will not squander the scarce resource of court time on a case they might not win. Some argue that the informal process has made our system more just. Given the immense pressure of limited resources, the argument goes, only rarely will an innocent person end up before a judge and jury.[17]

Law Enforcement Discretion The use of discretion in law enforcement is also widespread, and this informal decision making often directly impacts the public. For example, both New York and Los Angeles have local ordinances prohibiting pedestrians from *jaywalking*, or crossing the street outside of a crosswalk or against a traffic light. Although jaywalking is quite common in New York, police rarely issue tickets to punish such behavior. In Los Angeles, however, where an automobile culture dominates, police handed out more than 31,000 jaywalking citations over a recent six-month period in the downtown area alone.[18] Evidently, New York police officers are using their discretion to ignore this illegal behavior, while their counterparts in Los Angeles have decided to expend considerable resources in an effort to reduce it.

In Chapters 5, 6, and 7, we will examine many other circumstances that call for discretionary decision making by law enforcement officers. (See Figure 1.4 for a description of some of the important discretionary decisions that make up the informal criminal justice process.)

Formal Criminal Justice Process The model of the criminal justice process in which participants follow formal rules to create a smoothly functioning disposition of cases from arrest to punishment.

Discretion The ability of individuals in the criminal justice system to make operational decisions based on personal judgment instead of formal rules or official information.

Informal Criminal Justice Process A model of the criminal justice system that recognizes the informal authority exercised by individuals at each step of the criminal justice process.

FIGURE 1.4 Discretion in the Criminal Justice System

Criminal justice officials must make decisions every day concerning their duties. The officials listed below, whether they operate on a local, state, or federal level, rely heavily on discretion when meeting the following responsibilities.

Police	Judges
• Enforce laws • Investigate specific crimes • Search people or buildings • Arrest or detain people	• Set conditions for pretrial release • Accept pleas • Dismiss charges • Impose sentences
Prosecutors	**Correctional Officials**
• File charges against suspects brought to them by the police • Drop cases • Reduce charges	• Assign convicts to prison or jail • Punish prisoners who misbehave • Reward prisoners who behave well

The Pitfalls of Discretion Unfortunately, the informal criminal justice system does not always benefit from measured, rational decision making. Individual judgment can be tainted by personal bias, erroneous or irrational thinking, and plain ill will. When this occurs, discretion becomes "the power to *get away* with alternative decisions [emphasis added]."[19] Indeed, many of the rules of the formal criminal justice process are designed to keep its employees from substituting their own judgment for that of the general public, as expressed by the law.

Recently, the American Civil Liberties Union of Michigan accused police officers in Saginaw of improperly using their discretion to racially profile recipients of jaywalking citations.[20] As you will learn in Chapter 7, racial profiling is the police practice of improperly targeting members of minority groups based on personal characteristics such as race or ethnicity. Furthermore, associate Supreme Court justice Antonin Scalia has criticized discretion in the courts for its tendency to cause discriminatory and disparate criminal sentences, a subject we will discuss in Chapter 11. According to Scalia, the need for fairness and certainty in the criminal justice system outweighs the practical benefits of widespread and unpredictable discretionary decision making.[21]

Ethics and Justice

How can we reconcile the need for some sort of discretion in criminal justice with the ever-present potential for abuse? Part of the answer lies in our initial definition of discretion, which mentions not only individual judgment but also *conscience*. Ideally, actors in the criminal justice system will make moral choices about what is right and wrong based on the norms that have been established by society. In other words, they will behave *ethically*.

Ethics in criminal justice is closely related to the concept of justice. Because criminal justice professionals are representatives of the state, they have the power to determine whether the state is treating its citizens fairly. If some law enforcement officers in fact make the decision to issue a jaywalking citation on the basis of the offender's race, then they are not only acting unethically but also unjustly.

Ethics and the Law The line between ethics and justice is often difficult to discern, as ethical standards are usually not written into criminal statutes. Consequently, individuals must often "fill in" the ethical blanks. To make this point, ethics expert John Kleinig uses the real-life example of a police officer who refused to arrest a homeless

Ethics The moral principles that govern a person's perception of right and wrong.

person for sleeping in a private parking garage. A local ordinance clearly prohibited such behavior. The officer, however, felt it would be unethical to arrest a homeless person under those circumstances unless he or she was acting in a disorderly manner. The officer's supervisors were unsympathetic to this ethical stance, and he was suspended from duty without pay.[22] (To further consider the possible tensions between a police officer's personal values and the law, see the feature *Discretion in Action—Stirring the Pot.*)

Ethics and Critical Thinking Did the police officer in the preceding example behave ethically by inserting his own beliefs into the letter of the criminal law? Would an officer who arrested peaceful homeless trespassers be acting unethically? In some cases, the ethical decision will be *intuitive,* reflecting an automatic response determined by a person's background and experiences. In other cases, however, intuition is not enough. *Critical thinking* is needed for an ethical response. Throughout this textbook, we will use the principle of critical thinking—which involves developing analytical skills and reasoning—to address the many ethical challenges inherent in the criminal justice system.

EthicsChallenge

Refer back to this section's discussion of the police officer who refused to arrest the nonviolent homeless person for ethical reasons. Did the officer act properly in this situation, or should he have carried out the law regardless of his personal beliefs? Explain your answer. ■

Discretion in Action

Stirring the Pot

The Situation Several years ago, Washington residents voted to legalize the sale of small amounts of marijuana to adults in the state. Among those Washingtonians who oppose the new law are a large number of police officers, many of whom see it as a surrender to the criminal element. There is also a sense in the law enforcement community that the new law is unethical. Even though the legal sale of marijuana will certainly lead to profits for some and increased tax revenues, it will also allow more young people to gain access to the drug. As with cigarettes and alcohol, this access will have health and social consequences for the community.

The Law Washington police officers no longer have the ability to make arrests for possession of small amounts of marijuana. The public use of marijuana is, however, still illegal in the state. Consequently, if a law enforcement agent sees a person smoking pot in public, he or she has the discretion to issue that person a ticket. In Seattle, the fine for such behavior is $27.

What Would You Do? Suppose you are a Seattle police officer who strongly disagrees with the legalization of marijuana on ethical grounds. You can no longer make arrests for possession of small amounts of marijuana, but you have

LEARNING OBJECTIVE 7 Define ethics, and describe the role that it plays in discretionary decision making.

the discretion to issue tickets and fines for public use of the drug. Would you do so, even though such steps defy the spirit of the new law? (In the first six months of 2014, a single Seattle police officer wrote about 80 percent of the one hundred public marijuana use tickets issued in the city. Displeased, Seattle officials reassigned the officer—who felt the new law was "silly"—and rescinded all the fines he levied against public marijuana users.)

Criminal Justice Today

In describing the general direction of the criminal justice system as a whole, many observers point to two models introduced by Professor Herbert Packer: the *crime control model* and the *due process model*.[23] The underlying value of the **crime control model** is that the most important function of the criminal justice process is to punish and repress criminal conduct. The system must be quick and efficient, placing as few restrictions as possible on the ability of law enforcement officers to make discretionary decisions in apprehending criminals.

Although not in direct conflict with crime control, the underlying values of the **due process model** focus more on protecting the rights of the accused through formal, legal restraints on the police, courts, and corrections. That is, the due process model relies on the courts to make it more difficult to prove guilt. It rests on the belief that it is more desirable for society that ninety-nine guilty suspects go free than that a single innocent person be condemned.[24] (This chapter's *Mastering Concepts* feature provides a further comparison of the two models.)

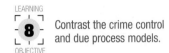

LEARNING **8** OBJECTIVE Contrast the crime control and due process models.

Crime and Law Enforcement: The Bottom Line

It is difficult to say which of Packer's two models has the upper hand today. As we will see throughout the textbook, homeland security concerns have brought much of the criminal justice system in line with crime control values. At the same time, decreasing arrest and imprisonment rates suggest that due process values are strong, as well. Indeed, national rates of violent and property crimes are at historically low levels.[25] In Chapter 3, we will discuss some of the reasons for this phenomenon, as well as concerns on the part of some experts that crime rates in the United States have "plateaued" and are likely to rise in the near future.[26]

Smarter Policing Just as law enforcement inevitably gets a great deal of the blame when crime rates are high, American police forces have received much credit for the apparent decline in criminality. The consensus is that the police have become smarter and more disciplined over the past two decades, putting into practice strategies that allow them to more effectively prevent crime. For example, the widespread use of *proactive policing* promotes more rigorous enforcement of minor offenses—such as drunkenness and public disorder—with an eye toward preventing more serious wrongdoing. In addition, *hot-spot policing* has law enforcement officers focusing on high-crime areas rather than spreading their resources evenly throughout metropolitan areas. These and other innovative policing strategies will be explored more fully in Chapter 6.

Identifying Criminals Technology has also played a significant role in improving law enforcement efficiency. Police investigators are enjoying the benefits of perhaps the most effective new crime-fighting tool since fingerprint identification: DNA profiling. This technology allows law enforcement agents to identify a suspect from body fluid evidence (such as blood, saliva, or semen) or biological evidence (such as hair strands or fingernail clippings). As we will also see in Chapter 6, by collecting DNA from convicts and storing the information in databases, investigators have been able to reach across hundreds of miles and back in time to catch wrongdoers.

Crime Control Model A criminal justice model that places primary emphasis on the right of society to be protected from crime and violent criminals.

Due Process Model A criminal justice model that places primacy on the right of the individual to be protected from the power of the government.

Crime Control Model

Due Process Model

Goal	Goal
• Deter crime by arresting and incarcerating criminals as quickly and efficiently as possible.	• Protect the individual charged with a crime against the immense and sometimes possibly unjust power of the state.

Methods	Methods
• Allow the police to "do their jobs" by limiting the amount of judicial oversight of law enforcement tactics.	• Assure the constitutional rights of those accused of crimes, at the hands of both the law enforcement officers who make the arrest and the prosecutors who prosecute the defendant in criminal court.
• Limit the number of rights and protections enjoyed by defendants in court.	• Whenever possible, allow nonviolent convicts to serve their sentences in the community rather than behind bars.
• Incarcerate criminals for lengthy periods of time by imposing harsh sentences, including the death penalty.	• Protect the civil rights of all inmates, and focus on rehabilitation rather than punishment in prisons and jails.

Law enforcement's ability to identify criminal suspects is set to receive another boost with the increased use of **biometrics.** The term refers to the various technological devices that read a person's unique physical characteristics and report his or her identity to authorities. The most common biometric devices record a suspect's fingerprints, but hand geometry, facial features, and the minute details of the human eye can also provide biometric identification.

Already, some banks are using biometrics in the form of voice recognition software to confirm clients' identities. Before long, smartphones and other electronic devices will be activated by facial recognition, and drivers will be able to start their cars with their fingerprints. In law enforcement, the FBI is consolidating all of its biometric information such as fingerprints and mug shots into a single database that will allow local police departments to verify the identities of more than 100 million Americans.[27] Using mobile biometrics systems, law enforcement agents in the field can now instantaneously determine whether a suspect is wanted for other criminal activity, a process that previously took hours or even days.[28] We will address the spread of this technology in greater detail in Chapter 7.

Biometrics Methods to identify a person based on his or her unique physical characteristics, such as fingerprints or facial configuration.

BOSS (Biometric Optical Surveillance System)

As far back as the 2001 Super Bowl, the federal government has been experimenting with facial recognition software that would allow video cameras to identify individuals within large crowds of people. Finally, it seems, the technology is close to becoming operational. The Biometric Optical Surveillance System (BOSS) uses 3-D cameras mounted on the top of two towers to take photos of a subject from different angles. A computer then reads the features of the subject's face and matches those features against those stored in a database.

The goal, according to researchers, is for BOSS to provide a near-instant match at a range of more than three hundred feet. The technology is being developed primarily for counterterrorism purposes. For example, BOSS could be used to search for terrorist suspects at a presidential inaugural parade or in an airport lounge.

Thinking about BOSS

How could local police departments implement BOSS to identify and apprehend criminal suspects or fugitives? Should law enforcement agencies wait until BOSS's successful match rate is close to 100 percent, or would an 80 or 90 percent certainty be acceptable? Explain your answer.

iStockPhoto.com/labsas

Continuing Challenges for Law Enforcement Due to economic concerns, according to one recent survey, about half of the nation's local law enforcement agencies have been subject to budget cuts in recent years.[29] The impact of these cuts, which include officer layoffs and resource reductions, could seriously hamper efforts regarding three of the major challenges facing today's police: gangs, guns, and strained community relations.

The Scourge of Street Gangs For many local law enforcement agencies, particularly those in large metropolitan areas, success is measured by their ability to control **street gangs.** These gangs are often identified as groups of offenders who band together to engage in violent, unlawful, or criminal activity. According to the most recent data, more than 30,000 gangs, with approximately 780,000 members, are criminally active in the United States. The same study estimates that the number of gangs has grown by nearly one-third since 2003, and that such groups are responsible for 12 percent of homicides in the United States.[30] The topic of youth gangs and efforts to combat their criminal activity will be covered more extensively in Chapter 15.

Gun Use and Crime Even though gangs are heavily involved in criminal activity, most gang-related homicides are not crime related. That is, the killings do not occur during drug deals or robberies "gone bad." Rather, according to data collected by the federal government, the great majority of gang deaths involve the deadly mix of inter-gang conflict (such as territorial or personal disputes) and firearms.[31] Overall, about 475,000 violent crimes are committed each year using a firearm, including over 10,000 homicides,[32] and illegally obtained firearms are a constant concern for law enforcement officials.

Street Gang A group of people, usually three or more, who share a common identity and engage in illegal activities.

At the same time, legal ownership of guns is widespread, with almost one-third of American households possessing at least one gun.[33] In 2008, the United States Supreme Court further solidified the legal basis for this practice by ruling that the U.S. Constitution protects an individual's right to "bear arms."[34] The Court's decision has done little to lessen the debate over **gun control,** or the policies that the government implements to keep firearms out of the hands of the wrong people. We will take a closer look at the divisive topic of gun control in the *CJ in Action* feature at the end of this chapter.

Issues of Race and Public Trust In the introduction to this chapter, we discussed the fallout after a grand jury decided that a white police officer should not face criminal charges for fatally shooting a young black man in Ferguson, Missouri. Shortly thereafter, in early December 2014, another grand jury similarly declined to charge a white New York City police officer who accidentally killed a black suspect named Eric Garner using a chokehold. For many African Americans, these two incidents seemed to underscore a growing mistrust between their communities and law enforcement in the United States.

According to a poll taken following the shooting of Michael Brown in Ferguson, nearly half of African American respondents said that they had experienced racial discrimination by a police officer. (Virtually none of the white respondents responded in the same manner.)[35] Examining racial tensions between blacks and law enforcement in Cleveland, a recent federal report stated that the city's police force sees itself as an "occupying force" and that the various local departments "must undergo a cultural shift at all levels to change an 'us-against-them' mentality."[36]

This mutual distrust was only reinforced when, on December 20, 2014, an African American named Ismaaiyl Brinsley killed two New York police officers, apparently in retaliation for the earlier deaths of Michael Brown and Eric Garner. Following the murders, a Baltimore, Maryland, police union official denounced the "dangerous political climate" caused by anti-police protests.[37] In Chapters 5 and 6, we will take a comprehensive look at the possible root causes of this climate, and explore some of the ways in which tensions between police and members of minority groups might be defused. In particular, we will focus on diversity in law enforcement, a crucial issue in today's criminal justice system.

Illegal Drugs in the United States

Another source of frustration for the African American community is the significant disparity in the rate that blacks and whites are arrested for illegal drug offenses,[38] a topic we will discuss in Chapter 3. Indeed, drug use plays a major role in the criminal justice system as a whole. Local police make about 1,500,000 arrests for drug law violations each year,[39] and more than six of every ten male adult arrestees in the United States test positive for at least one illegal drug in their systems at the time of arrest.[40]

The broadest possible definition of a **drug,** which includes alcohol, is any substance that modifies biological, psychological, or social behavior. In popular terminology, however, the word *drug* has a more specific connotation. When people speak of the "drug" problem, or the war on "drugs," or "drug" abuse, they are referring specifically to illegal **psychoactive drugs,** which affect the brain and alter consciousness or perception. Almost all of the drugs that we will be discussing in this textbook, such as marijuana, cocaine, heroin, and amphetamines, are illegal and psychoactive.

Marijuana Trends To the surprise of many criminal justice professionals, the final sentence in the previous section is no longer completely accurate. Numerous

Gun Control Efforts by a government to regulate or control the sale of guns.

Drug Any substance that modifies biological, psychological, or social behavior. In particular, an illegal substance with those properties.

Psychoactive Drugs Chemicals that affect the brain, causing changes in emotions, perceptions, and behavior.

state legislatures have decided to permit marijuana consumption under certain circumstances. As Figure 1.5 shows, thirty states allow the use of marijuana or THC—an active ingredient in marijuana—for medicinal purposes. The drug has also been *decriminalized* in fourteen states, meaning that its use is treated as an infraction similar to a traffic violation rather than as a crime. Finally, in 2014, Alaska, Oregon, and Washington, D.C., joined Colorado and Washington State by *legalizing* small amounts of marijuana sale and possession, a trend that is expected to continue in the near future. As mentioned earlier in the chapter, marijuana is still illegal under federal law, a situation that we will examine more closely later in this textbook.

High-Risk Behavior Generally speaking, the American public seems to support measures taken by states to reduce criminal sanctions for marijuana use.[41] Critics of these new measures, however, contend that the liberalization of marijuana laws will have unintended consequences when it comes to young people. College students are smoking marijuana at the highest levels in three decades.[42] About 6 percent of eight graders regularly smoke marijuana, and there has been a steady decline in the percentage of high school students who consider using the drug to be risky behavior.[43] These statistics are troubling because, as we will see when we look at the juvenile justice system in Chapter 15, drug abuse often leads to further criminal behavior in adolescents.

Unintended consequences have also played a role in the recent increase in heroin use in the United States. Over the past few years, federal law enforcement agencies have successfully cracked down on the illicit use of prescription painkillers such as OxyContin, Vicodin, and Percocet. These successes caused the black market prices of those drugs to soar, leaving heroin as a low-cost alternative. The result: a 100 percent increase in the number of heroin users between 2007 and 2012, with an annual toll of 3,000 deaths due to heroin overdoses.[44]

Homeland Security and Domestic Terrorism

Without question, the attacks of September 11, 2001—when terrorists hijacked four commercial airlines and used them to kill nearly three thousand people in New York City, northern Virginia, and rural Pennsylvania—were the most significant events of the first decade of the 2000s as far as crime fighting is concerned. As we will see throughout this textbook, the resulting **homeland security** movement has touched nearly every aspect

Homeland Security A concerted national effort to prevent terrorist attacks within the United States and reduce the country's vulnerability to terrorism.

FIGURE 1.5 Marijuana and Criminal Law

As this map shows, at the beginning of 2015 most states—representing about three-fourths of the population of the United States—allow for the use of marijuana under certain circumstances. Remember that *any* use of the drug is outlawed under federal law.

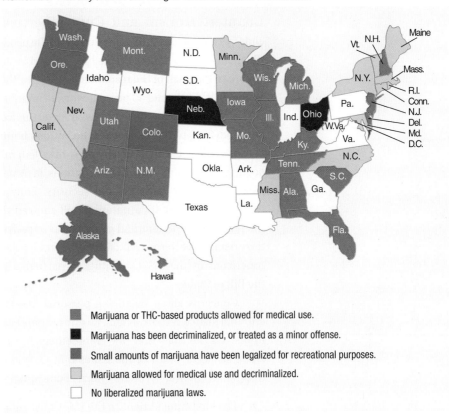

■ Marijuana or THC-based products allowed for medical use.

■ Marijuana has been decriminalized, or treated as a minor offense.

■ Small amounts of marijuana have been legalized for recreational purposes.

▫ Marijuana allowed for medical use and decriminalized.

□ No liberalized marijuana laws.

Explain the defining aspects LEARNING
of a terrorist act, and identify
one common misperception **9**
concerning domestic OBJECTIVE
terrorism.

of criminal justice. This movement has the ultimate goal of protecting America from **terrorism**, which can be broadly defined as the random use of staged violence to achieve political goals.

Counterterrorism and Civil Liberties

"September 11 is the day that never ends," wrote journalist Richard Cohen on the occasion of its tenth anniversary.[45] Certainly, the memory of that day's events has lingered in the public consciousness. In a recent survey, more than half of the respondents thought that a future terrorist attack was "very" or "somewhat" likely, and 40 percent worried about terrorism directly impacting themselves or their families.[46] Mobilized by such fears, the federal government spent about $560 billion from 2002 to 2015 to bolster the nation's homeland security apparatus.[47]

Several years ago, disclosures that federal antiterrorism agencies had secretly acquired the phone records of millions of Americans caused many to reassess their views on privacy and national security. Following these revelations, which we will explore in Chapter 16, a national poll showed that 47 percent of Americans said that the federal government had gone too far in restricting *civil liberties* in its efforts to fight terrorism.[48] The term **civil liberties** refers to the personal freedoms guaranteed to all Americans by the U.S. Constitution, particularly the first ten amendments, known as the Bill of Rights.

Concerns about balancing personal freedoms and personal safety permeate our criminal justice system. In fact, an entire chapter of this textbook—Chapter 7—is needed to discuss the rules that law enforcement must follow to protect the civil liberties of crime suspects. Many of the issues that we will address in these pages are particularly relevant to counterterrorism efforts. For example:

1. The First Amendment to the U.S. Constitution states that the government shall not interfere with citizens' "freedom of speech." Does this mean that individuals should be allowed to support terrorist causes on the Internet?
2. The Fourth Amendment protects against "unreasonable searches and seizures." Does this mean that law enforcement agents should be able to seize the computer of a terrorist subject without any actual proof of wrongdoing?
3. The Sixth Amendment guarantees a trial by jury to a person accused of a crime. Does this mean that the U.S. military can find a suspect guilty of terrorist actions without providing a jury trial?

Critics of counterterrorism measures that include increased surveillance of Internet activity (including e-mails), phone records, and citizens' daily movements believe that limits should be placed on the government's ability to collect "Big Data." Supporters counter that, for the most part, such tactics have been effective and therefore are worth any minimal privacy intrusions.

Domestic Terrorism

For most of the first decade of the 2000s, America's counterterrorism strategies focused on international terrorism, represented by foreign terrorist organizations that possess the resources to carry out large-scale, coordinated attacks. According to James Comey, director of the FBI, because of these strategies, "the risk of that spectacular attack in the homeland is significantly lower than it was before 9/11." At the same time, Comey warned against the "risk of smaller attacks" by *domestic terrorists*.[49] Though the label covers a variety of illegal activities, **domestic terrorism** generally refers to acts of terror that are carried out within one's own country, against one's own people, and with little or no direct foreign involvement.

Terrorism The use or threat of violence to achieve political objectives.

Civil Liberties The basic rights and freedoms for American citizens guaranteed by the U.S. Constitution, particularly in the Bill of Rights.

Domestic Terrorism Acts of terrorism that take place on U.S. soil without direct foreign involvement.

Domestic terrorists are often alienated individuals who become emboldened after meeting others who share their extreme views. In many instances, these views involve outrage over American military excursions against Muslims in the Middle East, as well as contempt for Western cultural norms at home. For example, Dzhokhar Tsarnaev told investigators that he and his brother Tamerlan planted pressure-cooker bombs near the finish of the 2013 Boston Marathon as a protest against U.S.-led wars in Iraq and Afghanistan.[50] Contrary to public perception, however, many domestic terrorists have no connection whatsoever to Islamic fundamentalism. According to one estimate, between 2009 and 2013 American law enforcement agents had forty "violent encounters" with anti-government extremists and white supremacists engaged in terrorist acts.[51] The FBI devotes significant resources to thwarting domestic threats such as the "sovereign citizens" movement, whose members reject government authority and plot to kill police officers as a form of protest.[52]

▲ Law enforcement agents console each other after the funeral of Las Vegas police officer Igor Soldo, who was fatally shot by Jerad Miller and his wife Amanda in June 2014. Miller, who did not survive the shootout, saw himself as an "anti-police" revolutionary and believed that "Satan runs our government." **Why is Miller considered a domestic terrorist?** Photo by Ethan Miller/Getty Images

The Emergence of Victims' Rights

In the debate over whether Anthony Elonis should be imprisoned for making online threats—discussed earlier in the chapter—much of the focus was on how his behavior impacted the mental well-being of the *victim* of this crime. At Elonis's trial, his ex-wife testified that she felt like Elonis was stalking her, and that she was "extremely afraid" for her own life and the lives of her children.[53] "There has been a huge movement in criminal law toward giving victims a voice in what happens—which provides both some solace and closure," notes Chicago Kent College of Law professor Doug Godfrey.[54] For our purposes, a **victim** is any person against whom a crime has been committed or who is directly or indirectly harmed by a criminal act.

Advocating for Crime Victims Widespread recognition of crime victims is a relatively recent phenomenon. It was not until the 1970s that victims' rights advocates began addressing what they perceived to be an imbalance in favor of criminal defendants in the criminal justice system. These activists pointed out that crime victims had virtually no rights under state or federal law. Therefore, they were forced to deal with the physical, emotional, and financial consequences of victimization on their own. As a presidential task force concluded in 1982, "The victims of crime have been transformed into a group oppressively burdened by a system designed to protect them. This oppression must be redressed."[55]

Legislative Efforts Over the past twenty years, all fifty states have redressed the situation by providing legal rights to victims in their statutory codes or state constitutions. Furthermore, in 2004, the U.S. Congress passed the Crime Victims' Rights Act.[56] These legislative actions have given victims a much greater presence in criminal proceedings, including the right to be heard in criminal court.[57] Various government agencies also provide a broad range of services to crime victims, from crisis intervention to emotional support to financial compensation. In Chapter 3, we will examine attempts by some university administrators and politicians to protect potential victims of sexual assault on college campuses.

Victim Any person who suffers physical, emotional, or financial harm as the result of a criminal act.

Not all observers believe that the emergence of victims' rights has had a positive impact. In many instances, these critics point out, the various legislative efforts have failed to protect victims' rights as promised. Furthermore, some feel that that the presence of victims in the courtroom adds an element of bias to criminal proceedings.[58] Throughout this textbook, we will examine the growing role of the victim in the criminal justice system to determine whether such criticisms are justified.

Inmate Population Trends

After increasing by 500 percent from 1980 to 2008, the inmate population in the United States has leveled off and, as you can see in Figure 1.6, has even decreased slightly since 2009. Certainly, this decrease has been small, and the American corrections system remains immense. More than 2.2 million offenders are in prison or jail in this country, and another 4.7 million are under community supervision.[59] Still, the new trend reflects a series of crucial changes in the American criminal justice system.

The Economics of Incarceration For many years, the growing prison population was fed by a number of "get tough on crime" laws passed by politicians in response to the crime wave of the late 1980s and early 1990s. These sentencing laws—discussed in Chapter 11—made it more likely that a person arrested for a crime would wind up behind bars and that, once there, he or she would not be back in the community for a long while. The recent reversal of this pattern has led some experts to suggest that the due process model, which favors rehabilitation over incarceration, has started to play a larger role in American criminal justice policy. "This is the beginning of the end of mass incarceration," predicts Natasha Frost of Northeastern University.[60]

There is no question that economic considerations have played a role in the nation's shrinking inmate population. Federal, state, and local governments spend $80 billion a year on prisons and jails, and many corrections officials are under pressure to decrease costs.[61] Increasingly, however, downsizing efforts reflect "the message that locking up a

FIGURE 1.6 Prison and Jail Populations in the United States, 1985–2013

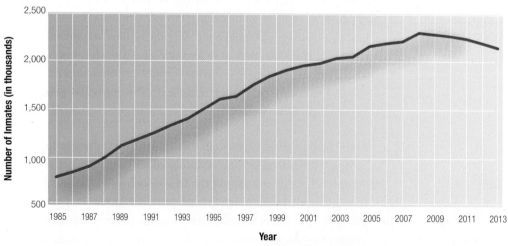

Sources: Bureau of Justice Statistics, *Correctional Populations in the United States, 1995* (Washington, D.C.: U.S. Department of Justice, June 1997), Table 1.1, page 12; and Bureau of Justice Statistics, *Correctional Populations in the United States, 2013* (Washington, D.C.: U.S. Department of Justice, December 2014), Table 1, page 2.

lot of people doesn't necessarily bring public safety," says Joan Petersilia, co-director of Stanford University's Criminal Justice Center.[62] To reduce prison populations, therefore, federal and state correctional officials are

1. Granting early release to nonviolent offenders, particularly low-level drug offenders,
2. Diverting offenders from jail and prison through special courts that promote rehabilitation rather than punishment, and
3. Implementing a number of programs to reduce the *recidivism* rate of ex-convicts.

Recidivism refers to the act of committing another crime (and possibly returning to incarceration) after a person has already been punished for previous criminal behavior. We will examine these policies and the ramifications for the nation's prisons and jails in Chapters 12, 13, and 14.

Declining Use of the Death Penalty Another interesting corrections trend involves death row inmates, who are in prison awaiting execution after having been found guilty of committing a **capital crime.** Near the end of 2014, the death row population in American prisons stood at 3,035, down from 3,653 in 2000.[63] During that same time period, the number of annual executions in this country dropped from 85 to 35, a twenty-year low.

Judges and juries, it seems, have become less willing to sentence the "worst of the worst" criminals to death. In 2014, only seventy-two offenders were sentenced to death, down from 315 in 1996.[64] Furthermore, Nebraska recently became the seventh state since 2007 to abolish the death penalty. We will further explore *capital punishment,* one of the most controversial areas of the criminal justice system, in Chapter 11.

Incarceration and Race One troublesome aspect of capital punishment is that a black defendant is much more likely to be sentenced to death for killing a white victim than a white defendant is for killing a black victim.[65] Indeed, looking at the general statistics, a bleak picture of minority incarceration emerges. Even though African Americans make up only 13 percent of the general population in the United States, the number of black men in state and federal prisons (526,000) is significantly larger than the number of white men (454,000).[66] In federal prisons, one in every three inmates is Hispanic,[67] a ratio that has increased dramatically over the past decade as law enforcement and homeland security agencies have focused on immigration law violations, a subject we will consider in Chapter 5. The question of whether these figures reflect purposeful bias on the part of certain members of the criminal justice community will be addressed at various points in this textbook.

Criminal Justice and the Mentally Ill

Another socially and statistically significant segment of the inmate population is the mentally ill. According to the National Alliance on Mental Illness, 40 percent of adults with serious mental health problems will be arrested at some point in their lives, often for petty crimes.[68] About 56 percent of all state prison inmates and 64 percent of all jail inmates are suffering from some sort of mental illness.[69] States reduced their spending on mental health services by about $5 billion from 2009 to 2012,[70] meaning that those suffering from poor mental health often wind up in the "care" of the criminal justice system. "We have replaced the hospital bed with the jail cell," says Tim Murphy, a Republican congressman from Pennsylvania.[71]

LEARNING **10** OBJECTIVE List the major issues in criminal justice today.

Recidivism The act of committing a new crime after a person has already been punished for a previous crime by being convicted and sent to jail or prison.

Capital Crime A criminal act that makes the offender eligible to receive the death penalty.

Prison programs have been shown to improve the situation, both for the corrections system and for those suffering from mental illness. When Georgia began providing comprehensive health services to mentally ill jail inmates, the state was able to reduce the number of days these inmates spent behind bars by 78 percent.[72] Such treatment also makes it less likely that these offenders will reoffend after being released back into the community. In Chapter 14, we will examine how prison and jail treatment programs impact the *reentry process* for the approximately 620,000 inmates who exit prisons in the United States each year.

▲ An inmate suffering from mental illness speaks to his attorney through a cell door at the Stanislaus County Public Safety Center in Modesto, California. **Why do many experts blame the large number of mentally ill jail and prison inmates on reductions in government spending on community mental health services?** Photo by Debbie Noda/ *Modesto Bee*/MCT via Getty Images

EthicsChallenge

Did our discussion in this section of the increased use of biometrics by law enforcement raise any ethical "red flags" for you? Consider, for example, technology that allows the police to scan crowds and pick out criminal suspects using facial recognition software. What are some of ways that this technology could be used to potentially infringe on Americans' civil liberties? ■

CJ IN ACTION

Gun Control versus Gun Rights

After 82 people were struck by gunfire—with fourteen suffering fatal wounds—over the 2014 Fourth of July weekend in Chicago, the debate over gun violence proceeded along predictable lines. "We can only hope that the bloody numbers help in tipping the balance toward eventual enactment of common-sense gun laws," wrote a *Washington Post* editorialist.[73] "Chicago has some of the strictest gun laws in the country," countered the *National Review*, pointing out the futility of gun control efforts.[74] Certainly, the vast majority of Americans who own guns are law-abiding citizens who keep their firearms at home for self-protection. This chapter's *CJ in Action* feature deals with the thorny issue of how best to protect the rights of this group while at the same time limiting the harm done by the illegal or improper use of firearms in the United States.

As American As . . .

The Second Amendment to the U.S. Constitution states, "A well regulated Militia, being necessary to the security of a free State, the right of the people to keep and bear Arms, shall not be infringed." Recently, the United States Supreme Court has tried to clarify this somewhat unclear language. Over the course of two separate rulings, the Court has stated that the Second Amendment provides individuals with a constitutional right to bear arms, and that this right must be recognized at all levels of government—federal, state, and local.[75]

Although the Supreme Court emphasized in both cases that states could continue to prohibit certain individuals—such as criminals and the mentally ill—from legally purchasing firearms, critics of our nation's relatively lax gun laws were disappointed with the results. Pointing out that people with mental health problems, such as Ivan Lopez, are often easily able to obtain firearms legally, these critics continue to argue for greater restrictions on gun ownership. (Lopez killed three U.S. military service members and wounded sixteen others in Killeen, Texas, on April 2, 2014, with a recently purchased handgun.) Opponents of stricter gun control laws reject the notion that firearms themselves are to blame for violent crime. Said one gun seller, "That's like pointing a finger at Ford and blaming them for car deaths."[76]

The Case for More Restrictive Gun Laws

- Each year, about 31,000 people in the United States die from gun violence, including about 20,000 suicides and 10,000 homicides.[77] About 70 percent of murders in the nation involve firearms.[78]

- The importance of guns for self-protection is overstated. Less than 1 percent of all gun deaths involve self-defense, with the rest being accidents, suicides, and homicides.[79]

- Considered too dangerous for public use, fully automatic weapons such as machine guns are already banned in the United States. For the same reason, the federal government should outlaw semiautomatic weapons, which can rapidly fire multiple rounds, and the high-capacity ammunition clips that allow them to do so.

The Case against More Restrictive Gun Laws

- Gun control laws do not decrease crime, for the simple reason that someone who is going to commit a crime with a gun is probably going to obtain that firearm illegally. Consequently, stricter gun control would "prevent only law-abiding citizens from owning handguns."[80] Furthermore, as we saw earlier in the chapter, violent crime is at historically low levels in the United States, belying the argument that the country needs to change its gun laws.[81]

- Firearms offer protection from criminal attacks beyond that provided by public law enforcement.

- About one-third of American households include someone who possesses a firearm, accounting for more than 310 million privately and legally owned guns in this country.[82] Putting restrictions on that ownership would create a huge new criminal class in this country, not to mention the anger toward the government that such measures would provoke.

Your Opinion—Writing Assignment

When it comes to allowing concealed weapons on college campuses, the United States is a nation divided. Twenty states ban the practice outright. Twenty-three states permit the schools to decide for themselves. Seven states—Colorado, Idaho, Kansas, Mississippi, Oregon, Utah, and Wisconsin—have passed bills expressly permitting the carrying of concealed weapons on campus grounds.[83] Should this practice be allowed? Does it make campuses safer or more dangerous? Would it be more desirable to have a single law that covered the entire nation? Before responding, you can review our discussions in the sections of this chapter concerning:

- Consensus and conflict models of crime ("What Is Crime?").

- Federalism and the structure of the criminal justice system ("The Structure of the Criminal Justice System").

- Gun sales and gun control ("Criminal Justice Today").

Your answer should include at least three full paragraphs.

Summary

For more information on these concepts, look back to the Learning Objective icons throughout the chapter.

 Describe the two most common models of how society determines which acts are criminal. The consensus model argues that the majority of citizens will agree on which activities should be outlawed and punished as crimes. It rests on the assumption that a diverse group of people can have similar morals. In contrast, the conflict model argues that in a diverse society, the dominant groups exercise power by codifying their value systems into criminal laws.

 Define *crime*. Crime is any action punishable under criminal statutes and is considered an offense against society. Therefore, alleged criminals are prosecuted by the state rather than by victims. Crimes are punishable by sanctions that bring about a loss of personal freedom or, in some cases, fines.

 Explain two main purposes of the criminal justice system. The first purpose of the criminal justice system is to provide justice to society by ensuring that all individuals are treated equally under criminal law. The second purpose is to protect society, a far-reaching objective that involves the fair treatment of crime victims and those who may or may not have committed criminal acts.

 Outline the three levels of law enforcement. Because we have a federal system of government, law enforcement occurs at the (a) national, or federal, level and the (b) state level and within the states at (c) local levels. Because crime is mostly a local concern, most employees in the criminal justice system work for local governments. Agencies at the federal level include the FBI, the DEA, and the U.S. Secret Service, among others.

 List the essential elements of the corrections system. Criminal offenders are placed on probation, incarcerated in a jail or prison, transferred to community-based corrections facilities, or released on parole.

 Explain the difference between the formal and informal criminal justice processes. The formal criminal justice process involves the somewhat mechanical steps that are designed to guide criminal defendants from arrest to possible punishment. For every step in the formal process, though, someone has discretion, and such discretion leads to an informal process. Even when prosecutors believe that a suspect is guilty, they have the discretion not to prosecute, for example.

 Define ethics, and describe the role that it plays in discretionary decision making. Ethics consist of the moral principles that guide a person's perception of right and wrong. Most criminal justice professionals have a great deal of discretionary leeway in their day-to-day decision making, and their ethical beliefs can help ensure that they make such decisions in keeping with society's established values.

 Contrast the crime control and due process models. The crime control model assumes that the criminal justice system is designed to protect the public from criminals. Thus, its most important function is to punish and repress criminal conduct. The due process model presumes that the accused are innocent and provides them with the most complete safeguards, usually within the court system.

 Explain the defining aspects of a terrorist act, and identify one common misperception concerning domestic terrorism. According to the federal government, the defining aspects of terrorism are (a) violence in the service of (b) intimidation or coercion, with the goal of furthering (c) political or social objectives. Terrorists need not represent a certain religion or support fundamentalist religious causes.

 List the major issues in criminal justice today. (a) Falling violent and property crime rates; (b) improved policing strategies; (c) street gangs; (d) gun sales and gun control; (e) social justice and law enforcement; (f) liberalization of state marijuana prohibition laws; (g) homeland security and civil liberties; (h) domestic terrorism; (i) America's shrinking, though still massive, inmate population; (j) cost-cutting measures in the corrections system; (k) possible bias against minorities in the criminal justice system; and (l) mental illness and crime.

Questions for Critical Analysis

1. How is it possible to have a consensus about what should or should not be illegal in a country with several hundred million adults from such diverse races, religions, and walks of life?

2. What would be some of the drawbacks of having the victims of a crime, rather than the state (through its public officials), prosecute criminals?

3. Do you agree that public order crimes such as prostitution and illegal gambling are "victimless" crimes? Why or why not?

4. Are you worried about being the victim of a terrorist attack? If so, why? If not, why not?

5. As noted earlier in the chapter, corrections officials are reducing prison budgets by releasing nonviolent offenders before their sentences are finished. What is your opinion of this strategy? What might be some of the consequences of large-scale early release programs for drug dealers and those convicted of property crimes?

Key Terms

assault   7
battery   7
biometrics   20
burglary   8
capital crime   27
civil liberties   24
conflict model   6
consensus model   5
crime   5
crime control model   19
criminal justice system   10
deviance   7
discretion   16

domestic terrorism   24
drug   22
due process model   19
ethics   17
federalism   11
formal criminal justice process   16
gun control   22
homeland security   23
informal criminal justice process   16
justice   10
larceny   8
morals   5
murder   7

organized crime   9
psychoactive drugs   22
public order crime   8
recidivism   27
robbery   7
sexual assault   7
street gang   21
system   15
terrorism   24
victim   25
white-collar crime   9

1. "Don't Shoot," *The Economist* (December 13, 2014), 27.

2. Missouri Revised Statutes, Section 563.046.2 (August 28, 2014).

3. Quoted in Ashby Jones, "Why Ferguson Officer Wasn't Charged: A Look at the 'Use of Force' Doctrine," *Wall Street Journal* (November 24, 2014), at **blogs.wsj.com/law/2014/11/24 /why-ferguson-officer-wasnt-charged-a -look-at-use-of-force-doctrine.**

4. Herman Bianchi, *Justice as Sanctuary: Toward a New System of Crime Control* (Bloomington: Indiana University Press, 1994), 72.

5. Tanzina Vega and Megan Thee-Brenan, "Polls Show National Unease with Missouri Unrest," *New York Times* (August 22, 2014), A14.

6. *2014 Report to the Nations: Occupational Fraud and Abuse* (Austin, Tex.: Association of Certified Fraud Examiners, 2014), 4.

7. "Defending the Digital Frontier" in "Special Report: Cyber Security," *The Economist* (July 24, 2014), 3.

8. Megan Kurlychek, "What Is My Left Hand Doing? The Need for Unifying Purpose and Policy in the Criminal Justice System," *Criminology & Public Policy* (November 2011), 909.

9. Quoted in Paula Mejia, "Supreme Court to Tackle Rap-Inspired Online Threats," *Newsweek.com* (November 30, 2014), at **www .newsweek.com/supreme-court-tackle -rap-inspired-online-threats-288060.**

10. *Gonzales v. Oregon,* 546 U.S. 243 (2006). Many United States Supreme Court cases will be cited in this book, and it is important to understand these citations. *Gonzales v. Oregon* refers to the parties in the case that the Court is reviewing. "U.S." is the abbreviation for *United States Reports,* the official publication of United States Supreme Court decisions. "546" refers to the volume of the *United States Reports* in which the case appears, and "243" is the page number. The citation ends with the year the case was decided, in parentheses. Most, though not all, Supreme Court case citations in this book will follow this formula.

11. Steve Nelson, "Bipartisan Task Force Looks to Cut List of 4,500 Federal Crimes," *U.S. News & World Report* (June 14, 2013), at **www.usnews .com/news/newsgram/articles/2013/06 /14/bipartisan-task-force-looks-to-cut -list-of-4500-federal-crimes.**

12. President's Commission on Law Enforcement and Administration of Justice, *The Challenge of Crime in a Free Society* (Washington, D.C.: Government Printing Office, 1967), 7.

13. John Heinz and Peter Manikas, "Networks among Elites in a Local Criminal Justice System," *Law and Society Review* 26 (1992), 831–861.

14. James Q. Wilson, "What to Do about Crime: Blaming Crime on Root Causes," *Vital Speeches* (April 1, 1995), 373.

15. Herbert Packer, *The Limits of the Criminal Sanction* (Stanford, Calif.: Stanford University Press, 1968), 154–173.

16. *Ibid.*

17. Daniel Givelber, "Meaningless Acquittals, Meaningful Convictions: Do We Reliably Acquit the Innocent?" *Rutgers Law Review* 49 (Summer 1997), 1317.

18. Donna Evans, "Police Crackdown on Jaywalking Means Tickets of Up to $250," *DT News* (December 9, 2013), at **www.la downtownnews.com/news/police-crack down-on-jaywalking-means-tickets-of -up-to/article_f7ebf922-5ec6-11e3-b537 -001a4bcf887a.html.**

19. George P. Fletcher, "Some Unwise Reflections about Discretion," *Law & Contemporary Problems* (Autumn 1984), 279.

20. "ACLU Asks Justice Department to Investigate Racially-Biased Police Practices in Saginaw," *aclu.org* (September 19, 2013), at **www .aclu.org/criminal-law-reform-prisoners -rights-racial-justice/aclu-asks-justice -department-investigate.**

21. Antonin Scalia, "The Rule of Law as a Law of Rules," *University of Chicago Law Review* 56 (1989), 1178–1180.

22. John Kleinig, *Ethics and Criminal Justice: An Introduction* (New York: Cambridge University Press, 2008), 33–35.

23. Packer, *op. cit.,* 154–173.

24. Givelber, *op. cit.,* 1317.

25. Federal Bureau of Investigation, *Crime in the United States 2013* (Washington, D.C.: U.S. Department of Justice, 2014) at **www.fbi.gov /about-us/cjis/ucr/crime-in-the-u.s/2013 /crime-in-the-u.s.-2013/cius-home.**

26. James Alan Fox, quoted in Donna Leinwand Leger, "Violent Crime Rises for 2nd Year," *USA Today* (October 25–27, 2013), 1A.

27. Federal Bureau of Investigation, "Next Generation Identification," at **www.fbi.gov /about-us/cjis/fingerprints_biometrics /ngi.**

28. Jeffrey A. Rose, "The Future of Corrections: How Can Mobile Biometric Technology Revolutionize the Arrest and Booking Process?" *The Police Chief* (December 2014), 68–72.

29. *Policing and the Economic Downturn: Striving for Efficiency Is the New Normal* (Washington, D.C.: Police Executive Research Forum, February 2013), 1.

30. National Gang Center, *2011 National Youth Gang Survey Analysis* (January 15, 2014), at **www.nationalgangcenter.gov /Survey-Analysis.**

31. Centers for Disease Control and Prevention, "Press Release: CDC Study Explores Role of Drugs, Drive-by Shootings, and Other Crimes in Gang Homicides" (January 26, 2012), at **www.cdc.gov/media/releases/2012 /p0126_gang_homicides.html.**

32. Michael Planty and Jennifer L. Truman, *Firearm Violence, 1993–2011* (Washington, D.C.: U.S. Department of Justice, May 2013), 1.

33. Pew Research Center, "Fact Tank: News in the Numbers" (July 15, 2014), at **www .pewresearch.org/fact-tank/2014/07/15 /the-demographics-and-politics-of-gun -owning-households.**

34. *District of Columbia v. Heller,* 554 U.S. 570 (2008).

35. Vega and Thee-Brennan, *op. cit.,* A14.

36. Quoted in Richard A. Oppel, Jr., "National Questions over Police Hit Home in Cleveland," *New York Times* (December 9, 2014), A16.

37. Quoted in Heather Haddon, "Killing of New York Police Officers Spark Backlash to Protests," *Wall Street Journal* (December 22, 2014), A1.

38. *Report of the Sentencing Project to the United Nations Human Rights Committee: Regarding Racial Disparities in the United States Criminal*

Justice System (Washington, D.C.: The Sentencing Project, August 2013), 4.

39. *Crime in the United States 2013, op. cit.*, Table 29.

40. Office of National Drug Control Policy, *ADAM II: 2013 Annual Report* (Washington, D.C.: Executive Office of the President, January 2014), vii.

41. Lydia Saad, "Gallup: Politics" (November 6, 2014), at **www.gallup.com/poll/179195 /majority-continues-support-pot -legalization.aspx**.

42. Press Release, "College Students Use of Marijuana on the Rise, Some Drugs Declining," *Michigan News: University of Michigan* (September 5, 2014), at **www.monitoring thefuture.org//pressreleases/September 14PR.pdf**.

43. National Institute of Drug Abuse, "Teen Prescription Opioid Abuse, Cigarette, and Alcohol Use Trends Down" (December 16, 2014), at **www.drugabuse.gov/news-events /news-releases/2014/12/teen-prescription -opioid-abuse-cigarette-alcohol-use -trends-down**.

44. "Heroin's Lethal Comeback," *The Week* (February 28, 2014), 11.

45. Quoted in "9/11: Ten Years Later, How America Has Changed," *The Week* (September 16, 2011), 18.

46. Lydia Saad, "Post-Boston, Half in U.S. Anticipate More Terrorism Soon," *Gallup Politics* (April 26, 2013), at **www.gallup.com /poll/162074/post-boston-half-anticipate -terrorism-soon.aspx**.

47. Department of Homeland Security, "DHS Budget" (March 18, 2014), at **www.dhs.gov /dhs-budget**.

48. Pew Research Center for the People & the Press, "Few See Adequate Limits on NSA Surveillance Program" (July 26, 2013), at **www.people-press.org/2013/07/26/few -see-adequate-limits-on-nsa-surveillance -program**.

49. Quoted in Timothy M. Phelps, "Terrorist Threat in U.S. Declining, FBI Directory Says," *Arizona Daily Star* (November 15, 2013), A15.

50. Greg Miller and Sari Horwitz, "Blasts Point to Gaps in U.S. Counterterror System," *Chicago Tribune* (May 6, 2013), 12.

51. Anti-Defamation League, "Officers Down: Right-Wing Extremists Attacking Police at a Growing Rate" (June 9, 2014), at **blog.adl .org/extremism/officers-down-right-wing -extremists-attacking-police-at-growing -rate**.

52. Federal Bureau of Investigation, "Domestic Terrorism: The Sovereign Citizen Movement" (April 13, 2010), at **www.fbi.gov/news/stories /2010/april/sovereigncitizens_041310**.

53. Quoted in Amy Howe, "Drawing a Line Between Therapy and Threats: In Plain English," *Supreme Court of the United States Blog* (November 24, 2014), at **www.scotus blog.com/2014/11/drawing-a-line -between-therapy-and-threats-in-plain -english**.

54. Quoted in Daniel B. Wood, "James Holmes Hearing: At Last, A Chance for Victims to Testify," *Christian Science Monitor* (January 7, 2013), at **www.csmonitor.com/USA/Justice /2013/0107/James-Holmes-hearing-At -last-a-chance-for-victims-to-testify**.

55. Lois Haight Herrington et al., *President's Task Force on Victims of Crime: Final Report* (1982), at **www.ojp.usdoj.gov/ovc/publications /presdntstskforcrprt/87299.pdf**.

56. 18 U.S.C. Section 3771 (2006).

57. Susan Herman, *Parallel Justice for Victims of Crime* (Washington, D.C.: The National Center for Victims of Crime, 2010), 46–47.

58. Danielle Levine, "Public Wrongs and Private Rights: Limiting the Victim's Role in a System of Public Prosecution," 104 *Northwestern University Law Review* (2010), 335–362.

59. Bureau of Justice Statistics, *Correctional Populations in the United States*, 2013 (Washington, D.C.: U.S. Department of Justice, December 2014), Table 1, page 1.

60. Quoted in Erica Goode, "U.S. Prison Populations Decline, Reflecting New Approach to Crime," *New York Times* (July 26, 2013), A11.

61. "One Nation, Behind Bars," *The Economist* (August 17, 2013), 12.

62. Quoted in Goode, *op. cit.*

63. Death Penalty Information Center, "Size of Death Row by Year—1968 to Present," at **www .deathpenaltyinfo.org/death-row-inmates -state-and-size-death-row-year#year**.

64. *The Death Penalty in 2014: Year End Report* (Washington, D.C.: Death Penalty Information Center, December 2014), 1.

65. Death Penalty Information Center, "National Statistics on Death Penalty and Race," at **www.deathpenaltyinfo.org/race -death-rowinmates-executed-1976**.

66. Bureau of Justice Statistics, *Prisoners in 2013* (Washington, D.C.: U.S. Department of Justice, September 2014), Table 7, page 8.

67. Federal Bureau of Prisons, "Inmate Ethnicity," at **www.bop.gov/about/statistics/statistics _inmate_ethnicity.jsp**.

68. *A Guide to Mental Illness and the Criminal Justice System* (Arlington, Va.: National Alliance on Mental Illness, 1993), iii.

69. Doris J. James and Lauren E. Glaze, *Mental Health Problems of Prison and Jail Inmates* (Washington, D.C.: U.S. Department of Justice, December 2006), 1.

70. Liz Szabo, "The Cost of Not Caring," *USA Today* (May 13, 2014), 1A.

71. Quoted in *ibid.*

72. *Fact Sheet: Assertive Community Treatment* (Arlington, Va.: National Alliance on Mental Illness, September 2007), 1.

73. "Maybe Chicago's Death Toll Will Help Stop the Madness on Gun Access," *Washington Post* (July 8, 2014), at **washingtonpost .com/opinions/maybe-chicagos-death -toll-will-help-stop-the-madness-on-gun -access/2014/07/08/10b1988a-06de-11e4 -bbf1-cc51275e7f8f_story.html**.

74. Rich Lowry, "Chicago's July Fourth Shooting Spree," *National Review* (July 8, 2014), at **www.nationalreview.com/article/382164 /chicagos-july-fourth-shooting-spree -rich-lowry**.

75. *District of Columbia v. Heller* (2008); and *McDonald v. Chicago*, 561 U.S. 742 (2010).

76. Quoted in Adam Magourney, "In an Ocean of Firearms, Tucson Is Far Away," *New York Times* (January 20, 2011), A15.

77. Donna L. Hoyert and Jiaquan Xu, "Deaths: Preliminary Data for 2011" in *National Vital Reports* (Washington, D.C.: National Center for Health Statistics, October 2012), 42, 60.

78. *Crime in the United States 2013, op. cit.*, Expanded Homicide Data Table 7.

79. Michael Grunwald, "The Tucson Tragedy: Fire Away," *Time* (January 24, 2011), 38.

80. Quoted in David Nakamura and Robert Barnes, "Appeals Court Rules D.C. Handgun Ban Unconstitutional," *Washington Post* (March 10, 2007), A1.

81. Harry Wilson, quoted in David Espo and Nancy Benac, "Gun Control Agenda Seems Futile Despite Tragedies," *Arizona Daily Star* (July 22, 2012), A10.

82. Bureau of Alcohol, Tobacco, Firearms and Explosives, *Firearms Commerce in the United States 2011* (Washington, D.C.: U.S. Department of Justice, August 2011), 15.

83. National Conference of State Legislators, "Guns on Campus: Overview" (March 7, 2014), at **www.ncsl.org/research/education/guns -on-campus-overview.aspx.**

Chapter One Appendix

How to Read Case Citations and Find Court Decisions

Many important court cases are discussed throughout this book. Every time a court case is mentioned, you will be able to check its citation using the endnotes on the final pages of the chapter. Court decisions are recorded and published on paper and on the Internet. When a court case is mentioned, the notation that is used to refer to, or to *cite,* the case denotes where the published decision can be found.

Decisions of state courts of appeals are usually published in two places, the state reports of that particular state and the more widely used *National Reporter System* published by West Group. Some states no longer publish their own reports. The *National Reporter System* divides the states into the following geographic areas: Atlantic (A. or A.2d), North Eastern (N.E. or N.E.2d), North Western (N.W. or N.W.2d), Pacific (P., P.2d, or P.3d), Southern (So., So.2d, or So.3d), and South Western (S.W., S.W.2d, or S.W.3d). The 2d and 3d in these abbreviations refer to the *Second Series* and *Third Series,* respectively.

Federal trial court decisions are published unofficially in West's *Federal Supplement* (F.Supp. or F.Supp.2d), and opinions from the circuit courts of appeals are reported unofficially in West's *Federal Reporter* (F., F.2d, or F.3d). Opinions from the United States Supreme Court are reported in the *United States Reports* (U.S.), the *Lawyers' Edition of the Supreme Court Reports* (L.Ed.), West's *Supreme Court Reporter* (S.Ct.), and other publications. The *United States Reports* is the official publication of United States Supreme Court decisions. It is published by the federal government. Many early decisions are missing from these volumes. The citations of the early volumes of the United States Reports include the names of the actual reporters, such as Dallas, Cranch, or Wheaton. *McCulloch v. Maryland,* for example, is cited as 17 U.S. (4 Wheat.) 316. Only after 1874 did the present citation system, in which cases are cited based solely on their volume and page numbers in the *United States Reports,* come into being. The *Lawyers' Edition of the Supreme Court Reports* is an unofficial and more complete edition of Supreme Court decisions. West's *Supreme Court Reporter* is an unofficial edition of decisions dating from October 1882. These volumes contain headnotes and numerous brief editorial statements of the law involved in a given case.

Citations to decisions of state courts of appeals give the name of the case; the volume, name, and page number of the state's official report (if the state publishes its own reports); and the volume, unit, and page number of the *National Reporter.* Federal court citations also give the name of the case and the volume, name, and page number of the reports. In addition to the citation, this textbook lists the year of the decision in parentheses. Consider, for example, the case *Miranda v. Arizona,* 384 U.S. 436 (1966). The Supreme Court's decision in this case may be found in volume 384 of the *United States Reports* on page 436. The case was decided in 1966.

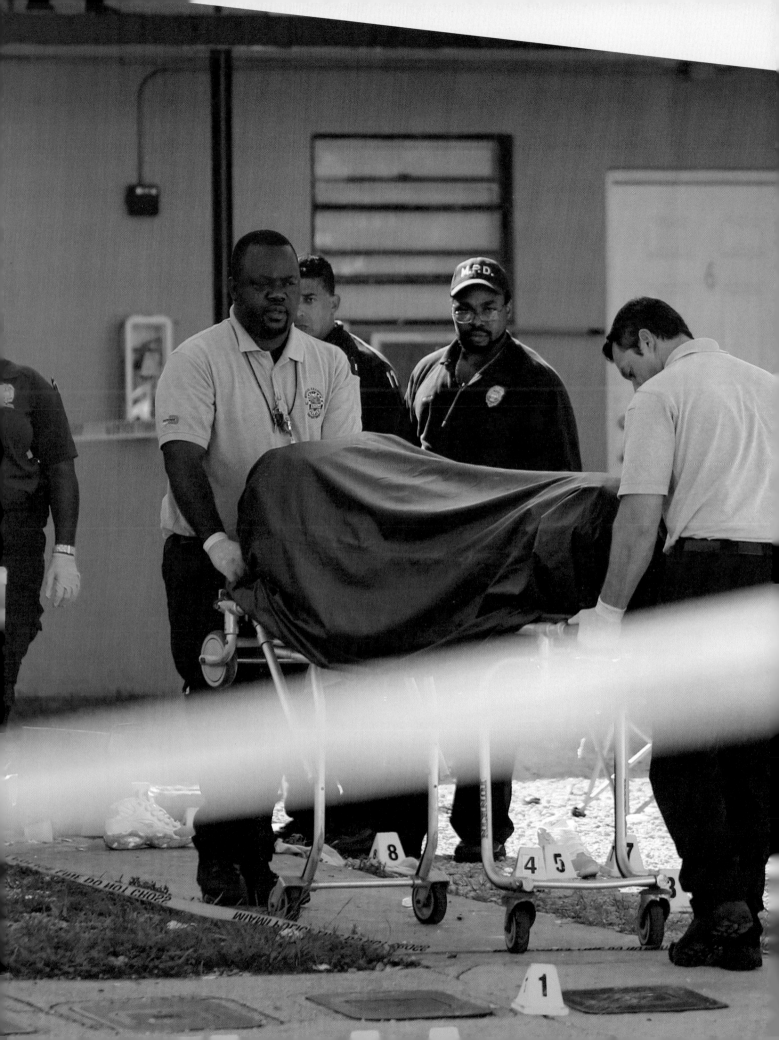

Causes of Crime

Chapter Outline		Corresponding Learning Objectives
The Role of Theory	**1**	Discuss the difference between a hypothesis and a theory in the context of criminology.
The Brain and the Body	**2**	Contrast positivism with classical criminology.
	3	Explain how brain-scanning technology is able to help scientists determine if an individual is at risk for criminal offending.
Bad Neighborhoods and Other Economic Disadvantages	**4**	List and describe the three theories of social structure that help explain crime.
	5	Describe the social conflict theory known as the social reality of crime.
Life Lessons and Criminal Behavior	**6**	List and briefly explain the three branches of social process theory.
	7	Describe the importance of early childhood behavior for those who subscribe to self-control theory.
The Link between Drugs and Crime	**8**	Contrast the medical model of addiction with the criminal model of addiction.
Criminology from Theory to Practice	**9**	Explain the theory of the chronic offender and its importance for the criminal justice system.

To target your study and review, look for these numbered Learning Objective icons throughout the chapter.

Photo by Angel Valentin/Getty Images

The **Hater**

while Elliot Rodger could be shy and withdrawn in the real world, he had no trouble expressing himself on the Internet. A self-labeled "incel," or "involuntary celibate," the twenty-two-year-old college dropout spent hours online ranting about his lack of success with the opposite sex. At one Web site, he exhorted his fellow incels to "start imagining a world where WOMEN FEAR YOU." At another, he posted a video titled "Why Do Girls Hate Me So Much?" that, according to one comment, made him look like a serial killer.

On the night of May 23, 2014, as reports of a shooting spree near the campus of the University of California, Santa Barbara, spread through the media, members of Rodger's online community speculated that he was the gunman. Their concerns were justified. Before taking his own life that night, Rodger killed six people and wounded thirteen others. Among his victims were two young women outside a sorority house. In an e-mail he sent out minutes before the carnage, Rodger vowed to kill "all those beautiful girls" that had rejected him and "make them suffer, just as they have made me suffer."

Looking back, Rodger's Internet postings were not the only warning signs of potential violence. He had been seeing therapists regularly since he was eight years old to help deal with a variety of emotional problems. Three weeks before the killings, Rodger's family contacted local law enforcement expressing concerns about his mental health. Six police officers visited Rodger's apartment to perform a "welfare check." They found Rodger "timid and polite," and concluded that there was no reason to search his home. Had they done so, they likely would have found the three semiautomatic weapons Rodger used in his rampage. "For a few horrible seconds I thought it was all over," Rodger admitted in his final e-mail. "When they left, the biggest wave of relief swept over me."

▲ Elliot Rodger, shown here in a photo released by the Santa Barbara Sheriff's Department, killed six people in Isla Vista, California, before committing suicide on May 23, 2014.

Robyn Beck/AFP/Getty Images

1. Many people post violent views on the Internet. At what point, if any, should these views alone allow law enforcement to take the poster into custody?

2. Given what they knew of the situation, should the police officers have searched Elliot Rodger's apartment? Why do you think they failed to do so?

3. Some experts have suggested that a psychiatric nurse accompany the police on all calls involving suspects with potential mental health problems. What are the pros and cons of this strategy?

The Role of Theory

The study of crime, or **criminology,** is rich with different explanations for why people commit crimes. At the same time, *criminologists,* or those who study the causes of crime, warn against using models or profiles to predict violent behavior. After all, not every sexually frustrated and depressed young man who spends an inordinate amount of time venting on the Internet should be treated as a future multiple-victim shooter. Most people with the same behavior patterns as Elliot Rodger "never act out in a violent way," says J. Reid Meloy, an editor at the *International Handbook of Threat Assessment.* "You can't predict who will or who won't."[1]

Still, in the case of Elliot Rodger, there did seem to be some connection between his characteristics and his violent outburst, particularly when one considers that he may have been suffering from mental illness. That is, there may have been a *correlation* between his behavior and his crimes, a concept that is crucial to criminology.

Correlation and Cause

Correlation between two variables means that they tend to vary together. **Causation,** in contrast, means that one variable is responsible for the change in the other. As we will see later in the chapter, there is a correlation between drug abuse and criminal behavior: statistically, many criminals are also drug abusers. But drug abuse does not cause crime: not everyone who abuses drugs is a criminal.

To give another example, a recent study led by Scott Wolfe, a criminologist at the University of South Carolina, looked at crime rates in counties where the megastore Walmart added new stores during the 1990s. Wolfe and his co-author found that crime rates in those counties were significantly higher than in those neighboring counties with no Walmart expansion.[2] Despite these results, few criminologists would assert that new Walmart stores *caused* the higher crime rates. Other factors, such as unemployment, poverty, and zoning patterns, must also be taken into account to get a fuller understanding of the crime picture in the studied areas.

So, correlation does not equal cause. Such is the quandary for criminologists. We can say that there is a correlation between many factors and criminal behavior, but it is quite difficult to prove that the factors directly cause criminal behavior. Consequently, the question that is the underpinning of criminology—What causes crime?—has yet to be definitively answered.

Criminological Theories

Criminologists have, however, uncovered a wealth of information concerning a different, and more practically applicable, inquiry: Given a certain set of circumstances, why do individuals commit criminal acts? This information has allowed criminologists to develop a number of *theories* concerning the causes of crime.

The Scientific Method Most of us tend to think of a *theory* as some sort of guess or a statement that is lacking in credibility. In the academic world, and therefore for our purposes, a **theory** is an explanation of a happening or circumstance that is based on observation, experimentation, and reasoning. Scientific and academic researchers observe facts and their consequences to develop *hypotheses* about what will occur when a similar fact pattern is present in the future. A **hypothesis** is a proposition that can be tested by researchers or observers to determine if it is valid. If enough authorities do find the hypothesis valid, it will be accepted as a theory. See Figure 2.1 for an

Criminology The scientific study of crime and the causes of criminal behavior.

Correlation The relationship between two measurements or behaviors that tend to move in the same direction.

Causation The relationship in which a change in one measurement or behavior creates a recognizable change in another measurement or behavior.

Theory An explanation of a happening or circumstance that is based on observation, experimentation, and reasoning.

Hypothesis A possible explanation for an observed occurrence that can be tested by further investigation.

 LEARNING OBJECTIVE **1** Discuss the difference between a hypothesis and a theory in the context of criminology.

FIGURE 2.1 The Scientific Method

The scientific method is a process through which researchers test the accuracy of a hypothesis. This simple example should provide an idea of how the scientific method works.

 Observation: I left my home at 7:00 this morning, and I was on time for class.

 Hypothesis: If I leave home at 7:00 every morning, then I will never be late for class. (Hypotheses are often presented in this "If . . . , then . . ." format.)

 Test: For three straight weeks, I left home at 7:00 every morning. Not one time was I late for class.

 Verification: Four of my neighbors have the same morning class. They agree that they are never late if they leave by 7:00 A.M.

 Theory: As long as I leave home at 7:00 A.M., I don't have to worry about being late for class.

 Prediction: Tomorrow morning I'll leave at 7:00, and I will be on time for my class.

Note that even a sound theory supported by the scientific method, such as this one, does not *prove* that the prediction will be correct. Other factors not accounted for in the test and verification stages, such as an unexpected traffic accident, may disprove the theory. Predictions based on complex theories, such as the criminological ones we will be discussing in this chapter, are often challenged in such a manner.

example of this process, known as the *scientific method,* in action.

Theory in Action Criminological theories are primarily concerned with attempting to determine the reasons for criminal behavior. For example, two criminologists from Arizona State University, Matthew Larson and Gary Sweeten, wanted to test their hypothesis that young people involved in romantic breakups are at high risk for destructive behavior. Relying on a survey of high school and college students who were asked about issues in their personal lives, Larson and Sweeten found some support for their hypothesis. According to the data, breakups do indeed correlate with higher rates of criminal offending and substance abuse among young men and higher rates of substance abuse among young women.[3]

The Brain and the Body

As you read this chapter, keep in mind that theories are not the same as facts, and most, if not all, of the criminological theories described in these pages have their detractors. Over the past century, however, a number of theories of crime have gained wide, if not total, acceptance. We now turn our attention to these theories, starting with those that focus on the psychological and physical aspects of criminal behavior.

Crime and Free Will: Choice Theories of Crime

For the purposes of the American criminal justice system, the answer to why a person commits a crime is rather straightforward: because that person chooses to do so. This application of **choice theory** to criminal law is not absolute. If a defendant can prove that she or he lacked the ability to make a rational choice, in certain circumstances the defendant will not be punished as harshly for a crime as would normally be the case. But such allowances are relatively recent. From the early days of this country, the general presumption in criminal law has been that behavior is a consequence of free will.

Theories of Classical Criminology An emphasis on free will and human rationality in the realm of criminal behavior has its roots in **classical criminology.** Classical theorists believed that crime was an expression of a person's rational decision-making process: before committing a crime, a person would weigh the benefits of the crime against the costs of being apprehended. Therefore, if punishments were stringent enough to outweigh the benefits of crime, they would dissuade people from committing the crime in the first place.

The earliest popular expression of classical theory came in 1764 when the Italian Cesare Beccaria (1738–1794) published his *Essays on Crime and Punishments.* Beccaria

Choice Theory A school of criminology based on the belief that individuals have free will to engage in any behavior, including criminal behavior.

Classical Criminology A school of criminology that holds that wrongdoers act as if they weigh the possible benefits of criminal or delinquent activity against the expected costs of being apprehended.

criticized existing systems of criminal law as irrational and argued that criminal procedures should be more consistent with human behavior. He believed that, to be just, criminal law should reflect three truths:

1. All decisions, including the decision to commit a crime, are the result of rational choice.
2. Fear of punishment can have a deterrent effect on the choice to commit crime.
3. The more swift and certain punishment is, the more effective it will be in controlling crime.[4]

Beccaria believed that any punishment that purported to do anything other than deter crime was cruel and arbitrary.

Positivism and Modern Rational Theory

By the end of the 1800s, the positivist school of criminologists had superseded classical criminology. According to **positivism,** criminal behavior is determined by biological, psychological, and social forces and is beyond the control of the individual. The Italian physician Cesare Lombroso (1835–1909), an early adherent of positivism who is known as the "Father of Criminology," believed that criminals were throwbacks to the savagery of early humankind and could therefore be identified by certain physical characteristics such as sharp teeth and large jaws. He also theorized that criminality was similar to mental illness and could be genetically passed down from generation to generation in families that had cases of insanity, syphilis, epilepsy, and even deafness. Such individuals, according to Lombroso and his followers, had no free choice when it came to wrongdoing—their criminality had been predetermined at birth.[5]

Positivist theory lost credibility as crime rates began to climb in the 1970s. If crime was caused by external factors, critics asked, why had the proactive social programs of the 1960s not brought about a decrease in criminal activity? An updated version of classical criminology, known as *rational choice theory,* found renewed acceptance. James Q. Wilson (1931–2012), one of the most prominent critics of the positivist school, summed up rational choice theory as follows:

> At any given moment, a person can choose between committing a crime and not committing it. The consequences of committing a crime consist of rewards (what psychologists call "reinforcers") and punishments; the consequences of not committing the crime also entail gains and losses. The larger the ratio of the net rewards of crime to the net rewards of [not committing a crime], the greater the tendency to commit a crime.[6]

In other words, a person, before committing a crime, acts as if she or he is weighing the benefits (which may be money, in the case of a robbery) against the costs (the possibility of being caught and going to prison or jail). If the perceived benefits are greater than the potential costs, the person is more likely to commit the crime.

"Thrill Offenders"

Expanding on rational choice theory, sociologist Jack Katz has stated that the "rewards" of crime may be sensual as well as financial. The inherent danger of criminal activity, according to Katz, increases the "rush" a criminal experiences on successfully committing a crime. Katz labels the rewards of this "rush" the *seduction of crime.*[7] For example, one of the three teenagers charged with randomly and fatally shooting a jogger in Duncan, Oklahoma, several years ago told police that he and his friends were "bored and didn't have anything to do, so we killed somebody."[8] Katz believes that such seemingly "senseless" crimes can be explained by rational choice theory only if the intrinsic (inner) reward of the crime itself is considered.

LEARNING **2** OBJECTIVE Contrast positivism with classical criminology.

Positivism A school of the social sciences that sees criminal and delinquent behavior as the result of biological, psychological, and social forces.

▲ Chancey Luna, standing, and Michael Jones, sitting, are two of the three "bored" teenagers charged with fatally shooting Australian Christopher Lane in Duncan, Oklahoma, on August 16, 2013. **How is the assumption that some people commit crimes for the "thrill of it" consistent with rational choice theory?** AP Images/ Sue Ogrocki

Choice Theory and Public Policy The theory that wrongdoers choose to commit crimes is a cornerstone of the American criminal justice system. Because crime is seen as the end result of a series of rational choices, policymakers have reasoned that severe punishment can deter criminal activity by adding another variable to the decision-making process. Supporters of the death penalty—now used by thirty-one states and the federal government—emphasize its deterrent effects, and legislators have used harsh mandatory sentences to control illegal drug use and trafficking.

"Born Criminal": Biological and Psychological Theories of Crime

As we have seen, Cesare Lombroso believed in the "criminal born" man and woman and was confident that he could distinguish criminals by their apelike physical features. Such far-fetched notions have long been relegated to scientific oblivion. Nevertheless, many criminologists do believe that *trait theories* have validity. These theories suggest that certain *biological* or *psychological* traits in individuals could incline them toward criminal behavior given a certain set of circumstances. **Biology** is a very broad term that refers to the scientific study of living organisms, while **psychology** pertains more specifically to the study of the mind and its processes. "All behavior is biological," pointed out geneticist David C. Rowe. "All behavior is represented in the brain, in its biochemistry, electrical activity, structure, and growth and decline."[9]

Genetics and Crime Criminologists who study biological theories of crime often focus on the effect that *genes* have on human behavior. Genes are coded sequences of DNA that control every aspect of our biology, from the color of our eyes and hair to the type of emotions we have. Every person's genetic makeup is determined by genes inherited from his or her parents. Consequently, when scientists study ancestral or evolutionary developments, they are engaging in **genetics,** a branch of biology that deals with traits that are passed from one generation to another through genes.

Twin and Adoption Studies Genetics is at the heart of criminology's "nurture versus nature" debate. In other words, are traits such as aggressiveness and antisocial behavior, both of which often lead to criminality, a result of a person's environment (nurture) or her or his genes (nature)? To tip the balance toward "nature," a criminologist must be able to prove that, all other things being equal, the offspring of aggressive or antisocial parents are at risk to exhibit those same traits.

Many criminologists have turned to *twin studies* to determine the relationship between genetics and criminal behavior. If the "nature" argument is correct, then twins should exhibit similar antisocial tendencies. The problem with twin studies is that most twins grow up in the same environment, so it is difficult, if not impossible, to determine whether their behavior is influenced by their genes or by their surroundings.[10] Because of the inconsistencies of twin studies, some criminologists have turned to *adoption studies,* which eliminate the problem of family members sharing the same environment.

Biology The science of living organisms, including their structure, function, growth, and origin.

Psychology The scientific study of mental processes and behavior.

Genetics The study of how certain traits or qualities are transmitted from parents to their offspring.

A number of well-received adoption studies have shown a correlation between rates of criminality among adopted children and antisocial or criminal behavior by their biological parents.[11]

The "Crime Gene" About twenty years ago, Dutch scientists claimed to have determined that males who possessed a mutant copy of the MAOA gene were abnormally aggressive.[12] Dubbed the "warrior gene," MAOA suddenly became the center of a great deal of criminological attention. Additional research, however, proved that this genetic mutation does not, by itself, lead to criminal behavior. Rather, a person with low levels of MAOA, which regulates emotion, exhibits an increased risk for violent behavior only when that person was also abused as a child.[13]

A 2014 study of nearly 900 prison inmates in Finland did find that those with a combination of mutated MAOA and another gene called CDH13 were strongly linked to "extremely violent behavior," defined as at least ten murders, attempted murders, or other attacks.[14] Keep in mind, however, that no single gene or trait has been proved to *cause* criminality. The lead author of the just-mentioned Finland study said that combination of the two genes increased only the "relative" risk of violent behavior. "The absolute risk is still very low," he cautioned.[15] The most that genetics can do, it seems, is raise the possibility for a predisposition toward aggression or violence in an individual based on her or his family background.

Hormones and Aggression Chemical messengers known as **hormones** have also been the subject of much criminological study. Criminal activity in males has been linked to elevated levels of hormones—specifically, **testosterone,** which controls secondary sex characteristics and has been associated with traits of aggression. Testing of inmate populations shows that those incarcerated for violent crimes exhibit higher testosterone levels than other prisoners.[16] Elevated testosterone levels have also been used to explain the age-crime relationship, as the average testosterone level of men under the age of twenty-eight is double that of men between thirty-one and sixty-six years old.[17]

A very specific form of female violent behavior is believed to stem from hormones. In 2014, Inakesha Armour was charged with attempted murder for throwing her three-month-old baby into a lake in Miramar, Florida. Armour's defense attorney claimed his client was suffering from *postpartum psychosis* at the time of her alleged crime. This temporary illness, believed to be caused partly by the hormonal changes that women experience after childbirth, triggers abnormal behavior in a small percentage of new mothers.[18]

The Brain and Crime Dr. Margaret Spinelli, a women's health expert at New York City's Columbia University, explains that during pregnancy, a pregnant woman's hormones increase "more than a hundredfold." Then, following birth, hormone levels plummet. This roller coaster of hormonal activity can "disrupt brain chemistry," contributing to postpartum psychosis.[19] The study of how genetics and brain activity influence criminal behavior is called *neurocriminology*. Its practitioners have contributed a great deal to the understanding of what predisposes humans to violent behavior.

Neurocriminology in Action Neurocriminology is based on the theory that criminal behavior is often the result of a combination of biological and environmental risk factors. For example, Jessica Wolpaw Reyes, an economist at Amherst College in Massachusetts, focused on the risks posed by lead to help explain the drop in crime rates over the past two decades, mentioned in the previous chapter.

Hormone A chemical substance, produced in tissue and conveyed in the bloodstream, that controls certain cellular and body functions such as growth and reproduction.

Testosterone The hormone primarily responsible for the production of sperm and the development of male secondary sex characteristics such as the growth of facial and pubic hair and the change of voice pitch.

Numerous studies have shown that exposure to lead damages the brains of children, causing them to have lower IQs, less impulse control, and a propensity for violent behavior. In the late 1970s, the federal government banned lead in gasoline and many types of paint. A generation of lead-free children has reached adulthood since then, and, Reyes believes, its nonviolent tendencies are responsible for half of the recent drop in violent crime rates.[20]

Mental Illness and Crime As we also mentioned in the previous chapter, more than half of all prison and jail inmates in the United States have mental health problems, with smaller percentages suffering from severe brain disorders.[21] In recent years, thanks to several high-profile murders, violent crime has been linked to *schizophrenia*, a chronic brain disorder that can lead to erratic, uncontrollable behavior. Persons suffering from this disease are at an unusually high risk for committing suicide or harming others. Psychiatrist E. Fuller Torrey estimates that schizophrenics commit about a thousand homicides each year.[22]

Further research shows that even moderate use of alcohol or drugs increases the chances that a schizophrenic will behave violently.[23] Still, it is important to note that about 3.5 million Americans—1 percent of the adult population—have been diagnosed with schizophrenia, and the vast majority of them will never become criminal offenders. Overall, according to Richard Friedman, a professor of clinical psychiatry at New York's Weill Cornell Medical College, only about 4 percent of violence in the United States can be attributed to those with mental illnesses.[24] Consequently, there may be a correlation between mental conditions such as schizophrenia and violence, but such conditions cannot be said to cause violent behavior.

CJ & Technology

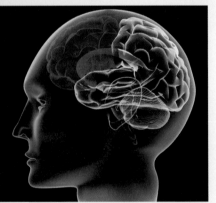

Yakobchuk Vasyl/ShutterStock.com

LEARNING OBJECTIVE **3** Explain how brain-scanning technology is able to help scientists determine if an individual is at risk for criminal offending.

Brain Science and Crime

Using various techniques, from X-ray technology to magnetic resonance imaging (MRI) to measuring oxygen flow, specialists have become quite skilled at mapping the human brain. Among other uses, these approaches can identify functional abnormalities and physical deformities in the brain that correlate with violent behavior.

For example, violent criminals tend to have impaired prefrontal cortexes—the part of the brain that manages our impulses and emotions. Furthermore, brain scanning shows that criminal behavior is often associated with a smaller-than-average amygdala, a cranial region that has been linked to moral decision making. Finally, Kent Kiehl of the University of New Mexico recently mapped the brains of ninety-six offenders in the state's prison system. Kiehl found that, in the four years after these men had been released from prison, those with low activity in the anterior cingulate cortex were twice as likely to commit a crime as those with high activity in this area of the brain.

Thinking about Brain Science and Crime

Brain scans cannot *predict* future criminal offending. They can only indicate a *possibility* of future criminal offending. With this proviso in mind, what use should the criminal justice system make of brain mapping technology, if any?

Psychology and Crime Like biological theories of crime, psychological theories of crime operate under the assumption that individuals have traits that make them more or less predisposed to criminal activity. To a certain extent, however, psychology rests more heavily on abstract ideas than does biology. Even Sigmund Freud (1856–1939), perhaps the most influential of all psychologists, considered the operations of the mind to be, like an iceberg, mostly hidden.

Freud's Psychoanalytic Theory For all his accomplishments, Freud rarely turned his attention directly toward the causes of crime. His **psychoanalytic theory,** however, has provided a useful approach for thinking about criminal behavior. According to Freud, most of our thoughts, wishes, and urges originate in the *unconscious* region of the mind, and we have no control—or even awareness of—these processes. Freud believed that, on an unconscious level, all humans have criminal tendencies and that each of us is continually struggling against these tendencies.

To explain this struggle, Freud devised three abstract systems that interact in the brain: the *id,* the *ego,* and the *superego.* The id is driven by a constant desire for pleasure and self-gratification through sexual and aggressive urges. The ego, in contrast, stands for reason and common sense, while the superego "learns" the expectations of family and society and acts as the conscience. When the three systems fall into disorder, the id can take control, causing the individual to act on his or her antisocial urges and, possibly, commit crimes.[25]

Social Psychology and "Evil" Behavior Another crucial branch of psychology—*social psychology*—focuses on human behavior in the context of how human beings relate to and influence one another. Social psychology rests on the assumption that the way we view ourselves is shaped to a large degree by how we think others view us. Generally, we act in the same manner as those we like or admire because we want them to like or admire us. Thus, to a certain extent, social psychology tries to explain the influence of crowds on individual behavior.

About three decades ago, psychologist Philip Zimbardo highlighted the power of group behavior in dramatic fashion. Zimbardo randomly selected some Stanford University undergraduate students to act as "guards" and other students to act as "inmates" in an artificial prison environment. Before long, the students began to act as if these designations were real, with the "guards" physically mistreating the "inmates," who rebelled with equal violence. Within six days, Zimbardo was forced to discontinue the experiment out of fear for its participants' safety.[26] One of the basic assumptions of social psychology is that people are able to justify improper or even criminal behavior by convincing themselves that it is actually acceptable behavior. This delusion, researchers have found, is much easier to accomplish with the support of others behaving in the same manner.[27]

Psychoanalytic Theory Sigmund Freud's theory that attributes our thoughts and actions to unconscious motives.

▼ On November 25, 2014, a firefighter surveys the rubble of a strip mall in Ferguson, Missouri. An angry crowd destroyed the property after learning that a local white police officer would not face criminal charges for killing an African American suspect. **How does social psychology explain acts of violence or disorder by large groups of people?** Scott Olson/Getty Images

Trait Theory and Public Policy Whereas choice theory justifies punishing wrongdoers, biological and psychological views of criminality suggest that antisocial behavior should be identified and treated before it manifests itself in first-time or further criminal activity. Though the focus on treatment diminished somewhat in the 1990s, rehabilitation practices in corrections have made somewhat of a comeback over the past decade. The primary motivation for this new outlook, as we will see in Chapters 11 through 14, is the pressing need to divert nonviolent offenders from the nation's overburdened prison and jail system.

EthicsChallenge

Suppose that a woman who harmed or even killed her newborn baby could be proven to be suffering from postpartum psychosis, as described in this section. Would it be ethical to punish her for a criminal act that she may not have had control over? Do you agree with the prosecutor who said, "The mere fact that you have a mental condition is not an excuse for a criminal act"? Explain your answer. ■

Bad Neighborhoods and Other Economic Disadvantages

For decades, the neighborhood of Liberty City in Miami, Florida, has endured one hardship after another. In the 1980s, it was racked by riots. In the 1990s, it was decimated by crack cocaine and AIDS. In the first decade of the 2000s, it was burdened by recession. Today, the area is marked by high levels of poverty, unemployment, and—not surprisingly—crime. After fifteen people were recently wounded during a shootout at a local nightclub, one resident reacted with resignation. "It's a shame," he said. "You hear gunshots every night and every day, and it becomes the norm."[28] Indeed, criminologists focusing on **sociology** have long argued that neighborhood conditions are perhaps the most important variable in predicting criminal behavior.

Sociological Theories of Crime

The problem with trait theory, many criminologists contend, is that it falters when confronted with certain crime patterns. Why is the crime rate in Liberty City so much higher than in other parts of Miami? Are its residents more likely to have abnormal brain activity or higher levels of testosterone? As no evidence has been found that would suggest that such biological factors can be easily influenced by the grid of a map, several generations of criminologists have instead focused on social and physical environmental factors in their study of criminal behavior.

The Chicago School The importance of sociology in the study of criminal behavior was established by a group of scholars who were associated with the Sociology Department at the University of Chicago in the early 1900s. These sociologists, known collectively as the Chicago School, gathered empirical evidence from the slums of the city that showed a correlation between conditions of poverty, such as inadequate housing and poor sanitation, and high rates of crime. Chicago School members Ernest Burgess (1886–1966) and Robert Ezra Park (1864–1944) argued that neighborhood conditions, be they of wealth or poverty, had a much greater determinant effect on criminal behavior than ethnicity, race, or religion.[29] The methods and theories of the Chicago School, which

Sociology The study of the development and functioning of groups of people who live together within a society.

stressed that humans are social creatures whose behavior reflects their environment, have had a profound effect on criminology over the past century.

The study of crime as correlated with social structure revolves around three specific theories: (1) social disorganization theory, (2) strain theory, and (3) cultural deviance theory.

Social Disorganization Theory Studies have shown that neighborhoods with high concentrations of liquor stores and payday lenders tend to have abnormally high levels of crime.[30] Again, to revisit a theme of this chapter, these studies do not suggest that such businesses cause crime. Rather, the availability of "take-away" alcohol and cash reflects other problems in the neighborhoods that have a more direct relationship to criminality.

 LEARNING **4** OBJECTIVE — List and describe the three theories of social structure that help explain crime.

The theory that crime is largely a product of unfavorable conditions in certain communities was popularized by Clifford Shaw and Henry McKay, contemporaries of the Chicago School mentioned previously.[31] Shaw and McKay's influence is shown in the widespread acceptance of **social disorganization theory** in contemporary criminology.

Disorganized Zones Studying juvenile delinquency in Chicago, Shaw and McKay discovered certain "zones" that exhibited high rates of crime. These zones were characterized by "disorganization," or a breakdown of the traditional institutions of social control such as family, school systems, and local businesses. In contrast, in the city's "organized" communities, residents had developed certain agreements about fundamental values and norms. Shaw and McKay found that residents in high-crime neighborhoods had to a large degree abandoned these fundamental values and norms. Also, a lack of social controls had led to increased levels of antisocial, or criminal, behavior.[32] According to social disorganization theory, factors that lead to crime in these neighborhoods are:

1. High levels of high school dropouts
2. Chronic unemployment
3. Deteriorating buildings and other infrastructures
4. Concentrations of single-parent families

(See Figure 2.2 to better understand social disorganization theory.)

The Value of Role Models In the late 1990s, sociologist Elijah Anderson of the University of Pennsylvania took Shaw and McKay's theories one step further. According to Anderson, residents in high-crime, African American "disorganized" zones separate themselves into two types of families: "street" and "decent." "Street" families are characterized by a lack of consideration for others and poorly disciplined children. In contrast, "decent" families are community minded, instill values of hard work and education in their children, and generally have "hope for the future."[33]

Spending time in these disadvantaged areas, Anderson discovered that most "decent" families included an older man who held a steady job, performed his duties as husband and father, and was interested in the community's well-being. When external factors such as racial discrimination and lack of employment opportunities reduce the presence of these traditional role models, Anderson theorizes, "street" codes fill the void and youth violence escalates.[34] In a study released several years ago, criminologists Eric A. Stewart and Ronald L. Simons tested Anderson's theories. They studied the behavior of more than seven hundred African American adolescents and found that, indeed, in

Social Disorganization Theory The theory that deviant behavior is more likely in communities where social institutions such as the family, schools, and the criminal justice system fail to exert control over the population.

FIGURE 2.2 The Stages of Social Disorganization Theory

Social disorganization theory holds that crime is related to the environmental pressures that exist in certain communities or neighborhoods. These areas are marked by the desire of many of their inhabitants to "get out" at the first possible opportunity. Consequently, residents tend to ignore the important institutions in the community, such as businesses and education, causing further erosion and an increase in the conditions that lead to crime.

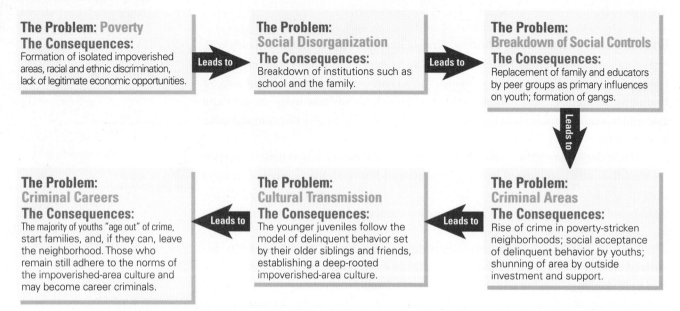

The Problem: Poverty
The Consequences:
Formation of isolated impoverished areas, racial and ethnic discrimination, lack of legitimate economic opportunities.

Leads to

The Problem: Social Disorganization
The Consequences:
Breakdown of institutions such as school and the family.

Leads to

The Problem: Breakdown of Social Controls
The Consequences:
Replacement of family and educators by peer groups as primary influences on youth; formation of gangs.

Leads to

The Problem: Criminal Careers
The Consequences:
The majority of youths "age out" of crime, start families, and, if they can, leave the neighborhood. Those who remain still adhere to the norms of the impoverished-area culture and may become career criminals.

Leads to

The Problem: Cultural Transmission
The Consequences:
The younger juveniles follow the model of delinquent behavior set by their older siblings and friends, establishing a deep-rooted impoverished-area culture.

Leads to

The Problem: Criminal Areas
The Consequences:
Rise of crime in poverty-stricken neighborhoods; social acceptance of delinquent behavior by youths; shunning of area by outside investment and support.

Source: Adapted from Larry J. Siegel, *Criminology,* 10th ed. (Belmont, CA: Thomson/Wadsworth, 2009), 180.

---

disorganized neighborhoods where a violent street culture dominates, juveniles are much more likely to commit acts of violent delinquency.[35]

Strain Theory Another self-perpetuating aspect of disorganized neighborhoods is that once residents gain the financial means to leave a high-crime community, they usually do so. This desire to escape the inner city is related to the second branch of social structure theory: **strain theory.** Most Americans have similar life goals, which include gaining a certain measure of wealth and financial freedom. The means of attaining these goals, however, are not universally available. Many citizens do not have access to the education or training necessary for financial success. This often results in frustration and anger, or *strain.*

Strain theory has its roots in the works of French sociologist Emile Durkheim (1858–1917) and his concept of *anomie* (derived from the Greek word for "without norms"). Durkheim believed that *anomie* resulted when social change threw behavioral norms into a flux, leading to a weakening of social controls and an increase in deviant behavior.[36] Another sociologist, American Robert K. Merton, expanded on Durkheim's ideas in his own theory of strain. Merton believed that *anomie* was caused by a social structure in which all citizens have similar goals without equal means to achieve them.[37] One way to alleviate this strain is to gain wealth by the means that are available to the residents of disorganized communities: drug trafficking, burglary, and other criminal activities.

In the 1990s, Robert Agnew of Emory University in Atlanta, Georgia, updated this line of criminology with his *general strain theory,* or GST.[38] Agnew reasoned that of all "strained" individuals, very few actually turn to crime to relieve the strain. GST tries to determine what factors, when combined with strain, actually lead to criminal activity. By the early 2000s, Agnew and other criminologists settled on the factor of negative

Strain Theory The assumption that crime is the result of frustration felt by individuals who cannot reach their financial and personal goals through legitimate means.

Anomie A condition in which the individual feels a disconnect from society due to the breakdown or absence of social norms.

Robert Agnew
Criminologist

When I first became interested in criminology, my research led me to "strain" or *anomie* theories that said when a person stumbles in achieving financial success or middle-class status due to social factors beyond his or her control, he or she may turn to crime. While strain theory made a lot of sense to me, I felt that the theory was incomplete. When I looked around me, it was easy to spot other sources of frustration and anger, such as harassment by peers, conflict with parents or romantic partners, poor grades in school, or poor working conditions.

I outlined sources of strain as the loss of "positively valued stimuli" such as romantic relationships, or the threat of "negatively valued stimuli" such as an insult or physical assault. I also pointed out that monetary success was just one among many "positively valued goals" that might cause strain when not achieved. Furthermore, I noted that people who experience strain may turn to crime for several reasons—crime might allow them to achieve their monetary and status goals, protect positively valued stimuli, escape negative stimuli, achieve revenge against wrongs, or simply deal with the strain (such as taking drugs to forget problems). I drew on these observations and my own experiences to develop a new "general strain theory."

> **SOCIAL MEDIA CAREER TIP** Find groups on Facebook and LinkedIn in which people are discussing the criminal justice career or careers that interest you. Participate in the discussions to get information and build contacts.

FASTFACTS

**Criminologist
Job description:**

- Work for local, state, and federal governments, on policy advisory boards, or for legislative committees. In some cases, he or she may work for privately funded think tanks or for a criminal justice or law enforcement agency. Most often, employment as a criminologist will be through a college or university, where both teaching and research will be conducted.

What kind of training is required?

- An advanced degree is required. Specifically, some combination of degrees in criminology, criminal justice, sociology, or psychology is preferable. Graduate level education is a must for any research position.

Annual salary range?

- $40,000–$122,000

---

emotionality, a term used to cover personality traits of those who are easily frustrated, quick to lose their tempers, and disposed to blame others for their own problems.[39] Thus, GST mixes strain theory with aspects of psychological theories of crime.

Cultural Deviance Theory Combining elements of social disorganization and strain theories, **cultural deviance theory** asserts that people adapt to the values of the subculture to which they belong. A **subculture** (a subdivision that exists within the dominant culture) has its own standards of behavior, or norms. By definition, a disorganized neighborhood is isolated from society at large, and the strain of this isolation encourages the formation of subcultures within its borders. According to cultural deviance theory, members of low-income subcultures are more likely to conform to value systems that celebrate behavior, such as violence, that directly confronts the value system of society at large and therefore draws criminal sanctions.

Social Structure Theory and Public Policy If criminal behavior can be explained by the conditions in which certain groups of people live, then it stands to reason that changing those conditions can prevent crime. Indeed, government programs to decrease unemployment, reduce poverty, and improve educational facilities in low-income neighborhoods have been justified as part of large-scale attempts at crime prevention.

Cultural Deviance Theory
A branch of social structure theory based on the assumption that members of certain subcultures reject the values of the dominant culture by exhibiting deviant behavior patterns.

Subculture A group exhibiting certain values and behavior patterns that distinguish it from the dominant culture.

Social Conflict Theories

Strain theory and the concept of *anomie* seem to suggest that the unequal structure of our society is, in part, to blame for criminal behavior. This argument forms the bedrock of **social conflict theories** of crime. These theories, which entered mainstream criminology in the 1960s, hold capitalism responsible for high levels of violence and crime because of the disparity of income that it encourages.

Marxism versus Capitalism The genesis of social conflict theory can be found in the political philosophy of a German named Karl Marx (1818–1883). Marx believed that capitalist economic systems necessarily produce income inequality and lead to the exploitation of the working classes.[40] Consequently, social conflict theory is often associated with a critique of our capitalist economic system. Capitalism is seen as leading to high levels of violence and crime because of the disparity of income that results. The poor commit property crimes for reasons of need and because, as members of a capitalist society, they desire the same financial rewards as everybody else. They commit violent crimes because of the frustration and rage they feel when these rewards seem unattainable.

Describe the social conflict theory known as the social reality of crime.

LEARNING 5 OBJECTIVE

It is important to note that, according to social conflict theory, power is not synonymous with wealth. Women and members of minority groups can be wealthy and yet still be disassociated from the benefits of power in our society. Richard Quinney, one of the most influential social conflict theorists of the past forty years, incorporates issues of race, gender, power, and crime in a theory known as the **social reality of crime**.[41] For Quinney, along with many of his peers, criminal law does not reflect a universal moral code, but instead is a set of "rules" through which those who hold power can control and subdue those who do not. Any conflict between the "haves" and the "have-nots," therefore, is bound to be decided in favor of the "haves," who make the law and control the criminal justice system. Following this reasoning, Quinney sees violations of the law not as inherently criminal acts, but rather as political ones—as revolutionary acts against the power of the state.

Patterns of Social Justice Those who perceive the criminal justice system as an instrument of social control point to a number of historical studies and statistics to support their argument. In the nineteenth century, nearly three-quarters of female inmates had been incarcerated for sexual misconduct. They were sent to institutions such as New York's Western House of Refuge at Albion to be taught the virtues of "true" womanhood.[42] Today, about two-thirds of the approximately 42,000 Americans arrested for prostitution each year are women.[43] After the Civil War (1861–1865), many African Americans were driven from the South by "Jim Crow laws" designed to keep them from attaining power in the postwar period. Today, the criminal justice system performs a similar function. One out of every ten black men in their thirties is in prison or jail on any given day,[44] and African American males are incarcerated at about 6.3 times the rate of white males.[45]

Issues of Race and Ethnicity Many Americans were taken aback by the intensity of the local protests in response to the August 2014 shooting of an unarmed African American teenager by a white police officer in Ferguson, Missouri. Residents of St. Louis—where Ferguson is located—were less surprised, given frustration in

Social Conflict Theories
A school of criminology that views criminal behavior as the result of class conflict.

Social Reality of Crime The theory that criminal laws are designed by those in power to help them keep power at the expense of those who do not have power.

the black community over the *segregation*, or the separation of the races, in the city. Indeed, in St. Louis the phenomenon even has a name: the Delmar Divide, for a major four-lane road called Delmar Boulevard. The area south of Delmar is 70 percent white and relatively wealthy. The area north of Delmar is 99 percent African American and marked by much higher levels of poverty and crime.[46]

Some residents south of the divide voluntarily pay higher taxes that cover the costs of hiring off-duty police officers to patrol the area. The unstated goal of this increased police presence, believe many of St. Louis's African Americans, is to keep them out of the neighborhood.[47] For social conflict experts, such efforts are an example of *racial threat theory* in action. This theory is based on the hypothesis that, as minority groups increase in population and expand geographically, the majority group employs the criminal justice system to oppress those minority groups.[48]

Racial threat theory is also applied in the context of Hispanic Americans, the largest minority group in the United States. In 2006, for example, the city of Hazleton, Pennsylvania, passed an ordinance that made it illegal to rent local housing to certain immigrants. City officials justified the ordinance, in part, as a response to rising crime rates caused by an influx of undocumented Mexicans.[49] The ordinance's constitutional flaws doomed it in federal court,[50] but it was also based on faulty criminology. Numerous studies show that high concentrations of immigrants result in lower neighborhood crime rates, not higher ones.[51]

▲ Two law enforcement officers investigate a murder in the Desire neighborhood of New Orleans. **How would a criminologist who advocates social conflict theories of criminal behavior explain high crime rates in low-income neighborhoods such as Desire?** Michael DeMocker/*The Times-Picayune*/Landov

Social Conflict Theory and Public Policy Given its radical nature, social conflict theory has had a limited impact on public policy. Even in the aftermath of situations in which class conflict has had serious and obvious repercussions, few observers feel that enough has been accomplished to improve the conditions that led to the violence. Indeed, many believe that the best hope for a shift in the power structure is the employment of more women and minorities in the criminal justice system itself.

Life Lessons and Criminal Behavior

Some criminologists find class theories of crime overly narrow. Surveys that ask people directly about their criminal behavior have shown that the criminal instinct is pervasive in middle- and upper-class communities, even if it is expressed differently. Anybody, these criminologists argue, has the potential to act out criminal behavior, regardless of class, race, or gender.

Family, Friends, and the Media: Social Processes of Crime

Philip Zimbardo conducted a well-known, if rather unscientific, experiment to show the broad potential for misbehavior. The psychologist placed an abandoned automobile with its hood up on the campus of Stanford University. The car remained in place, untouched, for a week. Then, Zimbardo smashed the car's window with a sledgehammer. Within minutes, passersby had joined in the destruction of the automobile, eventually stripping its valuable parts.[52] **Social process theories** function on the same basis as Zimbardo's "interdependence of decisions experiment": the potential for criminal behavior exists in everyone and will be realized depending on an individual's interaction with various institutions and processes of society. Social process theory has three main branches: (1) learning theory, (2) control theory, and (3) labeling theory.

LEARNING

List and briefly explain the three branches of social process theory.

6

OBJECTIVE

Learning Theory Popularized by Edwin Sutherland in the 1940s, **learning theory** contends that criminal activity is a learned behavior. In other words, a criminal is taught both the practical methods of crime (such as how to pick a lock) and the psychological aspects of crime (how to deal with the guilt of wrongdoing). Sutherland's *theory of differential association* held that individuals are exposed to the values of family and peers such as school friends or co-workers. If the dominant values one is exposed to favor criminal behavior, then that person is more likely to mimic such behavior.[53] Sutherland's focus on the importance of family relations in this area is underscored by research showing that sons of fathers who have been incarcerated are at an increased risk of delinquency and arrest.[54]

More recently, learning theory has been expanded to include the growing influence of the media. In the latest in a long series of studies, researchers released data in 2013 showing that children or adolescents who watched "excessive" amounts of violent television content faced an elevated risk of exhibiting antisocial behavior such as criminality in early adulthood.[55] Elliot Rodger, whose crimes were described at the beginning of this chapter, was obsessed with the violent video game World of Warcraft as a high school student. The issue of whether academic and anecdotal evidence can be used to conclusively link such games to violent behavior was addressed by the United States Supreme Court, as shown in the feature *Landmark Cases—Brown v. EMA*.

Control Theory Criminologist Travis Hirschi focuses on the reasons why individuals do not engage in criminal acts, rather than why they do. According to Hirschi, social bonds promote conformity to social norms. The stronger these social bonds—which include attachment to, commitment to, involvement with, and belief in societal values—the less likely that any individual will commit a crime.[56] **Control theory** holds that although we all have the potential to commit crimes, most of us are dissuaded from doing so because we care about the opinions of our family and peers. James Q. Wilson and George Kelling described control theory in terms of the "broken windows" effect. Neighborhoods in poor condition are filled with cues of lack of social control (for example, broken windows) that invite further vandalism and other deviant behavior.[57] If these cues are removed, according to Wilson and Kelling, so is the implied acceptance of crime within a community.

Janet Lauritsen, a criminologist at the University of Missouri–St. Louis, contends that familial control is more important than run-down surroundings in predicting

Social Process Theories A school of criminology that considers criminal behavior to be the predictable result of a person's interaction with his or her environment.

Learning Theory The theory that delinquents and criminals must be taught both the practical and the emotional skills necessary to participate in illegal activity.

Control Theory A series of theories that assume that all individuals have the potential for criminal behavior, but are restrained by the damage that such actions would do to their relationships with family, friends, and members of the community.

whether crime will occur. Lauritsen found that adolescents residing in two-parent households were victims of crime at similar rates, regardless of the levels of disadvantage in the neighborhoods in which they lived. By contrast, adolescents from single-parent homes who lived in highly disorganized neighborhoods were victimized at much higher rates than their counterparts in more stable locales. In Lauritsen's opinion, the support of a two-parent household offers crucial protection for children, whatever the condition of their neighborhood.[58]

Landmark Cases

Brown **v** Entertainment Merchants Association (EMA)

Reacting to studies linking violent video games to violent behavior in children, in 2006 then–California governor Arnold Schwarzenegger signed a bill prohibiting the sale or rental of games that portray "killing, maiming, dismembering or sexually assaulting an image of a human being" to people younger than eighteen years old. The law imposed a $1,000 fine on violators. Immediately, video game sellers sued the state, saying it had violated their constitutional right to freedom of speech. After two lower courts accepted this argument and invalidated California's law, the issue finally arrived before the United States Supreme Court.

Brown v. EMA
United States Supreme Court
559 S.Ct. 1448 (2010)

In the Words of the Court . . .
Justice Scalia, Majority Opinion

* * * *

Like the protected books, plays, and movies that preceded them, video games communicate ideas—and even social messages—through many familiar literary devices (such as characters, dialogue, plot, and music) and through features distinctive to the medium (such as the player's interaction with the virtual world). That suffices to confer First Amendment protection. Under our Constitution, "esthetic and moral judgments about art and literature * * * are for the individual to make, not for the Government to decree, even with the mandate or approval of a majority."

* * * *

No doubt a State possesses legitimate power to protect children from harm, but that does not include a free-floating power to restrict the ideas to which children may be exposed.

* * * *

California relies primarily on * * * research psychologists whose studies purport to show a connection between exposure to violent video games and harmful effects on children. These studies have been rejected by every court to consider them, and with good reason: They do not prove that violent video games *cause* minors to act aggressively (which would at least be a beginning). Instead, "[n]early all of the research is based on correlation, not evidence of causation * * * ." They show at best some correlation between exposure to violent entertainment and minuscule real-world effects, such as children's feeling more aggressive or making louder noises in the few minutes after playing a violent game than after playing a nonviolent game.

Decision
In the absence of any provable negative effects on minors from violent video games, the Court ruled that California's ban was unconstitutional and therefore could not be enforced.

For Critical Analysis
If states have the "legitimate power" to "protect children from harm," why did the Court invalidate California's violent video game law? How did Justice Scalia use the concepts of *cause* and *correlation* to support the Court's decision? (You can review those terms from our discussion earlier in the chapter.)

Labeling Theory The hypothesis that society creates crime and criminals by labeling certain behavior and certain people as deviant.

Life Course Criminology The study of crime based on the belief that behavioral patterns developed in childhood can predict delinquent and criminal behavior later in life.

Labeling Theory A third social process theory, **labeling theory,** focuses on perceptions of criminal behavior rather than the behavior itself. Labeling theorists study how being labeled a criminal—a "whore" or a "junkie" or a "thief"—affects that person's future behavior. Sociologist Howard Becker contends that deviance is

> a consequence of the application by others of rules and sanctions to an offender. The deviant is one to whom that label has successfully been applied; deviant behavior is behavior that people so label.[59]

Such labeling, some criminologists believe, becomes a self-fulfilling prophecy. Someone labeled a "junkie" will begin to consider himself or herself a deviant and continue the criminal behavior for which he or she has been labeled.

Following this line of reasoning, the criminal justice system is engaged in artificially creating a class of criminals by labeling victimless crimes such as drug use, prostitution, and gambling as "criminal." There are also practical consequences when a person is labeled a criminal, such as difficulty in finding employment. See this chapter's *CJ Policy— Your Take* to evaluate a federal law designed to protect minorities against job discrimination stemming from a criminal record.

Social Process Theory and Public Policy Because adult criminals are seen as too "hardened" to unlearn their criminal behavior, crime prevention policies associated with social process theory focus on juvenile offenders. Many youths, for example, are diverted from the formal juvenile justice process to keep them from being labeled "delinquent." Furthermore, many schools have implemented programs that attempt to steer children away from crime by encouraging them to "just say no" to drugs and stay in school. As we shall see in Chapter 6, implementation of Wilson and Kelling's "broken windows" principles has been credited with lowering the violent crime rate in New York and in a number of other major cities.

Looking Back to Childhood: Life Course Theories of Crime

If crime is indeed learned behavior, some criminologists are asking, shouldn't we be focusing on early childhood—the time when humans do the most learning? Many of the other theories we have studied in this chapter tend to attribute criminal behavior to factors—such as unemployment or poor educational performance—that take place long after an individual's personality has been established. Practitioners of **life course criminology** believe that lying, stealing, bullying, and other conduct problems that occur in childhood are the strongest predictors of future criminal behavior and have been seriously undervalued in the examination of why crime occurs.[60]

Self-Control Theory Focusing on childhood behavior raises the question of whether conduct problems established at a young age can be changed over time. Michael Gottfredson and Travis Hirschi, whose 1990 publication *A General Theory of Crime* is one of the foundations of life course criminology, think not.[61] Gottfredson and Hirschi believe that criminal behavior is linked to "low self-control," a personality trait that is formed before a child reaches the age of ten and can usually be attributed to poor parenting.[62]

In general, someone who has low self-control is:

1. Impulsive,
2. Thrill-seeking, and
3. Likely to solve problems with violence rather than her or his intellect.

Gottfredson and Hirschi think that once low self-control has been established, it will persist. In other words, childhood behavioral problems are not "solved" by positive developments later in life, such as healthy personal relationships or a good job.[63] Thus, these two criminologists ascribe to what has been called the *continuity theory of crime,* which essentially says that once negative behavior patterns have been established, they cannot be changed.

LEARNING
7
OBJECTIVE
Describe the importance of early childhood behavior for those who subscribe to self-control theory.

The Possibility of Change Not all of those who practice life course criminology follow the continuity theory. Terrie Moffitt, for example, notes that youthful offenders can be divided into two groups. The first group are life-course-persistent offenders: they are biting playmates at age five, skipping school at ten, stealing cars at sixteen, committing violent crimes at twenty, and perpetrating fraud and child abuse at thirty.[64] The second group are adolescent-limited offenders: as the name suggests, their "life of crime" is limited to the teenage years.[65] So, according to Moffitt, change is possible, if not for the life-course-persistent offenders (who are saddled with psychological problems that lead to continued social failure and misconduct), then for the adolescent-limited offenders.

Robert Sampson and John Laub take this line of thinking one step further. While acknowledging that "antisocial behavior is relatively stable" from childhood to old age, Sampson and Laub have gathered a great deal of data showing, in their opinion, that offenders may experience "turning points" when they are able to veer off the road from a life of crime.[66]

A good deal of research in this area has concentrated on the positive impact of getting married, having children, and finding a job,[67] but other turning points are also being explored. John F. Frana of Indiana State University and Ryan D. Schroeder of the University of Louisville argue that military service can act as a "rehabilitative agent."[68] Several researchers have studied the role that religion and spirituality can play as "hooks for change."[69] Furthermore, particularly for drug abusers, the death of a loved one or friend from shared criminal behavior can provide a powerful incentive to discontinue that behavior.

Life Course Theories and Public Policy Life course theories intersect with public policy mainly with regard to two crucial institutions that influence early childhood: parenting and school. In many jurisdictions, parenting-skills classes are available (or mandatory) for mothers and fathers of children with behavioral problems. Often, such problems are first identified by preschool teachers, and public school systems generally offer in-house intervention and counseling services. (See this chapter's *Mastering Concepts* for a review of theories discussed so far in this chapter.)

EthicsChallenge

In this section's *Landmark Cases* feature, you learned that the government cannot prohibit the sale of violent video games to minors. Even though the companies that produce these games are not *legally* required to censor their content, are there *ethical* reasons for doing so? What are the arguments for and against voluntarily removing graphic violence and abuse of women from these video games for the benefit of society? ▪

The Link between Drugs and Crime

Earlier in this chapter, we discussed the difference between correlations and causes. As you may recall, criminologists are generally reluctant to declare that any one factor

MasteringConcepts
The Causes of Crime

Choice Theories

Key Concept: Crime is the result of rational choices made by those who decide to engage in criminal activity for the rewards—financial and otherwise—that it offers.

Example: Montgomery County, Maryland, prosecutors charged Daniel Cleaves, who is HIV-positive, with a crime for having unprotected sex. In court, Cleaves apologized for knowingly placing his victim at risk of infection.

Biological and Psychological Trait Theories

Key Concept: Criminal behavior is explained by the biological and psychological attributes of an individual.

Example: A forty-year-old married schoolteacher in Virginia inexplicably began exhibiting aberrant sexual conduct, including trying to molest his stepdaughter. When a tumor in the part of the teacher's brain associated with social behavior was removed, his deviant actions stopped.

Sociological Theories

Key Concept: Crime is not something one is "born to do." Rather, crime is the result of the social conditions such as poverty, poor schools, unemployment, and discrimination with which a person lives.

Example: Researchers at the University of Texas at Dallas found that teens who expect to die young are more likely to commit serious crimes. In addition, these early-death expectations strongly correlated with adverse neighborhood living conditions.

Social Conflict Theories

Key Concept: Through criminal laws, the dominant members of society control the minority members, using institutions such as the police, courts, and prisons as tools of oppression.

Example: When making automobile stops from 2002 to 2013, police in Durham, North Carolina, searched African American male drivers at more than twice the rate of white male drivers. There was no difference in how often illicit materials such as illegal drugs were found on white and black drivers.

Social Process Theories

Key Concept: Family, friends, and peers have the greatest impact on an individual's behavior, and it is the interactions with these groups that ultimately determine whether a person will become involved in criminal behavior.

Example: According to the U.S. Department of Justice, nearly 50 percent of inmates in state prisons have relatives who have also been incarcerated.

Life Course Theories

Key Concept: Criminal and antisocial behavior is evident at each stage of a person's life. By focusing on such behavior in early childhood, criminologists may be able to better understand and predict offending patterns that emerge as a person grows older.

Example: Following the life course of more than seven thousand adolescents through adulthood, the American Psychological Association found that those repeatedly bullied as children were much more likely to go to prison than those who did not suffer repeated bullying.

causes a certain result. Richard B. Felson of Penn State University and Keri B. Burchfield of Northern Illinois University, however, believe that alcohol consumption has a causal effect on crime victimization under certain circumstances.[70] Felson and Burchfield found that "frequent and heavy" drinkers are at a great risk of assault when they are drinking, but do not show abnormal rates of victimization when sober. They hypothesize that consuming alcohol leads to aggressive and offensive behavior, particularly in men, which in turn triggers violent reactions from others.

According to the National Survey on Drug Use and Health, only 9.4 percent of those questioned had used an illegal drug in the past month. Even so, this means a significant number of Americans—about 24.6 million—are regularly using illegal drugs. That figure mushrooms when consumers of legal substances such as alcohol (137 million users) and tobacco (67 million users) are included.[71] (See Figure 2.3 for an overview of illegal drug use in the United States.) In this section, we will discuss two questions concerning these habits. First, why do people use drugs? Second, what are the consequences for the criminal justice system?

The Criminology of Drug Use

At first glance, the reason people use drugs, including legal drugs such as alcohol, is obvious: such drugs give the user pleasure and provide a temporary escape for those who may feel tension or anxiety. Ultimately, though, such explanations are unsatisfactory because they fail to explain why some people use drugs while others do not.

Theories of Drug Use Several of the theories we discussed earlier in the chapter have been used by experts to explain drug use. *Social disorganization theory* holds that rapid social change can cause people to become disaffiliated from mainstream society, causing them to turn to drugs. *Control theory* suggests that a lack of social control, as provided by entities such as the family or school, can lead to antisocial behavior.

Drugs and the "Learning Process" Focusing on the question of why first-time drug users become habitual users, sociologist Howard Becker sees three factors in the "learning process." He believes first-time users:

1. Learn the techniques of drug use.
2. Learn to perceive the pleasurable effects of drug use.
3. Learn to enjoy the social experience of drug use.[72]

Becker's assumptions are evident in the widespread belief that positive images of drug use in popular culture "teach" adolescents that such behavior is not only acceptable but desirable. The entertainment industry, in particular, has been criticized for glamorizing various forms of drug use.

FIGURE 2.3 Illegal Drug Use in the United States

In 2013, about 25 million Americans reported using an illegal drug at least once in the previous twelve months. As this graph shows, marijuana is by far the most popular illicit drug in the United States.

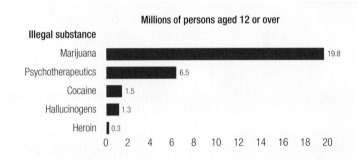

Marijuana: The most popular form of this drug is made using the dried, flowering tops of the cannabis plant, often mixed with tobacco, and smoked in the form of a cigarette. It primarily affects the central nervous system, causing feelings of relaxation, euphoria, and heightened sensory perception.

Psychotherapeutics: This term covers prescription drugs (pain relievers, tranquilizers, stimulants, and sedatives) used for non-medical purposes. It includes methamphetamine, a highly addictive stimulant that is manufactured using prescription and non-prescription drugs.

Cocaine: Derived from coca leaves, this stimulant is most commonly snorted as a powder, though it can be injected and, in a crystallized form known as "crack," smoked. Use of cocaine produces an instant euphoria, as well as numbness and feelings of increased energy and confidence.

Hallucinogens: A category that includes LSD, mescaline (from the peyote cactus), and PCP ("angel dust"). These drugs are known for their "psychedelic" effects, which cause users to experience reality in a distorted state.

Heroin: Derived from the poppy plant, this opioid is most commonly injected directly into the user's veins, though it can be snorted or smoked. Heroin use creates feelings of sedation and decreased anxiety, as well as a rush of euphoria.

Source: Substance Abuse and Mental Health Service Administration, *Results from the 2013 National Survey on Drug Use and Health: Summary of National Findings* (Washington, D.C.: National Institute of Drug Abuse, September 2014), Figure 2.1, page 16.

Drug Addiction and Dependency

Another theory rests on the assumption that some people possess overly sensitive drug receptors in their brains and are therefore biologically disposed toward drug use.[73] Though there is little conclusive evidence that biological factors can explain initial drug experimentation, scientific research has provided a great deal of insight into patterns of long-term drug use.

Drug Use and Drug Abuse

In particular, science has aided in understanding the difference between drug *use* and drug *abuse*. **Drug abuse** can be defined as the use of any drug—licit or illicit—that causes either psychological or bodily harm to the abuser or to third parties. Just as most people who drink beer or wine avoid abusing alcohol, most users of illegal substances are not abusers. For most drugs except nicotine, only between 7 and 20 percent of all users suffer from compulsive abuse.[74]

Despite their relatively small numbers, drug abusers have a disparate impact on the drug market. The 20 percent of Americans, for example, who drink the most consume more than 80 percent of all alcoholic beverages sold in the United States. The data are similar for illicit substance abusers, leading to the conclusion that, to a large extent, abusers and addicts sustain the market for illegal drugs.

Addiction Basics

The most extreme abusers are addicted to, or physically dependent on, a drug. To understand the basics of addiction and physical dependence, you must understand the role of *dopamine* in the brain. Dopamine is the neurotransmitter responsible for delivering pleasure signals to brain nerve endings in response to behavior—such as eating good food or engaging in sex—that makes us feel good. The bloodstream delivers drugs to the area of the brain that produces dopamine, thereby triggering the production of a large amount of the substance in the brain.

Over time, the continued use of drugs physically changes the nerve endings, called *receptors*. To continue operating in the presence of large amounts of dopamine, the receptors become less sensitive, meaning that greater amounts of any particular drug are required to create the amount of dopamine needed for the same levels of pleasure. When the supply of the drug is cut off, the brain strongly feels the lack of dopamine stimulation, and the abuser will suffer symptoms of withdrawal until the receptors readjust.[75]

Addiction and physical dependence are interrelated, though not exactly the same. Those who are physically dependent on a drug suffer withdrawal symptoms when they stop using it, but after a certain time period, they are generally able to emerge without further craving. Addicts, in contrast, continue to feel a need for the drug long after withdrawal symptoms have passed. For many years, researchers have been striving to determine if some people are more likely than others to become addicts for biological reasons. In 2008, a group of researchers from Peking University in China made significant headway toward doing so by showing that many addicts share a particular set of *enzymes*, or proteins that trigger chemical reactions in the body.[76]

▼ A young woman prepares to use heroin under a bridge in Portland, Maine. **Do you think that drug abusers should be treated as criminals to be punished or as ill people in need of treatment? Explain your answer.** Cheryl Senter/*The New York Times*/Redux

Crime and Health:
The Landscape of Drug Abuse

As we will see throughout this textbook, the prosecution of illegal drug users and suppliers has been one of the primary factors in the enormous growth of the American correctional industry. Of course, because many drugs are illegal, anybody who sells, uses, or in any way promotes any of these drugs is, under most circumstances, breaking the law. The drug-crime relationship goes well beyond the language of criminal drug statutes, however.

The Drug-Crime Relationship Studies that connect drug use to criminality can be problematic, mainly because such activity is likely one risk factor among many in a criminal user's life. Still, drugs and crime are related in three general ways:[77]

1. *Drug-defined offenses*, or violation of laws prohibiting the possession, use, distribution, or manufacture of illegal drugs. Examples include possession of marijuana or methamphetamine production.
2. *Drug-related offenses*, such as crimes motivated by drug abuse or committed to further the illegal drug trade. Examples include gang violence between rival drug dealers and theft to get money to buy illegal drugs.
3. *The drug-using lifestyle*, experienced by many drug abusers who do not participate in the legitimate economy and thus rely on crime for the means of survival. These users often support short-term goals with illegal activities such as prostitution and welfare fraud.

As we noted in Chapter 1, according to the federal government, at least two-thirds of all persons arrested in this country have illegal drugs in their systems when apprehended.[78] Legal drugs also play a role in the crime picture of the United States. About 37 percent of state prisoners and 33 percent of jail inmates incarcerated for a violent crime were under the influence of alcohol at the time of their arrest.[79] Richard Friedman, who studies the effect of drugs on behavior, estimates that abusing alcohol and other drugs increases the likelihood of violence by a factor of seven.[80]

Drugs and the National Health The laundry list of health problems associated with drug abuse is lengthy and sobering. It includes a weakened immune system, increased susceptibility to infection, heart conditions including heart attacks, liver damage, brain damage, and nausea, vomiting, and abdominal pain. Illegal drug users make about 525,000 costly emergency room visits each year.[81] About 40,000 fatal overdoses occur annually in the United States, half of which are attributed to prescription drugs.[82]

In the early days of the debate over the legalization of marijuana, the World Health Organization concluded widespread use of that drug was "unlikely to produce public health problems comparable in scale to those currently produced by alcohol and tobacco."[83] The scale of those health problems is, in fact, immense. The Centers for Disease Control estimates that six Americans die each day due to alcohol poisoning.[84] That federal agency also places the national annual death toll from tobacco-related causes at 480,000.[85]

Models of Addiction Is criminal conviction and incarceration the best way for society to deal with addicts? Those who follow the **medical model of addiction** believe that addicts are not criminals, but mentally or physically ill individuals who are forced

Medical Model of Addiction An approach to drug addiction that treats drug abuse as a mental illness and focuses on treating and rehabilitating offenders rather than punishing them.

LEARNING **8** OBJECTIVE Contrast the medical model of addiction with the criminal model of addiction.

into acts of petty crime to "feed their habit." Those who believe in the *enslavement theory of addiction* advocate treating addiction as a disease and hold that society should not punish addicts but rather attempt to rehabilitate them, as would be done for any other unhealthy person.[86]

Although a number of organizations, including the American Medical Association, recognize alcoholism and other forms of drug dependence as diseases, the criminal justice system tends to favor the **criminal model of addiction** over the medical model. The criminal model holds that illegal drug abusers and addicts endanger society with their behavior and should be punished the same as persons who commit non-drug-related crimes. (To learn how one European country employs a "harm reduction" model of addiction, which aims to reduce the negative consequences of drug use for addicts and for society, see the feature *Comparative Criminal Justice—Free Trade.*)

Marijuana Law Trends

How would the link between certain illegal drugs and crime change if those drugs were legalized? That is, what if a particular illegal drug was treated in the same manner as alcohol and tobacco—heavily regulated, but available to persons over the age of twenty-one? While these questions are not being asked with regard to "hard" drugs such as heroin and cocaine, the **legalization** of marijuana—America's most-used illicit drug—has become an important policy issue. Indeed, as we noted in Chapter 1, in 2014 Colorado and Washington became the first states to legalize the sale, possession, and use of small amounts of marijuana. The next year, Alaska and Oregon followed suit, and the District of Columbia approved possession but not sale of the drug.

Regulating Marijuana The four states (and one District) just mentioned chose the legalization of marijuana over its *decriminalization*. Favored in eighteen states, marijuana **decriminalization** policies treat marijuana use or possession as an infraction, similar to a parking ticket, and violators are spared a criminal record or threat of incarceration. To a certain extent, at least initially, decriminalization is an easier process than

Comparative Criminal Justice

Central Intelligence Agency

Free Trade

What is the best way to deal with hard-core heroin addicts who have failed to respond to medical care or incarceration? According to the Heroin Assisted Treatment (HAT) approach, the answer may be to give them free heroin and provide them with a clean, safe place to use it.

In the 1990s, the Netherlands adopted HAT as its national drug policy, and the results have been generally positive. With users shooting up in the presence of health-care professionals, heroin-related deaths and HIV infections have decreased dramatically. Since heroin users do not need to steal or sell their bodies to get funds for the drug, heroin-related crime rates have also fallen steeply. Finally, the black market heroin trade in the Netherlands has withered because, as the cliché goes, "you can't beat free."

For Critical Analysis

Recent government statistics show very few heroin users under the age of forty in the Netherlands, and almost no new annual users of any age. Given that HAT focuses on addicts, how might the policy lead to such a drastic reduction in the country's overall heroin consumption?

legalization, as the latter requires the creation of a new regulatory system. Given the complexities involved with legalization, early versions of the process are often marked by unexpected difficulties.

In Colorado, for example, state officials did not foresee the challenges posed by *edibles*, or products containing THC—the ingredient in marijuana that produces the "high"—that can be ingested. Edibles such as pot gummy bears, sodas, and chocolate bars apparently are popular among certain consumers because they do not involve the unpleasant aspects of smoking the drug. Inconveniently, however, it is difficult to gauge the strength of edibles, many of which have considerably more THC than a smoked marijuana cigarette. Also, one cannot identify an edible by looking it. In late 2014, after a series of accidental THC ingestions and the suicide of a college student who had just eaten marijuana-laced cookies, Colorado officials began considering how to regulate this unintended consequence of legalization.[87]

The Future of Legalization Another foreseeable problem with marijuana legalization is *diversion*. This occurs when marijuana from states where it is legal inevitably begins supplying the black market for the drug in other, non-legalized marijuana states. Of course, diversion would not exist if marijuana were legal throughout the United States, a contentious proposal we will address in the *CJ in Action* feature at the end of the chapter.

Practically speaking, whether or not the legalization movement spreads beyond Alaska, Colorado, Oregon, and Washington depends on what happens in those states. If they see a dramatic increase in underage pot use or drugged driving, or experience an unexpected rise in marijuana-related health problems, then the drug's "march toward the mainstream" could come to a halt. If, however, marijuana legalization has a primarily positive impact, particularly in areas such as tax revenue and crime reduction, then, in the words of one supporter, other states will "want to get rid of their prohibition laws, too."[88]

EthicsChallenge

Refer back to our description of Heroin Assisted Treatment (HAT) in this section's *Comparative Criminal Justice* feature. Do you think it is ethical for the government to provide free heroin to addicts? Why or why not? Explain any other ethical qualms you might have about this policy. ▪

Criminology from Theory to Practice

You have almost completed the only chapter in this textbook that deals primarily with theory. The chapters that follow will concentrate on the more practical and legal aspects of the criminal justice system: how law enforcement agencies fight crime, how our court systems determine guilt or innocence, and how we punish those who are found guilty. Criminology can, however, play a crucial role in the criminal justice system. "A lot of my colleagues just want to write scholarly articles for scholarly journals," notes Professor James Alan Fox of Northeastern University in Boston. "But I think if you're in a field with specialized knowledge that can be useful to the community, you should engage the public and policymakers."[89]

Criminology and the Chronic Offender

Perhaps the most useful criminological contribution to crime fighting in the past half century was *Delinquency in a Birth Cohort*, published by the pioneering trio of Marvin

Wolfgang, Robert Figlio, and Thorsten Sellin in 1972. This research established the idea of the **chronic offender,** or career criminal, by showing that a small group of juvenile offenders—6 percent—was responsible for a disproportionate amount of the violent crime attributed to a group of nearly 10,000 young males: 71 percent of the murders, 82 percent of the robberies, 69 percent of the aggravated assaults, and 73 percent of the rapes.[90]

Further research has supported the idea of a "chronic 6 percent,"[91] and law enforcement agencies and district attorneys' offices have devised specific strategies to apprehend and prosecute repeat offenders, with dozens of local police agencies forming career criminal units to deal with the problem. Legislators have also reacted to this research: habitual offender laws that provide harsher sentences for repeat offenders have become quite popular. We will discuss these statutes, including the controversial "three-strikes-and-you're-out" laws, in Chapter 11.

Criminology and the Criminal Justice System

There is a sense, however, that criminology has not done enough to make our country a safer place. Eminent criminologist James Q. Wilson, for one, criticized his peers for trying to understand crime rather than reduce it.[92] Many criminal justice practitioners also argue that too much of the research done by criminologists is inaccessible to them. As Sarah J. Hart, director of the National Institute of Justice, has noted, an overwhelmed police chief simply does not have the time or patience to wade through the many scientific journals in which crime research appears.[93]

This criticism may be too harsh. As we discuss further in Chapter 6, Wilson himself (in collaboration with George Kelling) developed the "broken windows" theory, which reshaped police strategy in the 1990s. Furthermore, as we will also see in Chapter 6, criminological theories about the "hot spots" in which crime takes place, also known as *applied geography,* have led dozens of police departments to adopt computer-based crime-mapping prevention strategies.[94]

David Kennedy, a criminologist at John Jay College in New York, has partnered with law enforcement agencies in a number of American cities to implement his drug-market intervention (DMI) initiative. As part of DMI, known drug dealers are approached by police and given a choice: stop dealing and we will help you turn your life around, or keep dealing and we will arrest you. Those who choose to participate in the program are offered educational classes, drug treatment, and job training and placement. Two years after DMI was initiated in high-crime East Austin, Texas, the operation resulted in nearly eighty narcotics arrests and is being credited for the neighborhood's burgeoning gentrification.[95] Indeed, in the opinion of many observers, researchers know more today about "what works" in criminology than at any other time in our nation's history.[96]

Chronic Offender A delinquent or criminal who commits multiple offenses and is considered part of a small group of wrongdoers who are responsible for a majority of the antisocial activity in any given community.

CJ IN ACTION

Legalizing Marijuana

The popularity of marijuana, the most commonly used illegal drug in the United States, is growing. Over the past seven years, the number of regular users has swollen from about 15 million to almost 20 million.[97] If, as some observers believe, the reason for this increase is pot's cultural acceptance in our society,[98] then we can expect the trend to continue. Four states recently have legalized the possession and sale of marijuana for personal use, the first four to do so. These steps reflect a growing "get soft" movement regarding the nation's marijuana laws that we now address in this chapter's *CJ in Action* feature.

Federal Law versus State Law

By allowing legitimate businesses to grow and sell marijuana, officials in Alaska, Colorado, Oregon, and Washington are—in the words of Mark Kleinman, a professor of public policy at the University of California, Los Angeles—"issuing licenses to commit a felony."[99] According to federal law, marijuana remains a Schedule I substance, which indicates the highest level of illegality. So, for example, Colorado allows its franchises to cultivate up to 10,200 marijuana plants at a time. The federal penalty for this activity is a minimum of ten years in prison and a fine of as much as $10 million.[100]

The administration of President Barack Obama has indicated that it will not interfere with state marijuana legalization as long as it produces no widespread negative criminal and health consequences.[101] Administrations change, however, and there is no guarantee that President Obama's successor will take the same lenient approach to the situation. Consequently, until the federal outlook on marijuana changes, many states will be unwilling to liberalize their criminal laws regarding the drug.

The Case for Federal Legalization

- The "peace dividend" of legalization would be substantial. On the one hand, about 750,000 Americans are arrested each year on marijuana-related charges. Removing these offenders from the criminal justice system would save U.S. taxpayers billions of dollars annually. On the other hand, the country would reap a windfall in taxes on the controlled sale of a previously illegal drug. One Harvard University economist has estimated that the net economic gain to the United States for legalizing marijuana would be between $10.1 billion and $13.9 billion a year.[102]

- Legalization would put the black market for marijuana—estimated at about $48 billion a year[103]—out of business, ending violent crime associated with the pot trade and depriving thousands of criminals of their livelihood.

- Legalization would result in a more efficient criminal justice system, as scarce law enforcement resources would be diverted away from marijuana offenses, and the pressure on both overloaded courts and overcrowded prisons would be alleviated.

The Case against Federal Legalization

- As one health professional puts it, "Marijuana is not good for you."[104] Frequent marijuana use has been linked to mental disorders such as depression and anxiety. It is also associated with respiratory problems, IQ reduction, and immune system weakness.[105]

- As with alcohol and tobacco, legalization of marijuana will increase the number of users and intensify the societal impact of the drug's negative consequences.

- Minors can often easily obtain legal but controlled drug products such as cigarettes and alcohol. If marijuana is legalized, we can expect that minors would have greater access to it as well.

Your Opinion—Writing Assignment

Several years ago, the Ending Federal Marijuana Prohibition Act was introduced before the U.S. Congress.[106] This bill, which never passed, would have (a) legalized marijuana by federal law, (b) required a federal permit for growing and selling the drug, and (c) regulated marijuana the same way, on the federal level, as alcohol. Should this proposed legislation become law? Why or why not? Before responding, you can review our discussions in the sections of this chapter concerning:

- The criminology of drug use ("The Link between Drugs and Crime").

- Crime, health, and drugs ("The Link between Drugs and Crime").

- Marijuana law trends ("The Link between Drugs and Crime").

Your answer should include at least three full paragraphs.

Summary

For more information on these concepts, look back to the Learning Objective icons throughout the chapter.

 Discuss the difference between a hypothesis and a theory in the context of criminology. A hypothesis is a proposition, usually presented in an "If . . . , then . . ." format, that can be tested by researchers. If enough different authorities are able to test and verify a hypothesis, it will usually be accepted as a theory. Because theories can offer explanations for behavior, criminologists often rely on them when trying to determine the causes of criminal behavior.

 Contrast positivism with classical criminology. Whereas classical theorists believe criminals make rational choices, those of the positivist school believe that criminal behavior is determined by psychological, biological, and social forces that the individual cannot control.

 Explain how brain-scanning technology is able to help scientists determine if an individual is at risk for criminal offending. Brain scanning technologies such as CAT scans, MRIs, and fMRIs provide scientists with detailed depictions of brain structure and brain activity. When these depictions show disease or dysfunction such as schizophrenia that is correlated with violent behavior, the subject is at greater risk of criminal offending.

 List and describe the three theories of social structure that help explain crime. Social disorganization theory states that crime is largely a product of unfavorable conditions in certain communities, or zones of disorganization. The strain theory argues that most people seek increased wealth and financial security and that the strain of not being able to achieve these goals through legal means leads to criminal behavior. Finally, cultural deviance theory asserts that people adapt to the values of the subculture—which has its own standards of behavior—to which they belong.

 Describe the social conflict theory known as the social reality of crime. This theory holds that criminal law, rather than being designed for the common good, is a set of "rules" put in place by those members of society who hold power to control and subdue those who do not.

 List and briefly explain the three branches of social process theory. (a) Learning theory, which contends that people learn to be criminals from their family and peers. (b) Control theory, which holds that most of us are dissuaded from a life of crime because we place importance on the opinions of family and peers. (c) Labeling theory, which holds that a person labeled a "junkie" or a "thief" will respond by becoming or remaining whatever she or he is labeled.

 Describe the importance of early childhood behavior for those who subscribe to self-control theory. Advocates of self-control theory believe that violent and antisocial behavior in adulthood can be predicted, to a large extent, by low levels of self-control in early childhood. Therefore, a child who is impulsive and tends to solve problems with violence is at risk for adult offending.

 Contrast the medical model of addiction with the criminal model of addiction. Those who support the former believe that addicts are not criminals, but mentally or physically ill individuals who are forced into acts of petty crime to "feed their habit." Those in favor of the criminal model of addiction believe that abusers and addicts endanger society with their behavior and should be treated like any other criminals.

 Explain the theory of the chronic offender and its importance for the criminal justice system. A chronic offender is a juvenile or adult who commits multiple offenses. According to research conducted by Marvin Wolfgang and others in the 1970s, chronic offenders are responsible for a disproportionately large percentage of all crime. In the decades since, law enforcement agencies and public prosecutors have developed strategies to identify and convict chronic offenders with the goal of lessening overall crime rates. In addition, legislators have passed laws that provide longer sentences for chronic offenders in an attempt to keep them off the streets.

Questions for Critical Analysis

1. Research shows that when levels of single-family mortgage foreclosures rise in a neighborhood, so do levels of violent crime. Explain the correlation between these two sets of statistics. Why is it false to say that single-family mortgage foreclosures *cause* violent crimes to occur?

2. Why would someone who subscribes to choice theory believe that increasing the harshness of a penalty for a particular crime would necessarily lead to fewer such crimes being committed?

3. Consider the following statement: "The government should protect the public from mentally ill persons who are potentially dangerous, even if that means hospitalizing those persons against their will." Do you agree or disagree? Why?

4. Review the theory of differential association in this chapter. Then, review the definition of white-collar crime in Chapter 1. How could the theory of differential association be used to describe high levels of white-collar crime in any particular business or industry?

5. Do you see illegal drug abuse as an illness or as a criminal activity? Explain your answer.

Key Terms

anomie 48
biology 42
causation 39
choice theory 40
chronic offender 62
classical criminology 40
control theory 52
correlation 39
criminal model of addiction 60
criminology 39
cultural deviance theory 49

decriminalization 60
drug abuse 58
genetics 42
hormone 43
hypothesis 39
labeling theory 54
learning theory 52
legalization 60
life course criminology 54
medical model of addiction 59
positivism 41

psychoanalytic theory 45
psychology 42
social conflict theories 50
social disorganization theory 47
social process theories 52
social reality of crime 50
sociology 46
strain theory 48
subculture 49
testosterone 43
theory 39

Notes

1. Quoted in Adam Nagourney, et al., "Before Brief, Deadly Spree, Trouble since Age 8," *New York Times* (June 2, 2014), A1.

2. Scott E. Wolfe and David C. Pyrooz, "Rolling Back Prices and Raising Crime Rates? The Walmart Effect on Crime in the United States," *The British Journal of Criminology* (March 2014), 199–221.

3. Matthew Larson and Gary Sweeten, "Breaking Up Is Hard to Do: Romantic Dissolution, Offending, and Substance Abuse During the Transition to Adulthood," *Criminology* (August 2012), 605–635.

4. James Q. Wilson and Richard J. Hernstein, *Crime and Human Nature: The Definitive Study of the Causes of Crime* (New York: Simon & Schuster, 1985), 515.

5. Cesare Lombroso, *Criminal Man,* eds. Mary Gibson and Nicole Hahn Rafter (Durham, N.C.: Duke University Press, 2006).

6. Wilson and Hernstein, *op. cit.,* 44.

7. Jack Katz, *Seductions of Crime: Moral and Sensual Attractions of Doing Evil* (New York: Basic Books, 1988).

8. Quoted in Matt Pearce, "Police: 'Bored' Oklahoma Teens Randomly Kill Australian Student," *Los Angeles Times* (August 20, 2013), A5.

9. David C. Rowe, *Biology and Crime* (Los Angeles: Roxbury, 2002), 2.

10. Callie H. Burt and Ronald L. Simons, "Pulling Back the Curtain on Heritability Studies: Biosocial Criminology in the Postgenomic Era," *Criminology* (May 2014), 223–262.

11. Raymond R. Crowe, "An Adoption Study of Antisocial Personality," *Archives of General Psychiatry* (1974), 785–791; Sarnoff A. Mednick, William F. Gabrielli, and Barry Hutchings, "Genetic Influences on Criminal Convictions: Evidence from an Adoption Cohort," *Science* (1994), 891–894; and Remi J. Cadoret, "Adoption Studies," *Alcohol Health & Research World* (Summer 1995), 195–201.

12. Hans G. Brunner et al., "Abnormal Behavior Associated with a Point Mutation in the Structural Gene for Monoamine Oxidase A," *Science* (October 22, 1993), 578–580.

13. Avshalom Caspi et al., "Role of Genotype in the Cycle of Violence in Maltreated Children," *Science* (August 2, 2002), 851–854.

14. Jari Tiihonen, et al., "Genetic Background of Extreme Violent Behavior," *Molecular Biology* (October 2014), 1–7.

15. Jari Tiihonen, quoted in Melissa Hogenboom, "Two Genes Linked with Violent Crime," *BBC News/Science and Environment* (October 28, 2014), at **www.bbc.com/news/science -environment-29760212**.

16. L. E. Kreuz and R. M. Rose, "Assessment of Aggressive Behavior and Plasma Testosterone in Young Criminal Population," *Psychosomatic Medicine* 34 (1972), 321–332.

17. H. Persky, K. Smith, and G. Basu, "Relation of Psychological Measures of Aggression and Hostility to Testosterone Production in Men," *Psychosomatic Medicine* 33 (1971), 265, 276.

18. Cindy-Lee Dennis and Simone N. Vigod, "The Relationship between Postpartum Depression, Domestic Violence, Childhood Violence, and Substance Use: Epidemiologic Study of a Large Community Sample," *Violence against Women* (April 2013), 503–517.

19. Quoted in Pam Belluck, "'Thinking of Ways to Harm Her': New Findings on Timing and Range of Maternal Mental Illness," *New York Times* (June 16, 2014), A1.

20. Jessica Wolpaw Reyes, *Environmental Policy as Social Policy? The Impact of Childhood Lead Exposure on Crime* (Cambridge, Mass.: National Bureau of Economic Research, May 2007), at **www.nber.org/papers/w13097 .pdf**.

21. Bureau of Justice Statistics, *Health Problems of Prison and Jail Inmates* (Washington, D.C.: U.S. Department of Justice, September 2006), 1.

22. Quoted in Eileen Sullivan, "Loners Like Tucson Gunman 'Fly below the Radar,'" *Associated Press* (January 17, 2011).

23. Herman Bianchi, *Justice as Sanctuary: Toward a New System of Crime Control* (Bloomington: Indiana University Press, 1994), 72.

24. Richard Friedman, "Why Can't Doctors Identify Killers?" *New York Times* (May 28, 2014), A21.

25. David G. Myers, *Psychology,* 7th ed. (New York: Worth Publishers, 2004), 576–577.

26. Philip Zimbardo, "Pathology of Imprison- ment," *Society* (April 1972), 4–8.

27. David Canter and Laurence Alison, "The Social Psychology of Crime: Groups, Teams, and Networks," in *The Social Psychology of Crime: Groups, Teams, and Networks,* ed. David Canter and Laurence Alison (Hanover, N.H.: Dartmouth, 2000), 3–4.

28. Quoted in Lizette Alvarez, "Club Shooting in Rough Miami Neighborhood Continues a Cycle of Violence," *New York Times* (September 30, 2014), A15.

29. Robert Park, Ernest Burgess, and Roderic McKenzie, *The City* (Chicago: University of Chicago Press, 1929).

30. Sam Bieler and John Roman, *Addressing Violence and Disorder around Alcohol Outlets* (Washington, D.C.: District of Columbia Crime Policy Institute, January 2013), 3–5.

31. Clifford R. Shaw, Henry D. McKay, and Leonard S. Cottrell, *Delinquency Areas* (Chicago: University of Chicago Press, 1929).

32. Clifford R. Shaw and Henry D. McKay, *Report on the Causes of Crime,* vol. 2: *Social Factors in Juvenile Delinquency* (Washington, D.C.: National Commission on Law Observance and Enforcement, 1931).

33. Elijah Anderson, *Code of the Street: Decency, Violence and the Moral Life of the Inner City* (New York: W. W. Norton, 2000), 35–65.

34. *Ibid.,* 180.

35. Eric A. Stewart and Ronald L. Simons, "Race, Code of the Street, and Violent Delinquency: A Multilevel Investigation of Neighborhood Street Culture and Individual Norms of Violence," *Criminology* (May 2010), 569–603.

36. Emile Durkheim, *The Rules of Sociological Method,* trans. Sarah A. Solovay and John H. Mueller (New York: Free Press, 1964).

37. Robert K. Merton, *Social Theory and Social Structure* (New York: Free Press, 1957). See the chapter on "Social Structure and Anomie."

38. Robert Agnew, "Foundation for a General Strain Theory of Crime and Delinquency," *Criminology* 30 (1992), 47–87.

39. Robert Agnew, Timothy Brezina, John Paul Wright, and Francis T. Cullen, "Strain, Personality Traits, and Delinquency: Extending General Strain Theory," *Criminology* (February 2002), 43–71.

40. Lawrence L. Shornack, "Conflict Theory and the Family," *International Social Science Review* 62 (1987), 154–157.

41. Richard Quinney, *The Social Reality of Crime* (Boston: Little, Brown, 1970).

42. Nicole Hahn Rafter, *Partial Justice: Women, Prisons, and Social Control* (New Brunswick, N.J.: Transaction Publishers, 1990).

43. Federal Bureau of Investigation, *Crime in the United States 2013* (Washington, D.C.: U.S. Department of Justice, 2014), at **www .fbi.gov/about-us/cjis/ucr/crime-in-the -u.s/2013/crime-in-the-u.s.-2013/tables /table-42/table_42_arrests_by_sex_2013 .xls**.

44. The Sentencing Project, at **www.sentencing project.org/template/page.cfm?id=122**.

45. Bureau of Justice Statistics, *Prisoners in 2013* (Washington, D.C.: U.S. Department of Justice, September 2014), Table 8, page 9.

46. Jason Purnell, Gabriela Camberos, and Robert Fields, *For the Sake of All* (St. Louis: Washington University in St. Louis and St. Louis University, November 2014), 29.

47. Chico Harlan, "In St. Louis, Delmar Boulevard Is the Line that Divides a City by Race and Perspective," *Washington Post* (August 22, 2014), A1.

48. Cindy Brooks Dollar, "Radical Threat Theory: Assessing the Evidence, Requesting Redesign," *Journal of Criminology* (July 2014), at **www.hindawi.com/journals /jcrim/2014/983026**.

49. Muzaffar Chishti and Claire Bergeron, "Hazleton Immigration Ordinance that Began with a Bang Goes Out with a Whimper," *Migration Policy Institute* (March 28, 2014), at **www.migrationpolicy.org /article/hazleton-immigration-ordinance -began-bang-goes-out-whimper**.

50. *Ibid.*

51. John H. MacDonald, John R. Hipp, and Charlotte Gill, "The Effect of Immigrant Concentration on Changes in Neighborhood Crime Rates," *Journal of Quantitative Criminology* (June 2012), 191–215.

52. Philip G. Zimbardo, "The Human Choice: Individuation, Reason, and Order versus Deindividuation, Impulse, and Chaos," in *Nebraska Symposium on Motivation,* eds. William J. Arnold and David Levie (Lincoln, Neb.: University of Nebraska Press, 1969), 287–293.

53. Edwin H. Sutherland, *Criminology,* 4th ed. (Philadelphia: Lippincott, 1947).

54. Michael E. Roettger and Raymond Swisher, "Associations of Fathers' History of Incarceration with Sons' Delinquency and Arrest among Black, White, and Hispanic Males in the United States," *Criminology* (November 2011), 1109–1147.

55. Lindsay A. Robertson, Helena M. McAnally, and Robert J. Hancox, "Childhood and Adolescent Television Viewing and Antisocial Behavior in Early Adulthood," *Pediatrics* (March 2013), 439–446.

56. Travis Hirschi, *Causes of Delinquency* (Berkeley: University of California Press, 1969).

57. James Q. Wilson and George L. Kelling, "Broken Windows," *Atlantic Monthly* (March 1982), 29.

58. Janet L. Lauritsen, *How Families and Communities Influence Youth Victimization* (Washington, D.C.: Office of Juvenile Justice and Delinquency Prevention, 2003).

59. Howard S. Becker, *Outsiders: Studies in the Sociology of Deviance* (New York: Free Press, 1963).

60. Francis T. Cullen and Robert Agnew, *Criminological Theory, Past to Present: Essential Readings,* 2d ed. (Los Angeles: Roxbury Publishing Co., 2003), 443.

61. Michael R. Gottfredson and Travis Hirschi, *A General Theory of Crime* (Stanford, Calif.: Stanford University Press, 1990).

62. *Ibid.*, 90.

63. *Ibid.*

64. Terrie Moffitt, "Adolescent-Limited and Life-Course-Persistent Antisocial Behavior: A Developmental Taxonomy," *Psychological Review* 100 (1993), 679–680.

65. *Ibid.*, 674.

66. Robert J. Sampson and John H. Laub, *Crime in the Making: Pathways and Turning Points through Life* (Cambridge, Mass.: Harvard University Press, 1993), 11.

67. *Ibid.*; John H. Laub and Robert J. Sampson, *Shared Beginnings, Divergent Lives: Delinquent Boys to Age 70* (Cambridge, Mass.: Harvard University Press, 2003); and Derek A. Kreager, Ross L. Matsueda, and Elena A. Erosheva, "Motherhood and Criminal Desistance in Disadvantaged Neighborhoods," *Criminology* (February 2010), 221–257.

68. John F. Frana and Ryan D. Schroeder, "Alternatives to Incarceration," *Justice Policy Journal* (Fall 2008), available at **www.cjcj .org/files/alternatives_to.pdf**.

69. Peggy C. Giordano, Monica A. Longmore, Ryan D. Schroeder, and Patrick M. Seffrin, "A Life-Course Perspective on Spirituality and Desistance from Crime," *Criminology* (February 2008), 99–132.

70. Richard B. Felson and Keri B. Burchfield, "Alcohol and the Risk of Physical and Sexual Assault Victimization," *Criminology* (November 1, 2004), 837.

71. Substance Abuse and Mental Health Services, *Results of the 2013 National Survey on Drug Use and Health: Summary of National Findings* (Washington, D.C.: National Institute on Drug Abuse, September 2014), 1, 35, 47.

72. Becker, *op. cit.*

73. Myers, *op. cit.*

74. Peter B. Kraska, "The Unmentionable Alternative: The Need for and Argument against the Decriminalization of Drug Laws," in *Drugs, Crime, and the Criminal Justice System,* ed. Ralph Weisheit (Cincinnati, Ohio: Anderson Publishing, 1990).

75. Anthony A. Grace, "The Tonic/Phasal Model of Dopamine System Regulation," *Drugs and Alcohol* 37 (1995), 111.

76. Li Chuan-Yun, Mao Xizeng, and Wei Liping, "Genes and (Common) Pathways Underlying Drug Addiction," *Public Library of Science*, at **www.ploscompbiol.org/articleinfo%3Ad oi%2F10.1371%2Fjournal.pcbi.0040002**.

77. Bureau of Justice Statistics, *Fact Sheet: Drug Related Crimes* (Washington, D.C.: U.S. Department of Justice, September 1994), 1.

78. *ADAM II: 2013 Annual Report* (Washington, D.C.: Office of National Drug Policy, January 2014), xi.

79. Bureau of Justice Statistics, "Alcohol and Crime: Data from 2002 to 2008," at **bjs.ojp .usdoj.gov/content/acf/29_prisoners _and_alcoholuse.cfm** and **bjs.ojp.usdoj .gov/content/acf/30_jails_and_alcohol use .cfm**.

80. Friedman, *op. cit.*

81. Gateway Foundation, "Effects of Drug Abuse and Addiction," at **recovergateway .org/substance-abuse-resources/drug -addiction-effects**.

82. Centers for Disease Control and Prevention, "Prescription Drug Overdose in the United States: Fact Sheet," at **www.cdc.gov/home andrecreationalsafety/overdose/facts .html**.

83. Wayne Hall, Robin Room, and Susan Bondy, World Health Organization, "A Comparative Appraisal of the Health and Psychological Consequences of Alcohol, Cannabis, Nicotine and Opiate Use" (August 28, 1995), at **www.druglibrary.org/schaffer/hemp /general/who-magnitude.htm**.

84. Centers for Disease Control, "Alcohol Poisoning Deaths" (January 2015), at **www .cdc.gov/vitalsigns/alcohol-poisoning -deaths/index.html**.

85. Centers for Disease Control, "Smoking & Tobacco Use: Fast Facts," at **www.cdc.gov /tobacco/data_statistics/fact_sheets /fast_facts**.

86. James A. Inciardi, *The War on Drugs: Heroin, Cocaine, and Public Policy* (Palo Alto, Calif.: Mayfield, 1986), 148.

87. Jack Healy, "New Scrutiny on Sweets with Ascent of Marijuana in Colorado," *New York Times* (October 30, 2014), A13.

88. Quoted in Matt Ferner, "Recreational Marijuana Shops Open in Colorado," *The Huffington Post* (January 1, 2014), at **www .huffingtonpost.com/2014/01/01 /marijuana-shops-open-colorado_n _4519506.html**.

89. Quoted in Timothy Egan, "After Seven Deaths, Digging for an Explanation," *New York Times* (June 25, 2006), 12.

90. Marvin Wolfgang, Robert Figlio, and Thorsten Sellin, *Delinquency in a Birth Cohort* (Chicago: University of Chicago Press, 1972).

91. Lawrence W. Sherman, "Attacking Crime: Police and Crime Control," in *Modern Policing,* ed. Michael Tonry and Norval Morris (Chicago: University of Chicago Press, 1992), 159.

92. James Q. Wilson, "What to Do about Crime," *Commentary* (September 1994), 25–34.

93. Sarah J. Hart, "A New Way of Doing Business at the NIJ," *Law Enforcement News* (January 15/31, 2002), 9.

94. David Weisburg, "Shifting Crime and Justice Resources from Prisons to Police: Shifting Police from People to Place," *Criminology & Public Policy* (February 2011), 153–163.

95. Amanda Brandeis, "Neighborhood Sees Change after APD's Drug Market Intervention Program," *KXAN* (October 25, 2014), at **kxan.com/2014/10/25/neighborhood -sees-change-after-apds-drug-market -intervention-program**.

96. Richard Rosenfeld, "Book Review: *The Limits of Crime Control,*" *Journal of Criminal Law and Criminology* (Fall 2002).

97. *Results of the 2013 National Survey on Drug Use and Health: Summary of National Findings, op. cit.*, Figure 2.1, page 16; and Tony Dokoupil, "High Times in America," *Newsweek* (October 29, 2012), 28.

98. David Frum, "Weed Whacked," *Newsweek* (December 17, 2012), 22.

99. Quoted in Patrick Radden Keefe, "Buzzkill," *The New Yorker* (November 18, 2013), 40.

100. David Firestone, "Let the States Decide on Marijuana," *New York Times* (July 27, 2014), SR10.

101. U.S. Department of Justice, "Justice Department Announces Update to Marijuana Enforcement Policy" (August 29, 2013), at **www.justice.gov/opa/pr/justice -department-announces-update -marijuana-enforcement-policy**.

102. Jeffrey A. Miron, "The Budgetary Implications of Marijuana Prohibition" (June 2005), at **www.prohibitioncosts.org/mironreport .html**.

103. Juliette Fairley, "$50 Billion in Pot Sold Annually Nationwide, Only $2.5 Billion Is Legal," *Main Street.com* (November 6, 2014), at **www.mainstreet.com/article/50-billion -in-pot-sold-annually-nationwide-only -25-billion-is-legal**.

104. Susan Weiss, policy chief for the National Institute on Drug Abuse, quoted in "Is Marijuana Bad for You?" *The Week* (November 30, 2012), 11.

105. *Fact Sheet: Office of National Drug Control Policy* (Washington, D.C.: Executive Office of the President, October 2010), 2.

106. Ending Federal Marijuana Prohibition Act of 2013, at **www.congress.gov/bill /113th-congress/house-bill/499**.

The Crime Picture:

Offenders and Victims

Chapter Outline		Corresponding Learning Objectives
Classifications of Crimes	**1**	Discuss the primary goals of civil law and criminal law and explain how these goals are realized.
	2	Explain the differences between crimes *mala in se* and *mala prohibita*.
Measuring Crime in the United States	**3**	Identify the publication in which the FBI reports crime data and list the two main ways in which the data are reported.
	4	Distinguish between the National Crime Victimization Survey (NCVS) and self-reported surveys.
Victims of Crime	**5**	Describe the three ways that victims' rights legislation increases the ability of crime victims to participate in the criminal justice system.
	6	Discuss one major concern regarding victim participation in the criminal justice process.
Crime Trends in the United States	**7**	Identify the three factors most often used by criminologists to explain changes in the nation's crime rate.
	8	Explain why income level appears to be more important than race or ethnicity when it comes to crime trends.
	9	Discuss the prevailing explanation for the rising number of women incarcerated in the United States.

To target your study and review, look for these numbered Learning Objective icons throughout the chapter.

David McNew/Getty Images

video Evidence

physical abuse that occurs within a spousal or romantic relationship, known as domestic violence or intimate partner violence, is perhaps the most hidden criminal activity in our society. Although the federal Centers for Disease Control estimates that this behavior impacts millions of victims in the United States each year, it is still often seen as a private matter, beyond the scope of the law. The veil that covers the problem was lifted, dramatically, in September 2014, when a video surfaced that showed professional football player Ray Rice brutally attacking his then-fianceé Janay Palmer in the elevator of an Atlantic City, New Jersey, casino.

▲ Janay Rice and her husband, Ray, answer questions regarding his domestic violence arrest at a press conference in Owings Mill, Maryland.

Rob Carr/Getty Images

In the national uproar that surrounded the incident, which actually took place seven months earlier, two related questions emerged. First, why wasn't Rice punished more severely for his actions? That May, he had pleaded guilty to felony assault charges and entered a pretrial diversion program that allowed him to avoid being incarcerated. Second, what can be done to better protect victims of intimate partner violence? By chance, the Rice video controversy coincided with the twentieth anniversary of the Violence Against Women Act (VAWA), signed in September 1994. That legislation, in part, made it easier for victims to file protection orders against their abusers. It also directed millions of dollars in federal funds toward training criminal justice professionals in intimate partner violence prevention.

VAWA is credited with contributing to an 83 percent decline in domestic violence victimization between 1994 and 2012. Not all of the law's provisions have had the intended effect, however. Through grant allocations, VAWA supported *mandatory arrest policies* throughout the nation, which require police officers to arrest suspects who have abused intimate partners. Contrary to expectations, recent research shows that domestic violence homicides have actually increased in states with these laws. The problem, it seems, is that victims are less likely to contact the police if they know such contact will result in the removal of the abuser from the family home.

1. It is not uncommon for American courts to steer first-time domestic violence offenders such as Ray Rice toward counseling rather than jail or prison. What are the arguments for and against this strategy?

2. Following the release of the Rice video, several New Jersey politicians suggested changing state law to require incarceration for first-time domestic violence offenders. Given the results of mandatory arrest policies described above, what might be some of the unintended consequences of this proposed legislation?

3. Janay Palmer Rice, who married Ray Rice six weeks after he punched her in the casino elevator, called the incident "a family matter." Why might a domestic violence victim reject interference by the criminal justice system in her or his abusive relationship?

Classification of Crimes

For a variety of reasons, many of which are evident in the Ray Rice case, the criminal justice system often struggles to find the proper response to intimate partner violence. Recognizing this, the original version of the Violence Against Women Act included a provision that allowed victims of domestic violence to sue their abusers in federal civil court for monetary damages. These lawsuits could go forward even if no criminal charges were filed in the matter.[1]

The United States Supreme Court eventually struck down this provision as unconstitutional.[2] Still, Congress's failed attempt to provide a separate remedy for intimate violence victims does, for our purposes, highlight the distinction between civil law and criminal law in the United States. We start this chapter with an explanation of this distinction, followed by a discussion of the differences between (a) felonies and misdemeanors and (b) crimes *mala in se* and *mala prohibita.*

Civil Law and Criminal Law

All law can be divided into two categories: civil law and criminal law. As U.S. criminal law has evolved, it has diverged from U.S. civil law. These two categories of law are distinguished by their primary goals. The criminal justice system is concerned with protecting society from harm by preventing and prosecuting crimes. A crime is an act so reprehensible that it is considered a wrong against society as a whole, as well as against the individual victim. Therefore, the state prosecutes a person who commits a criminal act. If the state is able to prove that a person is guilty of a crime, the government will punish her or him with imprisonment or fines, or both.

Civil law, which includes all types of law other than criminal law, is concerned with disputes between private individuals and between entities. Proceedings in civil lawsuits are normally initiated by an individual or a corporation (in contrast to criminal proceedings, which are initiated by public prosecutors). Such disputes may involve, for example, the terms of a contract, the ownership of property, or an automobile accident. Under civil law, the government provides a forum for the resolution of *torts*—or private wrongs—in which the injured party, called the **plaintiff,** tries to prove that a wrong has been committed by the accused party, or the **defendant.** (Note that the accused party in both criminal and civil cases is known as the *defendant.*)

 LEARNING OBJECTIVE 1 Discuss the primary goals of civil law and criminal law and explain how these goals are realized.

Guilt and Responsibility A criminal court is convened to determine whether the defendant is *guilty*—that is, whether the defendant has, in fact, committed the offense charged. In contrast, civil law is concerned with responsibility, a much more flexible concept. For example, nearly a decade ago Adam Jones started a melee in a Las Vegas strip club by tossing hundreds of dollar bills into the air. During the ensuing brawl, doorman Tommy Urbanski was shot and paralyzed from the waist down. Jones did not pull the trigger nor was he charged with any crime. Nonetheless, in 2015 a civil appeals court decided that he was **liable,** or legally responsible, for Urbanski's injuries because of his irresponsible behavior.

Most civil cases involve a request for monetary damages to compensate for the wrong that has been committed. Thus, the civil court ordered Jones to pay Tommy Urbanski and his ex-wife, Kathy, about $11.2 million to cover medical costs and loss of earnings, as well as for infliction of emotional distress.

Civil Law The branch of law dealing with the definition and enforcement of all private or public rights, as opposed to criminal matters.

Plaintiff The person or institution that initiates a lawsuit in civil court proceedings by filing a complaint.

Defendant In a civil court, the person or institution against whom an action is brought. In a criminal court, the person or entity who has been formally accused of violating a criminal law.

Liability In a civil court, legal responsibility for one's own or another's actions.

The Burden of Proof Although criminal law proceedings are completely separate from civil law proceedings in the modern legal system, the two systems do have some similarities. Both attempt to control behavior by imposing sanctions on those who violate society's definition of acceptable behavior. Furthermore, criminal and civil law often supplement each other. In certain instances, a victim may file a civil suit against an individual who is also the target of a criminal prosecution by the government.

Because the burden of proof is much greater in criminal trials than civil ones, it is almost always easier to win monetary damages than a criminal conviction. The most famous (or infamous) example of such a situation in recent memory occurred about twenty years ago. After former professional football player O. J. Simpson was acquitted of murder charges in the deaths of his ex-wife, Nicole, and Ronald Goldman, the families of the two victims sued Simpson. In 1997, a civil court jury found Simpson liable for the wrongful deaths of his ex-wife and Goldman, and ordered him to pay their families $33.5 million in damages.

During the criminal trial, the jury did not find enough evidence to prove **beyond a reasonable doubt** (the burden of proof in criminal cases) that Simpson was guilty of any crime. In contrast, the civil trial established by a **preponderance of the evidence** (the burden of proof in civil cases) that Simpson had killed his victims in a fit of jealous rage. (See this chapter's *Mastering Concepts* feature for a comparison of civil and criminal law.)

Felonies and Misdemeanors

Depending on their degree of seriousness, crimes are classified as *felonies* or *misdemeanors.* **Felonies** are crimes punishable by death or by imprisonment in a federal or state prison for one year or longer (though some states, such as North Carolina, consider felonies to be punishable by at least two years' incarceration). The Model Penal Code, a general guide for criminal law that you will learn more about in the next chapter, provides for four degrees of felony:

1. Capital offenses, for which the maximum penalty is death.
2. First degree felonies, punishable by a maximum penalty of life imprisonment.
3. Second degree felonies, punishable by a maximum of ten years' imprisonment.
4. Third degree felonies, punishable by a maximum of five years' imprisonment.

For the most part, felonies involve crimes of violence such as armed robbery or sexual assault, or other "serious" crimes such as stealing a large amount of money or selling illegal drugs.

▼ Police officers question two men suspected of shoplifting in National City, California. **Do you think that this crime, which involves stealing items from a store while posing as a customer, should be considered a felony or a misdemeanor? How does the value of the items stolen influence your answer?** Ricky Carioti/*The Washington Post* via Getty Images

Types of Misdemeanors Under federal law and in most states, any crime that is not a felony is considered a **misdemeanor.** Misdemeanors are crimes punishable by a fine or by confinement for up to a year. If imprisoned, the guilty party goes to a local jail instead of a prison. Disorderly conduct and trespassing are common misdemeanors. Most states distinguish between *gross misdemeanors,* which are offenses punishable by thirty days to a year in jail, and *petty misdemeanors,* or offenses punishable by fewer than thirty days in jail. Probation and community service are often imposed on those who commit misdemeanors, especially juveniles. As you will

Issue	Civil Law	Criminal Law
Area of concern	Rights and duties between individuals	Offenses against society as a whole
Wrongful act	Harm to a person or business entity	Violation of a statute that prohibits some type of activity
Party who brings suit	Person who suffered harm (plaintiff)	The state (prosecutor)
Party who responds	Person who supposedly caused harm (defendant)	Person who allegedly committed a crime (defendant)
Standard of proof	Preponderance of the evidence	Beyond a reasonable doubt
Remedy	Damages to compensate for the harm	Punishment (fine or incarceration)

see in Chapter 8, whether a crime is a felony or misdemeanor can also determine in which criminal court the case will be tried.

Infractions The least serious form of wrongdoing is often called an **infraction** and is punishable only by a small fine. Even though infractions such as parking tickets or traffic violations technically represent illegal activity, they generally are not considered "crimes." Therefore, infractions rarely lead to jury trials and are deemed to be so minor that they do not appear on the offender's criminal record. In some jurisdictions, the terms *infraction* and *petty offense* are interchangeable. In others, however, they are different. Under federal guidelines, for example, an infraction can be punished by up to five days behind bars, while a petty offender is only liable for a fine.[3] Finally, those who string together a series of infractions (or fail to pay the fines that come with such offenses) are in danger of being criminally charged. In Illinois, having three or more speeding violations in one year is considered criminal behavior.[4]

Mala in Se and *Mala Prohibita*

Criminologists often express the social function of criminal law in terms of *mala in se* or *mala prohibita* crimes. A criminal act is referred to as **mala in se** if it would be considered wrong even if there were no law prohibiting it. *Mala in se* crimes are said to go against "natural laws"—that is, against the "natural, moral, and public" principles of a society. Murder, rape, and theft are examples of *mala in se* crimes. These crimes are generally the same from country to country or culture to culture.

In contrast, the term **mala prohibita** refers to acts that are considered crimes only because they have been codified as such through statute—"human-made" laws. A *mala prohibita* crime is considered wrong only because it has been prohibited. It is not inherently wrong, though it may reflect the moral standards of a society at a given time. Thus, the definition of a *mala prohibita* crime can vary from country to country and even from state to state. Bigamy, or the offense of having two legal spouses, could be considered a *mala prohibita* crime.

Making the Distinction Some observers question the distinction between *mala in se* and *mala prohibita*. In many instances, it is difficult to define a "pure" *mala in se* crime. That is, it is difficult to separate a crime from the culture that has deemed

LEARNING
2
OBJECTIVE

Explain the differences between crimes *mala in se* and *mala prohibita*.

Infraction In most jurisdictions, a noncriminal offense for which the penalty is a fine rather than incarceration.

Mala in Se A descriptive term for acts that are inherently wrong, regardless of whether they are prohibited by law.

Mala Prohibita A descriptive term for acts that are made illegal by criminal statute and are not necessarily wrong in and of themselves.

CJ Policy—Your Take

Supporters of **legalized prostitution** point out that such a policy would provide tax revenues for state and county governments, and free up law enforcement to focus on more important, non-victimless criminal activity. It would also reduce the risk of sexually transmitted disease and violence for the prostitutes, who presently operate outside the protection of the law. Do you think these arguments are strong enough to start a "legalize prostitution" movement in the United States, as has been the case with marijuana? Why or why not?

it a crime.[5] Even murder, under certain cultural circumstances, is not considered a criminal act. In a number of poor, traditional areas of the Middle East and Asia, the law excuses "honor killings," in which men kill female family members suspected of sexual indiscretion.

Our own legal system excuses homicide in extreme situations, such as self-defense or when a law enforcement agent kills in the course of upholding the law. Therefore, "natural" laws can be seen as culturally specific. Similar difficulties occur in trying to define a "pure" *mala prohibita* crime. More than 150 countries, including most members of the European Union, have legalized prostitution. With the exception of seven rural counties of Nevada, prostitution is illegal in the United States. (The arguments for legalizing prostitution in this country are similar to those for legalizing drugs, which we discussed in the previous chapter. See this chapter's *CJ Policy—Your Take* feature to make your own judgment on the issue.)

The Drug Dilemma The *mala in se/mala prohibita* distinction helps explain a contradiction that we touched on in the previous chapter: Why has society prohibited the use of certain drugs, while allowing the use of others? The answer cannot be found in the risk of harm caused by the substances. Just as with illegal drugs, many legal drugs, if abused, can have serious consequences for the health of the user or of others. Improper consumption of the nonprescription pain reliever Tylenol (acctaminophen) is a leading cause of liver failure in the United States today,[6] and about 10,000 Americans are killed in alcohol-related car crashes each year.[7] Nor is illegality linked to the addictive quality of the drug. According to the American Medical Association, nicotine is the most habit-forming substance, with over two-thirds of people who smoke cigarettes becoming "hooked."[8] The next most addictive drug is heroin, followed by cocaine, alcohol, amphetamines, and marijuana, in that order. The drug most widely associated with violent behavior, especially domestic violence, is alcohol.[9] One professor of preventive medicine has concluded that "there are no scientific . . . or medical bases on which the legal distinctions between various drugs are made."[10]

If drug laws are not based on science or medicine, on what are they based? The answers lies in the concept of *mala prohibita:* certain drugs are characterized as illegal while others are not because of presiding social norms and values. Alcohol and tobacco are legal not because they have pharmacological effects that are considerably different or safer than those of illegal drugs, but rather because the law, as supported by society, says so.[11] Furthermore, as we saw in last chapter's discussion of the legalization of marijuana, sometimes certain segments of society challenge the status quo, placing pressure on criminal law to adjust accordingly.

Measuring Crime in the United States

So far in this textbook, you have been exposed to a number of studies relating to the criminal justice system. For the most part, these analyses have dealt with narrow topics such as the police response to jaywalking, the impact of Walmart expansion on offending, and the possible existence of a "crime gene." The best-known annual survey of criminal behavior, however, tries to answer the broadest of questions: How much crime is there in the United States?

The Uniform Crime Report

Suppose that a firefighter dies while fighting a fire at an office building. Later, police discover that the building manager intentionally set the fire. All of the elements of the crime of arson have certainly been met, but can the manager be charged with murder? In some jurisdictions, the act might be considered a form of murder, but according to the U.S. Department of Justice, arson-related deaths and injuries of police officers and firefighters due to the "hazardous natures of their professions" are not murders.[12]

The distinction is important because the Department of Justice provides us with the most far-reaching and oft-cited set of national crime statistics. Each year, the department releases the **Uniform Crime Report (UCR)**. Since its inception in 1930, the UCR has attempted to measure the overall rate of crime in the United States by organizing "offenses known to law enforcement."[13] To produce the UCR, the Federal Bureau of Investigation (FBI) relies on the voluntary participation of local law enforcement agencies. These agencies—approximately 18,400 in total, covering most of the population—base their information on three measurements:

1. The number of persons arrested.
2. The number of crimes reported by victims, witnesses, or the police themselves.
3. Police employee data.[14]

Once this information has been sent to the FBI, the agency presents the crime data in two important ways:

LEARNING OBJECTIVE 3 Identify the publication in which the FBI reports crime data and list the two main ways in which the data are reported.

1. As a *rate* per 100,000 people. So, for example, suppose the crime rate in a given year is 3,500. This means that, for every 100,000 inhabitants of the United States, 3,500 *Part I offenses* were reported to the FBI by local police departments. The crime rate is often cited by media sources when discussing the level of crime in the United States.
2. As a *percentage* change from the previous year or other time periods. From 2004 to 2013, there was a 14.5 percent decrease in violent crime and a 16.3 percent decrease in property crime. Thus, according to the UCR, that decade saw a significant reduction in criminal behavior in the United States.[15]

The Department of Justice publishes its data annually in *Crime in the United States*. Along with the basic statistics, this publication offers an exhaustive array of crime information, including breakdowns of crimes committed by city, county, and other geographic designations and by the demographics (gender, race, age) of the individuals who have been arrested for crimes.

Part I Offenses

The UCR divides the criminal offenses it measures into two major categories: Part I and Part II offenses. **Part I offenses** are those crimes that, due to their seriousness and frequency, are recorded by the FBI to give a general idea of the "crime picture" in the United States in any given year. For a description of the seven Part I offenses, see Figure 3.1.

Part I violent offenses are those most likely to be covered by the media and, consequently, inspire the most fear of crime in the population. These crimes have come to dominate crime coverage to such an extent that, for most Americans, the first image that comes to mind at the mention of "crime" is one person physically attacking another person or a robbery taking place with the use or threat of force.[16] Furthermore, in the stereotypical crime, the offender and the victim usually do not know each other.

Uniform Crime Report (UCR) An annual report compiled by the FBI to give an indication of criminal activity in the United States.

Part I Offenses Crimes reported annually by the FBI in its Uniform Crime Report. Part I offenses include murder, rape, robbery, aggravated assault, burglary, larceny, and motor vehicle theft.

FIGURE 3.1 Part I Offenses

Every month, local law enforcement agencies voluntarily provide information on serious offenses in their jurisdiction to the FBI. These serious offenses, known as Part I offenses, are defined here. (Arson is not included in the national crime report data, but it is sometimes considered a Part I offense nonetheless, so its definition is included here.) As the graph shows, most Part I offenses reported by local police departments in any given year are property crimes.

Murder. The willful (nonnegligent) killing of one human being by another.

Rape. The penetration, no matter how slight, of the vagina or anus with any body part or object, or oral penetration by a sex organ of another person, without the consent of the victim.

Robbery. The taking or attempting to take of anything of value from the care, custody, or control of a person or persons by force or threat of force or violence and/or by putting the victim in fear.

Aggravated assault. An unlawful attack by one person on another for the purpose of inflicting severe or aggravated bodily injury. This type of assault is usually accompanied by the use of a weapon or by means likely to produce death or great bodily harm.

Burglary—breaking or entering. The unlawful entry of a structure to commit a felony or a theft. Attempted forcible entry is included.

Larceny/theft (except motor vehicle theft). The unlawful taking, carrying, leading, or riding away of property from the possession or constructive possession of another.

Motor vehicle theft. The theft or attempted theft of a motor vehicle.

Arson. Any willful or malicious burning or attempt to burn, with or without intent to defraud, a dwelling house, public building, motor vehicle or aircraft, personal property of another, and the like.

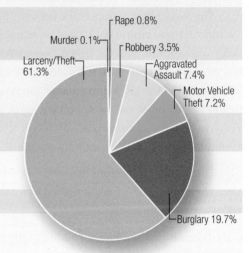

Murder 0.1% — Rape 0.8% — Robbery 3.5% — Aggravated Assault 7.4% — Motor Vehicle Theft 7.2% — Larceny/Theft 61.3% — Burglary 19.7%

Sources: Federal Bureau of Investigation, *Crime in the United States, 2013* (Washington, D.C.: U.S. Department of Justice, 2014), at **www.fbi.gov/about-us/cjis/ucr/crime-in-the-u.s/2013/crime-in-the-u.s.-2013/resource-pages/offense-definitions/13-offensedefinitions_final** and **www.fbi.gov/about-us/cjis/ucr/crime-in-the-u.s/2013/crime-in-the-u.s.-2013/tables/1tabledatadecoverviewpdf/table_1_crime_in_the_united_states_by_volume_and_rate_per_100000_inhabitants_1994-2013.xls.**

Given the trauma of violent crimes, this perception is understandable, but it is not accurate. According to UCR statistics, a relative or other acquaintance of the victim commits at least 45 percent of the homicides in the United States.[17] Furthermore, as is evident from Figure 3.1, the majority of Part I offenses committed are property crimes. Notice that 61 percent of all reported Part I offenses are larceny/thefts, and another 20 percent are burglaries.[18]

Part II Offenses

Not only do violent crimes represent the minority of Part I offenses, but Part I offenses are far outweighed by **Part II offenses,** which include all crimes recorded by the FBI that do not fall into the category of Part I offenses. While Part I offenses are almost always felonies, Part II offenses include criminal behavior that is often classified as a misdemeanor. Of the nineteen categories that make up Part II offenses, the most common are drug abuse violations, simple assaults (in which no weapons are used and no serious harm is done to the victim), driving under the influence, and disorderly conduct.[19]

Information gathered on Part I offenses reflects those offenses "known," or reported to the FBI by local agencies. Part II offenses, in contrast, are measured only by arrest data. In 2013, the FBI recorded about 2 million arrests for Part I offenses in the United States. That same year, about 9.3 million arrests for Part II offenses took place.[20] In other words, a Part II offense was four and one-half times more common than a Part I offense. Such statistics have prompted Marcus Felson, a professor at Rutgers University School of Criminal Justice, to comment that "most crime is very ordinary."[21]

Part II Offenses All crimes recorded by the FBI that do not fall into the category of Part I offenses. These crimes include both misdemeanors and felonies.

The UCR: A Flawed Method?

Even though the UCR is the predominant source of crime data in the country, there are numerous questions about the accuracy of its findings. For one, there is scattered evidence that some local police departments manipulate their crime reports. A recent *Los Angeles Times* investigation found that the Los Angeles Police Department misclassified nearly 1,200 violent offenses as minor crimes in 2013, severely distorting the city's crime reports for that year.[22] Furthermore, the UCR most likely suffers from the twin problems of underreporting and inconsistency.

Police Notification For the UCR to be accurate, citizens must report criminal activity to the police, and the police must then pass this information on to the FBI. Criminologists have long been aware that neither citizens nor police can be expected to perform these roles with consistency.[23] Citizens may not report a crime for any number of reasons, including fear of reprisal, embarrassment, or a personal bias in favor of the offender. Many also feel that police cannot do anything to help them in the aftermath of a crime, so they do not see the point of involving law enforcement agents in their lives. Surveys of crime victims reveal that only 46 percent of violent crimes and 36 percent of property crimes are reported to the police.[24] In general, people seem more willing to notify police about robberies and aggravated assaults by strangers than about rapes or violence that occurs within the family context.[25]

Problems with Discretion and Definitions Local police departments have a great deal of discretion in interpreting what constitutes a Part I offense, which can lead to inconsistencies. In Illinois, for example, if one person strikes another person but does not cause any harm, the offender is usually charged with a misdemeanor. If the victim is a police officer or a teacher, however, the misdemeanor becomes felony assault. So, in that state, an incident in which a teacher's finger is scratched and one where a victim is shot nonfatally could both be reported to the FBI as "aggravated assaults."[26]

Furthermore, the FBI and local law enforcement agencies do not always interpret Part I offenses in the same manner. In Chicago, for example, the police department routinely labels unsolved homicides as "noncriminal death investigations" rather than murders as defined by the UCR. This occurs even when a "willful killing" seems apparent, as was the case with one "noncriminal death" victim whose decomposed body was found with evidence that she had been tied to a chair with telephone wire.[27]

The National Incident-Based Reporting System

In the 1980s, well aware of the various criticisms of the UCR, the Department of Justice began seeking ways to revise its data-collecting system. The result was the National Incident-Based Reporting System (NIBRS). In the NIBRS, local agencies collect data on each single crime occurrence within twenty-three offense categories made up of forty-nine specific crimes called Group A offenses. These data are recorded on computerized record systems provided—though not completely financed—by the federal government.

The NIBRS became available to local agencies in 1989. Twenty-six years later, thirty-three states have been NIBRS certified, and fifteen of those states now submit all their crime data to the federal government using this program.[28] Criminologists are responding enthusiastically to the NIBRS because the system provides information about four "data sets"—offenses, victims, offenders, and arrestees—unavailable through the UCR.

Victim Surveys A method of gathering crime data that directly surveys participants to determine their experiences as victims of crime.

Dark Figure of Crime A term used to describe the actual amount of crime that takes place. The "figure" is "dark," or impossible to detect, because a great number of crimes are never reported to the police.

The NIBRS also presents a more complete picture of crime by monitoring all criminal "incidents" reported to the police, not just those that lead to an arrest. For example, the 2013 NIBRS, which recorded more than 5.6 million criminal incidents, found that sex offenses were most likely to take place between midnight and 12:59 A.M., and that nearly 100,000 aggravated assaults were the result of an argument.[29] (See Figure 3.2 to get a clearer sense of the differences between the UCR and the NIBRS.)

Victim Surveys

One alternative method of data collecting attempts to avoid the distorting influence of the "intermediary," or the local police agencies. In **victim surveys,** criminologists or other researchers ask the victims of crime directly about their experiences, using techniques such as interviews or e-mail and phone surveys. The first large-scale victim survey took place in 1966, when members of 10,000 households answered questionnaires as part of the President's Commission on Law Enforcement and the Administration of Justice. The results indicated a much higher victimization rate than had been previously expected, and researchers felt the process gave them a better understanding of the **dark figure of crime,** or the actual amount of crime that occurs in the country.

The National Crime Victimization Survey Criminologists were so encouraged by the results of the 1966 experiment that the federal government decided to institute an ongoing victim survey. The result was the National Crime Victimization Survey (NCVS), which started in 1972. Conducted by the U.S. Bureau of the Census in cooperation with the Bureau of Justice Statistics of the Justice Department, the NCVS conducts an annual survey of approximately 90,000 households with about 160,000 occupants over twelve years of age. Participants are interviewed twice a year concerning their experiences with crimes in the prior six months. As you can see in Figure 3.3, questions are quite detailed in determining the experiences of crime victims.

FIGURE 3.2 Comparing the UCR and the NIBRS

As the following scenario shows, the process of crime data collection under the NIBRS is much more comprehensive than the reporting system of the UCR.

At approximately 9:30 p.m. on March 22, 2015, two young males approach a thirty-two-year-old African American woman in the parking garage of a movie theater. The first man, who is white, puts a knife to the woman's throat and grabs her purse, which contains $150. The second man, who is Hispanic, then puts a gun to the woman's temple and rapes her. When he is finished, he shoots her in the chest, a wound that does not prove to be fatal. The two men flee the scene and are not apprehended by law enforcement.

	UCR	NIBRS
Crime reported to FBI	One rape. Under the UCR, when more than one crime is involved in a single incident, only the most serious is reported. Also, attempts are not recorded.	One rape, one robbery, and one attempted murder.
Age, sex, and race of the victim	Not recorded.	Recorded.
Age, sex, and race of the offenders	Not recorded.	Recorded.
Location and time of the attack	Not recorded.	Recorded.
Type and value of lost property	Not recorded.	Recorded.

Source: U.S. Department of Justice.

FIGURE 3.3 Sample Questions from the NCVS (National Crime Victimization Survey)

36a. Was something belonging to YOU stolen, such as
a. Things that you carry, like luggage, a wallet, purse, briefcase, book
b. Clothing, jewelry, or cell phone
c. Bicycle or sports equipment
d. Things in your home—like a TV, stereo, or tools
e. Things outside your home, such as a garden hose or lawn furniture
f. Things belonging to children in the household
g. Things from a vehicle, such as a package, groceries, camera, or CDs?

41a. Has anyone attacked or threatened you in any of these ways
a. With any weapon, for instance, a gun or knife
b. With anything like a baseball bat, frying pan, scissors, or stick
c. By something thrown, such as a rock or a bottle
d. Include any grabbing, punching, or choking
e. Any rape, attempted rape, or other type of sexual attack
f. Any face to face threats OR
g. Any attack or threat or use of force by anyone at all? Please mention it even if you are not certain it was a crime.

43a. Incidents involving forced or unwanted sexual acts are often difficult to talk about. Have you been forced or coerced to engage in unwanted sexual activity by
a. Someone you didn't know
b. A casual acquaintance OR
c. Someone you know well?

45. During the last six months, did anything you thought was a crime happen to YOU, but you did NOT report it to the police?
a. Yes
b. No

Source: Adapted from U.S. Department of Justice, *National Crime Victimization Survey 2009* (Washington, D.C.: Bureau of Justice Statistics, 2013).

Advantages and Disadvantages Proponents of the NCVS highlight a number of aspects in which the victim survey is superior to the UCR:

1. It measures both reported and unreported crime.
2. It is unaffected by police bias and distortions in reporting crime to the FBI.
3. It does not rely on victims directly reporting crime to the police.[30]

In the past, the NCVS was criticized for the use of confusing, technical jargon in its questions. As is clear from Figure 3.3, efforts have been made to simplify the survey's language so that it is more easily understood. Another problem with any victim survey is that the responses cannot be verified. If a participant, for whatever reason, fails to answer truthfully, the faulty response is recorded as fact.[31]

The Definition of Rape One of the most celebrated aspects of victim surveys is that they give the victim a "voice" in the criminal justice system. This voice was certainly heard in the recent debate concerning the federal government's definition of sexual assault. Up until 2013, the UCR defined rape as "the carnal knowledge of a female forcibly and against her will." Victims' rights groups had long argued that this definition omitted offenses involving male victims, oral and anal penetration, and a wide range of nonconsensual sexual activity. The "legacy" tradition would not, for example, cover the rape of any man or of a woman who was unconscious when she was sexually assaulted.

One victim survey, defining the crime as "forced penetration" or "attempted forced penetration," estimated that as many as 1.3 million American women are the victims of sexual assault each year—about fifteen times the standard UCR tally.[32] The new UCR definition of rape, included in Figure 3.2, is much more detailed and covers a broader spectrum of unwanted sexual activities.[33] Somewhat surprisingly, however, the 2013 UCR, using this new definition, showed a decrease of nearly 5,400 rapes from the previous year.[34]

Distinguish between the LEARNING
National Crime Victimization
Survey (NCVS) and self-
reported surveys. OBJECTIVE **4**

Self-Reported Surveys

Based on many of the same principles as victim surveys, but focusing instead on offenders, **self-reported surveys** are a third source of information for criminologists. In this form of data collection, persons are asked directly—through personal interviews or questionnaires, or over the telephone—about specific criminal activity to which they may have been a party. Self-reported surveys are most useful in situations in which the group to be studied is already gathered in an institutional setting, such as a juvenile facility or a prison. One of the most widespread self-reported surveys in the United States, the Drug Use Forecasting Program, collects information on narcotics use from arrestees who have been brought into booking facilities.

Because there is no penalty for admitting to criminal activity in a self-reported survey, subjects tend to be more forthcoming in discussing their behavior. Researchers often use self-reported studies to get a better idea of the actual amount of sexual assault that takes place in our society. These studies invariably show that many more rapes take place than are reported to the police.[35] Such conclusions underscore the most striking finding of self-reported surveys: the dark figure of crime, referred to earlier as the *actual* amount of crime that takes place, appears to be much larger than the UCR or NCVS would suggest.

Ethics Challenge

Given the importance placed on crime statistics by the public and the media, the temptation within local police departments to "doctor" these stats, described in this section, is inescapable. What steps could police administrators take to discourage this clearly unethical behavior? ■

Victims of Crime

It is no coincidence that the U.S. Department of Justice launched the first version of the National Crime Victimization Survey in the 1970s. The previous decade had seen a dramatic increase in the rights afforded to criminal defendants. To offset what they saw as a growing imbalance in the American criminal justice system, advocates had begun to argue that crime victims also needed greater protection under the law. Initially, the victims' rights movement focused on specific areas of crime, such as domestic violence, sexual assault, and, through the efforts of Mothers Against Drunk Driving, vehicular homicide.[36] Today, an emphasis on the rights of all crime victims has a profound impact on the workings of law enforcement, courts, and corrections in the United States.

Legal Rights of Crime Victims

Thirty years ago, a presidential task force invited federal and state legislatures to "address the needs of the millions of Americans and their families who are victimized by crime every year and who often carry its scars into the years to come."[37] This call to action was, in large part, a consequence of the rather peculiar position of victims in our criminal justice system. That is, once a crime has occurred, the victim is relegated to a single role: being a witness against the suspect in court. Legally, he or she has no say in the prosecution of the offender, or even whether such a prosecution is to take place. Such powerlessness can be extremely frustrating, particularly in the wake of a traumatic, life-changing event.

Self-Reported Survey A method of gathering crime data that relies on participants to reveal and detail their own criminal or delinquent behavior.

Legislative Action To remedy this situation, all states have passed legislation creating certain rights for victims. On a federal level, such protections are encoded in the Crime Victims' Rights Act of 2004 (CVRA), which gives victims "the right to participate in the system."[38] This participation primarily focuses on three categories of rights:

 LEARNING OBJECTIVE **5** Describe the three ways that victims' rights legislation increases the ability of crime victims to participate in the criminal justice system.

1. The right to be *informed*. This includes receiving information about victims' rights in general, as well as specific information such as the dates and time of court proceedings relating to the relevant crime.
2. The right to be *present*. This includes the right to be present at those court hearings involving the case at hand, as long as the victim's presence does not interfere with the rights of the accused.
3. The right to be *heard*. This includes the ability to consult with prosecutorial officials before the criminal trial (addressed in Chapter 9), to speak during the sentencing phase of the trial (Chapter 11), and to offer an opinion when the offender is scheduled to be released from incarceration (Chapter 12).[39]

Some jurisdictions also provide victims with the right of law enforcement protection from the offender during the time period before a criminal trial. In addition, most states require *restitution*, or monetary payment, from offenders to help victims repay any costs associated with the crime and rebuild their lives. In 2014, for instance, a federal judge ordered three men who illegally started a two-thousand-acre fire in Southern California to pay several million dollars to the residents whose homes the blaze destroyed. (To learn about one potential downside of the victims' rights movement, see the feature *A Question of Ethics: With a Vengeance.*)

Enforceability Although many victims have benefited from victims' rights legislation, advocates still find fault with the manner in which such legislation is applied. The main problem, they say, is that the federal and state laws do not contain sufficient enforcement mechanisms. That is, if a victim's rights are violated in some way, the victim has little recourse.

This situation is changing, gradually, thanks to state ballot initiatives, a process we will discuss in the next chapter. In 2008, for example, California voters passed "Marsy's Law," a ballot initiative named after a woman whose murderer was released from prison without state officials notifying that woman's family. Importantly, the law provides *legal standing* for crime victims. This means that, if a California crime victim believes that his or her rights have been violated, he or she can go to court to have those rights enforced.[40] In 2014, Illinois voters passed their own version of Marsy's Law,[41] and several other states are considering similar actions.

Victim Services

The consequences for crime victims go well beyond frustrations with the criminal justice system. Many feel some degree of anger, guilt, shame, and grief. In particular, victims of violent crimes are at a high risk of post-traumatic stress disorder (PTSD), a

▼ Crystal King, left, addresses a criminal court in Chardon, Ohio, during the sentencing of T. J. Lane for murdering her brother. **Should crime victims and their families have the "right" to participate in criminal justice proceedings? Why or why not?** AP Images/*The News-Herald,* Duncan Scott, Pool

condition that burdens sufferers with extreme anxiety and flashbacks relating to the traumatic event. Crime victims also experience higher-than-normal levels of depression, drug abuse, and suicidal tendencies.[42]

In addition to the emotional support of family and friends, a number of victim services exist to help with these symptoms of victimization. Hundreds of *crisis intervention centers* operate around the country, providing a wide range of aid. For example, the Donald W. Reynolds Crisis Intervention Center in Fort Smith, Arkansas, offers counseling, shelter, and relocation guidance to victims of domestic violence and sexual assault. These centers also allow for contact with *victim advocates,* or individuals that help victims gain access to public benefits, health care, employment and educational assistance, and numerous other services. The impact of such programs is, however, somewhat limited. Only about 9 percent of victims of violent crimes avail themselves of victim service agencies.[43]

The Risks of Victimization

Anybody can be a victim of crime. This does not mean, however, that everybody is at an equal risk of being victimized. In the previous chapter, for instance, we noted that residents of neighborhoods with heavy concentrations of payday lending businesses are targeted by criminals at unusually high rates.[44] To better explain the circumstances surrounding this type of victimization, criminologists Larry Cohen and Marcus Felson devised the *routine activities theory*. According to Cohen and Felson, most criminal acts require the following:

A Question of Ethics: With a Vengeance

LEARNING
6
OBJECTIVE

Discuss one major concern regarding victim participation in the criminal justice process.

The Situation During the recent trial of her son's murderer in Chardon, Ohio, Dina Parmertor pointed her finger at the defendant and said, "You don't deserve to be called human. You are a monster. You are a weak, pathetic, vile coward."

The Ethical Dilemma Such feelings are understandable, but they cause a certain amount of distrust regarding the victims' rights movement's impact on our criminal justice system. In most cases, victims cannot be expected to be objective or impartial. A victim would never, for example, be allowed to sit on a jury. Indeed, some worry that increasing the legal rights of victims creates an imbalance in our criminal justice system. According to one expert, this trends forces "prosecutors and judges [to] elevate victims over the defendant and the public" and "may threaten the fair and just adjudication of a crime case."

What Is the Solution? Does the concept of revenge have a place in the American criminal justice

system? Most observers would assert strongly that it does not. Ideally, criminal justice professionals have an ethical obligation to be fair, objective, and impartial, and to avoid the desire to inflict harm on a criminal for reasons of vengeance, no matter how heinous the crime.

What about victims of crime? During the colonial period of the 1600s, crime victims played a dominant role in the American criminal justice system. A victim would hire a sheriff to pursue and arrest the defendant, and pay court officials to run the trial. What are the disadvantages of such as system for society? Are there any advantages?

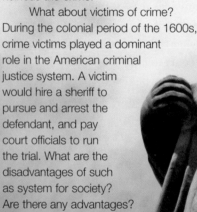

1. A likely offender.
2. A suitable target (a person or an object).
3. The absence of a capable guardian—that is, any person (not necessarily a law enforcement agent) whose presence or proximity prevents a crime from happening.[45]

Repeat Victimization The theory that certain people and places are more likely to be subject to repeated criminal activity and that past victimization is a strong indicator of future victimization.

When these three factors are present, the likelihood of crime rises. Cohen and Felson cite routine activities theory in explaining the link between payday lenders and crime. People who use payday lenders often leave those establishments with large sums of cash, late at night or during weekends when there is less street traffic. Consequently, they act as suitable targets, attracting likely offenders to neighborhoods where the payday lenders are located.[46]

Repeat Victimization Cohen and Felson also hypothesize that offenders attach "values" to suitable targets. The higher the value, the more likely that target is going to be the subject of a crime.[47] A gold watch, for example, would obviously have a higher value for a thief than a plastic watch and therefore is more likely to be stolen. Similarly, people who are perceived to be weak or unprotected can have high value for criminals. Law enforcement officials in southern Florida, for example, believe that undocumented immigrants in the area have elevated victimization rates because criminals know they are afraid to report crimes to authorities for fear of being removed from the country.

Resources such as the National Crime Victimization Survey provide criminologists with an important tool for determining which types of people are most valued as potential victims. Statistics clearly show that a relatively small number of victims are involved in a disproportionate number of crimes. These findings support an approach to crime analysis known as **repeat victimization.** This theory is based on the premise that certain populations—mostly low-income resident of urban areas—are more likely to be victims of crimes than others and, therefore, past victimization is a strong predictor of future victimization.[48] Further criminological research shows that factors such as drug and alcohol use and depression also increase the possibility that a crime victim will be revictimized.[49]

The Victim-Offender Connection Not only does past victimization seem to increase the risk of future victimization, but so does past criminal behavior. "The notion that [violent crimes] are random bolts of lightning, which is the commonly held image, is not the reality at all," says David Kennedy, a professor at New York's John Jay College of Criminal Justice.[50]

Kennedy's point is further made by Figure 3.4, which identifies young minority males from urban neighborhoods as the most common victims of crimes. This demographic, as will become clear later in the chapter, is also at the highest risk for criminal behavior. Increasingly, law enforcement agencies are applying the lessons of repeat victimization and other victim studies to concentrate their attention on "hot spots" of crime, a strategy we address in Chapter 6.

EthicsChallenge

Many state victims' rights acts include provisions protecting the privacy of victims and their families. Should these privacy provisions outweigh the public's "right to know" certain facts about crimes? For example, would it be unethical for the police to release photos of a murder victim from the crime scene, or toxicology reports indicating that he or she was drunk or under the influence of drugs at the time of death? Explain your answer. ■

Crime Trends in the United States

The UCR, NCVS, and other statistical measures we have discussed so far in this chapter, though important, represent only the tip of the iceberg of crime data. Thanks to the efforts of government law enforcement agencies, educational institutions, and private individuals, more information on crime is available today than at any time in the nation's history. When interpreting and predicting general crime trends, experts tend to rely on what University of California at Berkeley law professor Franklin Zimring calls the three "usual suspects" of crime fluctuation:

LEARNING OBJECTIVE 7 Identify the three factors most often used by criminologists to explain changes in the nation's crime rate.

1. *Imprisonment,* based on the principle that (a) an offender in prison or jail is unable to commit a crime on the street, and (b) a potential offender on the street will not commit a crime because he or she does not want to wind up behind bars.
2. *Youth populations,* because offenders commit fewer crimes as they grow older.
3. The *economy,* because when legitimate opportunities to earn income become scarce, some people will turn to illegitimate methods such as crime.[51]

Pure statistics do not always tell the whole story, however, and crime rates often fail to behave in the ways that the experts predict.

Looking Good: Crime in the 1990s and 2000s

In 1995, eminent crime expert James Q. Wilson, noting that the number of young males was set to increase dramatically over the next decade, predicted that "30,000 more young muggers, killers, and thieves" would be on the streets by 2000. "Get ready," he warned.[52] Other criminologists offered their own dire projections. John DiIulio foresaw a swarm of "juvenile super-predators" on the streets,[53] and James A. Fox prophesied a "blood bath" by 2005.[54] Given previous data, these experts could be fairly confident in their predictions. Fortunately for the country, they were wrong. As is evident from Figure 3.5, starting in 1994 the United States experienced a steep crime decline that we are still enjoying today.

The Great Crime Decline The crime statistics of the 1990s are startling. Even with the upswing at the beginning of the decade, from 1990 to 2000 the homicide rate dropped 39 percent, the robbery rate 44 percent, the burglary rate 41 percent, and the auto theft rate 37 percent. By most measures, this decline was the longest and deepest of the twentieth century.[55] In retrospect, the 1990s seem to have encompassed a "golden era" for the leading indicators of low crime rates. The economy was robust. The incarceration rate was skyrocketing. Plus, despite the misgivings of James Q. Wilson and many of his colleagues, the percentage of the population in the high-risk age bracket in 1995 was actually lower than it had been in 1980.[56]

FIGURE 3.4 Crime Victims in the United States

According to the U.S. Department of Justice, minorities, residents of urban areas, and young people are most likely to be victims of violent crime in this country.

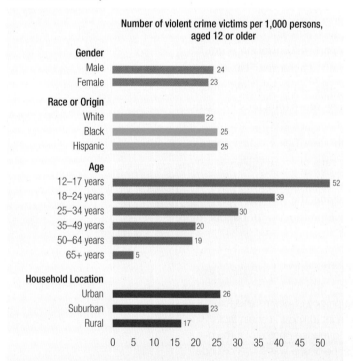

Number of violent crime victims per 1,000 persons, aged 12 or older

Gender
- Male: 24
- Female: 23

Race or Origin
- White: 22
- Black: 25
- Hispanic: 25

Age
- 12–17 years: 52
- 18–24 years: 39
- 25–34 years: 30
- 35–49 years: 20
- 50–64 years: 19
- 65+ years: 5

Household Location
- Urban: 26
- Suburban: 23
- Rural: 17

Source: Bureau of Justice Statistics, *Criminal Victimization, 2013* (Washington, D.C.: U.S. Department of Justice, September 2014), 9, 10.

FIGURE 3.5 Violent Crime in the United States, 1990–2013

According to statistics gathered each year by the FBI, American violent crime rates dropped steadily in the second half of the 1990s, leveled off for several years, and now have begun to decrease anew.

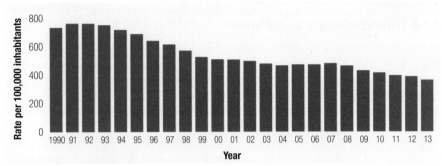

Source: Federal Bureau of Investigation.

Several other factors also seemed to favor lower crime rates. Police tactics, many of which we will discuss in Chapter 6, became more innovative—thanks in no small part to "zero-tolerance" policies inspired by Wilson's writings. Furthermore, many of those most heavily involved in a crack cocaine boom that shook the nation in the late 1980s had been killed or imprisoned, or were no longer offending. Without their criminal activity, the United States became a much safer place.[57]

Continuing Decreases According to the UCR, the United States is presently enjoying historically low levels of crime. Since the mid-1990s, the violent crime rate has declined by about 50 percent (see Figure 3.5), and the property crime rate has dropped about 40 percent.[58] Experts have put forth a number of theories to explain this fall in crime, including

1. Continued improvements in law enforcement, particularly DNA fingerprinting and information-based policing techniques that focus crime prevention tactics on "hot spots" of criminal activity.
2. An aging population: the median age in the United States is around thirty-seven years, the highest of any time in the nation's history.[59] As noted earlier, older people commit fewer crimes than younger people.
3. Improvements in digital technology that have increased the use and effectiveness of security cameras. Also, the public, armed with mobile phones with cameras, has become something of a complementary police force, sending immediate crime alerts and recording videos of criminal activity.
4. The gentrification of many formerly high-crime neighborhoods, which has contributed significantly to a 64 percent crime-rate reduction in America's largest cities.[60]

Another possible factor in the crime decline may be the large number of offenders who have been locked up in prison over the past two decades. The relationship between inmate populations and crime rates is controversial, however, and will be revisited in Chapter 13.

"We've plateaued," says James Alan Fox of Northeastern University in Boston regarding criminal activity in the United States. "The challenge will be making sure crime rates don't go back up."[61] One potential area of concern is the growing practice of releasing low-level criminals early from prison to reduce state inmate populations. In Chapter 13, we will take a closer look at the possible crime ramifications of these policies.

CJ & Technology

iStockPhoto.com/SteveStone

Engine Immobilizer Systems

It's a staple of television crime dramas: a crook needs to steal a car, and he or she easily does so by touching a couple of wires together, thus "hot wiring" the ignition. In the real world, such criminal ingenuity has become much more difficult. Starting in the late 1990s, automobile manufacturers began adding engine immobilizer systems to all new cars. This simple piece of technology makes it almost impossible to start a vehicle without an ignition key, each of which contains a microchip that the dealer programs to match the car.

Because of this innovation, the United States has seen a drop of 66 percent in the rate of motor vehicle theft since the early 1990s. In some cities, such as New York, the rate has decreased nearly 100 percent over that time period. The influence of engine immobilizer systems on car thieves is evident with regard to the Honda Accord, the most stolen car in this country. Of the 54,000 Accord thefts in 2013, 84 percent involved 1997 models or earlier. Not coincidentally, Accords started to be sold with new protection devices in 1998.

Thinking about Engine Immobilizer Systems

According to our discussion of victimization earlier in the chapter, criminals are more likely to target those people or items with the most "value." Why are Honda Accords manufactured before 1997 of less "value" to criminals, even though they are easier to steal? What impact could this fact have on national motor vehicle theft rates in the future?

Crime, Race, and Poverty

Although crime and victimization rates have decreased across racial lines over the past twenty years, the trends have been less positive for African Americans than for whites. For example, blacks are 6.3 times more likely to be homicide victims than whites,[62] and almost 20 percent more likely to be homicide offenders.[63] African Americans are particularly susceptible to gun violence, with firearm murder rates of 14.6 per 100,000 adults, compared to 1.9 for whites and 4.0 for Hispanics.[64] A large part of this violence is taking place within the African American community—nationwide, most murder victims are killed by someone of the same race (90 percent for blacks and 83 percent for whites).[65]

Race and Crime Homicide rates are not the only area in which there is a divergence in crime trends between the races. Official crime data seem to indicate a strong correlation between minority status and crime: African Americans—who make up 13 percent of the population—constitute 39 percent of those arrested for violent crimes and 29 percent of those arrested for property crimes.[66] In five states that recently reformed their drug laws, the Center of Juvenile and Criminal Justice found that African Americans were still five times more likely than all other races and ethnicities to be arrested for marijuana-related crimes.[67] (See the feature *Myth vs Reality—Race Stereotyping and Drug Crime* to further consider the intersection between drug crime and race.) Furthermore, a black juvenile in the United States is more than twice as likely as a white juvenile to wind up in delinquency court.[68]

Class and Crime The racial differences in the crime rate are one of the most controversial areas of the criminal justice system. At first glance, crime statistics seem to support the idea that the subculture of African Americans in the United States is disposed

Explain why income level appears to be more important than race or ethnicity when it comes to crime trends.
LEARNING
8
OBJECTIVE

toward criminal behavior. Not all of the data, however, support that assertion. A recent research project led by sociologist Ruth D. Peterson of Ohio State University gathered information on nearly 150 neighborhoods in Columbus, Ohio. Peterson and her colleagues separated the neighborhoods based on race and on levels of disadvantage such as poverty, joblessness, lack of college graduates, and high levels of female-headed families. She found that whether the neighborhoods were predominantly white or predominantly black had little impact on violent crime rates. Those neighborhoods with higher levels of disadvantage, however, had uniformly higher violent crime rates.[69]

Income Level and Crime Peterson's research suggests that, regardless of race, a person is at a much higher risk of violent offending or being a victim of violence if he or she lives in a disadvantaged neighborhood. Given that African Americans are two times more likely than whites to live in poverty and hold low-wage-earning jobs, they are, as a group, more susceptible to the factors that contribute to criminality.[70]

Indeed, a wealth of information suggests that income level is more important than skin color when it comes to crime trends. A 2002 study of nearly 900 African American children (400 boys and 467 girls) from neighborhoods with varying income levels showed that family earning power had the only significant correlation with violent behavior.[71] More recent research conducted by William A. Pridemore of Indiana University found a "positive and significant association" between poverty and homicide.[72] Lack of education, another handicap most often faced by low-income citizens, also seems to correlate with criminal behavior. Forty-one percent of all inmates in state and federal prisons failed to obtain a high school education, compared with 18 percent of the population at large.[73]

The Class-Crime Relationship The sociological theories of crime you studied in Chapter 2 predict that those without the financial means to acquire the consumer goods

Myth vs Reality

Race Stereotyping and Drug Crime

The Myth African Americans are sent to prison for drug crimes in greater numbers than whites because more of them buy, sell, and use drugs.

The Reality The use of illegal drugs by blacks and whites in the United States is roughly equal. According to data gathered by the federal government, about 11 percent of African Americans and about 10 percent of whites admit to using drugs within the previous month. A recently released study conducted by Duke University researchers showed that black adolescents are only about half as likely as their white counterparts to become dependent on illegal drugs and alcohol.

These figures are not reflected in criminal justice trends. African Americans who use drugs are arrested at about three times the rate of whites who use drugs. Furthermore, although blacks account for only 31 percent of all drug arrests, they represent 44 percent of those convicted of drug crimes and 40 percent of all Americans sentenced for drug crimes. Finally, more than four out of every five drug arrests are for possession of the banned substance, not for its sale or manufacture. Thus, the racial disparity in arrests cannot be due to a large class of African American drug dealers.

Although these statistics leave the criminal justice system open to charges of institutionalized racism, the disparities are possibly the result of practical considerations. Several years ago, criminologists Robin Engel, Michael Smith, and Francis Cullen compared police deployment patterns and drug arrests in Seattle. They found that, as police presence is necessarily greater in crime-prone areas, the numbers of drug arrests in those areas were higher than normal. Because crime-prone areas have large concentrations of minority residents, that population is subject to greater law enforcement scrutiny. The authors concluded, therefore, that citizens' demand for protection played a much more significant role than possible police bias in the disproportionate drug arrest rates for African Americans in the city.

For Critical Analysis
Heather Mac Donald, a crime expert at the Manhattan Institute in New York, suggests that the racial disparities in the "war on drugs" make sense because the urban street trade often leads to violence and other crimes that harm inner-city communities. Drug use by whites, in contrast, generally takes place in suburban homes, hidden from view, without the same level of negative side effects. What is your opinion of Mac Donald's theory?

and services that dominate our society will turn to illegal methods to "steal" purchasing power. But, logic aside, many criminologists are skeptical of such an obvious class-crime relationship. After all, poverty does not *cause* crime. The majority of residents in low-income neighborhoods are law-abiding. Furthermore, self-reported surveys indicate that high-income citizens are involved in all sorts of criminal activities[74] and are far more likely to commit white-collar crimes, which are not included in national crime statistics. These facts tend to support the theory that high crime rates in low-income communities are at least partly the result of a greater willingness of police to arrest poor citizens and of the court system to convict them.

Ethnicity and Crime Another point to remember when reviewing statistical studies of minority offenders and victims is that they tend to focus on race, which distinguishes groups based on physical characteristics such as skin color, rather than *ethnicity,* which denotes national or cultural background. Thus, the bulk of criminological research in this area has focused on the differences between European Americans and African Americans, both because the latter have been the largest minority group in the United States for most of its history and because the racial differences between the two groups are easily identifiable.

Americans of Hispanic descent have either been excluded from many crime studies or been linked with whites or blacks based on racial characteristics. The UCR, for example, does not gather statistics on Hispanic Americans for most of its categories of criminal behavior. Other minority groups, such as Asian Americans, Native Americans, and immigrants from the South Pacific or Eastern Europe, have been similarly underreported in crime studies.

This state of affairs will more than likely change in the near future. At present rates of growth, the Hispanic population will triple by 2050, when it will account for approximately one-third of the total U.S. population. Hispanics are also the fastest-growing minority group in the U.S. prison population.[75] Because of an increased emphasis on immigration law enforcement, more than half of the inmates in federal prisons in this country today are Hispanic.[76]

▼ A member of Prince George's County's Anti-Gang Unit makes an arrest during a crackdown on Hispanic gangs in Langley Park, Maryland. **Why is it likely that crime experts will increase their focus on issues of Hispanic offenders and victims in the United States over the next few decades?** Photo by Robert Nickelsberg/Getty Images

In fact, crime experts have already begun to focus on issues of Hispanic criminality. For example, Robert J. Sampson of Harvard University, examining the criminal behavior of more than 11,000 residents of 180 Chicago neighborhoods, found lower rates of violence among Mexican Americans than among either whites or blacks. Sampson and his colleagues theorize that strong social ties in immigrant populations create an environment that is incompatible with crime.[77] At the same time, the firearm homicide victimization rate for Hispanics in this country is more than twice that as whites,[78] and, as you can see in Figure 3.4, their overall victimization rates are equal to that of African Americans.

Courtesy Anne Seymour

Anne Seymour
National Victim Advocate

The aspect of my job that I enjoy the most is my direct work with crime victims and survivors. These are people who have been severely traumatized by pain and suffering and loss, and I consider it a true honor to be able to assist them. I'll never forget the day I met a young survivor who had been abducted, beaten within an inch of her life, raped, and then left to die in the forest. This young woman became one of my closest friends, and I helped her to speak out in her state and at the national level. Every time she does so, she has a powerful impact on our society. So my help in turning a victim/survivor into a stellar victim advocate/activist began on the day I met her, and it continues.

Victim advocacy is one of the most exciting and rewarding careers you could ever embark on, though it is not one that you should get into because of the money. (Few victim advocates become rich doing this work!) Every day is unique and different, reflecting the people I assist and the colleagues with whom I interact. I am never, ever bored and never will be. AND I go to bed every single day knowing that I have done at least one thing—and often many more than one!—to promote social justice and to help someone who is hurting. It's an amazing feeling!

> **SOCIAL MEDIA CAREER TIP** Social media technologies are about connecting and sharing information—which means privacy is an important issue. Make sure you understand who can see the material you post and how you can control it. Facebook has numerous privacy settings, for example, as does Google+.

FASTFACTS

National victim advocate Job description:
- Provide direct support, advocacy, and short-term crisis counseling to crime victims.

What kind of training is required?
- Bachelor's degree in criminal justice, social work/ psychology, or related field.
- A minimum of two years' experience in the criminal justice system, one year of which must have involved direct services with victims.

Annual salary range?
- $45,000–$65,000

Women and Crime

To put it bluntly, crime is an overwhelmingly male activity. Almost 62 percent of all murders involve a male victim and a male perpetrator, and in only 2.5 percent of homicides are both the offender and the victim female.[79] Only 14 percent of the national jail population and 7 percent of the national prison population are female, and in 2013 only 26 percent of all arrests involved women.[80]

A Growing Presence The statistics cited previously fail to convey the startling rate at which the female presence in the criminal justice system has been increasing. Between 1991 and 2013, the number of men arrested each year declined about 12 percent. Over that time period, annual arrests for women increased by 34 percent.[81] In 1970, there were about 6,000 women in federal and state prisons, but today, there are more than 111,000.[82] There are two possible explanations for these increases. Either (1) the life circumstances and behavior of women have changed dramatically in the past forty years, or (2) the criminal justice system's attitude toward women has changed over that time period.[83]

In the 1970s, when female crime rates started surging upward, many observers accepted the former explanation. "You can't get involved in a bar fight if you're not allowed in the bar," said feminist theorist Freda Adler in 1975.[84] It has become clear, however, that a significant percentage of women arrested are involved in a narrow band

LEARNING
9
OBJECTIVE

Discuss the prevailing explanation for the rising number of women incarcerated in the United States.

of wrongdoing, mostly drug- and alcohol-related offenses or property crimes.[85] Research shows that as recently as the 1980s, many of the women now in prison would not have been arrested or would have received lighter sentences for their crimes.[86] Consequently, more scholars are convinced that rising female criminality is the result of a criminal justice system that is "more willing to incarcerate women."[87]

Women as Crime Victims In contrast to male dominance of criminal violent offender statistics, men and women are victims of violent crimes at almost the same rate.[88] The most striking aspect of women as victims of crime is the extent to which such victimization involves a prior relationship. According to the National Crime Victimization Survey, a male is twice as likely as a female to experience violence at the hands of a stranger.[89] With regard to intimate partner violence—involving a spouse, ex-spouse, boyfriend, girlfriend, ex-boyfriend, or ex-girlfriend—the gender difference is even more pronounced. Women are about five times more likely then men to be victims of intimate partner violence.[90]

Common Crimes against Women In general, about six of every ten crimes in the United States are committed by someone known to the victim. Those crimes that usually involve strangers, such as robbery and assault, most often target male victims. In contrast, women have a greater chance of being victimized in nonstranger crimes, such as sexual assault.[91] Indeed, women are the victims in 86 percent of all intimate partner violence prosecutions.[92] The highest rate of victimization occurs among women between the ages of twelve and thirty-four, and one study estimates that between one-fifth and one-quarter of female college students have experienced a rape or attempted rape.[93] (The feature *Discretion in Action—"Yes" Means "Yes"* explores efforts to reduce the incidence of sexual assault on college campuses.)

Statistically, women are also at a greater risk of being victims of **domestic violence.** This umbrella term covers a wide variety of maltreatment, including physical violence and psychological abuse, inflicted among family members and others in close relationships. Though government data show that women are significantly more likely to be victims of domestic violence than men, these findings are not unquestioned. Men, many observers assume, are less likely to report abuse because of the social stigma surrounding female-on-male violence.[94] In the opening of this chapter, when discussing the Ray Rice videotape, we saw that domestic violence presents a number of challenges for the criminal justice system. We will continue to explore this subject in the *CJ in Action* feature at the end of the chapter.

A third crime that appears to mainly involve female victims is **stalking,** or a course of conduct directed at a person that would reasonably cause that person to feel fear. Such behavior includes unwanted phone calls, following or spying, and a wide range of online activity that we will address in Chapter 16. Stalkers target women at about three times the rate they target men, and seven out of ten stalking victims have had some prior relationship with their stalkers.[95]

Increased Exposure Previously, we noted that women's changing place in American society over the past four decades is believed to have contributed to climbing female arrest and incarceration numbers. Some criminologists contend that these changing circumstances are similarly responsible for a shift in female victimization characteristics. Since 1970, the number of women in the workplace has increased significantly, as has the participation of women in the political arena. As a result, women more commonly

Domestic Violence The act of willful neglect or physical violence that occurs within a familial or other intimate relationship.

Stalking The criminal act of causing fear in a person by repeatedly subjecting that person to unwanted or threatening attention.

Discretion in Action

"Yes" Means "Yes"

The Situation According to a White House task force, nearly one in five college female students have been the victims of sexual assault, with only 12 percent of those cases reported to school authorities. Attempts to reduce campus sexual assaults have generally relied on educating incoming students about the problem and discouraging binge drinking. As these efforts seem to have failed, victims' rights advocates are demanding stronger measures.

The Law As we saw earlier in the chapter, the legal definition of rape hinges on the concept of consent. If both parties to sexual activity are willing, then no crime has occurred. If one party is unwilling, then perhaps there has been a crime. Given the complexity of sexual relationships, school administrators and student disciplinary bodies often find it difficult to determine whether a rape has taken place, and whether the perpetrator should be expelled. In response, about eight hundred postsecondary institutions have implemented *affirmative consent* policies on their campuses. These policies are designed to make consent obvious by requiring each party to indicate—either verbally with a "yes" or through actions—that she or he is willing to engage in sexual activity.

What Would You Do? Assume you are a politician in a state that has recently gone through several on-campus sexual assault controversies. One of your colleagues has proposed a bill making affirmative consent state law, meaning that all postsecondary school students would be required to actively indicate willingness to sex on campus. Proponents insist that, by removing the possibility that "silence equals consent," the proposed legislation would reduce the incidence of coerced sex and remove the burden from victims of having to prove that they said "no." Opponents counter that it is unrealistic to expect sex partners to ask, "Can I do this now?" and that the proposed bill unfairly shifts the burden to the accused. Would you support the proposed affirmative consent legislation? Explain your answer.

[To see how one state has reacted to the problem of sexual assault on campus, go to Example 3.1 in Appendix B.]

---

find themselves at work or other activities away from home that expose them to stranger violence.[96] And, indeed, although women are still at much less risk for stranger violence than men, the gap between the sexes has been steadily shrinking since at least the early 1990s.[97]

Mental Illness and Crime

On November 20, 2014, Myron May shot three people on the campus of Florida State University in Tallahassee. According to a journal kept by May, who was killed by police during the incident, he believed himself to be under constant surveillance by the government. Following the shooting, the Tallahassee chief of police said that May was "not what most people would refer to as normal."[98] Such incidents draw national public attention and create the assumption that "not normal" people such as May pose a particular danger to society. The reality concerning mental illness and crime is much more nuanced and complex.

Risk Factors for Violent Crime In the context of the criminal justice system, the term *mental illness* covers a wide variety of symptoms, ranging from recurring depression and anger to hallucinations and schizophrenia (described in Chapter 2). It also indicates recent treatment from a mental health care practitioner. Government research shows that, using these descriptions, about 11 percent of Americans over the age of eighteen suffer from some form of mental illness.[99] Does this mean that 26 million adults in this country are at a high risk for violent behavior? Not necessarily.

Gun Control After Adam Lanza killed twenty children and six adults at an elementary school in Newtown, Connecticut, on December 14, 2012, many observers called for stricter laws to keep guns out of the hands of the mentally ill. Although Lanza had never been diagnosed with any specific mental illness, at least half a dozen states moved to revise their mental health laws to that effect. Maryland, for example, now bars anyone with a "mental disorder" who has a history of violence from owning firearms.[100] California similarly prohibits firearm ownership for mentally ill persons who pose a threat to themselves or others, or communicate a violent threat to a third party in the presence of licensed psychotherapist.[101]

In New York, the legislature passed a bill requiring mental health practitioners to report potentially dangerous clients to gun control authorities. By 2014, the database of New Yorkers banned from owning firearms for reasons of mental health had grown to 34,000.[102] Overall, forty-four states regulate the sale of firearms to the mentally ill, and the federal government bars such sales to any person who is a "mental defective."[103]

Drug Abuse Critics say that the emphasis on the mentally ill in the gun control debate is unfair and inaccurate. Of the tens of thousand of gun deaths that occur in this country, few are caused by people with mental illness.[104] Furthermore, a 2006 study published in the *American Journal of Psychiatry* claimed that only 4 percent of violent crime in the United States can be attributed to people with a mental illness.[105] Although the possibility of violent behavior increases for those with serious conditions such as schizophrenia or bipolar disorder,[106] the most significant risk factor for the mentally ill is substance abuse. Between 80 and 90 percent of all mentally ill inmates in American prisons and jails are abusers of alcohol or other drugs.[107]

Risk Factors for Victimization Those who suffer from mental illness are much more likely to be victims of crime than perpetrators. There are several reasons for this high victimization risk:

1. Mental illness often interferes with a person's ability to find and keep employment, and therefore leads to poverty, which, we have seen, correlates with victimization.
2. The mentally ill are more likely to be homeless, a circumstance that leaves them particularly susceptible to crime.[108]
3. Mental illness can interfere with a person's ability to make prudent decisions in potentially dangerous situations, increasing her or his chances of being assaulted.[109]

One review of the subject found that rates of victimization among people with mental illness are as much as 140 percent higher than in the general population.[110]

Mental health advocates insist that increasing services such as treatment and temporary housing for America's mentally ill will reduce the harm they cause themselves and others. The prohibitive costs of such services, however, seem to guarantee that mental illness will continue to be a problem for the criminal justice system, and for society at large, a subject we will explore more fully in Chapter 12.

EthicsChallenge

According to one commentator, "The disproportionate amount of African Americans playing criminals in Hollywood fuels the racial stereotype that black men are dangerous and have zero respect for the law." What is your opinion of this statement, in light of our discussion in this section on race stereotyping and drug crime? Is it unethical for film and television producers to cast minorities as drug users and outlaws? Why or why not? ■

CJ IN ACTION

Victims of Domestic Violence

On March 26, 2014, an Atlantic County, New Jersey, grand jury indicted Ray Rice on third degree aggravated assault charges for punching his fiancée, Janay Palmer, in a casino elevator, an incident described in the opening of this chapter. On March 27, Rice and Palmer became husband and wife. Several months later, Janay—who consistently said she did not want Ray to be charged with any crime—apologized for "the role I played in the incident."[111] Janay's actions underscore the often contradictory relationship between victims of domestic violence and the criminal justice system. In this chapter's *CJ in Action,* we address the debate surrounding one widespread method of dealing with a crime where the defendant and victim frequently live together.

No-Drop Policies

Legally, crime victims are not the clients of public prosecutors. That is, as you will see in Chapter 9, prosecutors have the ultimate authority to decide when to bring a case to court, regardless of the victim's wishes. In practice, domestic violence cases unfold somewhat differently. Because the victim is usually the only witness to the violence, if she or he refuses to participate, such cases can be very difficult to prosecute successfully.[112] For a number of reasons, domestic violence victims such as Janay Palmer Rice frequently choose not to side with law enforcement against their abusers. These reasons include fear of retaliation, financial dependence on the offender, issues of custody and child support, and complex emotional ties.[113]

Faced with uncooperative victims, prosecutors will consistently "drop" domestic violence cases. To remedy this situation, many jurisdictions in the United States have implemented "no-drop" policies. Such policies require prosecutors to carry through with a domestic violence case once an arrest has been made, even if this goes against the wishes of the victim. There is little question that no-drop policies increase the prosecution and conviction rates of domestic violence offenders.[114] The question is, do such policies actually benefit domestic violence victims?

The Case for No-Drop Policies

- If a domestic violence victim decides to cooperate with law enforcement officials, she or he becomes more vulnerable to retaliatory attacks by the abuser. By taking this decision out of the victim's hands, no-drop policies remove the dangerous tag of "snitch" from the victim.[115]

- Without no-drop policies, prosecutors dismiss 50 to 80 percent of all domestic violence charges. With such policies, dismissal rates fall to 10 to 35 percent. Therefore, no-drop policies show a commitment to treat domestic violence as a serious crime.[116]

- No-drop policies deter domestic violence by increasing the likelihood that offenders will be prosecuted and punished.

The Case against No-Drop Policies

- No-drop policies send the paternalistic message that victims of domestic violence cannot make rational choices about themselves and their futures.[117]

- Domestic violence victims are in a better position than public officials to determine the risk of continued abuse. If a victim feels that prosecuting the abuser will only increase the likelihood of further violence, prosecutors should respect her or his decision to forgo such action.[118]

- Several studies show that no-drop policies increase the risk of victimization. This can be attributed to "separation assault," which is violence that occurs as retaliation after a victim is separated from her or his abuser. Such separation is a common result of no-drop policies.[119]

Your Opinion—Writing Assignment

No-drop policies certainly increase the chances that an offender will be convicted and punished. The policies do not, however, make the punishment more severe. Most domestic violence charges are misdemeanors, not felonies, and therefore offenders such as Ray Rice are usually sentenced to little or no jail time.[120] Does this leniency change your opinion of no-drop policies? Why or why not? Do you feel such policies properly balance the needs of society and the needs of domestic violence victims? Before responding, you can review our discussions in the sections of this chapter concerning:

- Felonies and misdemeanors ("Classification of Crimes").

- Legal rights of victims ("Victims of Crime").

- Women as crime victims ("Crime Trends in the United States").

Your answer should include at least three full paragraphs.

Summary

For more information on these concepts, look back to the Learning Objective icons throughout the chapter.

 Discuss the primary goals of civil law and criminal law and explain how these goals are realized. Civil law is designed to resolve disputes between private individuals and other entities such as corporations. In these disputes, one party, called the plaintiff, tries to gain monetary damages by proving that the accused party, or defendant, is to blame for a tort, or wrongful act. In contrast, criminal law exists to protect society from criminal behavior. To that end, the government prosecutes defendants, or persons who have been charged with committing a crime.

 Explain the differences between crimes *mala in se* and *mala prohibita*. A criminal act is *mala in se* if it is inherently wrong, while a criminal act *mala prohibita* is illegal only because it is prohibited by the laws of a particular society. It is sometimes difficult to distinguish between these two sorts of crimes because it is difficult to define a "pure" *mala in se* crime—that is, it is difficult to separate a crime from the culture that has deemed it a crime.

 Identify the publication in which the FBI reports crime data and list the two main ways in which the data are reported. Every year the FBI releases the Uniform Crime Report (UCR), in which it presents different crimes as (a) a rate per 100,000 people and (b) a percentage change from the previous year.

 Distinguish between the National Crime Victimization Survey (NCVS) and self-reported surveys. The NCVS involves an annual survey of more than 40,000 households conducted by the Bureau of the Census along with the Bureau of Justice Statistics. The survey queries citizens on crimes that have been committed against them. As such, the NCVS includes crimes not necessarily reported to police. Self-reported surveys, in contrast, involve asking individuals about criminal activity to which they may have been a party.

 Describe the three ways that victims' rights legislation increases the ability of crime victims to participate in the criminal justice system. (a) The right to be informed of victims' rights in general and of specific information relating to the relevant criminal case; (b) the right to be present at court proceedings involving the victim; and (c) the right to be heard on matters involving the prosecution, punishment, and release of the offender.

 Discuss one major concern regarding victim participation in the criminal justice process. Criminal justice professionals have an ethical obligation to be fair, objective, and impartial in their duties. Understandably, crime victims are usually not impartial toward an offender who has allegedly wronged them. Therefore, by allowing crime victims to participate, public officials allow a measure of partiality into criminal justice proceedings.

 Identify the three factors most often used by criminologists to explain changes in the nation's crime rate. (a) Levels of incarceration, because an offender behind bars cannot commit any additional crimes and the threat of imprisonment acts as a deterrent to criminal behavior; (b) the size of the youth population, because those under the age of twenty-four commit the majority of crimes in the United States; and (c) the health of the economy, because when income and employment levels fall, those most directly affected may turn to crime for financial gain.

 Explain why income level appears to be more important than race or ethnicity when it comes to crime trends. Criminologists have found that the most consistent indicators of criminal behavior are circumstances such as low family earning power and the absence of a parent. In addition, failure to obtain a high school diploma appears to have a positive correlation with criminal activity, regardless of the race or ethnicity of the individual. Finally, some believe that high arrest rates in low-income minority neighborhoods can be attributed to a willingness of police to arrest residents of these communities and of the court system to convict them.

 Discuss the prevailing explanation for the rising number of women incarcerated in the United States. Experts believe that many women are arrested and given harsh punishment for activity that would not have put them behind bars several decades ago. For the most part, this activity is nonviolent: the majority of female arrestees are involved in drug- and alcohol-related offenses and property crimes.

Questions for Critical Analysis

1. Give an example of how one person could be involved in a civil lawsuit and a criminal lawsuit for the same action.

2. For nearly eight decades until 2013, the federal government defined rape as sex with "a female forcibly and against her will." Compare this definition with the new definition in Figure 3.1. Which do you think is more representative of the crime, and why? What are the consequences of removing "forcibly" and "against her will" from the previous definition?

3. Assume that you are a criminologist who wants to determine the extent to which high school students engage in risky behavior such as abusing alcohol and illegal drugs, carrying weapons, and contemplating suicide. How would you go about gathering these data?

4. Research shows that female college students who have been the victim of rape or attempted rape are at an unusually high risk of repeat victimization if they engage in binge alcohol drinking. What victim services should colleges provide to reduce the chances that this group of victims will be revictimized?

5. Critics of laws that limit ownership of firearms for people with mental illness claim that these laws discourage such people from seeking treatment. Why would this be the case?

Key Terms

beyond a reasonable doubt   72
civil law   71
dark figure of crime   78
defendant   71
domestic violence   90
felony   72
infraction   73

liability   71
mala in se   73
mala prohibita   73
misdemeanor   72
Part I offenses   75
Part II offenses   76
plaintiff   71

preponderance of the evidence   72
repeat victimization   83
self-reported survey   80
stalking   90
Uniform Crime Report (UCR)   75
victim surveys   78

Notes

1. 42 U.S.C. Section 13981.

2. *United States v. Morrison*, 529 U.S. 598 (2000).

3. *Federal Criminal Rules Handbook*, Section 2.1 (West 2008).

4. 625 Illinois Compiled Statutes Annotated Section 5/16-104 (West 2002).

5. Johannes Andenaes, "The Moral or Educative Influence of Criminal Law," *Journal of Social Issues* 27 (Spring 1971), 17, 26.

6. Mayo Clinic, "Disease and Conditions: Acute Liver Failure," at **www.mayoclinic.org/diseases-conditions/liver-failure/basics/causes/con-20030966**.

7. Centers for Disease Control, "Impaired Driving: Get the Facts," at **www.cdc.gov/Motorvehiclesafety/impaired_driving/impaired-drv_factsheet.html**.

8. John Slade, "Health Consequences of Smoking: Nicotine Addiction," *Hearings before the Subcommittee on Health and the Environment of the House Committee on Energy and Commerce* (Washington, D.C.: U.S. Government Printing Office, 1988), 163–164.

9. Ethan Nadelmann, "Should We Legalize Drugs? History Answers: Yes," *Hofstra Law Review* 18 (1990), 41.

10. Steven Jonas, "Solving the Drug Problem: A Public Health Approach to the Reduction of the Use and Abuse of Both Legal and Recreational Drugs," *Hofstra Law Review* 18 (1990), 753.

11. Douglas N. Husak, *Drugs and Rights* (New York: Cambridge University Press, 2002), 21.

12. Federal Bureau of Investigation, *Uniform Crime Reporting Handbook* (Washington, D.C.: U.S. Department of Justice, 2004), 74.

13. Federal Bureau of Investigation, *Crime in the United States 2013* (Washington, D.C.: U.S. Department of Justice, 2014), at **www.fbi.gov/about-us/cjis/ucr/crime-in-the-u.s/2013/crime-in-the-u.s.-2013/about-cius**.

14. *Ibid.*

15. *Ibid.*, Table 1.

16. Jeffrey Reiman, *The Rich Get Richer and the Poor Get Prison*, 4th ed. (Boston: Allyn & Bacon, 1995), 59–60.

17. *Crime in the United States 2013, op. cit.*, Expanded Homicide Data Table 10.

18. *Ibid.*, Table 1.

19. *Ibid.*, Offense Definitions.

20. *Ibid.*, Table 29.

21. Marcus Felson, *Crime in Everyday Life* (Thousand Oaks, Calif.: Pine Forge Press, 1994), 3.

22. Joel Rubin and Ben Poston, "LAPD Targets Crime Statistics," *Los Angeles Times* (December 17, 2014), A12.

23. Eric P. Baumer and Janet L. Lauritsen, "Reporting Crime to the Police, 1973–2005: A Multivariate Analysis of Long-Term Trends in the National Crime Survey (NCS) and National Crime Victimization Survey (NCVS)," *Criminology* (February 2010), 132–133.

24. Bureau of Justice Statistics, *Crime Victimization, 2013* (Washington, D.C.: U.S. Department of Justice, September 2014), Table 6, page 7.

25. Lynn Langton et al., *Victimizations Not Reported to the Police, 2006–2010* (U.S. Department of Justice, August 2012), 4.

26. Dave Gathman, "Counting Crime in the Smaller Towns," *Courier News* (Elgin, Ill.) (November 14, 2012), 8.

27. David Bernstein and Noah Isackson, "The Truth about Chicago's Crime Rates," *Chicago Magazine* (April 7, 2014), at **www.chicago mag.com/Chicago-Magazine/May-2014 /Chicago-crime-rates**.

28. *Crime in the United States 2013, op. cit.*, at **www.fbi.gov/about-us/cjis/ucr/nibrs/2013 /resources/nibrs-participation-by-state**.

29. *Ibid.*, at **www.fbi.gov/about-us/cjis/ucr /nibrs/2013/data-tables**.

30. Victor E. Kappeler, Mark Blumberg, and Gary W. Potter, *The Mythology of Crime and Criminal Justice*, 2d ed. (Prospect Heights, Ill.: Waveland Press, 1993), 31.

31. Frank A. Hagan, *Introduction to Criminology: Theories, Methods, and Criminal Behavior* 7th ed. (Thousand Oaks, Calif.: Sage Publications, 2011), 41.

32. M. C. Black et al., *The National Intimate Partner and Sexual Violence Survey: 2010 Summary Report* (Atlanta, Ga.: National Center for Injury Prevention and Control, 2011), 3.

33. *Crime in the United States 2013, op. cit.*, at Offense Definitions.

34. *Ibid.*, Table 1.

35. David Lisak and Paul M. Miller, "Repeat Rape and Multiple Offending among Undetected Rapists," *Violence & Victims* (2002), 73–84.

36. Lynne N. Henderson, "The Wrongs of Victims' Rights," 37 *Stanford Law Review* (1985), 947–948.

37. Lois H. Harrington et al., *President's Task Force on Victims of Crime: Final Report* (Washington, D.C.: U.S. Department of Justice, December 1982), viii.

38. 18 U.S.C. Section 3771 (2006).

39. Susan Herman, *Parallel Justice for Victims of Crime* (Washington, D.C.: The National Center for Victims of Crime, 2010), 45–48.

40. State of California, Department of Justice Office of the Attorney General, "Victims' Bill of Rights," at **oag.ca.gov/victimservices /content/bill_of_rights**.

41. Ballotpedia, "Illinois Crime Victims' Bill of Rights Amendment (2014)," at **ballotpedia .org/Illinois_Crime_Victims'_Bill_of _Rights_Amendment_(2014)**.

42. Herman, *op. cit.*, 17–21.

43. Lynn Langton, *Use of Victim Service Agencies by Victims of Serious Violent Crime, 1993–2009* (Washington, D.C.: U.S. Department of Justice, August 2011), 1.

44. Chris E. Kubrin, et al., "Does Fringe Banking Exacerbate Neighborhood Crime Rates?" *Criminology and Public Policy* (May 2011), 437–464.

45. Larry Cohen and Marcus Felson, "Social Change and Crime Rate Trends: A Routine Activity Approach," *American Sociological Review* (1979), 588–608.

46. Kubrin, et al., *op. cit.*, 441.

47. Cohen and Felson, *op. cit.*

48. Herman, *op. cit.*, 13–16.

49. R. Barry Ruback, Valerie A. Clark, and Cody Warner, "Why Are Crime Victims at Risk of Being Victimized Again? Substance Use, Depression, and Offending as Mediators of the Victimization-Revictimization Link," *Journal of Interpersonal Violence* (January 2014), 157–185.

50. Quoted in Kevin Johnson, "Criminals Target Each Other, Trend Shows," *USA Today* (August 31, 2007), 1A.

51. Franklin E. Zimring, *The Great American Crime Decline* (New York: Oxford University Press, 2007), 45–72.

52. James Q. Wilson, "Concluding Essay in Crime," in James Q. Wilson and Joan Petersilia, eds., *Crime* (San Francisco: Institute for Contemporary Studies Press, 1995), 507.

53. John DiIulio, *How to Stop the Coming Crime Wave* (New York: Manhattan Institute, 1996), 4.

54. James Fox, *Trends in Juvenile Violence* (Boston: Northeastern University Press, 1996), 1.

55. Zimring, *op. cit.*, 6.

56. *Ibid.*, 197–198.

57. *Ibid.*, 82.

58. *Crime in the United States 2013, op. cit.*, Table 1.

59. Andrew Mach, "Violent Crime Rates in the U.S. Drop, Approach Historical Lows," *msnbc. com* (June 11, 2012), at **usnews.nbcnews .com/_news/2012/06/11/12170947-fbi -violent-crime-rates-in-the-us-drop -approach-historic-lows?lite**.

60. "Where Have All the Burglars Gone?" *The Economist* (July 20, 2013), 21–23.

61. Quoted in Donna L. Leger, "Violent Crime Rises for 2nd Year," *USA Today* (October 25–27, 2013), 1A.

62. Erica L. Smith and Alexia Cooper, *Homicide in the U.S. Known to Law Enforcement, 2011* (Washington, D.C.: U.S. Department of Justice, December 2013), 1.

63. *Crime in the United States 2013, op. cit.*, Expanded Homicide Data Table 3.

64. Michael Planty and Jennifer L. Truman, *Firearm Violence, 1993–2011* (Washington, D.C: U.S. Department of Justice, May 2013), 5.

65. *Crime in the United States 2013, op. cit.*, Expanded Homicide Data Table 6.

66. *Ibid.*, Table 43.

67. Mark Males and Lizzie Buchen, *Reforming Marijuana Laws: Which Approach Best Reduces the Harms of Criminalization* (San Francisco, Calif.: Center of Juvenile and Criminal Justice, September 2014), 5–6.

68. Sarah Hockenberry and Charles Puzzanchera, *Juvenile Court Statistics, 2013* (Washington, D.C.: National Center for Juvenile Justice, July 2014), 20.

69. Ruth D. Peterson, "The Central Place of Race in Crime and Justice—The American Society of Criminology's 2011 Sutherland Address," *Criminology* (May 2012), 303–327.

70. Patricia Y. Warren, "Inequality by Design: The Connection between Race, Crime, Victimization, and Social Policy," *Criminology & Public Policy* (November 2010), 715.

71. Eric A. Stewart, Ronald L. Simons, and Rand D. Donger, "Assessing Neighborhood and Social Psychological Influence on Childhood Violence in an African American Sample," *Criminology* (November 2002), 801–829.

72. William Alex Pridemore, "A Methodological Addition to the Cross-National Empirical Literature on Social Structure and Homicide: A First Test of the Poverty-Homicide Thesis," *Criminology* (February 2008), 133.

73. Caroline Wolf Harlow, *Education and Correctional Populations* (Washington, D.C.: Bureau of Justice Statistics, January 2003), 1.

74. Charles Tittle and Robert Meier, "Specifying the SES/Delinquency Relationship," *Criminology* 28 (1990), 270–301.

75. Marguerite Moeller, *America's Tomorrow: A Profile of Latino Youth* (New York: National Council of La Raza, 2010).

76. *2013 Sourcebook of Federal Sentencing Statistics* (Washington, D.C.: U.S. Sentencing Commission, 2014), Table 4, at **www.ussc.gov/sites/default/files/pdf/research-and-publications/annual-reports-and-sourcebooks/2013/Table04.pdf**.

77. Robert J. Sampson, Jeffrey Morenoff, and Stephen W. Raudenbush, "Social Anatomy of Racial and Ethnic Disparities in Violence," *American Journal of Public Health* 95 (2005), 231.

78. *Hispanic Victims of Lethal Firearms Violence in the United States* (Washington D.C.: Violent Policy Center, April 2014), i.

79. *Crime in the United States, op. cit.*, Expanded Homicide Table 6.

80. Bureau of Justice Statistics, *Jail Inmates at Midyear 2013—Statistical Tables* (Washington, D.C.: U.S. Department of Justice, May 2014), Table 2, page 6; Bureau of Justice Statistics, *Prisoners in 2013* (Washington, D.C.: U.S. Department of Justice, September 2014), Table 1, page 2; and *Crime in the United States 2013, op. cit., Table 33*.

81. Federal Bureau of Justice, *Crime in the United States, 2000* (Washington, D.C.: U.S. Department of Justice, 2001), Table 33, page 221; and *Crime in the United States 2013, op. cit.*, Table 33.

82. *Prisoners in 2013, op. cit.*, Table 1, page 2.

83. Jennifer Schwartz and Bryan D. Rookey, "The Narrowing Gender Gap in Arrests: Assessing Competing Explanations Using Self-Report, Traffic Fatality, and Official Data on Drunk Driving, 1980–2004," *Criminology* (August 2008), 637–638.

84. Quoted in Barry Yeoman, "Violent Tendencies: Crime by Women Has Skyrocketed in Recent Years," *Chicago Tribune* (March 15, 2000), 3.

85. *Crime in the United States 2013, op. cit.*, Table 42.

86. Schwarz and Rookey, *op. cit.*, 637–671.

87. Meda Chesney-Lind, "Patriarchy, Prisons, and Jails: A Critical Look at Trends in Women's Incarceration," *Prison Journal* (Spring/Summer 1991), 57.

88. Bureau of Justice Statistics, *Criminal Victimization, 2013* (Washington, D.C.: U.S. Department of Justice, September 2014), Table 5, page 6.

89. Erika Harrell, *Violent Victimization Committed by Strangers, 1993–2010* (Washington, D.C.: U.S. Department of Justice, December 2012), 2.

90. Shannan Catalano, *Intimate Partner Violence, 1993–2010* (Washington, D.C.: U.S. Department of Justice, November 2012), Table 1, page 2.

91. Harrell, *op. cit.*, Table 1, page 2.

92. Bureau of Justice Statistics, *Female Victims of Violence* (Washington, D.C.: U.S. Department of Justice, September 2009), Table 2, page 5.

93. Bonnie S. Fisher, Francis T. Cullen, and Michael G. Turner, *The Sexual Victimization of College Women* (Washington, D.C.: U.S. Department of Justice, December 2000), 10.

94. Eve S. Buzawa, "Victims of Domestic Violence," in Robert C. Davis, Arthur Lurigio, and Susan Herman, eds., *Victims of Crime*, 4th ed. (Los Angeles: Sage, 2013), 36–37.

95. Shannan Catalano, *Stalking Victims in the United States—Revised* (Washington, D.C.: U.S. Department of Justice, September 2012), 1, 5.

96. Min Xie, Karen Heimer, and Janet L. Lauritsen, "Violence against Women in U.S. Metropolitan Areas: Changes in Women's Status and Risk, 1980–2004," *Criminology* (February 2012), 106–107, 131.

97. Harrell, *op. cit.*, Figure 2, page 2.

98. Quoted in Sean Rossman, "Shooting at Strozier Library Stuns Florida State," *Tallahassee Democrat* (November 21, 2014), A1.

99. Doris J. James and Lauren E. Glaze, *Mental Heath Problems of Prison and Jail Inmates* (Washington, D.C.: U.S. Department of Justice, September 2006), 3.

100. Maryland Public Safety Code Section 5–133.

101. Law Center to Prevent Gun Violence, "Mental Health-Related Prohibited Categories in California" (January 12, 2015), at **smartgunlaws.org/mental-health-related-prohibited-categories-in-california**.

102. Anemona Hartocollis, "Mental Health Issues Put 34,500 on New York's No Guns List," *New York Times* (October 19, 2014), A1.

103. National Conference of State Legislatures, "Possession of Firearms by People with Mental Illness," at **www.ncsl.org/research/civil-and-criminal-justice/possession-of-a-firearm-by-the-mentally-ill.aspx**.

104. Richard A. Friedman, "In Gun Debate, a Misguided Focus on Mental Illness," *New York Times* (December 18, 2012), D5.

105. Seena Fazel and Martin Grann, "The Population Impact of Severe Mental Illness on Violent Crime," *American Journal of Psychiatry* (August 2006), 1397–1403.

106. Jeffrey W. Swanson et al., "Violence and Psychiatric Disorder in the Community: Evidence from the Epidemiologic Catchment Area Surveys," *Hospital & Community Psychiatry* (July 1990), 761–770.

107. James and Glaze, *op. cit.*, 6.

108. Arthur J. Lurigio, Kelli E. Canada, and Matthew W. Epperson, "Crime Victimization and Mental Illness" in *Victims of Crime, op. cit.*, 216–217.

109. *Ibid.*, 217–218.

110. Roberto Maniglio, "Severe Mental Illness and Criminal Victimization: A Systematic Review," *Acta Psychiactra Scandinavica* 119 (2009), 180–191.

111. Quoted in John Breech, "Ray Rice's Wife: 'I Deeply Regret the Role I Played in the Incident'" (May 23, 2014), at **www.cbssports.com/nfl/eye-on-football/24571153/ray-rices-wife-i-deeply-regret-the-role-i-played-in-the-incident**.

112. Naomi R. Cahn, "Innovative Approaches to the Prosecution of Domestic Violence Crimes: An Overview," in Eve S. Buzawa and Carl G. Buzawa, eds., *Domestic Violence: The Changing Criminal Justice Response* (Santa Barbara, Calif.: Praeger, 1992), 163.

113. Erin L. Han, "Mandatory Arrest and No-Drop Policies: Victim Empowerment in Domestic Violence Cases," 23 *Boston College Third World Law Journal* (2003), 159–192.

114. Andrew R. Klein, *Practical Implications of Current Domestic Violence Research: For Law Enforcement, Prosecutors, and Judges* (Washington, D.C.: National Institute of Justice, June 2009), 44, 45.

115. Malinda L. Seymore, "Isn't It a Crime?: Feminist Perspectives on Spousal Immunity and Spousal Violence," 90 *Northwestern University Law Review* (1996), 1079–1080.

116. Kalyani Robbins, "No-Drop Prosecution of Domestic Violence: Just Good Policy, or Equal Protection Mandate?" 52 *Stanford Law Review* (1999), 205–233.

117. Jessica Dayton, "The Silencing of a Woman's Choice: Mandatory Arrest and No Drop Prosecution Policies in Domestic Violence Cases," 9 *Cardozo Women's Law Journal* (2003), 281.

118. Tamara L. Kuennen, "Private Relationships and Public Problems: Applying Principles of Relational Contract Theory to Domestic Violence," *Brigham Young University Law Review* (2010), 528–530.

119. *Ibid.*, 529–530.

120. *Ibid.*, 574–575.

4

Inside Criminal Law

Chapter Outline		Corresponding Learning Objectives
The Development of American Criminal Law	**1**	List the four written sources of American criminal law.
	2	Explain precedent and the importance of the doctrine of *stare decisis*.
The Purposes of Criminal Law	**3**	Explain the two basic functions of criminal law.
The Elements of a Crime	**4**	Delineate the elements required to establish *mens rea* (a guilty mental state).
	5	Explain how the doctrine of strict liability applies to criminal law.
Defenses under Criminal Law	**6**	List and briefly define the most important excuse defenses for crimes.
	7	Discuss a common misperception concerning the insanity defense in the United States.
	8	Describe the four most important justification criminal defenses.
Procedural Safeguards	**9**	Distinguish between substantive and procedural criminal law.
	10	Explain the importance of the due process clause in the criminal justice system.

To target your study and review, look for these numbered Learning Objective icons throughout the chapter.

when dogs Attack

according to witnesses who testified at his murder trial, Alex Jackson's dogs had menaced or bitten people near his home in Littlerock, California, on at least nine different occasions. One witness, an animal control officer, said that Jackson told him, "If you mess with me, you're coming into the lion's den." So, prosecutors argued, it could hardly have been a surprise to the defendant when four of his pit bulls leaped over the fence and attacked and killed sixty-three-year-old retiree Pamela Devitt during her morning walk.

About thirty people die from dog attacks each year in the United States, but criminal charges against the owners of these animals are rare. To gain conviction in such cases, prosecutors must prove both that the defendants knew that their pets were dangerous and failed to control them. In September 2014, a jury decided that Jackson had consciously disregarded the threat his dogs posed to the community, and found him guilty of second degree murder. A judge subsequently sentenced him to fifteen years behind bars.

Depending on the circumstances, other dog-related deaths may not warrant such serious punishment. One month after Jackson's conviction, a Saline County, Arkansas, judge sentenced Brande Coy to sixty days in jail when a bull mastiff she was looking after killed a neighbor. Unlike Jackson, Coy was apparently unaware that the dog had any violent tendencies. Similarly, that summer Steven Hayashi of Concord, California, was sent to jail for one year after his three pit bulls mauled his grandson to death. Previously, those dogs had only attacked other animals. Besides being criminally careless, the three defendants discussed here had one other characteristic in common: they had no intent to harm their dogs' victims. "This isn't anything I orchestrated or planned," said Jackson during his trial. "I feel terrible about it."

▲ One of Alex Jackson's pit bulls is held at a Lancaster, California, animal shelter following its owner's arrest on murder charges.

AP Images/The Antelope Valley Press, Claudia Lopez

1. Do you think it is fair that criminal law holds Alex Jackson, Brande Coy, and Steven Hayashi accountable for deaths caused by dogs under their control? Why or why not?

2. Do you think that the judge was correct in sentencing Alex Jackson to fifteen years in prison? How does society benefit, if at all, from such a harsh punishment in a case that involves a dog killing?

3. During trial, prosecutors claimed that Jackson used the dogs to guard his marijuana-growing operation. In what ways could this evidence have helped convince the jury to find Jackson guilty of second degree murder rather than a lesser crime?

The Development of American Criminal Law

Given the various functions of *law,* a single definition of this term is difficult to establish. To the Greek philosopher Aristotle (384–322 B.C.E.), law was a "pledge that citizens of a state will do justice to one another." Aristotle's mentor, Plato (427–347 B.C.E.), saw the law as primarily a form of social control. The British jurist Sir William Blackstone (1723–1780) described law as "a rule of civil conduct prescribed by the supreme power in a state, commanding what is right, and prohibiting what is wrong." In the United States, jurist Oliver Wendell Holmes, Jr. (1841–1935), contended that law was a set of rules that allowed one to predict how a court would resolve a particular dispute.

The Conception of Law

Although these definitions vary in their particulars, they are all based on the following general observation: law consists of enforceable rules governing relationships among individuals and between individuals and their society.[1] Searching back into history, several sources for modern American law can be found in the rules laid out by ancient societies. One of the first known examples of written law was created during the reign of Hammurabi (1792–1750 B.C.E.), the sixth king of the ancient empire of Babylon. The Code of Hammurabi set out crimes and their punishments based on *lex Talionis,* or "an eye for an eye." This concept of retribution is still important and will be discussed in Chapter 11.

Another ancient source of law can be found in the Mosaic Code of the Israelites (1200 B.C.E.). According to tradition, Moses—acting as an intermediary for God—presented the code to the tribes of Israel. The two sides entered into a covenant, or contract, in which the Israelites agreed to follow the code and God agreed to protect them as the chosen people. Besides providing the basis for Judeo-Christian teachings, the Mosaic Code is also reflected in modern American law, as evident in similar prohibitions against murder, theft, adultery, and perjury.

Modern law also owes a debt to the Code of Justinian, promulgated throughout the Roman Empire in the sixth century. This code collected many of the laws that Western society had produced. It was influential in the development of the legal systems of the European continent. To some extent, it also influenced the common law of England.

English Common Law

The English system of law as it stands today was solidified during the reign of Henry II (1154–1189). Henry sent judges on a specific route throughout the country, known as a circuit. These circuit judges established a **common law** in England. In other words, they solidified a national law in which legal principles applied to all citizens equally, no matter where they lived or what the local customs had dictated in the past. When confusion about any particular law arose, the circuit judges could draw on English traditions, or they could borrow from legal decisions made in other European countries.

Once a circuit judge made a ruling, other circuit judges faced with similar cases generally followed that ruling. Each interpretation became part of the law on the subject and served as a legal **precedent**—a decision that furnished an example or authority for deciding subsequent cases involving similar legal principles or facts. Over time, a body of general rules that prescribed social conduct and that was applied throughout the entire English realm was established, and subsequently it was passed on to British colonies,

Common Law The body of law developed from custom or judicial decisions in English and U.S. courts and not attributable to a legislature.

Precedent A court decision that furnishes an example or authority for deciding subsequent cases involving similar facts.

Rule of Law The principle that the rules of a legal system apply equally to all persons, institutions, and entities—public or private—that make up a society.

Constitutional Law Law based on the U.S. Constitution and the constitutions of the various states.

including those in the New World that would eventually become the thirteen original United States.

What is important about the formation of the common law is that it developed from the customs of the populace rather than simply the will of a ruler. As such, the common law came to reflect the social, religious, economic, and cultural values of the people. In any society that is, like our own, governed by the **rule of law,** all persons and institutions, including the government itself, must abide by the law. Furthermore, the law must be applied equally and enforced fairly, and must not be altered arbitrarily by any individual or group, no matter how powerful.

Written Sources of American Criminal Law

LEARNING **1** OBJECTIVE

List the four written sources of American criminal law.

Originally, common law was *uncodified.* That is, it relied primarily on judges following precedents, and the body of the law was not written down in any single place. Uncodified law, however, presents a number of drawbacks. For one, if the law is not recorded in a manner or a place in which the citizenry has access to it, then it is difficult, if not impossible, for people to know exactly which acts are legal and which acts are illegal. Furthermore, citizens have no way of determining or understanding the procedures that must be followed to establish innocence or guilt. Consequently, U.S. history has seen the development of several written sources of American criminal law, also known as "substantive" criminal law. These sources include:

1. The U.S. Constitution and the constitutions of the various states.
2. Statutes, or laws, passed by Congress and by state legislatures, plus local ordinances.
3. Regulations, created by regulatory agencies, such as the federal Food and Drug Administration.
4. Case law (court decisions).

We describe each of these important written sources of law in the remainder of this section. (For a preview, see Figure 4.1.)

Constitutional Law The federal government and the states have separate written constitutions that set forth the general organization and powers of, and the limits on, their respective governments. **Constitutional law** is the law as expressed in these constitutions.

The U.S. Constitution is the supreme law of the land. As such, it is the basis of all law in the United States. Any law that violates the Constitution, as ultimately determined by the United States Supreme Court, will be declared unconstitutional and will not be enforced. The Tenth Amendment, which defines the powers and limitations of the federal government, reserves to the states all powers not granted to the federal government. Under our system of federalism (see Chapter 1), each state also has its own constitution. Unless they conflict with the U.S. Constitution or a federal law, state constitutions are supreme within their respective borders. (You will learn more about how constitutional law applies to our criminal justice system throughout this textbook.)

▼ George Washington, standing at right, presided over the constitutional convention of 1787. The convention resulted in the U.S. Constitution, the source of a number of laws that continue to form the basis of our criminal justice system today. Bettmann/Corbis

FIGURE 4.1 Sources of American Law

Constitutional law	**Definition:** The law as expressed in the U.S. Constitution and the various state constitutions.	**Example:** The Fifth Amendment to the U.S. Constitution states that no person shall "be compelled in any criminal case to be a witness" against himself or herself.
Statutory law	**Definition:** Laws or *ordinances* created by federal, state, and local legislatures and governing bodies.	**Example:** Texas state law considers the theft of cattle, horses, or exotic livestock or fowl a felony.
Administrative law	**Definition:** The rules, orders, and decisions of federal or state government administrative agencies.	**Example:** The federal Environmental Protection Agency's rules criminalize the use of lead-based paint in a manner that causes health risks to the community.
Case law	**Definition:** Judge-made law, including judicial interpretations of the other three sources of law.	**Example:** A federal judge overturns a Nebraska state law making it a crime for sex offenders to use social networking sites on the ground that the statute violated the constitutional right of freedom of speech.

Statutory Law Statutes enacted by legislative bodies at any level of government make up another source of law, which is generally referred to as **statutory law.** *Federal statutes* are laws that are enacted by the U.S. Congress. *State statutes* are laws enacted by state legislatures, and statutory law also includes the ordinances passed by cities and counties. A federal statute, of course, applies to all states. A state statute, in contrast, applies only within that state's borders. City or county ordinances (statutes) apply only to those jurisdictions where they are enacted.

The Model Penal Code Until the mid-twentieth century, state criminal statutes were disorganized, inconsistent, and generally inadequate for modern society. In 1952, the American Law Institute began to draft a uniform penal code in the hopes of solving this problem. The first **Model Penal Code** was released ten years later and has had a broad effect on state statutes.[2] Though not a law itself, the Code defines the general principles of criminal responsibility. The majority of states have adopted parts of the Model Penal Code into their criminal statutes, and some states, such as New York, have adopted a large portion of the Code.

Legal Supremacy It is important to keep in mind that there are essentially fifty-two different criminal codes in this country—one for each state, the District of Columbia, and the federal government. Originally, the federal criminal code was quite small. The U.S. Constitution mentions only three federal crimes: treason, piracy, and counterfeiting. Today, according to a recent study, federal law includes about 4,500 offenses that carry criminal penalties.[3] Inevitably, these federal criminal statutes are bound to overlap or even contradict state statutes. In such cases, thanks to the **supremacy clause** of the Constitution, federal law will almost always prevail. Simply put, the supremacy clause holds that federal law is the "supreme law of the land."

So, for example, at least 330 individuals have been charged with violating federal law for possessing or selling medical marijuana in states where such use is legal under state law.[4] As we discussed earlier in the textbook, marijuana use—for medicinal purposes or otherwise—remains illegal under federal law, and, in the words of one federal judge, "we are all bound by federal law, like it or not."[5] Along the same lines, any statutory law—federal or state—that violates the Constitution will be overturned. In the late 1980s, for example, the United States Supreme Court ruled that any state laws banning the burning of the American flag were unconstitutional because they impinged on the individual's right to freedom of expression.[6]

Statutory Law The body of law enacted by legislative bodies.

Model Penal Code A statutory text created by the American Law Institute that sets forth general principles of criminal responsibility and defines specific offenses.

Supremacy Clause A clause in the U.S. Constitution establishing that federal law is the "supreme law of the land" and shall prevail when in conflict with state constitutions or statutes.

▲ In Oregon, because of a ballot initiative, any person who fails a field sobriety test, such as the one shown here, and is convicted of drunk driving for a third time must spend ninety days in jail. **What are some of the pros and cons of using ballot initiatives to create criminal law?** Joe Raedle/Getty Images

Ballot Initiatives On a state and local level, voters can write or rewrite criminal statutes through a form of direct democracy known as the **ballot initiative.** In this process, a group of citizens draft a proposed law and then gather a certain number of signatures to get the proposal on that year's ballot. If a majority of the voters approve the measure, it is enacted into law. Currently, twenty-four states and the District of Columbia accept ballot initiatives, and these special elections have played a crucial role in shaping criminal law in those jurisdictions. In this textbook, we have already discussed how ballot initiatives changed state law regarding assisted suicide, marijuana legalization, and victims' rights.

Like other state laws, laws generated by ballot initiatives are not immune from review by state and federal courts. In late 2014, for example, Oklahoma and Nebraska filed a joint lawsuit asking the United States Supreme Court to find Colorado's recreational marijuana law, passed as a ballot initiative, unconstitutional. The two states claimed that marijuana flowing from Colorado over their borders has unfairly "stressed" state and local law enforcement resources.[7]

Administrative Law A third source of American criminal law consists of **administrative law**—the rules, orders, and decisions of *regulatory agencies.* A regulatory agency is a federal, state, or local government agency established to perform a specific function. The Occupational Safety and Health Administration (OSHA), for example, oversees the safety and health of American workers. The Environmental Protection Agency (EPA) is concerned with protecting the natural environment, and the Food and Drug Administration (FDA) regulates food and drugs produced in the United States.

Disregarding certain laws created by regulatory agencies can be a criminal violation. Federal statutes, such as the Clean Water Act, authorize a specific regulatory agency, such as the EPA, to enforce regulations to which criminal sanctions are attached.[8] So, in 2014, following a criminal investigation led by EPA agents, a Longview, Washington, septic tank pumping business was found to have illegally dumped two million gallons of pollutants and waste into the city's sewage system. A federal judge sentenced the business's owner to twenty-seven months in prison and a fine of $250,000.

Case Law As is evident from the earlier discussion of the common law tradition, another basic source of American law consists of the rules of law announced in court decisions, or precedents. These rules of law include interpretations of constitutional provisions, of statutes enacted by legislatures, and of regulations created by administrative agencies. Today, this body of law is referred to variously as the common law, judge-made law, or **case law.**

Case law is the basis for a doctrine called *stare decisis* ("to stand on decided cases"). Under this doctrine, judges are obligated to follow the precedents established within their jurisdiction. For example, any decision of a particular state's highest court will control the outcome of future cases on that issue brought before all the lower courts within that same state. Per the supremacy clause, discussed earlier, all U.S. Supreme Court decisions involving the U.S. Constitution are binding on *all* courts, because the U.S. Constitution is the supreme law of the land.

LEARNING
Explain precedent and the
importance of the doctrine of **2**
stare decisis.
OBJECTIVE

Ballot Initiative A procedure in which the citizens of a state, by collecting enough signatures, can force a public vote on a proposed change to state law.

Administrative Law The body of law created by administrative agencies (in the form of rules, regulations, orders, and decisions) in order to carry out their duties and responsibilities.

Case Law The rules of law announced in court decisions.

Stare Decisis (pronounced *ster*-ay dih-*si*-ses). A legal doctrine under which judges are obligated to follow the precedents established under prior decisions.

The doctrine of *stare decisis* does not require the U.S. Supreme Court *always* to follow its own precedent, though the Court often does so. At times, a change in society's values will make an older ruling seem obsolete, at least in the eyes of the Supreme Court justices. In 1986, for example, the Court upheld a state law that banned certain homosexual acts that were lawful when performed by a man and a woman.[9] Seventeen years later, the Court overturned that decision, ruling that the government does not have the ability to treat one class of citizens differently from the rest of society when it comes to sexual practices between consenting adults. The original case "was not correct when it was decided, and it is not correct today," wrote Justice Anthony Kennedy.[10]

The Purposes of Criminal Law

Why do societies need laws? Many criminologists believe that criminal law has two basic functions: one relates to the legal requirements of a society, and the other pertains to the society's need to maintain and promote social values.

LEARNING **3** OBJECTIVE

Explain the two basic functions of criminal law.

Protect and Punish: The Legal Function of the Law

The primary legal function of the law is to maintain social order by protecting citizens from *criminal harm.* This term refers to a variety of harms that can be generalized to fit into two categories:

1. Harms to individual citizens' physical safety and property, such as the harm caused by murder, theft, or arson.
2. Harms to society's interests collectively, such as the harm caused by unsafe foods or consumer products, a polluted environment, or poorly constructed buildings.[11]

Because criminal law has the primary goal of protecting people from harm, new criminal laws are often passed in response to specific acts. For example, in May 2014, an otherwise healthy eighteen-year-old high school senior in LaGrange, Ohio, died from a caffeine powder overdose. Before the end of the year, U.S. Senator Richard Blumenthal, a Democrat from Connecticut, had begun work on a bill that would ban the unregulated dietary supplement nationwide.[12]

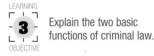

CJ & Technology

Revenge Porn

Consider the following scenario: Jasmine, a graduate school student, exchanges intimate photos with Josh, her boyfriend. Then they break up. Several months later, Josh begins posting nude pictures of Jasmine online. Although she is mortified, there is little Jasmine can do to stop Josh, because such behavior is not illegal in most of the United States. For the most part, Web site operators are not responsible for content provided by others, unless that content happens to be in violation of federal law, such as child pornography.

Technology often moves faster than criminal law, allowing for behavior that seems like it should be illegal but is not. In December 2014, Illinois became the fourteenth state in the previous two years to ban "revenge porn," or the "non-consensual dissemination of private

iStockPhoto.com/Yuri_Arcurs

(continued)

sexual images." Under the state law, a person convicted of sharing such images online faces one to three years in prison and a maximum $25,000 fine.

Thinking about Revenge Porn
Notice that Illinois's revenge porn law has no provision for intent, as is the case in other states. For example, in California the crime requires "the intent to cause serious emotional distress." Why might civil liberties advocates support the inclusion of an intent provision? Which version of revenge porn legislation—Illinois's or California's—do you favor? Why?

Maintain and Teach: The Social Function of the Law

If criminal laws against acts that cause harm or injury to others are almost universally accepted, the same cannot be said for laws that criminalize "morally" wrongful activities that may do no obvious, physical harm outside the families of those involved. Why criminalize gambling or prostitution if the participants are consenting?

Expressing Public Morality The answer lies in the social function of criminal law. Many observers believe that the main purpose of criminal law is to reflect the values and norms of society, or at least of those segments of society that hold power. Legal scholar Henry Hart has stated that the only justification for criminal law and punishment is "the judgment of community condemnation."[13]

Take, for example, the misdemeanor of bigamy, which occurs when someone knowingly marries a second person without terminating her or his marriage to an original husband or wife. Apart from moral considerations, there would appear to be no victims in a bigamous relationship, and indeed many societies have allowed and continue to allow bigamy to exist. In the American social tradition, however, as John L. Diamond of the University of California's Hastings College of the Law points out:

> Marriage is an institution encouraged and supported by society. The structural importance of the integrity of the family and a monogamous marriage requires unflinching enforcement of the criminal laws against bigamy. The immorality is not in choosing to do wrong, but in transgressing, even innocently, a fundamental social boundary that lies at the core of social order.[14]

Of course, public morals are not uniform across the entire nation, and a state's criminal code often reflects the values of its residents. In Kentucky, for example, someone who uses a reptile as part of a religious service is subject to up to $100 in fines, and New Hampshire prohibits any person or agency from introducing a wolf into the state's wilds.[15] Sometimes, local values and federal law will conflict with one another. Nine states, mostly in the western half of the country, have passed "nullification" laws that seek to void federal gun legislation within their borders.[16] For example, in 2014, Idaho passed a new law under which state law enforcement officers could be charged with a misdemeanor and fined up to $1,000 dollars for enforcing a federal gun law.[17]

Teaching Societal Boundaries Some scholars believe that criminal laws not only express the expectations of society, but "teach" them as well. Professor Lawrence M. Friedman of Stanford University thinks that just as parents teach children behavioral norms through punishment, criminal justice "'teaches a lesson' to the people it punishes, and to society at large." Making burglary a crime, arresting burglars, putting them in jail—each step in the criminal justice process reinforces the idea that burglary is unacceptable and is deserving of punishment.[18]

This teaching function can also be seen in traffic laws. There is nothing "natural" about most traffic laws: Americans drive on the right side of the street, the British on the left side, with no obvious difference in the results. These laws, such as stopping at intersections, using headlights at night, and following speed limits, do lead to a more orderly flow of traffic and fewer accidents—certainly socially desirable goals. The laws can also be updated when needed. Over the past few years, several states have banned the use of handheld cell phones while driving because of the safety hazards associated with that behavior. Various forms of punishment for breaking traffic laws teach drivers the social order of the road.

EthicsChallenge

Coyote-hunting contests, in which prizes are given to those who kill the most coyotes over a certain period of time, are becoming increasingly popular in the western United States. In your opinion, is this activity an acceptable way to control the coyote population, or is it unethical? Should coyote-hunting contests be prohibited by law, as is the case in California? Why or why not? ■

The Elements of a Crime

In fictional accounts of police work, the admission of guilt is often portrayed as the crucial element of a criminal investigation. Although an admission is certainly useful to police and prosecutors, it alone cannot establish the innocence or guilt of a suspect. Criminal law normally requires that the **corpus delicti,** a Latin phrase for "the body of the crime," be proved before a person can be convicted of wrongdoing.[19]

Corpus delicti can be defined as "proof that a specific crime has actually been committed by someone."[20] It consists of the elements of any crime, which include:

1. The *actus reus,* or guilty act,
2. The *mens rea,* or guilty intent,
3. Concurrence, or the coming together of the criminal act or the guilty mind,
4. A link between the act and the legal definition of the crime,
5. Any attendant, or accompanying, circumstances, and
6. The harm done by the crime.

(See this chapter's *Mastering Concepts* for an example showing the three basic elements of a crime.)

Criminal Act: *Actus Reus*

Suppose Mr. Smith walks into a police department and announces that he just killed his wife. In and of itself, the confession is insufficient for conviction unless the police

▲ Many gun rights activists, such as these two demonstrators outside the Idaho State Capitol in Boise, support state "nullification" laws that aim to void federal gun legislation. **Why does the supremacy clause, discussed earlier in the chapter, make it unlikely that such state laws would survive a court challenge?** Chris Butler/*Idaho Statesman*/MCT via Getty Images

Corpus Delicti The body of circumstances that must exist for a criminal act to have occurred.

Carl Robert Winchell walked into the SunTrust Bank in Volusia County, Florida, and placed a bag containing a box on a counter. Announcing that the box held a bomb, he demanded to be given an unspecified amount of cash. After receiving several thousand dollars in cash, Winchell fled, leaving the box behind. A Volusia County Sheriff's Office bomb squad subsequently determined that the box did not in fact contain any explosive device. Winchell was eventually arrested and charged with robbery.

Winchell's actions were criminal because they satisfy the three basic elements of a crime:

1. *Actus Reus:* Winchell **physically** committed the crime of bank robbery.
2. *Mens Rea:* Winchell **intended** to commit the crime of bank robbery.
3. *Concurrence:* Winchell's intent to rob the bank and his use of the false bomb threat* **came together** to create a criminal act.

*Note that the fact that there was no bomb in the box has no direct bearing on the three elements of the crime. It could, however, lead to Winchell's receiving a lighter punishment than if he had used a real bomb.

find Mrs. Smith's corpse, for example, with a bullet in her brain and establish through evidence that Mr. Smith fired the gun. (This does not mean that an actual dead body has to be found in every homicide case. Rather, it is the fact of the death that must be established in such cases.)

Most crimes require an act of *commission,* meaning that a person must *do* something in order to be accused of a crime. The prohibited act is referred to as the **actus reus,** or guilty act. Furthermore, the act of commission must be voluntary. For example, if Mr. Smith had an epileptic seizure while holding a hunting rifle and accidentally shot his wife, he normally would not be held criminally liable for her death.

A Legal Duty In some cases, an act of *omission* can be a crime, but only when a person has a legal duty to perform the omitted act. One such legal duty is assumed to exist based on a "special relationship" between two parties, such as a parent and child, adult children and their aged parents, and spouses.[21] Those persons involved in contractual relationships with others, such as physicians and lifeguards, must also perform legal duties to avoid criminal penalty. Hawaii, Minnesota, Rhode Island, Vermont, and Wisconsin have even passed "duty to aid" statutes requiring their citizens to report criminal conduct and help victims of such conduct if possible.[22] Another example of a criminal act of omission is failure to file a federal income tax return when required by law to do so.

A Plan or Attempt The guilty act requirement is based on one of the premises of criminal law—that a person is punished for harm done to society. Planning to kill someone or to steal a car may be wrong, but the thoughts do no harm and are therefore not criminal until they are translated into action. Of course, a person can be punished for *attempting* murder or robbery, but normally only if he or she took substantial steps toward the criminal objective and the prosecution can prove that the desire to commit the crime was present. Furthermore, the punishment for an **attempt** normally is less severe than if the act had succeeded.

Actus Reus (pronounced *ak*-tus *ray*-uhs). A guilty (prohibited) act.

Attempt The act of taking substantial steps toward committing a crime while having the ability and the intent to commit the crime, even if the crime never takes place.

Mental State: *Mens Rea*

A wrongful mental state—*mens rea*—is usually as necessary as a wrongful act in determining guilt. The mental state, or requisite *intent*, required to establish guilt of a crime is indicated in the applicable statute or law. For theft, the wrongful act is the taking of another person's property, and the required mental state involves both the awareness that the property belongs to another and the desire to deprive the owner of it.

The Categories of *Mens Rea* A guilty mental state includes elements of purpose, knowledge, negligence, and recklessness.[23] A defendant is said to have *purposefully* committed a criminal act when he or she desires to engage in certain criminal conduct or to cause a certain criminal result. For a defendant to have *knowingly* committed an illegal act, he or she must be aware of the illegality, must believe that the illegality exists, or must correctly suspect that the illegality exists but fail to do anything to dispel (or confirm) his or her belief.

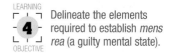

LEARNING OBJECTIVE 4 Delineate the elements required to establish *mens rea* (a guilty mental state).

Negligence Criminal **negligence** involves the mental state in which the defendant grossly deviates from the standard of care that a reasonable person would use under the same circumstances. The defendant is accused of taking an unjustified, substantial, and foreseeable risk that resulted in harm.

In 2015, for example, Greeley, Colorado, prosecutors charged Kristen Braig and her boyfriend, Dustin Blanchard, with negligent homicide after the death of Braig's three-year-old daughter in a mobile home fire. Just before the fire started, Braig and Blanchard, who had been drinking and smoking marijuana, left the child alone in the mobile home to visit a neighbor. The couple obviously did not intend for Braig's daughter to die. At the same time, there is a foreseeable risk in leaving a child of that age unattended for any amount of time, especially when one's judgment is impaired by alcohol and marijuana.

Recklessness A defendant who commits an act recklessly is more blameworthy than one who is criminally negligent. The Model Penal Code defines criminal **recklessness** as "consciously disregard[ing] a substantial and unjustifiable risk."[24] So, in 2015, Ryan Jorgenson pleaded guilty to reckless homicide in an Oshkosh, Wisconsin, court for causing the death of his fiancée's three-year-old daughter. Jorgenson, annoyed that the little girl would not stop crying, had fatally pushed her down a flight of stairs. Although Jorgenson—like Kristen Braig and Dustin Blanchard in the previous example—had no intention of killing his victim, the substantial risk of harm in treating a child in such a manner is evident to any reasonable person.

Degrees of Crime In the previous chapter, you learned that crimes are graded by degree. Generally speaking, the degree of a crime is a reflection of the seriousness of that crime, and is used to determine the severity of any subsequent punishment.

With many crimes, degree is a function of the criminal act itself, as determined by statute. For example, most criminal codes consider a burglary that involves a nighttime forced entry into a home to be a burglary in the first degree. If the same act takes place during the day and involves a nonresidential building, then it is burglary in the second degree. As you might expect, burglary in the first degree carries a harsher penalty than burglary in the second degree.

Mens Rea (pronounced mehns ray-uh). Mental state, or intent. A wrongful mental state is usually as necessary as a wrongful act to establish criminal liability.

Negligence A failure to exercise the standard of care that a reasonable person would exercise in similar circumstances.

Recklessness The state of being aware that a risk does or will exist and nevertheless acting in a way that consciously disregards this risk.

First Degree Murder With murder, the degree of the crime is, to a large extent, determined by the mental state of the offender. Murder is generally defined as the willful killing of a human being. It is important to emphasize the word *willful*, as it precludes homicides caused by accident or negligence. A death that results from negligence or accident generally is considered a private wrong and therefore a matter for civil law.

In addition, criminal law punishes those who plan and intend to do harm more harshly than it does those who act wrongfully because of strong emotions or other extreme circumstances. First degree murder—usually punishable by life in prison or the death penalty—occurs under two circumstances:

1. When the crime is premeditated, or contemplated beforehand by the offender, instead of being a spontaneous act of violence.
2. When the crime is deliberate, meaning that it was planned and decided on after a process of decision making. Deliberation does not require a lengthy planning process. A person can be found guilty of first degree murder even if she or he made the decision to kill only seconds before committing the crime.

Second Degree Murder As you may recall, in this chapter's opening we discussed Alex Jackson, who was convicted of second degree murder for failing to control his dangerous dogs. In California, where Jackson's case was tried, second degree murder is defined as any murder that is not first degree murder.[25] Jackson's behavior does, nonetheless, fall within the boundaries set by the two general definitions of second degree murder:

1. An intentional killing in which no premeditation or deliberation was present, and
2. A killing resulting from the offender's dangerous conduct and an obvious lack of concern for human life.

Second degree murder is usually punishable by fifteen to twenty-five years in prison.

The difference between first and second degree murder is illustrated in a case involving a California man who beat a neighbor to death with a partially full brandy bottle. The crime took place after Ricky McDonald, the victim, complained to Kazi Cooksey, the offender, about the noise coming from a late-night barbecue Cooksey and his friends were holding. The jury could not find sufficient evidence that Cooksey's actions were premeditated, but he certainly acted with wanton disregard for his victim's safety. Therefore, the jury convicted Cooksey of second degree murder rather than first degree murder.

Types of Manslaughter A homicide committed without *malice* toward the victim is known as *manslaughter* and is commonly punishable by up to fifteen years in prison. (*Malice* means "wrongful intention" or "the desire to do evil.") **Voluntary manslaughter** occurs when the intent to kill may be present, but malice is lacking. Voluntary manslaughter covers crimes of passion, in which the emotion of an argument between two friends may lead to a homicide. Voluntary manslaughter can also occur when the victim provoked the offender to act violently.

Involuntary manslaughter covers incidents in which the offender's acts may have been careless, but he or she had no intent to kill. In 2014, for instance, a grand jury charged Hillary Schwartz with involuntary manslaughter following a fatal train collision. Schwartz was the assistant director on *Midnight Rider*, a film being made in rural Wayne

Voluntary Manslaughter A homicide in which the intent to kill was present in the mind of the offender, but malice was lacking.

Involuntary Manslaughter A homicide in which the offender had no intent to kill her or his victim.

County, Georgia. The filmmakers had been refused legal permission to shoot a scene on a particular railroad bridge, but, with Schwartz behind the camera, the decision was made to do so anyway. A freight train then crashed into the film set on the bridge, killing a camera assistant named Sarah Jones.

Although Schwartz had certainly not intended for Jones to die in the accident, local law enforcement authorities believed that she and several other members of the production crew were criminally responsible for the woman's death. (As the feature *Discretion in Action—Murder or Manslaughter?* shows, the distinction between various homicide charges is not always clear, and often rests on the issue of intent.)

Strict Liability For certain crimes, criminal law holds the defendant to be guilty even if intent to commit the offense is lacking. These acts are known as **strict liability crimes** and generally involve endangering the public welfare in some way.[26] Drug-control statutes, health and safety regulations, and traffic laws are all strict liability laws.

Protecting the Public To a certain extent, the concept of strict liability is inconsistent with the traditional principles of criminal law, which hold that *mens rea* is required for an act to be criminal. The goal of strict liability laws is to protect the public by eliminating the possibility that wrongdoers could claim ignorance or mistake to absolve themselves of criminal responsibility.[27] Thus, a person caught dumping waste in a protected pond or driving 70 miles per hour in a 55 miles-per-hour zone cannot plead a lack of intent in his or her defense.

The principle is often applied in more serious situations as well. Several years ago, Cody Trailes was charged with first degree murder in connection with the heroin

Strict Liability Crimes Certain crimes, such as traffic violations, in which the defendant is guilty regardless of her or his state of mind at the time of the act.

LEARNING
5
OBJECTIVE
Explain how the doctrine of strict liability applies to criminal law.

Discretion in Action

Murder or Manslaughter?

The Situation It is after midnight, and George, drunk and angry, decides to pay a visit to Yeardley, his ex-girlfriend. When Yeardley refuses to let George in her apartment, he kicks the door down, grabs Yeardley by the neck, and wrestles her to the floor before leaving. Several hours later, Yeardley's roommate finds her dead, lying face down on a pillow soaked with blood.

The Law George can be charged with one of three possible crimes: (1) first degree murder, which is premeditated and deliberate; (2) second degree murder,

which means he acted with wanton disregard for the consequences of his actions; or (3) involuntary manslaughter, which involves extreme carelessness but no intent to kill.

What Would You Do? Further investigation shows that, two years prior to Yeardley's death, a jealous George put her in a chokehold in public. Furthermore, just days before breaking into her apartment, George sent Yeardley an e-mail in which he reacted to news that she was dating someone else by

threatening, "I should have killed you." In his defense, George says that although he did have a physical confrontation with Yeardley, she did not seem injured when he left the apartment. George's lawyer claims that Yeardley died from suffocation, not from any wound caused by George. If it were your decision, would you charge George with first degree murder, second degree murder, or involuntary manslaughter? Why?

[To see how a Charlottesville, Virginia, jury responded to a similar situation, see Example 4.1 in Appendix B.]

overdose death of John Simmons, Jr. There was no evidence that Trailes intended for Simmons to die, or even knew him. He did, however, supply Simmons with the heroin that led to the overdose. In most jurisdictions, Trailes would only be charged with a drug offense under these circumstances. Under New Jersey law, however, strict liability murder is imposed on anybody who helps another person obtain drugs that lead to a fatal overdose.[28] As a result, Trailes's *mens rea* concerning Simmons's death was irrelevant.

Protecting Minors One of the most controversial strict liability crimes is **statutory rape,** in which an adult engages in a sexual relationship with a minor. In most states, even if the minor consents to the sexual act, the crime still exists because, being underage, he or she is considered incapable of making a rational decision on the matter.[29] Therefore, statutory rape has been committed even if the adult was unaware of the minor's age or was misled to believe that the minor was older.

Accomplice Liability

Under certain circumstances, a person can be charged with and convicted of a crime that he or she did not actually commit. This occurs when the suspect has acted as an *accomplice,* helping another person commit the crime. Generally, to be found guilty as an accomplice, a person must have had "dual intent." This level of *mens rea* includes *both:*

1. The intent to aid the person who committed the crime, and
2. The intent that such aid would lead to the commission of the crime.[30]

So, assume that Jerry drives Jason to a bank that Jason intends to rob. If Jerry had no knowledge of Jason's criminal plan, he would not fulfill the second prong of the "dual intent" test. As for the *actus reus,* the accomplice must have helped the primary actor in either a physical sense (for example, by providing the getaway car) or a psychological sense (for example, by encouraging her or him to commit the crime).[31]

In some states, a person can be convicted as an accomplice even without intent if the crime was a "natural and probable consequence" of his or her actions.[32] This principle has led to a proliferation of **felony-murder** legislation. Felony-murder is a form of first degree murder that applies when a person participates in any of a list of serious felonies that results in the death of a human being. Under felony-murder law, if two men rob a bank, and the first man intentionally kills a security guard, the second man can be convicted of first degree murder as an accomplice to the bank robbery, even if he had no intent to hurt anyone.

Along these same lines, if a security guard accidentally shoots and kills a customer during a bank robbery, the bank robbers can be charged with first degree murder because they committed the underlying felony. These kinds of laws have come under criticism because they punish individuals for an unintended act or acts committed by others. Nevertheless, the criminal codes of more than thirty states include some form of the felony-murder rule.

Concurrence

According to criminal law, there must be *concurrence* between the guilty act and the guilty intent. In other words, the guilty act and the guilty intent must occur together.[33] Suppose, for example, that a woman intends to murder her husband with poison in

Statutory Rape A strict liability crime in which an adult engages in a sexual act with a minor.

Felony-Murder An unlawful homicide that occurs during the attempted commission of a felony.

Courtesy Diana Tabor

Diana Tabor
Crime Scene Photographer

A crime scene photographer's job is invaluable to those who are not present at the scene, yet need to be able to observe the scene as accurately as possible. I like the variety of my work. No two scenes are exactly alike, and the conditions pose different challenges. I have photographed scenes in cramped mobile homes, spacious homes, and out in the woods where we had to hike because there were no roads leading directly to the scene. I've been really hot and sweaty, fogging up the viewfinder. Then I have been so cold that I had to go sit in the van to let my hands and the camera warm up because they had stopped working.

Vozks/Stockphoto

I do wonder what the people at the gas stations think when we come in there after we're done to clean up and get something to drink. Fingerprint powder gets everywhere—I have found that nothing less than a shower really gets rid of it completely. It is sometimes difficult to accept that there is nothing to prevent the crime that has already happened, but I take pride in representing the victim when he or she cannot speak.

SOCIAL MEDIA CAREER TIP Don't forget about your phone! Every week, call at least three people from your social media networks and talk with them about your career interests. This kind of personal contact can be far more useful than an exchange of posts.

FASTFACTS

Crime scene photographer Job description:
- Photograph physical evidence and crime scenes related to criminal investigations.
- Also must be able to compose reports, testify in court, and understand basic computer software and terminology.

What kind of training is required?
- One year in law enforcement or commercial photography OR a degree or certificate in photography and darkroom techniques OR some combination of the above training or experience totaling one year.

Annual salary range?
- $45,780–$53,290

order to collect his life insurance. Every evening, this woman drives her husband home from work. On the night she plans to poison him, however, she swerves to avoid a cat crossing the road and runs into a tree. She survives the accident, but her husband is killed. Even though her intent was realized, the incident would be considered an accidental death because she had not planned to kill him by driving the car into a tree.

Causation

Criminal law also requires that the criminal act cause the harm suffered. In 1998, for example, thirteen-year-old Don Collins doused eight-year-old Robbie Middleton with gasoline and set him on fire, allegedly to cover up a sexual assault. Thirteen years later, after years of skin grafts and other surgeries, Middleton died from his burns. In 2014, a Montgomery County, Texas, judge ruled that, despite the passage of time, Collins could be charged with Middleton's murder.

Attendant Circumstances The facts surrounding a criminal event that must be proved to convict the defendant of the underlying crime.

Hate Crime Law A statute that provides for greater sanctions against those who commit crimes motivated by bias against an individual or a group based on race, ethnicity, religion, gender, sexual orientation, disability, or age.

Attendant Circumstances

In certain crimes, **attendant circumstances**—also known as accompanying circumstances—are relevant to the *corpus delicti*. Most states, for example, differentiate between simple assault and the more serious offense of aggravated assault depending on the attendant circumstance of whether the defendant used a weapon such as a gun or a knife while committing the crime. Criminal law also classifies degrees of property crimes based on the attendant circumstance of the amount stolen. According to federal statutes, the theft of less than $1,000 from a bank is a misdemeanor, while the theft of any amount over $1,000 is a felony.[34] (To get a better understanding of the role of attendant circumstances in criminal statutes, see Figure 4.2.)

Requirements of Proof and Intent Attendant circumstances must be proved beyond a reasonable doubt, just like any other element of a crime.[35] Furthermore, the *mens rea* of the defendant regarding each attendant circumstance must be proved as well. Consider the case of Ronald Thompson, who was charged several years ago with multiple crimes for taking underwater photos of children wearing swimsuits at a San Antonio, Texas, water park. Thompson had broken a state "upskirt" law prohibiting photography or video recordings taken "with the intent to arouse or gratify the sexual desire of the defendant."

In 2014, a Texas appeals court struck down the part of the law dealing with the defendant's intentions. The court ruled that it would be difficult, if not impossible, for prosecutors to prove beyond a reasonable doubt exactly what Thompson was thinking while he was taking the photos. Therefore, the *mens rea* requirement was unfair.[36] In general, if state legislatures want to ban "upskirting" or "downblousing" or other similar behavior, they must remove intent requirements. For example, a new Massachusetts law makes "the secret photographing, videotaping, or electronically surveilling of another person's sexual or other inmate parts" a crime.[37]

Hate Crime Laws In most cases, a person's motive for committing a crime is irrelevant—a court will not try to read the accused's mind. Over the past few decades, however, nearly every state and the federal government have passed *hate crime laws* that make the suspect's motive an important attendant circumstance to his or her criminal act. In general, **hate crime laws** provide for greater sanctions against those who commit crimes motivated by bias against a person based on race, ethnicity, religion, gender, sexual orientation, disability, or age. According to the federal government's Crime Victimization Survey, nearly 300,000 nonfatal hate crime offenses take place each year.[38] The concept of a hate crime as measurable, definable criminal behavior is a relatively new one and, as we will see in the *CJ in Action* feature at the end of this chapter, has its detractors.

FIGURE 4.2 Attendant Circumstances in Criminal Law

Most criminal statutes incorporate three of the elements we have discussed in this section: the act (*actus reus*), the intent (*mens rea*), and attendant circumstances. This diagram of the federal false imprisonment statute should give you an idea of how these elements combine to create the totality of a crime.

| Intent | Act | Attendant Circumstances |

Whoever intentionally confines, restrains, or detains another against that person's will is guilty of felony false imprisonment.

Harm

For most crimes to occur, some harm must have been done to a person or to property. A certain number of crimes are actually categorized depending on the harm done to the victim, regardless of the intent behind the criminal act. Take two offenses, both of which involve one person hitting another in the back of the head with a tire iron. In the first instance, the victim dies, and the offender is charged with murder. In the second, the victim is only knocked unconscious, and the offender is charged with battery. Because the harm in the second instance was less severe, so was the crime with which the offender was charged, even though the act was exactly the same. Furthermore, most states have different degrees of battery depending on the extent of the injuries suffered by the victim.

Many acts are deemed criminal if they could do harm that the laws try to prevent. Such acts are called **inchoate offenses.** They exist when only an attempt at a criminal act was made. If Jenkins solicits Peterson to murder Jenkins's business partner, this is an inchoate offense on the part of Jenkins, even though Peterson fails to carry out the act. Threats and *conspiracies* also fall into the category of inchoate offenses. In 2014, two teenage boys were arrested on suspicion of **conspiracy** and making criminal threats after local officials found evidence online that they were planning a mass shooting at South Pasadena High School in southern California. The United States Supreme Court has ruled that a person could be convicted of criminal conspiracy even though police intervention made the completion of the illegal plan impossible.[39]

EthicsChallenge

Consider a situation in which Lisa sets fire to the house of her boyfriend, Andre, who has been cheating on her. The fire spreads out of control, burning down the house of George, Andre's next door neighbor. A week later, George dies of a heart attack caused by the stress of losing all his worldly possessions. Under what legal concept discussed in this section could Lisa be charged with first degree murder for George's death? Would it be ethical for prosecutors to do so, given that Lisa had no intent of harming George? Explain why or why not. ■

Defenses under Criminal Law

Several years ago, sixteen-year-old Ethan Couch, driving with a blood-alcohol level three times the legal limit, killed four pedestrians in Burleson, Texas. During Couch's trial, a psychiatrist testified that the teenager should receive a lenient sentence because he suffered from "affluenza," a condition that "afflicts" irresponsible children of rich, lenient parents.

Although the "spoiled brat" excuse has not been embraced in the American legal system, defendants can raise a number of other, established defenses for wrongdoing in our criminal courts. These defenses generally rely on one of two arguments: (1) the defendant is not responsible for the crime, or (2) the defendant was justified in committing the crime.

Criminal Responsibility and the Law

The idea of responsibility plays a significant role in criminal law. In certain circumstances, the law recognizes that even though an act is inherently criminal, society will not punish the actor because he or she does not have the requisite mental condition. In other words, the law "excuses" the person for his or her behavior. Insanity, intoxication,

Inchoate Offenses Conduct deemed criminal without actual harm being done, provided that the harm that would have occurred is one the law tries to prevent.

Conspiracy A plot by two or more people to carry out an illegal or harmful act.

List and briefly define the
most important excuse
defenses for crimes.

LEARNING
6
OBJECTIVE

and mistake are the most important excuse defenses today, but we start our discussion of the subject with one of the first such defenses recognized by American law: infancy.

Infancy Under the earliest state criminal codes of the United States, children younger than seven years of age could never be held legally accountable for crimes. Those between seven and fourteen years old were presumed to lack the capacity for criminal behavior, while anyone over the age of fourteen was tried as an adult. Thus, early American criminal law recognized **infancy** as a defense in which the accused's wrongdoing is excused because he or she is too young to fully understand the consequences of his or her actions.

With the creation of the juvenile justice system in the early 1900s, the infancy defense became redundant, as youthful delinquents were automatically treated differently than adult offenders. Today, most states either designate an age (eighteen or under) under which wrongdoers are sent to juvenile court or allow judges and prosecutors to decide whether a minor will be charged as an adult on a case-by-case basis. We will explore the concept of infancy as it applies to the modern American juvenile justice system in much greater detail in Chapter 15.

Insanity After Cody Metzker-Madsen beat his five-year-old brother with a brick and drowned him, the Iowa teenager told law enforcement agents that he thought he had been doing battle with a goblin. In 2014, a district court judge ruled Metzker-Madsen suffered from a severe mental illness that prevented him from knowing that his actions were wrong. As a result, Metzker-Madsen was sent to a psychiatric hospital rather than prison. Thus, **insanity** may be a defense to a criminal charge when the defendant's state of mind is such that she or he cannot claim legal responsibility for her or his actions.

Measuring Sanity The general principle of the insanity defense is that a person is excused for his or her criminal wrongdoing if, as a result of a mental disease or defect, he or she

- Does not perceive the physical nature or consequences of his or her conduct;
- Does not know that his or her conduct is wrong or criminal; or
- Is not sufficiently able to control his or her conduct so as to be held accountable for it.[40]

Although criminal law has traditionally accepted the idea that an insane person cannot be held responsible for criminal acts, society has long debated what standards should be used to measure sanity for the purposes of a criminal trial. This lack of consensus is reflected in the diverse tests employed by different American jurisdictions to determine insanity. The tests include the following:

1. *The* M'Naghten *rule.* Derived from an 1843 British murder case, the **M'Naghten rule** states that a person is legally insane and therefore not criminally responsible if, at the time of the offense, he or she was not able to distinguish between right and wrong.[41] As Figure 4.3 shows, half of the states still use a version of the *M'Naghten* rule. One state, New Hampshire, uses a slightly different version of this rule called the "product test." Under this standard, a defendant is not guilty if the unlawful act was the product of a mental disease or defect.

2. *The ALI/MPC test.* In the early 1960s, the American Law Institute (ALI) included an insanity standard in its Model Penal Code (MPC), discussed earlier in the chapter. Also known as the **substantial-capacity test,** the **ALI/MPC test** requires that the

Infancy A condition that, under early American law, excused young wrongdoers of criminal behavior because presumably they could not understand the consequences of their actions.

Insanity A defense for criminal liability that asserts a lack of criminal responsibility due to mental instability

M'Naghten Rule A common law test of criminal responsibility, derived from *M'Naghten's* Case in 1843, that relies on the defendant's inability to distinguish right from wrong.

Substantial-Capacity Test (ALI/MPC Test) A test for the insanity defense that states that a person is not responsible for criminal behavior when he or she "lacks substantial capacity" to understand that the behavior is wrong or to know how to behave properly.

FIGURE 4.3 Insanity Defenses

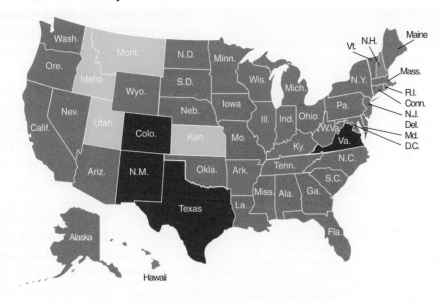

■ **M'Naghten:** "Didn't know what he was doing or didn't know it was wrong."

■ **M'Naghten plus irresistible impulse:** "Could not control his conduct."

■ **ALI/MPC:** "Lacks substantial capacity to appreciate the wrongfulness of his conduct or to control it."

■ **Product test:** "No criminal responsibility if the unlawful act is the product of a mental disease or defect."

■ **No insanity defense** established by state legislature.

defendant lack "substantial capacity" to either "appreciate the wrongfulness" of his or her conduct or to conform that conduct "to the requirements of the law."[42]

3. *The irresistible-impulse test.* Under the **irresistible-impulse test,** a person may be found insane even if he or she was aware that a criminal act was "wrong," provided that some "irresistible impulse" resulting from a mental deficiency drove him or her to commit the crime.[43]

The ALI/MPC test is considered the easiest standard of the three for a defendant to meet because the defendant needs only to show a lack of "substantial capacity" to be released from criminal responsibility. Defense attorneys generally consider it more difficult to prove that the defendant could not distinguish "right" from "wrong" or that he or she was driven by an irresistible impulse.

Determining Competency Whatever the standard, the insanity defense is rarely entered and is even less likely to result in an acquittal, as it is difficult to prove.[44] (See the feature *Myth vs Reality—Are Too Many Criminals Found Not Guilty by Reason of Insanity?*) Psychiatry is far more commonly used in the courtroom to determine the "competency" of a defendant to stand trial. If a judge believes that the defendant is unable to understand the nature of the proceedings or to assist in his or her own defense, the trial will not take place.

When **competency hearings** (which may also take place after the initial arrest and before sentencing) reveal that the defendant is in fact incompetent, criminal proceedings come to a halt. For example, in November 2014, a San Diego, California, judge ruled

Irresistible-Impulse Test A test for the insanity defense under which a defendant who knew his or her action was wrong may still be found insane if he or she was unable, as a result of a mental deficiency, to control the urge to complete the act.

Competency Hearing A court proceeding to determine whether the defendant is mentally well enough to understand the charges filed against him or her and cooperate with a lawyer in presenting a defense.

Myth vs Reality

Are Too Many Criminals Found Not Guilty by Reason of Insanity?

Discuss a common misperception concerning the insanity defense in the United States. LEARNING OBJECTIVE 7

To many Americans, it seems likely that any person who commits a gruesome murder or any other sort of violent crime has psychological problems. The question, then, is, how do we balance the need to punish such a person with the possibility that he or she may be seriously ill?

The Myth The American system of criminal justice answers this question by stating that a person may not be tried for an offense if that person cannot be held legally responsible for her or his actions. Because of the publicity surrounding the insanity defense, many people are under the impression that it is a major loophole in our system, allowing criminals to be "let off" no matter how heinous their crimes.

The Reality In fact, the insanity defense is raised in only about 1 percent of felony trials, and it is successful only one out of every four times it is raised. The reason: it is extremely difficult to prove insanity under the law. For example, Andre Thomas cut out the hearts of his wife, their young son, and her thirteen month-old daughter. Before his murder trial, Thomas pulled his right eye out of its socket. (Several years later, while on death row, he ripped out the other eye and apparently ate it.) Nonetheless, prosecutors were able to convince a Texas jury that Brown understood the difference between right and wrong at the time of the murders, and an appeals court upheld the conviction. Thomas is "clearly 'crazy,'" said one of the appellate judges who heard his case, "but he is also 'sane' under Texas law."

Even if Thomas had succeeded with the insanity defense, he would not have been "let off" in the sense that he would have been set free. Many defendants found not guilty by reason of insanity spend more time in mental hospitals than criminals who are convicted of similar acts spend in prison.

For Critical Analysis

What do the relatively limited use and success rate of the insanity defense indicate about the impact of public opinion on criminal law?

that because Carlo Mercado suffered from severe mental illness, he was not fit to stand trial. Mercado was charged with three counts of murder resulting from a shooting spree outside a shopping mall the previous Christmas Eve. As a result of the judge's decision, Mercado would receive psychiatric treatment to restore his competency. When this goal was achieved, the criminal proceedings would continue.

Guilty but Mentally Ill Public backlash against the insanity defense caused six state legislatures to pass "guilty but mentally ill" statutes. Under these laws, a defendant is guilty but mentally ill if

> at the time of the commission of the act constituting the offense, he [or she] had the capacity to distinguish right from wrong . . . but because of mental disease or defect he [or she] lacked sufficient capacity to conform his [or her] conduct to the requirements of the law.[45]

In other words, the laws allow a jury to determine that a defendant is "mentally ill," though not insane, and therefore criminally responsible for her or his actions. Defendants found guilty but mentally ill generally spend the early years of their sentences in a psychiatric hospital and the rest of the time in prison, or they receive treatment while in prison.

Intoxication The law recognizes two types of **intoxication,** whether from drugs or from alcohol: *voluntary* and *involuntary.*

Involuntary Intoxication Involuntary intoxication occurs when a person is physically forced to ingest or is injected with an intoxicating substance, or is unaware that a substance contains drugs or alcohol. Involuntary intoxication is a viable defense to a crime if the substance leaves the person unable to form the mental state necessary to understand that the act committed while under the influence was wrong.[46] For example, Montana's Supreme Court recently ruled that a woman had wrongly been denied the ability to present the involuntary intoxication defense to counter a drunken driving charge. The defendant claimed that she had unwittingly consumed a drink laced with GHB, known as the "date rape drug," before being arrested during her drive home from a bar.[47]

Intoxication A defense for criminal liability in which the defendant claims that the taking of intoxicants rendered him or her unable to form the requisite intent to commit a criminal act.

Voluntary Intoxication Voluntary drug or alcohol intoxication is also used to excuse a defendant's actions, though it is not a defense in itself. Rather, it is used when the defense attorney wants to show that the defendant was so intoxicated that *mens rea* was negated. In other words, the defendant could not possibly have had the state of mind that a crime requires. Many courts are reluctant to allow voluntary intoxication arguments to be presented to juries, however. After all, the defendant, by definition, voluntarily chose to enter an intoxicated state.

Thirteen states have eliminated voluntary intoxication as a possible defense, a step that has been criticized by many legal scholars but was upheld by the United States Supreme Court in *Montana v. Egelhoff* (1996).[48] In 2014, Wisconsin repealed its voluntary intoxication law, mostly due to the grassroots efforts of a murder victim's loved ones. A year earlier, attorneys for Brian Cooper successfully argued that their client was too drunk to have intentionally strangled twenty-one-year-old Alisha Bromfield to death. Afterward, Sherry Anicich, Bromfield's mother, walked out of the courtroom and told her husband, "We're changing this law."[49] Following a campaign of online petitions, letter writing, and meetings with state legislators by Bromfield's family and friends, the voluntary intoxication defense was no longer part of Wisconsin's criminal code.

▲ In 2014, Kerry Kennedy exits a White Plains, New York, courtroom after a jury acquitted her of driving while impaired. Several years earlier, Kennedy drove her car into another vehicle because, she claims, she mistakenly took a sleeping pill instead of her thyroid medication. **Why do you think Kennedy was able to successfully raise the involuntary intoxication defense?** Reuters/Eduardo Munoz

Mistake Everyone has heard the saying, "Ignorance of the law is no excuse." Ordinarily, ignorance of the law or a *mistaken idea* about what the law requires is not a valid defense. Such was the case when retired science teacher Eddie Leroy Anderson and his son dug for arrowheads near their favorite campground site in Idaho, unaware that the land was a federally protected archaeological site. Facing two years in prison for this mistake, they pleaded guilty and were given a year's probation and a $1,500 fine each. "Folks need to pay attention to where they are," said U.S. attorney Wendy Olson.[50]

Mistake of Law As the above example suggests, strict liability crimes specifically preclude the *mistake of law* defense, because the offender's intent is irrelevant. For practical reasons, the mistake of law defense is rarely allowed under any circumstances. If "I didn't know" was a valid defense, the courts would be clogged with defendants claiming ignorance of all aspects of criminal law. In some rare instances, however, people who claim that they honestly did not know that they were breaking a law may have a valid defense if (1) the law was not published or reasonably known to the public or (2) the person relied on an official statement of the law that was erroneous.[51]

Mistake of Fact A *mistake of fact,* as opposed to a *mistake of law,* operates as a defense if it negates the mental state necessary to commit a crime. If, for example, Oliver mistakenly walks off with Julie's briefcase because he thinks it is his, there is no theft. Theft requires knowledge that the property belongs to another. The mistake-of-fact defense has proved very controversial in rape and sexual assault cases, in which the accused claims a mistaken belief that the sex was consensual, while the victim insists that he or she was coerced.

Justification Criminal Defenses and the Law

Describe the four most important justification criminal defenses.
LEARNING
8
OBJECTIVE

In certain instances, a defendant will accept responsibility for committing an illegal act, but contend that—given the circumstances—the act was justified. In other words, even though the guilty act and the guilty intent are present, the particulars of the case relieve the defendant of criminal liability. In 2013, for example, there were 742 "justified" killings of those who were in the process of committing a felony: 461 were killed by law enforcement officers and 281 by private citizens.[52] Four of the most important justification defenses are duress, self-defense, necessity, and entrapment.

Duress **Duress** exists when the *wrongful* threat of one person induces another person to perform an act that she or he would otherwise not perform. In such a situation, duress is said to negate the *mens rea* necessary to commit a crime. For duress to qualify as a defense, the following requirements must be met:

1. The threat must be of serious bodily harm or death.
2. The harm threatened must be greater than the harm caused by the crime.
3. The threat must be immediate and inescapable.
4. The defendant must have become involved in the situation through no fault of his or her own.[53]

Note that some scholars consider duress to be an excuse defense, because the threat of bodily harm negates any guilty intent on the part of the defendant.[54]

When ruling on the duress defense, courts often examine whether the defendant had the opportunity to avoid the threat in question. Two narcotics cases illustrate this point. In the first, the defendant claimed that an associate threatened to kill him and his wife unless he participated in a marijuana deal. Although this contention was proved true during the course of the trial, the court rejected the duress defense because the defendant made no apparent effort to escape, nor did he report his dilemma to the police. In sum, the drug deal was avoidable—the defendant could have made an effort to extricate himself, but he did not, thereby surrendering the protection of the duress defense.[55]

In the second case, a taxi driver in Bogotá, Colombia, was ordered by a passenger to swallow cocaine-filled balloons and take them to the United States. The taxi driver was warned that if he refused, his wife and three-year-old daughter would be killed. After a series of similar threats, the taxi driver agreed to transport the drugs. On arriving at customs at the Los Angeles airport, the defendant consented to have his stomach X-rayed, which led to discovery of the contraband and his arrest. During his trial, the defendant told the court that he was afraid to notify the police in Colombia because he believed them to be corrupt. The court accepted his duress defense, on the grounds that it met the four requirements listed above and the defendant had notified American authorities when given the opportunity to do so.[56]

Justifiable Use of Force—Self-Defense A person who believes he or she is in danger of being harmed by another is justified in defending himself or herself with the use of force, and any criminal act committed in such circumstances can be justified as **self-defense.** Other situations that also justify the use of force include the defense of another person, the defense of one's dwelling or other property, and the prevention of a crime. In all these situations, it is important to distinguish between deadly and nondeadly force. Deadly force is likely to result in death or serious bodily harm.

The Amount of Force Generally speaking, people can use the amount of nondeadly force that seems necessary to protect themselves, their dwellings, or other property or to

Duress Unlawful pressure brought to bear on a person, causing the person to perform an act that he or she would not otherwise perform.

Self-Defense The legally recognized privilege to protect one's self or property from injury by another.

prevent the commission of a crime. Deadly force can be used in self-defense if there is a *reasonable belief* that imminent death or bodily harm will otherwise result, if the attacker is using unlawful force (an example of lawful force is that exerted by a police officer), if the defender has not initiated or provoked the attack, and if there is no other possible response or alternative way out of the life-threatening situation.[57]

Duty to Retreat The requirement that a person claiming self-defense prove that she or he first took reasonable steps to avoid the conflict that resulted in the use of deadly force.

Deadly force normally can be used to defend a dwelling only if the unlawful entry is violent and the person believes deadly force is necessary to prevent imminent death or great bodily harm. In some jurisdictions, it is also a viable defense if the person believes deadly force is necessary to prevent the commission of a felony (such as arson) in the dwelling. Authorities will often take an expansive view of lawful deadly force when it is used to protect another person. So, in 2014, a New Orleans man was not charged with any crime after he fatally shot an offender who was sexually assaulting a woman—the first man's companion—at gunpoint.

The Duty to Retreat When a person is outside the home or in a public space, the rules for self-defense change somewhat. Until relatively recently, almost all jurisdictions required someone who is attacked under these circumstances to "retreat to the wall" before fighting back. In other words, under this **duty to retreat** one who is being assaulted may not resort to deadly force if she or he has a reasonable opportunity to "run away" and thus avoid the conflict. Only when this person has run into a "wall," literally or otherwise, may deadly force be used in self-defense.

Recently, however, several states have changed their laws to eliminate this duty to retreat. For example, a Florida law did away with the duty to retreat outside the home, stating that citizens have "the right to stand [their] ground and meet force with force, including deadly force," if they "reasonably" fear for their safety.[58] The Florida law also allows a person to use deadly force against someone who unlawfully intrudes into her or his house (or vehicle), even if that person does not fear for her or his safety.[59] More than thirty states now have passed legislation that removes the duty to retreat before using force in self-defense.

Debating Self-Defense "Stand your ground" statutes gained national attention when, in February 2012, George Zimmerman shot and killed unarmed seventeen-year-old Trayvon Martin in Sanford, Florida. Zimmerman told police that he had encountered Martin during his rounds as a neighborhood watchman, and that he had pulled the trigger only after being attacked by the younger man. Zimmerman was eventually acquitted of second degree murder when a jury decided that he could have been acting reasonably by defending himself against great bodily harm or death.[60]

During the furor that surrounded this case—caused in large measure because Zimmerman is Hispanic and Martin was black—"stand your ground" laws came under a great deal of criticism. According to one opponent, they have created a "nation where disputes are settled by guns instead of gavels, and where suspects are shot by civilians instead of arrested by the police."[61] In Texas, which passed its version of this legislation in 2007, the number of justifiable homicides increased from eighteen in 1999 to sixty-two in 2013.[62]

Proponents of "stand your ground" laws contend that they allow people who face serious bodily harm or death the opportunity to defend themselves without first having to retreat as far as possible. Supporters also argue that the laws strengthen the concept of self-defense by making it less likely that a person defending him- or herself will be charged with a crime. In this chapter's *CJ Policy—Your Take* feature, you can make up your own mind about "stand your ground" laws.

CJ Policy—Your Take

At 4 A.M., Ronald Westbrook, lost and suffering from Alzheimer's disease, tried to open Joe Hendrix's front door. Armed with a handgun, Hendrix, unaware of the intruder's condition, came outside and shouted at Westbrook, who was carrying an unlit flashlight. Westbrook did not respond, but instead began walking toward the other man. Hendrix fatally shot Westbrook. Citing Georgia's **"stand your ground" law,** prosecutors decided not to charge Hendrix with any crime. What is your opinion of the prosecutors' decision in this case, and of "stand your ground" laws in general?

Necessity A defense against criminal liability in which the defendant asserts that circumstances required her or him to commit an illegal act.

Entrapment A defense in which the defendant claims that he or she was induced by a public official—usually an undercover agent or police officer—to commit a crime that he or she would otherwise not have committed.

Substantive Criminal Law Law that defines the rights and duties of individuals with respect to one another.

Procedural Criminal Law Rules that define the manner in which the rights and duties of individuals may be enforced.

Necessity The **necessity** defense requires courts to weigh the harm caused by the crime actually committed against the harm that would have been caused by the criminal act avoided. If the avoided harm is greater than the committed harm, then the defense has a chance of succeeding. A San Francisco jury, for example, acquitted a defendant of illegally carrying a concealed weapon because he was avoiding the "greater evil" of getting shot himself. The defendant had testified that he needed the gun for protection while entering a high-crime neighborhood to buy baby food and diapers for his crying niece.[63] Murder is the one crime for which the necessity defense is not applicable under any circumstances.

Entrapment **Entrapment** is a justification defense that criminal law allows when a police officer or government agent deceives a defendant into wrongdoing. Although law enforcement agents can legitimately use various forms of subterfuge—such as informants or undercover agents—to gain information or apprehend a suspect in a criminal act, the law places limits on these strategies. Police cannot persuade an innocent person to commit a crime, nor can they coerce a suspect into doing so, even if they are certain she or he is a criminal.

The guidelines for determining entrapment were established in the 1932 case of *Sorrells v. United States.*[64] The case, which took place during Prohibition, when the sale of alcoholic beverages was illegal, involved a federal law enforcement agent who repeatedly urged the defendant to sell him bootleg whiskey. The defendant initially rejected the agent's overtures, stating that he "did not fool with whiskey." Eventually, however, he sold the agent a half-gallon of the substance and was summarily convicted of violating the law. The United States Supreme Court held that the agent had improperly induced the defendant to break the law and reversed his conviction.

This case set the precedent for focusing on the defendant's outlook in entrapment cases. In other words, the Court decided that entrapment occurs if a defendant who is not predisposed to commit the crime is convinced to do so by an agent of the government.[65] (For an overview of justification and excuse defenses, see Figure 4.4.)

EthicsChallenge

Over the past decade, federal law enforcement agents have conducted more than 350 "stash-house stings." In these operations, an undercover agent pretending to be a drug courier tells a group of suspected criminals about a fictitious, heavily guarded warehouse filled with illegal drugs. When the suspects arm themselves to raid the stash house and steal the contraband, they are arrested. Is this entrapment? Is it an ethical way to round up criminal conspirators? Explain your answers. ■

Procedural Safeguards

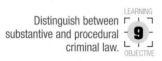
LEARNING
9
OBJECTIVE
Distinguish between substantive and procedural criminal law.

To this point, we have focused on **substantive criminal law**, which defines the acts that the government will punish. We will now turn our attention to **procedural criminal law**. (The section that follows will provide only a short overview of criminal procedure. In later chapters, many other constitutional issues will be examined in more detail.)

Criminal law brings the force of the state, with all its resources, to bear against the individual. Criminal procedures, drawn from the ideals stated in the Bill of Rights, are designed to protect the constitutional rights of individuals and to prevent the arbitrary use of this power by the government.

FIGURE 4.4 Excuse and Justification Defenses

Excuse Defenses: Based on a defendant's admitting that she or he committed the criminal act, but asserting that she or he cannot be held criminally responsible for the act due to lack of criminal intent.

	The defendant must prove that:	Example
INFANCY	Because he or she was under a statutorily determined age, he or she did not have the maturity to make the decisions necessary to commit a criminal act.	A thirteen-year-old takes a handgun from his backpack at school and begins shooting at fellow students, killing three. (In such cases, the offender is often processed by the juvenile justice system rather than the criminal justice system.)
INSANITY	At the time of the criminal act, he or she did not have the necessary mental capacity to be held responsible for his or her actions.	A man with a history of mental illness pushes a woman in front of an oncoming subway train, which kills her instantly.
INTOXICATION	She or he had diminished control over her or his actions due to the influence of alcohol or drugs.	A woman who had been drinking malt liquor and vodka stabs her boyfriend to death after a domestic argument. She claims to have been so drunk as to not remember the incident.
MISTAKE	He or she did not know that his or her actions violated a law (this defense is very rarely even attempted), or that he or she violated the law believing a relevant fact to be true when, in fact, it was not.	A woman, thinking that her divorce in another state has been finalized when it has not, marries for a second time, thereby committing bigamy.

Justification Defenses: Based on a defendant's admitting that he or she committed the particular criminal act, but asserting that, under the circumstances, the criminal act was justified.

	The defendant must prove that:	Example
DURESS	She or he performed the criminal act under the use or threat of use of unlawful force against her or his person that a reasonable person would have been unable to resist.	A mother assists her boyfriend in committing a burglary after he threatens to kill her children if she refuses to do so.
SELF-DEFENSE	He or she acted in a manner to defend himself or herself, others, or property, or to prevent the commission of a crime.	A husband awakes to find his wife standing over him, pointing a shotgun at his chest. In the ensuing struggle, the firearm goes off, killing the wife.
NECESSITY	The criminal act he or she committed was necessary in order to avoid a harm to himself or herself or another that was greater than the harm caused by the act itself.	Four people physically remove a friend from her residence on the property of a religious cult, arguing that the crime of kidnapping was justified in order to remove the victim from the damaging influence of cult leaders.
ENTRAPMENT	She or he was encouraged by agents of the state to engage in a criminal act she or he would not have engaged in otherwise.	The owner of a boat marina agrees to allow three federal drug enforcement agents, posing as drug dealers, to use his dock to unload shipments of marijuana from Colombia.

The Bill of Rights

For various reasons, proposals related to the rights of individuals were rejected during the framing of the U.S. Constitution in 1787. In fact, the original constitution contained only three provisions that referred to criminal procedure. Article I, Section 9, Clause 2, states that the "Privilege of the Writ of Habeas Corpus shall not be suspended." As will be discussed in Chapter 10, a writ of *habeas corpus* is an order that requires jailers to bring a person before a court or judge and explain why the person is being held in prison. Article I, Section 9, Clause 3, holds that no "Bill of Attainder or ex post facto Law shall be passed." A bill of attainder is a legislative act that targets a particular person or group for punishment without a trial, while an *ex post facto* law operates retroactively, making an event or action illegal though it took place before the law was passed. Finally, Article III, Section 2, Clause 3, maintains that the "Trial of all Crimes" will be by jury and "such Trial shall be held in the State where the said crimes shall have been committed."

Amending the Constitution The need for a written declaration of rights of individuals eventually caused the first Congress to draft twelve amendments to the Constitution and submit them for approval by the states. Ten of these amendments, commonly known as the **Bill of Rights,** were adopted in 1791. Since then, seventeen more amendments have been added.

The Bill of Rights, as interpreted by the United States Supreme Court, has served as the basis for procedural safeguards of the accused in this country. These safeguards include the following:

1. The Fourth Amendment protection from unreasonable searches and seizures.
2. The Fourth Amendment requirement that no warrants for a search or an arrest can be issued without probable cause.
3. The Fifth Amendment requirement that no one can be deprived of life, liberty, or property without "due process" of law.
4. The Fifth Amendment prohibition against *double jeopardy* (trying someone twice for the same criminal offense).
5. The Fifth Amendment guarantee that no person can be required to be a witness against (incriminate) himself or herself.
6. The Sixth Amendment guarantees of a speedy trial, a trial by jury, a public trial, the right to confront witnesses, and the right to a lawyer at various stages of criminal proceedings.
7. The Eighth Amendment prohibitions against excessive bails and fines and cruel and unusual punishments. (For the full text of the Bill of Rights, see Appendix A.)

▼ Why do most Americans accept certain security precautions taken by the federal government—such as full body scans at airports— that restrict our individual freedom or compromise our privacy? John Moore/Getty Images

Expanding the Constitution The Bill of Rights initially offered citizens protection only against the federal government. Over the years, however, the procedural safeguards of most of the provisions of the Bill of Rights have been applied to the actions of state governments through the Fourteenth Amendment.[66] Furthermore, the states, under certain circumstances, have the option to grant even more protections than are required by the federal Constitution. As these protections are crucial to criminal justice procedures in the United States, they will be afforded much more attention in Chapter 7, with regard to police action, and in Chapter 10, with regard to the criminal trial.

In 2013, several members of Congress introduced a proposed Victims' Rights Amendment to the U.S. Constitution.[67] This proposed amendment would contain many of the same rights that are present in state victims' rights laws and the federal Victims' Rights Act, as discussed in Chapter 3. The difference, claim its supporters, is that such an amendment would give some "teeth" to protections that are now, as you also learned in Chapter 3, mostly discretionary.[68] Victims' rights supporters have been trying, without success, to amend the Constitution in favor of victims since 1996, showing just how important constitutional protections are in the criminal justice system.

Due Process

Both the Fifth and Fourteenth Amendments provide that no person should be deprived of "life, liberty, or property without due process of law." This **due process clause** basically requires that the government not act unfairly or arbitrarily. In other words, the government cannot rely on individual judgment and impulse when making decisions, but must stay within the boundaries of reason and the law. Not surprisingly, disagreements as to the meaning of these provisions have plagued courts, politicians, and citizens since this nation was founded, and will undoubtedly continue to do so.

To understand due process, it is important to consider its two types: procedural due process and substantive due process.

Procedural Due Process   According to **procedural due process,** the law must be carried out by a *method* that is fair and orderly. It requires that certain procedures be followed in administering and executing a law so that an individual's basic freedoms are not violated.

The American criminal justice system's adherence to due process principles is evident in its treatment of the death penalty. To ensure that the process is fair, as we will see in Chapter 11, a number of procedural safeguards have been built into capital punishment. Much to the dismay of many victims' groups, these procedures make the process expensive and lengthy. The average time between sentencing and execution for those convicted of capital crimes is almost sixteen years, and some inmates spend well over twenty years on death row.[69] (Concepts of due process can become muddied when it comes to fighting terrorism, as detailed in the feature *A Question of Ethics: Due Justice?*)

Procedural Due Process
A provision in the Constitution that states that the law must be carried out in a fair and orderly manner.

LEARNING
10
OBJECTIVE
Explain the importance of the due process clause in the criminal justice system.

A Question of Ethics: Due Justice?

The Situation   The U.S. government has learned the precise location of an Islamist cleric in the Middle Eastern country of Yemen. This cleric has been linked to more than a dozen terrorist operations, including a failed plot to blow up cargo airplanes bound for the United States, and his online sermons in English contain numerous threats to Americans. Using a Predator drone—a remote-controlled unmanned aircraft armed with missiles—the U.S. military has the ability to target and kill the cleric. There is one problem, however: he was born in New Mexico and is therefore a citizen of the United States.

The Ethical Dilemma   The U.S. Constitution forbids the conviction and execution of American citizens without due process of law, which usually means a criminal trial.

What Is the Solution?   In 2011, an American Predator drone missile killed Anwar al-Awlaki, the U.S. citizen Islamist cleric described above. Legal expert Glenn Greenwald echoed the sentiments of a number of critics by arguing this action was inherently unfair. Awlaki had not been charged with any crime, and he had not been afforded a trial to prove his innocence. "[Awlaki] was simply ordered killed by [President Barack Obama]: his judge, jury, and executioner," Greenwald said.

Federal counterterrorism officials defended the drone strike as "'legal,' 'ethical,' and 'wise.'" According to the Obama administration, Awlaki was no ordinary American citizen. Rather, he was a member of terrorist organizations that were, essentially, at war with the United States. Furthermore, several years ago federal lawyers justified targeted assassinations of suspected terrorists—including U.S. citizens—as "lawful acts of self-defense." After reviewing our discussion of self-defense earlier in this chapter, what is your opinion of this argument? Do you think that the assassination of U.S. citizens without due process is acceptable? Explain your answer.

Substantive Due Process Fair procedures would obviously be of little use if they were used to administer unfair laws. For example, suppose a law requires everyone to wear a red shirt on Mondays. You wear a blue shirt on Monday, and you are arrested, convicted, and sentenced to one year in prison. The fact that all proper procedures were followed and your rights were given their proper protections would mean very little because the law that you broke was unfair and arbitrary.

Thus, **substantive due process** requires that the laws themselves be reasonable. The idea is that if a law is unfair or arbitrary, even if properly passed by a legislature, it must be declared unconstitutional. In the 1930s, for example, Oklahoma instituted the Habitual Criminal Sterilization Act. Under this statute, a person who had been convicted of three felonies could be "rendered sexually sterile" by the state (that is, the person would no longer be able to produce children). The United States Supreme Court held that the law was unconstitutional, as there are "limits to the extent which a legislatively represented majority may conduct biological experiments at the expense of the dignity and personality and natural powers of a minority."[70]

The Judicial System's Role in Due Process As the last example suggests, the United States Supreme Court often plays the important role of ultimately deciding when due process has been violated and when it has not. (See Figure 4.5 for a list of important Supreme Court due process cases.)

The Court is also called on from time to time to determine whether a due process right exists in the first place. For example, in Figure 4.3 from earlier in the chapter, you will notice that four states—Idaho, Kansas, Montana, and Utah—do not provide defendants with access to the insanity defense. In 2007, John Delling killed two men in Idaho whom he believed had conspired to steal his soul. Because Idaho does not allow the insanity defense, Delling pleaded guilty to the murders and was sentenced to life in prison. In 2012, his lawyers asked the Supreme Court to rule that the insanity defense was a constitutional right that should be available to all defendants in the United States. The Court refused to do so, allowing individual states to prohibit the insanity defense if they so wish.[71]

FIGURE 4.5 Important United States Supreme Court Due Process Decisions

YEAR	ISSUE	AMENDMENT INVOLVED	COURT CASE
1948	Right to a public trial	VI	*In re Oliver*, 333 U.S. 257
1952	Police searches cannot be so invasive as to "shock the conscience"	IV	*Rochin v. California*, 342 U.S. 165
1961	Exclusionary rule	IV	*Mapp v. Ohio*, 367 U.S. 643
1963	Right to a lawyer in all criminal felony cases	VI	*Gideon v. Wainwright*, 372 U.S. 335
1964	No compulsory self-incrimination	V	*Malloy v. Hogan*, 378 U.S. 1
1964	Right to have counsel when taken into police custody and subjected to questioning	VI	*Escobedo v. Illinois*, 378 U.S. 478
1965	Right to confront and cross-examine witnesses	VI	*Pointer v. Texas*, 380 U.S. 400
1966	Right to an impartial jury	VI	*Parker v. Gladden*, 385 U.S. 363
1966	Confessions of suspects not notified of due process rights ruled invalid	V	*Miranda v. Arizona*, 384 U.S. 436
1967	Right to a speedy trial	VI	*Klopfer v. North Carolina*, 386 U.S. 21
1967	Juveniles have due process rights, too	V	*In re Gault*, 387 U.S. 1
1968	Right to a jury trial ruled a fundamental right	VI	*Duncan v. Louisiana*, 391 U.S. 145
1969	No double jeopardy	V	*Benton v. Maryland*, 395 U.S. 784

Society's Best Interests The due process clause does not automatically doom laws that may infringe on procedural or substantive rights. In certain circumstances, the lawmaking body may be able to prove that its interests are greater than the due process rights of the individual, and in those cases the statute may be upheld. Several years ago, for example, a U.S. appellate court upheld the immediate suspension of a kindergarten student who said "I'm going to shoot you" to classmates during recess. Although a school generally must follow certain steps before suspending a student, the court felt that in this instance the kindergarten's interest in limiting this kind of violent speech was more important than the student's due process rights.[72]

Due Process and National Security The U.S. court system, including the Supreme Court, is put under particular pressure when national security is threatened. Certainly, as was clear in the earlier *A Question of Ethics* feature concerning Predator drones, many of the controversies concerning antiterrorism strategies that we will discuss in this textbook have their basis in due process concerns.

To give another example, in 2014 a federal judge ruled that the Department of Homeland Security's "no fly" list was plagued by significant constitutional problems. The list, which bans those on it from most air travel involving American airports, was established in the aftermath of the September 11, 2001, terrorist attacks and contains about 20,000 names. The judge ruled that there was, in practice, no way for people on the list to challenge their inclusion, which violated the Fifth Amendment's guarantee of due process.[73] We will cover the U.S. Constitution's role in the fight against terrorism much more extensively in Chapter 16.

▲ Spectators line up to enter the U.S. Supreme Court building in Washington, D.C. The Court recently upheld a federal law broadening the government's power to eavesdrop on international e-mails and phone calls. **Why might the Court tend to defer to the federal government where questions of national security are concerned?** Mark Wilson/Getty Images

CJ IN ACTION

Hate Crime Laws

Like many other shoppers, on November 28, 2014—"Black Friday"—Chris Bujaj and Ardijan Mehaj went to the Palisades Center Mall in West Nyack, New York. While at the mall, the two teenagers—screaming "dirty Jews!"—attacked two Orthodox Jewish men. As a result, local prosecutors charged Bujaj and Mehaj with third degree assault as a *hate crime*. This meant that they each faced a maximum sentence of seven years behind bars instead of the relatively short jail term (no longer than one year) or probation usually handed down for this offense.[74] The philosophy behind hate crime legislation, which punishes the defendant not only for acts but also for motives, is the subject of this chapter's *CJ in Action* feature.

Punishing Bias

Nearly every state and the federal government have hate crime laws that, as noted earlier in the text, apply when the underlying crime is committed because of the victim's race, color, religion, ancestry, national origin, political affiliation, gender, sexual orientation, age, or disability. These laws are based on a model created by the Anti-Defamation League (ADL) in 1981. The ADL model was centered on the concept of "penalty enhancement": just as someone who robs a convenience store using a gun will face a greater penalty than if he or she had been unarmed, so will someone who commits a crime because of prejudice against her or his victim or victims.[75]

Critics of hate crime laws feel that such "penalty enhancements" rest on shaky legal grounds. It is one thing to prove that a robber used a gun, but it is another thing to prove what was in a defendant's mind. Even when an offender's bias is obvious, as is the case with Chris Bujaj and Ardijan Mehaj, should it affect how many years they spend behind bars? Despite these misgivings, the United States Supreme Court has upheld the constitutionality of hate crime laws as long as the prohibited motive (1) is specifically listed in the legislation as an attendant circumstance, defined earlier in the chapter, and (2) is proved beyond a reasonable doubt during the trial.[76]

The Case for Hate Crime Laws

- Hate crimes target groups, not just an individual—if one Muslim or Hindu in New York is attacked, for example, then all Muslims or Hindus in New York suffer intimidation and fear. Thus, such acts need to be punished more harshly.

- Historically, the groups listed in hate crime legislation have received inadequate protection from the American criminal justice system. Hate crime laws redress these shortcomings.

- Hate crime laws do not punish a defendant's speech or beliefs, which are protected by the U.S. Constitution. Rather, they allow jurors to learn whether the defendant's speech or beliefs were the reason for the choice of victim.

The Case against Hate Crime Laws

- Hate crime laws punish political views that, though unpopular and even appalling, are protected by the First Amendment, which states that the government shall make no law "abridging the freedom of speech."

- For the most part, motive is irrelevant in criminal law. Defendants are punished for what they did, not for why they did it.

- Hate crime laws indicate that some victims are worthy of more protection than others. It is unjust that Chris Bujaj and Ardijan Mehaj would receive lesser sentences if their victims were not members of a minority group.[77]

Your Opinion—Writing Assignment

Harold, who is white, is at a party, and he is drunk. He sees Mary, his ex-girlfriend, talking with James, who is African American. Harold knows that Mary and James have been dating for several weeks. Harold shouts racial epithets at James and is thrown out of the party. Later that night, Harold stalks James and attacks him with a baseball bat.

Did Harold commit a hate crime deserving of a harsher penalty? How does this case influence your opinion of hate crime laws in general? Before responding, you can review our discussion in the sections of this chapter concerning:

- The purposes of criminal law ("The Purposes of Criminal Law").

- *Mens rea* and criminal acts ("The Elements of a Crime").

- Attendant circumstances ("The Elements of a Crime").

Your answer should include at least three full paragraphs.

Summary

For more information on these concepts, look back to the Learning Objective icons throughout the chapter.

 List the four written sources of American criminal law. (a) The U.S. Constitution and state constitutions; (b) statutes passed by Congress and state legislatures (plus local ordinances); (c) administrative agency regulations; and (d) case law.

 Explain precedent and the importance of the doctrine of *stare decisis*. Precedent is a common law concept in which one decision becomes the example or authority for deciding future cases with similar facts. Under the doctrine of *stare decisis,* judges in a particular jurisdiction are bound to follow precedents of that same jurisdiction. The doctrine of *stare decisis* leads to efficiency in the judicial system.

 Explain the two basic functions of criminal law. The primary function is to protect citizens from harms to their safety and property and from harms to society's interest collectively. The second function is to maintain and teach social values as well as social boundaries—for example, speed limits and laws against bigamy.

 Delineate the elements required to establish *mens rea* (a guilty mental state). (a) Purpose, (b) knowledge, (c) negligence, and (d) recklessness.

 Explain how the doctrine of strict liability applies to criminal law. Strict liability crimes do not allow the alleged wrongdoer to claim ignorance or mistake to avoid criminal responsibility—for example, exceeding the speed limit and statutory rape.

 List and briefly define the most important excuse defenses for crimes. Insanity—different tests of insanity can be used, including (a) the *M'Naghten* rule (right-wrong test); (b) the ALI/MPC test, also known as the substantial-capacity test; and (c) the irresistible-impulse test. **Intoxication**—voluntary and involuntary, the latter being a possible criminal defense. **Mistake**—sometimes valid if the law was not published or reasonably known or if the alleged offender relied on an official statement of the law that was erroneous. Also, a mistake of fact may negate the mental state necessary to commit a crime.

 Discuss a common misperception concerning the insanity defense in the United States. Contrary to popular opinion, the insanity defense is not an oft-used loophole that allows criminals to avoid responsibility for committing heinous crimes. Insanity defenses are difficult to mount and very rarely succeed. Even when a defendant is found not guilty by reason of insanity, she or he does not "go free." Instead, such defendants are sent to mental health care institutions.

 Describe the four most important justification criminal defenses. Duress—requires that (a) the threat is of serious bodily harm or death, (b) the harm is greater than that caused by the crime; (c) the threat is immediate and inescapable; and (d) the defendant became involved in the situation through no fault of his or her own. **Justifiable use of force**—the defense of one's person, dwelling, or property, or the prevention of a crime. **Necessity**—justifiable if the harm sought to be avoided is greater than that sought to be prevented by the law defining the offense charged. **Entrapment**—that the criminal action was induced by certain governmental persuasion or trickery.

 Distinguish between substantive and procedural criminal law. The former concerns questions about what acts are actually criminal. The latter concerns procedures designed to protect the constitutional rights of individuals and to prevent the arbitrary use of power by the government.

LEARNING OBJECTIVE 10 **Explain the importance of the due process clause in the criminal justice system.** The due process clause acts to limit the power of government. In the criminal justice system, the due process clause requires that certain procedures be followed to ensure the fairness of criminal proceedings and that all criminal laws be reasonable and in the interest of the public good.

Questions for Critical Analysis

1. Give an example of a criminal law whose main purpose seems to be teaching societal boundaries rather than protecting citizens from harm. Do you think this behavior should be illegal? Explain your answer.

2. Nine-year-old Savannah lies to her grandmother Jessica about eating candy bars. As punishment, Jessica forces Savannah to run for three hours without a rest. Severely dehydrated, the girl has a seizure and dies. What should be the criminal charge against Jessica, and why?

3. What is your opinion of the voluntary intoxication defense?

4. Gerald, whose house has been burgled four times in previous weeks, sets a trap for future intruders by placing his wife's purse in clear view of a window in his garage. Then he leaves the garage door slightly open, and hides in the shadows with his shotgun. If Gerald shoots and kills a would-be burglar who takes the bait, would he be protected from murder charges by Florida's "stand your ground" law? Why or why not?

5. Suppose that Louisiana's legislature passes a law allowing law enforcement officers to forcibly remove residents from their homes in the face of an imminent hurricane. Why might a court uphold this law even though, in most circumstances, such forcible removal would violate the residents' due process rights? If you were a judge, would you uphold Louisiana's new law?

Key Terms

actus reus 108	entrapment 122	procedural criminal law 122
administrative law 104	felony-murder 112	procedural due process 125
attempt 108	hate crime law 114	recklessness 109
attendant circumstances 114	inchoate offenses 115	rule of law 102
ballot initiative 104	infancy 116	self-defense 120
Bill of Rights 124	insanity 116	*stare decisis* 104
case law 104	intoxication 118	statutory law 103
common law 101	involuntary manslaughter 110	statutory rape 112
competency hearing 117	irresistible-impulse test 117	strict liability crimes 111
conspiracy 115	*mens rea* 109	substantial-capacity test
constitutional law 102	*M'Naghten* rule 116	(ALI/MPC test) 116
corpus delicti 107	Model Penal Code 103	substantive criminal law 122
due process clause 124	necessity 122	substantive due process 126
duress 120	negligence 109	supremacy clause 103
duty to retreat 121	precedent 101	voluntary manslaughter 110

Notes

1. Roger LeRoy Miller and Gaylord A. Jentz, *Business Law Today, Comprehensive Edition,* 7th ed. (Cincinnati, Ohio: South-Western, 2007), 2–3.

2. Joshua Dressler, *Understanding Criminal Law,* 2d ed. (New York: Richard D. Irwin, 1995), 22–23.

3. John S. Baker, Jr., *Measuring the Explosive Growth of Federal Crime Legislation* (Washington, D.C.: The Federalist Society for Law and Public Policy Studies, 2008), 1.

4. "US Court Records Show Nearly 500 Years in Prison Time for Medical Marijuana Offenses," *California NORML* (June 13, 2013), at **www.canorml.org/costs/Nearly_500 _Years_Prison_Time_for_Medical _Marijuana_Offenses**.

5. Quoted in "Judge: Federal Law Trumps Montana's Medical Pot Law," *Associated Press* (January 23, 2012).

6. *Texas v. Johnson,* 491 U.S. 397 (1989).

7. *States of Nebraska and Oklahoma v. State of Colorado* (December 2014), at **www .scribd.com/doc/250506006/Nebraska -Oklahoma-lawsuit**.

8. Clean Water Act Section 309, 33 U.S.C.A. Section 1319 (1987).

9. *Bowers v. Hardwick,* 478 U.S. 186 (1986)

10. *Lawrence v. Texas,* 539 U.S., 558, 578 (2003).

11. Joel Feinberg, *The Moral Limits of the Criminal Law: Harm to Others* (New York: Oxford University Press, 1984), 221–232.

12. Anna Merriman, "U.S. Senator Seeks National Caffeine Powder Ban after Keystone

Student's Death," *The Chronicle-Telegram* (Elyria, OH) (August 30, 2014), at **chronicle .northcoastnow.com/2014/08/30/u-s -senator-seeks-national-caffeine -powder-ban**.

13. Henry M. Hart, Jr., "The Aims of the Criminal Law," *Law & Contemporary Problems* 23 (1958), 405–406.

14. John L. Diamond, "The Myth of Morality and Fault in Criminal Law Doctrine," *American Criminal Law Review* 34 (Fall 1996), 111.

15. Kentucky Statutes Section 437.060; and New Hampshire Revised Statutes Section 207:61.

16. Robby Korth and Jessica Boehm, "Butt Out: State Legislatures Move to Nullify Federal Gun Laws," *NBCNews.com* (August 21, 2014), at **www.nbcnews.com/news /investigations/butt-out-state-legislatures -move-nullify-federal-gun-laws-n185326**.

17. Idaho Senate Bill 1332 (March 19, 2014), at **legislature.idaho.gov/legislation/2014 /S1332.htm**.

18. Lawrence M. Friedman, *Crime and Punishments in American History* (New York: Basic Books, 1993), 10.

19. Thomas A. Mullen, "Rule without Reason: Requiring Independent Proof of the *Corpus Delicti* as a Condition of Admitting Extrajudicial Confession," *University of San Francisco Law Review* 27 (1993), 385.

20. *Hawkins v. State*, 219 Ind. 116, 129, 37 N.E.2d 79 (1941).

21. David C. Biggs, "'The Good Samaritan Is Packing': An Overview of the Broadened Duty to Aid Your Fellowman, with the Modern Desire to Possess Concealed Weapons," *University of Dayton Law Review* 22 (Winter 1997), 225.

22. Terry Halbert and Elaine Ingulli, *Law and Ethics in the Business Environment*, 6th ed. (Mason, Ohio: South-Western Cengage Learning, 2009), 8.

23. Model Penal Code Section 2.02.

24. Model Penal Code Section 2.02(c).

25. California Penal Code Section 189.

26. *Black's Law Dictionary*, 1423.

27. *United States v. Dotterweich*, 320 U.S. 277 (1943).

28. New Jersey Statutes Annotated Section 2C:35-9 (West 2004).

29. *State v. Stiffler*, 763 P.2d 308, 311 (Idaho Ct.App. 1988).

30. *State v. Harrison*, 425 A.2d 111 (1979).

31. Richard G. Singer and John Q. LaFond, *Criminal Law: Examples and Explanations* (New York: Aspen Law & Business, 1997), 322.

32. *State v. Linscott*, 520 A.2d 1067 (1987).

33. *Morissette v. United States*, 342 U.S. 246, 251–252 (1952).

34. Federal Bank Robbery Act, 18 U.S.C.A. Section 2113.

35. *In re Winship*, 397 U.S. 358, 364, 368–369 (1970).

36. Cindy George, "Texas Court Throws Out 'Upskirt' Photo Law," *Houston Chronicle* (September 18, 2014), 6A.

37. Massachusetts Statutes, Chapter 272, Section 105, at **www.womenslaw.org/statutes _detail.php?statute_id=7544#statute-top**.

38. Bureau of Justice Statistics, *Hate Crime Victimization, 2004–2012, Statistical Tables* (Washington, D.C.: U.S. Department of Justice, February 2014), 1.

39. *United States v. Jiminez Recio*, 537 U.S. 270 (2003).

40. Paul H. Robinson, *Criminal Law Defenses* (St. Paul, Minn.: West, 2008), Section 173, Ch. 5Bl.

41. *M'Naghten's* Case, 10 Cl.&F. 200, Eng.Rep. 718 (1843). Note that the name is also spelled M'Naughten and McNaughten.

42. Model Penal Code Section 401 (1952).

43. Joshua Dressler, *Cases and Materials on Criminal Law*, 2d ed. (St. Paul, Minn.: West Group, 1999), 599.

44. Ronald Schouten, "The Insanity Defense: An Intersection of Morality, Public Policy, and Science," *Psychology Today* (August 16, 2012), at **www.psychologytoday.com /blog/almost-psychopath/201208/the -insanity-defense**.

45. South Carolina Code Annotated Section 17-24-20(A) (Law. Co-op. Supp. 1997).

46. Lawrence P. Tiffany and Mary Tiffany, "Nosologic Objections to the Criminal Defense of Pathological Intoxication: What Do the Doubters Doubt?" *International Journal of Law and Psychiatry* 13 (1990), 49.

47. *City of Missoula v. Paffhausen*, 289 P.3d 149-150 (Mont. 2012).

48. 518 U.S. 37 (1996).

49. Quoted in Geoff Ziezulewicz, "Mom of Slain Daughter Helps Change Wis. Law," *Arizona Daily Star* (May 11, 2014), A5.

50. Quoted in Gary Fields and John R. Emshwiller, "As Criminal Laws Proliferate, More Are Ensnared," *Wall Street Journal* (July 23, 2011), at **online.wsj.com/article/SB100 0142405274870374950457617271418460 1654.html**.

51. *Lambert v. California*, 335 U.S. 225 (1957).

52. Federal Bureau of Investigation, *Crime in the United States 2013* (Washington, D.C.: U.S. Department of Justice, 2014), at **www .fbi.gov/about-us/cjis/ucr/crime-in -the-u.s/2013/crime-in-the-u.s.-2013**, Expanded Homicide Table 14 and Expanded Homicide Table 15.

53. Craig L. Carr, "Duress and Criminal Responsibility," *Law and Philosophy* 10 (1990), 161.

54. Arnold N. Enker, "In Supporting the Distinction between Justification and Excuse," *Texas Tech Law Review* 42 (2009), 277.

55. *United States v. May*, 727 F.2d 764 (1984).

56. *United States v. Contento-Pachon*, 723 F.2d 691 (1984).

57. *People v. Murillo*, 587 N.E.2d 1199, 1204 (Ill. App.Ct. 1992).

58. Florida Statutes Section 776.03 (2005).

59. *Ibid.*

60. Molly Hennessy-Fiske and Michael Muskal, "Jury Finds George Zimmerman Not Guilty," *Los Angeles Times* (July 13, 2013), A1.

61. Michael Bloomberg, quoted in "A Lethal Right to Self-Defense," *The Week* (May 4, 2012), 13.

62. Kevin Schwaller, "Justifiable Homicides Rise in Texas," *KXAN.com* (January 8, 2015), at **kxan.com/2015/01/08/justifiable -homicides-rise-in-texas**.

63. "Man Acquitted of Concealed Weapon Charge on 'Necessity' Defense," *San Francisco Examiner* (July 10, 2011), at **www .sfexaminer.com/local/crime/2011/07 /man-acquitted-concealed-weapon -charge-necessity-defense**.

64. 287 U.S. 435 (1932).

65. Kenneth M. Lord, "Entrapment and Due Process: Moving toward a Dual System of Defenses," *Florida State University Law Review* 25 (Spring 1998), 463.

66. Henry J. Abraham, *Freedom and the Court: Civil Liberties in the United States*, 7th ed. (New York: Oxford University Press, 1998), 38–41.

67. National Victims' Constitutional Amendment Passage, "House Joint Resolution 40" (April 23, 2013), at **www.nvcap.org /legis/113/VRAtext.html**.

68. Paul G. Cassell, "The Victims' Rights Amendment: A Sympathetic, Clause-by-Clause Analysis," *Phoenix Law Review* (Spring 2012), 301.

69. Bureau of Justice Statistics, *Capital Punishment, 2012—Statistical Tables* (Washington, D.C.: U.S. Department of Justice, May 2014), Table 10, page 14.

70. *Skinner v. Oklahoma*, 316 U.S. 535, 546–547 (1942).

71. Jonathan Stempel, "Supreme Court Declines to Review Insanity Defense Appeal," *Reuters* (November 26, 2012).

72. "*S.G.V. Sayreville Board of Education et al.*," No. 02-2384," *New Jersey Law Journal* (July 14, 2003), 139.

73. *Latif et al. v. Holder et al.*, No. 3:10-cv-00750, 2014 WL 2871346 (D.Or. June 24, 2014).

74. Article 485—NY Penal Law, at **ypdcrime .com/penal.law/article485.htm**.

75. Steve M. Freeman, "Hate Crime Laws: Punishment Which Fits the Crime," *Annual Survey of American Law* 4 (1992/1993), 581–585.

76. *Wisconsin v. Mitchell*, 508 U.S. 476 (1993); and *Apprendi v. New Jersey*, 530 U.S. 466 (2000).

77. Richard Cohen, "When Thought Becomes a Crime," *Washington Post* (October 19, 2010), at **www.realclearpolitics.com/articles /2010/10/19/punish_crime_not _thought_107629.html**.

Law Enforcement Today

Chapter Outline	Corresponding Learning Objectives
The Responsibilities of the Police	**1** List the four basic responsibilities of the police.
A Short History of the American Police	**2** Tell how the patronage system affected policing.
	3 Explain how intelligence-led policing works and how it benefits modern police departments.
Recruitment and Training: Becoming a Police Officer	**4** Identify the differences between the police academy and field training as learning tools for recruits.
Women and Minorities in Policing Today	**5** Explain how consent decrees make law enforcement agencies more diverse.
	6 Describe the challenges facing women who choose law enforcement as a career.
Public and Private Law Enforcement	**7** Indicate some of the most important law enforcement agencies under the control of the Department of Homeland Security.
	8 Identify the duties of the FBI.
	9 Analyze the importance of private security today.

To target your study and review, look for these numbered Learning Objective icons throughout the chapter.

Bill Clark/CQ Roll Call/Getty Images

Starting Over

year after year, Camden, New Jersey—population 77,000—ranked as one of the nation's most violent and dangerous cities. Illegal drug buyers and sellers would commute using light rail to take advantage of the city's nearly two hundred open drug markets. Residents spent most of their days safely inside homes barricaded by iron bars, known as "bird cages." In 2011, a bad situation became worse when city officials were forced to lay off half of Camden's police force due to budget cuts. In response, local drug dealers printed tee-shirts that read, "It's Our Time."

A number of the social factors linked to crime are present in Camden, such as high unemployment, urban blight, and youth gangs. For many, however, the local police department was a significant part of the problem. After the layoffs, the city had only 230 active officers. Understaffed, the Camden police stopped responding to 911 calls and let shooting investigations lag. Asked one frustrated observer, "What happens when the city can no longer pay" to fight crime?

In May 2013, Camden officials responded by disbanding the city's entire police department. This unprecedented step allowed Camden County to hire a completely new force without the restrictions of the previous department's police union labor contract. As a result, per officer costs were cut in half, and the city was eventually able to nearly double its number of police officers. Law enforcement officials also increased the use of crime-fighting technology and trained the new officers to be more involved in the community. By the summer of 2014, even though the city's murder rate was still considerably higher than the national average, shootings were down 43 percent and overall violent crime was down 22 percent from two years earlier. "A lot of the old officers, all they did was ride around and not do anything," said one Camden resident. "These are soldiers we have here now."

▲ Camden, New Jersey, police officers interact with residents during a day dedicated to cleaning up local parks.

Andrew Burton/Getty Images

1. The new Camden County Police Department is focusing on making more traffic stops and issuing tickets for minor violations such as tinted windows and broken headlights. How might this strategy contribute to lower violent crime rates?

2. Ninety-five percent of Camden's residents are either African American or Hispanic. These minorities make up only 45 percent of Camden's new police force. What impact could this have on the police department's effectiveness?

3. Under the circumstances, do you think that Camden's plan to lay off an entire police force for financial reasons was ethical? Why or why not?

The Responsibilities of the Police

Before the city's "reboot" of its police department, residents of Whitman Park, a high-crime neighborhood in Camden, New Jersey, would shout obscenities at patrol cars. After the changes, the locals were more welcoming. One little girl even yelled out, "Hi, cop!" when she saw an officer approaching her family's front porch.[1] The difference in attitudes is important, as police officers are the most visible representatives of our criminal justice system. Indeed, they symbolize the system for many Americans who may never see the inside of a courtroom or a prison cell. Still, the general perception of a "cop's life" is often shaped by television dramas such as the *CSI* series and *Hawaii Five-O*. In reality, police spend a great deal of time on such mundane tasks as responding to noise complaints, confiscating firecrackers, and poring over paperwork.

Sociologist Egon Bittner warned against the tendency to see the police primarily as agents of law enforcement and crime control. A more inclusive accounting of "what the police do," Bittner believed, would recognize that they provide "situationally justified force in society."[2] In other words, the function of the police is to solve any problem that may *possibly*, though not *necessarily*, require the use of force.

Within Bittner's rather broad definition of "what the police do," we can pinpoint four basic responsibilities of the police:

1. To enforce laws.
2. To provide services.
3. To prevent crime.
4. To preserve the peace.

LEARNING OBJECTIVE 1 — List the four basic responsibilities of the police.

As will become evident over the next two chapters, there is a great deal of debate among legal and other scholars and law enforcement officers over which responsibilities deserve the most police attention and what methods should be employed by the police in meeting those responsibilities.

Enforcing Laws

In the public mind, the primary role of the police is to enforce society's laws—hence, the term *law enforcement officer*. In their role as "crime fighters," police officers have a clear mandate to seek out and apprehend those who have violated the law. The crime-fighting responsibility is so dominant that all police activity—from the purchase of new automobiles to a plan to hire more minority officers—must often be justified in terms of its law enforcement value.[3]

Police officers also see themselves primarily as crime fighters, or "crook catchers," a perception that often leads people into what they believe will be an exciting career in law enforcement. Although the job certainly offers challenges unlike any other, police officers normally do not spend the majority of their time in law enforcement duties. After surveying a year's worth of dispatch data from the Wilmington (Delaware) Police Department, researchers Jack Greene and Carl Klockars found that officers spent only about half of their time enforcing the law or dealing with crimes. The rest of their time was spent on order maintenance, service provision, traffic patrol, and medical assistance.[4]

Furthermore, information provided by the Uniform Crime Report shows that most arrests are made for "crimes of disorder" or public annoyances rather than violent or property crimes.[5] In 2013, for example, police made about 9.3 million arrests for drunkenness, liquor law violations, disorderly conduct, vagrancy, loitering, and other minor offenses, but only about 480,000 arrests for violent crimes.[6] (See the feature *Discretion in Action—Soft Power* to consider one of the many challenges police face in trying to enforce criminal laws.)

Providing Services

The popular emphasis on crime fighting and law enforcement tends to overshadow the fact that a great deal of a police officer's time is spent providing services for the community. The motto "To Serve and Protect" has been adopted by thousands of local police departments, and the *Law Enforcement Code of Ethics* recognizes the duty "to serve the community" in its first sentence.[7] The services that police provide are numerous—a partial list would include directing traffic, performing emergency medical procedures, counseling those involved in domestic disputes, providing directions to tourists, and finding lost children.

As we will see in the next section, many police departments have adopted a strategy called *community policing*. This strategy requires officers to provide assistance in areas that are not, at first glance, directly related to law enforcement. Often, regardless of official policy, the police are forced into providing certain services. For example, in many instances, law enforcement officers are first on the scene when a person has been seriously injured. As a result, officers increasingly are becoming proficient in emergency medical procedures. Some cities even allow police officers to take injured persons to the hospital in a squad car rather than wait for an ambulance.[8]

Also, because of changes in American national health-service policy, law enforcement agents find themselves on the front lines when it comes to dealing with mental illness and substance abuse. The Tucson (Arizona) Police Department, for example, receives more calls about mental illness than about stolen cars or burglaries.[9] Police

Discretion in Action

Soft Power

The Situation Every day, about fifty men gather in a small park, waiting to get picked up by employers for hourly menial work. The situation at this impromptu day-laborer camp has become chaotic and, at times, dangerous. Many of the men are homeless, and use the park as a bedroom and as a toilet. Prostitutes frequent the area, as do alcohol sellers and drug dealers. You are a police sergeant, and your superiors have ordered you to "clean up" the park.

The Law These men are committing numerous infractions and minor crimes, including disorderly conduct, vagrancy, drunkenness, and public urination. Once

arrested, the offenders—most of whom are recent immigrants, in the country illegally—could be reported to the federal government and potentially removed from the country.

What Would You Do? Many of the day workers are breaking the law, and you would be justified in having the police officers under your command make a sweep of arrests. In the long term, however, this strategy is problematic. Because their offenses are minor, most of the men would be released quickly, and, needing work, would find their way back to the park. Also, as you will see later in the chapter, the federal government

is focusing on removing undocumented immigrants who have committed serious crimes, not petty offenders.

When faced with a similar problem, police officers in Kansas City, Missouri, decided to use a less confrontational approach. They helped set up a day-laborer program at a nearby community center that provided the men with bathrooms, showers, food, and help finding work. Within a year, 911 calls in the area went down by more than 50 percent. "We couldn't arrest our way out of the problem," one Kansas City police officer told a reporter. "[So] we started treating them like human beings."

officers in numerous cities now carry naloxone, a drug that can instantly reverse the effects of a heroin overdose. Police in Quincy, Massachusetts, saved 211 lives using naloxone between 2011 and 2014.[10]

Preventing Crime

Perhaps the most controversial responsibility of the police is to *prevent* crime. According to Jerome Skolnick, co-director of the Center for Research in Crime and Justice at the New York University School of Law, there are two predictable public responses when crime rates begin to rise in a community. The first is to punish convicted criminals with stricter laws and more severe penalties. The second is to demand that the police "do something" to prevent crimes from occurring in the first place. Is it, in fact, possible for the police to "prevent" crimes? The strongest response that Professor Skolnick is willing to give to this question is "maybe."[11]

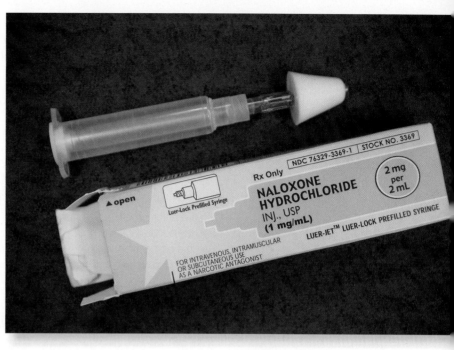

▲ Nationwide, thousands of police officers are carrying naloxone kits such as the one shown here as part of an effort to prevent heroin overdoses. **What are the benefits and drawbacks of having law enforcement agents provide health-related service to the community?** Andrew Burton/Getty Images

On a limited basis, police can certainly prevent some crimes. If a rapist is dissuaded from attacking a solitary woman because a patrol car is cruising the area, then the police officer behind the wheel has prevented a crime. Furthermore, exemplary police work can have a measurable effect. "Quite simply, cops count," says William Bratton, who has directed police departments in Boston, Los Angeles, and New York. "[T]he quickest way to impact crime is with a well-led, managed, and appropriately resourced police force."[12] In Chapter 6, we will study a number of policing strategies that have been credited, by some, for decreasing crime rates in the United States.

In general, however, the deterrent effects of police presence are unclear. One recent study found no relationship between the size of the police presence in a neighborhood and the residents' perceived risk of being arrested for wrongdoing.[13] Furthermore, Carl Klockars has written that the "war on crime" is a war that the police cannot win because they cannot control the factors—such as unemployment, poverty, immorality, inequality, political change, and lack of educational opportunities—that contribute to criminal behavior in the first place.[14]

Preserving the Peace

To a certain extent, the fourth responsibility of the police, that of preserving the peace, is related to preventing crime. Police have the legal authority to use the power of arrest, or even force, in situations in which no crime has yet occurred, but might occur in the immediate future.

In the words of James Q. Wilson, the police's peacekeeping role (which Wilson believed to be the most important role of law enforcement officers) often takes on a pattern of simply "handling the situation."[15] For example, when police officers arrive on the scene of a loud, late-night house party, they may feel the need to disperse the party and even arrest some of the partygoers for disorderly conduct. By their actions, the officers have lessened the chances of serious and violent crimes taking place later in the evening. The same principle is often used when dealing with domestic disputes, which, if escalated, can lead to homicide. Such situations are in need of, to use Wilson's terminology again, "fixing up," and police can use the power of arrest, or threat, or coercion, or sympathy, to do just that.

The basis of Wilson and George Kelling's zero-tolerance theory is similar: street disorder—such as public drunkenness, urination, and loitering—signals to both law-abiding citizens and criminals that the law is not being enforced and therefore leads to more violent crime. Hence, if police preserve the peace and "crack down" on the minor crimes that make up street disorder, they will in fact be preventing serious crimes that would otherwise occur in the future.[16]

EthicsChallenge

Do law enforcement agents have an ethical obligation to provide offenders with medical assistance? What if a police officer's partner has been killed by a suspect during a shootout, and the suspect—also shot—is bleeding profusely nearby? Ethically, must that officer do everything in his or her power to save the suspect's life? Why or why not? ■

A Short History of the American Police

Although modern society relies on law enforcement officers to control and prevent crime, in the early days of this country police services had little to do with crime control. The policing efforts in the first American cities were directed toward controlling certain groups of people (mostly slaves and Native Americans), delivering goods, regulating activities such as buying and selling in the town market, maintaining health and sanitation, controlling gambling and vice, and managing livestock and other animals.[17] Furthermore, these police services were for the most part performed by volunteers, as a police force was an expensive proposition. Often, the volunteers were organized using the **night watch system,** brought over from England by colonists in the seventeenth century. Under this system, all physically fit males were required to offer their services to protect the community on a rotating nightly basis.[18]

The Evolution of American Law Enforcement

The night watch system did not ask much of its volunteers, who were often required to do little more than loudly announce the time and the state of the weather. Furthermore, many citizens avoided their duties by hiring others to "go on watch" in their place, and those who did serve frequently spent their time on watch sleeping and drinking.[19] Eventually, as the populations of American cities grew in the late eighteenth and early nineteenth centuries, so did the need for public order and the willingness to devote public resources to the establishment of formal police forces. The night watch system was insufficient to meet these new demands, and its demise was inevitable.

Early Police Departments In 1829, the British home secretary Sir Robert "Bobbie" Peel took a dramatic step to organize law enforcement in London—then as now one of the largest cities in the Western world. He pushed the Metropolitan Police Act through Parliament, forming the London Metropolitan Police. One thousand strong at first, the members of this police force were easily recognizable in their uniforms that featured blue coats and top hats. Under Peel's direction, the "bobbies," as the police were called in honor of their founder, did not carry any firearms and were assigned to specific

Night Watch System An early form of American law enforcement in which volunteers patrolled their community from dusk to dawn to keep the peace.

areas, or "beats," to prevent crime. Peel also believed that the police should be organized along military lines under the control of local, elected officials.[20]

London's police operation was so successful that it was soon imitated in smaller towns throughout England and, eventually, in the United States. In 1833, Philadelphia became the first city to employ both day and night watchmen. Five years later, working from Peel's model, Boston formed the first organized police department, consisting of six full-time officers. In 1844, New York City laid the foundation for the modern police department by combining its day and night watches under the control of a single police chief. By the onset of the Civil War in 1861, a number of American cities, including Baltimore, Boston, Chicago, Cincinnati, New Orleans, and Philadelphia, had similarly consolidated police departments, modeled on the Metropolitan Police of London.[21]

▲ A horse-drawn police wagon used by the New York City Police Department, circa 1886. **Why might this new form of transportation have represented a "revolution" for early American police forces?** Corbis/Bettmann

The Political Era Like their modern counterparts, many early police officers were hard working, honest, and devoted to serving and protecting the public. On the whole, however, in the words of historian Samuel Walker, "The quality of American police service in the nineteenth century could hardly have been worse."[22] This poor quality can be attributed to the fact that the recruitment and promotion of police officers were intricately tied to the politics of the day. Police officers received their jobs as a result of political connections, not because of any particular skills or knowledge. Whichever political party was in power in a given city would hire its own cronies to run the police department. Consequently, the police were often more concerned with serving the interests of the political powers than with protecting the citizens.[23]

Corruption was rampant during this *political era* of policing, which lasted roughly from 1840 to 1930. Police salaries were relatively low, and many police officers saw their positions as opportunities to make extra income through any number of illegal activities. Bribery was common, as police would use their close proximity to the people to request "favors," which went into the police officers' own pockets or into the coffers of the local political party as "contributions."[24] This was known as the **patronage system,** or the "spoils system," because to the political victors went the spoils.

The political era also saw police officers take an active role in providing social services for their bosses' constituents. In many instances, this role even took precedence over law enforcement duties. Politicians realized that they could attract more votes by offering social services to citizens than by arresting them, and they required the police departments under their control to act accordingly.

LEARNING **2** OBJECTIVE Tell how the patronage system affected policing.

The Reform Era The abuses of the political era of policing did not go unnoticed. Nevertheless, it was not until 1929 that President Herbert Hoover appointed the national Commission on Law Observance and Enforcement to assess the American criminal

Patronage System A form of corruption in which the political party in power hires and promotes police officers and receives job-related "favors" in return.

justice system. The Wickersham Commission, named after its chairman, George Wickersham, focused on two areas of American policing that were in need of reform: (1) police brutality and (2) "the corrupting influence of politics." According to the commission, this reform should come about through higher personnel standards, centralized police administrations, and the increased use of technology.[25] Reformers of the time took the commission's findings as a call for the professionalization of American police and initiated the progressive (or *reform*) era in American policing.

Professionalism and Administrative Reforms Many of the Wickersham Commission's recommendations echoed the opinions of one of its contributors—August Vollmer, the police chief of Berkeley, California, from 1905 to 1932.[26] Along with his protégé O. W. Wilson, Vollmer promoted a style of policing known as the **professional model.** Under the professional model, police chiefs, who had been little more than figureheads during the political era, took more control over their departments. A key to these efforts was the reorganization of police departments in many major cities. To improve their control over operations, police chiefs began to add midlevel positions to the force. These new officers, known as majors or assistant chiefs, could develop and implement crime-fighting strategies and more closely supervise individual officers. Police chiefs also tried to consolidate their power by bringing large areas of a city under their control so that no local ward, neighborhood, or politician could easily influence a single police department.

The professionalism trend benefited law enforcement agents in a number of ways. Salaries and working conditions improved, and for the first time, women and members of minority groups were given opportunities—albeit limited—to serve.[27] At the same time, police administrators controlled officers to a much greater extent than in the past, expecting them to meet targets for arrests and other numerical indicators that were seen as barometers of effectiveness. Any contact with citizens that did not explicitly relate to law enforcement was considered "social work" and discouraged.[28] As police expert Chris Braiden puts it, American police officers were expected to "park their brains at the door of the stationhouse" and simply "follow orders like a robot."[29]

The isolation of officers from the public was made complete by an overreliance on the patrol car, a relatively new technological innovation at the time. In the political era, officers walked their beats, interacting with citizens. In the reform era, they were expected to stay inside their "rolling fortresses," driving from one call to the next without wasting time or resources on public relations.[30]

CJ & Technology

Michael Hanson/*New York Times*/Redux

High-Tech Cops

When patrol cars came into common use by police departments in the 1930s, they changed the face of American policing. Nine decades later, the technology associated with patrol cars continues to evolve. Today, approximately 80 percent of all police cars in the United States are equipped with on-board computers with which officers can immediately retrieve a suspect's criminal record or access neighborhood crime data. The majority of police departments also attach video cameras to their patrol automobiles, and many are able to "live stream" video content from these devices. Another mounted camera commonly found on police autos automatically reads the license plates of nearby vehicles and performs an instant background check on both car and driver.

In addition to their sophisticated transportation, today's police officers enjoy a multitude of other technological advantages. A new generation of apps helps law enforcement agents locate the source of 911 calls and "tagged" tweets on their smartphones and tablet computers. As we saw in Chapter 1, mobile biometric technology provides officers with the ability to immediately identify a suspect using her or his fingerprints or facial features. Advances in through-the-wall sensor devices are increasingly allowing law enforcement agents to track people's movements within buildings.

Thinking about Police Technology
Google is in the process of developing Glass, an optical head-mounted display that essentially transforms the wearer's eyes into mobile, visual computers. At some point, Google Glass will enable users to immediately identify every object—or person—in his or her field of vision. How could this technology eventually benefit law enforcement?

Turmoil in the 1960s and 1970s By the 1950s, America prided itself on having the most modern and professional police force in the world. As efficiency became the goal of the reform-era police chief, however, relations with the community suffered. Instead of being members of the community, police officers were now seen almost as intruders, patrolling the streets in the anonymity of their automobiles. The drawbacks of this perception—and of the professional model in general—became evident in the 1960s, one of the most turbulent decades in American history. The civil rights movement, though not inherently violent, intensified feelings of helplessness and impoverishment in African American communities. These frustrations resulted in civil unrest, and many major American cities experienced race riots in the middle years of the decade. Concurrently, America was experiencing rising crime rates and often violent protests against U.S. involvement in the war in Vietnam (1964–1975).

By the early 1970s, many observers believed that poor policing was contributing to the national turmoil. The National Advisory Commission on Civil Disorders stated bluntly that poor relations between the police and African American communities were partly to blame for the violence that plagued many of those communities.[31] In striving for professionalism, the police appeared to have lost touch with the citizens they were supposed to be serving. To repair their damaged relations with a large segment of the population, police would have to rediscover their community roots.

The Community Era The beginning of the *community era* may be traced to several government initiatives that took place in 1968. Of primary importance was the Omnibus Crime Control and Safe Streets Act, which was passed that year.[32] Under this act, the federal government provided state and local police departments with funds to create a wide variety of police-community programs. Most large-city police departments established entire units devoted to community relations, implementing programs that ranged from summer recreation activities for inner-city youths to "officer-friendly" referral operations that encouraged citizens to come to the police with their crime concerns.

In the 1970s, as this vital rethinking of the role of the police was taking place, the country was hit by a crime wave. Thus, police administrators were forced to combine efforts to improve community relations with aggressive and innovative crime-fighting strategies. As we will see in Chapter 6 when we discuss these strategies in more depth, the police began to focus on stopping crimes before they occur, rather than concentrating only on solving crimes that have already been committed. A dedication to such proactive strategies led to widespread acceptance of *community policing* in the 1980s and 1990s.

Community policing is based on the notion, mentioned in the chapter-opening discussion of policing in Camden, New Jersey, that meaningful interaction between officers and citizens will lead to a partnership in preventing and fighting crime.[33] Though the idea of involving members of the community in this manner is hardly new—a similar principle was set forth by Sir Robert Peel in the 1820s—community policing has had a major impact on the culture of American law enforcement by asking the average police officer to be a problem solver as well as a crime fighter.[34] (See Figure 5.1 for an overview of the three eras of policing described in this section.)

Policing Today: Intelligence, Terrorism, and Technology

Many law enforcement experts believe that the events of September 11, 2001, effectively ended the community era of policing.[35] Though police departments have not, in general, abandoned the idea of partnering with the community, their emphasis has shifted toward developing new areas of expertise, including counterterrorism and surveillance through technology. In particular, the process of collecting, analyzing, and mapping crime data has become a hallmark of law enforcement in the twenty-first century.

FIGURE 5.1 **The Three Eras of American Policing**

George L. Kelling and Mark H. Moore have separated the history of policing in the United States from 1840 to 2000 into three distinct periods. Below is a brief summarization of these three eras.

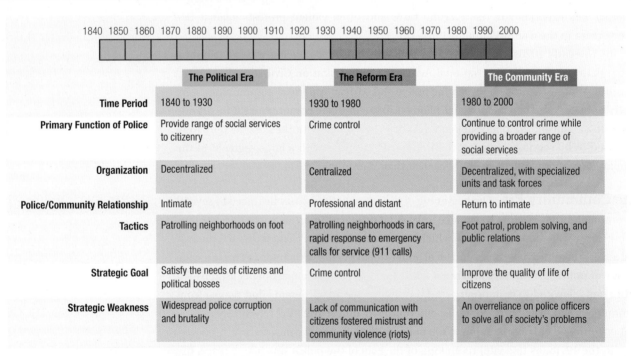

	The Political Era	The Reform Era	The Community Era
Time Period	1840 to 1930	1930 to 1980	1980 to 2000
Primary Function of Police	Provide range of social services to citizenry	Crime control	Continue to control crime while providing a broader range of social services
Organization	Decentralized	Centralized	Decentralized, with specialized units and task forces
Police/Community Relationship	Intimate	Professional and distant	Return to intimate
Tactics	Patrolling neighborhoods on foot	Patrolling neighborhoods in cars, rapid response to emergency calls for service (911 calls)	Foot patrol, problem solving, and public relations
Strategic Goal	Satisfy the needs of citizens and political bosses	Crime control	Improve the quality of life of citizens
Strategic Weakness	Widespread police corruption and brutality	Lack of communication with citizens fostered mistrust and community violence (riots)	An overreliance on police officers to solve all of society's problems

Sources: Adapted from George L. Kelling and Mark H. Moore, "From Political to Reform to Community: The Evolving Strategy of Police," in *Community Policing: Rhetoric or Reality*, eds. Jack R. Greene and Stephen D. Mastrofski (New York: Praeger Publishers, 1991), 14–15, 22–23; plus authors' updates. Reproduced with permission of Greenwood Publishing Group, Inc., Westport, Connecticut.

Intelligence-Led Policing "Humans are not nearly as random as we think," says Jeff Brantingham, an anthropologist at the University of California, Los Angeles. "Crime is a physical process, and if you can explain how offenders move and how they mix with victims, you can understand an incredible amount."[36] Relying on this basic principle, Brantingham and several colleagues developed PredPol, a software program that strives to predict when and where crimes are most likely to occur. Each day, the software identifies a geographic area—sometimes as small as 500 square feet—most likely to experience a certain type of criminal activity. So, for example, within six months of applying PredPol to a neighborhood in the foothills of Los Angeles, local police reported a 12 percent drop in property crimes when compared to the previous year.[37]

The PredPol approach is known as predictive policing, or **intelligence-led policing** (IPL), because it relies on data—or intelligence—concerning past crime patterns to predict future crime patterns. In theory, IPL is relatively simple. Just as commercial fishers are most successful when they concentrate on the areas of the ocean where the fish are, law enforcement does well to focus its scarce resources on the areas where the most crime occurs. With programs such as PredPol and other "hot spot" technologies that we will discuss in the next chapter, police administrators are able to deploy small forces to specific locations, rather than blanketing an entire city with random patrols. Doing "more with less" in this manner is a particularly important consideration as police budgets shrink around the country.[38]

The Challenges of Counterterrorism When basic IPL principles are applied to the issue of terrorism, it quickly becomes clear that terrorists, like other criminals, are likely to choose targets close to their homes. At the same time, when terrorist attacks occur great distances from those homes, the attacks are more deadly. Consequently, counterterrorism provides three specific challenges for American law enforcement:

1. The need to focus scarce resources to prevent and fight crimes that are relatively uncommon,
2. The scrutiny that comes with crimes that sometimes have international implications, and
3. The difficult task of gathering information, or intelligence, about crimes before they happen.[39]

The only way to meet these challenges, clearly, is for a level of cooperation between federal and local law enforcement that was not required in previous eras of policing.

Fusion Centers This cooperation relies on each level of law enforcement taking advantage of its strengths while relying on help from the other levels to shore up its weaknesses. Although they are proficient at gathering intelligence on domestic and, especially, foreign terrorist suspects, federal law enforcement agencies only have several thousand agents available for counterterrorism duties.

This is not enough to protect Americans on a local level. So, the federal antiterrorism agencies must enlist the aid of the country's nearly 800,000 local and state police officers. To this aim, the federal government has created seventy-seven fusion centers across the United States. The centers are designed to enable intelligence sharing between all levels of law enforcement on homeland security matters.

An Evolving Threat Each year, the U.S. Department of Homeland Security awards about $1.5 billion in grants for homeland security preparedness.[40] These funds have helped support more than one hundred local and state police intelligence units, with

Intelligence-Led Policing An approach that measures the risk of criminal behavior associated with certain individuals or locations so as to predict when and where such criminal behavior is most likely to occur in the future.

 LEARNING OBJECTIVE 3 Explain how intelligence-led policing works and how it benefits modern police departments.

▲ On February 12, 2014, a survivor of the Boston Marathon bombing makes his way toward the courthouse where suspect Dzhokhar Tsarnaev had his initial hearings. Dzhokhar was apprehended (and his brother Tamerlan killed) after being discovered by Watertown, Massachusetts, police following their alleged bombing of the event ten months earlier. **Why are local police departments so important to national counterterrorism efforts?** Pat Greenhouse/*The Boston Globe* via Getty Images

at least one in each state. The New York Police Department, in a class by itself, has more than one thousand personnel assigned to homeland security and has stationed agents in six foreign countries. The Los Angeles Police Department operates the National Counter-Terrorism Academy, offering a five-month course that trains police officers to prevent, rather than respond to, terrorist attacks.

The shifting nature of terrorism makes such training a necessity. Initially, the primary homeland security concern was a large-scale attack such as those that occurred in September 2001. Then, law enforcement attention shifted to "lone wolf" domestic terrorists motivated by grievances nurtured on the Internet. Now, homeland security officials in the United States and Europe are also focusing on citizens who receive training from extremists in the Middle East but return home to carry out their plans. In response to these various threats, all police officers are expected to prepare for a terrorist attack in their communities, and counterterrorism has become part of the day-to-day law enforcement routine.

Law Enforcement 2.0 Fortunately, just as more intelligence has become crucial to police work, the means available to gather such intelligence have also increased greatly. Nearly every successful anti-terrorism investigation has relied on information gathered from the Internet. To give just one example, Christopher Cornell drew the attention of federal law enforcement agents with a series of tweets expressing support for the terrorist organization Islamic State of Iraq and the Levant. In 2015, Cornell was arrested for planning to attack the U.S. Capitol Building in Washington, D.C.

Online Investigations and Intelligence Just like the rest of American society, criminals are active on social networking sites, providing police officers with a wealth of potential evidence, including messages, chat logs, tweets, photos, videos, tags, "likes," profiles, lists of friends, locations, and more.[41] Police can also use social media to enlist the help of civilian "cyber sleuths." A series of retweeted surveillance camera photos recently led to the arrests of three men suspected of committing an anti-homosexual hate crime in Philadelphia.

At least 90 percent of law enforcement agencies monitor social media to find leads on criminal activity.[42] Several years ago, for instance, the New York Police Department set up a new unit dedicated to preventing violence between groups of neighborhood adolescents knows as "crews." Because most of these youths use social media to communicate with each other, police officers monitoring Facebook and Twitter are often able to learn about potential conflicts before they take place. New York officials credit Operation Crew Cut with contributing to a record-low number of murders in the city in 2013.[43]

Technology on the Beat As the leaders of the reform movement envisioned, technology also continues to improve the capabilities of officers in the field. In this section's *CJ & Technology* feature, we saw that law enforcement agents can use smartphones and tablets to access a wealth of crime information and have turned their patrol cars into command centers on wheels. Officers are also able to use less lethal weapons such as laser beams (discussed in Chapter 6), monitor suspects via satellite (discussed in Chapter 7), and incorporate dozens of other technological innovations into their day-to-day-duties.

Some law enforcement veterans are concerned that the "art" of policing is being lost in an era of intelligence-led policing and increased reliance on technology. "If it becomes all about the science," says Los Angeles Police Department Deputy Chief Michael Downing, "I worry we'll lose the important nuances."[44] As the remainder of this chapter and the two that follow show, however, the human element continues to dominate all aspects of policing in America.

Recruitment and Training: Becoming a Police Officer

In 1961, police expert James H. Chenoweth commented that the methods used to hire police officers had changed little since 1829 when the Metropolitan Police of London was created.[45] The past half-century, however, has seen a number of improvements in the way that police administrators handle the task of **recruitment,** or the development of a pool of qualified applicants from which to select new officers. Efforts have been made to diversify police rolls, and recruits in most police departments undergo a substantial array of tests and screens—discussed next—to determine their aptitude. Furthermore, annual starting salaries that can exceed $70,000, along with the opportunities offered by an interesting profession in the public service field, have attracted a wide variety of applicants to police work.

Basic Requirements

The selection process involves a number of steps, and each police department has a different method of choosing candidates. Most agencies, however, require at a minimum that a police officer:

- Be a U.S. citizen.
- Not have been convicted of a felony.
- Have or be eligible to have a driver's license in the state where the department is located.
- Be at least twenty-one years of age.
- Meet weight and eyesight requirements.

In addition, few departments will accept candidates older than forty-five years of age.

Background Checks and Tests Beyond these minimum requirements, police departments usually engage in extensive background checks, including drug tests; a review of the applicant's educational, military, and driving records; credit checks; interviews with spouses, acquaintances, and previous employers; and a background search to determine whether the applicant has been convicted of any criminal acts. Police agencies generally require certain physical attributes in applicants: normally, they must be able to pass a physical agility or fitness test. (For an example of one such test, see Figure 5.2).

In some departments, particularly those that serve large metropolitan areas, the applicant must take a psychological screening test to determine if he or she is suited to law enforcement work. Generally, such suitability tests measure the applicant's ability to handle stress, follow rules, use good judgment, and avoid off-duty behavior that would reflect negatively on the department.[46]

Along these same lines, more than one-third of American police agencies now review an applicant's social media activity on sources such as Facebook, Instagram,

Recruitment The process by which law enforcement agencies develop a pool of qualified applicants from which to select new employees.

FIGURE 5.2 Physical Agility Exam for the Henrico County (Virginia) Division of Police

Those applying for the position of police officer must finish this physical agility exam within 3 minutes, 30 seconds. During the test, applicants are required to wear the equipment (with a total weight of between 9 and 13 pounds) worn by patrol officers, which includes the police uniform, leather gun belt, firearm, baton, portable radio, and ballistics vest.

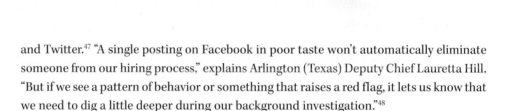

1. Applicant begins test seated in a police vehicle, door closed, seat belt fastened.
2. Applicant must exit vehicle and jump or climb a six-foot barrier.
3. Applicant then completes a one-quarter mile run or walk, making various turns along the way, to simulate a pursuit run.
4. Applicant must jump a simulated five-foot culvert/ditch.
5. Applicant must drag a "human simulator" (dummy) weighing 175 pounds a distance of 50 feet (to simulate a situation in which an officer is required to pull or carry an injured person to safety).
6. Applicant must draw his or her weapon and fire five rounds with the strong hand and five rounds with the weak hand.

and Twitter.[47] "A single posting on Facebook in poor taste won't automatically eliminate someone from our hiring process," explains Arlington (Texas) Deputy Chief Lauretta Hill. "But if we see a pattern of behavior or something that raises a red flag, it lets us know that we need to dig a little deeper during our background investigation."[48]

Educational Requirements One of the most dramatic differences between today's police recruits and those of several generations ago is their level of education. In the 1920s, when August Vollmer began promoting the need for higher education in police officers, few had attended college. In the 2000s, 82 percent of all local police departments require at least a high school diploma, and 9 percent require a degree from a two-year college.[49] Although a four-year degree is necessary for certain elite law enforcement positions such as Federal Bureau of Investigation special agent, only about 5 percent of large local police departments have such a requirement.[50] Those officers with four-year degrees do, however, generally enjoy an advantage in hiring and promotion, and often receive higher salaries than their less educated co-employees.

Not all police observers believe that education is a necessity for police officers, however. In the words of one police officer, "Effective street cops learn their skills on the job, not in a classroom."[51] By emphasizing a college degree, say some, police departments discourage those who would make solid officers but lack the education necessary to apply for positions in law enforcement.

Training

LEARNING OBJECTIVE 4 Identify the differences between the police academy and field training as learning tools for recruits.

If an applicant successfully navigates the application process, he or she will be hired on a *probationary* basis. During this **probationary period,** which can last from six to eighteen months depending on the department, the recruit is in jeopardy of being fired without cause if he or she proves inadequate to the challenges of police work. Almost every state requires that police recruits pass through a training period while on probation. During this time, they are taught the basics of police work and are under constant supervision by superiors. The training period usually has two components: the police academy and field training. On average, local police departments serving populations of 250,000 or more require 1,648 hours of training—972 hours in the classroom and 676 hours in the field.[52]

Probationary Period A period of time at the beginning of a police officer's career during which she or he may be fired without cause.

Academy Training The *police academy,* run by either the state or a police agency, provides recruits with a controlled, militarized environment in which they receive their introduction to the world of the police officer. They are taught the laws of search, seizure, arrest, and interrogation; how and when to use weapons; the procedures of securing a crime scene and interviewing witnesses; first aid; self-defense; and other essentials of police work. Nine in ten police academies also provide terrorism-related training to teach recruits how to respond to terrorist incidents, including those involving weapons of mass destruction.[53] Academy instructors evaluate the recruits' performance and send intermittent progress reports to police administrators.

▲ A recruit goes through an exercise routine at a police academy for the U.S. Capitol Police in Cheltenham, Maryland. **Why are police academies an important part of the learning process for a potential police officer?** Tom Williams/CQ Roll Call/Getty Images

In the Field **Field training** takes place outside the confines of the police academy. A recruit is paired with an experienced police officer known as a field training officer (FTO). The goal of field training is to help rookies apply the concepts they have learned in the academy "to the streets," with the FTO playing a supervisory role to make sure that nothing goes awry. According to many, the academy introduces recruits to the formal rules of police work, but field training gives the rookies their first taste of the informal rules. In fact, the initial advice to recruits from some FTOs is often along the lines of "O.K., kid. Forget everything you learned in the classroom. You're in the real world now." Nonetheless, the academy is a critical component in the learning process, as it provides rookies with a road map to the job.

EthicsChallenge

How much impact do you think ethics training in a police academy will have on the future ethical behavior of recruits? Can ethics be taught, or is each person's concept of "right and wrong" permanently shaped in childhood? Explain your answer. ▪

Women and Minorities in Policing Today

For most of this nation's history, the typical American police officer was white and male. As recently as 1968, African Americans represented only 5 percent of all sworn officers in the United States, and the percentage of "women in blue" was even lower.[54] Only within the past thirty years has this situation been addressed, with many police departments actively trying to recruit women, African Americans, Hispanics, Asian Americans, and members of other minority groups. The result, as you will see, has been a steady though not spectacular increase in the diversity of the nation's police forces. When it comes to issues of gender, race, and ethnicity, however, mere statistics rarely tell the entire story.

Field Training The segment of a police recruit's training in which he or she is removed from the classroom and placed on the beat, under the supervision of a senior officer.

Antidiscrimination Law and Affirmative Action

To a certain extent, external forces have driven law enforcement agencies to increase the number of female and minority recruits. The 1964 Civil Rights Act and its 1972 amendments guaranteed members of minority groups and women equal access to jobs in law enforcement, partly by establishing the Equal Employment Opportunity Commission (EEOC) to ensure fairness in hiring practices. The United States Supreme Court has also ruled on several occasions that **discrimination** by law enforcement agencies violates federal law.[55] In legal terms, discrimination occurs when hiring and promotion decisions are based on individual characteristics such as gender or race, and not on job-related factors.

Consent Decrees Since the early 1970s, numerous law enforcement agencies have instituted **affirmative action** programs to increase the diversity of their employees. These programs are designed to give women and members of minority groups certain advantages in hiring and promotion to remedy the effects of past discrimination and prevent future discrimination. Often, affirmative action programs are established voluntarily. Sometimes, however, they are the result of lawsuits brought by employees or potential employees who believe that the employer has discriminated against them.

In such instances, if the court finds that discrimination did occur, it will implement a *consent decree* to remedy the situation. Under a consent decree, the law enforcement agency often agrees to meet certain numerical goals in hiring women and members of minority groups. If it fails to meet these goals, it is punished with a fine or some other sanction.[56] One study found that the rate of female employment increased significantly in police agencies under a consent degree, only to return to average after the consent degree expired.[57]

Explain how consent decrees make law enforcement agencies more diverse. LEARNING **5** OBJECTIVE

Recruiting Challenges Over the past two decades, the EEOC has brought about two dozen discrimination lawsuits against local and state law enforcement agencies on behalf of wronged individuals. In almost every case, the agency agreed to resolve the problem through a consent decree.[58] As the Rochester (New York) Police Department (RPD) has learned, however, simply being willing to increase diversity in recruiting may not be enough. The RPD is operating under a voluntary consent decree that requires at least one in four new hires to come from a minority group. Despite an affirmative action program and a population of potential recruits that is 52 percent nonwhite, from 2009 to 2013, the number of African American and Hispanic officers with the RDP actually declined by 10.[59]

Police agencies do face a number of roadblocks when it comes to increasing diversity. For example, educational requirements often disqualify members of minority groups. The Cleveland Heights, Ohio, Police Department, which had twenty-two black officers out of 102 in 2014, created a two-tier recruiting process to alleviate this problem. The upper tier requires a college degree, while the lower, called "basic patrol," does not. When a basic patrol recruit is hired, the city provides financial assistance for that recruit to earn his or her degree and eventually reach the upper tier.[60]

Regardless of creative recruiting methods by individual police departments, too often the "multiple hurdles" of the police recruiting process discourage or disqualify women and minorities from police work. In the *CJ in Action* feature at the end of this chapter, we will examine the controversial practice of lowering these hurdles to help diversify American police departments.

Discrimination The illegal use of characteristics such as gender or race by employers when making hiring or promotion decisions.

Affirmative Action A hiring or promotion policy favoring those groups, such as women, African Americans, or Hispanics, who have suffered from discrimination in the past or continue to suffer from discrimination.

Working Women: Gender and Law Enforcement

In 1987, about 7.6 percent of all local police officers were women. Twenty-six years later, that percentage had risen to almost 12 percent—17 percent in departments serving populations of more than one million people.[61] That increase seems less impressive, however, when one considers that women make up more than half of the population of the United States, meaning that they are severely underrepresented in law enforcement.

Added Scrutiny There are several reasons for the low levels of women serving as police officers. First, relatively few women hold positions of high rank in American police departments,[62] and only about 3 percent of the police chiefs in the United States are women.[63] Consequently, female police officers have few superiors who might be able to mentor them in what can be a hostile work environment.

LEARNING
6
OBJECTIVE
Describe the challenges facing women who choose law enforcement as a career.

In addition to the dangers and pressures facing all law enforcement agents, which we will discuss in the next chapter, women must deal with an added layer of scrutiny. Many male police officers feel that their female counterparts are mentally soft, physically weak, and generally unsuited for the rigors of the job. At the same time, male officers often try to protect female officers by keeping them out of hazardous situations, thereby denying the women the opportunity to prove themselves.[64]

Tokenism Women in law enforcement also face the problem of *tokenism,* or the belief that they have been hired or promoted to fulfill diversity requirements and have not earned their positions. Tokenism creates pressure to prove the stereotypes wrong. When comparing the arrest patterns of male and female officers over a twelve-month period in Cincinnati, Ohio, for example, researchers noted several interesting patterns. Although overall arrest rates were similar, female officers were much more likely than their male counterparts to arrest suspects who were "non-deferential" or hostile. Also, the presence of a supervisor greatly increased the likelihood that a female officer would make an arrest.

Such patterns, the researchers concluded, show that female officers feel pressure to demonstrate that they are "good cops" who cannot be intimidated because of their gender.[65] One officer said that her female colleagues "go into that physical-arrest mode quicker [because] you want to prove that you can do it."[66] Similarly, women who rise through the law enforcement ranks often face questions concerning their worthiness. According to Tampa (Florida) police chief Jane Castor, "No matter how qualified you are or how much experience you have . . . people will say that you were promoted—in part, if not fully—because you're a woman."[67]

In fact, most of the negative attitudes toward women police officers are based on prejudice rather than actual experience. A number of studies have shown that there is very little difference between the performances of men and women in uniform.[68] (For more on this topic, see the feature *Myth vs Reality—Women Make Bad Cops.*)

Sexual Harassment According to a female officer interviewed by researcher Teresa Lynn, "The guys can view you as a sex object."[69] Anecdotal evidence suggests that this attitude is commonplace in police departments and often leads to **sexual harassment** of female police officers. Sexual harassment refers to a pattern of behavior that is sexual in nature, such as inappropriate touching or lewd jokes, and is unwelcome by its target. Such conduct can impact the recipient's career. One victim of sexual comments and physical contact by a superior said that when she rebuffed his advances, "he would

Sexual Harassment A repeated pattern of unwelcome sexual advances and/or obscene remarks in the workplace. Under certain circumstances, sexual harassment is illegal and can be the basis for a civil lawsuit.

Myth vs Reality

Women Make Bad Cops

Since the formation of the earliest police departments in the nineteenth century, policing has been seen as "man's work." Only men were considered to have the physical strength necessary to deal with the dangers of the street.

The Myth The perception that women are not physically strong enough to be effective law enforcement officers prevails both in the public mind and within police forces themselves. Criminologist Susan Martin has found that policewomen are under "constant pressure to demonstrate their competence and effectiveness vis-à-vis their male counterparts." One female police officer describes her experience:

> I was the smallest person . . . . [The male officers] didn't feel I could do the job. They tried to get me into fighting situations to see if I would back down. They told me, "You know, if you aren't strong enough or are going to be a coward, we have to find out fast and get you out of here."

The Reality Female police officers are certainly capable of acts of bravery and physical prowess. In fact, a number of studies have shown that policewomen can be as effective as men in most situations, and often more so. Citizens appear to prefer dealing with a female police officer rather than a male during service calls—especially those that involve domestic violence. In general, policewomen are less aggressive and more likely to reduce the potential for a violent situation by relying on verbal skills rather than their authority as law enforcement agents. According to one large-scale study of local police departments in the southeast United States, women made up 12.4 percent of the sworn officer work force and accounted for only 5.7 percent of misconduct allegations.

For Critical Analysis

Do you believe that female police officers can be just as effective as men in protecting citizens from criminal behavior? Why or why not?

▲ A female member of the Miami (Florida) Police Department provides security during a public event. Joe Raedle/Getty Images

retaliate by criticizing my reports or judgment."[70]

Over a nine-month period in 2010, the National Police Misconduct Statistics and Reporting Project confirmed eighty-six incidents of sexual harassment in police departments nationwide.[71] Self-reported surveys, however, suggest that the actual incidence is much higher, with most incidents going unreported.[72] Despite having to deal with problems such as sexual harassment, outdated stereotypes, and tokenism, female police officers have generally shown that they are capable law enforcement officers, willing to take great risks if necessary to do their job. The names of nearly three hundred women are included on the National Law Enforcement Memorial in Washington, D.C.

Minority Report: Race and Ethnicity in Law Enforcement

Like women, members of minority groups have been slowly increasing their presence in local police departments since the late 1980s. The latest available data show that African American officers comprise about 12 percent of the nation's police officers; Hispanic officers, about 10 percent; and other minority groups such as Asians, American Indians, and Pacific Islanders, about 3 percent.[73] By some measures, members of minority groups are better represented than women in policing. Cities such as Detroit and Washington have local police departments that closely match their civilian populations in terms of diversity, and in recent years, a majority of police recruits in New York City have been members of minority groups. On other measures, such as promotion, minorities in law enforcement continue to seek parity.[74]

Double Marginality According to Peter C. Moskos, a professor at the John Jay College of Criminal Justice in New York, "Black and white police officers remain two distinct shades of blue, with distinct attitudes toward each other and the communities they serve."[75] While that may be true, minority officers generally report that they have good relationships with their white fellow officers.[76] Often, though, members of minority groups in law enforcement—particularly African Americans and Hispanics—do face the problem of **double marginality.** This term refers to a situation in which minority officers are viewed with suspicion by both sides:

Double Marginality The double suspicion that minority law enforcement officers face from their white colleagues and from members of the minority community to which they belong.

1. White police officers believe that minority officers will give members of their own race or ethnicity better treatment on the streets.
2. Those same minority officers face hostility from members of their own community who are under the impression that black and Hispanic officers are traitors to their race or ethnicity.

In response, minority officers may feel the need to act more harshly toward minority offenders to prove that they are not biased in favor of their own racial or ethnic group.[77]

The Benefits of a Diverse Police Force In 1986, Supreme Court justice John Paul Stevens spoke for many in the criminal justice system when he observed that "an integrated police force could develop a better relationship [with a racially diverse citizenry] and therefore do a more effective job of maintaining law and order than a force composed of white officers."[78] Indeed, despite the effects of double marginality, African American officers may have more credibility in a predominantly black neighborhood than white police officers, leading to better community-police relations and a greater ability to solve and prevent crimes.

Certainly, in the Mexican American communities typical of border states such as Arizona, Texas, and California, many Hispanic officers are able to gather information that would be very difficult for non-Spanish-speaking officers to collect. Finally, however, the best argument for a diverse police force is that members of minority groups represent a broad source of talent in this country, and such talent can only enhance the overall effectiveness of American law enforcement. The lack of such diversity in a number of jurisdictions, underscored by the information in Figure 5.3, continues to be a problem for the criminal justice system.

FIGURE 5.3 Police Diversity in American Cities

This graph shows the five cities in the United States with the largest negative gaps between the percentage of African American residents and the percentage of African Americans working as officers with the local police department.

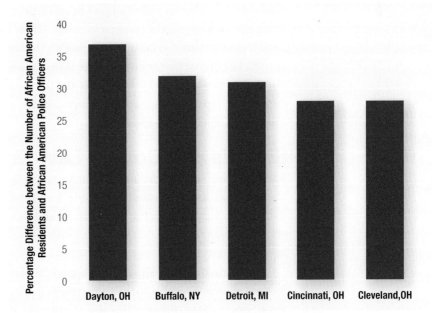

Source: U.S. Census Bureau and *USA Today.*

Public and Private Law Enforcement

On September 12, 2014, Eric Frein allegedly killed Corporal Bryon Dickson and wounded Trooper Alex Douglass with a high-powered rifle outside a state police barracks in northeastern Pennsylvania. Over the next forty-eight days, hundreds of law enforcement agents took part in the manhunt for Frein, including officers from the Federal Bureau of Investigation; the U.S. Marshals Service; the New Jersey, New York, and Pennsylvania state police; and sheriffs' departments in Monroe County (Penn.) and Schuyler County (N.Y.). Frein was finally captured by three deputy U.S. marshals at an abandoned airstrip near Tannersville, Pennsylvania.

As the effort to capture Frein shows, Americans are served by a multitude of police organizations. Overall, there are about 18,000 law enforcement agencies in the United States, employing about 880,000 officers.[79] For the most part, these agencies operate on three different levels: local, state, and federal. Each level has its own set of responsibilities, which we shall discuss starting with local police departments.

Municipal Law Enforcement Agencies

According to federal statistics, there is one local or state police officer for every 400 residents of the United States.[80] About two-thirds of all *sworn officers,* or those officers with arrest powers, work in small- and medium-sized police departments serving cities with populations from 10,000 to one million.[81] While the New York City Police Department employs about 35,000 police personnel, 50 percent of all local police departments have ten or fewer law enforcement officers.[82]

Of the three levels of law enforcement, municipal agencies have the broadest authority to apprehend criminal suspects, maintain order, and provide services to the community. Whether the local officer is part of a large force or the only law enforcement officer in the community, he or she is usually responsible for a wide spectrum of duties, from responding to noise complaints to investigating homicides. Larger police departments will often assign officers to specialized task forces or units that deal with a particular crime or area of concern. For example, in Washington, D.C., the police department features a Gay and Lesbian Liaison Unit that deals with anti-homosexual crimes in the city. The Knoxville (Tennessee) Police Department has a squad devoted to combating Internet crimes against children, while the three hundred officers assigned to the New York Police Department's Emergency Services Unit are trained in suicide rescue, hostage negotiation, and SCUBA operations.

Sheriffs and County Law Enforcement

The **sheriff** is a very important figure in American law enforcement. Almost every one of the more than three thousand counties in the United States (except those in Alaska) has a sheriff. In every state except Rhode Island and Hawaii, sheriffs are elected by members of the community for two- or four-year terms and are paid a salary set by the state legislature or county board.

As elected officials who do not necessarily need a background in law enforcement, modern sheriffs resemble their counterparts from the political era of policing in many ways. Simply stated, the sheriff is also a politician. When a new sheriff is elected, she or he will sometimes repay political debts by appointing new deputies or promoting those who have given her or him support.

Sheriff The primary law enforcement officer in a county, usually elected to the post by a popular vote.

Size and Responsibility of Sheriffs' Departments Like municipal police forces, sheriffs' departments vary in size. The largest is the Los Angeles County Sheriff's Department, with more than 9,000 deputies. Of the 3,063 sheriffs' departments in the country, thirteen employ more than 1,000 officers, while forty-five have only one.[83]

Keep in mind that cities, which are served by municipal police departments, often exist within counties, which are served by sheriffs' departments. Therefore, police officers and sheriffs' deputies often find themselves policing the same geographical areas. Police departments, however, are generally governed by a local political entity such as a mayor's office, while most sheriffs' departments are assigned their duties by state law. About 80 percent of all sheriffs' departments are responsible for investigating violent crimes in their jurisdictions. Other common responsibilities of a sheriff's department include:

▲ Lane County (Oregon) sheriff's deputies take part in an "active shooter" training exercise to protect local grade school students. **Why do sheriffs' departments and municipal police agencies often find themselves policing the same geographical areas?** AP Images/*The Register-Guard*, Brian Davies

- Investigating drug crimes.
- Maintaining the county jail.
- Carrying out civil and criminal processes within county lines, such as serving eviction notices and court summonses.
- Keeping order in the county courthouse.
- Enforcing orders of the court, such as overseeing the isolation of a jury during a trial.[84]

It is easy to confuse sheriffs' departments and local police departments. Both law enforcement agencies are responsible for many of the same tasks, including crime investigation and routine patrol. There are differences, however. Sheriffs' departments are more likely to be involved in county court and jail operations and to perform certain services such as search and rescue. Local police departments, for their part, are more likely to perform traffic-related functions than are sheriffs' departments.[85]

The County Coroner Another elected official on the county level is the **coroner,** or medical examiner. Duties vary from county to county, but the coroner has a general mandate to investigate "all sudden, unexplained, unnatural, or suspicious deaths" reported to the office. The coroner is ultimately responsible for determining the cause of death in these cases. Coroners also perform autopsies and assist other law enforcement agencies in homicide investigations. For example, after actor Philip Seymour Hoffman died in February 2014 of an apparent heroin overdose, the New York City medical examiner needed to determine the exact cause of death. After a two-month investigation, the medical examiner confirmed that Hoffman had died because of a toxic mix of heroin and other drugs such as cocaine and amphetamines.

State Police and Highway Patrols

The most visible state law enforcement agency is the state police or highway patrol agency. Historically, state police agencies were created for three reasons:

Coroner The medical examiner of a county, usually elected by popular vote.

▲ A state highway patrol officer gives advice to a motorist stuck in a snowstorm on Hammond Road in Raleigh, North Carolina. **Why is it beneficial for states to have separate law enforcement agencies that focus primarily on major roadways?** Travis Long/*Raleigh News & Observer*/MCT via Getty Images

1. To assist local police agencies, which often did not have adequate resources or training to handle their law enforcement tasks.
2. To investigate criminal activities that crossed jurisdictional boundaries (such as when bank robbers committed a crime in one county and then fled to another part of the state).
3. To provide law enforcement in rural and other areas that did not have local or county police agencies.

The Difference between State Police and Highway Patrols Today, there are twenty-three state police agencies and twenty-six highway patrols in the United States. State police agencies have statewide jurisdiction and are authorized to perform a wide variety of law enforcement tasks. Thus, they provide the same services as city or county police departments and are restricted only by the boundaries of the state. In contrast, highway patrols have limited authority. Their duties are generally defined either by their jurisdiction or by the specific types of offenses they have the authority to control. As their name suggests, most highway patrols concentrate primarily on regulating traffic. Specifically, they enforce traffic laws and investigate traffic accidents. Furthermore, they usually limit their activity to patrolling state and federal highways.

Trying to determine what state agency has which duties can be confusing. The Washington State Highway Patrol, despite its name, also has state police powers. In addition, thirty-five states have investigative agencies that are independent of the state police or highway patrol. Such agencies are usually found in states with highway patrols, and they have the primary responsibility of investigating criminal activities. For example, in addition to its highway patrol, Oklahoma runs a State Bureau of Investigation and a State Bureau of Narcotics and Dangerous Drugs. Each state has its own methods of determining the jurisdictions of these various organizations.

Limited-Purpose Law Enforcement Agencies Even with the agencies just discussed, a number of states have found that certain law enforcement areas need more specific attention. As a result, a wide variety of limited-purpose law enforcement agencies have sprung up in the fifty states. For example, most states have an alcoholic beverage control commission (ABC), or a similarly named organization, which monitors the sale and distribution of alcoholic beverages. The ABC monitors alcohol distributors to ensure that all taxes are paid on the beverages and is responsible for revoking or suspending the liquor licenses of establishments that have broken relevant laws.

Many states have fish and game warden organizations that enforce all laws relating to hunting and fishing. Motor vehicle compliance (MVC) agencies monitor interstate carriers or trucks to make sure that they are in compliance with state and federal laws. MVC officers generally operate the weigh stations that are commonly found on interstate highways. Other limited-purpose law enforcement agencies deal with white-collar and computer crime, regulate nursing homes, and provide training to local police departments.

Federal Law Enforcement Agencies

Statistically, employees of federal agencies do not make up a large part of the nation's law enforcement force. In fact, the New York City Police Department has about one-fifth as many employees as all of the federal law enforcement agencies combined. Nevertheless, the influence of these federal agencies is substantial.

Unlike local police departments, which must deal with all forms of crime, federal agencies have been authorized, usually by Congress, to enforce specific laws or attend to specific situations. The U.S. Coast Guard, for example, patrols the nation's waterways, while U.S. Postal inspectors investigate and prosecute crimes perpetrated through the use of the U.S. mails. In this section, you will learn the elements and duties of the most important federal law enforcement agencies, which are grouped according to the federal department or bureau to which they report. (See Figure 5.4 for the current federal law enforcement "lineup.")

FIGURE 5.4 Federal Law Enforcement Agencies

A number of federal agencies employ law enforcement officers who are authorized to carry firearms and make arrests. The most prominent ones are under the control of the U.S. Department of Homeland Security, the U.S. Department of Justice, and the U.S. Department of the Treasury.

Department of Homeland Security

DEPARTMENT NAME	APPROXIMATE NUMBER OF OFFICERS	MAIN RESPONSIBILITIES
U.S. Customs and Border Protection (CBP)	37,000	• (1) Prevent the illegal flow of people and goods across America's international borders; (2) facilitate legal trade and travel
U.S. Immigration and Customs Enforcement (ICE)	12,400	• Uphold public safety and homeland security by enforcing the nation's immigration and customs laws
U.S. Secret Service	4,500	• (1) Protect the president, the president's family, former presidents and their families, and other high-ranking politicians; (2) combat currency counterfeiters

Department of Justice

DEPARTMENT NAME	APPROXIMATE NUMBER OF OFFICERS	MAIN RESPONSIBILITIES
Federal Bureau of Investigation (FBI)	13,600	• (1) Protect national security by fighting international and domestic terrorism; (2) enforce federal criminal laws such as those dealing with cyber crime, public corruption, and civil rights violations
Drug Enforcement Administration (DEA)	4,700	• Enforce the nation's laws regulating the sale and use of drugs
Bureau of Alcohol, Tobacco, Firearms and Explosives (ATF)	2,500	• (1) Combat the illegal use and trafficking of firearms and explosives; (2) investigate the illegal diversion of alcohol and tobacco products
U.S. Marshals Service	4,000	• (1) Provide security at federal courts; (2) protect government witnesses; (3) apprehend fugitives from the federal court or corrections system

Department of the Treasury

DEPARTMENT NAME	APPROXIMATE NUMBER OF OFFICERS	MAIN RESPONSIBILITIES
Internal Revenue Service (IRS)	2,500	• Investigate potential criminal violations of the nation's tax code

Indicate some of the most important law enforcement agencies under the control of the Department of Homeland Security.

LEARNING

7

OBJECTIVE

The Department of Homeland Security Comprising twenty-two federal agencies, the Department of Homeland Security (DHS) coordinates national efforts to protect the United States against international and domestic terrorism. While most of the agencies under DHS control are not specifically linked with the criminal justice system, the department does oversee three agencies that play an important role in counterterrorism and fighting crime: U.S. Customs and Border Protection, U.S. Immigration and Customs Enforcement, and the U.S. Secret Service.

U.S. Customs and Border Protection (CBP) The federal government spends about $18 billion annually to enforce immigration law.[86] A large chunk of these funds go to **U.S. Customs and Border Protection (CBP),** which polices the flow of goods and people across the United States' international borders. In general terms, this means that the agency has two primary goals:

1. To keep undocumented immigrants, illegal drugs, and drug traffickers from crossing our borders; and
2. To facilitate the smooth flow of legal trade and travel.

Consequently, CBP officers are stationed at every port of entry and exit to the United States. The officers have widespread authority to investigate and search all international passengers, whether they arrive on airplanes, ships, or other forms of transportation.

To ensure that those coming into the United States from abroad have permission to do so, CBP officers check documents such as passports and *visas*. (A **visa** is a document issued by the U.S. State Department that indicates the conditions under which a holder can enter and travel within the United States.) The officers also have the responsibility of inspecting luggage and cargo to ensure compliance with immigration and trade laws.

Under the Office of Biometric Identity Management program, most foreigners entering the United States on visas are subject to fingerprinting and a facial scan using digital photography. Their names are also checked against criminal records and watch lists for suspected terrorists. Although the program has been effective in recording the entry of foreigners, it has been less successful in following their movements once they are in the United States. Without the cooperation of the visitor, federal officials are unable to confirm when, or if, a foreign visitor has left the country. As a result, about 4.4 million of the nearly 11 million undocumented immigrants living in the United States have overstayed their visa.[87]

Unregulated Border Entry The U.S. Border Patrol, a branch of the CBP, has the burden of policing the Mexican and Canadian borders between official ports of entry. Every year, hundreds of thousands of non-U.S. citizens, unable to legally obtain visas, attempt to enter the country illegally by crossing these large, underpopulated regions, particularly in the southern part of the country. In 2013, Border Patrol agents apprehended about 490,000 illegal border crossers, down from a high of nearly 1.7 million in 2000.[88]

To a large degree, this decrease reflects the recent economic downturn, which has removed some of the monetary incentives for foreign nationals looking for work in the United States. In addition, CBP has "shrunk" the border, focusing the efforts of many of the nation's 20,000 Border Patrol agents on areas where illegal crossings are most likely to occur. Agents working those areas are supported by helicopters, surveillance towers, reconnaissance planes with infrared radar, and highly-sensitive cameras. Eventually, CBP hopes is to cover 45 percent of the border with these "dense" arrays of agents and technology, while monitoring the remaining, lightly-trafficked 55 percent of the U.S.-Mexican border primarily with surveillance drones.[89]

U.S. Customs and Border Protection (CBP) The federal agency responsible for protecting U.S. borders and facilitating legal trade and travel across those borders.

Visa Official authorization allowing a person to travel to and within the issuing country.

U.S. Immigration and Customs Enforcement (ICE) The CBP shares responsibility for locating and apprehending those persons illegally in the United States with special agents from **U.S. Immigration and Customs Enforcement (ICE).** While the CBP focuses almost exclusively on the nation's borders, ICE has a broader mandate to investigate and to enforce our country's immigration and customs laws. Simply stated, the CBP covers the borders, and ICE covers everything else. The latter agency's duties include detaining undocumented aliens and deporting (removing) them from the United States, ensuring that those without permission do not work or gain other benefits in this country, and disrupting human trafficking operations.

Recently, ICE has been aggressively removing undocumented immigrants from the United States. In 2014, for example, the agency conducted about 315,000 removals, 56 percent of which involved those who had been convicted of a crime.[90] Critics pointed out, however, that many of those crimes were minor, belying an assurance by President Barack Obama that, under his leadership, ICE would mainly focus on "criminals, gang bangers, [and] people who are hurting the community."[91] The Obama administration responded to this criticism with an initiative called the Priority Enforcement Program, addressed in this chapter's *CJ Policy—Your Take* feature. This new directive requires ICE to center its removal efforts solely on those undocumented immigrants who have been convicted of serious crimes or pose a danger to national security.[92]

The U.S. Secret Service When it was created in 1865, the **U.S. Secret Service** was primarily responsible for combating currency counterfeiters. In 1901, the agency was given the added responsibility of protecting the president of the United States, the president's family, the vice president, the president-elect, and former presidents. These duties have remained the cornerstone of the agency, with several expansions. After a number of threats against presidential candidates in the 1960s and early 1970s, including the shootings of Robert Kennedy of New York and Governor George Wallace of Alabama, in 1976 Secret Service agents became responsible for protecting those political figures as well.

In addition to its special plainclothes agents, the agency also directs two uniformed groups of law enforcement officers. The Secret Service Uniformed Division protects the grounds of the White House and its inhabitants, and the Treasury Police Force polices the Treasury Building in Washington, D.C. To aid its battle against counterfeiters and forgers of government bonds, the agency has the use of a laboratory at the Bureau of Engraving and Printing in the nation's capital.

Additional DHS Agencies Besides the three already discussed—CBP, ICE, and the U.S. Secret Service—three other DHS agencies play a central role in preventing and responding to crime and terrorist-related activity:

- The *U.S. Coast Guard* defends the nation's coasts, ports, and inland waterways. It also combats illegal drug shipping and enforces immigration law at sea.
- The *Transportation Security Administration* is responsible for the safe operation of our airline, rail, bus, and ferry services. It also operates the Federal Air Marshals program that places undercover federal agents on commercial flights.
- The *Federal Emergency Management Agency* holds a position as the lead federal agency in preparing for and responding to disasters such as hurricanes, floods, terrorist attacks, and *infrastructure* concerns. Our national **infrastructure** includes all of the facilities and systems that provide the daily necessities of modern life, such as electric power, food, water, transportation, and telecommunications.

CJ Policy—**Your Take**

Technically, almost every immigrant who is in the United States illegally is **eligible for removal** by U.S. Immigrations and Customs Enforcement. What is your opinion of the recent decision to focus removal efforts only on those undocumented immigrants who have committed a serious crime or are considered a threat to national security? What might be some of the practical reasons behind this new policy?

U.S. Immigration and Customs Enforcement (ICE) The federal agency that enforces the nation's immigration and customs laws.

U.S. Secret Service A federal law enforcement organization with the primary responsibility of protecting the president, the president's family, the vice president, and other important political figures.

Infrastructure The services and facilities that support the day-to-day needs of modern life, such as electricity, food, transportation, and water.

Careers in CJ

Courtesy FBI.gov

Arnold E. Bell
Federal Bureau of Investigation (FBI) Agent

I came to the FBI from the U.S. Army, where I worked as a crewman on a UH-1 helicopter and subsequently as a special agent with the U.S. Army Criminal Investigation Command. My work experience in the U.S. Army and degree from St. Leo College (now University) provided the educational foundation that allowed entry into the FBI. After graduating from the FBI Academy in Quantico, Virginia, I was assigned to our Los Angeles division, where I spent the next twelve years. It was a particularly interesting time to be working in Los Angeles, which was experiencing a boom in bank robberies. During the most intense stretches, we were averaging between five and seven bank robberies a day! When I wasn't chasing down a bank robber, I had my hands full with hunting down fugitives, working against organized crime, and dealing with public corruption.

I am currently assigned to the FBI's cyber division as an assistant section chief. The primary mission of my division is to combat cyber-based terrorism and hostile-intelligence operations conducted via the Internet, and to address general cyber crime. Since September 11, 2001, our primary focus has shifted from criminal work to counterterrorism. This has been a difficult transformation for many of us "old-timers" because we grew up in the Bureau doing criminal work. We all recognize, however, the importance of this new challenge, and, despite the difficulties, I believe we have been successful in fulfilling both missions.

fbi.gov

> **SOCIAL MEDIA CAREER TIP** Be aware of your e-mail address/screen name/login name and what it represents. Stay away from nicknames. Use a professional and unique name to represent yourself consistently across social media platforms.

The Department of Justice

The U.S. Department of Justice, created in 1870, is still the primary federal law enforcement agency in the country. With the responsibility of enforcing criminal law and supervising the federal prisons, the Justice Department plays a leading role in the American criminal justice system. To carry out its responsibilities to prevent and control crime, the department has a number of law enforcement agencies, including the Federal Bureau of Investigation, the federal Drug Enforcement Administration, the Bureau of Alcohol, Tobacco, Firearms and Explosives, and the U.S. Marshals Service.

The Federal Bureau of Investigation (FBI)

Initially created in 1908 as the Bureau of Investigation, this agency was renamed the **Federal Bureau of Investigation (FBI)** in 1935. One of the primary investigative agencies of the federal government, the FBI has jurisdiction over nearly two hundred federal crimes, including white-collar crimes, espionage (spying), kidnapping, extortion, interstate transportation of stolen property, bank robbery, interstate gambling, and civil rights violations.

With its network of agents across the country and the globe, the FBI is also uniquely positioned to combat worldwide criminal activity such as terrorism and drug trafficking. In fact, since 2001, the agency has shifted its focus from traditional crime to national

LEARNING
Identify the duties of the FBI. — **8** —
OBJECTIVE

Federal Bureau of Investigation (FBI) The branch of the Department of Justice responsible for investigating violations of federal law.

security. Between that year and 2009, the FBI doubled its roster of counterterrorism agents, while reducing its number of criminal investigations. In 2014, the agency even officially changed its primary function from "law enforcement" to "national security."[93]

The FBI and Local Cooperation The FBI is also committed to providing valuable support for local and state law enforcement agencies. Its Identification Division maintains a large database of fingerprint information and offers assistance in finding missing persons and identifying the victims of fires, airplane crashes, and other disfiguring disasters. The services of the FBI Laboratory, the largest crime laboratory in the world, are available at no cost to other agencies. Finally, the FBI's National Crime Information Center (NCIC) provides lists of stolen vehicles and firearms, missing license plates, vehicles used to commit crimes, and other information to local and state law enforcement officers.

The FBI's latest information-sharing program, the Law Enforcement National Data Exchange (N-DEx), acts as an electronic search engine for suspected criminals. So, for example, when Philadelphia police were unable to find a suspect in a local home invader/murder investigation, they turned to N-DEx for help. The N-DEx search indicated that the suspect had been involved in a domestic violence incident in Wilmington, Delaware. With the aid of Wilmington law enforcement, Philadelphia police were subsequently able to learn the suspect's home address and arrest him.[94]

The Drug Enforcement Administration (DEA) The mission of the **Drug Enforcement Administration (DEA)** is to enforce domestic drug laws and regulations and to assist other federal and foreign agencies in combating illegal drug manufacture and trade on an international level. The agency also enforces the provisions of the Controlled Substances Act (CSA). The CSA specifies five categories for drugs and the penalties for the manufacture, sale, distribution, possession, or consumption of these drugs, based on the substances' medical use, potential for abuse, and addictive qualities.[95] (See Figure 5.5 for an overview of the CSA. Notice that, despite the various changes in state law that we discussed earlier in this textbook, the DEA is still legally required to treat marijuana as one of the most dangerous drugs on the black market.)

FIGURE 5.5 Schedules of Narcotics as Defined by the Federal Controlled Substances Act

The Comprehensive Drug Abuse Prevention and Control Act of 1970 continues to be the basis for the regulation of drugs in the United States. Substances named by the act were placed under direct regulation of the Drug Enforcement Administration (DEA). The act "ranks" drugs from I to V, with Schedule I drugs being the most heavily controlled and carrying the most severe penalties for abuse.

	Criteria	Examples
SCHEDULE I	Drugs with high abuse potential that are lacking therapeutic utility or adequate safety for use under medical supervision.	Marijuana, heroin, LSD, peyote, PCP, mescaline
SCHEDULE II	Drugs with high abuse potential that are accepted in current medical practice despite high physical and psychological dependence potential.	Opium, cocaine, morphine, Benzedrine, methadone, methamphetamine
SCHEDULE III	Drugs with moderate abuse potential that are utilized in current medical practice despite dependence potential.	Barbiturates, amphetamine
SCHEDULE IV	Drugs with low abuse potential that are accepted in current medical practice despite limited dependence potential.	Valium, Darvon, phenobarbital
SCHEDULE V	Drugs with minimal abuse potential that are used in current medical practice despite limited dependence potential.	Cough medicine with small amounts of narcotic

Source: The Comprehensive Drug Abuse Prevention and Control Act of 1970.

Like the FBI, the DEA operates a network of six regional laboratories used to test and categorize seized drugs. Local law enforcement agencies have access to the DEA labs and often use them to ensure that information about particular drugs that will be presented in court is accurate and up to date. In recent years, Congress has given the FBI more authority to enforce drug laws, and the two agencies now share a number of administrative controls.

The Bureau of Alcohol, Tobacco, Firearms and Explosives (ATF) As its name suggests, the Bureau of Alcohol, Tobacco, Firearms and Explosives (ATF) is primarily concerned with the illegal sale, possession, and use of firearms and the control of untaxed tobacco and liquor products. The Firearms Division of the agency has the responsibility of enforcing the Gun Control Act of 1968, which sets the circumstances under which firearms may be sold and used in this country. The bureau also regulates all gun trade between the United States and foreign nations and collects taxes on all firearm importers, manufacturers, and dealers. In keeping with these duties, the ATF is also responsible for policing the illegal use and possession of explosives. Furthermore, the ATF is charged with enforcing federal gambling laws.

Because it has jurisdiction over such a wide variety of crimes, especially those involving firearms and explosives, the ATF is a constant presence in federal criminal investigations. So, following Elliot Rodger's May 2014 shooting spree in Isla Vista, California (described in Chapter 2), ATF agents searched his parents' house to determine whether the guns Rodger used were legally obtained. Furthermore, the ATF is engaged in an ongoing and crucial operation to keep American firearms out of the hands of Mexican drug cartels. The ATF has also formed multijurisdictional antigang task forces with other federal and local law enforcement agencies to investigate gang-related crimes involving firearms.

The U.S. Marshals Service The oldest federal law enforcement agency is the U.S. Marshals Service. In 1789, President George Washington assigned thirteen U.S. Marshals to protect his attorney general. That same year, Congress created the office of the U.S. Marshals and Deputy Marshals. Originally, the U.S. Marshals acted as the main law enforcement officers in the western territories. Following the Civil War (1861–1865), when most of these territories had become states, these agents were assigned to work for the U.S. district courts, where federal crimes are tried. The relationship between the U.S. Marshals Service and the federal courts continues today and forms the basis for the officers' main duties, which include:

1. Providing security at federal courts for judges, jurors, and other courtroom participants.
2. Controlling property that has been ordered seized by federal courts.
3. Protecting government witnesses who put themselves in danger by testifying against the targets of federal criminal investigations. This protection is sometimes accomplished by relocating the witnesses and providing them with different identities.
4. Transporting federal prisoners to detention institutions.
5. Investigating violations of federal fugitive laws.[96]

The Department of the Treasury The Department of the Treasury, formed in 1789, is mainly responsible for all financial matters of the federal government. It pays all the federal government's bills, borrows funds, collects taxes, mints coins, and prints paper currency. The largest bureau of the Treasury Department, the Internal Revenue Service (IRS), is concerned with violations of tax laws and regulations. The bureau has three divisions, only one of which is involved in criminal investigations. The examination branch of the IRS audits the tax returns of corporations and individuals. The collection division attempts to collect taxes from corporations or citizens who have failed to pay the taxes they owe. Finally, the criminal investigation division investigates cases of tax evasion and tax fraud. Criminal investigation agents can make arrests.

The IRS has long played a role in policing criminal activities such as gambling and selling drugs for one simple reason: those who engage in such activities almost never report any illegally gained income on their tax returns. Therefore, the IRS is able to apprehend them for tax evasion. The most famous example took place in the early 1930s, when the IRS finally arrested famed crime boss Al Capone—responsible for numerous violent crimes—for not paying his taxes.

Private Security

Even with increasing numbers of local, state, and federal law enforcement officers, the police do not have the ability to prevent every crime. Recognizing this, many businesses and citizens have decided to hire private guards for their properties and homes. In fact, according to a 2013 study released by ASIS International, an industry-research firm, demand for **private security** generates revenues of more than $300 billion a year.[97] More than 10,000 firms employing around 1.9 million people provide private security services in this country, compared with about 1.1 million public law enforcement employees.

Privatizing Law Enforcement As there are no federal regulations regarding private security, each state has its own rules for this form of employment. In several states, including California and Florida, prospective security guards must have at least forty hours of training. Ideally, a security guard—lacking the extensive training of a law enforcement agent—should only observe and report criminal activity unless use of force is needed to prevent a felony.[98]

As a rule, private security is not designed to replace law enforcement. It is intended to deter crime rather than stop it. A uniformed security guard patrolling a shopping mall parking lot or a bank lobby has one primary function—to convince a potential criminal to search out a shopping mall or bank that does not have private security. For the same reason, many citizens hire security personnel to drive marked cars through their neighborhoods, making them a less attractive target for burglaries, robberies, vandalism, and other crimes.

Secondary Policing Although many states have minimum training requirements for private security officers, such training lags far behind the requirements to be a public officer. Consequently, there is a high demand for **secondary policing,** an umbrella term that covers the work that off-duty cops do when "moonlighting" for private companies or government agencies.

Generally speaking, police officers operate under the same rules whether they are off duty or

LEARNING
9 Analyze the importance of private security today.
OBJECTIVE

▼ A private security guard patrols the Manhattan Mall in New York City. **Why is being visible such an important aspect of many private security jobs?** Mario Tama/Getty Images News/Getty Images

on duty. In addition, 83 percent of local police departments in the United States have written policies for secondary policing.[99] For example, among other restrictions, Seattle police officers cannot work (on duty or off duty) longer than eighteen consecutive hours in a twenty-four-hour period and must clear all private employment with a superior.[100] Off-duty police officers commonly provide traffic control and pedestrian safety at road construction sites, or crowd control at large-scale functions such as music festivals or sporting events. They are also often hired to protect private properties and businesses, just like their nonpublic counterparts.[101]

Continued Health of the Industry Indicators point to continued growth for the private security industry. The *Hallcrest Report II,* a far-reaching overview of private security trends funded by the National Institute of Justice, identifies four factors driving this growth:

1. An increase in fear on the part of the public triggered by media coverage of crime.
2. The problem of crime in the workplace. According to the University of Florida's National Retail Security Survey, American retailers lose about $34 billion a year because of shoplifting and employee theft.
3. Budget cuts in states and municipalities that have forced reductions in the number of public police, thereby raising the demand for private ones.
4. A rising awareness of private security products (such as home burglar alarms) and services as cost-effective protective measures.[102]

Another reason for the industry's continued health is terrorism. Private security is responsible for protecting more than three-fourths of the nation's likely terrorist targets such as power plants, financial centers, dams, malls, oil refineries, and transportation hubs.

EthicsChallenge

Lisa, a sheriffs' deputy, sometimes moonlights as a private security guard for the Mardi Gras Saloon. Suppose that Lisa, while working at the bar, gets in an altercation with Perry, who is drunk. Perry hits Lisa on the head with a beer bottle. Would it be proper to charge Perry with assault upon a law enforcement officer, which carries a greater punishment than "regular" assault? Why or why not? What other ethical issues arise with regard to secondary policing?

CJ IN ACTION

Affirmative Action in Law Enforcement

Even before the killing of an unarmed black man by a white police officer in August 2014, racial tensions between the community and law enforcement were simmering in Ferguson, Missouri. African American residents would carpool for daily errands because they did not want to risk being harassed by the police. "That community doesn't like police," said Darren Wilson—the white officer who fatally shot Michael Brown—of Ferguson.[103] Part of the problem, it seems, is that two-thirds of Ferguson's population is African American, but only three of its fifty-three police officers are black. Should the Ferguson city government—also mostly white—force its police force to diversify through an affirmative action program? In this *CJ in Action* feature, we will attempt to answer two questions concerning such programs. First, do they work? Second, and just as important, are they fair?

Strategies for Diversity

For potential female police officers, the physical fitness test often poses the greatest barrier to hiring. In Pennsylvania, for example, all applicants to the state police department must pass a physical exam that includes sit-ups, push-ups, vertical jumps, a 300-meter run, and a 1.5-mile run. Between 2009 and 2012, approximately 98 percent of male applicants and 71 percent of female applicants were able to pass this test.[104] Some police departments, however, adjust their physical fitness tests to level the playing field. The New York State Police, for example, require male applicants under the age of thirty to run 1.5 miles in 10:47 minutes and female applicants under thirty to complete the distance in 13:35 minutes.[105] Thus, affirmative action programs represent an "active effort" to support the employment of women and members of minority groups in law enforcement.

The Case for Affirmative Action in Law Enforcement

- For most of the nation's history, women and minorities suffered from widespread discrimination in policing. Affirmative action remedies these past wrongs.

- The existence of a diverse police force improves community-police relations and makes it easier for all officers to do their jobs because it assures the community that the police will not act in a discriminatory manner.

- Affirmative action works. In Pittsburgh, the percentage of female police officers rose from 1 percent to 27 percent after an affirmative action program went into effect, but

it began to decline as soon as the program ended.[106] In Chicago, the African American share of new police hires rose from 10 percent to 40 percent in just two years after the implementation of a consent decree.[107]

The Case against Affirmative Action in Law Enforcement

- A stigma is attached to persons perceived to have benefited from affirmative action. "I don't want to be in a department where I was hired because of my skin color," said one African American applicant in Dayton, Ohio. "I want it because I earned it."[108]

- Public safety requires that all police officers be the most competent and skilled people available, regardless of their gender, race, or ethnicity.

- There are no "special skills" unique to women or minority law enforcement agents. Studies show that, for the most part, "cops act like cops."[109]

Your Opinion—Writing Assignment

The city of Springfield wants to test seventy-seven of its police officers for possible promotion to lieutenant. The exam—part written multiple choice and part oral—is specifically designed to avoid bias against minority candidates. Of the seventy-seven candidates, forty-three are white, nineteen are black, and fifteen are Hispanic. All of the top ten performers on the exam, immediately eligible for promotion, are white.

A city official argues that these results should be disregarded because black and Hispanic candidates have been unfairly excluded from the opportunity for promotion. What do you think of this argument? Would it be fair to the successful white candidates to invalidate the results? What would be in the best interests of the citizens of Springfield? Before responding, you can review our discussions in the sections of this chapter concerning:

- The reform era of policing ("A Short History of the American Police").

- Antidiscrimination law and affirmative action ("Women and Minorities in Policing Today").

- Gender, race, and ethnicity in law enforcement ("Women and Minorities in Policing Today").

Your answer should include at least three full paragraphs.

Summary

For more information on these concepts, look back to the Learning Objective icons throughout the chapter.

 List the four basic responsibilities of the police. (a) To enforce laws, (b) to provide services, (c) to prevent crime, and (d) to preserve the peace.

 Tell how the patronage system affected policing. During the political era of policing (1840–1930), bribes paid by citizens and business owners often went into the coffers of the local political party. This became known as the patronage system.

 Explain how intelligence-led policing works and how it benefits modern police departments. Intelligence-led policing uses past crime patterns to predict when and where crime will occur in the future. In theory, intelligence-led policing allows police administrators to use fewer resources because it removes costly and time-consuming "guesswork" from the law enforcement equation.

 Identify the differences between the police academy and field training as learning tools for recruits. The police academy is a controlled environment where police recruits learn the basics of policing from instructors in classrooms. In contrast, field training takes place in the "real world": the recruit goes on patrol with an experienced police officer.

 Explain how consent decrees make law enforcement agencies more diverse. A consent degree is part of the settlement of a discrimination lawsuit brought against a law enforcement agency. Generally, as part of this decree, the agency will agree to follow a court-sponsored plan to increase its hiring of women or members of minority groups.

 Describe the challenges facing women who choose law enforcement as a career. Many male officers believe that their female counterparts are not physically or mentally strong enough for police work, which puts pressure on women officers to continually prove themselves. Female officers must also deal with tokenism, or the stigma that they were hired only to fulfill diversity requirements, and sexual harassment in the form of unwanted advances or obscene remarks.

 Indicate some of the most important law enforcement agencies under the control of the Department of Homeland Security. (a) U.S. Customs and Border Protection, which polices the flow of goods and people across the United States' international borders and oversees the U.S. Border Patrol; (b) U.S. Immigration and Customs Enforcement, which investigates and enforces our nation's immigration and customs laws; and (c) the U.S. Secret Service, which protects high-ranking federal government officials and federal property.

 Identify the duties of the FBI. The FBI has jurisdiction to investigate hundreds of federal crimes, including white-collar crime, kidnapping, bank robbery, and civil rights violations. The FBI is also heavily involved in combating terrorism and drug-trafficking operations in the United States and around the world. Finally, the agency provides support to state and local law enforcement agencies through its crime laboratories and databases.

 Analyze the importance of private security today. In the United States, businesses and citizens spend billions of dollars each year on private security. Heightened fear of crime and increased crime in the workplace have fueled the growth in spending on private security.

Questions for Critical Analysis

1. Which of the four basic responsibilities of the police do you think is most important? Why?

2. Should law enforcement agencies have the same physical agility and fitness requirements for male and female applicants? Explain your answer.

3. Review the discussion of double marginality in this chapter. Why would members of a minority community think that police officers of the same race or ethnicity were "traitors"? What can police departments do to dispel this misperception?

4. One of the major differences between a local police chief and a sheriff is that the sheriff is elected, while the police chief is appointed. What are some of the possible problems with having a law enforcement official who, like any other politician, is responsible to voters? What are some of the possible benefits of this situation?

5. Twenty-nine states do not require any specific training for private security personnel. What are the arguments for and against requiring at least forty hours of training, as is the case in California and Florida?

Key Terms

affirmative action   148
coroner   153
discrimination   148
double marginality   151
Drug Enforcement Administration (DEA)   159
Federal Bureau of Investigation (FBI)   158
field training   147

infrastructure   157
intelligence-led policing   143
night watch system   138
patronage system   139
private security   161
probationary period   146
professional model   140
recruitment   145
secondary policing   161

sexual harassment   149
sheriff   152
U.S. Customs and Border Protection (CBP)   156
U.S. Immigration and Customs Enforcement (ICE)   157
U.S. Secret Service   157
visa   156

Notes

1. Kate Zernike, "Camden Turns Around with New Police Force," *New York Times* (September 1, 2014), A1.

2. Egon Bittner, *The Functions of Police in a Modern Society*, Public Health Service Publication No. 2059 (Chevy Chase, Md.: National Institute of Mental Health, 1970), 38–44.

3. Carl Klockars, "The Rhetoric of Community Policing," in *Community Policing: Rhetoric or Reality*, eds. Jack Greene and Stephen Mastrofski (New York: Praeger Publishers, 1991), 244.

4. Jack R. Greene and Carl B. Klockars, "What Do Police Do?" in *Thinking about Police*, 2d ed., ed. Carl B. Klockars and Stephen D. Mastrofski (New York: McGraw-Hill, 1991), 273–284.

5. John S. Dempsey and Linda S. Forst, *An Introduction to Policing*, 6th ed. (Clifton Park, N.Y.: Delmar Cengage Learning, 2012), 380–381.

6. Federal Bureau of Investigation, *Crime in the United States 2013* (Washington, D.C.: U.S. Department of Justice, 2014), at **www .fbi.gov/about-us/cjis/ucr/crime-in-the -u.s/2013/crime-in-the-u.s.-2013**, Table 29.

7. Reprinted in *The Police Chief* (January 1990), 18.

8. Jason Busch, "Shots Fired: When a Police Car Becomes an Ambulance," *Law Enforcement Technology* (September 2013), 8–10.

9. Darren DaRonco and Carli Brosseau, "Hundreds in Mental Crisis Call Police," *Arizona Daily Star* (April 14, 2013), C1.

10. Donna L. Leger, "Police Armed with Heroin Antidote," *USA Today* (January 31, 2014), 3A.

11. Jerome H. Skolnick, "Police: The New Professionals," *New Society* (September 5, 1986), 9–11.

12. Quoted in Nancy Ritter, ed., "LAPD Chief Bratton Speaks Out: What's Wrong with Criminal Justice Research—and How to Make It Right," *National Institute of Justice Journal* 257 (2007), 29.

13. Gary Kleck and J.C. Barnes, "Do More Police Lead to More Crime Deterrence?" *Crime & Delinquency* (August 2014), 716–738.

14. Klockars, *op. cit.*, 250.

15. James Q. Wilson, *Varieties of Police Behavior: The Management of Law and Order in Eight Communities* (Cambridge, Mass.: Harvard University Press, 1968).

16. James Q. Wilson and George L. Kelling, "Broken Windows," *Atlantic Monthly* (March 1982), 29.

17. M. K. Nalla and G. R. Newman, "Is White-Collar Crime Policing, Policing?" *Policing and Society* 3 (1994), 304.

18. Mitchell P. Roth, *Crime and Punishment: A History of the Criminal Justice System*, 2d ed. (Belmont, Calif.:: Wadsworth Cengage Learning, 2011), 65.

19. *Ibid.*

20. Peter K. Manning, *Police Work* (Cambridge, Mass.: MIT Press, 1977), 82.

21. Mark H. Moore and George L. Kelling, "'To Serve and Protect': Learning from Police History," *Public Interest* 70 (1983), 53.

22. Samuel Walker, *The Police in America: An Introduction* (New York: McGraw-Hill, 1983), 7.

23. Moore and Kelling, *op. cit.*, 54.

24. Mark H. Haller, "Chicago Cops, 1890–1925," in *Thinking about Police*, eds. Carl Klockars and Stephen Mastrofski (New York: McGraw-Hill, 1990), 90.

25. William J. Bopp and Donald O. Shultz, *A Short History of American Law Enforcement* (Springfield, Ill.: Charles C Thomas, 1977), 109–110.

26. Roger G. Dunham and Geoffrey P. Alpert, *Critical Issues in Policing: Contemporary Issues* (Prospect Heights, Ill.: Waveland Press, 1989).

27. Ken Peak and Emmanuel P. Barthe, "Community Policing and CompStat: Merged, or Mutually Exclusive?" *The Police Chief* (December 2009), 73.

28. *Ibid.*, 74.

29. Quoted in *ibid.*

30. Peter K. Manning, "The Police: Mandate, Strategies, and Appearances," in *Crime and Justice in American Society,* ed. Jack D. Douglas (Indianapolis, Ind.: Bobbs-Merrill, 1971), 149–163.

31. National Advisory Commission on Civil Disorder, *Report* (Washington, D.C.: U.S. Government Printing Office, 1968), 157–160.

32. 18 U.S.C.A. Sections 2510–2521.

33. Jayne Seagrave, "Defining Community Policing," *American Journal of Police* 1 (1996), 1–22.

34. Peak and Barthe, *op. cit.*, 78.

35. Jason Vaughn Lee, "Policing after 9/11: Community Policing in an Age of Homeland Security," *Police Quarterly* (November 2010), 351–353.

36. Quoted in Ronnie Garrett, "Predict and Serve," *Law Enforcement Technology* (January 2013), 19.

37. Scott Harris, "Product Feature: Predictive Policing Helps Law Enforcement 'See Around the Corners'," *The Police Chief* (October 2014), 44–45.

38. Charlie Beck and Colleen McCue, "Predictive Policing: What Can We Learn from Wal-Mart and Amazon about Fighting Crime in a Recession?" *The Police Chief* (November 2009), 19.

39. Gary LaFree, *Policing Terrorism* (Washington, D.C.: The Police Foundation, 2012), 1.

40. Federal Emergency Management Agency, "Information Bulletin No. 398: Fiscal Year 2014 DHS Preparedness Grant Programs Allocation Announcement" (July 25, 2014), at **www.fema.gov/media-library-data/14 06300071406-69f388acb175b5226 b828476d462a5ce/GPD%20IB%20 Allocation%20Announcement_Final.pdf.**

41. Adrian Fontecilla, "The Ascendance of Social Media as Evidence," *Criminal Justice* (Spring 2013), 55.

42. *How Are Innovations in Technology Transforming Policing?* (Washington, D.C.: Police Executive Research Forum, January 2012), 2.

43. Joseph Goldstein and J. David Goodman, "Frisking Tactic Yields to a Focus on Youth Gangs," *New York Times* (September 13, 2013), A1.

44. Quoted in Joel Rubin, "Stopping Crime before It Starts," *Los Angeles Times* (August 21, 2010), A17.

45. James H. Chenoweth, "Situational Tests: A New Attempt at Assessing Police Candidates," *Journal of Criminal Law, Criminology and Police Science* 52 (1961), 232.

46. Yossef S. Ben-Porath et al., "Assessing the Psychological Suitability of Candidates for Law Enforcement Positions," *The Police Chief* (August 2011), 64-70.

47. D. P. Hinkle, "College Degree: An Impractical Prerequisite for Police Work," *Law and Order* (July 1991), 105.

48. Quoted in *How Are Innovations in Technology Transforming Policing?, op. cit.*, 10.

49. Bureau of Justice Statistics, *Local Police Departments, 2007* (Washington, D.C.: U.S. Department of Justice, December 2010), Table 5, page 11.

50. Kevin Johnson, "Police Agencies Find It Hard to Require Degrees," *USA Today* (September 18, 2006), 3A.

51. Hinkle, *op. cit.*

52. *Local Police Departments, 2007, op. cit.*, 12.

53. Bureau of Justice Statistics, *State and Local Law Enforcement Training Academies, 2006* (Washington, D.C.: U.S. Department of Justice, February 2009), 7.

54. National Advisory Commission on Civil Disorder, *Report* (Washington, D.C.: U.S. Government Printing Office, 1968), Chapter 11.

55. *Griggs v. Duke Power Co., 401 U.S. 424 (1971); and Abermarle Paper Co. v. Moody,* 422 U.S. 405 (1975).

56. Gene L. Scaramella, Steven M. Cox, and William P. McCamey, *Introduction to Policing* (Thousand Oaks, Calif.: Sage Publications, 2011), 30–31.

57. National Center for Women and Policing, "Under Scrutiny: The Effect of Consent Decrees on the Representation of Women in Sworn Law Enforcement, Spring 2003," at **www.womenandpolicing.org/pdf/Full consentdecreestudy.pdf.**

58. Lucas Sullivan, "Black Applicants Protest Lowering Scores," *Dayton (OH) Daily News* (March 6, 2011), A13.

59. "Diversity of Police Departments in New York," *Democrat & Chronicle* (Rochester, N.Y.) (2014), at **rocdocs.com/database /diversity-police-departments-new-york.**

60. Shaila Dewan, "Mostly White Forces in Mostly Black Towns: Police Struggle with Racial Diversity," *New York Times* (September 10, 2014), A1.

61. *Crime in the United States 2013, op. cit.*, Table 74.

62. Marisa Silvestri, "Doing Time: Becoming a Police Leader," *International Journal of Police Science & Managements* (November 2005), 266–281.

63. Dorothy Schulz, quoted in Talk of the Nation, "What Changes as Women Rise through Law Enforcement's Ranks," *NPR* (April 2, 2013), at **www.npr.org/2013/04/02/176037643 /what-changes-as-women-rise-through -law-enforcements-ranks.**

64. Scaramella, Cox, and McCamey, *op. cit.*, 318.

65. Kenneth J. Novak, Robert A. Brown, and James Frank, *Women on Patrol: An Analysis of Differences in Officer Arrest Behavior* (Bingley, United Kingdom: Emerald Group Publishing Ltd., 2006), 21–27.

66. Quoted in Robin N. Haarr and Merry Morash, "The Effect of Rank on Police Women Coping with Discrimination and Harassment," *Police Quarterly* (December 2013), 403.

67. Quoted in Talk of the Nation, *op. cit.*

68. Katherine Stuart van Wormer and Clemens Bartollas, *Women and the Criminal Justice System,* 3d ed. (Upper Saddle River, N.J.: Pearson Education, 2011), 318–319.

69. Quoted in Teresa Lynn Wertsch, "Walking the Thin Blue Line: Policewomen and Tokenism Today," *Women and Criminal Justice* (1998), 35–36.

70. Quoted in Kimberly A. Lonsway, Rebecca Paynich, and Jennifer N. Hall, "Sexual Harassment in Law Enforcement: Incidence, Impact, and Perception," *Police Quarterly* (June 2013), 196.

71. The Cato Institute, "National Police Misconduct Statistics and Reporting Project: 2010 Quarterly Q3 Report," at **www .policemisconduct.net/statistics /2010-quarterly-q3-report.**

72. Lonsway, Paynich, and Hall, *op. cit.*, 179–180.

73. *Local Police Departments, 2007, op. cit.*,14.

74. David Alan Sklansky, "Not Your Father's Police Department: Making Sense of the New Demographics of Law Enforcement," *Journal of Criminal Law and Criminology* (Spring 2006), 1209–1243.

75. Peter C. Moskos, "Two Shades of Blue: Black and White in the Blue Brotherhood," *Law Enforcement Executive Forum* (2008), 57.

76. Scaramella, Cox, and McCamey, *op. cit.*, 324.

77. Dempsey and Forst, *op. cit.*, 183.

78. *Wygant v. Jackson Board of Education,* 476 U.S. 314 (1986).

79. Bureau of Justice Statistics, *Census of State and Local Law Enforcement Agencies, 2008* (Washington, D.C.: U.S. Department of Justice, July 2011), 1; and Bureau of Justice Statistics, *Federal Law Enforcement Officers, 2008* (Washington, D.C.: U.S. Department of Justice, June 2012), 1.

80. *Census of State and Local Law Enforcement Agencies, 2008, op. cit.*, 3.

81. *Local Police Departments, 2007, op. cit.*, Table 3, page 9.

82. *Census of State and Local Law Enforcement Agencies, 2008, op. cit.*, 4.

83. *Ibid.*, Table 4, page 5.

84. Bureau of Justice Statistics, *Sheriffs' Offices, 2003* (Washington, D.C.: U.S. Department of Justice, May 2006), 15–18.

85. Bureau of Justice Statistics, *Sheriffs' Departments, 1997* (Washington, D.C.: U.S. Department of Justice, February 2000), 14.

86. Doris Meissner et al., *Immigration Enforcement in the United States: The Rise of a Formidable Machinery* (Washington, D.C.: Migration Policy Institute, January 2013), 2.

87. Sara Murray, "Many in U.S. Illegally Overstayed Their Visas," *Wall Street Journal* (April 7, 2013), A7.

88. United States Border Patrol, "Nationwide Illegal Alien Apprehensions Fiscal Years 1925–2014," at **www.cbp.gov/sites/default /files/documents/BP%20Total%20 Apps%20FY1925-FY2014_0.pdf.**

89. Julia Preston, "Border Patrol Seeks to Add Digital Eyes to Its Ranks," *New York Times* (March 22, 2014), A11.

90. U.S. Immigration and Customs Enforcement, "FY 2014 ICE Immigration Removals," at **www.ice.gov/removal-statistics**.

91. Quoted in Ginger Thompson and Sarah Cohen, "More Deportations Follow Minor Crimes, Records Show," *New York Times* (April 6, 2014), A1.

92. Jeh Charles Johnson, "Memorandum: Secure Communities" (November 20, 2014), at **www.dhs.gov/sites/default/files/publications/14_1120_memo_secure_communities.pdf**.

93. John Hudson, "FBI Drops Law Enforcement as 'Primary' Mission," *Foreign Policy* (January 5, 2014), at **foreignpolicy.com/2014/01/05/fbi-drops-law-enforcement-as-primary-mission**.

94. Charlie Bush, "Enhancing Criminal Justice and Homeland Security Capabilities: N-DEx Fulfilling Its Vision to Support Law Enforcement," *The Police Chief* (February 2013), 34–37.

95. Uniform Controlled Substances Act (1994), Section 201(h).

96. United States Marshals Service, "Fact Sheet," at **www.justice.gov/marshals/duties/fact sheets/general-1209.html**.

97. *The United States Security Industry* (Alexandria, Va.: ASIS International, 2013), 1.

98. John B. Owens, "Westec Story: Gated Communities and the Fourth Amendment," *American Criminal Law Review* (Spring 1997), 1138.

99. *Local Policy Departments, 2007, op. cit.*, Table 8, page 13.

100. Seattle Police Department, Seattle Police Manual, "5.120—Secondary Employment" (Updated March 19, 2014), at **www.seattle.gov/police/publications/manual/05_120_Secondary_Employment.html**.

101. Michael J. Palmiotto, *Policing: Concepts, Strategies and Current Issues in American Police Forces*, 3d ed. (San Bernadino, Calif.: CreateSpace Independent, 2014), 76–77.

102. William C. Cunningham, John J. Strauchs, and Clifford W. Van Meter, *The Hallcrest Report II: Private Security Trends, 1970 to 2000* (Boston: Butterworth-Heinemann, 1990), 236.

103. Quoted in Manny Fernandez, "Police Face a Long and Complex Task to Mend Distrust Deepened by Killings," *New York Times* (December 8, 2014), A13.

104. Marc Levy, "U.S. Sues Pa. State Police, Saying Physical Fitness Test Discriminates against Women," *Associated Press* (July 30, 2014).

105. New York State Police Recruitment Center, "Physical Fitness Levels," at **nytrooper.com/fitness_levels.cfm**.

106. Kim Lonsway et al., "Under Scrutiny: The Effect of Consent Decrees on the Representation of Women in Sworn Law Enforcement," National Center for Women and Policing (2003), at **www.womenandpolicing.org/pdf/Fullconsentdecreestudy.pdf**.

107. Justin McCrary, "The Effect of Court-Ordered Hiring Quotas on the Composition and Quality of Police," National Bureau of Economic Research (2006), at **www.nber.org/papers/w12368**.

108. Quoted in Sullivan, *op. cit.*

109. Sklansky, *op. cit.*, 1224–1228.

6

Problems and Solutions

in Modern Policing

Chapter Outline		Corresponding Learning Objectives
The Role of Discretion in Policing	**1**	Explain why police officers are allowed discretionary powers.
Police Organization and Field Operations	**2**	List the three primary purposes of police patrol.
	3	Indicate some investigation strategies that are considered aggressive.
	4	Describe how forensic experts use DNA fingerprinting to solve crimes.
Police Strategies: What Works	**5**	Explain why differential response strategies enable police departments to respond more efficiently to 911 calls.
	6	Explain community policing and its contribution to the concept of problem-oriented policing.
"Us versus Them": Issues in Modern Policing	**7**	Determine when police officers are justified in using deadly force.
Police Misconduct and Ethics	**8**	Identify the three consent decree requirements commonly made of local police departments that have exhibited patterns of civil rights violations.
	9	Explain what an ethical dilemma is and name four categories of ethical dilemmas that a police officer typically may face.

To target your study and review, look for these numbered Learning Objective icons throughout the chapter.

the **Camera's Eye**

the video starts with Albuquerque, New Mexico, police officer Matthew Fisher in his squad car, his rifle drawn. "Did you guys see him go into that . . .? Is he up on that street?" Fisher asks his colleagues about John Okeefe, a convicted felon with narcotics and armed robbery charges dating back fifteen years. The video then shows Fisher jumping out of his car and running. "Show me your hands!" Fisher yells several times before several faint pops of gunfire are audible. Fisher responds by shooting his rifle a total of eight times before calling for an ambulance. "He [expletive] shot at us," Fisher says. "I think he shot at us."

The January 2015 recording of this incident, in which Okeefe was killed, came from a small video camera that Fisher was wearing on his lapel. Albuquerque is one of dozens of police departments—including those in large cities such as Houston, New York, and Los Angeles—that require its officers to wear such video cameras on their uniforms. At a time of often tense community-police relations, these devices seem to promise much-needed transparency and accountability for American law enforcement. "When you put a camera on a police officer, they tend to behave a little better," says Rialto, California, police chief William Farrar. "And if a citizen knows the officer is wearing a camera, chances are the citizen will behave a little better."

As documents of "the truth," police videos can be somewhat ambiguous. For example, the footage described above does not actually show Okeefe fleeing or shooting at Officer Fisher. One day before that incident, however, prosecutors did decide to pursue murder charges against two other Albuquerque police officers whose killing of a homeless man was captured by a helmet camera. "Everyone here agrees that that the officer-worn video made the difference," said one observer of that decision. "Now, the public will get to see the evidence and judge for [themselves.]"

▲ A Washington, D.C., police officer models one of her department's new body-worn cameras, designed to record officer interactions with the public.

Win McNamee/Getty Images

1. Should evidence of police shootings taken by officer-worn video cameras be made available to the public? Why or why not?

2. In the first year after Rialto, California, police officers began using body-worn cameras, citizen complaints against officers decreased by 88 percent. How might the cameras help explain this statistic?

3. In most cases, police officers control when their body-worn cameras start recording. Under what circumstances should an officer be required to turn on her or his camera? Why might any such regulations be difficult to enforce? Explain your answers.

The Role of Discretion in Policing

One of the ironies of law enforcement is that patrol officers—often the lowest-paid members of an agency with the least amount of authority—have the greatest amount of discretionary power. Part of the explanation for this is practical. Patrol officers spend most of the day on the streets, beyond the control of their supervisors. Usually, only two people are present when a patrol officer must make a decision: the officer and the possible wrongdoer. In most cases, the law enforcement officer has a great deal of freedom to take the action that he or she feels the situation requires.

Without this freedom, many police officers might find their duties unrewarding. Indeed, numerous studies have shown that higher levels of officer autonomy are reflected in higher levels of officer job satisfaction.[1] At the same time, discretion can lead to second-guessing on the part of the public, an officer's superiors, and the officer him- or herself. Certainly, the Albuquerque police officers just discussed would have preferred not to have shot and killed the suspects in the videotaped incidents, regardless of the consequences. Their decisions were made in a split second, under stressful circumstances, and without the benefit of hindsight.

Justification for Police Discretion

Despite the possibility of mistakes, courts generally have upheld the patrol officer's freedom to decide "what law to enforce, how much to enforce it, against whom, and on what occasions."[2] This judicial support of police discretion is based on the following factors:

LEARNING OBJECTIVE 1 Explain why police officers are allowed discretionary powers.

- Police officers are considered trustworthy and are therefore assumed to make honest decisions, regardless of contradictory testimony by a suspect.
- Experience and training give officers the ability to determine whether certain activity poses a threat to society, and to take any reasonable action necessary to investigate or prevent such activity.
- Due to the nature of their jobs, police officers are extremely knowledgeable in human, and, by extension, criminal, behavior.
- Police officers may find themselves in danger of personal, physical harm and must be allowed to take reasonable and necessary steps to protect themselves.[3]

Dr. Anthony J. Pinizzotto, a psychologist with the Federal Bureau of Investigation (FBI), and Charles E. Miller, an instructor in the bureau's Criminal Justice Information Services Division, take the justification for discretion one step further. These two experts argue that many police officers have a "sixth sense" that helps them handle on-the-job challenges. Pinizzotto and Miller believe that although "intuitive policing" is often difficult to explain to those outside law enforcement, it is a crucial part of policing and should not be discouraged by civilian administrators.[4]

Factors of Police Discretion

There is no doubt that subjective factors influence police discretion. The officer's beliefs, values, personality, and background all enter into his or her decisions. To a large extent, however, a law enforcement agent's actions are determined by the rules of policing set down in the U.S. Constitution and enforced by the courts. These rules are of paramount importance and will be discussed in great detail in Chapter 7.

Elements of Discretion Assuming that most police officers stay on the right side of the Constitution in most instances, four other factors generally enter the discretion equation in any particular situation. First, and most important, is the nature of the criminal act. The less serious a crime, the more likely a police officer is to ignore it. A person driving 60 miles per hour in a 55-miles-per-hour zone, for example, is much less likely to be ticketed than someone doing 80 miles per hour. A second element often considered is the attitude of the wrongdoer toward the officer. A motorist who is belligerent toward a highway patrol officer is much more likely to be ticketed than one who is contrite and apologetic. Third, the relationship between the victim and the offender can influence the outcome. If the parties are in a familial or other close relationship, police officers may see the incident as a personal matter and be hesitant to make an arrest.

Limiting Police Discretion The fourth factor of the discretion equation is departmental policy.[5] A **policy** is a set of guiding principles that law enforcement agents must adhere to in stated situations. If a police administrator decides that all motorists who exceed the speed limit by 10 miles per hour will be ticketed, that policy will certainly influence the patrol officer's decisions. Policies must be flexible enough to allow for officer discretion, but at the same time be specific enough to provide the officer with a clear sense of her or his duties and obligations.

In Chapter 3, we discussed *mandatory arrest policies* that instruct police officers to arrest a suspect who has likely committed an act of domestic violence. In addition, nearly every local police department in the United States has a policy limiting their officers' discretion to engage in high-speed automobile chases of suspects, which can place other drivers and pedestrians in grave danger.[6] The success of such policies can be seen in the results from Los Angeles, which features more high-speed chases than any other city in the country by a wide margin. In 2003, Los Angeles police officers were ordered to conduct dangerous pursuits only if the fleeing driver was suspected of a serious crime. Within a year, the number of high-speed pursuits decreased by 62 percent, and injuries to third parties dropped by 58 percent.[7]

The New York Police Department's policy prohibiting chokeholds became a source of controversy when, in July 2014, cellphone video surfaced of an officer using the technique against Eric Garner. As we will see later in the chapter, Garner died as a result of the encounter. (See the feature *CJ Policy—Your Take*, which serves as an introduction to the crucial issue of use of force in law enforcement.)

Discretion and Body-Worn Cameras Policies regarding the use of body-worn police cameras vary, as law enforcement experts have not yet reached a consensus on how best to implement this new technology. Many departments have no body-worn camera policy whatsoever, allowing the devices to be employed at the discretion of the officer.[8] This lack of standards can be problematic, as it leaves the police open to charges of selectively recording only those incidents free of any officer wrongdoing.

One civil liberties expert believes that officers should be required to turn the cameras on during all traffic stops and arrests, as these often are the situations in which use of force can occur.[9] The Albuquerque Police Department goes even further. Its policy orders officers to record almost all interactions with the public. In December 2014, Albuquerque officials dismissed an officer for insubordination because he consistently failed to turn on his lapel recording device as required. Eight months earlier, the officer's camera was off when he fatally shot a nineteen-year-old woman suspected of stealing a truck.[10]

Police Organization and Field Operations

Albuquerque police administrators placed Officer Matthew Fisher, whose fatal shooting of suspect John Okeefe was discussed in the opening of this chapter, on *administrative leave* pending an investigation into the incident. In other words, Fisher was temporarily relieved of his duties, with pay. This step does not imply that Fisher was suspected of any wrongdoing. Most law enforcement agencies react similarly when a firearm is fired in the line of duty, both to allow for a full investigation of the event and to give the officer a chance to recover from what can be a traumatic experience.

Administrative leave is a *bureaucratic* response to an officer-involved shooting. In a **bureaucracy**, formal rules govern an individual's actions and relationships with co-employees. The ultimate goal of any bureaucracy is to reach its maximum efficiency—in the case of a police department, to provide the best service for the community within the confines of its limited resources such as staff and budget. Although some police departments are experimenting with alternative structures based on a partnership between management and the officers in the field, most continue to rely on the hierarchical structure described below.

The Structure of the Police Department

Each police department is organized according to its environment: the size of its jurisdiction, the type of crimes it must deal with, and the demographics of the population it must police. The Metropolitan Police Department of Washington, D.C., operates an Asian Liaison Unit that works within that city's Asian community, while the Evansville, Indiana, Police Department has set up a "No Meth" task force. Geographic location also influences police organization. The San Diego Police Department has a Harbor Patrol Unit, which would be unproductive in Grand Forks, North Dakota—as would be the Grand Forks Police Department's snowmobile patrol in Southern California.

Chain of Command Whatever the size or location of a police department, it needs a clear rank structure and strict accountability to function properly. One of the goals of the police reformers, especially beginning in the 1950s, was to lessen the corrupting influence of politicians. The result was a move toward a militaristic organization of police.[11] As you can see in Figure 6.1, a typical police department is based on a "top-down" chain of command that leads from the police chief down to detectives and patrol officers. In this formalized structure, all persons are aware of their place in the chain and of their duties and responsibilities within the organization.

Delegation of authority is a critical component of the chain of command, especially in larger departments. The chief of police delegates authority to division chiefs, who delegate authority to commanders, and on down through the organization. This structure creates a situation in which nearly every member of a police department is directly accountable to a superior. As was the original goal of police reformers, these links encourage discipline and control and lessen the possibility that any individual police employee will have the unsupervised freedom to abuse her or his position.[12] Furthermore, experts suggest that no single supervisor should be responsible for too many employees. The ideal number of subordinates for a police sergeant, for example, is eight to ten patrol officers. This number is often referred to as the *span of control*. If the span of control rises above fifteen, then it is assumed that the superior officer will not be able to effectively manage his or her team.[13]

Bureaucracy A hierarchically structured administrative organization that carries out specific functions.

Delegation of Authority The principles of command on which most police departments are based, in which personnel take orders from and are responsible to those in positions of power directly above them.

FIGURE 6.1 A Typical Police Department Chain of Command

Most American police departments follow this model of the chain of command, though smaller departments with fewer employees often eliminate several of these categories.

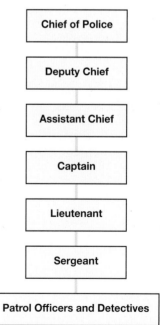

Chief of Police

Deputy Chief

Assistant Chief

Captain

Lieutenant

Sergeant

Patrol Officers and Detectives

▲ A lieutenant (in the white shirt) gives instructions to two sergeants. On his left, a patrol officer appears to be awaiting instructions. **How do the delegation of authority and the chain of command contribute to police efficiency?** Elyse Rieder/ScienceSource

Organizing by Area and Time In most metropolitan areas, police responsibilities are divided according to zones known as *beats* and *precincts*. A beat is the smallest stretch that a police officer or a group of police officers regularly patrol. A precinct—also known as a *district* or a *station*—is a collection of beats. A precinct commander, or captain, is held responsible by his or her superiors at police headquarters for the performance of the officers in that particular precinct.[14]

Police administrators must also organize their personnel by time. Most departments separate each twenty-four-hour day into three eight-hour *shifts,* also called *tours* or *platoons.* The night shift generally lasts from midnight to 8 A.M., the day shift from 8 A.M. to 4 P.M., and the evening shift from 4 P.M. to midnight. Officers either vary their hours by, say, working days one month and nights the next, or they have fixed tours in which they consistently take day, night, or evening shifts.[15] A number of police departments have implemented compressed workweeks, in which officers work longer shifts (ten or twelve hours) and fewer days. Such schedules are believed to improve the officers' quality of life by providing more substantial blocks of time off the job to recover from the stresses of police work.[16]

Law Enforcement in the Field To a large extent, the main goal of any police department is the most efficient organization of its *field services.* Also known as "operations" or "line services," field services include patrol activities, investigations, and special operations. According to Henry M. Wrobleski and Karen M. Hess, most police departments are "generalists." Thus, police officers are assigned to general areas and perform all field service functions within the boundaries of their beats. Larger departments may be more specialized, with personnel assigned to specific types of crime, such as illegal drugs or white-collar crime, rather than geographic locations. Smaller departments, which make up the bulk of local law enforcement agencies, rely almost exclusively on general patrol.[17]

Police on Patrol: The Backbone of the Department

Every police department has a patrol unit, and patrol is usually the largest division in the department. More than two-thirds of the sworn officers, or those officers authorized to make arrests and use force, in local police departments in the United States have patrol duties.[18]

"Life on the street" is not easy. Patrol officers must be able to handle any number of difficult situations, and experience is often the best and, despite training programs, the only teacher. As one patrol officer commented:

> You never stop learning. You never get your street degree. The person who says . . . they've learned it all is the person that's going to wind up dead or in a very compromising position. They've closed their minds.[19]

It may take a patrol officer years to learn when a gang is "false flagging" (trying to trick rival gang members into the open) or what to look for in a suspect's eyes to sense if he or she is concealing a weapon. This learning process is the backdrop to a number of different general functions that a patrol officer must perform on a daily basis.

The Purpose of Patrol In general, patrol officers do not spend most of their shifts chasing, catching, and handcuffing suspected criminals. The vast majority of patrol shifts are completed without a single arrest.[20] Officers spend a great deal of time meeting with other officers, completing paperwork, and patrolling with the goal of preventing crime in general rather than focusing on any specific crime or criminal activity.

As police accountability expert Samuel Walker has noted, the basic purposes of the police patrol have changed very little since 1829, when Sir Robert Peel founded the modern police department. These purposes include:

1. The deterrence of crime by maintaining a visible police presence.
2. The maintenance of public order and a sense of security in the community.
3. The twenty-four-hour provision of services that are not crime related.[21]

The first two goals—deterring crime and keeping order—are generally accepted as legitimate police functions. The third, however, has been more controversial.

Community Concerns As noted in Chapter 5, the community era saw a resurgence of the patrol officer as a provider of community services, many of which have little to do with crime. The extent to which noncrime incidents dominate patrol officers' time is evident in the Police Services Study, a survey of 26,000 calls to police in sixty different neighborhoods. The study found that only one out of every five calls involved the report of criminal activity.[22] (See Figure 6.2 for the results of another survey of crime calls.)

There is some debate over whether community services should be allowed to dominate patrol officers' duties. The question, however, remains: If the police do not handle these problems, who will? Few cities have the financial resources to hire public servants to deal specifically with, for example, finding shelter for homeless persons. Furthermore, the police are on call twenty-four hours a day, seven days a week, making them uniquely accessible to citizen needs.

Law Enforcement and Mental Illness Of particular concern is the frequency with which police officers on patrol find themselves acting as psychiatric social workers. According to various studies, between 7 percent and 10 percent of all police-public contacts involve people with mental illness.[23] If law enforcement officers are not properly trained or otherwise prepared for these encounters, the results can be disastrous. By one estimate, at least half of the people justifiably killed by the police each year are mentally ill.[24]

A number of law enforcement agencies have set up *crisis intervention teams,* designed to improve this situation. Although the programs vary, many of them include:

1. Specialized training for law enforcement officers in managing encounters with mentally ill members of the community,
2. Access to mental health professionals who are "on call" to respond to police requests for assistance, and

▼ Given that most patrol shifts end without an officer making a single arrest, what activities take up most of a patrol officer's time?
Rod Lamkey Jr/AFP/Getty Images

FIGURE 6.2 Calls for Service

Over a period of two years, the Project on Policing Neighborhoods gathered information on calls for service in Indianapolis, Indiana, and St. Petersburg, Florida. As you can see, the largest portion of these calls involved disputes where no violence or threat of violence existed. Be aware also that nearly two-thirds of the nonviolent dispute calls and nearly half of the assault calls answered by police dealt with domestic confrontations.

Description of Violation	Percentage of Total Calls
NONSERIOUS CRIME CALLS	
Nonviolent disputes	42
Public disorder (examples: drunk, disorderly, begging, prostitution)	22
Assistance (examples: missing persons, traffic accident, damaged property)	10
Minor violations (examples: shoplifting, trespassing, traffic/parking offense, refusal to pay)	4
SERIOUS CRIME CALLS	
Assaults (examples: using violence against a person, kidnapping, child abuse)	26
Serious theft (examples: motor vehicle theft, burglary, purse snatching)	5
General disorder (examples: illicit drugs, fleeing police, leaving the scene of an accident)	2

Source adapted from: Stephen D. Mastrofski, Jeffrey B. Snipes, Roger B. Parks, and Christopher D. Maxwell, "The Helping Hand of the Law: Police Control of Citizens on Request," *Criminology* 38 (May 2000), Table 5, page 328.

3. Drop-off locations, such as hospitals or mobile crisis vehicles, that provide mental health services beyond the expertise of law enforcement agencies.[25]

On the positive side, it appears that the crisis intervention model is favorably viewed by police officers and can result in reduced arrest rates of the mentally ill.[26] At the same time, such programs may be beyond the limited financial and personnel resources of small law enforcement agencies in rural areas.

Patrol Activities To recap, the purposes of police patrols are to prevent and deter crime and also to provide social services. How can the police best accomplish these goals? Of course, each department has its own methods and strategies, but William Gay, Theodore Schell, and Stephen Schack are able to divide routine patrol activity into four general categories:[27]

1. *Preventive patrol.* By maintaining a presence in a community, either in a car or on foot, patrol officers attempt to prevent crime from occurring. This strategy, which O. W. Wilson called "omnipresence," was a cornerstone of early policing philosophy and still takes up roughly 40 percent of patrol time.
2. *Calls for service.* Patrol officers spend nearly a quarter of their time responding to 911 calls for emergency service or other citizen problems and complaints.
3. *Administrative duties.* Paperwork takes up nearly 20 percent of patrol time. In Albuquerque, officers now spend 15 percent to 20 percent of their shifts saving and logging footage from their lapel cameras.[28]
4. *Officer-initiated activities.* Incidents in which the patrol officer initiates contact with citizens, such as stopping motorists and pedestrians and questioning them, account for 15 percent of patrol time.

The category estimates made by Gay, Schell, and Schack are not universally accepted. Professor of law enforcement Gary W. Cordner argues that administrative duties account for the largest percentage of patrol officers' time. According to Cordner, when officers are not consumed with paperwork and meetings, they are either answering calls for service (which takes up 67 percent of the officers' time on the street) or initiating activities themselves (the remaining 33 percent).[29]

Detective Investigations

Investigation is the second main function of police, along with patrol. Whereas patrol is primarily preventive, investigation is reactive. After a crime has been committed and the patrol officer has gathered the preliminary information from the crime scene, the responsibility of finding "who dunnit" is delegated to the investigator, generally known as the **detective.** The most common way for someone to become a detective is to be promoted from patrol officer. Detectives have not been the focus of nearly as much reform attention as their patrol counterparts, mainly because the scope of the detective's job is limited to law enforcement, with less emphasis given to social services or order maintenance.

The detective's job is not quite as glamorous as it is sometimes portrayed by the media. Detectives spend much of their time investigating common crimes such as burglaries and are more likely to be tracking down stolen property than a murderer. They must also prepare cases for trial, which involves a great deal of time-consuming paperwork. Furthermore, a landmark RAND Corporation study estimated that more than 97 percent of cases that are "solved" can be attributed to a patrol officer making an arrest at the scene, witnesses or victims identifying the perpetrator, or detectives undertaking routine investigative procedures that could easily be performed by clerical personnel.[30]

"There is no Sherlock Holmes," said one investigator. "The good detective on the street is the one who knows all the weasels and one of the weasels will tell him who did it."[31] Citizen tips can also be helpful. For example, for a month in the spring of 2014 an unidentified sniper terrorized residents of Kansas City, Missouri. Despite the efforts of a number of local police departments, the FBI, and the Bureau of Alcohol, Tobacco, and Firearms, the suspect was identified only after a suspicious citizen wrote down his license plate number.

Aggressive Investigation Strategies

Detective bureaus also have the option of implementing aggressive strategies. For example, if detectives suspect that a person was involved in the robbery of a Mercedes-Benz parts warehouse, one of them might pose as a "fence"—or purchaser of stolen goods. In what is known as a "sting" operation, the suspect is deceived into thinking that the detective (fence) wants to buy stolen car parts. After the transaction takes place, the suspect can be arrested.

Undercover Operations Perhaps the most dangerous and controversial operation a law enforcement agent can undertake is to go *undercover,* or to assume a false identity in order to obtain information concerning illegal activities. Though each department has its own guidelines on when undercover operations are necessary, all that is generally required is the suspicion that illegal activity is taking place. Today, undercover officers are commonly used to infiltrate large-scale narcotics operations or those run by organized crime.

In some situations, a detective bureau may not want to take the risk of exposing an officer to undercover work or may believe that an outsider cannot infiltrate an

LEARNING **3** OBJECTIVE Indicate some investigation strategies that are considered aggressive.

Detective The primary police investigator of crimes.

▲ For more than a decade, the New York Police Department (NYPD) has been persuading Muslims in the city's jails to act as informants concerning possible terrorist activity in their communities. **What is your opinion of this strategy? Why do you think the NYPD has come under criticism, such as in the demonstration shown here, for these kinds of tactics?** Timothy Clary/AFP/Getty Images

organized crime network. When the police need access and information, they have the option of turning to a **confidential informant (CI)**. A CI is a person who is involved in criminal activity and gives information about that activity and those who engage in it to the police. As many as 80 percent of all illegal drug cases in the United States involve confidential informants. "They can get us into places we can't go," says one police administrator. "Without them, narcotics cases would practically cease to function."[32]

Preventive Policing and Domestic Terrorism Aggressive investigative strategies also play a crucial role in the federal government's efforts to combat domestic terrorism. Because would-be terrorists often need help to procure the weaponry necessary for their schemes, they are natural targets for well-placed informants and undercover agents. According to the Center on Law and Security at New York University, about two-thirds of the federal government's major terrorism prosecutions have relied on evidence provided by informants.[33]

The recent arrest of Christopher Cornell provides an example of *preventive policing*, a popular counterterrorism strategy employed by the federal government. On January 14, 2015, FBI agents arrested Cornell in the parking lot of a Cincinnati gun shop where he had just purchased two semiautomatic rifles and six hundred rounds of ammunition. About a month earlier, Cornell had met with an FBI informant and discussed plans to attack "enemies" working in the U.S. Capitol Building.[34]

With preventive policing, then, the goal is not to solve the crime after it has happened. Rather, the goal is to prevent the crime from happening in the first place. Inevitably, such tactics raise the issue of entrapment. As you learned in Chapter 4, entrapment is a possible defense for criminal behavior when a government agent plants the idea of committing a crime in the defendant's mind. In the Cornell case, the suspect's father claimed that his son could not have afforded to purchase the weaponry he was caught with, and that the funds to do so must have been provided by the FBI.[35] Although the entrapment defense has been raised often in domestic terrorism cases involving informants and undercover agents, it has yet to succeed. The government has been uniformly successful in proving that these defendants were predisposed to commit the crime regardless of any outside influence.

Clearance Rates and Cold Cases

The ultimate goal of all law enforcement activity is to *clear* a crime, or secure the arrest and prosecution of the offender. Even a cursory glance at **clearance rates,** which show the percentage of reported crimes that have been cleared, reveals that investigations succeed only part of the time. In 2013, just 64 percent of homicides and 46 percent of total violent crimes were solved, while police cleared only 20 percent of property crimes.[36] For the most part, the different clearance rates for different crimes reflect the resources that

Confidential Informant (CI)
A human source for police who provides information concerning illegal activity in which he or she is involved.

Clearance Rate A comparison of the number of crimes cleared by arrest and prosecution with the number of crimes reported during any given time period.

a law enforcement agency expends on each type of crime. The police generally investigate a murder or a rape more vigorously than the theft of an automobile or a computer.

As a result of low clearance rates, police departments are saddled with an increasing number of **cold cases,** or criminal investigations that are not cleared after a certain amount of time. (The length of time before a case becomes "cold" varies from department to department. In general, a cold case must be "somewhat old" but not "so old that there can be no hope of ever solving it."[37]) Even using the various technologies we will explore in the next section, cold case investigations rarely succeed. A RAND study found that only about one in twenty cold cases results in an arrest, and only about one in a hundred results in a conviction.[38]

Forensic Investigations and DNA

Although the crime scene typically offers a wealth of evidence, some of it is incomprehensible to a patrol officer or detective without assistance. For that aid, law enforcement officers rely on experts in **forensics,** or the practice of using science and technology to investigate crimes. Forensic experts apply their knowledge to items found at the crime scene to determine crucial facts such as:

- The cause of death or injury.
- The time of death or injury.
- The type of weapon or weapons used.
- The identity of the crime victim, if that information is unavailable.
- The identity of the offender (in the best-case scenario).[39]

To assist forensic experts, many police departments operate or are affiliated with approximately 400 publicly funded crime laboratories in the United States. As we noted in the previous chapter, the FBI also offers the services of its crime lab to agencies with limited resources. The FBI's aid in this area is crucial, given that the nation's crime labs are burdened with a crippling backlog of hundreds of thousands of requests for forensic services.[40]

Crime Scene Forensics The first law enforcement agent to reach a crime scene has the important task of protecting any **trace evidence** from contamination. Trace evidence is generally very small—often invisible to the naked human eye—and often requires technological aid for detection. Hairs, fibers, blood, fingerprints, broken glass, and footprints are all examples of trace evidence. A study released by the National Institute of Justice confirmed that when police are able to link such evidence to a suspect, the likelihood of a conviction rises dramatically.[41]

Police will also search a crime scene for bullets and spent cartridge casings. These items can provide clues as to how far the shooter was from the target. They can also be compared with information stored in national firearms databases to determine, under some circumstances, the gun used and its most recent owner. The study of firearms and its application to solving crimes goes under the general term **ballistics.** A new generation of ballistics technology allows technicians to create a 3D image of a bullet and match that image to the gun from which the original was fired.

For more than a century, the most important piece of trace evidence has been the human fingerprint. Because no two fingerprints are alike, they are considered reliable sources of identification. Forensic scientists compare a fingerprint lifted from a crime scene with that of a suspect and declare a match if there are between eight and sixteen

Cold Case A criminal investigation that has not been solved after a certain amount of time.

Forensics The application of science to establish facts and evidence during the investigation of crimes.

Trace Evidence Evidence such as a fingerprint, blood, or hair found in small amounts at a crime scene.

Ballistics The study of firearms, including the firing of the weapon and the flight of the bullet.

Courtesy Martha Blake

Martha Blake
Forensic Scientist

In high school, I was interested in science, but didn't want to end up being a technician doing the same thing every day. I was looking in college catalogues and came across criminalistics at U.C. Berkeley. The coursework included such courses as microscopy, instrumental analysis, trace evidence, criminal law, and statistics, and it sounded fascinating. I decided in my senior year of high school to become a forensic scientist.

As quality assurance manager at the San Francisco Police Department's crime lab, I am often called to criminal court to testify about evidence that has passed through our lab. I am always nervous when I testify, and I think it is healthy to be a little nervous. As an expert witness, the most challenging part of my testimony is describing my findings to a jury of primarily nonscientists in a way that will make my testimony understandable and credible. I've found that juries tend to understand evidence that is part of their lives. Everyone can identify the writing of a family member or spouse, so describing how handwriting is identified is not too hard. Explaining how DNA analysis works is more difficult.

SOCIAL MEDIA CAREER TIP When people search for you online, they won't click past the first page. Check to see where your material appears on a regular basis.

"points of similarity." This method of identification is not infallible, however. It is often difficult to lift a suitable print from a crime scene, and researchers have uncovered numerous cases in which innocent persons were convicted based on evidence obtained through faulty fingerprinting procedures.[42]

The DNA Revolution The technique of **DNA fingerprinting,** or using a suspect's DNA to match the suspect to a crime, emerged in the mid-1990s and has now all but replaced fingerprint evidence in many types of criminal investigations. The shift has been a boon to crime fighters: one law enforcement agent likened DNA fingerprinting to "the finger of God pointing down" at a guilty suspect.[43]

DNA, which is the same in each cell of a person's body, provides a "genetic blueprint" or "code" for every living organism. DNA fingerprinting is useful in criminal investigations because no two people, save for identical twins, have the same genetic code. Therefore, lab technicians, using the process described in Figure 6.3, can compare the DNA sample of a suspect to the evidence found at the crime scene. If the match is negative, it is certain that the two samples did not come from the same source. If the match is positive, the lab will determine the odds that the DNA sample could have come from someone other than the suspect. Those odds are so high—sometimes reaching 30 billion to one—that a match is practically conclusive.[44]

The initial use of DNA to establish criminal guilt took place in Britain in 1986. The FBI used it for the first time in the United States two years later. The process begins

Describe how forensic experts use DNA fingerprinting to solve crimes.

LEARNING **4** OBJECTIVE

DNA Fingerprinting The identification of a person based on a sample of her or his DNA, the genetic material found in the cells of all living things.

FIGURE 6.3 Unlocking Evidence in DNA

Deoxyribonucleic acid, or DNA, is the genetic material that carries the code for all living cells. Through DNA profiling, a process explained here, forensic scientists test DNA samples to see if they match the DNA profile of a known criminal or other test subject.

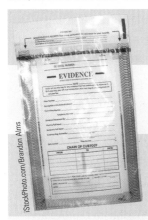

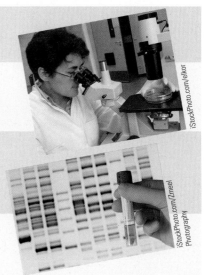

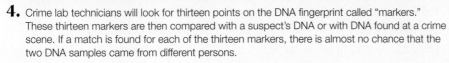

1. DNA samples can be taken from a number of sources, including saliva, blood, hair, or skin. These samples are labeled and shipped to a forensic lab.

2. The DNA is extracted from the cells of the sample using complex proteins known as enzymes. An electrical charge is then sent through the resulting DNA fragments to separate them according to size.

3. Another set of enzymes is added to the now separate DNA fragments. These enzymes attach themselves to different categories of genetic material within the DNA fragments and become distinct when exposed to photographic film. The "photograph" of this visible pattern is the DNA fingerprint.

4. Crime lab technicians will look for thirteen points on the DNA fingerprint called "markers." These thirteen markers are then compared with a suspect's DNA or with DNA found at a crime scene. If a match is found for each of the thirteen markers, there is almost no chance that the two DNA samples came from different persons.

when forensic technicians gather blood, semen, skin, saliva, or hair from the scene of a crime. Blood cells and sperm are rich in DNA, making them particularly useful in murder and rape cases, but DNA has also been extracted from sweat on dirty laundry, skin cells on eyeglasses, and saliva on used envelope seals. Once a suspect is identified, her or his DNA can be used to determine whether she or he can be placed at the crime scene. In 2014, for example, investigators connected Dennis Wilson to a bank robbery in Ansonia, Connecticut, by obtaining his DNA from a cigarette left in the abandoned getaway car.

DNA in Action The ability to "dust" for genetic information on such a wide variety of evidence, as well as that evidence's longevity and accuracy, greatly increases the chances that a crime will be solved. Indeed, police no longer need a witness or even a suspect in custody to solve crimes. What they do need is a piece of evidence and a database.

In 1974, for example, Eileen Ferro was stabbed to death in her Shrewsbury, Massachusetts, home. For four decades, local police were unable to establish any useful leads concerning Ferro's killer. In 2014, however, investigators asked a crime lab to reevaluate evidence from the crime scene for the presence of DNA. The traces they found matched a sample recently taken from parole violator Lonzo Guthrie in California. Due to the match, Guthrie—who had delivered furniture to Ferro's house the day before her death—was arrested for murder.

Databases and Cold Hits The identification of Lonzo Guthrie is an example of what police call a **cold hit,** which occurs when law enforcement finds a suspect "out of nowhere" by comparing DNA evidence from a crime scene against the contents of a database. The largest and most important database is the National Combined DNA Index System (CODIS). Operated by the FBI since 1998, CODIS gives local and state law enforcement agencies access to the DNA profiles of almost 13.5 million people who have been connected to criminal activity. As of January 2015, the database had produced about 270,300 cold hits nationwide.[45]

Cold Hit The establishment of a connection between a suspect and a crime, often through the use of DNA evidence, in the absence of an ongoing criminal investigation.

New Developments DNA fingerprinting has been widely available for a relatively short time, and the scope of its investigative uses continues to expand. For example, a new rapid-testing device reduces the time needed to process DNA samples from at least two weeks to ninety minutes. This technology, which several states started using in late 2014, will aid law enforcement immensely by quickly matching suspects to crimes.[46] Other recent developments involving DNA fingerprinting technology include:

1. *Touch DNA,* which allows investigators to test for the presence of DNA by scraping items such as a piece of food or an article of clothing for microscopic cells left behind by the suspect.
2. *Familial searches,* based on the premise that parents, siblings, and other relatives have DNA similar to that of suspects whose identity might be unknown or who might be unavailable for testing.
3. *DNA fog,* a security system that, when triggered by an alarm, marks intruders with genetic material derived from plants that it is almost impossible to remove and links suspects to crime scenes.
4. The possible use of DNA as a *genetic witness* by providing law enforcement with a physical description of a suspect, including her or his age or eye, skin, and hair color.[47]

Furthermore, because of its cost, DNA fingerprinting has traditionally been used mostly in conjunction with "important" violent crime investigations. The National Institute of Justice has found, however, that not only was using DNA testing in property crimes cost effective, but it also dramatically increased the police's ability to identify burglary and theft suspects.[48] Because many property offenders commit violent crimes as well, it seems logical that apprehending "unimportant" burglars and thieves would prevent a significant amount of serious criminal activity.[49]

DNA Collection Policies Authorities in all fifty states are required to collect DNA samples from offenders who have been convicted of felonies. In addition, more than half the states authorize the collection of DNA from those who have been arrested for a crime but not yet convicted. Indeed, the FBI's CODIS database contains more than 1.3 million DNA profiles of arrestees. As the example of Lonzo Guthrie—who had been arrested for a parole violation—from earlier in the section shows, this policy provides a valuable tool for cold case investigators. But is it fair to arrestees who may not have committed a crime? We examine how the United States Supreme Court answered that question in the feature *Landmark Cases*—Maryland v. King.

EthicsChallenge

In speaking with a domestic terrorism suspect, an undercover FBI agent says, "Allah has more work for you to do," adding, "Revelation is going to come in your dreams that you have to do this thing." The "thing" is to shoot down American military airplanes with handheld missiles. Is this ethical behavior on the part of the FBI agent? What should happen to the suspect if he proceeds to purchase a handheld missile launcher on the black market? ■

Police Strategies: What Works

How important are police when it comes to preventing crime? According to the RAND Institute, a 10 percent increase in police staffing in an average city lowers the annual murder rate by 9 percent, the annual robbery rate by 6 percent, and the annual vehicle theft rate by 4 percent.[50] Using the RAND study to argue that her city should hire more law enforcement agents, Oakland (California) mayor Libby Schaaf concluded, "Police are expensive, but worth it."[51]

Budget cuts are commonplace in today's law enforcement environment, and many law enforcement agencies find themselves having to do more with less.[52] In this section, we will examine those strategies being used by police departments to improve efficiency regardless of the limitations placed on their resources.

Calls for Service

While law enforcement officers do not like to think of themselves as being at the "beck and call" of citizens, that is the operational basis of much police work. All police departments practice **incident-driven policing,** in which calls for service are the primary instigators of action. Between 40 and 60 percent of police activity is the result of 911 calls or

Incident-Driven Policing
A reactive approach to policing that emphasizes a speedy response to calls for service.

Landmark Cases

Maryland **v** King

After Maryland resident Alonzo King was arrested for threatening a group of people with a shotgun, local police took a swab of DNA from his cheek. When the sample matched evidence from an unsolved rape case in the state DNA database, King was eventually convicted of that crime and sentenced to life in prison. He challenged this outcome, focusing on the unfairness of a Maryland law that allows for DNA fingerprinting of those who have been arrested, but not yet convicted, of violent crimes. King's challenge gave the United States Supreme Court a chance to decide a crucial question: is taking DNA samples from arrestees (a) merely the equivalent of traditional fingerprinting or (b) an unacceptable invasion of privacy of the potentially innocent?

Maryland v. King
United States Supreme Court
133 S.Ct. 1980 (2013)

In the Words of the Court . . .
Justice Kennedy, Majority Opinion

* * * *

At issue is a standard, expanding technology already in widespread use throughout the Nation.

* * * *

DNA identification is an advanced technique superior to fingerprinting in many ways, so much so that to insist on fingerprints as the norm would make little sense to either the forensic expert or a layperson. The additional intrusion upon the arrestee's privacy beyond that associated with fingerprinting is not significant . . . and DNA is a markedly more accurate form

of identifying arrestees. A suspect who has changed his facial features to evade photographic identification or even one who has undertaken the more arduous task of altering his fingerprints cannot escape the revealing power of his DNA. * * * The only difference between DNA analysis and fingerprint databases is the unparalleled accuracy DNA provides.

* * * *

The expectations of privacy of an individual taken into police custody "necessarily [are] of a diminished scope . . . ." "[B]oth the person and the property in his immediate possession may be searched at the station house." * * * A suspect's criminal history is a critical part of his identity that officers should know when processing him for detention. It is a common occurrence that "[p]eople detained for minor offenses can turn out to be the most devious and dangerous criminals."

Decision
The Court upheld Maryland's ability to take DNA samples from people arrested for serious crimes and, in the process, validated similar laws in twenty-seven other states. The decision was not, however, based on cold case concerns. Instead, the Court justified the practice as necessary to help police identify suspects in custody.

For Critical Analysis
In his dissent, Justice Scalia argued, "[B]ecause of today's decision, your DNA can be taken and entered into a national database if you are ever arrested, rightly or wrongly, and for whatever reason." Do you agree with Scalia that the Court erred in upholding arrestee-DNA testing laws? Why or why not?

other citizen requests, which means that police officers in the field initiate only about half of such activity.[53]

Response Time and Efficiency The speed with which the police respond to calls for service has traditionally been seen as a crucial aspect of crime fighting and crime prevention. In incident-driven policing, the ideal scenario is as follows: a citizen sees a person committing a crime and calls 911, and the police arrive quickly and catch the perpetrator in the act. Alternatively, a citizen who is the victim of a crime, such as a mugging, calls 911 as soon as possible, and the police arrive to catch the mugger before she or he can flee the immediate area of the crime.

Although such scenarios are quite rare in real life, **response time,** or the time elapsed between the instant a call for service is received and the instant the police arrive on the scene, has become a benchmark for police efficiency. As a measure of the successful reformation of the Camden County Police Department, discussed in the opening of Chapter 5, city officials pointed to an average response time of 4.4 minutes. Under the previous regime, those times had lagged to more than an hour.[54] Of course, Camden needed to nearly double the size of its force to bring about this improvement. Indeed, many police administrators believe that maintaining acceptable response times is primarily a function of the number of police officers available to respond.

CJ & Technology

Jahi Chikwendiu/ *The Washington Post*/Getty Images

Gunshot Detection Systems

For reasons ranging from disinterest to fear to laziness, the general public fails to report about eighty percent of gunfire incidents to police. Now, thanks to ShotSpotter, a gunshot detection system, law enforcement has the means to overcome this civic shortcoming. Placed on a rooftop, a ShotSpotter sensor unit uses microphones, computer software, a clock, and satellite positioning technology to pinpoint the precise time and location of gunfire.

When a unit detects gunfire, it sends an image of the sound wave to the local police department, where a specialist confirms that a weapon has been fired. (The sound wave of a gun blast looks something like a Christmas tree.) Ideally, police officers are dispatched to the scene within forty seconds of the initial shot. Between 2006 and 2014, ShotSpotter detected about 39,000 shooting incidents in Washington, D.C., helping the police fight violent crime and providing valuable information about gun use in the city.

Thinking about Gunshot Detection Systems

As you will see in the next chapter, many cities have placed surveillance cameras in high-crime neighborhoods. How can ShotSpotter be linked with these cameras to provide further evidence of criminal activity?

Improving Response Time Efficiency Many police departments have come to realize that overall response time is not as critical as response time for the most important calls. For this reason, a number of metropolitan areas have introduced 311 nonemergency call systems to reduce the strain on 911 operations. Another popular

Response Time The rapidity with which calls for service are answered.

FIGURE 6.4 Putting the Theory of Differential Response into Action

Differential response strategies are based on a simple concept: treat emergencies like emergencies and nonemergencies like nonemergencies. As you see, calls for service that involve "hot crimes" will be dealt with immediately, while those that report "cold crimes" will be dealt with at some point in the future.

"HOT" CALLS FOR SERVICE—IMMEDIATE RESPONSE	
Complaint to 911 Officer	**Rationale**
"I just got home from work, and I can see someone in my bedroom through the window."	Possibility that the intruder is committing a crime.
"My husband has a baseball bat, and he says he's going to kill me."	Crime in progress.
"A woman in a green jacket just grabbed my purse and ran away."	Chances of catching the suspect are increased with immediate action.

"COLD" CALLS FOR SERVICE—ALTERNATIVE RESPONSE	
"I got to my office about two hours ago, but I just noticed that the laser printer was stolen during the night."	The crime occurred at least two hours earlier.
"The guy in the apartment above me has been selling pot for years, and I'm sick and tired of it."	Not an emergency situation.
"My husband came home late two nights ago with a black eye, and I finally got him to admit that he didn't run into a doorknob. Larry Smith smacked him."	Past crime with a known suspect who is unlikely to flee.

Source: Adapted from John S. Dempsey and Linda S. Forst, *An Introduction to Policing*, 7th ed. (Clifton Park, NY: Delmar Cengage Learning, 2014), 269–271.

method of improving performance in this area is a **differential response** strategy, in which the police distinguish among different calls for service so that they can respond more quickly to the most serious incidents.

Suppose, for example, that a police department receives two calls for service at the same time. The first caller reports that a burglar is in her house, and the second says that he has returned home from work to find his automobile missing. If the department employs differential response, the burglary in progress—a "hot" crime—will receive immediate attention. The missing automobile—a "cold" crime that could have been committed several hours earlier—will receive attention "as time permits," and the caller may even be asked to make an appointment to come to the police station to formally report the theft. (See Figure 6.4 for possible responses to calls to a 911 operator.)

LEARNING OBJECTIVE **5** Explain why differential response strategies enable police departments to respond more efficiently to 911 calls.

911 Technology Automatic differential response is an integral part of **computer-aided dispatch (CAD)** systems, used by nearly every police department in the country. With CAD, a 911 dispatcher enters the information from a caller into his or her computer, which prioritizes the emergency based on its nature. CAD also verifies the caller's address and phone number, and determines the closest patrol unit to the site of the emergency. In many jurisdictions, the details, including any previous 911 calls from the location, are then sent to a *mobile digital terminal* in the police officer's patrol car.

Next Generation 911 A growing number of 911 calls come from mobile phones rather than landlines. In fact, four in ten American homes now use these devices only, a figure that is sure to increase in the near future.[55] This trend has forced police departments across the country to adopt Next Generation 911 systems, which make it possible for officers to receive text messages, videos, photos, and location data about crime incidents. For example, a store clerk who has just been robbed at gunpoint will be able to take a photo of the offender's getaway car and send that photo to police along with the emergency call for service.[56]

Differential Response A strategy for answering calls for service in which response time is adapted to the seriousness of the call.

Computer-Aided Dispatch (CAD) A method of dispatching police patrols units to the site of 911 emergencies with the assistance of a computer program.

Reverse 911 Communication technology now allows public officials to contact citizens in a certain geographic area when the need arises. In 2014, for example, the Jefferson County (Colorado) Sheriff's Department sent out **reverse 911** calls to local residents warning them that two armed suspects were attempting to carjack vehicles on a stretch of the I-70 freeway. These systems have proved particularly helpful during natural disasters such as tornadoes and floods, when officials need to get pertinent information to the community. Reverse 911 is also commonplace at colleges and universities, where it is used to alert employees and students of campus emergencies.

Patrol Strategies

Many experts believe that, in the words of Grand Rapids (Michigan) police chief Kevin Belk, an overreliance on calls for service "tends to make you a reactive department," rather than a police force that prevents crimes from happening in the first place.[57] Similarly, another traditional police strategy, *random patrol,* is increasingly felt to be an inefficient use of law enforcement resources.[58] **Random patrol** refers to police officers making the rounds of a specific area with the general goal of detecting and preventing crime. Every police department in the United States randomly patrols its jurisdiction using automobiles. In addition, 53 percent utilize foot patrols, 32 percent bicycle patrols, 16 percent motorcycle patrols, 4 percent boat patrols, and 1 percent horse patrols.[59]

Testing Random Patrol Police researchers have been questioning the effectiveness of random patrols since the influential Kansas City Preventive Patrol Experiment of the early 1970s. As part of this experiment, different neighborhoods in the city were subjected to three different levels of patrol: random patrol by a single police car, random patrol by multiple police cars, and no random patrol whatsoever. The results of the Kansas City experiment were somewhat shocking. Researchers found that increasing or decreasing preventive patrol had little or no impact on crimes, public opinion, the effectiveness of the police, police response time, traffic accidents, or reports of crime to police.[60]

For some, the Kansas City experiment and other similar data prove that patrol officers, after a certain threshold, are not effective in preventing crime and that scarce law enforcement resources should therefore be diverted to other areas. "It makes about as much sense to have police patrol routinely in cars to fight crime as it does to have firemen patrol routinely in fire trucks to fight fire," said University of Delaware professor Carl Klockars.[61] Still, random patrols are important for maintaining community relations, and they have been shown to reduce fear of crime in areas where police have an obvious presence.[62]

Directed Patrols In contrast to random patrols, **directed patrols** target specific areas of a city and often attempt to prevent a specific type of crime. Directed patrols have found favor among law enforcement experts as being a more efficient use of police resources than random patrols, as indicated by the Philadelphia Foot Patrol Experiment. During this experiment, extra foot patrols were utilized in sixty Philadelphia locations plagued by high levels of violent crime. During three months of directed patrols, arrests increased by 13 percent in the targeted areas, and violent crime decreased by 23 percent. In addition, an estimated fifty-three violent crimes were prevented over the three-month period.[63]

Predictive Policing and Crime Mapping

In the previous chapter, we discussed how predictive, or intelligence-led, policing strategies help law enforcement agencies anticipate patterns of criminal activity,

Reverse 911 A mobile phone-based communications system that allows public officials to send outbound messages in the event of an emergency.

Random Patrol A patrol strategy that relies on police officers monitoring a certain area with the goal of detecting crimes in progress or preventing crime due to their presence. Also known as *general* or *preventive patrol.*

Directed Patrol A patrol strategy that is designed to focus on a specific type of criminal activity in a specific geographic area.

allowing them to respond to, or even prevent, crime more effectively. Predictive policing is increasingly attractive to police administrators because, in theory, it requires fewer resources than traditional policing.

For example, due to budget cuts and attrition, the Modesto (California) Police Department has been operating below ideal staff levels for several years. At the same time, crime rates in the city are dropping, thanks to the department's use of a computer program initially designed to predict earthquakes. Using recent criminal behavior as a guide, the program indicates areas where the next crime is most likely to occur by placing a small red box around that area on a computerized grid of the city. When not responding to calls, Modesto police officers prioritize the "red boxed" areas instead of having fixed patrol beats.[64]

Finding "Hot Spots" As was the case in Modesto, predictive policing strategies are strongly linked with directed patrols, which seek to improve on random patrols by targeting specific high-crime areas already known to law enforcement. The target areas for directed patrols are often called **hot spots** because they contain greater numbers of criminals and have higher-than-average levels of victimization. Needless to say, police administrators are no longer sticking pins in maps to determine where hot spots exist. Rather, police departments are using **crime mapping** technology to locate and identify hot spots and "cool" them down. Crime mapping uses geographic information systems (GIS) to track criminal acts as they occur in time and space. Once sufficient information has been gathered, it is analyzed to predict future crime patterns.

Why does hot spot policing work? Criminologists Lawrence Sherman and David Weisburd provided a clue more than twenty years ago by observing the anti-crime impact of patrol officers. Sherman and Weisburd observed that after a police officer left a certain high-crime area, about fifteen minutes elapsed before criminal activity occurred at that spot.[65] Therefore, a police officer on patrol is most efficient when she or he spends a certain amount of time at a hot spot and then returns after fifteen minutes.

A recent experiment involving the Sacramento Police Department supports this hypothesis. Over a three-month period, twenty-one crime hot spots in the city received fifteen-minute randomized patrols, while another twenty-one crime hot spots received normal random patrols. Using calls for service as a measuring stick, the hot spots subject to fifteen-minute patrols were found to experience much less criminal activity.[66]

The Rise of CompStat Computerized crime mapping was popularized when the New York Police Department launched CompStat in the mid-1990s. Still in use, CompStat starts with police officers reporting the exact location of crime and other crime-related information to department officials. These reports are then fed into a computer, which prepares grids of a particular city or neighborhood and highlights areas with a high incidence of serious offenses. (See Figure 6.5 for an example of a GIS crime map.)

In New York and many other cities, the police department holds "Crime Control Strategy Meetings" during which precinct commanders are held accountable for CompStat's data-based reports in their districts. In theory, this system provides the police with accurate information about patterns of crime and gives them the ability to "flood" hot spots with officers at short notice. About two-thirds of large departments now employ some form of computerized crime mapping,[67] and Wesley Skogan, a criminologist at Northwestern University, believes that CompStat and similar technologies are the most likely cause of recent declines in big-city crime.[68]

Hot Spots Concentrated areas of high criminal activity that draw a directed police response.

Crime Mapping Technology that allows crime analysts to identify trends and patterns of criminal behavior within a given area.

FIGURE 6.5 A GIS Crime Map for a Neighborhood in New Orleans

This crime map shows the incidence of various crimes during a two-week period in a neighborhood near downtown New Orleans.

The Omega Group/crimemapping.com

Arrest Strategies

Like patrol strategies, arrest strategies can be divided into two categories that reflect the intent of police administrators. **Reactive arrests** are those arrests made by police officers, usually on general patrol, who observe a criminal act or respond to a call for service. **Proactive arrests** occur when the police take the initiative to target a particular type of criminal or behavior. Proactive arrests are often associated with directed patrols of hot spots, and thus are believed by many experts to have a greater influence on an area's crime rates.[69]

Quality-of-Life Crimes To a certain extent, the popularity of proactive theories was solidified by a magazine article that James Q. Wilson and George L. Kelling wrote in 1982.[70] In their piece, entitled "Broken Windows," Wilson and Kelling argued that reform-era policing strategies focused on violent crime to the detriment of the vital police role of promoting the quality of life in neighborhoods. As a result, many communities, particularly in large cities, had fallen into a state of disorder and disrepute, with two very important consequences.

First, these neighborhoods—with their broken windows, dilapidated buildings, and lawless behavior by residents—were sending out "signals" that criminal activity is tolerated. Second, this disorder was spreading fear among law-abiding citizens, dissuading them from leaving their homes or attempting to improve their surroundings. Thus, the **broken windows theory** is based on "order maintenance" of neighborhoods by cracking down on "quality-of-life" crimes such as panhandling, public drinking and urinating, loitering, and graffiti painting.

The Broken Windows Effect Only by encouraging directed arrest strategies with regard to quality-of-life crime, Wilson and Kelling argued, could American cities be

Reactive Arrests Arrests that come about as part of the ordinary routine of police patrol and responses to calls for service.

Proactive Arrests Arrests that occur because of concerted efforts by law enforcement agencies to respond to a particular type of criminal or criminal behavior.

Broken Windows Theory Wilson and Kelling's theory that a neighborhood in disrepair signals that criminal activity is tolerated in the area. By cracking down on quality-of-life crimes, police can reclaim the neighborhood and encourage law-abiding citizens to live and work there.

rescued from rising crime rates. Along with CompStat, the implementation of this theory has been given a great deal of credit for crime decreases in the United States (particularly New York) over the past three decades.[71] It continues to influence police strategy: several years ago, the Cincinnati Police Department cracked down on traffic accidents in "micro" hot spots of criminal activity such as intersections and street corners. Within twelve months, the impacted areas had experienced a significant decrease in both traffic crashes and crime.[72]

Some experts question how much impact broken windows strategies actually have, pointing out that violent crime rates have also dropped in cities that do not implement this approach.[73] Critics also contend that instituting "zero-tolerance" arrest policies for lesser crimes in low-income neighborhoods not only discriminates against the poor and minority groups but also fosters a strong mistrust of police.[74] Such criticism was fueled by the July 2014 death of Eric Garner, a black man who was unintentionally killed by a New York police officer while resisting arrest for selling seventy-five cent "loosies"— individual, untaxed cigarettes. Speaking at one of the many demonstrations in the city's African American communities that followed this incident, Garner's sister asked, "A cigarette? Are you serious?"[75]

Community Policing and Problem Solving

In "Broken Windows," Wilson and Kelling insisted that, to reduce fear and crime in high-risk neighborhoods, police had to rely on the cooperation of citizens. For all its drawbacks, the political era of policing (see Chapter 5) did have characteristics that observers such as Wilson and Kelling have come to see as advantageous. During the nineteenth century, the police were much more involved in the community than they were after the reforms. Officers performed many duties that today are associated with social services, such as operating soup kitchens and providing lodging for homeless people. They also played a more direct role in keeping public order by "running in" drunks and intervening in minor disturbances.[76] To a certain extent, **community policing** advocates a return to this understanding of the police mission.

Return to the Community Community policing can be defined as an approach that promotes community-police partnerships, proactive problem solving, and community engagement to address issues such as fear of crime and the causes of such fear in a particular area. Neighborhood watch programs, in which police officers and citizens work together to prevent local crime and disorder, are a popular version of a community policing initiative.

Under community policing, patrol officers have the freedom to improvise. They are expected to develop personal relationships with residents and to encourage those residents to become involved in making the community a safer place. As part of Operation Heat Wave, for instance, Dallas detectives go door-to-door in neighborhoods plagued by burglary and auto theft. During these face-to-face meetings, the detectives are able to gather information concerning recent victimizations and encourage attendance at community crime-watch meetings.[77]

Collaborative Reform More than half of all American police departments mention community policing in their mission statements, and a majority of the departments in large cities offer community police training for employees.[78] At the same time, as the federal government has shifted local grant funds to fighting terrorism, community policing programs have declined, as have the number of full-time community policing

LEARNING **6** OBJECTIVE Explain community policing and its contribution to the concept of problem-oriented policing.

Community Policing
A policing philosophy that emphasizes community support for and cooperation with the police in preventing crime.

▲ Two Washington, D.C., police officers offer suggestions to a six-year-old during the annual "Shop with a Cop" event in the nation's capital. **How can establishing friendly relations with citizens help law enforcement agencies reduce crime?** Andrew Harnik/*Washington Times*/Landov

officers nationwide.[79] The result seems to be a growing lack of trust between law enforcement and the public, particularly in minority communities. One resident of a mixed-race Cleveland, Ohio, neighborhood says that the police "don't make an effort to know us. They're trying to get a bust or a collar."[80]

To improve trust within their communities, a number of police departments have turned to *collaborative reform.* In this offshoot of community policing, law enforcement officials form partnerships with local leaders to address difficult issues such as police use of force and arrest policies. Policing experts call this strategy "putting good will in the bank" for use at times of crisis.[81] In South Los Angeles, for example, officers are in constant contact with community organizers and church leaders. These efforts were partially credited for the public reaction in August 2014 when Los Angeles police officers fatally shot an unarmed African American. Although local residents expressed concern, the response was relatively calm in comparison to other cities that had experienced similar incidents that year.

Problem-Oriented Policing

Several years ago, the city of Glendale, Arizona, was experiencing property crime levels that were 63 percent above the national average. Using crime mapping, the Glendale police found that a disproportionate amount of the city's property offenses were taking place at ten Circle K convenience stores. After analyzing the situation, the police determined that Circle K management practices such as inadequate staffing, failure to respond to panhandling, and poor lighting were making the stores breeding grounds of property crime.

By working with Circle K to resolve these issues, as well as putting a proactive arrest strategy into effect in the stores, the Glendale police reduced property crime at the stores by 42 percent in a single year.[82] These efforts are an example of **problem-oriented policing**, a strategy based on the premise that police departments devote too many of their resources to reacting to calls for service and too few to "acting on their own initiative to prevent or reduce community problems."[83] To rectify this situation, problem-oriented policing moves beyond simply responding to incidents and attempts instead to control or even solve the root causes of criminal behavior.

Problem-oriented policing encourages police officers to stop looking at their work as a day-to-day proposition. Rather, they should try to shift the patterns of criminal behavior in a positive direction. For example, instead of responding to a 911 call concerning illegal drug use by simply arresting the offender—a short-term response—the patrol officers should also look at the long-term implications of the situation. They should analyze the pattern of similar arrests in the area and interview the arrestee to determine the reasons, if any, that the site was selected for drug activity.[84] Then additional police action should be taken to prevent further drug sales at the identified location. Research shows that, when properly implemented, problem-oriented policing can be even more effective than directed patrols in reducing "hot spot" crime.[85] (See Figure 6.6 for an example of problem-oriented policing in action.)

Problem-Oriented Policing A policing philosophy that requires police to identify potential criminal activity and develop strategies to prevent or respond to that activity.

FIGURE 6.6 The SARA Model of Problem-Oriented Policing

The reaction of the Boston Police Department (BPD) to a surge in violent crime in the early 2000s gives an example of the four-step SARA (scanning, analysis, response, assessment) model of problem-oriented policing.

Step 1: *Scanning (identifying the problem).* The number of shootings, fatal and non-fatal, in Boston increased 133 percent from 2000 to 2006.

Step 2: *Analysis (researching the problem).* Gun violence "hot spots" covered 5.1 percent of Boston's square mileage and accounted for 53 percent of shooting incidents.

Step 3: *Response (finding a solution to the problem).* The BPD created Safe Street Teams (SSTs) consisting of a sergeant and six patrol officers to work each gun violence hot spot. These SSTs sought to improve the appearance of the neighborhoods by removing graffiti and trash and repairing lighting systems. They also operated directed patrols and improved social services in the areas.

Step 4: *Assessment (determining whether the solution was effective).* Violent crimes declined by 17.3 percent over a three-year period in the targeted hot spots.

Source: Adapted from Bureau of Justice Assistance, *Boston, Massachusetts Smart Policing Initiative* (Washington, D.C.: U.S. Department of Justice, August 2012).

"Us versus Them": Issues in Modern Policing

On December 3, 2014, a grand jury cleared Daniel Pantaleo of the New York Police Department in the chokehold death of Eric Garner, as mentioned in the previous section. Seventeen days later, a vigilante assassinated New York police officers Wenjian Liu and Rafael Ramos as they sat in their patrol car. Earlier, the killer had posted, "I'm Putting Wings on Pigs Today. They Take 1 of Ours . . . Let's Take 2 of Theirs," on social media.[86] Reacting to the officers' murders, a New York police union official said that there was "blood on many hands."[87] Specifically, he was referring to New York mayor Bill de Blasio, who many law enforcement agents felt had gone too far in supporting anti-police protests following the grand jury's decision not to charge Pantaleo with a crime.

In the weeks to come, New York police officers used their discretion to ignore low-level offenses in the city. As a result of this work slowdown, the number of summonses for minor crimes and traffic violations dropped more than 90 percent below normal.[88] Hundreds of these officers also turned their backs on Mayor de Blasio during Lui's and Ramos's funerals. These conflicts highlight many of the on-the-job issues that bind police officers together while at the same time potentially alienating them from the society that they are sworn to protect and serve.

Police Subculture

As a rule, police officers do not appreciate being second-guessed when it comes to their decisions on when to use force against a civilian. "A majority of people don't understand what officers face on a daily basis," said one retired detective. "There were a lot of situations where I almost got killed."[89] Feelings of frustration and mistrust toward civilians are hallmarks of **police subculture,** a broad term used to describe the basic assumptions and values that permeate law enforcement agencies and are taught to new members of a law enforcement agency as the proper way to think, perceive, and act.

Every organization has a subculture, with values shaped by the particular aspects and pressures of that organization. In the police subculture, those values are formed in an environment characterized by danger, stress, boredom, and violence.

Police Subculture The values and perceptions that are shared by members of a police department and, to a certain extent, by all law enforcement agents.

The Core Values of Police Subculture From the first day on the job, rookies begin the process of **socialization,** in which they are taught the values and rules of police work. This process is aided by a number of rituals that are common to the law enforcement experience. Police theorist Harry J. Mullins believes that the following rituals are critical to the police officer's acceptance, and even embrace, of police subculture:

- Attending a police academy.
- Working with a senior officer, who passes on the "lessons" of police work and life to the younger officer.
- Making the initial felony arrest.
- Using force to make an arrest for the first time.
- Using or witnessing deadly force for the first time.
- Witnessing major traumatic incidents for the first time.[90]

Each of these rituals makes it clear to the police officer that this is not a "normal" job. The only other people who can understand the stresses of police work are fellow officers, and consequently law enforcement officers tend to insulate themselves from civilians. Eventually, the insulation breeds mistrust, and the police officer develops an "us versus them" outlook toward those outside the force. In turn, this outlook creates what sociologist William Westly called the **blue curtain,** also known as the "blue wall of silence" or simply "the code."[91] This curtain separates the police from the civilians they are meant to protect.

Police Cynicism A cynic is someone who universally distrusts human motives and expects nothing but the worst from human behavior. *Police cynicism* is characterized by a rejection of the ideals of truth and justice—the very values that an officer is sworn to uphold.[92] As cynical police officers lose respect for the law, they replace legal rules with those learned in the police subculture, which are believed to be more reflective of "reality." The implications for society can be an increase in police misconduct, corruption, and brutality.[93]

Police cynicism is exacerbated by a feeling of helplessness—to report another officer's wrongdoing is a severe breach of the blue wall of silence. As one officer told a columnist for the *New York Times,* the prevailing attitude among law enforcement officers is that, as long as one's supervisors accept a certain form of questionable behavior without comment, there is no reason to curtail that behavior. Indeed, according to the officer, any hint of disapproval can lead to accusations of being a "rat." "You've gotta work with a lot of these guys," the officer explained. "You go on a gun job, the next thing you know, you got nobody following you up the stairs."[94]

The officer's statement highlights one of the reasons why the police subculture resonates beyond department walls—he has basically admitted that he will not report wrongdoing by his peers. In this manner, the police subculture influences the actions of police officers, sometimes to the detriment of society. In the next sections, we will examine two areas of the law enforcement work environment that help create the police subculture and must be fully understood if the cynical nature of the police subculture is ever to be changed: (1) the dangers of police work and (2) the need for police officers to establish and maintain authority.

The Physical Dangers of Police Work

As described at the beginning of this section, New York police officers Wenjian Liu and Rafael Ramos were sitting in a parked patrol car when an assailant took their lives. As these shootings show, there is no such thing as a "routine" day on the job as a law enforcement agent.

Socialization The process through which a police officer is taught the values and expected behavior of the police subculture.

Blue Curtain A metaphorical term used to refer to the value placed on secrecy and the general mistrust of the outside world shared by many police officers.

Officers Killed and Assaulted According to the Officer Down Memorial Page, Officers Liu and Ramos were two of 121 law enforcement agents who died in the line of duty in 2014, and two of forty-seven who were killed by hostile gunfire that year.[95] In addition, about 50,000 assaults were committed against police officers in 2013, with 29 percent of these assaults resulting in an injury.[96] These numbers are hardly surprising. As police experts John S. Dempsey and Linda S. Forst point out, police "deal constantly with what may be the most dangerous species on this planet—the human being."[97]

At the same time, Dempsey and Forst note that according to data compiled by the federal government, citizens and the police come into contact about 40 million times a year.[98] Given this figure, the police have relatively low death and injury rates. The statistical safety of police officers can be attributed to two factors. First, police academies emphasize officer safety, focusing on areas such as self-defense, firearm proficiency, arrest tactics, and nonlethal weapons (which will be addressed later in the chapter).

Second, police officers take extraordinary precautions to protect their physical safety, including wearing protective **body armor** underneath their clothing. The body armor most widely used by American police officers is made of Kevlar, a high-strength fiber discovered in 1964 by a chemist named Stephanie Kwolek. Low-level Kevlar can stop .357 and .9mm shots, while high-level "tactical armor" can deflect rifle and machine gun bullets. Ninety-two percent of all police departments require their officers to wear body armor, which has saved at least 3,000 law enforcement lives since 1987.[99]

Accidental Deaths Despite perceptions to the contrary, a high percentage of deaths and injuries suffered by police officers are not the result of assaults by criminal suspects. Generally speaking, half of all law enforcement officer injuries are due to accidents, and about two-thirds of those injuries occur when officers are doing something other than making an arrest.[100] In particular, traffic accidents cause as many line-of-duty deaths as do firearms.[101] One reason for the fatalities is that a number of law enforcement officers do not take simple precautions when behind the wheel. A recent study conducted by the National Highway Traffic Safety Administration found that 42 percent of police officers killed in vehicle crashes were not wearing seat belts.[102]

Also, as Craig Floyd of the National Law Enforcement Officers Memorial Fund points out, nearly every police officer will be involved in a high-speed automobile response or chase during her or his career, but only 10 percent will be involved in a gunfight. Yet firearms training is common, while driver training is not. Furthermore, although great strides have been made in protective body armor for police officers, the same cannot be said for safety measures in patrol cars.[103]

Stress and the Mental Dangers of Police Work

In addition to physical dangers, police work entails considerable mental pressure and stress. Professor John Violanti and

Body Armor Protective covering that is worn under a police officer's clothing and designed to minimize injury from being hit by a fired bullet.

▼ Fellow officers escort the casket of Ogden City, Utah, police officer Jared Francom, who was shot and killed while trying to apprehend a suspect. **How might violence against police officers contribute to the "blue curtain" between law enforcement and the public?** George Frey/Reuters/Landov

his colleagues at the University at Buffalo have determined that police officers experience unusually high levels of *cortisol,* otherwise known as the "stress hormone," which is associated with serious health problems such as diabetes and heart disease.[104] "Intervention is necessary to help officers deal with this difficult and stressful occupation," says Violanti. "[Police officers] need to learn how to relax, how to think differently about things they experience as a cop."[105]

Police Stressors The conditions that cause stress—such as worries over finances or relationships—are known as **stressors.** Each profession has its own set of stressors, but police are particularly vulnerable to occupational pressures and stress factors such as the following:

- The constant fear of being a victim of violent crime.
- Exposure to violent crime and its victims.
- The need to comply with the law in nearly every job action.
- Lack of community support.
- Negative media coverage.

Police officers may face a number of internal pressures as well, including limited opportunities for career advancement, excessive paperwork, and low wages and benefits.[106]

Both male and female law enforcement agents experience these stressors, as well as others such as lack of sleep and chaotic private lives. Some stressors are, however, unique to female police officers, for reasons we touched on last chapter. These challenges include sexism, sexual harassment, the constant demand to prove one's self, and lack of acceptance in the male-dominated police subculture.[107]

The Consequences of Police Stress Police stress can manifest itself in different ways. The University at Buffalo study cited above found that the stresses of law enforcement often lead to high blood pressure and heart problems.[108] Other research shows that 18 percent of male police officers and 16 percent of female police officers report "adverse consequences" from alcohol use.[109]

If stress becomes overwhelming, an officer may suffer from **burnout,** becoming listless and ineffective as a result of mental and physical exhaustion. Another problem related to stress is *post-traumatic stress disorder (PTSD).* Often recognized in war veterans and rape victims, PTSD is a reaction to a traumatic event that evokes significant stress. For police officers, such events might include the death of a fellow agent or the shooting of a civilian. An officer suffering from PTSD will:

1. Re-experience the traumatic event through nightmares and flashbacks.
2. Become less and less involved in the outside world by withdrawing from others and refusing to participate in normal social interactions.
3. Experience "survival guilt," which may lead to loss of sleep and memory impairment.[110]

Several years ago, Columbia (South Carolina) police chief Randy Scott resigned after struggling with PTSD related to the fatal automobile crash of a fellow officer.

To put it bluntly, law enforcement officers are exposed to more disturbing images—of violent death, bloody crime scenes, horrible accidents, and human cruelty—in their first few years on the job than most people will see in a lifetime. Though some studies suggest that police officers have higher rates of suicide than the general population, it appears that most develop an extraordinary ability to handle the difficulties of the profession and persevere.[111]

Stressors The aspects of police work and life that lead to feelings of stress.

Burnout A mental state that occurs when a person suffers from exhaustion and has difficulty functioning normally as a result of overwork and stress.

Authority and the Use of Force

If the police subculture is shaped by the dangers of the job, it often finds expression through authority. The various symbols of authority that decorate a police officer—including the uniform, badge, nightstick, and firearm—establish the power she or he holds over civilians. For better or for worse, both police officers and civilians tend to equate terms such as *authority* and *respect* with the ability to use force.

It is generally accepted that not only is police use of force inevitable, but that law enforcement agents who are unwilling to use force cannot do their jobs effectively. "The police officer always causes the trouble," stated an appeals court in one well-known use-of-force case. "But it is trouble which the police officer is sworn to cause, which society pays him to cause and which, if kept within constitutional limits, society praises the officer for causing."[112]

Use of Force in Law Enforcement In general, the use of physical force by law enforcement personnel is very rare, occurring in only about 1.4 percent of the 40 million annual police-public encounters mentioned earlier. Still, the Department of Justice estimates that law enforcement officers threaten to use force or use force in encounters with 770,000 civilians a year, and nearly 14 percent of those incidents result in an injury.[113] Federal authorities also report that about 690 deaths occur in the process of an arrest on an annual basis.[114] Of course, police officers are often justified in using force to protect themselves and other citizens. As we noted previously, they are the targets of tens of thousands of assaults each year. Law enforcement agents are also usually justified in using force to make an arrest, to prevent suspects from escaping, to restrain suspects or other individuals for their own safety, or to protect property.[115]

At the same time, few observers would be naïve enough to believe that the police are *always* justified in the use of force. A survey of emergency room physicians found that 98 percent believed that they had treated patients who were victims of excessive police force.[116] How, then, is "misuse" of force to be defined? To provide guidance for officers in this tricky area, nearly every law enforcement agency designs a *use of force matrix*. As the example in Figure 6.7 shows, such a matrix presents officers with the proper force options for different levels of contact with a civilian. (In the *CJ in Action* feature at the end of the chapter, we will the examine the impact of police militarization on the national use-of-force debate.)

Types of Force To comply with the various, and not always consistent, laws concerning the use of force, a police officer must

FIGURE 6.7 The Orlando (Florida) Police Department's Use of Force Matrix

Like most local law enforcement agencies, the Orlando Police Department has a policy to guide its officers' use of force. These policies instruct an officer on how to react to an escalating series of confrontations with a civilian and are often expressed visually, as shown here.

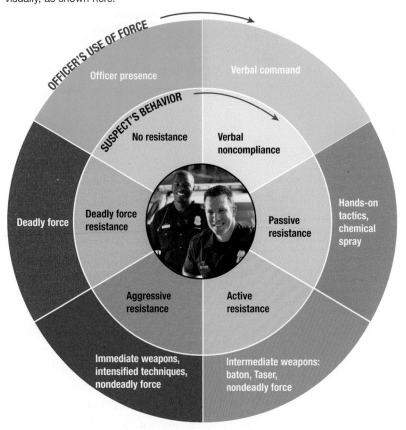

OFFICER'S USE OF FORCE

SUSPECT'S BEHAVIOR

- Officer presence / No resistance
- Verbal command / Verbal noncompliance
- Hands-on tactics, chemical spray / Passive resistance
- Intermediate weapons: baton, Taser, nondeadly force / Active resistance
- Immediate weapons, intensified techniques, nondeadly force / Aggressive resistance
- Deadly force / Deadly force resistance

Source: Michael E. Miller, "Taser Use and the Use-of-Force Continuum," *Police Chief* (September 2010), 72. Photo credit: iStockPhoto.com/Susan Chiang

understand that there are two kinds of force: *nondeadly force* and *deadly force*. Most force used by law enforcement is nondeadly force. In most states, the use of nondeadly force is regulated by the concept of **reasonable force,** which allows the use of non-deadly force when a reasonable person would assume that such force was necessary. Police officers act within the law when they use reasonable force in making an arrest. For example, Daniel Pantaleo, the New York police officer who killed Eric Garner with a chokehold, could not reasonably have been expected to know that Garner suffered from health issues such as asthma that made his death more likely. This is the likely reason that a grand jury decided Pantaleo was not criminally responsible for killing Garner.[117]

In contrast, **deadly force** is force that an objective police officer realizes will place the subject in direct threat of serious injury or death. A law enforcement agent is justi-fied in using deadly force if she or he reasonably believes that such force is necessary to protect herself, himself, or another person from serious harm.[118] Generally speaking, the key question in use-of-force cases is: did the officer behave reasonably, under the circumstances?

The United States Supreme Court and Use of Force The United States Supreme Court set the standards for the use of deadly force by law enforcement officers in *Tennessee v. Garner* (1985).[119] The case involved an incident in which Memphis police officer Elton Hymon shot and killed a suspect who was trying to climb over a fence after stealing ten dollars from a residence. Hymon testified that he had been trained to shoot to keep a suspect from escaping, and indeed Tennessee law at the time allowed police officers to apprehend fleeing suspects in this manner.

In reviewing the case, the Supreme Court focused not on Hymon's action but on the Tennessee statute itself, ultimately finding it unconstitutional:

> When the suspect poses no immediate threat to the officer and no threat to others, the use of deadly force is unjustified. . . . It is not better that all felony suspects die than that they escape.[120]

The Court's decision forced twenty-three states to change their fleeing felon rules, but it did not completely eliminate police discretion in such situations. Police officers still may use deadly force if they have probable cause to believe that the fleeing suspect poses a threat of serious injury or death to the officers or others. (We will discuss the concept of probable cause in the next chapter.)

In essence, the Court recognized that police officers must be able to make split-second decisions without worrying about the legal ramifications. Four years after the *Garner* case, the Court tried to clarify this concept in *Graham v. Connor* (1989), stating that the use of any force should be judged by the "reasonableness of the officer on the scene, rather than with the 20/20 vision of hindsight."[121] In 2004, the Court modified this rule by suggest-ing that an officer's use of force could be "reasonable" even if, by objective measures, the force was not needed to protect the officer or others in the area.[122] (See the feature *Discre-tion in Action—High-Speed Force.*)

Less Lethal Weapons Regardless of any legal restrictions, violent confronta-tions between officers and suspects are inevitable. To decrease the likelihood that such confrontations will result in death or serious injury, many police departments use *less lethal weapons,* which are designed to subdue but not seriously harm suspects. The most common less lethal weapon is Oleoresin Capsicum, or OC pepper spray, which is used by 97 percent of all local police departments.[123] An organic substance that combines ingredients such as resin and cayenne pepper, OC causes a sensation similar to having

Reasonable Force The degree of force that is appropriate to protect the police officer or other citizens and is not excessive.

Deadly Force Force applied by a police officer that is likely or intended to cause death.

Discretion in Action

High-Speed Force

The Situation You are a sheriff's deputy, and you have just pulled over a driver named Rickar whom you suspect of being impaired by alcohol. When you ask Rickar for his license, he takes off and, weaving through traffic, leads you and five other deputies on a dangerous automobile chase with speeds reaching 100 miles per hour. Eventually, you and your colleagues corner Rickar in a parking lot. Instead of surrendering, he smashes into several of the other patrol cars and creates an opening to escape down a side street. From your position, you have the opportunity to shoot Rickar as he speeds away.

The Law The use of deadly force by a law enforcement officer is based on the concept of reasonableness. In other words, would a reasonable police officer in this situation be justified in using force?

What Would You Do? Do you fire your service weapon? On the one hand, by his actions Rickar is certainly placing

LEARNING **7** OBJECTIVE | Determine when police officers are justified in using deadly force.

you, your colleagues, pedestrians, and other drivers in imminent threat of serious bodily injury. On the other hand, if you let him escape, this threat of harm will be significantly reduced.

[To see how a law enforcement officer in West Memphis, Arkansas, reacted in similar circumstances, go to Example 6.1 in Appendix B.]

---

sand or needles in the eyes when sprayed into a suspect's face. Other common less lethal weapons include tear gas, water cannons, and **conducted energy devices (CEDs)**, which rely on an electrical shock to incapacitate uncooperative suspects.

The best-known, and most controversial, CED is the Taser—a handheld electrical stun gun that fires blunt darts up to 21 feet at speeds of 200 to 220 feet per second. The darts deliver 50,000 volts into the target for a span of about five seconds. Nationally, more than 17,000 law enforcement agencies deploy Tasers, and, when properly used, the devices increase the safety of both officers and suspects.[124] According to a study conducted by researchers at Wake Forest University, 99.7 percent of people shocked by Tasers had minor or no injuries.[125] Nevertheless, according to the human rights organization Amnesty International, as of 2012 more than 500 people have died after being Tasered by police.[126] Often, these deaths occurred because the target had a weakened heart or was in ill health because of drug use.[127]

EthicsChallenge

In this section, you learned that many members of the New York Police Department recently engaged in an unofficial "work slowdown" to protest a perceived lack of support from the city government. Was this an ethical response to the situation surrounding the deaths of Eric Garner and Officers Rafael Ramos and Wenjian Liu? Why or why not? ■

Police Misconduct and Ethics

If police culture is, as we noted earlier, marked by a certain mistrust of the public, it is only fair to note that the reverse is often true as well. Police are held to a high standard of behavior that can be summarized by the umbrella term **professionalism**. A professional law enforcement agent is expected to be honest, committed to ideals of justice, respectful of the law, and intolerant of misconduct by his or her fellow officers. When police act

Conducted Energy Device (CED) A less lethal weapon designed to disrupt a target's central nervous system by means of a charge of electrical energy.

Professionalism Adherence to a set of values that show a police officer to be of the highest moral character.

unprofessionally, or are perceived to have done so, then their relationship with the community will inevitably suffer.

Indeed, Yale University professor Tom Tyler believes that the public's perception of police *legitimacy* is the basis of law enforcement–community relations. That is, if citizens fail to see their moral and social norms reflected in police behavior, then they will be less likely to respect criminal law themselves or aid the police in fighting crime.[128]

Racial and Ethnic Biases in Policing

On November 22, 2014, two white Cleveland police officers took a "Code 1" call—indicating the highest level of urgency—from a dispatcher about "a guy with a pistol." Two seconds after arriving on the scene, they fatally shot twelve-year-old African American Tamir Rice, who, as it turned out, was holding a pellet gun that fired plastic bullets. When Rice's fourteen-year-old sister rushed to help him, the officers tackled her to the ground and placed her in handcuffs. They also failed to provide medical aid for Tamir, who died soon thereafter.

Such incidents contribute to the perception among minorities that they do not receive equal treatment from the criminal justice system. One African American woman said that, when she heard that a young boy had been fatally shot by the police while wielding a toy gun, her first reaction was, "Is he black?"[129] When polled, African Americans consistently express less confidence in the police than do whites (see Figure 6.8). Consequently, the legitimacy of the police for many minorities is compromised by the specter of bias.

Perceived Bias In the next chapter's discussion of racial profiling, we will see that many African Americans believe that they are often targeted for a particular "offense"—DWB, or "driving while black." To a certain extent, statistics bear out these suspicions. A recent Justice Department study reports that although police pull over black, white, and Hispanic drivers at similar rates, blacks and Hispanics are almost three times more likely to be searched following the stop.[130]

In Ferguson, Missouri, the site of another recent racially charged police shooting, African Americans make up 65 percent of the population while accounting for 86 percent of traffic stops, 93 percent of arrests, and 92 percent of searches after stops by local law enforcement.[131] Nationwide, African Americans are about four times as likely to be arrested for marijuana possession as whites.[132] These data reinforce the notion that police bias is responsible for the disproportionate numbers of minorities in American prisons and jails discussed throughout this textbook.

Police Attitudes and Discretion

Although everyone would agree that some individual officers may be influenced by prejudice,

FIGURE 6.8 Racial Attitudes toward the Police

As these polls conducted by the federal government show, members of minority groups are more likely than whites to have negative views of the police.

Q: How do you rate the honesty and ethical standards of the police?

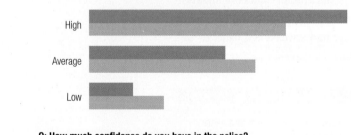

Q: How much confidence do you have in the police?

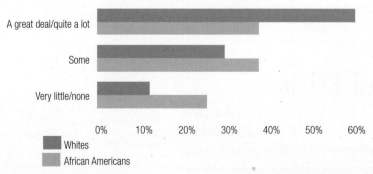

Whites

African Americans

Source: Gallup, 2014.

the greater police presence and arrest rates in minority neighborhoods should not be accepted as automatic evidence of law enforcement discrimination. As we learned earlier in the chapter, the primary operational tactic of all metropolitan police forces is responding to calls for service. According to research by law enforcement expert Richard J. Ludman, the greater police presence in these communities is mainly the result of calls for service from residents, which, in turn, are caused by higher local crime rates. Indeed, Randall Kennedy believes that such "selective law enforcement" should be, and for the most part is, welcomed by those who live in high-crime areas and appreciate the added protection.[133]

Furthermore, as several experts point out, cultural differences often exist between police officers and the residents of the neighborhoods they patrol. One survey found that police working in minority areas perceived higher levels of abuse and less respect from those citizens than from those in nonminority areas.[134] Another found that drivers pulled over by law enforcement agents of the same race or ethnicity were more likely to think that the stop was legitimate than when the race or ethnicity of the driver and the officer was different.[135] Judging someone's demeanor is often a subjective task and can be influenced by a lack of communication between two people of different backgrounds—another reason why it is so important for police departments to attract members of minority groups, as noted in our discussion of recruiting strategies in the previous chapter.

Police Corruption

Police *corruption* has been a concern since the first organized American police departments. As you recall from Chapter 5, a desire to eradicate, or at least limit, corruption was one of the motivating factors behind the reform movement of policing. For general purposes, **police corruption** can be defined as the misuse of authority by a law enforcement officer "in a manner designed to produce personal gain."

In the 1970s, a police officer named Frank Serpico went public about corruption in the New York Police Department. City authorities responded by establishing the Knapp Commission to investigate Serpico's claims. The inquiry uncovered widespread institutionalized corruption in the department. In general, the Knapp Commission report divided corrupt police officers into two categories: "grass eaters" and "meat eaters." "Grass eaters" are involved in passive corruption—they simply accept the payoffs and opportunities that police work can provide. As the name implies, "meat eaters" are more aggressive in their quest for personal gain, initiating and going to great lengths to carry out corrupt schemes.[136]

Types of Corruption Specifically, the Knapp Commission's investigation identified three basic, traditional types of police corruption:

1. *Bribery,* in which the police officer accepts money or other forms of payment in exchange for "favors," which may include allowing a certain criminal activity to continue or misplacing a key piece of evidence before a trial. Related to bribery are *payoffs,* in which an officer demands payment from an individual or a business in return for certain services.
2. *Shakedowns,* in which an officer attempts to coerce money or goods from a citizen or criminal.
3. *Mooching,* in which the police officer accepts free "gifts" such as cigarettes, liquor, or services in return for favorable treatment of the gift giver.[137]

Additionally, corrupt police officers have many opportunities to engage in theft or burglary by taking money or property in the course of their duties. Vice investigations,

▲ Philadelphia Police Commissioner Charles Ramsey, left, takes questions during a 2014 press conference after the FBI arrested six of his officers for stealing cash and drugs from suspects. **Why do you think federal law enforcement agents are often in the best position to carry out investigations of local police corruption?** AP Images/Matt Rourke

for example, often uncover temptingly large amounts of illegal drugs and cash. Several years ago, six Philadelphia police officers were arrested for improperly "confiscating" $500,000 in cash, drugs, and personal property such as Rolex watches from suspects.

Another scenario involves police misconduct that becomes pervasive, infecting a group of officers. In 2015, federal agents began investigating the Calexico, California, police department's detective unit for using recently purchased surveillance equipment to extort local politicians. The department's police chief accused his own detectives of "acting like the mob."[138]

Theories of Police Corruption Not all police corruption is for personal gain. As we will discuss further in Chapter 10, *wrongful convictions* are sometimes the result of officers manipulating evidence or coercing false confessions. "Bad cops give the system what it wants—convictions," says one police corruption expert.[139] In addition, a recent study found a strong correlation between police misconduct and the violent crime rate in the area being policed. Criminologists theorize that officers who patrol high-crime neighborhoods start seeing crime as the norm. Eventually, these officers come to believe, cynically, that residents of such neighborhoods, including crime victims, are less deserving of "good" policing.[140]

In general, there is no single reason why police misconduct occurs. Certain types of officers do, however, seem more likely to engage in corruption—the young, the relatively uneducated (lacking a college degree), those with records of prior criminality and citizens' complaints, and those unlikely to be promoted.[141] Criminologists Christopher Donner and Wesley Jennings believe that the roots of police misbehavior are similar to the roots of criminal misbehavior. In Chapter 2, we saw that criminality has been linked to "low self-control," or a predisposition to seek pleasure through deviance. Researching the behavior of nearly two thousand Philadelphia police officers, Donner and Jennings identified low self-control as a "significant predictor" of citizen complaints for physical and verbal abuse and departmental investigations of misconduct.[142]

Police Accountability

Even in a police department with excellent recruiting methods, state-of-the-art ethics and discretionary training programs, and a culturally diverse workforce that nearly matches the makeup of the community, the problems discussed earlier in this chapter are bound to occur. The question then becomes—given the inevitability of excessive force, corruption, and other misconduct—*who shall police the police?*

Inside the Department Placing body-worn cameras on police officers, discussed at the opening of this chapter, is a management strategy designed to hold law enforcement officers accountable for their actions. Randy Sutton, a former police officer and ethics expert, recognizes three components of accountability within law enforcement agencies:

1. *Self-accountability.* Each officer is responsible for his or her actions, and must be aware that these actions impact the integrity of the agency as a whole.
2. *Supervisory accountability.* Supervisors, such as sergeants, are often in the best position to observe the activities of officers under their command. By being swift and firm with advice or discipline, they can "set the tone" for ethical behavior in a department.
3. *Administrative accountability.* Given the nature of departmental hierarchies, those at the top of the command structure are in a crucial position to implement policies that promote accountability. They must also "walk the walk," ethically, so as to set a good example.[143]

When corruption or misbehavior is uncovered within a department, the first step is generally disciplinary. Such discipline includes the officer being placed on administrative leave, suspended, or fired. During this process, the officer is generally represented by her or his police union and afforded the due process protections due all civil servants.[144]

The mechanism for investigations within a police department is the **internal affairs unit (IAU).** In many smaller police departments, the police chief conducts internal affairs investigations, while midsized and large departments have a team of internal affairs officers. The New York Police Department's IAU has an annual budget of nearly $62 million and consists of 650 officers.

Outside the Department
Many communities also rely on an external procedure for handling citizen complaints against the police, known as **citizen oversight.** In this process, citizens—people who are not sworn officers and, by inference, not biased in favor of law enforcement officers—review allegations of police misconduct or brutality. According to data gathered by police accountability expert Samuel Walker, nearly one hundred cities now operate some kind of review procedure by an independent body.[145]

For the most part, citizen review boards can only recommend action to the police chief or other executive. They do not have the power to discipline officers directly. Police officers generally resent this intrusion by civilians, and most studies have shown that civilian review boards are not widely successful in their efforts to convince police chiefs to take action against their subordinate officers.[146] From the beginning of 2009 to June 2014, for example, the New York Police Department's Civil Complaint Review Board received just over one thousand complaints concerning police officers using chokeholds. The Board confirmed only ten of those complaints, and none of the officers involved received serious punishment.[147]

Police Liability
The American court system also plays a role in policy accountability. To start, police officers can be held criminally liable for misconduct, as we saw at the beginning of this chapter with regard to the two Albuquerque officers charged with murder for allegedly killing a homeless man.

Civil Liability
Local prosecutors and grand juries are, however, sometimes reluctant to charge police officers with criminal wrongdoing for on-the-job activity. Consequently, alleged victims of police misconduct often rely on the **civil liability** of police officers. That is, they sue the officer or the agency responsible for the officer in state or federal court.

So, even before the Cuyahoga County Sheriff's Office decided whether to file criminal charges against the officer who killed twelve-year-old Tamir Rice, discussed earlier, the boy's family filed a civil wrongful death lawsuit against the city of Cleveland

Internal Affairs Unit (IAU) A division within a police department that receives and investigates complaints of wrongdoing by police officers.

Citizen Oversight The process by which citizens review complaints brought against individual police officers or police departments.

Civil Liability The potential responsibility of police officers, police departments, or municipalities to defend themselves against civil lawsuits.

in December 2014. These lawsuits can prove costly, if not for the officer then for local taxpayers. In 2013, the city of New York spent $428 million to settle a series of civil lawsuits against its police officers.[148]

Civil Rights Violations Keep in mind that police officers generally cannot be charged with a crime or sued simply because they used poor judgment in their discretionary decisions.[149] Rather, they usually face criminal or civil sanctions for negligence on the job or for intentional *civil rights violations*. A **civil rights violation** involves denial of the rights afforded to all Americans by the United States Constitution. Because the Constitution prohibits government officials from discriminating against citizens on the basis of race or ethnicity, many police lawsuits involve members of minority groups.[150]

Also, the U.S. Department of Justice has the power to investigate cities for law enforcement civil rights violations.[151] If, following the investigation, the federal government finds the pattern of such violations to be pervasive, it can enter into a consent decree (see previous chapter) with the city to improve the situation. In general, under these consent decrees, a local police department agrees to:

Identify the three consent decree requirements commonly made of local police departments that have exhibited patterns of civil rights violations.

LEARNING **8** OBJECTIVE

1. Implement policies and training that minimize the use of force,
2. Set up tracking systems to identify and discipline those officers most often involved in use-of-force incidents, and
3. Improve community relations, particularly by providing effective protocols for responding to citizen complaints.

Since 2008, the Justice Department has opened civil rights investigations in about twenty cities, including Albuquerque, New Orleans, Portland, Oregon, and, in September 2014, Ferguson, Missouri.

Ethics in Law Enforcement

Police corruption is intricately connected with the ethics of law enforcement officers. As you saw in Chapter 1, ethics has to do with fundamental questions of the fairness, justice, rightness, or wrongness of any action. Given the significant power that police officers hold, society expects very high standards of ethical behavior from them.

Ethical Dilemmas Some police actions are obviously unethical, such as the behavior of the Philadelphia police officers who stole cash and jewelry from suspects, described in a previous section. The majority of ethical dilemmas that a police officer will face are not so clear cut. Criminologists Joycelyn M. Pollock and Ronald F. Becker define an ethical dilemma as a situation in which law enforcement officers:

- Do not know the right course of action;
- Have difficulty doing what they consider to be right; and/or
- Find the wrong choice very tempting.[152]

Because of the many rules that govern policing—the subject of the next chapter—police officers often find themselves tempted by a phenomenon called **noble cause corruption.** This type of corruption occurs when, in the words of John P. Crank and Michael A. Caldero, "officers do bad things because they believe the outcomes will be good."[153] Examples include planting evidence or lying in court to help convict someone the officer knows to be guilty, and the situation discussed in the feature *A Question of Ethics: The "Dirty Harry" Problem.*

Elements of Ethics Pollock and Becker, both of whom have extensive experience as ethics instructors for police departments, further identify four categories of ethical dilemmas, involving discretion, duty, honesty, and loyalty.[154]

- *Discretion.* The law provides rigid guidelines for how police officers must act and how they cannot act, but it does not offer guidelines for how officers *should act* in many circumstances. As mentioned at the beginning of this chapter, police officers often use discretion to determine how they should act, and ethics plays an important role in guiding discretionary actions.
- *Duty.* The concept of discretion is linked with **duty,** or the obligation to act in a certain manner. Society, by passing laws, can make a police officer's duty clearer and, in the process, help eliminate discretion from the decision-making process. But an officer's duty will not always be obvious, and ethical considerations can often supplement "the rules" of being a law enforcement agent.
- *Honesty.* Of course, honesty is a critical attribute for an ethical police officer. A law enforcement agent must make hundreds of decisions in a day, and most of them require him or her to be honest in order to properly do the job.
- *Loyalty.* What should a police officer do if he or she witnesses a partner using excessive force on a suspect? The choice often sets loyalty against ethics, especially if the officer does not condone the violence.

Although an individual's ethical makeup is determined by a multitude of personal factors, police departments can create an atmosphere that is conducive to professionalism.

Duty The moral sense of a police officer that she or he should behave in a certain manner.

LEARNING **9** OBJECTIVE Explain what an ethical dilemma is and name four categories of ethical dilemmas that a police officer typically may face.

A Question of Ethics: The "Dirty Harry" Problem

The Situation A young girl has been kidnapped by a psychotic killer named Scorpio. Demanding a $200,000 ransom, Scorpio has buried the girl alive, leaving her with just enough oxygen to survive for a few hours. Detective Harry Callahan manages to find Scorpio, but the kidnapper stubbornly refuses to reveal the location of the girl. Callahan comes to the conclusion that the only way he can get this information from Scorpio in time is to beat it out of him.

The Ethical Dilemma The U.S. Constitution, as interpreted by the United States Supreme Court, forbids the torture of criminal suspects. Following proper procedure, Callahan should arrest Scorpio and advise him of his constitutional rights. If Scorpio requests an attorney, Callahan must comply. If the attorney then advises Scorpio to remain silent, there is nothing Callahan can do. Of course, after all this time, the girl will certainly be dead.*

What Is the Solution? What should Detective Callahan do? According to the late Carl B. Klockars of the University of Delaware, "Each time a police officer considers deceiving a suspect into confessing by telling him that his [or her] fingerprints were found at the scene or that a conspirator has already confessed, each time a police officer considers adding some untrue details to his [or her] account of a probable cause to legitimate a crucial stop or search [that police officer] faces" the same problem as Detective Callahan. Are police ever justified in using unlawful methods, no matter what good may ultimately be achieved?

* This scenario is taken from *Dirty Harry* (1971), one of the most popular police dramas of all time. In the film, Detective Callahan, played by Clint Eastwood, shoots Scorpio and then tortures him. Although Callahan eventually gets the information he needs, it is too late to save the girl.

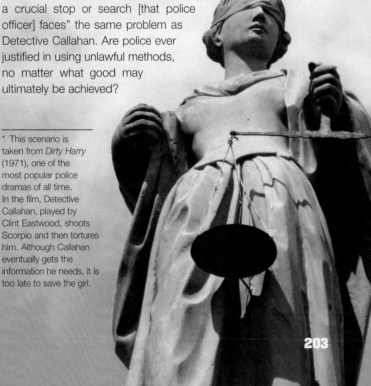

▲ Vice President Joseph Biden presents Kitsap County (Washington) deputy sheriff Krista McDonald with the Public Safety Officer Medal of Valor. McDonald earned the honor for placing herself in the line of fire to rescue two fellow deputies who had been wounded in a shootout with a suspected sex offender. **What role does the concept of duty play in a law enforcement agent's decision, regardless of her or his own safety, to protect the life of another person?** Mandel Ngan/AFP/Getty Images

Brandon V. Zuidema and H. Wayne Duff, both captains with the Lynchburg (Virginia) Police Department, believe that law enforcement administrators can encourage ethical policing by:

1. Incorporating ethics into the department's mission statement.
2. Conducting internal training sessions in ethics.
3. Accepting "honest mistakes" and helping the officer learn from those mistakes.
4. Adopting a zero-tolerance policy toward unethical decisions when the mistakes are not so honest.[155]

EthicsChallenge

Several years ago, a Daytona Beach, Florida, police officer was fired for a post on his Facebook page that said of Trayvon Martin's killing (discussed in Chapter 4), "Another thug gone. Pull up your pants and be respectful." What is your opinion of this punishment? What ethical responsibilities do law enforcement agents have when using social media? ■

CJ IN ACTION

Militarizing Local Police

As residents watched in awe, the BearCat—an eight-ton, ten-foot high, bullet-proof attack truck with rotating roof hatch and multiple gun ports—rumbled down NE 204th Street in Miami, Florida. The massive military machine, filled with local police officers, was headed toward the home of Antonio Cardoza, who had barricaded himself inside. "When I saw the [BearCat], I thought . . . are they going to war or something?" said one of Cardoza's neighbors.[156] After a brief exchange of gunfire, Cardoza was injured and taken to a nearby hospital. The incident, in which no officers were wounded, aptly summarizes the militarization of local police departments in the United States, the controversial subject of this chapter's *CJ in Action* feature.

The Growth of SWAT

The military model of local police departments started with the Los Angeles Police Department's first Special Weapons and Tactics (SWAT) units in the late 1960s. These units, trained and armed like special military forces, were initially designed to deal with extreme circumstances such as riots, hostage situations, or active-shooter scenarios. Today, SWAT teams are used around 50,000 times a year, most often to serve drug-related warrants in private homes.[157]

The trend toward SWAT unit militarization intensified after the terrorist attacks of September 11, 2001, when the federal government began to consider local police as the "front lines" of a new kind of war. Since 2001, the Department of Defense has donated military equipment worth more than $4 billion to local police departments in all fifty states. In addition, the Department of Defense has distributed more than $34 billion in "terrorism grants" to local departments to purchase military gear.[158] This largesse went relatively unnoticed by the public until August 2014. That month, local officers in full body armor, including a sniper in a BearCat, confronted unarmed protestors in Ferguson, Missouri, a situation discussed in Chapter 1. Suddenly, the "blurring lines between military and local law enforcement" were the focus of a national debate.[159]

The Case for Militarizing Local Police

- Police officers risk their lives every day, and this equipment helps protect them. "There's violence in schools, there's violence on the streets," says one sheriff. "If driving a military vehicle is going to protect officers, that's what I'm going to do."[160]

- The possibility that military equipment places innocent citizens in danger is exaggerated. Even during the heated Ferguson confrontations, no officer fired a lethal weapon at protestors.

- Local police departments need to be prepared for the worst-case terrorism scenario, even if it has not yet occurred in their jurisdictions.

The Case against Militarizing Local Police

- "Neighborhoods are not war zones," said the American Civil Liberties Union in a report, "and our police officers should not be treating us like wartime enemies."[161]

- The potential for abuse is too great. According to one estimate, more than fifty people have been killed during SWAT raids for nonviolent wrongdoing such as illegal drug use or gambling.[162]

- The use of military equipment by police disproportionately occurs in minority communities, increasing distrust of law enforcement where trust is most needed.

Your Opinion—Writing Assignment

In one poll following the Ferguson protests, the only shared ground between African American and white respondents was the subject of police militarization. Two-thirds of both groups agreed that military weapons "should be reserved for the military."[163] What is your opinion of this statement? Also, given that local police departments are likely to continue using military equipment, how can they be made more accountable when doing so? Which of the accountability mechanisms covered in this chapter, including body cameras, would be most effective in this area? Why? Before responding, you can review our discussions in the sections of this chapter concerning:

- Police use of force ("Us versus Them": Issues in Modern Policing").

- Racial and ethnic biases in policing ("Police Misconduct and Ethics").

- Police accountability ("Police Misconduct and Ethics").

Your answer should include at least three full paragraphs.

Summary

For more information on these concepts, look back to the Learning Objective icons throughout the chapter.

 Explain why police officers are allowed discretionary powers. Police officers are considered trustworthy and able to make honest decisions. They have experience and training. They are knowledgeable in criminal behavior. Finally, they must have the discretion to take reasonable steps to protect themselves.

 List the three primary purposes of police patrol. (a) The deterrence of crime, (b) the maintenance of public order, and (c) the provision of services that are not related to crime.

 Indicate some investigation strategies that are considered aggressive. Using undercover officers is considered an aggressive (and often dangerous) investigative technique. The use of informants is also aggressive, but involves danger for those who inform.

 Describe how forensic experts use DNA fingerprinting to solve crimes. Law enforcement agents gather trace evidence such as blood, semen, skin, and hair from the crime scene. Because these items are rich in DNA, which provides a unique genetic blueprint for every living organism, crime labs can create a DNA profile of the suspect and test it against other such profiles stored in databases. If the profiles match, then law enforcement agents have found a strong suspect for the crime.

 Explain why differential response strategies enable police departments to respond more efficiently to 911 calls. A differential response strategy allows a police department to distinguish among calls for service so that officers may respond to important calls more quickly. Therefore, a "hot" crime, such as a burglary in progress, will receive more immediate attention than a "cold" crime, such as a missing automobile that disappeared several days earlier.

 Explain community policing and its contribution to the concept of problem-oriented policing. Community policing involves proactive problem solving and a community-police partnership in which the community engages itself along with the police to address crime and the fear of crime in a particular geographic area. By establishing a cooperative presence in a community, police officers are better able to recognize the root causes of criminal behavior there and apply problem-oriented policing methods when necessary.

 Determine when police officers are justified in using deadly force. Police officers must make a reasonable judgment in determining when to use force that will place the suspect in threat of injury or death. That is, given the circumstances, the officer must reasonably assume that the use of such force is necessary to avoid serious injury or death to the officer or someone else.

 Identify the three consent decree requirements commonly made of local police departments that have exhibited patterns of civil rights violations. Generally, such consent decrees require the local agency to (a) improve use-of-force training programs, (b) "red-flag" officers mostly likely to be improperly using force, and (c) upgrade its response to citizen complaints.

 Explain what an ethical dilemma is and name four categories of ethical dilemmas that a police officer typically may face. An ethical dilemma is a situation in which police officers (a) do not know the right course of action, (b) have difficulty doing what they consider to be right, and/or (c) find the wrong choice very tempting. The four types of ethical dilemmas involve (a) discretion, (b) duty, (c) honesty, and (d) loyalty.

Questions for Critical Analysis

1. Suppose a state legislator proposed a bill to limit the amount of time a law enforcement officer would be allowed to go undercover. What might be the reasoning behind this legislation?

2. Criminologists John and Emily Beck suggest that crime reduction strategies should treat crime as if it were a form of pollution. How does this comparison make sense in the context of predictive policing and crime mapping?

3. In many large cities, "hot spots" of crime are located in low-income, minority neighborhoods. Given this reality, how might such data-driven policing contribute to tensions between the police and members of minority groups?

4. Suppose that a high-crime neighborhood is plagued by numerous abandoned homes and malfunctioning streetlights. Applying the "broken windows" theory, what steps should local politicians take to reduce crime in the area? Why?

5. The International Association of Chiefs of Police's *Code of Conduct* states that law enforcement agents should "never allow personal feelings, animosities, or friendships to influence official conduct." Is this standard for police behavior realistic? Explain your answer.

Key Terms

ballistics   179

blue curtain   192

body armor   193

broken windows theory   188

bureaucracy   173

burnout   194

citizen oversight   201

civil liability   201

civil rights violation   202

clearance rate   178

cold case   179

cold hit   181

community policing   189

computer-aided dispatch (CAD)   185

conducted energy device (CED)   197

confidential informant (CI)   178

crime mapping   187

deadly force   196

delegation of authority   173

detective   177

differential response   185

directed patrol   186

DNA fingerprinting   180

duty   203

forensics   179

hot spots   187

incident-driven policing   183

internal affairs unit (IAU)   201

noble cause corruption   202

police corruption   199

police subculture   191

policy   172

proactive arrests   188

problem-oriented policing   190

professionalism   197

random patrol   186

reactive arrests   188

reasonable force   196

response time   184

reverse 911   186

socialization   192

stressors   194

trace evidence   179

Notes

1. Richard R. Johnson, "Police Officer Job Satisfaction: A Multidimensional Analysis," *Police Quarterly* (June 2012), 158–160.

2. Kenneth Culp David, *Police Discretion* (St. Paul, Minn.: West Publishing Co., 1975).

3. C. E. Pratt, "Police Discretion," *Law and Order* (March 1992), 99–100.

4. "More than a Hunch," *Law Enforcement News* (September 2004), 1.

5. Herbert Jacob, *Urban Justice* (Boston: Little, Brown, 1973), 27.

6. Bureau of Justice Statistics, *Local Police Departments, 2003* (Washington, D.C.: U.S. Department of Justice, May 2006), 24.

7. Jack Richter, "Number of Police Pursuits Drop Dramatically in Los Angeles," *Los Angeles Police Department Press Release* (August 20, 2003).

8. Lindsay Miller and Jessica Toliver, *Implementing a Body-Worn Camera Program* (Washington, D.C.: Police Executive Research Forum, 2014), 12–14.

9. Quoted in Ryan Boetel, "APD Chief, IRO Often at Odds over Lapel Video," *Albuquerque Journal* (December 27, 2014), A1.

10. Nicole Perez, "Officer Who Shot Mary Hawkes Fired for Insubordination," *Albuquerque Journal* (December 1, 2014), at **www .abqjournal.com/503875/news/lawyer -albuquerque-officer-in-shooting-fired .html**.

11. Samuel Walker, *The Police in America: An Introduction*, 2d ed. (New York: McGraw-Hill, 1992), 16.

12. George L. Kelling and Mark H. Moore, "From Political to Reform to Community: The Evolving Strategy of Police," in *Community Policing: Rhetoric or Reality*, ed. Jack Greene and Stephen Mastrofski (New York: Praeger Publishers, 1988), 13.

13. Michael White, *Controlling Officer Behavior in the Field* (New York: John Jay College of Criminal Justice, 2011), 19.

14. John S. Dempsey and Linda S. Forst, *An Introduction to Policing*, 7th ed. (Clifton Park, N.Y.: Delmar Cengage Learning, 2014), 91.

15. *Ibid.*, 93–95.

16. Karen L. Amendola, "Schedule Matters: The Movement to Compressed Work Weeks," *The Police Chief* (May 2012), 30–35.

17. Henry M. Wrobleski and Karen M. Hess, *Introduction to Law Enforcement and Criminal Justice*, 7th ed. (Belmont, Calif.: Wadsworth/Thomson Learning, 2003), 119.

18. Bureau of Justice Statistics, *Local Police Departments, 2007* (Washington, D.C.: U.S. Department of Justice, December 2010), 6.

19. Connie Fletcher, "What Cops Know," *On Patrol* (Summer 1996), 44–45.

20. David H. Bayley, *Police for the Future* (New York: Oxford University Press, 1994), 20.

21. Walker, *op. cit.*, 103.

22. Eric J. Scott, *Calls for Service: Citizens Demand an Initial Police Response* (Washington, D.C.: National Institute of Justice, 1981), 28–30.

23. Vivian B. Lord, et al., "Factors Influencing the Response of Crisis Intervention Team–Certified Law Enforcement Officers," *Police Quarterly* (December 2011), 388.

24. E. Fuller Torrey, *Justifiable Homicides by Law Enforcement Officers: What Is the Role of Mental Illness?* (Arlington, Va.: Treatment Advocacy Center, September 2013), 3.

25. Lord, et al., *op. cit.*, 390–391.

26. *Ibid.*, 391–392.

27. William G. Gay, Theodore H. Schell, and Stephen Schack, *Routine Patrol: Improving Patrol Productivity*, vol. 1 (Washington, D.C.: National Institute of Justice, 1977), 3–6.

28. Boetel, *op. cit.*

29. Gary W. Cordner, "The Police on Patrol," in *Police and Policing: Contemporary Issues*, ed. Dennis Jay Kenney (New York: Praeger Publishers, 1989), 60–71.

30. Peter W. Greenwood and Joan Petersilia, *The Criminal Investigation Process: Summary and Policy Implications* (Santa Monica, Calif.: RAND Corporation, 1975).

31. Fletcher, *op. cit.*, 46.

32. Quoted in Sarah Stillman, "The Throwaways," *New Yorker* (September 3, 2012), 38–39.

33. Center on Law and Security, *Terrorist Trial Report Card: September 11, 2001–September 11, 2009* (New York: New York University School of Law, January 2010), 42–44.

34. Kimball Perry and Patrick Brennan, "Father: Terror Plot Suspect Was a 'Momma's Boy,'" *Cincinnati Enquirer* (January 24, 2015), A1.

35. "Dad Accuses FBI of Setting Up 'Mommy's Boy' Son in Bomb Plot," *ABC News* (January 15, 2015), at **abcnews.go.com/US/dad -accuses-fbi-setting-son-bomb-plot /story?id=28240751.**

36. Federal Bureau of Investigation, *Crime in the United States 2013* (Washington, D.C.: U.S. Department of Justice, 2014), at **www .fbi.gov/about-us/cjis/ucr/crime-in-the -u.s/2013/crime-in-the-u.s.-2013/cius -home**, Table 25.

37. James M. Cronin, Gerard R. Murphy, Lisa L. Spahr, Jessica I. Toliver, and Richard E. Weger, *Promoting Effective Homicide Investigations* (Washington, D.C.: Police Executive Research Forum, August 2007), 102–103.

38. Robert C. Davis, Carl Jenses, and Karin E. Kitchens, *Cold Case Investigations: An Analysis of Current Practices and Factors Associated with Successful Outcomes* (Santa Monica, Calif.: RAND Corporation, 2011), xii.

39. Ronald F. Becker, *Criminal Investigations*, 2d ed. (Sudbury, Mass.: Jones & Bartlett, 2004), 7.

40. Bureau of Justice Statistics, *Census of Publicly Funded Forensic Crime Laboratories, 2009* (Washington, D.C.: U.S. Department of Justice, August 2012), 1.

41. Joseph Peterson, Ira Sommers, Deborah Baskin, and Donald Johnson, *The Role and Impact of Forensic Evidence in the Criminal Justice Process* (Washington, D.C.: National Institute of Justice, September 2010), 8–9.

42. Simon A. Cole, "More Than Zero: Accounting for Error in Latent Fingerprinting Identification," *Journal of Criminal Law and Criminology* (Spring 2005), 985–1078.

43. Quoted in "New DNA Database Helps Crack 1979 N.Y. Murder Case," *Miami Herald* (March 14, 2000), 18A.

44. Judith E. Lewter, "The Use of Forensic DNA in Criminal Cases in Kentucky as Compared with Other Selected States," *Kentucky Law Journal* (1997–1998), 223.

45. "CODIS—NDIS Statistics," at **www.fbi.gov /about-us/lab/biometric-analysis/codis /ndis-statistics.**

46. Annette Summers and Stephanie Yeung, "Speeding Up DNA Analysis," *Police* (February 6, 2014), at **www.policemag.com/channel /technology/articles/2014/02/speeding -up-dna-analysis.aspx.**

47. Gautam Naik, "To Sketch a Thief: Genes Draw Likeness of Suspects," *Wall Street Journal* (March 29, 2009), A9.

48. Nancy Ritter, "DNA Solves Property Crimes (But Are We Ready for That?)," *NIJ Journal* (October 2008), 2–12.

49. Phil Bulman, "DNA and Property Crimes," *The Police Chief* (April 2013), 16.

50. Paul Heaton, *Hidden in Plain Sight: What Cost-of-Crime Research Can Tell Us about Investing in Police* (Santa Monica, Calif.: RAND Corporation, 2010).

51. Libby Schaaf, "How New York Cut Crime," *San Francisco Chronicle* (April 23, 2013), A8.

52. *Policing and the Economic Downturn* (Washington, D.C.: Police Executive Research Forum, February 2013), 1–4.

53. Wrobleski and Hess, *op. cit.*, 173.

54. Kate Zernike, "Camden Turns Around with New Police Force," *New York Times* (September 1, 2014), A1.

55. Stephen J. Blumberg and Julian V. Luke, "Wireless Substitution: Early Release of Estimates from the National Health Interview Survey, July–December 2013," *National Health Interview Survey* (Centers for Disease Control and Prevention, July 2014), 1.

56. Eddie Reyes, "Next Generation 9-1-1: What It Is—and Why Police Chiefs Should Care," *The Police Chief* (December 2012), 86–87.

57. Quoted in Carl Bialik, "Detroit Police Response Times No Guide to Effectiveness," *Wall Street Journal* (August 2, 2013), at **online.wsj.com/news/articles/SB10001424127887323997004578642250518125898.**

58. Cody W. Telep and David Weisburd, "What Is Known about the Effectiveness of Police Practices in Reducing Crime and Disorder?" *Police Quarterly* (December 2012), 344.

59. *Local Police Departments, 2007, op. cit.,* Table 12, page 15.

60. George L. Kelling, Tony Pate, Duane Dieckman, and Charles Brown, *The Kansas City Preventive Patrol Experiment: A Summary Report* (Washington, D.C.: The Police Foundation, 1974), 3–4.

61. Carl B. Klockars and Stephen D. Mastrofski, "The Police and Serious Crime," in *Thinking about Police,* ed. Carl B. Klockars and Stephen Mastrofski (New York: McGraw-Hill, 1990), 130.

62. Anthony M. Pate, "Experimenting with Foot Patrol: The Newark Experience," in Dennis P. Rosenbaum, ed., *Community Crime Prevention: Does It Work?* (Newbury Park, Calif.: Sage, 1986).

63. Jerry H. Ratcliffe, et al., "The Philadelphia Foot Patrol Experiment: A Randomized Controlled Trial of Police Patrol Effectiveness in Violent Crime Hotspots," *Criminology* (August 2011), 795–830.

64. Nick James, "Despite Fewer Cops On Streets, Modesto Police Reduce Crime Thanks to Predictive Policing," *CBS Sacramento* (November 12, 2014), at **sacramento.cbslocal.com/2014/11/12/despite-fewer-cops-on-streets-modesto-police-reduce-crime-thanks-to-predictive-policing.**

65. Lawrence W. Sherman and David Weisburd, "General Deterrent Effects of Police Patrol in Crime 'Hot Spots': A Randomized Controlled Trial," *Justice Quarterly* (December 1995), 625–648.

66. Renée J. Mitchell, "Hot-Spot Randomized Control Works for Sacramento," *The Police Chief* (February 2013), 12.

67. David Weisburd and Cynthia Lum, "The Diffusion of Computerized Crime Mapping in Policing: Linking Research and Practice," *Police Practice and Research* 6 (2005), 419–434.

68. Quoted in "New Model Police," *The Economist* (June 9, 2007), 29.

69. Lawrence W. Sherman, "Policing for Crime Prevention," in *Contemporary Policing: Controversies, Challenges, and Solutions,* eds. Quint C. Thurman and Jihong Zhao (Los Angeles: Roxbury Publishing Co., 2004), 63–66.

70. *Ibid.,* 65.

71. William Sousa and George L. Kelling, "Of 'Broken Windows,' Criminology, and Criminal Justice," in *Police Innovation: Contrasting Perspectives,* eds. David L. Weisburd and Anthony A. Braga (New York: Cambridge University Press, 2006), 77–97.

72. Daniel W. Gerard, "Cincinnati HAZARD: A Place-Based Traffic Enforcement and Violent Crime Strategy," *The Police Chief* (July 2013), 44–46.

73. Richard Rosenfeld, "Crime Decline in Context," *Contexts* (Spring 2002), 25–34.

74. Ralph B. Taylor, "Incivilities Reduction Policing, Zero Tolerance, and the Retreat from Coproduction: Weak Foundations and Strong Pressures," in *Police Innovation: Contrasting Perspectives,* eds. David L. Weisburd and Anthony A. Braga (New York: Cambridge University Press, 2006), 133–153.

75. Quoted in Joseph Goldstein and Nate Schweber, "Complaints about Chokeholds Focus of Study," *New York Times* (July 20, 2014), A19.

76. Mark H. Moore and George L. Kelling, "'To Serve and Protect': Learning from Police History," *Public Interest* (Winter 1983), 54–57.

77. Brigitte Gassaway, Steven Armon, and Dana Perez, "Engaging the Community: Operation Heat Wave," *Geography and Public Safety* (October 2011), 8–9.

78. *Local Police Departments, op. cit.,* 26.

79. *Ibid.,* 28.

80. Quoted in Richard A. Oppel, Jr., "National Questions over Police Hit Home in Cleveland," *New York Times* (December 9, 2014), A16.

81. Dennis Rosenbaum, quoted in Jon Schuppe, "Can Smarter Police Work Prevent Another Ferguson?" *NBC News* (August 15, 2014), at **www.nbcnews.com/storyline/michael-brown-shooting/can-smarter-police-work-prevent-another-ferguson-n180841.**

82. Michael D. White and Charles M. Katz, "Policing Convenience Store Crime: Lessons from the Glendale, Arizona Smart Policing Initiative," *Police Quarterly* (September 2013), 305–322.

83. Herman Goldstein, "Improving Policing: A Problem-Oriented Approach," *Crime and Delinquency* 25 (1979), 236–258.

84. Bureau of Justice Assistance, *Problem-Oriented Drug Enforcement: A Community-Based Approach for Effective Policing* (Washington, D.C.: Office of Justice Programs, 1993), 5.

85. Christopher S. Koper, Bruce Taylor, and Jamie Roush, "What Works Best at Violent Crime Hot Spots? A Test of Directed Patrol and Problem-Solving Approaches in Jacksonville, Florida," *The Police Chief* (October 2013), 12–13.

86. Larry Celona, et al., "Gunman Executes 2 NYPD Cops in Garner 'Revenge,'" *New York Post* (December 20, 2014), at **nypost.com/2014/12/20/2-nypd-cops-shot-execution-style-in-brooklyn**.

87. Quoted in Al Baker and J. David Goodman, "New Fight for a Police Bullhorn after 2 Killings," *New York Times* (December 24, 2012), A1.

88. Al Baker and J. David Goodman, "Arrests and Summonses Rise in New York City, but Fall Short of Pre-Slowdown Levels," *New York Times* (January 13, 2015), A21.

89. Quoted in Benjamin Mueller, "Outcome of Eric Garner Case Bares a Staten Island Divide," *New York Times* (December 5, 2014), A30.

90. Harry J. Mullins, "Myth, Tradition, and Ritual," *Law and Order* (September 1995), 197.

91. William Westly, *Violence and the Police: A Sociological Study of Law, Custom, and Morality* (Cambridge, Mass.: MIT Press, 1970).

92. Wallace Graves, "Police Cynicism: Causes and Cures," *FBI Law Enforcement Bulletin* (June 1996), 16–21.

93. Robert Regoli, *Police in America* (Washington, D.C.: R. F. Publishing, 1977).

94. Bob Herbert, "A Cop's View," *New York Times* (March 15, 1998), 17.

95. Officer Down Memorial Page, at **www.odmp.org/search/year?year=2014.**

96. Federal Bureau of Investigation, *Law Enforcement Officers Killed and Assaulted, 2011* (Washington, D.C.: U.S. Department of Justice, 2012), at **www.fbi.gov/about-us/cjis/ucr/leoka/2013/officers-assaulted/assaults_topic_page_-2013.**

97. Dempsey and Forst, *op. cit.,* 180.

98. Bureau of Justice Statistics, *Contacts between Police and the Public, 2008* (Washington, D.C.: U.S. Department of Justice, October 2011), 1.

99. Nathan James, "Body Armor for Law Enforcement Officers: In Brief," *Congressional Research Service* (May 13, 2014).

100. Steven G. Brandl and Meghan S. Stroshine, "The Physical Hazards of Police Work Revisited," *Police Quarterly* (September 2012), 263.

101. The Officer Down Memorial Page; and Craig W. Floyd and Kevin P. Morrison, "Officer Safety on Our Roadways: What the Numbers

Say about Saving Lives," *The Police Chief* (July 2010), 28.

102. National Highway Traffic Safety Administration, *Characteristics of Law Enforcement Officers' Fatalities in Motor Vehicle Crashes* (Washington, D.C.: U.S. Department of Transportation, January 2011), Figure 15, page 25.

103. Rebecca Kanable, "Going Home at Night," *Law Enforcement Technology* (January 2009), 23–24.

104. University at Buffalo, "Impact of Stress on Police Officers' Physical and Mental Health," *Science Daily* (September 29, 2008), at **www.buffalo.edu/news/releases /2008/09/9660.html.**

105. Quoted in *ibid.*

106. Gail A. Goolsakian, et al., *Coping with Police Stress* (Washington, D.C.: National Institute of Justice, 1985).

107. Kim S. Ménard and Michael L. Arter, "Stress, Coping, Alcohol Use, and Posttraumatic Stress Disorder among an International Sample of Police Officers: Does Gender Matter?" *Police Quarterly* (December 2014), 309–310.

108. "Impact of Stress on Police Officers' Physical and Mental Health," *op. cit.*

109. James F. Ballenger, et al., "Patterns and Predictors of Alcohol Use in Male and Female Urban Police Officers," *American Journal on Addictions* (January–February 2011), 21–29.

110. M. J. Horowitz, N. Wilner, N. B. Kaltreider, and W. Alvarez, "Signs and Symptoms of Post Traumatic Stress Disorder," *Archives of General Psychiatry* 37 (1980), 85–92.

111. Daniel W. Clark, Elizabeth K. White, and John M. Violanti, "Law Enforcement Suicide: Current Knowledge and Future Directions," *The Police Chief* (May 2012), 48.

112. *Plakas v. Drinksi,* 19 F.3d 1143, 1150 (7th Cir.) (1994).

113. Bureau of Justice Statistics, *Contacts between Police and the Public, 2008, op. cit.,* 14.

114. Bureau of Justice Statistics, *Arrest-Related Deaths, 2003–2009, Statistical Tables* (Washington, D.C.: U.S. Department of Justice, November 2011), 1.

115. David J. Spotts, "Reviewing Use-of-Force Practices," *The Police Chief* (August 2012), 12.

116. H. Range Hutson, Deirdre Anglin, Phillip Rice, Demetrious N. Kyriacou, Michael Guirguis, and Jared Strote, "Excessive Use of Force by Police: A Survey of Academic Emergency Physicians," *Emergency Medicine Journal* (January 2009), 20–22.

117. Columbia Law School, "Professors Fagan and Harcourt Provide Facts on Grand Jury Practice after Staten Island Decision" (January 23, 2015), at **www.law.columbia.edu /media_inquiries/news_events/2014 /december2014/garner-grand-jury-facts.**

118. *Scott v. Harris,* 127 S.Ct. 1779 (2007).

119. 471 U.S. 1 (1985).

120. 471 U.S. 1, 11 (1985).

121. 490 U.S. 386 (1989).

122. *Brosseau v. Haugen,* 543 U.S. 194 (2004).

123. *Local Police Departments, 2007, op. cit.,* Table 14, page 17.

124. Geoffrey P. Alpert, et al., *Police Use of Force, Tasers, and Other Less-than-Lethal Weapons* (Washington, D.C.: National Institute of Justice, 2011), 1–3.

125. William P. Bozeman, et al., "Safety and Injury Profile of Conducted Electrical Weapons Used by Law Enforcement Officers against Criminal Suspects," *Annals of Emergency Medicine* 53 (2009), 480–489.

126. Amnesty International, Press Release, "Amnesty International Urges Stricter Limits on Police Taser Use as U.S. Death Toll Reaches 500" (February 15, 2012), at **www .amnestyusa.org/news/press-releases /amnesty-international-urges-stricter -limits-on-police-taser-use-as-us-death -toll-reaches-500.**

127. Michael D. White, et al., "An Incident-Level Profile of TASER Device Deployments in Arrest-Related Deaths," *Police Quarterly* (March 2013), 97–98.

128. Tom Tyler, "Legitimacy and Cooperation: Why Do People Help the Police Fight Crime in Their Communities?" *Yale Law School Legal Scholarship Repository* (January 2008), 234–236.

129. Quoted in Michael Wines, "Reaction to Ferguson Decision Shows Racial Divide Remains over Views of Justice," *New York Times* (November 26, 2014), A1.

130. Bureau of Justice Statistics, *Police Behavior during Traffic and Street Stops, 2011* (Washington, D.C.: U.S. Department of Justice, September 2013), Table 5, page 7, and Table 7, page 9.

131. Missouri Attorney General Chris Koster, "MO Stops Report," at **ago.mo.gov/Vehicle Stops/Reports.php?lea=161.**

132. American Civil Liberties Union, "Billions of Dollars Wasted on Racially Biased Arrests," at **www.aclu.org/billions-dollars-wasted -racially-biased-arrests.**

133. Randall L. Kennedy, "*McClesky v. Kemp,* Race, Capital Punishment, and the Supreme Court," *Harvard Law Review* 101 (1988), 1436–1438.

134. Douglas A. Smith, "Minorities and the Police: Attitudinal and Behavioral Questions," in *Race and Criminal Justice,* eds. Michael J. Lynch and E. Britt Patterson (New York: Harrow & Heston, 1991), 28–30.

135. *Police Behavior during Traffic and Street Stops, 2011, op. cit.,* 1.

136. Anthony V. Bouza, *The Police Mystique: An Insider's Look at Cops, Crime, and the Criminal Justice System* (New York: Plenum Books, 1990), 72.

137. Knapp Commission, *Report on Police Corruption* (New York: Brazilier, 1973).

138. Quoted in Jill Replogle, "Calexico Police Department under Fire and Under Investigation," *KPBOS.com* (January 6, 2015), at **www .kpbs.org/news/2015/jan/06/calexico -police-department-under-fire-alleged -crim.**

139. Lonnie Soury, quoted in Hella Winston, "Why Do Bad Cops Escape Punishment?" *The Crime Report* (January 26, 2015), at **www.thecrimereport.org/news/inside -criminal-justice/2015-01-why-do-bad -cops-escape-punishment.**

140. David Eitle, Stewart J. D'Alessio, and Lisa Stolzenberg, "The Effect of Organizational and Environmental Factors in Police Misconduct," *Police Quarterly* (June 2014), 103–126.

141. Robert J. Kane and Michael D. White, "Bad Cops: A Study of Career-Ending Misconduct among New York City Police Officers," *Criminology & Public Policy* (November 2009), 764.

142. Christopher M. Donner and Wesley G. Jennings, "Low Self-Control and Police Deviance: Applying Gottfredson and Hirschi's General Theory to Officer Misconduct," *Police Quarterly* (September 2014), 203–225.

143. Randy Sutton, "Policing with Honor," *PoliceOne.com* (December 28, 2009), at **www .policeone.com/patrol-issues/articles /1983356-Policing-with-honor-The -three-levels-of-accountability.**

144. Dempsey and Forst, *op. cit.,* 245.

145. "Roster of Civilian Oversight Agencies in the U.S.," National Association for Civilian Oversight of Law Enforcement, at **www .nacole.org.**

146. Hazel Glenn Beh, "Municipal Liability for Failure to Investigate Citizen Complaints against Police," *Fordham Urban Law Journal* 23 (Winter 1998), 209.

147. J. David Goodman, "Some New York Police Officers Were Quick to Resort to Chokeholds, Inspector General Finds," *New York Times* (January 12, 2015), A15.

148. Drake Bennett, "Building a Better Police Department," *BusinessWeek* (December 15–December 21, 2014), 27.

149. *Town of Castle Rock v. Gonzales,* 545 U.S. 748 (2005).

150. Dempsey and Forst, *op. cit.,* 248–249.

151. 42 U.S.C. Section 14141 (2006).

152. Jocelyn M. Pollock and Ronald F. Becker, "Ethics Training Using Officers' Dilemmas," *FBI Law Enforcement Bulletin* (November 1996), 20–28.

153. Quoted in Thomas J. Martinelli, "Dodging the Pitfalls of Noble Cause Corruption and the Intelligence Unit," *The Police Chief* (October 2009), 124.

154. Pollock and Becker, *op. cit.,* 20–28.

155. Brandon V. Zuidema and H. Wayne Duff, "Organizational Ethics through Effective Leadership," *Law Enforcement Bulletin* (March 2009), 8–9.

156. Quoted in Charles Rabin, "Miami-Dade Cops Roll Out 8-Ton Tank-Like Military Machine to Confront Hiding Suspects," *Miami Herald* (March 15, 2014), A6.

157. "Cops or Soldiers?" *The Economist* (March 22, 2014), 27.

158. "The Flow of Money and Equipment to Local Police," *New York Times* (December 1, 2014), at **www.nytimes.com/interactive /2014/08/23/us/flow-of-money-and -equipment-to-local-police.html?_r=0.**

159. John F. Kirby, quoted in Matt Apuzzo and Michael S. Schmidt, "In Washington, Second Thoughts on Arming Police," *New York Times* (August 24, 2014), A1.

160. Quoted in "Indiana Sheriff on MRAP Purchase: 'America Has Become a War Zone,'" *Washington Times* (June 10, 2014), at **www.washingtontimes.com/news/2014 /jun/10/indiana-sheriff-mrap-purchase -america-has-become-w.**

161. *War Comes Home: The Excessive Militarization of American Policing* (New York: American Civil Liberties Union, June 2014), 2.

162. Radley Balko, "The Rise of the Warrior Cop," *Wall Street Journal* (July 20–21, 2013), C1.

163. Tanzina Vega and Megan Thee-Brenan, "Polls Shows National Unease with Missouri Unrest," *New York Times* (August 22, 2014), A14.

Police and the Constitution:
The Rules of Law Enforcement

Chapter Outline		Corresponding Learning Objectives
The Fourth Amendment	**1**	Outline the four major sources that may provide probable cause.
	2	Explain the exclusionary rule and the exceptions to it.
Lawful Searches and Seizures	**3**	List the four categories of items that can be seized by use of a search warrant.
	4	Explain when searches can be made without a warrant.
	5	Describe the plain view doctrine and indicate one of its limitations.
Stops and Frisks	**6**	Distinguish between a stop and a frisk, and indicate the importance of the case *Terry v. Ohio*.
Arrests	**7**	List the four elements that must be present for an arrest to take place.
The Interrogation Process and *Miranda*	**8**	Explain why the U.S. Supreme Court established the *Miranda* warnings.
	9	Indicate situations in which a *Miranda* warning is unnecessary.
The Identification Process	**10**	List the three basic types of police identification.

To target your study and review, look for these numbered Learning Objective icons throughout the chapter.

AP Images/*The Albuquerque Journal*, Roberto E. Rosales

Sniff Search

when the Miami-Dade County (Florida) Police Department received an anonymous tip that Joelis Jardines was growing marijuana in his home, they sent Franky to verify. After circling for a few minutes on Jardines's front porch, Franky, a chocolate Labrador trained to sniff out illegal drugs, sat down near the front door. This was a signal to the two officers on the scene that the dog smelled something suspicious. Relying on Franky's expertise, the officers obtained permission from a judge to search Jardines's home. They found nearly 180 marijuana plants having an estimated street value of about $700,000.

Jardines eventually pleaded not guilty to drug trafficking charges. At trial, his lawyers claimed that—by allowing Franky to sniff around the outside of Jardines's home—the Miami police had used improper means to justify their search. Several years ago, the United States Supreme Court agreed. To come to this conclusion, the Court relied on a concept called the *expectation of privacy*, which we will address later in this chapter. Historically, Americans have enjoyed a strong expectation of privacy inside their homes and on their *curtilage*, or the area in which they live their lives.

Under certain circumstances, the Court recognized, we tolerate the presence of uninvited visitors on our property. Such visitors include Girl Scouts selling cookies, trick-or-treaters, and salespeople. This tolerance does not, however, extend to law enforcement agents with drug-sniffing dogs. "The police cannot . . . hang around on the lawn or in the side garden, trawling for evidence and perhaps peering into the windows of the home," said Justice Antonin Scalia. "And the officers [in the Jardines case] had all four of their feet and all four of their companion's planted firmly on that curtilage—the front porch is the classic example of an area intimately associated with the life of the home."

▲ The Supreme Court has ruled that the U.S. Constitution limits the ability of law enforcement to gather evidence of criminal behavior by using narcotics-sniffing police dogs.

Matthew Staver/Bloomberg via Getty Images

1. Do you agree that one's home should receive added protection from police searches under American criminal law? Why or why not?

2. If you were to argue *against* the Supreme Court's decision in this case, how could you use the fact that mail carriers are customarily allowed on private property?

3. What if a police officer had come to Joelis Jardines's front door to get information about a missing child in the neighborhood and noticed a strong smell of marijuana? Why might the Court allow a search based on this scenario?

The Fourth Amendment

In *Florida v. Jardines,* the Supreme Court did not address whether Joelis Jardines was guilty or innocent of the charges against him. That was for the trial court to decide. Rather, the Court ruled that the Miami narcotics officers had overstepped the boundaries of their authority by using a drug-sniffing dog to detect the smell of marijuana from Jardines's front porch.[1] In the previous chapter, we discussed the importance of discretion for police officers. This discretion, as we noted, is not absolute. A law enforcement agent's actions are greatly determined by the rules for policing set down in the U.S. Constitution and enforced by the courts.

To understand these rules, law enforcement officers must understand the Fourth Amendment, which reads as follows:

> The right of the people to be secure in their persons, houses, papers, and effects, against unreasonable searches and seizures, shall not be violated, and no Warrants shall issue, but upon probable cause, supported by Oath or affirmation, and particularly describing the place to be searched, and the persons or things to be seized.

This amendment contains two critical legal concepts: a prohibition against *unreasonable* searches and seizures and the requirement of probable cause to issue a warrant.

Reasonableness

Law enforcement personnel use searches and seizures to look for and collect the evidence prosecutors need to convict individuals suspected of crimes. As you have just read, when police are conducting a search or seizure, they must be *reasonable*. Though courts have spent innumerable hours scrutinizing the word, no specific meaning for *reasonable* exists. A thesaurus can provide useful synonyms—logical, practical, sensible, intelligent, plausible—but because each case is different, those terms are relative.

In the *Jardines* case, the Supreme Court accepted the argument that the search had been so unreasonable as to violate the Fourth Amendment's prohibition against unreasonable searches and seizures. That does not mean that the police officers' actions would have been unreasonable under any circumstances. The Court has allowed evidence of illegal drugs uncovered by trained dogs sniffing the exterior of luggage in an airport and the outside of a car that the police have stopped for a traffic violation.[2] According to American case law, searches in those public places are more likely to be found reasonable than searches of the home, "the most private . . . of all the places and things the Fourth Amendment protects."[3]

Probable Cause

The concept of reasonableness is linked to probable cause. The Supreme Court has ruled, for example, that any arrest or seizure is unreasonable unless it is supported by probable cause.[4] The burden of probable cause requires more than mere suspicion on a police officer's part. The officer must know of facts and circumstances that would reasonably lead to "the belief that an offense has been or is being committed."[5]

Sources of Probable Cause If no probable cause existed when a police officer took a certain action, it cannot be retroactively applied. If, for example, a police officer stops a person for jaywalking and then finds several ounces of marijuana in that person's pocket, the arrest for marijuana possession would probably be disallowed. Remember, suspicion does not equal probable cause. If, however, an informant had tipped the officer

Searches and Seizures The legal term, as found in the Fourth Amendment to the U.S. Constitution, that generally refers to the searching for and the confiscating of evidence by law enforcement agents.

Probable Cause Reasonable grounds to believe the existence of facts warranting certain actions, such as the search or arrest of a person.

Careers in CJ

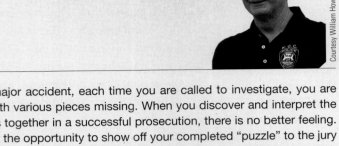

Courtesy William Howe

William Howe
Police Detective

Each crime scene, each major accident, each time you are called to investigate, you are presented with a puzzle with various pieces missing. When you discover and interpret the interlocking missing pieces together in a successful prosecution, there is no better feeling. The payoff is when you get the opportunity to show off your completed "puzzle" to the jury and they agree that the pieces fit. When I once thrilled at the chase of the bad guy through the alleys and neighborhoods, I now enjoy even more pursuing them with the mental skills I have developed—accident reconstruction, fingerprint identification, and the interpretation of crime scenes. This can be every bit as rewarding as the foot pursuit, not to mention ever so much easier on the body.

Having been in police work for thirty-five years, I have been assaulted only four times on the job (two of which were at gunpoint). This confirmed for me, once and for all, the importance of being able to use your mind rather than your size to, first, talk your way out of trouble and, second, talk the bad guys into going along with your plans for them.

SOCIAL MEDIA CAREER TIP For your profile photo, stick with a close-up, business-appropriate photo in which you are smiling and wearing something you would wear as a potential employee. Avoid symbols, party photos, long-distance shots, or baby pictures.

off that the person was a drug dealer, probable cause might exist and the arrest could be valid. Several sources that may provide probable cause include:

LEARNING OBJECTIVE 1
Outline the four major sources that may provide probable cause.

1. *Personal observation.* Police officers may use their personal training, experience, and expertise to infer probable cause from situations that may not be obviously criminal. If, for example, a police officer observes several people in a car slowly circling a certain building in a high-crime area, that officer may infer that the people are "casing" the building in preparation for a burglary. Probable cause could be established for detaining the suspects.

2. *Information.* Law enforcement officers receive information from victims, eyewitnesses, informants, and official sources such as police bulletins or broadcasts. Such information, as long as it is believed to be reliable, is a basis for probable cause.

3. *Evidence.* In certain circumstances, which will be examined later in this chapter, police have probable cause for a search or seizure based on evidence—such as a shotgun—in plain view.

4. *Association.* In some circumstances, if the police see a person with a known criminal background in a place where criminal activity is openly taking place, they have probable cause to stop that person. Generally, however, association is not adequate to establish probable cause.[6]

The Probable Cause Framework In a sense, the concept of probable cause allows police officers to do their job effectively. Most arrests are made without written permission from a judge called a *warrant* because most arrests are the result of quick police reaction to the commission of a crime. Indeed, it would not be practical to expect a police officer to obtain a warrant before making an arrest on the street. Thus, probable cause provides a framework that limits the situations in which police officers can make arrests, but also gives officers the freedom to act within that framework. In 2003, the Supreme Court reaffirmed this freedom by ruling that Baltimore (Maryland) police officers acted properly when they arrested all three passengers of a car in which cocaine had been hidden in the back seat. "A reasonable officer," wrote Chief Justice William H. Rehnquist, "could conclude that there was probable cause to believe" that the defendant, who had been sitting in the front seat, was in "possession" of the illicit drug despite his protestations to the contrary.[7]

Once an arrest is made, the arresting officer must prove to a judge that probable cause existed. In *County of Riverside v. McLaughlin* (1991),[8] the Supreme Court held that this judicial determination of probable cause must be made within forty-eight hours after the arrest, even if this two-day period includes a weekend or holiday.

The Exclusionary Rule

Historically, the courts have looked to the Fourth Amendment for guidance in regulating the activity of law enforcement officers, as the language of the Constitution does not expressly do so. The courts' most potent legal tool in this endeavor is the **exclusionary rule,** which prohibits the use of illegally seized evidence. According to this rule, any evidence obtained by an unreasonable search or seizure is inadmissible (may not be used) against a defendant in a criminal trial.[9] Even highly incriminating evidence, such as a knife stained with the victim's blood, usually cannot be introduced at a trial if illegally obtained. (Due to the Supreme Court's ruling explained at the beginning of this chapter, evidence of the marijuana plants in Joelis Jardines's house was excluded from his trial because of the improper search.)

Furthermore, any physical or verbal evidence police are able to acquire by using illegally obtained evidence is known as the **fruit of the poisoned tree** and is also inadmissible. For example, if the police use the existence of the bloodstained knife to get a confession out of a suspect, that confession will be excluded as well.

One of the implications of the exclusionary rule is that it forces police to gather evidence properly. If they follow appropriate procedures, they are more likely to be rewarded with a conviction. If they are careless or abuse the rights of the suspect, they are unlikely to get a conviction. A strict application of the exclusionary rule, therefore, will permit guilty people to go free because of police carelessness or honest errors. In practice, relatively few apparently guilty suspects

Exclusionary Rule A rule under which any evidence that is obtained in violation of the accused's rights, as well as any evidence derived from illegally obtained evidence, will not be admissible in criminal court.

Fruit of the Poisoned Tree Evidence that is acquired through the use of illegally obtained evidence and is therefore inadmissible in court.

▼ Suppose that this gun—used by a defendant to murder a victim—was found as the result of an improper police search. **Why might the exclusionary rule keep evidence of the gun's existence out of court? What is your opinion of the exclusionary rule?**
Gary W. Green/*Orlando Sentinel*/Getty Images

benefit from the exclusionary rule. Research shows that about 3 percent of felony arrestees avoid incarceration because of improper police searches and seizures.[10]

Explain the exclusionary rule and the exceptions to it.

LEARNING
2
OBJECTIVE

The "Inevitable Discovery" Exception Critics of the exclusionary rule maintain that, regardless of statistics, the rule hampers the police's ability to gather evidence and causes prosecutors to release numerous suspects before their cases make it to court. Several Supreme Court decisions have mirrored this view and provided exceptions to the exclusionary rule.

The **"inevitable discovery" exception** was established in the wake of the disappearance of ten-year-old Pamela Powers of Des Moines, Iowa, on Christmas Eve, 1968. The primary suspect in the case, a religious fanatic named Robert Williams, was tricked by a detective into leading police to the site where he had buried Powers. The detective convinced Williams that if he did not lead police to the body, he would soon forget where it was buried. This would deny his victim a "Christian burial." Initially, in *Brewer v. Williams* (1977),[11] the Court ruled that the evidence (Powers's body) had been obtained illegally because Williams's attorney had not been present during the interrogation that led to his admission. Several years later, in *Nix v. Williams* (1984),[12] the Court reversed itself, ruling that the evidence was admissible because the body would have eventually ("inevitably") been found by lawful means.

The "Good Faith" Exception The scope of the exclusionary rule has been further diminished by two cases involving faulty warrants. In the first, *United States v. Leon* (1984),[13] the police seized evidence on authority of a search warrant that had been improperly issued by a judge. In the second, *Arizona v. Evans* (1995),[14] due to a computer error, a police officer detained Isaac Evans on the mistaken belief that he was subject to an arrest warrant. As a result, the officer found a marijuana cigarette on Evans's person and, after a search of his car, discovered a bag of marijuana.

In both cases, the Court allowed the evidence to stand under a **"good faith" exception** to the exclusionary rule. Under this exception, evidence acquired by a police officer using a technically invalid warrant is admissible if the officer was unaware of the error. In these two cases, the Court said that the officers acted in "good faith." By the same token, if police officers use a search warrant that they know to be technically incorrect, the good faith exception does not apply, and the evidence can be suppressed.

EthicsChallenge

Explain the exclusionary rule in terms of its impact on the ethical behavior of law enforcement agents. ■

Lawful Searches and Seizures

How far can law enforcement agents go in searching and seizing private property? Consider the steps taken by Jenny Stracner, an investigator with the Laguna Beach (California) Police Department. After receiving information that a suspect, Greenwood, was engaged in drug trafficking, Stracner enlisted the aid of the local trash collector in procuring evidence. Instead of taking Greenwood's trash bags to be incinerated, the collector agreed to give them to Stracner. The officer found enough drug paraphernalia in the garbage to obtain a warrant to search the suspect's home. Subsequently, Greenwood was arrested and convicted on narcotics charges.[15]

"Inevitable Discovery" Exception The legal principle that illegally obtained evidence can be admissible in court if police using lawful means would have "inevitably" discovered it.

"Good Faith" Exception The legal principle that evidence obtained with the use of a technically invalid search warrant is admissible during trial if the police acted in good faith when they sought the warrant from a judge.

Remember, the Fourth Amendment is quite specific in forbidding unreasonable searches and seizures. Were Stracner's search of Greenwood's garbage and her seizure of its contents "reasonable"? The Supreme Court thought so, holding that Greenwood's garbage was not protected by the Fourth Amendment.[16]

Search The process by which police examine a person or property to find evidence that will be used to prove guilt in a criminal trial.

The Role of Privacy in Searches

A crucial concept in understanding search and seizure law is *privacy*. By definition, a **search** is a governmental intrusion on a citizen's reasonable expectation of privacy. The recognized standard for a "reasonable expectation of privacy" was established in *Katz v. United States* (1967).[17] The case dealt with the question of whether the defendant was justified in his expectation of privacy in the calls he made from a public phone booth. The Supreme Court held that "the Fourth Amendment protects people, not places," and Katz prevailed.

In his concurring opinion, Justice John Harlan, Jr., set a two-pronged test for a person's expectation of privacy:

1. The individual must prove that she or he expected privacy, and
2. Society must recognize that expectation as reasonable.[18]

Accordingly, the Court agreed with Katz's claim that he had a reasonable right to privacy in a public phone booth. Even though the phone booth was a public place, accessible to anyone, Katz had taken clear steps to protect his privacy.

A Legitimate Privacy Interest Despite the *Katz* ruling, simply taking steps to protect one's privacy is not enough to protect against law enforcement intrusion. The steps must be reasonably certain to ensure privacy. If a person is unreasonable or mistaken in expecting privacy, he or she may forfeit that expectation. For instance, in *California v. Greenwood* (1988),[19] described at the beginning of this section, the Court did not believe that the suspect had a reasonable expectation of privacy when it came to his garbage bags. The Court noted that when we place our trash on a curb, we expose it to any number of intrusions by "animals, children, scavengers, snoops, and other members of the public."[20] In other words, if Greenwood had truly intended for the contents of his garbage bags to remain private, he would not have left them on the side of the road.

In *Florida v. Jardines*, the Supreme Court case that opened this chapter, four of the nine justices believed that the Court had gone too far in protecting the defendant's expectation of privacy. As recently as 2011, these justices noted, the Court had found that people have no such expectation regarding marijuana smells coming from their homes that can be detected by a human being.[21] Why, they asked, should the nose of a drug-sniffing dog be any different?[22]

Privacy and Satellite Monitoring As you can see, a number of factors go into determining whether a reasonable expectation of

▼ Should law enforcement be able to use police helicopters such as the one shown here to determine if people are carrying out illegal behavior in their fenced-in back yards? Why or why not? Ricky Carioti/ *The Washington Post*/ Getty Images

privacy exists. In *United States v. Jones* (2012),[23] the U.S. Supreme Court emphasized the important roles that time and technology play in this equation. The Court's ruling invalidated the efforts of federal agents who had placed a GPS tracking device on the car of Antoine Jones, a Washington, D.C., nightclub owner suspected of drug trafficking. Using the device, which relies on satellite transmissions to determine location, the agents were able to follow Jones's movements for a month. This evidence helped bring about Jones's conviction for conspiring to distribute cocaine.

The Court found that the government had "physically occupied" private property—Jones's car—for an unreasonably long amount of time. As a result, all evidence gathered by the GPS device was ruled inadmissible. Several Supreme Court justices also pointed out that most citizens do not expect the police to be monitoring every drive they make over the course of twenty-eight days.[24] As one commentator stated, the ruling seemed to acknowledge that just because technology now permits greater levels of surveillance, this "does not mean that society has decided there's no such thing as privacy anymore."[25] (See the feature *A Question of Ethics: Fake Friends* to learn more about expectation of privacy issues on the Internet.)

Search and Seizure Warrants

The Supreme Court's ruling in the case of Antoine Jones does not mean that law enforcement officers can *never* track someone for a month using a GPS device or any other technology. Rather, it means that, to do so, they need to obtain a **search warrant**, a step that

A Question of Ethics: Fake Friends

The Situation During its investigation of Sondra Arquiett for cocaine-related crimes, the Drug Enforcement Administration (DEA) seized the suspect's phone and downloaded its contents. Afterward, a DEA agent used photos from the phone—including one of Arquiett in her underwear—to create a fake Facebook page designed to "friend" other suspects. Similarly, law enforcement officers investigating a string of burglaries in New Jersey set up an undercover Instagram account that was "followed" by suspect Daniel Gatson. This gave the investigators access to Gatson's own Instagram account, which featured photos of cash and jewelry—and led to his eventual arrest.

The Ethical Dilemma The user agreements of Facebook and Instagram both ban law enforcement agents from going "undercover" online by impersonating others or setting up fake accounts. As you have just seen, this has not stopped numerous police officers from engaging in the practice. For American courts, then, the question becomes, do social media users have a reasonable expectation that information they post on "private" or "friends only" sites will be free from law enforcement intrusions? In general, courts have not found that such a reasonable expectation exists.

Consequently, law enforcement officers are for the most part permitted to use fake identities online, just as undercover officers routinely use fake identities in the real world.

What Is the Solution? In 2015, the federal government paid Sondra Arquiett $134,000 to settle a lawsuit she brought for invasion of privacy. A few months earlier, a federal judge ruled that, because Daniel Gatson voluntarily followed the fake Instagram account, he had no expectation of privacy regarding any information he unwittingly shared with the police. What is your opinion of the outcomes of these two cases? Is it ethical for police officers to use fake social media identities to trick criminal suspects? Why or why not?

the federal agents failed to take before beginning their surveillance of Jones. A search warrant is a court order that authorizes police to search a certain area. Before a judge or magistrate will issue a search warrant, law enforcement officers must provide:

- Information showing probable cause that a crime has been or will be committed.
- Specific information on the premises to be searched, the suspects to be found and the illegal activities taking place at those premises, and the items to be seized.

The purpose of a search warrant is to establish, before the search takes place, that a *probable cause to search* justifies infringing on the suspect's reasonable expectation of privacy.

Particularity of Search Warrants The members of the First Congress specifically did not want law enforcement officers to have the freedom to make "general, exploratory" searches through a person's belongings.[26] Consequently, the Fourth Amendment requires that a warrant describe with "particularity" the place to be searched and the things—either people or objects—to be seized.

This "particularity" requirement places a heavy burden on law enforcement officers. Before going to a judge to ask for a search warrant, they must prepare an **affidavit** in which they provide specific, written information on the property that they wish to search and seize. They must know the specific address of any place they wish to search. General addresses of apartment buildings or office complexes are not sufficient. Furthermore, courts generally frown on vague descriptions of goods to be seized. For example, several years ago, a federal court ruled that a warrant permitting police to search a home for "all handguns, shotguns and rifles" and "evidence showing street gang membership" was too broad. As a result, the seizure of a shotgun was disallowed for lack of a valid search warrant.[27]

A **seizure** is the act of taking possession of a person or property by the government because of a (suspected) violation of the law. In general, four categories of items can be seized by use of a search warrant:

1. Items resulting from the crime, such as stolen goods.
2. Items that are inherently illegal for anybody to possess (with certain exceptions), such as narcotics and counterfeit currency.
3. Items that can be called "evidence" of the crime, such as a bloodstained sneaker or a ski mask.
4. Items used in committing the crime, such as an ice pick or a printing press used to make counterfeit bills.[28]

See Figure 7.1 for an example of a search warrant.

Reasonableness during a Search and Seizure No matter how "particular" a warrant is, it cannot provide for all the conditions that are bound to come up during its service. Consequently, the law gives law enforcement officers the ability to act "reasonably" during a search and seizure in the event of unforeseeable circumstances. For example, if a police officer is searching an apartment for a stolen MacBook Pro

Affidavit A written statement of facts, confirmed by the oath or affirmation of the party making it and made before a person having the authority to administer the oath or affirmation.

Seizure The forcible taking of a person or property in response to a violation of the law.

LEARNING OBJECTIVE **3** List the four categories of items that can be seized by use of a search warrant.

FIGURE 7.1 Example of a Search Warrant

United States District Court
DISTRICT OF

In the Matter of the Search of
(Name, address or brief description of person or property to be searched)

SEARCH WARRANT

CASE NUMBER:

TO: _____ and any Authorized Officer of the United States

Affidavit(s) having been made before me by _____ who has reason to
believe that ☐ on the person of or ☐ on the premises known as (name, description and/or location)

in the _____ District of _____ there is now
concealed a certain person or property, namely (describe the person or property)

I am satisfied that the affidavit(s) and any recorded testimony establish probable cause to believe that the person or property so described is now concealed on the person or premises above-described and establish grounds for the issuance of this warrant.

YOU ARE HEREBY COMMANDED to search on or before _____
Date
(not to exceed 10 days) the person or place named above for the person or property specified, serving this warrant and making the search (in the daytime — 6:00 A.M. to 10:00 P.M.) (at any time in the day or night as I find reasonable cause has been established) and if the person or property be found there to seize same, leaving a copy of this warrant and receipt for the person or property taken, and prepare a written inventory of the person or property seized and promptly return this warrant to _____
U.S Judge or Magistrate
as required by law.

Date and Time Issued _____ at _____
City and State

Name and Title of Judicial Officer _____ Signature of Judicial Officer _____

laptop computer and notices a vial of crack cocaine sitting on the suspect's bed, that contraband is considered to be in "plain view" and can be seized.

Note that if law enforcement officers have a search warrant that authorizes them to search for a stolen laptop computer, they would not be justified in opening small drawers. Because a computer could not fit in a small drawer, an officer would not have a basis for reasonably searching one. Hence, officers are restricted in terms of where they can look by the items they are searching for.

Searches and Seizures without a Warrant

LEARNING
4
OBJECTIVE

Explain when searches can be made without a warrant.

Although the Supreme Court has established the principle that searches conducted without warrants are *per se* (by definition) unreasonable, it has set "specifically established" exceptions to the rule.[29] In fact, most searches take place in the absence of a judicial order. Warrantless searches and seizures can be lawful when police are in "hot pursuit" of a subject or when they search bags of trash left at the curb for regular collection. Because of the magnitude of smuggling activities in "border areas" such as airports, seaports, and international boundaries, a warrant normally is not needed to search property in those places.

Furthermore, in 2006 the Court held unanimously that police officers do not need a warrant to enter a private home in an emergency, such as when they reasonably fear for the safety of the inhabitants.[30] The two most important circumstances in which a warrant is not needed, though, are (1) searches incidental to an arrest and (2) consent searches.

Searches Incidental to an Arrest The most frequent exception to the warrant requirement involves **searches incidental to arrests,** so called because nearly every time police officers make an arrest (a procedure discussed in detail later in the chapter), they also search the suspect. As long as the original arrest was based on probable cause, these searches are valid for two reasons, established by the Supreme Court in *United States v. Robinson* (1973):

1. The need for a police officer to find and confiscate any weapons a suspect may be carrying.
2. The need to protect any evidence on the suspect's person from being destroyed.[31]

Law enforcement officers are, however, limited in the searches they may make during an arrest. These limits were established by the Supreme Court in *Chimel v. California* (1969).[32] In that case, police arrived at Chimel's home with an arrest warrant but not a search warrant. Even though Chimel refused their request to "look around," the officers searched the entire three-bedroom house for nearly an hour, finding stolen coins in the process. Chimel was convicted of burglary and appealed, arguing that the evidence of the coins should have been suppressed.

The Supreme Court held that the search was unreasonable. In doing so, the Court established guidelines as to the acceptable extent of searches incidental to an arrest. Primarily, the Court ruled that police may search any area within the suspect's "immediate control" to confiscate any weapons or evidence that the suspect could destroy. The Court found, however, that there was no justification

for routinely searching rooms other than that in which the arrest occurs—or, for that matter, for searching through all desk drawers or other closed or concealed areas in that room itself. Such searches, in the absence of well-recognized exceptions, may be made only under the authority of a search warrant.[33]

Searches Incidental to Arrests Searches for weapons and evidence that are conducted on persons who have just been arrested.

The exact interpretation of the "area within immediate control" has been left to individual courts, but in general it has been taken to mean the area within the reach of the arrested person. Thus, the Court is said to have established the "arm's reach doctrine" in its *Chimel* decision.

Searches with Consent

Consent searches, the second most common type of warrantless searches, take place when individuals voluntarily give law enforcement officers permission to search their persons, homes, or belongings. The most relevant factors in determining whether consent is voluntary are

1. The age, intelligence, and physical condition of the consenting suspect;
2. Any coercive behavior by the police, such as the language used to request consent; and
3. The length of the questioning and its location.[34]

If a court finds that a person has been physically threatened or otherwise coerced into giving consent, the search is invalid.[35] Furthermore, the search consented to must be reasonable. In 2007, the North Carolina Supreme Court invalidated a consent search that turned up a packet of cocaine. As part of this search, the police had pulled down the suspect's underwear and shone a flashlight on his groin. The court ruled that a reasonable person in the defendant's position would not consent to such an intrusive examination.[36]

The standard for consent searches was set in *Schneckcloth v. Bustamonte* (1973),[37] in which, after being asked, the defendant told police officers to "go ahead" and search his car. A packet of stolen checks found in the trunk was ruled valid evidence because the driver consented to the search. As the feature *Myth vs Reality—Consent to Search Automobiles* explains, as a general rule, drivers are not required to agree to such searches.[38]

Numerous court decisions have also supported the "knock and talk" strategy, in which the law enforcement agent simply walks up to the door of a residence, knocks, and asks to come in and talk to the resident.[39] The officer does not need reasonable suspicion or probable cause that a crime has taken place in this situation because the decision to cooperate rests with the civilian.

Recent Developments

Because warrantless searches are relatively commonplace—and crucial for law enforcement—defense attorneys are constantly testing their limits. In recent years, for instance, American courts have determined the constitutionality of warrantless searches of:

1. *Digital devices on the border.* Do the traditional reasons for allowing warrantless searches at entry points—combating smuggling

Consent Searches Searches by police that are made after the subject of the search has agreed to the action. In these situations, consent, if given of free will, validates a warrantless search.

Myth vs Reality

Consent to Search Automobiles

The Myth If a police officer pulls over a driver and issues a speeding ticket, and then asks to search the car, the driver must agree to the officer's request and submit to a vehicle search.

The Reality In fact, in this scenario, the driver is well within his or her rights to refuse an officer's request to search his or her car. As long as police officers do not improperly coerce a suspect to cooperate, however, they are not required to inform the person that he or she has a choice in the matter. In *Ohio v. Robinette* (1996), the U.S. Supreme Court held that police officers do not need to notify people that they are "free to go" after an initial stop when no arrest is involved. This lack of notification has significant consequences. In the two years leading up to the *Robinette* case, four hundred Ohio drivers were convicted of narcotics offenses that resulted directly from search requests that could have been denied but were not.

For Critical Analysis
Do you think police officers should be required to tell drivers that permission to search a vehicle can be denied? Why or why not?

and terrorism—also apply to warrantless searches of laptop computers and cell phones owned by people crossing the border? A federal court has said no, as a search of a car is not nearly as "comprehensive and intrusive" as a search of the data stored in an electronic device.[40]

2. *Blood used as evidence in drunk driving cases.* The natural dissipation of alcohol in the bloodstream is not enough, according to the United States Supreme Court, for police officers to draw a drunk driving suspect's blood without consent or a warrant. Other factors, however, such as slurred speech and the smell of alcohol, may be enough for such a "bodily intrusion" without a warrant.[41]

3. *Homes over the objection of an absent resident.* Walter Fernandez refused to consent to a warrantless search of his Los Angeles home in connection with a robbery. Police then arrested Fernandez for abusing his domestic partner, who consented to the search while Fernandez was being booked at the local jail. In 2014, the Supreme Court upheld this strategy, ruling that any occupant's consent is sufficient.[42]

Figure 7.2 provides an overview of the circumstances under which warrantless searches have traditionally been allowed.

Searches of Automobiles

In *Carroll v. United States* (1925),[43] the Supreme Court ruled that the law could distinguish among automobiles, homes, and persons in questions involving police searches. In the years since its *Carroll* decision, the Court has established that the Fourth Amendment does not require police to obtain a warrant to search automobiles or other movable vehicles when they have probable cause to believe that a vehicle contains contraband or evidence of criminal activity.[44]

The reasoning behind such leniency is straightforward: requiring a warrant to search an automobile places too heavy a burden on police officers. By the time the officers could communicate with a judge and obtain the warrant, the suspects could have driven away and destroyed any evidence. Consequently, the Court has consistently held that someone in a vehicle does not have the same reasonable expectation of privacy as someone at home or even in a phone booth.

FIGURE 7.2 Exceptions to the Requirement That Officers Have a Search Warrant

In many instances, it would be impractical for police officers to leave a crime scene, go to a judge, and obtain a search warrant before conducting a search. Therefore, under the following circumstances, a search warrant is not required.

INCIDENT TO LAWFUL ARREST
Police officers may search the area within immediate control of a person after they have arrested him or her.

CONSENT
Police officers may search a person without a warrant if that person voluntarily agrees to be searched and has the legal authority to authorize the search.

STOP AND FRISK
Police officers may frisk, or "pat down," a person if they suspect that the person may be involved in criminal activity or pose a danger to those in the immediate area.

HOT PURSUIT
If police officers are in "hot pursuit" or chasing a person they have probable cause to believe committed a crime, and that person enters a building, the officers may search the building without a warrant.

AUTOMOBILE EXCEPTION
If police officers have probable cause to believe that an automobile contains evidence of a crime, they may, in most instances, search the vehicle without a warrant.

PLAIN VIEW
If police officers are legally engaged in police work and happen to see evidence of a crime in "plain view," they may seize it without a warrant.

ABANDONED PROPERTY
Any property, such as a hotel room that has been vacated or contraband that has been discarded, may be searched and seized by police officers without a warrant.

BORDER SEARCHES
Law enforcement officers on border patrol do not need a warrant to search vehicles crossing the border.

Warrantless Searches of Automobiles For nearly three decades, police officers believed that if they lawfully arrested the driver of a car, they could legally make a warrantless search of the car's entire front and back compartments. This understanding was based on the Supreme Court's ruling in *New York v. Benton* (1981),[45] which seemed to allow this expansive interpretation of the "area within immediate control" with regard to automobiles.

In *Arizona v. Gant* (2009), however, the Court announced that its *Benton* decision had been misinterpreted. Such warrantless searches are only allowed if

1. The person being arrested is close enough to the car to grab or destroy evidence or a weapon inside the car, or
2. The arresting officer reasonably believes that the car contains evidence pertinent to the same crime for which the arrest took place.[46]

So, for example, police will no longer be able to search an automobile for contraband if the driver has been arrested for failing to pay previous speeding tickets—unless the officer reasonably believes the suspect has the ability to reach and destroy any such contraband.

Significant Powers As you can imagine, the law enforcement community reacted negatively to the new restrictions outlined in the *Gant* decision.[47] Police officers, however, still can conduct a warrantless search of an automobile based on circumstances other than the incidental-to-an-arrest doctrine. These circumstances include probable cause of criminal activity, consent of the driver, and "protective searches" to search for weapons if police officers have a reasonable suspicion that such weapons exist.[48]

The Supreme Court even allows warrantless searches of automobiles when the law enforcement agent has a mistaken notion of the law. For instance, several years ago a police officer in North Carolina stopped a car for having a broken brake light. The resulting consensual search of the automobile uncovered a sandwich bag of cocaine. North Carolina law only requires a single working brake light, however, meaning that the officer should not have made the traffic stop in the first place. Nonetheless, in 2014, the Court ruled that, because the officer's mistake was objectively reasonable (that is, the type of mistake than any reasonable officer might make), his search was valid.[49]

Pretextual Stops What if the officer in the previous example was just using the mistaken traffic violation as an excuse to stop the car and do a drug search? It is important to understand that, as long as an officer has probable cause to believe that a traffic law has been broken, her or his "true" motivation for making a stop is irrelevant.[50] So, even if the police officer does not have a legally sufficient reason to search for evidence of a crime such as drug trafficking, the officer can use a minor traffic violation to pull over the car and investigate his or her "hunch." (To learn more about such "pretextual stops," see the feature *Discretion in Action—A Valid Pretext?*)

Container Searches In keeping with the principles of the "movable vehicle" exception, the Supreme Court has also provided law enforcement agents with a great deal of leeway for warrantless searches of containers within a vehicle. In one case, Washington, D.C., detectives received a reliable tip that a man known as the "Bandit" was selling drugs from his car. Without first getting a warrant, the detectives searched the Bandit's trunk and found heroin in a closed paper bag. The Court refused to suppress the evidence, ruling that in such situations police officers can search every part of the vehicle that might

Discretion in Action

A Valid Pretext?

The Situation You are a police officer patrolling an area of Washington, D.C., that is marked by extremely high rates of drug-related crime. You become suspicious of a truck with temporary plates being driven slowly by a young African American male. Although you do not consider yourself as being racially biased, you are well aware, from experience, that in this neighborhood many young black men in these types of cars with temporary plates are drug dealers. These suspicions do not, however, reach the level of probable cause needed to pull over the truck. Then, the driver fails to signal while making a right turn.

The Law As far as Fourth Amendment law is concerned, any subjective reasons that a police officer might have for stopping a suspect, including any motives based on racial stereotyping or bias, are irrelevant. As long as the officer has objective probable cause to believe a traffic violation or other wrongdoing has occurred, the stop is valid.

What Would You Do? You are convinced that the driver of the truck is selling illegal drugs, and you want to stop and search him. The "failure to signal" gives you a valid pretext to pull over the truck, even though your real reasons for the stop would be its slow pace, its temporary plates, the race of its driver, and the level of drug crime in the neighborhood. What do you do?

[To see how the United States Supreme Court reacted to an officer's decision in a similar situation, got to Example 7.1 in Appendix B.]

---

contain the items they are seeking, as long as they have probable cause to believe that the items are somewhere in the car.[51]

Nevertheless, there are limits to what can be searched. As Justice John Paul Stevens stated in his opinion, "[P]robable cause to believe that undocumented aliens are being transported in a van will not justify a warrantless search of a suitcase" in that van.[52] By the same token, if the tipster had told the police specifically that "Bandit has a bag of heroin in his trunk," they would not have been justified in searching the front area of the car without a warrant or probable cause.[53]

The Plain View Doctrine

Describe the plain view doctrine and indicate one of its limitations. **5** LEARNING OBJECTIVE

As we have already seen several times in this chapter, the Constitution, as interpreted by our courts, provides very little protection to evidence *in plain view*. For example, suppose a traffic officer pulls over a person for speeding, looks in the driver's side window, and clearly sees what appears to be a bag of heroin resting on the passenger seat. In this instance, under the **plain view doctrine,** the officer would be justified in seizing the drugs without a warrant.

The plain view doctrine was first put forward by the Supreme Court in *Coolidge v. New Hampshire* (1971).[54] The Court ruled that law enforcement officers may make a warrantless seizure of an item if four criteria are met:

1. The item is positioned so as to be detected easily by an officer's sight or some other sense.
2. The officer is legally in a position to notice the item in question.
3. The discovery of the item is inadvertent. That is, the officer had not intended to find the item.
4. The officer immediately recognizes the illegal nature of the item. No interrogation or further investigation is allowed under the plain view doctrine.

Plain View Doctrine The legal principle that objects in plain view of a law enforcement agent who has the right to be in a position to have that view may be seized without a warrant and introduced as evidence.

Advances in technology that allow law enforcement agents to "see" beyond normal human capabilities have raised new issues in regard to plain view principles. *Thermal imagers,* for example, measure otherwise invisible levels of infrared radiation. These devices are particularly effective in detecting marijuana plants grown indoors because of the heat thrown off by the "grow lights" that the plants need to survive. The question for the courts has been whether a warrantless search of a dwelling through its walls by means of a thermal imager violates Fourth Amendment protections of privacy. According to the Supreme Court, an item is not in plain view if law enforcement agents need the aid of this technology to "see" it.[55] Thus, information from a thermal imager is not by itself justification for a warrantless search.

CJ &Technology

Through-the-Wall Sensors

If law enforcement agents need a warrant to use thermal imagers, what about radar that can "see" through walls? Such devices, employed by numerous law enforcement agencies in the United States, use radio waves to detect movement from a distance of more than fifty feet. A display shows the movement, giving officers an idea—though not an actual picture—of human activity on the other side of the wall.

In December 2014, these radar devices were mentioned for the first time during a criminal case. U.S. marshals, after tracking a fugitive to a home in Wichita, Kansas, used a sensor to establish "reasonable suspicion" that the suspect was inside before forcing the door open. A judge upheld the suspect's eventual conviction, but warned that "the government's warrantless use of such a powerful tool to search inside homes poses grave Fourth Amendment questions."

Thinking about Through-the-Wall Sensors

In this chapter, we have studied Supreme Court rulings disallowing warrantless searches based on drug dog sniffs and thermal imaging devices. Given these precedents, how do you think the Court would rule on the use of a through-the-wall sensor to justify a warrantless search?

Donna Miles/Department of Defense

Electronic Surveillance

During the course of a criminal investigation, law enforcement officers may decide to use **electronic surveillance,** or electronic devices such as wiretaps or hidden microphones ("bugs"), to monitor and record conversations, observe movements, and trace or record telephone calls.

Basic Rules: Consent and Probable Cause Given the invasiveness of electronic surveillance, the Supreme Court has generally held that the practice is prohibited by the Fourth Amendment. In *Burger v. New York* (1967),[56] however, the Court ruled that it was permissible under certain circumstances. That same year, *Katz v. United States* (discussed at the beginning of this section) established that recorded conversations are inadmissible as evidence unless certain procedures are followed.

Electronic Surveillance The use of electronic equipment by law enforcement agents to record private conversations or observe conduct that is meant to be private.

In general, law enforcement officers can use electronic surveillance only if consent is given by one of the parties to be monitored, or, in the absence of such consent, with a warrant.[57] For the warrant to be valid, it must:

1. Detail with "particularity" the conversations that are to be overheard.
2. Name the suspects and the places that will be under surveillance.
3. Show probable cause to believe that a specific crime has been or will be committed.[58]

Once the specific information has been gathered, the law enforcement officers must end the electronic surveillance immediately.[59] In any case, the surveillance cannot last more than thirty days without a judicial extension.

Force Multiplying Pervasive forms of electronic surveillance are allowed under the theory that people who are in public places have no reasonable expectation of privacy. This theory, generally upheld by American courts,[60] allows for the use of a number of technological *force multipliers,* or devices that allow law enforcement agencies to expand their capabilities without a significant increase in personnel. Perhaps the most pervasive force multiplier is closed-circuit television surveillance (CCTV). This form of surveillance relies on strategically placed video cameras to record and transmit all activities in a targeted area. New York City's CCTV system uses about 3,000 cameras to cover much of that city's midtown and downtown areas, and other large cities such as Boston and Los Angeles employ hundreds of public surveillance cameras.

Another popular force multiplier involves computerized infrared cameras that take digital photos of license plates. Usually mounted on police cars, these *automatic license place recognition (ALPR)* devices convert the images to text. Then the numbers are instantly checked against databases that contain records of the license plates of stolen cars and automobiles driven by a wide variety of targets, from wanted felons to citizens with unpaid parking tickets. In heavy-traffic areas, ALPR units can check thousands of license plates each hour.

Constitutional Concerns Privacy advocates worry that technologically advanced force multipliers are giving the government—through law enforcement—a "way to track all Americans all the time, regardless of whether they're accused of any crime."[61] The Supreme Court's ruling in *United States v. Jones,* the GPS monitoring case discussed earlier in the chapter, did little to clarify this area of the law, as it applies only to lengthy periods of surveillance. Generally speaking, law enforcement agents do not need a search warrant when using CCTV, ALPR, or other surveillance technologies that record short periods of time in public places. As noted earlier, no reasonable expectation of privacy exists in such situations. American courts have been less consistent in determining the constitutionality of another increasingly common forms of police surveillance: tracking a suspect's movements by his or her use of a mobile phone.

Cell Phones and the Fourth Amendment

Given the pervasiveness of cell phones in everyday life and the amount of information stored on these "mobile computers," it should come as no surprise that the devices raise a number of questions about privacy and police searches.

Tracking Cell Phones The ability to track cell phone records certainly has been a boon for law enforcement. To provide just one example of many, in October 2014, police were able to find alleged serial killer Darren Vann in an Indiana hotel room by tracing his cell phone records. Still, courts must decide whether the Fourth Amendment requires a warrant under such circumstances. The situation becomes even more complex due to technology such the StingRay, a device that mimics the signal sent out by a cell phone tower to "trick" cell phones in the area into providing their locations and other identifying information.

The Federal Bureau of Investigation (FBI), the DEA, and nearly fifty local police departments have been using the StingRay to carry out warrantless searches on cell phone data for several years.[62] The legal justification for this practice rests on the assumption that people do not have a reasonable expectation that the location of their cell phone use will be kept private. In 2013, the New Jersey Supreme Court rejected that assumption, holding that local police needed a warrant before asking a cell phone provider for information on the whereabouts of a burglary suspect.[63] Other courts have ruled that warrants are not required to track cell phones, setting up a probable United States Supreme Court decision on the matter.

▲ In 2014, the Supreme Court required police officers to obtain a warrant before searching the contents of a cell phone confiscated during an arrest—except in the event of an emergency. **Name one "emergency" circumstance in which you think a police officer would be justified in searching the contents of an arrestee's cell phone without a warrant or without the owner's consent.** AP Images/Jose Luis Magana

Searching Cell Phones In 2014, the Supreme Court ruled, unanimously, that police officers do need a warrant to search the contents of cell phones belonging to suspects they have just arrested.[64] As we saw earlier in this section, law enforcement agents may, in many instances, carry out a warrantless search on an arrestee's body following an arrest. Because of the vast amounts of personal information on cell phones, the Court decided that these items were deserving of greater protections than items such as wallets or cigarette packets. Furthermore, once a cell phone has been secured by police, the arrestee will not be able to "delete incriminating data" and the "data on the phone can endanger no one"—the two primary justifications for warrantless searches incidental to an arrest.[65]

In his opinion, Chief Justice John G. Roberts acknowledged that the Court's decision would "have an impact on the ability of law enforcement to combat crime." But, he added, "Privacy comes at a cost."[66] Practically, the ruling does not mean the end of cell phone searches. Rather, it means that police will need to get a warrant before engaging in such searches. Or, they will need the consent of the cell phone owner. As we saw earlier in the chapter, such consent is often given despite it being against a suspect's best interests.

EthicsChallenge

In an e-mail, a Sarasota, Florida, police officer told other officers to conceal the fact that they had used a StingRay, the cell phone monitoring tool described in this section, during an investigation. Instead, he suggested that the officers say they received the StingRay information from "a confidential source." What are some of the reasons that law enforcement agents might not want to reveal the use of a new technology to gather evidence? Is such concealment ethical? Why or why not? ■

Stops and Frisks

Two experienced Chicago police officers were standing by their patrol car when a woman approached. She told the officers that she had just purchased illegal drugs from a man and provided them with the suspect's physical description and the location of his drug-selling activity. The police officers went to the location—in an area known to both as a hotspot for drug dealing—and saw a man matching the woman's description clasp hands with another man. Believing that they had just witnessed a drug deal, the officers stopped the suspect, patted him down, and, after finding heroin, made an arrest.

Under the circumstances, these two law enforcement agents believed that they had *reasonable suspicion* that the man had committed a crime. When reasonable suspicion exists, police officers may *stop and frisk* a suspect. In a stop and frisk, law enforcement officers (1) briefly detain a person they reasonably believe to be suspicious, and (2) if they believe the person to be armed, proceed to pat down, or "frisk," that person's outer clothing.[67]

The Elusive Definition of Reasonable Suspicion

Like so many elements of police work, the decision of whether to stop a suspect is based on the balancing of conflicting priorities. On the one hand, a police officer feels a sense of urgency to act when he or she believes that criminal activity is occurring or is about to occur. On the other hand, law enforcement agents do not want to harass innocent individuals, especially if doing so runs afoul of the U.S. Constitution. In stop-and-frisk law, this balancing act rests on the fulcrum of reasonable suspicion.

 Distinguish between a stop and a frisk, and indicate the importance of the case *Terry v. Ohio*. LEARNING **6** OBJECTIVE

Terry v. Ohio The precedent for the ever-elusive definition of a "reasonable" suspicion in stop-and-frisk situations was established in *Terry v. Ohio* (1968).[68] In that case, a detective named McFadden observed two men (one of whom was Terry) acting strangely in downtown Cleveland. The men would walk past a certain store, peer into the window, and then stop at a street corner and confer. While they were talking, another man joined the conversation and then left quickly. Several minutes later, the three men met again at another corner a few blocks away. Detective McFadden believed the trio was planning to break into the store. He approached them, told them who he was, and asked for identification. After receiving a mumbled response, the detective frisked the three men and found handguns on two of them, who were tried and convicted of carrying concealed weapons.

The Supreme Court upheld the conviction, ruling that Detective McFadden had reasonable cause to believe that the men were armed and dangerous and that swift action was necessary to protect himself and other citizens in the area.[69] The Court accepted McFadden's interpretation of the unfolding scene as based on objective facts and practical conclusions. It therefore concluded that his suspicion was reasonable.

The "Totality of the Circumstances" Test For the most part, the judicial system has refrained from placing restrictions on police officers' ability to make stops. In the *Terry* case, the Supreme Court did say that an officer must have "specific and articulable facts" to support the decision to make a stop, but added that the facts may be "taken together with rational inferences."[70] The Court has consistently ruled that because of their practical experience, law enforcement agents are in a unique position to make such inferences and should be given a good deal of freedom in doing so.

In the years since the *Terry* case was decided, the Court has settled on a "totality of the circumstances" test to determine whether a stop is based on reasonable suspicion.[71] In 2002, for example, the Court ruled that a U.S. Border Patrol agent's stop of a minivan in Arizona was reasonable.[72] On being approached by the Border Patrol car, the driver had stiffened, slowed down his van, and avoided making eye contact with the agent. Furthermore, the children in the van waved at the officer in a mechanical manner, as if ordered to do so. The agent pulled over the van and found 128 pounds of marijuana.

In his opinion, Chief Justice William Rehnquist pointed out that such conduct might have been unremarkable on a busy city highway, but on an unpaved road thirty miles from the Mexican border it was enough to reasonably arouse the agent's suspicion.[73] The justices also made clear that the need to prevent terrorist attacks is part of the "totality of the circumstances," and, therefore, law enforcement agents will have more leeway to make stops near U.S. borders.

A Stop

The terms *stop* and *frisk* are often used in concert, but they describe two separate acts. A **stop** takes place when a law enforcement officer has reasonable suspicion that criminal activity has taken place or is about to take place. Because an investigatory stop is not an arrest, there are limits to the extent police can detain someone who has been stopped. For example, in one situation an airline traveler and his luggage were detained for ninety minutes while the police waited for a drug-sniffing dog to arrive. The Supreme Court ruled that the initial stop of the passenger was constitutional, but that the ninety-minute wait was excessive.[74]

In 2004, the Court held that police officers could require suspects to identify themselves during a stop that is otherwise valid under the *Terry* ruling.[75] The case involved a Nevada rancher who was fined $250 for refusing to give his name to a police officer investigating a possible assault. The defendant argued that such requests force citizens to incriminate themselves against their will, which is prohibited, as we shall see later in the chapter, by the Fifth Amendment. Justice Anthony Kennedy wrote, however, that "asking questions is an essential part of police investigations" that would be made much more difficult if officers could not determine the identity of a suspect.[76] The ruling validated "stop-and-identify" laws in twenty states and numerous cities and towns.

A Frisk

The Supreme Court has stated that a **frisk** should be a protective measure. Police officers cannot conduct a frisk as a "fishing expedition" simply to try to find items besides weapons, such as illegal narcotics, on a suspect.[77] A frisk does not necessarily follow a stop and in fact may occur only when the officer is justified in thinking that the safety of police officers or other citizens may be endangered. So, in the case of the two Chicago police officers that opened this section, an Illinois appeals court ruled that while the initial stop was acceptable, the officers had violated the

Stop A brief detention of a person by law enforcement agents for questioning.

Frisk A pat-down or minimal search by police to discover weapons.

▼ A police officer frisks a suspect in San Francisco, California. **What is the main purpose behind a frisk? When are police justified in frisking someone?** Mark Richards/PhotoEdit

suspect's right by frisking him. The state court was unwilling to accept the contention that "drugs and guns go together" as sufficient grounds for a pat-down.[78]

As with stops, frisks must be supported by reasonable suspicion. The Illinois court rejected the argument that the Chicago police officers had objective reasons to fear for their safety. In the *Terry* case, by contrast, the Supreme Court accepted that Detective McFadden reasonably believed that the three suspects posed a threat. The suspects' refusal to answer McFadden's questions, though within their rights because they had not been arrested, provided him with sufficient motive for the frisk. In 2009, the Court extended the "stop-and-frisk" authority by ruling that a police officer could order a passenger in a car that had been pulled over for a traffic violation to submit to a pat-down.[79] To do so, the officer must have a reasonable suspicion that the suspect may be armed and dangerous.

Race and Reasonable Suspicion

By the letter of the law, a person's race or ethnicity alone cannot provide reasonable suspicion for stops and frisks.[80] Some statistical measures, however, seem to show that these factors do, at times, play a troubling role in this area of policing. Exploring all traffic stops made by Rhode Island police over a one-year period, Leo Carroll and M. Lilliana Gonzalez of the University of Rhode Island found that

1. African American drivers are more likely to be frisked and searched,
2. This racial disparity is even greater with frisks than with searches,
3. The racial disparity of frisks depends on the racial makeup of the community where the traffic stop takes place, and
4. The race of the driver has no impact on how often frisks successfully uncover evidence of criminal wrongdoing.[81]

Furthermore, as you will recall from last chapter, on a national level, police officers are almost three times as likely to search members of minority groups than whites after a traffic stop.[82]

Racial Profiling Such statistics are often seen as proof that some police departments or officers use **racial profiling** in deciding which suspects to stop. Racial profiling occurs when a police action is based on the race, ethnicity, or national origin of the suspect rather than any reasonable suspicion that he or she has broken the law. As you may recall from our discussion of pretextual stops earlier in the chapter, as long as a police officer can provide a valid reason for a stop, any racial motivation on his or her part is often legally irrelevant. When data show that a law enforcement agency is improperly focusing its attention on members of minority groups, the remedies include

1. A civil lawsuit against the law enforcement agency for violating provisions of the U.S. Constitution that require all citizens to be treated fairly and equally by the government,
2. Law enforcement agency policies designed to stop the practice.

Both remedies came into play recently in New York City, where police officials had encouraged aggressive stops and frisks for nearly a decade. In 2013, a federal judge found that members of minority groups living in the city were "likely targeted for stops based on a lesser degree of objectively founded suspicion than whites" and therefore that the New York Police Department's stop-and-frisk tactics violated the Fourth Amendment.[83] After the department instituted new measures designed to discourage the practice, the

Racial Profiling The practice of targeting people for police action based solely on their race, ethnicity, or national origin.

number of overall stops in New York declined from 16,000 a week in January 2013 to fewer than 2,000 per week at the end of 2013.[84]

Immigration Law and Profiling Racial profiling has also played a role in the contentious national debate over immigration policy. In 2010, Arizona passed a law aimed at policing its large number of undocumented immigrants. The legislation, known as S.B. 1070, *requires* state and local police officers, "when practicable," to check the immigration status of someone they have a reasonable suspicion is in the country illegally.[85]

The language of Arizona's law does prohibit officers from using a suspect's race or ethnicity as the sole consideration in determining reasonable suspicion. Furthermore, officers can inquire about immigration status only after a suspect has been stopped for another reason, such as a traffic violation. The law's critics, however, believe that police will have no choice but to focus on Arizona's Hispanic population, as determined primarily by skin color.

Much to the disappointment of these critics, in 2012 the U.S. Supreme Court upheld the so-called "papers, please" provision of the Arizona law.[86] The Court based its ruling on the fact that state and local police officers are not actually enforcing immigration law, which is the domain of the federal government. Rather, they are notifying federal immigration officials about the presence of undocumented immigrants who have been detained for other forms of misconduct. If, however, the implementation of S.B 1070 and similar laws in five other states does lead to blatant levels of racial profiling, experts believe that the Court will revisit the constitutionality of these laws.[87] We will take a closer look at the practice of racial profiling in the *CJ in Action* feature at the end of the chapter.

▲ A U.S. Border Patrol agent checks the identifications of passengers on a train stopped in upstate New York, near the Canadian border. **What strategies could law enforcement agents employ to avoid racial profiling when searching for undocumented immigrants in these circumstances?** John Moore/Getty Images

Arrests

As happened in the *Terry* case discussed earlier, a stop and frisk may lead to an **arrest**. An arrest is the act of apprehending a suspect for the purpose of detaining him or her on a criminal charge. It is important to understand the difference between a stop and an arrest. In the eyes of the law, a stop is a relatively brief intrusion on a citizen's rights, whereas an arrest—which involves a deprivation of liberty—is deserving of a full range of constitutional protections (see this chapter's *Mastering Concepts—The Difference between a Stop and an Arrest*). Consequently, while a stop can be made based on reasonable suspicion, a law enforcement officer needs probable cause, as defined earlier, to make an arrest.[88]

Elements of an Arrest

When is somebody under arrest? The easy—and incorrect—answer would be whenever the police officer says so. In fact, the state of being under arrest is dependent not only on the actions of the law enforcement officers but also on the perception of the suspect. Suppose Mr. Smith is stopped by plainclothes detectives, driven to the police station,

Arrest To deprive the liberty of a person suspected of criminal activity.

PhotoDisc

Both stops and arrests are considered seizures because both police actions involve the restriction of an individual's freedom to "walk away." Both must be justified by a showing of reasonableness as well. You should be aware, however, of the differences between a stop and an arrest. **During a stop,** police can interrogate the person and make a limited search of his or her outer clothing. If anything occurs during the stop, such as the discovery of an illegal weapon, then officers may arrest the person. **If an arrest is made,** the suspect is now under police control and is protected by the U.S. Constitution in a number of ways that will be discussed later in the chapter.

	Stop	Arrest
Justification	Reasonable suspicion only	Probable cause
Warrant	None	Required in some, but not all, situations
Intent of Officer	To investigate suspicious activity	To make a formal charge against the suspect
Search	May frisk, or "pat down," for weapons	May conduct a full search for weapons or evidence
Scope of Search	Outer clothing only	Area within the suspect's immediate control or "reach"

and detained for three hours for questioning. During this time, the police never tell Mr. Smith he is under arrest, and in fact, he is free to leave at any time. But if Mr. Smith or any other reasonable person *believes* he is not free to leave, then, according to the Supreme Court, that person is in fact under arrest and should receive the necessary constitutional protections.[89]

Criminal justice professor Rolando V. del Carmen of Sam Houston State University has identified four elements that must be present for an arrest to take place:

LEARNING
7
OBJECTIVE

List the four elements that must be present for an arrest to take place.

1. The *intent* to arrest. In a stop, though it may entail slight inconvenience and a short detention period, there is no intent on the part of the law enforcement officer to deprive the suspect of her or his freedom. Therefore, there is no arrest. As intent is a subjective term, it is sometimes difficult to determine whether the police officer intended to arrest. In situations when the intent is unclear, courts often rely—as in our hypothetical case of Mr. Smith—on the perception of the arrestee.[90]

2. The *authority* to arrest. State laws give police officers the authority to place citizens under custodial arrest, or take them into *custody,* a concept defined later in the chapter.

3. *Seizure or detention.* A necessary part of an arrest is the detention of the subject. Detention is considered to have occurred as soon as the arrested individual submits to the control of the officer, whether peacefully or under the threat or use of force.

4. The *understanding* of the person that she or he has been arrested. Through either words—such as "you are now under arrest"—or actions, the person taken into custody must understand that an arrest has taken place. When a suspect has been forcibly subdued by the police, handcuffed, and placed in a patrol car, he or she is believed to understand that an arrest has been made. This understanding may be lacking if the person is intoxicated, insane, or unconscious.[91]

Arrests with a Warrant

When law enforcement officers have established probable cause to arrest an individual who is not in police custody, they obtain an **arrest warrant** for that person. An arrest warrant, similar to a search warrant, contains information such as the name of the person suspected and the crime he or she is suspected of having committed. (See Figure 7.3 for an example of an arrest warrant.) Judges or magistrates issue arrest warrants after first determining that the law enforcement officers have indeed established probable cause.

FIGURE 7.3 Example of an Arrest Warrant

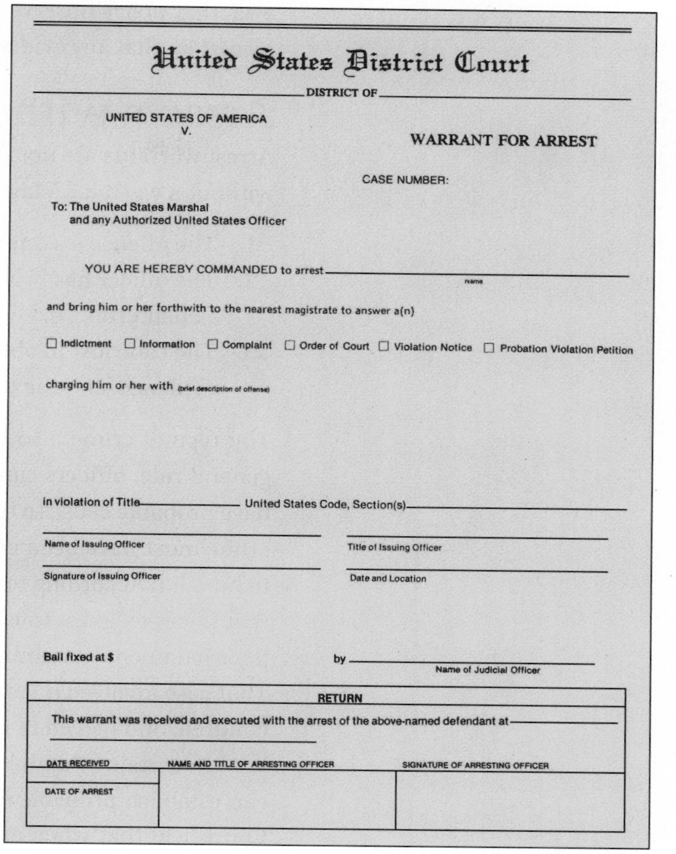

United States District Court

DISTRICT OF

UNITED STATES OF AMERICA
V.

WARRANT FOR ARREST

CASE NUMBER:

To: The United States Marshal
and any Authorized United States Officer

YOU ARE HEREBY COMMANDED to arrest ______ name

and bring him or her forthwith to the nearest magistrate to answer a(n)

☐ Indictment ☐ Information ☐ Complaint ☐ Order of Court ☐ Violation Notice ☐ Probation Violation Petition

charging him or her with (brief description of offense)

in violation of Title ______ United States Code, Section(s) ______

Name of Issuing Officer | Title of Issuing Officer

Signature of Issuing Officer | Date and Location

Bail fixed at $ ______ by ______ Name of Judicial Officer

RETURN

This warrant was received and executed with the arrest of the above-named defendant at ______

DATE RECEIVED	NAME AND TITLE OF ARRESTING OFFICER	SIGNATURE OF ARRESTING OFFICER
DATE OF ARREST		

Entering a Dwelling There is a perception that an arrest warrant gives law enforcement officers the authority to enter a dwelling without first announcing themselves. This is not accurate. In *Wilson v. Arkansas* (1995),[92] the Supreme Court reiterated the common law requirement that police officers must knock and announce their identity and purpose before entering a dwelling. Under certain conditions, known as **exigent circumstances,** law enforcement officers need not announce themselves. As determined by the courts, these circumstances include situations in which the officers have a reasonable belief of any of the following:

- The suspect is armed and poses a strong threat of violence to the officers or others inside the dwelling.
- Persons inside the dwelling are in the process of destroying evidence or escaping because of the presence of the police.
- A felony is being committed at the time the officers enter.[93]

According to Peter Kraska, a professor at Eastern Kentucky University, the number of no-knock police raids based on exigent circumstances has increased from 2,000 to 3,000 per year in the mid-1980s to 50,000 per year today.[94] As we noted last chapter in our discussion of police militarization, critics worry that with these tactics police are increasingly endangering citizens, some of whom may be innocent.[95] In 2014, a SWAT team in Habersham County, Georgia, severely burned an infant by throwing a flash-bang grenade into its crib during a "no-knock" drug raid.

The Waiting Period The Supreme Court severely weakened the practical impact of the "knock-and-announce" rule with its decision in *Hudson v. Michigan* (2006).[96] In that case, Detroit police did not knock before entering the defendant's home with a warrant. Instead, they announced themselves and then waited only three to five seconds before making their entrance, not the fifteen to twenty seconds suggested by a prior Court ruling.[97] Hudson argued that the drugs found during the subsequent search were inadmissible because the law enforcement agents did not follow proper procedure.

By a 5–4 margin, the Court disagreed. In his majority opinion, Justice Antonin Scalia stated that an improper "knock and announce" is not unreasonable enough to provide defendants with a "get-out-of-jail-free card" by disqualifying evidence uncovered on the basis of a valid search warrant.[98] Thus, the exclusionary rule, discussed earlier in this

Arrest Warrant A written order, based on probable cause and issued by a judge or magistrate, commanding that the person named on the warrant be arrested by the police.

Exigent Circumstances Situations that require extralegal or exceptional actions by the police.

chapter, would no longer apply under such circumstances. Legal experts still advise, however, that police observe a reasonable waiting period after knocking and announcing to be certain that any evidence found during the subsequent search will stand up in court.[99]

Arrests without a Warrant

Arrest warrants are not always required, and in fact, most arrests are made on the scene without a warrant. A law enforcement officer may make a **warrantless arrest** if:

1. The offense is committed in the presence of the officer; or
2. The officer has probable cause to believe that the suspect has committed a particular crime; or
3. The time lost in obtaining a warrant would allow the suspect to escape or destroy evidence, and the officer has probable cause to make an arrest.[100]

The type of crime also comes to bear in questions of arrests without a warrant. As a general rule, officers can make a warrantless arrest for a crime they did not see if they have probable cause to believe that a felony has been committed. For misdemeanors, the crime must have been committed in the presence of the officer for a warrantless arrest to be valid. According to a 2001 Supreme Court ruling, even an arrest for a misdemeanor that involves "gratuitous humiliations" imposed by a police officer "exercising extremely poor judgment" is valid as long as the officer can satisfy probable cause requirements.[101] That case involved a Texas mother who was handcuffed, taken away from her two young children, and placed in jail for failing to wear her seat belt.

In certain situations, warrantless arrests are unlawful even though a police officer can establish probable cause. In *Payton v. New York* (1980),[102] for example, the Supreme Court held that when exigent circumstances do not exist and the suspect does not give consent to enter a dwelling, law enforcement officers cannot force themselves in for the purpose of making a warrantless arrest. A year after the *Payton* ruling, the Court expanded its holding to cover the homes of third parties.[103] So, if police wish to arrest a criminal suspect in another person's home, they cannot enter that home to arrest the suspect without first obtaining a search warrant, a process we discussed earlier in the chapter.

The Interrogation Process and *Miranda*

After the Pledge of Allegiance, there is perhaps no recitation that comes more readily to the American mind than the *Miranda* warning:

> You have the right to remain silent. If you give up that right, anything you say can and will be used against you in a court of law. You have the right to speak with an attorney and to have the attorney present during questioning. If you so desire and cannot afford one, an attorney will be appointed for you without charge before questioning.

The *Miranda* warning is not a mere prop. It strongly affects one of the most important aspects of any criminal investigation—the **interrogation,** or questioning of a suspect from whom the police want to get information concerning a crime and perhaps a confession.

The Legal Basis for *Miranda*

The Fifth Amendment guarantees protection against self-incrimination. In other words, as we shall see again in Chapter 10, a defendant cannot be required to provide information about his or her own criminal activity. A defendant's choice *not* to incriminate

Warrantless Arrest An arrest made without first seeking a warrant for the action.

Interrogation The direct questioning of a suspect to gather evidence of criminal activity and to try to gain a confession.

himself or herself cannot be interpreted as a sign of guilt by a jury in a criminal trial. A confession, or admission of guilt, is by definition a statement of self-incrimination. How, then, to reconcile the Fifth Amendment with the critical need of law enforcement officers to gain confessions? The answer lies in the concept of **coercion,** or the use of physical or psychological duress to obtain a confession.

Setting the Stage for *Miranda* The Supreme Court first ruled that a confession could not be physically coerced in a 1936 case concerning a defendant who was beaten and whipped until he confessed to a murder.[104] It was not until 1964, however, that the Court specifically recognized that the accused's due process rights should be protected during interrogation.

That year, the Court heard the case of *Escobedo v. Illinois,*[105] which involved a convicted murderer who had incriminated himself during a four-hour questioning session at a police station. Police officers ignored the defendant's requests to speak with his lawyer, who was actually present at the station while his client was being interrogated. The Court overturned the conviction, setting forth a five-pronged test in the process. This test established that if police are interrogating a suspect in custody, they cannot deny the suspect's request to speak with an attorney and must warn the suspect of his or her constitutional right to remain silent under the Fifth Amendment. If any one of the five prongs was not satisfied, the suspect had effectively been denied his or her right to counsel under the Sixth Amendment.[106]

The *Miranda* Case The limitations of the *Escobedo* decision quickly became apparent. All five of the prongs had to be satisfied for the defendant to enjoy the Sixth Amendment protections it offered. In fact, the accused rarely requested counsel, rendering the *Escobedo* test irrelevant no matter what questionable interrogation methods the police used to elicit confessions. Consequently, two years later, the Supreme Court handed down its *Miranda* decision,[107] establishing the **Miranda rights** and introducing the concept of what University of Columbia law professor H. Richard Uviller called *inherent coercion.* This term refers to the assumption that even if a police officer does not lay a hand on a suspect, the general atmosphere of an interrogation is in and of itself coercive.[108]

Though the *Miranda* case is best remembered for the procedural requirement it spurred, at the time the Supreme Court was more concerned about the treatment of suspects during interrogation. (See the feature *Landmark Cases*—Miranda v. Arizona.) The Court found that routine police interrogation strategies, such as leaving suspects alone in a room for several hours before questioning them, were inherently coercive. Therefore, the Court reasoned, every suspect needed protection from coercion, not just those who had been physically abused. The *Miranda* warning is a result of this need. In theory, if the warning is not given to a suspect before an interrogation, the fruits of that interrogation, including a confession, are invalid.

When a *Miranda* Warning Is Required

As we shall see, a *Miranda* warning is not necessary under several conditions, such as when no questions are asked of the suspect. Generally, *Miranda* requirements apply only when a suspect is in **custody.** In a series of rulings since *Miranda,* the Supreme Court has defined custody as an arrest or a situation in which a reasonable person would not feel free to leave.[109] Consequently, a **custodial interrogation** occurs when a suspect is under arrest or is deprived of her or his freedom in a significant manner. Remember, a *Miranda* warning is only required before a custodial interrogation takes place. For example, if four

Coercion The use of physical force or mental intimidation to compel a person to do something—such as confess to committing a crime—against her or his will.

Miranda Rights The constitutional rights of accused persons taken into custody by law enforcement officials, such as the right to remain silent and the right to counsel.

Custody The forceful detention of a person, or the perception that a person is not free to leave the immediate vicinity.

Custodial Interrogation The questioning of a suspect after that person has been taken into custody. In this situation, the suspect must be read his or her *Miranda* rights before interrogation can begin.

police officers enter a suspect's bedroom at 4:00 A.M., wake him, and form a circle around him, then they must give him a *Miranda* warning before questioning. Even though the suspect has not been arrested, he will "not feel free to go where he please[s]."[110]

The concept of custody is a fluid one, as the Court demonstrated with a 2012 ruling involving an imprisoned convict suspected of committing additional sex crimes. The inmate was taken from his prison cell to a conference room on a different floor, where he was questioned for five to seven hours without being read his *Miranda* rights. Even though the inmate was under armed guard and still in prison, the Court ruled that he was not in "custody" because the door to the room was open and he was told several times during the session that he was free to leave.[111]

Landmark Cases

Miranda **v** Arizona

Explain why the U.S. Supreme Court established the *Miranda* warnings. **LEARNING OBJECTIVE 8**

In 1963, a rape and kidnapping victim identified produce worker Ernesto Miranda as her assailant in a lineup. Phoenix detectives questioned Miranda for two hours concerning the crimes, at no time informing him that he had a right to have an attorney present. When the police emerged from the session, they had a signed statement by Miranda confessing to the crimes. He was subsequently convicted and sentenced to twenty to thirty years in prison. After the conviction was confirmed by the Arizona Supreme Court, Miranda appealed to the United States Supreme Court, claiming that he had not been warned that any statement he made could be used against him, and that he had a right to counsel during the interrogation.

Miranda v. Arizona
United States Supreme Court
384 U.S. 436 (1966)

In the Words of the Court . . .
Chief Justice Warren, Majority Opinion

* * * *

The cases before us raise questions which go to the roots of our concepts of American criminal jurisprudence: the restraints society must observe consistent with the Federal Constitution in prosecuting individuals for crime. More specifically, we deal with the admissibility of statements obtained from an individual who is subjected to custodial police interrogation and the necessity for procedures which assure that the individual is accorded his privilege under the Fifth Amendment to the Constitution not to be compelled to incriminate himself.

* * * *

It is obvious that such an interrogation environment is created for no purpose other than to subjugate the individual to the will of his examiner. This atmosphere carries its own badge of intimidation. To be sure, this is not physical intimidation, but it is equally destructive of human dignity. The current practice of incommunicado interrogation is at odds with one of our Nation's most cherished principles—that the individual may not be compelled to incriminate himself. Unless adequate protective devices are employed to dispel the compulsion inherent in custodial surroundings, no statement obtained from the defendant can truly be the product of his free choice.

Decision
The Court overturned Miranda's conviction, stating that police interrogations are, by their very nature, coercive and therefore deny suspects their constitutional right against self-incrimination by "forcing" them to confess. Consequently, any person who has been arrested and placed in custody must be informed of his or her right to be free from self-incrimination and to be represented by counsel during any interrogation. In other words, suspects must be told that they *do not have* to answer police questions. To accomplish this, the Court established the *Miranda* warning, which must be read prior to questioning a suspect in custody.

For Critical Analysis
What is meant by the phrase "coercion can be mental as well as physical"? What role does the concept of "mental coercion" play in Chief Justice Warren's opinion?

When a *Miranda* Warning Is Not Required

A *Miranda* warning is not necessary in a number of situations:

LEARNING
9
OBJECTIVE
Indicate situations in which a *Miranda* warning is unnecessary.

1. When the police do not ask the suspect any questions that are *testimonial* in nature. Such questions are designed to elicit information that may be used against the suspect in court. Note that "routine booking questions," such as the suspect's name, address, height, and eye color, do not require a *Miranda* warning. Even though answering these questions may provide incriminating evidence (especially if the person answering is a prime suspect), the Supreme Court has held that they are absolutely necessary if the police are to do their jobs.[112] (Imagine the officer not being able to ask a suspect her or his name.)

2. When the police have not focused on a suspect and are questioning witnesses at the scene of a crime.

3. When a person volunteers information before the police have asked a question.

4. When the suspect has given a private statement to a friend or some other acquaintance. *Miranda* does not apply to these statements so long as the government did not orchestrate the situation.

5. During a stop and frisk, when no arrest has been made.

6. During a traffic stop.[113]

In 1984, the Supreme Court also created a "public-safety exception" to the *Miranda* rule. The case involved a police officer who, after feeling an empty shoulder holster on a man he had just arrested, asked the suspect the location of the gun without informing him of his *Miranda* rights. The Court ruled that the gun was admissible as evidence because the police's duty to protect the public is more important than a suspect's *Miranda* rights.[114] In April 2013, federal law enforcement agents relied on this exception to question Boston Marathon bomber Dzhokhar Tsarnaev from a hospital bed without first "Mirandizing" him. Once the agents were satisfied that Tsarnaev knew of no other active plots or threats to public safety, they read the suspect his *Miranda* rights in the presence of a lawyer.[115]

▼ Study the details of this photo of an Aspen, Colorado, police officer and a suspect. **Why must the officer "Mirandize" the suspect before asking him any questions, even if the officer never formally places the suspect under arrest?** Chris Hondros/Getty Images

Waiving *Miranda* Suspects can *waive* their Fifth Amendment rights and speak to a police officer, but only if the waiver is made voluntarily. Silence on the part of a suspect does not mean that his or her *Miranda* protections have been relinquished. To waive their rights, suspects must state—either in writing or orally—that they understand those rights and that they will voluntarily answer questions without the presence of counsel.

To ensure that the suspect's rights are upheld, prosecutors are required to prove by a preponderance of the evidence that the suspect "knowingly and intelligently" waived his or her *Miranda* rights.[116] To make the waiver perfectly clear, police will ask suspects two questions in addition to giving the *Miranda* warning:

1. Do you understand your rights as I have read them to you?
2. Knowing your rights, are you willing to talk to another law enforcement officer or me?

If the suspect indicates that she or he does not want to speak to the officer, thereby invoking her or his right to silence, the officer must *immediately* stop any questioning.[117] Similarly, if the suspect requests a lawyer, the police can ask no further questions until an attorney is present.[118]

Clear Intent The suspect must be absolutely clear about her or his intention to stop the questioning or have a lawyer present. In *Davis v. United States* (1994),[119] the Supreme Court upheld the interrogation of a suspect after he said, "Maybe I should talk to a lawyer." The Court found that this statement was too ambiguous, saying that it did not want to force police officers to "read the minds" of suspects who make vague declarations. Along these same lines, in *Berghuis v. Thompkins* (2010),[120] the Court upheld the conviction of a suspect who implicated himself in a murder after remaining mostly silent during nearly three hours of police questioning. The defendant claimed that he had invoked his *Miranda* rights by being uncommunicative with the interrogating officers. The Court disagreed, saying that silence is not enough—a suspect must actually state that he or she wishes to cut off questioning for the *Miranda* protections to apply.

The Weakening of *Miranda*

"*Miranda* has become embedded in routine police practice to the point where the warnings have become part of our national culture," wrote Chief Justice William Rehnquist over a decade ago.[121] This may be true, but, at the same time, many legal scholars believe that a series of Supreme Court rulings have eroded *Miranda*'s protections. "It's death by a thousand cuts," says Jeffrey L. Fisher of the National Association of Criminal Defense Lawyers, who believes the Court is "doing everything it can to ease the admissibility of confessions that police wriggle out of suspects."[122]

One such exception, created by the Supreme Court in 2004, is crucial to understanding the status of *Miranda* rights in current criminal law. The case involved a Colorado defendant who voluntarily told the police the location of his gun (which, being an ex-felon, he was not allowed to possess) without being read his rights.[123] The Court upheld the conviction, finding that the *Miranda* warning is merely *prophylactic*. In other words, it is only intended to prevent violations of the Fifth Amendment. Because only the gun, and not the defendant's testimony, was presented at trial, the police had not violated the defendant's constitutional rights.

In essence, the Court was ruling that the "fruit of the poisoned tree" doctrine, discussed earlier in this chapter, does not bar the admission of physical evidence that is discovered based on voluntary statements by a suspect who has not been "Mirandized." (See Figure 7.4 for a rundown of several other significant Court rulings that have weakened the *Miranda* requirements over the past decades.)

False Confessions

While observing more than two hundred interrogations over a nine-month period in northern California, University of San Francisco law professor Richard Leo noted that more than 80 percent of the suspects waived their *Miranda* rights.[124] Apparently, the suspects wanted to appear cooperative, a "willingness to please" that contributes to the troubling phenomenon of *false confessions* in the American criminal justice system.

FIGURE 7.4 Supreme Court Decisions Eroding *Miranda* Rights

Moran v. Burbine (475 U.S. 412 [1986]). **This case established that police officers are not required to tell suspects undergoing custodial interrogation that their attorney is trying to reach them.** The Court ruled that events that the suspect could have no way of knowing about have no bearing on his ability to waive his *Miranda* rights.

Arizona v. Fulminante (499 U.S. 279 [1991]). **In this very important ruling, the Court held that a conviction is not automatically overturned if the suspect was coerced into making a confession.** If the other evidence introduced at the trial is strong enough to justify a conviction without the confession, then the fact that the confession was illegally gained can be, for all intents and purposes, ignored.

Texas v. Cobb (532 U.S. 162 [2001]). When a suspect refuses to waive his or her *Miranda* rights, a police officer cannot lawfully continue the interrogation until the suspect's attorney arrives on the scene. In this case, however, **the Court held that a suspect may be questioned without having a lawyer present if the interrogation does not focus on the crime for which he or she was arrested,** even though it does touch on another, closely related, offense.

Florida v. Powell (559 U.S. 50 [2010]). Florida's version of the *Miranda* warning informs suspects that they have a right "to talk with an attorney," but does not clearly inform them of the right to a lawyer during any police interrogation. The Court upheld Florida's warning, **ruling that different jurisdictions may use whatever version of the *Miranda* warning they please, as long as it reasonably conveys the essential information about a suspect's rights.**

Maryland v. Shatzer (559 U.S. 98 [2010]). **The Court announced a new rule that permits police to resume questioning of a suspect two weeks after that suspect has invoked her or his *Miranda* rights and been released from custody.** The Court reasoned that fourteen days "provides plenty of time for the suspect to get reacclimated to his normal life . . . and to shake off any residual coercive effect of his prior custody."

Coercion and False Confessions A false confession occurs when a suspect admits to a crime that she or he did not actually commit. Given that juries tend to place a great deal of weight on admissions, sometimes to the exclusion of other evidence, false confessions can have disastrous consequences for the defendant in court.[125] About 30 percent of wrongful convictions overturned by DNA evidence were at least partially the result of a false confession.[126]

The Reid Technique According to Saul Kassin, a professor of psychology at Williams College in Williamstown, Massachusetts, there are three general types of false confessions:

1. *Voluntary.* The suspect is seeking attention, or is delusional and thinks he or she did commit the crime.
2. *Internalized.* The suspect is a vulnerable person, suffering from the stress of the interrogation, who comes to believe that he or she committed the crime.
3. *Compliant.* The suspect knows he or she is innocent, but decides—under police influence—that it is in his or her best interests to confess to the crime.

Kassin believes that last two categories of false confessions are often "coerced."[127] Indeed, the Reid Technique, used widely by American law enforcement, is premised on the assumption that all interrogation subjects are guilty. Police officers trained in this method reject any denials during the interrogation. They are also taught to minimize the moral seriousness of the crime, and to present the suspect's actions as the lesser of two evils. ("Was this your idea, or did your buddies talk you into it?") When the suspect finally does admit to the crime, he or she is to be congratulated and immediately asked for corroborating details.[128]

Pressure Points Critics believe that the Reid Technique creates feelings of helplessness in the suspect, and turns a confession into an "escape hatch" from the unpleasantness of

False Confession An admission of guilt when the confessor did not, in fact, commit the crime.

the interrogation.[129] In 1983, for example, after five hours of questioning with no lawyer present, Henry Lee McCollum told police that he was involved in the rape and murder of an eleven-year-old girl. He was eventually sentenced to death for the crimes. "I had never been under this much pressure, with a person hollering at me and threatening me," McCollum said in 2014, when a North Carolina judge declared him innocent and released him from prison. "I just made up a story and gave it to them so they would let me go home."[130]

Another potential problem with the Reid Technique, noted earlier, is that it is predicated on the assumption that the suspect is guilty.[131] Because both guilty and innocent suspects show stress when being interrogated by police, the interrogator may be "fooled" by an innocent person's evasive and nervous behavior. An alternative method of police interrogation, which resembles a journalistic interview rather than psychological combat, is the subject of this chapter's *CJ Policy—Your Take* feature.

Recording Confessions As with body-worn cameras (discussed in the previous chapter), the mandatory videotaping of interrogations has been offered as a means to promote police accountability. Nearly 900 law enforcement agencies, including the FBI and the DEA, now regularly record police interviews, particularly as part of felony investigations.[132]

In theory, such recordings will make clear any improper tactics used by law enforcement to gain a confession. In reality, this strategy might not live up to reformers' expectations. As Professor Jennifer Mnookin of the University of California, Los Angeles, points out, there is no guarantee that "judges or jurors can actually tell the difference between true and false confessions, even with the more complete record of interactions that recorded interrogations provide."[133]

EthicsChallenge

Several years ago, police in Troy, New York, told a suspect that his son's life could be saved only if the suspect explained how the boy had injured his head. In fact, the child was already brain dead, which the suspect did not known when he admitted to slamming his son's head against a mattress. Law enforcement agents can use deception when interviewing suspects to gain a confession. Even so, did the Troy police behave ethically in this instance? Explain your answer. ▪

The Identification Process

A confession is a form of self-identification; the suspect has identified herself or himself as the guilty party. If police officers are unable to gain a confession, they must use other methods to link the suspect with the crime. In fact, to protect against false admissions, police must use these other methods even if the suspect confesses.

Essential Procedures

Unless police officers witness the commission of the crime themselves, they must establish the identity of the suspect using three basic types of identification procedures:

List the three basic types of police identification. **10** LEARNING OBJECTIVE

1. *Showups,* which occur when a suspect who matches the description given by witnesses is apprehended near the scene of the crime within a reasonable amount of time after the crime has been committed. The suspect is usually returned to the crime scene for possible identification by witnesses.

2. *Photo arrays,* which occur when no suspect is in custody but the police have a general description of the person. Witnesses and victims are shown "mug shots" of people with police records that match the description. Police will also present witnesses and victims with pictures of people they believe might have committed the crime.

3. *Lineups,* which entail lining up several physically similar people, one of whom is the suspect, in front of a witness or victim. The police may have each member of the lineup wear clothing similar to that worn by the criminal and say a phrase that was used during the crime. These visual and oral cues are designed to help the witness identify the suspect.

As with the other procedures discussed in this chapter, constitutional law governs the identification process, though some aspects are more tightly restricted than others. The Sixth Amendment right to counsel, for example, does not apply during showups or photo arrays. In showups, the police often need to establish a suspect quickly, and it would be unreasonable to expect them to wait for an attorney to arrive. According to the Supreme Court in *United States v. Ash* (1973),[134] however, the police must be able to prove this need for immediate identification, perhaps by showing that it was necessary to keep the suspect from fleeing the state.

As for photo arrays, courts have found that any procedure that does not require the suspect's presence does not require the presence of his or her attorney.[135] The lack of an attorney does not mean that police can "steer" a witness toward a positive identification with statements such as "Are you sure this isn't the person you saw robbing the grocery store?" Such actions would violate the suspect's due process rights.

Nontestimonial Evidence

Some observers feel that the standard **booking** procedure—the process of recording information about the suspect immediately after arrest—infringes on a suspect's Fifth Amendment rights. During booking, the suspect is photographed and fingerprinted, and blood samples may be taken. If these samples lead to the suspect's eventual identification, according to some, they amount to self-incrimination.

In *Schmerber v. California* (1966),[136] however, the Supreme Court held that such tests are not the equivalent of *testimonial* self-incrimination (where the suspect testifies verbally against himself or herself) and therefore do not violate the Fifth Amendment. Using similar legal reasoning, the Court has also determined that voice and handwriting samples gathered by police may be used to identify a suspect.[137]

Booking The process of entering a suspect's name, offense, and arrival time into the police log following her or his arrest.

▼ Fort Bend County (Texas) authorities arrested Ronald Curtis for a string of robberies after a dog identified him by his smell, even though store videos showed that Curtis bore little resemblance to the suspect. **What might be some of the drawbacks of using "scent" lineups, in which a police dog smells the crime scene and is then expected to choose that same smell out of a group of suspects?** Daniel Kramer/*The New York Times*/Redux Pictures

CJ IN ACTION

Racial Profiling and the Constitution

If Pima County (Arizona) sheriff's deputy Brad Gill sees a person near the U.S.-Mexico border who is carrying a backpack and looks dirty from trekking across the desert, he will assume that person is in the United States illegally. "All of that adds up to a kind of profiling, [and] there's value to that," says Gill. "But I'm not judging . . . I'm doing my job efficiently."[138] Gill fails to mention that most of the people he finds in such a condition are also Hispanic. In this *CJ in Action* feature, we explore the difficult question of whether judging a person by his or her skin color in a law enforcement context can ever be justified.

A Valid Strategy?

The Fourth Amendment protects persons against "unreasonable searches and seizures." Intuitively, it would seem that when the police search or detain a person because of his or her race, an unreasonable search or seizure has taken place. Nevertheless, as detailed in the chapter, such profiling does seem to occur. Between 2004 and 2012, for example, New York Police Department (NYPD) officers made almost 5 million stops. About 83 percent of those stops involved African Americans and Hispanics, even though those two groups make up only about half the city's residents.[139] In these cases, as you learned earlier, as long as a police officer has probable cause that actual wrongdoing has occurred, any "racist intent" on his or her part is often irrelevant.

Regardless of wrongdoing, federal agents are still permitted by law to consider race and ethnicity at immigration checkpoints, border crossings, and airports, if the investigation involves national security. In defending this policy, one official said that Border Patrol agents "have a very short period of time to make an assessment as to whether further inquiry needs to be given."[140] Does this mean that racial profiling can be a valid law enforcement strategy?

The Case for Racial Profiling

- Crime rates are racially disproportionate. Young African American males are often more likely than other age and racial groups to commit drug-related crimes. Hispanics are more likely than other ethnic groups to have violated immigration laws. To ignore such evidence in the name of cultural sensitivity does a disservice to law-abiding citizens of all races.[141]

- Racial profiling sometimes can seem to work. In the decade that the NYPD implemented its Stop, Question, and Frisk policy, the city experienced a "historic" crime decline, and officers have confiscated 6,000 firearms.[142] At the same time, the murder rate in Philadelphia jumped by 10 percent in the first year after the city reined in its own aggressive stop-and-frisk policy.[143]

- Racial profiling is necessary to protect against terrorist acts, which, at present, have mostly been committed by men of Middle Eastern background. "We're at war with a terrorist network," says one commentator. "Are we really supposed to ignore the one identifiable fact that we know about them?"[144]

The Case against Racial Profiling

- Racial profiling is indistinguishable from racism and humiliates thousands of innocent people.

- If members of minority groups are more likely to be carrying illegal drugs than are whites, then police should find drugs more often on them than on whites after a stop and search. In fact, such "hit rates" are remarkably similar among the races.[145]

- If terrorist groups know in advance that law enforcement agencies are focusing on certain races or ethnic groups, they will simply select individuals of different races or ethnic groups for future attacks.

Your Opinion—Writing Assignment

In 2014, the NYPD shut down its Demographic Squad, a group of plainclothes detectives who would eavesdrop on conversations in Muslim neighborhoods, hoping to gain intelligence about possible terrorist activities. Under this program, the NYPD also assembled databases on where Muslims lived, worked, and prayed, and placed informants in hundreds of Muslim student groups and mosques. Do you agree with the decision to terminate the Demographic Squad? Are there any circumstances under which a suspect's race or ethnicity can be used to establish reasonable suspicion or probable cause in counterterrorism operations? Or, do you think that law enforcement should always be "color blind"? Before responding, you can review our discussions in the sections of this chapter concerning:

- Probable cause ("The Fourth Amendment").

- Race and reasonable suspicion ("Stops and Frisks").

- The elements of an arrest ("Arrests").

Your answer should include at least three full paragraphs.

Summary

For more information on these concepts, look back to the Learning Objective icons throughout the chapter.

 Outline the four major sources that may provide probable cause. (a) Personal observation, usually due to an officer's personal training, experience, and expertise; (b) information, gathered from informants, eyewitnesses, victims, police bulletins, and other sources; (c) evidence, which often has to be in plain view; and (d) association, which generally must involve a person with a known criminal background who is seen in a place where criminal activity is openly taking place.

 Explain the exclusionary rule and the exceptions to it. This rule prohibits illegally seized evidence, or evidence obtained by an unreasonable search and seizure in an inadmissible way, from being used against the accused in criminal court. Exceptions to the exclusionary rule are the "inevitable discovery" exception established in *Nix v. Williams* and the "good faith" exception established in *United States v. Leon* and *Arizona v. Evans.*

 List the four categories of items that can be seized by use of a search warrant. (a) Items resulting from a crime, such as stolen goods; (b) inherently illegal items; (c) evidence of the crime; and (d) items used in committing the crime.

 Explain when searches can be made without a warrant. Searches and seizures can be made without a warrant if they are incidental to an arrest (but they must be reasonable); when they are made with voluntary consent; when they involve the "movable vehicle" exception; when property has been abandoned; and when items are in plain view, under certain restricted circumstances (see *Coolidge v. New Hampshire*).

 Describe the plain view doctrine and indicate one of its limitations. Under the plain view doctrine, police officers are justified in seizing an item if (a) the item is easily seen by an officer who is legally in a position to notice it; (b) the discovery of the item is unintended; and (c) the officer, without further investigation, immediately recognizes the illegal nature of the item.

An item is not in plain view if the law enforcement agent needs to use technology such as a thermal imager to "see" it.

 Distinguish between a stop and a frisk, and indicate the importance of the case *Terry v. Ohio.* Though the terms *stop* and *frisk* are often used in concert, a stop is the separate act of detaining a suspect when an officer reasonably believes that a criminal activity is about to take place. A frisk is the physical "pat-down" of a suspect. In *Terry v. Ohio,* the Supreme Court ruled that an officer must have "specific and articulable facts" before making a stop, but those facts may be "taken together with rational inferences."

 List the four elements that must be present for an arrest to take place. (a) Intent, (b) authority, (c) seizure or detention, and (d) the understanding of the person that he or she has been arrested.

 Explain why the U.S. Supreme Court established the *Miranda* warnings. The Supreme Court recognized that police interrogations are, by their nature, coercive. Consequently, to protect a suspect's constitutional rights during interrogation, the Court ruled that the suspect must be informed of those rights before being questioned.

 Indicate situations in which a *Miranda* warning is unnecessary. (a) When no questions that are testimonial in nature are asked of the suspect; (b) when there is no suspect and witnesses in general are being questioned at the scene of a crime; (c) when a person volunteers information before the police ask anything; (d) when a suspect has given a private statement to a friend without the government orchestrating it; (e) during a stop and frisk when no arrests have been made; (f) during a traffic stop; and (g) when a threat to public safety exists.

 List the three basic types of police identification. (a) Showups, (b) photo arrays, and (c) lineups.

Questions for Critical Analysis

1. What are the two most significant legal concepts contained in the Fourth Amendment, and why are they important?

2. Using e-mail communications and their handheld smartphones or computer tablets, police can sometimes get an electronic warrant from a judge in as little as

fifteen minutes. How might this technological upgrade of the warrant process influence police officers' ability to conduct warrantless searches and seizures?

3. The Washington State Court of Appeals recently compared text messages to voice mail messages that can be overheard by anybody in a room. Using this logic, the court upheld a conviction based on text messages seized by police. Do you agree that people do not have a reasonable expectation of privacy when it comes to their text messaging? Why or why not?

4. A suspect discards his half-smoked cigarette on the sidewalk. The cigarette is picked up by a police officer, and the saliva on it allows law enforcement to obtain a sample of the suspect's DNA. Without a search warrant, should this evidence be allowed in court? Why or why not?

5. If, during questioning, a suspect says, "Maybe I should talk to a lawyer," should police immediately stop the interrogation? Why or why not? (To see how the Supreme Court ruled on this matter, search for *Davis v. United States* [1994] online.)

Key Terms

affidavit   221
arrest   233
arrest warrant   235
booking   243
coercion   237
consent searches   223
custodial interrogation   237
custody   237
electronic surveillance   227
exclusionary rule   217

exigent circumstances   235
false confession   241
frisk   231
fruit of the poisoned tree   217
"good faith" exception   218
"inevitable discovery" exception   218
interrogation   236
Miranda rights   237
plain view doctrine   226

probable cause   215
racial profiling   232
search   219
searches and seizures   215
searches incidental to arrests   222
search warrant   220
seizure   221
stop   231
warrantless arrest   236

Notes

1. *Florida v. Jardines*, 569 U.S. _____ (2013).
2. *United States v. Place*, 462 U.S. 696 (1983); and *Illinois v. Caballes*, 543 U.S. 405 (2005).
3. *Jardines, op. cit.,* at ____.
4. *Michigan v. Summers*, 452 U.S. 692 (1981).
5. *Brinegar v. United States*, 338 U.S. 160 (1949).
6. Rolando V. del Carmen, *Criminal Procedure for Law Enforcement Personnel* (Monterey, Calif.: Brooks/Cole Publishing Co., 1987), 63–64.
7. *Maryland v. Pringle*, 540 U.S. 366 (2003).
8. 500 U.S. 44 (1991).
9. *United States v. Leon*, 468 U.S. 897 (1984).
10. Thomas Y. Davis, "A Hard Look at What We Know (and Still Need to Learn) about the 'Costs' of the Exclusionary Rule: The NIJ Study and Other Studies of 'Lost' Arrests," *A.B.F. Research Journal* (1983), 680.
11. 430 U.S. 387 (1977).
12. 467 U.S. 431 (1984).
13. 468 U.S. 897 (1984).
14. 514 U.S. 1 (1995).
15. *California v. Greenwood*, 486 U.S. 35 (1988).
16. *Ibid.*
17. 389 U.S. 347 (1967).
18. *Ibid.*, 361.
19. 486 U.S. 35 (1988).

20. *Ibid.*
21. *Kentucky v. King*, 563 U.S. _____ (2011).
22. *Jardines, op. cit.,* at ____.
23. 565 U.S. _____ (2012).
24. *Ibid.*
25. Quoted in James Vicini, "Supreme Court Limits Police Use of GPS to Track Suspects," *Reuters* (January 23, 2012).
26. *Coolidge v. New Hampshire*, 403 U.S. 443, 467 (1971).
27. *Millender v. Messerschmidt*, 620 F.3d 1016 (9th Cir. 2010).
28. del Carmen, *op. cit.,* 158.
29. *Katz v. United States*, 389 U.S. 347, 357 (1967).
30. *Brigham City v. Stuart*, 547 U.S. 398 (2006).
31. 414 U.S. 234–235 (1973).
32. 395 U.S. 752 (1969).
33. *Ibid.*, 763.
34. Carl A. Benoit, "Questioning 'Authority': Fourth Amendment Consent Searches," *FBI Law Enforcement Bulletin* (July 2008), 24.
35. *Bumper v. North Carolina*, 391 U.S. 543 (1968).
36. *State v. Stone*, 362 N.C. 50, 653 S.E.2d 414 (2007).
37. 412 U.S. 218 (1973).
38. *Ohio v. Robinette*, 519 U.S. 33 (1996).

39. Jayme W. Holcomb, "Knock and Talks," *FBI Law Enforcement Bulletin* (August 2006), 22–32.
40. *United States v. Cotterman*, 709 F.3d. 952 (9th Cir. 2013).
41. *Missouri v. McNeely*, 569 U.S. _____ (2013).
42. *Fernandez v. California*, 571 U.S. ____ (2014).
43. 267 U.S. 132 (1925).
44. *United States v. Ross*, 456 U.S. 798, 804–809 (1982); and *Chambers v. Maroney*, 399 U.S. 42, 44, 52 (1970).
45. 453 U.S. 454 (1981).
46. *Arizona v. Gant*, 556 U.S. 332 (2009).
47. Adam Liptak, "Justices Significantly Cut Back Officers' Searches of Cars of People They Arrest," *New York Times* (April 22, 2009), A12.
48. Dale Anderson and Dave Cole, "Search and Seizure after *Arizona v. Gant*," *Arizona Attorney* (October 2009), 15.
49. *Heien v. North Carolina*, 574 U.S. _____ (2014).
50. *Whren v. United States*, 517 U.S. 806 (1996).
51. *United States v. Ross*, 456 U.S. 798 (1982).
52. *Ibid.*, 824.
53. *California v. Acevedo*, 500 U.S. 565 (1991).
54. 403 U.S. 443 (1971).
55. *Kyollo v. United States*, 533 U.S. 27 (2001).

56. 388 U.S. 42 (1967).

57. 18 U.S.C. Sections 2510(7), 2518(1)(a), 2516 (1994).

58. Christopher K. Murphy, "Electronic Surveillance," in "Twenty-Sixth Annual Review of Criminal Procedure," *Georgetown Law Journal* (April 1997), 920.

59. *United States v. Nguyen,* 46 F.3d 781, 783 (8th Cir. 1995).

60. Joseph Siprut, "Privacy through Anonymity: An Economic Argument for Expanding the Right of Privacy in Public Places," *Pepperdine Law Review* 33 (2006), 311, 320.

61. Catherine Crump, quoted in Elizabeth Weise and Greg Toppo, "License-Plates Scanners: Love 'Em or Loathe 'Em," *USA Today* (July 19, 2013), 3A.

62. "Cops Use Military Gear to Track Cell Phones," *Businessweek* (October 16, 2014), 30.

63. *State v. Earls,* 214 N.J. 564, 70 A.3d 630 (2013).

64. *California v. Riley,* 134 S.Ct. 2473 (2014).

65. Ibid., 2485.

66. Ibid., 2473.

67. Karen M. Hess and Henry M. Wrobleski, *Police Operation: Theory and Practice* (St. Paul, Minn.: West Publishing Co., 1997), 122.

68. 392 U.S. 1 (1968).

69. Ibid., 20.

70. Ibid., 21.

71. See *United States v. Cortez,* 449 U.S. 411 (1981); and *United States v. Sokolow,* 490 U.S. 1 (1989).

72. *United States v. Arvizu,* 534 U.S. 266 (2002).

73. Ibid., 270.

74. *United States v. Place,* 462 U.S. 696 (1983).

75. *Hibel v. Sixth Judicial District Court,* 542 U.S. 177 (2004).

76. Ibid., 182.

77. *Minnesota v. Dickerson,* 508 U.S. 366 (1993).

78. *People v. Powell,* Ill.App.1st 122275 (2014).

79. *Arizona v. Johnson,* 555 U.S. 328 (2009).

80. *United States v. Avery,* 137 F.3d 343, 353 (6th Cir. 1997).

81. Leo Carroll and M. Lilliana Gonzalez, "Out of Place: Racial Stereotypes and the Ecology of Frisks and Searches Following Traffic Stops," *Journal of Research in Crime and Delinquency* (August 2014), 559–584.

82. Lynn Langton and Matthew Durose, *Police Behavior during Traffic and Street Stops* (Washington, D.C.: U.S. Department of Justice, September 2013), Table 7, page 9.

83. Joseph Goldstein, "Judge Rejects New York's Stop-and-Frisk Policy," *New York Times* (August 13, 2013), A1.

84. Mike Bostock and Ford Fessenden, "'Stop-and-Frisk' Is All But Gone from New York," *New York Times* (September 19, 2014), at **www.nytimes.com/interactive/2014/09 /19/nyregion/stop-and-frisk-is-all-but -gone-from-new-york.html**.

85. Arizona Revised Statutes Sections 11-1051(B), 13-1509, 13-2929(C).

86. *Arizona v. United States,* 567 U.S. ___ (2012).

87. Julia Preston, "Immigration Ruling Leaves Issues Unresolved," *New York Times* (June 27, 2012), A14.

88. Rolando V. del Carmen and Jeffrey T. Walker, *Briefs of Leading Cases in Law Enforcement,* 2d ed. (Cincinnati, Ohio: Anderson, 1995), 38–40.

89. *Florida v. Royer,* 460 U.S. 491 (1983).

90. See also *United States v. Mendenhall,* 446 U.S. 544 (1980).

91. del Carmen, op. cit., 97–98.

92. 514 U.S. 927 (1995).

93. Linda J. Collier and Deborah D. Rosenbloom, *American Jurisprudence,* 2d ed. (Rochester, N.Y.: Lawyers Cooperative Publishing, 1995), 122.

94. "Cops or Soldiers?" *The Economist* (March 22, 2014), 27.

95. Radley Balco, *Rise of the Warrior Cop: The Militarization of America's Police Forces* (New York: PublicAffairs, 2013), 239–308.

96. 547 U.S. 586 (2006).

97. *United States v. Banks,* 540 U.S. 31, 41 (2003).

98. *Hudson v. Michigan,* 547 U.S. 586, 593 (2006).

99. Tom Van Dorn, "Violation of Knock-and-Announce Rule Does Not Require Suppression of All Evidence Found in Search," *The Police Chief* (October 2006), 10.

100. "Warrantless Searches and Seizures" in *Georgetown Law Journal Annual Review of Criminal Procedure, 2011* (Washington, D.C.: Georgetown Law Journal, 2011), 955.

101. *Atwater v. City of Lago Vista,* 532 U.S. 318, 346–347 (2001).

102. 445 U.S. 573 (1980).

103. *Steagald v. United States,* 451 U.S. 204 (1981).

104. *Brown v. Mississippi,* 297 U.S. 278 (1936).

105. 378 U.S. 478 (1964).

106. Ibid., 490–491.

107. *Miranda v. Arizona,* 384 U.S. 436 (1966).

108. H. Richard Uviller, *Tempered Zeal* (Chicago: Contemporary Books, 1988), 188–198.

109. *Orozco v. Texas,* 394 U.S. 324 (1969); *Oregon v. Mathiason,* 429 U.S. 492 (1977); and *California v. Beheler,* 463 U.S. 1121 (1983).

110. *Orozco,* op. cit., 325.

111. *Howes v. Fields,* 132 S.Ct. 1181 (2012).

112. *Pennsylvania v. Muniz,* 496 U.S. 582 (1990).

113. del Carmen, op. cit., 267–268.

114. *New York v. Quarles,* 467 U.S. 649 (1984).

115. Ethan Bronner and Michael S. Schmidt, "In Questions at First, No *Miranda* for Suspect," *New York Times* (April 23, 2013), A13.

116. *Moran v. Burbine,* 475 U.S. 412 (1986).

117. *Michigan v. Mosley,* 423 U.S. 96 (1975).

118. *Fare v. Michael C.,* 442 U.S. 707, 723–724 (1979).

119. 512 U.S. 452 (1994).

120. 560 U.S. 370 (2010).

121. *Dickerson v. United States,* 530 U.S. 428 (2000).

122. Quoted in Jesse J. Holland, "High Court Trims *Miranda* Warning Rights Bit by Bit," *Associated Press* (August 2, 2010).

123. *United States v. Patane,* 542 U.S. 630 (2004).

124. Richard A. Leo, "Inside the Interrogation Room," *Journal of Criminal Law and Criminology* (1996), 266.

125. Saul M. Kassin and Lawrence S. Wrightsman, "Prior Confessions and Mock Juror Verdicts," *Journal of Social Psychology* (1980), 133–146.

126. The Innocence Project, "False Confessions & Mandatory Recording of Interrogations," at **www.innocenceproject.org/fix/False -Confessions.php**.

127. Saul M. Kassin, "Internalized False Confessions," in Michael P. Toglia, et al., eds., *Handbook of Eyewitness Psychology, Vol. 1* (New York: Psychology Press, 2007), 171.

128. Douglas Starr, "The Interview: Do Police Interrogation Techniques Produce False Confessions?" *The New Yorker* (December 9, 2013), 43–44.

129. Ibid., 44.

130. "Death Row Interview with Henry McCollum," *News and Observer* (Raleigh, N.C.) (August 30, 2014), at **www.youtube.com /watch?v=NxV6PWfa7i8**.

131. Gregg McCrary, quoted in Starr, op. cit., 46.

132. The Innocence Project, op. cit.

133. Jennifer L. Mnookin, "Can a Jury Believe What It Sees?" *New York Times* (July 14, 2014), A19.

134. 413 U.S. 300 (1973).

135. *United States v. Barker,* 988 F.2d 77, 78 (9th Cir. 1993).

136. 384 U.S. 757 (1966).

137. *United States v. Dionisio,* 410 U.S. 1 (1973); and *United States v. Mara,* 410 U.S. 19 (1973).

138. Quoted in Mario Koran, "Near the Border, a Few Deputies Are Outnumbered by Drugs and Bodies," *New York Times* (June 10, 2013), A10.

139. Goldstein, op. cit.

140. Quoted in Matt Apuzzo and Michael A. Schmidt, "U.S. to Continue Racial, Ethnic Profiling in Border Policy," *New York Times* (December 6, 2014), A1.

141. Dinesh D'Souza, *The End of Racism: Principles for a Multicultural Society* (New York: Free Press, 1995), 260–261.

142. "Spread 'Em!" *The Economist* (June 2, 2012), 36–37.

143. Ibid., 37.

144. Michael Kinsley, "When Is Racial Profiling Okay?" *Washington Post* (September 30, 2001), A1.

145. Bureau of Justice Statistics, *Contacts between Police and the Public, 2005* (Washington, D.C.: U.S. Department of Justice, April 2007).

8

Courts and the Quest for Justice

Chapter Outline		Corresponding Learning Objectives
Functions of the Courts	**1**	Define and contrast the four functions of the courts.
The Basic Principles of the American Judicial System	**2**	Define *jurisdiction* and contrast geographic and subject-matter jurisdiction.
	3	Explain the difference between trial and appellate courts.
State Court Systems	**4**	Outline the several levels of a typical state court system.
The Federal Court System	**5**	Outline the federal court system.
	6	Explain briefly how a case is brought to the Supreme Court.
Judges in the Court System	**7**	Explain the difference between the selection of judges at the state level and at the federal level.
	8	Describe one alternative, practiced in other countries, to the American method of choosing judges.
The Courtroom Work Group	**9**	List and describe the members of the courtroom work group.
	10	List the three basic features of an adversary system of justice.

To target your study and review, look for these numbered Learning Objective icons throughout the chapter.

Business as Usual

on the afternoon of October 21, 2014, without much fanfare, Ahmed Abu Khattala made his first appearance in a federal courthouse in Washington, D.C. Unshackled, wearing a black, zip-up hooded sweatshirt, unencumbered by any extra security, he heard the charges against him and swore to tell the truth, just like any other person charged with a crime. His public defender told the judge that Khattala was not guilty, bemoaning the "utter lack of evidence" against him, as she would for any client.

▲ In 2014, Ahmed Abu Khattala was transferred to an American courtroom to face charges for directing this terrorist attack on the U.S. Consulate in Benghazi, Libya, two years earlier.

Khattala was not, however, your average criminal defendant. He was facing the death penalty for being the alleged ringleader of a 2012 terrorist attack that killed the U.S. ambassador and three other Americans in Benghazi, Libya. Had Khattala been captured five years earlier, there likely would have been an extensive debate over whether he should have been tried in a civilian criminal court. The alternative of sending him to the U.S. Naval Base at Guantánamo Bay, Cuba (GTMO), to appear before a military tribunal, would have been presented as the better national security alternative. Such tribunals offer fewer protections to suspected terrorists than those offered in civilian courts, and were therefore seen as more of a "sure thing" for gaining convictions.

This has not turned out to be the case. As of 2015, military tribunals have convicted only eight GTMO detainees. Furthermore, the military's efforts to prosecute Khalid Sheikh Mohammed, the self-proclaimed mastermind behind the September 11, 2001, terrorist attacks, have been plagued by numerous missteps and delays, with no end in sight. Conversely, from 2001 to 2014, federal prosecutors operating in civilian criminal courts convicted sixty-seven terrorist defendants captured on foreign soil. Voicing his support for the criminal justice system's counterterrorism role at the time of Khattala's arrest, then–U.S. Attorney General Eric Holder said, "We have shown, time and again, that upholding the rule of law is not inconsistent with safeguarding our national security."

1. Do you think that foreign terrorist suspects like Ahmed Abu Khattala should receive the same rights under the U.S. Constitution as other criminal suspects? Explain your answer.

2. Critics of using the criminal justice system to prosecute terrorist suspects often point to the drawbacks of reading such suspects their *Miranda* rights, discussed in the previous chapter. Why might that procedure endanger national security?

3. In 2013, the military tribunal proceedings against Khalid Sheikh Mohammed were delayed when federal agents admitted to setting up secret microphones in rooms used by Mohammed and his lawyers. What do you think the agents hoped to accomplish with this strategy? Why is it unfair to Mohammed?

Functions of the Courts

In 2014, angered by the slow pace of military tribunal hearings involving alleged September 11 mastermind Khalid Sheikh Mohammed, Charlie Clyne called the proceedings "a farce." "These parasites did it. They're guilty," said Clyne, whose wife was killed in the 2001 terrorist attacks. "Let's try them, fairly. And then kill them."[1] Clyne's frustrations—and those of many other September 11 victims and their families—are centered on the belief that *justice* has not yet been done in the case of Mohammed and his co-conspirators.

Famed jurist Roscoe Pound once characterized "justice" as society's demand "that serious offenders be convicted and punished," while at the same time "the innocent and unfortunate are not oppressed."[2] This somewhat idealistic definition obscures the fact that there are two sides to each court proceeding. While Clyne understandably has strong feelings about Mohammed's fate, American legal traditions allow a person accused of any crime, no matter how heinous, the chance to prove his or her innocence before a neutral decision maker. On a more practical level, then, a court is a place where arguments are settled. At best, the court provides a just environment in which the basis of the argument can be decided through the application of the law.

Courts have extensive powers in our criminal justice system: they can bring the authority of the state to seize property and to restrict individual liberty. Given that the rights to own property and to enjoy personal freedom are enshrined in the U.S. Constitution, a court's *legitimacy* in taking such measures must be unquestioned by society. This legitimacy is based on two factors: impartiality and independence.[3] In theory, each party involved in a courtroom dispute must have an equal chance to present its case and must be secure in the belief that no outside factors are going to influence the decision rendered by the court. In reality, as we shall see over the next four chapters, it does not always work that way.

LEARNING

1

OBJECTIVE

Define and contrast the four functions of the courts.

Due Process and Crime Control in the Courts

As mentioned in Chapter 1, the criminal justice system has two sets of underlying values: due process and crime control. Due process values focus on protecting the rights of the individual, whereas crime control values stress the punishment and repression of criminal conduct. The competing nature of these two value systems is often evident in the nation's courts.

▼ Why is it important that American criminal courtrooms, such as this one in Cape May, New Jersey, are places of impartiality and independence?
AP Images/*The Press of Atlantic City*, Dale Gerhard

The Due Process Function

The primary concern of early American courts was to protect the rights of the individual against the power of the state. Memories of injustices suffered at the hands of the British monarchy were still strong, and most of the procedural rules that we have discussed in this textbook were created with the express purpose of giving the individual a "fair chance" against the government in any courtroom proceedings. Therefore, the due process function of the courts is to

protect individuals from the unfair advantages that the government—with its immense resources—automatically enjoys in legal battles.

Seen in this light, constitutional guarantees such as the right to counsel, the right to a jury trial, and protection from self-incrimination are equalizers in the "contest" between the state and the individual. The idea that the two sides in a courtroom dispute are adversaries is, as we shall discuss in the next chapter, fundamental in American courts.

The Crime Control Function Advocates of crime control distinguish between the court's obligation to be fair to the accused and its obligation to be fair to society. The crime control function of the courts emphasizes punishment and retribution—criminals must suffer for the harm done to society, and it is the courts' responsibility to see that they do so. Given this responsibility to protect the public, deter criminal behavior, and "get criminals off the streets," the courts should not be concerned solely with giving the accused a fair chance. Rather than using due process rules as "equalizers," the courts should use them as protection against blatantly unconstitutional acts. For example, a detective who beats a suspect with a tire iron to get a confession has obviously infringed on the suspect's constitutional rights. If, however, the detective uses trickery to gain a confession, the court should allow the confession to stand because it is not in society's interest that law enforcement agents be deterred from outwitting criminals.

The Rehabilitation Function

A third view of the court's responsibility is based on the "medical model" of the criminal justice system. In this model, criminals are analogous to patients, and the courts perform the role of physicians who dispense "treatment."[4] The criminal is seen as sick, not evil, and therefore treatment is morally justified. Of course, treatment varies from case to case, and some criminals require harsh penalties such as incarceration. In other cases, however, it may not be in society's best interest for the criminal to be punished according to the formal rules of the justice system. Perhaps the criminal can be rehabilitated to become a productive member of society and thus save taxpayers the costs of incarceration or other punishment.

The Bureaucratic Function

To a certain extent, the crime control, due process, and rehabilitation functions of a court are secondary to its bureaucratic function. In general, a court may have the goal of protecting society or protecting the rights of the individual, but on a day-to-day basis that court has the more pressing task of dealing with the cases brought before it. Like any bureaucracy, a court is concerned with speed and efficiency, and loftier concepts such as justice can be secondary to a judge's need to wrap up a particular case before six o'clock so that administrative deadlines can be met. Indeed, many observers feel that the primary adversarial relationship in the courts is not between the two parties involved but between the ideal of justice and the reality of bureaucratic limitations.[5]

The Basic Principles of the American Judicial System

One of the most often cited limitations of the American judicial system is its complex nature. In truth, the United States does not have a single judicial system, but fifty-two different systems—one for each state, the District of Columbia, and the federal government.

As each state has its own unique judiciary with its own set of rules, some of which may be in conflict with the federal judiciary, it is helpful at this point to discuss some basics—jurisdiction, trial and appellate courts, and the dual court system.

Jurisdiction

In Latin, *juris* means "law," and *diction* means "to speak." Thus, **jurisdiction** literally refers to the power "to speak the law." Before any court can hear a case, it must have jurisdiction over the persons involved in the case or its subject matter. The jurisdiction of every court, even the United States Supreme Court, is limited in some way.

Geographic Jurisdiction One limitation is geographic. Generally, a court can exercise its authority over residents of a certain area. A state trial court, for example, normally has jurisdictional authority over crimes committed in a particular area of the state, such as a county or a district. A state's highest court (often called the state supreme court) has jurisdictional authority over the entire state, and the United States Supreme Court has jurisdiction over the entire country. For the most part, criminal jurisdiction is determined by legislation. The U.S. Congress or a state legislature can determine what acts are illegal within the geographic boundaries it controls, thus giving federal or state courts jurisdiction over those crimes.

Federal versus State Jurisdiction Most criminal laws are state laws, so the majority of all criminal trials are heard in state courts. Many acts that are illegal under state law, however, are also illegal under federal law. What happens when more than one court system has jurisdiction over the same criminal act? As a general rule, when Congress "criminalizes" behavior that is already prohibited under a state criminal code, the federal and state courts both have jurisdiction over that crime unless Congress states otherwise in the initial legislation. Thus, **concurrent jurisdiction,** which occurs when two different court systems have simultaneous jurisdiction over the same case, is quite common.

For instance, both the federal courts and the Massachusetts state court system have jurisdiction over Dzokhar Tsarnaev, suspected of carrying out the Boston Marathon bombings of April 2013. First, in 2015, Tsarnaev faced federal terrorism charges in federal court. At the conclusion of this federal trial, state officials have the option to try him in state court for the killing of Massachusetts Institute of Technology police officer Sean Collier, even if they must take him from a federal prison cell to do so.

State versus State Jurisdiction Multiple states can also claim jurisdiction over the same defendant or criminal act, depending on state legislation and the circumstances of the crime. For example, if Billy is standing in State A and shoots Frances, who is standing in State B, the two states could have concurrent jurisdiction to try Billy for murder. Similarly, if a property theft takes places in State A but police recover the stolen goods in State B, concurrent jurisdiction could exist. Some states have also passed laws stating that they have jurisdiction

Jurisdiction The authority of a court to hear and decide cases within an area of the law or a geographic territory.

Concurrent Jurisdiction The situation that occurs when two or more courts have the authority to preside over the same criminal case.

LEARNING

2

OBJECTIVE

Define *jurisdiction* and contrast geographic and subject-matter jurisdiction.

▼ Following an extensive dogfighting investigation, animal rescue workers load pit bulls into a mobile trailer in Nathalie, Virginia. The dogs' owners were charged with violating federal dogfighting laws and faced those charges in federal criminal court. **Do you think that the federal government should have jurisdiction over a local activity like dogfighting? Why or why not?** AP Images/Steven Mantilla

over their own citizens who commit crimes in other states, even if there is no other connection between the home state and the criminal act.[6]

The concept of jurisdiction encourages states to cooperate with each other regarding fugitives from the law. In 2014, for example, Michael Leday was suspected of killing two people by running them over with his car in Tucson, Arizona. Leday fled to Kansas City, Missouri, where police apprehended him by following his girlfriend to a hideout. Missouri officials subsequently *extradited* Leday back to Tucson to stand trial for the two murders. **Extradition** is the formal process by which one legal authority, such as a state or a nation, transfers a fugitive or a suspect to another legal authority that has a valid claim on that person.

Multiple Trials When different courts share jurisdiction over the same defendant, multiple trials can result. In 2014 and 2015, for example, former professional football player Darren Sharper faced court proceedings in three different states—Arizona, California, and Louisiana—related to charges that he had drugged and raped a number of different women. Because officials in each state had probable cause that he had committed crimes within state limits, each state had jurisdiction over him and the right to conduct a criminal trial.

Although some believe that such multiple trials are a waste of taxpayer money, state and county prosecutors often argue that local victims of crimes deserve the "sense of closure" that comes with criminal proceedings.[7] In addition, as we will see in Chapter 10, guilty verdicts can be appealed and reversed, and extra convictions serve as "insurance" against that possibility. In most situations, however, convictions in one jurisdiction end the prosecution of the same case in another jurisdiction.

Tribal Jurisdiction The 310 Native American reservations in the United States operate under an interesting geographic jurisdictional framework. Because of treaties with the federal government, tribes enjoy a considerable amount of self-rule on reservation land. Leaders of the Yakama Nation in Washington, for example, will not adhere to the recent state law legalizing marijuana.[8] Furthermore, tribal courts have jurisdiction to prosecute tribal members for crimes committed on tribal property.[9] These courts cannot, however, sentence most convicted defendants to more than three years in prison. Consequently, tribal leaders often ask the U.S. Department of Justice to prosecute serious crimes such as murder and rape that take place on reservations in federal court.

International Jurisdiction Under international law, each country has the right to create and enact criminal law for its territory. Therefore, the notion that a nation has jurisdiction over any crimes committed within its borders is well established. The situation becomes more delicate when one nation feels the need to go outside its own territory to enforce its criminal law. International precedent does, however, provide several bases for expanding jurisdiction across international borders.

For example, anti-terrorism efforts have been aided by the principle that the United States has jurisdiction over persons who commit crimes against Americans even when the former are citizens of foreign countries and live outside the United States. In 2012, British authorities extradited Mostafa Kamel Mostafa to New York City to face eleven different terrorism-related charges, including helping to orchestrate the kidnapping of American citizens in the Middle East. Three years later, a federal judge sentenced the British cleric to life in prison for his crimes.

Extradition The process by which one jurisdiction surrenders a person accused or convicted of violating another jurisdiction's criminal law to the second jurisdiction.

The extradition of Mostafa occurred only because American officials agreed not to seek his execution, a form of punishment prohibited in Great Britain. Indeed, some countries, for legal and political reasons, will not extradite criminal suspects to the United States. Nevertheless, the federal government feels it is legally justified in claiming jurisdiction over persons who commit crimes against U.S. citizens, even if these suspects live in a foreign country.[10] Such was the case with the drone attack that killed Anwar al-Awlaki in Yemen, an event discussed in Chapter 4. Yemeni officials had resolutely refused to extradite Awlaki to the United States. Furthermore, some behavior, such as piracy and genocide, is considered a crime against all nations collectively and, according to the principles of *universal jurisdiction,* can be prosecuted by any nation having custody of the wrongdoer.

▲ In 2014, Honduras extradited suspected drug dealer Carlos Lobo, shown here with members of the Honduran military police, to the United States. **Should the possibility that Lobo was shipping cocaine into this country give the American court system jurisdiction over him? Why or why not?** Orlando Sierra/Getty Images

Subject-Matter Jurisdiction Jurisdiction over subject matter also acts as a limitation on the types of cases a court can hear. State court systems include courts of *general* (unlimited) *jurisdiction* and courts of *limited jurisdiction.* Courts of general jurisdiction have no restrictions on the subject matter they may address, and therefore deal with the most serious felonies and civil cases. Courts of limited jurisdiction, also known as lower courts, handle misdemeanors and civil matters under a certain amount, usually $1,000.

As we will discuss later in the chapter, many states have created special subject-matter courts that only dispose of cases involving a specific crime. For example, a number of jurisdictions have established drug courts to handle an overload of illicit narcotics arrests. Furthermore, under the Uniform Code of Military Justice, the U.S. military has jurisdiction over active personnel who commit crimes, even if those crimes occur outside the course of duty.[11] In such cases, military officials can either attempt to *court-martial* the suspect in military court or allow civilian prosecutors to handle the case in state or federal court. Congress has also passed legislation giving the military jurisdiction over certain foreign-born terrorist suspects,[12] as detailed at the beginning of this chapter.

Trial and Appellate Courts

Another distinction is between courts of original jurisdiction and courts of appellate, or review, jurisdiction. Courts having *original jurisdiction* are courts of the first instance, or **trial courts.** Almost every case begins in a trial court. It is in this court that a trial (or a guilty plea) takes place, and the judge imposes a sentence if the defendant is found guilty. Trial courts are primarily concerned with *questions of fact.* They are designed to determine exactly what events occurred that are relevant to questions of the defendant's guilt or innocence.

Courts having *appellate jurisdiction* act as reviewing courts, or **appellate courts.** In general, cases can be brought before appellate courts only on appeal by one of the parties in the trial court. (Note that because of constitutional protections against being tried twice for the same crime, prosecutors who lose in criminal trial court *cannot* appeal the verdict.) An appellate court does not use juries or witnesses to reach its decision. Instead, its judges make a decision on whether the case should be *reversed* and *remanded,* or sent back to the court of original jurisdiction for a new trial. Appellate judges present written

LEARNING
3 Explain the difference between trial and appellate courts.
OBJECTIVE

Trial Courts Courts in which most cases usually begin and in which questions of fact are examined.

Appellate Courts Courts that review decisions made by lower courts, such as trial courts; also known as *courts of appeals.*

Opinions Written statements by appellate judges expressing the reasons for the court's decision in a case.

Dual Court System The separate but interrelated court system of the United States, made up of the courts on the national level and the courts on the state level.

explanations for their decisions, and these **opinions** of the court are the basis for a great deal of the precedent in the criminal justice system.

It is important to understand that appellate courts do not determine the defendant's guilt or innocence—they only make judgments on questions of procedure. In other words, they are concerned with *questions of law* and normally accept the facts as established by the trial court. Only rarely will an appeals court question a jury's decision. Instead, the appellate judges will review the manner in which the facts and evidence were provided to the jury and rule on whether errors were made in the process.

The Dual Court System

As we saw in Chapter 1, America's system of federalism allows the federal government and the governments of the fifty states to hold authority in many areas. As a result, the federal government and each of the fifty states, as well as the District of Columbia, have their own separate court systems. Because of the split between the federal courts and the state courts, this is known as the **dual court system.** (See Figure 8.1 to get a better idea of how federal and state courts operate as distinct yet parallel entities.)

Federal and state courts both have limited jurisdiction. Generally, federal courts preside over cases involving violations of federal law, and state courts preside over cases involving violations of state law. The distinction is not always clear, however. Federal courts have jurisdiction over more than 4,500 crimes, many of which also can be found in state criminal codes. As we saw earlier in this section, when such *concurrent jurisdiction* exists, both sides can try the defendant under their own laws, or one side can step aside and let the other decide the fate of the defendant. Because the federal court system has greater resources than most state court systems, federal criminal charges often take precedence over state criminal charges for practical reasons.

EthicsChallenge

In 2003, the U.S. military opened fire on a hotel in Baghdad, Iraq, believing that enemy troops were hiding in the building. During the battle, a Spanish journalist named José Couso was killed in the hotel. Eight years later, a Spanish judge indicted three U.S. soldiers in connection with Couso's death. Would it have been ethical for the American government to send the soldiers to Spain for a criminal trial? Why or why not? ■

FIGURE 8.1 The Dual Court System

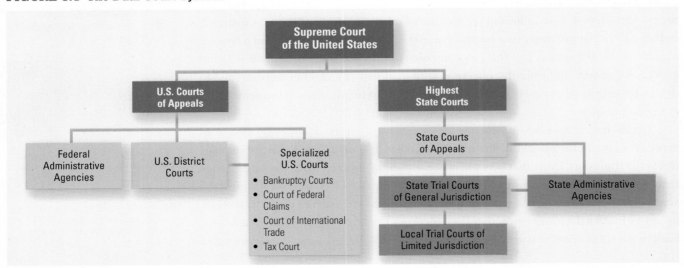

State Court Systems

Typically, a state court system includes several levels, or tiers, of courts. State courts may include:

LEARNING **4** OBJECTIVE Outline the several levels of a typical state court system.

1. Lower courts, or courts of limited jurisdiction,
2. Trial court of general jurisdiction,
3. Appellate courts, and
4. The state's highest court.

As previously mentioned, each state has a different judicial structure, in which different courts have different jurisdictions, but there are enough similarities to allow for a general discussion. Figure 8.2 shows a typical state court system.

Courts of Limited Jurisdiction

Most states have local trial courts that are limited to trying cases involving minor criminal matters, such as traffic violations, prostitution, and drunk and disorderly conduct. Although these minor courts usually keep no written record of the trial proceedings and cases are decided by a judge rather than a jury, defendants have the same rights as those

FIGURE 8.2 A Typical State Court System

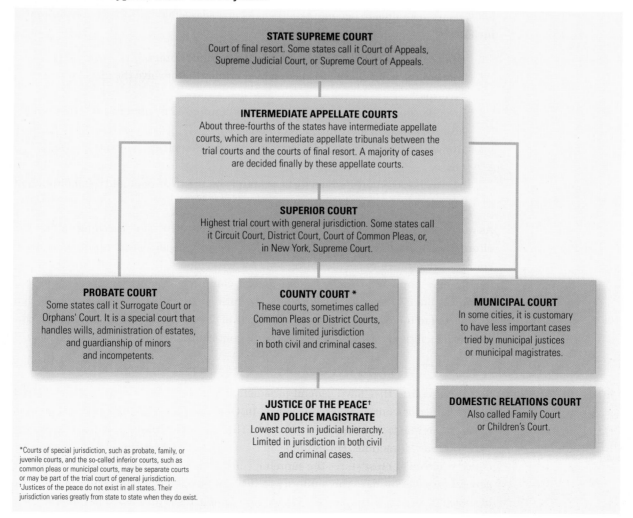

STATE SUPREME COURT
Court of final resort. Some states call it Court of Appeals, Supreme Judicial Court, or Supreme Court of Appeals.

INTERMEDIATE APPELLATE COURTS
About three-fourths of the states have intermediate appellate courts, which are intermediate appellate tribunals between the trial courts and the courts of final resort. A majority of cases are decided finally by these appellate courts.

SUPERIOR COURT
Highest trial court with general jurisdiction. Some states call it Circuit Court, District Court, Court of Common Pleas, or, in New York, Supreme Court.

PROBATE COURT
Some states call it Surrogate Court or Orphans' Court. It is a special court that handles wills, administration of estates, and guardianship of minors and incompetents.

COUNTY COURT *
These courts, sometimes called Common Pleas or District Courts, have limited jurisdiction in both civil and criminal cases.

MUNICIPAL COURT
In some cities, it is customary to have less important cases tried by municipal justices or municipal magistrates.

**JUSTICE OF THE PEACE†
AND POLICE MAGISTRATE**
Lowest courts in judicial hierarchy. Limited in jurisdiction in both civil and criminal cases.

DOMESTIC RELATIONS COURT
Also called Family Court or Children's Court.

*Courts of special jurisdiction, such as probate, family, or juvenile courts, and the so-called inferior courts, such as common pleas or municipal courts, may be separate courts or may be part of the trial court of general jurisdiction.
†Justices of the peace do not exist in all states. Their jurisdiction varies greatly from state to state when they do exist.

in other trial courts. The majority of all minor criminal cases are decided in these lower courts. Courts of limited jurisdiction can also be responsible for the preliminary stages of felony cases. Arraignments, bail hearings, and preliminary hearings often take place in these lower courts.

Magistrate Courts One of the earliest courts of limited jurisdiction was the justice court, presided over by a *justice of the peace,* or JP. In the early days of this nation, JPs were found everywhere in the country. One of the most famous JPs was Judge Roy Bean, the "hanging judge" of Langtry, Texas, who presided over his court at the turn of the twentieth century. Today, more than half the states have abolished justice courts, though JPs still serve a useful function in some cities and rural areas, notably in Texas.

The jurisdiction of justice courts is limited to minor disputes between private individuals and to crimes punishable by small fines or short jail terms. The equivalent of a county JP in a city is known as a **magistrate** or, in some states, a municipal court judge. Magistrate courts have the same limited jurisdiction as do justice courts in rural settings. In most jurisdictions, magistrates are responsible for providing law enforcement agents with search and seizure warrants, discussed in Chapter 7.

Specialty Courts As mentioned earlier, many states have created **problem-solving courts** that have jurisdiction over very narrowly defined areas of criminal justice. Not only do these courts remove many cases from the existing court systems, but they also allow court personnel to become experts in a particular subject. Problem-solving courts include:

1. Drug courts, which deal only with illegal substance crimes.
2. Gun courts, which have jurisdiction over crimes that involve the illegal use of firearms.
3. Juvenile courts, which specialize in crimes committed by minors. (We will discuss juvenile courts in more detail in Chapter 15.)
4. Domestic violence courts, which deal with crimes such as child and spousal abuse.
5. Mental health courts, which focus primarily on the treatment and rehabilitation of offenders with mental health problems.

As we will see in Chapter 12, many state and local governments are searching for cheaper alternatives to locking up nonviolent offenders in prison or jail. Because problem-solving courts offer a range of treatment options for wrongdoers, these courts are becoming increasingly popular in today's more budget-conscious criminal justice system. For example, about 3,000 drug courts are now operating in the United States, a number that is expected to increase as the financial benefits of diverting drug law violators from correctional facilities become more attractive to politicians.

Trial Courts of General Jurisdiction

State trial courts that have general jurisdiction may be called county courts, district courts, superior courts, or circuit courts. In Ohio, the name is the court of common pleas and in Massachusetts, the trial court. (The name sometimes does not correspond with the court's functions. For example, in New York the trial court is called the supreme court, whereas in most states the supreme court is the state's highest court.) Courts of general jurisdiction have the authority to hear and decide cases involving many types of subject matter, and they are the setting for criminal trials (discussed in Chapter 10).

Magistrate A public civil officer or official with limited judicial authority within a particular geographic area, such as the authority to issue an arrest warrant.

Problem-Solving Courts Lower courts that have jurisdiction over one specific area of criminal activity, such as illegal drugs or domestic violence.

State Courts of Appeals

Every state has at least one court of appeals (known as an appellate, or reviewing, court), which may be an intermediate appellate court or the state's highest court. About three-fourths have intermediate appellate courts. The highest appellate court in a state is usually called the supreme court, but in both New York and Maryland, the highest state court is called the court of appeals. The decisions of each state's highest court on all questions of state law are final. Only when issues of federal law or constitutional procedure are involved can the United States Supreme Court overrule a decision made by a state's highest court. (See the feature *Discretion in Action—Eyewitness Identification* for an example of how the appeals process works.)

The Federal Court System

The federal court system is basically a three-tiered model consisting of (1) U.S. district courts (trial courts of general jurisdiction) and various courts of limited jurisdiction, (2) U.S. courts of appeals (intermediate courts of appeals), and (3) the United States Supreme Court.

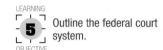

LEARNING
5 Outline the federal court system.
OBJECTIVE

Unlike state court judges, who are usually elected, federal court judges—including the justices of the Supreme Court—are appointed by the president of the United States, subject to the approval of the Senate. All federal judges receive lifetime appointments (because under Article III of the Constitution they "hold their offices during Good Behavior").

Discretion in Action

Eyewitness Identification

The Situation Getting ready for bed one night at an Oregon campsite, Sheryl was shot in the chest and her husband, Noris, killed by an assailant with a hunting rifle. At the scene, Sheryl told rescuers that she had not seen the shooter. On two occasions soon thereafter, police showed Sheryl a photo array that included the image of Samuel Lawson. She failed to recognize Lawson either time. Two years later, Lawson was arrested for the attack at the campsite, and a detective took Sheryl to his pretrial hearing. She then identified Lawson in a photo lineup, saying, "I'll never forget his face as long as I live." With little physical evidence linking him to the crime, Lawson was convicted

of murder and sentenced to life in prison on the strength of Sheryl's testimony.

The Law According to previous Oregon court cases, the fact that a police officer uses "suggestive" methods to gain an eyewitness identification does not mean such evidence should be excluded from a trial. As long as the witness makes the identification with a degree of certainty "independent of the suggestive procedure," it is valid. Following this precedent, the Oregon Court of Appeals upholds Lawson's conviction.

What Would You Do? Lawson's lawyers have appealed the lower court's decision to the Oregon Supreme Court,

on which you sit. His lawyers argue that Sheryl's testimony is unreliable and that state case law fails to reflect the findings of more than two thousand studies showing how memories are prone to suggestion and distortion. They also point out that eyewitness identification has played a role in nearly three-quarters of all wrongful convictions in the United States. Do you vote to uphold Lawson's conviction or, by overturning it, indicate that state case law in this area is flawed and should be changed? Explain your answer.

[To see how the Oregon Supreme Court ruled on a similar case, go to Example 8.1 in Appendix B.]

U.S. District Courts

On the lowest tier of the federal court system are the U.S. district courts, or federal trial courts. These are the courts in which cases involving federal laws begin, and a judge or jury decides the case (if it is a jury trial). Every state has at least one federal district court, and there is one in the District of Columbia. The number of judicial districts varies over time, primarily owing to population changes and corresponding caseloads. At the present time, there are ninety-four judicial districts. The federal system also includes other trial courts of limited jurisdiction, such as the Tax Court and the Court of International Trade.

U.S. Courts of Appeals

In the federal court system, there are thirteen U.S. courts of appeals—also referred to as U.S. circuit courts of appeals. The federal courts of appeals for twelve of the circuits hear appeals from the district courts located within their respective judicial circuits (see Figure 8.3). The Court of Appeals for the Thirteenth Circuit, called the Federal Circuit, has national appellate jurisdiction over certain types of cases, such as cases in which the U.S. government is a defendant. The decisions of the circuit courts of appeals are final unless a further appeal is pursued and granted. In that case, the matter is brought before the Supreme Court.

FIGURE 8.3 Geographic Boundaries of the Federal Circuit Courts of Appeals

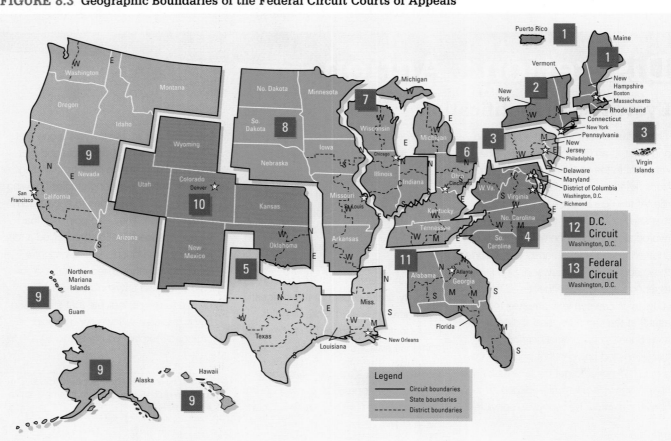

Source: Administrative Office of the United States Courts, January 1994.

The United States Supreme Court

Alexander Hamilton, writing in *Federalist Paper* No. 78 (1788), predicted that the United States Supreme Court would be the "least dangerous branch" of the federal government because it had neither the power of the purse nor the power of the sword (that is, it could not raise any revenue, and it lacked an enforcement agency).[13] Unless the other two branches of the government—the president and Congress—would accept its decisions, the Court would be superfluous.

In the Supreme Court's earliest years, it appeared that Hamilton's prediction would come true. The first chief justice of the Supreme Court, John Jay, resigned to become governor of New York because he thought the Court would never play an important role in American society. The next chief justice, Oliver Ellsworth, quit to become an envoy to France. In 1801, when the federal capital was moved to Washington, D.C., no one remembered to include the Supreme Court in the plans. It did not have its own meeting space until 1835.[14]

Interpreting and Applying the Law Despite these early bouts of inconsequence, the Supreme Court has come to dominate the country's legal culture. Although the Court reviews a minuscule percentage of the cases decided in the United States each year, its decisions profoundly affect our lives. The impact of Court decisions on the criminal justice system is equally far reaching: *Gideon v. Wainwright* (1963)[15] established every American's right to be represented by counsel in a criminal trial; *Miranda v. Arizona* (1966)[16] transformed pretrial interrogations; *Furman v. Georgia* (1972)[17] ruled that the death penalty was unconstitutional; and *Gregg v. Georgia* (1976)[18] spelled out the conditions under which it could be allowed. As you have no doubt noticed from references in this textbook, the Court has addressed nearly every important facet of criminal law.

Judicial Review The Supreme Court "makes" criminal justice policy in two important ways: through *judicial review* and through its authority to interpret the law. **Judicial review** refers to the power of the Court to determine whether a law or action by the other branches of the government is constitutional. In 2005, for example, Congress passed the Stolen Valor Act, which made it a crime punishable by up to six months in prison for someone to falsely claim that he or she had earned military honors or medals.[19]

Several years after passage of this legislation, Xavier Alvarez was sentenced to three years probation and given a $5,000 fine for lying about having received the Medal of Honor. In 2012, the Court overturned Alvarez's conviction and invalidated the federal law on the ground that a false statement that does no obvious harm is protected by the First Amendment's freedom of expression.[20] (A year later, Congress passed a new version of the Stolen Valor Act that made it a crime to lie about earning military honors "with the intent to obtain money, property, or some other tangible benefit.")[21]

Statutory Interpretation As the final interpreter of the Constitution, the Supreme Court must also determine the meaning of certain statutory provisions when applied to specific situations. In 1994, for example, Congress passed a law that gives a victim of child pornography the ability to seek restitution from offenders to the extent that he or she has been harmed by the illegal behavior.[22] Twenty years later, the Court overturned a $3.4 million award to a woman whose childhood rape had been videotaped and widely disseminated on the Internet. The Court ruled that, under the 1994 law, a single offender who had just two images of the victim on his computer could not be held responsible for all of the damages she had suffered.[23]

Judicial Review The power of a court—particularly the United States Supreme Court—to review the actions of the executive and legislative branches and, if necessary, declare those actions unconstitutional.

Explain briefly how a case is brought to the Supreme Court.

▼ John G. Roberts, Jr., pictured here, is the seventeenth chief justice of the United States Supreme Court. **What does it mean to say that Roberts and the eight associate members of the Court "make criminal justice policy"?** AP Images/Lawrence Jackson, File

Jurisdiction of the Supreme Court

The United States Supreme Court consists of nine justices—a chief justice and eight associate justices. The Supreme Court has original, or trial, jurisdiction only in rare instances (set forth in Article III, Section 2, of the Constitution). In other words, only rarely does a case originate at the Supreme Court level. Most of the Court's work is as an appellate court. It has appellate authority over cases decided by the U.S. courts of appeals, as well as over some cases decided in the state courts when federal questions are at issue.

Which Cases Reach the Supreme Court?

There is no absolute right to appeal to the United States Supreme Court. Although thousands of cases are filed with the Supreme Court each year, in 2013–2014 the Court heard only seventy-five. With a **writ of *certiorari*** (pronounced sur-shee-uh-*rah*-ree), the Supreme Court orders a lower court to send it the record of a case for review. A party can petition the Supreme Court to issue a writ of *certiorari*, but whether the Court will do so is entirely within its discretion. More than 90 percent of the petitions for writs of *certiorari* (or "certs," as they are popularly called) are denied. A denial is not a decision on the merits of a case, nor does it indicate agreement with the lower court's opinion. Therefore, the denial of the writ has no value as a precedent.

The Court will not issue a writ unless at least four justices approve of it. This is called the **rule of four**. Although the justices are not required to give their reasons for refusing to hear a case, most often the discretionary decision is based on whether the legal issue involves a "substantial federal question." Often, such questions arise when lower courts split on a particular issue. For example, different federal and state courts had produced varying opinions on the question of whether an anonymous tip provides reasonable suspicion for police officers to pull over a driver that the officers do not actually see breaking any traffic laws. To clear up confusion on this question—important because, as we saw in Chapter 7, such stops can lead to warrantless searches—the Court agreed to consider the matter. In 2014, it ruled that that law enforcement agents can stop drivers based on nothing more than a 911 tip phoned in by an anonymous caller.[24]

Practical considerations aside, if the justices feel that a case does not address an important federal law or constitutional issue, they will vote to deny the writ of *certiorari*.

Supreme Court Decisions

Like all appellate courts, the Supreme Court normally does not hear any evidence. The Court's decision in a particular case is based on the written record of the case and the written arguments (briefs) that the attorneys submit. The attorneys also present **oral arguments**—arguments presented in person rather than on paper—to the Court, after which the justices discuss the case in *conference*. The conference is strictly private—only the justices are allowed in the room.

Majorities and Pluralities When the Court has reached a decision, the chief justice, if in the majority, assigns the task of writing the Court's opinion to one of the justices. When the chief justice is not in the majority, the most senior justice voting with the majority assigns the writing of the Court's opinion. The opinion outlines the reasons for the Court's decision, the rules of law that apply, and the decision.

From time to time, the justices agree on the outcome of a case, but no single reason for that outcome gains five votes. When this occurs, the rationale that gains the most votes is called the *plurality* opinion. Plurality opinions are problematic, because they do not provide a strong precedent for lower courts to follow. Although still relatively rare, the incidence of plurality opinions has increased over the past fifty years as the Court has become more ideologically fractured.[25]

Concurrence and Dissent Often, one or more justices who agree with the Court's decision may do so for different reasons than those outlined in the majority opinion. These justices may write **concurring opinions** setting forth their own legal reasoning on the issue. Frequently, one or more justices disagree with the Court's conclusion. These justices may write **dissenting opinions** outlining the reasons why they feel the majority erred. Although a dissenting opinion does not affect the outcome of the case before the Court, it may be important later. In a subsequent case concerning the same issue, a justice or attorney may use the legal reasoning in the dissenting opinion as the basis for an argument to reverse the previous decision and establish a new precedent.

Concurring Opinions Separate opinions prepared by judges who support the decision of the majority of the court but who want to make or clarify a particular point or to voice disapproval of the grounds on which the decision was made.

Dissenting Opinions Separate opinions in which judges disagree with the conclusion reached by the majority of the court and expand on their own views about the case.

Judges in the Court System

Supreme Court justices are the most visible and best-known American jurists, but in many ways they are unrepresentative of the profession as a whole. Few judges enjoy three-room office suites fitted with a fireplace and a private bath, as do the Supreme Court justices. Few judges have four clerks to assist them. Few judges get a yearly vacation that stretches from July through September. Most judges, in fact, work at the lowest level of the system, in criminal trial courts, where they are burdened with overflowing caseloads and must deal daily with the pettiest of criminals.

One attribute a Supreme Court justice and a criminal trial judge in any small American city do have in common is the expectation that they will be just. Of all the participants in the criminal justice system, no single person is held to the same high standards as the judge. From her or his lofty perch in the courtroom, the judge is counted on to be "above the fray" of the bickering defense attorneys and prosecutors. When the other courtroom contestants rise at the entrance of the judge, they are placing the burden of justice squarely on the judge's shoulders.

The Roles and Responsibilities of Trial Judges

One of the reasons that judicial integrity is considered so important is the amount of discretionary power a judge has over the court proceedings. Figure 8.4 shows that nearly every stage of the trial process includes a decision or action to be taken by the presiding judge.

Before the Trial A great deal of the work done by a judge takes place before the trial even starts, free from public scrutiny. These duties, some of which you have seen from a different point of view in the section on law enforcement agents, include determining the following:

FIGURE 8.4 The Role of the Judge in the Criminal Trial Process

In the various stages of a felony case, judges must undertake the actions described here.

David Young-Wolff/The Image Bank/Getty Images

1. Pre-Arrest
- Decide whether law enforcement officers have provided sufficient probable cause to justify a search or arrest warrant.

2. Initial Appearance
- Inform the suspect of the charges against him or her and of his or her rights.
- Review the charges to see if probable cause exists that the suspect committed the crime. If not, the judge will dismiss the case.
- Set the amount of bail (or deny bail) and determine any other conditions of pretrial release.

3. Preliminary Hearing
- Based on evidence provided by the prosecution and defense, decide whether there is probable cause that the suspect committed the crime.
- Continue to make sure that the defendant's constitutional rights are not being violated.

4. Arraignment
- Ensure that the defendant has been informed of the charges against him or her.
- Ensure that the defendant understands the plea choices before him or her (to plead guilty, not guilty, or *nolo contendere*).

5. Plea Bargain
- Assist with the plea bargaining process, if both sides are willing to "make a deal."
- If the defendant decides to plead guilty in return for charges being lessened, ensure that the defendant understands the nature of the plea bargain and has not been pressured into pleading guilty by his or her attorney.

6. Pretrial Motions
- Rule on pretrial motions presented by the defense.
- Decide whether to grant continuances (the postponement of the trial to allow more time for gathering evidence).

7. Trial
- Ensure that proper procedure is followed in jury selection.
- "Officiate" at the trial, making sure that both the prosecutor and the defense follow procedural rules in presenting evidence and questioning witnesses.
- Explain to the jury points of law that affect the case.
- Provide jury instructions, or instruction to jurors on the meaning of the laws applicable to the case.
- Receive the jury's final verdict of guilty or not guilty.

8. Sentencing
- If the verdict is "guilty," impose the sentence on the convict.

---

1. Whether there is sufficient probable cause to issue a search or arrest warrant.
2. Whether there is sufficient probable cause to authorize electronic surveillance of a suspect.
3. Whether enough evidence exists to justify the temporary incarceration of a suspect.
4. Whether a defendant should be released on bail, and if so, the amount of the bail.
5. Whether to accept pretrial motions by prosecutors and defense attorneys.
6. Whether to accept a plea bargain.

During these pretrial activities, the judge takes on the role of the *negotiator*.[26] As most cases are decided through plea bargains rather than through trial proceedings, the judge often offers his or her services as a negotiator to help the prosecution and the defense "make a deal." The amount at which bail is set is often negotiated as well. Throughout the trial process, the judge usually spends a great deal of time in his or her *chambers,* or office, negotiating with the prosecutors and defense attorneys.

During the Trial When the trial starts, the judge takes on the role of *referee*. In this role, she or he is responsible for seeing that the trial unfolds according to the dictates of the law and that the participants in the trial do not overstep any legal or ethical bounds. Furthermore, the judge is expected to be neutral, determining the admissibility of testimony and evidence on a completely objective basis. The judge also acts as a *teacher* during the trial, explaining points of law to the jury. If the trial is not a jury trial, then the judge must also make decisions concerning the guilt or innocence of the defendant.

At the close of the trial, if the defendant is found guilty, the judge must decide on the length of the sentence and the type of sentence. (Different types of sentences, such as incarceration, probation, and other forms of community-based corrections, will be discussed in Chapters 11 and 12.) The sentencing phase also gives the judge a chance to make personal comments about the proceedings, if he or she wishes. While sentencing a confessed sex offender to five years' probation in 2014, Texas district judge Jeanine Howard opened herself up to criticism by implying that his fourteen-year-old victim "wasn't the victim she claimed to be" because of her promiscuity. "There are rape cases that deserve life. There are rape cases that deserve 20 years," the judge added. "Every now and then you have one of those that deserve probation. This is one of those, and I stand by it."[27]

The Administrative Role Judges are also *administrators* and are responsible for the day-to-day functioning of their courts. A primary administrative task of a judge is scheduling. Each courtroom has a **docket,** or calendar of cases, and it is the judge's responsibility to keep the docket current. This entails not only scheduling the trial, but also setting pretrial motion dates and deciding whether to grant attorneys' requests for *continuances,* or additional time to prepare for the trial.

Judges must also keep track of the immense paperwork generated by each case and manage the various employees of the court. Some judges are even responsible for the budgets of their courtrooms.[28] In 1939, Congress, recognizing the burden of such tasks, created the Administrative Office of the United States Courts to provide administrative assistance for federal court judges.[29] Most state court judges, however, do not have the luxury of similar aid, though they are supported by a court staff.

Docket The list of cases entered on a court's calendar and thus scheduled to be heard by the court.

CJ & Technology

Lie Detection in Court

During a polygraph test, rubber tubes are placed on a person's chest and abdominal area to record his or her breathing patterns. In addition, two small metal plates are attached to the subject's fingers to measure sweat levels, and a blood pressure cuff indicates her or his heart rate. The examiner asks a series of questions, keeping track of changes in the body's responses to determine if the subject is telling the truth. Law enforcement agents routinely employ polygraphs in the course of criminal investigations, and the technology is widely used by the government to test job applicants and those seeking a security clearance.

In criminal courtrooms, however, polygraph exams are surprisingly absent. The decision to allow evidence of such exams rests primarily with the judge, particularly in federal court. In exercising this discretion, the judge must decide whether the results of the exam are reliable. Even though properly administered polygraphs are, by some measures, accurate about 75 percent of the time, many judges are suspicious of what they believe to be "junk science" and therefore are reluctant to allow it in their courtrooms.

AP Images/Cecil Whig, Matthew Given

Thinking about Polygraph Exams

In particular, polygraph exams are popular with defendants who want to use the tests to prove their innocence. Assuming that such exams do have 75 percent accuracy rates, are judges justified in keeping the results out of court? Explain your answer.

Explain the difference between the selection of judges at the state level and at the federal level.

LEARNING OBJECTIVE

7

Selection of Judges

In the federal court system, all judges are appointed by the president and confirmed by the Senate. It is difficult to make a general statement about how judges are selected in state court systems, however, because the procedure varies widely from state to state. In some states, such as New Jersey, all judges are appointed by the governor and confirmed by the upper chamber of the state legislature. In other states, such as Alabama, **partisan elections** are used to choose judges. In these elections, a judicial candidate declares allegiance to a political party, usually the Democrats or the Republicans, before the election. States such as Kentucky that conduct **nonpartisan elections** do not require a candidate to affiliate herself or himself with a political party in this manner. Finally, some states, such as Missouri, select judges based on a subjective definition of merit.

The two key concepts in discussing methods of selecting judges are *independence* and *accountability*.[30] Those who feel that judicial fairness is dependent on the judges' belief that they will not be removed from office as the result of an unpopular ruling support methods of selection that include appointment.[31] In contrast, some observers feel that judges are "politicians in robes" who make policy decisions every time they step to the bench. Following this line of thought, judges should be held accountable to those who are affected by their decisions and therefore should be chosen through elections, as legislators are.[32]

The most independent, and therefore least accountable, judges are those who hold lifetime appointments. They are influenced neither by the temptation to make popular decisions to impress voters nor by the need to follow the ideological or party line of the politicians who provided them with their posts.

Appointment of Judges Article II, Section 2, of the Constitution authorizes the president to appoint the justices of the Supreme Court with the advice and consent of the Senate. Subsequent laws enacted by Congress provide that the same procedure is used for appointing judges to the lower federal courts as well.

Federal Appointments On paper, the federal appointment process is relatively simple. After selecting a nominee, the president submits the name to the Senate for approval. The Senate Judiciary Committee then holds hearings and makes its recommendation to the Senate, where a majority vote is needed to confirm the nomination.

In practice, the process does not always proceed smoothly. Given the importance of the Supreme Court in shaping the nation's laws and values, the appointment process for its justices is highly politicized. Presidents choose candidates who reflect the political beliefs of their party, and members of the opposing party in the Senate do their best to discredit these individuals. In recent years, heated debate over controversial issues such as abortion and gay rights has characterized the proceedings to the point that one commentator likens them to elections rather than the appointments envisioned by the nation's founders.[33]

Patronage Issues Five states, as well as Puerto Rico, employ similar selection methods, with the governor offering nominees for the approval of the state legislature. Judges in these states, as would be expected, serve longer terms than their counterparts in nonappointment judicial systems.[34] They are also regarded as products of *patronage*, as are judges appointed to federal positions by the president. In other words, appointed judges often obtain their positions because they belong to the same political party as the president (or governor, at the state level) and also have been active in supporting the candidates and

Partisan Elections Elections in which candidates are affiliated with and receive support from political parties.

Nonpartisan Elections Elections in which candidates are presented on the ballot without any party affiliation.

ideology of the party in power. One of the most prevalent criticisms of appointing judges is that the system is based on "having friends in high places" rather than on merit.[35]

Election of Judges Most states moved from an appointive to an elective system for judges in the mid-nineteenth century. The reasoning behind the move was to make judges more representative of the communities in which they served. Today, all but eleven states choose at least some of their judges through elections.[36] Nearly 90 percent of all state judges face elections at some point in their judicial careers.[37] Even though the practice is widespread, as we will see in the *CJ in Action* feature at the end of the chapter, many observers feel that judicial elections raise unavoidable questions about the impartiality that lies at the heart of the profession.

Merit Selection In 1940, Missouri became the first state to combine appointment and election in a single merit selection. When all jurisdiction levels are counted, nineteen states and the District of Columbia now utilize the **Missouri Plan,** as merit selection has been labeled. The Missouri Plan consists of three basic steps:

- When a vacancy on the bench arises, candidates are nominated by a nonpartisan committee of citizens.
- The names of the three most qualified candidates are sent to the governor or executive of the state judicial system, and that person chooses who will be the judge.
- A year after the new judge has been installed, a "retention election" is held so that voters can decide whether the judge deserves to keep the post.[38]

The goal of the Missouri Plan is to eliminate partisan politics from the selection procedure, while at the same time giving the citizens a voice in the process. Regardless of how they are selected, the average term for state judges in this country is about seven years.[39] (For a review of the selection processes, see this chapter's *Mastering Concepts—The Selection of State and Federal Judges.*)

The Removal of Judges Besides losing an election, sitting judges can be removed from office for **judicial misconduct,** or behavior that diminishes public confidence in the judiciary. Nearly every state has a *judicial conduct commission,* which consists of lawyers, judges, and other prominent citizens and is often a branch of the state's highest court. This commission investigates charges of judicial misconduct and may recommend removal if warranted. The final decision to discipline a judge generally is made by the state supreme court.[40]

Several state judges are removed from office each year. A recent example is Marion County (Indiana) judge Kimberly Brown, whom the state supreme court found engaged in forty-six different forms of "significant judicial misconduct." Brown's unprofessional behavior included failure to complete paperwork, insufficient supervision of staff, calling a defense lawyer "a moron," and "crassly" remarking about a deputy prosecutor's weight.[41]

The Impeachment Process Such transgressions as those committed by Kimberly Brown, however deplorable, would be unlikely to result in a similar outcome if committed by a federal judge. Appointed under Article II of the U.S. Constitution, federal judges can be removed from office only if found guilty of "Treason, Bribery, or other high Crimes and Misdemeanors." Before a federal judge can be **impeached,** the U.S. House of Representatives must be presented with specific charges of misconduct and vote on whether

Missouri Plan A method of selecting judges that combines appointment and election.

Judicial Misconduct A general term describing behavior—such as accepting bribes or consorting with known felons—that diminishes public confidence in the judiciary.

Impeachment The formal process by which a public official is charged with misconduct that could lead to his or her removal from office.

Federal Judges	State Judges	

Federal Judges

1. The president nominates a candidate and presents the nominee to the U.S. Senate.
2. The Senate Judiciary Committee holds hearings concerning the qualifications of the candidate and makes its recommendation to the full Senate.
3. The full Senate votes to confirm or reject the president's nominee.

State Judges

Partisan Elections
- Judicial candidates, supported by and affiliated with political parties, place their names before the voters for consideration for a particular judicial seat.
- The electorate votes to decide who will retain or gain the seat.

Executive Appointment
- The governor nominates a candidate to the state legislature.
- The legislature votes to confirm or reject the governor's nominee.

Nonpartisan Elections
- Judicial candidates, not supported by or affiliated with political parties, place their names before the voters for consideration for a particular judicial seat.
- The electorate votes to decide who will retain or gain the seat.

Missouri Plan
- A nominating commission provides a list of worthy candidates.
- An elected official (usually the governor) chooses from the list submitted by the commission.
- A year later, a "retention election" is held to allow voters to decide whether the judge will stay on the bench.

these charges merit further action. If the House votes to impeach by a simple majority (more than 50 percent), the U.S. Senate—presided over by the chief justice of the United States Supreme Court—holds a trial on the judge's conduct. At the conclusion of this trial, a two-thirds majority vote is required in the Senate to remove the judge.

This disciplinary action is extremely rare: only eight federal judges have been impeached and convicted in the nation's history. Most recently, in 2010 U.S. District Court Judge G. Thomas Porteous was removed from office for accepting tens of thousands of dollars in cash from lawyers to pay gambling debts and then lying about his misbehavior to federal investigators. (See the feature *Comparative Criminal Justice—Back to School* to learn about France's preferred method for producing ethical judges.)

Diversity on the Bench

According to the Brennan Center for Justice in New York City, "Americans who enter the courtroom often face a predictable presence on the bench: a white male."[42] Overall, about two-thirds of all state appellate judges are white males, and women in particular are notably absent from the highest courts of most states.[43] In many states, members of minority groups are underrepresented in comparison to the demographics of the general population. California, for example, is nearly 38 percent Hispanic and 16 percent Asian American. The state judiciary, however, is only 8.3 percent Hispanic and 4.4 percent Asian American.[44] New York is 67 percent white and 52 percent female, and its judiciary is 81 percent white and 35 percent female.[45]

Federal Diversity Members of minority groups are also underrepresented in the federal judiciary, though not to the same extent as in the states. Of the approximately 870 federal judges in this country, about 24 percent are African American, 14 percent are Hispanic, and less than 5 percent are Asian American. Furthermore, about 45 percent are women.[46] Of the 111 justices who have served on the United States Supreme Court, two have been African American: Thurgood Marshall (1970–1991) and Clarence Thomas

Comparative Criminal Justice

Back to School

LEARNING OBJECTIVE 8 Describe one alternative, practiced in other countries, to the American method of choosing judges.

Elections for judges are extremely rare outside the United States. Indeed, only two nations—Japan and Switzerland—engage in the practice, and then only in very limited situations. To the rest of the world, according to one expert, "American adherence to judicial elections is as incomprehensible as our rejection of the metric system." Much more common, for example, is the French system, crafted to provide extensive training for potential judges.

French judicial candidates must pass two exams. The first, open to law school graduates only, combines oral and written sections and lasts at least four days. In some years, only 5 percent of the applicants overcome this hurdle. Not surprisingly, the pressure is intense. "It gives you nightmares for years afterwards," says Jean-Marc Baissus, a judge in Toulouse. "You come out of [the exam] completely shattered." Those who do survive the first test enter a two-year program at the École Nationale de la Magistrature, a judicial training academy. This school is similar to a police training academy in the United States, in that candidates spend half of their time in the classroom and the other half in the courtroom.

At the end of this program, judicial candidates are subject to a second examination. Only those who pass the exam may become judges. The result, in the words of Mitchell Lasser, a law professor at Cornell University, is that French judges "actually know what the hell they are doing. They've spent years in school taking practical and theoretical courses on how to be a judge." The French also pride themselves on creating judges who are free from the kind of political pressures faced by American judges who must go before the voters.

For Critical Analysis

Do you think that the French system of training judges is superior to the American system of electing them? Before explaining your answer, consider that French judges lack the practical courtroom experience of American judges, many of whom served as lawyers earlier in their careers.

(1991–present). In 2009, Sonia Sotomayor became the first Hispanic appointed to the Court and the third woman, following Sandra Day O'Connor (1981–2006) and Ruth Bader Ginsburg (1993–present). A year later, Elena Kagan became the fourth woman appointed to the Court.

Promoting Judicial Diversity Edward Chen, a federal judge for the Northern District of California, identifies a number of reasons for the low minority representation on the bench. Past discrimination in law schools has limited the pool of experienced minority attorneys who have the political ties, access to "old boy" networks, and career opportunities that lead to judgeships.[47] Only recently, as increased numbers of minorities have graduated from law schools, have rates of minority judges begun to creep slowly upward. Of the state judicial selection methods discussed in the previous section, those that rely on elected officials result in the highest levels of judicial diversity.[48] Given that the federal judiciary is also relatively diverse (at least compared with many state judiciaries), this suggests that politicians are more likely than voters to choose judges that are members of minority groups or women.

To further promote judicial diversity, the Brennan Center for Justice suggests that state judicial bodies:

1. Increase recruitment of minorities and women for open judicial seats,
2. Raise judicial salaries to attract diverse candidates from the legal community, and
3. Appoint a diversity compliance officer to oversee efforts to include more minorities and women in the selection process.[49]

CJ Policy—Your Take

In his first six years in office, 42 percent of President Barack Obama's **judicial nominations to federal courts** were women. During the same time period, 36 percent were members of racial and ethnic minority groups. Twenty-two percent of the new federal judges were women and 19 percent were minorities under George W. Bush, the previous president. Do you think that politicians should make a concerted effort to appoint greater numbers of minorities and women as judges? Why or why not?

This chapter's *CJ Policy—Your Take* addresses the politics of judicial appointments concerning racial and ethnic minorities and women.

The Benefits of Judicial Diversity There is a sense among criminal justice professionals that citizens are more likely to recognize the legitimacy of a diverse judiciary. That is, people tend to trust judges that resemble themselves.[50] Along those lines, Sherrilyn A. Ifill of the University of Maryland School of Law believes that "diversity on the bench" enriches our judiciary by introducing a variety of voices and perspectives into positions of power. By the same token, Ifill credits the lack of diversity in many trial and appeals courts with a number of harmful consequences, such as more severe sentences for minority youths than for white youths who have committed similar crimes, disproportionate denial of bail to minority defendants, and the disproportionate imposition of the death penalty on minority defendants accused of killing white victims.[51]

EthicsChallenge

In a dissent, U.S. Supreme Court justice Sonya Sotomayor described the actions of an Alabama judge who, facing reelection, sentenced a white defendant to be executed. "If I had not imposed the death sentence," said the anonymous judge, "I would have sentenced three black people to death and no white people." How is the judge justifying his obviously unethical behavior? ■

The Courtroom Work Group

Television dramas often depict the courtroom as a battlefield, with prosecutors and defense attorneys spitting fire at each other over the loud and insistent protestations of a frustrated judge. Consequently, many people are somewhat disappointed when they witness a real courtroom at work. Rarely does anyone raise his or her voice, and the courtroom professionals appear—to a great extent—to be cooperating with each other. In Chapter 6, we discussed the existence of a police subculture, based on the shared values of law enforcement agents. A courtroom subculture exists as well, centered on the **courtroom work group.**

The most important feature of any work group is that it is a *cooperative* unit, whose members establish shared values and methods that help the group efficiently reach its goals. Though cooperation is not a concept usually associated with criminal courts, it is in fact crucial to the adjudication process.

Members of the Courtroom Work Group

The courtroom work group is made up of those individuals who are involved with the defendant from the time she or he is arrested until sentencing. The most prominent members are the judge, the prosecutor, and the defense attorney (the latter two will be discussed in detail in the next chapter). Three other court participants complete the work group:

1. The *bailiff of the court* is responsible for maintaining security and order in the judge's chambers and the courtroom. Bailiffs lead the defendant in and out of the courtroom and attend to the needs of the jurors during the trial. A bailiff, often a member of the local sheriff's department but sometimes an employee of the court, also delivers summonses in some jurisdictions.

LEARNING
9
OBJECTIVE

List and describe the members of the courtroom work group.

Courtroom Work Group The social organization consisting of the judge, prosecutor, defense attorney, and other court workers.

(Courtesy Shawn Davis)

Shawn Davis
Bailiff

Basically, there are two kinds of bailiffs: administrative bailiffs and criminal bailiffs. An administrative bailiff will handle paperwork, set up court dates, and answer questions about filings that the attorneys may have. A criminal bailiff is responsible for bringing the court to session, directing jurors, and overseeing court security, which involves keeping everybody—judges, attorneys, jurors, spectators, witnesses, and defendants—safe. In my case, I do double duty as an administrative and criminal bailiff.

Violence in the courtroom is rare. Most inmates are on their best behavior in front of the judge. It can flare up in an instant, however, and you have to be constantly on guard. One time, an inmate under my control made a run for it as we were transporting him back to the jail from his court appearance. His leg shackles broke, giving him a short-lived sense of freedom. We were able to tackle him in front of the courthouse just before he could jump into a waiting convertible. We later learned that the accomplice—the inmate's brother—was supposed to bring a handgun and shoot us as part of the escape plan. Another time, a defendant started taking off his shirt and tried to attack the victim, who had just given testimony. He was quickly tackled, cuffed, and carted off to jail.

SOCIAL MEDIA CAREER TIP Networking is crucial. Develop as many useful social media contacts as possible, and cultivate those contacts. Also, reciprocate. If you help others establish online contacts, they are likely to remember you and return the favor.

FASTFACTS

Bailiff
Job description:
- Maintain order and provide security in the courtroom during trials.
- Open and close court, call cases, call witnesses, and the like.
- Escort and guard juries, prevent juries from having contact with the public.

What kind of training is required?
- At a minimum, a high school diploma or GED.

Annual salary range?
- $25,000–$67,000

2. The *clerk of the court* has an exhausting list of responsibilities. Any plea, motion, or other matter to be acted on by the judge must go through the clerk. The large amount of paperwork generated during a trial, including transcripts, photographs, evidence, and any other records, is maintained by the clerk. The clerk also issues subpoenas for jury duty and coordinates the jury selection process. In the federal court system, judges select clerks, while state clerks are either appointed or, in nearly a third of the states, elected.

3. *Court reporters* record every word that is said during the course of the trial. They also record any *depositions,* or pretrial question-and-answer sessions in which a party or a witness answers an attorney's questions under oath.

Formation of the Courtroom Work Group

The premise of the work group is based on constant interaction that fosters relationships among the members. As legal scholar David W. Neubauer describes:

> Every day, the same group of courthouse regulars assembles in the same courtroom, sits or stands in the same places, and performs the same tasks as the day before. The types of defendants and the nature of the crimes they are accused of committing also remain constant. Only the names of the victim, witnesses, and defendants are different.[52]

▲ Three trial lawyers confer as the judge waits at the Sedgwick County Courthouse in Wichita, Kansas. **How is working in a courtroom similar to working in a corporate office? How is it different?** Jaime Oppenheimer/MCT/Landov

After a period of time, the members of a courtroom work group learn how the others operate. The work group establishes patterns of behavior and norms, and cooperation allows the adjudication process to function informally and smoothly.[53] In some cases, the members of the work group may even form personal relationships, which only strengthen the courtroom culture.

One way in which the courtroom work group differs from a traditional work group at a company such as Facebook, Inc., is that each member answers to a different sponsoring organization. Although the judge has ultimate authority over a courtroom, he or she is not the "boss" of the attorneys. The prosecutor is hired by the district attorney's office, the defense attorney by a private individual or the public defender's office, and the judge by the court system itself.

The Judge in the Courtroom Work Group

The judge is the dominant figure in the courtroom and therefore exerts the most influence over the values and norms of the work group. A judge who runs a "tight ship" follows procedure and restricts the freedom of attorneys to deviate from regulations, while a *"laissez-faire"* judge allows more leeway to members of the work group. A judge's personal philosophy also affects the court proceedings. If a judge has a reputation for being "tough on crime," both prosecutors and defense attorneys will alter their strategies accordingly. In fact, a lawyer may be able to manipulate the system to "shop" for a judge whose philosophy best fits the attorney's goals in a particular case.[54] If a lawyer is caught trying to influence the assignment of judges, however, she or he is said to be "corrupting judicial independence" and may face legal proceedings.

Although preeminent in the work group, a judge must still rely on other members of the group. To a certain extent, the judge is the least informed member of the trio. Like a juror, the judge learns the facts of the case as they are presented by the attorneys. If the attorneys do not properly present the facts, then the judge is hampered in making rulings. Furthermore, if a judge deviates from the norms of the work group—by, for example, refusing to grant continuances—the other members of the work group can "discipline" the judge. Defense attorneys and prosecutors can request further continuances, fail to produce witnesses in a timely manner, and slow down the proceeding through a general lack of preparedness. The delays caused by such acts can ruin a judge's calendar—especially in large courts—and bring pressure from the judge's superiors.

The Adversary System

Two members of the courtroom work group—the prosecutor and the defense attorney—stand opposite each other in court and have opposing goals. That is, generally speaking, the goal of the prosecutor is to prove the defendant guilty, and the goal of the defense attorney is to prove the defendant innocent. For this reason, the American court system is often called an *adversary system*.

In strictly legal terms, three basic features characterize the **adversary system:**

1. A neutral and passive decision maker, either the judge or the jury.
2. The presentation of evidence from both parties.
3. A highly structured set of procedures (in the form of constitutional safeguards) that must be followed in the presentation of that evidence.[55]

LEARNING **10** OBJECTIVE List the three basic features of an adversary system of justice.

"Ritualized Aggression"? Some critics of the American court system believe that it has been tainted by overzealous prosecutors and defense attorneys. Gordon Van Kessel, a professor at Hastings College of Law in California, complains that American lawyers see themselves as "prize fighters, gladiators, or, more accurately, semantic warriors in a verbal battle," and bemoans the atmosphere of "ritualized aggression" that exists in the courts.[56]

Our recent portrayal of the courtroom work group, however, seems to contradict this image of "ritualized aggression." As political scientists Herbert Jacob and James Eisenstein have written, "[P]ervasive conflict is not only unpleasant; it also makes work more difficult."[57] The image of the courtroom work group as "negotiators" rather than "prize fighters" seems to be supported by the fact that more than nine out of every ten cases conclude with negotiated "deals" rather than trials. (We will cover these plea bargain procedures in the next chapter.)

Jerome Skolnick of the University of California at Berkeley found that work group members grade each other according to "reasonableness"[58]—a concept criminal justice scholar Abraham S. Blumberg embellished by labeling the defense attorney a "double agent." Blumberg believed that a defense attorney is likely to cooperate with the prosecutor in convincing a client to accept a negotiated plea of guilty because the defense attorney's main object is to finish the case quickly so as to collect the fee and move on.[59]

Truth versus Victory Perhaps the most useful definition of the adversary process tempers Professor Van Kessel's criticism with the realities of the courtroom work group. University of California at Berkeley law professor Malcolm Feeley observes:

> In the adversary system the goal of the advocate is not to determine truth but to win, to maximize the interests of his or her side within the confines of the norms governing the proceedings. This is not to imply that the theory of the adversary process has no concern for the truth. Rather, the underlying assumption of the adversary process is that truth is most likely to emerge as a by-product of vigorous conflict between intensely partisan advocates, each of whose goal is to win.[60]

Blumberg took a more cynical view when he called the court process a "confidence game" in which "victory" is achieved when a defense attorney—with the implicit aid of the prosecutor and judge—is able to persuade the defendant to plead guilty.[61] As you read the next chapter, which deals with the various pretrial strategies employed by the prosecution and the defense, keep in mind Feeley's and Blumberg's contentions concerning "truth" and "victory" in the American courts.

Adversary System A legal system in which the prosecution and defense are opponents, or adversaries, and present their cases in the light most favorable to themselves.

EthicsChallenge

In this section, we quoted a legal expert as saying, "In the adversary system the goal of the advocate is not to determine the truth but to win . . . ." Does this mean that prosecutors and defense attorneys should behave unethically in court? Why or why not? ■

CJ IN ACTION

Electing Judges

The television advertisement started by telling viewers that West Virginia Supreme Court justice Warren McGraw voted to release a sex offender from prison. "Worse," the voiceover continued, "McGraw agreed to let this convicted child rapist work as a janitor in a West Virginia school."[62] The ad was part of a $3 million effort by a group called "For the Sake of the Kids" to remove McGraw from office. Its success in doing so shows the power of outside interests to influence judicial elections, the subject of this chapter's *CJ in Action* feature.

Popularity and Accountability

"For the Sake of the Kids" was created and financed by a coal mining executive who wanted Warren McGraw off the West Virginia Supreme Court because of an unrelated business matter. The fact that the focus of the negative campaign was on McGraw's decision regarding a sex offender rather than a fraudulent coal supply contract is hardly surprising. Attack ads in judicial campaigns often focus on crime. The subject is seen as a "hot button issue" that will anger voters and, at least theoretically, get them to the polls.

Proponents of judicial elections insist that unless judges are regularly forced to submit themselves to the will of the electorate, there is no way to hold them accountable for their actions. Critics, such as Hans A. Linde, a retired justice of the Oregon Supreme Court, counter, "'Judicial accountability' has a virtuous ring to it until one asks, accountability for what?"[63] The answer to Linde's rhetorical question, at least in his mind, is that the public will hold a judge accountable for making unpopular rulings, but not necessarily for making "incorrect" ones. If Linde's assertion is true, the negative impact will fall most heavily on defendants in criminal trials, who are among the most unpopular participants in the judicial process. One recent study claims that state supreme court judges are more likely to rule against criminal defendants when they are involved in elections featuring heavy rotations of television advertising.[64]

The Case for Judicial Elections

- In a democracy, voters have the right to select government officials such as judges who make important policy decisions.

- Elections ensure that the people have a measure of control over the judiciary. If a judge repeatedly makes unpopular decisions involving the punishment of criminals or other important issues, he or she deserves to be voted out of office.

- Campaigning requires judges to interact with the community, thereby broadening their perspective. One judicial candidate noted that he was forced to "leave his comfort zone of similarly minded lawyers" and talk to "nurses in Pearland [Texas], stay-at-home moms in Galveston, shrimpers in Chambers County, doctors in Houston's vast medical center, [and] farmers in Sealy."[65]

The Case against Judicial Elections

- Judges are not like politicians. They must be neutral in applying the law to the facts, regardless of any political consequences. In other words, "courts are supposed to do what is right, not what is popular."[66]

- The need to raise funds for judges' election campaigns raises concerns of undue influence by major contributors such as lawyers and other special interests. In one poll, more than a quarter of 2,428 state judges felt that campaign contributions had some influence on judges' decisions.[67]

- Voters not only lack knowledge of the issues of a judicial election, but do not even know who the candidates are. A poll in Michigan found that nine out of ten voters could not identify a single sitting state supreme court justice.[68]

Your Opinion—Writing Assignment

In the criminal justice context, under what circumstances, if any, should a judge be required to remove himself or herself from a trial because of statements made or contributions accepted during a campaign? Note that, according to the Model Code of Judicial Conduct, "A judge shall disqualify himself or herself in a proceeding in which the judge's impartiality might reasonably be questioned."[69] Before completing this assignment, you can review our discussions in the sections of this chapter concerning:

- The legitimacy of courts ("Functions of the Courts").

- The roles and responsibilities of trial judges ("Judges in the Court System").

- Selection of judges ("Judges in the Court System").

Your answer should include at least three full paragraphs.

Summary

For more information on these concepts, look back to the Learning Objective icons throughout the chapter.

 Define and contrast the four functions of the courts. The four functions are (a) due process, (b) crime control, (c) rehabilitation, and (d) bureaucratic. The most obvious contrast is between the due process and crime control functions. The former is mainly concerned with the procedural rules that allow each accused individual to have a "fair chance" against the government in a criminal proceeding. For crime control, the courts are supposed to impose enough "pain" on convicted criminals to deter criminal behavior. For the rehabilitation function, the courts serve as "doctors" who dispense "treatment." In their bureaucratic function, courts are more concerned with speed and efficiency.

 Define *jurisdiction* and contrast geographic and subject-matter jurisdiction. Jurisdiction relates to the power of a court to hear a particular case. Courts are typically limited in geographic jurisdiction—for example, to a particular state. Some courts are restricted in subject matter, such as a small claims court, which can hear only cases involving civil matters under a certain monetary limit.

 Explain the difference between trial and appellate courts. Trial courts are courts of the first instance, where a case is first heard. Appellate courts review the proceedings of a lower court. Appellate courts do not have juries.

 Outline the several levels of a typical state court system. (a) At the lowest level are courts of limited jurisdiction, (b) next are trial courts of general jurisdiction, (c) then appellate courts, and (d) finally, the state's highest court.

 Outline the federal court system. (a) At the lowest level are the U.S. district courts in which trials are held, as well as various minor federal courts of limited jurisdiction; (b) next are the U.S. courts of appeals, otherwise known as circuit courts of appeals; and (c) finally, the United States Supreme Court.

 Explain briefly how a case is brought to the Supreme Court. Cases decided in U.S. courts of appeals, as well as cases decided in the highest state courts (when federal questions arise), can be appealed to the Supreme Court. If at least four justices approve of a case filed with the Supreme Court, the Court will issue a writ of *certiorari,* ordering the lower court to send the Supreme Court the record of the case for review.

 Explain the difference between the selection of judges at the state level and at the federal level. The president nominates all judges at the federal level, and the Senate must approve the nominations. A similar procedure is used in some states. In other states, all judges are elected on a partisan ballot or on a nonpartisan ballot. Some states use merit selection, or the Missouri Plan, in which a citizen committee nominates judicial candidates, the governor or executive of the state judicial system chooses among the top three nominees, and a year later a "retention election" is held.

 Describe one alternative, practiced in other countries, to the American method of choosing judges. The practice of electing judges is quite rare, with the United States being one of the few countries that allows it. Other nations, including France, require candidates for judicial positions (generally law school graduates) to complete an academic program that includes several difficult exams and has a low success rate.

 List and describe the members of the courtroom work group. (a) The judge; (b) the prosecutor, who brings charges in the name of the people (the state) against the accused; (c) the defense attorney; (d) the bailiff, who is responsible for maintaining security and order in the judge's chambers and the courtroom; (e) the clerk, who accepts all pleas, motions, and other matters to be acted on by the judge; and (f) court reporters, who record what is said during a trial as well as at depositions.

 List the three basic features of an adversary system of justice. (a) A neutral decision maker (judge or jury); (b) presentation of evidence from both parties; and (c) a highly structured set of procedures that must be used when evidence is presented.

Questions for Critical Analysis

1. "The primary adversarial relationship in the courts is not between the plaintiff (prosecutor, or state) and defendant, but rather between the ideal of justice and the reality of bureaucratic limitations." Explain why you agree or disagree with this statement.

2. In 2010, authorities in Thailand extradited Russian citizen and alleged international arms dealer Viktor Bout to the United States. The evidence against Bout included an audio recording of a conversation he had with American agents posing as Colombian rebels. During this conversation, Bout agreed to furnish the "revolutionaries" with weapons for the purpose of killing American pilots. How does this evidence give the United States jurisdiction over Bout?

3. In 2012, the United States Supreme Court "denied cert" in the case of Joel Tenenbaum, who had been ordered to pay a recording company $675,000 in fines for illegally downloading thirty-one songs using a file-sharing Web site. Tenenbaum claimed that the fine was excessive and unfair. What does it mean for the Court to "deny cert"? In this instance, what might have been some reasons for the Court's refusal to consider Tenenbaum's case?

4. The United States Supreme Court does not allow its proceedings to be televised. Do you think that doing so would increase or diminish public confidence in the Court? Why?

5. Why do federal judges have more job security than state judges? How does this give them more freedom to make unpopular decisions?

Key Terms

adversary system 273
appellate courts 255
concurrent jurisdiction 253
concurring opinions 263
courtroom work group 270
dissenting opinions 263
docket 265
dual court system 256

extradition 254
impeachment 267
judicial misconduct 267
judicial review 261
jurisdiction 253
magistrate 258
Missouri Plan 267
nonpartisan elections 266

opinions 256
oral arguments 262
partisan elections 266
problem-solving courts 258
rule of four 262
trial courts 255
writ of *certiorari* 262

Notes

1. Quoted in Carol Rosenberg, "Guantanamo Trial Delays Frustrate 9/11 Relatives," *Miami Herald* (April 17, 2014), A1.

2. Roscoe Pound, "The Administration of Justice in American Cities," *Harvard Law Review* 12 (1912).

3. Russell Wheeler and Howard Whitcomb, *Judicial Administration: Text and Readings* (Englewood Cliffs, N.J.: Prentice Hall, 1977), 3.

4. Larry J. Siegel, *Criminology: Instructor's Manual*, 6th ed. (Belmont, Calif.: West/Wadsworth Publishing Co., 1998), 440.

5. Gerald F. Velman, "Federal Sentencing Guidelines: A Cure Worse Than the Disease," *American Criminal Law Review* 29 (Spring 1992), 904.

6. Wayne R. LaFave, "Section 4.6. Multiple Jurisdiction and Multiple Prosecution," *Substantive Criminal Law*, 2d ed. (C.J.S. Criminal Section 254), 2007.

7. William Wan, "Snipers to Be Tried in Maryland," *Baltimore Sun* (May 11, 2005), 1A.

8. Maria L. La Ganga, "Tribe Just Says No to Legal Pot," *Los Angeles Times* (December 22, 2013), A1.

9. Public Law Number 111-211, 124 Statute 2258, 2279 (2010).

10. Anthony J. Colangelo, "Constitutional Limits on Extraterritorial Jurisdiction: Terrorism and the Intersection of National and International Law," *Harvard International Law Journal* 48 (2007), 121–122.

11. 18 U.S.C. Section 3231; and *Solorio v. United States*, 483 U.S. 435 (1987).

12. 18 U.S.C.A. Section 1951.

13. Alexander Hamilton, *Federalist Paper* No. 78, in *The Federalist Papers*, ed. Clinton Rossiter (New York: New American Library, 1961), 467–470.

14. G. Edward White, *History of the Supreme Court*, vols. 3–4: *The Marshall Court and Cultural Change* (New York: Oxford University Press, 1988), 157–200.

15. 372 U.S. 335 (1963).

16. 384 U.S. 436 (1966).

17. 408 U.S. 238 (1972).

18. 428 U.S. 153 (1976).

19. 18 U.S.C.A. Section 704.

20. *U.S. v. Alvarez*, 132 S.Ct. 2537 (2012).

21. 18 U.S.C.A. Section 704(a).

22. Public Law Number 103-322, Section 16001, 108 Statute 2036 (1994); codified as amended at 18 U.S.C. Section 2259.

23. *Paroline v. United States*, 134 S.Ct. 1710 (2014).

24. *Navarette v. California*, 562 U.S. ____ (2014).

25. David R. Stras and James F. Spriggs II, "Explaining Plurality Opinions," *Georgetown Law Journal* 99 (March 2010), 519.

26. Barry R. Schaller, *A Vision of American Law: Judging Law, Literature, and the Stories We Tell* (Westport, Conn.: Praeger, 1997).

27. Quoted in Jennifer Emily, "Judge Says Sexually Assaulted 14-Year-Old 'Wasn't the Victim She Claimed to Be,'" *Dallas Morning News* (May 2, 2014), A1.

28. Harlington Wood, Jr., "Judiciary Reform: Recent Improvements in Federal Judicial Administration," *American University Law Review* 44 (June 1995), 1557.

29. Pub. L. No. 76-299, 53 Stat. 1223, codified as amended at 28 U.S.C. Sections 601–610 (1988 & Supp. V 1993).

30. Patrick Emery Longan, "Judicial Professionalism in a New Era of Judicial Selection," *Mercer Law Review* (Spring 2005), 913.

31. Andrew F. Hanssen, "Learning about Judicial Independence: Institutional Change in the State Courts," *Journal of Legal Studies* (2004), 431–474.

32. Brian P. Anderson, "Judicial Elections in West Virginia," *West Virginia Law Review* (Fall 2004), 243.

33. Richard Davis, *Electing Justice: Fixing the Supreme Court Nomination Process* (New York: Oxford University Press, 2005), 6–9.

34. Daniel R. Deja, "How Judges Are Selected: A Survey of the Judicial Selection Process in the United States," *Michigan Bar Journal* 75 (September 1996), 904.

35. Edmund V. Ludwig, "Another Case against the Election of Trial Judges," *Pennsylvania Lawyer* 19 (May/June 1997), 33.

36. American Judicature Society, "Methods of Judicial Selection," at **www.judicial selection.us/judicial_selection/methods /selection_of_judges.cfm?state=.**

37. David K. Scott, "Zero-Sum Judicial Elections: Balancing Free Speech and Impartiality through Recusal Reform," *Brigham Young University Law Review* (2009), 481, 485.

38. James E. Lozier, "The Missouri Plan a.k.a. Merit Selection Is the Best Solution for Selecting Michigan's Judges," *Michigan Bar Journal* 75 (September 1996), 918.

39. Ron Malega and Thomas H. Cohen, *State Court Organization, 2011* (Washington, D.C.: U.S. Department of Justice, November 2013), 8.

40. John Gardiner, "Preventing Judicial Misconduct: Defining the Role of Conduct Organizations," *Judicature* 70 (1986), 113–121.

41. Debra Cassens Weiss, "Indiana Judge Is Removed from Office for Rude Conduct, Delayed Dispositions and Retaliation," *ABA Journal* (March 5, 2014), at **www.aba journal.com/news/article/indiana_judge _is_removed_from_office_for_rude _conduct_delayed_dispositions_/.**

42. Ciara Torres-Spelliscy, Monique Chase, and Emma Greenman, *Improving Judicial Diversity*, 2d ed. (New York: Brennan Center for Justice, 2010), 1.

43. *Ibid.*

44. Maura Dolan, "Diversity Rises among California Judges," *Los Angeles Times* (February 28, 2013), at **articles.latimes.com/2013 /feb/28/local/la-me-judges-20130301.**

45. New York State Bar Association Executive Committee, *Judicial Diversity: A Work in Progress* (Albany, N.Y.: New York State Bar Association, September 2014), Table 1, page 5.

46. Federal Judicial Center, "Diversity on the Bench," at **www.fjc.gov/history/home.nsf /page/judges_diversity.html.**

47. Edward M. Chen, "The Judiciary, Diversity, and Justice for All," *California Law Review* (July 2003), 1109.

48. Malia Reddick, Michael J. Nelson, and Rachel Paine Caufield, "Racial and Gender Diversity on State Courts: An AJS Study," *The Judges' Journal* (Summer 2009), 29–30.

49. New York State Bar Executive Committee, *op. cit.*, 2.

50. Spelliscy, Chase, and Greenman, *op. cit.*, 36–42.

51. Sherrilyn A. Ifill, "Racial Diversity on the Bench: Beyond Role Models and Public Confidence," *Washington and Lee Law Review* (Spring 2000), 405.

52. David W. Neubauer, *America's Courts and the Criminal Justice System*, 5th ed. (Belmont, Calif.: Wadsworth Publishing Co., 1996), 41.

53. Alissa P. Worden, "The Judge's Role in Plea Bargaining: An Analysis of Judges' Agreement with Prosecutors' Sentencing Recommendations," *Justice Quarterly* 10 (1995), 257–278.

54. Kimberly Jade Norwood, "Shopping for Venue: The Need for More Limits," *University of Miami Law Review* 50 (1996), 295–298.

55. Johannes F. Nijboer, "The American Adversary System in Criminal Cases: Between Ideology and Reality," *Cardozo Journal of International and Comparative Law* 5 (Spring 1997), 79.

56. Gordon Van Kessel, "Adversary Excesses in the American Criminal Trial," *Notre Dame Law Review* 67 (1992), 403.

57. James Eisenstein and Herbert Jacob, *Felony Justice* (Boston: Little, Brown, 1977), 24.

58. Jerome Skolnick, "Social Control in the Adversary System," *Journal of Conflict Resolution* 11 (1967), 52–70.

59. Abraham S. Blumberg, "The Practice of Law as Confidence Game: Organizational Cooption of a Profession," *Law and Society Review* 4 (June 1967), 115–139.

60. Malcolm Feeley, "The Adversary System," in *Encyclopedia of the American Judicial System*, ed. Robert J. Janosik (New York: Scribners, 1987), 753.

61. Blumberg, *op. cit.*, 115.

62. "Don Blankenship Ad against Warren McGraw," *YouTube*, at **www.youtube.com /watch?v=cmatV0myFjA&NR=1.**

63. Quoted in Daniel Burke, "Code of Judicial Conduct Canon 7B(1)(c): Toward the Proper Regulation of Speech in Judicial Campaigns," *Georgetown Journal of Legal Ethics* 81 (Summer 1993), 181.

64. Joanna Shepherd and Michael S. Kang, "Skewed Justice," *American Constitution Society* (2014), at **skewedjustice.org.**

65. Martin J. Siegel, "In Defense of Judicial Election (Sort Of)," *Litigation* (Summer 2010), 24–25.

66. Owen Fiss, "The Right Degree of Independence," in *The Law As It Could Be* (New York: New York University Press, 2003), 61.

67. Justice at Stake Campaign, "Justice at Stake—State Judges Frequency Questionnaire" (2002), at **www.justiceatstake.org /media/cms/JASJudgesSurveyResults _EA8838C0504A5.pdf.**

68. William Ballenger, "In Judicial Wilderness, Even Brickley's Not Safe," *Michigan Politics* 28 (1996), 1–3.

69. *Model Code of Judicial Conduct*, Canon 3(E)(1) (2007).

Pretrial Procedures:
The Adversary System in Action

Chapter Outline		Corresponding Learning Objectives
The Prosecution	**1**	List the different names given to public prosecutors and indicate the general powers that they have.
	2	Contrast the prosecutor's roles as an elected official and as a crime fighter.
The Defense Attorney	**3**	Delineate the responsibilities of defense attorneys.
	4	Explain why defense attorneys must often defend clients they know to be guilty.
Pretrial Detention	**5**	Identify the steps involved in the pretrial criminal process.
	6	Indicate the three influences on a judge's decision to set bail.
Establishing Probable Cause	**7**	Identify the main difference between an indictment and an information.
The Prosecutorial Screening Process	**8**	Explain how a prosecutor screens potential cases.
Pleading Guilty	**9**	Indicate why prosecutors, defense attorneys, and defendants often agree to plea bargains.

To target your study and review, look for these numbered Learning Objective icons throughout the chapter.

Trading Paint

in the high-risk, high-speed world of sprint car racing, it is not uncommon for two automobiles to bump into each other, or "trade paint." So, when Tony Stewart pinched Kevin Ward, Jr., against the frontstretch wall at the Canandaigua (New York) Motorsports Park on the night of August 9, 2014, causing Ward's car to crash, the incident could not have been considered out of the ordinary. Ward was, however, outraged. With the race suspended under a yellow caution flag, he exited his car and, wearing a dark suit, walked out onto the muddy track to confront Stewart. One driver swerved to avoid Ward, but Stewart's sprint car fishtailed and struck him. Soon thereafter, Ward died of "massive blunt force trauma."

The initial investigation by the Ontario County Sheriff's Department found that Stewart, a well-known NASCAR driver, did not intend to kill Ward. Still, there were concerns that Stewart had wanted to intimidate Ward and, in the words of one observer, "went over the line." Consequently, Michael Tantillo, the local district attorney, sent the matter to a grand jury to decide whether criminal charges should be filed against Stewart. In theory, the jurors could have found that Stewart "recklessly caused the death of another person," the definition of second degree manslaughter in New York.

Instead, the grand jury—composed of at least sixteen members of the community—determined that there was no evidence that Stewart committed a criminal act. Although the details of such proceedings are kept secret, it seems likely that the fact that Ward was under the influence of marijuana at the time of the accident played a role in the decision. Not surprisingly, the outcome displeased Ward's family. "This matter is not at rest, and we will pursue all remedies in fairness to Kevin," said his father.

▲ In September 2014, an Ontario County (New York) grand jury decided that professional stock car racer Tony Stewart, shown here, was not criminally responsible for killing his colleague Kevin Ward, Jr.

1. Why might it be difficult for Kevin Ward's family to win a civil wrongful death lawsuit against Tony Stewart? Even discounting that Ward was under the influence of marijuana during the race, in what other ways did he contribute to his own death?

2. Why do you think the Ontario County Sheriff's Department did not arrest Stewart following the race?

3. If you were a member of the grand jury, would you have voted to charge Stewart with committing a criminal act? Why or why not? What kind of evidence would you have needed to hear to find that he might have recklessly caused Ward's death?

The Prosecution

Under the circumstances, there seemed to be little possibility that a grand jury was going to find Tony Stewart criminally liable for Kevin Ward, Jr.'s, death. Indeed, many observers felt that, by sending the case to the grand jury, the local prosecutor was simply protecting himself against any suspicion that he was providing preferential treatment to a celebrity suspect.[1] Still, Stewart's defense attorneys weren't taking any chances. They hired a consultant to reconstruct film of the accident for the grand jury, showing—frame by frame—why Stewart was not at fault.

As this example shows, the American adversary system is set in motion well before a criminal trial even starts. In fact, cases rarely make it as far as trial. Instead, the issue of guilt or innocence is usually negotiated beforehand, with the terms largely dictated by government lawyers called **public prosecutors**.

Prosecutorial Duties

The public prosecutor in federal criminal cases is called a U.S. attorney. In cases tried in state or local courts, the public prosecutor may be referred to as a *prosecuting attorney, state attorney, district attorney, county attorney,* or *city attorney.* Given their great autonomy, prosecutors are generally considered the most dominant figures in the American criminal justice system.

 LEARNING OBJECTIVE 1 List the different names given to public prosecutors and indicate the general powers that they have.

A Duty of Fairness In some jurisdictions, the district attorney is the chief law enforcement officer, with broad powers over police operations. Prosecutors have the power to bring the resources of the state against the individual and hold the legal keys to meting out or withholding punishment. Ideally, this power is balanced by a duty of fairness and a recognition that the prosecutor's ultimate goal is not to win cases, but to see that justice is done. In *Berger v. United States* (1935), Justice George Sutherland called the prosecutor

> in a peculiar and very definite sense the servant of the law, the twofold aim of which is that guilt shall not escape or innocence suffer. He may prosecute with earnestness and vigor—indeed, he should do so. But, while he may strike hard blows, he is not at liberty to strike foul ones. It is as much his duty to refrain from improper methods calculated to produce a wrongful conviction as it is to use every legitimate means to bring about a just one.[2]

The Brady Rule To lessen the opportunity for "foul" behavior by prosecutors, the United States Supreme Court established the *Brady rule* more than half a century ago. This rule holds that prosecutors are not permitted to keep evidence from the defendant and her or his attorneys that may be useful in showing innocence.[3]

For example, in 2000 former state trooper George Martin was convicted of burning his wife to death in Mobile, Alabama. The only eyewitness to the crime gave conflicting reports to police, including calling the killer "a big man" (Martin is 5 feet, 6 inches tall) and pointing to a different suspect in a photo lineup. Obviously, Martin's defense attorneys could have used this information to create reasonable doubt concerning their client's guilt in court. Prosecutors, however, failed to tell the defense about the eyewitness's inconsistent testimony. Consequently, in 2013 a Mobile County judge overturned Martin's conviction and ordered a new trial.[4]

Public Prosecutors Individuals, acting as trial lawyers, who initiate and conduct cases in the government's name and on behalf of the people.

The Office of the Prosecutor

When he or she is acting as an *officer of the law* during a criminal trial, there are limits on the prosecutor's conduct, as we shall see in the next chapter. During the pretrial process, however, prosecutors hold a great deal of discretion in deciding the following:

1. Whether an individual who has been arrested by the police will be charged with a crime.
2. The level of the charges to be brought against the suspect.
3. If and when to stop the prosecution.[5]

There are more than eight thousand prosecutor's offices around the country, serving state, county, and municipal jurisdictions. Even though the **attorney general** is the chief law enforcement officer in any state, she or he has limited (and in some states, no) control over prosecutors within the state's boundaries.

Each jurisdiction has a chief prosecutor, who is sometimes appointed but more often elected. As an elected official, he or she typically serves a four-year term, though in some states, such as Alabama, the term is six years. In smaller jurisdictions, the chief prosecutor has several assistants, and they work closely together. In larger ones, the chief prosecutor may have numerous *assistant prosecutors,* many of whom he or she rarely meets. Assistant prosecutors—for the most part, young attorneys recently graduated from law school—may be assigned to particular sections of the organization, such as criminal prosecutions in general or areas of *special prosecution,* such as narcotics or gang crimes. (See Figure 9.1 for the structure of a typical prosecutor's office.)

The Prosecutor as Elected Official

The chief prosecutor's autonomy is not absolute. As an elected official, she or he must answer to the voters. (There are exceptions: U.S. attorneys are nominated by the president and approved by the Senate, and chief prosecutors in Alaska, Connecticut, New Jersey, Rhode Island, and the District of Columbia are either appointed or hired as members of the attorney general's office.) The prosecutor may be part of the political machine. In many jurisdictions, the prosecutor must declare a party affiliation and is expected to reward fellow party members with positions in the district attorney's office if elected.

The post of prosecutor is also considered a "stepping-stone" to higher political office, and many prosecutors have gone on to serve in legislatures or as judges. Sonia Sotomayor, the first Hispanic member of the United States Supreme Court, started her legal career in 1979 as an assistant district attorney in New York City. While at that job, she first came to public attention by helping to prosecute the "Tarzan Murderer," an athletic criminal responsible for at least twenty burglaries and four killings.

FIGURE 9.1 The Baltimore City State's Attorney's Office

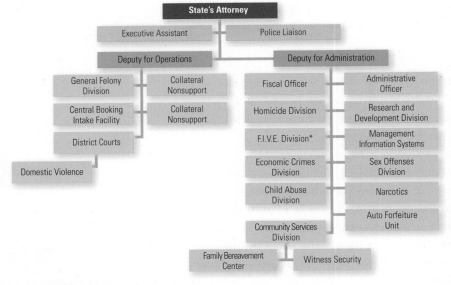

*F.I.V.E. is an acronym for "Firearms Investigation Violence Enforcement."

Source: Baltimore City State's Attorney's Office.

Elections and Impartiality Just as judicial elections can raise concerns that judges' decisions may be influenced by politics, as we discussed in the previous chapter, the specter of an upcoming election can cast doubt on the impartiality of a prosecutor's decisions. For example, researchers have determined that during an election year, incumbent prosecutors in North Carolina are more likely to take cases to trial and less likely to allow defendants to plead guilty. In contrast, when that state's prosecutors do not face an election, fewer cases are taken to trial and more are plea bargained.[6] Similar research in New York found that convictions won by prosecutors within six months of an election are 5 to 7 percent more likely to be later overturned by an appeals court. This is interpreted as evidence that prosecutors under electoral pressure are more apt to make mistakes while aggressively trying to win cases and attract positive publicity.[7]

Community Pressures A prosecutor's electability is often enhanced by her or his involvement in high-profile cases. Such cases can be challenging for prosecutors to navigate, as was evident in the recent controversy surrounding the alleged rape of a fourteen-year-old girl in Maryville, Missouri. When, in January 2012, Matt Barnett, a high school senior, was arrested for having sex with the girl, who was too drunk to consent, local sheriff Darren White said the evidence gathered would "absolutely" result in a prosecution.[8] Two months later, however, Nodaway County prosecutor Robert Rice dropped all charges against Barnett, calling the incident nothing more than a case of "incorrigible teenagers" drinking alcohol and having sex.[9]

Maryville residents suspected that Rice's decision had been influenced by the fact that Barnett, besides being a popular football player, was the grandson of a prominent local political figure. After the *Kansas City Star* ran an article on the situation—which included details such as the suspect leaving the lightly dressed alleged victim passed out on her front lawn in freezing weather[10]—Rice began to receive a great deal of criticism. In October 2013, he relented and asked a judge to appoint a special prosecutor to reopen the case. Finally, in January 2014, the special prosecutor declined to bring sexual assault charges against Barnett, saying that there was "insufficient evidence" of any criminal behavior."[11]

▲ Give several reasons why experience as a prosecutor would make someone such as United States Supreme Court justice Sonia Sotomayor a more effective judge. AP Images/Pablo Martinez Monsivais

The Prosecutor as Crime Fighter

One of the reasons the prosecutor's post is a useful first step in a political career is that it is linked to crime fighting. Thanks to savvy public relations efforts and television police dramas such as *Law & Order*—with its opening line, "In the criminal justice system, the people are represented by two separate yet equally important groups: the police who investigate crime and the district attorneys who prosecute the offenders"—prosecutors are generally seen as law enforcement agents. Indeed, the prosecutors and the police do have a symbiotic relationship. Prosecutors rely on police to arrest suspects and gather sufficient evidence, and police rely on prosecutors to convict those who have been apprehended.

LEARNING
2
OBJECTIVE
Contrast the prosecutor's roles as an elected official and as a crime fighter.

Prosecutors and Police Despite, or perhaps because of, this mutual dependency, the relationship between the two branches of law enforcement is often strained. Part of this can be attributed to different backgrounds. Most prosecutors come from middle- or upper-class families, while police are often recruited from the working class. Furthermore, prosecutors are required to have a level of education that is not attained by most police officers. More important, however, is a basic divergence in the concept of guilt. For a police officer, a suspect is guilty if he or she has in fact committed a crime. For a prosecutor, a suspect is guilty if enough evidence can be legally gathered to prove such guilt in a court of law.

In other words, police officers often focus on *factual guilt,* whereas prosecutors are ultimately concerned with *legal guilt.*[12] Thus, police officers will feel a great deal of frustration when a suspect they "know" to be guilty is set free. Similarly, a prosecutor may become annoyed when police officers do not follow the letter of the law in gathering evidence, thereby greatly reducing the chances of conviction. To alleviate this tension, the Mecklenburg County (North Carolina) District Attorney's Office holds regular "roundtable" meetings with local police to discuss the fate of recently arrested violent offenders.[13]

Prosecutors and Victims Because prosecutors have the responsibility of trying and convicting offenders, crime victims often see themselves as being on "the same side" as the prosecution. This perception is only strengthened when prosecutors publicly align themselves with victims. In fact, prosecutors do not represent crime victims. Understandably, most victims are focused primarily on the fate of the defendant who caused them harm. Prosecutors, in contrast, must balance the rights of the victims with those of the accused and the best interests of the public at large. Indeed, if a prosecutor becomes too involved in the personal tragedies of crime victims, he or she runs the risk of losing the neutrality that is the hallmark of the office.[14]

A prosecutor's duty of neutrality does not mean that he or she should ignore crime victims or their wishes. Practically, prosecutors rely on victims as sources of information and valuable witnesses. Believable victims are also quite helpful if a case goes to trial, as they may be able to elicit a sympathetic response from the jury.[15] Furthermore, as we saw in Chapter 3, federal and state victims' rights legislation requires the prosecutor to confer with victims at various stages of the criminal justice process.

CJ & Technology

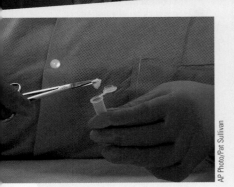

AP Photo/Pat Sullivan

Untested Rape Kits

In 2010, the Wayne County Prosecutor's Office found 11,000 untested rape kits in a Detroit police storage unit. These kits are prepared by forensic medical experts in the hours following a sexual assault, and often contain DNA left by the offender. In the five years following this discovery, prosecutor Kym Worthy arranged for 2,000 of the kits to be tested, identifying 188 serial rapists and obtaining fifteen convictions in the process. Though the pace of Worthy's efforts may seem slow, it isn't. A crime lab can take weeks to extract usable DNA evidence from a rape kit, at a cost of up to $1,500.

Nationwide, there is a backlog of 400,000 to 500,000 untested rape kits, meaning that innumerable sexual assault offenders have escaped arrest and conviction. Given that most crime labs in the country are already overwhelmed with requests to test evidence, it seems that technology offers the best hope of reducing this backlog. Presently, lab technicians must laboriously separate the DNA of the victim from the DNA from the offender by slicing the cells of material in the rape kit such as blood, semen, skin, or saliva. A new process called *pressure cycling* immediately identifies the offender's semen, which significantly lessens the amount of time needed to get a usable DNA sample for database-matching purposes.

Thinking about Untested Rape Kits
How might the massive backlog of untested rape kits in this country discourage victims of sexual assault from reporting the crime to police?

The Defense Attorney

The media provide most people's perception of defense counsel: the idealistic public defender who nobly serves the poor, the "ambulance chaser," or the celebrity attorney in the $3,000 suit. These stereotypes, though not entirely fictional, tend to obscure the crucial role that the **defense attorney** plays in the criminal justice system. Most persons charged with crimes have little or no knowledge of criminal procedure. Without assistance, they would be helpless in court. By acting as a staunch advocate for her or his client, the defense attorney (ideally) ensures that the government proves every point against that client beyond a reasonable doubt, even for cases that do not go to trial. In sum, the defense attorney provides a counterweight against the state in our adversary system.

The Responsibilities of the Defense Attorney

The Sixth Amendment right to counsel is not limited to the actual criminal trial. In a number of instances, the United States Supreme Court has held that defendants are entitled to representation as soon as their rights may be denied, which, as we have seen, includes the custodial interrogation and lineup identification procedures.[16] Therefore, an important responsibility of the defense attorney is to represent the defendant at the various stages of the custodial process, such as arrest, interrogation, lineup, and arraignment. Other responsibilities include:

LEARNING
3
OBJECTIVE
Delineate the responsibilities of defense attorneys.

- Investigating the incident for which the defendant has been charged.
- Communicating with the prosecutor, which includes negotiating plea bargains.
- Preparing the case for trial.
- Submitting defense motions, including motions to suppress evidence.
- Representing the defendant at trial.
- Negotiating a sentence, if the client has been convicted.
- Determining whether to appeal a guilty verdict.[17]

Defending the Guilty

At one time or another in their careers, all defense attorneys will face a difficult question: Must I defend a client whom I know to be guilty? According to the American Bar Association's code of legal ethics, the answer is almost always, "yes."[18] The most important responsibility of the criminal defense attorney is to be an advocate for her or his client. As such, the attorney is obligated to use all ethical and legal means to achieve the client's desired goal, which is usually to avoid or lessen punishment for the charged crime.

As Supreme Court justice Byron White once noted, defense counsel has no "obligation to ascertain or present the truth." Rather, our adversary system insists that the defense attorney "defend the client whether he is innocent or guilty."[19] Indeed, if defense attorneys refused to represent clients whom they believed to be guilty, the Sixth

Defense Attorney The lawyer representing the defendant.

Public Defenders Court-appointed attorneys who are paid by the state to represent defendants who cannot afford private counsel.

Amendment guarantee of a criminal trial for all accused persons would be rendered meaningless. (To learn more about the difficult situations that can arise with a guilty defendant, see the feature *A Question of Ethics: The Right Decision?*)

The Public Defender

Generally speaking, there are two different types of defense attorneys: (1) private attorneys, who are hired by individuals, and (2) **public defenders,** who work for the government. The distinction is not absolute, as many private attorneys accept employment as public defenders, too. The modern role of the public defender was established by the Supreme Court's interpretation of the Sixth Amendment in *Gideon v. Wainwright* (1963).[20]

In that case, the Court ruled that no defendant can be "assured a fair trial unless counsel is provided for him," and therefore the state must provide a public defender to those who cannot afford to hire one for themselves. Subsequently, the Court extended this protection to juveniles in *In re Gault* (1967)[21] and those faced with imprisonment for committing misdemeanors in *Argersinger v. Hamlin* (1972).[22] The impact of these decisions has been substantial: about 90 percent of all criminal defendants in the United States are represented by public defenders or other appointed counsel.[23]

A Question of Ethics: The Right Decision?

The Situation Gerard Marrone is the defense attorney for Levi Aron, charged with kidnapping, murdering, and dis-

 LEARNING **4** OBJECTIVE Explain why defense attorneys must often defend clients they know to be guilty.

membering eight-year-old Leiby Kletzky in Brooklyn, New York. There is little question of Aron's guilt, as he provided the police with a signed confession and has no alibi for his whereabouts at the time of the crime. Marrone is uncertain about whether he wants to continue representing this "horrific" client. "You can't look at your kids and then look at yourself in the mirror, knowing that a little boy, who's close in age to my eldest son, was murdered so brutally," Marrone said about his conflicting feelings.

The Ethical Dilemma The criminal justice system would not be able to function if lawyers refused to represent clients they knew to be guilty. At the same time, a lawyer must be guided by his or her own conscience. If a client is so repugnant to the lawyer as to impair the quality of representation, then perhaps the lawyer should drop the case.

What Is the Solution? What would you do in Marrone's shoes? Several years ago, he decided that his conscience prevented him

from representing Aron, and he withdrew from the case. His replacement, Jennifer McCann, criticized Marrone's actions. "To sit there and say, 'This is a hard case, I don't want to take it,'" McCann said, "that's for somebody else; that's not who I am." She added, "It's not about defending [Aron's] actions. It's about defending his rights."

Defense attorneys Pierre Bazile, right, and Jennifer McCann appear with their client Levi Aron at the State Supreme Court in Brooklyn in New York. Jesse Ward/*The New York Times*/Redux Pictures

Eligibility Issues Although the Supreme Court's *Gideon* decision obligated the government to provide attorneys for poor defendants, it offered no guidance on just how poor the defendant needs to be to qualify for a public defender. In theory, counsel should be provided for those who are unable to hire an attorney themselves without "substantial hardship."[24] In reality, each jurisdiction has its own guidelines, and a defendant refused counsel in one area might be entitled to it in another. A judge in Kittitas County, Washington, to give an extreme example, would frequently deny public counsel for college student defendants. This judge believed that any person who chooses to go to school rather than work automatically falls outside the *Gideon* case's definition of indigence.[25]

Defense Counsel Programs In most areas, the county government is responsible for providing indigent defendants with attorneys. Three basic types of programs are used to allocate defense counsel:

1. *Assigned counsel programs,* in which local private attorneys are assigned clients on a case-by-case basis by the county.
2. *Contracting attorney programs,* in which a particular law firm or group of attorneys is hired to regularly assume the representative and administrative tasks of indigent defense.
3. *Public defender programs,* in which the county assembles a salaried staff of full-time or part-time attorneys and creates a public (taxpayer-funded) agency to provide services.[26]

Much to the surprise of many indigent defendants, these programs are not entirely without cost. Government agencies can charge fees for "free" legal counsel when the fees will not impose a "significant legal financial hardship" on the defendant. In at least forty-three states and the District of Columbia, therefore, local public defender offices have the option of charging some form of so-called cost recoupment.[27] Florida, North Carolina, and Virginia have mandatory public defender fees, meaning that judges cannot waive such costs under any circumstances. In Virginia, indigent defendants may be charged up to $1,235 per count for certain felonies.[28]

Effectiveness of Public Defenders Under the U.S. Constitution, a defendant who is paying for her or his defense attorney has a right to choose that attorney without interference from the court.[29] This right of choice does not extend to indigent defendants. According to the United States Supreme Court, "[A] defendant may not insist on an attorney he cannot afford."[30] In other words, an indigent defendant must accept the public defender provided by the court system. (Note that, unless the presiding judge rules otherwise, a person can waive her or his Sixth Amendment rights and act as her or his own defense attorney.) This lack of control contributes to the widespread belief that public defenders do not provide an acceptable level of defense to indigents.

Statistics show, however, that conviction rates of defendants with private counsel and those represented by publicly funded attorneys are generally the same.[31] The main difference seems to be between private attorneys who are assigned indigent clients and full-time public defenders. A study of 3,412 Philadelphia indigent murder defendants found that, compared with private appointed counsel, public defenders reduce the conviction rate by 19 percent and the overall expected time served in prison by 24 percent.[32]

The main reason for this discrepancy, at least in Philadelphia, appears to be financial. Court-appointed defense attorneys in that city receive a flat fee for each client, which essentially works out to an average of $2 an hour. Furthermore, they are afforded

Annika Carlsten
Public Defender

Courtesy Annika Carlsten

FASTFACTS

**Public defender
Job description:**

- Interview low-income applicants for legal services; advise and counsel individuals and groups regarding their legal rights; handle a reasonable caseload; and, where necessary, engage in the negotiation, trial, and/or appeal of legal issues that have a substantial impact on the rights of eligible clients.

What kind of training is required?

- A law degree and membership in the relevant state bar association.

Annual salary range?

- $44,000–$92,000

My very first day on the job, I watched another attorney conduct *voir dire* (see Chapter 10) on a domestic violence assault. I wondered if I would ever be that comfortable and confident in court. Many years later, the cases have started to blur in my memory. That said, I will always remember my very first "not guilty" verdict. I was utterly convinced of my client's innocence, and very emotionally invested in winning the case for him. At the other end of the spectrum, I will never forget having to explain court proceedings to a man only hours after he accidentally shot and killed his child. Nothing in law school prepares you for that conversation. Nothing in life prepares you for that conversation.

Most of all, I believe passionately in the idea of what I do, in the principle of equal justice for everyone, regardless of money or circumstance. On a good day, I see that ideal fulfilled. On a great day, I feel like I personally have done something to make it so.

> **SOCIAL MEDIA CAREER TIP** You need to differentiate yourself from everyone else on line by providing unique, relevant, high-quality content on a regular basis. You should network with a purpose, not just to share fun things.

limited public funds to investigate their client's innocence. Philadelphia's public defenders, by contrast, are paid an annual salary and supported by a staff of investigators and various experts.[33]

Unreasonable Caseloads The American Bar Association recommends that a public defender handle no more than 150 felony cases and 400 misdemeanor cases each year. Nationwide, about three-quarters of all county-based public defender programs exceed these limits.[34] Public defenders working in the Washington cities of Mount Vernon and Burlington, for example, typically have 500 clients at any given time and "often meet their clients for the first time in the courtroom."[35]

Public defender offices increasingly are turning to the courts for relief from excessive caseloads. In 2013, the Florida Supreme Court ruled that public defenders in the state could decline new clients to ensure proper representation for existing ones.[36] In 2014, New York state settled a lawsuit by agreeing to cap the number of criminal cases for its court-appointed lawyers.[37] That same year, a federal judge in Washington state appointed a monitor to ensure that indigent defendants in Burlington and Mount Vernon are receiving adequate representation from public defenders.[38]

The *Strickland* Standard In one Louisiana murder trial, not only did the court-appointed defense attorney spend only eleven minutes preparing for trial on a charge that carries a mandatory life sentence, but she also represented the victim's father and had been representing the victim at the time of his death. Not surprisingly, her defendant was found guilty. Such behavior raises a critical question: When a lawyer does such a poor job, has the client essentially been denied his or her Sixth Amendment right to assistance of counsel? In *Strickland v. Washington* (1984),[39] the Supreme Court set up a two-pronged test to determine whether constitutional requirements have been met. To prove that prior counsel was not sufficient, a defendant must show that:

1. The attorney's performance was deficient, *and*
2. This deficiency *more likely than not* caused the defendant to lose the case.

In practice, it has been very difficult to prove the second prong of this test. A prosecutor can always argue that the defendant would have lost the case even if his or her lawyer had not been inept. Sometimes, however, such ineptness is so intolerable that it meets the *Strickland* standard and a new trial is required. Several years ago, the Kansas Supreme Court overturned the capital conviction of Phillip Cheatham, Jr., for the shooting deaths of two Topeka women a decade earlier. Most crucially, Cheatham's defense attorney had failed to present evidence that his client was driving to Chicago at the time of the shootings. The lawyer also spent only sixty hours preparing for the trial (being busy running for governor at the time) and referred to Cheatham as a "professional drug dealer" and "shooter of people" in court.[40]

▲ Public defender Megan Downing makes a point to the jury during a trial in Brighton, Colorado. **What would be the benefits and drawbacks of allowing an indigent defendant to choose her or his public defender rather than being assigned one by the court system?** Andy Cross/*The Denver Post* via Getty Images

The Attorney-Client Relationship

The implied trust between an attorney and her or his client usually is not in question when the attorney has been hired directly by the defendant—as an "employee," the attorney well understands her or his duties. Relationships between public defenders and their clients, however, are often marred by suspicion on both sides. As Northwestern University professor Jonathan D. Casper discovered while interviewing indigent defendants, many of them feel a certain amount of respect for the prosecutor. Like police officers, prosecutors are just "doing their job" by trying to convict the defendant. In contrast, the defendants' view of their own attorneys can be summed up in the following exchange between Casper and a defendant:

> Did you have a lawyer when you went to court the next morning?
> No, I had a public defender.[41]

This attitude is somewhat understandable. Given the caseloads that most public defenders carry, they may have as little as five or ten minutes to spend with a client before appearing in front of a judge. How much, realistically, can a public defender learn about the defendant in that time? Furthermore, the defendant is well aware that the public defender is being paid by the same source as the prosecutor and the judge. "Because you're part of the system, your indigent client doesn't trust you," admitted one court-appointed attorney.[42]

The situation handcuffs the public defenders as well. With so little time to spend on each case, they cannot validate the information provided by their clients. If the defendant says he or she has no prior offenses, the public defender often has no choice but to believe the client. Consequently, many public defenders later find that their clients have deceived them. Along with the high pressures of the job, a client's lack of cooperation and disrespect can limit whatever satisfaction a public defender may find in the profession.

Attorney-Client Privilege

To defend a client effectively, a defense attorney must have access to all the facts concerning the case, even those that may be harmful to the defendant. To promote the unrestrained flow of information between the two parties, legislatures and lawyers themselves have constructed rules of **attorney-client privilege**. These rules require that communications between a client and his or her attorney be kept confidential, unless the client consents to the disclosure.

The Privilege and Confessions Attorney-client privilege does not stop short of confessions. Indeed, if, on hearing any statement that points toward guilt, the defense attorney could alert the prosecution or try to resign from the case, attorney-client privilege would be rendered meaningless. Even if the client says, "I have just killed seventeen women. I selected only pregnant women so I could torture them and kill two people at once. I did it. I liked it. I enjoyed it," the defense attorney must continue to do his or her utmost to serve that client.[43]

Without attorney-client privilege, observes legal expert John Kaplan, lawyers would be forced to give their clients the equivalent of the *Miranda* warning before representing them.[44] In other words, lawyers would have to make clear what clients could or could not say in the course of preparing for trial, because any incriminating statement might be used against the client in court. Such a development would have serious ramifications for the criminal justice system.

The Exception to the Privilege The scope of attorney-client privilege is not all encompassing. In *United States v. Zolin* (1989),[45] the Supreme Court ruled that lawyers may disclose the contents of a conversation with a client if the client has provided information concerning a crime that has yet to be committed. This exception applies only to communications involving a crime that is ongoing or will occur in the future.

If the client reveals a past crime, the privilege is still in effect, and the attorney may not reveal any details of that particular criminal act. This aspect of the privilege can, admittedly, have tragic consequences. In 1956, for example, Darrel Parker was convicted of raping and killing his wife in Lincoln, Nebraska. These crimes had actually been committed by Wesley Peery, who admitted as much to his attorney. Parker spent fourteen years in prison, however, and was not exonerated until Peery died of a heart attack, allowing his attorney to make the confession public.

EthicsChallenge

Suppose a public defender named Jones is assigned to represent Carmichael, who has been charged with raping a nurse and then fatally shooting her with a handgun. Carmichael informs Jones that although he did sexually assault the nurse, he didn't kill her. Instead, according to Carmichael, the nurse—distraught after being raped—grabbed the gun out of his hands and killed herself. Carmichael wants to tell this story, which Jones does not believe, to the jury during his trial. Is Jones ethically obligated to let Carmichael take the stand, or is she ethically obliged to keep him from testifying? Explain your answer. ■

Pretrial Detention

After police arrested Darren Vann on suspicion of killing a nineteen-year-old woman in northwest Indiana, he proved a helpful suspect. First, Vann admitted to the initial murder. Then, he identified the bodies of six women in various nearby abandoned buildings, confessing to have murdered each one. When, however, Vann made his first court appearance a week later, he refused to speak. "You might want to explain to your client that he stays in jail for the rest of his life until we have this hearing," a frustrated judge told Vann's public defender.[46]

LEARNING **5** OBJECTIVE Identify the steps involved in the pretrial criminal process.

Once a suspect is arrested and booked, her or his fate is decided not by law enforcement officers but by officers of the court. As Figure 9.2 shows, each suspect must navigate a series of pretrial procedures, with the help of an attorney, as part of the process of determining his or her innocence or guilt.

The Initial Appearance

After a suspect has been booked, she or he is brought before a magistrate (see Chapter 8) for the **initial appearance**. During this brief proceeding, the magistrate informs the defendant of the charges that have been brought against him or her and explains his or her constitutional rights—particularly, the right to remain silent (under the Fifth Amendment) and the right to be represented by counsel (under the Sixth Amendment). At this point, if the defendant cannot afford to hire a private attorney, a public defender may be appointed, or private counsel may be hired by the state to represent the defendant. As the U.S. Constitution does not specify how soon a defendant must be brought before a magistrate after arrest, it has been left to the judicial branch to determine the timing of the initial appearance. The Supreme Court has held that the initial appearance must occur "promptly," which in most cases means within forty-eight hours of booking.[47]

In misdemeanor cases, a defendant may decide to plead guilty and be sentenced during the initial appearance. Otherwise, the magistrate will usually release those charged with misdemeanors on their promise to return at a later date for further proceedings. For felony cases, however, the defendant is not permitted to make a plea at the initial appearance because a magistrate's court does not have jurisdiction to decide felonies.

Bail

At the initial appearance, in most cases the defendant will be released only if she or he posts **bail**—an amount paid by the defendant to the court and retained by the court until the defendant returns for further proceedings. Defendants who cannot afford bail are generally kept in a local jail or lockup until the date of their trial, though many jurisdictions are searching for alternatives to this practice because of overcrowded incarceration facilities. Just under two-thirds of felony defendants in state courts are released before their trials. Not surprisingly, release is more likely for defendants charged with property, public order, or drug crimes than for defendants charged with violent crimes.[48]

Setting Bail Bail is provided for under the Eighth Amendment. The amendment does not, however, guarantee the right to bail. Instead, it states that "excessive bail shall not be required." This has come to mean that the bail amount must be reasonable compared with the seriousness of the wrongdoing. It does *not* mean that the amount of bail must be within the defendant's ability to pay. Indeed, one of the most consistent criticisms of bail is that the system is biased against low-income defendants who may

Initial Appearance An accused's first appearance before a judge or magistrate following arrest.

Bail The dollar amount or conditions set by the court to ensure that an individual accused of a crime will appear for further criminal proceedings.

FIGURE 9.2 The Steps Leading to a Trial

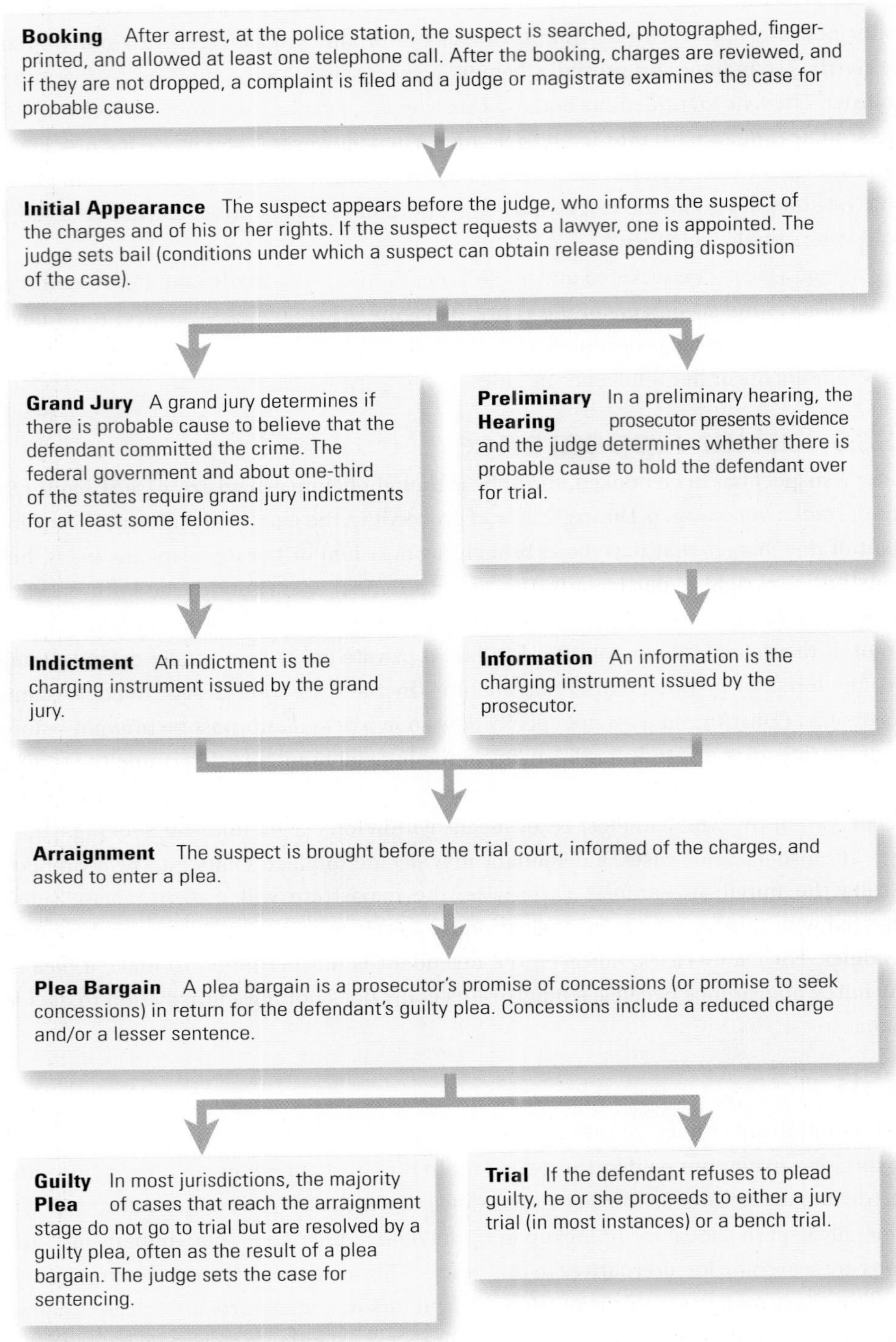

Booking After arrest, at the police station, the suspect is searched, photographed, finger-printed, and allowed at least one telephone call. After the booking, charges are reviewed, and if they are not dropped, a complaint is filed and a judge or magistrate examines the case for probable cause.

Initial Appearance The suspect appears before the judge, who informs the suspect of the charges and of his or her rights. If the suspect requests a lawyer, one is appointed. The judge sets bail (conditions under which a suspect can obtain release pending disposition of the case).

Grand Jury A grand jury determines if there is probable cause to believe that the defendant committed the crime. The federal government and about one-third of the states require grand jury indictments for at least some felonies.

Preliminary Hearing In a preliminary hearing, the prosecutor presents evidence and the judge determines whether there is probable cause to hold the defendant over for trial.

Indictment An indictment is the charging instrument issued by the grand jury.

Information An information is the charging instrument issued by the prosecutor.

Arraignment The suspect is brought before the trial court, informed of the charges, and asked to enter a plea.

Plea Bargain A plea bargain is a prosecutor's promise of concessions (or promise to seek concessions) in return for the defendant's guilty plea. Concessions include a reduced charge and/or a lesser sentence.

Guilty Plea In most jurisdictions, the majority of cases that reach the arraignment stage do not go to trial but are resolved by a guilty plea, often as the result of a plea bargain. The judge sets the case for sentencing.

Trial If the defendant refuses to plead guilty, he or she proceeds to either a jury trial (in most instances) or a bench trial.

not have the financial means to "buy" their temporary freedom. Numerous studies show that defendants detained in jail have worse trial outcomes than those who are able to gain pretrial release.[49]

There is no uniform system for pretrial detention. Each jurisdiction has its own *bail tariffs,* or general guidelines concerning the proper amount of bail. For misdemeanors, the police usually follow a preapproved bail schedule created by local judicial authorities. In felony cases, the primary responsibility to set bail lies with the judge. Figure 9.3 shows typical bail amounts for violent offenses.

Bail guidelines can be quite extensive. In Illinois, for example, a judge is required to take thirty-eight different factors into account when setting bail: fourteen involve the crime itself, two refer to the evidence gathered, four to the defendant's record, nine to the defendant's flight risk and immigration status, and nine to the defendant's general character.[50] For the most part, however, judges are free to use such tariffs as loose guidelines, and they have a great deal of discretion in setting bail according to the circumstances in each case.

Judges and Bail Extralegal factors may also play a part in bail setting. University of New Orleans political scientist David W. Neubauer has identified three contexts that may influence a judge's decision-making process:[51]

1. *Uncertainty.* To a certain extent, predetermined bail tariffs are unrealistic, given that judges are required to set bail within forty-eight hours of arrest. It is often difficult to get information on the defendant in that period of time, and even if a judge can obtain a "rap sheet," or list of prior arrests ("priors"), she or he will probably not have an opportunity to verify its accuracy. Due to this uncertainty, most judges have no choice but to focus primarily on the seriousness of the crime in setting bail.

2. *Risk.* There is no way of knowing for certain whether a defendant released on bail will return for his or her court date, or whether he or she will commit a crime while free. Judges are aware of the criticism they will come under from police groups, prosecutors, the press, and the public if a crime is committed during that time. Consequently, especially if she or he is up for reelection, a judge may prefer to "play it safe" and set a high bail to detain a suspect or refuse outright to offer bail when legally able to do so. In general, risk aversion also dictates why those who are charged with a violent crime such as murder are usually less likely to be released prior to trial than those who are charged with property crimes such as larceny or motor vehicle theft.

3. *Overcrowded jails.* As we will discuss in detail in Chapter 13, many of the nation's jails are overcrowded. This may force a judge to make a difficult distinction between those suspects she or he believes must be detained and those who might need to be detained. To save jail space, a judge might be more lenient in setting bail for members of the latter group.[52]

Gaining Pretrial Release

If a judge decides that the defendant is not a risk to "jump" bail or get rearrested while awaiting trial, that judge has several options regarding pretrial release. One of the most popular is **release on recognizance (ROR),** in which the defendant is set free at no cost with the understanding that he or she will return at the time of the trial. The Vera Institute, a nonprofit organization in New York City, introduced the concept of ROR as part of the Manhattan Bail Project in the 1960s, and such programs are now found in nearly every jurisdiction. When properly administered, ROR programs seem to be successful, with less than 5 percent of the participants failing to show for trial.[53]

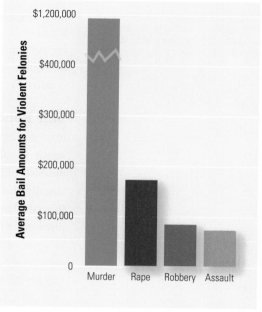

FIGURE 9.3 **Average Bail Amounts for Violent Felonies**

These figures represent the mean bail figures for the seventy-five largest counties in the nation.

Source: Adapted from Bureau of Justice Statistics, *Felony Defendants in Large Urban Counties, 2009–Statistical Tables* (Washington, D.C.: U.S. Department of Justice, December 2013), Table 16, page 19.

LEARNING **6** OBJECTIVE Indicate the three influences on a judge's decision to set bail.

Release on Recognizance (ROR) A judge's order that releases an accused from jail with the understanding that he or she will return of his or her own will for further proceedings.

Property Bond An alternative to posting bail in cash, in which the defendant gains pretrial release by providing the court with property as assurance that he or she will return for trial.

Bail Bond Agent A businessperson who agrees, for a fee, to pay the bail amount if the accused fails to appear in court as ordered.

Posting Bail Those suspected of committing a felony, however, are rarely released on recognizance. These defendants may post, or pay, the full amount of the bail in cash to the court. The money will be returned when the suspect appears for trial. Given the large amount of funds required, and the relative lack of wealth of many criminal defendants, a defendant can rarely post bail in cash. Another option is to use real property, such as a house, instead of cash as collateral. These **property bonds** are also rare because most courts require property valued at double the bail amount. Thus, if bail is set at $5,000, the defendant (or the defendant's family and friends) will have to produce property valued at $10,000.

Bail Bond Agents If unable to post bail with cash or property, a defendant may arrange for a **bail bond agent** to post a bail bond on the defendant's behalf. The bond agent, in effect, promises the court that he or she will turn over to the court the full amount of bail if the defendant fails to return for further proceedings. The defendant usually must give the bond agent a certain percentage of the bail (frequently 10 percent) in cash. This amount, which is often not returned to the defendant later, is considered payment for the bond agent's assistance and assumption of risk. Depending on the amount of the bail bond, the defendant may also be required to sign over to the bond agent rights to certain property (such as a car, a valuable watch, or other asset) as security for the bond.

Although bail bond agents obviously provide a service for which there is demand, the process is widely viewed with distaste. Indeed, the Philippines is the only other nation where bail bonding is an accepted part of the pretrial release process. Four states—Illinois, Kentucky, Oregon, and Wisconsin—have abolished bail bonding for profit. The rationale for such reform focuses on three perceived problems with the practice:

1. Bail bond agents provide opportunities for corruption, as they may improperly influence officials who are involved in setting bail to inflate the bail.
2. Because they can refuse to post a bail bond, bail bond agents are, in essence, making a business decision concerning a suspect's pretrial release. This is considered the responsibility of a judge, not a private individual with a profit motive.[54]

▼ If a defendant "skips" bail by failing to appear at trial, the bail bond agent sometimes will hire a fugitive-recovery agent to find the defendant and return him or her to court. **Are there any circumstances under which a fugitive-recovery agent should be allowed to use deadly force in apprehending a runaway defendant? Explain your answer.**
Chris Johnson/Getty Images/RF

3. About 40 percent of defendants released on bail are eventually found not guilty of any crime. These people, although innocent, have had to pay what amounts to a bribe if they wanted to stay out of jail before their trial.[55]

The states that have banned bail bond agents have established an alternative known as *ten percent cash bail.* This process, pioneered in Chicago in the early 1960s, requires the court, in effect, to take the place of the bond agent. An officer of the court will accept a deposit of 10 percent of the bail amount, refundable when the defendant appears at the assigned time. A number of jurisdictions allow for both bail bond agents and ten percent cash bail, with the judge deciding whether a defendant is eligible for the latter.

Bail and Community Safety

The vagueness of the Eighth Amendment's requirement that "excessive bail shall not be required" allows the practice to serve another purpose: the protection of the community. That is, if a judge feels that the defendant poses a threat should he or she be released before trial, the judge will set bail at a level the suspect cannot possibly afford. In July 2013, for example, a King County, Washington, district court judge set bail at $2 million for indigent defendant Justin Jasper, accused of planning to firebomb three college campuses in the Seattle area.

Preventive Detention Alternatively, more than thirty states have passed **preventive detention** legislation to protect the community. These laws allow judges to act "in the best interests of the community" by denying bail to arrestees with prior records of violence, thus keeping them in custody prior to trial. The federal Bail Reform Act of 1984 similarly affirms that federal offenders can be held without bail to ensure "the safety of any other person and the community."[56] Critics of the 1984 act believe that it violates the U.S. Constitution by allowing the freedom of a citizen to be restricted before he or she has been proved guilty in a court of law.

False Positives For many, preventive detention also brings up the troubling issue of *false positives*—erroneous predictions that defendants, if given pretrial release, would commit a crime, when in fact they would not. In *United States v. Salerno* (1987),[57] however, the Supreme Court upheld the federal Bail Reform Act. Then Chief Justice William Rehnquist wrote that preventive detention was not a "punishment for dangerous individuals" but a "potential solution to a pressing social problem." Therefore, "there is no doubt that preventing danger to the community is a legitimate . . . goal."

In fact, about 17 percent of released defendants are rearrested before their trials begin, most of them for missing a scheduled court appearance. Only about 8 percent are rearrested for committing a felony while free on bail.[58] (As the feature *Discretion in Action—Bail Out?* shows, the seriousness of the underlying crime is a crucial factor in the judge's decision regarding pretrial release.)

Preventive Detention The retention of an accused person in custody due to fears that she or he will commit a crime if released before trial.

Discretion in Action

Bail Out?

The Situation Nine-year-old Savannah lied to her grandmother Joyce about eating candy bars. As punishment, Joyce forced Savannah to run three hours without a rest. Severely dehydrated, the girl had a seizure and died. Alabama authorities have charged Joyce, forty-eight years old and in poor health, with capital murder, meaning she is eligible for the death penalty. Her lawyers request that Joyce be freed on bail to help prepare for her trial.

The Law By statute, any person charged with a capital crime in Alabama can be denied bail. When considering whether to impose preventive detention, the judge usually focuses on the threat the defendant would pose to the community if she or he were set free.

What Would You Do? If you were the judge presiding over these proceedings, would you give Joyce her pretrial release? If so, what would her bail amount be? Or, would you take advantage of the state's preventive detention law and deny Joyce bail? Explain your answers.

[To see how an Alabama judge ruled in this situation, go to Example 9.1 in Appendix B.]

Establishing Probable Cause

Once the initial appearance has been completed and bail has been set, the prosecutor must establish *probable cause.* In other words, the prosecutor must show that a crime was committed and link the defendant to that crime. There are two formal procedures for establishing probable cause at this stage of the pretrial process: preliminary hearings and grand juries.

The Preliminary Hearing

During the **preliminary hearing,** the defendant appears before a judge or magistrate who decides whether the evidence presented is sufficient for the case to proceed to trial. Normally, every person arrested has a right to this hearing within a reasonable amount of time after his or her initial arrest—usually, no later than ten days if the defendant is in custody or within thirty days if he or she has gained pretrial release.

The Preliminary Hearing Process The preliminary hearing is conducted in the manner of a mini-trial. Typically, a police report of the arrest is presented by a law enforcement officer, supplemented with evidence provided by the prosecutor. Because the burden of proving probable cause is relatively light (compared with proving guilt beyond a reasonable doubt), prosecutors rarely call witnesses during the preliminary hearing, saving them for the trial.

During this hearing, the defendant has a right to be represented by counsel, who may cross-examine witnesses and challenge any evidence offered by the prosecutor. In most states, defense attorneys can take advantage of the preliminary hearing to begin the process of **discovery,** in which they are entitled to have access to any evidence in the possession of the prosecution relating to the case. Discovery is considered a keystone in the adversary process, as it allows the defense to see the evidence against the defendant prior to making a plea.

Waiving the Hearing The preliminary hearing often seems rather perfunctory. It usually lasts no longer than five minutes, and the judge or magistrate rarely finds that probable cause does not exist. For this reason, defense attorneys commonly advise their clients to waive their right to a preliminary hearing. Once a judge has ruled affirmatively, in many jurisdictions the defendant is bound over to the **grand jury,** a group of citizens called to decide whether probable cause exists. In other jurisdictions, the prosecutor issues an **information,** which replaces the police complaint as the formal charge against the defendant for the purposes of a trial.

The Grand Jury

As we saw at the beginning of the chapter, some jurisdictions require a grand jury to make the decision as to whether a case should go to trial. The grand jury does not

Preliminary Hearing An initial hearing in which a magistrate decides if there is probable cause to believe that the defendant committed the crime with which he or she is charged.

Discovery Formal investigation by each side prior to trial.

Grand Jury The group of citizens called to decide whether probable cause exists to believe that a suspect committed the crime with which she or he has been charged.

Information The formal charge against the accused issued by the prosecutor after a preliminary hearing has found probable cause.

determine the guilt or innocence of the defendant. Rather, it determines whether the evidence presented by the prosecution is sufficient to provide reasonable cause that a crime occurred. If a majority of the jurors find sufficient evidence, the grand jury will issue an **indictment** (pronounced in-*dyte*-ment). Like an information in a preliminary hearing, the indictment becomes the formal charge against the defendant.

LEARNING **7** OBJECTIVE Identify the main difference between an indictment and an information.

The federal government and about one-third of the states require grand jury indictments to bring felony charges. In most of the other states, a grand jury is optional. When a grand jury is not used, the discretion of whether to charge is left to the prosecutor, who must then present his or her argument at the preliminary hearing (discussed earlier in the chapter).

Special Features of Grand Juries Grand juries are *impaneled*, or created, for a period of time usually not exceeding three months. For the most part, grand jury proceedings are dominated by the prosecution, which can present a wide variety of evidence against the defendant, including photographs, documents, tangible objects, and the testimony of witnesses. Generally speaking, grand juries differ from trials, which we will discuss in the next chapter, in that:

1. Jurors can ask the district attorney and the judge questions about relevant law, and can request that witnesses be recalled to the stand to testify a second time.
2. The defense cannot cross-examine prosecution witnesses, though it can present its own witnesses.
3. The proceedings are closed (secret). Witnesses can speak publicly, but only about their own testimony. Members of the grand jury are not allowed to speak to the media.

The confidential nature of grand jury proceedings tends to come under criticism during high-profile cases such as the 2014 shooting death of Michael Brown by police officer Darren Wilson, covered in Chapter 1. After a grand jury failed to indict Wilson, the St. Louis County prosecutor decided to make public thousands of documents related to the hearings in an effort to demonstrate that the hearings had been fair and balanced.

This unusual strategy backfired. The transcripts showed prosecutors giving deference to Wilson and aggressively challenging witnesses who contradicted the officer's version of the events leading to Brown's death.[59] In addition, an anonymous grand juror, frustrated by the gag rule, sued the St. Louis county prosecutor for the right to speak, an issue covered in this chapter's *CJ Policy—Your Take feature.*

A "Rubber Stamp" Following the release of the grand jury documents in the Michael Brown case, a lawyer for the Brown family made a familiar complaint about the process. "If you present evidence to indict, you get an indictment," he said. "If you present evidence not to indict, you don't get an indictment."[60] Certainly, the procedural rules of the grand jury favor prosecutors. The exclusionary rule (see Chapter 7) does not apply in grand jury investigations, so prosecutors can present evidence that would be disallowed at any subsequent trial. Furthermore, the grand jury is given the prosecution's version of the facts, with the defense having only a limited ability to offer counterarguments.

In the words of one observer, a grand jury would indict a "ham sandwich" if the government asked it to do so.[61] Overall, defendants are indicted at a rate of more than 99 percent,[62] leading to the common characterization of the grand jury as little more than a "rubber stamp" for the prosecution.

CJ Policy—Your Take

There are several reasons for **grand jury secrecy,** including protecting the identity of witnesses who might otherwise be reluctant to testify. Following a grand jury's decision not to indict police officer Darren Wilson for the shooting death of Michael Brown, however, one of the jurors sued the county for the right to speak to the media about the case. This juror apparently wanted to contradict the community's assumption that the grand jury's decision had been unanimous. Would you be in favor of legislation that allows grand jury members to go public? Why or why not?

Indictment A charge or written accusation, issued by a grand jury, that probable cause exists to believe that a named person has committed a crime.

The Prosecutorial Screening Process

Some see the high government success rates in pretrial proceedings as proof that prosecutors successfully screen out weak cases before they get to a grand jury or preliminary hearing. If, however, grand juries have indeed abandoned their traditional duties in favor of "rubber stamping" most cases set in front of them, and preliminary hearings are little better, what is to keep prosecutors from using their charging powers indiscriminately?

Nothing, say many observers. Once the police have initially charged a defendant with committing a crime, the prosecutor can prosecute the case as it stands, reduce or increase the initial charge, file additional charges, or dismiss the case. In a system of government and law that relies on checks and balances, asked legal expert Kenneth Culp Davis, why should the prosecutor be "immune to review by other officials and immune to review by the courts?"[63] (For information on another prosecutor-friendly system, see the feature *Comparative Criminal Justice—Japan's All-Powerful Prosecutors.*) Though American prosecutors have far-ranging discretionary charging powers, it is not entirely correct to say that they are unrestricted. Controls are indirect and informal, but they do exist.

Comparative Criminal Justice

Central Intelligence Agency

Japan's All-Powerful Prosecutors

Prosecutors in the United States are generally believed to have a great deal of charging discretion. The discretionary power of American prosecutors, however, does not equal that of their Japanese counterparts. With the ability to "cherry pick" their cases, prosecutors in Japan routinely have annual conviction rates of about 99 percent.

The "Confession Mill"

One observer described the Japanese courts as a "confession mill." Unlike the American system, Japan has no arraignment procedure during which the accused can plead guilty or innocent. Instead, the focus of the Japanese criminal justice system is on extracting confessions of guilt: police can hold and question suspects for up to twenty-three days without pressing charges. Furthermore, the suspect has no absolute right to counsel during the interrogation, and police are often able to get confessions that make for open-and-shut convictions. The prosecutor also has the "benevolent" discretion to drop the case altogether if the suspect expresses remorse.

In addition, the extraordinarily high conviction rate is a product of Japanese culture. To fail in an attempt to convict results in a loss of face, not only for the individual prosecutor but also for the court system as a whole. The Japanese

Justice Ministry estimates that, to avoid the risk of losing, prosecutors decline to press charges against 35 percent of indictable suspects each year. Japanese judges—there are almost no juries—contribute to the high conviction rate by rarely questioning the manner in which prosecutors obtain confessions.

No Plea Bargaining

Interestingly, given the amount of prosecutorial discretion, the Japanese criminal justice system does not allow for plea bargaining. The Japanese see the practice of "trading" a guilty plea for a lesser sentence as counterproductive, as a defendant may be tempted to confess to crimes she or he did not commit if the prosecution has a strong case. For the Japanese, a confession extracted after, say, twenty-three days of interrogation may be "voluntary," but a confession gained through a promise of leniency is "forced" and therefore in conflict with the system's goals of truth seeking and accuracy.

For Critical Analysis

Explain the fundamental differences between the American and Japanese criminal justice systems. Do you think the lack of a comparable adversary system weakens or strengthens the Japanese system in comparison with the American one?

Case Attrition

Prosecutorial discretion includes the power *not* to prosecute cases. Figure 9.4 depicts the average outcomes of one hundred felony arrests in the United States. As you can see, of the sixty-five adult arrestees brought before the district attorney, only thirty-five are prosecuted, and only eighteen of these prosecutions lead to incarceration. Consequently, fewer than one in three adults arrested for a felony sees the inside of a prison or jail cell. This phenomenon is known as **case attrition,** and it is explained in part by prosecutorial discretion.

Scarce Resources About half of those adult felony cases brought to prosecutors by police are dismissed through a *nolle prosequi* (Latin for "unwilling to pursue"). Why are these cases "nolled," or not prosecuted by the district attorney? In the section on law enforcement, you learned that the police do not have the resources to arrest every lawbreaker in the nation. Similarly, district attorneys do not have the resources to prosecute every arrest. They must choose how to distribute their scarce resources.

In some cases, the decision is made for prosecutors, such as when police break procedural law and negate important evidence. This happens rarely—less than 3 percent of felony arrests are dropped because of the exclusionary rule, and almost all of these are the result of illegal drug searches.[64]

Case Attrition The process through which prosecutors, by deciding whether to prosecute each person arrested, effect an overall reduction in the number of persons prosecuted.

FIGURE 9.4 **Following One Hundred Felony Arrests: The Criminal Justice Funnel**

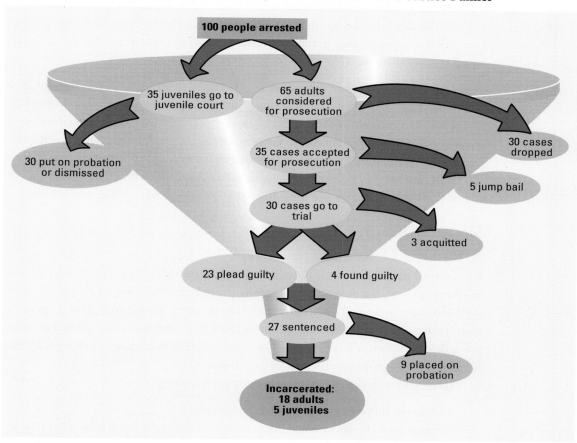

Source: Adapted from Todd R. Clear, George F. Cole, and Michael D. Reisig, *American Corrections,* 9th ed. (Belmont, CA: Wadsworth, 2011), 134.

LEARNING
8
OBJECTIVE

Screening Factors Most prosecutors have a *screening* process for deciding when to prosecute and when to "noll." This process varies a bit from jurisdiction to jurisdiction, but most prosecutors consider several factors in making the decision:[65]

- The most important factor in deciding whether to prosecute is not the prosecutor's belief in the guilt of the suspect, but whether there is *sufficient evidence for conviction.* If prosecutors have strong physical evidence and a number of reliable and believable witnesses, they are quite likely to prosecute.

- Prosecutors also rely heavily on *offense seriousness* to guide their priorities, preferring to take on felony offenses rather than misdemeanors. In other words, everything else being equal, a district attorney will prosecute a rapist instead of a jaywalker because the former presents a greater threat to society than does the latter. A prosecutor will also be more likely to prosecute someone with an extensive record of wrongdoing than a first-time offender.

- Sometimes a case is dropped even when it involves a serious crime and a wealth of evidence exists against the suspect. These situations usually involve *uncooperative victims.* As you saw in Chapter 3, domestic violence cases are particularly difficult to prosecute because the victims may want to keep the matter private, fear reprisals, or have a strong desire to protect their abuser. In some jurisdictions, as many as 80 percent of domestic violence victims refuse to cooperate with the prosecution.[66]

- *Unreliability of victims* can also affect a charging decision. If the victim in a rape case is a crack addict and a prostitute, while the defendant is a decorated military veteran, prosecutors may be hesitant to have a jury decide which one is more trustworthy.

- A prosecutor may be willing to drop a case or reduce the charges against *a defendant who is willing to testify against other offenders.* Federal law encourages this kind of behavior by offering sentencing reductions to defendants who provide "substantial assistance in the investigation or prosecution of another person who has committed an offense."[67]

Often, prosecutors are motivated by a sense of doing "the right thing" for their communities. In 2014, for example, Bristol County (Massachusetts) district attorney Sam Sutter dropped conspiracy charges against two environmental activists who used illegal means to block a shipment of coal to the Brayton Point Power Station. Sutter justified his decision by stating that he supported the defendants' goal of lessening climate change, "one of the gravest crises our planet has ever faced."[68] (To get a better idea of the difficulty of some charging decisions, see the feature *Discretion in Action—A Battered Woman.*)

Prosecutorial Charging and the Defense Attorney

For the most part, there is little the defense attorney can do when the prosecutor decides to charge a client. If a defense attorney feels strongly that the charge has been made in violation of the defendant's rights, he or she can, however, submit *pretrial motions* to the court requesting that a particular action be taken to protect his or her client. For example, a defense attorney has the option of filing a motion to dismiss the charges against her or his client completely because of lack of evidence.

Other common pretrial motions include the following:

1. Motions to suppress evidence obtained illegally.
2. Motions for a change of venue because the defendant cannot receive a fair trial in the original jurisdiction.

Discretion in Action

A Battered Woman

The Situation For more than twenty years, John regularly beat his wife, Judy. He even put out cigarettes on her skin and slashed her face with glass. John was often unemployed and forced Judy into prostitution to earn a living. He regularly denied her food and threatened to maim or kill her. Judy left home several times, but John always managed to find her, bring her home, and punish her. Finally, Judy took steps to get John put in a psychiatric hospital. He told her that if anybody came for him, he would "see them coming" and cut her throat before they arrived. That night, Judy shot John three times in the back of the head while he was asleep, killing him. You are the prosecutor with authority over Judy.

The Law In your jurisdiction, a person can use deadly force in self-defense if it is necessary to kill an unlawful aggressor to save himself or herself from imminent death. (See Chapter 4 for a review of self-defense.) Voluntary manslaughter is the intentional killing of another human being without malice. It covers crimes of passion. First degree murder is premeditated killing, with malice. (Also, see Chapter 4 for a review of the different degrees of murder.)

What Would You Do? Will you charge Judy with voluntary manslaughter or first degree murder? Alternatively, do you believe she was acting in self-defense, in which case you will not charge her with any crime? Explain your choice.

[To see how a Rutherford County, North Carolina, prosecutor decided a case with similar facts, go to Example 9.2 in Appendix B.]

---

3. Motions to invalidate a search warrant.
4. Motions to dismiss the case because of a delay in bringing it to trial.
5. Motions to obtain evidence that the prosecution may be withholding.

As we shall soon see, defense attorneys sometimes use these pretrial motions to pressure the prosecution into offering a favorable deal for their client.

EthicsChallenge

What are the potential ethical pitfalls of the practice, common among prosecutors, of reducing the charges against a defendant who is willing to testify against other offenders? ■

Pleading Guilty

Based on the information (delivered during the preliminary hearing) or indictment (handed down by the grand jury), the prosecutor submits a motion to the court to order the defendant to appear before the trial court for an **arraignment.** Due process of law, as guaranteed by the Fifth Amendment, requires that a criminal defendant be informed of the charges brought against her or him and be offered an opportunity to respond to those charges. The arraignment is one of the ways in which due process requirements are satisfied by criminal procedure law.

At the arraignment, the defendant is informed of the charges and must respond by pleading not guilty or guilty. In some but not all states, the defendant may also enter a plea of *nolo contendere,* which is Latin for "I will not contest it." The plea of *nolo contendere* is neither an admission nor a denial of guilt. (The consequences for someone who pleads guilty and for someone who pleads *nolo contendere* are the same in a criminal trial, but the latter plea cannot be used in a subsequent civil trial as an admission of guilt.) Most frequently, the defendant pleads guilty to the initial charge or to a lesser charge that has been agreed on through *plea bargaining*

Arraignment A court proceeding in which the suspect is formally charged with the criminal offense stated in the indictment.

Nolo Contendere Latin for "I will not contest it." A criminal defendant's plea, in which he or she chooses not to challenge, or contest, the charges brought by the government.

between the prosecutor and the defendant. If the defendant pleads guilty, no trial is necessary, and the defendant is sentenced based on the crime he or she has admitted committing.

Plea Bargaining in the Criminal Justice System

Plea bargaining most often takes place after the arraignment and before the beginning of the trial. In its simplest terms, it is a process by which the accused, represented by the defense counsel, and the prosecutor work out a mutually satisfactory disposition of the case, subject to court approval.

Usually, plea bargaining involves the defendant's pleading guilty to the charges against her or him in return for a lighter sentence, but other variations are possible as well. The defendant can agree to plead guilty in exchange for having the charge against her or him reduced from, say, felony burglary to the lesser offense of breaking and entering. Or a person charged with multiple counts may agree to plead guilty if the prosecutor agrees to drop one or more of the counts. Whatever the particulars, the results of a plea bargain are generally the same: the prosecutor gets a conviction, and the defendant a lesser punishment.

In *Santobello v. New York* (1971),[69] the Supreme Court held that plea bargaining "is not only an essential part of the process but a highly desirable part for many reasons." Some observers would agree, but with ambivalence. They understand that plea bargaining offers the practical benefit of saving court resources, but question whether it is the best way to achieve justice.[70] We will address the question of whether plea bargaining is an acceptable means of determining the defendant's fate in the *CJ in Action* feature at the end of the chapter.

Motivations for Plea Bargaining

Indicate why prosecutors, defense attorneys, and defendants often agree to plea bargains.
LEARNING
9
OBJECTIVE

Given the high rate of plea bargaining—accounting for 97 percent of criminal convictions in state courts[71]—it follows that the prosecutor, defense attorney, and defendant each have strong reasons to engage in the practice.

Prosecutors and Plea Bargaining In most cases, a prosecutor has a single goal after charging a defendant with a crime: conviction. If a case goes to trial, no matter how certain a prosecutor may be that the defendant is guilty, there is always a chance that a jury or judge will disagree. Plea bargaining removes this risk. Furthermore, the prosecutorial screening process described earlier in the chapter is not infallible. Sometimes, a prosecutor will find that the evidence against the accused is weaker than first thought or will uncover new information that changes the complexion of the case. In these situations, the prosecutor may decide to drop the charges or, if he or she still feels that the defendant is guilty, turn to plea bargaining to "save" a questionable case.

The prosecutor's role as an administrator also comes into play. She or he may be interested in the quickest, most efficient manner to dispose of caseloads, and plea bargains reduce the time and money spent on each case. Personal philosophy can affect the proceedings as well. A prosecutor who feels that a mandatory minimum sentence for a particular crime, such as marijuana possession, is too strict may plea bargain in order to lessen the penalty. Similarly, some prosecutors will consider plea bargaining only in certain instances—for burglary and theft, for example, but not for more serious felonies such as rape and murder.

Plea Bargaining The process by which the accused and the prosecutor work out a mutually satisfactory conclusion to the case, subject to court approval.

Defense Attorneys and Plea Bargaining

Political scientist Milton Heumann has said that a defense attorney's most important lesson is that "most of his [or her] clients are guilty."[72] Given this stark reality, favorable plea bargains are often the best a defense attorney can do for clients, aside from helping them to gain acquittals. Some have suggested that defense attorneys have other, less savory motives for convincing a client to plead guilty, such as a desire to increase profit margins by quickly disposing of cases[73] or a wish to ingratiate themselves with the other members of the courtroom work group by showing their "reasonableness."[74]

Defendants and Plea Bargaining The plea bargain allows the defendant a measure of control over his or her fate. In August 2014, for example, Miranda Barbour and her husband, Elytte, pleaded guilty to second degree murder in a Northumberland County (Pennsylvania) court for killing a man they had arranged to meet using the online classified site Craigslist. Had the case gone to trial, the couple risked being convicted of first degree murder and given the death penalty. Instead, under the terms of the plea agreement, the Barbours will spend the rest of their lives in jail. As Figure 9.5 shows, defendants who plea bargain receive significantly lighter sentences on average than those who are found guilty at trial.

▲ Why did Miranda Barbour, shown here being escorted out of a Sunbury, Pennsylvania, courtroom, agree to plead guilty to second degree murder for killing a man she met on Craigslist? What incentives might local prosecutors have had for accepting Barbour's guilty plea and declining to seek her execution? AP Images/PennLive.com, Christine Baker, File

Victims and Plea Bargaining One of the major goals of the victims' rights movement has been to increase the role of victims in the plea bargaining process. In recent years, the movement has had some success in this area. About half of the states now allow for victim participation in plea bargaining. Many have laws similar to North Carolina's statute that requires the district attorney's office to offer victims "the opportunity to consult with the prosecuting attorney" and give their views on "plea possibilities."[75] On the federal level, the Crime Victims' Rights Act grants victims the right to be "reasonably heard" during the process.[76]

Crime victims often have mixed emotions regarding plea bargains. On the one hand, any form of "negotiated justice" that lessens the offender's penalty may add insult to the victim's emotional and physical injuries. "No punishment will ever be long enough, harsh enough," said the widow of Miranda and Elytte Barbour's murder victim after the couple was sentenced to life in prison, as described earlier in this section.[77] On the other hand, trials can bring up events and emotions that some victims would rather not have to reexperience. District Attorney Ann Targonski said that she allowed the Barbours' guilty plea to spare the victim's family the trauma of court proceedings that could have lasted decades.[78]

Plea Bargaining and the Adversary System

One criticism of plea bargaining is that it subverts the adversary system, the goal of which is to determine innocence or guilt. Although plea bargaining does value negotiation over conflict, it is important to remember that it does so in a context in which legal guilt has already been established. Even within this context, plea bargaining is not completely divorced from the adversary process.

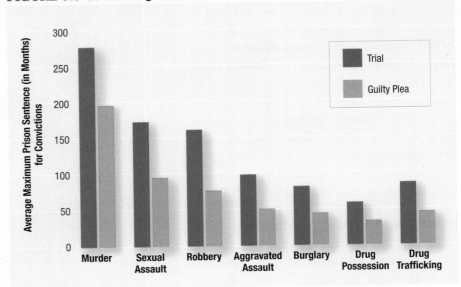

FIGURE 9.5 Sentencing Outcomes for Guilty Pleas

Source: Bureau of Justice Statistics, *Felony Sentences in State Courts, 2006—Statistical Tables* (Washington, D.C.: U.S. Department of Justice, December 2009), Table 4.3.

Strategies to Induce a Plea Bargain Earlier, we pointed out that the most likely reason why a prosecutor does not bring charges is the lack of a strong case. This is also the most common reason why a prosecutor agrees to a plea bargain once charges have been brought. Defense attorneys are well aware of this fact and often file numerous pretrial motions in an effort to weaken the state's case. Even if the judge does not accept the motions, the defense may hope that the time required to process them will wear on the prosecutor's patience. As one district attorney has said, "[T]he usual defense strategy today is to bring in a stack of motions as thick as a Sunday newspaper; defense attorneys hope that we won't have the patience to ride them out."[79]

Prosecutors have their own methods of inducing a plea bargain. The most common is the ethically questionable practice of *overcharging*—that is, charging the defendant with more counts than may be appropriate. There are two types of overcharging:

1. In *horizontal overcharging*, the prosecutor brings a number of different counts for a single criminal incident.
2. In *vertical overcharging*, the prosecutor raises the level of a charge above its proper place.

After overcharging, prosecutors allow themselves to be "bargained down" to the correct charge, giving the defense attorney and the defendant the impression that they have achieved some sort of victory.

Protecting the Defendant Watching the defense attorney and the prosecutor maneuver in this manner, the defendant often comes to the conclusion that the plea bargaining process is a sort of game with sometimes incomprehensible rules. The Supreme Court is also aware of the potential for taking advantage of the defendant in plea bargaining and has taken steps to protect the accused. (For a summary of notable Supreme Court cases involving plea bargaining procedures, see Figure 9.6.) Until *Boykin*

FIGURE 9.6 Notable United States Supreme Court Decisions on Plea Bargaining

The constitutional justification of the plea bargain as an accepted part of the criminal justice process has been fortified by these Supreme Court rulings.

Brady v. United States (397 U.S. 742 [1970]). In this case the defendant entered a guilty plea in order to avoid the death penalty. In allowing this action, the Court ruled that **plea bargains are a legitimate part of the adjudication process as long as they are entered into voluntarily and the defendant has full knowledge of the consequences of pleading guilty.**

North Carolina v. Alford (400 U.S. 25 [1970]). Although maintaining he was innocent of the first degree murder with which he was charged, Alford pleaded guilty to second degree murder in order to avoid the possibility of the death penalty that came with the original charges. After being sentenced to thirty years in prison, Alford argued that he was forced to plea bargain because of the threat of the death penalty.

The Court refused to invalidate Alford's guilty plea, stating that **plea bargains are valid even if the defendant claims innocence, as long as the plea was entered into voluntarily.**

Santobello v. New York (404 U.S. 257 [1971]). This case focused on the prosecutor's role in the plea bargain process. The Court ruled that **if a prosecutor promises a more lenient sentence in return for the defendant's guilty plea, the promise must be kept.**

Ricketts v. Adamson (483 U.S. 1 [1987]). In return for a reduction of charges, Ricketts agreed to plead guilty and to testify against a co-defendant in a murder case. When the co-defendant's conviction was reversed on appeal, Ricketts refused to testify a second

time. Therefore, the prosecutor rescinded the offer of leniency. The Court ruled that the prosecutor's action was justified, and that **defendants must uphold their side of the plea bargain in order to receive its benefits.**

United States v. Mezzanatto (513 U.S. 196 [1995]). The Court ruled that a prosecutor can refuse to plea bargain with a defendant unless the defendant agrees that any statements made by him or her during the bargaining process can be used against him or her in a possible trial. In other words, **if the defendant admits to committing the crime during plea bargain negotiations, and then decides to plead not guilty, the prosecution can use the admission as evidence during the trial.**

---

v. Alabama (1969),[80] judges would often accept the defense counsel's word that the defendant wanted to plead guilty. In that case, the Court held that the defendant must make a clear statement that he or she accepts the plea bargain. As a result, many jurisdictions now ask the accused to sign a *Boykin* **form** waiving his or her right to a trial.

Faulty Advice In 2012, the Supreme Court dramatically affected plea bargaining law by ruling that defendants have a constitutional right to effective representation during plea negotiations.[81] That year, the Court considered the plight of Anthony Cooper, who had shot a woman in Detroit. Based on faulty legal advice from his attorney, Cooper rejected a plea bargain that called for a sentence of four to seven years behind bars. Instead, he lost at trial and was sentenced to fifteen to thirty years. After hearing Cooper's appeal, the Court found that, in essence, defendants have a constitutional right to effective counsel during plea bargaining, just as they do during a trial.

A Second Chance to Plead Because of the Supreme Court's ruling, defendants like Anthony Cooper now have the opportunity to argue that had they received proper legal advice, they would have accepted the plea bargain rather than risk a trial. If a defendant successfully proves ineffective counsel during plea bargaining, he or she will be given another chance to make a favorable plea.[82] The four members of the Court who dissented from this decision warned that it would give defendants who lose at trial an unfair opportunity to revisit a rejected plea bargain. "It's going to be tricky," agrees Stephanos Bibas, a law professor at the University of Pennsylvania. "There are going to be a lot of defendants who say after they're convicted that they really would have taken the plea."[83]

Pleading Not Guilty

Despite the large number of defendants who eventually plead guilty, the plea of not guilty is fairly common at the arraignment. This is true even when the facts of the case seem

Boykin Form A form that must be completed by a defendant who pleads guilty. The defendant states that she or he has done so voluntarily and with full comprehension of the consequences.

stacked against the defendant. Generally, a not guilty plea in the face of strong evidence is part of a strategy to

1. Gain a more favorable plea bargain,
2. Challenge a crucial part of the evidence on constitutional grounds, or
3. Submit one of the affirmative defenses that we discussed in Chapter 4.

Of course, if either side is confident in the strength of its arguments and evidence, it will obviously be less likely to accept a plea bargain. Both prosecutors and defense attorneys may favor a trial to gain publicity, and sometimes public pressure after an extremely violent or high-profile crime will force a chief prosecutor (who is, remember, normally an elected official) to take a weak case to trial. Also, some defendants may insist on their right to a trial, regardless of their attorneys' advice. In the next chapter, we will examine what happens to the roughly 3 percent of indictments that do lead to the courtroom.

CJ IN ACTION

The Plea Bargain Puzzle

In June 2014, Thomas Neely pleaded guilty to attempted first degree murder for stabbing his wife, Elizabeth Allen, multiple times in their Union County (North Carolina) home. As part of the plea agreement, he was sentenced to fifteen years in prison, rather than the forty years he could have received if he had been found guilty at trial. For her part, Allen was not pleased with the result. "What he did was so bad, how could he get such a little bit of time?" she asked.[84] Prosecutor Trey Robison defended the deal, saying that "the vast majority of cases we handle we seek some kind of compromise resolution, if one can be reached, because we simply don't have the court resources to try every case."[85] In this *CJ in Action* feature, we will examine the pros and cons of plea bargaining, a source of constant frustration for defendants, attorneys, and victims that the American court system apparently cannot live without.

Adversarial and Inevitable

Those who support plea bargaining often do so because they fear the alternative. In 1970, Supreme Court chief justice Warren Burger warned that "a reduction from 90 percent to 80 percent in guilty pleas requires the assignment of twice the judicial manpower and facilities—judges, court reporters, bailiffs, clerks, jurors, and courtrooms." Burger added, "A reduction to 70 percent trebles this demand."[86] This practicality bothers some observers. "Because of plea bargaining, I guess we can say, 'Gee, the trains run on time,'" notes criminologist Franklin Zimring. "But do we like where they're going?"[87]

The Case for Plea Bargaining

- Plea bargaining provides prosecutors and defense attorneys with the flexibility to quickly dispose of some cases while allocating scarce resources to the cases that require them.

- Because of mandatory minimum sentencing, which you will study in Chapter 11, criminal defendants who go to trial risk very harsh punishments if they lose. Plea bargaining allows them to mitigate that risk and accept a lesser sentence.

- The practice spares victims from reliving the horrors of their victimization as courtroom witnesses.

The Case against Plea Bargaining

- Plea bargaining gives innocent people an incentive to plead guilty if they feel that there is even a slight chance that a jury or judge might decide against them. "I tell people, 'If you think ten years is too long to serve and the other option is to get twenty, I want you to think, how would you feel nine years from now?'" said one public defender. "Those aren't the options people should have."[88]

- Plea bargaining gives prosecutors too much power to coerce defendants, either by overcharging or by claiming to have evidence that the prosecutor knows would actually be inadmissible at trial, such as contraband gained by an illegal search. (Incidentally, the Supreme Court has ruled that prosecutors are within their rights to threaten defendants with harsher sentences to induce a guilty plea.)[89]

- The practice allows dangerous criminals to "beat the system" by negotiating for lighter sentences than they deserve. Consequently, it undermines the deterrent effects of punishment and the public's confidence in the criminal justice system.

Your Opinion—Writing Assignment

About fifteen years ago, Shelby County (Tennessee) district attorney General Bill Gibbons instituted a "no deals" policy for certain crimes prosecuted by his office. The policy covers many violent crimes, including first degree murder, second degree murder, aggravated robbery, aggravated rape, carjacking, and attempted first degree murder. The idea is simple: should a defendant in Shelby County be indicted for one of these, he or she will not get the "benefit" of a plea bargain for a lesser punishment or a lesser charge.

What is your opinion of "no deals" policies for specific crimes? What impact do such policies have on prosecutors, defense attorneys, and defendants? If you agree with this strategy, to which crimes would you apply it and why? Before responding, you can review our discussions in the sections of this chapter concerning:

- Case attrition ("The Prosecutorial Screening Process").

- Motivations for plea bargaining ("Pleading Guilty").

- Plea bargaining and the adversary system ("Pleading Guilty").

Your answer should include at least three full paragraphs.

Summary

For more information on these concepts, look back to the Learning Objective icons throughout the chapter.

 List the different names given to public prosecutors and indicate the general powers that they have. At the federal level, the prosecutor is called the U.S. attorney. In state and local courts, the prosecutor may be referred to as the prosecuting attorney, state attorney, district attorney, county attorney, or city attorney. Prosecutors in general have the power to decide when and how the state will pursue an individual suspected of criminal wrongdoing. In some jurisdictions, the district attorney is also the chief law enforcement officer, holding broad powers over police operations.

 Contrast the prosecutor's roles as an elected official and as a crime fighter. In most instances, the prosecutor is elected and therefore may feel obliged to reward members of her or his party with jobs. To win reelection or higher political office, the prosecutor may feel a need to bow to community pressures. As a crime fighter, the prosecutor is dependent on the police, and indeed prosecutors are generally seen as law enforcement agents. Prosecutors, however, generally pursue cases only when they believe there is sufficient legal guilt to obtain a conviction.

 Delineate the responsibilities of defense attorneys. (a) Representation of the defendant during the custodial process; (b) investigation of the supposed criminal incident; (c) communication with the prosecutor (including plea bargaining); (d) preparation of the case for trial; (e) submission of defense motions; (f) representation of the defendant at trial; (g) negotiation of a sentence after conviction; and (h) appeal of a guilty verdict.

 Explain why defense attorneys must often defend clients they know to be guilty. In our adversary system, the most important responsibility of a defense attorney is to be an advocate for her or his client. This means ensuring that the client's constitutional rights are protected during criminal justice proceedings, regardless of whether the client is guilty or innocent.

 Identify the steps involved in the pretrial criminal process. (a) Suspect taken into custody or arrested; (b) initial appearance before a magistrate, at which time the defendant is informed of his or her constitutional rights and a public defender may be appointed or private counsel may be hired by the state to represent the defendant; (c) the posting of bail or release on recognizance; (d) preventive detention, if deemed necessary to ensure the safety of other persons or the community, or regular detention, if the defendant is unable to post bail; (e) preliminary hearing (mini-trial), at which the judge rules on whether there is probable cause and the prosecutor issues an information; or in the alternative (f) grand jury hearings, after which an indictment is issued against the defendant if the grand jury finds probable cause; (g) arraignment, in which the defendant is informed of the charges and must respond by pleading not guilty or guilty (or in some cases *nolo contendere*); and (h) plea bargaining.

 Indicate the three influences on a judge's decision to set bail. (a) Uncertainty about the character and past criminal history of the defendant; (b) the risk that the defendant will commit another crime if out on bail; and (c) overcrowded jails, which may influence a judge to release a defendant on bail.

 Identify the main difference between an indictment and an information. An indictment is the grand jury's declaration that probable cause exists to charge a defendant with a specific crime. In jurisdictions that do not use grand juries, the prosecution issues an information as the formal charge of a crime.

 Explain how a prosecutor screens potential cases. (a) Is there sufficient evidence for conviction? (b) What is the priority of the case? The more serious the alleged crime, the higher the priority. The more extensive the defendant's criminal record, the higher the priority. (c) Are the victims cooperative? Violence against family members often yields uncooperative victims, so these cases are rarely prosecuted. (d) Are the victims reliable? (e) Might the defendant be willing to testify against other offenders?

 Indicate why prosecutors, defense attorneys, and defendants often agree to plea bargains. For prosecutors, a plea bargain removes the risk of losing the case at trial, particularly if the evidence against the defendant is weak. For defense attorneys, the plea bargain may be the best deal possible for a potentially guilty client. For defendants, plea bargains give a measure of control over a highly uncertain future.

Questions for Critical Analysis

1. According to the United States Supreme Court, prosecutors cannot face civil lawsuits for misconduct, even if they have deliberately sent an innocent person to prison. In practical terms, why do you think prosecutors are protected in this manner? Do you think the Supreme Court should lift this immunity for prosecutors? Why or why not?

2. Why might the practice of charging low-income defendants fees for the services of public defenders go against the Supreme Court's ruling in *Gideon v. Wainwright*?

3. Preventive detention laws raise the troubling issue of *false positives*, or erroneous predictions that defendants, if released before trial, would commit a crime when in fact they would not. Why do you think that legislators, judges, and citizens are willing to accept the possibility of false positives when denying pretrial release to certain defendants?

4. In practice, the constitutional right to a lawyer does not cover initial bail hearings. What are the disadvantages for an indigent defendant who is not represented by a lawyer at this point in the pretrial process?

5. Review the Supreme Court's ruling, discussed in the last section of this chapter, that defendants have a constitutional right to effective representation during plea negotiations. Do you think the Court made the proper ruling? Why or why not?

Key Terms

arraignment   301
attorney-client privilege   290
attorney general   282
bail   291
bail bond agent   294
Boykin form   305
case attrition   299

defense attorney   285
discovery   296
grand jury   296
indictment   297
information   296
initial appearance   291
nolo contendere   301

plea bargaining   302
preliminary hearing   296
preventive detention   295
property bond   294
public defenders   286
public prosecutors   281
release on recognizance (ROR)   293

Notes

1. Jerry Bonkowski, "Tony Stewart Awaits District Attorney's Review of Kevin Ward Jr. Case," *Motor Sports Talk* (September 15, 2014), at **motorsportstalk.nbcsports .com/2014/09/15/what-might-happen -to-tony-stewart-when-district-attorneys -review-of-kevin-ward-jr-case-is -completed/**.

2. 295 U.S. 78 (1935).

3. *Brady v. Maryland*, 373 U.S. 83 (1963).

4. Brendan Kirby, "Judge Overturns 13-Year-Old Capital Murder Conviction of Mobile-Based State Trooper," *AL.com* (September 4, 2013), at **blog.al.com/live/2013/09/judge _overturns_13-year-old_ca.html**.

5. Celesta Albonetti, "Prosecutorial Discretion: The Effects of Uncertainty," *Law and Society Review* 21 (1987), 291–313.

6. Siddhartha Bandyopadhyay and Bryan C. McCannon, "The Effect of the Election of Public Prosecutors on Criminal Trials," Working Paper (October 12, 2010), at **editorial express.com/cgi-bin/conference/down load.cgi?db_name=res2011&paper _id=436**.

7. Bryan C. McCannon, "Prosecutor Elections, Mistakes, and Appeals," 7th Annual Conference on Empirical Legal Studies Paper (July 3, 2012), at **papers.ssrn.com/sol3/papers .cfm?abstract_id=2099730**.

8. Quoted in Dugan Arnett, "Nightmare in Maryville: Teens' Sexual Encounter Ignites a Firestorm against Family," *Kansas City Star* (October 24, 2013), at **www.kansascity .com/2013/10/12/4549775/nightmare -in-maryville-teens-sexual.html**.

9. Quoted in *ibid*.

10. *Ibid*.

11. Stephanie Slifer, "Daisy's Mom Disappointed over Charge in Maryville Case," *CBS News* (January 9, 2014), at **www.cbsnews.com /news/daisys-mom-disappointed-over -charge-in-maryville-case/**.

12. Herbert Packer, *Limits of the Criminal Sanction* (Stanford, Calif.: Stanford University Press, 1968), 166–167.

13. William T. Stetzer, "A Collaborative Approach to Plea Offers," *The Police Chief* (April 2014), 26–29.

14. Bennett L. Gershman, "Prosecutorial Ethics and Victims' Rights: The Prosecutor's Duty of Neutrality," *Lewis & Clark Law Review* 9 (2005), 561.

15. Gershman, *op. cit*., 560–561.

16. *Gideon v. Wainwright,* 372 U.S. 335 (1963); *Massiah v. United States,* 377 U.S. 201 (1964); *United States v. Wade,* 388 U.S. 218 (1967); *Argersinger v. Hamlin,* 407 U.S. 25 (1972); and *Brewer v. Williams,* 430 U.S. 387 (1977).

17. Larry Siegel, *Criminology,* 6th ed. (Belmont, Calif.: West/Wadsworth Publishing Co., 1998), 487–488.

18. Center for Professional Responsibility, *Model Rules of Professional Conduct* (Washington, D.C.: American Bar Association, 2003), Rules 1.6 and 3.1.

19. *United States v. Wade,* 388 U.S. 218, 256–258 (1967).

20. 372 U.S. 335 (1963).

21. 387 U.S. 1 (1967).

22. 407 U.S. 25 (1972).

23. Laurence A. Benner, "Eliminating Excessive Public Defender Workloads," *Criminal Justice* (Summer 2011), 25.

24. American Bar Association, "Providing Defense Services," Standard 5-7.1, at **www.abanet.org/crimjust/standards/defsvcs _blk.html#7.1.**

25. Robert C. Boruchowitz, "The Right to Counsel: Every Accused Person's Right," *Washington State Bar Association Bar News* (January 2004), at **www.wsba.org /media/publications/barnews/2004 /jan-04-boruchowitz.htm.**

26. Bureau of Justice Statistics, *County-Based and Local Public Defender Offices, 2007* (Washington, D.C.: U.S. Department of Justice, September 2010), 3.

27. "State-by-State Court Fees," *npr.org* (May 19, 2014), at **www.npr.org/2014/05/19 /312455680/state-by-state-court-fees.**

28. Alicia Bannon, Mitali Nagrecha, and Rebekah Diller, *Criminal Justice Debt: A Barrier to Reentry* (New York: Brennan Center for Justice, October 2010), 12.

29. *United States v. Gonzalez-Lopez,* 548 U.S. 140 (2006).

30. *Wheat v. United States,* 486 U.S. 153, 159 (1988).

31. Bureau of Justice Statistics, *Defense Counsel in Criminal Cases* (Washington, D.C.: U.S. Department of Justice, 2000), 3.

32. James M. Anderson and Paul Heaton, *Measuring the Effect of Defense Counsel on Homicide Case Outcomes: Executive Summary* (Santa Monica, Calif.: RAND Corporation, December 2012), 1.

33. Peter A. Joy and Kevin C. McMunigal, "Does a Lawyer Make a Difference? Public Defender v. Appointed Counsel," *Criminal Justice* (Spring 2012), 46–47.

34. *County-Based and Local Public Defender Offices, 2007, op. cit.,* 1.

35. Adam Liptak, "Need-Blind Justice," *New York Times* (January 5, 2014), SR4.

36. *Public Defender, Eleventh Judicial Circuit of Florida v. State of Florida,* 115 So. 3d 261 (Fla. 2013).

37. Daniel Wiessner, "New York State to Settle Landmark Suit over Public Defenders," *Reuters* (October 21, 2014).

38. Liptak, *op. cit.*

39. 466 U.S. 668 (1984).

40. Sherman Smith, "Cheatham 'Elated' by Court's Decision to Give Him New Trial," *Topeka Capital Journal (Kansas)* (January 26, 2013), A1.

41. Jonathan D. Casper, *American Criminal Justice: The Defendant's Perspective* (Englewood Cliffs, N.J.: Prentice Hall, 1972), 101.

42. Quoted in Mark Pogrebin, *Qualitative Approaches to Criminal Justice* (Thousand Oaks, Calif.: Sage Publications, 2002), 173.

43. Randolph Braccialarghe, "Why Were Perry Mason's Clients Always Innocent?" *Valparaiso University Law Review* (Fall 2004), 65.

44. John Kaplan, "Defending Guilty People," *University of Bridgeport Law Review* (1986), 223.

45. 491 U.S. 554 (1989).

46. Quoted in Mitch Smith and Julie Bosman, "Despite Earlier Confessions, Suspect in Indiana Killings Refuses to Speak in Court," *New York Times* (October 23, 2014), A16.

47. *Riverside County, California v. McLaughlin,* 500 U.S. 44 (1991).

48. Bureau of Justice Statistics, *Felony Defendants in Large Urban Counties, 2009—Statistical Tables* (Washington, D.C.: U.S. Department of Justice, December 2013), 15.

49. *Bail Fail: Why the U.S. Should End the Practice of Using Money for Bail* (Washington, D.C.: Justice Policy Institute, September 2012), 13.

50. Illinois Annotated Statutes Chapter 725, Paragraph 5/110-5.

51. David W. Neubauer, *America's Courts and the Criminal Justice System,* 5th ed. (Belmont, Calif.: Wadsworth Publishing Co., 1996), 179–181.

52. Roy Flemming, C. Kohfeld, and Thomas Uhlman, "The Limits of Bail Reform: A Quasi Experimental Analysis," *Law and Society Review* 14 (1980), 947–976.

53. Michael R. Jones, *Unsecured Bonds: The As Effective and Most Efficient Pretrial Release Option* (Washington, D.C.: Pretrial Justice Institute, October 2013), 10–20.

54. John S. Goldkamp and Michael R. Gottfredson, *Policy Guidelines for Bail: An Experiment in Court Reform* (Philadelphia: Temple University Press, 1985), 18.

55. Adam Liptak, "Illegal Globally, Bail Profit Remains Pillar of U.S. Justice," *New York Times* (January 28, 2008), A1.

56. 18 U.S.C. Sections 3141–3150 (Supp. III 1985).

57. 481 U.S. 739 (1987).

58. Bureau of Justice Statistics, *Felony Defendants in Large Urban Counties, 2009—Statistical Tables* (Washington, D.C.: U.S. Department of Justice, December 2013), Table 18, page 21; and Table 19, page 21.

59. Julie Bosman, et al., "Amid Conflicting Accounts, Trusting Darren Wilson," *New York Times* (November 26, 2014), A1.

60. Quoted in *ibid.*

61. New York Court of Appeals Judge Sol Wachtler, quoted in David Margolik, "Law Professor to Administer Courts in State," *New York Times* (February 1, 1985), B2.

62. Sam Skolnick, "Grand Juries: Power Shift?" *The Legal Times* (April 12, 1999), 1.

63. Kenneth C. Davis, *Discretionary Justice: A Preliminary Inquiry* (Baton Rouge, La.: Louisiana State University Press, 1969), 189.

64. Milton Hirsh and David Oscar Markus, "Fourth Amendment Forum," *Champion* (December 2002), 42.

65. Bruce Frederick and Don Stemen, *The Anatomy of Discretion: An Analysis of Prosecutorial Decision Making—Summary Report* (New York: Vera Institute of Justice, December 2012), 4–16.

66. Tom Lininger, "Evidentiary Issues in Federal Prosecutions of Violence against Women," *Indiana Law Review* 36 (2003), 709.

67. 18 U.S.C. Section 3553(e) (2006).

68. Quoted in David Abel, "Bristol DA Drops Charges, Says Protesters Were Right," *Boston Globe* (September 9, 2014), A8.

69. 404 U.S. 257 (1971).

70. Fred C. Zacharias, "Justice in Plea Bargaining," *William and Mary Law Review* 39 (March 1998), 1121.

71. Bureau of Justice Statistics, *Prosecutors in State Courts, 2007—Statistical Tables* (Washington, D.C.: U.S. Department of Justice, December 2011), 2.

72. Milton Heumann, *Plea Bargaining: The Experiences of Prosecutors, Judges, and Defense Attorneys* (Chicago: University of Chicago Press, 1978), 58.

73. Albert W. Alschuler, "The Defense Attorney's Role in Plea Bargaining," *Yale Law Journal* 84 (1975), 1200.

74. Stephen J. Schulhofer, "Plea Bargaining as Disaster," *Yale Law Journal* 101 (1992), 1987.

75. North Carolina General Statutes Section 15A-832(f) (2003).

76. 18 U.S.C. Section 3771 (2004).

77. Quoted in John Beauge, "Widow to Pa. Craigslist Killer: 'No Punishment Will Ever Be Long Enough,'" *PennLive* (September 18, 2014), at **www.pennlive.com/midstate /index.ssf/2014/09/widows_says _craigslist_killers.html#incart_story _package**.

78. John Beauge, "Couple Avoid Death Penalty, Face Life in Prison for Pleading Guilty to Craigslist Murder," *PennLive* (August 26, 2014), at **www.pennlive.com/midstate /index.ssf/2014/08/couple_pleads _guilty_in_sunbur_1.html**.

79. Albert W. Alschuler, "The Prosecutor's Role in Plea Bargaining," *University of Chicago Law Review* 36 (1968), 53.

80. 395 U.S. 238 (1969).

81. *Lafler v. Cooper,* 132 S.Ct. 1376 (2012); and *Missouri v. Frye,* 132 S.Ct. 1399 (2012).

82. Laurence Benner, "Expanding the Right to Effective Counsel at Plea Bargaining," *Criminal Justice* (Fall 2012), 4-11.

83. Quoted in Adam Liptak, "Justices' Ruling Expands Rights of Accused in Plea Bargains," *New York Times* (March 22, 2012), A1.

84. Quoted in "Plea Deal Angers Stabbing Victim," *Enquirer-Journal* (Monroe, NC) (June 12, 2014), at **www.enquirerjournal .com/news/x2105769767/Plea-deal -angers-stabbing-victim**.

85. Quoted in *ibid.*

86. Warren Burger, "Address to the American Bar Association Annual Convention," *New York Times* (August 11, 1970), 24.

87. Quoted in "Is Plea Bargaining a Cop-Out?" *Time* (August 28, 1978), at **www.time .com/time/magazine/article/0,9171,91 6340-3,00.html**.

88. Quoted in Erik Eckholm, "Prosecutors Draw Fire for Sentences Called Harsh," *New York Times* (December 6, 2013), A19.

89. *Bordenkircher v. Hayes,* 434 U.S. 357 (1978).

The Criminal Trial

Chapter Outline	Corresponding Learning Objectives
Special Features of Criminal Trials	**1** Identify the basic protections enjoyed by criminal defendants in the United States.
	2 Explain what "taking the Fifth" really means.
Jury Selection	**3** List the requirements normally imposed on potential jurors.
	4 Contrast challenges for cause and peremptory challenges during *voir dire*.
The Trial	**5** List the standard steps in a criminal jury trial.
	6 Explain the difference between testimony and real evidence, between lay witnesses and expert witnesses, and between direct and circumstantial evidence.
	7 Identify the primary method that defense attorneys use in most trials to weaken the prosecution's case against their client.
The Final Steps of the Trial and Postconviction Procedures	**8** Delineate circumstances in which a criminal defendant may be tried a second time for the same act.
	9 List the five basic steps of an appeal.

To target your study and review, look for these numbered Learning Objective icons throughout the chapter.

the Love Defense

gigi jordan never denied killing Jude, her eight-year-old son. Her justification for giving the boy a lethal dose of drugs at a luxury midtown Manhattan hotel was, however, quite unusual. "She did it because she loved Jude," said Alan Brenner, Jordan's defense attorney. Specifically, Jordan claimed that her first husband was planning to murder her, leaving Jude in the custody of her second husband, his father. This man, she was convinced, would sexually abuse the boy, who suffers from autism, a developmental disorder that impairs one's ability to communicate.

Generally speaking, of course, love is not an acceptable legal excuse for homicide. Nevertheless, at Jordan's 2014 trial in New York City, her lawyers asked the jury to find her guilty of manslaughter rather than second degree murder. The lesser crime was appropriate, they argued, because Jordan had been under the influence of an "extreme emotional disturbance" when she killed her son. To succeed with this defense, which is normally used for murders committed in a jealous rage, Jordan's attorneys needed to prove that, in an unstable mental state, Jordan believed that her behavior was reasonable.

Prosecutors scoffed at the notion that Jude's killing was a poignant, impulsive act of mercy. They pointed out that Jordan had not seen her ex-husbands for months and could offer no proof that either man was planning to harm her or her son. A witness for the prosecution also testified that Jordan had told her about plans to commit suicide and "take [Jude] with me" if chemotherapy treatments did not alleviate the boy's symptoms. Even so, the jury accepted Jordan's explanation for ending Jude's life and found her guilty of manslaughter instead of murder. According to one juror, Jordan's beliefs may have been irrational or incorrect, but her actions met the definition of extreme emotional disturbance. "It was clear that she believed these stories," said the juror, explaining why the defendant did not deserve to spend the rest of her life in prison.

▲ In 2014, Gigi Jordan was convicted of manslaughter for intentionally killing her eight-year-old son in a Manhattan hotel room four years earlier.

Jefferson Siegel/NY Daily News via Getty Images

1. Do you agree with the jury's decision in the case of Gigi Jordan? Why or why not?

2. Taking the witness stand, Jordan said that her son had typed out detailed accusations of his father's sexual abuse using a computer. In this manner, Jude also accused twenty other people of sexually abusing him, including several babysitters, his grandfather, and an uncle. If you were the prosecutor, how would you use this testimony against the defendant?

3. Jordan also tried, unsuccessfully, to argue that she had acted in self-defense and under duress. After reviewing these defenses in Chapter 4, do you think either applies in this case? Explain your answer.

Special Features of Criminal Trials

Not surprisingly, given the extraordinary nature of the case and the defendant's significant personal wealth, estimated at more than $50 million, Gigi Jordan's murder trial attracted national attention. Those who followed the proceedings might have gotten a skewed version of how the criminal justice system works. According to the *"wedding cake" model* of our court system, only the top, and smallest, "layer" of trials comes close to meeting constitutional standards of procedural justice.[1] In these celebrity trials, such as Jordan's, committed (and expensive) attorneys argue minute technicalities for days, with numerous (and expensive) expert witnesses taking the stand for both sides.

On the bottom, largest layer of the wedding cake, the vast majority of defendants are dealt with informally, and the end goal seems to be speed rather than justice. Indeed, misdemeanor cases comprise about 80 percent of criminal court dockets, and for these defendants "convictions are largely a function of being selected for arrest."[2] Ideally, of course, criminal trial procedures are designed to protect *all* criminal defendants against the power of the state by providing them with a number of rights. Many of the significant rights of the accused are spelled out in the Sixth Amendment, which reads, in part, as follows:

> In all criminal prosecutions, the accused shall enjoy the right to a speedy and public trial, by an impartial jury of the State and the district wherein the crime shall have been committed, . . . and to be informed of the nature and cause of the accusation; to be confronted with the witnesses against him; to have compulsory process for obtaining witnesses in his favor; and to have the Assistance of Counsel for his defense.

 LEARNING OBJECTIVE 1 Identify the basic protections enjoyed by criminal defendants in the United States.

In the last chapter, we discussed the Sixth Amendment's guarantee of the right to counsel. In this section, we will examine the other important aspects of the criminal trial, beginning with two protections explicitly stated in the Sixth Amendment: the right to a speedy trial by an impartial jury.

A "Speedy" Trial

As you have just read, the Sixth Amendment requires a speedy trial for those accused of a criminal act. The reason for this requirement is obvious: depending on various factors, the defendant may lose his or her right to move freely and may be incarcerated prior to trial. Also, the accusation that a person has committed a crime jeopardizes that person's reputation in the community. If the defendant is innocent, the sooner the trial is held, the sooner his or her innocence can be established in the eyes of the court and the public.

The Definition of a Speedy Trial The Sixth Amendment does not specify what is meant by the term *speedy*. The United States Supreme Court has refused to quantify "speedy" as well, ruling instead in *Barker v. Wingo* (1972)[3] that only in situations in which the delay is unwarranted and proved to be prejudicial can the accused claim a violation of Sixth Amendment rights.

Speedy-Trial Laws To meet constitutional requirements, all fifty states have their own speedy-trial statutes. For example, the Illinois Speedy Trial Act holds that a defendant must be tried within 120 days of arrest unless both the prosecution and the defense agree otherwise.[4] Keep in mind, however, that a defendant does not automatically go free if her or his trial is not "speedy" enough. There must be judicial action, which is rare but does occur from time to time. In 2014, for example, the Indiana Supreme Court overturned a child molestation conviction because the defendant's trial was not held until 1,291 days after his arrest. The court called the delay, "considerable, unfortunate and inexcusable."[5] Nearly half of all criminal trials in state courts are settled within three months of the defendant's arrest. About 15 percent take more than a year to adjudicate.[6]

At the national level, the Speedy Trial Act of 1974[7] (amended in 1979) specifies the following time limits for those in the federal court system:

1. No more than thirty days between arrest and indictment.
2. No more than ten days between indictment and arraignment.
3. No more than sixty days between arraignment and trial.

Federal law allows extra time for hearings on pretrial motions, mental competency examinations, and other procedural actions.

Note that the Sixth Amendment's guarantee of a speedy trial does not apply until a person has been accused of a crime. Citizens are protected against unreasonable delays before accusation by **statutes of limitations,** which are legislative time limits that require prosecutors to charge a defendant with a crime within a certain amount of time after the illegal act took place. If the statute of limitations on a particular crime is ten years, and the police do not identify a suspect until ten years and one day after the criminal act occurred, then that suspect cannot be charged with that particular offense.

In general, prosecutions for murder and other offenses that carry the death penalty do not have a statute of limitations. This exception provides police with the ability to conduct cold case investigations that last for decades. In 2014, for example, because of a DNA "cold hit," as we saw in Chapter 6, Georgia authorities arrested Lonzo Guthrie for the murder of Eileen Ferro in Shrewsbury, Massachusetts, forty years earlier. The problem with prosecuting such cases, of course, is that so much time has passed since the criminal act that witnesses may be missing or dead, memories may be unreliable, and other evidence may have been lost.

The Role of the Jury

The Sixth Amendment also states that anyone accused of a crime shall be judged by "an impartial jury." In *Duncan v. Louisiana* (1968),[8] the Supreme Court solidified this right by ruling that in all felony cases, the defendant is entitled to a **jury trial.** The Court has, however, left it to the individual states to decide whether juries are required for misdemeanor cases.[9] If the defendant waives her or his right to trial by jury, a **bench trial** takes place in which a judge decides questions of legality and fact, and no jury is involved.

▼ Nearly three dozen alumni of the Horace Mann preparatory school in New York City, including the man showed here with his attorney, claim that they were sexually molested by a music teacher from the 1960s to the 1990s. Because the state's statute of limitation bans prosecution of such crimes after the accuser turns twenty-three years old, in 2013 the Bronx district attorney's office decided not to pursue any criminal charges against the alleged abuser. **What are the arguments for and against statutes of limitations in sexual abuse cases?** Rob Kim/Getty Images

Jury Size The predominant American twelve-person jury is not the result of any one law—the Constitution does not require that the jury be a particular size. Historically, the number was inherited from the size of English juries, which was fixed at twelve during the fourteenth century.

In 1970, responding to a case that challenged Florida's practice of using a six-person jury in all but capital cases, the Supreme Court ruled that the accused did not have the right to be tried by a twelve-person jury. Indeed, the Court labeled the number twelve "a historical accident, wholly without significance except to mystics." [10] In *Ballew v. Georgia* (1978),[11] however, the Court did strike down attempts to use juries with fewer than six members, stating that a jury's effectiveness was severely hampered below that limit. About half the states allow fewer than twelve persons on criminal juries, though rarely for serious felony cases. In federal courts, defendants are entitled to have the case heard by a twelve-member jury unless both parties agree in writing to a smaller jury.

Unanimity In most jurisdictions, jury verdicts in criminal cases must be *unanimous* for **acquittal** or conviction. As will be explained in more detail later, if the jury cannot reach unanimous agreement on whether to acquit or convict the defendant, the result is a *hung jury,* and the judge may order a new trial. The Supreme Court has held that unanimity is not a rigid requirement. It declared that jury verdicts must be unanimous in federal criminal trials, but has given states leeway to set their own rules.[12] As a result, Louisiana and Oregon continue to require only ten votes for conviction in criminal cases.

The Privilege against Self-Incrimination

In addition to the Sixth Amendment, which specifies the protections we have just discussed, the Fifth Amendment to the Constitution also provides important safeguards for the defendant. The Fifth Amendment states that no person "shall be compelled in any criminal case to be a witness against himself." Therefore, a defendant has the right not to testify at his or her own trial—in popular parlance, to "take the Fifth." Because defense attorneys often are wary of exposing their clients to prosecutor's questions in court, defendants rarely take the witness stand.

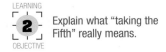

LEARNING **2** OBJECTIVE Explain what "taking the Fifth" really means.

Prejudicing the Jury It is important to note that not only does the defendant have the right to "take the Fifth," but also that the decision to do so should not prejudice the jury in the prosecution's favor. The Supreme Court came to this controversial decision while reviewing *Adamson v. California* (1947),[13] a case involving the convictions of two defendants who had declined to testify in their own defense against charges of robbery, kidnapping, and murder. The prosecutor in the *Adamson* proceedings frequently and insistently brought this silence to the notice of the jury in his closing argument, insinuating that if the pair had been innocent, they would not have been afraid to testify.

The Court ruled that such tactics effectively invalidated the Fifth Amendment by using the defendants' refusal to testify as a ploy to insinuate guilt. Now judges are required to inform the jury that an accused's decision to remain silent cannot be held against him or her. This protection only covers post-arrest and trial silence, however. In 2013, the Supreme Court ruled that prosecutors can inform a jury that a defendant refused to answer police questions *before* being arrested, a process detailed in Chapter 6.[14]

Witnesses in Court Witnesses are also protected by the Fifth Amendment and may refuse to testify on the ground that such testimony would reveal their own criminal wrongdoing. In practice, however, witnesses are sometimes granted *immunity* before testifying, meaning that no information they disclose can be used to bring criminal charges against them. Witnesses who have been granted immunity cannot refuse to answer questions in court on the basis of self-incrimination.

Acquittal A declaration following a trial that the individual accused of the crime is innocent in the eyes of the law and thus is absolved from the charges.

The Presumption of a Defendant's Innocence

The presumption in criminal law is that a defendant is innocent until proved guilty. The burden of proving guilt falls on the state (the public prosecutor). Even if a defendant did in fact commit the crime, she or he will be "innocent" in the eyes of the law unless the prosecutor can substantiate the charge with sufficient evidence to convince a jury (or judge in a bench trial) of the defendant's guilt.

Sometimes, especially when a case involves a high-profile violent crime, pretrial publicity may have convinced many members of the community—including potential jurors—that a defendant is guilty. In these instances, a judge has the authority to change the venue of the trial to increase the likelihood of an unbiased jury. In 2014, for example, Dzokhar Tsarnaev's defense attorneys requested a change of venue from Boston to Washington, D.C., for their client's trial on charges relating to the 2013 Boston Marathon bombings. They argued that "an extraordinarily high number" of Boston residents had either attended the marathon or knew someone else who had, and would therefore be "less able to set aside preconceived notions regarding guilt and punishment."[15]

The presiding judge refused this request, stating, "It is doubtful whether a jury could be selected anywhere in the country whose members were wholly unaware of the marathon bombings."[16] (The feature *Discretion in Action—Local Hero* gives another example of how pretrial publicity can bring the impartiality of a local jury into question.)

A Strict Standard of Proof

In a criminal trial, the defendant is not required to prove his or her innocence. As mentioned earlier, the burden of proving the defendant's guilt lies entirely with the state. Furthermore, the state must prove the defendant's guilt *beyond a reasonable doubt*. In other words, the prosecution must show that, based on all the evidence, the defendant's guilt is clear and unquestionable. In *In re Winship* (1970),[17] a case involving the due process rights of juveniles, the Supreme Court ruled that the Constitution requires the

Discretion in Action

Local Hero

The Situation Several years ago, Eddie Ray Routh fatally shot Chris Kyle at a gun range in Stephenville, Texas. As Routh's 2015 murder trial was set to open in Stephenville, *American Sniper*—a movie about Kyle's experiences as one of the deadliest soldiers in U.S. military history—was playing at a multiplex located just three miles from the courthouse. A nearby western-style clothing store was selling Chris Kyle baseball caps. The governor had just declared the two-year anniversary of

the shooting "Chris Kyle Day" in Texas. Almost everybody in Stephenville, including potential jurors, had seen the movie, which ends with footage from Kyle's funeral. "The death happening here, that makes it more personal," said one local resident. "[The prosecutors] aren't seeking the death penalty [for Routh], which I think is hogwash."

The Law Generally speaking, a judge can, at her or his discretion, move the venue of a trial if the defendant cannot

obtain a "fair and impartial" hearing in the region where the crime took place.

What Would You Do? Routh's lawyers asked District Judge Jason Cashon to move the trial to a different county and postpone it until public interest in *American Sniper* had died down. The judge refused both requests. Addressing the publicity surrounding Kyle and the film, Cashon ordered jurors to "stay away from it." Do you agree with the decision to keep the trial in Stephenville? Why or why not?

reasonable doubt standard because it reduces the risk of convicting innocent people and therefore reassures Americans of the law's moral force and legitimacy.

This high standard of proof in criminal cases reflects a fundamental social value—the belief that it is worse to convict an innocent individual than to let a guilty one go free. The consequences to the life, liberty, and reputation of an accused person from an erroneous conviction for a crime are substantial, and this has been factored into the process. Placing a high standard of proof on the prosecutor reduces the margin of error in criminal cases (at least in one direction).

Jury Selection

The initial step in a criminal trial involves choosing the jury. The framers of the Constitution ensured that the importance of the jury would not be easily overlooked. The right to a trial by jury is explicitly mentioned no fewer than three times in the Constitution: in Section 2 of Article III, in the Sixth Amendment, and again in the Seventh Amendment. The use of a peer jury not only provided safeguards against the abuses of state power that the framers feared, but also gave Americans a chance—and a duty—to participate in the criminal justice system.

In the early years of the country, a jury "of one's peers" meant a jury limited to white, landowning males. Now, as the process has become fully democratized, there are still questions about what "a jury of one's peers" actually means and how effective the system has been in providing the necessary diversity in juries.

Initial Steps: The Master Jury List and *Venire*

The main goal of jury selection is to produce a cross section of the population in the jurisdiction where the crime was committed. As we saw earlier, sometimes a defense attorney may argue that his or her client's trial should be moved to another community to protect against undue prejudice. In practice, judges, mindful of the intent of the Constitution, are hesitant to grant such pretrial motions.

A Jury of Peers This belief that trials should take place in the community where the crime was committed is central to the purpose of selecting a jury of the defendant's "peers." The United States is a large, diverse nation, and the outlook of its citizens varies accordingly. Two very different cases, one tried in rural Maine and the other in San Francisco, illustrate this point.[18]

In Maine, the defendant had accidentally shot and killed a woman standing in her backyard because he had mistaken her white mittens for a deer's tail. His attorney argued that it was the responsibility of the victim to wear bright-colored clothing in the vicinity of hunters during hunting season. The jury agreed, and the defendant was acquitted of manslaughter. In the San Francisco case, two people were charged with distributing sterile needles to intravenous drug users. Rather than denying that the defendants had distributed the needles, the defense admitted the act but insisted that it was necessary to stem the transmission of AIDS and, thus, to save lives. The jury voted 11–1 to acquit, causing a mistrial.

These two outcomes may surprise or even anger people in other parts of the country, but they reflect the values of the regions where the alleged crimes were committed. Thus, a primary goal of the jury selection process is to ensure that the defendant is judged by members of her or his community—peers in the true sense of the word.

▲ A Boston jury waits to be dismissed after finding Christian K. Gerhartsreiter guilty of kidnapping his seven-year-old daughter during a supervised visit. **Why is it important for a defendant to be tried by a jury of her or his "peers"?** AP Images/CJ Gunther, Pool

The Master Jury List Besides having to live in the jurisdiction where the case is being tried, there are very few restrictions on eligibility to serve on a jury. State legislatures generally set the requirements, and they are similar in most states. For the most part, jurors must be

1. Citizens of the United States.
2. Eighteen years of age or over.
3. Free of felony convictions.
4. Healthy enough to function in a jury setting.
5. Sufficiently intelligent to understand the issues of a trial.
6. Able to read, write, and comprehend the English language (with one exception—New Mexico does not allow non-English-speaking citizens to be eliminated from jury lists simply because of their lack of English-language skills).

The **master jury list,** sometimes called the *jury pool,* is made up of all the eligible jurors in a community. This list is usually drawn from voter-registration lists or driver's license rolls, which have the benefit of being easily available and timely.

List the requirements normally imposed on potential jurors. **LEARNING 3 OBJECTIVE**

Venire The next step in gathering a jury is to draw together the **venire** (Latin for "to come"). The *venire* is composed of all those people who are notified by the clerk of the court that they have been selected for jury duty. Those selected to be part of the *venire* are ordered to report to the courthouse on the date specified by the notice.

Some people are excused from answering this summons. Persons who do not meet the qualifications just listed either need not appear in court or, in some states, must appear only in order to be officially dismissed by court officials. Also, people in some professions, including teachers, physicians, and judges, can receive exemptions due to the nature of their work. Each court sets its own guidelines for the circumstances under which it will excuse jurors from service, and these guidelines can be as strict or as lenient as the court desires.

Voir Dire

At the courthouse, prospective jurors are gathered, and the process of selecting those who will actually hear the case begins. This selection process is not haphazard. The court ultimately seeks jurors who are free of any biases that may affect their willingness to listen to the facts of the case impartially. To this end, both the prosecutor and the defense

Master Jury List The list of citizens in a court's district from which a jury can be selected; compiled from voter-registration lists, driver's license lists, and other sources.

Venire The group of citizens from which the jury is selected.

attorney have some input into the ultimate makeup of the jury. Each attorney questions prospective jurors in a proceeding known as *voir dire* (French for "to speak the truth"). During *voir dire,* jurors are required to provide the court with a significant amount of personal information, including home address, marital status, employment status, arrest record, and life experiences.

Questioning Potential Jurors The *voir dire* process involves both written and oral questioning of potential jurors. Attorneys fashion their inquiries in such a manner as to uncover any biases on the parts of prospective jurors and to find persons who might identify with the plights of their respective sides. As one attorney noted, though a lawyer will have many chances to talk to a jury as a whole, *voir dire* is his or her only chance to talk with the individual jurors. (To better understand the specific kinds of questions asked during this process, see Figure 10.1.)

During this process, the judge can, at her or his own discretion, dismiss any potential jurors who seem unable to apply the law impartially to the case at hand. So, for example, before the trial of Eddie Ray Routh for murdering Chris Kyle, described in an earlier *Discretion in Action* feature, Judge Jason Cashon dismissed twelve potential jurors who admitted that they were biased against the defendant.[19] Similarly, the judge in the trial of Dzokhar Tsarnaev, also discussed earlier, dismissed a potential juror who had been the neighbor of one of the victims of the Boston Marathon bombing.

Challenging Potential Jurors During *voir dire,* the attorney for each side may exercise a certain number of challenges to prevent particular persons from serving on the jury. Both sides can exercise two types of challenges: challenges "for cause" and peremptory challenges.

Challenges for Cause If a defense attorney or prosecutor concludes that a prospective juror is unfit to serve, the attorney may exercise a **challenge for cause** and request that that person not be included on the jury. Attorneys must provide the court with a sound, legally justifiable reason for why potential jurors are "unfit" to serve. For example, jurors can be challenged for cause if they are mentally incompetent, do not understand English, or are proved to have a prior link—be it personal or financial—with the defendant or victim.

FIGURE 10.1 Sample Juror Questionnaire

In 2015, Aaron Hernandez went on trial for murdering Odin Lloyd in North Attleborough, Massachusetts, two years earlier. As the following excerpt from the juror questionnaire shows, lawyers in the case were interested in determining whether potential jurors had any biases that could keep them from objectively deciding the defendant's fate.

30. Do you believe that Mr. Hernandez is more likely to be guilty of the charges in this case because he has tattoos than an individual without tattoos would be?

31. Mr. Hernandez, the defendant, is Hispanic and the decedent, Odin Lloyd, was African American. Is there anything about those facts that would interfere with your ability to render a fair and just verdict?

37. Are you a fan of the New England Patriots?

39. In this case, you will hear evidence that the defendant was a professional football player for the New England Patriots. Is there anything about that fact that would impair your ability to be fair and impartial?

John Tlumacki/*The Boston Globe* via Getty Images

Source: Bristol County, Massachusetts, Superior Court.

Jurors can also be challenged if they express opinions that would prejudice them for or against the defendant. In addition, the Supreme Court has ruled that individuals may be legally excluded from a jury in a capital case if they would under no circumstances vote for a guilty verdict if it carried the death penalty.[20] At the same time, potential jurors cannot be challenged for cause if they have "general objections" or have "expressed conscientious or religious scruples" against capital punishment.[21] The final responsibility for deciding whether a potential juror should be excluded rests with the judge, who may choose not to act on an attorney's request.

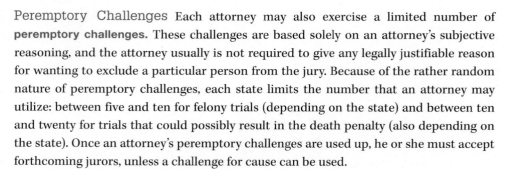

LEARNING
4
OBJECTIVE

Contrast challenges for cause and peremptory challenges during *voir dire*.

Peremptory Challenges Each attorney may also exercise a limited number of **peremptory challenges**. These challenges are based solely on an attorney's subjective reasoning, and the attorney usually is not required to give any legally justifiable reason for wanting to exclude a particular person from the jury. Because of the rather random nature of peremptory challenges, each state limits the number that an attorney may utilize: between five and ten for felony trials (depending on the state) and between ten and twenty for trials that could possibly result in the death penalty (also depending on the state). Once an attorney's peremptory challenges are used up, he or she must accept forthcoming jurors, unless a challenge for cause can be used.

An attorney's decision to exclude a juror may sometimes seem whimsical. One state prosecutor who litigated drug cases was known to use a peremptory challenge whenever he saw a potential juror with a coffee mug or backpack bearing the insignia of the local public broadcasting station. The attorney presumed that this was evidence that the potential juror had donated funds to the public station, and that anybody who would do so would be too "liberal" to give the government's case against a drug offender a favorable hearing.[22] Lawyers have been known to similarly reject potential jurors for reasons of demeanor, dress, and posture.

Jury Consultants To ensure that the jury is as sympathetic to their clients as possible, trial lawyers sometimes will hire a *jury selection consultant* to help with the *voir dire* process. These experts provide a number of services, from investigating the background of potential jurors to running mock trials that assist in determining what types of jurors will be most likely to provide the desired outcome.[23] As you might imagine, these services can be quite expensive, with fees reaching tens of thousands of dollars. A less costly alternative for attorneys is to conduct their own research by scouring Facebook and Twitter for valuable information on potential jurors' media habits, interests, hobbies, and religious affiliations.

Race and Gender Issues in Jury Selection

For many years, prosecutors used their peremptory challenges as an instrument of segregation in jury selection. Prosecutors were able to keep African Americans off juries in cases in which an African American was the defendant. The argument that African Americans—or members of any other minority group—would be partial toward one of their own was tacitly supported by the Supreme Court. Despite its own assertion, made in *Swain v. Alabama* (1965),[24] that blacks have the same right to appear on a jury as whites, the Court mirrored the apparent racism of society as a whole by protecting the questionable actions of many prosecutors.

The *Batson* Reversal The Supreme Court reversed this policy in 1986 with *Batson v. Kentucky*.[25] In that case, the Court declared that the Constitution prohibits prosecutors

Peremptory Challenges *Voir dire* challenges to exclude potential jurors from serving on the jury without any supporting reason or cause.

Courtesy Collins E. Ijoma

Collins E. Ijoma
Trial Court Administrator

As the trial court administrator, I serve principally as the chief administrative officer for the largest trial and municipal court system in New Jersey. We provide technical and managerial support to the court (more than sixty superior court judges and thirty-six municipal court judges) on such matters as personnel, program development, case flow, resources, and facilities management. This description may sound "highfalutin" considering that most people can only describe a court in terms of a judge, one or two courtroom staff, and a few other employees associated with the visible activities in the courthouse. Obviously, there is a lot more going on behind the scenes of which the average citizen is not aware.

One thing that keeps me going and enthused about this profession is the resolve and dedication of our judges and staff. The family division embraces a host of issues, and in some cases those who seek help are hurting and desperate. The court may be their only hope.

SOCIAL MEDIA CAREER TIP Many businesses and organizations have their own career Web sites for potential employees. Some have even set up *talent communities* to interact with applicants. Explore these options if you have a specific job in mind.

FASTFACTS

**Trial court administrator
Job description:**

- Oversees court operations, budget and accounting, technology, emergency management, and human resources.

**What kind of
training is required?**

- A B.A. in court administration, management, or a related area, and five years of professional experience in court administration or government administration, plus five years in a supervisory capacity.

Annual salary range?

- $30,000–$90,000

---

from using peremptory challenges to strike possible jurors on the basis of race. Under the *Batson* ruling, the defendant must prove that the prosecution's use of a peremptory challenge was racially motivated. Doing so requires a number of legal steps:[26]

1. First, the defendant must make a *prima facie* case that there has been discrimination during *venire*. (*Prima facie* is Latin for "at first sight." Legally, it refers to a fact that is presumed to be true unless contradicted by evidence.)

2. To do so, the defendant must show that he or she is a member of a recognizable racial group and that the prosecutor has used peremptory challenges to remove members of this group from the jury pool.

3. Then, the defendant must show that these facts and other relevant circumstances raise the possibility that the prosecutor removed the prospective jurors solely because of their race.

4. If the court accepts the defendant's charges, the burden shifts to the prosecution to prove that its peremptory challenges were race neutral. If the court finds against the prosecution, it rules that a *Batson* violation has occurred.

The Court has revisited the issue of race a number of times in the years since its *Batson* decision. In *Powers v. Ohio* (1991),[27] it ruled that a defendant may contest race-based peremptory challenges even if the defendant is not of the same race as the excluded jurors. In *Georgia v. McCollum* (1992),[28] the Court placed defense attorneys under the same restrictions as prosecutors when making race-based peremptory challenges. Finally, in 2008, the Court, reaffirming its *Batson* decision of twenty-two years earlier, overturned the conviction of an African American death row inmate because a Louisiana prosecutor improperly picked an all-white jury for his murder trial.[29]

These rulings do not mean that a black defendant can never be judged by a jury made up entirely of whites. Rather, they indicate that attorneys cannot use peremptory challenges to reject a prospective juror because of her or his race. Indeed, there is evidence that African Americans are still being kept off juries, particularly in parts of the South.[30] A study conducted by researchers at Michigan State University found that, from 1990 to 2010, African Americans were more than twice as likely as whites to be struck from juries in trials with black defendants facing the death penalty.[31] "Anyone with any sense at all can think up a race-neutral reason [to exclude a potential minority juror] and get away with it," says Atlanta defense attorney Stephen B. Bright.[32]

Women on the Jury In *J.E.B. v. Alabama ex rel. T.B.* (1994),[33] the Supreme Court extended the principles of the *Batson* ruling to cover gender bias in jury selection. The case was a civil suit for paternity and child support brought by the state of Alabama. Prosecutors used nine of their ten challenges to remove men from the jury, while the defense made similar efforts to remove women. When challenged, the state defended its actions by referring to what it called the rational belief that men and women might have different views on the issues of paternity and child support. The Court disagreed and held this approach to be unconstitutional.

Alternate Jurors

Because unforeseeable circumstances or illness may necessitate that one or more of the sitting jurors be dismissed, the court may also seat several *alternate jurors* who will hear the entire trial. Depending on the rules of the particular jurisdiction, two or three alternate jurors may be present throughout the trial. If a juror has to be excused in the middle of the trial, an alternate may take his or her place without disrupting the proceedings.

EthicsChallenge

During *voir dire* for a 2014 trial featuring a white defendant who allegedly fatally shot a black victim in Wayne County (Michigan), each of the defense attorney's five peremptory challenges removed a potential African American juror. The defense attorney claimed to have race-neutral reasons for dismissing all five, including that one had relatives killed in gunfire and another had slept during jury selection. Even if these reasons are valid, how does this situation underscore the potential for unethical behavior by lawyers in their use of peremptory challenges? ■

The Trial

Once the jury members have been selected, the judge swears them in and the trial itself can begin. (See Figure 10.2 for a preview of the stages of a jury trial that will be detailed in this section.) A rather pessimistic truism among attorneys is that every case "has been won or lost when the jury is sworn." This reflects the belief that a juror's values are the major, if not dominant, factor in the decision of guilt or innocence.[34]

In actuality, it is difficult to predict how a jury will go about reaching a decision. Despite a number of studies on the question, researchers have not been able to identify any definitive consistent patterns of jury behavior. Sometimes, jurors in a criminal trial will follow instructions to find a defendant guilty unless there is a reasonable doubt, and sometimes they seem to follow instinct or prejudice and apply the law any way they choose.

List the standard steps in a criminal jury trial.

LEARNING **5** OBJECTIVE

FIGURE 10.2 The Steps of a Jury Trial

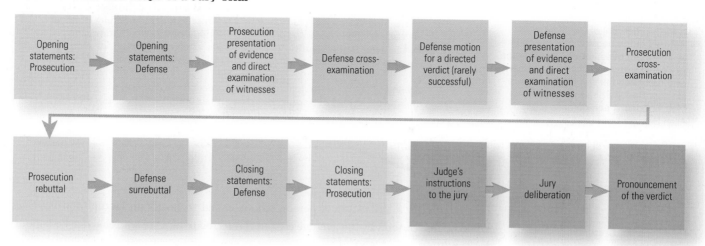

Opening statements: Prosecution → Opening statements: Defense → Prosecution presentation of evidence and direct examination of witnesses → Defense cross-examination → Defense motion for a directed verdict (rarely successful) → Defense presentation of evidence and direct examination of witnesses → Prosecution cross-examination →

Prosecution rebuttal → Defense surrebuttal → Closing statements: Defense → Closing statements: Prosecution → Judge's instructions to the jury → Jury deliberation → Pronouncement of the verdict

Opening Statements

Attorneys may choose to open the trial with a statement to the jury, though they are not required to do so. In these **opening statements,** the attorneys give a brief version of the facts and the supporting evidence that they will present during the trial. Because some trials can drag on for weeks or even months, it is extremely helpful for jurors to hear a summary of what will unfold. In short, the opening statement is a kind of "road map" that describes the destination that each attorney hopes to reach and outlines how she or he plans to reach it.

The danger for attorneys is that they will offer evidence during the trial that might contradict an assertion made during the opening statement. This may cause jurors to disregard the evidence or shift their own thinking further away from the narrative being offered by the attorney.[35] (For an example of an opening statement, see Figure 10.3.)

The Role of Evidence

Once the opening statements have been made, the prosecutor begins the trial proceedings by presenting the state's evidence against the defendant. Courts have complex rules about what types of evidence may be presented and how the evidence may be brought out during the trial. **Evidence** is anything that is used to prove the existence or nonexistence of a fact. For the most part, evidence can be broken down into two categories: testimony and real evidence. **Testimony** consists of statements by competent witnesses. **Real evidence,** presented to the court in the form of exhibits, includes any physical items—such as the murder weapon or a bloodstained piece of clothing—that affect the case.

Rules of evidence are designed to ensure that testimony and exhibits presented to the jury are relevant, reliable, and not unfairly prejudicial against the defendant. One of the tasks of the defense attorney is to challenge evidence presented by the prosecution by establishing that the evidence is not reliable. Of course, the prosecutor also tries to demonstrate the irrelevance or unreliability of evidence presented by the defense. The final decision on whether evidence is allowed before the jury rests with the judge, in keeping with his or her role as the "referee" of the adversary system.

Opening Statements The attorneys' statements to the jury at the beginning of the trial.

Evidence Anything that is used to prove the existence or nonexistence of a fact.

Testimony Verbal evidence given by witnesses under oath.

Real Evidence Evidence that is brought into court and seen by the jury, as opposed to evidence that is described for a jury.

LEARNING **6** OBJECTIVE

Explain the difference between testimony and real evidence, between lay witnesses and expert witnesses, and between direct and circumstantial evidence.

FIGURE 10.3 The Opening Statement

In the murder trial of Gigi Jordan, featured at the beginning of the chapter, an important question was whether the jury could feel sympathy for a mother who had killed her own eight-year-old son. Recognizing this, prosecutor Matt Bogdanos and defense attorney Allan Brenner both used their opening statements to describe the defendant's actions in the worst (or best) possible light.

> **Bogdanos:** Two fresh bruises on [the victim's] nose, fresh bruises on his chin and chest suggest [Jordan] got on top of him and, hopefully while he was asleep, filled a syringe with the poisonous concoction and pressed that plunger into his body. His fate was sealed. He didn't die fast. One by one, his vital organs shut down. It didn't take minutes. It took hours to die.
>
> **Brenner:** [Jordan had] no malice. No murderous intent, only the firm love and devotion that everyone who came into contact with [Jordan and her son] will swear to. She protected him from the animals she couldn't keep from the door.

Testimonial Evidence A person who is called to testify on factual matters that would be understood by the average citizen is referred to as a **lay witness**. If asked about the condition of a victim of an assault, for example, a lay witness could relate certain facts, such as "she was bleeding from her forehead" or "she was unconscious on the ground for several minutes." A lay witness could not, however, give information about the medical extent of the victim's injuries, such as whether she suffered from a fractured skull or internal bleeding. Coming from a lay witness, such testimony would be inadmissible.

Expert Witnesses When the matter in question requires scientific, medical, or technical skill beyond the scope of the average person, prosecutors and defense attorneys may call an **expert witness** to the stand. The expert witness is an individual who has professional training, advanced knowledge, or substantial experience in a specialized area, such as medicine, computer technology, or ballistics. The rules of evidence state that expert witnesses may base their opinions on three types of information:

1. Facts or data of which they have personal knowledge.
2. Material presented at trial.
3. Secondhand information given to the expert outside the courtroom.[36]

Expert witnesses are considered somewhat problematic for two reasons. First, they may be chosen for their "court presence"—whether they speak well or will appear sympathetic to the jury—rather than their expertise. Second, attorneys pay expert witnesses for their services. Given human nature, the attorneys expect a certain measure of cooperation from an expert they have hired, and an expert witness has an interest in satisfying the attorneys so that he or she will be hired again.[37] Under these circumstances, some have questioned whether the courts can rely on the professional nonpartisanship of expert witnesses.[38]

Challenging Expert Testimony If a trial lawyer wants to challenge an expert witness's validity or reliability, he or she must follow guidelines established by a Supreme Court decision from 1993. These guidelines call on the judge to determine whether the technique on which the expert witness is relying has been accepted by the scientific community at large.[39] Such challenges are fairly commonplace and have been used to question expert analysis of DNA evidence (see Chapter 6) and polygraph tests (see Chapter 8).

This procedure has also been employed in efforts to undermine the legitimacy of fingerprint matches. The predominant method of fingerprint identification, known as ACE-V (Analysis Comparison Evaluation Verification), relies on infrared or X-ray imaging of secretions from the body to produce fingerprint matches. If these samples are

Lay Witness A witness who can truthfully and accurately testify on a fact in question without having specialized training or knowledge.

Expert Witness A witness with professional training or substantial experience qualifying her or him to testify on a certain subject.

incomplete or in some way damaged, a faulty match between the print lifted from a crime scene and that of a suspect may result. Several scientific studies have shown that fingerprint matching is not infallible, though error rates are quite low at less than 1 percent.[40]

Because of the such small error rates, challenges of the reliability of fingerprint matches almost always fail.[41] Defense attorneys have, however, had success questioning the link between their clients and fingerprints found on movable objects. In these cases, since prosecutors cannot prove *when* a fingerprint was left on an object, courts have found that a match does not prove the defendant's presence at a crime scene beyond a reasonable doubt.[42]

Direct versus Circumstantial Evidence
Two types of testimonial evidence may be brought into court: direct evidence and circumstantial evidence. **Direct evidence** is evidence that has been witnessed by the person giving testimony. "I saw Bill shoot Chris" is an example of direct evidence. **Circumstantial evidence** is indirect evidence that, even if believed, does not establish the fact in question but only the degree of likelihood of the fact. In other words, circumstantial evidence can create an inference that a fact exists.

Suppose, for example, that the defendant owns a gun that shoots bullets of the type found in the victim's body. This circumstantial evidence, by itself, does not establish that the defendant committed the crime. Combined with other circumstantial evidence, however, it may do just that. For instance, if other circumstantial evidence indicates that the defendant had a motive for harming the victim and was at the scene of the crime when the shooting occurred, the jury might conclude that the defendant committed the crime.

The "CSI Effect"
When possible, defense attorneys will almost always make the argument that the state has failed to present any evidence other than circumstantial evidence against their client. Recently, this tactic has been aided by a phenomenon known as the "CSI effect," taking its name from the popular television series *CSI: Crime Scene Investigation* and its spin-offs. According to many prosecutors, these shows have fostered unrealistic notions among jurors as to what high-tech forensic science can accomplish as part of a criminal investigation.

In reality, the kind of physical evidence used to solve crimes on *CSI* is often not available to the prosecution, which must rely instead on witnesses and circumstantial evidence. To test the CSI effect, researchers surveyed more than one thousand jurors in Washtenaw County, Michigan, and found that nearly half "expected the prosecutor to present scientific evidence in every criminal case." This expectation was particularly strong in rape trials and trials lacking direct evidence of a crime.[43]

Relevance
Evidence will not be admitted in court unless it is relevant to the case being considered. **Relevant evidence** is evidence that tends to prove or disprove a fact in question. Forensic proof that the bullets found in a victim's body were fired from a gun discovered in the suspect's pocket at the time of arrest, for example, is certainly relevant. The suspect's prior record, showing a conviction for armed robbery ten years earlier, is, as we shall soon see, irrelevant to the case at hand and in most instances will be ruled inadmissible by the judge.

Prejudicial Evidence
Evidence may be excluded if it would tend to distract the jury from the main issues of the case, mislead the jury, or cause jurors to decide the issue on an emotional basis.

Direct Evidence Evidence that establishes the existence of a fact that is in question without relying on inference.

Circumstantial Evidence Indirect evidence that is offered to establish, by inference, the likelihood of a fact that is in question.

Relevant Evidence Evidence tending to make a fact in question more or less probable than it would be without the evidence. Only relevant evidence is admissible in court.

Real Evidence In most cases involving a violent crime, prosecutors try to offer as much physical evidence of the crime as possible. Such evidence often includes heartwarming photographs of the victim before the crime and graphic photos of the victim after the crime, bloody pieces of clothing, and other evocative items. Defense attorneys usually try to exclude these items on the ground that they unfairly prejudice the jury against the defendant.

Judges generally will permit such evidence so long as it is not blatantly prejudicial. In 2014, for example, the Mississippi Supreme Court overturned LeDarius Bond's murder conviction because the prosecution showed the jury a photo of the victim's badly decomposed, "maggot-infested skull and facial area." The court found that prosecutors could have used other means to prove the angle of the bullet wound that killed the victim and, therefore, ruled that the photograph's prejudicial effect outweighed its value as evidence.[44]

Evil Character Defense attorneys are likely to have some success precluding prosecutors from using prior purported criminal activities or actual convictions to show that the defendant has criminal propensities or an "evil character."[45] Along the same lines, courts also frown on the defense practice of portraying the alleged victim in a negative light. For example, before George Zimmerman's murder trial, described in Chapter 4, the judge barred a great deal of evidence concerning the past of alleged victim Trayvon Martin. This evidence included:

1. A photo of Martin showing his gold teeth to the camera while sticking up his middle fingers,

2. School records indicating that Martin had been suspended for marijuana possession,

3. Texts and videos suggesting that Martin was involved in organized fights, and

4. A text from Martin to a friend that read, "U gotta gun?"

Such information, according to the judge, was irrelevant to the altercation between Zimmerman and Martin and would only serve to prejudice the jury against Martin.[46]

These concerns are codified in the Federal Rules of Evidence, which state that evidence of "other crimes, wrongs, or acts is not admissible to prove the character of a person in order to show action in conformity therewith." Such evidence is allowed only when it does not apply to character construction and focuses instead on "motive, opportunity, intent, preparation, plan, knowledge, identity, or absence of mistake or accident."[47]

Although this legal concept has come under a great deal of criticism, it is consistent with the presumption-of-innocence standards discussed earlier. Arguably, if a prosecutor is allowed to establish that the defendant has shown antisocial or even violent traits in the past, this will prejudice the jury against the defendant in the present trial. Even if the judge instructs jurors that this prior evidence is irrelevant, human nature dictates that

▼ Review the list of information concerning Trayvon Martin that was barred by the judge during the murder trial of George Zimmerman. **Do you agree that this evidence would have unfairly prejudiced the jury against Martin, whose likeness is reproduced on a tee shirt in this photo? Explain your answer.** Ron T. Ennis/*Fort Worth Star-Telegram*/MCT via Getty Images

it will probably have a "warping influence" on the jurors' perception of the defendant.[48] Therefore, whenever possible, defense attorneys will keep such evidence from the jury.

The Prosecution's Case

Because the burden of proof is on the state, the prosecution is generally considered to have a more difficult task than the defense. The prosecutor attempts to establish guilt beyond a reasonable doubt by presenting the *corpus delicti* ("body of the offense" in Latin) of the crime to the jury. The *corpus delicti* is simply a legal term that refers to the substantial facts that show a crime has been committed. By establishing such facts through the presentation of relevant and nonprejudicial evidence, the prosecutor hopes to convince the jury of the defendant's guilt.

Direct Examination of Witnesses Witnesses are crucial to establishing the prosecutor's case against the defendant. The prosecutor will call witnesses to the stand and ask them questions pertaining to the sequence of events that the trial is addressing. This form of questioning is known as **direct examination.** During direct examination, the prosecutor will usually not be allowed to ask *leading questions*—questions that might suggest to the witness a particular desired response.

A leading question might be something like "So, Mrs. Williams, you noticed the defendant threatening the victim with a broken beer bottle?" If Mrs. Williams answers "yes" to this question, she has, in effect, been "led" to the conclusion that the defendant was, in fact, threatening with a broken beer bottle. The fundamental purpose behind testimony is to establish what actually happened, not what the trial attorneys would like the jury to believe happened. (A properly worded query would be, "Mrs. Williams, please describe the defendant's manner toward the victim during the incident.")

Competence and Reliability of Witnesses The rules of evidence include certain restrictions and qualifications pertaining to witnesses. Witnesses must have sufficient mental competence to understand the significance of testifying under oath. They must also be reliable in the sense that they are able to give a clear and reliable description of the events in question. If not, the prosecutor or defense attorney will make sure that the jury is aware of these shortcomings through *cross-examination.*

Cross-Examination

After the prosecutor has directly examined her or his witnesses, the defense attorney is given the chance to question the same witnesses. The Sixth Amendment states, "In all criminal prosecutions, the accused shall enjoy the right . . . to be confronted with witnesses against him." This **confrontation clause** gives the accused, through his or her attorneys, the right to cross-examine witnesses. **Cross-examination** refers to the questioning of an opposing witness during trial, and both sides of a case are allowed to do so.

Questioning Witnesses Cross-examination allows the attorneys to test the truthfulness of opposing witnesses and usually entails efforts to create doubt in the jurors' minds that the witness is reliable (see Figure 10.4). After the defense has cross-examined a prosecution witness, the prosecutor may want to reestablish any reliability that might have been lost. The prosecutor can do so by again questioning the witness, a process known as *redirect examination.* Following the redirect examination, the defense attorney will be given the opportunity to ask further questions of prosecution witnesses, or

Direct Examination The examination of a witness by the attorney who calls the witness to the stand to testify.

Confrontation Clause The part of the Sixth Amendment that guarantees all defendants the right to confront witnesses testifying against them during the criminal trial.

Cross-Examination The questioning of an opposing witness during trial.

FIGURE 10.4 The Cross-Examination

During Michael Dunn's 2014 trial for the murder of Jordan Davis outside a convenience store in Jacksonville, Florida, the defendant claimed he fatally shot Davis in self-defense. Crucially, Dunn insisted that Davis had pointed a shotgun at him, though no such weapon was found at the crime scene. When Dunn took the stand, the prosecution cross-examined him about what he said to his fiancée, Rhonda Rouer, following the shooting.

Prosecutor: How did you describe the weapon [to her]? Did you say [Davis and his friends] had a sword? Did you say they had a machete?

Dunn: Gun.

Prosecutor: A gun. You used the word "gun"?

Dunn: Multiple times.

Later in the trial, the prosecution called Rouer (pictured here) as a witness. In her testimony, she stated that Dunn never mentioned that he had been threatened with a shotgun, or any other kind of weapon, during the confrontation.

AP Images/The Florida Times-Union, Bob Mack, Pool

recross-examination. Thus, each side has two opportunities to question a witness. The attorneys need not do so, but only after each side has been offered the opportunity will the trial move on to the next witness or the next stage.

Hearsay Cross-examination is also linked to problems presented by *hearsay* evidence. **Hearsay** can be defined as any testimony given about a statement made by someone else. An example of hearsay would be: "Jenny told me that Bill told her that he was the killer." Literally, it is what someone heard someone else say. For the most part, hearsay is not admissible as evidence. When a witness offers hearsay, the person making the original remarks is not in court and therefore cannot be cross-examined. If such testimony were allowed, the defendant's Sixth Amendment right to confront witnesses against him or her would be violated.

There are a number of exceptions to the hearsay rule, and as a result a good deal of hearsay evidence finds its way into criminal trials. For example, a hearsay statement is usually admissible if there seems to be little risk of a lie. Therefore, a statement made by someone who believes that his or her death is imminent—a "dying declaration" or a suicide note—is often allowed in court even though it is hearsay.[49] Similarly, the rules of most states allow hearsay when the statement contains an admission of wrongdoing *and* the speaker is not available to testify in court. The logic behind this exception is that a person generally does not make a statement against her or his own best interests unless it is true.[50]

Motion for a Directed Verdict

After the prosecutor has finished presenting evidence against the defendant, the government will inform the court that it has rested the people's case. At this point, the defense may make a **motion for a directed verdict** (now also known as a *motion for judgment as a matter of law* in federal courts). Through this motion, the defense is basically saying that the prosecution has not offered enough evidence to prove that the accused is guilty beyond a reasonable doubt. If the judge grants this motion, which rarely occurs, then a judgment will be entered in favor of the defendant, and the trial is over.

Hearsay An oral or written statement made by an out-of-court speaker that is later offered in court by a witness (not the speaker) concerning a matter before the court.

Motion for a Directed Verdict A motion requesting that the court grant judgment in favor of the defense on the ground that the prosecution has not produced sufficient evidence to support the state's claim.

The Defendant's Case

Assuming that the motion for a directed verdict is denied, the defense attorney may offer the defendant's case. Because the burden is on the state to prove the accused's guilt, the defense is not required to offer any case at all. It can simply "rest" without calling any witnesses or producing any real evidence, and ask the jury to decide the merits of the case on what it has seen and heard from the prosecution.

Placing the Defendant on the Stand If the defense does present a case, its first—and often most important—decision is whether the defendant will take the stand in her or his own defense. Because of the Fifth Amendment protection against self-incrimination, the defendant is not required to testify. Therefore, the defense attorney must make a judgment call. He or she may want to put the defendant on the stand if the defendant is likely to appear sympathetic to the jury, or is well spoken and able to aid the defense's case. With a less sympathetic or less effective defendant, the defense attorney may decide that exposing the defendant before the jury presents too large a risk.

Also, if the defendant testifies, she or he is open to cross-examination under oath from the prosecutor. In Gigi Jordan's murder trial, described at the beginning of this chapter, prosecutors took advantage of her willingness to testify by focusing on the speculative nature of her fears concerning her son's well-being. When asked whether she had any proof that her ex-husband had sexually abused Jude, she admitted that she did not.[51] In the end, however, Jordan's testimony helped her cause by showing jurors the extent to which she was suffering from "extreme emotional disturbance" when she killed her son.

Creating a Reasonable Doubt Defense lawyers most commonly defend their clients by attempting to expose weaknesses in the prosecutor's case. Remember that if the defense attorney can create reasonable doubt concerning the client's guilt in the mind of just a single juror, the defendant has a good chance of gaining an acquittal or at least a *hung jury,* a circumstance explained later in the chapter.

Even if the prosecution can present seemingly strong evidence, a defense attorney may succeed by creating reasonable doubt. In an illustrative case, Jason Korey bragged to his friends that he had shot and killed Joseph Brucker in Pittsburgh, Pennsylvania, and a great deal of circumstantial evidence linked Korey to the killing. The police, however, could find no direct evidence: they could not link Korey to the murder weapon, nor could they match his footprints to those found at the crime scene. Michael Foglia, Korey's defense attorney, explained his client's bragging as an attempt to gain attention, not a true statement. Though this explanation may strike some as unlikely, in the absence of physical evidence it did create doubt in the jurors' minds, and Korey was acquitted. (For a better idea of how this strategy works in court, see the feature *Discretion in Action— Murder or Suicide?*)

Reasonable Doubt and Sexual Assault Creating reasonable doubt is also very effective in cases that essentially rely on the word of the defendant against the word of the victim. In sexual-assault cases, for example, if the defense attorneys can create doubt about the victim's credibility—in other words, raise the possibility that he or she is lying—then they may prevail at trial. According to the Alcohol and Rape Study, carried out by researchers at Rutgers University and the University of New Hampshire, juries acquit about 90 percent of the time when the defendant says the sex was consensual and there is evidence that the alleged victim was drinking alcohol before the incident in

Discretion in Action

Murder or Suicide?

The Situation Your client is Michelle, who dialed 911 several years ago, hysterical, screaming, "My husband was shot. Somebody was in the house." When police arrived, they found her husband, Greg, lying in bed with a fatal gunshot wound to the back of his head. First, Michelle said that an intruder had knocked her unconscious and killed her husband. The police found no evidence of a forced entry. After several hours of questioning, Michelle changed her story, claiming that Greg had committed suicide and she had wiped down the crime scene—and then lied to police—to spare the couple's young daughter from knowing that her father had killed himself. Forensics showed, however, that the muzzle of the .45-caliber pistol was too far from Greg's head when it fired for him to have shot himself. Subsequently, Michelle was arrested and charged with murdering her husband.

The Law To find a defendant guilty, a jury must find *beyond a reasonable doubt* that he or she committed the crime.

What Would You Do? As a defense attorney, your job is to create reasonable doubt in the jurors' minds that Michelle killed her husband. Besides the circumstantial evidence presented above, other important details about this case include the following: (1) the murder weapon was found near Greg's body, clean of any fingerprints; (2) Greg was heavily in debt at the time of his death; and (3) Greg's life insurance policy contained a suicide clause, meaning Michelle was not eligible to receive a payout if he took his own life. What argument will you make before the jury to create reasonable doubt?

LEARNING **7** OBJECTIVE — Identify the primary method that defense attorneys use in most trials to weaken the prosecution's case against their client.

[To see how a Fort Worth, Texas, defense attorney argued in a case with similar facts, go to Example 10.1 in Appendix B.]

---

question.[52] (The *CJ in Action* feature at the end of this chapter explores issues concerning evidence in sexual-assault cases in more detail.)

Other Defense Strategies The defense can choose among a number of strategies to generate reasonable doubt in the jurors' minds. It can present an *alibi defense,* by submitting evidence that the accused was not at or near the scene of the crime at the time the crime was committed. Another option is to attempt an *affirmative defense,* by presenting additional facts to the ones offered by the prosecution. Possible affirmative defenses, which we discussed in detail in Chapter 4, include the following:

1. Self-defense   2. Insanity   3. Duress   4. Entrapment

With an affirmative defense strategy, the defense attempts to prove that the defendant should be found not guilty because of certain circumstances surrounding the crime. An affirmative strategy can be difficult to carry out because it forces the defense to prove the reliability of its own evidence, not simply disprove the evidence offered by the prosecution.

The defense is often willing to admit that a certain criminal act took place, especially if the defendant has already confessed. In this case, the primary question of the trial becomes not whether the defendant is guilty, but what the defendant is guilty of. In these situations, the defense strategy focuses on obtaining the lightest possible penalty for the defendant. As we saw in the last chapter, this strategy is responsible for the high percentage of proceedings that end in plea bargains.

Rebuttal and Surrebuttal

After the defense closes its case, the prosecution is permitted to bring new evidence forward that was not used during its initial presentation to the jury. This is called the rebuttal stage of the trial. When the rebuttal stage is finished, the defense is given the opportunity to cross-examine the prosecution's new witnesses and introduce new witnesses of its own. This final act is part of the *surrebuttal*. After these stages have been completed, the defense may offer another motion for a directed verdict, asking the judge to find in the defendant's favor. If this motion is rejected, and it almost always is, the case is closed, and the opposing sides offer their closing arguments.

Rebuttal Evidence given to counteract or disprove evidence presented by the opposing party.

Closing Arguments Arguments made by each side's attorney after the cases for the plaintiff and defendant have been presented.

Closing Arguments

In their closing arguments, the attorneys summarize their presentations and argue one final time for their respective cases. In most states, the defense attorney goes first, and then the prosecutor. (In Colorado, Kentucky, and Missouri, the order is reversed.) An effective closing argument includes all of the major points that support the government's or the defense's case. It also emphasizes the shortcomings of the opposing party's case. Jurors will view a closing argument with some skepticism if it merely recites the central points of a party's claim or defense without also responding to the unfavorable facts or issues raised by the other side. Of course, neither attorney wants to focus too much on the other side's position, but the elements of the opposing position do need to be acknowledged and their flaws highlighted. (For an example of opposing closing arguments, see Figure 10.5.)

One danger in the closing arguments is that an attorney will become too emotional and make remarks that are later deemed by appellate courts to be prejudicial. Furthermore, lawyers are not permitted to introduce any additional facts during a closing statement. If allowed to do so, lawyers would be able to "sneak in" new evidence without giving the opposing party a chance to challenge that evidence.[53] Once both attorneys have completed their remarks, the case is submitted to the jury, and the attorneys' role in the trial is, for the moment, complete.

FIGURE 10.5 The Closing Argument

Defense attorneys for Keith Kidwell, charged with murdering convenience store worker Crayton Nelms in Bull City, North Carolina, argued that the case against their client was "flawed to the core." In her closing argument, District Attorney Tracey Cline focused on one particular piece of evidence to contradict this assertion:

> Inside that [store] that morning, there were footprints, shoe impressions. All the ones that were in blood—and I'm not talking about what the kids put on their face at Halloween. Real blood. Blood that had once run warm inside a body. But all of the shoe prints in blood can be traced to Mr. Kidwell's shoes. Outside sole design, same physical size, general wear, similar features. Scientific words. You, each of you, had in your hands the picture of that bloody shoe print on Mr. Nelms' back and matched it up—I said matched—with [Kidwell's] shoe. Coincidence?

The jury found Kidwell guilty of first degree murder, and he was sentenced to life in prison without the possibility of parole.

Source: For a complete transcript of Cline's closing argument, go to **media2.newsobserver.com/smedia/2011/09/05/09/47/qSaKF .So.156.pdf**.

As you learned in this section, expert witnesses are paid for their testimony by either the prosecution or the defense. In your opinion, what ethical problems, if any, does this common practice raise? What role does cross-examination play in limiting any potential problems with partisan expert witnesses? ■

The Final Steps of the Trial and Postconviction Procedures

After closing arguments, the outcome of the trial is in the hands of the jury. In this section, we examine the efforts to give jurors the means necessary to make informed decisions about the guilt or innocence of the accused. We also look at the posttrial motions that can occur when the defense feels that the jurors, prosecution, or trial judge made errors that necessitate remedial legal action.

Jury Instructions

Before the jurors begin their deliberations, the judge gives the jury a **charge,** summing up the case and instructing the jurors on the rules of law that apply to the issues in the case. These charges, also called jury instructions, are usually prepared during a special *charging conference* involving the judge and the trial attorneys. In this conference, the attorneys suggest the instructions they would like to see be sent to the jurors, but the judge makes the final decision as to the charges submitted. If the defense attorney disagrees with the charges sent to the jury, he or she can enter an objection, thereby setting the stage for a possible appeal.

The judge usually begins by explaining basic legal principles, such as the need to find the defendant guilty beyond a reasonable doubt. Then the jury instructions narrow to the specifics of the case at hand, and the judge explains to the jurors what facts the prosecution must have proved to obtain a conviction. If the defense strategy centers on an affirmative defense such as insanity or entrapment, the judge will discuss the relevant legal principles that the defense must have proved to obtain an acquittal.

The final segment of the charges discusses possible verdicts. These always include "guilty" and "not guilty," but some cases also allow for the jury to find "guilt by reason of insanity" or "guilty but mentally ill." Juries are often charged with determining the seriousness of the crime as well, such as deciding whether a homicide is murder in the first degree, murder in the second degree, or manslaughter.

Jury Deliberation

After receiving the charge, the jury begins its deliberations. Jury deliberation is a somewhat mysterious process, as it takes place in complete seclusion. Most of what is known about how a jury deliberates comes from mock trials or interviews with jurors after the verdict has been reached. A general picture of the deliberation process constructed from this research shows that jurors are not necessarily predisposed to argue with one another over the fate of the defendant. In approximately three out of every ten cases, the initial vote by the jury led to a unanimous decision. In 90 percent of the remaining cases, the majority eventually dictated the decision.[54]

One of the most important instructions that a judge normally gives the jurors is that they should seek no outside information during deliberation. The idea is that jurors

Charge The judge's instructions to the jury following the attorneys' closing arguments.

should base their verdict *only* on the evidence that the judge has deemed admissible. In extreme cases, the judge will order that the jury be *sequestered,* or isolated from the public, during the trial and deliberation stages of the proceedings. **Sequestration** is used when deliberations are expected to be lengthy, or the trial is attracting a high amount of interest and the judge wants to keep the jury from being unduly influenced. Juries are usually sequestered in hotels and kept under the watch and guard of officers of the court.

The importance of *total* sequestration is reflected in a recent Colorado Supreme Court decision to overturn the death penalty of a man who was sentenced after the jurors consulted a Bible during deliberations. The court held that a Bible constituted an improper outside influence and a reliance on a "higher authority." [55]

CJ & Technology

Wireless Devices in the Courtroom

One former juror, fresh from trial, complained that the members of the courtroom work group had not provided the jury with enough information to render a fair verdict. "We felt deeply frustrated at our inability to fill those gaps in our knowledge," he added. Until recently, frustrated jury members have lacked the means to carry out their own investigations in court. Today, however, jurors with smartphones and tablet computers can easily access news stories and online research tools. With these wireless devices, they can look up legal terms, blog and tweet about their experiences, and sometimes even try to contact other participants in the trial through "friend" requests on social media Web sites.

This access can cause serious problems for judges, whose responsibility it is to ensure that no outside information taints the jury's decision. Following a Vermont trial of an immigrant from the African country of Somalia for the sexual assault of a child, one juror went online to research certain aspects of Somali culture and religion. During deliberation, the juror relied on this research to argue his position that the defendant was guilty. The judge had no choice but to overturn the defendant's eventual conviction, as this juror misconduct could have improperly influenced the final verdict.

Champion Studio/ShutterStock.com

Thinking about Wireless Devices in the Courtroom

The Sixth Amendment guarantees the accused the right to trial by an "impartial jury." How does the use of wireless devices in the courtroom threaten this right?

The Verdict

Once it has reached a decision, the jury issues a **verdict.** The most common verdicts are guilty and not guilty, though, as we have seen, juries may signify different degrees of guilt if instructed to do so. Following the announcement of a guilty or not guilty verdict, the jurors are discharged, and the jury trial proceedings are finished.

Hung Juries When a jury in a criminal trial is unable to agree on a unanimous verdict—or a majority in certain states—it returns with no decision. This is known as a **hung jury.** Following a hung jury, the judge will declare a mistrial, and the case will be tried again in front of a different jury if the prosecution decides to pursue the matter a second time. A judge can do little to reverse a hung jury, considering that "no decision" is just as legitimate a verdict as guilty or not guilty.

Sequestration The isolation of jury members during a trial to ensure that their judgment is not tainted by information other than what is provided in the courtroom.

Verdict A formal decision made by the jury.

Hung Jury A jury whose members are so irreconcilably divided in their opinions that they cannot reach a verdict.

In some states, if there are only a few dissenters to the majority view, a judge can send the jury back to the jury room under a set of rules set forth more than a century ago by the Supreme Court in *Allen v. United States* (1896).[56] The **Allen charge,** as this instruction is called, asks the jurors in the minority to reconsider the majority opinion. Many jurisdictions do not allow *Allen* charges on the ground that they improperly coerce jurors with the minority opinion to change their minds.[57]

Jury Nullification For all of the attention they receive, hung juries are relatively rare. Juries are unable to come to a decision in only about 6 percent of all cases.[58] Furthermore, juries may be more lenient (or easy to "trick") than is generally perceived. One study found that juries were six times more likely than judges (in bench trials) to acquit a person who turns out to be guilty.[59] This statistic raises the question of *jury nullification,* which occurs when jurors "nullify" by using their own judgment to reach a verdict rather than following judicial instructions or the law.

Although there is no way to measure the amount of jury nullification in American courts, it is believed to occur most often in cases involving controversial issues such as race, the death penalty, or drug offenses. In 2012, New Hampshire's legislature passed "fully informed jury" legislation giving defense attorneys the ability to tell a jury that it is permitted to nullify a conviction that it feels would be unjust.[60] That same year, following a trial for marijuana possession in Laconia, the judge gave the following jury instruction, as requested by the defense:

> Even if you find that the State has proven each and every element of the offense charged beyond a reasonable doubt, you may still find the defendant not guilty if you have a conscientious feeling that a not guilty verdict would be a fair result in this case.[61]

The jury acquitted the defendant, who had rejected a plea bargain and claimed that the fifteen marijuana plants growing in his backyard were for personal, medicinal use only. As this chapter's *CJ Policy—Your Take* feature shows, some New Hampshire lawmakers would like to further strengthen support for jury nullification in state courts.

Appeals

Even if a defendant is found guilty, the trial process is not necessarily over. In our criminal justice system, a person convicted of a crime has a right to appeal. An **appeal** is the process of seeking a higher court's review of a lower court's decision for the purpose of correcting or changing the lower court's judgment. A defendant who loses a case in a trial court cannot automatically appeal the conviction. The defendant normally must first be able to show that the trial court acted improperly on a question of law. Common reasons for appeals include the introduction of tainted evidence by the prosecution or faulty jury instructions delivered by the trial judge. In federal courts, about 18 percent of criminal convictions are appealed.[62]

Double Jeopardy The appeals process is available only to the defense. If a jury finds the accused not guilty, the prosecution cannot appeal to have the decision reversed. To do so would infringe on the defendant's Fifth Amendment rights against multiple trials for the same offense. This guarantee against being tried a second time for the same crime is known as protection from **double jeopardy.** The prohibition against double jeopardy means that once a criminal defendant is found not guilty of a particular crime, the government may not reindict the person and retry him or her for the same crime. (Some nations allow for such retrials, as explained in the feature *Comparative Criminal Justice—Double Trouble.*)

Allen **Charge** An instruction by a judge to a deadlocked jury with only a few dissenters that asks the jurors in the minority to reconsider the majority opinion.

Appeal The process of seeking a higher court's review of a lower court's decision for the purpose of correcting or changing this decision.

Double Jeopardy To twice place at risk (jeopardize) a person's life or liberty. Constitutional law prohibits a second prosecution in the same court for the same criminal offense.

Comparative Criminal Justice

Double Trouble

American college student Amanda Knox's long Italian nightmare began in Perugia on November 6, 2007. That day, she was arrested, along with her boyfriend, for killing her British roommate, Meredith Kercher. In 2009, Knox (pictured at right) was convicted of murder, on the theory that Kercher's death was the result of a drug-fed orgy gone wrong. In 2011, an Italian appellate court overturned this conviction. The court based its ruling on shoddy investigative techniques by Italian law enforcement, which misread DNA evidence at the crime scene that pointed to a drug dealer named Rudy Guede as the obvious wrongdoer. After serving four years of a twenty-six-year prison sentence, Knox was freed and returned home to continue her education at the University of Washington in Seattle.

In March 2013, however, Italy's Court of Cassation reversed Knox's 2011 acquittal and ordered that her case be reviewed. This created the possibility that she would face a new trial and be convicted, again, for the same crime. In Italy, prosecutors routinely appeal acquittals. In the United States, because of constitutional protections against double jeopardy, defendants almost never face a second trial for the same crime. On January 30, 2014, an Italian appellate court convicted Knox for a second time of murdering Kercher and sentenced her to twenty-eight and a half years in prison. Following this verdict, Knox vowed that she would "never go willingly back" to Italy.

AP Images/Mark Lennihan

For Critical Analysis

In March 2015, nearly eight years after the initial crime, Italy's highest court annulled Knox's murder conviction, thus ending her involvement with the Italian legal system. How does Knox's ordeal bolster the theory behind America's prohibition of double jeopardy?

The basic idea behind the double jeopardy clause, in the words of Supreme Court Justice Hugo Black, is that the state should not be allowed to

> make repeated attempts to convict an individual for an alleged offense, thereby subjecting him to embarrassment, expense, and ordeal and compelling him to live in a continuing state of anxiety and insecurity, as well as enhancing the possibility that though innocent he may be found guilty.[63]

The American prohibition against double jeopardy is not, however, absolute. There are several circumstances in which, for practical purposes, a defendant can find herself or himself back in court after a jury has failed to find her or him guilty of committing a particular crime:

1. One state's prosecution will not prevent a different state or the federal government from prosecuting the same crime.

2. Acquitted defendants can be sued in *civil court* for circumstances arising from the alleged wrongdoing on the theory that they are not being tried for the same *crime* twice.

3. A hung jury is not an acquittal for purposes of double jeopardy. So, if a jury is deadlocked, the government is free to set a new trial.

LEARNING **8** OBJECTIVE

Delineate circumstances in which a criminal defendant may be tried a second time for the same act.

As a consequence of the final listed exception to double jeopardy, Michael Dunn found himself back in court only seven months after a hung jury in his murder trial for fatally shooting Jordan Davis outside a Jacksonville, Florida, convenience store. At Dunn's first trial, referenced earlier in Figure 10.4, the jury could not decide whether he acted in self-defense. In November 2014, however, a second jury rejected his self-defense claim and convicted Dunn of first degree murder, sending to him prison for the remainder of his life.

The Appeals Process There are two basic reasons for the appeals process. The first is to correct an error made during the initial trial. The second is to review policy. Because of this second function, the appellate courts are an important part of the flexible nature of the criminal justice system. When existing law has ceased to be effective or no longer reflects the values of society, an appellate court can effectively change the law through its decisions and the precedents that it sets.[64] A classic example was the *Miranda v. Arizona* decision (see Chapter 7), which, although it failed to change the fate of the defendant (he was found guilty on retrial), had a far-reaching impact on custodial interrogation of suspects.

It is also important to understand that once the appeals process begins, the defendant is no longer presumed innocent. The burden of proof has shifted, and the defendant is obligated to prove that her or his conviction should be overturned. The method of filing an appeal differs slightly among the fifty states and the federal government, but the five basic steps are similar enough for summarization in Figure 10.6. For the most part, defendants are not required to exercise their right to appeal. The one exception involves the death sentence. Given the seriousness of capital punishment, the defendant is required to appeal the case, regardless of his or her wishes.

List the five basic steps of an appeal.

LEARNING 9 OBJECTIVE

Wrongful Convictions

The appeals process is primarily concerned with "legal innocence." That is, appeals courts focus on how the law was applied in a case, rather than on the facts of the case. But what if a defendant who is factually innocent has been found guilty at trial? For the most part, such **wrongful convictions** can be righted only with the aid of new evidence suggesting that the defendant was not, in fact, guilty. When such new evidence is uncovered, a prosecutor's office can choose to reopen the case and redress the initial injustice.

FIGURE 10.6 The Steps of an Appeal

1. The defendant, or *appellant,* files a **notice of appeal**—a short written statement outlining the basis of the appeal.

2. The appellant transfers the trial court record to the appellate court. This record contains items such as evidence and a transcript of the testimony.

3. Both parties file **briefs.** A brief is a written document that presents the party's legal arguments.

4. Attorneys from both sides present **oral arguments** before the appellate court.

5. Having heard from both sides, the judges of the appellate court retire to deliberate the case and make their decision. As described in Chapter 8, this decision is issued as a **written opinion.** Appellate courts generally do one of the following:

   • **Uphold** the decision of the lower court.

   • **Modify** the lower court's decision by changing only a part of it.

   • **Reverse** the decision of the lower court.

   • **Reverse and remand** the case, meaning that the matter is sent back to the lower court for further proceedings.

DNA Exoneration In Chapter 6, we saw how DNA fingerprinting has been a boon for law enforcement. According to the Innocence Project, a New York–based legal group, as of March 2015, the procedure has also led to the exoneration of 325 convicts in the United States.[65] For example, in 1997 Jamie Lee Peterson was wrongly convicted of raping and murdering sixty-eight-year-old Geraldine Montgomery in Kalkaska, Michigan. Peterson subsequently spent seventeen years in prison before testing of the original rape kit and DNA on the victim's shirt showed conclusively that another man had committed the crimes. Acting on this new evidence, in August 2014, Kalkaska County prosecutors dropped the original charges against Peterson, and he was released from prison.

The Causes of Wrongful Convictions Jamie Lee Peterson was in jail for an unrelated sex crime when an inmate informant told police that Peterson claimed to have killed Geraldine Montgomery. After a lengthy series of interrogations, Peterson then confessed to the crime, though he withdrew this confession several days later. Furthermore, although DNA testing excluded Peterson as the source of the DNA on the victim's body, prosecutors argued that his DNA was on the victim's shirt collar, which could not be tested conclusively at the time.

Peterson's case highlights three of the five most common reasons[66] for wrongful convictions later overturned by DNA evidence:

1. *Eyewitness misidentification,* which may occur in as many as one-third of all cases in which it is used to identify criminal suspects.[67]
2. *False confessions,* which are often the result of overly coercive police interrogation techniques (see Chapter 7) or a suspect's mental illness.
3. *Faulty forensic evidence* produced by crime labs, which analyze evidence from bite marks to handwriting samples to ballistics.
4. *False informant testimony,* provided by "jailhouse snitches" and other offenders who are motivated to lessen their own punishment by incriminating other suspects.
5. *Law enforcement misconduct* by overzealous or corrupt police officers and prosecutors.

Numerous jurisdictions are taking steps to lessen the probability that these factors will result in wrongful convictions. District attorney offices in Cook County, Illinois, and Dallas County, Texas, among others, have formed Conviction Integrity Units to review and reinvestigate questionable convictions. The supreme courts of New Jersey and Oregon (as we saw in Chapter 8) now require state judges to determine whether eyewitness testimony is unfairly prejudicial, just like any other piece of evidence.[68] Several years ago, Texas legislators enacted a "Junk Science Writ" that allows inmates to challenge faulty forensic evidence from their prison cells.[69]

Habeas Corpus In 2009, the United States Supreme Court ruled that convicts have no constitutional right to DNA testing that may prove their innocence.[70] Nonetheless, most states allow prisoners access to such testing if there is a reasonable possibility of a wrongful conviction.

In addition, even after the appeals process is exhausted, a convict may have access to a procedure known as **habeas corpus** (Latin for "you have the body"). *Habeas corpus* is a judicial order that commands a corrections official to bring a prisoner before a federal court so that the court can hear the convict's claim that he or she is being held illegally. A writ of *habeas corpus* differs from an appeal in that it can be filed only by someone who is imprisoned. In recent years, defense attorneys have successfully used the *habeas corpus*

Habeas Corpus An order that requires corrections officials to bring an inmate before a court or a judge and explain why he or she is being held in prison.

▲ After spending nearly forty years behind bars, Ricky Jackson was freed from the Ohio corrections system when a key witness admitted that Cleveland police detectives had coerced him into identifying Jackson as a murder suspect in 1975. **Should prosecutors be disciplined for mistakenly bringing charges against innocent defendants such as Jackson, pictured here on November 20, 2014, following his release? Why or why not?**
AP Images/Phil Long

procedure for a number of their death row clients who have new DNA evidence proving their innocence.[71]

According to federal law, *habeas corpus* petitions must be filed no later than a year after the date of conviction. This restriction has proved problematic for inmates and their lawyers who may come across evidence of innocence after the deadline has passed. In 2013, the Supreme Court provided an exception to the one-year deadline rule in situations where the convict can prove that "it is more likely than not that no reasonable juror would have convicted him in light of the new evidence."[72]

EthicsChallenge

Suppose that, after Theodore is acquitted of murdering his wife at trial, a district attorney finds photos that, if shown to the jury, would likely have led to Theodore being convicted. Should Theodore be retried, despite prohibitions against double jeopardy? What if Theodore had *bribed* the district attorney to keep the photos out of court? Should Theodore face another trial under those circumstances? Explain your answers. ■

Rape Shield Laws

Historically, the courtroom has been a hostile environment for victims of sexual assault. Because of a pervasive attitude labeled the "chastity requirement" by Professor Michelle Anderson of the City University of New York School of Law, rape victims who were perceived to be sexually virtuous were much more likely to be believed by jurors than those who had been sexually active.[73] If a woman had consented to sex before, so the line of thought went, she was more likely to do so again. Consequently, defense attorneys invariably and successfully focused on the accuser's sexual past, convincing juries that consent had been given in the present instance by establishing a pattern of consent in past ones. As we close this chapter, we will examine much-debated legislative efforts to make the courtroom "safe" for rape victims.

"Unchastity" Evidence

Rape shield laws keep specific evidence, including evidence about the victim's reputation and previous sexual conduct, out of the courtroom, except under certain circumstances.[74] Today, every state except Arizona has a rape shield law. (In Arizona, well-established case law, rather than a statute, declares evidence of the accuser's "unchastity" inadmissible.)[75] In 1978, Congress also imposed a rape shield law in federal courts.[76]

Rape shield laws do contain certain exceptions that allow the defense to use evidence of the accuser's prior sexual conduct to undermine the credibility of his or her testimony. For example, Federal Rule 412 states that evidence of "other sexual behavior" or the "sexual disposition" of a rape complainant is inadmissible *unless* it is offered *either* (1) to prove that a person other than the accused was the source of semen, injury, or other physical evidence, *or* (2) to prove consent *and* involves previous sexual behavior by the alleged victim with the defendant. In addition, the defense must show that the exclusion of the evidence would violate the constitutional rights of the defendant.[77]

The Case for Rape Shield Laws

- Without these laws, defense attorneys may subject victims of sexual assault to embarrassing and degrading cross-examination concerning their personal lives.

- These laws ensure that defendants are convicted or acquitted based on the relevant evidence, not the prejudices of jurors more focused on the sexual history of the accuser than on the facts of the case.

- Only about a third of rapes are reported to police.[78] These laws encourage victims to report these crimes by ensuring that their privacy will be protected in court.

The Case against Rape Shield Laws

- The confrontation clause of the Sixth Amendment gives all defendants the right to question their accusers. By limiting this right, rape shield laws leave defendants in sexual-assault cases at the mercy of juries that do not know all the facts.

- In many instances, the victim's prior sexual history is relevant to the issue of whether she or he consented to the incident in question. These facts should not be hidden from the jury simply because they may cause an emotional reaction or deal with sexual issues.

- The many exceptions to rape shield laws, mentioned earlier, have effectively rendered them meaningless.

Your Opinion—Writing Assignment

A woman accuses two men of raping her in the back seat of a car. Both defendants claim that the sexual activity was consensual. At their trial, they want to present the following evidence from that night: (1) a fourth person had witnessed the accuser flirting aggressively with numerous men at a local bar; (2) the accuser had openly tried to seduce the older brother of one of the defendants; and (3) another witness had seen the accuser sitting on a soda crate in front of the defendants, one of whom was zipping up his pants.

Given the goals of rape shield laws and their exceptions discussed in this feature, which evidence, if any, concerning the above incident should be admitted before the jury? In cases such as this one, do you feel that rape shield laws properly balance the rights of the accuser and the rights of the accused? Before responding, you can review our discussions in the sections of this chapter concerning:

- Relevant and prejudicial evidence ("The Trial").

- The prosecutor's case ("The Trial").

- The defendant's case ("The Trial").

Your answer should include at least three full paragraphs.

Summary

For more information on these concepts, look back to the Learning Objective icons throughout the chapter.

 Identify the basic protections enjoyed by criminal defendants in the United States. According to the Sixth Amendment, a criminal defendant has the right to a speedy and public trial by an impartial jury in the physical location where the crime was committed. Additionally, a person accused of a crime must be informed of the nature of the crime and be confronted with the witnesses against him or her. Further, the accused must be able to summon witnesses in her or his favor and have the assistance of counsel.

 Explain what "taking the Fifth" really means. The Fifth Amendment states that no person "shall be compelled in any criminal case to be a witness against himself." Thus, defendants do not have to testify if their testimony would implicate them in the crime. Witnesses may refuse to testify on this same ground. (Witnesses, though, are often granted immunity and thereafter can no longer take the Fifth.) In the United States, silence on the part of a defendant cannot be used by the jury in forming its opinion about guilt or innocence.

 List the requirements normally imposed on potential jurors. They must be (a) citizens of the United States; (b) over eighteen years of age; (c) free of felony convictions; (d) healthy enough to function on a jury; (e) sufficiently intelligent to understand the issues at trial; and (f) able to read, write, and comprehend the English language.

 Contrast challenges for cause and peremptory challenges during *voir dire*. A challenge for cause occurs when an attorney provides the court with a legally justifiable reason why a potential juror should be excluded—for example, the juror does not understand English. In contrast, peremptory challenges do not require any justification by the attorney and are usually limited to a small number. They cannot, however, be based, even implicitly, on race or gender.

 List the standard steps in a criminal jury trial. (a) Opening statements by the prosecutor and the defense attorney; (b) presentation of evidence, usually in the form of questioning by the prosecutor, known as direct examination; (c) cross-examination by the defense attorney of the same witnesses; (d) at the end of the prosecutor's presentation of evidence, motion for a directed verdict by the defense (also called a motion for judgment as a matter of law in the federal courts), which is normally denied by the judge; (e) presentation of the defendant's case, which may include putting the defendant on the stand and direct examination of the defense's witnesses; (f) cross-examination by the prosecutor; (g) after the defense closes its case, rebuttal by the prosecution, which may involve new evidence that was not used initially by the prosecution; (h) cross-examination of the prosecution's new witnesses by the defense and introduction of new witnesses of its own, called the surrebuttal; (i) closing arguments by both the defense and the prosecution; (j) the charging of the jury by the judge, during which the judge sums up the case and instructs the jurors on the rules of law that apply; (k) jury deliberations; and (l) presentation of the verdict.

 Explain the difference between testimony and real evidence, between lay witnesses and expert witnesses, and between direct and circumstantial evidence. Testimony consists of statements by competent witnesses, whereas real evidence includes physical items that affect the case. A lay witness is an "average person," whereas an expert witness speaks with the authority of one who has professional training, advanced knowledge, or substantial experience in a specialized area. Direct evidence is evidence presented by witnesses as opposed to circumstantial evidence, which can create an inference that a fact exists, but does not directly establish the fact.

 Identify the primary method that defense attorneys use in most trials to weaken the prosecution's case against their client. To find a defendant guilty, a jury must believe beyond a reasonable doubt that he or she committed the crime. Therefore, defense attorneys will often present arguments and evidence designed to raise a reasonable doubt of guilt in the jurors' minds.

 Delineate circumstances in which a criminal defendant may be tried a second time for the same act. A defendant who is acquitted in a criminal trial may be sued in a civil case for essentially the same act. When an act is a crime under both state and federal law, a defendant who is acquitted in state court may be tried in federal court for the same act, and vice versa.

LEARNING 9 OBJECTIVE **List the five basic steps of an appeal.** (a) The filing of a notice of appeal; (b) the transfer of the trial court record to the appellate court; (c) the filing of briefs; (d) the presentation of oral arguments; and (e) the issuance of a written opinion by the appellate judges, upholding the decision of the lower court, modifying part of the decision, reversing the decision, or reversing and remanding the case to the trial court.

Questions for Critical Analysis

1. Why is it important for the judge to tell jurors that a defendant's decision to remain silent during the trial cannot be taken as a sign of guilt?

2. During the trial of George Zimmerman (described in Chapter 4), a defense attorney joked, "Knock, knock. Who's there? George Zimmerman. George Zimmerman who? All right, good, you're on the jury." Explain the point behind this attempt at courtroom humor.

3. Police find a critically wounded man lying in the parking lot of a gas station. When they ask him what happened, he indicates that Mr. X shot him. Then, the man dies. Should the dead man's identification of Mr. X be allowed in court? Or is it inadmissible hearsay? Explain your answer. (To see how the United States Supreme Court ruled in a similar case, go to **www.scotusblog.com/case-files/cases/michigan-v-bryant**.)

4. Texas has a law called the Timothy Cole Compensation Act, under which people who are wrongfully convicted of crimes may collect $80,000 from the state for each year of unwarranted imprisonment. Do you think this is fair? Why or why not? What are the goals of this kind of legislation?

5. Why is the appeals process so important to the American criminal justice system? What would be some of the consequences if criminal defendants did not have the ability to appeal questionable convictions?

Key Terms

acquittal   317
Allen charge   336
appeal   336
bench trial   316
challenge for cause   321
charge   334
circumstantial evidence   327
closing arguments   333
confrontation clause   329
cross-examination   329
direct evidence   327
direct examination   329

double jeopardy   336
evidence   325
expert witness   326
habeas corpus   339
hearsay   330
hung jury   335
jury trial   316
lay witness   326
master jury list   320
motion for a directed verdict   330
opening statements   325
peremptory challenges   322

real evidence   325
rebuttal   333
relevant evidence   327
sequestration   335
statute of limitations   316
testimony   325
venire   320
verdict   335
voir dire   321
wrongful conviction   338

Notes

1. Lawrence M. Friedman and Robert V. Percival, *The Roots of Justice* (Chapel Hill, N.C.: University of North Carolina Press, 1981).

2. Alexandra Natapoff, "Misdemeanors," *Southern California Law Review* 85 (2012), 105.

3. 407 U.S. 514 (1972).

4. 725 Illinois Compiled Statutes Section 5/103-5 (1992).

5. Jeff Parrott, "Indiana Supreme Court Overturns Elkhart Man's Child Molestation Conviction Because of Speedy Trial Violation," *The Elkhart (IN) Truth* (September 26, 2014), at **www.elkharttruth.com/news /crime-fire-courts/2014/09/26/Indiana -Supreme-Court-overturns-molestation -charge.html**.

6. Bureau of Justice Statistics, *Felony Defendants in Large Urban Counties, 2009— Statistical Tables* (Washington, D.C.: U.S. Department of Justice, December 2013), Table 20, page 23.

7. 18 U.S.C. Section 3161.

8. 391 U.S. 145 (1968).

9. *Blanton v. Las Vegas,* 489 U.S. 538 (1989).

10. *Williams v. Florida,* 399 U.S. 102 (1970).

11. 435 U.S. 223 (1978).

12. *Apodaca v. Oregon,* 406 U.S. 404 (1972); and *Lee v. Louisiana,* No. 07-1523 (2008).

13. 332 U.S. 46 (1947).

14. *Salinas v. Texas,* 570 U.S. _____ (2013).

15. Judy Clarke, quoted in Katharine Q. Seelye, "Boston Bombing Suspect Seeking Change of Trial Venue," *New York Times* (June 19, 2014), A16.

16. Quoted in Milton J. Valencia, "Judge Denies Tsarnaev Request for Change of Venue," *Boston Globe* (September 25, 2014), A1.

17. 397 U.S. 358 (1970).

18. James P. Levine, "The Impact of Local Political Cultures on Jury Verdicts," *Criminal Justice Journal* 14 (1992), 163–164.

19. Manny Fernandez and Kathryn Jones, "'American Sniper' Trial Sets Town on Edge," *New York Times* (February 10, 2015), A10.

20. *Lockhart v. McCree,* 476 U.S. 162 (1986).

21. *Witherspoon v. Illinois,* 391 U.S. 510 (1968).

22. John Kaplan and Jon R. Waltz, *The Trial of Jack Ruby* (New York: Macmillan, 1965), 91–94.

23. John W. Clark III, "The Utility of Jury Consultants in the Twenty-First Century," *Criminal Law Bulletin* (Spring 2006), 3.

24. 380 U.S. 224 (1965).

25. 476 U.S. 79 (1986).

26. Eric L. Muller, "Solving the *Batson* Paradox: Harmless Error, Jury Representation, and the Sixth Amendment," *Yale Law Journal* 106 (October 1996), 93.

27. 499 U.S. 400 (1991).

28. 502 U.S. 1056 (1992).

29. *Snyder v. Louisiana,* 552 U.S. 472 (2008).

30. *Illegal Racial Discrimination in Jury Selection: A Continuing Legacy* (Montgomery, Ala.: Equal Justice Initiative, August 2010).

31. Catherine M. Grosso and Barbara O'Brien, "A Stubborn Legacy: The Overwhelming Importance of Race in Jury Selection in 173 Post-*Batson* North Carolina Capital Trials," *Iowa Law Review* 97 (2012), 1531.

32. Quoted in Shaila Dewan, "Study Finds Blacks Blocked from Southern Juries," *New York Times* (June 2, 2010), 14.

33. 511 U.S. 127 (1994).

34. Harry Kalven and Hans Zeisel, *The American Jury* (Boston: Little, Brown, 1966), 163–167.

35. Nancy Pennington and Reid Hastie, "The Story Model for Juror Decision Making," in *Inside the Juror: The Psychology of Juror Decision Making* (Cambridge, Mass.: Harvard University Press, 1983), 192, 194–195.

36. Federal Rule of Evidence 703.

37. Richard A. Epstein, "Judicial Control over Expert Testimony: Of Deference and Education," *Northwestern University Law Review* 87 (1993), 1156.

38. L. Timothy Perrin, "Expert Witnesses under Rules 703 and 803(4) of the Federal Rules of Evidence: Separating the Wheat from the Chaff," *Indiana Law Journal* 72 (Fall 1997), 939.

39. *Daubert v. Merrell Dow Pharmaceuticals,* 509 U.S. 579 (1993).

40. Committee on Identifying the Needs of the Forensic Science Community, *Strengthening Forensic Science in the United States: A Path Forward* (Washington, D.C.: National Academies Press, 2009), 269–278; Bradford T. Ulery, et al., "Accuracy and Reliability of Forensic Latent Fingerprint Decisions, *Proceedings of the National Academy of Sciences Early Edition* (April 5, 2011), 1–6; and Jason M. Tanger, Matthew B. Thompson, and Duncan J. McCarthy, "Identifying Fingerprint Expertise," *Psychological Science* (August 16, 2011), 995–997.

41. Lyn Haber and Ralph Norman Haber, "Scientific Validation of Fingerprint Evidence under *Daubert,*" *Law, Probability, and Risk* 7 (2008), 87–109.

42. "Highlighting the Limits to Fingerprint Evidence," *Federal Evidence Review* (February 26, 2014), at **federalevidence.com/blog /2014/march/noting-limits-fingerprint -evidence**.

43. Donald E. Shelton, "Juror Expectations for Scientific Evidence in Criminal Cases: Perceptions and Reality about the 'CSI Effect' Myth," *Thomas M. Cooley Law Review* 27 (2010), at **www.npr.org/documents/2011 /feb/shelton-CSI-study.pdf**.

44. *Bonds v. Mississippi,* Number 2012-CT-00640-SCT (May 22, 2014).

45. Thomas J. Reed, "Trial by Propensity: Admission of Other Criminal Acts Evidenced in Federal Criminal Trials," *University of Cincinnati Law Review* 50 (1981), 713.

46. Tracy Connor, "Jury's Look into Travyon Martin's Past Has Its Limits," *NBC News* (June 7, 2013), at **usnews.nbcnews.com /_news/2013/06/07/18832092-jurys -look-into-trayvon-martins-past-has-its -limits?lite**.

47. Reed, *op. cit.,* 713.

48. *People v. Zackowitz,* 254 N.Y. 192 (1930).

49. Federal Rules of Procedure, Rule 804(b)(2).

50. Arthur Best, *Evidence: Examples and Explanations,* 4th ed. (New York: Aspen Law & Business, 2001), 89–90.

51. "Multimillionaire Mom Who Killed 8-Year-Old Autistic Son Admits She Had No Proof He Was Abused by Father," *New York Daily News* (October 11, 2014), at **www .nydailynews.com/new-york/nyc-crime /mom-killed-autistic-son-admits-no -proof-abused-article-1.1970812**.

52. Douglas D. Koski, "Alcohol and Rape Study," *Criminal Law Bulletin* 38 (2002), 21–159.

53. *United States v. Wright,* 625 F.3d 583, 611 (9th Cir. 2010).

54. David W. Broeder, "The University of Chicago Jury Project," *Nebraska Law Review* 38 (1959), 744–760.

55. *People v. Haran,* 109 P.3d 616 (Colo. 2005).

56. 164 U.S. 492 (1896).

57. *United States v. Fioravanti,* 412 F.2d 407 (3d Cir. 1969).

58. William S. Neilson and Harold Winter, "The Elimination of Hung Juries: Retrials and Nonunanimous Verdicts," *International Review of Law and Economics* (March 2005), 2.

59. Joseph L. Gastwirth and Michael D. Sinclair, "Diagnostic Test Methodology in the Design and Analysis of Judge-Jury Agreement Studies," *Jurimetrics Journal* 39 (Fall 1998), 59.

60. New Hampshire Revised Statute 519:23-a (2013).

61. Hilary Hanson, "Doug Darrell Acquitted of Marijuana Charges through Jury Nullification in New Hampshire," *The Huffington Post* (September 19, 2012), at **www.huffington post.com/2012/09/17/doug-darrell -marijuana-jury-nullification_n_1890824 .html**.

62. Bureau of Justice Statistics, *Federal Justice Statistics, 2010* (Washington, D.C.: U.S. Department of Justice, December 2013), 17, 26.

63. *Green v. United States,* 355 U.S. 184 (1957).

64. David W. Neubauer, *America's Courts and the Criminal Justice System,* 5th ed. (Belmont, Calif.: Wadsworth Publishing Co. 1996), 254.

65. The Innocence Project, "Know the Cases," at **www.innocenceproject.org/know**.

66. Michigan Law School & Northwestern Law School, "The National Registry of Exonerations," at **www.law.umich.edu/special/exoneration/Pages/browse.aspx**.

67. "Brief for the American Psychological Association as Amici Curiae Supporting Petitioner," *Perry v. New Hampshire,* 132 S. Ct. 716 (2012).

68. *State v. Henderson,* 27 A.3d 872 (N.J. 2011); *State v. Lawson,* 291 P.3d 673 (Or. 2012).

69. Rick Jervis, "Texas Leads National Trend in Challenging Forensic Evidence," *USA Today* (December 17, 2013), 3A.

70. *District Attorney's Office v. Osborne,* 557 U.S. 52 (2009).

71. Theresa Hsu Schriever, "In Our Own Backyard: Why California Should Care about Habeas Corpus," *McGeorge Law Review* 45 (2014), 764–798.

72. *McQuiggin v. Perkins,* 133 S.Ct. 1924, 1932 (2013).

73. Michelle J. Anderson, "From Chastity Requirement to Sexuality License: Sexual Consent and a New Rape Shield Law," *George Washington Law Review* (February 2002), 51.

74. Michigan Compiled Laws Annotated Section 750.520j (West 1991).

75. *State ex rel. Pope v. Superior Court,* 545 P.2d 946, 953 (Ariz. 1996).

76. Federal Rule of Evidence 412(a)(1)–(2).

77. Federal Rule of Evidence 412(b)(1)(A)–(C).

78. Bureau of Justice Statistics, *Criminal Victimization, 2013* (Washington, D.C.: U.S. Department of Justice, September 2014), Table 6, page 7.

Punishment and Sentencing

Chapter Outline		Corresponding Learning Objectives
The Purpose of Sentencing	**1**	List and contrast the four basic philosophical reasons for sentencing criminals.
The Structure of Sentencing	**2**	Contrast indeterminate with determinate sentencing.
	3	Explain why there is a difference between the sentence imposed by a judge and the actual sentence served by the prisoner.
	4	State who has input into the sentencing decision and list the factors that determine a sentence.
Inconsistencies in Sentencing	**5**	Explain some of the reasons why sentencing reform has occurred.
Sentencing Reform	**6**	Identify the arguments for and against the use of victim impact statements during sentencing hearings.
Capital Punishment	**7**	Identify the two stages that make up the bifurcated process of death penalty sentencing.
	8	Explain why the U.S. Supreme Court abolished the death penalty for juvenile offenders.
	9	Describe the main issues of the death penalty debate.

To target your study and review, look for these numbered Learning Objective icons throughout the chapter.

iStockPhoto.com/Montes-Bradley

A Long Time Gone

in 1991, Timothy Tyler was arrested for selling five grams of the hallucinogenic drug LSD to a friend who was working as an informant for the federal government. In 1996, Scott Walker was arrested for being a low-level pusher of LSD, cocaine, marijuana, and methamphetamine. If their arrests for these nonviolent offenses had happened today, Tyler and Walker—lacking criminal records—would have been punished with relatively short prison sentences. Instead, both of them are still behind bars, and can expect to spend the rest of their lives there.

"Over the years, the absolute nature of his sentence has often weighed on my mind," wrote John Gilbert, the judge who sentenced Walker, in 2012. Gilbert did not, however, have any choice in the matter. Under a formula adopted by the United States government in 1987, federal judges could not deviate from strict sentencing guidelines for nonviolent crimes. This discretion was returned to them by the United States Supreme Court in 2005, but the consequences of harsh federal and state sentencing laws are still evident in our corrections system. According to the American Civil Liberties Union, more than 3,200 inmates presently are serving life prison sentences without the possibility of parole for nonviolent drug and property crimes.

For these offenders, the best hope for freedom is clemency, a process through which the president of the United States or a state governor essentially forgives an inmate's wrongdoing and sets her or him free from prison. In 2014, recognizing the unfair nature of many life prison sentences, the federal government announced changes to its clemency criteria. The new regulations offer federal prisoners a chance at freedom if they are low-level, nonviolent offenders who have served at least ten years of their sentences, with no history of violence before or during their prison terms. Scott Walker hopes that he can benefit from the updated clemency standards. "I believe in my right to liberty," he says, "and I continue to wait for the moment when I receive the call."

Nancy Stone/MCT/Newscom

▲ Reynolds Wintersmith, sentenced to life in prison without parole on a nonviolent drug charge, spent twenty years behind bars before being freed by presidential clemency in 2014.

1. Are there any circumstances under which you think a nonviolent criminal deserves to spend his or her life in prison? Explain your answer.

2. What is your opinion of the North Dakota law that gives judges discretion to sentence an offender to life in prison for selling at least two grams of cocaine in a designated "school zone"?

3. Do you think a judge should be able to overrule a sentencing law—created by elected politicians—that he or she feels is too harsh or too lenient? Why or why not?

The Purpose of Sentencing

Professor Herbert Packer has said that punishing criminals serves two ultimate purposes: the "deserved infliction of suffering on evil doers" and "the prevention of crime."[1] Even this straightforward assessment raises several questions. How does one determine the sort of punishment that is "deserved"? How can we be sure that certain penalties "prevent" crime? Should criminals be punished solely for the good of society, or should their well-being also be taken into consideration? Why are Timothy Tyler and Scott Walker spending their lives in prison for nonviolent drug offenses committed in the 1990s, when those same crimes committed in the 2010s would be punished much less harshly?

Sentencing laws indicate how any given group of people has answered these questions, but do not tell us why they were answered in that manner. To understand why, we must first consider the four basic philosophical reasons for sentencing—retribution, deterrence, incapacitation, and rehabilitation.

Retribution

The oldest and most common justification for punishing someone is that he or she "deserved it"—as the Old Testament states, "an eye for an eye and a tooth for a tooth." Under a system of justice that favors **retribution,** a wrongdoer who has freely chosen to violate society's rules must be punished for the infraction. Retribution relies on the principle of **just deserts,** which holds that the severity of the punishment must be in proportion to the severity of the crime. Retributive justice is not the same as *revenge*. Whereas revenge implies that the wrongdoer is punished only with the aim of satisfying a victim or victims, retribution is more concerned with the needs of society as a whole.

The *principle of willful wrongdoing* is central to the idea of retribution. According to this principle, society is morally justified in punishing someone only if that person was aware that he or she committed a crime. Therefore, animals, children, and the mentally incapacitated are not responsible for their criminal actions, even though they may be a threat to the community.[2] Furthermore, the principles of retribution reject any wide-reaching social benefit as a goal of punishment. The philosopher Immanuel Kant (1724–1804), an early proponent of retribution in criminal justice, believed that punishment by a court

> can never be inflicted merely as a means to promote some other good for the criminal himself or for civil society. It must always be inflicted upon him only because he has committed a crime. For a man can never be treated merely as a means to the purposes of another.[3]

In other words, punishment is an end in itself and cannot be justified by any future good that may result from a criminal's suffering.

One problem with retributive ideas of justice lies in proportionality. Whether or not one agrees with the death penalty, the principle behind it is easy to fathom: the punishment (death) often fits the crime (murder). But what about the theft of an automobile? How does one fairly determine the amount of time the thief must spend in prison for that crime? Should the type of car or the wealth of the car owner matter? Theories of retribution often have a difficult time providing answers to such questions.

Deterrence

The concept of **deterrence** (as well as incapacitation and rehabilitation) takes a different approach than does retribution. That is, rather than seeking only to punish the wrongdoer, the goal of sentencing should be to prevent future crimes. By "setting an example,"

LEARNING OBJECTIVE **1** List and contrast the four basic philosophical reasons for sentencing criminals.

Retribution The philosophy that those who commit criminal acts should be punished for breaking society's rules to the extent required by just deserts.

Just Deserts A sanctioning philosophy based on the assertion that criminal punishment should be proportionate to the severity of the crime.

Deterrence The strategy of preventing crime through the threat of punishment.

▲ In March 2014, former Florida A&M University band member Jessie Baskin, right, pleaded guilty to manslaughter and was sentenced to nearly a year in jail for his role in the hazing death of drum major Robert Champion. **How does the theory of deterrence justify Baskin's punishment?** AP Images/*Orlando Sentinel*, George Skene, Pool

society is sending a message to potential criminals that certain actions will not be tolerated. Jeremy Bentham, a nineteenth-century British reformer who first articulated the principles of deterrence, felt that retribution was counterproductive because it does not serve the community. He believed that a person should be punished only when doing so is in society's best interests and that the severity of the punishment should be based on its deterrent value, not on the severity of the crime.[4]

General and Specific Deterrence Deterrence can take two forms: general and specific. The basic idea of *general deterrence* is that by punishing one person, others will be discouraged from committing a similar crime. *Specific deterrence* assumes that an individual, after being punished once for a certain act, will be less likely to repeat that act because she or he does not want to be punished again.[5] Proponents of harsh sentences for nonviolent drug crimes, addressed in the opening of this chapter, often rely on general deterrence principles to argue that such punishments discourage illegal drug possession and distribution by others.[6]

Both forms of deterrence have proved problematic in practice. General deterrence assumes that a person commits a crime only after a rational decision-making process, in which he or she implicitly weighs the benefits of the crime against the possible costs of the punishment. This is not necessarily the case, especially for young offenders who tend to value the immediate rewards of crime over the possible future consequences. The argument for specific deterrence is somewhat weakened by the fact that a relatively small number of habitual offenders are responsible for the majority of certain criminal acts.

Low Probability of Punishment Another criticism of deterrence is that for most crimes, wrongdoers are unlikely to be caught, sentenced, and imprisoned. According to the National Crime Victimization Survey, only 46 percent of all violent crimes and 36 percent of all property crimes are even reported to the police.[7] Of those reported, only 46 percent of violent crimes and 20 percent of property crimes result in an arrest.[8] Then, as we saw in Chapter 9, case attrition further whittles down the number of arrestees who face trial and the possibility of imprisonment.

Furthermore, studies show that potential offenders are generally unaware of the likely punishment for any given crime, and they underestimate the already low probability of being caught by law enforcement.[9] Professors Paul H. Robinson of the University of Pennsylvania Law School and John M. Darley of Princeton University note that this low probability of punishment could be offset by making the punishment so severe that even the slightest chance of apprehension could act as a deterrent—for example, an eighty-five-year prison term for shoplifting or the loss of a hand for burglary.[10] Or punishments could be "advertised" to have a greater deterrent impact. In Iran, criminals are sometimes hanged in public, and Chinese authorities broadcast death sentence proceedings on national television. Our society is, however, unwilling to accept these possibilities.

Incapacitation

"Wicked people exist," said James Q. Wilson. "Nothing avails except to set them apart from innocent people."[11] Wilson's blunt statement summarizes the justification for **incapacitation** as a form of punishment. As a purely practical matter, incarcerating criminals guarantees that they will not be a danger to society, at least for the length of their prison terms. Such reasoning is partially responsible for the dramatic increase of life sentences without the possibility of parole in the criminal justice system. Since 1984, the inmate population serving life without parole has quadrupled, to nearly 160,000, encompassing one of every nine individuals behind bars in the United States.[12] (See the feature *Comparative Criminal Justice—Whole-Life Tariffs* to learn about Europe's philosophy regarding the incapacitation of violent offenders for life.)

Incapacitation A strategy for preventing crime by detaining wrongdoers in prison, thereby separating them from the community and reducing criminal opportunities.

The Impact of Incapacitation Several studies do support incapacitation's efficacy as a crime-fighting tool. Criminologist Isaac Ehrlich of the University at Buffalo estimated that a 1 percent increase in sentence length will produce a 1 percent decrease in the crime rate.[13] More recently, Avinash Singh Bhati of the Urban Institute in Washington, D.C., found that higher levels of incarceration lead to fewer violent crimes but have little impact on property crime rates.[14]

Incapacitation as a theory of punishment does suffer from several weaknesses. Unlike retribution, it offers no proportionality with regard to a particular crime. Giving a burglar a life sentence would certainly ensure that she or he would not commit another burglary. Does that justify such a severe penalty? Furthermore, incarceration protects society only until the criminal is freed. Many studies have shown that, on release, offenders may actually be more likely to commit crimes than before they were imprisoned.[15] In that case, incapacitation may increase likelihood of crime, rather than diminish it.

Comparative Criminal Justice

Central Intelligence Agency

Whole-Life Tariffs

In England, life prison sentences, called "whole-life tariffs," are reserved for "exceptionally" serious crimes. In fact, the country has only fifty-two offenders presently serving whole-life tariffs. Recently, three of these English "lifers" challenged their punishments in the European Court of Human Rights (ECHR), which oversees the provisions of a human rights treaty signed by most countries in Europe. At the ECHR, located in Strasbourg, France, the lawyer representing these offenders argued that a whole-life tariff "crushes human dignity from the outset" and leaves the inmate in a "position of hopelessness whereby he cannot progress whatever occurs."

The three inmates involved in this case are hardly sympathetic figures. One killed his wife and a work colleague, another murdered five members of his family, and the third is a serial killer of homosexual men. Nonetheless, the ECHR judges ruled sixteen to one in their favor. The Court found that England's whole-life tariffs amount to inhuman and degrading treatment because such sentences offer no hope of release or rehabilitation. The ECHR ordered England to provide those serving life terms a "right to review" after twenty-five years to determine whether their continued imprisonment is still justified. In response, British politicians are considering replacing whole-life tariffs with one-hundred-year sentences (technically not "whole-life") that include periodical reviews of the inmates' continued potential for violence.

For Critical Analysis

In the opening of this chapter, we discussed life sentences for nonviolent offenders. In Europe, as this feature highlights, such punishments for even the most violent offenders are considered "inhuman and degrading." What is your opinion of the European philosophy regarding life sentences?

Selective and Collective Incapacitation Some observers believe that strategies of *selective incapacitation* should be favored over strategies of *collective incapacitation* for the best results. With collective incapacitation, all offenders who have committed a similar crime are imprisoned for the same time period. Selective incapacitation, in contrast, provides longer sentences for individuals, such as career criminals, who are considered more likely to commit further crimes if and when they are released. The problem with selective incapacitation, however, lies in the difficulty of predicting just who is at the greatest risk to commit future crimes. Studies have shown that even the most effective methods of trying to predict future criminality are correct less than half of the time.[16]

Rehabilitation

For many, **rehabilitation** is the most "humane" goal of punishment. This line of thinking reflects the view that crime is a "social phenomenon" caused not by the inherent criminality of a person, but by factors in that person's surroundings. By removing wrongdoers from their environment and intervening to change their values and personalities, the rehabilitative model suggests that criminals can be "treated" and possibly even "cured" of their proclivities toward crime. Although studies of the effectiveness of rehabilitation are too varied to be easily summarized, it does appear that, in most instances, criminals who receive treatment are less likely to reoffend than those who do not.[17]

For the better part of the past three decades, the American criminal justice system has been characterized by a notable rejection of many of the precepts of rehabilitation in favor of retributive, deterrent, and incapacitating sentencing strategies that "get tough on crime." Recently, however, more jurisdictions are turning to rehabilitation as a cost-effective (and, possibly, crime-reducing) alternative to punishment, a topic that we will explore more fully in the next few chapters. Furthermore, the American public may be more accepting of rehabilitative principles than many elected officials think. A recent national survey by the Pew Research Center found that 67 percent of Americans think the government should provide treatment for users of illegal drugs such as heroin and cocaine, compared to 26 percent who feel that such offenders should be prosecuted and imprisoned.[18] (See this chapter's first *Mastering Concepts* feature for an overview of the four main sentencing philosophies discussed in this chapter.)

Restorative Justice

On many reservations across the United States, Native Americans practice a "peacemaking" approach to criminal justice. Unlike the adversary system of the mainstream court system, peacemaking focuses on dispute resolution and the needs of the community rather than the rights of individual offenders. In a Navajo peacemaking session, members of the community, including the victim, describe the harm suffered because of the act in question. Then, the participants, as a group, decide on the proper *nalyeeh,* loosely translated as payment, that the offender (or the offender's family) owes the community.[19]

The goal of *nalyeeh,* which may or may not include money, is to make the injured party and the community "feel better," in the words of one judge from a Navajo tribe.[20] In Native American jurisdictions, these principles have been applied to resolve criminal issues from domestic violence to gang activity to driving while intoxicated. They are also spreading to the nontribal criminal justice system as part of the **restorative justice** movement in this country.

Rehabilitation The philosophy that society is best served when wrongdoers are provided the resources needed to eliminate criminality from their behavioral pattern.

Restorative Justice An approach to punishment designed to repair the harm done to the victim and the community by the offender's criminal act.

Several years ago, Judge Vic VanderSchoor sentenced Dennis Huston to sixteen years in prison for embezzling nearly $3 million from government agencies in Franklin County, Washington. Although Huston's defense attorney asked for a lighter punishment because of his client's age (sixty-six years), the judge's decision was in keeping with the four main philosophies of sentencing.

Philosophy	Basic Principle	Explanation
Retribution	Punishment is society's means of expressing condemnation of illegal acts such as embezzlement.	Dennis Huston "violated the trust of each and every citizen of the county," according to Judge VanderSchoor.
Deterrence	Harsh sentences for embezzlement may convince others not to engage in that illegal behavior.	Prosecutors said that Huston's example would prevent other government employees "from going down that same road."
Incapacitation	Incarcerated criminals are not a threat to the general society for the duration of their time behind bars.	While in prison, Huston will be unable to commit embezzlement or any other white-collar crime.
Rehabilitation	Prison programs can help inmates change their behavior so that they no longer pose a threat to themselves or others.	Huston reportedly used the stolen money to fuel his cocaine and gambling habits. While in prison, he can receive treatment and training to address these problems.

Source: Kristen M. Kraemer, "Huston Sentenced to 16 Years in Franklin County Embezzlement Scandal," *Tri-City Herald* (Kennewick, WA) (March 27, 2013), at **www.tri-cityherald .com/2013/03/27/2331438/huston-sentenced-to-16-years.html.**

A Different Approach Restorative justice strategies attempt to repair the damage that a crime does to the victim, the victim's family, and society as a whole. This outlook relies on the efforts of the offender to "undo" the harm caused by the criminal act through an apology and **restitution,** or monetary compensation for losses suffered by the victim(s). Restorative justice has five separate components that differentiate it from the mainstream criminal justice system:

1. *Offender involvement.* Offenders are given the opportunity to take responsibility for and address the reasons behind their behavior in ways that do not involve the corrections system.

2. *Victim involvement.* Victims have a voice in determining how the offender should atone for her or his crime.

3. *Victim-offender interaction.* On a voluntary basis, victims and offenders meet to discuss and better understand the circumstances of the crime. This meeting allows the victim to express her or his feelings related to the offense.

4. *Community involvement.* Community members also affected by the crime can participate in the process and request an apology and restitution from the offender.

5. *Problem-solving practices.* Participants in the process—including victims, offenders, and community members—can develop strategies for solving the problems that led to the crime in question.[21]

Although restorative justice is theoretically available for all types of criminal behavior, it almost always involves property crime, public order crime, and, particularly, offenses committed by juveniles. Rarely, if ever, will restorative justice principles be applied to violent crime.

Restorative Justice Legislation Nearly forty states have passed legislation that relies on restorative justice principles and uses the language of the movement. For the

Restitution Monetary compensation for damages done to the victim by the offender's criminal act.

Indeterminate Sentencing An indeterminate term of incarceration in which a judge determines the minimum and maximum terms of imprisonment.

most part, these laws involve alternatives to the state juvenile justice system, victim participation in the justice process, and the requirement that offenders pay restitution directly to victims or into a victim's fund.[22] On the federal level, the Victims of Crime Act of 1984 established the Crime Victims Fund to provide financial aid for crime victims.[23] This program—financed by fines and penalties assessed on convicted federal offenders—distributes grants to state governments, which in turn pass the funds on to victims. In 2012, the fund took in nearly $2.8 billion and distributed nearly $1.2 billion to crime victims to help cover expenses such as medical costs and lost wages.[24]

Victim-Offender Dialogue Principles of restorative justice are also infiltrating the American corrections system. For example, the practice of *victim-offender dialogue* (VOD) encourages face-to-face meetings between victims and offenders in a secure setting at the offender's prison. VOD allows the victims to speak directly to offenders about the criminal incident and how it has affected their lives. It also gives the offender a chance to apologize directly to the victim. Today, more than half of state corrections departments support VOD programs within their prisons.[25]

Furthermore, state corrections systems in California and Massachusetts are experimenting with an in-prison program called the Victim Offender Education Group. This intensive, thirty-four-week program encourages participating inmates, as part of their rehabilitation, to take accountability for the harm they have caused. Although restorative justice still suffers from the suspicion among criminal justice professionals that it is too vague and "touchy-feely" to be useful,[26] that perception is changing. According to Stanley Garnett, a district attorney in Boulder, Colorado, "[S]tats don't lie—recidivism drops significantly when restorative justice processes are employed."[27]

EthicsChallenge

In Iran, convicted criminals can buy their freedom from their victims. In 2014, for example, a man found guilty of murdering a rival during a knife fight had the charges against him dropped after he paid the victim's family $50,000. Does this practice have any ethical benefits for society? How does it differ from the American practice of restitution, described in this section? Explain your answers. ■

The Structure of Sentencing

Philosophy not only is integral to explaining *why* we punish criminals, but also influences *how* we do so. The history of criminal sentencing in the United States has been characterized by shifts in institutional power among the three branches of the government. When public opinion moves toward more severe strategies of retribution, deterrence, and incapacitation, *legislatures* have responded by asserting their power over determining sentencing guidelines. In contrast, periods of rehabilitation are marked by a transfer of this power to the *administrative* and *judicial* branches.

Legislative Sentencing Authority

Because legislatures are responsible for making laws, these bodies are also initially responsible for passing the criminal codes that determine the length of sentences.

Indeterminate Sentencing Penal codes with **indeterminate sentencing** policies set a minimum and maximum amount of time that a person must spend in prison. For example, the indeterminate sentence for aggravated assault could be three to nine years,

LEARNING
2
OBJECTIVE

Contrast indeterminate with determinate sentencing.

or six to twelve years, or twenty years to life. Within these parameters, a judge can prescribe a particular term, after which an administrative body known as the *parole board* decides at what point the offender is to be released. A prisoner is aware that he or she is eligible for *parole* as soon as the minimum time has been served and that good behavior can further shorten the sentence.

Determinate Sentencing

Disillusionment with the somewhat vague nature of indeterminate sentencing often leads politicians to support **determinate sentencing,** or fixed sentencing. As the name implies, in determinate sentencing an offender serves exactly the amount of time to which she or he is sentenced (minus "good time," described below). For example, if the legislature deems that the punishment for a first-time armed robber is ten years, then the judge has no choice but to impose a sentence of ten years, and the criminal will serve ten years minus good time before being freed.

"Good Time" and Truth in Sentencing

Often, the amount of time prescribed by a judge bears little relation to the amount of time the offender actually spends behind bars. In states with indeterminate sentencing, parole boards have broad powers to release prisoners once they have served the minimum portion of their sentence. Furthermore, most states offer prisoners the opportunity to reduce their sentences by doing **"good time"**—or behaving well—as determined by prison administrators. (See Figure 11.1 for an idea of the effects of good-time regulations and other early-release programs on state prison sentences.)

Sentence-reduction programs promote discipline within a correctional institution and reduce overcrowding, so many prison officials welcome them. The public, however, may react negatively to news that a violent criminal has served a shorter term than ordered by a judge and pressure elected officials to "do something." In Illinois, for example, some inmates were serving less than half their sentences by receiving a one-day reduction in their term for each day of "good time." Under pressure from victims' groups, the state legislature passed a **truth-in-sentencing law** in 1995 that requires murderers and others convicted of serious crimes to complete at least 85 percent of their sentences with no time off for good behavior.[28]

Determinate Sentencing A period of incarceration that is fixed by a sentencing authority and cannot be reduced by judges or other corrections officials.

"Good Time" A reduction in time served by prisoners based on good behavior, conformity to rules, and other positive behavior.

Truth-in-Sentencing Laws Legislative attempts to ensure that convicts will serve approximately the terms to which they were initially sentenced.

 LEARNING **3** OBJECTIVE Explain why there is a difference between the sentence imposed by a judge and the actual sentence served by the prisoner.

FIGURE 11.1 Average Sentence Length and Estimated Time to Be Served in State Prison

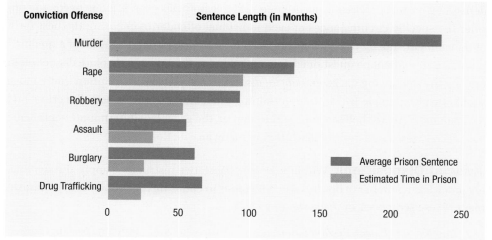

Source: Bureau of Justice Statistics, *National Corrections Reporting Program: Sentence Length of State Prisoners, by Offense, Admission Type, Sex, and Race* (January 20, 2011), "Table 9: First Releases from State Prison, 2008," at **bjs.ojp.usdoj.gov/index.cfm?ty=pb detail&iid=2056**.

As their name suggests, the primary goal of these laws is to provide the public with more accurate information about the actual amount of time an offender will spend behind bars. The laws also keep convicts incapacitated for longer periods of time. Fifteen years after Illinois passed its truth-in-sentencing law, those murderers subject to the legislation were spending an average of seventeen years more in prison than those not subject to the legislation. For sex offenders in the state, the difference was 3.5 years.[29] Today, forty states have instituted some form of truth-in-sentencing laws, though the continued popularity of such statutes is being undermined by the pressures of overflowing prisons.

Administrative Sentencing Authority

Parole is a condition of early release in which a prisoner is released from a correctional facility but is not freed from the legal custody and supervision of the state. Generally, after an inmate has been released on parole, he or she is supervised by a parole officer for a specified amount of time. The decision of whether to parole an inmate lies with the parole board. Parole is a crucial aspect of the criminal justice system and will be discussed in detail in Chapter 12.

For now, it is important to understand the role rehabilitation theories play in *administrative sentencing authority.* The formation in 1910 of the U.S. Parole Commission and similar commissions in the fifty states implied that the judge, though a legal expert, was not trained to determine when an inmate had been rehabilitated. Therefore, the commission argued, sentencing power should be given to experts in human behavior, who were qualified to determine whether a convict was fit to return to society.[30]

Judicial Sentencing Authority

During the pretrial procedures and the trial itself, the judge's role is somewhat passive and reactive. She or he is primarily a "procedural watchdog," ensuring that the rights of the defendant are not infringed while the prosecutor and defense attorney dictate the course of action. At a traditional sentencing hearing, however, the judge is no longer an arbiter between the parties. She or he is now called on to exercise the ultimate authority of the state in determining the defendant's fate.

From the 1930s to the 1970s, when theories of rehabilitation held sway over the criminal justice system, indeterminate sentencing practices were guided by the theory of "individualized justice." Just as a physician gives specific treatment to individual patients depending on their particular health needs, the hypothesis goes, a judge needs to consider the specific circumstances of each individual offender in choosing the best form of punishment. Taking the analogy one step further, just as the diagnosis of a qualified physician should not be questioned, a qualified judge should have absolute discretion in making the sentencing decision. *Judicial discretion* rests on the assumption that a judge should be given ample leeway in determining punishments that fit both the crime and the criminal.[31] As we shall see later in the chapter, the growth of determinate sentencing has severely restricted judicial discretion in many jurisdictions.

Judicial Dispositions Within whatever legislative restrictions apply, the sentencing judge has a number of options when it comes to choosing the proper form of punishment. These sentences, or *dispositions,* include:

1. *Capital punishment.* Reserved normally for those who commit first degree murder—that is, a premeditated killing—capital punishment is a sentencing option in thirty-one states. It is also an option in federal court, where a defendant can be put to

death for murder, as well as for trafficking in a large amount of illegal drugs, *espionage* (spying), and *treason* (betraying the United States).

2. *Imprisonment.* Whether for the purpose of retribution, deterrence, incapacitation, or rehabilitation, a common form of punishment in American history has been imprisonment. In fact, it is used so commonly today that judges—and legislators—are having to take factors such as prison overcrowding into consideration when making sentencing decisions. The issues surrounding imprisonment will be discussed in Chapters 13 and 14.

3. *Probation.* One of the effects of prison overcrowding has been a sharp rise in the use of probation, in which an offender is permitted to live in the community under supervision and is not incarcerated. (Probation is covered in Chapter 12.) *Alternative sanctions* (also discussed in Chapter 12) combine probation with other dispositions such as electronic monitoring, house arrest, boot camps, and shock incarceration.

4. *Fines.* Fines can be levied by judges in addition to incarceration and probation or independently of other forms of punishment. When a fine is the only punishment, it usually reflects the judge's belief that the offender is not a threat to the community and does not need to be imprisoned or supervised. In some instances, mostly involving drug offenders, a judge can order the seizure of an offender's property, such as his or her home.

Other Forms of Punishment Whereas fines are payable to the government, restitution and community service are seen as reparations to the injured party or to the community. As noted earlier, restitution is a direct payment to the victim or victims of a crime. Community service consists of "good works"—such as cleaning up highway litter or tutoring disadvantaged youths—that benefit the entire community. Along with restitution, *apologies* play an important role in restorative justice, discussed previously in this chapter. An apology is seen as an effort by the offender to recognize the wrongness of her or his conduct and acknowledge the impact that it has had on the victim and the community.

In some jurisdictions, judges have a great deal of discretionary power and can impose sentences that do not fall into any of these categories. This "creative sentencing," as it is sometimes called, has produced some interesting results. A judge in South Euclid, Ohio, ordered a man who had harassed his neighbor for fifteen years to stand at a local intersection carrying a sign that said, "I AM A BULLY! I pick on children that are disabled, and I am intolerant of those that are different from myself."[32] In Broward County, Florida, a man who shoved his wife was sentenced to "take her to Red Lobster," go bowling with her, and then undergo marriage counseling.[33] Though these types of punishments are often ridiculed, many judges see them as a viable alternative to incarceration for less dangerous offenders.

▼ After Jason Householder, left, and John Stockum were convicted of criminal damaging for throwing beer bottles at a car, municipal court judge David Hostetler of Coshocton, Ohio, gave them a choice: jail time or a walk down Main Street in women's clothing. As you can see, they chose the dresses. **What reasons might a judge have for handing down this sort of "creative" sentence?**
AP Images/Dante Smith/*Coshocton Tribune*

The Sentencing Process

The decision of how to punish a wrongdoer is the end result of what Yale Law School professor Kate Stith and federal appeals court judge José A. Cabranes call the "sentencing ritual."[34] The two main participants in this ritual are the judge and the defendant, but prosecutors,

State who has input into the sentencing decision and list the factors that determine a sentence.

LEARNING
4
OBJECTIVE

defense attorneys, and probation officers also play a role in the proceedings. Individualized justice requires that the judge consider all the relevant circumstances in making sentencing decisions. Therefore, judicial discretion is often tantamount to *informed* discretion—without the aid of the other members of the courtroom work group, the judge would not have sufficient information to make the proper sentencing choice.

The Presentence Investigative Report For judges operating under various states' indeterminate sentencing guidelines, information in the **presentence investigative report** is a valuable component of the sentencing ritual. Compiled by a probation officer, the report describes the crime in question, notes the suffering of any victims, and lists the defendant's prior offenses (as well as any alleged but uncharged criminal activity). The report also contains a range of personal data such as family background, work history, education, and community activities—information that is not admissible as evidence during trial. In putting together the presentence investigative report, the probation officer is supposed to gain a "feel" for the defendant and communicate these impressions of the offender to the judge.

The report also includes a sentencing recommendation. This aspect has been criticized as giving probation officers too much power in the sentencing process, because less diligent judges would simply rely on the recommendation in determining punishment.[35] For the most part, however, judges do not act as if they were bound by the presentence investigative report.

The Prosecutor and Defense Attorney To a certain extent, the adversary process does not end when the guilt of the defendant has been established. Both the prosecutor and the defense attorney are interviewed in the process of preparing the presentence investigative report, and both will try to present a version of the facts consistent with their own sentencing goals. The defense attorney in particular has a duty to make sure that the information contained in the report is accurate and not prejudicial toward his or her client. Depending on the norms of any particular courtroom work group, prosecutors and defense attorneys may petition the judge directly for certain sentences.

Sentencing and the Jury Juries also play an important role in the sentencing process. As we will see later in the chapter, it is the jury, and not the judge, who generally decides whether a convict eligible for the death penalty will in fact be executed. Additionally, six states—Arkansas, Kentucky, Missouri, Oklahoma, Texas, and Virginia—allow juries, rather than judges, to make the sentencing decision even when the death penalty is not an option. In these states, the judge gives the jury instructions on the range of penalties available, and then the jury makes the final decision.[36]

Juries have traditionally been assigned a relatively small role in felony sentencing, largely out of concern that jurors' lack of experience and legal expertise leaves them unprepared for the task. When sentencing by juries is allowed, the practice is popular with prosecutors because jurors are more likely than judges to give harsh sentences, particularly for drug crimes, sexual assault, and theft.[37]

Factors of Sentencing

The sentencing ritual strongly lends itself to the concept of individualized justice. With inputs—sometimes conflicting—from the prosecutor, attorney, and probation officer, the judge can be reasonably sure of getting the "full picture" of the crime and the

Presentence Investigative Report An investigative report on an offender's background that assists a judge in determining the proper sentence.

Courtesy Ellen Kalama Clark

Ellen Kalama Clark
Superior Court Judge

My favorite thing about my work is making a difference in people's lives. This is especially true in juvenile court, which is my favorite assignment. For example, early one morning I was walking to the juvenile court building when I saw a group of teenage boys heading toward me. Some of them I recognized from being in court, and they recognized me. A couple avoided eye contact, one looked me straight in the eye rather defiantly, and the last one kind of smirked. As we got closer to each other, the last boy—a tall, stocky kid— stopped, and the group just about blocked the sidewalk. It made me nervous.

The boy then leaned forward toward me and said, not in an intimidating manner but certainly meaning to get my attention, "Hey, Judge." I said good morning. He then broke into a big smile and said, "I got my GED [general equivalency diploma]! And I'm staying out of trouble." I didn't remember his name or his offense, but I was absolutely thrilled that he had accomplished those things, that he would want me to know that, and that he was bragging about it in front of his friends. I consider this a great success story.

SOCIAL MEDIA CAREER TIP Think about your online presence as your online personal brand. You create this online personal brand through the sum of all the posts you make on different Web sites and social media tools.

FASTFACTS

Judge
Job description:
- Preside over trials and hearings in federal, state, and local courts.

What kind of training is required?
- A law degree and several years of legal experience.
- Judges are either appointed or elected.

Annual salary range?
- $104,000–$178,000

criminal. In making the final decision, however, most judges consider two factors above all others: the seriousness of the crime and any mitigating or aggravating circumstances.

The Seriousness of the Crime As would be expected, the seriousness of the crime is the primary factor in a judge's sentencing decision. The more serious the crime, the harsher the punishment, for society demands no less. Each judge has his or her own methods of determining the seriousness of the offense. Many judges simply consider the "conviction offense," basing their sentence on the crime for which the defendant was convicted.

Other judges—some mandated by statute—focus instead on the **"real offense"** in determining the punishment. The "real offense" is based on the actual behavior of the defendant, regardless of the official conviction. For example, through a plea bargain, a defendant may plead guilty to simple assault when in fact he hit his victim in the face with a baseball bat. A judge, after reading the presentence investigative report, could decide to sentence the defendant as if he had committed aggravated assault, which is the "real offense." Though many prosecutors and defense attorneys are opposed to "real offense" procedures, which can render a plea bargain meaningless, there is considerable belief in criminal justice circles that they bring a measure of fairness to the sentencing decision.[38]

Mitigating and Aggravating Circumstances When deciding the severity of punishment, judges and juries are often required to evaluate the *mitigating* and

"Real Offense" The actual offense committed, as opposed to the charge levied by a prosecutor as the result of a plea bargain.

Mitigating Circumstances Any circumstances accompanying the commission of a crime that may justify a lighter sentence.

Aggravating Circumstances Any circumstances accompanying the commission of a crime that may justify a harsher sentence.

aggravating circumstances surrounding the case. **Mitigating circumstances** are those circumstances, such as the fact that the defendant was coerced into committing the crime, that allow a lighter sentence to be handed down. In contrast, **aggravating circumstances,** such as a prior record, blatant disregard for the safety of others, or the use of a weapon, can lead a judge or jury to inflict a harsher penalty than might otherwise be warranted (see Figure 11.2).

Aggravating circumstances play an important role in a prosecutor's decision to charge a suspect with capital murder. The criminal code of every state that employs the death penalty contains a list of aggravating circumstances that make an offender eligible for execution. Most of these codes require that the murder take place during the commission of a felony, or create a grave risk of death for multiple victims, or interfere with the duties of law enforcement. (For a comprehensive rundown, go to **www.death penaltyinfo.org/aggravating-factors-capital-punishment-state.**) As you will see later in the chapter, mitigating factors such as mental illness and youth can spare an otherwise death-eligible offender from capital punishment.

Judicial Philosophy Most states and the federal government spell out mitigating and aggravating circumstances in statutes, but there is room for judicial discretion in applying the law to particular cases. Judges are not uniform, or even consistent, in their opinions of which circumstances are mitigating or aggravating. One judge may believe that a fourteen-year-old is not fully responsible for his or her actions, while another may believe that teenagers should be treated as adults by criminal courts. A recent study in the journal *Science* found that, faced with a hypothetical situation in which a defendant suffered from brain damage, judges reduced the length of the sentence by about 7 percent.[39]

Often, a judge's personal philosophy will place her or him at odds with prosecutors. In July 2014, for example, teenager Latrez Cummings pleaded guilty in Detroit for participating in a violent attack on a man who accidentally struck a ten-year-old child with his

FIGURE 11.2 Aggravating and Mitigating Circumstances

Aggravating Circumstances	Mitigating Circumstances
• An offense involved multiple participants, and the offender was the leader of the group. • A victim was particularly vulnerable. • A victim was treated with particular cruelty for which an offender should be held responsible. • The offense involved injury or threatened violence to others and was committed to gratify an offender's desire for pleasure or excitement. • The degree of bodily harm caused, attempted, threatened, or foreseen by an offender was substantially greater than average for the given offense. • The degree of economic harm caused, attempted, threatened, or foreseen by an offender was substantially greater than average for the given offense. • The amount of contraband materials possessed by the offender or under the offender's control was substantially greater than average for the given offense.	• An offender acted under strong provocation, or other circumstances in the relationship between the offender and the victim make the offender's behavior less serious and therefore less deserving of punishment. • An offender played a minor or passive role in the offense or participated under circumstances of coercion or duress. • An offender, because of youth or physical impairment, lacked substantial capacity for judgment when the offense was committed. 

iStockphoto.com/mactrunk

Source: American Bar Association.

pickup truck. Prosecutors wanted Cummings to receive a one-to-three-year sentence, but Judge James Callahan decided that the defendant should spend only six months behind bars. The judge's ruling seemed to be influenced, at least in part, by sympathy for the defendant's fatherless upbringing. "That's what you have needed in your life is a father," he told Cummings, "somebody to beat the hell out of you when you made a mistake."[40]

EthicsChallenge

Defendant A broke into an unoccupied house and stole $1,000 in cash to buy food for his family. Defendant B broke into an unoccupied house and stole $1,000 in cash to feed his methamphetamine habit. If you were a judge, would you sentence Defendant A less harshly than Defendant B? Why or why not? ■

Inconsistencies in Sentencing

For some, the natural differences in judicial philosophies, when combined with a lack of institutional control, raise important questions. Why should a bank robber in South Carolina and a bank robber in Michigan receive different sentences? Even federal indeterminate sentencing guidelines seem overly vague: a bank robber can receive a prison term from one day to twenty years, depending almost entirely on the judge.[41] Furthermore, if judges have freedom to use their discretion, do they not also have the freedom to misuse it?

Purported improper judicial discretion is often the first reason given for two phenomena that plague the criminal justice system: *sentencing disparity* and *sentencing discrimination*. Though the two terms are often used interchangeably, they describe different statistical occurrences—the causes of which are open to debate.

LEARNING **5** OBJECTIVE
Explain some of the reasons why sentencing reform has occurred.

Sentencing Disparity

Justice would seem to demand that those who commit similar crimes should receive similar punishments. **Sentencing disparity** occurs when this expectation is not met in one of three ways:

1. Criminals receive similar sentences for different crimes of unequal seriousness.
2. Criminals receive different sentences for similar crimes.
3. Mitigating or aggravating circumstances have a disproportionate effect on sentences.

Most of the blame for sentencing disparities is placed at the feet of the judicial profession. Even with the restrictive presence of the sentencing reforms we will discuss shortly, judges have a great deal of influence over the sentencing decision, whether they are making that decision themselves or instructing the jury on how to do so. Like other members of the criminal justice system, judges are individuals, and their discretionary sentencing decisions reflect that individuality. Besides judicial discretion, several other causes have been offered as explanations for sentencing disparity, including differences between geographic jurisdictions and between federal and state courts.

Geographic Disparities For offenders, the amount of time spent in prison often depends as much on where the crime was committed as on the crime itself. A comparison of the sentences for drug trafficking reveals that someone convicted of the crime in Oregon faces an average of 69 months in prison, whereas a similar offender in eastern North Carolina can expect an average of 128 months.[42] The average sentences imposed

Sentencing Disparity A situation in which those convicted of similar crimes do not receive similar sentences.

in the Fourth Circuit, which includes North Carolina, South Carolina, Virginia, and West Virginia, are consistently harsher than those in the Ninth Circuit, comprising most of the western states: 42 months longer for convictions related to firearms and 43 months longer for all offenses.[43] Such disparities can be attributed to a number of different factors, including local attitudes toward crime and available financial resources to cover the expenses of incarceration.

Federal versus State Court Disparities Because of different sentencing guidelines the punishment for the same crime in federal and state courts can also be dramatically different. In North Carolina, for example, a defendant convicted of distributing child pornography in state court will rarely face a prison sentence of more than two years. If it is a first offense, he or she will most likely be placed on probation. Federal courts, however, have a mandatory five-year minimum prison term for any child pornography distribution conviction, with punishments often reaching twenty years because of aggravating circumstances.[44] Figure 11.3 shows the sentencing disparities for certain crimes in the two systems.

Sentencing Discrimination

Sentencing discrimination occurs when disparities can be attributed to extralegal variables such as the defendant's gender, race, or economic standing.

Race and Sentencing At first glance, racial discrimination would seem to be rampant in sentencing practices. Research by Cassia Spohn of Arizona State University and David Holleran of the College of New Jersey suggests that minorities pay a "punishment penalty" when it comes to sentencing.[45] In Chicago, Spohn and Holleran found that convicted African Americans were 12.1 percent more likely and convicted Hispanics were 15.3 percent more likely to go to prison than convicted whites. Another report released

FIGURE 11.3 Average Maximum Sentences for Selected Crimes in State and Federal Courts

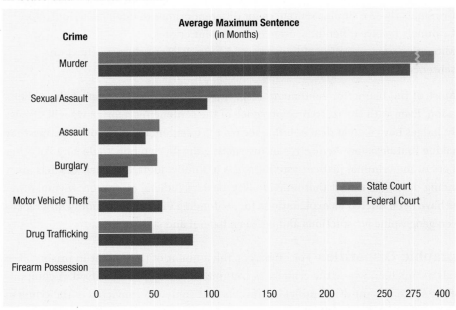

Source: Bureau of Justice Statistics, *Felony Sentences in State Courts, 2006—Statistical Tables* (Washington, D.C.: U.S. Department of Justice, December 2009), Table 1.6, page 9.

by the Illinois Disproportionate Justice Impact Study Commission found that African Americans were nearly five times more likely to be sentenced to prison than whites for low-level drug crimes in that state.[46]

Nationwide, about 38 percent of all inmates in state and federal prisons are African American,[47] even though members of that minority group make up only about 13 percent of the country's population and represent 28 percent of those arrested.[48] In federal prisons, nearly seven out of every ten inmates is either African American or Hispanic.[49]

Sentencing Bias? Such numbers, while drastic, may not be the result of blatant sentencing bias. For example, the large numbers of Hispanics in federal prison are a direct result of immigration laws, which disproportionately target that demographic. Furthermore, Spohn and Holleran found that the rate of imprisonment rose significantly for minorities who were young and unemployed. This led them to conclude that the disparities between races were not the result of "conscious" discrimination on the part of the sentencing judges. Rather, faced with limited time to make decisions and limited information about the offenders, the judges would resort to stereotypes, considering not just race, but age and unemployment as well.[50]

Another study, published in 2006, found that older judges and judges who were members of minority groups in Pennsylvania were less likely to send offenders to prison, regardless of their race.[51] Such research findings support the argument in favor of diversity among judges, discussed in Chapter 8. (This chapter's *CJ Policy—Your Take* examines an innovative strategy that several state governments have put in place to reduce bias in their sentencing processes.)

Length of Sentence Further evidence suggests that race has an impact on length of sentences. About 65 percent of those inmates serving life sentences without parole for nonviolent offenses are African American. In Louisiana, that number is 91 percent.[52] Over the past decade, the issue of crack cocaine sentencing has placed a particularly harsh spotlight on racial disparity in the criminal justice system. Powder cocaine and crack, a crystallized form of the drug that is smoked rather than inhaled, are chemically identical. Under federal legislation passed in 1986, however, sentences for crimes involving crack were, in some instances, one hundred times more severe than for crimes involving powder cocaine.[53]

Because blacks are more likely to use crack, with white users favoring powder cocaine, these laws had a disproportionate impact on the African American community in the United States. About 80 percent of federal crack defendants are black and therefore received considerably more severe punishments than their powder-favoring, mostly white, counterparts.[54] In 2010, Congress reduced the crack/powder cocaine disparity,[55] and in 2014 the Obama administration urged federal inmates sentenced under the old guidelines to apply for a reduction in their sentences. "[These are] low-level, nonviolent drug offenders who remain in prison, and who would likely have received a substantially lower sentence if convicted of precisely the same offenses today," said one federal official. "This is not fair, and it harms our criminal justice system."[56]

Women and Sentencing Few would argue that race or ethnicity should be a factor in sentencing decisions—the system should be "color-blind." Does the same principle apply to women? In other words, should the system be "gender-blind" as well—at least on a policy level? Congress answered that question in the Sentencing Reform Act of 1984, which emphasized the ideal of gender-neutral sentencing.[57]

CJ Policy—Your Take

Three states—Connecticut, Iowa, and Oregon—require **racial impact statements** for all new sentencing laws. These statements are designed to highlight the intended and unintended racial impacts of any such legislation, including how it might disproportionately impact members of minority groups. Suppose one of these states is considering a new law that increases penalties for selling illegal drugs within 1,000 feet of a school. What factors would a racial impact statement look at to determine whether the proposed statute unfairly targets minorities?

▲ A judge in Pontiac, Michigan, gave seventy-five-year-old Sandra Layne a harsher sentence than required by state guidelines for the second-degree murder of her seventeen-year-old grandson. **How might a woman's gender work against her in sentencing situations involving family-related violent crimes?** AP Images/Rich Pedroncelli

Gender Differences In practice, however, this has not occurred. Women who are convicted of crimes are less likely to go to prison than men, and those who are incarcerated tend to serve shorter sentences. According to government data, on average, a woman receives a sentence that is twenty-nine months shorter than that of a man for a violent crime and nine months shorter for a property crime.[58] When adjusting for comparable arrest offenses, criminal histories, and other presentencing factors, Sonja B. Starr of the University of Michigan Law School found that male convicts receive sentences that are 60 percent more severe than those for women.[59] One study attributes these differences to the elements of female criminality: in property crimes, women are usually accessories, and in violent crimes, women are usually reacting to physical abuse. In both situations, the mitigating circumstances lead to lesser punishment.[60]

The Chivalry Effect Other evidence also suggests that a *chivalry effect,* or the idea that women should be treated more leniently than men, plays a large role in sentencing decisions. Several self-reported studies have shown that judges may treat female defendants more "gently" than males and that with women, judges are influenced by mitigating factors such as marital status and family background that they would ignore with men.[61]

In certain situations, however, a woman's gender can work against her. Several years ago, for example, seventy-five-year-old Sandra Layne was convicted of second degree murder for fatally shooting her seventeen-year-old grandson. According to state sentencing guidelines, discussed in the next section, Layne, who had no criminal history, deserved to spend twelve to twenty years in prison. Oakland County (Michigan) judge Denise Langford, however, sentenced Layne to twenty-to-forty years behind bars, saying, "Grandmothers are supposed to protect."[62] According to Keith Crew, a professor of sociology and criminology at the University of Northern Iowa, defendants who are seen as bad mothers (or grandmothers) often "get the hammer" from judges and juries.[63]

Sentencing Reform

Judicial discretion, then, has both positive and negative aspects. Although it allows judges to impose a wide variety of sentences to fit specific criminal situations, it appears to fail to rein in a judge's subjective biases, which can lead to disparity and perhaps discrimination. Critics of judicial discretion believe that its costs (the lack of equality) outweigh its benefits (providing individualized justice). As Columbia law professor John C. Coffee noted:

> If we wish the sentencing judge to treat "like cases alike," a more inappropriate technique for the presentation could hardly be found than one that stresses a novelistic portrayal of each offender and thereby overloads the decisionmaker in a welter of detail.[64]

In other words, Professor Coffee feels that judges are given too much information in the sentencing process, making it impossible for them to be consistent in their decisions. It follows that limiting judicial discretion would not only simplify the process but lessen the opportunity for disparity or discrimination. This attitude has spread through state and federal legislatures, causing extensive changes in sentencing procedures within the American criminal justice system.

Sentencing Guidelines

In an effort to eliminate the inequities of disparity by removing judicial bias from the sentencing process, many states and the federal government have turned to **sentencing guidelines,** which require judges to dispense legislatively determined sentences based on factors such as the seriousness of the crime and the offender's prior record.

State Sentencing Guidelines In 1978, Minnesota became the first state to create a Sentencing Guidelines Commission with a mandate to construct and monitor the use of a determinate sentencing structure. The Minnesota Commission left no doubt as to the philosophical justification for the new sentencing statutes, stating unconditionally that retribution was its primary goal.[65] Today, about twenty states employ some form of sentencing guidelines with similar goals.

In general, these guidelines remove discretionary power from state judges by turning sentencing into a mathematical exercise. Members of the courtroom work group are guided by a *grid,* which helps them determine the proper sentence. Figure 11.4 shows the grid established by the Massachusetts sentencing commission. As in the grids used by most states, one axis ranks the type of crime, while the other refers to the offender's criminal history. In the grid for Massachusetts, the pink boxes indicate the "incarceration zone." A prison sentence is required for crimes in this zone. The yellow boxes delineate a "discretionary zone," in which the judge can decide between incarceration or intermediate sanctions, which you will learn about in the next chapter. The green boxes indicate the "intermediate sanction zone," in which only intermediate sanctions are to be levied.

Certain crimes are "staircased" in the Massachusetts grid, meaning that the same crime can result in different punishments based on other factors.[66] For example, assault and battery with a dangerous weapon (A&B DW) resulting in no injury or a minor injury is at offense seriousness level 3. When the crime results in a moderate but not life-threatening injury, it is at offense seriousness level 4. But when the injury is life threatening, the crime is at offense seriousness level 6—squarely in the "incarceration zone" regardless of the defendant's criminal history.

Federal Sentencing Guidelines In 1984, Congress passed the Sentencing Reform Act (SRA),[67] paving the way for federal sentencing guidelines that went into effect three years later. Similar in many respects to the state guidelines, the SRA also eliminated parole for federal prisoners and severely limited early release from prison due to good behavior.[68] The impact of the SRA and the state guidelines has been dramatic. Sentences have become harsher—by 2004, the average federal prison sentence was fifty months, more than twice as long as in 1984.[69]

Much to the disappointment of supporters of sentencing reform, a series of United States Supreme Court decisions handed down midway though the first decade of the 2000s held that federal sentencing guidelines were advisory only.[70] Five years after these Court decisions, according to the U.S. Sentencing Commission, African American defendants were receiving sentences about 20 percent longer than white males that were convicted of similar crimes.[71] Similarly, a 2012 study by the Transactional Records Access Clearinghouse found widespread sentencing disparities in federal courts, particularly in drug, weapons, and white-collar cases.[72]

Sentencing Guidelines
Legislatively determined guidelines that judges are required to follow when sentencing those convicted of specific crimes.

FIGURE 11.4 Massachusetts's Sentencing Guidelines

Sentencing Guidelines Grid

Level	Illustrative Offenses	Sentence Range				
9	Murder	Life	Life	Life	Life	Life
8	Manslaughter (Voluntary) Rape of a Child with Force Aggravated Rape Armed Burglary	96–144 Months	108–162 Months	120–180 Months	144–216 Months	204–306 Months
7	Armed Robbery Rape Mayhem	60–90 Months	68–102 Months	84–126 Months	108–162 Months	160–240 Months
6	Manslaughter (Involuntary) Armed Robbery (No Gun) A&B DW* (Significant Injury)	40–60 Months	45–67 Months	50–75 Months	60–90 Months	80–120 Months
5	Unarmed Robbery Unarmed Burglary Stalking in Violation of Order Larceny ($50,000 and over)	12–36 Months IS-IV IS-III IS-II	24–36 Months IS-IV IS-III IS-II	36–54 Months	48–72 Months	60–90 Months
4	Larceny (from a Person) A&B DW (Moderate Injury)* B&E** (Dwelling) Larceny ($10,000 to $50,000)	0–24 Months IS-IV IS-III IS-II	3–30 Months IS-IV IS-III IS-II	6–30 Months IS-IV IS-III IS-II	20–30 Months	24–36 Months
3	A&B DW (Minor or No Injury) B&E (Not Dwelling) Larceny ($250 to $10,000)	0–12 Months IS-IV IS-III IS-II IS-I	0–15 Months IS-IV IS-III IS-II IS-I	0–18 Months IS-IV IS-III IS-II IS-I	0–24 Months IS-IV IS-III IS-II	6–24 Months IS-IV IS-III IS-II
2	Assault Larceny (under $250)	IS-III IS-II IS-I	0–6 Months IS-III IS-II IS-I	0–6 Months IS-III IS-II IS-I	0–9 Months IS-IV IS-III IS-II IS-I	0–12 Months IS-IV IS-III IS-II IS-I
1	Driving after Suspended License Disorderly Conduct Vandalism	IS-II IS-I	IS-III IS-II IS-I	IS-III IS-II IS-I	0–3 Months IS-IV IS-III IS-II IS-I	0–6 Months IS-IV IS-III IS-II IS-I
	Criminal History Scale	**A** No/Minor Record	**B** Moderate Record	**C** Serious Record	**D** Violent/Repetitive	**E** Serious Violent

*A&B DW = Assault and Battery, Dangerous Weapon
**B&E = Breaking and Entering

The numbers in each cell represent the range from which the judge selects the maximum sentence ("not more than"). The minimum sentence ("not less than") is two-thirds of the maximum sentence and constitutes the initial parole eligibility date.

Sentencing Zones

☐ Incarceration Zone
☐ Discretionary Zone (incarceration/intermediate sanction)
☐ Intermediate Sanction Zone

Intermediate Sanction Levels

IS-IV   24-Hour Restriction
IS-III   Daily Accountability
IS-II   Standard Supervision
IS-I   Financial Accountability

www.mass.gov/courts/formsandguidelines/sentencing/grid.html

Departure A stipulation in many federal and state sentencing guidelines that allows a judge to adjust his or her sentencing decision based on the special circumstances of a particular case.

Judicial Departures In essence, the Supreme Court decisions just mentioned returned to federal judges the ability to "depart" from federal sentencing guidelines. Federal judges are taking advantage of this discretion, deviating from sentencing guidelines in almost half of all cases before them.[73] This "escape hatch" of judicial discretion is called a **departure,** and is available to state judges as well as their federal counterparts. Judges in Massachusetts, for example, can depart from the grid in Figure 11.4 if a case involves mitigating or aggravating circumstances.[74]

Mandatory Sentencing Guidelines

In an attempt to close even the limited loophole of judicial discretion offered by departures, politicians (often urged on by their constituents) have passed sentencing laws even more contrary to the idea of individualized justice. These **mandatory** (minimum) **sentencing guidelines** further limit a judge's power to deviate from determinate sentencing laws by setting firm standards for certain crimes.

State and Federal Mandatory Minimums The mandatory minimum "movement" started in the early 1970s in New York state, which was experiencing a wave of heroin-related crime. Governor Nelson Rockefeller pushed through a series of mandatory drug sentences, the most draconian being a fifteen-years-to-life punishment for anyone convicted of possessing four ounces of any illegal narcotic other than marijuana.[75] Today, nearly every state has mandatory sentencing laws, most related to crimes involving the sale or possession of illegal drugs.

The federal government passed its Anti-Drug Abuse Act[76] in the mid-1980s, in response to the cocaine overdose death of a well-known basketball player named Len Bias. Federal mandatory minimums are guided by a set of "triggers" based on the amount of drugs involved, the offender's criminal history, and many other attendant circumstances (see Chapter 4). These triggers include selling drugs to someone under twenty-one years of age, using a minor as part of "drug operations," and carrying a firearm during the drug-related crime.[77] This legislation has given a great deal of power to federal prosecutors, who, by using their discretion to add penalty enhancements, are able to coerce defendants into plea bargaining rather than risking a lengthy prison sentence.[78]

"Three-Strikes" Legislation **Habitual offender laws** are a form of mandatory sentencing found in twenty-six states and used by the federal government. Also known as "three-strikes-and-you're-out" laws, these statutes require that any person convicted of a third felony must serve a lengthy prison sentence. In many cases, the crime does not have to be of a violent or dangerous nature. Under Washington's habitual offender law, for example, a "persistent offender" is automatically sentenced to life even if the third felony offense happens to be "vehicular assault" (an automobile accident that causes injury), unarmed robbery, or attempted arson, among other lesser felonies.[79] Consequently, two-thirds of all inmates serving life without parole in that state were sentenced for a third strike.[80] In California, convicts have been sent to prison for life for third offenses that include shoplifting a pair of tube socks, stealing a slice of pizza, and possessing .14 grams of methamphetamine.[81]

The Supreme Court validated the most punitive aspects of habitual offender laws with its decision in *Lockyer v. Andrade* (2003).[82] That case involved the sentencing under California's "three-strikes" law of Leandro Andrade to fifty years in prison for stealing $153 worth of videotapes. Writing for the majority in a bitterly divided 5–4 decision, Justice Sandra Day O'Connor concluded that Andrade's punishment was not so "objectively" unreasonable that it violated the Constitution.[83] Basically, the justices who upheld the law said that if the California legislature—and by extension the California voters—felt that the law was reasonable, then the judicial branch was in no position to disagree.

Mandatory Sentencing Guidelines Statutorily determined punishments that must be applied to those who are convicted of specific crimes.

Habitual Offender Laws Statutes that require lengthy prison sentences for those who are convicted of multiple felonies.

Reforming Mandatory Minimums Somewhat ironically, in 2012 California voters decided that the state's three-strikes law was indeed unreasonable. That year, by a two-thirds vote, Californians passed a ballot initiative revising the law. Now, a life sentence will be imposed only when the third felony conviction is for a serious or violent crime. Furthermore, the measure authorizes judges to resentence those approximately 3,000 inmates who are serving life prison terms in California prisons because of a non-violent "third strike."[84]

The California ballot initiative reflects nationwide discontent with mandatory minimum sentencing statutes. As we saw with the judge who was forced to sentence Scott Walker to life in prison at the beginning of the chapter, these laws are often unpopular with judges. They are also seen as contributing heavily to the explosive, and costly, growth of the U.S. prison population since the 1980s, which we will discuss in Chapter 13. In addition, the country's minority population seems to have borne the brunt of harsh sentencing legislation—nearly 70 percent of all convicts subject to mandatory minimum sentences are African American or Hispanic.[85]

In response to these issues, nearly thirty states have reformed their mandatory sentencing laws since 2000. In general, these reforms take one of three approaches:[86]

1. *Expanding judicial discretion.* In Connecticut, judges can depart from mandatory minimum sentences for certain drug crimes when no violence or threat of violence was present.[87]
2. *Limiting habitual offender "triggers."* In Nevada, misdemeanor convictions no longer count toward a five-year mandatory minimum sentence for a third conviction.[88]
3. *Repealing or revising mandatory minimum sentences.* In 2009, New York repealed the "Rockefeller drug laws," eliminating mandatory minimum sentences for low-level drug offenders.[89]

On the federal level, the U.S. Congress is considering several bills that would allow federal judges to depart from mandatory minimum sentences for nonviolent drug offenses.[90] Absent legislative reform, the U.S. Department of Justice has asked federal prosecutors to avoid charging nonviolent drug offenders with the penalty enhancements that lead to long prison terms.[91]

Victim Impact Evidence

The final piece of the sentencing puzzle involves victims and victims' families. As mentioned in Chapter 3, crime victims traditionally were banished to the peripheries of the criminal justice system. This situation has changed dramatically with the emergence of the victims' rights movement over the past few decades. Victims are now given the opportunity to testify—in person or through written testimony—during sentencing hearings about the suffering they experienced as the result of the crime. These **victim impact statements (VISs)** have proved extremely controversial, however, and legal experts have had a difficult time determining whether they cause more harm than good.

Balancing the Process The Crime Victims' Rights Act provides victims the right to be reasonably heard during the sentencing process,[92] and many state victims' rights laws contain similar provisions.[93] In general, these laws allow a victim (or victims) to tell his or her "side of the story" to the sentencing body, be it a judge, jury, or parole officer. In nonmurder cases, the victim can personally describe the physical, financial, and

Victim Impact Statement (VIS) A statement to the sentencing body (judge, jury, or parole board) in which the victim is given the opportunity to describe how the crime has affected her or him.

emotional impact of the crime. When the charge is murder or manslaughter, relatives or friends can give personal details about the victim and describe the effects of her or his death. In almost all instances, the goal of the VIS is to increase the harshness of the sentence.

Most of the debate surrounding VISs centers on their use in the sentencing phases of death penalty cases. Supporters point out that the defendant has always been allowed to present character evidence in the hopes of dissuading a judge or jury from capital punishment. According to some, a VIS balances the equation by giving survivors a voice in the process. Presenting a VIS is also said to have psychological benefits for victims, who are no longer forced to sit in silence as decisions that affect their lives are made by others.[94] Finally, on a purely practical level, a VIS may help judges and juries make informed sentencing decisions by providing them with an understanding of all of the consequences of the crime. (For an example of a victim impact statement from a recent death penalty case, see Figure 11.5.)

The Risks of Victim Evidence Opponents of the use of VISs claim that they interject dangerously prejudicial evidence into the sentencing process, which should be governed by reason, not emotion. The inflammatory nature of VISs, they say, may distract judges and juries from the facts of the case, which should be the only basis for a sentence.[95] Furthermore, critics contend that a VIS introduces the idea of "social value" into the courtroom. In other words, judges and juries may feel compelled to base the punishment on the "social value" of the victim (his or her standing in the community, role as a family member, and the like) rather than the circumstances of the crime.

LEARNING OBJECTIVE 6 Identify the arguments for and against the use of victim impact statements during sentencing hearings.

FIGURE 11.5 Victim Impact Statement (VIS)

In 2013, an Arizona jury found Jodi Arias guilty of first degree murder for killing Travis Alexander, her ex-boyfriend. Arias stabbed Alexander twenty-seven times, slashed his throat, and, after he had already died, shot him. During the sentencing phase of the trial, Steven Alexander, Travis's brother (see photo), gave a VIS as part of the prosecution's argument that Arias should receive the death penalty. A portion of that VIS is reprinted here.

AP Images

The nature of my brother's murder has had a major impact on me. It has even invaded my dreams. I have nightmares about someone coming after me with a knife and then going after my wife and my daughter. When I wake up I cannot establish what is real and what is a dream. . . . It may sound childish, but I cannot sleep alone in the dark anymore. I've had dreams of my brother, all curled up in the shower, thrown in there, left to rot, for days, all alone. I don't want these nightmares anymore. I don't want to have to see my brother's murderer anymore.

In fact, research has shown that hearing victim impact evidence makes jurors more likely to impose the death penalty.[96] The Supreme Court, however, has given its approval to the use of VISs, allowing judges to decide whether the statements are admissible on a case-by-case basis, just as they do with any other type of evidence.[97]

Capital Punishment

"You do not know how hard it is to let a human being die," Abraham Lincoln (1809–1865) once said, "when you feel that a stroke of your pen will save him." Despite these misgivings, during his four years in office Lincoln approved the execution of 267 soldiers, including those who had slept at their posts.[98] Our sixteenth president's ambivalence toward **capital punishment** is reflected in America's continuing struggle to reconcile the penalty of death with the morals and values of society. Capital punishment has played a role in sentencing since the earliest days of the Republic and—having survived a brief period of abolition between 1972 and 1976—continues to enjoy public support.

Still, few topics in the criminal justice system inspire such heated debate. Death penalty opponents such as legal expert Stephen Bright wonder whether "there comes a time when a society gets beyond some of the more primitive forms of punishment."[99] They point out that only twenty-three countries still employ the death penalty and that the United States is the sole Western democracy that continues the practice. Critics also claim that a process whose subjects are chosen by "luck and money and race" cannot serve the interests of justice.[100] Proponents believe that the death penalty serves as the ultimate deterrent for violent criminal behavior and that the criminals who are put to death are the "worst of the worst" and deserve their fate.

Today, about 3,000 convicts are living on "death row" in American prisons, meaning they have been sentenced to death and are awaiting execution. In the 1940s, as many as two hundred people were put to death in the United States in one year. As Figure 11.6 shows, the most recent high-water mark was ninety-eight in 1999. Despite declines since then, certain states and the federal government still regularly seek the death penalty for those offenders convicted of capital crimes. Consequently, the questions that surround the death penalty—Is it fair? Is it humane? Does it deter crime?—will continue to mobilize both its supporters and its detractors.

Methods of Execution

In its early years, when the United States adopted the practice of capital punishment from England, it also adopted English methods, which included drawing and quartering and boiling the convict alive. By the nineteenth century, these techniques had been deemed "barbaric" and were replaced by hanging. Indeed, the history of capital punishment in America is marked by attempts to make the act more humane. The 1890s saw the introduction of electrocution as a less painful method of execution than hanging, and in 1890 in Auburn Prison, New York, William Kemmler became the first American to die in an electric chair.

Capital Punishment The use of the death penalty to punish wrongdoers for certain crimes.

FIGURE 11.6 Executions in the United States, 1976 to 2014

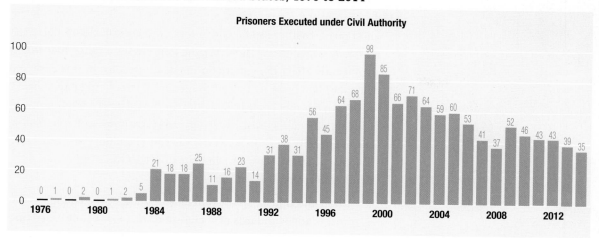

Prisoners Executed under Civil Authority

Source: Death Penalty Information Center.

The "chair" remained the primary form of execution until 1977, when Oklahoma became the first state to adopt lethal injection. Today, this method dominates executions in all thirty-one states that employ the death penalty. Fourteen states authorize at least two different methods of execution, meaning that electrocution (eight states), lethal gas (three states), hanging (three states), and the firing squad (two states) are still used on very rare occasions.[101]

For most of the past three decades, states have used a similar three-drug process to carry out lethal injections. The process—which involves a sedative, a paralyzing agent, and a drug that induces heart failure—was designed to be as painless as possible for the condemned convict. Over the past five years, however, the companies that manufacture these three drugs have increasingly refused to sell them for execution purposes. This has forced state officials to experiment with untested replacement drugs, a development that—as we shall soon see—has added an element of uncertainty to capital punishment in the United States.

The Death Penalty and the Supreme Court

In 1890, William Kemmler challenged his sentence to die in New York's new electric chair (for murdering his mistress) on the grounds that electrocution infringed on his Eighth Amendment rights against cruel and unusual punishment.[102] Kemmler's challenge is historically significant in that it did not implicate the death penalty itself as being cruel and unusual, but only the method by which it was carried out. Many constitutional scholars believe that the framers never questioned the necessity of capital punishment, as long as due process is followed in determining the guilt of the suspect.[103] Accordingly, the Supreme Court rejected Kemmler's challenge, stating:

> Punishments are cruel when they involve torture or a lingering death; but the punishment of death is not cruel, within the meaning of that word as used in the Constitution. It implies there something inhuman and barbarous, something more than the mere extinguishment of life.[104]

Thus, the Court set a standard that it has followed to this day. No *method* of execution has ever been found to be unconstitutional by the Supreme Court.

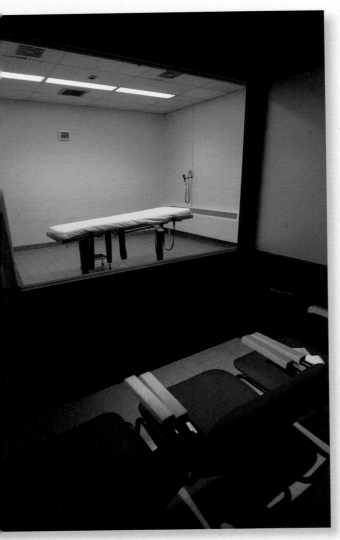

▲ This photo shows the death chamber at the Southern Ohio Correctional Facility in Lucasville, Ohio—site of convicted murderer Dennis McGuire's January 2014 execution. During the lethal injection process, which took twenty-six minutes, McGuire choked several times and appeared to clench his fists in discomfort. **Do you think that offenders convicted of capital crimes are entitled to a pain-free execution? Why or why not?**
AP Images

The *Weems* Standard For nearly eight decades following its decision in the *Kemmler* case, the Supreme Court was silent on the question of whether capital punishment was constitutional. In *Weems v. United States* (1910),[105] however, the Court made a ruling that would significantly affect the debate on the death penalty. In this case, the defendant had been sentenced to fifteen years of hard labor, a heavy fine, and a number of other penalties for the relatively minor crime of falsifying official records. The Court overturned the sentence, ruling that the penalty was too harsh considering the nature of the offense. Ultimately, in the *Weems* decision, the Court set three important precedents concerning sentencing:

1. Cruel and unusual punishment is defined by the changing norms and standards of society and therefore is not based on historical interpretations.
2. Courts may decide whether a punishment is unnecessarily cruel with regard to physical pain.
3. Courts may decide whether a punishment is unnecessarily cruel with regard to psychological pain.[106]

"Cruel and Unusual" Concerns In *Baze v. Rees* (2008),[107] the Supreme Court ruled that the mere possibility of pain "does not establish the sort of 'objectively intolerable risk of harm' that qualifies as cruel and unusual" punishment. That ruling, however, applied to the three-drug process described earlier, which has become difficult to implement because of supply issues.

Furthermore, there is some evidence that the replacement lethal injection methods used by various states, most of which use a drug called midazolam, may carry a "risk of harm." In January 2014, Michael Lee Wilson said, "I feel my whole body burning" as he was executed in Oklahoma.[108] Four months later, Oklahoma officials appeared to botch the execution of Clayton Lockett, who writhed in evident discomfort for forty-three minutes before dying. As a result, in early 2015 the Supreme Court agreed to determine whether the state's new midazolam-based lethal drug "cocktail" is a constitutionally acceptable method of execution.[109]

Death Penalty Sentencing

In the 1960s, the Supreme Court became increasingly concerned about what it saw as serious flaws in the way the states administered capital punishment. Finally, in 1967, the Court put a moratorium on executions until it could "clean up" the process. The chance to do so came with the *Furman v. Georgia* case, decided in 1972.[110]

The Bifurcated Process In its *Furman* decision, by a 5–4 margin, the Supreme Court essentially held that the death penalty, as administered by the states, violated the Eighth Amendment. Justice Potter Stewart was particularly eloquent in his concurring opinion, stating that the sentence of death was so arbitrary as to be comparable to "being struck by lightning."[111] Although the *Furman* ruling invalidated the death penalty for more than six hundred offenders on death row at the time, it also provided the states with a window to make the process less arbitrary, therefore bringing their death penalty statutes up to constitutional standards.

Identify the two stages that make up the bifurcated process of death penalty sentencing.

LEARNING
7
OBJECTIVE

The result was a two-stage, or *bifurcated,* procedure for capital cases. In the first stage, a jury determines the guilt or innocence of the defendant for a crime that has, by state statute, been determined to be punishable by death. If the defendant is found guilty, the jury reconvenes in the second stage and considers all aggravating and mitigating factors to decide whether the death sentence is in fact warranted. (See this chapter's second *Mastering Concepts* feature to get a better idea of how these two stages work.) Therefore, even if a jury finds the defendant guilty of a crime, such as first degree murder, that *may be* punishable by death, in the second stage it can decide that the circumstances surrounding the crime justify only a punishment of life in prison.

Today, thirty-one states and the federal government have capital punishment laws based on the bifurcated process. State governments are responsible for almost all executions in this country. The federal government has carried out only three death sentences since 1963, and usually seeks capital punishment only for high-profile defendants such as Dzokhar Tsarnaev, convicted of bombing the Boston Marathon in April 2013.

The Jury's Role The Supreme Court reaffirmed the important role of the jury in death penalties in *Ring v. Arizona* (2002).[112] The case involved Arizona's bifurcated process: after the jury determined a defendant's guilt or innocence, it would be dismissed, and the judge alone would decide whether execution was warranted. The Court found that this procedure violated the defendant's Sixth Amendment right to a jury trial, ruling that juries must be involved in *both* stages of the bifurcated process. The decision invalidated death penalty laws in Arizona, Colorado, Idaho, Montana, and Nebraska, forcing legislatures in those states to hastily revamp their procedures. (To learn how a jury makes this difficult decision, see the feature *Discretion in Action—Life or Death?*)

Alabama is the only state that routinely allows a measure of judicial discretion when it comes to capital punishment. Alabama juries only *recommend* a sentence of death or life in prison. If the judge feels that the sentence is unreasonable, he or she can override the jury. This unusual policy has come under criticism because, between 1976 and 2013, Alabama judges rejected a life sentence in favor of execution ninety-five times (compared to only nine overrides in the other direction).[113] The Supreme Court recently refused to accept a case challenging the practice, however, ensuring that it will continue.[114]

Mitigating Circumstances Several mitigating circumstances will prevent a defendant found guilty of first degree murder from receiving the death penalty.

Insanity In 1986, the United States Supreme Court held that the Constitution prohibits the execution of a person who is insane. The Court failed to provide a test for insanity

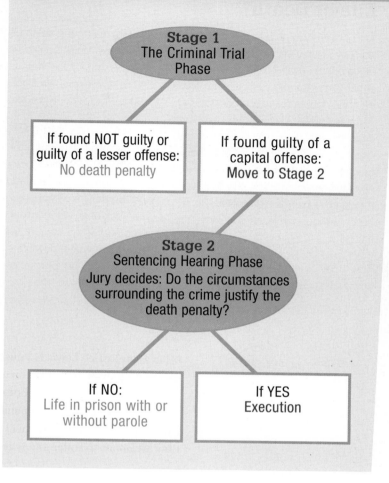

Mastering**Concepts**
The Bifurcated Death Penalty Process

Stage 1
The Criminal Trial Phase

If found NOT guilty or guilty of a lesser offense:
No death penalty

If found guilty of a capital offense:
Move to Stage 2

Stage 2
Sentencing Hearing Phase
Jury decides: Do the circumstances surrounding the crime justify the death penalty?

If NO:
Life in prison with or without parole

If YES
Execution

Discretion in Action

Life or Death?

The Situation In a fit of extreme jealousy, twenty-seven-year-old Jodi drove one thousand miles to the home of her thirty-year-old ex-boyfriend, Travis. After the couple had sex, Jodi stabbed Travis twenty-seven times and left him for dead in the shower. You are part of the jury that found Jodi guilty of first degree murder. You and your fellow jurors must now decide whether she should receive the death penalty, or, alternately, life in prison without parole, as punishment for her crime.

The Law Jurors must weigh aggravating factors against mitigating factors during the death penalty phase of criminal trials. If you believe that the aggravating factors surrounding Jodi's crime outweigh the mitigating factors, you must vote for her to be executed.

What Would You Do? In arguing for her client's life, Jodi's attorney raises a number of mitigating factors, including the childhood abuse that Jodi suffered, her borderline personality disorder, and her lack of a prior criminal record. Jodi also addresses the jury, telling you that her death would devastate her family. "I'm asking you, please, please don't do that to them. I've already hurt them so badly," Jodi says. Finally, Jodi describes several volunteer prison programs she would like to participate in, and speaks of her desire to bring "people together in a positive and constructive way" behind bars. The prosecutor counters that the violent nature of Jodi's crime outweighs any mitigating factors, and members of Travis's family ask you to sentence her to death (see Figure 11.5 from earlier in the chapter). Do you think Jodi should receive the death penalty or life in prison? Why?

[To see whether an Arizona jury chose the death sentence in similar circumstances, go to Example 11.1 in Appendix B.]

---

other than Justice Lewis F. Powell's statement that the Eighth Amendment "forbids the execution only of those who are unaware of the punishment they are about to suffer and why they are to suffer it." [115] Consequently, each state must come up with its own definition of "insanity" for death penalty purposes. A state may also force convicts on death row to take medication that will make them sane enough to be aware of the punishment they are about to suffer and why they are about to suffer it. [116]

Mental Handicap The Supreme Court's change of mind on the question of whether a mentally handicapped convict may be put to death underscores the continuing importance of the *Weems* test. In 1989, the Court rejected the argument that execution of a mentally handicapped person was "cruel and unusual" under the Eighth Amendment. [117] At the time, only two states barred execution of the mentally handicapped. Thirteen years later, eighteen states had such laws, and the Court decided that this increased number reflected "changing norms and standards of society." In *Atkins v. Virginia* (2002), [118] the Court used the *Weems* test as the main rationale for barring the execution of the mentally handicapped.

The *Atkins* ruling did not end controversy in this area, however, as it allowed state courts to make their own determinations concerning which inmates qualified as "mentally impaired" for death penalty purposes. In 2014, the Supreme Court disallowed one method of doing so by ruling that states cannot designate a fixed IQ score to determine whether a capital offender is mentally disabled. While overturning Florida's "inflexible bright-line cutoff" of an IQ below 71, Justice Anthony Kennedy wrote that, "Intellectual disability is a condition, not a number." [119]

Age Following the *Atkins* case, many observers, including four Supreme Court justices, hoped that the same reasoning would be applied to the question of whether convicts who committed the relevant crime when they were juveniles may be executed. These hopes were realized in 2005 when the Court issued its *Roper v. Simmons* decision, which effectively ended the execution of those who committed crimes as juveniles.[120] As in the *Atkins* case, the Court relied on the "evolving standards of decency" test, noting that a majority of the states, as well as every other civilized nation, prohibited the execution of offenders who committed their crimes before the age of eighteen. (See the feature *Landmark Cases*—Roper v. Simmons.) The *Roper* ruling required that seventy-two convicted murderers in twelve states be resentenced and took the death penalty "off the table" for dozens of pending cases in which prosecutors were seeking capital punishment for juvenile criminal acts.

Landmark Cases

Roper **v** Simmons

Explain why the U.S. Supreme Court abolished the death penalty for juvenile offenders. **LEARNING 8 OBJECTIVE**

When he was seventeen years old, Christopher Simmons abducted Shirley Cook, used duct tape to cover her eyes and mouth and bind her hands, and threw her to her death in a river. Although he bragged to his friends that he would "get away with it" because he was a minor, he was found guilty of murder and sentenced to death by a Missouri court. After the United States Supreme Court held, in 2002, that "evolving standards of decency" rendered the execution of mentally retarded persons unconstitutional, Simmons appealed his own sentence. His case gave the Court a chance to apply the "evolving standards of decency" test to death sentences involving offenders who were juveniles at the time they committed the underlying capital crime.

Roper v. Simmons
United States Supreme Court
543 U.S. 551 (2005)

In the Words of the Court . . .
Justice Kennedy, Majority Opinion

* * * *

The evidence of national consensus against the death penalty for juveniles is similar, and in some respects parallel, to the evidence *Atkins* held sufficient to demonstrate a national consensus against the death penalty for the mentally retarded.

* * * *

Three general differences between juveniles under 18 and adults demonstrate that juvenile offenders cannot with reliability be classified among the worst offenders. First, as any parent knows and as the scientific and sociological studies * * * tend to confirm, "[a] lack of maturity and an underdeveloped sense of responsibility are found in youth more often than in adults and are more understandable among the young. These qualities often result in impetuous and ill-considered actions and decisions." * * * In recognition of the comparative immaturity and irresponsibility of juveniles, almost every State prohibits those under 18 years of age from voting, serving on juries, or marrying without parental consent.

The second area of difference is that juveniles are more vulnerable or susceptible to negative influences and outside pressures, including peer pressure. * * * The third broad difference is that the character of a juvenile is not as well formed as that of an adult. The personality traits of juveniles are more transitory, less fixed.

These differences render suspect any conclusion that a juvenile falls among the worst offenders. * * * Retribution is not proportional if the law's most severe penalty is imposed on one whose culpability or blameworthiness is diminished, to a substantial degree, by reason of youth and immaturity.

Decision
The Court found that, applying the Eighth Amendment in light of "evolving standards of decency," the execution of offenders who were under the age of eighteen when their crimes were committed was cruel and unusual punishment and therefore unconstitutional.

For Critical Analysis
In his majority opinion, Justice Kennedy noted that a number of countries, including China, Iran, and Pakistan, had recently ended the practice of executing juveniles, leaving the United States "alone in a world that has turned its face against the practice." What impact, if any, should international customs have on American criminal law?

Debating the Sentence of Death

Of the topics covered in this textbook, few inspire such passionate argument as the death penalty. Many advocates believe that execution is "just deserts" for those who commit heinous crimes. In the words of sociologist Ernest van den Haag, death is the "only fitting retribution for murder that I can think of."[121] Opponents worry that retribution is simply another word for vengeance and that "the use of the death penalty by the state will increase the acceptance of revenge in our society and will give official sanction to a climate of violence."[122] As the debate over capital punishment continues, it tends to focus on several key issues: deterrence, fallibility, arbitrariness, and discrimination.

Deterrence Those advocates of the death penalty who wish to show that the practice benefits society often turn to the idea of deterrence. In other words, they believe that by executing convicted criminals, the criminal justice system discourages potential criminals from committing similar violent acts. (When people speak of "deterrence" with regard to the death penalty, they are usually referring to general deterrence rather than specific deterrence.) Deterrence was the primary justification for the frequent public executions carried out in this country before the 1830s and for the brutality of those events.

For Deterrence In 1975, Isaac Ehrlich, an economist then at the University of Chicago, estimated that if all those eligible for the death penalty had been executed, each additional execution that would have taken place between 1933 and 1967 could have saved the lives of as many as eight murder victims.[123] Ehrlich's data were subjected to heavy criticism, but researchers, relying on statistical comparisons of death sentences, executions, and homicide rates in particular geographic areas, continue to find statistical proof of the deterrent effect of capital punishment. Several reports released in the first decade of the 2000s claim that each convict executed deters between three and eighteen future homicides.[124] More recent research suggests that if the death penalty does have a deterrent effect, it is small and relatively short-lived, influencing behavior only for about a month after an execution takes place.[125]

Against Deterrence The main problem with studies that support the death penalty, say its critics, is that there are too few executions carried out in the United States each year to adequately determine their impact.[126] (In 2013, there was one execution in the United States for every 292 murder arrests.) Furthermore, each study that "proves" the deterrent effect of the death penalty seems be matched by one that "disproves" the same premise.[127] In 2004, for example, criminal justice professors Lisa Stolzenberg and Stewart J. D'Alessio of Florida International University found no evidence that the number of executions had any effect on the incidence of murder in the Houston, Texas, area over a five-year period.[128]

In the end, the deterrence debate follows a familiar pattern. Opponents of the death penalty claim that murderers rarely consider the consequences of their act, and therefore it makes no difference whether capital punishment exists or not. Proponents counter that this proves the death penalty's deterrent value, because if the murderers *had* considered the possibility of execution, they would not have committed their crimes. (For a discussion of the moral component to this argument, see the feature *CJ in Action* at the end of the chapter.)

Fallibility In a sense, capital punishment acts as the ultimate deterrent by rendering those executed incapable of committing further crimes. Incapacitation as a justification for the death penalty, though, rests on two questionable assumptions: (1) every convicted murderer is likely to recidivate, and (2) the criminal justice system is *infallible*. In other words, the system never convicts someone who is actually not guilty.

Wrongful Deaths? Although several executions from the 1980s and 1990s are coming under increased scrutiny,[129] no court has ever found that an innocent person has been executed in the United States. According to the Death Penalty Information Center, however, between 1973, when the Supreme Court had temporarily suspended capital punishment, and March 2015, 150 American men and women who had been convicted of capital crimes and sentenced to death—though not executed—were later found to be innocent. Over that same time period, 1,402 executions took place, meaning that for about every nine convicts put to death during that period, about one death row inmate has been found innocent.[130]

Defense Issues The single factor that contributes the most to the criminal justice system's fallibility in this area is widely believed to be unsatisfactory legal representation. Many states and counties cannot or will not allocate adequate funds for death penalty cases, meaning that indigent capital defendants are often provided with a less-than-vigorous defense.

The case of convicted murderer Ronald Rompilla highlights the consequences of poor counsel in a capital case. During the sentencing phase of his trial, Rompilla's lawyers made two serious errors. First, they failed to challenge the prosecution's characterization of Rompilla's previous conviction for rape and assault. In fact, they never even looked at the file of that case. Second, they failed to provide the Pennsylvania jury with mitigating factors that would argue against a death sentence, such as their client's troubled childhood, severe alcoholism, and other mental illnesses. Not surprisingly, the jury ordered Rompilla's execution, a sentence that was eventually overturned by the United States Supreme Court due to ineffective counsel.[131]

Arbitrariness As noted earlier, one of the reasons it is so difficult to determine the deterrent effect of the death penalty is that it is rarely meted out. Despite the bifurcated process required by the Supreme Court's *Furman* ruling (discussed earlier in the chapter), a significant amount of arbitrariness appears to remain in the system. Only 2 percent of all defendants convicted of murder are sentenced to death, and relatively few of those on death row are ever executed.[132]

The chances of a defendant in a capital trial being sentenced to death seem to depend heavily on, as we have just seen, the quality of the defense counsel and the jurisdiction where the crime was committed. As Figure 11.7 shows, a convict's likelihood of being executed is strongly influenced by geography. Five states (Florida, Missouri, Oklahoma, Texas, and Virginia) account for more than two-thirds of all executions, while nineteen states and the District of Columbia do not provide for capital punishment within their borders. In addition, because the decision to seek the death penalty is made on a local level by local prosecutors, the practice is not consistent within states that allow it. According to the Death Penalty Information Center, just four counties are responsible for more than half of the executions carried out in Texas since 1976.[133]

Discriminatory Effect Whether or not capital punishment is imposed arbitrarily, some observers claim that it is not done without bias. A disproportionate number of those executed since 1976—just over one-third—have been African American, and today

FIGURE 11.7 Executions by State, 1976–2014

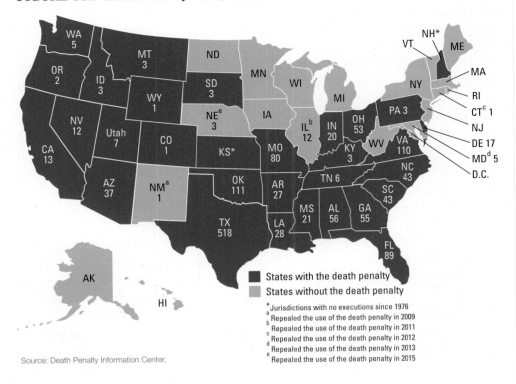

States with the death penalty

States without the death penalty

* Jurisdictions with no executions since 1976
a Repealed the use of the death penalty in 2009
b Repealed the use of the death penalty in 2011
c Repealed the use of the death penalty in 2012
d Repealed the use of the death penalty in 2013
e Repealed the use of the death penalty in 2015

Source: Death Penalty Information Center.

42 percent of all inmates on death row are black.[134] Another set of statistics also continues to be problematic: in 269 cases involving interracial murders in which the defendant was executed between 1976 and February 2014, the defendant was African American and the victim was white. Over that same time period, only 20 cases involved a white defendant and a black victim.[135] In fact, although slightly less than half of murder victims are white, three out of every four executions involve white victims.[136]

In *McCleskey v. Kemp* (1987),[137] the defense attorney for an African American sentenced to death for killing a white police officer used similar statistics to challenge Georgia's death penalty law. A study of two thousand Georgia murder cases showed that although African Americans were the victims of six out of every ten murders in the state, more than 80 percent of the cases in which death was imposed involved murders of whites.[138] In a 5–4 decision, the United States Supreme Court rejected the defense's claims, ruling that statistical evidence did not prove discriminatory intent on the part of Georgia's lawmakers.

The Future of the Death Penalty

As noted earlier in the chapter, the number of executions carried out each year in the United States has decreased dramatically since 1999. Other statistics also indicate a decline in death penalty activity. In 2014, only 72 people were sentenced to death, compared with 277 in 1999.[139] That same year, Texas, the most active state when it comes to capital punishment, executed thirty-five convicts and sentenced another forty-eight to death. By 2014, those numbers had dropped to ten and eleven, respectively.[140]

The Decline in Executions We have already addressed some of the reasons for the diminishing presence of executions in the criminal justice system. With its decisions in the *Atkins* (2002) and *Roper* (2005) cases, the United States Supreme Court removed the possibility that hundreds of mentally handicapped and juvenile offenders could be sentenced to death. The availability and reliability of drugs used in lethal injections have also become an issue. In 2015, at least four states—Arizona, Florida, Ohio, and Oklahoma—temporarily shut down their death chambers, either to reassess their drug protocols or in anticipation of the Supreme Court's ruling on Oklahoma's lethal injection procedures.

Other factors in the declining use of capital punishment in the United States include:

1. *The life-without-parole alternative.* In the early 1970s, only seven states allowed juries to sentence offenders to life in prison without parole instead of death. Now, every state provides this option, and juries seem to prefer this form of incapacitation to execution.[141]

2. *Plummeting murder rates.* The number of murders committed in this country is currently half what it was in the early 1990s.[142] As murder is the most common capital crime, this reduction has led to a decline in the number of offenders eligible for the death penalty.

3. *High costs.* Because of the costs of intensive law enforcement investigations, extensive *voir dire* (see Chapter 10), and lengthy appellate reviews, pursuing capital punishment can be very expensive for states. Nevada recently determined that its death penalty cases cost twice as much as similar cases without the death penalty, resulting in a $76 million price tag for state taxpayers since 1976.[143]

Public Opinion and the Death Penalty In July 2014, a federal judge declared that California's death penalty system had become so arbitrary and unpredictable that it was unconstitutional. The state has the nation's largest death row population at around 750, but—because of procedural problems—has not carried out an execution since 2006. As a result, said the judge, those on California's death row are experiencing a punishment that "no rational jury or legislature could ever impose: life in prison, with the remote possibility of death."[144]

As a consequence of this ruling, California joined the four states mentioned earlier in suspending its death penalty operations in 2015. Furthermore, also in 2015, Nebraska became the seventh state in eight years to end capital punishment, along with Connecticut, Illinois, Maryland, New Jersey, New Mexico, and New York. Does this mean society's "standards of decency" are changing to the point that the death sentence is in danger of being completely abolished in the United States? Probably not. The Supreme Court has shown no interest in holding that the death penalty itself is unconstitutional. In addition to its *Baze* decision (discussed earlier in this section), in 2007 the Court made it easier for prosecutors to seek the death penalty by allowing them to remove potential jurors who express reservations about the practice.[145]

Although public support for the death penalty has been steadily dropping since the mid-1990s, one poll taken in 2014 showed that 63 percent of Americans still favor the practice. (That percentage does, however, drop to about 50 percent when the choice is between execution and a sentence of life in prison without parole.)[146] Taking a closer look at the numbers, however, it becomes evident that support for capital punishment is stronger among older, white Americans than it is among younger generations and members of minority groups.[147] Thus, in the future, the continued use of the death penalty in the United States may come under threat from a majority of voters who oppose this method of criminal punishment.

CJ IN ACTION

The Morality of the Death Penalty

On August 31, 1984, gang members killed Kermit Alexander's mother, sister, and two young nephews in Los Angeles when they targeted the wrong home for a hit. Tiequon Cox, one of the gang members involved in the crimes, was eventually convicted of four counts of murder and sentenced to death. In 2014, however, when a federal judge ruled that capital punishment in California was unconstitutional, Cox's execution was put on hold. "I'm saddened, deeply saddened," by the ruling, said Alexander. "I though we had reached a point in society where [murderers] could be held accountable."[148] Like many Americans, Alexander does not see the death penalty in terms of the Eighth Amendment, "changing norms and standards," or the bifurcated sentencing process. Rather, he sees it as a matter of right and wrong, a viewpoint we will examine in this *CJ in Action* feature.

The "Life-Life Trade-Off"

In academic circles, discussion about the morality of the death penalty has generally focused on two concepts. Those who take a *utilitarian* approach believe that the "cost" of each execution is acceptable because of the "benefit" to society, usually expressed in terms of deterrence of future crimes. Those who favor the *deontological* approach reject this cost-benefit analysis on the grounds that an individual's right to life should never be sacrificed, not even for the greater good.

Robert Blecker, a professor at New York Law School, sees such arguments as too esoteric to explain our country's somewhat unique relationship with the death penalty. Blecker believes that, for many Americans, capital punishment is an expression of hatred toward the offender and the "wrongness" of his or her crime.[149] Viewed in this light, the death penalty, still popular in the United States, can be seen as an expression of society's collective moral judgment on those who commit murder.

The Case for Execution as a Moral Act

- If the death penalty can prevent even a single future murder, then it is morally justifiable and perhaps even required by the government.

- Some crimes are so horrible that executing the person responsible is the only fitting response.

- The victim's family members often say that a murderer's execution brings them a sense of "closure" by allowing them to come to terms with their grief.

The Case against Execution as a Moral Act

- The death penalty is an inherently cruel and barbaric act, and it is improper for the government of a civilized nation to kill its own citizens.

- Just as we would not permit a physician to remove the organs of a living person to save the lives of others who need organ transplants, we should not execute a criminal based on the principle that the act would save the lives of others.[150]

- Problems of arbitrariness, discrimination, and wrongful convictions rob the death penalty of any moral justification, leaving it nothing more than the pointless infliction of violence by the government.

Your Opinion—Writing Assignment

Patrick O. Kennedy spent five years on Louisiana's death row for raping his eight-year-old stepdaughter so violently that she required emergency surgery. Louisiana was one of six states that allowed the death penalty for certain sex crimes, mostly involving minors. In 2008, the United States Supreme Court found these laws to be unconstitutional, labeling as "cruel and unusual" any punishment that is not proportionate to the crime.[151] Kennedy's sentence was reduced to life in prison without parole.

How do the arguments concerning the morality of the death penalty apply when the punishment extends to other crimes besides murder? In general, do you think an argument can be made that people who rape children should be executed? Before responding, you can review our discussions in the sections of this chapter concerning:

- Retribution, deterrence, and incapacitation ("The Purpose of Sentencing").

- The issues of the death penalty debate ("Capital Punishment").

- The future of the death penalty in the United States ("Capital Punishment").

Your answer should include at least three full paragraphs.

Summary

For more information on these concepts, look back to the Learning Objective icons throughout the chapter.

 List and contrast the four basic philosophical reasons for sentencing criminals. (a) Retribution, (b) deterrence, (c) incapacitation, and (d) rehabilitation. Under the principle of retributive justice, the severity of the punishment is in proportion to the severity of the crime. Punishment is an end in itself. In contrast, the deterrence approach seeks to prevent future crimes by setting an example. Such punishment is based on its deterrent value and not necessarily on the severity of the crime. The incapacitation theory of punishment simply argues that a criminal in prison cannot inflict further harm on society. In contrast, the rehabilitation theory asserts that criminals can be rehabilitated in the appropriate prison environment.

 Contrast indeterminate with determinate sentencing. Indeterminate sentencing follows from legislative penal codes that set minimum and maximum amounts of incarceration time. Determinate sentencing carries a fixed amount of time, although this may be reduced for "good time."

 Explain why there is a difference between the sentence imposed by a judge and the actual sentence served by the prisoner. Although judges may decide on indeterminate sentencing, thereafter it is parole boards that decide when prisoners will be released after the minimum sentence is served.

 State who has input into the sentencing decision and list the factors that determine a sentence. The prosecutor, defense attorney, probation officer, and judge provide inputs. The factors considered in sentencing are (a) the seriousness of the crime, (b) mitigating circumstances, (c) aggravating circumstances, and (d) judicial philosophy.

 Explain some of the reasons why sentencing reform has occurred. One reason is sentencing disparity, which is indicative of a situation in which those convicted of similar crimes receive dissimilar sentences (often due to a particular judge's sentencing philosophy). Sentencing discrimination has also occurred on the basis of defendants' gender, race, or economic standing. An additional reason for sentencing reform has been a general desire to "get tough on crime."

 Identify the arguments for and against the use of victim impact statements during sentencing hearings. Proponents of victim impact statements believe that they allow victims to provide character evidence in the same manner as defendants have always been allowed to do and that they give victims a therapeutic "voice" in the sentencing process. Opponents argue that the statements bring unacceptable levels of emotion into the courtroom and encourage judges and juries to make sentencing decisions based on the "social value" of the victim rather than the facts of the case.

 Identify the two stages that make up the bifurcated process of death penalty sentencing. The first stage of the bifurcated process requires a jury to find the defendant guilty or not guilty of a crime that is punishable by execution. If the defendant is found guilty, then, in the second stage, the jury reconvenes to decide whether the death sentence is warranted.

 Explain why the U.S. Supreme Court abolished the death penalty for juvenile offenders. In its *Roper v. Simmons* decision, the Supreme Court ruled that national "evolving standards of decency" no longer justified the execution of juvenile offenders. Such offenders are understood to be less blameworthy than adults because of various issues relating to immaturity and irresponsibility.

 Describe the main issues of the death penalty debate. Many of those who favor capital punishment believe that it is "just deserts" for the most violent of criminals. Those who oppose it see the act as little more than revenge. There is also disagreement over whether the death penalty acts as a deterrent. The relatively high number of death row inmates who have been found innocent has raised questions about the fallibility of the process, while certain statistics seem to show that execution is rather arbitrary. Finally, many observers contend that capital punishment is administered unfairly with regard to members of minority groups.

Questions for Critical Analysis

1. Suppose that the U.S. Congress passed a new law that punished shoplifting with a mandatory eighty-five-year prison term. What would be the impact of the new law on shoplifting nationwide? Would such a harsh law be justified by its deterrent effect? What about imposing a similarly extreme punishment on a more serious crime—a mandatory sentence of life in prison for, say, drunk driving? Would such a law be in society's best interest? Why or why not?

2. Why are truth-in-sentencing laws generally popular among victims' rights advocates? Why might these laws not be so popular with prison administrators or government officials charged with balancing a state budget?

3. Harold is convicted of unarmed burglary after a trial in Boston, Massachusetts. He has no prior convictions. According to the grid in Figure 11.4, what punishment do the state guidelines require? What would his punishment be if he had a previous conviction for armed robbery, which means that he has a "serious" criminal record?

4. Refer to the victim impact statement in Figure 11.5. How might Steven Alexander's words be helpful to jurors trying to decide whether the defendant should be executed? Do you think this statement is unfairly prejudicial against the defendant? Why or why not?

5. Supporters of the death penalty often use the principles of retribution and deterrence to argue in favor of the practice. How are these arguments affected by the long period of time (often fifteen years or more) from conviction to execution for many death row inmates in this country?

Key Terms

aggravating circumstances   360
capital punishment   370
departure   366
determinate sentencing   355
deterrence   349
"good time"   355
habitual offender laws   367
incapacitation   351

indeterminate sentencing   354
just deserts   349
mandatory sentencing guidelines   367
mitigating circumstances   360
presentence investigative report   358
"real offense"   359
rehabilitation   352

restitution   353
restorative justice   352
retribution   349
sentencing discrimination   362
sentencing disparity   361
sentencing guidelines   365
truth-in-sentencing laws   355
victim impact statement (VIS)   368

Notes

1. Herbert L. Packer, "Justification for Criminal Punishment," in *The Limits of Criminal Sanction* (Palo Alto, Calif.: Stanford University Press, 1968), 36–37.

2. Jami L. Anderson, "Reciprocity as a Justification for Retributivism," *Criminal Justice Ethics* (Winter/Spring 1997), 13–14.

3. Immanuel Kant, *Metaphysical First Principles of the Doctrine of Right*, trans. Mary Gregor (Cambridge, UK: Cambridge University Press, 1991), 331.

4. Jeremy Bentham, *An Introduction to the Principles of Morals and Legislation 1789* (New York: Hafner Publishing Corp., 1961).

5. Brian Forst, "Prosecution and Sentencing," in *Crime*, eds. James Q. Wilson and Joan Petersilia (San Francisco: ICS Press, 1995), 376.

6. Frank O. Bowman III, "Playing '21' with Narcotics Enforcement: A Response to Professor Carrington," *Washington and Lee Law Review* 52 (1995), 972.

7. Bureau of Justice Statistics, *Criminal Victimization, 2013* (Washington, D.C.: U.S. Department of Justice, September 2014), Table 6, page 7.

8. Federal Bureau of Investigation, *Crime in the United States, 2013* (Washington, D.C.: U.S. Department of Justice, 2012), at **www.fbi.gov/about-us/cjis/ucr/crime-in-the-u.s/2013/crime-in-the-u.s.-2013**, Table 25.

9. Daniel Nagin, "Deterrence in the 21st Century: A Review of the Evidence," in ed. Michael Tonry, *Crime and Justice in America: 1975–2025, Vol. 42* (Chicago: University of Chicago Press, 2013), 199–263; and Gary Kleck and J. C. Barnes, "Deterrence and Macro-Level Perceptions of Punishment Risks: Is There a Collective Wisdom?" *Crime & Delinquency* (October 2013), 1006–1035.

10. Paul H. Robinson and John M. Darley, "The Utility of Desert," *Northwestern University Law Review* 91 (Winter 1997), 453.

11. James Q. Wilson, *Thinking about Crime* (New York: Basic Books, 1975), 235.

12. Ashley Nellis, *Life Goes On: The Historic Rise of Life Sentences in America* (Washington, D.C.: The Sentencing Project, September 2013), 1.

13. Isaac Ehrlich, "Participation in Illegitimate Activities: A Theoretical and Empirical Investigation," *Journal of Political Economy* 81 (May/June 1973), 521–564.

14. Avinash Singh Bhati, *An Information Theoretic Method for Estimating the Number of Crimes Averted by Incapacitation* (Washington, D.C.: Urban Institute, July 2007), 18–33.

15. Todd Clear, *Harm in Punishment* (Boston: Northeastern University Press, 1980).

16. Jan Chaiken, Marcia Chaiken, and William Rhodes, "Predicting Violent Behavior and Classifying Violent Offenders," in *Understanding and Preventing Violence,* eds. Albert J. Reiss, Jr., and Jeffrey A. Roth (Washington, D.C.: National Academy Press, 1994).

17. Patricia M. Clark, "An Evidence-Based Intervention for Offenders," *Corrections Today* (February/March 2011), 62–64.

18. "America's New Drug Policy Landscape," *Pew Research Center* (April 2, 2014), at **www .people-press.org/2014/04/02/americas -new-drug-policy-landscape.**

19. Robert V. Wolf, *Widening the Circle: Can Peacemaking Work Outside of Tribal Communities?* (New York: Center for Court Innovation, 2012), 2–8.

20. Quoted in *ibid.,* 8.

21. Kimberly S. Burke, *An Inventory and Examination of Restorative Justice Practices for Youth in Illinois* (Chicago: Illinois Criminal Justice Information Authority, April 2013), 6–7.

22. "Legislation," *Restorative Justice Online*, at **www.restorativejustice.org/university -classroom/02world/nothamcar /legislation.**

23. 42 U.S.C. Section 10601 (2006).

24. Office for Victims of Crime, "Crime Victims Fund" (June 2013), at **www.ovc.gov/pubs /crimevictimsfundfs/intro.html.**

25. Josh Allen, "Jon Wilson Helps Crime Victims Talk with Their Offenders," *The Christian Science Monitor Weekly* (April 9, 2012), 45.

26. Leena Kurki, "Restorative and Community Justice in the United States," in *Crime and Justice: A Review of Research,* vol. 27, ed. Michael Tonry (Chicago: University of Chicago Press, 2000), 253–303.

27. Quoted in Molly Rowan Leach, "The Political Rise of Restorative Justice," *The Huffington Post* (March 26, 2014), at **www.huffington post.com/molly-rowan-leach/the -political-rise-of-res_b_5029413.html.**

28. Gregory W. O'Reilly, "Truth-in-Sentencing: Illinois Adds Yet Another Layer of 'Reform' to Its Complicated Code of Corrections," *Loyola University of Chicago Law Journal* (Summer 1996), 986, 999–1000.

29. David E. Olson, et al., *Final Report: The Impact of Illinois' Truth-in-Sentencing Law on Sentence Lengths, Time to Serve and Disciplinary Incidents of Convicted Murderers and Sex Offenders* (Chicago: Illinois Criminal Justice Information Authority, June 2009), 4–5.

30. Marvin Zalman, "The Rise and Fall of the Indeterminate Sentence," *Wayne Law Review* 24 (1977), 45, 52.

31. Paul W. Keve, *Crime Control and Justice in America: Searching for Facts and Answers* (Chicago: American Library Association, 1995), 77.

32. Adam Ferrise, "Man Ordered by Judge to Hold Sign Saying He Bullied Disabled Children Starts His Five-Hour Shift," *Cleveland .com* (April 13, 2014), at **www.cleveland .com/metro/index.ssf/2014/04/man _ordered_by_judge_to_hold_s.html.**

33. Danielle A. Alvarez, "Flowers, Dinner, Bowling—and Counseling—Ordered by Broward Judge in Domestic Case," *Sunsentinel .com* (February 7, 2012), at **articles.sun -sentinel.com/2012-02-07/news/fl -flowers-food-bowling-20120207_1 _red-lobster-broward-judge-judge -johnjay-hurley.**

34. Kate Stith and José A. Cabranes, "Judging under the Federal Sentencing Guidelines," *Northwestern University Law Review* 91 (Summer 1997), 1247.

35. Mark M. Lanier and Claud H. Miller III, "Attitudes and Practices of Federal Probation Officers towards Pre-Plea/Trial Investigative Report Policy," *Crime & Delinquency* 41 (July 1995), 365–366.

36. Nancy J. King and Rosevelt L. Noble, "Felony Jury Sentencing in Practice: A Three-State Study," *Vanderbilt Law Review* (2004), 1986.

37. Jena Iontcheva, "Jury Sentencing as Democratic Practice," *Virginia Law Review* (April 2003), 325.

38. Julie R. O'Sullivan, "In Defense of the U.S. Sentencing Guidelines Modified Real-Offense System," *Northwestern University Law Review* 91 (1997), 1342.

39. Lisa G. Aspinwall, Teneille R. Brown, and James Tabery, "The Double-Edged Sword: Does Biomechanism Increase or Decrease Judges' Sentencing of Psychopaths?" *Science* (August 2012), 846–849.

40. Quoted in Robert Allen, "6-Month Sentence for Driver's Attacker Angers Prosecutor," *Detroit Free Press* (July 17, 2014), at **www.usatoday.com/story/news/nation /2014/07/17/steven-utash-detroit -beating-sentencing/12783233/.**

41. 18 U.S.C. Section 2113(a) (1994).

42. U.S. Sentencing Commission, "Statistical Information Packet, Fiscal Year 2013, Oregon," Table 7, at **www.ussc.gov/sites/default /files/pdf/research-and-publications /federal-sentencing-statistics/state -district-circuit/2013/or13.pdf;** and "Statistical Information Packet, Fiscal Year 2013, Eastern District of North Carolina," Table 7, at **www.ussc.gov/sites/default/files/pdf /research-and-publications/federal -sentencing-statistics/state-district -circuit/2013/nce13.pdf.**

43. U.S. Sentencing Commission, "Statistical Information Packet, Fiscal Year 2012, Fourth Circuit," Table 7, at **www.ussc.gov /sites/default/files/pdf/research-and**

-publications/federal-sentencing -statistics/state-district-circuit/2013 /4c13.pdf; and "Statistical Information Packet, Fiscal Year 2012, Ninth Circuit," Table 7, at **www.ussc.gov/sites/default /files/pdf/research-and-publications /federal-sentencing-statistics/state -district-circuit/2013/9c13.pdf.**

44. Keith Williams, "Practical Child Porn Defense: Fighting the Pitchfork Mentality," *Aspatore* (July 2012), 3911.

45. Cassia Spohn and David Holleran, "The Imprisonment Penalty Paid by Young, Unemployed Black and Hispanic Male Offenders," *Criminology* 35 (2000), 281.

46. Illinois Disproportionate Justice Impact Study Commission, "Key Findings and Recommendations" (2011), at **www.illinois senatedemocrats.com/phocadownload /PDF/Attachments/2011/djisfactsheet .pdf.**

47. Bureau of Justice Statistics, *Prisoners in 2013* (Washington, D.C.: U.S. Department of Justice, September 2014), Table 14, page 16.

48. Nellis, *op. cit.,* 10.

49. Bureau of Justice Statistics, *Federal Statistics, 2010* (Washington, D.C.: U.S. Department of Justice, December 2013), Table 14, page 24.

50. Spohn and Holleran, *op. cit.,* 301.

51. Brian Johnson, "The Multilevel Context of Criminal Sentencing: Integrating Judge- and County-Level Influences," *Criminology* (May 2006), 259–298.

52. *A Living Death: Life without Parole for Nonviolent Offenses* (New York: American Civil Liberties Union, November 2013), Table 10, page 28.

53. Anti-Drug Abuse Act of 1986, Pub. L. No. 99-570, 100 Stat. 3207 (1986).

54. Solomon Moore, "Justice Department Seeks Equity in Sentences for Cocaine," *New York Times* (April 30, 2009), A17.

55. Pub. L. No. 111-220, Section 2, 124 Stat. 2372.

56. Quoted in Matt Apuzzo, "Justice Dept. Starts Quest for Inmates to Be Freed," *New York Times* (January 31, 2014), A13.

57. 28 U.S.C. Section 991 (1994).

58. Bureau of Justice Statistics, *Felony Sentences in State Courts, 2006—Statistical Tables* (Washington, D.C.: U.S. Department of Justice, December 2009), Table 3.5, page 20.

59. Sonja B. Starr, "Estimating Gender Disparities in Federal Criminal Cases," *University of Michigan Law and Economics Research Paper* (August 29, 2012), at **papers.ssrn.com /sol3/papers.cfm?abstract_id=2144002.**

60. Clarice Feinman, *Women in the Criminal Justice System,* 3d ed. (Westport, Conn.: Praeger, 1994), 35.

61. Darrell Steffensmeier, John Kramer, and Cathy Streifel, "Gender and Imprisonment Decisions," *Criminology* 31 (1993), 411.

62. Quoted in L.L. Brasier, "Sandra Layne Sentenced to 20–40 Years in Death of Grandson," *Detroit Free Press* (April 18, 2013), at **archive.freep.com/article/20130418/NEWS03/304180154/sandra-layne-sentencing-oakland-county-jonathan-hoffman-west-bloomfield.**

63. Quoted in Kareem Fahim and Karen Zraick, "Seeing Failure of Mother as Factor in Sentencing," *New York Times* (November 17, 2008), A24.

64. John C. Coffee, "Repressed Issues of Sentencing," *Georgetown Law Journal* 66 (1978), 987.

65. J. S. Bainbridge, Jr., "The Return of Retribution," *ABA Journal* (May 1985), 63.

66. The Massachusetts Court System, "Introduction: Sentencing Guidelines," at **www.mass.gov/courts/formsandguidelines/sentencing/step1.html#step1.**

67. Pub. L. No. 98-473, 98 Stat. 1987, codified as amended at 18 U.S.C. Sections 3551–3742 and 28 U.S.C. Sections 991–998 (1988).

68. Julia L. Black, "The Constitutionality of Federal Sentences Imposed under the Sentencing Reform Act of 1984 after *Mistretta v. United States,*" *Iowa Law Review* 75 (March 1990), 767.

69. *Fifteen Years of Guidelines Sentencing: An Assessment of How Well the Federal Criminal Justice System Is Achieving the Goals of Sentencing Reform* (Washington, D.C.: U.S. Sentencing Commission, November 2004), 46.

70. *Blakely v. Washington,* 542 U.S. 296 (2004); *United States v. Booker,* 543 U.S. 220 (2005); and *Gall v. United States,* 552 U.S. 38 (2007).

71. *Demographic Differences in Federal Sentencing Practices: An Update of the Booker Report's Multivariate Regression Analysis* (Washington, D.C.: U.S. Sentencing Commission, March 2010), C-3.

72. Transactional Records Access Clearinghouse, "Wide Variations Seen in Federal Sentencing" (March 5, 2012), at **trac.syr.edu/whatsnew/email.120305.html.**

73. U.S. Sentencing Commission, "Table N: National Comparison of Sentence Imposed and Position Relative to the Guideline Range, Fiscal Year 2013," *FY 2013 Sourcebook,* at **www.ussc.gov/Research_and_Statistics/Annual_Reports_and_Sourcebooks/2012/TableN.pdf.**

74. Neal B. Kauder and Brian J. Ostrom, *State Sentencing Guidelines: Profiles and Continuum* (Williamsburg, Va.: National Center for State Courts, 2008), 15.

75. N.Y. Penal Law Sections 220.21, 60.5, 70.0(3) (1973).

76. Public Law Number 99–570 (1986).

77. 21 U.S.C. Section 859(b) (1986); 21 U.S.C. Section 861(a) (1986); and 18 U.S.C. Section 924(c)(1)(A)(i) (1998).

78. Todd R. Clear, George F. Cole, and Michael D. Reisig, *American Corrections,* 7th ed. (Belmont, Calif.: Thomson Wadsworth, 2006), 68–69.

79. Washington Revised Code Annotated Section 9.94A.030.

80. Nellis, *op. cit.,* 16.

81. Matt Taibbi, "Cruel and Unusual Punishment: The Shame of Three Strikes Laws," *Rolling Stone* (March 27, 2013), at **www.rollingstone.com/politics/news/cruel-and-unusual-punishment-the-shame-of-three-strikes-laws-20130327.**

82. *Lockyer v. Andrade,* 270 F.3d 743 (9th Cir. 2001).

83. *Ibid.,* 76.

84. Marisa Lagos and Ellen Huet, "'Three Strikes' Law Changes Approved by Wide Margin," *San Francisco Chronicle* (November 7, 2012), A14.

85. *United States Sentencing Commission, Report to Congress: Mandatory Minimum Penalties in the Federal Criminal Justice System* (Washington, D.C.: United States Sentencing Commission, October 2011), xxviii.

86. Ram Subramanian and Ruth Delaney, *Playbook for Change? States Reconsider Mandatory Sentences* (New York: Vera Institute of Justice, February 2014), 8–12.

87. Connecticut Senate Bill Number 1160 (2001).

88. Nevada House Bill Number 239 (2009).

89. Jim Parsons, et al., *End of an Era? The Impact of Drug Reform in New York City* (New York: Vera Institute of Justice, 2015).

90. Evan Bernick and Paul J. Larkin, Jr., *Reconsidering Mandatory Minimum Sentences: The Arguments For and Against Potential Reforms* (Washington, D.C.: The Heritage Foundation, February 10, 2014), 1.

91. Erick Eckhold, "Prosecutors Draw Fire for Sentences Called Harsh," *New York Times* (December 6, 2013), A19.

92. Justice for All Act of 2004, Pub. L. No. 108-405, 118 Stat. 2260.

93. Paul G. Cassell, "In Defense of Victim Impact Statements," *Ohio State Journal of Criminal Law* (Spring 2009), 614.

94. Edna Erez, "Victim Voice, Impact Statements, and Sentencing: Integrating Restorative Justice and Therapeutic Jurisprudence Principles in Adversarial Proceedings," *Criminal Law Bulletin* (September/October 2004), 495.

95. Bryan Myers and Edith Greene, "Prejudicial Nature of Impact Statements," *Psychology, Public Policy, and Law* (December 2004), 493.

96. Bryan Myers and Jack Arbuthnot, "The Effects of Victim Impact Evidence on the Verdicts and Sentencing Judgments of Mock Jurors," *Journal of Offender Rehabilitation* (1999), 95–112.

97. *Payne v. Tennessee,* 501 U.S. 808 (1991).

98. Walter Berns, "Abraham Lincoln (Book Review)," *Commentary* (January 1, 1996), 70.

99. Comments made at the Georgetown Law Center, "The Modern View of Capital Punishment," *American Criminal Law Review* 34 (Summer 1997), 1353.

100. David Bruck, quoted in Bill Rankin, "Fairness of the Death Penalty Is Still on Trial," *Atlanta Journal-Constitution* (July 29, 1997), A13.

101. Bureau of Justice Statistics, *Capital Punishment, 2012* (Washington, D.C.: U.S. Department of Justice, May 2014), Table 2, page 6.

102. Larry C. Berkson, *The Concept of Cruel and Unusual Punishment* (Lexington, Mass.: Lexington Books, 1975), 43.

103. John P. Cunningham, "Death in the Federal Courts: Expectations and Realities of the Federal Death Penalty Act of 1994," *University of Richmond Law Review* 32 (May 1998), 939.

104. *In re Kemmler,* 136 U.S. 447 (1890).

105. 217 U.S. 349 (1910).

106. Pamela S. Nagy, "Hang by the Neck until Dead: The Resurgence of Cruel and Unusual Punishment in the 1990s," *Pacific Law Journal* 26 (October 1994), 85.

107. 553 U.S. 35 (2008).

108. Quoted in Dan Frosch and Sabrina Tavernise, "Judge Rejects Execution Delay Over Use of Compounded Drug," *New York Times* (January 27, 2014), A11.

109. Adam Liptak and Erik Eckholm, "Justices to Hear Case over Drugs Used in Executions," *New York Times* (January 23, 2015), A1.

110. 408 U.S. 238 (1972).

111. 408 U.S. 309 (1972) (Stewart, concurring).

112. 536 U.S. 584 (2002).

113. Adam Liptak, "Alabama Judges Retain the Right to Override Juries in Capital Sentencing," *New York Times* (November 19, 2013), A15.

114. *Woodward v. Alabama,* 134 S.Ct. 405 (2013).

115. *Ford v. Wainwright,* 477 U.S. 399, 422 (1986).

116. Vidisha Barua, "'Synthetic Sanity': A Way around the Eighth Amendment?" *Criminal Law Bulletin* (July/August 2008), 561–572.

117. *Penry v. Lynaugh,* 492 U.S. 302 (1989).

118. 536 U.S. 304 (2002).

119. *Hall v. Florida,* 134 S.Ct. 1986, 2001 (2014).

120. 543 U.S. 551 (2005).

121. Ernest van den Haag, "The Ultimate Punishment: A Defense," *Harvard Law Review* 99 (1986), 1669.

122. *The Death Penalty: The Religious Community Calls for Abolition* (pamphlet published by the National Coalition to Abolish the Death Penalty and the National Interreligious Task Force on Criminal Justice, 1988), 48.

123. Isaac Ehrlich, "The Deterrent Effect of Capital Punishment: A Question of Life and Death," *American Economic Review* 65 (June 1975), 397–417.

124. Hashem Dezhbakhsh, Paul H. Rubin, and Joanna M. Shepherd, "Does Capital Punishment Have a Deterrent Effect? New Evidence from Postmoratorium Panel Data," *American Law and Economics Review* 5 (2003), 344–376; H. Naci Mocan and R. Kaj Gittings, "Getting Off Death Row: Commuted Sentences and the Deterrent Effect of Capital Punishment," *Journal of Law and Economics* 46 (2003), 453–478; Joanna M. Shepherd, "Deterrence versus Brutalization: Capital Punishment's Differing Impact among States," *Michigan Law Review* 104 (2005), 203–255; and Paul R. Zimmerman, "State Executions, Deterrence, and the Incidence of Murder," *Journal of Applied Economics* 7 (2005), 163–193.

125. Kenneth C. Land, Raymond H. C. Teske, Jr., and Hui Zheng, "Overview of: 'The Differential Short-Term Impacts of Executions on Felony and Non-Felony Homicides,'" *Criminology & Public Policy* (August 2012), 539–563.

126. Richard Berk, "Can't Tell: Comments on 'Does the Death Penalty Save Lives?'" *Criminology and Public Policy* (November 2009), 845–851.

127. Aaron Chalfin, Amelia M. Haviland, and Steven Raphael, "What Do Panel Studies Tell Us About a Deterrent Effect of Capital Punishment? A Critique of the Literature," *Journal of Quantitative Criminology* (March 2013), 5–43.

128. Lisa Stolzenberg and Stewart J. D'Alessio, "Capital Punishment, Execution Publicity, and Murder in Houston, Texas," *Journal of Criminal Law and Criminology* (Winter 2004), 351–379.

129. Roger C. Barnes, "Death Penalty Undermines Justice," *San Antonio Express-News* (July 12, 202), 6B.

130. Death Penalty Information Center, "Innocence and the Death Penalty," at **www.deathpenaltyinfo.org/innocence-and-death-penalty.**

131. *Rompilla v. Beard,* 545 U.S. 375 (2005).

132. Adam Liptak, "Geography and the Machinery of Death," *New York Times* (February 5, 2007), A10.

133. Richard C. Dieter, *The 2% Penalty: How a Minority of Counties Produce Most Death Cases at Enormous Costs to All* (Washington, D.C.: Death Penalty Information Center, October 2013), 5.

134. Deborah Fins, *Death Row U.S.A.* (New York: NAACP Legal Defense and Educational Fund, Fall 2014), 1.

135. Death Penalty Information Center, "National Statistics on the Death Penalty and Race," at **www.deathpenaltyinfo.org/race-death-row-inmates-executed-1976#defend.**

136. *Ibid.*

137. 481 U.S. 279 (1987).

138. David C. Baldus, George Woodworth, and Charles A. Pulaski, *Equal Justice and the Death Penalty: A Legal and Empirical Analysis* (Boston: Northeastern University Press, 1990), 140–197, 306.

139. *The Death Penalty in 2014: Year End Report* (Washington, D.C.: Death Penalty Information Center, December 2014), 1.

140. *Ibid.,* 2.

141. "The Slow Death of the Death Penalty," *The Economist* (April 26, 2014), 27.

142. Federal Bureau of Investigation, *Crime in the United States 2013* (Washington, D.C.: U.S. Department of Justice, 2014), at **www.fbi.gov/about-us/cjis/ucr/crime-in-the-u.s/2013/crime-in-the-u.s.-2013,** Table 1.

143. Legislative Auditor, *Performance Audit: Fiscal Costs of the Death Penalty* (Carson City, Nev.: State of Nevada, 2014), 1.

144. *Jones v. Chappell* (C.D. Cal. 2014), available at **documents.latimes.com/judge-orders-californias-death-penalty-unconstitutional/.**

145. *Uttecht v. Brown,* 551 U.S. 1 (2007).

146. Gallup, "Americans' Support for Death Penalty Stable," (October 23, 2014), at **www.gallup.com/poll/178790/americans-support-death-penalty-stable.aspx.**

147. Pew Research Center, "Shrinking Majority of Americans Support Death Penalty" (March 28, 2014), at **www.pewforum.org/2014/03/28/shrinking-majority-of-americans-support-death-penalty/.**

148. Quoted in Samia Khan, "Families of Death Row Inmate Victims Upset over Judge's Death Penalty Ruling," *NBC Los Angeles* (July 17, 2014), at **www.nbclosangeles.com/news/local/Families-of-Death-Row-Inmate-Victims-Upset-Over-Judges-Death-Penalty-Ruling-267475651.html.**

149. Quoted in Andrea Weigl, "Father Wants Killer to Die," *Raleigh (N.C.) News & Observer* (April 23, 2007), A1.

150. Claire Finkelstein, "A Contractarian Argument against the Death Penalty," *New York University Law Review* (October 2006), 1283.

151. *Kennedy v. Louisiana,* 554 U.S. 407 (2008).

Probation, Parole, and Intermediate Sanctions

Chapter Outline		Corresponding Learning Objectives
The Justifications for Community Corrections	**1**	Explain the justifications for community-based corrections programs.
Probation: Doing Time in the Community	**2**	Explain several alternative sentencing arrangements that combine probation with incarceration.
	3	Specify the conditions under which an offender is most likely to be denied probation.
	4	Describe the three general categories of conditions placed on a probationer.
The Parole Picture	**5**	Identify the main differences between probation and parole.
	6	Explain which factors influence the decision to grant parole.
Intermediate Sanctions	**7**	Contrast day reporting centers with intensive supervision probation.
	8	List the three levels of home monitoring.
The Paradox of Community Corrections	**9**	Summarize the paradox of community corrections.

To target your study and review, look for these numbered Learning Objective icons throughout the chapter.

Travis Dove/The New York Times/Redux

Family Ties

returning home from a barbecue at 3 A.M. in rural Philo, Illinois, twenty-four-year-old Katie Daly skidded on wet gravel and lost control of the all-terrain vehicle she was driving. Her nineteen-year-old cousin, Annie Daly, was thrown from the passenger seat and died in a hospital four hours later. At the time of the accident, Katie's blood alcohol level was well over the state's legal limit, and she was charged with felony aggravated driving under the influence (DUI). Given her family connection to the victim, local prosecutors agreed to a plea deal in which Katie would be spared prison, instead receiving a punishment of probation for her crime.

Champaign County judge Richard Klaus had other ideas. Despite impassioned pleas for leniency from Annie's parents and brother, Klaus rejected the plea bargain and sentenced Katie to three and a half years in prison for reckless homicide. "Under the law, it is not a mitigating factor that a family member died. The loss to society is the same whether Annie was killed by a family member or a stranger," Klaus explained. "This is absolutely a deterrable crime and it must be deterred. It is the duty of the court to see that it is deterred."

Prosecutors and Katie's defense attorneys joined forces to appeal Klaus's decision. Noting Katie's youth, her lack of a criminal record, and the effect of the incarceration on her family, including her infant son, the appeals brief stated, "A prison sentence in this case would not be of any benefit to society, the defendant, or to our system of justice." In December 2014, an Illinois appellate court agreed, ruling that Klaus had abused his discretion by putting the defendant behind bars. After six months in prison, Katie was freed and resentenced to thirty months of probation. According to state's attorney Julia Reitz, the intent of the appellate court "was not to minimize the seriousness of the DUI aspect but more to focus on Katie's rehabilitative potential."

▲ Katie Daly was eventually sentenced to probation for killing her cousin Annie in an alcohol-related accident involving an all-terrain vehicle such as the one shown here.

iStockPhoto.com/Gaffizone

1. What is your opinion of Judge Richard Klaus's justification for sentencing Katie Daly to prison rather than probation?

2. "We need to have Katie here to help us heal," Annie Daly's mother told the court. Should a victim's wishes influence the judge's sentencing decision? Why or why not?

3. What do you think prosecutor Julia Reitz meant when she referred to Katie's "rehabilitative potential"?

The Justifications for Community Corrections

In overturning Judge Richard Klaus's sentence of Katie Daly, the Fourth District Appellate Court of Illinois scolded the judge for focusing on incarceration and ignoring the "range of sentencing possibilities" called for by the facts of the case.[1] As this chapter will make clear, the range of sentencing possibilities for American judges includes numerous options that keep offenders out of prison and jail. For instance, about 3.9 million offenders such as Daly are presently serving their sentences in the community on *probation* rather than behind bars. In addition, approximately 850,000 convicts in the United States have been *paroled,* meaning that they are finishing their prison sentences "on the outside" under the supervision of correctional officers.[2]

America, says University of Minnesota law professor Michael Tonry, is preoccupied with the "absolute severity of punishment" and the "widespread view that only imprisonment counts."[3] Consequently, **community corrections** such as probation and parole are often considered a less severe, and therefore a less worthy, alternative to imprisonment. In reality, community corrections are crucial to our criminal justice system. One in fifty adults in this country is living under community supervision,[4] and few criminal justice matters are more pressing than the need to successfully reintegrate these offenders into society.

LEARNING OBJECTIVE 1 Explain the justifications for community-based corrections programs.

Reintegration

A very small percentage of all convicted offenders have committed crimes that warrant life imprisonment or capital punishment. Most, at some point, will return to the community. Consequently, according to one group of experts, the task of the corrections system

> includes building or rebuilding solid ties between the offender and the community, integrating or reintegrating the offender into community life—restoring family ties, obtaining employment and an education, securing in the larger sense a place for the offender in the routine functioning of society.[5]

Considering that some studies have shown higher recidivism rates for offenders who are subjected to prison culture, a frequent justification of community-based corrections is that they help to reintegrate the offender into society.

Reintegration has a strong theoretical basis in rehabilitative theories of punishment. An offender is generally considered to be "rehabilitated" when he or she no longer represents a threat to other members of the community and therefore is believed to be fit to live in that community. In the context of this chapter and the two that follow, it will also be helpful to see reintegration as a process through which criminal justice officials such as probation and parole officers provide the offender with incentives to follow the rules of society.

These incentives can be positive, such as enrolling the offender in a drug treatment program. They can also be negative—in particular, the threat of return to prison or jail for failure to comply. In all instances, criminal justice professionals must carefully balance the needs of the individual offender against the rights of law-abiding members of the community.

Diversion

Another justification for community-based corrections, based on practical considerations, is **diversion.** As you are already aware, many criminal offenses fall into the

Community Corrections The correctional supervision of offenders in the community as an alternative to sending them to prison or jail.

Reintegration A goal of corrections that focuses on preparing the offender for a return to the community unmarred by further criminal behavior.

Diversion In the context of corrections, a strategy to divert those offenders who qualify away from prison and jail and toward community-based and intermediate sanctions.

▲ In Dallas, street prostitutes such as the two shown here are often treated as crime victims and offered access to treatment and rehabilitation programs. **How might society benefit if such offenders are kept out of jail or prison through these kinds of diversion programs?** AP Images/LM Otero

category of "petty," and it is well-nigh impossible, as well as unnecessary, to imprison every offender for every offense. Community-based corrections are an important means of diverting criminals to alternative modes of punishment so that scarce incarceration resources are consumed by only the most dangerous criminals.

In his "strainer" analogy, corrections expert Paul H. Hahn likens this process to the workings of a kitchen strainer. With each "shake" of the corrections "strainer," the less serious offenders are diverted from incarceration. At the end, only the most serious convicts remain in prison.[6] (The concept of diversion is closely linked to that of selective incapacitation, mentioned in Chapter 11.)

The diversionary role of community-based punishments has become more pronounced as prisons and jails have filled up over the past three decades. In fact, probationers and parolees now account for about 70 percent of all adults in the American corrections systems.[7] (To learn about another form of diversion, which focuses on the mental health system rather than the criminal justice system, see the *CJ in Action* feature at the end of this chapter.)

The "Low-Cost Alternative"

Not all of the recent expansion of community corrections can be attributed to acceptance of its theoretical underpinnings. Many politicians and criminal justice officials who do not look favorably on ideas such as reintegration and diversion have embraced programs to keep nonviolent offenders out of prison. The reason is simple: economics. The cost of constructing and maintaining prisons and jails, as well as housing and caring for inmates, has placed a great deal of pressure on corrections budgets across the country. States spend an estimated $52 billion a year on their corrections systems, most of which goes to prison operating costs.[8]

Community corrections offer an enticing financial alternative to imprisonment. The Bureau of Prisons estimates that the federal government saves about $25,600 annually by shifting a nonviolent offender from incarceration to supervised release.[9] The average yearly cost of housing an inmate in Nebraska is $35,169, compared to $3,760 for community corrections.[10] Prison admissions in North Carolina declined by 21 percent from 2011 to 2014, as state corrections officials moved nonviolent offenders to probation and parole. In the process, the state's annual corrections budget shrank by $50 million.[11]

EthicsChallenge

In a number of jurisdictions, those offenders serving community corrections sentences are responsible for financing their own supervision. Oklahoma probationers, for example, annually pay more than $15 million to local district attorney's offices statewide. If these offenders fail to make their payments, they can be incarcerated (or reincarcerated). What are some of the ethical problems with this practice? ■

Probation: Doing Time in the Community

As Figure 12.1 shows, **probation** is the most common form of punishment in the United States. Although it is administered differently in various jurisdictions, probation can be generally defined as

> the legal status of an offender who, after being convicted of a crime, has been directed by the sentencing court to remain in the community under the supervision of a probation service for a designated period of time and subject to certain conditions imposed by the court or by law.[12]

The theory behind probation is that certain offenders can be treated more economically and humanely by putting them under controls while still allowing them to live in the community. One of the advantages of probation has been that it provides for the rehabilitation of the offender while saving society the costs of incarceration. Despite probation's widespread use, certain participants in the criminal justice system question its ability to reach its rehabilitative goals. Critics point to the immense number of probationers and the fact that many of them are violent felons as evidence that the system is "out of control." Supporters contend that nothing is wrong with probation in principle, but admit that its execution must be adjusted to meet the goals of modern corrections.[13]

FIGURE 12.1 Probation in American Corrections

As you can see, the majority of convicts under the control of the American corrections system are on probation.

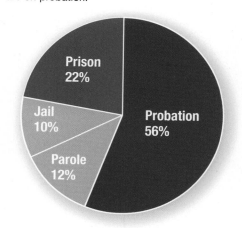

Source: Bureau of Justice Statistics, *Correctional Populations in the United States, 2013* (Washington, D.C.: U.S. Department of Justice, December 2014), Table 1, page 2.

Sentencing and Probation

Probation is basically an arrangement between sentencing authorities and the offender. In traditional probation, the offender agrees to comply with certain terms for a specified amount of time in return for serving the sentence in the community. One of the primary benefits for the offender, besides not getting sent to a correctional facility, is that the length of the probationary period is usually considerably shorter than the length of a prison term (see Figure 12.2).

The traditional form of probation is not the only arrangement that can be made. A judge can hand down a **suspended sentence,** under which a defendant who has been convicted and sentenced to be incarcerated is not required to serve the sentence. Instead, the judge puts the offender on notice, keeping open the option of reinstating the original sentence and sending the offender to prison or jail if he or she reoffends. In practice, suspended sentences are quite similar to probation.

 LEARNING OBJECTIVE 2 Explain several alternative sentencing arrangements that combine probation with incarceration.

Alternative Sentencing Arrangements Judges can also combine probation with incarceration. Such sentencing arrangements include:

- *Split sentences.* In **split sentence probation,** also known as *shock probation,* the offender is sentenced to a specific amount of time in prison or jail, to be followed by a period of probation.
- *Shock incarceration.* In this arrangement, an offender is sentenced to prison or jail with the understanding that after a period of time, she or he may petition the court to be released on probation. Shock incarceration is discussed more fully later in the chapter.
- *Intermittent incarceration.* With intermittent incarceration, the offender spends a certain amount of time each week, usually during the weekend, in a jail, workhouse, or other government institution.

Probation A criminal sanction in which a convict is allowed to remain in the community rather than be imprisoned.

Suspended Sentence A judicially imposed condition in which an offender is sentenced after being convicted of a crime, but is not required to begin serving the sentence immediately.

Split Sentence Probation A sentence that consists of incarceration in a prison or jail, followed by a probationary period in the community.

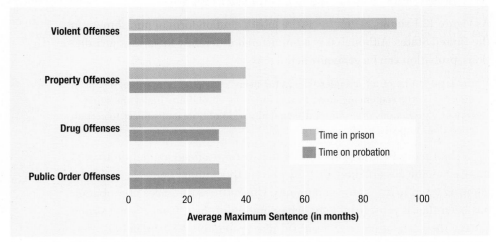

FIGURE 12.2 Average Length of Sentence: Prison versus Probation

As you can see, the average probation sentence is much shorter than the average prison sentence for most crimes.

Source: Bureau of Justice Statistics, *Felony Defendants in State Courts, 2009—Statistical Tables* (Washington, D.C.: U.S. Department of Justice, December 2013), Table 25, page 30; and Table 27, page 31.

Split sentences are popular with judges, as they combine the "treatment" aspects of probation with the "punishment" aspects of incarceration. According to the U.S. Department of Justice, about a fifth of all probationers are also sentenced to some form of incarceration.[14]

Choosing Probation Generally, research has shown that offenders are most likely to be denied probation if they:

- Are convicted on multiple charges.
- Were on probation or parole at the time of the arrest.
- Have two or more prior convictions.
- Are addicted to narcotics.
- Seriously injured the victim of the crime.
- Used a weapon during the commission of the crime.[15]

As might be expected, the chances of a felon being sentenced to probation are highly dependent on the seriousness of his or her crime. Only 19 percent of probationers in the United States have committed a violent crime, including domestic violence and sex offenses. The majority of probationers have been convicted of property crimes, drug offenses, or public order crimes such as drunk driving.[16]

Probation permits the judicial system to recognize that some offenders are less blameworthy than others. Several years ago, for example, a judge in Arizona found himself with the difficult task of punishing eighty-six-year-old George Sanders for fatally shooting Virginia, his eighty-one-year-old wife. Virginia, who was suffering from a painful health condition, had begged George to end her life. In handing down his sentence of two years' probation, Judge John Ditsworth said that his decision tempered "justice with mercy."[17]

Probation Demographics As in other areas of the criminal justice system, African Americans make up a higher percentage of the national probation population (30 percent) than the general population (13 percent). Fifty-four percent of probationers

Specify the conditions under which an offender is most likely to be denied probation.

LEARNING OBJECTIVE **3**

are white, and 14 percent are Hispanic.[18] The percentage of female probationers is significantly higher than female prison inmates (25 percent to 7 percent),[19] which is in keeping with the gender sentencing trends we discussed in the previous chapter. More detailed surveys of probationers reveal that they tend to be between the ages of twenty-one and thirty-nine, single, high school graduates, and have annual incomes of less than $20,000.[20]

Revocation The formal process that follows the failure of a probationer or parolee to comply with the terms of his or her probation or parole, often resulting in the probationer's incarceration.

Conditions of Probation

A judge may decide to impose certain conditions as part of a probation sentence. These conditions represent a "contract" between the judge and the offender, in which the latter agrees that if she or he does not follow certain rules, probation may be *revoked* (see Figure 12.3). **Revocation** is the formal process by which probation is ended and a probationer is punished for his or her wrongdoing, often by being sent to jail or prison for the original term decided by the court.

Judges have a great deal of discretion to impose any terms of probation that they feel are necessary. In the case that opened this chapter, for example, Champaign County (Illinois) judge Tom Difanis ordered Katie Daly not to use any alcohol or illegal drugs during her thirty-month probationary period. He also prohibited her from entering an establishment whose primary purpose is selling alcohol, and required her to wear an alcohol-monitoring device for the first year of her supervised sentence.

Principles of Probation A judge's personal philosophy is often reflected in the probation conditions that she or he creates for probationers. In *In re Quirk* (1997),[21] for example, the Louisiana Supreme Court upheld the ability of a trial judge to impose church attendance as a condition of probation. Though judges have a great deal of discretion in setting the conditions of probation, they do operate under several guiding principles. First, the conditions must be related to the dual purposes of probation, which most federal and state courts define as (1) the rehabilitation of the probationer and (2) the protection of the community. Second, the conditions must not violate the U.S. Constitution, as probationers are generally entitled to the same constitutional rights as other prisoners.[22]

Of course, probationers do give up certain constitutional rights when they

FIGURE 12.3 Conditions of Probation

UNITED STATES DISTRICT COURT
FOR THE
DISTRICT OF COLUMBIA

To: _____ No. 84-417
Address: 1440 N St., N.W., #10, Wash., D.C.

In accordance with authority conferred by the United States Probation Law, you have been placed on probation this date, January 25, 2016 for a period of one year by the Hon. Thomas F. Hogan United States District Judge, sitting in and for this District Court at Washington, D.C.

CONDITIONS OF PROBATION

It is the order of the Court that you shall comply with the following conditions of probation:

(1)-You shall refrain from violation of any law (federal, state, and local). You shall get in touch immediately with your probation officer if arrested or questioned by a law enforcement officer.

(2)-You shall associate only with law-abiding persons and maintain reasonable hours.

(3)-You shall work regularly at a lawful occupation and support your legal dependents, if any, to the best of your ability. When out of work you shall notify your probation officer at once. You shall consult him prior to job changes.

(4)-You shall not leave the judicial district without permission of the probation officer.

(5)-You shall notify your probation officer immediately of any change in your place of residence.

(6)-You shall follow the probation officer's instructions.

(7)-You shall report to the probation officer as directed.

(8)-You shall not possess a firearm (handgun or rifle) for any reason.

The special conditions ordered by the Court are as follows:
  Imposition of sentence suspended, one year probation, Fine of $75 on each count.

I understand that the Court may change the conditions of probation, reduce or extend the period of probation, and at any time during the probation period or within the maximum probation period of 5 years permitted by law, may issue a warrant and revoke probation for a violation occurring during the probation period.

I have read or had read to me the above conditions of probation. I fully understand them and I will abide by them.

_____ Date _____
Probationer

You will report as follows: _____ as directed by your Probation Officer

_____ Date _____
U.S. Probation Officer

consent to the terms of probation. Most probationers, for example, agree to spot checks of their homes for contraband such as drugs or weapons, and they therefore have a diminished expectation of privacy.

In *United States v. Knights* (2001),[23] the United States Supreme Court upheld the actions of deputy sheriffs in Napa County, California, who searched a probationer's home without a warrant or probable cause. The unanimous decision was based on the premise that because those on probation are more likely to commit crimes, law enforcement agents "may therefore justifiably focus on probationers in a way that [they do] not on the ordinary citizen."[24]

Types of Conditions Obviously, probationers who break the law are very likely to have their probation revoked. Other, less serious infractions may also result in revocation. The conditions placed on a probationer fall into three general categories:

Describe the three general categories of conditions placed on a probationer.

LEARNING
4
OBJECTIVE

- *Standard conditions*, which are imposed on all probationers. These include reporting regularly to the probation officer, notifying the agency of any change of address, not leaving the jurisdiction without permission, and remaining employed.
- *Punitive conditions*, which usually reflect the seriousness of the offense and are intended to increase the punishment of the offender. Such conditions include fines, community service, restitution, drug testing, and home confinement (discussed later).
- *Treatment conditions*, which are imposed to reverse patterns of self-destructive behavior. Such treatment generally includes counseling for drug and alcohol abuse, anger management, and mental health issues, and is a component of approximately 27 percent of probation sentences in this country.[25]

Some observers feel that judges have too much discretion in imposing overly restrictive conditions that no person, much less one who has exhibited antisocial tendencies, could meet. Citing prohibitions on drinking liquor, gambling, and associating with "undesirables," as well as requirements such as meeting early curfews, the late University of Delaware professor Carl B. Klockars claimed that if probation rules were taken seriously, "very few probationers would complete their terms without violation."[26]

As the majority of probationers do complete their terms successfully,[27] Klockars's statement suggests that either probation officers are unable to determine that violations are taking place, or many of them are exercising a great deal of discretion in reporting minor probation violations. Perhaps the officers realize that violating probationers for every single "slip-up" is unrealistic and would add to the already significant problem of jail and prison overcrowding.

The Supervisory Role of the Probation Officer

The probation officer has two basic roles. The first is investigative and consists of conducting the presentence investigation (PSI), which was discussed in Chapter 11. The second is supervisory and begins as soon as the offender has been sentenced to probation. In smaller probation agencies, individual officers perform both tasks. In larger jurisdictions, the trend has been toward separating the responsibilities, with *investigating officers* handling the PSI and *line officers* concentrating on supervision.

Supervisory policies vary and are often a reflection of whether the authority to administer probation services is *decentralized* (under local, judicial control) or *centralized* (under state, administrative control). In any circumstance, however, certain

Courtesy Peggy McCarthy

Peggy McCarthy
Lead Probation Officer

The best thing about my job is that every day is different. I may be in court first thing in the morning, and then in my office meeting with defendants or developing case plans. In the afternoon, I may be at the jail taking statements for court reports or out in the field seeing my defendants. If I work a late shift, I may be visiting counseling agencies or talking to collateral sources or doing surveillance. I may be organizing a search on a defendant's home or making an arrest. I may be working with the police to solve crimes or locate absconders. Or I may simply be completing administrative duties like filing or returning phone calls to defendants and/or their family members. Anything can happen at any time, and I have to be ready to respond. If a probation officer gets bored, something is wrong.

I take a great deal of pride in assisting defendants with the difficult task of making positive change in their lives. The rewards may be few and far between, but when a defendant with a history of substance abuse stays clean and sober for a year, when a gang-affiliated defendant secures a job and no longer associates with negative peers, or when a defendant who admittedly never liked school obtains a GED or diploma, that is when I realize that what I'm doing day in and day out is 100 percent worthwhile.

SOCIAL MEDIA CAREER TIP Manage your online reputation—or someone else will do it for you. Monitor your profile using tools such as iSearch, Pipl, and ZabaSearch. Check BoardTracker, BoardReader, and Omgili for information on what people are saying about you on message boards.

FASTFACTS

**Lead probation officer
Job description:**

- Work with offenders or clients who have been sentenced to probation.
- Work with the courts. Investigate backgrounds, write presentence reports, and recommend sentences.

What kind of training is required?

- Bachelor's degree in criminal justice, social work/psychology, or related field.
- Must be at least 21 years of age, have no felony convictions, and have strong writing and interview skills. Experience in multicultural outreach a plus.

Annual salary range?

- $30,000–$80,000

---

basic principles of supervision apply. Starting with a preliminary interview, the probation officer establishes a relationship with the offender. This relationship is based on the mutual goal of both parties: the successful completion of the probationary period. Just because the line officer and the offender have the same goal, however, does not necessarily mean that cooperation will be a feature of probation.

The Use of Authority Not surprisingly, research shows that the ideal officer-offender relationship is based on mutual respect, honesty, and trust.[28] In reality, these qualities are often hard to maintain between probation officers and their clients. Any incentive an offender might have to be completely truthful with a line officer is marred by one simple fact: self-reported wrongdoing can be used to revoke probation. Even probation officers whose primary mission is to rehabilitate are under institutional pressure to punish their clients for violating conditions of probation. One officer deals with this situation by telling his clients

> that I'm here to help them, to get them a job, and whatever else I can do. But I tell them too that I have a family to support and that if they get too far off track, I can't afford to put my job on the line for them. I'm going to have to violate them.[29]

In the absence of trust, most probation officers rely on their **authority** to guide an offender successfully through the sentence. An officer's authority, or ability to influence a person's actions without resorting to force, is based partially on her or his power to

Authority The power designated to an agent of the law over a person who has broken the law.

revoke probation. It also reflects her or his ability to impose a number of lesser sanctions. For example, if a probationer fails to attend a required alcohol treatment program, the officer can send him or her to a "lockup," or detention center, overnight. To be successful, a probation officer must establish this authority early in the relationship because it is the primary tool for persuading the probationer to behave in an acceptable manner.

The Caseload Dilemma Even the most balanced, "firm but fair" approach to probation can be defeated by the problem of excessive *caseloads*. A **caseload** is the number of clients a probation officer is responsible for at any one time. Heavy probation caseloads seem inevitable: unlike a prison cell, a probation officer can always take "just one more" client. Furthermore, the ideal caseload size is very difficult to determine because different offenders require different levels of supervision.[30]

The consequences of disproportionate probation officer–probationer ratios are self-evident, however. When burdened with large caseloads, probation officers find it practically impossible to rigorously enforce the conditions imposed on their clients. Lack of surveillance leads to lack of control, which can undermine the very basis of a probationary system.

Between 2003 and 2014, the number of federal probation officers declined by 5 percent. Due to the stricter federal sentencing guidelines discussed in the previous chapter, the number of federal probationers increased by 19 percent over that time period. Furthermore, the rolls of federal probationers with mental health treatment conditions and substance abuse treatment conditions expanded significantly, placing even more time pressure on federal probation officers.[31]

Revocation of Probation

The probation period can end in one of two ways. Either the probationer successfully fulfills the conditions of the sentence, or the probationer misbehaves and probation is revoked, resulting in a prison or jail term. The decision of whether to revoke after a **technical violation**—such as failing to report a change of address or testing positive for drug use—is often made at the discretion of the probation officer and therefore the focus of controversy. (See the feature *Discretion in Action—A Judgment Call* to learn more about the issues surrounding revocation.)

Probation and the Constitution As we have seen, probationers do not always enjoy the same protections under the U.S. Constitution as other members of society. The United States Supreme Court has not stripped these offenders of all rights, however. In *Mempa v. Rhay* (1967),[32] the Court ruled that probationers were entitled to an attorney during the revocation process. Then, in *Morrissey v. Brewer* (1972) and *Gagnon v. Scarpelli* (1973),[33] the Court established a three-stage procedure by which the "limited" due process rights of probationers must be protected in potential revocation situations:

- *Preliminary hearing.* In this appearance before a "disinterested person" (often a judge), the facts of the violation or arrest are presented, and it is determined whether probable cause for revoking probation exists. This hearing can be waived by the probationer.
- *Revocation hearing.* During this hearing, the probation agency presents evidence to support its claim of violation, and the probationer can attempt to refute this evidence. The probationer has the right to know the charges being brought against him or her. Furthermore, probationers can testify on their own behalf and

Caseload The number of individual probationers or parolees under the supervision of a probation or parole officer.

Technical Violation An action taken by a probationer or parolee that, although not criminal, breaks the terms of probation or parole as designated by the court.

Discretion in Action

A Judgment Call

The Situation You are a probation officer. Your client, Alain, was convicted of selling drugs and given a split sentence—three years in prison and three years on probation. You meet Alain for the first time two days after his release, and you are immediately concerned about his mental health. His mother confirms your worries, telling you that Alain needs help. You refer him to a psychiatric hospital, but the officials there determine that he "does not require mental health treatment at this time." Several weeks later, Alain's mother tells you that he is staying out late at night and "hanging out with the wrong crowd," both violations of his probation agreement. After he tests positive for marijuana, you warn Alain that, after one more violation, you will revoke his probation and send him back to prison. He tells you that he is "feeling agitated" and "having intermittent rage." You refer him to a substance abuse and mental health treatment facility, where he tests positive for marijuana once again.

The Law For any number of reasons, but particularly for the failed drug tests, you can start revocation proceedings against Alain. These proceedings will almost certainly conclude with his return to prison.

What Would You Do? On the one hand, Alain has violated the terms of his probation agreement numerous times. On the other hand, he has been convicted of only one crime—a drug violation—and you have no evidence that he is behaving violently or poses a danger to himself or others. Furthermore, Alain has strong family support and is willing to enter treatment for his substance abuse problems. Do Alain's technical violations cause you to begin the revocation process? Why or why not?

[To see how a Fairfield County, Connecticut, probation officer dealt with a similar situation, go to Example 12.1 in Appendix B.]

---

present witnesses in their favor, as well as confront and cross-examine adverse witnesses. A "neutral and detached" body must hear the evidence and rule on the validity of the proposed revocation.

- *Revocation sentencing.* If the presiding body rules against the probationer, then the judge must decide whether to impose incarceration and for what length of time. In a revocation hearing dealing with technical violations, the judge will often reimpose probation with stricter terms or intermediate sanctions.

In effect, this is a "bare-bones" approach to due process. Most of the rules of evidence that govern regular trials do not apply to revocation hearings. Probation officers are not, for example, required to read offenders their *Miranda* rights before questioning them about crimes they may have committed during probation. In *Minnesota v. Murphy* (1984),[34] the Supreme Court ruled that a meeting between probation officer and client does not equal custody and, therefore, the Fifth Amendment protection against self-incrimination does not apply, either.

Limiting Revocation Probation (and parole) revocation accounts for a significant portion of prison admissions in many states. Research also shows that revoking probation for technical violations does not increase community safety. Indeed, a low-level offender sent to prison for a technical violation is more likely to reoffend than if he or she is able to avoid incarceration.[35]

Consequently, policy makers recently have been focusing on **graduated sanctions** to keep those who violate the terms of their probation out of jail or prison. These sanctions move upward on a scale of severity, punishing offenders more harshly with each misstep. So, for example, in Kansas, at the discretion of a judge, a probationer's:

Graduated Sanctions A series of punishments that become more severe with each subsequent act of wrongdoing.

1. First technical violation = a modification of the terms of probation.
2. Second technical violation = a short stint in jail, not more than six days per month for three consecutive months.
3. Third technical violation = imprisonment for three months.
4. Fourth technical violation = imprisonment for four months.
5. Fifth technical violation = parole revocation and restoration of original sentence.[36]

Kansas also offers certain low-level offenders the chance to finish their probationary term after one year, regardless of the length of the sentence, if they have complied with their conditions during that time.[37] A number of states offer similar incentives, which serve the dual purpose of providing motivation for good behavior and reducing probation officer caseloads.

Does Probation Work?

On March 11, 2014, police in Berkeley County, West Virginia, arrested William Jackson for placing a plastic bag over seventy-two-year-old Martha Tyler's head and suffocating her to death. At the time of the murder, Jackson was on probation for drug charges and grand larceny. Indeed, probationers are responsible for a significant amount of crime. According to the most recent data, 11 percent of all suspects arrested for violent crimes (and 13 percent of those arrested for murder) were on probation at the time of their apprehension.[38] Such statistics raise a critical question—is probation worthwhile?

To measure the effectiveness of probation, one must first establish its purpose. Generally, as we saw earlier, the goal of probation is to reintegrate and divert as many offenders as possible while at the same time protecting the public. Specifically, probation and other community corrections programs are evaluated by their success in preventing *recidivism*—the eventual rearrest of the probationer.[39] Given that most probationers are first-time, nonviolent offenders, the system is not designed to prevent relatively rare outbursts of violence, such as the murder committed by William Jackson.

Risk Factors for Recidivism About 15 percent of all probationers are returned to prison or jail before the end of their probationary terms.[40] There are several risk factors that make a probationer more likely to recidivate, including

1. *Antisocial personality patterns,* meaning that the probationer is impulsive, pleasure seeking, restlessly aggressive, or irritable.
2. *Procriminal attitudes* such as negative opinions of authority and the law, as well as a tendency to rationalize one's prior criminal behavior.
3. *Social supports for crime,* including friends who are offenders and a living environment lacking in positive role models.[41]

Other important risk factors for recidivism include substance abuse and unemployment. By concentrating resources on those probationers who exhibit these risk factors, probation departments can succeed in lowering caseloads and overall recidivism rates.

Jurisdictions are increasingly using crime-prediction software to determine which probationers are at the greatest risk of recidivating and therefore need greater levels of supervision. Before implementing a risk-prediction tool called "Random Forest Modeling," for example, Philadelphia's Adult Probation and Parole Department (APPD) had each offender meet with his or her probation officer for about half an hour once each month. Using factors such as the probationer's criminal history, number of years since the last serious offense, and ZIP code, the APPD now assigns each offender to one of three risk categories. Its high-risk probationers are thirteen times more likely to recidivate than low-risk probationers, and are supervised accordingly.[42]

"Swift and Certain" One of the problems with traditional methods of sanctioning probation violations is the length of the proceedings. If, for example, a probationer fails a drug test, it may take months before a penalty is enforced, weakening the link between wrongdoing and punishment. As criminologist James Q. Wilson pointed out, one does not discipline a child by saying, "Because [you've misbehaved], you have a 50-50 chance nine months from now of being grounded."[43]

A number of probation departments have implemented strategies that operate on the principle of providing "swift and certain" sanctions for probation violations. Perhaps the most successful of these strategies is Hawaii's Opportunity Probation with Enforcement (HOPE) program. The rules of HOPE are simple. Each substance abuse probationer must call the courthouse every day to learn if she or he is required to come in for urine tests for drugs, or *urinalysis*. If drugs are found in the probationer's system during one of these frequent tests, a short jail term—one to two weeks—is automatically served.[44] HOPE has resulted in large reductions in positive drug tests by probationers, and its 1,500 participants are significantly less likely to be rearrested than those not in the program.[45]

Following the HOPE model, South Dakota's 24/7 Sobriety Project requires probationers convicted of alcohol-related offenses to wear alcohol-monitoring bracelets or submit to daily breathalyzer tests. Offenders who skip or fail these tests are immediately sent to jail for a short stay. Data show that, from 2005 to 2010, when more than 17,000 South Dakota residents participated in the program, repeat DUI arrests in the state declined 12 percent and domestic violence arrests declined 9 percent.[46]

EthicsChallenge

You may have noticed that one of the factors used in Philadelphia to determine a probationer's risk category is his or her residential ZIP code. Why have some observers criticized this tactic as a form of racial and ethnic discrimination? Should the use of ZIP codes in offender risk assessment strategies be prohibited because it is unethical? Explain your answer. ■

The Parole Picture

At any given time, about 850,000 Americans are living in the community on **parole,** or the *conditional* release of a prisoner after a portion of his or her sentence has been served behind bars. Parole allows the corrections system to continue to supervise an offender who is no longer incarcerated. As long as parolees follow the conditions of their parole, they are allowed to finish their terms outside the prison. If parolees break the terms of their early release, however, they face the risk of being returned to a penal institution.

Parole is based on three concepts:[47]

1. *Grace.* The prisoner has no right to be given an early release, but the government has granted her or him that privilege.
2. *Contract of consent.* The government and the parolee enter into an arrangement whereby the latter agrees to abide by certain conditions in return for continued freedom.
3. *Custody.* Technically, though no longer incarcerated, the parolee is still the responsibility of the state. Parole is an extension of corrections.

Parole The conditional release of an inmate before his or her sentence has expired.

Parole Contract An agreement between the state and the offender that establishes the conditions of parole.

Because of good-time credits and parole, most prisoners do not serve their entire sentence in prison. In fact, the average felon serves only about half of the term handed down by the court.

Comparing Probation and Parole

Identify the main differences between probation and parole.

Both probation and parole operate under the basic assumption that the offender serves her or his time in the community rather than in a prison or jail. The main differences between the two concepts—which sound confusingly similar—involve their circumstances. Probation is a sentence handed down by a judge following conviction and usually does not include incarceration. Parole is a conditional release from prison and occurs after an offender has already served some time in a correctional facility. (See *Mastering Concepts—Probation versus Parole* for clarification.)

Conditions of Parole In many ways, parole supervision is similar to probation supervision. Like probationers, offenders who are granted parole are placed under the supervision of community corrections officers and required to follow certain conditions. Parole conditions often mirror probation conditions. All parolees, for example, must comply with the law, and they are generally responsible for reporting to their parole officer at certain intervals.

The frequency of these visits, along with the other terms of parole, is spelled out in the **parole contract,** which sets out the agreement between the state and the paroled offender. Under the terms of the contract, the state agrees to conditionally release the inmate, and the future parolee agrees that her or his conditional release will last only as long as she or he abides by the contract. (See Figure 12.4 for a list of standard parole conditions.)

Parole Revocation About a quarter of parolees return to prison before the end of their parole period, most because they were convicted of a new offense or had their parole revoked.[48] Property crimes are the most common reason that both male and female parolees return to incarceration, and men on parole are twice as likely as their female counterparts to have their parole revoked for a violent crime.[49] Parole revocation is similar in many aspects to probation revocation. If the parolee commits a new crime, then a return to prison is very likely. If, however, the individual commits a technical violation by breaking a condition of parole, then parole authorities have discretion as to whether revocation proceedings should be initiated. A number of states, including Michigan, Missouri, and New York, have taken steps to avoid reincarcerating parolees for technical violations as part of their continuing efforts to reduce prison populations.[50]

When authorities do attempt to revoke parole for a technical violation, they must provide the parolee with a revocation hearing.[51] Although this hearing does not provide the same due process protections as a criminal trial, the parolee does have the right to be notified of the charges, to present witnesses, to speak in his or her defense, and to question any hostile witnesses (so long as such questioning would not place these witnesses in danger). In the first stage of the hearing, the parole authorities determine whether there is probable cause that a violation occurred. Then, they decide whether to return the parolee to prison.

FIGURE 12.4 Standard Conditions of Parole

The parolee must do the following:
- Stay within a certain area.
- Obtain permission before changing residence or employment.
- Obtain and maintain employment.
- Maintain acceptable, nonthreatening behavior.
- Not possess firearms or weapons.
- Report any arrest within twenty-four hours.
- Not use illegal drugs or alcohol or enter drinking establishments.
- Not break any state or local laws.
- Allow contacts by parole officers at home or employment without obstruction.
- Submit to search of person, residence, or motor vehicle at any time by parole officers.

Probation and parole have many aspects in common. In fact, probation and parole are so similar that many jurisdictions combine them into a single agency. There are, however, some important distinctions between the two systems, as noted below.

	Probation	Parole
Basic Definition	An **alternative to imprisonment** in which a person who has been convicted of a crime is allowed to serve his or her sentence in the community subject to certain conditions and supervision by a probation officer.	An **early release** from a correctional facility, in which the convicted offender is given the chance to spend the remainder of her or his sentence under supervision in the community.
Timing	The offender is sentenced to a probationary term in place of a prison or jail term. If the offender breaks the conditions of probation, he or she is sent to prison or jail. Therefore, **probation generally occurs *before* imprisonment.**	Parole is a form of early release. Therefore, **parole occurs *after* an offender has spent time behind bars.**
Authority	**Probation is under the domain of the judiciary.** A judge decides whether to sentence a convict to probation, and a judge determines whether a probation violation warrants revocation and incarceration.	**Parole often falls under the domain of the parole board.** This administrative body determines whether the prisoner qualifies for early release and the conditions under which the parole must be served.
Characteristics of Offenders	As a number of studies have shown, probationers are normally less involved in the criminal lifestyle. Most of them are **first-time offenders who have committed nonviolent crimes.**	Many parolees have **spent months or even years in prison** and, besides abiding by conditions of parole, must make the difficult transition to "life on the outside."

Probation and Parole Officers Unlike police officers or sheriffs' deputies, probation and parole officers generally do not wear uniforms. Instead, they have badges that identify their position and agency. The duties of probation officers and parole officers are so similar that many small jurisdictions combine the two posts into a single position.

Given the supervisory nature of their professions, probation and parole officers are ultimately responsible for protecting the community by keeping their clients from committing crimes. There is also an element of social work in their duties, and these officers must constantly balance the needs of the community with the needs of the offender.[52] Parole officers in particular are expected to help the parolee readjust to life outside the correctional institution by helping her or him find a place to live and a job, and seeing that she or he receives any treatment that may be necessary.

Discretionary Release

As you may recall from Chapter 11, corrections systems are classified by sentencing procedure—indeterminate or determinate. Indeterminate sentencing occurs when the legislature sets a range of punishments for particular crimes, and the judge and the parole board exercise discretion in determining the actual length of the prison term. For that reason, states with indeterminate sentencing are said to have systems of **discretionary release**.

Eligibility for Parole Under indeterminate sentencing, parole is not a right but a privilege. This is a crucial point, as it establishes the terms of the relationship between the inmate and the corrections authorities during the parole process. In *Greenholtz v.*

Discretionary Release The release of an inmate into a community supervision program at the discretion of the parole board within limits set by state or federal law.

Inmates of the Nebraska Penal and Correctional Complex (1979),[53] the Supreme Court ruled that inmates do not have a constitutionally protected right to expect parole, thereby giving states the freedom to set their own standards for determining parole eligibility. In most states that have retained indeterminate sentencing, a prisoner is eligible to be considered for parole release after serving a legislatively determined percentage of the minimum sentence—usually one-half or two-thirds—less any good time or other credits.

Not all convicts are eligible for parole. As we saw in Chapter 11, offenders who have committed the most serious crimes often receive life sentences without the possibility of early release. In general, life without parole is reserved for those who have committed first degree murder or are defined by statute as habitual offenders. As was also discussed in Chapter 11, however, about 3,300 inmates convicted of nonviolent drug and property crimes have also received this sentence.[54] Today, about one-third of convicts serving life sentences have no possibility of parole.[55] (To give your opinion on a parole strategy that goes somewhat in the opposite direction, see this chapter's *CJ Policy—Your Take* feature.)

Parole Procedures A convict does not apply for parole. Rather, different jurisdictions have different procedures for determining discretionary release dates. In many states, the offender is eligible for discretionary release at the end of his or her minimum sentence minus good-time credits (see Chapter 11). In 2014, for example, Glenwood Carr was sentenced to six to twelve years in prison for fleeing the scene of a fatal accident that he caused by driving drunk in Clay, New York. This means that Carr will become eligible for parole after serving six years, less good time. In other states, parole eligibility is measured at either one-third or one-half of the maximum sentence, or it is a matter of discretion for the parole authorities.

In most, but not all, states, the responsibility for making the parole decision falls to the **parole board,** whose members are generally appointed by the governor. According to the American Correctional Association, the parole board has four basic roles:

1. To decide which offenders should be placed on parole.
2. To determine the conditions of parole and aid in the continuing supervision of the parolee.
3. To discharge the offender when the conditions of parole have been met.
4. If a violation occurs, to determine whether parole privileges should be revoked.[56]

Most parole boards are small, made up of three to seven members. In many jurisdictions, board members' terms are limited to between four and six years. The requirements for board members vary. Nearly half the states have no prerequisites, while others require a bachelor's degree or some expertise in the field of criminal justice.

The Parole Decision Parole boards use a number of criteria to determine whether a convict should be given discretionary release. These criteria include:

1. The nature and circumstances of the underlying offense and the offender's current attitude toward it.
2. The offender's prior criminal record.
3. The offender's attitude toward the victim and the victim's family members.
4. The offender's physical, mental, and emotional health.
5. The offender's behavior behind bars, including his or her participation in programs for self-improvement.[57]

Parole Board A body of appointed civilians that decides whether a convict should be granted conditional release before the end of his or her sentence.

In a system that uses discretionary parole, the actual release decision is made at a **parole grant hearing.** During this hearing, the entire board or a subcommittee reviews relevant information on the convict. Sometimes, but not always, the offender is interviewed.

Because the board members have only limited knowledge of each offender, key players in the case are often notified in advance of the parole hearing and asked to provide comments and recommendations. These participants include the sentencing judge, the attorneys at the trial, the victims, and any law enforcement officers who may be involved. After these preparations, the typical parole hearing itself is very short—usually lasting just a few minutes.

As parole has become a more important tool for reducing prison populations, corrections authorities are making greater efforts to ensure that the process does not endanger the community. Four-fifths of the parole boards in the United States now use risk assessment technology to help with the parole decision.[58] These tools generally increase a state's number of parolees, as parole board members—left to their own devices—may be hesitant to grant parole if there is even the slightest hint that an offender will recidivate. Texas, for example, used its risk assessment software to release 10,000 more inmates onto parole in 2012 than in 2005. Similarly, with the aid of this technology Michigan decreased its prison population by more than 15 percent between 2007 and 2013.[59]

Parole Denial When parole is denied, the reasons usually involve poor prison behavior by the offender and/or the severity of the underlying crime.[60] After a parole denial, the entire process will generally be replayed at the next "action date," which depends on the nature of the offender's crimes and all relevant laws. In February 2014, for example, Herman Bell was denied parole for the sixth time. More than four decades earlier, Bell had been convicted of murder for his involvement in the execution-style killings of two New York City police officers and sentenced to twenty-five years to life in prison. Although Bell was sixty-six years old at the time of his latest parole grant hearing, the state parole board told him that "if released at this time, there is a reasonable probability that you would not live and remain at liberty without again violating the law."[61]

On rare occasions, a state governor will veto the decision of a parole board to grant supervised release. In 2014, for example, a California parole board granted the release of seventy-one-year-old Bruce Davis, who had spent forty-three years behind bars for a double murder that took place in 1960. The board cited Davis's age, his religious conversion, and his role as a counselor to other inmates as factors in its decision. California governor Jerry Brown blocked Davis's parole, however, calling him an "unreasonable danger to society."[62] (See the feature *Discretion in Action—Cause for Compassion?* to learn more about the process of discretionary release.)

Parole Guidelines

Nearly twenty states have moved away from discretionary release systems to procedures that provide for **mandatory release.** Under mandatory release, offenders leave prison only when their prison terms

Parole Grant Hearing A hearing in which the entire parole board or a subcommittee reviews information, meets the offender, and hears testimony from relevant witnesses to determine whether to grant parole.

Mandatory Release Release from prison that occurs when an offender has served the full length of his or her sentence, minus any adjustments for good time.

▼ Parole board members discuss the case of thirty-two-year-old Jeffrey Dingman at the state prison in Concord, New Hampshire. In 2014, the board paroled Dingman, who had spent nearly two decades behind bars for helping his older brother kill their parents in 1996. **Do you think the age of the offender at the time of his or her offense should be taken into consideration as part of the parole decision? Why or why not?** AP Images/Jim Cole

Discretion in Action

Cause for Compassion?

The Situation Thirty-seven years ago, Susan was convicted of first degree murder and sentenced to life in prison for taking part in a grisly killing spree in Los Angeles. Over the course of two days, Susan and her accomplices killed seven people. Susan stabbed one of the victims—a pregnant woman—sixteen times and wrote the word "PIG" on a door using another victim's blood. During her trial, Susan testified that she "was stoned, man, stoned on acid" at the time of her crimes. Now sixty-one years old, Susan is before your parole board, requesting release from prison. For most of her time behind bars, she has been a model prisoner, and she has apologized numerous times for her wrongdoing. Furthermore, her left leg has been amputated, the left side of her body is paralyzed, and she has been diagnosed with terminal brain cancer.

The Law You have a great deal of discretion in determining whether a prisoner should be paroled. Some of the factors you should consider are the threat the prisoner would pose to the community if released, the nature of the offense, and the level of remorse. In addition, California allows for "compassionate release" when an inmate is "terminally ill."

LEARNING OBJECTIVE **6** Explain which factors influence the decision to grant parole.

What Would You Do? Susan obviously poses no threat to the community and is a viable candidate for compassionate release. Should she be set free on parole? Or are some crimes so horrific that the convict should never be given parole, no matter what the circumstances? Explain your vote.

[To see how a California parole board voted in a similar situation, go to Example 12.2 in Appendix B.]

---

have expired, minus adjustments for good time. No parole board is involved in this type of release, which is designed to eliminate discretion from the process.

Instead, in mandatory release, corrections officials rely on **parole guidelines** to determine the early release date. Similar to sentencing guidelines (see Chapter 11), parole guidelines determine a potential parolee's risk of recidivism using a mathematical equation. Under this system, inmates and corrections authorities know the *presumptive parole date* soon after the inmate enters prison. So long as the offender does not experience any disciplinary or other problems while incarcerated, he or she can be fairly sure of the time of release.

Note that a number of states and the federal government claim to have officially "abolished" parole through truth-in-sentencing laws. (As described in Chapter 11, this form of legislation requires certain statutorily determined offenders to serve at least 85 percent of their prison terms.) For the most part, however, these laws simply emphasize prison terms that are "truthful," not necessarily "longer." Mechanisms for parole, by whatever name, are crucial to the criminal justice system for several reasons. First, they provide inmates with an incentive to behave properly in the hope of an early release. Second, they reduce the costs related to incarceration by keeping down the inmate population, a critical concern for prison administrators.[63]

Victims' Rights and Parole

Herman Bell's chances of being granted parole, described earlier in this section, are certainly not helped by the sentiments of Diane Piagentini, the widow of one of his victims. According to Piagentini, Bell should remain behind bars "until the end of time."[64] Over the past several decades, the community corrections system has expanded to better encompass the wants and needs of victims. Many probation and parole departments now have employees responsible for assisting victims in areas such as collecting restitution or compensation and providing information about the status and location of offenders.[65]

Parole Guidelines Standards that are used in the parole process to measure the risk that a potential parolee will recidivate.

The federal Crime Victims' Rights Act provides victims with the right to be reasonably notified of any parole proceedings and the right to attend and be reasonably heard at such proceedings.[66] A number of states offer similar assurances of victim participation in the parole process. Generally, victim testimony before a parole board focuses on the emotional, physical, and financial hardship experienced by the victim or the victim's family because of the offender's criminal act. Given the moral power of such testimony, it is somewhat surprising to learn that victim input appears to have little effect on the parole decision. Instead, parole boards prefer to rely on the traditional criteria for determining parole, described earlier in this section.[67]

Intermediate Sanctions

Many observers feel that the most widely used sentencing options—imprisonment and probation—fail to reflect the immense diversity of crimes and criminals. **Intermediate sanctions** provide a number of additional sentencing options for those wrongdoers who require stricter supervision than that supplied by probation, but for whom imprisonment would be unduly harsh and counterproductive. The intermediate sanctions discussed in this section are designed to match the specific punishment and treatment of an individual offender with a corrections program that reflects that offender's situation.

Dozens of different variations of intermediate sanctions are handed down each year. To cover the spectrum succinctly, two general categories of such sanctions will be discussed in this section: those administered primarily by the courts and those administered primarily by corrections departments, including day reporting centers, intensive supervision probation, shock incarceration, and home confinement. Remember that none of these sanctions are exclusive. They are often combined with imprisonment and probation and parole, and with each other.

Judicially Administered Sanctions

The lack of sentencing options is most frustrating for the person who, in the majority of cases, does the sentencing—the judge. Consequently, when judges are given the discretion to "color" a punishment with intermediate sanctions, they will often do so. In addition to imprisonment and probation, a judge has five sentencing options:

1. Fines.
2. Community service.
3. Restitution.
4. Pretrial diversion programs.
5. Forfeiture.

Fines, community service, and restitution were discussed in Chapter 11. In the context of intermediate sanctions, it is important to remember that these punishments are generally combined with incarceration or probation. For that reason, some critics feel the retributive or deterrent impact of such punishments is severely limited. Many European countries, in contrast, rely heavily on fines as the sole sanctions for a variety of crimes. (See the feature *Comparative Criminal Justice—Swedish Day-Fines.*)

Pretrial Diversion Programs Not every criminal violation requires the courtroom process. Consequently, some judges have the discretion to order an offender into a **pretrial diversion program** during the preliminary hearing. (Prosecutors can also offer an offender the opportunity to join such a program in return for reducing or dropping the initial

Intermediate Sanctions
Sanctions that are more restrictive than probation and less restrictive than imprisonment.

Pretrial Diversion Program An alternative to trial offered by a judge or prosecutor, in which the offender agrees to participate in a specified counseling or treatment program in return for withdrawal of the charges.

Comparative **Criminal Justice**

Swedish Day-Fines

Few ideals are cherished as highly in our criminal justice system as equality. Most Americans take it for granted that individuals guilty of identical crimes should face identical punishments. From an economic perspective, however, this emphasis on equality renders our system decidedly unequal. Take two citizens, one a millionaire investment banker and the other a checkout clerk earning the minimum wage. Driving home from work one afternoon, each is caught by a traffic officer doing 80 miles per hour in a 55-mile-per-hour zone. The fine for this offense is $150. This amount, though equal for both, has different consequences: it represents mere pocket change for the investment banker, but a significant chunk out of the checkout clerk's weekly paycheck.

Restricted by a "tariff system" that sets specific amounts for specific crimes, regardless of the financial situation of the convict, American judges often refrain from using fines as a primary sanction. They either assume that poor offenders cannot pay the fine or worry that a fine will allow wealthier offenders to "buy" their way out of a punishment.

Paying for Crime

In searching for a way to make fines more effective sanctions, many reformers have seized on the concept of the "day-fine,"

as practiced in Sweden and several other European countries. In this system, which was established in the 1920s and 1930s, the fine amount is linked to the monetary value of the offender's daily income. Depending on the seriousness of the crime, a Swedish offender will be sentenced to 1 to 120 day-fines or, as combined punishment for multiple crimes, up to 200 day-fines.

For each day-fine unit assessed, the offender is required to pay one-thousandth of her or his annual gross income (minus a deduction for basic living expenses, as determined by the Prosecutor General's Office) to the court. Consequently, the day-fine system not only reflects the degree of the crime, but also ensures that the economic burden will be equal for those with different incomes.

Swedish police and prosecutors can levy day-fines without court involvement. As a result, plea bargaining is nonexistent, and more than 80 percent of all offenders are sentenced to intermediate sanctions without a trial. The remaining cases receive full trials, with a non-conviction rate of only 6 percent, compared with 26 percent in the United States.

For Critical Analysis

Do you think a "day-fine" system would be feasible in the United States? Why might it be difficult to implement in this country?

---

charges.) These programs represent an "interruption" of the criminal proceedings and are generally reserved for young or first-time offenders who have been arrested on charges of illegal drug use, child or spousal abuse, or sexual misconduct. Pretrial diversion programs usually include extensive counseling, often in a treatment center. If the offender successfully follows the conditions of the program, the criminal charges are dropped.

Problem-Solving Courts Many judges have found opportunities to divert low-level offenders by presiding over problem-solving courts. In these comparatively informal courtrooms, judges attempt to address problems such as drug addiction, mental illness, and homelessness that often lead to the eventual rearrest of the offender.

Drug Courts About three thousand problem-solving courts are operating in the United States. Although these specialized courts cover a wide variety of subjects, from domestic violence to juvenile crime to mental illness, the most common problem-solving courts are drug courts.

Although the specific procedures of drug courts vary widely, most follow a general pattern. Either after arrest or on conviction, the offender is given the option of entering a drug court program or continuing through the standard courtroom process. Those who choose the former come under the supervision of a judge who will oversee a mixture of treatment and sanctions designed to cure their addiction. When offenders successfully complete the program, the drug court rewards them by dropping all charges.

Drug courts operate on the assumption that when a criminal addict's drug use is reduced, his or her drug-fueled criminal activity will also decline.

The success of drug courts has led state legislatures to target other areas of criminality for similar treatment. In 2013, new state laws were passed allowing prostitutes access to mental health courts (Illinois), authorizing problem-solving courts as a condition of a misdemeanor sentence (Indiana), and permitting any jurisdiction in the state to create a problem-solving court (Washington).[68]

Diversion and Restorative Justice Judges are also taking advantage of the positive policy implications of specialty courts to insert principles of restorative justice, which we discussed in Chapter 11, into their diversion efforts. For example, more judges are using *community dispute resolution centers* to move certain misdemeanors and minor criminal matters out of the court system completely. At these centers, specialists help the parties involved in a dispute—such as one involving vandalism or noise complaints—by *mediating*, or negotiating, a satisfactory outcome for both sides. In 2011, New York judges, prosecutors, and police officers referred more than 3,100 criminal cases to community dispute resolution centers, thus diverting the participants from the formal court system.[69]

▲ In Pinellas County, Florida, Judge Dee Anna Farnell congratulates graduates of her drug court program. **How does society benefit when an offender successfully completes a drug court program rather than being sent to prison or jail?** Scott Keeler/ *Tampa Bay Times*/ZUMAPRESS.com/Newscom

Forfeiture In 1970, Congress passed the Racketeer Influenced and Corrupt Organizations Act (RICO) in an attempt to prevent the use of legitimate business enterprises as shields for organized crime.[70] As amended, RICO and other statutes give judges the ability to implement *forfeiture* proceedings in certain criminal cases. **Forfeiture** is a process by which the government seizes property gained from or used in criminal activity. For example, if a person is convicted for smuggling cocaine into the United States from South America, a judge can order the seizure of not only the narcotics, but also the speedboat the offender used to deliver the drugs to a pickup point off the coast of South Florida. In *Bennis v. Michigan* (1996),[71] the Supreme Court ruled that a person's home or car could be forfeited even though the owner was unaware that the property was connected to illegal activity.

Once property is forfeited, the government has several options. It can sell the property, with the proceeds going to the state and/or federal law enforcement agencies involved in the seizure. Alternatively, the government agency can use the property directly in further crime-fighting efforts or award it to a third party, such as an informant. In Harris County, Texas, for example, law enforcement officials purchased about eight hundred body-worn cameras for local police officers (discussed in Chapter 6) using funds from civil forfeitures.

Forfeiture is financially rewarding for both federal and local law enforcement agencies. The U.S. Marshals Service manages about $2.2 billion worth of contraband and property impounded from criminals and criminal suspects. In 2014, the agency shared about $487 million of these funds with state and local law enforcement agencies, with an additional $1.9 billion going to crime victims.[72]

Day Reporting Centers

First used in Great Britain, **day reporting centers (DRCs)** are mainly tools to reduce jail and prison overcrowding. Although the offenders are allowed to live in the community rather

Forfeiture The process by which the government seizes private property attached to criminal activity.

Day Reporting Center (DRC) A community-based corrections center to which offenders report on a daily basis for treatment, education, and rehabilitation.

than jail or prison, they must spend all or part of each day at a reporting center. In general, being sentenced to a DRC is an extreme form of supervision. With offenders under a single roof, they are much more easily monitored and controlled. (According to critics of DRCs, they are also more easily able to "network" with other individuals who have criminal histories and drug and alcohol abuse issues.)[73]

DRCs are instruments of rehabilitation as well. They often feature treatment programs for drug and alcohol abusers and provide counseling for a number of psychological problems, such as depression and anger management. Many of those found guilty in the Roanoke (Virginia) Drug Court, for example, are ordered to participate in a yearlong day reporting program. At the center, offenders meet with probation officers, submit to urine tests, and attend counseling and education programs, such as parenting and life-skills classes. After the year has passed, if the offender has completed the program to the satisfaction of the judge and has found employment, the charges will be dropped.[74]

Intensive Supervision Probation

Over the past several decades, a number of jurisdictions have turned to **intensive supervision probation (ISP)** to solve the problems associated with burdensome caseloads we discussed earlier in the chapter. ISP offers a more restrictive alternative to regular probation, with higher levels of face-to-face contact between offenders and officers and frequent modes of control such as urine tests for drugs. In New Jersey, for example, ISP officers have caseloads of only 20 offenders (compared with 115 for other probation officers in the state) and are provided with additional resources to help them keep tabs on their charges.[75] Different jurisdictions have different methods of determining who is eligible for ISP, but a majority of states limit ISP to offenders who do not have prior probation violations.

LEARNING
Contrast day reporting centers with intensive supervision probation. **7** OBJECTIVE

The main goal of ISP is to provide prisonlike control of offenders while keeping them out of prison. Critics of ISP believe that it "causes" high failure rates, as more supervision increases the chances that an offender will be caught breaking conditions of probation.[76] One comparison of ISP with DRCs, however, found the intensive supervision of ISP to be more effective. In the six months following termination of the program, DRC participants were more likely to be convicted for a new offense and to test positive for drugs than their ISP counterparts. The study suggests that when combined with services such as outpatient drug treatment and educational training, ISP can be effective in producing low rates of recidivism.[77]

Shock Incarceration

As the name suggests, **shock incarceration** is designed to "shock" criminals into compliance with the law. Following conviction, the offender is first sentenced to a prison or jail term. Then, usually within ninety days, he or she is released and resentenced to probation. The theory behind shock incarceration is that by getting a taste of the brutalities of the daily prison grind, the offender will be shocked into a crime-free existence.

In the past, shock incarceration was targeted primarily toward youthful, first-time offenders, who were thought to be more likely to be "scared straight" by a short stint behind bars. Recent data show, however, that 20 percent of all adults sentenced to probation spend some time in jail or prison before being released into the community.[78] Critics of shock incarceration are dismayed by this trend. They argue that the practice needlessly disrupts the lives of low-level offenders who would not otherwise be eligible for incarceration and exposes them to the mental and physical hardships of prison life (which we will discuss in Chapter 14).[79] Furthermore, there is little evidence that shock probationers fare any better than regular probationers when it comes to recidivism rates.[80]

Intensive Supervision Probation (ISP) A punishment-oriented form of probation in which the offender is placed under stricter and more frequent surveillance and control than in conventional probation.

Shock Incarceration A short period of incarceration that is designed to deter further criminal activity by "shocking" the offender with the hardships of imprisonment.

Impact incarceration programs, or *boot camps,* are a variation on traditional shock incarceration. Instead of spending the "shock" period of incarceration in prison or jail, offenders are sent to a boot camp. Modeled on military basic training, these camps are generally located within prisons and jails, though some can be found in the community. The programs emphasize strict discipline, manual labor, and physical training. They are designed to instill self-responsibility and self-respect in participants, thereby lessening the chances that they will return to a life of crime. More recently, boot camps have also emphasized rehabilitation, incorporating such components as drug and alcohol treatment programs, anger-management courses, and vocational training.

▲ Inmates engage in morning calisthenics at the Impact Incarceration Program in Illinois. **In theory, why would boot camps like this one benefit first-time nonviolent offenders more than a jail or prison sentence?** *Journal Courier/ The Image Works*

Home Confinement and Electronic Monitoring

Various forms of **home confinement**—in which offenders serve their sentences not in a government institution but at home—have existed for centuries. It has often served, and continues to do so, as a method of political control, used by totalitarian regimes to isolate and silence dissidents. For purposes of general law enforcement, home confinement was impractical until relatively recently. After all, one could not expect offenders to keep their promises to stay at home, and the personnel costs of guarding them were prohibitive.

In the 1980s, however, with the advent of **electronic monitoring,** or using technology to guard the prisoner, home confinement became more viable. Today, all fifty states and the federal government have home monitoring programs with about 200,000 offenders, including probationers and parolees, participating at any one time.[81]

The Levels of Home Monitoring Home monitoring has three general levels of restriction:

LEARNING **8** OBJECTIVE List the three levels of home monitoring.

1. *Curfew,* which requires offenders to be in their homes at specific hours each day, usually at night.
2. *Home detention,* which requires that offenders remain home at all times, with exceptions being made for education, employment, counseling, and other specified activities such as the purchase of food or, in some instances, attendance at religious services.
3. *Home incarceration,* which requires the offender to remain home at all times, save for medical emergencies.

Under ideal circumstances, home confinement serves many of the goals of intermediate sanctions. It protects the community. It saves public funds and space in correctional facilities by keeping convicts out of institutional incarceration. It meets public expectations of punishment for criminals. Uniquely, home confinement also recognizes that convicts, despite their crimes, play important roles in the community, and allows them to continue in those roles. An offender, for example, may be given permission to leave confinement to care for elderly parents.

Home Confinement A community-based sanction in which offenders serve their terms of incarceration in their homes.

Electronic Monitoring A technique of probation supervision in which the offender's whereabouts are kept under surveillance by an electronic device.

▲ Offenders who are confined to their homes are often monitored by electronic devices like this one, which fits around the ankle. **What are some of the benefits of electronic monitoring as an intermediate sanction?** AP Images/ Wilfredo Lee

Home confinement is also lauded for giving sentencing officials the freedom to match the punishment with the needs of the offender. In 2014, for example, a sixty-four-year-old Maine businessman was sentenced to six months of home confinement for tax fraud. He was, however, allowed to return to his office during the day to earn the money needed to pay nearly $140,000 in court-ordered fines. The offender was also allowed to leave home for doctor's appointments and to buy groceries.

Types of Electronic Monitoring According to some reports, the inspiration for electronic monitoring was a *Spider-Man* comic book in which the hero was trailed by the use of an electronic device on his arm. In 1979, a New Mexico judge named Jack Love, having read the comic, convinced an executive at Honeywell, Inc., to begin developing similar technology to supervise convicts.[82]

Two major types of electronic monitoring have grown out of Love's initial concept. The first is a "programmed contact" program, in which the offender is contacted periodically by voice or text to verify his or her whereabouts. Verification is obtained via a computer that uses voice or visual identification techniques or by requiring the offender to enter a code in an electronic box when called. The second is a "continuously signaling" device, worn around the convict's wrist, ankle, or neck. A transmitter in the device sends out a continuous signal to a "receiver-dialer" device located in the offender's dwelling. If the receiver device does not detect a signal from the transmitter, it informs a central computer, and the police are notified.

Technological Advances in Electronic Monitoring As electronic monitoring technology has evolved, the ability of community corrections officials to target specific forms of risky behavior has greatly increased. Michigan courts, for example, routinely place black boxes in the automobiles of repeat traffic law violators. Not only do these boxes record information about the offenders' driving habits for review by probation officers, but they also emit a loud beep when the car goes too fast or stops too quickly. Another device—an ankle bracelet—is able to test a person's sweat for alcohol levels and transmit the results over the Internet.

Effectiveness of Home Confinement Because most participants in home confinement programs are low-risk offenders, their recidivism rates are quite low. Indeed, these programs appear to be no more or less effective than those that rely on human supervision, with most of their upside coming from the benefits mentioned earlier, such as cost savings and offender freedom. One concern about home confinement is that offenders are often required to defray program costs, which can be over $200 a month.[83] Consequently, those who cannot afford to pay for electronic monitoring may not be eligible.

This form of intermediate sanction may also cause problems in the personal and financial lives of offenders. Forty-three percent of those placed on electronic monitoring surveyed in Florida complained that the devices had a negative effect on their relationships with intimate partners. A number of these respondents noted the sense of shame such devices cause, given that most people assume that those who wear them are sex offenders. In addition, the visibility of the devices makes job interviews awkward, and 22 percent of the Florida offenders said they had lost their employment because of electronic monitoring requirements.[84]

Global Positioning System (GPS)

Global positioning system (GPS) technology is a form of tracking technology that relies on twenty-four military satellites orbiting thousands of miles above the earth. The satellites transmit signals to each other and to a receiver on the ground, allowing a monitoring station to determine the location of a receiving device to within a few feet. GPS provides a much more precise level of supervision than regular electronic monitoring. The offender wears a transmitter, similar to a traditional electronic monitor, around his or her ankle or wrist. This transmitter communicates with a portable tracking device, a small box that uses military satellites to determine the probationer's movements.

AP Images/Jeff T. Green

GPS technology can be used either "actively" to constantly monitor the subject's whereabouts, or "passively" to ensure that the offender remains within the confines of a limited area determined by a judge or probation officer. Inclusion and exclusion zones are also important to GPS supervision. Inclusion zones are areas such as a home or workplace where the offender is expected to be at certain times. Exclusion zones are areas such as parks, playgrounds, and schools where the offender is not permitted to go. GPS-linked computers can alert officials immediately when an exclusion zone has been breached and create a computerized record of the probationer's movements for review at a later time. Despite the benefits of this technology, it is rarely implemented. According to the Bureau of Justice Statistics, only about eight thousand probationers are currently being tracked by GPS.

Thinking about GPS
How might GPS monitoring be used to improve and overhaul the American bail system, covered in Chapter 9?

Widening the Net

As we have seen, most of the convicts chosen for intermediate sanctions are low-risk offenders. From the point of view of the corrections official doing the choosing, this makes sense. Such offenders are less likely to commit crimes and attract negative publicity. This selection strategy, however, appears to invalidate one of the primary reasons intermediate sanctions exist: to reduce prison and jail populations. If most of the offenders in intermediate sanctions programs would otherwise have received probation, then the effect on these populations is nullified. Indeed, studies have shown this to be the case.[85]

At the same time, intermediate sanctions broaden the reach of the corrections system. In other words, they increase rather than decrease the amount of control the state exerts over the individual. Suppose a person is arrested for a misdemeanor such as shoplifting and, under normal circumstances, would receive probation. With access to intermediate sanctions, the judge may add a period of home confinement to the sentence. Critics contend that such practices **widen the net** of the corrections system by augmenting the number of citizens who are under the control and surveillance of

Widen the Net The criticism that intermediate sanctions designed to divert offenders from prison actually increase the number of citizens who are under the control and surveillance of the American corrections system.

▲ Explain the possible connection between higher levels of surveillance by probation and parole officers and greater numbers of probationers and parolees being incarcerated. Los Angeles County Probation Department

the state and also *strengthen the net* by increasing the government's power to intervene in the lives of its citizens.[86] Technological advances—such as the black boxes in automobiles, sweat-testing ankle bracelets, and GPS devices mentioned in this chapter—will only accelerate the trend.

The Paradox of Community Corrections

Despite their many benefits, including cost savings, treatment options, and the ability to divert hundreds of thousands of nonviolent wrongdoers from prisons and jails, community-based corrections programs suffer from a basic paradox: the more effectively offenders are controlled, the more likely they are to be caught violating the terms of their conditional release. As you may have noticed, the community supervision programs discussed in this chapter are evaluated according to rates of recidivism and revocation, with low levels of each reflecting a successful program. Increased control and surveillance, however, will necessarily raise the level of violations, thus increasing the probability that any single violation will be discovered. Therefore, as factors such as the number of conditions placed on probationers and the technological proficiency of electronic monitoring devices increase, so, too, will the number of offenders who fail to meet the conditions of their community-based punishment.

One observer calls this the "quicksand" effect of increased surveillance. Instead of helping offenders leave the corrections system, increased surveillance pulls them more deeply into it.[87] Given that, as we have noted throughout this chapter, policymakers are relying on community corrections to *decrease* the costs associated with corrections, many states are taking active steps to counteract the quicksand effect.

For example, North Carolina has successfully kept thousands of parole and probation violators out of expensive prison cells. Similar to Hawaii's HOPE program discussed earlier in the chapter, those offenders who do violate the terms of their supervised freedom often are sent to jail for 90 days, rather than having their parole or probation revoked. As part of its "justice reinvestment" strategy, North Carolina has used some of the savings produced by these tactics to hire nearly two hundred new probation and parole officers which, state officials hope, will further improve the quality of its community corrections system.[88]

Summarize the paradox of community corrections.

LEARNING **9** OBJECTIVE

EthicsChallenge

With criminal forfeiture, as described in this section, a defendant must be convicted of committing a crime before her or his property is confiscated. Under *civil* forfeiture, as implemented by the federal government and almost every state government, law enforcement agencies can confiscate property without the criminal conviction of its owner and can keep that property, even if the owner is ultimately found to be innocent of the crime. The government need only prove a "substantial connection" between the property and underlying crime for civil forfeiture to apply. How might this practice provide law enforcement agencies with a motive to commit "legalized theft," in the words of one critic? ■

CJ IN ACTION

Involuntary Commitment of the Mentally Ill

Most people who suffer from mental illness are not criminals, and most criminals are not mentally ill. As we saw in Chapter 2, however, there appears to be a correlation between mental illness and violent behavior. So, under certain circumstances that we will explore in this *CJ in Action* feature, mental health professionals have the same powers as criminal justice professionals—they can restrict the freedom of potentially dangerous individuals for the good of society. As in the criminal justice system, however, this power is fraught with controversy and fears of making the wrong decision.

The Need for Treatment

Before killing six people, injuring thirteen others, and committing suicide in Isla Vista, California (an incident described in the opening of Chapter 2), Elliot Rodger behaved erratically and menacingly. When some of this behavior—in particular, a YouTube video in which he described his upcoming "Day of Retribution"—became known to the public, many community members wondered why Rodger had not been locked up by authorities. California, like every other state, has an involuntary civil commitment law, under which mentally ill individuals can be held in custody and committed to a psychiatric hospital against their wishes. Involuntary commitment, like imprisonment for criminals, raises due process concerns because it involves a significant deprivation of liberty.[89] Therefore, states must devise procedures that protect the rights of mentally ill individuals during this process.

California has one of the strictest involuntary commitment laws in the nation. The person in question must be judged "a danger to others, or to himself or herself, or gravely disabled" by a qualified medical or psychological expert after being detained for at least seventy-two hours.[90] Rodger's mother actually had warned law enforcement about her son's deteriorating mental condition, but his actions never reached the level necessary to be held for a psychiatric evaluation. When discussing issues of mental health and crime, then, one question inevitably arises: should we make it easier to involuntarily commit mentally ill individuals, for their safety and our own?

The Case for Lenient Involuntary Commitment Standards

- More lenient standards would allow for the care and rehabilitation of individuals who need treatment and are not receiving it.

- Such standards would protect society from the dangers posed by the untreated mentally ill.

- Treatment before arrest would also prevent many criminal acts from taking place and spare society the costs of incarceration.[91]

The Case against Lenient Involuntary Commitment Standards

- Such standards infringe on the rights of the mentally ill. As the United States Supreme Court has stated, "[T]he mere presence of mental illness does not disqualify a person from preferring his home to the comforts of an institution."[92]

- Only a small percentage of people with mental illnesses behave violently, and it is very difficult to predict whether a person will present a future danger. More lenient commitment standards would strip many harmless people of their freedoms unnecessarily.[93]

- States do not have the funds or the capacity to treat a large influx of new psychiatric patients.

Writing Assignment—Your Opinion

As you have seen throughout this textbook, substance abuse has a strong connection to criminality. For that reason, the American corrections system routinely mandates substance abuse treatment for those under community supervision or behind bars. But what if alcohol or drug problems could be addressed before the first arrest? Research shows that early treatment improves an addict's ability to stay off drugs and alcohol, and therefore lessens the chances of future wrongdoing.[94]

Would you support a law, similar to Arizona's involuntary commitment law, that would allow concerned parties—family members, co-workers, or friends—to petition a court for involuntary substance abuse treatment? In other words, the law would permit one adult to force another adult, with judicial approval, to get treatment for drug or alcohol abuse. How could such a law be written to balance individual rights and society's need for protection? Would it successfully divert potential offenders from the criminal justice system? Before responding, you can review our discussions in the sections of this chapter concerning:

- Diversion ("The Justifications for Community Corrections").

- Drug courts ("Intermediate Sanctions").

- Widening the net ("Intermediate Sanctions").

Your answer should include at least three full paragraphs.

Summary

For more information on these concepts, look back to the Learning Objective icons throughout the chapter.

 Explain the justifications for community-based corrections programs. One justification involves reintegration of the offender into society. Reintegration restores family ties, encourages employment and education, and secures a place for the offender in the routine functioning of society. Other justifications involve diversion and cost savings. By diverting criminals to alternative modes of punishment, further overcrowding of jail and prison facilities can be avoided, as can the costs of incarcerating the offenders.

 Explain several alternative sentencing arrangements that combine probation with incarceration. With a suspended sentence, a convicted offender is not required to serve the sentence, but the judge has the option of reinstating the sentence if the person reoffends. In addition, there are three other general types of sentencing arrangements: (a) split sentence probation, in which the judge specifies a certain time in jail or prison followed by a certain time on probation; (b) shock incarceration, in which a judge sentences an offender to be incarcerated, but allows that person to petition the court to be released on probation; and (c) intermittent incarceration, in which an offender spends a certain amount of time each week in jail or in a halfway house or another government institution.

 Specify the conditions under which an offender is most likely to be denied probation. The offender (a) has been convicted of multiple charges, (b) was on probation or parole when arrested, (c) has two or more prior convictions, (d) is addicted to narcotics, (e) seriously injured the victim of the crime, or (f) used a weapon while committing the crime.

 Describe the three general categories of conditions placed on a probationer. (a) Standard conditions, such as requiring that the probationer notify the agency of a change of address, not leave the jurisdiction without permission, and remain employed; (b) punitive conditions, such as restitution, community service, and home confinement; and (c) treatment conditions, such as required drug or alcohol treatment.

 Identify the main differences between probation and parole. Probation is a sentence handed down by a judge that generally acts as an alternative to incarceration. Parole is a form of early release from prison determined by a parole authority, often a parole board. Probationers are usually first-time offenders who have committed nonviolent crimes, while parolees have often spent significant time in prison.

 Explain which factors influence the decision to grant parole. In deciding whether to grant parole, parole board members primarily consider the severity of the underlying crime and the threat the offender will pose to the community if released. Other factors include the offender's level of remorse and his or her behavior while incarcerated.

 Contrast day reporting centers with intensive supervision probation. In a day reporting center, the offender is allowed to remain in the community, but must spend all or part of each day at the reporting center. While at the center, offenders meet with probation officers, submit to drug tests, and attend counseling and education programs. With intensive supervision probation (ISP), more restrictions are imposed, and there is more face-to-face contact between offenders and probation officers. ISP may also include electronic surveillance.

 List the three levels of home monitoring. (a) Curfew, which requires that the offender be at home during specified hours; (b) home detention, which requires that the offender be at home except for education, employment, and counseling; and (c) home incarceration, which requires that the offender be at home at all times except for medical emergencies.

 Summarize the paradox of community corrections. The more effective a probation or parole department is in controlling and supervising its clients, the more likely it is that those clients will be caught violating the conditions of their supervision. This makes it more likely the probationer or parolee will be incarcerated, thus defeating the diversion and treatment purposes of community corrections.

Questions for Critical Analysis

1. In this chapter, you learned about the sentence of two years' probation given to an eighty-six-year-old man who was found guilty of fatally shooting his eighty-one-year-old wife. As you might recall, the victim was suffering from a painful health condition and had begged her husband to end her life. Do you agree with the judge's sentencing decision in this case? Why or why not?

2. Why might probationers and parolees want to limit their social media activity? Give an example of a circumstance in which a Facebook posting could cause probation or parole to be revoked.

3. Review our discussion of Hawaii's Opportunity Probation with Enforcement (HOPE) from earlier in the chapter. What might be some of the reasons participants in the program are less likely to fail a second urinalysis test?

4. In many jurisdictions, parolees can be stopped and searched by parole or police officers at any time, even if there is no probable cause that the parolee has committed a crime. How can these types of stops and searches be justified?

5. In your own words, explain what the phrase "widening the net" means. What might be some of the unintended consequences of increasing the number of offenders who are supervised by corrections officers in the community?

Key Terms

authority   395
caseload   396
community corrections   389
day reporting center (DRC)   407
discretionary release   401
diversion   389
electronic monitoring   409
forfeiture   407
graduated sanctions   397
home confinement   409

intensive supervision probation (ISP)   408
intermediate sanctions   405
mandatory release   403
parole   399
parole board   402
parole contract   400
parole grant hearing   403
parole guidelines   404
pretrial diversion program   405

probation   391
reintegration   389
revocation   393
shock incarceration   408
split sentence probation   391
suspended sentence   391
technical violation   396
widen the net   411

Notes

1. Mary Schenk and Michael Howie, "Reckless Homicide Sentence Reduced to Probation," *The News-Gazette* (Champaign, Ill.) (December 2, 2014), at **www.news-gazette.com /news/local/2014-12-02/reckless -homicide-sentence-reduced-probation .html.**

2. Bureau of Justice Statistics, *Correctional Populations in the United States, 2013* (Washington, D.C.: U.S. Department of Justice, December 2014), Table 1, page 2.

3. Michael Tonry, *Sentencing Matters* (New York: Oxford Press, 1996), 28.

4. *Correctional Populations in the United States, 2013, op. cit.*, 1.

5. Corrections Task Force of the President's Commission on Law Enforcement and Administration of Justice (1967).

6. Paul H. Hahn, *Emerging Criminal Justice: Three Pillars for a Proactive Justice System* (Thousand Oaks, Calif.: Sage Publications, 1998), 106–108.

7. *Correctional Populations in the United States, 2013, op. cit.*, Table 1, page 2.

8. Pew Center on the States, *State of Recidivism: The Revolving Door of America's Prisons* (Washington, D.C.: The Pew Charitable Trusts, April 2011).

9. "Supervision Costs Significantly Less than Incarceration in Federal System," *United States Courts* (July 18, 2013), at **news.uscourts.gov /supervision-costs-significantly-less -incarceration-federal-system.**

10. Ram Subramanian and Rebecca Tublitz, *Realigning Justice Resources: A Review of Population Spending Shifts in Prison and Community Corrections* (New York: Vera Institute of Justice, 2012), 32, 33.

11. Erik Eckholm, "North Carolina Cuts Prison Time for Probation Violators, and Costs," *New York Times* (September 12, 2014), A14.

12. Paul W. Keve, *Crime Control and Justice in America* (Chicago: American Library Association, 1995), 183.

13. Gerald Bayens and John Ortiz Smykla, *Probation, Parole, & Community-Based Corrections* (New York: McGraw-Hill, 2013), 186–217.

14. Bureau of Justice Statistics, *Probation and Parole in the United States, 2010* (Washington, D.C.: U.S. Department of Justice, December 2011), Appendix table 3, page 31.

15. Joan Petersilia and Susan Turner, *Prison versus Probation in California: Implications for Crime and Offender Recidivism* (Santa Monica, Calif.: RAND Corporation, 1986).

16. Bureau of Justice Statistics, *Probation and Parole in the United States, 2013* (Washington, D.C.: U.S. Department of Justice, October 2014), Appendix table 3, page 17.

17. Brian Skoloff, "George Sanders Gets Probation in Mercy Killing," *Associated Press* (March 29, 2013).

18. *Probation and Parole in the United States, 2013, op. cit.*, Appendix table 3, page 17.

19. *Ibid.*; and Bureau of Justice Statistics, *Prisoners in 2013* (Washington, D.C.: U.S. Department of Justice, September 2014), Table 1, page 2.

20. Sharyn Adams, Lindsay Bostwick, and Rebecca Campbell, *Examining Illinois Probationer Characteristics and Outcomes* (Chicago: Illinois Criminal Justice Information Authority, September 2011), Table 1, pages 16–17.

21. 705 So.2d 172 (La. 1997).

22. Neil P. Cohen and James J. Gobert, *The Law of Probation and Parole* (Colorado Springs, Colo.: Shepard's/McGraw-Hill, 1983), Section 5.01, 183–184; Section 5.03, 191–192.

23. 534 U.S. 112 (2001).

24. *Ibid.*, 113.

25. Bureau of Justice Statistics, *Felony Defendants in Large Urban Counties, 2009—Statistical Tables* (Washington, D.C.: U.S. Department of Justice, December 2013), Table 28, page 32.

26. Carl B. Klockars, Jr., "A Theory of Probation Supervision," *Journal of Criminal Law, Criminology, and Police Science* 63 (1972), 550–557.

27. *Probation and Parole in the United States, 2013, op. cit.*, Table 4, page 5.

28. Gwen Robinson, "What Works in Offender Management?" *The Howard Journal of Criminal Justice* 44 (2005), 307–318.

29. Klockars, *op. cit.*, 551.

30. Matthew T. DeMichele, *Probation and Parole's Growing Caseloads and Workload Allocation: Strategies for Managerial Decision Making* (Lexington, Ky.: American Probation and Parole Association, May 2007).

31. "Rise in Number of Serious Offenders Takes Toll on Supervision Resources," *United States Courts* (October 15, 2014), at **news.uscourts.gov/rise-numbers-serious-offenders-takes-toll-supervision-resources.**

32. 389 U.S. 128 (1967).

33. *Morrissey v. Brewer,* 408 U.S. 471 (1972); and *Gagnon v. Scarpelli,* 411 U.S. 778 (1973).

34. 465 U.S. 420 (1984).

35. L.M. Vieraitis, et al., "The Criminogenic Effects of Imprisonment: Evidence from State Panel Data, 1974–2002," *Criminology and Public Policy* 6 (2007), 589–622.

36. Kansas House Bill 2170 (2013).

37. *Ibid.*

38. *Felony Defendants in Large Urban Counties, 2009—Statistical Tables, op. cit.*, Table 6, page 10.

39. Jennifer L. Skeem and Sarah Manchak, "Back to the Future: From Klockars' Model of Effective Supervision to Evidence-Based Practice in Probation," *Journal of Offender Rehabilitation* 47 (2008), 231.

40. *Probation and Parole, 2013, op. cit.*, Table 4, page 5.

41. Pamela M. Casey, Roger K. Warren, and Jennifer K. Elek, *Using Offender Risk and Needs Assessment Information at Sentencing* (Williamsburg, Va.: National Center for State Courts, 2011), Table 1, page 5.

42. Nancy Ritter, "Predicting Recidivism Risk: New Tool in Philadelphia Shows Great Promise," *NIJ Journal* (February 2013), 4–13.

43. James Q. Wilson, "Making Justice Swifter," *City Journal* 7 (1997), 4.

44. Graeme Wood, "Prison without Walls," *The Atlantic* (September 2010), 92–93.

45. Angela Hawken and Mark Kleiman, *Managing Drug Involved Probationers and Swift and Certain Sanctions: Evaluating Hawaii's HOPE* (Washington, D.C.: U.S. Department of Justice, December 2009), 4.

46. Beau Kilmer, et al., "Efficacy of Frequent Monitoring with Swift, Certain, and Modest Sanctions for Violations: Insights from South Dakota's 24/7 Sobriety Project," *American Journal of Public Health* (January 2013), e37–e43.

47. Todd R. Clear, George F. Cole, and Michael D. Reisig, *American Corrections,* 9th ed. (Belmont, Calif.: Wadsworth Cengage Learning, 2011), 408.

48. *Probation and Parole in the United States, 2013, op. cit.*, Appendix table 7, page 21.

49. Bureau of Justice Statistics, *Probation and Parole in the United States, 2012* (Washington, D.C.: U.S. Department of Justice, December 2013), Table 7, page 9.

50. Joseph Walker, "Rules May Help Parolees Avoid Jail for Small Errors," *New York Times* (January 5, 2012), at **cityroom.blogs.nytimes.com/2012/01/05/rating-a-parolees-risk-before-a-return-to-prison.**

51. *Morrissey v. Brewer,* 408 U.S. 471 (1972).

52. Todd R. Clear and Edward Latessa, "Probation Officer Roles in Intensive Supervision: Surveillance versus Treatment," *Justice Quarterly* 10 (1993), 441–462.

53. 442 U.S. 1 (1979).

54. American Civil Liberties Union, *A Living Death: Life without Parole for Nonviolent Offenses* (November 2013), 2.

55. Marie Gottschalk, "Days without End: Life Sentences and Penal Reform," *Prison Legal News* (April 11, 2013), at **www.prisonlegalnews.org/24102_displayArticle.aspx.**

56. William Parker, *Parole: Origins, Development, Current Practices, and Statutes* (College Park, Md.: American Correctional Association, 1972), 26.

57. Clear, Cole, and Reisig, *op. cit.*, 387.

58. "Prison Breakthrough," *The Economist* (April 19, 2014), 29.

59. Joseph Walker, "State Parole Boards Use Software to Decide Which Inmates to Release," *Wall Street Journal* (October 11, 2013), A8.

60. Clear, Cole, and Reisig, *op. cit.*, 389.

61. Quoted in Thomas Tracy, "Cop-Killer Herman Bell Denied Parole in Murder of Two NYPD Officers in 1971," *New York Daily News* (February 25, 2014), at **www.nydailynews.com/new-york/nyc-crime/cop-killer-herman-bell-denied-parole-article-1.1701111.**

62. Quoted in "Governor Denies Parole to a Follower of Manson," *Associated Press* (August 9, 2014).

63. Mark P. Rankin, Mark H. Allenbaugh, and Carlton Fields, "Parole's Essential Role in Bailing Out Our Nation's Criminal Justice Systems," *Champion* (January 2009), 47–48.

64. Quoted in Tracy, *op. cit.*

65. Council of State Government/American Probation and Parole Association, "Fact Sheet 1: The Role of Community Corrections in Victim Services" (2012), at **www.appa-net.org/eWeb/docs/APPA/pubs/PVRPPP-FACTSHEET-1.pdf.**

66. 18 U.S.C. Section 3771(a)(4) (2006).

67. Joel M. Caplan, "Parole Release Decisions: Impact of Victim Input on a Representative Sample of Inmates," *Journal of Criminal Justice* (May–June 2010), 291–300.

68. Ram Subramanian, Rebecka Moreno, and Sharyn Broomhead, *Recalibrating Justice: A Review of 2013 State Sentencing and Corrections Trends* (New York: Vera Institute of Justice, July 2014), 20–21.

69. *Community Dispute Resolution Centers Program: Annual Report 2010–2011* (New York: New York State Unified Court System, February 2012), 14.

70. 18 U.S.C. Sections 1961–1968.

71. 516 U.S. 442 (1996).

72. U.S. Marshals, "Fact Sheet: Asset Forfeiture 2015," at **www.usmarshals.gov/duties/factsheets/asset_forfeiture.pdf.**

73. Douglas J. Boyle, et al., "Overview of: 'An Evaluation of Day Reporting Centers for Parolees: Outcomes of a Randomized Trial,'" *Criminology & Public Policy* (February 2013), 136.

74. Model State Drug Court Legislation Committee, *Model State Drug Court Legislation: Model Drug Offender Accountability and Treatment Act* (Alexandria, Va.: National Drug Court Institute, May 2004), 42.

75. *ISP Fact Sheet: Intensive Supervision Program* (Trenton, N.J.: Administrative Office of the Courts, February 2015), 1–2.

76. Joan Petersilia and Susan Turner, "Intensive Probation and Parole," *Crime and Justice* 17 (1993), 281–335.

77. Douglas J. Boyle, et al., *Outcomes of a Randomized Trial of an Intensive Community Corrections Program—Day Reporting Center—for Parolees, Final Report for the National Institute*

of Justice (Washington, D.C.: U.S. Department of Justice, October 2011), 3–4.

78. *Probation and Parole in the United States, 2010,* Appendix table 3, page 31.

79. Clear, Cole, and Reisig, *op. cit.,* 125.

80. Paul Stageberg and Bonnie Wilson, *Recidivism among Iowa Probationers* (Des Moines, Iowa: The Iowa Division of Criminal and Juvenile Justice Planning, July 2005); and Paul Koniceck, *Five Year Recidivism Follow-Up Offender Releases* (Columbus, Ohio: Ohio Department of Rehabilitation and Correction, August 1996).

81. Todd R. Clear, et al., *American Corrections in Brief,* 2nd ed. (Belmont, Calif.: Wadsworth Cengage Learning, 2014), 102.

82. Josh Kurtz, "New Growth in a Captive Market," *New York Times* (December 31, 1989), 12.

83. William Bales, et al., *A Quantitative and Qualitative Assessment of Electronic Monitoring* (Tallahassee, Fla.: The Florida State University College of Criminology and Criminal Justice, January 2010), 102.

84. National Institute of Justice, *Electronic Monitoring Reduces Recidivism* (Washington, D.C.: U.S. Department of Justice, 2011), 2.

85. Michael Tonry and Mary Lynch, "Intermediate Sanctions," in *Crime and Justice,* vol. 20, ed. Michael Tonry (Chicago: University of Chicago Press, 1996), 99.

86. Dennis Palumbo, Mary Clifford, and Zoann K. Snyder-Joy, "From Net Widening to Intermediate Sanctions: The Transformation of Alternatives to Incarceration from Benevolence to Malevolence," in *Smart Sentencing: The Emergence of Intermediate Sanctions,* eds. James M. Byrne, Arthur Lurigio, and Joan Petersilia (Newbury Park, Calif.: Sage, 1992), 231.

87. Keve, *op. cit.,* 207.

88. Eckholm, *op. cit.*

89. *Addington v. Texas,* 441 U.S. 418, 425 (1979).

90. "California," Treatment Advocacy Center, at **www.treatmentadvocacycenter.org/legal-resources/california.**

91. Andrew P. Wilper, et al., "The Health and Health Care of U.S. Prisoners: Results of a National Survey," *American Journal of Public Health* (April 2009), 673–679.

92. *O'Connor v. Donaldson,* 422 U.S. 563, 575 (1975).

93. Jacob Sullum, "The Slippery Slope of Locking Up Loons," *Chicago Sun-Times* (January 19, 2011), 27.

94. David Farabee, et al., "The Effectiveness of Coerced Treatment for Drug-Abusing Offenders," *Federal Probation* 2 (1998), 3–7.

Prisons and Jails

Chapter Outline		Corresponding Learning Objectives
A Short History of American Prisons	**1**	Contrast the Pennsylvania and the New York penitentiary theories of the 1800s.
	2	Explain the three general models of prisons.
Prison Organization and Management	**3**	Describe the formal prison management system, and indicate the three most important aspects of prison governance.
	4	List and briefly explain the four types of prisons.
Inmate Population Trends	**5**	List the factors that have caused the prison population to grow dramatically in the last several decades.
	6	Indicate some of the consequences of our high rates of incarceration.
The Emergence of Private Prisons	**7**	Describe the arguments for and against private prisons.
Jails	**8**	Summarize the distinction between jails and prisons, and indicate the importance of jails in the American corrections system.
	9	Explain why the U.S. Supreme Court upheld the practice of strip searching all jail inmates, including those who have not been charged with a crime.

To target your study and review, look for these numbered Learning Objective icons throughout the chapter.

Nick Oxford/*The New York Times*/Redux

A Trend Indeed?

the ballot initiative offered a dramatic solution to the problem of California's overcrowded prisons and jails. Called Proposition 47, it proposed to downgrade a number of nonviolent felonies involving less than $950—including grand theft, shoplifting, writing bad checks, receiving stolen property, and drug possession—to misdemeanors. As a result of this change, offenders convicted of these crimes would probably not wind up behind bars. In November 2014, nearly 60 percent of California voters approved Proposition 47. Three months after the new law went into effect, the jail populations of Los Angeles, Orange, and San Diego counties dropped by 20 percent, 22 percent, and 16 percent, respectively.

California is hardly the only state that recently has taken steps to reduce both its inmate population and the costs associated with its corrections system. In 2013, six states closed correctional facilities, with North Carolina alone estimating a resulting $40 million in savings. In 2014, thirty states passed legislation designed to lower incarceration rates, often by steering nonviolent offenders to community supervision. These policy choices reflect a small but significant trend in American corrections: fewer inmates. Before a slight (0.3 percent) rise in 2013, the total U.S. prison population declined each year from 2010 to 2012, the first time that had happened in nearly four decades.

To be sure, these decreases do little to threaten our nation's title as "the globe's leading incarcerator." About 2.2 million Americans are in prison and jail. The United States locks up six times as many of its citizens as Canada does, and eight times as many as a number of European democracies. Still, the fact that politicians are willing to accept policies that reduce the number of inmates represents a sea change in the country's corrections strategies. "People want their government to make a distinction in the public safety area between those who have to be locked up and those who can serve their sentence in less expensive, more humane, and more effective ways," says former California state representative Darrel Steinberg, who pushed for Proposition 47's approval. "That's what the people want."

▲ About 2.2 million inmates are incarcerated in the United States, including these prisoners working in the bakery of the Richard J. Donovan Correctional Facility in San Diego, California.

Sam Hodgson/Bloomberg/Getty Images

1. Sacramento County district attorney Jan Scully predicts that Proposition 47 will lead to increased crime rates in California by "reducing the consequences of crime." Do you agree? Why or why not?

2. Many of the diversion programs discussed in the previous chapter rely on defendants agreeing to treatment in exchange for reduced penalties. How might Proposition 47 lessen participation in California drug courts and other state offender treatment programs?

3. How do you think declining national crime rates over the past two decades, as discussed in Chapter 3, have contributed to an atmosphere in which politicians are less worried about being depicted as "soft on crime"?

A Short History of American Prisons

Today's high rates of imprisonment—often referred to as evidence of "mass incarceration" in the United States—are the result of many criminal justice strategies that we have discussed in this textbook. These include truth-in-sentencing guidelines, relatively long sentences for gun and drug crimes, "three-strikes" habitual offender laws, and judicial freedom to incarcerate convicts for relatively minor criminal behavior. At the base of all these policies is a philosophy that sees prisons primarily as instruments of punishment. The loss of freedom imposed on inmates is the penalty for the crimes they have committed. Punishment has not, however, always been the main reason for incarceration in this country.

English Roots

The prisons of eighteenth-century England, known as "bridewells" after London's Bridewell Palace, had little to do with punishment. These facilities were mainly used to hold debtors or those awaiting trial, execution, or banishment from the community. (In many ways, as will be made clear, these facilities resembled the modern jail.) English courts generally imposed one of two sanctions on convicted felons: they turned them loose, or they executed them.[1] To be sure, most felons were released, pardoned either by the court or the clergy after receiving a whipping or a branding.

The correctional system in the American colonies differed very little from that of their motherland. If anything, colonial administrators were more likely to use corporal punishment than their English counterparts, and the death penalty was not uncommon in early America. The one dissenter was William Penn, who adopted the "Great Law" in Pennsylvania in 1682. Based on Quaker ideals of humanity and rehabilitation, this criminal code forbade the use of torture and mutilation as forms of punishment. Instead, felons were ordered to pay restitution of property or goods to their victims. If the offenders did not have sufficient property to make restitution, they were placed in a prison, which was primarily a "workhouse."[2] The death penalty was still allowed under the "Great Law," but only in cases of premeditated murder. Penn proved to be an exception, however, and the path to reform was much slower in the colonies than in England.

Walnut Street Prison: The First Penitentiary

On William Penn's death in 1718, the "Great Law" was rescinded in favor of a harsher criminal code, similar to those of the other colonies. At the time of the American Revolution, however, the Quakers were instrumental in the first broad swing of the incarceration pendulum from punishment to rehabilitation. In 1776, Pennsylvania passed legislation ordering that offenders be reformed through treatment and discipline rather than simply beaten or executed.[3] Several states, including Massachusetts and New York, quickly followed Pennsylvania's example.

Pennsylvania continued its reformist ways by opening the country's first **penitentiary** in a wing of Philadelphia's Walnut Street Jail in 1790. The penitentiary operated on the assumption that silence and labor provided the best hope of rehabilitating the criminal spirit. Remaining silent would force the prisoners to think about their crimes, and eventually the weight of conscience would lead to repentance. At the same time, enforced labor would attack the problem of idleness—regarded as the main cause of crime by penologists of the time.[4] Consequently, inmates at Walnut Street were isolated from one another in solitary rooms and kept busy with constant menial chores.

Penitentiary An early form of correctional facility that emphasized separating inmates from society and from each other.

Contrast the Pennsylvania and the New York penitentiary theories of the 1800s.

LEARNING OBJECTIVE 1

Eventually, the penitentiary at Walnut Street succumbed to the same problems that continue to plague institutions of confinement: overcrowding and excessive costs. As an influx of inmates forced more than one person to be housed in a room, maintaining silence became nearly impossible. By the early 1800s, officials could not find work for all of the convicts, so many were left idle.

The Great Penitentiary Rivalry: Pennsylvania versus New York

The apparent lack of success at Walnut Street did little to dampen enthusiasm for the penitentiary concept. Throughout the first half of the nineteenth century, a number of states reacted to prison overcrowding by constructing new penitentiaries. Each state tended to have its own peculiar twist on the roles of silence and labor, and two such systems—those of Pennsylvania and New York—emerged to shape the debate over the most effective way to run a prison.

The Pennsylvania System After the failure of Walnut Street, Pennsylvania constructed two new prisons: the Western Penitentiary near Pittsburgh (opened in 1826) and the Eastern Penitentiary in Cherry Hill, near Philadelphia (1829). The Pennsylvania system took the concept of silence as a virtue to new extremes. Based on the idea of **separate confinement**, these penitentiaries were constructed with back-to-back cells facing outward from the center. (See Figure 13.1 for the layout of the original Eastern Penitentiary.) To protect each inmate from the corrupting influence of the others, prisoners worked, slept, and ate alone in their cells. Their only contact with other human beings came in the form of religious instruction from a visiting clergyman or prison official.[5]

The New York System If Pennsylvania's prisons were designed to transform wrongdoers into honest citizens, those in New York focused on obedience. When New York's Newgate Prison (built in 1791) became overcrowded, the state authorized the construction of Auburn Prison, which opened in 1816. Auburn initially operated under many of the same assumptions that guided the penitentiary at Walnut Street. Solitary confinement, however, seemed to lead to an inordinate amount of sickness, insanity, and even suicide among inmates, and it was abandoned in 1822. Nine years later, Elam Lynds became warden at Auburn and instilled the **congregate system**, also known as the Auburn system. Like Pennsylvania's separate confinement system, the congregate system was based on silence and labor. At Auburn, however, inmates worked and ate together, with silence enforced by prison guards.[6]

If either state can be said to have "won" the debate, it was New York. The Auburn system proved more popular, and a majority of the new prisons built during the first half of the nineteenth century followed New York's lead, though mainly for economic reasons rather than philosophical ones. New York's penitentiaries were cheaper to build because they did not require so much space. Furthermore, inmates in New York were employed in workshops, whereas those in Pennsylvania toiled alone in their cells. Consequently, the Auburn system was better positioned to exploit prison labor in the early years of widespread factory production.

FIGURE 13.1 The Eastern Penitentiary

As you can see, the Eastern Penitentiary was designed in the form of a "wagon wheel," known today as the radial style. The back-to-back cells in each "spoke" of the wheel faced outward from the center to limit contact between inmates.

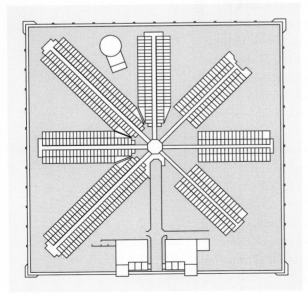

The Reformers and the Progressives

The Auburn system did not go unchallenged. In the 1870s, a group of reformers argued that fixed sentences, imposed silence, and isolation did nothing to improve prisoners. These critics proposed that penal institutions should offer the promise of early release as a prime tool for rehabilitation. Echoing the views of the Quakers a century earlier, the reformers presented an ideology that would heavily influence American corrections for the next century.

This "new penology" was put into practice at New York's Elmira Reformatory in 1876. At Elmira, good behavior was rewarded by early release, and misbehavior was punished with extended time under a three-grade system of classification. On entering the institution, the offender was assigned a grade of 2. If the inmate followed the rules and completed work and school assignments, after six months he was moved up to grade 1, the necessary grade for release. If, however, the inmate broke institutional rules, he was lowered to grade 3. A grade 3 inmate needed to behave properly for three months before he could return to grade 2 and begin to work back toward grade 1 and eventual release.[7]

Although other penal institutions did not adopt the Elmira model, its theories came into prominence in the first two decades of the twentieth century thanks to the Progressive movement in criminal justice. The Progressives—linked to the positivist school of criminology discussed in Chapter 2—believed that criminal behavior was caused by social, economic, and biological factors and, therefore, a corrections system should have a goal of treatment, not punishment. Consequently, they trumpeted a **medical model** for prisons, which held that institutions should offer a variety of programs and therapies to cure inmates of their "ills," whatever the root causes. The Progressives were largely responsible for the spread of indeterminate sentences (Chapter 11), probation (Chapter 12), intermediate sanctions (Chapter 12), and parole (Chapter 12) in the first half of the twentieth century.

▲ Inmates of the Elmira Reformatory in New York attend a presentation at the prison auditorium. **To what extent do you believe that treatment should be a part of the incarceration of criminals?** Historical/Corbis

The Reassertion of Punishment

Even though the Progressives had a great influence on the corrections system as a whole, their theories had little impact on the prisons themselves. Many of these facilities had been constructed in the nineteenth century and were impervious to change. More important, prison administrators usually did not agree with the Progressives and their followers, so the day-to-day lives of most inmates varied little from the congregate system of Auburn Prison.

Academic attitudes began to shift away from the Progressives in the mid-1960s. Then, in 1974, the publication of Robert Martinson's famous "What Works?" essay provided opponents of the medical model with statistical evidence that rehabilitation efforts did nothing to lower recidivism rates.[8] This is not to say that Martinson's findings went unchallenged. A number of critics argued that rehabilitative programs could be successful.[9] In fact, Martinson himself retracted most of his claims in a little-noticed

Medical Model A model of corrections in which the psychological and biological roots of an inmate's criminal behavior are identified and treated.

article published five years after his initial report.[10] Attempts by Martinson and others to "set the record straight" went largely unnoticed, however, as crime rose sharply in the early 1970s. This trend led many criminologists and politicians to champion "get tough" measures to deal with criminals they now considered "incurable." By the end of the 1980s, the legislative, judicial, and administrative strategies that we have discussed throughout this text had positioned the United States for an explosion in inmate populations and prison construction unparalleled in the nation's history.

The Role of Prisons in Modern Society

For reasons that we will explain later in the chapter, the number of federal and state prisoners quadrupled between 1980 and 2010.[11] This increase reflects the varied demands placed on the modern American penal institution. As University of Connecticut sociologist Charles Logan once noted, Americans expect prisons to "correct the incorrigible, rehabilitate the wretched . . . restrain the dangerous, and punish the wicked."[12] Basically, prisons exist to make society a safer place. Whether this is to be achieved through retribution, deterrence, incapacitation, or rehabilitation—the four justifications of corrections introduced in Chapter 11—depends on the operating philosophy of the individual penal institution.

Three general models of prisons have emerged to describe the different schools of thought behind prison organization:

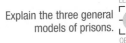

Explain the three general models of prisons. LEARNING OBJECTIVE 2

- The *custodial model* is based on the assumption that prisoners are incarcerated for reasons of incapacitation, deterrence, and retribution. All decisions within the prison—such as what form of recreation to provide the inmates—are made with an eye toward security and discipline, and the daily routine of the inmates is highly controlled. The custodial model has dominated the most restrictive prisons in the United States since the 1930s.
- The *rehabilitation model* stresses the ideals of individualized treatment that we discussed in Chapter 11. Security concerns are often secondary to the well-being of the individual inmate, and a number of treatment programs are offered to aid prisoners in changing their criminal and antisocial behavior. The rehabilitation model came into prominence during the 1950s and enjoyed widespread popularity until it began to lose general acceptance in the 1970s and 1980s.
- In the *reintegration model,* the correctional institution serves as a training ground for the inmate to prepare for existence in the community. Prisons that have adopted this model give the prisoners more responsibility during incarceration and offer halfway houses and work programs (both discussed in Chapter 14) to help them reintegrate into society. This model is becoming more influential, as corrections officials react to problems such as prison overcrowding.[13]

Critical views of the prison's role in society are at odds with these three "ideal" perspectives. Professor Alfred Blumstein argues that prisons create new criminals, especially with regard to nonviolent drug offenders. Not only do these nonviolent felons become socialized to the criminal lifestyle while in prison, but the stigma of incarceration makes it more difficult for them to obtain employment on release. Their only means of sustenance "on the outside" is to apply the criminal methods they learned in prison.[14] A study by criminal justice professors Cassia Spohn of Arizona State University and David Holleran of the College of New Jersey found that convicted drug offenders who were sentenced to prison were 2.2 times more likely to be incarcerated for a new offense than those sentenced to probation.[15]

The federal government pays inmates wages as low as twenty-five cents an hour to make goods for the U.S. military and other federal agencies. Should inmates be paid a reasonable minimum wage for any work that they do? Why or why not? Why might competing private companies think that prison labor at such low wages is unethical? ■

Prison Organization and Management

The United States has a dual prison system that parallels its dual court system, which we discussed in Chapter 8. The Federal Bureau of Prisons (BOP) currently operates about one hundred confinement facilities, ranging from prisons to immigration detention centers to community corrections institutions.[16] In the federal corrections system, a national director, appointed by the president, oversees six regional directors and a staff of nearly 40,000 employees. All fifty states also operate state prisons, which number about 1,700 and make up more than 90 percent of the country's correctional facilities.[17] Governors are responsible for the organization and operation of state corrections systems, which vary widely based on each state's geography, *demographics* (population characteristics), and political culture.

Generally, those offenders sentenced in federal court for breaking federal law serve their time in federal prisons, and those offenders sentenced in state court for breaking state law serve their time in state prisons. As you can see in Figure 13.2, federal prisons hold relatively few violent felons, because relatively few federal laws involve violent crime. At the same time, federal prisons are much more likely to hold public order offenders, a group that includes violators of federal immigration law.

FIGURE 13.2 Types of Offenses of Federal and State Prison Inmates

As the comparison below shows, state prisoners are most likely to have been convicted of violent crimes, while federal prisoners are most likely to have been convicted of drug and public order offenses.

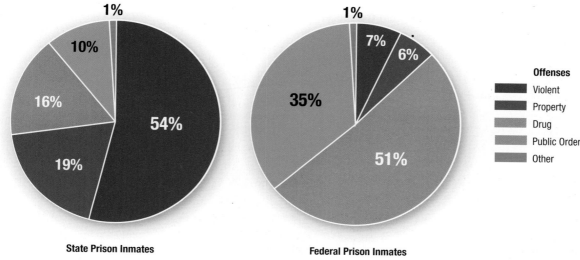

State Prison Inmates

Federal Prison Inmates

Offenses
- Violent
- Property
- Drug
- Public Order
- Other

Source: Bureau of Justice Statistics, *Prisoners in 2013* (Washington, D.C.: U.S. Department of Justice, September 2014), Table 13, page 5; and Table 16, page 17.

Warden The prison official who is ultimately responsible for the organization and performance of a correctional facility.

Prison Administration

Whether the federal government or a state government operates a prison, its administrators have the same general goals, summarized by Charles Logan as follows:

> The mission of a prison is to keep prisoners—to keep them in, keep them safe, keep them in line, keep them healthy, and keep them busy—and to do it with fairness, without undue suffering and as efficiently as possible.[18]

Considering the environment of a prison—an enclosed world inhabited by people who are generally violent and angry and would rather be anywhere else—Logan's mission statement is somewhat unrealistic. A prison staff must supervise the daily routines of hundreds or thousands of inmates, a duty that includes providing them with meals, education, vocational programs, and different forms of leisure. The smooth operation of this supervision is made more difficult—if not, at times, impossible—by budgetary restrictions, overcrowding, and continual inmate turnover.

Formal Prison Management In some respects, the management structure of a prison is similar to that of a police department, as discussed in Chapter 6. Both systems rely on a hierarchical (top-down) *chain of command* to increase personal responsibility. Both assign different employees to specific tasks, though prison managers have much more direct control over their subordinates than do police managers. The main difference is that police departments have a *continuity of purpose* that is sometimes lacking in prison organizations. All members of a police force are, at least theoretically, working to reduce crime and apprehend criminals. In a prison, this continuity is less evident. An employee in the prison laundry service and one who works in the visiting center have little in common. In some instances, employees may even have cross-purposes: a prison guard may want to punish an inmate, while a counselor in the treatment center may want to rehabilitate her or him.

Consequently, a strong hierarchy is crucial for any prison management team that hopes to meet Charles Logan's expectations. As Figure 13.3 shows, the **warden** (also known as a superintendent) is ultimately responsible for the operation of a prison. He or she oversees deputy wardens, who in turn manage the various organizational lines of the institution. The custodial employees, who deal directly with the inmates and make up more than half of a prison's staff, operate under a militaristic hierarchy, with a line of command passing from the deputy warden to the captain to the correctional officer.

Describe the formal prison management system, and indicate the three most important aspects of prison governance.
LEARNING **3** OBJECTIVE

FIGURE 13.3 Organizational Chart for a Typical Correctional Facility

Warden

Deputy Warden: Custody
1. Security
2. Guard Forces
3. Training
4. Safety
5. Prisoner Discipline
6. Investigations
7. Visiting Schedules

Deputy Warden: Management
1. Budget
2. Accounting
3. Purchasing
4. Warehouse
5. Commissary
6. Food Service
7. Clothing and Laundry
8. Grounds Maintenance

Deputy Warden: Programs
1. Treatment Programs
2. Medical Services
3. Mental Health
4. Recreation
5. Classification
6. Volunteers
7. Religious Services

Deputy Warden: Industry and Agriculture
1. Prison Work Programs
2. Prison Farm Programs

Courtesy Berry Larson

Berry Larson
Prison Warden

Before I began my career as a correctional officer for the Arizona Department of Corrections, I had several people question my desire to work inside a prison. Why would I want to stick myself somewhere so unpleasant and stressful? While at the training academy, however, we were taught that "approach determines response." I found that to be very true during my time as a correctional officer. It is all about the way you carry yourself and the way you relate to the inmates. An inmate can tell if you are trying to be someone you are not. They can also tell if you are afraid. I never had to use physical force once in all the time I was a correctional officer—officer presence and nonverbal/verbal communication is usually sufficient to handle any situation, as long as you keep control of your emotions.

As warden of the Arizona State Prison Complex–Lewis, my duties include touring the units; attending special events such as inmate graduations for GED and vocational programs; managing emergency situations such as power outages, fights and assaults, and staff injuries; and eradicating all criminal activity from the facility. Many, if not most, of our inmates came to us in pretty bad shape—little or no education, a substance abuse history, or mental health or behavioral issues. These young men have spent their lives watching television and playing video games and simply do not have the skills to be successful in life. We try to remedy the situation by providing them with educational and vocational programs and "life-skills" classes that promote civil and productive behavior.

SOCIAL MEDIA CAREER TIP Regularly reevaluate your social media tools and the methods you use to keep up to date in your fields of interest. If you are still using the same tools as a year ago, you probably aren't keeping up with the latest developments in Internet technology.

FASTFACTS

**Prison warden
Job description:**

- A prison warden is the chief managing officer of an adult correctional institution.

What kind of training is required?

- Bachelor's degree in criminal justice, corrections, law enforcement, or a related field.
- One or more years of work experience in the management of a major division of a correctional institution.

Annual salary range?

- $38,000–$100,000 (depending on size of institution and geographic region)

Governing Prisons The implications of prison mismanagement can be severe. While studying a series of prison riots, sociologists Bert Useem and Peter Kimball found that breakdown in managerial control commonly preceded such acts of mass violence.[19] During the 1970s, for example, conditions at the State Penitentiary in New Mexico deteriorated significantly. Inmates were increasingly the targets of random and harsh treatment at the hands of the prison staff, while at the same time a reduction in structured activities left prison life "painfully boring."[20] The result, in 1980, was one of the most violent prison riots in the nation's history.

What sort of prison management is most suited to avoid such situations? Most prisons in the United States operate under an authoritarian management structure, characterized by a strong leader, extensive control of the prison environment, and harsh discipline for misbehaving inmates.[21] Political scientist John DiIulio believes that, in general, the sound governance of correctional facilities is a matter of order, amenities, and services:

- *Order* can be defined as the absence of misconduct such as murder, assault, and rape. Many observers, including DiIulio, believe that, having incarcerated a person, the state has a responsibility to protect that person from disorder in the correctional institution.
- *Amenities* are those comforts that make life "livable," such as clean living conditions, acceptable food, and entertainment. One theory of incarceration holds

Classification The process through which prison officials screen each incoming inmate to best determine that inmate's security and treatment needs.

Custody Level As a result of the classification process, the security designation given to new inmates, crucial in helping corrections officials determine which correctional facility is best suited to the individual offender.

that inmates should not enjoy a quality of life comparable to life outside prison. Without the basic amenities, however, prison life becomes unbearable, and inmates are more likely to lapse into disorder.

- *Services* include programs designed to improve an inmate's prospects on release, such as vocational training, remedial education, and drug treatment. Again, many feel that a person convicted of a crime does not deserve to participate in these kinds of programs, but they have two clear benefits. First, they keep the inmate occupied and focused during her or his sentence. Second, they reduce the chances that the inmate will go back to a life of crime after she or he returns to the community.[22]

According to DiIulio, in the absence of order, amenities, and services, inmates will come to see their imprisonment as not only unpleasant but unfair, and they will become much more difficult to control.[23] Furthermore, weak governance encourages inmates to come up with their own methods of regulating their lives. As we shall see in the next chapter, the result is usually high levels of violence and the expansion of prison gangs and other unsanctioned forms of authority.

Classification One of the most important aspects of prison administration occurs soon after a defendant has been convicted of a crime and sentenced to be incarcerated. In this **classification** process, an inmate's mental, physical, and security needs are evaluated to help determine the best correctional facility "fit." The classification process usually takes four to eight weeks, and is overseen by a corrections counselor, also known as a case manager. During this period, the inmate undergoes numerous tests and interviews to identify education levels, medical issues, drug/alcohol addictions, and any behavioral "red flags."

Taking the results of the process into consideration, prison administrators generally rely on three broad criteria for classification purposes:

1. The seriousness of the crime committed.
2. The risk of future criminal or violent conduct.
3. The need for treatment and rehabilitation programs.[24]

Classification is not a one-time operation. Inmates can, and often do, change their behavior patterns during the course of their incarceration. If an inmate acts more violently, or, conversely, shows an increasingly positive attitude, that inmate will need to be *reclassified*. Furthermore, the successful completion of prison rehabilitation programs may require an adjustment in the inmate's release plan, discussed in the next chapter.[25]

Types of Prisons

Following the classification process, an inmate is assigned a **custody level.** Corrections officials rely on this custody level to place the inmate in the appropriate correctional facility. In the federal prison system, an offender's custody level determines whether she or he is sent to one of six different types of prisons. Inmates in level 1 facilities are usually nonviolent and require the least amount of security, while inmates in level 6 facilities are the most dangerous and require the harshest security measures. (Many states also use the six-level system, an example of which can be seen in Figure 13.4.)

To simplify matters, most correctional facilities are designated as being one of three security levels—minimum, medium, or maximum. A fourth level—the supermaximum-security prison, known as the "supermax"—is relatively rare and extremely controversial due to its hyperharsh methods of punishing and controlling the most dangerous prisoners.

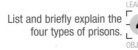

List and briefly explain the four types of prisons.

LEARNING
4
OBJECTIVE

FIGURE 13.4 Security Levels of Correctional Facilities in Virginia

The security levels of correctional facilities in Virginia are graded from level 1 to level 6. As you can see, level 1 facilities are for those inmates who pose the least amount of risk to fellow inmates, staff members, and themselves. Level 6 facilities are for those who are considered the most dangerous by the Virginia Department of Corrections.

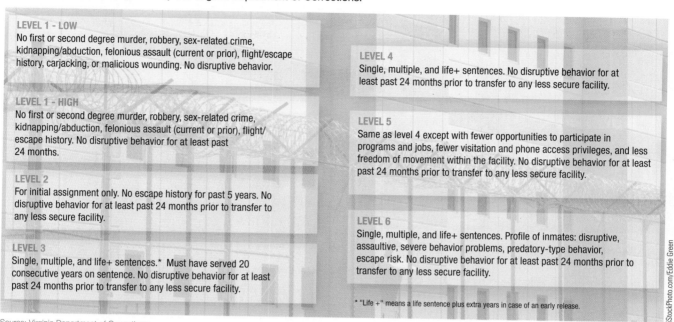

LEVEL 1 - LOW
No first or second degree murder, robbery, sex-related crime, kidnapping/abduction, felonious assault (current or prior), flight/escape history, carjacking, or malicious wounding. No disruptive behavior.

LEVEL 1 - HIGH
No first or second degree murder, robbery, sex-related crime, kidnapping/abduction, felonious assault (current or prior), flight/escape history. No disruptive behavior for at least past 24 months.

LEVEL 2
For initial assignment only. No escape history for past 5 years. No disruptive behavior for at least past 24 months prior to transfer to any less secure facility.

LEVEL 3
Single, multiple, and life+ sentences.* Must have served 20 consecutive years on sentence. No disruptive behavior for at least past 24 months prior to transfer to any less secure facility.

LEVEL 4
Single, multiple, and life+ sentences. No disruptive behavior for at least past 24 months prior to transfer to any less secure facility.

LEVEL 5
Same as level 4 except with fewer opportunities to participate in programs and jobs, fewer visitation and phone access privileges, and less freedom of movement within the facility. No disruptive behavior for at least past 24 months prior to transfer to any less secure facility.

LEVEL 6
Single, multiple, and life+ sentences. Profile of inmates: disruptive, assaultive, severe behavior problems, predatory-type behavior, escape risk. No disruptive behavior for at least past 24 months prior to transfer to any less secure facility.

* "Life +" means a life sentence plus extra years in case of an early release.

Source: Virginia Department of Corrections.

Maximum-Security Prisons In a certain sense, the classification of prisoners today owes a debt to the three-grade system developed at the Elmira Reformatory, discussed earlier in the chapter. Once wrongdoers enter a corrections facility, they are constantly graded on behavior. Those who serve "good time," as we have seen, are often rewarded with early release. Those who compile extensive misconduct records are usually housed, along with violent and repeat offenders, in **maximum-security prisons.** The names of these institutions—Folsom, San Quentin, Sing Sing, Attica—conjure up foreboding images of concrete and steel jungles, with good reason.

Maximum-security prisons are designed with full attention to security and surveillance. In these institutions, inmates' lives are programmed in a militaristic fashion to keep them from escaping or from harming themselves or the prison staff. About a quarter of the prisons in the United States are classified as maximum security, and these institutions house about a third of the country's prisoners.

The Design Maximum-security prisons tend to be large—holding more than a thousand inmates—and they have similar features. The entire operation is usually surrounded by concrete walls that stand twenty to thirty feet high and have also been sunk deep into the ground to deter tunnel escapes. Fences reinforced with razor-ribbon barbed wire that can be electrically charged may supplement these barriers. The prison walls are studded with watchtowers, from which guards armed with shotguns and rifles survey the movement of prisoners below. The designs of these facilities, though similar, are not uniform. Though correctional facilities built using the radial design pioneered by the Eastern Penitentiary still exist, several other designs have become prominent in more recently constructed institutions. For an overview of these designs, including the radial design, see Figure 13.5.

Inmates live in cells, most of them with similar dimensions to those found in the Topeka Correctional Facility, a maximum-security prison in Topeka, Kansas: eight feet by fourteen feet with cinder block walls. The space contains bunks, a toilet, a sink, and possibly

Maximum-Security Prison
A correctional institution designed and organized to control and discipline dangerous felons, as well as prevent escape.

FIGURE 13.5 Prison Designs

The Radial Design

The wagon wheel form of the radial design was created with the dual goals of separation and control. Inmates are separated from one another in their cells on the "spokes" of the wheel, and prison officials can control the activities of the inmates from the control center in the "hub" of the wheel.

The Telephone-Pole Design

The main feature of this design is a long central corridor that serves as a means for transporting inmates from one part of the facility to another. Branching off from this main corridor are the functional areas of the facility: housing, food services, workshops, a treatment programs room, and other services.

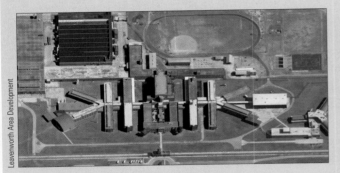

Source: Text adapted from Todd R. Clear, George F. Cole, and Michael D. Reisig, *American Corrections*, 9th ed. (Belmont, Calif.: Cengage Learning, 2010), 267–268.

The Courtyard Style

In the courtyard-style prison, a courtyard replaces the transportation function of the "pole" in the telephone-pole prison. The prison buildings form a square around the courtyard, and to get from one part of the facility to another, the inmates go across the courtyard.

The Campus Style

Some of the newer minimum-security prisons have adopted the campus style, which had previously been used in correctional facilities for women and juveniles. As on a college campus, housing units are scattered among functional units such as the dining room, recreation area, and treatment centers.

a cabinet or closet. Cells are located in rows of *cell blocks,* each of which forms its own security unit, set off by a series of gates and bars. A maximum-security institution is essentially a collection of numerous cell blocks, each constituting its own prison within a prison.

Most prisons, regardless of their design, have cell blocks that open into sprawling prison yards, where the inmates commingle daily. The "prison of the future," however, rejects this layout. Instead, it relies on a podular design, as evident at the Two Rivers Correctional Institution in Umatilla, Oregon. At Two Rivers, which opened in 2007, fourteen housing pods contain ninety-six inmates each. Each unit has its own yard, so inmates rarely, if ever, interact with members of other pods. This design gives administrators the flexibility to, for example, place violent criminals in pod A and white-collar criminals in pod B without worrying about mixing the two different security levels.[26]

Security Measures Within maximum-security prisons, inmates' lives are dominated by security measures. Whenever they move from one area of the prison to another, they do so in groups and under the watchful eye of armed correctional officers. Television surveillance cameras may be used to monitor their every move, even when sleeping, showering, or using the toilet. They are subject to frequent pat-downs or strip searches at the guards' discretion. Constant "head counts" ensure that every inmate is where he or she should be. Tower guards—many of whom have orders to shoot to kill in the case of a disturbance or escape attempt—constantly look down on the inmates as they move around outdoor areas of the facility.

CJ & Technology

Tracking Inmates

Technology has added significantly to the overall safety of maximum-security prisons. Walk-through metal detectors and X-ray body scanners, for example, can detect weapons or other contraband hidden on the body of an inmate. The most promising new technology in this field, however, relies on radio frequency identification (RFID). About the size of two grains of rice, an RFID tag consists of a glass capsule that contains a computer chip, a tiny copper antenna, and an electrical device known as a "capacitor" that transmits the data in the chip to an outside scanner. In the prison context, RFID works as a high-tech head count: inmates wear bracelets tagged with the microchips while correctional officers wear small RFID devices resembling smartphones.

Guided by a series of radio transmitters and receivers, the system is able to pinpoint the location of inmates and guards within twenty feet. Every two seconds, radio signals "search out" the location of each inmate and guard, and relay this information to a central computer. On a grid of the prison, an inmate shows up as a yellow dot and a correctional officer as a blue dot. Many RFID systems also store all movements in a database for future reference. "[RFID] completely revolutionizes a prison because you know where everyone is—not approximately but exactly where they are," remarked an official at the National Institute of Justice.

Black Creek/TSI PRISM

Thinking about RFID Tracking

Review the discussion of crime mapping and "hot spots" in Chapter 6. Drawing on your knowledge of crime-mapping technology, discuss how RFID technology can reduce violence and other misconduct such as drug sales in prisons.

Supermax Prisons About thirty states and the Federal Bureau of Prisons (BOP) operate **supermax** (short for supermaximum security) **prisons,** which are supposedly reserved for the "worst of the worst" of America's corrections population. Many of the inmates in these facilities are deemed high risks to commit murder behind bars—about a quarter of the occupants of the BOP's U.S. Penitentiary Administrative Maximum (ADX) in Florence, Colorado, have killed other prisoners or assaulted correctional officers elsewhere.

Supermax prisons are also used as punishment for offenders who commit serious disciplinary infractions in maximum-security prisons, or for those inmates who become involved with prison gangs. In addition, a growing number of supermax occupants are either high-profile individuals who would be at constant risk of attack in a general prison population or convicted terrorists such as Zacarias Moussaoui, who helped plan the attacks of September 11, 2001; Ted "the Unabomber" Kaczynski; and Terry Nichols,

Supermax Prison A highly secure, freestanding correctional facility—or such a unit within a correctional facility—that manages offenders who would pose a threat to the security and safety of other inmates and staff members if housed in the general inmate population.

Lockdown A disciplinary action taken by prison officials in which all inmates are ordered to their quarters and nonessential prison activities are suspended.

Medium-Security Prison A correctional institution that houses less dangerous inmates and therefore uses less restrictive measures to prevent violence and escapes.

who was involved in the bombing of a federal office building in Oklahoma City in 1995. Although different jurisdictions have different definitions of what constitutes a super-max, the most reliable surveys estimate that about sixty such facilities exist in the United States, holding approximately 25,000 inmates.[27]

A Controlled Environment The main purpose of a supermax prison is to strictly control the inmates' movement, thereby limiting (or eliminating) situations that could lead to breakdowns in discipline. The conditions at California's Security Housing Unit (SHU) at Pelican Bay State Prison are representative of most supermax institutions. Prisoners are confined to their one-person cells for twenty-three hours each day under video camera surveillance. They receive meals through a slot in the door. The cells measure eight by ten feet in size and are windowless. Fluorescent lights are continuously on, day and night, making it difficult for inmates to enjoy any type of privacy or sleep.[28]

For the most part, supermax prisons operate in a state of perpetual lockdown, in which all inmates are confined to their cells and social activities such as meals, recreational sports, and treatment programs are nonexistent. For the sixty minutes of each day that SHU inmates are allowed out of their cells (compared with twelve to sixteen hours in regular maximum-security prisons), they may either shower or exercise in an enclosed, concrete "yard" covered by plastic mesh. Prisoners are strip-searched before and after leaving their cells, and are placed in waist restraints and handcuffs on their way to and from the "yard" and showers.[29]

Supermax Syndrome Many prison officials support the proliferation of supermax prisons because they provide increased security for the most dangerous inmates. These proponents believe that the harsh reputation of the facilities will deter convicts from misbehaving for fear of transfer to a supermax. Nevertheless, the supermax has aroused a number of criticisms. Amnesty International and other human rights groups assert that the facilities violate standards for proper treatment of prisoners. At Wisconsin's Supermax Correctional Facility, for example, the cells have no air-conditioning or windows, and average temperatures during the summer top 100 degrees.[30]

Furthermore, while studying prisoners at California's Pelican Bay facility, a Harvard University psychiatrist found that 80 percent suffered from what he called "SHU [security housing unit] syndrome," a condition brought on by long periods of isolation.[31] Further research on SHU syndrome shows that supermax inmates manifest a number of psychological problems, including massive anxiety, hallucinations, and acute confusion.[32] We will take a closer look at the merits and drawbacks of solitary confinement, a method of inmate punishment that extends well beyond supermax prisons, in the *CJ in Action* feature that ends this chapter.

▼ What security measures can you identify from this photo of a cell block at Arizona State Prison in Florence? AP Images/Matt York

Medium- and Minimum-Security Prisons Medium-security prisons hold about 45 percent of the prison population and minimum-security prisons 20 percent. Inmates at medium-security prisons have for

the most part committed less serious crimes than those housed in maximum-security prisons and are not considered high risks for escaping or causing harm. Consequently, medium-security institutions are not designed for control to the same extent as maximum-security prisons and have a more relaxed atmosphere. These facilities also offer more educational and treatment programs and allow for more contact between inmates. Medium-security prisons are rarely walled, relying instead on high fences. Prisoners have more freedom of movement within the structures, and the levels of surveillance are much lower. Living quarters are less restrictive as well—many of the newer medium-security prisons provide dormitory housing.

A **minimum-security prison** seems at first glance to be more like a college campus than an incarceration facility. Most of the inmates at these institutions are first-time offenders who are nonviolent and well behaved. A high percentage are white-collar criminals. Indeed, inmates are often transferred to minimum-security prisons as a reward for good behavior in other facilities. Therefore, security measures are lax compared with even medium-security prisons. Unlike medium-security institutions, minimum-security prisons do not have armed guards. Prisoners are provided with amenities such as television sets and computers in their rooms. They also enjoy freedom of movement, and are allowed off prison grounds for educational or employment purposes to a much greater extent than those held in more restrictive facilities.

Some critics have likened minimum-security prisons to "country clubs," but in the corrections system, everything is relative. A minimum-security prison may seem like a vacation spot when compared with the horrors of Sing Sing, but it still represents a restriction of personal freedom and separates the inmate from the outside world. (The feature *Comparative Criminal Justice—Prison Lite* provides a look at Norway's approach to incarceration, in which even the worst offenders are afforded the minimum-security experience.)

Minimum-Security Prison A correctional institution designed to allow inmates, most of whom pose low security risks, a great deal of freedom of movement and contact with the outside world.

Comparative Criminal Justice

Central Intelligence Agency

Prison Lite

In Norway, incarceration is based on the premise that loss of liberty is punishment enough for offenders. Consequently, the prisons themselves are made as pleasant as possible. For example, Halden prison, which houses murderers and rapists, provides amenities such as a recording studio, a "kitchen laboratory" for cooking classes, and a two-bedroom house where inmates can house their families for overnight visits. An inmate at the Skien maximum-security island prison compares his incarceration to "living in a village." He adds, "Everybody has to work. But we have free time so we can do some fishing, or in summer we can swim off the beach. We know we are prisoners but here we feel like people."

Norway's methods have, it appears, created certain expectations among its inmates. After spending several

months behind bars following a conviction on multiple counts of murder, one Norwegian prisoner wrote a letter to authorities protesting the conditions of his imprisonment. Among the complaints: not enough butter for his bread, cold coffee, and no skin moisturizer. By at least one measurement, however, Norway's "prison lite" strategy is effective, as the country has one of the lowest recidivism rates in the world.

For Critical Analysis

In the United States, life behind bars has long been predicated on the *principle of least eligibility,* which holds that the least advantaged members of society outside prison should lead a better existence than any prison or jail inmate. Do you favor the American or the Norwegian approach to prison conditions? Why?

Inmate Population Trends

As Figure 13.6 shows, the number of Americans in prison or jail has increased dramatically in the past three decades. This growth can be attributed to a number of factors, starting with the enhancement and stricter enforcement of the nation's illegal drug laws.

Factors in Prison Population Growth

List the factors that have caused the prison population to grow dramatically in the last several decades. **LEARNING** **5** OBJECTIVE

There are more people in prison and jail for drug offenses today than there were for *all* offenses in the early 1970s.[33] In 1980, about 19,000 drug offenders were incarcerated in state prisons and 4,800 drug offenders were in federal prisons. Thirty-three years later, state prisons held about 210,000 inmates who had been arrested for drug offenses, and the number of drug offenders in federal prisons had risen to approximately 98,000 (representing about half of all inmates in federal facilities).[34]

Increased Probability of Incarceration The growth of America's inmate population also reflects the reality that the chance of someone who is arrested going to prison today is much greater than it was thirty years ago. Most of this growth took place in the 1980s, when the likelihood of incarceration in a state prison after arrest increased fivefold for drug offenses, threefold for weapons offenses, and twofold for crimes such as sexual assault, burglary, auto theft, and larceny.[35] For federal crimes, the proportion of convicted defendants being sent to prison rose from 54 percent in 1988 to 88 percent in 2013.[36]

Inmates Serving More Time In Chapter 11, we discussed a number of "get tough" sentencing laws passed in reaction to the crime wave of the 1970s and 1980s. These measures, including sentencing guidelines, mandatory minimum sentences, and truth-in-sentencing laws, have significantly increased the length of prison terms in the United States.[37] Overall, inmates released from state prison in 2009 spent an average of nine months—about 36 percent—longer behind bars than those inmates released in

FIGURE 13.6 The Inmate Population of the United States

The total number of inmates in the United States has risen from 744,208 in 1985 to about 2.2 million in 2014.

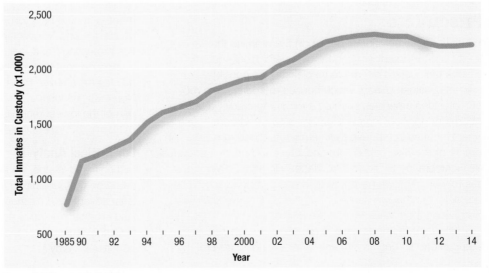

Source: U.S. Department of Justice.

1990.[38] On the federal level, in the fifteen years after the passage of the Sentencing Reform Act of 1984, the average time served in federal prison increased more than 50 percent.[39]

Federal Prison Growth Even though, as noted earlier in the chapter, the overall U.S. prison population rose slightly in 2013, the number of federal prisoners dropped—by about 2,000—for the first time in thirty-four years.[40] This decrease is too small, however, to offset the recent expansion of the federal corrections system. Between 2000 and 2013, the federal prison population grew 56 percent, from about 125,000 to just over 195,000.[41]

As already mentioned, an increase in federal drug offenders is largely responsible for the growth of the federal prison population. Because of mandatory minimum sentencing laws, federal drug traffickers spend an average of seventy-four months behind bars, considerably longer than those sentenced to state prisons.[42] Other factors driving federal prison population growth include:

▲ Immigration detainees exercise at the federal Adelanto Detention Center in Adelanto, California. Why have efforts to enforce immigration law increased the inmate population at federal prisons, while having little or no impact on the inmate populations of state prisons? Getty Images

1. Starting in 1987, Congress *abolished parole* in the federal corrections system, meaning that federal inmates must serve their entire sentences, minus good time credits.[43]
2. The number of federal inmates sentenced for *immigration violations* (covered by federal law rather than state law) increased by 30 percent from 2001 to 2013.[44]
3. In 2015, approximately 14,000 *female offenders* were behind bars in federal prison, about double their numbers in 1995.[45] Indeed, there were about the same number of women in federal prison for drug offenses in 2012 as there were for all offenses in 1995.[46]

Decarceration

As recently as 2007, one expert lamented the unwillingness of corrections authorities in the United States to reduce their prison populations, calling such efforts "practically virgin territory."[47] This is no longer the case, as the high cost of imprisonment—which reached $52.4 billion for the fifty states in 2012[48]—has caused policymakers to embrace strategies of *decarceration,* or the lowering of incarceration rates. In general, decarceration policies rely on three methods to reduce the number of offenders in prison:

1. Decreasing the probability that nonviolent offenders will be sentenced to prison.
2. Increasing the rate of release of nonviolent offenders from prison.
3. Decreasing the rate of imprisonment for probation and parole violators.[49]

With Proposition 47, as we saw at the beginning of this chapter, California voters chose the first decarceration approach just listed. The federal government is focusing on the early release of nonviolent drug offenders from prisons, a strategy we discussed in Chapter 11. States increasingly are relying on *evidence-based strategies,* or those strategies supported by statistical research, to decarcerate. Since 2005, fifteen states have lowered their recidivism rates using well-tested tactics such as community corrections, prison treatment programs, and risk assessment planning.[50]

Myth vs Reality

Does Putting Criminals in Prison Reduce Crime?

The Myth Since the early 1990s, crime rates in the United States have been stable or declining. During most of that same period, as seen in Figure 13.6 earlier in the chapter, the number of imprisoned Americans climbed precipitously. Thus, it seems clear that crime falls when the prison population rises.

This perception is supported by the theories of deterrence and incapacitation, which we covered in Chapter 11. First, the threat of prison deters would-be criminals from committing crimes. Second, a prison inmate is incapable of committing crimes against the public because he or she has been separated from the community.

The Reality Numerous statistical examples discredit a direct, sustained link between decreased crime rates and increased prison populations. Canada, for example, experienced a decline in crime rates similar to the United States in the 1990s without any increase in national incarceration levels. Furthermore, between 1999 and 2012, New York and New Jersey reduced their prison populations by 26 percent. During this period of time, violent and property crime rates in the two states fell at a greater rate than the national average.

According to one theory, massive incarceration accounted for about a quarter of the crime drop of the 1990s, as many of the most violent offenders were removed from society and remain behind bars. Since then, however, a large percentage of new prison admissions have been drug law offenders and probation/parole violators. The data tell us that removing these sorts of criminals from the community has a relatively limited effect on violent and property crime rates. In fact, their absence from their homes may even contribute to criminal activity. As we discussed in Chapter 2, many criminologists believe that widespread family disruption greatly increases the incidence of crime in a community.

Additionally, some experts believe that prisons are "schools of crime" that "teach" low-level offenders to be habitual criminals. If this is true, many inmates are more likely to commit crimes after their release from prison than they would have been if they had never been incarcerated in the first place.

For Critical Analysis

How might implementation of California Proposition 47, discussed in the opening of this chapter, give criminologists a chance to test theories regarding the correlation between incarceration levels and crime rates?

In response to a U.S. Supreme Court ruling that we will discuss in the next chapter, California has implemented a "realignment" strategy to reduce rates of imprisonment for low-level criminals. As a result, from 2011 to 2012, the number of offenders admitted to California prisons dropped by nearly 19 percent, and the state's prison population fell from 164,200 to 135,800.[51] In fact, some observers point out that the decrease in the nation's prison population from 2010 to 2012 was almost entirely the result of California's court-mandated decarceration efforts. When that state's inmate number rose slightly in 2013, so did the number of inmates nationwide.[52] (To better understand the possible impact of decarceration on crime rates, see the feature *Myth vs Reality—Does Putting Criminals in Prison Reduce Crime?*)

The Consequences of America's High Rates of Incarceration

Despite the conclusions drawn in this chapter's *Myth vs Reality* feature, many observers believe that America's high rate of incarceration has contributed significantly to the drop in the country's crime rates.[53] Putting that particular debate aside, however, criminologists are well aware of a number of negative consequences related to this country's immense prison and jail population.

Indicate some of the consequences of our high rates of incarceration.

LEARNING 6 OBJECTIVE

For one, incarceration can have severe social repercussions for communities and the families that make up those communities. About 2.7 million minors in this country—one in twenty-eight—have a parent in prison.[54] These children are at an increased risk of suffering from poverty, depression, and academic problems, as well as higher levels of juvenile delinquency and eventual incarceration themselves.[55] Studies also link high imprisonment rates to increased incidence of sexually transmitted diseases and teenage pregnancy, as the separation caused by incarceration wreaks havoc on interpersonal relationships.[56] Incarceration also has a harmful impact on offenders themselves. After being released from prison or jail, these men and women suffer from a higher rate of physical and mental health problems than the rest of the population, and are more likely to struggle with addiction, unemployment, and homelessness.[57]

Because of the demographics of the U.S. prison population, these problems have a disproportionate impact on members of minority groups. African American males are incarcerated at a rate more than six times that of white males and about two and a half times that of Hispanic males.[58] With more black men behind bars than enrolled in the nation's colleges and universities, Marc Mauer of the Sentencing Project, a nonprofit research group in Washington, D.C., believes that the "ripple effect on their communities and on the next generation of kids, growing up with their fathers in prison, will certainly be with us for at least a generation."[59] (This chapter's *CJ Policy—Your Take* feature highlights another hardship faced by this nation's offender population: loss of the right to vote.)

The Emergence of Private Prisons

As the prison population soared at the end of the twentieth century, state corrections officials faced a serious problem: too many inmates, not enough prisons. "States couldn't build space fast enough," explains corrections expert Martin Horn. "And so they had to turn to the private sector."[60] With corrections exhibiting all appearance of "a recession-proof industry," American businesses eagerly entered the market.

Today, **private prisons,** or prisons run by private firms to make a profit, are an important part of the criminal justice system. About two dozen private companies operate more than two hundred facilities across the United States. The two largest corrections firms, Corrections Corporation of America (CCA) and the GEO Group, Inc., manage approximately 160 correctional facilities and generate about $2.5 billion in annual revenue combined.[61] By 2013, private penal institutions housed about 133,000 inmates, representing 8.4 percent of all prisoners in the state and federal corrections systems.[62]

Why Privatize?

It would be a mistake to automatically assume that private prisons are less expensive to run than public ones. Nevertheless, the incentive to privatize is primarily financial.

Cost Efficiency In the 1980s and 1990s, a number of states and cities reduced operating costs by transferring government-run services such as garbage collection and road maintenance to the private sector. Similarly, private prisons can often be run more cheaply and efficiently than public ones for the following reasons:

- *Labor costs.* The wages of public employees account for nearly two-thirds of a prison's operating expenses. Although private corrections firms pay base salaries comparable to those enjoyed by public prison employees, their nonunionized staffs receive lower levels of overtime pay, workers' compensation claims, sick leave, and health-care insurance.
- *Competitive bidding.* Because of the profit motive, private corrections firms have an incentive to buy goods and services at the lowest possible price.
- *Less red tape.* Private corrections firms are not part of the government bureaucracy and therefore do not have to contend with the massive amount of paperwork that can clog government organizations.[63]

In 2005, the National Institute of Justice released the results of a five-year study comparing low-security public and private prisons in California. The government agency found that private facilities cost taxpayers between 6 and 10 percent less than public ones.[64] More recent research conducted at Vanderbilt University found that states saved

LEARNING
7
OBJECTIVE

Describe the arguments for and against private prisons.

Private Prisons Correctional facilities operated by private corporations instead of the government and, therefore, reliant on profits for survival.

about $15 million annually when they supplemented their corrections systems with privately managed institutions.[65]

Overcrowding and Outsourcing Private prisons are becoming increasingly attractive to state governments faced with the competing pressures of tight budgets and overcrowded corrections facilities. Lacking the funds to alleviate overcrowding by building more prisons, state officials are turning to the private institutions for help. In Oklahoma, for example, where corrections officials are sending prison inmates to local jails due to lack of prison space, more than a quarter of the state's prisoners—about 5,800 inmates—are housed in private facilities.[66] Often, the private prison is out of state, which leads to the "outsourcing" of inmates. California has alleviated its chronic overcrowding problems by sending about 9,000 inmates to private institutions in Arizona, Mississippi, and Oklahoma.[67]

The Argument against Private Prisons

The assertion that private prisons offer economic benefits is not universally accepted. A number of studies have found that private prisons are no more cost-effective than public ones.[68] Furthermore, opponents of private prisons worry that, despite the assurances of corporate executives, private corrections companies will "cut corners" to save costs, denying inmates important security guarantees in the process.

Safety Concerns Criticism of private prisons is somewhat supported by the anecdotal evidence. Certainly, these institutions have been the setting for a number of violent incidents over the past several years. In 2012, the Adams County Correctional Center in Natchez, Mississippi—operated by CCA—experienced a riot that ended with the death of a correctional officer and twenty other injuries. During this disturbance, three hundred inmates used broomsticks and other homemade weapons to control the facility for nearly eight hours.[69] In 2014, the federal government launched an investigation into management practices at the Idaho Correctional Center (ICC), another CCA facility. Understaffing had created such a violent atmosphere in the ICC that inmates had nicknamed it "Gladiator School."[70]

Apart from anecdotal evidence, various studies have also uncovered disturbing patterns of misbehavior at private prisons. For example, in the year after CCA took over operations of Ohio's Lake Erie Correctional Institution from the state corrections department, the number of assaults against correctional officers and inmates increased by over 40 percent.[71] In addition, research conducted by Curtis R. Blakely of the University of South Alabama and Vic W. Bumphus of the University of Tennessee at Chattanooga found that a prisoner in a private correctional facility was twice as likely to be assaulted by a fellow inmate as a prisoner in a public one.[72]

Philosophical Concerns Other critics see private prisons as inherently unjust, even if they do save tax dollars or provide enhanced services. These observers believe that corrections is not simply another industry, like garbage collection or road maintenance, and that only the government has the authority to punish wrongdoers. In the words of John DiIulio:

▼ In 2014, the state of Idaho took over management of the Idaho Correctional Center—located south of Boise—from the Corrections Corporation of America. The private prison had been beset by problems such as inmate violence, gang activity, understaffing, and contract fraud. **How can state corrections departments ensure that private prisons are operating properly?** AP Images/Charlie Litchfield, File

IDAHO DEPARTMENT OF CORRECTION

IDAHO CORRECTIONAL CENTER
Operated by Corrections Corporation of America

It is precisely because corrections involves the deprivation of liberty, precisely because it involves the legally sanctioned exercise of coercion by some citizens over others, that it must remain wholly within public hands.[73]

Furthermore, some observers note, if a private corrections firm receives a fee from the state for each inmate housed in its facility, does that not give management an incentive to increase the amount of time each prisoner serves? Though government parole boards make the final decision on an inmate's release from private prisons, the company could manipulate misconduct and good behavior reports to maximize time served and, by extension, higher profits.[74] "You can put a dollar figure on each inmate that is held at a private prison," says Alex Friedmann of *Prison Legal News*. "They are treated as commodities. And that's very dangerous and troubling when a company sees the people it incarcerates as nothing more than a money stream."[75]

The Future of Private Prisons

The number of inmates in private prisons declined by 3 percent from 2012 to 2013,[76] largely as a result of a reduction in the number of federal prisoners noted earlier in the chapter. Still, the private prison industry will continue to play an important role in American corrections, for two reasons. First, states experiencing shrinking corrections budgets and congested prisons rely on private correctional institutions to handle their inmate population overflow. Second, the federal government houses about 25,000 noncitizens—many of whom have violated immigration laws—in thirteen privately operated "Criminal Alien Requirement" correctional facilities across the country.[77]

EthicsChallenge

Several private prisons have been criticized for accepting only inmates who are in relatively good health. If true, why would this strategy make financial sense? What ethical questions does it raise concerning private prisons? ■

Jails

Although prisons and prison issues dominate the public discourse on corrections, there is an argument to be made that jails are the dominant penal institutions in the United States. In general, a prison is a facility designed to house people convicted of felonies for lengthy periods of time, while a **jail** is authorized to hold pretrial detainees and offenders who have committed misdemeanors. On any given day, about 730,000 inmates are in jail in this country, and jails admit approximately 11.7 million persons over the course of an entire year.[78] Nevertheless, jail funding is often the lowest priority for the tight budgets of local governments, leading to severe overcrowding and other dismal conditions.

Many observers see this negligence as having far-reaching consequences for criminal justice. Jail is often the first contact that citizens have with the corrections system. It is at this point that treatment and counseling have the best chance to deter future criminal behavior.[79] By failing to take advantage of this opportunity, says Professor Franklin Zimring of the University of California at Berkeley School of Law, corrections officials have created a situation in which "today's jail folk are tomorrow's prisoners."[80] (To better understand the role that these two correctional institutions play in the criminal justice system, see *Mastering Concepts—The Main Differences between Prisons and Jails*.)

LEARNING **8** OBJECTIVE

Summarize the distinction between jails and prisons, and indicate the importance of jails in the American corrections system.

Jail A facility, usually operated by the county government, used to hold persons awaiting trial or those who have been found guilty of less-serious felonies or misdemeanors.

	Prisons		Jails
1.	. . . are operated by the federal and state governments.		. . . are operated by county and city governments.
2.	. . . hold inmates who may have lived quite far away before being arrested.		. . . hold mostly inmates from the local community.
3.	. . . house only those who have been convicted of a crime.		. . . house those who are awaiting trial or have recently been arrested, in addition to convicts.
4.	. . . generally hold inmates who have been found guilty of serious crimes and received sentences of longer than one year.		. . . generally hold inmates who have been found guilty of minor crimes and are serving sentences of less than a year.
5.	. . . often offer a wide variety of rehabilitation and educational programs for long-term prisoners.		. . . due to smaller budgets, tend to focus only on the necessities of safety, food, and clothing.

The Jail Population

Like their counterparts in state prisons, jail inmates are overwhelmingly young male adults. About 47 percent of jail inmates are white, 36 percent are African American, and 15 percent are Hispanic.[81] The main difference between state prison and jail inmates involves their criminal activity. As Figure 13.7 shows, jail inmates are more likely to have been convicted of nonviolent crimes than their counterparts in state prison.

Pretrial Detainees A significant number of those detained in jails technically are not prisoners. They are **pretrial detainees** who have been arrested by the police and, for a variety of reasons that we discussed in Chapter 9, are unable to post bail. Pretrial detainees are, in many ways, walking legal contradictions. According to the U.S. Constitution, they are innocent until proved guilty. At the same time, by being incarcerated while awaiting trial, they are denied a number of personal freedoms and are subjected to the poor conditions of many jails.

In *Bell v. Wolfish* (1979), the Supreme Court rejected the notion that this situation is inherently unfair by refusing to give pretrial detainees greater legal protections than sentenced jail inmates have.[82] In essence, the Court recognized that treating pretrial detainees differently from convicted jail inmates would place too much of a burden on corrections officials and was therefore impractical.[83] (To learn about another area where the courts have deferred to jail authorities, see the feature *A Question of Ethics: The Strip Search.*)

Sentenced Jail Inmates According to the U.S. Department of Justice, about 40 percent of those in jail have been convicted of their current charges.[84] In other words, they have been found guilty of a crime, usually a misdemeanor, and sentenced to time in jail. The typical jail term lasts between thirty and ninety days, and rarely does a prisoner spend more than one year in jail for any single crime. Often, a judge will credit the length of time the convict has spent in detention waiting for trial—known as **time served**—toward his or her sentence. This practice acknowledges two realities of jails:

Pretrial Detainees Individuals who cannot post bail after arrest and are therefore forced to spend the time prior to their trial incarcerated in jail.

Time Served The period of time a person denied bail (or unable to pay it) has spent in jail prior to his or her trial.

FIGURE 13.7 Types of Offenses of Prison and Jail Inmates

As the comparison below shows, jail inmates are more likely than state prisoners to have been convicted of nonviolent crimes. This underscores the main function of jails: to house less serious offenders for a relatively short period of time.

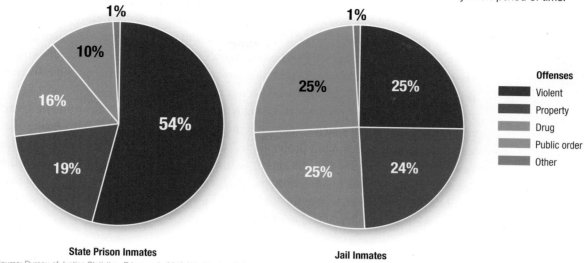

State Prison Inmates

Jail Inmates

Offenses
- Violent
- Property
- Drug
- Public order
- Other

Source: Bureau of Justice Statistics, *Prisoners in 2013* (Washington, D.C.: U.S. Department of Justice, September 2014), Table 13, page 15; and Bureau of Justice Statistics, *Profile of Jail Inmates, 2002* (Washington, D.C.: U.S. Department of Justice, July 2004), 1.

1. Terms are generally too short to allow the prisoner to gain any benefit (that is, rehabilitation) from the jail's often limited or nonexistent treatment facilities. Therefore, the jail term can serve no purpose except to punish the wrongdoer. (Judges who believe jail time can serve purposes of deterrence and incapacitation may not agree with this line of reasoning.)
2. Jails are chronically overcrowded, and judges need to clear space for new offenders.

Other Jail Inmates Pretrial detainees and those convicted of misdemeanors make up the majority of the jail population. Jail inmates also include probation and parole violators, the mentally ill, juveniles awaiting transfer to juvenile authorities, and immigration law violators being held for the federal government. Increasingly, jails are also called on to handle the overflow from state prisons. To comply with a United States Supreme Court order to reduce its prison population, California corrections officials diverted thousands of low-level offenders from its prisons to its jails. This strategy, in turn, led to such severe overcrowding of local jails that, by 2014, these institutions were releasing 13,500 inmates a month, a 34 percent increase from three years earlier.[85]

The Sociology of Jail According to sociologist John Irwin, the unofficial purpose of a jail is to manage society's "rabble," so called because

> [they] are not well integrated into conventional society, they are not members of conventional social organizations, they have few ties to conventional social networks, and they are carriers of unconventional values and beliefs.[86]

In Irwin's opinion, rabble who act violently are arrested and sent to prison. The jail is reserved for merely offensive rabble, whose primary threat to society lies in their failure to conform to its behavioral norms. This concept of rabble has been used by some critics of American corrections to explain the disproportionate number of poor and minority groups who may be found in the nation's jails at any time.

Jail Administration

About 3,300 jails are in operation in the United States. The vast majority of these are managed on a county level by an elected sheriff. Most of the remainder are under the control of the federal government or local municipalities, and six state governments (Alaska, Connecticut, Delaware, Hawaii, Rhode Island, and Vermont) also manage jails. The capacity of jails varies widely. The Los Angeles County Men's Central Jail holds nearly seven thousand people, but jails that large are the exception rather than the rule. Forty percent of all jails in this country house fewer than fifty inmates.[87]

Many jails operate on the principle of a **fee system,** in which a government agency reimburses the sheriff's department for the daily cost of housing and feeding each inmate. This practice is often problematic, because once the daily fee per inmate has been established (at, say $8), the sheriff is free to divert some of those funds to other areas of need in her or his department. Also, it is not uncommon for sheriffs' departments to charge inmates "pay-to-stay" fees for aspects of their incarceration such as food, clothing, and medical and dental care.

The "Burden" of Jail Administration Given that the public's opinion of jails ranges from negative to indifferent, some sheriffs neglect their jail management duties. Instead, they focus on high-visibility issues such as putting more law enforcement officers on the streets and improving security in schools. In fact, a jail usually receives publicity only after an escape or an incident in which inmates are abused by jailers.

A Question of Ethics: The Strip Search

The Situation During a stop, New Jersey police officers determined that Albert Florence had an outstanding warrant for an unpaid fine related to a previous traffic infraction. Even though this is not a criminal offense, the officers arrested Florence and took him to the Burlington County Jail. At the jail, correctional officers subjected him to a strip search, a highly invasive procedure that includes a shower and a search of the suspect's genitals and rectum.

The Ethical Dilemma Jail officials routinely strip search new entrants to (1) detect lice and other contagious medical conditions, (2) look for evidence of gang membership such as tattoos, and (3) prevent smuggling of drugs or weapons. As with Florence, however, the subject of the strip search often has not been charged with committing a crime. In such cases, say some observers, strip searches represent "a serious affront to human dignity and to individual privacy" and should be used only when there is reasonable suspicion that the inmate is carrying contraband.

What Is the Solution? The U.S. Supreme Court has ruled that jail authorities may, using their discretion, conduct strip searches whenever they see fit, even if the inmate is not suspected of committing a crime and there is no evidence that he or she is carrying contraband. Justice Anthony Kennedy pointed out that "people detained for minor offenses can turn out to be the most devious and dangerous criminals." Do you agree that noncriminals such as Florence, detained for traffic violations and not suspected of any other wrongdoing, should be subjected to strip searches in jails? Why or why not?

Nonetheless, with their complex and diverse populations, jails are often more difficult to manage than prisons. Jails hold people who have never been incarcerated before and who exhibit a range of violent behavior—from nonexistent to extreme—that only adds to the unpredictable atmosphere. Jail inmates have a number of other problems, including:

1. *Mental illness.* About 60 percent of jail inmates have a history of mental illness, including symptoms of schizophrenia, depression, hallucinations, and suicidal tendencies.[88]

2. *Physical health problems.* More than one-third of jail inmates report having a current medical problem such as an injury or ailments such as arthritis, asthma, or sexually transmitted diseases.[89]

3. *Substance abuse and dependency.* About two-thirds of jail inmates are dependent on alcohol or other drugs, and half of all convicted jail inmates were under the influence of drugs or alcohol at the time of their arrest.[90]

Given that most jails lack the resources and facilities to properly deal with these problems, the task of managing jail inmate populations falls disproportionately on untrained prison staff. Speaking of mentally ill inmates at Rikers Island, New York City's main jail complex, one corrections official said, "They need medication, treatment, psychological help. They don't need a corrections officer."[91]

The Challenges of Overcrowding Overcrowding exacerbates the difficulties involved in jail management. Cells intended to hold one or two people are packed with up to six. Inmates are forced to sleep in hallways. Treatment facilities, when they exist, are overwhelmed. In such stressful situations, tempers flare, leading to violent, aggressive behavior. The jails most likely to suffer from such issues are those in heavily populated metropolitan areas with large numbers of "pass through" pretrial detainees.[92]

Given the emphasis on reducing prison populations discussed throughout this chapter, there are concerns that jails will be forced to house more low-level offenders in the future than they have in the past. As most jurisdictions do not have the resources to build new jails, administrators will have to come up with creative ways to alleviate possible overcrowding. Two possible solutions involve pretrial procedures we discussed in Chapter 9:

1. Increasing options for pretrial release, and
2. Speeding up trials so that detainees do not need to spend as much time waiting in jail for court proceedings to begin.[93]

Also, community corrections—the subject of the previous chapter—can be useful in reducing jail inmate populations. In 2013, nearly 60,000 offenders sentenced to jail terms were supervised in the community, with nearly a quarter subjected to electronic monitoring.[94]

New-Generation Jails

For most of the nation's history, the architecture of a jail was secondary to its purpose of keeping inmates safely locked away. Consequently, most jails in the United States continue to resemble those from the days of the Walnut Street Jail in Philadelphia. In this *traditional,* or *linear design,* jail cells are located along a corridor. To supervise the inmates while they are in their cells, custodial officers must walk up and down the corridor, so the number of prisoners they can see at any one time is severely limited. With this limited supervision, inmates can more easily break institutional rules.

Podular Design In the 1970s, planners at the Bureau of Federal Prisons decided to upgrade the traditional jail design with the goal of improving conditions for both the staff and the inmates. The result was the **new-generation jail,** which differs significantly from its predecessors.[95] The layout of the new facilities makes it easier for the staff to monitor cell-confined inmates. The basic structure of the new-generation jail is based on a podular design. Each "pod" contains "living units" for individual prisoners. These units, instead of lining up along a straight corridor, are often situated in a triangle so that a staff member in the center of the triangle has visual access to nearly all the cells.

Daily activities such as eating and showering take place in the pod, which also has an outdoor exercise area. Treatment facilities are also located in the pod, allowing greater access for the inmates. During the day, inmates stay out in the open and are allowed back in their cells only when given permission. The officer locks the door to the cells from his or her control terminal.

▼ How does the layout of this direct supervision jail differ from that of the maximum-security prison pictured earlier in the chapter? What do these differences tell you about the security precautions needed for jail inmates as opposed to prison inmates? Photo courtesy Bergen County Sheriff's Office, Bergen, NJ

Direct Supervision Approach The podular design also enables a new-generation jail to be managed using a **direct supervision approach.**[96] One or more jail officers are stationed in the living area of the pod and are therefore in constant interaction with all prisoners in that particular pod. Some new-generation jails even provide a desk in the center of the living area, which sends a very different message to the prisoners than the traditional control booth. Theoretically, jail officials who have constant contact with inmates will be able to stem misconduct quickly and efficiently, and will also be able to recognize "danger signs" from individual inmates and stop outbursts before they occur. (As noted earlier in the chapter, corrections officials are using aspects of podular design when building new prisons, for many of the same reasons that the trend has been popular in jails.)

EthicsChallenge

Local officials recently started charging inmates at the Elko County (Nevada) Jail about $7 a day for their meals, to be paid when the inmate is released. In this section, you learned that many jail inmates are awaiting trial. Is it ethical for the county to require these inmates to pay for meals when they have not yet been found guilty of any crime? Why or why not? What should Elko County do with the meal funds collected from an inmate who is eventually found not guilty? ■

CJ IN ACTION

Solitary Confinement: Senseless Suffering?

After "some rat" told a correctional officer that an inmate named King had been selling marijuana to other prisoners, King found himself in the Special Housing Unit (SHU) of Fishkill Correctional Facility in upstate New York. King spent seventy-five days in "the Box"—a seven-by-ten foot cell with a bed and a toilet—listening to other inmates screaming "all day, every day." Four years after his release, he still felt the effects of his time in SHU. "[I've] got my back to the door when I take the train. I can't have anyone behind me. I hate being in crowds," King said.[97] In this *CJ in Action* feature, we will examine the widespread practice of solitary confinement, condemned by critics as inhumane but heralded by supporters as an invaluable tool of prison management.

Enforced Isolation

Although conditions of solitary confinement vary, in general the term refers to the confinement of an inmate alone in a small cell for most or all of the day with minimal environmental stimulation and social interaction. Most solitary confinement cells measure approximately ten feet by six feet. Furnished with only a sink, toilet, and concrete bed, they have no windows or barred doors that would let in natural light.

As a rule, inmates are not sentenced to solitary confinement by a judge, and the assignment has no connection to the severity of the original offense. Rather, these isolation cells are reserved for prisoners who commit disciplinary violations once in prison or are deemed a security risk to themselves or others. According to estimates, at least 25,000 inmates—and probably significantly more—are in solitary confinement in American prisons at any given time.[98]

The Case for Solitary Confinement

- Prison officials see the threat of solitary confinement as a vital tool in maintaining order and discipline. Because human contact is one of the few privileges that inmates enjoy, they have a strong incentive to conform to the rules of the institution rather than risk losing that privilege.

- Solitary confinement protects prison staff and inmates alike by removing violent convicts from the general inmate population.

- Solitary confinement can be a form of rehabilitation, as it separates the inmate from negative influences. Also, because of the sparseness of the cells, inmates who otherwise would harm themselves with items used in everyday prison life are unable to do so.

The Case against Solitary Confinement

- Solitary confinement causes severe damage to the mental health of prisoners. Researchers have identified a number of resulting symptoms, including intense anxiety, hallucinations, violent fantasies, and reduced impulse control.[99]

- The majority of inmates who suffer the psychological harm of solitary confinement will eventually be returned to society, which will have to bear the burden of their mental illness.[100]

- Because prison officials have unfettered discretion in deciding who gets sent to solitary confinement and for how long, the practice is rife with abuse.

Your Opinion—Writing Assignment

To many observers, the drawbacks of solitary confinement lie in its practice, not its principles. Although they may be useful in controlling inmate populations, solitary confinement procedures suffer from failure to properly monitor the medical and psychological state of those in "the Hole," use of confinement for trivial offenses like "talking back" to corrections officials, and unacceptably long periods of isolation. The courts have shown no inclination to rein in these abuses, as judges tend to be extremely deferential to the decisions and policies of prison officials.

Today, no federal laws control the use of solitary confinement. Only one state, Washington, places a limit—twenty days—on the length of time an inmate may be kept in isolation.[101] If you were to draft a law regulating the use of solitary confinement, what elements would your law contain? Would you, like the courts, give prison officials a "free hand," or would you restrict their discretion? Would you allow prisoners to challenge their solitary confinement in court? Before responding, you can review our discussions in the sections of this chapter concerning:

- The three general models of prison organization ("A Short History of American Prisons").

- Prison administration ("Prison Organization and Management").

- Maximum-security and supermax prisons ("Prison Organization and Management").

Your answer should include at least three full paragraphs.

Summary

For more information on these concepts, look back to the Learning Objective icons throughout the chapter.

 Contrast the Pennsylvania and the New York penitentiary theories of the 1800s. Basically, the Pennsylvania system imposed total silence on its prisoners. Based on the concept of separate confinement, penitentiaries were constructed with back-to-back cells facing both outward and inward. Prisoners worked, slept, and ate alone in their cells. In contrast, New York used the congregate system: silence was imposed, but inmates worked and ate together.

 Explain the three general models of prisons. (a) The custodial model assumes the prisoner is incarcerated for reasons of incapacitation, deterrence, and retribution. (b) The rehabilitation model puts security concerns second and the well-being of the individual inmate first. As a consequence, treatment programs are offered to prisoners. (c) The reintegration model sees the correctional institution as a training ground for preparing convicts to reenter society.

 Describe the formal prison management system, and indicate the three most important aspects of prison governance. A formal system is militaristic with a hierarchical (top-down) chain of command; the warden (or superintendent) is on top, then deputy wardens, and last, custodial employees. Sound governance of a correctional facility requires officials to provide inmates with a sense of order, amenities such as clean living conditions and acceptable food, and services such as vocational training and remedial education programs.

 List and briefly explain the four types of prisons. (a) Maximum-security prisons, which are designed mainly with security and surveillance in mind. Such prisons are usually large and consist of cell blocks, each of which is set off by a series of gates and bars. (b) Medium-security prisons, which offer considerably more educational and treatment programs and allow more contact between inmates. Such prisons are usually surrounded by high fences rather than by walls. (c) Minimum-security prisons, which permit prisoners to have television sets and computers and often allow them to leave the grounds for educational and employment purposes. (d) Supermaximum-security (supermax) prisons, in which prisoners are confined to one-person cells for up to twenty-three hours per day under constant video camera surveillance.

 List the factors that have caused the prison population to grow dramatically in the last several decades. (a) The enhancement and stricter enforcement of the nation's drug laws; (b) increased probability of incarceration; (c) inmates serving more time for each crime; (d) federal prison growth; and (e) rising incarceration rates for women.

 Indicate some of the consequences of our high rates of incarceration. Some people believe that the reduction in the country's crime rate is a direct result of increased incarceration rates. Others believe that high incarceration rates are having increasingly negative social consequences, such as financial hardships, reduced supervision and discipline of children, and a general deterioration of the family structure when one parent is in prison.

 Describe the arguments for and against private prisons. Proponents of private prisons contend that they can be run more cheaply and efficiently than public ones. Opponents of prison privatization dispute such claims, and argue that private prisons are financially motivated to deny inmates the same protections and rights they receive in public correctional facilities.

 Summarize the distinction between jails and prisons, and indicate the importance of jails in the American corrections system. Generally, a prison is for those convicted of felonies who will serve lengthy periods of incarceration, whereas a jail is for those who have been convicted of misdemeanors and will serve less than a year of incarceration. Jails also hold individuals awaiting trial, juveniles awaiting transfer to juvenile authorities, probation and parole violators, and the mentally ill. In any given year, approximately 12 million people are admitted to jails, and therefore jails often provide the best chance for treatment or counseling that may deter future criminal behavior by these low-level offenders.

 Explain why the U.S. Supreme Court upheld the practice of strip searching all jail inmates, including those who have not been charged with a crime. In general, American courts are reluctant to require jail authorities to have different policies for different classes of jail inmates. When it comes to strip searches, the Supreme Court ruled that jail authorities may, at their discretion, strip search any inmate for reasons relating to jail hygiene and security.

Questions for Critical Analysis

1. By most measures, the United States imprisons more of its citizens than any other country in the world. Economic considerations aside, what is your opinion of our dramatically high incarceration rates?

2. Supermax prisons operate in a state of perpetual lockdown. Why might a warden institute a lockdown in a maximum-security prison?

3. Do you agree with the argument that private prisons are inherently unjust, no matter what costs they may save taxpayers? Why or why not?

4. Why have pretrial detainees been called "walking legal contradictions"? What are the practical reasons why pretrial detainees will continue to be housed in jails prior to trial, regardless of whether their incarceration presents any constitutional irregularities?

5. Experience shows that building new jails does little or nothing to alleviate jail overcrowding. Why might this be the case?

Key Terms

classification   428
congregate system   422
custody level   428
direct supervision approach   444
fee system   442
jail   439
lockdown   432

maximum-security prison   429
medical model   423
medium-security prison   432
minimum-security prison   433
new-generation jail   444
penitentiary   421
pretrial detainees   440

private prisons   437
separate confinement   422
supermax prison   431
time served   440
warden   426

Notes

1. James M. Beattie, *Crime and the Courts in England, 1660–1800* (Princeton, N.J.: Princeton University Press, 1986), 506–507.

2. Samuel Walker, *Popular Justice* (New York: Oxford University Press, 1980), 11.

3. Michael Meranze, *Laboratories of Virtue: Punishment, Revolution, and Authority in Philadelphia, 1760–1835* (Chapel Hill, N.C.: University of North Carolina Press, 1996), 55.

4. Negley K. Teeters, *The Cradle of the Penitentiary: The Walnut Street Jail at Philadelphia, 1773–1835* (Philadelphia: Pennsylvania Prison Society, 1955), 30.

5. Negley K. Teeters and John D. Shearer, *The Prison at Philadelphia's Cherry Hill* (New York: Columbia University Press, 1957), 142–143.

6. Henry Calvin Mohler, "Convict Labor Policies," *Journal of the American Institute of Criminal Law and Criminology* 15 (1925), 556–557.

7. Zebulon Brockway, *Fifty Years of Prison Service* (Montclair, N.J.: Patterson Smith, 1969), 400–401.

8. Robert Martinson, "What Works? Questions and Answers about Prison Reform," *Public Interest* 35 (Spring 1974), 22.

9. See Ted Palmer, "Martinson Revisited," *Journal of Research on Crime and Delinquency* (1975), 133; and Paul Gendreau and Bob Ross, "Effective Correctional Treatment: Bibliotherapy for Cynics," *Crime & Delinquency* 25 (1979), 499.

10. Robert Martinson, "New Findings, New Views: A Note of Caution Regarding Sentencing Reform," *Hofstra Law Review* 7 (1979), 243.

11. Byron Eugene Price and John Charles Morris, eds., *Prison Privatization: The Many Facets of a Controversial Industry, Volume 1* (Santa Barbara, Calif.: Praeger, 2012), 58.

12. Charles H. Logan, *Criminal Justice Performance Measures in Prisons* (Washington, D.C.: U.S. Department of Justice, 1993), 5.

13. Todd R. Clear and George F. Cole, *American Corrections,* 4th ed. (Belmont, Calif.: Wadsworth Publishing Co., 1997), 245–246.

14. Alfred Blumstein, "Prisons," in *Crime,* eds. James Q. Wilson and Joan Petersilia (San Francisco: ICS Press, 1995), 392.

15. Cassia Spohn and David Holleran, "The Effect of Imprisonment on Recidivism Rates of Felony Offenders: A Focus on Drug Offenders," *Criminology* (May 1, 2002), 329–357.

16. Bureau of Justice Statistics, *Census of State and Federal Correctional Facilities, 2005* (Washington, D.C.: U.S. Department of Justice, October 2008), 2.

17. *Ibid.*

18. Charles H. Logan, "Well Kept: Comparing Quality of Confinement in a Public and Private Prison," *Journal of Criminal Law and Criminology* 83 (1992), 580.

19. Bert Useem and Peter Kimball, *Stages of Siege: U.S. Prison Riots, 1971–1986* (New York: Oxford University Press, 1989).

20. Bert Useem, "Disorganization and the New Mexico Prison Riot of 1980," *American Sociology Review* 50 (1985), 685.

21. Peter M. Carlson and John J. DiIulio, Jr., "Organization and the Management of the Prison," in *Prison and Jail Administration: Practice and Theory*, 3rd ed., ed. Peter M. Carlson (Burlington, Mass.: Jones & Bartlett Learning, 2015), 272.

22. John J. DiIulio, *Governing Prisons* (New York: Free Press, 1987), 12.

23. *Ibid.*

24. Todd R. Clear, George F. Cole, and Michael D. Reisig, *American Corrections*, 9th ed. (Belmont, Calif.: Wadsworth Cengage Learning, 2010), 162.

25. Peter M. Carlson, "Inmate Classification," in *Prison and Jail Administration: Practice and Theory*, 3rd ed., *op. cit.*, 53–57.

26. Douglas Page, "The Prison of the Future," *Law Enforcement Technology* (January 2012), 11–13.

27. Daniel P. Mears, "Supermax Prisons: The Policy and the Evidence," *Criminology and Public Policy* (November 2013), 684.

28. Keramet Reiter, *Parole, Snitch, or Die: California's Supermax Prisons and Prisoners, 1987–2007* (Berkeley, Calif.: University of California Institute for the Study of Social Change, 2010), 1.

29. "Facts about Pelican Bay's SHU," *California Prisoner* (December 1991).

30. *Jones-El et al. v. Berge and Lichter,* 164 F.Supp.2d 1096 (2001).

31. Robert Perkinson, "Shackled Justice: Florence Federal Penitentiary and the New Politics of Punishment," *Social Justice* (Fall 1994), 117–123.

32. Terry Kuppers, *Prison Madness: The Mental Health Crisis behind Bars and What We Must Do about It* (San Francisco: Jossey-Bass, 1999), 56–64.

33. Steven D. Levitt, "Understanding Why Crime Fell in the 1990s: Four Factors That Explain the Decline and Six That Do Not," *Journal of Economic Perspectives* (Winter 2004), 177.

34. Bureau of Justice Statistics, *Prisoners in 2013* (Washington, D.C.: U.S. Department of Justice, September 2014), Table 13, page 15; and Table 16, page 17.

35. Allen J. Beck, "Growth, Change, and Stability in the U.S. Prison Population, 1980–1995," *Corrections Management Quarterly* (Spring 1997), 9–10.

36. U.S. District Courts, "Criminal Defendants Sentenced after Conviction, by Offense, during the 12-Month Period Ending September 30, 2013" at **www.uscourts.gov /uscourts/Statistics/JudicialBusiness /2013/appendices/D05Sep13.pdf.**

37. Joan Petersilia, "Beyond the Prison Bubble," *Wilson Quarterly* (Winter 2011), 27.

38. *Time Served: The High Cost, Low Return of Longer Prison Terms* (Washington, D.C.: The Pew Center on the States, June 2012), 2.

39. *Fifteen Years of Guidelines Sentencing: An Assessment of How Well the Federal Criminal Justice System Is Achieving the Goals of Sentencing Reform* (Washington, D.C.: U.S. Sentencing Commission, November 2004), 46.

40. *Prisoners in 2013, op. cit.*, Table 1, page 2.

41. *Ibid.*, Table 3, page 4.

42. Julie Samuels, Nancy La Vigne, and Samuel Taxy, *Stemming the Tide: Strategies to Reduce the Growth and Cut the Cost of the Federal Prison System* (Washington, D.C.: Urban Institute, November 2013), 1.

43. Comprehensive Crime Control Act of 1984, Public Law Number 98-473.

44. *Prisoners in 2013, op. cit.*, Table 15, page 17.

45. Federal Bureau of Prisons, "Inmate Gender" (January 25, 2015), at **www.bop.gov/about /statistics/statistics_inmate_gender.jsp.**

46. Bureau of Justice Statistics, *Prisoners in 2012: Trends in Admissions and Releases, 1991–2012* (Washington, D.C.: U.S. Department of Justice, December 2013), Appendix table 10, page 43; and Bureau of Justice Statistics, *Prison and Jail Inmates 1995* (Washington, D.C.: U.S. Department of Justice, August 1996), Table 6, page 6.

47. James B. Jacobs, "Finding Alternatives to the Carceral State," *Social Research* (Summer 2007), 695.

48. *State Spending for Corrections: Long Term Trends and Recent Criminal Justice Policy Reforms* (Washington, D.C.: The National Association of State Budget Officers, September 2013), 1.

49. Rosemary Gartner, Anthony N. Doob, and Franklin E. Zimring, "The Past as Prologue? Decarceration in California Then and Now," *Criminology & Public Policy* (May 2011), 294–296.

50. Council of State Governments Justice Center, *Reducing Recidivism: States Deliver Results* (New York: Council of State Governments Justice Center, June 2014), 1–23.

51. Bureau of Justice Statistics, *Prisoners in 2011* (Washington, D.C.: U.S. Department of Justice, December 2012), Table 3, page 5; and Mike Males, *Update: Eight Months in Realignment: Dramatic Reductions in California's Prisoners* (San Francisco, Calif.: Center on Juvenile & Criminal Justice, June 2012), 4.

52. Joan Petersilia and Francis T. Cullen, "Liberal but Not Stupid: Meeting the Promise of Downsizing Prisons," *Stanford Journal of Criminal Law and Criminal Policy* (Winter 2014–2015), 13–17.

53. Dan Seligman, "Lock 'Em Up," *Forbes* (May 23, 2005), 216–217.

54. Bruce Western and Becky Pettit, *Collateral Costs: Incarceration's Effect on Economic Mobility* (Washington, D.C.: The Pew Charitable Trusts, 2010), 4.

55. John Tierney, "Prison and the Poverty Trap," *New York Times* (February 19, 2013), D1.

56. *Ibid.*

57. *Rethinking the Blues: How We Police in the U.S. and at What Cost* (Washington, D.C.: Justice Policy Institute, May 2012), 34.

58. *Prisoners in 2012: Trends in Admissions and Releases, 1991–2012, op. cit.*, Table 18, page 25.

59. Quoted in Fox Butterfield, "Study Finds 2.6% Increase in U.S. Prison Population," *New York Times* (July 28, 2003), A8.

60. Quoted in Scott Cohn, "Private Prison Industry Grows Despite Critics," *cnbc.com* (October 18, 2011), at **www.nbcnews.com /id/44936562/ns/business-cnbc_tv/t /private-prison-industry-grows-despite -critics/#.UW6vC7_zdzU.**

61. Thierry Godard, "The Economics of the American Prison System," *SmartAsset.com* (January 23, 2015), at **smartasset.com /insights/the-economics-of-the-american -prison-system.**

62. *Prisoners in 2013, op. cit.*, Table 12, page 14.

63. "A Tale of Two Systems: Cost, Quality, and Accountability in Private Prisons," *Harvard Law Review* (May 2002), 1872.

64. Douglas C. McDonald and Kenneth Carlson, *Contracting for Imprisonment in the Federal Prison System: Cost and Performance of the Privately Operated Taft Correctional Institution* (Cambridge, Mass.: Abt Associates, Inc., October 2005), vii.

65. Vanderbilt University Law School, "New Study Shows Benefits of Having Privately and Publicly Managed Prisons in the Same State" (November 25, 2008), at **law .vanderbilt.edu/article-search/article -detail/index.aspx?nid=213.**

66. Clifton Adcock, "State Weighs Moving More Inmates to Private Prisons, or Buying a Private Prison," *Oklahoma Watch* (January 9, 2014), at **oklahomawatch.org/2014/01/09 /with-overcrowded-prisons-state-looks -at-moving-more-inmates-to-private -prisons-or-buying-a-private-prison.**

67. "California Prisoners Could Be Moved Out of State Due to Overcrowding," *Associated Press* (January 8, 2014).

68. Gerald G. Gaes, "The Current Status of Prison Privatization Research on American Prisons" (2012), at **works.bepress.com /gerald_gaes_1/.**

69. Robbie Brown, "Mississippi Prison on Lockdown after Guard Dies," *New York Times* (May 23, 2012), A12.

70. "FBI Investigates Company Running 'Gladiator School' Prison," *Associated Press* (March 7, 2014).

71. Gregory Geisler, *CIIC: Lake Erie Correctional Institution* (Columbus, Ohio: Correctional Institution Inspection Committee, January 2013), 16.

72. Curtis R. Blakely and Vic W. Bumphus, "Private and Public Sector Prisons," *Federal Probation* (June 2004), 27.

73. John DiIulio, "Prisons, Profits, and the Public Good: The Privatization of Corrections," in *Criminal Justice Center Bulletin* (Huntsville, Tex.: Sam Houston State University, 1986).

74. Richard L. Lippke, "Thinking about Private Prisons," *Criminal Justice Ethics* (Winter/Spring 1997), 32.

75. Quoted in Cohn, *op. cit.*

76. *Prisoners in 2013, op. cit.*, Table 12, page 14.

77. *Warehoused and Forgotten: Immigrants Trapped in Our Shadow Private Prison System* (New York: American Civil Liberties Union, June 2014), 6.

78. Bureau of Justice Statistics, *Jail Inmates at Midyear 2013—Statistical Tables* (Washington, D.C.: U.S. Department of Justice, May 2014), 1, 4.

79. Arthur Wallenstein, "Jail Crowding: Bringing the Issue to the Corrections Center Stage," *Corrections Today* (December 1996), 76–81.

80. Quoted in Fox Butterfield, "'Defying Gravity,' Inmate Population Climbs," *New York Times* (January 19, 1998), A10.

81. *Jail Inmates at Midyear 2013—Statistical Tables, op. cit.*, Table 2, page 6.

82. 441 U.S. 520 (1979).

83. *Ibid.*, at 546.

84. *Jail Inmates at Midyear 2013—Statistical Tables, op. cit.*, 1.

85. Paige St. John, "Early Jail Releases Have Surged Since California's Prison Realignment," *Los Angeles Times* (August 16, 2014), at **www.latimes.com/local/crime/la-me-ff-early-release-20140817-story.html#page=1.**

86. John Irwin, *The Jail: Managing the Underclass in American Society* (Berkeley, Calif.: University of California Press, 1985), 2.

87. Bureau of Justice Statistics, *Census of Jail Facilities, 2006* (Washington, D.C.: U.S. Department of Justice, December 2011), 14.

88. Doris J. James and Lauren E. Glaze, *Bureau of Justice Statistics Special Report: Mental Health Problems of Prison and Jail Inmates* (Washington, D.C.: U.S. Department of Justice, September 2006), 1.

89. Laura M. Maruschak, *Bureau of Justice Statistics Special Report: Medical Problems of Jail Inmates* (Washington, D.C.: U.S. Department of Justice, November 2006), 1.

90. Jennifer C. Karberg and Doris J. James, *Bureau of Justice Statistics Special Report: Substance Dependence, Abuse, and Treatment of Jail Inmates, 2002* (Washington, D.C.: U.S. Department of Justice, July 2005), 1.

91. Quoted in Michael Schwirtz, "Rikers Island Struggles with a Surge in Violence and Mental Illness," *New York Times* (March 19, 2014), A1.

92. Todd R. Clear, George F. Cole, and Michael D. Reisig, *American Corrections,* 10th ed. (Belmont, Calif.: Wadsworth Cengage Learning, 2013), 180.

93. Mark Cuniff, *Jail Crowding: Understanding Jail Population Dynamics* (Washington, D.C.: National Institute of Corrections, January 2002), 36.

94. *Jail Inmates at Midyear 2013—Statistical Tables, op. cit.*, Table 9, page 10.

95. R. L. Miller, "New Generation Justice Facilities: The Case for Direct Supervision," *Architectural Technology* 12 (1985), 6–7.

96. David Bogard, Virginia A. Hutchinson, and Vicci Persons, *Direct Supervision Jails: The Role of the Administrator* (Washington, D.C.: National Institute of Corrections, February 2010), 1–2.

97. Quoted in Shruti Ravindran, "Going Crazy in Solitary," *The Week* (March 28, 2014), 40.

98. Erica Goode, "Prisons Rethink Isolation, Saving Money, Lives, and Sanity," *New York Times* (March 11, 2012), A1.

99. Bruce Arrigo and Jennifer Leslie Bullock, "The Psychological Effects of Solitary Confinement on Prisoners in Supermax Units," *International Journal of Offender Therapy and Comparative Criminology* (December 2008), 622–640.

100. Matthew Lowen and Caroline Isaacs, *Lifetime Lockdown: How Isolation Conditions Impact Prisoner Reentry* (Tucson, Ariz.: American Friends Service Committee, August 2012).

101. Washington Revised Code Section 10.64.060 (2005).

14

The Prison Experience and Prisoner Reentry

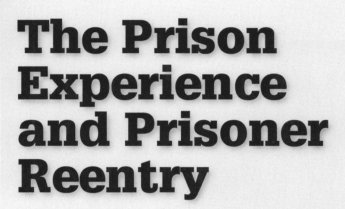

John Moore/Getty Images News/Getty Images

Chapter Outline		Corresponding Learning Objectives
Prison Culture	**1**	Explain the concept of prison as a total institution.
	2	Describe a risk run by corrections officials who fail to provide adequate medical care to the inmates under their control.
Prison Violence	**3**	Indicate some of the reasons for violent behavior in prisons.
Correctional Officers and Discipline	**4**	List the three goals of prison disciplinary strategies.
	5	Describe the hands-off doctrine of prisoner law and indicate two standards used to determine if prisoners' rights have been violated.
Inside a Women's Prison	**6**	Explain the aspects of imprisonment that prove challenging for incarcerated mothers and their children.
Return to Society	**7**	Contrast parole, expiration release, pardon, and furlough.
	8	Explain the goal of prisoner reentry programs.
	9	Indicate typical conditions for release for a paroled child molester.

To target your study and review, look for these numbered Learning Objective icons throughout the chapter.

the "**Wildest** show in the South"

two of the inmates sitting at the poker table had been convicted of murder. Two others were doing time for armed robbery. The fifth player in the "game"—a large, angry bull—rammed the table, and then turned its attention to the inmates, kicking its hind legs and swinging its massive horns with violent intent. The last prisoner of the four brave enough to remain seated during the bull's rampage was declared the winner, taking $200 back to his cell for his troubles.

"Convict Poker" is one of the most popular competitions at the Angola Prison Rodeo, which celebrated its fiftieth anniversary in 2014. Dubbed the "Wildest Show in the South," the tournament draws thousands of spectators to the Louisiana State Penitentiary each year and raises millions of dollars for the prison's educational and recreational programs. Warden Burl Cain promotes the rodeo as a highly anticipated perk for the inmates, who spend most of their days working in the prison's farming operations picking wheat, corn, and cotton. The rodeo also encourages discipline at the nation's largest maximum security prison, which houses most of Louisiana's violent offenders. Inmates know that, if they misbehave, they won't be allowed to participate in the event, which includes an arts-and-crafts fair open to the public.

Critics of the rodeo see it as an unseemly ritual in which untrained inmates are subjected to the risk (and reality) of serious injury for the amusement of tourists and the profit of the penitentiary. At a time when many prisoners across the country are denied amenities such as weightlifting, television, magazines, and conjugal visits, however, the Angola Prison Rodeo is a rare exception to the "no frills" movement in American corrections. Furthermore, the inmates are eager to take part. "[The rodeo] make me feel like somebody," says one who is serving a life sentence for murder. "It gives me a chance . . . to entertain the people and just have fun."

▲ An inmate is struck by a bull during the "Guts and Glory" event at the Louisiana State Penitentiary's annual Angola Prison Rodeo.

Cooper Neill/Getty Images Entertainment/Getty Images

1. Fifty percent of the inmates at the Louisiana State Penitentiary have been convicted of murder. Another 16 percent are rapists. Should these offenders be given the chance to "have fun" at a prison rodeo? Why or why not?

2. In the "Guts and Glory" event, inmates risk serious injury trying to grab a $500 poker chip tied to the forehead of an enraged, two-thousand pound bull. Are there any ethical problems with allowing prisoners to participate in such a dangerous competition before paying customers? Explain your answer.

3. Most of the inmates at Angola will die behind bars. How do you think this influences their attitude toward participating in the rodeo?

Prison Culture

In this chapter, we will look at the life of the imprisoned convict, starting with the realities of an existence behind bars and finishing with the challenges of returning to free society. Along the way, we will discuss violence in prison, correctional officers, women's prisons, different types of release, and several other issues that are at the forefront of American corrections today. To start, we must understand the forces that shape prison culture and how those forces affect the overall operation of the correctional facility.

Any institution, whether a school, a bank, or a police department, has an organizational culture—a set of values that help the people in the organization understand what actions are acceptable and what actions are unacceptable. According to a theory put forth by the influential sociologist Erving Goffman, prison cultures are unique because prisons are **total institutions** that encompass every aspect of an inmate's life. Unlike a student or a bank teller, a prisoner cannot leave the institution or have any meaningful interaction with outside communities. Others arrange every aspect of daily life, and all prisoners are required to follow this schedule in the same manner.[1]

Inmates develop their own argot, or language (see Figure 14.1). They create their own economy, which, in the absence of currency, is based on the barter of valued items such as food, contraband, and sexual favors. They establish methods of determining power, many of which, as we shall see, involve violence. Isolated and heavily regulated, prisoners create a social existence that is, out of both necessity and design, separate from the outside world.

Adapting to Prison Society

On arriving at prison, each convict attends an orientation session and receives a "Resident's Handbook." The handbook provides information such as meal and official count times, disciplinary regulations, and visitation guidelines. The norms and values of the prison society, however, cannot be communicated by the staff or learned from a handbook. As first described by Donald Clemmer in his classic 1940 work, *The Prison Community,* the process of **prisonization**—or adaptation to the prison culture—advances as the inmate gradually understands what constitutes acceptable behavior in the institution, as defined not by the prison officials but by other inmates.[2]

In studying prisonization, criminologists have focused on two areas: how prisoners change their behavior to adapt to life behind bars, and how life behind bars has changed because of inmate behavior. Sociologist John Irwin has identified several patterns of inmate behavior, each one driven by the inmate's personality and values:

Total Institution An institution, such as a prison, that provides all of the necessities for existence to those who live within its boundaries.

Prisonization The socialization process through which a new inmate learns the accepted norms and values of the prison culture.

LEARNING **1** OBJECTIVE

Explain the concept of prison as a total institution.

FIGURE 14.1 Prison Slang

All day A life sentence, as in "I'm here all day."

All day and a night A life-without-parole sentence.

Bit Prison sentence, usually relatively short, as in "I've got a three-year bit."

Carga Heroin.

Catch a ride A request to another inmate to get high.

Cakero Description of a convict who rapes weaker inmates.

Fire on the line A warning that a correctional officer is in the area.

Fish A new arrival, unschooled in the ways of prison life.

Grandma's (or Grandma's House) A prison gang's meeting place, or the cell of the gang leader.

Mud Coffee.

Mule Someone who smuggles drugs into the institution.

N.G. "No Good," as in "He's N.G." (meaning the inmate in question is not trustworthy).

Neutron Term used by gang members to describe an inmate not affiliated with a gang.

Old School Description of an older prisoner, usually with respect.

Square Cigarette.

Three knee deep To stab someone so that they're injured, but not killed, as a warning.

1. Professional criminals adapt to prison by "doing time." In other words, they follow the rules and generally do whatever is necessary to speed up their release and return to freedom.

2. Some convicts, mostly state-raised youths or those frequently incarcerated in juvenile detention centers, are more comfortable inside prison than outside. These inmates serve time by "jailing," or establishing themselves in the power structure of prison culture.

3. Other inmates take advantage of prison resources such as libraries or drug treatment programs by "gleaning," or working to improve themselves to prepare for a return to society.

4. Finally, "disorganized" criminals exist on the fringes of prison society. These inmates may have mental impairments or low levels of intelligence, and find it impossible to adapt to prison culture on any level.[3]

The process of categorizing prisoners has a theoretical basis, but it serves a practical purpose as well, allowing administrators to reasonably predict how different inmates will act in certain situations. An inmate who is "doing time" generally does not present the same security risk as one who is "jailing."

Who Is in Prison?

The culture of any prison is heavily influenced by its inmates. Their values, beliefs, and experiences will be reflected in the social order that exists behind bars. As we noted in the last chapter, the past three decades have seen incarceration rates of women and minority groups rise sharply. Furthermore, the arrest patterns of inmates have changed over that time period. A prisoner today is much more likely to have been incarcerated on a drug charge or immigration violation than was the case in the 1980s. Today's inmate is also more likely to behave violently behind bars—a situation that will be addressed shortly.

An Aging Inmate Population In recent years, the most significant demographic change in the prison population involves age. Though the majority of inmates are still under thirty-four years old, the number of state and federal prisoners over the age of forty has increased dramatically since the mid-1990s, as you can see in Figure 14.2. Several factors have contributed to this upsurge, including longer prison terms, mandatory prison terms, recidivism, and higher levels of crimes—particularly violent crimes—committed by older offenders.[4] For example, in Angola State Prison, featured at the beginning of this chapter, the average sentence for those inmates not serving life-without-parole is ninety-one years.[5]

An Ailing Inmate Population Overall, about half of those incarcerated in the United States (including federal and state prisoners and jail inmates) report having a chronic medical condition such as cancer, high blood pressure, diabetes, or asthma.[6]

FIGURE 14.2 The Aging Prison Population

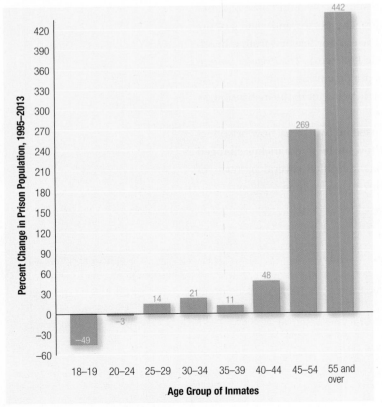

Sources: Bureau of Justice Statistics, *Prisoners in 2003* (Washington, D.C.: U.S. Department of Justice, November 2004), Table 10, page 8; Bureau of Justice Statistics, *Prisoners in 2013* (Washington, D.C.: U.S. Department of Justice, September 2014), Table 7, page 8.

Furthermore, given the frailties of older inmates, prisons and jails are now holding more people with medical issues than in the past. Poor health is the cause of nine of ten inmate deaths in state prisons, with heart disease and cancer accounting for just over half of these fatalities.[7] Not surprisingly, the mortality rates of inmates fifty-five and older from heart disease and cancer are significantly higher than those of any other age group.[8]

Corrections budgets are straining under the financial pressures caused by the health-care needs of aging inmates. Nationwide, an inmate aged fifty years or older is three times more expensive to incarcerate than a younger prisoner.[9] In Virginia, inmates fifty years or older have average annual medical expenses of about $5,372, compared with an average annual medical expense of $795 for those prisoners under fifty.[10] Given the burden of inmate medical costs, state corrections officials may be tempted to cut such services whenever possible. As the feature *Landmark Cases*—Brown v. Plata shows, however, prisoners have a constitutional right to adequate health care.

Mental Illness behind Bars Another factor in rising correctional health-care costs is the high incidence of mental illness in American prisons and jails. During the 1950s and 1960s, nearly 600,000 mental patients lived in public hospitals, often against their will. A series of scandals spotlighting the poor medical services and horrendous living conditions in these institutions led to their closure and the elimination of much of the nation's state-run mental health infrastructure.[11] Many mentally ill people now receive no supervision whatsoever, and some inevitably commit deviant or criminal acts.

As a result, in the words of criminal justice experts Katherine Stuart van Wormer and Clemens Bartollas, jails and prison have become "the dumping grounds for people whose bizarre behavior lands them behind bars."[12] On any given day, for example, the Cook County Jail in Chicago houses between 2,000 and 2,500 inmates who have been diagnosed with a mental illness.[13] Nearly 10 percent of all federal inmates receive medications to treat illnesses such as depression and bipolar disorder.[14] As with aging and ailing prisoners, correctional facilities are required by law to provide treatment to mentally ill inmates, thus driving the costs associated with their confinement well above the average. For reasons that should become clear over the course of this chapter, correctional facilities are not designed to foster mental well-being, and indeed inmates with mental illnesses often find that their problems are exacerbated by the prison environment.[15]

Rehabilitation and Prison Programs

In Chapter 11, we saw that rehabilitation is one of the basic theoretical justifications for punishment. **Prison programs,** which include any organized activities designed to foster rehabilitation, benefit inmates in several ways. On a basic level, these programs get prisoners out of their cells and alleviate the boredom that marks prison and jail life. The programs also help inmates improve their health and skills, giving them a better chance of reintegration into society after release. Consequently, nearly every federal and state prison in the United States offers some form of rehabilitation.[16]

Prison programs are limited, however. Many state inmates suffering from mental illness would benefit from medication and twenty-four-hour psychiatric care. Yet these services are quite rare behind bars, mostly due to their high costs.[17] In addition, as many state prison systems face budget restraints, rehabilitation programs are increasingly subject to a *cost-benefit* analysis. In other words, for each dollar spent on a program, how many dollars are saved? These savings can be difficult to calculate, but researchers have become skilled at measuring reductions in future criminal behavior—and the costs such behavior would have imposed on society—to determine the usefulness of prison programs.

Prison Programs Organized activities for inmates that are designed to improve their physical and mental health, provide them with vocational skills, or simply keep them busy while incarcerated.

Landmark Cases

Brown **v** Plata

Describe a risk run by LEARNING corrections officials who fail **2** to provide adequate medical care to the inmates under OBJECTIVE their control.

California's thirty-three prisons are designed to hold 80,000 inmates. For most of the first decade of the 2000s, these facilities housed around 160,000 inmates. "It's an unacceptable working environment for everyone," said a former state corrections official. "It leads to greater violence, more staff overtime, and a total inability to deal with health care and mental illness issues." In 2009, a federal court agreed, ordering the state to reduce its prison population by 30,000 in two years. California officials appealed, giving the U.S. Supreme Court a chance to rule on the importance of medical care for inmates in this country.

Brown v. Plata
United States Supreme Court
131 S.Ct. 1910 (2011)

In the Words of the Court . . .
Justice Kennedy, Majority Opinion

* * * *

For years the medical and mental health care provided by California's prisons has fallen short of minimum constitutional requirements and has failed to meet prisoners' basic health needs. Needless suffering and death have been the well documented result.

* * * *

Prisoners are crammed into spaces neither designed nor intended to house inmates. As many as 200 prisoners may live in a gymnasium, monitored by as few as two or three correctional officers. * * * The consequences of overcrowding include "increased, substantial risk for transmission of infectious illness" and a suicide rate "approaching an average of one per week." * * * A correctional officer testified that, in one prison, up to 50 sick inmates may be held together in a 12- by 20-foot cage for up to five hours awaiting treatment. The number of staff is inadequate, and prisoners face significant delays in access to care. A prisoner with severe abdominal pain died after a 5-week delay in referral to a specialist; a prisoner with "constant and extreme" chest pain died after an 8-hour delay in evaluation by a doctor; and a prisoner died of testicular cancer after a "failure of MDs to work up for cancer in a young man with 17 months of testicular pain."

* * * *

A prison that deprives prisoners of basic sustenance, including adequate medical care, is incompatible with the concept of human dignity and has no place in civilized society.

Decision
The Court found that severe overcrowding in California state prisons denied inmates satisfactory levels of mental and physical health care and therefore amounted to unconstitutional cruel and unusual punishment. It ordered the state to reduce the prison population to 137.5 percent of capacity—about 110,000 inmates—by June 2013. (As of May 2015, California's prison population stood at nearly 130,000.)

For Critical Analysis
In his dissent, Justice Alito wrote, "I fear that today's decision will lead to a grim roster of victims." What might be some of the reasons behind this fear? What steps could California corrections officials take to alleviate Alito's worries?

Substance Abuse Treatment As we have seen throughout this textbook, there is a strong link between crime and abuse of drugs and alcohol. According to the National Center on Addiction and Substance Abuse (CASA) at New York's Columbia University, 1.5 million prison and jail inmates in the United States meet the medical criteria for substance abuse or addiction. Also according to CASA, only 11 percent of these inmates have received any type of professional treatment behind bars.[18] The most effective substance abuse programs for prisoners require trained staff, lengthy periods of therapy, expensive medication, and community aftercare, but such programs carry a price tag of nearly $10,000 per inmate. If every eligible prisoner in the United States received such treatment, the cost would be $12.6 billion.

Researchers at CASA contend, however, that "the nation would break even in a year" if just one in ten of these inmates remained substance and crime free and employed for one year after release from prison.[19] One method that seems to have had success in this area is **therapeutic community (TC)** treatment, in which former substance abusers help current addicts change the harmful behavior patterns that lead to drug and alcohol abuse. The Cornerstone program in Oregon, for example, provides prerelease TC to inmates, followed by a six-month program in the community. Full-term participants have showed considerably lower recidivism rates than those who dropped out of Cornerstone before finishing the program.[20]

Therapeutic Community (TC)
A group-based form of substance abuse treatment that focuses on identifying the underlying social and psychological problems of abusers to help change negative behaviors linked to drug and alcohol addiction.

Vocational and Educational Programs Even if an ex-convict does stay substance free, he or she will have a difficult time finding a steady paycheck. Employers are only about half as likely to hire job applicants with criminal records as they are those with "clean sheets."[21] To overcome this handicap, more than half of all American prisons offer *vocational* training, or prison programs that provide inmates with skills necessary to find a job. Such programs commonly provide instruction in blue-collar fields such as landscaping, automobile repair, and electrical work. Nine out of ten prisons also attempt to educate their inmates, offering literacy training, GED (general equivalency degree) programs, and other types of instruction.[22]

Some evidence suggests that such efforts can have a positive effect on rates of reoffending. A recent study by the nonprofit Rand Corporation, summarizing thirty years of research, found that ex-inmates who participated in education programs from behind bars had a 43 percent lower chance of reoffending within three years after release than those who did not.[23] In addition, the same study found that participation in vocational training improved an inmate's chances of finding post-release employment by 28 percent.[24] Proponents of such efforts also point to their potential financial benefits. Researchers at the Washington State Institute for Public Policy estimate that every $1,182 spent for inmate vocational training saves $6,806 in future criminal justice costs and that every $962 spent on inmate education saves $5,306 in future criminal justice costs.[25]

At one time, the federal government provided grants that helped eligible inmates earn college degrees while in prison. This Pell Grant program was discontinued as part of the "no frills" movement mentioned in the opening of the chapter, after critics successfully argued that any available educational funds should go to non-prisoners.[26] Today, fewer than 3,000 inmates earn their associate's or bachelor's degree behind bars each year. Not only do most correctional facilities lack the financial resources to provide such postsecondary degrees, but they also lack facilities, technology (for online classes), and qualified instructors.[27]

EthicsChallenge

Do you feel that corrections officials are ethically obligated to provide all necessary health care to inmates? Consider the case of Prisoner X, who is serving life in prison for murder. He has fallen ill, and only a $1 million heart transplant will save his life. Should taxpayers pay for the heart transplant? Should Prisoner X receive the transplant instead of other, law-abiding citizens who also need a new heart? Explain your answers. ■

Prison Violence

Prisons and jails are dangerous places to live. Prison culture is predicated on violence—one observer calls the modern institution an "unstable and violent jungle."[28] Correctional

Deprivation Model A theory that inmate aggression is the result of the frustration inmates feel at being deprived of freedom, consumer goods, sex, and other staples of life outside the institution.

Relative Deprivation The theory that inmate aggression is caused when freedoms and services that the inmate has come to accept as normal are decreased or eliminated.

officers use the threat of violence (and, at times, actual violence) to control the inmate population. Sometimes, the inmates strike back. According to the National Institute of Justice, about 2,000 correctional officers are injured by inmates annually in the United States.[29]

Among the prisoners, violence is used to establish power and dominance. On occasion, this violence leads to death. About seventy inmates in state prisons and twenty inmates in local jails are murdered by fellow inmates each year.[30] (Note, though, that this homicide rate is lower than the national average.) With nothing but time on their hands, prisoners have been known to fashion deadly weapons out of everyday items such as toothbrushes and mop handles. Many inmates also bring the "code of the street," with its fixation on "respect, toughness, and retribution," into prison, making them likely both to engage in violent acts behind bars and to be victims of such violence.[31]

Violence in Prison Culture

LEARNING
Indicate some of the reasons for violent behavior in prisons.
3
OBJECTIVE

Until the 1970s, prison culture emphasized "noninterference" and did not support inmate-on-inmate violence. Prison "elders" would themselves punish any of their peers who showed a proclivity toward assaulting fellow inmates. Today, in contrast, violence is used to establish the prisoner hierarchy by separating the powerful from the weak. Humboldt State University's Lee H. Bowker has identified several other reasons for violent behavior:

- It provides a deterrent against being victimized, as a reputation for violence may eliminate an inmate as a target of assault.
- It enhances self-image in an environment that does not respect other attributes, such as intelligence.
- In the case of rape, it gives sexual relief.
- It serves as a means of acquiring material goods through extortion or outright robbery.[32]

The **deprivation model** can be used to explain the high level of prison violence. According to this model, the stressful and oppressive conditions of prison life lead to aggressive behavior on the part of inmates. Prison researcher Stephen C. Light found that when conditions such as overcrowding worsen, inmate misconduct often increases.[33] In these circumstances, the violent behavior may not have any express purpose—it may just be a means of relieving tension.

▼ A correctional official displays a set of homemade knives, also known as *shivs,* made by inmates at Attica Correctional Facility in Attica, New York. **What are some of the reasons that violence flourishes behind bars?** AP Images/ David Duprey

Riots

The deprivation model is helpful, though less convincing, in searching for the roots of collective violence. As far back as the 1930s, sociologist Frank Tannenbaum noted that harsh prison conditions can cause tension to build among inmates until it eventually explodes in the form of mass violence.[34] Living conditions among prisons are fairly constant, however, so how can the seemingly spontaneous outbreak of prison riots be explained?

Researchers have addressed the seeming randomness of prison violence by turning to the concept of **relative deprivation.** These theories focus on the gap between what is expected in a certain situation and what is achieved. Criminologist Peter C. Kratcoski has argued that because prisoners enjoy such meager privileges to begin with, any further deprivation can spark disorder.[35] A number of prison experts have noted that collective violence occurs in response to heightened measures of security at corrections facilities.[36] Thus, the violence is primarily a reaction to additional reductions in freedom for inmates, who enjoy very little freedom to begin with.

Riots, which have been defined as situations in which a number of prisoners are beyond institutional control for a significant amount of time, are relatively rare. These incidents are marked by extreme levels of inmate-on-inmate violence and can often be attributed, at least in part, to poor living conditions and inadequate prison administration. For example, a 2012 riot at the Adams County Correctional Center in Natchez, Mississippi, that left one correctional officer dead and twenty others injured was sparked by inmate protests over poor food and lack of medical care. Afterwards, a prisoner said, "The guard that died yesterday was a sad tragedy, but the situation is simple: if you treat a human as an animal for over two years, the response will be as an animal."[37]

Prison Rape

In contrast to riots, the problem of sexual assault in prisons receives relatively little attention from corrections officials and media sources. To remedy this situation, in 2003 Congress passed the Prison Rape Elimination Act, which mandates that prison officials collect data on the extent of the problem in their facilities.[38] According to a recent survey conducted because of this legislation, about 8,800 state prisoners reported having been sexually victimized by other inmates or prison staff during the previous year.[39]

Prison rape, like rape in general, is considered primarily an act of violence rather than sex. Inmates subject to rape ("punks") are near the bottom of the prison power structure and, in some instances, may accept rape by one particularly powerful inmate in return for protection from others.[40] Abused inmates often suffer from rape trauma syndrome and a host of other psychological ailments, including suicidal tendencies. Many prisons do not offer sufficient medical treatment for rape victims, nor does the prison staff take the necessary measures to protect obvious targets of rape—young, slightly built, nonviolent offenders. Furthermore, correctional officials are rarely held responsible for inmate-on-inmate violence.

Issues of Race and Ethnicity

On the morning of March 11, 2014, a melee involving two hundred African American and Mexican American inmates broke out in the yard of Calipatria State Prison in Calipatria, California. Race plays a major role in prison life, and prison violence is often an outlet for racial tension. As prison populations have changed over the past three decades, with African Americans and Hispanics becoming the majority in many penal institutions, issues of race and ethnicity have become increasingly important to prison administrators and researchers.

Separate Worlds As early as the 1950s, researchers were noticing different group structures in inmate life. At that time, for example, prisoners at California's Soledad Prison informally segregated themselves according to geography as well as race: Tejanos (Mexicans raised in Texas), Chicanos, blacks from California, blacks from the South and Southwest, and the majority whites all formed separate social worlds.[41] Leo Carroll, professor of sociology at the University of Rhode Island, has written extensively about how today's prisoners are divided into hostile groups, with race determining nearly every aspect of an inmate's life, including friends, job assignments, and cell location.[42]

Prison Segregation More than four decades ago, the United States Supreme Court put an end to the widespread practice of **prison segregation,** under which

Prison Segregation The practice of separating inmates based on a certain characteristic, such as age, gender, type of crime committed, or race.

correctional officials would place inmates in cells or blocks with those of a similar race or ethnicity.[43] According to the Supreme Court, prison segregation was unconstitutional because government officials were discriminating against individuals based on their skin color.

Years after this ruling, however, the California Department of Corrections began implementing an unwritten policy of putting all new and transferred male inmates in cells with inmates of the same race or ethnicity for the first sixty days of incarceration. The goal of this policy was to determine if an inmate was a member of a race-based gang before allowing him to live in integrated quarters. In 2005, the Supreme Court struck down California's version of prison segregation.[44] The Court did, however, leave prison officials with an "out": they can still segregate prisoners in an "emergency situation."[45]

Prison Gangs and Security Threat Groups (STGs)

In 2014, in response to legal action, the California Department of Corrections agreed to refrain from segregating inmates by race, even during an "emergency situation."[46] The lawsuit was brought by inmates claiming that state corrections officials unfairly used race to determine which of them was involved in *prison gang* activity. In reality, corrections officials routinely rely on racial and ethnic identification as a shortcut to identify members of **prison gangs,** or cliques of inmates who join together in an organizational structure to engage in illegal activity. Gang affiliation is often the cause of inmate-on-inmate violence. For decades, the California prison system has been plagued by feuds involving various gangs such as the Mexican Mafia, composed of U.S.-born inmates of Mexican descent, and their enemies, a spin-off organization called La Nuestra Familia.

In part, the prison gang is a natural result of life in the modern prison. As one expert says of these gangs:

> Their members have done in prison what many people do elsewhere when they feel personally powerless, threatened, and vulnerable. They align themselves with others, organize to fight back, and enhance their own status and control through their connection to a more powerful group.[47]

In addition to their important role in the social structure of correctional facilities, prison gangs participate in a wide range of illegal economic activities within these institutions, including prostitution, drug selling, gambling, and loan sharking. A study released in 2011 by Alan J. Drury and Matt DeLisi of Iowa State University found that gang members were more likely to be involved in prison misconduct than those inmates who had been convicted of murder.[48]

The Prevalence of Prison Gangs The most recent research places the rate of gang membership at 11.7 percent in federal prisons, 13.4 percent in state prisons, and 15.6 percent in jails.[49] When the National Gang Crime Research Center surveyed prison administrators, however, almost 95 percent said that gang recruitment took place at their institutions, so the overall prevalence of gangs is probably much higher.[50] Los Angeles correctional officials believe that eight out of every ten inmates in their city jails are gang affiliated.

▼ A member of the Aryan Brotherhood in California's Calipatria State Prison. This particular prison gang espouses white supremacy, but for the most part its leadership focuses on illegal activities such as extortion and drug trafficking. **Why might an inmate join a prison gang?** Mark Allen Johnson/Zumapress.com/Newscom

In many instances, prison gangs are extensions of street gangs. In fact, with the help of corrupt correctional officers and using contraband cell phones, gang members "at sea" (behind bars) often are able to coordinate criminal activities with gang members "on land" (on the streets). Though the stereotypical gang is composed of African Americans or Hispanics, the majority of large prisons also have white, or "Aryan," gangs. One of the largest federal capital prosecutions in U.S. history, involving thirty-two counts of murder, focused on a major prison gang known as the Aryan Brotherhood. (See Figure 14.3 for a rundown of several major prison gangs presently active in the American corrections system.)

FIGURE 14.3 The Top Prison Gangs in the United States

Certain prison gangs, such as the Crips and the Bloods, are offshoots of street gangs and gained influence behind bars because so many of their members have been incarcerated. Others, such as the Aryan Brotherhood and the Mexican Mafia, formed in prison and expanded to the streets. Listed here are seven of the most dangerous gangs operating in the American prison system today.

Aryan Brotherhood

White

Origins: Prison gang, formed in San Quentin State Prison in 1967, as white protection against blacks.

Allies: Mexican Mafia

Rivals: Black Guerrilla Family

Darren Hauck/Reuters/Landov

Signs/Symbols: Swastika, SS lightning bolts, numbers "666" (Satan, evil) and "88" (to signify the eighth letter of the alphabet, or HH), HH for "Heil Hitler," letters "AB," shamrock (a symbol of their original Irish membership), Nordic dagger on shield with lightning bolts.

Black Guerrilla Family

African American

Origins: Prison gang, founded by incarcerated Black Panthers in San Quentin State Prison in the mid-1960s.

Allies: La Nuestra Familia

Rivals: Aryan Brotherhood

Signs/Symbols: Crossed sabers, machetes, rifles, shotguns with the letters "B G F." A black dragon squeezing the life out of a prison guard by a prison tower.

Bloods

African American

Origins: Street gang, formed in Los Angeles in the 1960s, as a defense against the Crips.

Allies: People Nation (Chicago gang), La Nuestra Familia

Rivals: Crips, Aryan Brotherhood

Signs/Symbols: The color red, red bandannas or rags, the word "Piru" (the original Blood gang), crossed-out "c" in words as disrespect for Crips, other anti-Crip graffiti, hand signal spells "blood."

Crips

African American

Origins: Street gang, formed in the Central Avenue area of Los Angeles in the late 1960s.

Allies: Black Guerrilla Family, La Nuestra Familia

Rivals: Bloods, Aryan Brotherhood, Vice Lords

Signs/Symbols: The color blue, blue bandannas and rags, use the letter "c" in place of "b" in writing as disrespect for Bloods, calling each other "Cuzz," calling themselves "Blood Killas" (BK), wearing British Knight (BK) tennis shoes.

Mexican Mafia (EMC)

Mexican American/Hispanic

Origins: Prison gang, formed in Los Angeles in the Deuel Vocational Institution in the late 1950s. Foot soldiers and related Southern California street gangs are called Sureños.

Allies: Aryan Brotherhood

Rivals: Black Guerrilla Family, La Nuestra Familia

Signs/Symbols: The national symbol of Mexico, an eagle and a snake, on a flaming circle, lying on crossed knives. The color blue, the number 13.

Mara Salvatrucha 13 (MS-13)

Hispanic

Origins: Largest street gang in North America, originated in El Salvador and formed in Los Angeles in the 1980s.

Allies: Mexican Mafia

Rivals: MS-18 (LA gang)

Yuri Cortez/AFP/Getty Images

Signs/Symbols: Most Mara Salvatrucha members are covered in tattoos, even on their faces. Common markings include "MS," "13," "Salvadorian Pride," "Devil Horns."

La Nuestra Familia

Mexican American/Hispanic

Origins: Prison gang, formed in Soledad Prison in the late 1960s, as a reaction to the Mexican Mafia. Based in Northern California, foot soldiers outside of prison are called Norteños.

Allies: Black Guerrilla Family, Bloods, Crips

Rivals: Mexican Mafia, Mara Salvatrucha

Signs/Symbols: Large tattoos, often on the entire back. The initials NF, LNF, ENE, and F. The number 14 for "N," the fourteenth letter in the alphabet, stands for Norte or Norteño. The color red, Nebraska cornhuskers' caps with the letter N. A sombrero with a dagger is a common NF symbol.

Sources: "Gangs or Us," at **www.gangsorus.com/index.html**; and "Prison Gang Profiles," at **www.insideprison.com/prison_gang_profiles.asp**.

Combating Prison Gangs In their efforts to combat the influence of prison gangs, over the past decade correctional officials have increasingly turned to the **security threat group (STG)** model. Generally speaking, an STG is an identifiable group with three or more individuals and a leadership structure that poses a threat to the safety of other inmates or members of the corrections community. About two-thirds of all prisons have a correctional officer who acts as an STG coordinator.[51] This official is responsible for the classification of individuals who are likely to be involved in STG (though not necessarily prison gang) activity and for taking measures to protect the prison community from these individuals.

In many instances, these measures are punitive. Prison officials, for example, have reduced overall levels of violence significantly by putting gang members in solitary confinement, away from the general prison population. Other punitive measures include restrictions on privileges such as family visits and prison program participation, as well as delays of parole eligibility.[52] Treatment philosophies also have a place in these strategies. New York prison administrators have increased group therapy and anger-management classes for STGs, a decision they credit for low murder rates in their state prisons.[53]

CJ & Technology

AP Images/Associated Press/Mel Evans

Contraband Cell Phones

One piece of technology has made the task of controlling prison gangs extremely difficult: the cell phone. Although inmates are prohibited from possessing these devices, cell phones are routinely used to arrange attacks, plan escapes, and operate illegal money-making schemes from behind bars. The phones are usually smuggled in by visitors, who hide them in locations as varied as babies' diapers, food packages, soda cans, and body cavities. Each year, Florida corrections staff confiscate more than 4,000 cell phones from prisoners and, as one state official points out, "We know that's not all of them."

Several years ago, forty-four inmates and correctional officers at the Baltimore City Detention Center were arrested for helping to operate the Black Guerrilla Family gang from within the prison using cell phones. In response, the state of Maryland started a managed access program to deal with the problem. This "cellular umbrella" antenna technology is designed to analyze all calls made from the prison and instantly block any that originate from a contraband phone. During a test run at a California prison, over the course of eleven days a managed access system blocked 24,190 call attempts from 2,593 unauthorized devices.

Thinking about Contraband Cell Phones

How might correctional officials use confiscated contraband cell phones to combat criminal activity by inmates?

Correctional Officers and Discipline

Ideally, the presence of correctional officers—the standard term used to describe prison guards—has the effect of lessening violence in American correctional institutions. Practically speaking, this is indeed the case. Without correctional officers, the prison would be a place of anarchy. But in the highly regulated, oppressive environment of the prison, correctional officers must use the threat of violence, if not actual violence, to instill discipline and keep order. Thus, the relationship between prison staff and inmates is marked by mutual distrust. Consider the two following statements, the first made by a correctional officer and the second by a prisoner:

[My job is to] protect, feed, and try to educate scum who raped and brutalized women and children . . . who, if I turn my back, will go into their cell, wrap a blanket around their cell-mate's legs, and threaten to beat or rape him if he doesn't give sex, carry contraband, or fork over radios, money, or other goods willingly. And they'll stick a shank in me tomorrow if they think they can get away with it.[54]

The pigs in the state and federal prisons . . . treat me so violently, I cannot possibly imagine a time I could ever have anything but the deepest, aching, searing hatred for them. I can't begin to tell you what they do to me. If I were weaker by a hair, they would destroy me.[55]

It may be difficult for an outsider to understand the emotions that fuel such sentiments. French philosopher Michel Foucault points out that discipline, both in prison and in the general community, is a means of social organization as well as punishment.[56] Discipline is imposed when a person behaves in a manner that is contrary to the values of the dominant social group. Correctional officers and inmates have different concepts of the ideal structure of prison society, and, as the two quotations just cited demonstrate, this conflict generates intense feelings of fear and hatred, which often lead to violence.

Prison Employment

Explaining a situation in which a number of Texas correctional officers had been caught smuggling contraband cell phones into prison for inmates, one state official pointed out that state entry-level officers only make about $29,000 a year. Consequently, payment for one smuggled cell phone could earn them 10 percent of their annual salaries.[57] Despite the negative publicity that surrounds this type of misconduct, there are numerous benefits to a career as a correctional officer. Because the position is a civil service (government) job, it offers steady benefits and employment security. In some states, such as California and New York, salaries can reach $70,000. Furthermore, because of a professionalism movement in hiring, the standards of correctional officers have risen dramatically in the past few decades.[58]

Becoming a Correctional Officer Most prospective correctional officers are required to pass the civil service exam in their state of employment. Furthermore, as with police cadets (see Chapter 5), correctional officers usually go through a military-style training program prior to deployment in a prison. This program incorporates class-work and physical training, including instruction in areas such as self-defense, inmate control, and protection against communicable disease. Like police cadets, correctional officer trainees also go through a period of supervision with an experienced co-worker, in which they learn not only the job's specific techniques and procedures, but also about the prison environment and subculture.[59]

Correctional Officer Diversity In the not-too-distant past, prisons and jails drew their employees mainly from the communities in which they were located. Given that these rural areas were (and still are) mostly white and non-Hispanic, so were the vast majority of correctional officers.[60] (Women, as we will soon discuss, were also eliminated from most recruiting efforts.) Today, for many of the same reasons detailed in Chapter 5 regarding law enforcement officers, the field is considerably more diverse. According

▲ In high-security prisons, correctional officers such as these two at the supermax prison in Tamms, Illinois, monitor even the most mundane of inmate activities, including working, exercising, eating, and showering. **How might this constant surveillance contribute to tension between correctional officers and prisoners?** John Smierciak/*Chicago Tribune*/MCT/Landov

to the U.S. Bureau of Labor Statistics, about 24 percent of correctional officers are African American and 21 percent are Hispanic.[61]

Rank and Duties The custodial staff at most prisons is organized according to four general ranks—captain, lieutenant, sergeant, and officer. In keeping with the militaristic model, captains are primarily administrators who deal directly with the warden on custodial issues. Lieutenants are the disciplinarians of the prison, responsible for policing and transporting the inmates. Sergeants oversee platoons of officers in specific parts of the prison, such as various cell blocks or work spaces.

Lucien X. Lombardo, professor of sociology and criminal justice at Old Dominion University, has identified six general job categories among correctional officers:[62]

1. *Block officers.* These employees supervise cell blocks containing as many as four hundred inmates, as well as the correctional officers on block guard duty. In general, the block officer is responsible for the well-being of the inmates. He or she tries to ensure that the inmates do not harm themselves or other prisoners and also acts as something of a camp counselor, dispensing advice and seeing that inmates understand and follow the rules of the facility.

2. *Work detail supervisors.* In many penal institutions, the inmates work in the cafeteria, the prison store, the laundry, and other areas. Work detail supervisors oversee small groups of inmates as they perform their tasks.

3. *Industrial shop and school officers.* These officers perform maintenance and security functions in workshop and educational programs. Their primary responsibility is to make sure that inmates are on time for these programs and do not cause any disturbances during the sessions.

4. *Yard officers.* Officers who work the prison yard usually have the least seniority, befitting the assignment's reputation as dangerous and stressful. These officers must be constantly on alert for breaches in prison discipline or regulations in the relatively unstructured environment of the prison yard.

5. *Tower guards.* These officers spend their entire shifts, which usually last eight hours, in isolated, silent posts high above the grounds of the facility. Although their only means of communication are walkie-talkies or cellular devices, the safety benefits of the position can outweigh the loneliness that comes with the job.

6. *Administrative building assignments.* Officers who hold these positions provide security at prison gates, oversee visitation procedures, act as liaisons for civilians, and handle administrative tasks such as processing the paperwork when an inmate is transferred from another institution.

Discipline

Inmate discipline policies have three general goals:

1. To ensure a safe and orderly living environment,
2. To instill respect for authority of correctional officers and administrators, and

3. To teach values and respectful behavior that influence the inmate's attitude when she or he is released from prison.[63]

As Erving Goffman noted in his essay on the "total institution," in the general society adults are rarely placed in a position where they are "punished" as a child would be.[64] Therefore, the strict disciplinary measures imposed on prisoners come as something of a shock and can provoke strong defensive reactions. Correctional officers who must deal with these responses often find that disciplining inmates is the most difficult and stressful aspect of their job.

Sanctioning Prisoners As mentioned earlier, one of the first things that an inmate receives on entering a correctional facility is a manual that details the rules of the prison or jail, along with the punishment that will result from rule violations. These handbooks can be quite lengthy—running one hundred pages in some instances—and specific. Not only will a prison manual prohibit obvious misconduct such as violent or sexual activity, gambling, and possession of drugs or currency, but it also addresses matters of daily life such as personal hygiene, dress codes, and conduct during meals.

Correctional officers enforce the prison rules in much the same way that a highway patrol officer enforces traffic regulations. For a minor violation, the inmate may be "let off easy" with a verbal warning. More serious infractions will result in a "ticket," or a report forwarded to the institution's disciplinary committee.[65] The disciplinary committee generally includes several correctional officers and, in some instances, outside citizens or even inmates. Although, as we shall see, the United States Supreme Court has ruled that an inmate must be given a "fair hearing" before being disciplined, the Court denied inmates the ability to confront adverse witnesses or access to a lawyer during these hearings.[66] In practice, then, an inmate has very little ability to challenge the committee's decision. Depending on the seriousness of the violation, sanctions can range from a loss of privileges such as visits from family members to the unpleasantness of solitary confinement, discussed in the previous chapter.

Most correctional officers prefer to rely on the "you scratch my back and I'll scratch yours" model for controlling inmates. In other words, as long as the prisoner makes a reasonable effort to conform to institutional rules, the correctional officer will refrain from taking disciplinary steps. Of course, the staff-inmate relationship is not always marked by cooperation, and correctional officers often find themselves in situations where they must use force.

Use of Force Generally, courts have been unwilling to put too many restrictions on the use of force by correctional officers. As we saw with police officers in Chapter 6, correctional officers are given great leeway to use their experience to determine when force is warranted. In *Whitley v. Albers* (1986),[67] the Supreme Court held that the use of force by prison officials violates an inmate's Eighth Amendment protections only if the force amounts to "the unnecessary and wanton infliction of pain." Excessive force can be considered "necessary" if the legitimate security interests of the penal institution are at stake. Consequently, an appeals court ruled that when officers at a Maryland prison formed an "extraction team" to remove the leader of a riot from his cell, beating him in the process, the use of force was justified given the situation.[68]

Legitimate Security Interests Courts have found that the "legitimate security interests" of a prison or jail justify the use of force when the correctional officer is

1. Acting in self-defense.
2. Acting to defend the safety of a third person, such as a member of the prison staff or another inmate.
3. Upholding the rules of the institution.
4. Preventing a crime such as assault, destruction of property, or theft.
5. Preventing an escape effort.[69]

In addition, most prisons and jails have written policies that spell out the situations in which their employees may use force against inmates. (The feature *Discretion in Action— Spitting Mad* gives an example of a use-of-force situation involving correctional officers in which the response, though nonlethal, is bound to come under scrutiny.)

The "Malicious and Sadistic" Standard The judicial system has not, however, given correctional officers total freedom of discretion to apply force. In *Hudson v. McMillan* (1992),[70] the Supreme Court ruled that minor injuries suffered by a convict at the hands of a correctional officer following an argument did violate the inmate's rights, because there was no security concern at the time of the incident. In other words, the issue is not *how much* force was used, but whether the officer used the force as part of a good faith effort to restore discipline or acted "maliciously and sadistically" to cause harm. This "malicious and sadistic" standard has been difficult for aggrieved prisoners to meet: in the ten years following the *Hudson* decision, only about 20 percent of excessive force lawsuits against correctional officials were successful.[71]

Mental Illness and Prison Discipline Mentally ill inmates, who, as already noted, make up a significant percentage of this country's inmate population, present particular challenges when it comes to prison discipline. These inmates often respond erratically or defiantly to the punitive nature of life behind bars, and may at times have trouble

Discretion in Action

Spitting Mad

The Situation During a fit of depression caused by the breakup of his marriage, a state prison inmate named Schmidt purposefully tears at a previous wound in his arm. Correctional officers, following the orders of Deputy Warden Wasserman, strap Schmidt into a chair that restricts the inmate's ability to move. As he is being restrained, Schmidt becomes agitated and curses the correctional officers. Then, he spits at a nurse trying to treat his injuries. Wasserman reacts by discharging a can of pepper spray at Schmidt. (When aimed at the face, pepper spray is a nonlethal weapon that causes

a sensation similar to having sand or needles in the eyes.) Wasserman then places a spit mask on Schmidt, which traps the chemicals against the offender's skin. Schmidt is not allowed to clean his eyes and nose for nearly half an hour but suffers no lasting physical harm as a result of the pepper spray.

The Law In most cases, correctional officers are justified in using force against inmates so long as that force does not cause "unnecessary and wanton" pain. (*Wanton* means "deliberate and unprovoked.")

What Would You Do? Suppose you are the warden at the prison where this incident took place. Would you discipline Deputy Warden Wasserman for his use of force against Schmidt? Do you think that the steps Wasserman took to restrain Schmidt were justified? What about the use of pepper spray? Keep in mind that a spitting inmate may pose a danger to correctional officers if the inmate has a communicable disease.

[To see how state prison officials in Maine handled a similar situation, go to Example 14.1 in Appendix B.]

understanding orders given by correctional officers. This, in turn, leads to disciplinary measures, including use of force. A study by New York health officials found that, in one eleven-month period, seventy-seven of the 129 Rikers Island jail inmates who suffered serious injuries at the hands of correctional guards had received a mental illness diagnosis.[72]

In 2014, California's Department of Corrections introduced guidelines for the use of force against mentally ill inmates, which make up nearly 30 percent of the state's inmate population. This new policy requires a mental health practitioner to conduct an evaluation of the inmate's ability to understand and comply with correctional officers' orders before force can be used against the inmate. Furthermore, a high-level prison official must approve the deployment of pepper spray on mentally ill offenders, and such inmates cannot be forcibly extracted from their cells to receive medical treatment.[73]

Female Correctional Officers

Security concerns were the main reason that, for many years, prison administrators refused to hire women as correctional officers in men's prisons. The consensus was that women were not physically strong enough to subdue violent male inmates and that their mere presence in the predominantly masculine prison world would cause disciplinary breakdowns.[74] As a result, in the 1970s a number of women brought lawsuits against state corrections systems, claiming that they were being discriminated against on the basis of their gender. For the most part, these legal actions were successful in opening the doors to men's prisons for female correctional officers (and vice versa).[75] Today, more than 150,000 women work in correctional facilities, many of them in constant close contact with male inmates.[76]

As it turns out, female correctional officers have proved just as effective as their male counterparts in maintaining discipline in men's prisons. Furthermore, evidence shows that women prison staff can have a calming influence on male inmates, thus lowering levels of prison violence.[77] The primary problem caused by women working in male prisons, it seems, involves sexual misconduct. According to the federal government, nearly 55 percent of prison staff members who engage in sexual misconduct are female, with a disturbing 84 percent of those sexual encounters considered consensual.[78] As we will see in the next section, similar issues exist between male correctional officers and female inmates, though in those cases the sexual contact is much more likely to be coerced.

Protecting Prisoners' Rights

The general attitude of the law toward inmates is summed up by the Thirteenth Amendment to the U.S. Constitution:

> Neither slavery nor involuntary servitude, except as a punishment for crime whereof the party shall have been duly convicted, shall exist within the United States.

In other words, inmates do not have the same guaranteed rights as other Americans. For most of

▼ About a quarter of the security staff at Sing Sing Correctional Facility in Ossining, New York—shown here—are women. **What are some of the challenges that face female correctional officers who work in a men's maximum-security prison?** Susan Farley/*New York Times*/Redux

the nation's history, courts have followed the spirit of this amendment by applying the **"hands-off" doctrine** of prisoner law. This (unwritten) doctrine assumes that the care of inmates should be left to prison officials and that it is not the place of judges to intervene in penal administrative matters.

At the same time, the United States Supreme Court has stated that "[t]here is no iron curtain between the Constitution and the prisons of this country."[79] Consequently, like so many other areas of the criminal justice system, the treatment of prisoners is based on a balancing act—here, between the rights of prisoners and the security needs of the correctional institutions. Of course, as just noted, inmates do not have the same civil rights as do other members of society. In 1984, for example, the Supreme Court ruled that arbitrary searches of prison cells are allowed under the Fourth Amendment because inmates have no reasonable expectation of privacy[80] (see Chapter 7 for a review of this expectation).

The "Deliberate Indifference" Standard As for those constitutional rights that inmates do retain, in 1976 the Supreme Court established the **"deliberate indifference"** standard. In the case in question, *Estelle v. Gamble,*[81] an inmate had claimed to be the victim of medical malpractice. In his majority opinion, Justice Thurgood Marshall wrote that prison officials violated a convict's Eighth Amendment rights if they "deliberately" failed to provide him or her with necessary medical care. At the time, the decision was hailed as a victory for prisoners' rights, and it continues to ensure that a certain level of health care is provided. Several years ago, for example, a U.S. district court ruled that prison officials at the Louisiana State Penitentiary, site of the prison rodeo discussed at the beginning of the chapter, were "deliberately indifferent" in allowing the heat in that facility's death row to reach levels causing "cruel and unusual" punishment.[82]

In general, however, courts have found it difficult to define "deliberate" in this context. Does it mean that prison officials "should have known" that an inmate was placed in harm's way, or does it mean that officials purposefully placed the inmate in that position?

The Supreme Court seems to have taken the latter position. In *Wilson v. Seiter* (1991),[83] for example, inmate Pearly L. Wilson filed a lawsuit alleging that certain conditions of his confinement—including overcrowding; excessive noise; inadequate heating, cooling, and ventilation; and unsanitary bathroom and dining facilities—were cruel and unusual. The Court ruled against Wilson, stating that he had failed to prove that these conditions, even if they existed, were the result of "deliberate indifference" on the part of prison officials.

"Identifiable Human Needs" In its *Wilson* decision, the Supreme Court created the **"identifiable human needs"** standard for determining Eighth Amendment violations. The Court asserted that a prisoner must show that the institution has denied her or him a basic need such as food, warmth, or exercise.[84] The Court mentioned only these three needs, however, forcing the lower courts to determine for themselves what other needs, if any, fall into this category.

Because of the Supreme Court's *Estelle* decision described above, prisoners do have a well-established right to "adequate" medical care. "Adequate" has been interpreted to mean a level of care comparable to what the inmate would receive if he or she were not behind bars.[85] This concept has not always proved popular with the general public. In 2012, a federal judge in Boston commanded Massachusetts to cover the costs of gender reassignment surgery for a male inmate who had murdered his wife twelve years earlier. After numerous complaints from taxpayers, the judge rescinded his order. Furthermore, as noted earlier in the chapter, several years ago the Supreme

Describe the hands-off doctrine of prisoner law and indicate two standards used to determine if prisoners' rights have been violated.

LEARNING **5** OBJECTIVE

"Hands-Off" Doctrine The unwritten judicial policy that favors noninterference by the courts in the administration of prisons and jails.

"Deliberate Indifference" The standard for establishing a violation of an inmate's Eighth Amendment rights, requiring that prison officials were aware of harmful conditions in a correctional institution *and* failed to take steps to remedy those conditions.

"Identifiable Human Needs" The basic human necessities that correctional facilities are required by the Constitution to provide to inmates.

Court asserted, controversially, that the overcrowding of California's state prisons was so severe that it denied inmates satisfactory levels of health care.[86]

The First Amendment in Prison The First Amendment reads, in part, that the federal government "shall make no law respecting an establishment of religion, or prohibiting the free exercise thereof; or abridging the freedom of speech." In the 1970s, the prisoners' rights movement forced open the "iron curtain" to allow the First Amendment behind bars. In 1974, for example, the Supreme Court held that prison officials can censor inmate mail only if doing so is necessary to maintain prison security.[87] The decade also saw court decisions protecting inmates' access to group worship, instruction by clergy, special dietary requirements, religious publications, and other aspects of both mainstream and nonmainstream religions.[88]

Judges will limit some of these protections when an obvious security interest is at stake. In 2010, for example, a Pennsylvania prison was allowed to continue banning religious headscarves because of legitimate concerns that the scarves could be used to conceal drugs or strangle someone.[89] Such was not the case in 2013, however, when a California appeals court ruled that a supermax inmate had a First Amendment right to read a paperback novel that depicted sex between werewolves and humans. A warden had banned the novel, *The Silver Crown*, as obscene and tending to incite violence.[90] (This chapter's *CJ Policy—Your Take* examines the First Amendment issues raised by religion and inmate facial hair.)

Inside a Women's Prison

When the first women's prison in the United States opened in 1839 on the grounds of New York's Sing Sing institution, the focus was on rehabilitation. Prisoners were prepared for a return to society with classes on reading, knitting, and sewing. Early women's reformatories had few locks or bars, and several included nurseries for the inmates' young children. Today, the situation is dramatically different. "Women's institutions are literally men's institutions, only we pull out the urinals," remarks Meda Chesney-Lind, a criminologist at the University of Hawaii.[91] Following a recently concluded, decade-long study of conditions in women's prisons, researchers at the University of Cincinnati identified six specific concerns relating to female inmates:

1. They often suffer from lack of *self-efficacy,* meaning that they do not feel able to meet personal goals, and believe that they are not in control of their own lives.
2. Their criminal behavior is linked to *parental stress*—specifically, the financial strain of raising children and the possibility of losing custody of children due to antisocial behavior such as crime and substance abuse.
3. They are more likely than male offenders to suffer from *mental health problems* such as depression, anxiety, and self-injurious behaviors.
4. They are more likely than male offenders to have been *victims of physical and sexual abuse* as children and adults.
5. Before arrest, they were involved in *unhealthy relationships* with family members, spouses, or romantic partners that contributed to their criminal behavior.
6. Their lives are marked by *poverty and homelessness,* often brought on by substance abuse, child care responsibilities, and lack of educational and work skills.[92]

These concerns—when combined with the fact that most female inmates are nonviolent offenders—suggest that women's prisons require a different management style than men's prisons.

FIGURE 14.4 Female Prisoners in the United States by Race, Ethnicity, and Age

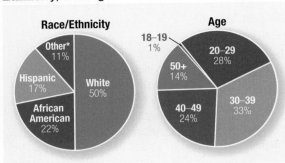

*Includes American Indians, Alaska Natives, Native Hawaiians, other Pacific Islanders, and persons identifying two or more races.

Source: Bureau of Justice Statistics, *Prisoners in 2013* (Washington, D.C.: U.S. Department of Justice, September 2014), Table 7, page 8.

Characteristics of Female Inmates

Male inmates outnumber female inmates by approximately nine to one, and there are only about a hundred women's correctional facilities in the United States. Consequently, most research concerning the American corrections system focuses on male inmates and men's prisons. Enough data exist, however, to provide a useful portrait of women behind bars. Female inmates are typically low income and undereducated, and have a history of unemployment. Female offenders are much less likely than male offenders to have committed a violent offense. Most are incarcerated for a nonviolent drug or property crime.[93] As Figure 14.4 shows, the demographics of female prisoners are similar to those of their male counterparts. That is, the majority of female inmates are under the age of forty, and the population is disproportionately African American.

A History of Abuse The single factor that most distinguishes female prisoners from their male counterparts is a history of physical or sexual abuse. A self-reported study conducted by the federal government indicates that 55 percent of female jail inmates have been abused at some point in their lives, compared with only 13 percent of male jail inmates.[94] Fifty-seven percent of women in state prisons and 40 percent of women in federal prisons report some form of past abuse—both figures are significantly higher than those for male prisoners.[95] Health experts believe that these levels of abuse are related to the significant amount of drug and/or alcohol addiction that plagues the female prison population, as well as to the mental illness problems that such addictions can cause or exacerbate.[96]

Other Health Problems In fact, about 25 percent of women in state prisons have been diagnosed with mental disorders such as post-traumatic stress disorder (PTSD), depression, and substance abuse. PTSD, in particular, is found in women who have experienced sexual or physical abuse.[97] Furthermore, more women than men enter prisons and jails with health problems due to higher instances of poverty, inadequate health care, and substance abuse.[98] Not only do women prisoners have high rates of breast and cervical cancer, but they are also 50 percent more likely than men to be HIV positive and are at significantly greater risk for lung cancer.[99] All these data suggest that administrators at women's prisons should focus less on security than their counterparts at male correctional institutions, and more on treatment and rehabilitation.[100]

The Motherhood Problem

Drug and alcohol use within a women's prison can be a function of the anger and depression many inmates experience due to being separated from their children. An estimated seven out of every ten female prisoners have at least one minor child. About 1.7 million American children have a mother who is under correctional supervision.[101] Given the scarcity of women's correctional facilities, inmates are often housed at great distances from their children. One study found that almost two-thirds of women in federal prison are more than five hundred miles from their homes.[102]

Further research indicates that an inmate who serves her sentence more than fifty miles from her residence is much less likely to receive phone calls or personal visits from family members. For most inmates and their families, the costs of "staying in touch" are too high.[103] This kind of separation can have serious consequences for the children of inmates. When a father goes to prison, his children are likely to live with their mother.

LEARNING OBJECTIVE 6 Explain the aspects of imprisonment that prove challenging for incarcerated mothers and their children.

When a mother is incarcerated, however, her children are likely to live with other relatives or, in about 11 percent of the cases, be sent to foster care.[104] Only nine states provide facilities where inmates and their infant children can live together, and even in these facilities nursery privileges generally end once the child is eighteen months old.

The Culture of Women's Prisons

After spending five years visiting female inmates in the Massachusetts Correctional Institution (MCI) at Framingham, journalist Cristina Rathbone observed that the medium-security facility seemed "more like a high school than a prison."[105] The prisoners were older and tougher than high school girls, but they still divided into cliques, with the "lifers" at the top of the hierarchy and "untouchables" such as child abusers at the bottom. Unlike in men's prisons, where the underground economy revolves around drugs and weapons, at MCI-Framingham the most treasured contraband items are clothing, food, and makeup.[106]

The Pseudo-Family Although both men's and women's prisons are organized with the same goals of control and discipline, the cultures within the two institutions are generally very different. As we have seen, male prison society operates primarily on the basis of power. Deprived of the benefits of freedom, male prisoners tend to create a violent environment that bears little relation to life on the outside.[107] In contrast, researchers have found that women prisoners prefer to re-create their outside identities by forming social networks that resemble, as noted earlier, high school cliques or, more commonly, the traditional family structure.[108] In these pseudo-families, inmates often play specific roles, with the more experienced convicts acting as "mothers" to younger, inexperienced "daughters." As one observer noted, the younger women rely on their "moms" for emotional support, companionship, loans, and even discipline.[109]

Such a family unit may have a "married" couple at its head, sometimes with a lesbian assuming the role of the father figure. Indeed, homosexuality in women's prisons often manifests itself through the formation of another traditional family model: the monogamous couple.[110] For the most part, sex between inmates plays a different role in women's prisons than in men's prisons. In the latter, rape is an act of aggression and power rather than sex, and "true" homosexuals are relegated to the lowest rungs of the social hierarchy. By contrast, women inmates who engage in sexual activity are not automatically labeled homosexual, and lesbians are not hampered in their social-climbing efforts.[111]

▼ Female inmates at the Women's Eastern Reception, Diagnostic and Correctional Center in Vandalia, Missouri, visit with their daughters and granddaughters. **Why is it difficult for many mothers behind bars to see their children?** AP Images/Whitney Curtis

Sexual Violence and Prison Staff

Compared with men's prisons, women's prisons have extremely low levels of race-based, gang-related physical aggression.[112] Furthermore, though rates of sexual victimization can be high, most such episodes involve abusive sexual contacts such as unwanted touching rather than sexual assault or rape.[113] One form of serious prison violence that does plague women prisoners, however, is sexual misconduct by prison staff. Although no large-scale study on sexual abuse of female inmates by male correctional officers exists, a number of state-level studies suggest that it is widespread.[114] Dr. Kerry Kupers, who has studied the effects of prison sexual assault, believes that it contributes to the PTSD, depression, anxiety, and other mental illnesses suffered by so many women prisoners.[115]

EthicsChallenge

A number of states place pregnant inmates in handcuffs or other forms of restraint as part of the procedure for childbirths that take place while the inmates are incarcerated. What might be some of the reasons for this practice? Do you feel it is an ethical way to treat these women during and after labor? Why or why not? ■

Return to Society

On June 16, 2014, police arrested Gary Moran for killing a priest with a handgun in the courtyard of the Mother of Mercy Mission in Phoenix, Arizona. Moran, homeless, had been released from prison only six weeks earlier after serving eight years for aggravated assault with a deadly weapon. In contrast, on his release from California's San Quentin State Prison in 2013, multiple drug offender Eddie Griffin earned an internship with a software firm in San Francisco. After a year of working with him, Griffin's boss praised the ex-inmate's "great work ethic, strong progress, and positive attitude."[116]

Each year, about 630,000 inmates are released from American prisons. The challenge for ex-inmates is to ensure that their post-release experience mirrors that of Eddie Griffin rather than that of Gary Moran. More so than in the past, however, ex-convicts are not facing this challenge alone. Given the benefits to society of reducing recidivism, corrections officials and community leaders are making unprecedented efforts to help newly released prisoners establish crime-free lives.

Types of Prison Release

The majority of all inmates leaving prison—about two-thirds—do so through one of the parole mechanisms discussed in Chapter 12. Of the remaining third, most are given an **expiration release**.[117] Also known as "maxing out," expiration release occurs when an inmate has served the maximum amount of time on the initial sentence, minus reductions for good-time credits, and is not subjected to community supervision. Another, quite rare unconditional release is a **pardon**, a form of executive clemency. The president (on the federal level) and the governor (on the state level) can grant a pardon, or forgive a convict's criminal punishment. Most states have a board of pardons—affiliated with the parole board—that makes recommendations to the governor in cases in which it believes a pardon is warranted. The majority of pardons involve obvious miscarriages of justice, though sometimes a governor will pardon an individual to remove the stain of conviction from her or his criminal record.

Certain temporary releases also exist. Some inmates, who qualify by exhibiting good behavior and generally proving that they do not represent a risk to society, are allowed to leave the prison on **furlough** for a certain amount of time, usually between a day and a week. At times, a furlough is granted because of a family emergency, such as a funeral. Furloughs can be particularly helpful for an inmate who is nearing release and can use them to ease the readjustment period. Finally, *probation release* occurs following a short period of incarceration at the back end of shock probation, which we discussed in Chapter 12. Generally, however, as you have seen, probationers experience community supervision in place of a prison term.

Contrast parole, expiration release, pardon, and furlough.

LEARNING OBJECTIVE 7

Expiration Release The release of an inmate from prison at the end of his or her sentence without any further correctional supervision.

Pardon An act of executive clemency that overturns a conviction and erases mention of the crime from the person's criminal record.

Furlough Temporary release from a prison for purposes of vocational or educational training, to ease the shock of release, or for personal reasons.

The Challenges of Reentry

What steps can corrections officials take to lessen the possibility that ex-convicts will reoffend following their release? Efforts to answer that question have focused on programs that help inmates make the transition from prison to the outside. In past years, these programs would have come under the general heading of "rehabilitation," but today corrections officials and criminologists refer to them as part of the strategy of **prisoner reentry.** The concept of reentry has come to mean many things to many people. For our purposes, keep in mind the words of Joan Petersilia of the University of California at Irvine, who defines *reentry* as encompassing "all activities and programming conducted to prepare ex-convicts to return safely to the community and to live as law abiding citizens."[118] In other words, whereas rehab is focused on the individual offender, *reentry* encompasses the released convict's relationship with society.

Barriers to Reentry Perhaps the largest obstacle to successful prisoner reentry is the simple truth that life behind bars is very different from life on the outside. As one inmate explains, the "rules" of prison survival are hardly compatible with good citizenship:

> An unexpected smile could mean trouble. A man in uniform was not a friend. Being kind was a weakness. Viciousness and recklessness were to be respected and admired.[119]

The prison environment also insulates inmates. They are not required to make the day-to-day decisions that characterize a normal existence beyond prison bars. Depending on the length of incarceration, a released inmate must adjust to an array of economic, technological, and social changes that took place while she or he was behind bars. Common acts such as using an ATM or a smartphone may be completely alien to someone who has just completed a long prison term.

Challenges of Release Other obstacles hamper reentry efforts. Housing can be difficult to secure, as many private property owners refuse to rent to someone with a criminal record, and federal and state laws restrict public housing options for ex-convicts. A criminal past also limits the ability to find employment, as does the lack of job skills of someone who has spent a significant portion of his or her life in prison. Research conducted by the Urban Institute found that only about 45 percent of ex-inmates are able to secure employment eight months after being released.[120] Furthermore, these released offenders generally have no means of transporation and no place to live.

These economic barriers can be complicated by the physical and mental condition of the freed convict. We have already discussed the high incidence of substance abuse among prisoners and the health-care needs of aging inmates. In addition, one study concluded that as many as one in five Americans leaving jail or prison is seriously mentally ill.[121] (See Figure 14.5 for a list of the hardships commonly faced by former inmates in their first year out of prison.)

The Threat of Relapse All of these problems conspire to make successful reentry difficult to achieve. Perhaps it is not surprising that research conducted by the Pew Center on the States found that 43 percent of ex-prisoners are back in prison or jail within three years of their release dates.[122] These figures highlight the problem of recidivism among those released from incarceration.

Even given the barriers to reentry we have discussed, these rates of recidivism seem improbably high. Regardless of their ability to find a job or housing, many ex-convicts

Prisoner Reentry A corrections strategy designed to prepare inmates for a successful return to the community and to reduce their criminal activity after release.

FIGURE 14.5 Prisoner Reentry Issues

Researchers from the Urban Institute in Washington, D.C., asked nearly three hundred former prisoners (all male) in the Cleveland, Ohio, area about the most pressing issues they faced in their first year after release. The answers provide a useful snapshot of the many challenges of reentry.

1. *Housing.* Nearly two-thirds of the men were living with family members, and about half considered their housing situation "temporary." Many were concerned about their living environment: half said that drug dealing was a major problem in their neighborhoods, and almost 25 percent were living with drug and alcohol abusers.

2. *Employment.* After one year, only about one-third of the former inmates had a full-time job, and another 11 percent were working part-time.

3. *Family and friends.* One in four of the men identified family support as the most important thing keeping them from returning to criminality. Another 16 percent said that avoiding certain people and situations was the most crucial factor in their continued good behavior.

4. *Programs and services.* About two-thirds of the former inmates had taken part in programs and services such as drug treatment and continuing education.

5. *Health.* More than half of the men reported suffering from a chronic health condition, and 29 percent showed symptoms of depression.

6. *Substance use.* About half of the men admitted to weekly drug use or alcohol intoxication. Men who had strong family ties and those who were required to maintain telephone contact with their parole officers were less likely to engage in frequent substance use.

7. *Parole violation and recidivism.* More than half of the former inmates reported that they had violated the conditions of their parole, usually by drug use or having contact with other parolees. Fifteen percent of the men returned to prison in the year after release. Four out of five of the returns were the result of a new crime.

Source: Christy A. Visher and Shannon M. E. Courtney, *One Year Out: Experience of Prisoners Returning to Cleveland* (Washington, D.C.: Urban Institute, April 2007), 2.

are fated to run afoul of the criminal justice system. Psychologists Edward Zamble and Vernon Quinsey explain the phenomenon as a *relapse process.*[123] Take the hypothetical example of an ex-convict who gets in a minor automobile accident while driving from his home to his job one morning. The person in the other car gets out and starts yelling at the ex-convict, who "relapses" and reacts just as he would have in prison—by punching the other person in the face. The ex-convict is then convicted of assault and battery and given a harsh prison sentence because of his criminal record.

Promoting Desistance One ex-inmate compared the experience of being released to entering a "dark room, knowing that there are steps in front of you and waiting to fall."[124] The goal of reentry is to act as a flashlight for convicts by promoting **desistance**, a general term used to describe the continued abstinence from offending and the reintroduction of offenders into society. Certainly, the most important factor in the process is the individual convict. She or he has to *want* to desist and take steps to do so. In most cases, however, ex-inmates are going to need help—help getting an education, help finding and keeping a job, and help freeing themselves from harmful addictions to drugs and alcohol. Corrections officials are in a good position to offer this assistance, and their efforts in doing so form the backbone of the reentry movement.

Reentry planning starts behind bars. In addition to the rehabilitation-oriented prison programs discussed earlier in the chapter, most correctional facilities offer "life skills" classes to inmates. This counseling covers topics such as finding and keeping a job, locating a residence, understanding family responsibilities, and budgeting. After release, however, former inmates often find it difficult to continue with educational programs and counseling as they struggle to readjust to life outside prison. Consequently, parole supervising agencies operate a number of programs to facilitate offenders' desistance efforts while, at the same time, protecting the community to the greatest extent possible.

Community-Based Reentry Programs As is made clear in Figure 14.5, work and lodging are crucial components of desistance. Corrections officials have several options in helping certain parolees—usually low-risk offenders—find employment and a place to live during the supervision period. Nearly a third of correctional facilities

LEARNING

8

OBJECTIVE

Explain the goal of prisoner reentry programs.

Desistance The process through which criminal activity decreases and reintegration into society increases over a period of time.

offer **work release programs,** in which prisoners nearing the end of their sentences are given permission to work at paid employment in the community.[125]

Inmates on work release either return to the correctional facility in the evening or, under certain circumstances, live in community residential facilities known as **halfway houses.** These facilities, also available to other parolees and those who have finished their sentences, are often remodeled hotels or private homes. They provide a less institutionalized living environment than a prison or jail for a small number of offenders (usually between ten and twenty-five). Halfway houses can be tailored to the needs of the former inmate. Many communities, for example, offer substance-free transitional housing for those whose past criminal behavior was linked to drug or alcohol abuse.

▲ Homeboy Industries, which operates this bakery in downtown Los Angeles, provides former gang members and recently released ex-convicts with job training opportunities and other reentry programs. **Why is finding employment such an important part of the desistance process?** AP Images/Damian Dovarganes

What Works in Reentry Recently, a study by the Pennsylvania Corrections Department established that about 67 percent of inmates sent to private halfway houses in the state were rearrested within three years.[126] Noting that this percentage was higher than the recidivism rate of those inmates released without supervision, one state official said, "The focus has been on filling up beds [rather than] producing results."[127] In general, reentry planning "produces results" when it focuses on reducing substance abuse and promoting employment. To that end, a number of jurisdictions have established *reentry courts,* in which a judge ensures that the inmate has been following her or his reentry requirements.

As noted earlier in the chapter, the reluctance of employers to consider hiring an ex-convict is a severe hurdle for many released inmates. Two policies have emerged to remedy this situation:

1. Expungement laws, which allow low-level criminals to remove offenses from their criminal records so that these crimes will not be uncovered by employer background checks.
2. "Ban the box" laws, which prohibit public employers from inquiring into the criminal backgrounds of potential employees by having a "criminal history box" on their application forms.[128]

Even though companies such as Walmart, Target, and Home Depot have adopted their own "ban the box" policies, the practice is not universally applauded in the private sector. "Does everybody deserve a second chance? Of course," says a spokesman for the National Federation of Independent Businesses. "But it's up to me as the guy taking the risk to decide that this person is worth taking the risk. The fact that they have a criminal record proves that at one point in their lives they weren't trustworthy."[129]

The Special Case of Sex Offenders

Despite the beneficial impact of reentry efforts, one group of wrongdoers has consistently been denied access to such programs: those convicted of sex crimes. The eventual

Work Release Program
Temporary release of convicts from prison for purposes of employment. The offenders may spend their days on the job, but must return to the correctional facility at night and during the weekend.

Halfway House A community-based form of early release that places inmates in residential centers and allows them to reintegrate with society.

Careers in CJ

Courtesy Julie Howe

Julie Howe
Halfway House Program Manager

Early on in my career, I felt a bit intimidated by the clients simply because of my discomfort, not by their behavior. I started out very stern and learned later that it was better to start strong and to lighten up later rather than the reverse. The clients respect you more and know to take you seriously. My first client as a case manager was a real eye-opener. He was in his fifties, and I was in my early twenties. Earning his trust was quite a challenge. In the end, he learned to respect me, and I learned different techniques when working with offenders.

My favorite part of my job is that I know that I have an impact on people's lives. If I can assist someone to become sober, responsible, employed, and self-sufficient, I am also having an impact on the community and those whom my clients' lives touch. I never get tired of hearing clients say thanks and knowing their lives are forever changed when they realize their potential and value. I also love that I have the opportunity to influence the behavior of others and shape their future. What an awesome responsibility!

SOCIAL MEDIA CAREER TIP Don't misrepresent facts or tell lies of omission online. Doing so in front of millions of online viewers virtually ensures you will be caught, and such untruths can fatally damage career possibilities.

---

return of these offenders to society causes such high levels of community anxiety that the criminal justice system has not yet figured out what to do with them.

Fear of Sex Offenders When sixty-three-year-old Christopher Hubbart, called the "Pillowcase Rapist" because he used that item to muffle the screams of his nearly forty victims, was released in Antelope Valley, California, in 2014, community members were outraged. "It scares the hell out of me," said one resident. "He's going to attack somebody again, and he's going to take someone's life."[130] To a large degree, this attitude reflects the widespread belief that convicted sex offenders cannot be "cured" of their criminality and therefore are destined to continue committing sex offenses after their release from prison.

It is true that the medical health profession has had little success in treating the "urges" that lead to sexually deviant or criminal behavior.[131] This has not, however, translated into rampant recidivism among sex offenders when compared to other types of criminals. According to the U.S. Department of Justice, the rearrest rates of rapists (46 percent) and those convicted of other forms of sexual assault (41 percent) are among the lowest for all offenders.[132] Furthermore, after analyzing eighty-two recidivism studies, Canadian researchers R. Karl Hanson and Kelly Morton-Bourgon found that only 14 percent of sex offenders were apprehended for another sex crime after release from prison or jail. On average, such offenders were significantly more likely to be rearrested for nonsexual criminal activity, if they were rearrested at all.[133]

Conditions of Release Whatever their recidivism rates, sex offenders are subject to extensive community supervision after being released from prison. Generally, they are supervised by parole officers and live under the same threat of revocation as other parolees. Specifically, many sex offenders—particularly child molesters—have the following special conditions of release:

LEARNING OBJECTIVE **9** Indicate typical conditions for release for a paroled child molester.

- No contact with children under the age of eighteen.
- Psychiatric treatment.
- Must stay a certain distance from schools or parks where children are present.
- Cannot own toys that may be used to lure children.
- Cannot have a job or participate in any activity that involves children.

As you will see in the *CJ in Action* feature at the end of this chapter, more than half of the states and hundreds of municipalities have passed *residency restrictions* for convicted sex offenders. These laws ban sex offenders from living within a certain distance of places where children naturally congregate.

Sex Offender Notification Laws Perhaps the most dramatic step taken by criminal justice authorities to protect the public from sex crimes involves *sex offender registries,* or databases that contain sex offenders' names, addresses, photographs, and other information. The movement to register sex offenders started about two decades ago, after seven-year-old Megan Kanka of Hamilton Township, New Jersey, was raped and murdered by a twice-convicted pedophile (an adult sexually attracted to children) who had moved into her neighborhood after being released from prison on parole. The next year, in response to public outrage, the state passed a series of laws known collectively as the New Jersey Sexual Offender Registration Act, or "Megan's Law."[134] Today, all fifty states and the federal government have their own version of Megan's Law, or a **sex offender notification law,** which requires local law authorities to alert the public when a sex offender has been released into the community.

Active and Passive Notification No two sex offender notification laws have exactly the same provisions, but all are designed with the goal of allowing the public to learn the identities of convicted sex offenders living in their midst. In general, the laws demand that a paroled sex offender notify local law enforcement authorities on taking up residence in a state. In Georgia, for example, paroled sex offenders are required to present themselves to both the local sheriff and the superintendent of the public school district where they plan to live.[135] This registration process must be renewed every time the parolee changes address.

The authorities, in turn, notify the community of the sex offender's presence through the use of one of two models. Under the "active" model, the authorities directly notify the community or community representatives. Traditionally, this notification has taken the form of bulletins or posters, distributed and posted within a certain distance from the offender's home. Now, however, a number of states use e-mail alerts to fulfill notification obligations. In the "passive" model, information on sex offenders is made open and available for public scrutiny.

Prevalence of Sex Offender Registries In 2006, Congress passed the Adam Walsh Child Protection and Safety Act, which established a national registry of sex offenders.[136] In addition, all fifty states operate sex offender registries with data on registered sex offenders in their jurisdictions. (For an idea of how this process works, you can visit the Federal Bureau of Investigation's Sex Offender Registry Web site.) The total number of registered sex offenders in the United States is about 800,000. These registries are quite

Sex Offender Notification Law Legislation that requires law enforcement authorities to notify people when convicted sex offenders are released into their neighborhood or community.

popular with the public and even appear to affect property values. Homes in the proximity of a registered sex offender lose about $5,500 in value.[137]

▲ Residents of Phelan, California, protest the opening of a proposed group home for sex offenders in their neighborhood. **What are some of the reasons that community members fear the nearby presence of freed sex offenders? Are these fears justified? Why or why not?** AP Images/Francis Specker

Civil Confinement To many, any type of freedom, even if encumbered by notification requirements, is too much freedom for a sex offender. "The issue is, what can you do short of putting them all in prison for the rest of their lives?" complained one policymaker.[138]

In fact, a number of states have devised a legal method to keep sex offenders off the streets for, if not their entire lives, then close to it. These **civil confinement** laws allow corrections officials to keep sex offenders locked up in noncorrectional facilities such as psychiatric hospitals after the conclusion of their prison terms. Under these laws, which we first encountered in Chapter 12 in connection with the mentally ill, corrections officials can keep sexual criminals confined indefinitely, as long as they are deemed a danger to society. In practice, civil confinement laws essentially give the state the power to detain this class of criminal indefinitely—a power upheld by the United States Supreme Court in 2010.[139]

EthicsChallenge

What role do you think ethics training should play in the reentry process? How would you design a class that strives to improve the ethical decision-making skills of inmates? ■

A Second Look at Residency Laws

Unlike most released convicts, Kenneth Rozier sometimes wishes he were still incarcerated. "When I was in prison, I had somewhere to sleep, a roof, food," says Rozier, who had been living in a parking lot near some train tracks in Miami-Dade County, Florida. "Out here, I don't have any of that. I have to pee in a cup at night."[140] In the spring of 2014, Rozier, who forced a fifteen-year-old girl to have sex with him when he was twenty-one, and nearly sixty other sex offenders called the parking lot "home." This situation arose because of the county's residency law, an increasingly common and popular method for protecting children that, as we will discuss in this *CJ in Action* feature, may have unexpected consequences.

Zoning Restrictions for Sex Offenders

More than half of the states and hundreds of municipalities have passed residency restrictions for convicted sex offenders. These laws ban sex offenders from living within a certain distance from places where children naturally congregate. In New Jersey, for example, "high-risk" offenders cannot take up residence within 3,000 feet of any school, park or campground, church, theater, bowling alley, library, or convenience store.[141] (For medium- and low-risk offenders, the distances are 2,500 feet and 1,000 feet, respectively.) The overlapping "off-limits zones" created by residency requirements can dramatically limit where a sex offender can find affordable housing, as was the case with Kenneth Rozier and the other sex offenders living in the Miami-Dade County parking lot.

The Case for Sex Offender Residency Restrictions

- Forbidding sex offenders from residing near schools and other areas that attract large groups of children decreases their access to these children, thus reducing the risk that they will reoffend. Research conducted by Jeffrey Walker of the University of Arkansas found that child molesters are nearly twice as likely to live near schools as offenders convicted of sexually assaulting adults.[142]

- The residency requirements are reassuring to parents and are generally very popular with the public.

- The right of convicted sex offenders to choose where they live is less important than the protection of law-abiding citizens.

The Case against Sex Offender Residency Restrictions

- The laws push sex offenders into less populated areas or homelessness, which makes it much more difficult for law enforcement and corrections agents to keep tabs on them. "Probation and parole supervisors cannot effectively monitor offenders who are living under bridges, in parking lots, in tents at parks or interstate truck stops," says Elizabeth Barnhill of the Iowa Coalition against Sexual Assault.[143]

- The laws are inadequate. Studies have shown that strangers commit only about 10 percent of all sexual offenses against children. The perpetrators of such crimes are much more likely to be family members, friends, or other acquaintances.[144]

- The laws create a false sense of security. If a sex offender wants to get to a child, a residency requirement cannot stop him or her from simply getting in a car or walking to find a victim.

Your Opinion—Writing Assignment

Many residence requirements prohibit convicted sex offenders from living within a certain distance of a public park. To force these offenders out of their neighborhoods, many communities are building small "pocket" parks, some of them so tiny as to barely have enough room for a swing set. What is your opinion of this strategy? How do you feel about residency laws in general? Do these regulations constitute extra punishment for convicts who have already, at least in theory, paid their debt for their crimes?

As an alternative, should certain sex offenders be sentenced to life in prison without parole, sparing the criminal justice system the need to create awkward laws like residency requirements and civil confinement? Before responding, you can review our discussions in the sections of this chapter concerning:

- Barriers to reentry ("Return to Society").

- Fear of sex offenders ("Return to Society").

- Civil confinement ("Return to Society").

Your answer should include at least three full paragraphs.

Summary

For more information on these concepts, look back to the Learning Objective icons throughout the chapter.

 Explain the concept of prison as a total institution. Though many people spend time in partial institutions—schools, companies where they work, and religious organizations—only in prison is every aspect of an inmate's life controlled, and that is why prisons are called total institutions. Every detail for every prisoner is fully prescribed and managed.

 Describe a risk run by corrections officials who fail to provide adequate medical care to the inmates under their control. In the first decade of the 2000s, medical care for inmates in California's prison system was severely compromised by extreme overcrowding. As a result, the U.S. Supreme Court ordered state corrections officials to release 30,000 inmates so that standards of health care in the prison could be more compatible "with the concept of human dignity."

 Indicate some of the reasons for violent behavior in prisons. (a) To separate the powerful from the weak and establish a prisoner hierarchy; (b) to minimize one's own probability of being a target of assault; (c) to enhance one's self-image; (d) to obtain sexual relief; and (e) to obtain material goods through extortion or robbery.

 List the three goals of prison disciplinary strategies. (a) Ensure a safe living environment for inmates; (b) instill a respect of authority; and (c) modify behavior so that the inmates will display proper values when they leave the correctional facility.

 Describe the hands-off doctrine of prisoner law and indicate two standards used to determine if prisoners' rights have been violated. The hands-off doctrine assumes that the care of prisoners should be left to prison officials and that it is not the place of judges to intervene. Nonetheless, the Supreme Court has created two standards to be used by the courts in determining whether a prisoner's Eighth Amendment protections against cruel and unusual punishment have been

violated. Under the "deliberate indifference" standard, prisoners must show that prison officials were aware of harmful conditions at the facility and failed to remedy them. Under the "identifiable human needs" standard, prisoners must show that they were denied a basic need such as food, warmth, or exercise.

 Explain the aspects of imprisonment that prove challenging for incarcerated mothers and their children. Besides the anxiety that results from any separation of parent and child, incarcerated mothers often find it difficult to stay in contact with their children due to long distances between the prison and home. Furthermore, when a mother is imprisoned, her children are more likely not only to be separated from their father, but also to wind up in foster care.

 Contrast parole, expiration release, pardon, and furlough. Parole is an early release program for those incarcerated. Expiration release occurs when the inmate has served the maximum time for her or his initial sentence minus good-time credits. A pardon can be given only by the president or one of the fifty governors. Furlough is a temporary release while in jail or prison.

 Explain the goal of prisoner reentry programs. Based on the ideals of promoting desistance, these programs have two main objectives: (a) to prepare a prisoner for a successful return to the community, and (b) to protect the community by reducing the chances that the ex-convict will continue her or his criminal activity after release from prison.

 Indicate typical conditions for release for a paroled child molester. (a) Have no contact with children under the age of eighteen; (b) continue psychiatric treatment; (c) keep away from schools or parks where children are present; (d) cannot own toys that may be used to lure children; and (e) cannot have a job or participate in any activity that involves children.

Questions for Critical Analysis

1. Can prison treatment and rehabilitation programs be justified for reasons that have nothing to do with their potential cost and safety benefits for society? In other words, does the American criminal justice system have a responsibility to individual inmates to "improve" them during incarceration?

2. Several years ago, an inmate sued the Florida Department of Corrections, claiming that his soy-based diet was cruel and unusual punishment. Under what circumstances, if any, do you think that unpleasant prison food can violate an inmate's constitutional rights?

3. Do you agree with prison policies that prohibit male correctional officers from patting down and strip-searching female inmates? Why or why not? Under what circumstances might such policies be unrealistic?

4. How does the process of prisonization differ between male and female inmates?

5. What is the main justification for legislation that prohibits convicted sex offenders from accessing Facebook and online video games? What is your opinion of such legislation?

Key Terms

civil confinement 478
"deliberate indifference" 468
deprivation model 458
desistance 474
expiration release 472
furlough 472
halfway house 475

"hands-off" doctrine 468
"identifiable human needs" 468
pardon 472
prisoner reentry 473
prison gang 460
prisonization 453
prison programs 455

prison segregation 459
relative deprivation 458
security threat group (STG) 462
sex offender notification law 477
therapeutic community (TC) 457
total institution 453
work release program 475

Notes

1. Erving Goffman, "On the Characteristics of Total Institutions," in *Asylums: Essays on the Social Situation of Mental Patients and Other Inmates* (New York: Doubleday, 1961), 6.

2. Donald Clemmer, *The Prison Community* (Boston: Christopher, 1940).

3. John Irwin, *Prisons in Turmoil* (Boston: Little, Brown, 1980), 67.

4. *Old Behind Bars: The Aging Prison Population in the United States* (New York: Human Rights Watch, 2012), 24–42.

5. "Life, Death, and Raging Bulls," *The Economist* (May 10, 2014), 30.

6. Bureau of Justice Statistics, *Medical Problems of State and Federal Prisoners and Jail Inmates, 2011–12* (Washington, D.C.: U.S. Department of Justice, February 2015), 1.

7. Bureau of Justice Statistics, *Mortality in Local Jails and State Prisons, 2000–2012—Statistical Tables* (Washington, D.C.: U.S. Department of Justice, October 2014), Table 21, page 20.

8. *Ibid.*

9. Kevin E. McCarthy and Carrie Rose, *State Initiatives to Address Aging Prisoners* (Hartford, Conn.: Connecticut General Assembly, Office of Legislative Research, 2013), 3.

10. *Managing Prison Health Care Spending* (Philadelphia: The Pew Charitable Trusts, October 2013), 11.

11. Michael Vitiello, "Addressing the Special Problems of Mentally Ill Prisoners: A Small Piece of the Solution to Our Nation's Prison Crisis," *Denver University Law Review* (Fall 2010), 57–62.

12. Katherine Stuart van Wormer and Clemens Bartollas, *Women and the Criminal Justice System*, 3d ed. (Upper Saddle River, N.J.: Pearson Education, 2011), 143.

13. "Locked In," *The Economist* (August 3, 2013), 24.

14. Kevin Johnson, "Mentally Ill Fill Crowded Prisons," *USA Today* (July 25, 2014), 5A.

15. William Kanapaux, "Guilty of Mental Illness," *Psychiatric Times* (January 1, 2004), at **www.psychiatrictimes.com/forensic-psych/content/article/10168/47631.**

16. Bureau of Justice Statistics, *Census of State and Federal Correctional Facilities, 2005* (Washington, D.C.: U.S. Department of Justice, October 2008), 6.

17. Todd R. Clear, George F. Cole, and Michael D. Reisig, *American Corrections*, 9th ed (Belmont, Calif.: Wadsworth Cengage Learning, 2011), 381.

18. *Behind Bars II: Substance Abuse and America's Prison Population* (New York: The National Center on Addiction and Substance Abuse at Columbia University, February 2010), 4.

19. *Ibid.*, 83–84.

20. James A. Inciardi, James E. Rivers, and Duane C. McBride, "Drug Treatment," in *Prison and Jail Administration: Practice and Theory*, 3rd ed., ed. Peter M. Carlson (Burlington, Mass.: Jones & Bartlett Learning, 2015), 202–204.

21. Devah Pager and Bruce Western, *Investigating Prisoner Reentry: The Impact of Conviction Status on the Employment Prospects of Young Men* (Washington, D.C.: National Institute of Justice, October 2009), 6.

22. *Census of State and Federal Correctional Facilities, 2005, op. cit.*, 6.

23. Lois M. Davis, et al., *Evaluating the Effectiveness of Correctional Education* (Santa Monica, Calif.: The Rand Corporation, 2013), xvi.

24. *Ibid.*, xvii.

25. Steve Aos, Marna Miller, and Elizabeth Drake, *Evidence-Based Public Policy Options to Reduce Future Prison Construction, Criminal Justice Costs, and Crime Rates* (Olympia, Wash.: Washington State Institute for Public Policy, 2006), Exhibit 4, page 9.

26. Wendy Erisman and Jeanne B. Contardo, *Learning to Reduce Recidivism: A 50-State Analysis of Postsecondary Correctional Education Policy* (Washington, D.C.: Institute for Higher Education Policy, 2005), 1.

27. Laura E. Gorgol and Brian A. Sponsler, *Unlocking Potential: Results of a National Survey of Postsecondary Education in State Prisons* (Washington, D.C.: Institute for Higher Education Policy, May 2011), 10–15.

28. Robert Johnson, *Hard Time: Understanding and Reforming the Prison*, 2d ed. (Belmont, Calif.: Wadsworth, 1996), 133.

29. Paul J. Biermann, *Improving Correctional Officer Safety: Reducing Inmate Weapons* (Washington, D.C.: National Institute of Justice, 2007), 23.

30. *Mortality in Local Jails and State Prisons, 2000–2012—Statistical Tables, op. cit.*, Table 1, page 6; and Table 15, page 19.

31. Daniel P. Mears, et al., "The Code of the Street and Inmate Violence: Investigating the Salience of Imported Belief Systems," *Criminology* (August 2013), 695–728.

32. Lee H. Bowker, *Prison Victimization* (New York: Elsevier, 1981), 31–33.

33. Stephen C. Light, "The Severity of Assaults on Prison Officers: A Contextual Analysis," *Social Science Quarterly* 71 (1990), 267–284.

34. Frank Tannenbaum, *Crime and Community* (Boston: Ginn & Co., 1938).

35. Randy Martin and Sherwood Zimmerman, "A Typology of the Causes of Prison Riots and an Analytical Extension to the 1986 Virginia Riot," *Justice Quarterly* 7 (1990), 711–737.

36. Bert Useem, "Disorganization and the New Mexico Prison Riot of 1980," *American Sociological Review* 50 (1985), 677–688.

37. Quoted in R. L. Nave, "Private Prisons, Public Problems," *Jackson (MS) Free Press* (June 6, 2012), at **www.jacksonfreepress.com/news/2012/jun/06/private-prisons-public-problems.**

38. 42 U.S.C. Sections 15601–15609 (2006).

39. Bureau of Justice Statistics, *Sexual Victimization Reported by Adult Correctional Authorities, 2009–11* (Washington, D.C.: U.S. Department of Justice, January 2014), 1.

40. James E. Robertson, "The Prison Rape Elimination Act of 2003: A Primer," *Criminal Law Bulletin* (May/June 2004), 270–273.

41. Irwin, *op. cit.*, 47.

42. Leo Carroll, "Race, Ethnicity, and the Social Order of the Prison," in *The Pains of Imprisonment*, eds. R. Johnson and H. Toch (Beverly Hills, Calif.: Sage, 1982).

43. *Lee v. Washington*, 390 U.S. 333 (1968).

44. *Johnson v. California*, 543 U.S. 499 (2005).

45. *Ibid.*, at 508.

46. Paige St. John, "California Prisons to End Race-Based Policy for Inmate Violence," *Los Angeles Times* (October 23, 2014), at **www.latimes.com/local/lanow/la-me-ln-california-prisons-race-policy-inmate-violence-20141023-story.html.**

47. Craig Haney, "Psychology and the Limits of Prison Pain," *Psychology, Public Policy, and Law* (December 1977), 499.

48. Alan J. Drury and Matt DeLisi, "Gangkill: An Exploratory Empirical Assessment of Gang Membership, Homicide Offending, and Prison Misconduct," *Crime & Delinquency* (January 2011), 130–146.

49. *A Study of Gangs and Security Threat Groups in America's Adult Prisons and Jails* (Indianapolis: National Major Gang Task Force, 2002).

50. George W. Knox, "The Problem of Gangs and Security Threat Groups (STGs) in American Prisons Today: Recent Research Findings from the 2004 Prison Gang Survey," available at **www.ngcrc.com/corr2006.html.**

51. *Ibid.*

52. John Winterdyk and Rick Ruddell, "Managing Prison Gangs: Results from a Survey of U.S. Prison Systems," *Journal of Criminal Justice* 38 (2010), 733–734.

53. Alan Gomez, "States Make Prisons Far Less Deadly," *USA Today* (August 22, 2008), 3A.

54. Quoted in John J. DiIulio, Jr., *No Escape: The Future of American Corrections* (New York: Basic Books, 1991), 268.

55. Jack Henry Abbott, *In the Belly of the Beast* (New York: Vintage Books, 1991), 54.

56. Michel Foucault, *Discipline and Punish: The Birth of the Prison* (New York: Pantheon Books, 1977), 128.

57. Edgar Walters, "In Cases of Smuggled Cellphones, Few Prosecutions," *New York Times* (May 4, 2014), A31.

58. Clear, Cole, and Reisig, *op. cit.*, 333.

59. *Ibid.*, 335.

60. Peter M. Carlson and Lindsey Battles, "Changing Diversity of Correctional Officers," in *Prison and Jail Administration: Practice and Theory*, 3rd ed., *op. cit.*, 260.

61. *BLS Reports: Labor Force Characteristics by Race and Ethnicity, 2013* (Washington, D.C.: U.S. Bureau of Labor Statistics, August 2014), Table 8, page 27.

62. Lucien X. Lombardo, *Guards Imprisoned: Correctional Officers at Work* (Cincinnati, Ohio: Anderson Publishing Co., 1989), 51–71.

63. Clair A. Crip, "Inmate Disciplinary Procedures," in *Prison and Jail Administration: Practice and Theory*, 3rd ed., *op. cit.*, 344.

64. Goffman, *op. cit.*, 7.

65. Clear, Cole, and Reisig, *op. cit.*, 333.

66. *Wolff v. McDonnell*, 418 U.S. 539 (1974).

67. 475 U.S. 312 (1986).

68. *Stanley v. Hejirika*, 134 F.3d 629 (4th Cir. 1998).

69. Christopher R. Smith, *Law and Contemporary Corrections* (Belmont, Calif.: Wadsworth, 1999), Chapter 6.

70. 503 U.S. 1 (1992).

71. Darrell L. Ross, "Assessing *Hudson v. McMillan* Ten Years Later," *Criminal Law Bulletin* (September/October 2004), 508.

72. Michael Winerip and Michael Schwirtz, "Rikers: Where Mental Illness Meets Brutality in Jail," *New York Times* (July 14, 2014), A1.

73. Erica Goode, "California Revises Policy on Mentally Ill Inmates," *New York Times* (August 3, 2014), A22.

74. Van Wormer and Bartollas, *op. cit.*, 387.

75. Cristina Rathbone, *A World Apart: Women, Prison, and a Life behind Bars* (New York: Random House, 2006), 46.

76. Carl Nink et al., *Women Professionals in Corrections: A Growing Asset* (Centerville, Utah: MTC Institute, August 2008), 1.

77. Michael H. Jaime and Armand R. Burruel, "Labor Relations in Corrections," in *Prison and Jail Administration: Practice and Theory*, 3rd ed., *op. cit.*, 264.

78. *Sexual Victimization Reported by Adult Correctional Authorities, 2009–11, op. cit.*, Table 10, page 12; and page 17.

79. *Wolff v. McDonnell*, 539.

80. *Hudson v. Palmer*, 468 U.S. 517 (1984).

81. 429 U.S. 97 (1976).

82. "Judge Orders Air Conditioning for Angola Prison's Death Row," *Associated Press* (May 24, 2014).

83. 501 U.S. 294 (1991).

84. *Wilson v. Seiter*, 501 U.S. 294, 304 (1991).

85. *Woodall v. Foti*, 648 F.2d, 268, 272 (5th Cir. 1981).

86. *Brown v. Plata*, 563 U.S. ____ (2011).

87. *Procunier v. Martinez*, 416 U.S. 396 (1974).

88. *Cruz v. Beto*, 405 U.S. 319 (1972); *Gittlemacker v. Prasse*, 428 F.2d 1 (3d Cir. 1970); and *Kahane v. Carlson*, 527 F.2d 492 (2d Cir. 1975).

89. Maryclaire Dale, "Court Says Pa. Prison Can Ban Muslim Scarf," *Associated Press* (August 2, 2010).

90. Bob Egelko, "Warden Can't Ban Werewolf Novel, Court Rules," *San Francisco Chronicle* (June 5, 2013), at **www.sfgate.com/crime/article/Warden-can-t-ban-werewolf-novel-court-rules-4581024.php.**

91. Quoted in Alexandra Marks, "Martha Checks in Today," *Seattle Times* (October 8, 2004), A8.

92. Emily M. Wright, et al., "Gender-Responsive Lessons Learned and Policy Implications for Women in Prison: A Review," *Criminal Justice and Behavior* (September 2012), 1612–1632.

93. Bureau of Justice Statistics, *Sourcebook of Criminal Justice*, 3d ed. (Washington, D.C.: U.S. Department of Justice, 2003), Table 6.56, page 519; and Bureau of Justice Statistics, *Prisoners in 2013* (Washington, D.C.: U.S. Department of Justice, September 2014), Table 13, page 15.

94. Bureau of Justice Statistics, *Profile of Jail Inmates, 2002* (Washington, D.C.: U.S. Department of Justice, July 2004), 10.

95. Bureau of Justice Statistics, *Prior Abuse Reported by Inmates and Probationers* (Washington, D.C.: U.S. Department of Justice, April 1999), 2.

96. *Caught in the Net: The Impact of Drug Policies on Women and Families* (Washington, D.C.: American Civil Liberties Union, 2004), 18–19.

97. Allen J. Beck and Laura M. Maruschak, *Mental Health Treatment in State Prisons, 2000* (Washington, D.C.: U.S. Department of Justice, July 2001), 1.

98. Barbara Bloom, Barbara Owen, and Stephanie Covington, *Gender Responsive Strategies: Research, Practice, and Guiding Principles for Women Offenders* (Washington, D.C.: National Institute of Corrections, 2003), 6.

99. *Ibid.*, 7.

100. Wright, et al., *op. cit.*, 1618–1624.

101. Sarah Schirmer, Ashley Nellis, and Marc Mauer, *Incarcerated Parents and Their Children: Trends 1991–2007* (Washington, D.C.: The Sentencing Project, February 2009), 2.

102. Kelly Bedard and Eric Helland, "Location of Women's Prisons and the Deterrent Effect of 'Harder' Time," *International Review of Law and Economics* (June 2004), 152.

103. *Ibid.*

104. Schirmer, Nellis, and Mauer, *op. cit.*, 5.

105. Rathbone, *op. cit.*, 4.

106. *Ibid.*, 158.

107. Van Wormer and Bartollas, *op. cit.*, 137–138.

108. Barbara Bloom and Meda Chesney-Lind, "Women in Prison," in *It's a Crime: Women and Justice*, 4th ed., ed. Roslyn Muraskin (Upper Saddle River, N.J.: Prentice Hall, 2007), 542–563.

109. Piper Kerman, *Orange Is the New Black: My Year in a Women's Prison* (New York: Spiegal and Grau, 2011), 131.

110. Esther Heffernan, *Making It in Prison: The Square, the Cool, and the Life* (New York: Wiley, 1972), 91.

111. Leanne F. Alarid, "Female Inmate Subcultures," in *Corrections Contexts: Contemporary and Classical Readings*, ed. James W. Marquart and Jonathan R. Sorenson (Los Angeles: Roxbury Publishing Co., 1997), 136–137.

112. Barbara Owen et al., *Gendered Violence and Safety: A Contextual Approach to Improving Security in Women's Facilities*, December 2008, 12–14, at **www.ncjrs.gov/pdffiles1/nij/grants/225340.pdf.**

113. Nancy Wolff, Cynthia Blitz, Jing Shi, Jane Siegel, and Ronet Bachman, "Physical Violence inside Prisons: Rates of Victimization," *Criminal Justice and Behavior* 34 (2007), 588–604.

114. Van Wormer and Bartollas, *op. cit.*, 146–148.

115. Cited in Bloom, Owen, and Covington, *op. cit.*, 26.

116. Hamed Aleaziz, "Optimism for Ex-Inmates' 2nd Chance at Redemption," *San Francisco Chronicle* (November 10, 2014), A1.

117. Bureau of Justice Statistics, *Prisoners in 2012: Trends in Admissions and Releases, 1991–2012* (Washington, D.C.: U.S. Department of Justice, December 2013), Table 2, page 4.

118. Joan Petersilia, *When Prisoners Come Home: Parole and Prisoner Reentry* (New York: Oxford University Press, 2003), 39.

119. Victor Hassine, *Life without Parole: Living in Prison Today*, eds. Thomas J. Bernard and Richard McCleary (Los Angeles: Roxbury Publishing Co., 1996), 12.

120. Christy Visher, Sara Debus, and Jennifer Yahner, *Employment after Prison: A Longitudinal Study of Releases in Three States* (Washington, D.C.: Urban Institute, October 2008), 1.

121. *Ill Equipped: U.S. Prisons and Offenders with Mental Illness* (New York: Human Rights Watch, 2003).

122. Pew Center on the States, *State of Recidivism: The Revolving Door of America's Prisons* (Washington, D.C.: The Pew Charitable Trusts, April 2011), 2.

123. Edward Zamble and Vernon Quinsey, *The Criminal Recidivism Process* (Cambridge, England: Cambridge University Press, 1997).

124. Quoted in Kevin Johnson, "After Years of Solitary, Freedom Is Hard to Grasp," *USA Today* (June 9, 2005), 2A.

125. *Census of State and Federal Correctional Facilities, 2005, op. cit.*, Table 6, page 5.

126. Nicolette Bell, et al., *Recidivism Report 2013* (Mechanicsburg, Pa.: Pennsylvania Department of Corrections, February 28, 2013), Table 25, page 29.

127. Quoted in Sam Dolnick, "Pennsylvania Study Finds Halfway Houses Don't Reduce Recidivism," *New York Times* (March 25, 2013), A17.

128. *The State of Sentencing 2014: Developments in Policy and Practice* (Washington, D.C.: The Sentencing Project, February 2015), 8–9.

129. Quoted in Timothy Williams and Tanzina Vega, "A Plan to Cut Costs and Crime: End Hurdle to Job after Prison," *New York Times* (October 24, 2014), A1.

130. Quoted in "'Pillowcase Rapist' Released to Live in Los Angeles Community," *Associated Press* (July 9, 2014).

131. Belinda Brooks Gordon and Charlotte Bilby, "Psychological Interventions for Treatment of Adult Sex Offenders," *British Medical Journal* (July 2006), 5–6.

132. Bureau of Justice Statistics, *Recidivism of Prisoners Released in 1994* (Washington, D.C.: U.S. Department of Justice, June 2002), Table 9, page 8.

133. R. Karl Hanson and Kelly Morton-Bourgon, "The Characteristics of Persistent Sexual Offenders: A Meta-Analysis of Recidivism Studies, *Journal of Consulting and Clinical Psychology* 73 (2005), 1154–1163.

134. New Jersey Revised Statute Section 2C:7-8(c) (1995).

135. Georgia Code Annotated Section 42-9-44.1(b)(1).

136. Public Law Number 109-248, Section 116, 120 Statute 595 (2006).

137. Leigh Linden and Jonah Rockoff, "Estimates of the Impact of Crime Risk on Property Values from Megan's Laws," *American Economic Review* 98 (2008), 1103–1127.

138. Abby Goodnough, "After Two Cases in Florida, Crackdown on Molesters," *Law Enforcement News* (May 2004), 12.

139. *United States v. Comstock*, 560 U.S. 126 (2010).

140. Quoted in Terrence McCoy, "Miami Sex Offenders Live on Train Tracks Thanks to Draconian Restrictions," *Miami New Times* (March 13, 2014), at **www.miaminewtimes.com/2014-03-13/news/miami-sex-offenders-train-tracks/2/.**

141. New Jersey Statutes Annotated Section 2C: 7-3.

142. Wendy Kock, "Sex-Offender Residency Laws Get a Second Look," *USA Today* (February 26, 2007), 1A.

143. Quoted in Jenifer Warren, "Sex Crime Residency Laws Exile Offenders," *Los Angeles Times* (October 30, 2006), 1.

144. Bureau of Justice Statistics, *Recidivism of Sex Offenders Released from Prison in 1994* (Washington, D.C.: U.S. Department of Justice, November 2003), 36; and Luis Rosell, "Sex Offenders: Pariahs of the 21st Century?" *William Mitchell Law Review* (2005), 419.

The Juvenile Justice System

Chapter Outline		Corresponding Learning Objectives
The Evolution of American Juvenile Justice	**1**	Describe the child-saving movement and its relationship to the doctrine of *parens patriae.*
	2	List the four major differences between juvenile courts and adult courts.
	3	Identify and briefly describe the single most important U.S. Supreme Court case with respect to juvenile justice.
Determining Delinquency Today	**4**	Describe the reasoning behind recent U.S. Supreme Court decisions that have lessened the harshness of sentencing outcomes for violent juvenile offenders.
Trends in Juvenile Delinquency	**5**	Explain how law enforcement's emphasis on domestic violence has influenced female juvenile arrest patterns.
Factors in Juvenile Delinquency	**6**	Describe the one variable that always correlates highly with juvenile crime rates.
First Contact: The Police and Pretrial Procedures	**7**	List the factors that normally determine what police do with juvenile offenders.
	8	Describe the four primary stages of pretrial juvenile justice procedure.
Trying and Punishing Juveniles	**9**	Explain the distinction between an adjudicatory hearing and a disposition hearing.

To target your study and review, look for these numbered Learning Objective icons throughout the chapter.

Pat Greenhouse/*The Boston Globe*/Getty Images

Life Lessened

when Ronald Salazar's mother and father left their native El Salvador to come to the United States, they decided that their son was too young to make the journey. So, they left him behind. For next the twelve years, Salazar was raised by grandparents who abused him, living in dire poverty and running with street gangs. By the time he finally joined his parents in Miami, they had three other daughters and seemingly little affection for the long-lost "black sheep" of the family. Salazar responded by acting violently and, at the age of fourteen, was briefly hospitalized for a psychological evaluation after threatening to kill himself and his three sisters.

In 2005, on returning home from the hospital, Salazar did kill his eleven-year-old sister, Marina, strangling and raping her before slitting her throat. He was convicted of first degree murder and, under Florida law, given an automatic sentence of life in prison without the possibility of parole. Salazar seemed fated to spend the rest of his days behind bars until 2012, when the United States Supreme Court banned mandatory life sentences without parole for juvenile murderers. With its ruling, the Court opened the possibility that all such sentences be reevaluated to determine whether the offender deserved a lesser punishment.

Consequently, in 2015, a tearful twenty-four-year-old Salazar found himself back in state court, telling Circuit Judge Ellen Sue Venzer, "My whole life has been messed up." Prosecutors argued strenuously against showing Salazar any leniency, comparing him to a character from a "bad slasher movie" who should never be let "loose on the streets." Following the hearing, however, Judge Venzer reduced Salazar's sentence to forty years in prison, meaning that he will likely go free in his mid-fifties. "You would have to admit that [this] fourteen-year-old kid had a horrific first fourteen years," said the judge, explaining her decision.

▲ In 2015, a Florida judge reduced the sentence of Ronald Salazar, shown here, from life without parole to forty years for raping and killing his sister when he was fourteen years old.

1. What is your opinion of judge Ellen Sue Venzer's choice to reduce Ronald Salazar's sentence from life without parole to forty years?

2. In its ruling, the Supreme Court stated that juveniles who commit murder should be given a chance to rehabilitate themselves because they were too young to fully appreciate the magnitude of their crimes. Do you agree with this reasoning? Why or why not?

3. After killing his sister, Salazar wiped clean the murder weapon—a knife—and returned it to a kitchen drawer. He then concocted a story about two strangers breaking into the house and killing and raping his sister. If you were a prosecutor arguing against a reduction of Salazar's sentence, how would you use this information?

The Evolution of American Juvenile Justice

A difficult question—asked every time a younger offender such as Ronald Salazar commits a heinous act of violence—lies at the heart of the juvenile justice debate: Should such acts by youths be given the same weight as those committed by adults, or should they be seen as "mistakes" that can be corrected by care and counseling?

From its earliest days, the American juvenile justice system has operated as an uneasy compromise between "rehabilitation and punishment, treatment and custody."[1] At the beginning of the 1800s, juvenile offenders were treated the same as adult offenders—they were judged by the same courts and sentenced to the same severe penalties. This situation began to change soon after, as urbanization and industrialization created an immigrant underclass that was, at least in the eyes of many reformers, predisposed to deviant activity. Certain members of the Progressive movement, known as the child savers, began to take steps to "save" children from these circumstances, introducing the idea of rehabilitating delinquents in the process.

The Child-Saving Movement

In general, the child savers favored the doctrine of *parens patriae,* which holds that the state has not only a right but also a duty to care for children who are neglected, delinquent, or in some other way disadvantaged. Juvenile offenders, the child savers believed, required treatment, not punishment, and they were horrified at the thought of placing children in prisons with hardened adult criminals. In 1967, then Supreme Court justice Abe Fortas said of the child savers:

> They believed that society's role was not to ascertain whether the child was "guilty" or "innocent," but "What is he, how has he become what he is, and what had best be done in his interest and in the interest of the state to save him from a downward career." The child— essentially good, as they saw it—was made "to feel that he is the object of [the government's] care and solicitude," not that he was under arrest or on trial.[2]

LEARNING OBJECTIVE 1 Describe the child-saving movement and its relationship to the doctrine of *parens patriae*.

Child-saving organizations convinced local legislatures to pass laws that allowed them to take control of children who exhibited criminal tendencies or had been neglected by their parents. To separate these children from the environment in which they were raised, the organizations created a number of institutions, the best known of which was New York's House of Refuge. Opening in 1825, the House of Refuge implemented many of the same reformist measures popular in the penitentiaries of the time, meaning that its charges were subjected to the healthful influences of hard study and labor. Although the House of Refuge was criticized for its harsh discipline (which caused many boys to run away), similar institutions sprang up throughout the Northeast during the middle of the 1800s.

The Illinois Juvenile Court

The efforts of the child savers culminated with the passage of the Illinois Juvenile Court Act in 1899. The Illinois legislature created the first court specifically for juveniles, guided by the principles of *parens patriae* and based on the belief that children are not fully responsible for criminal conduct and are capable of being rehabilitated.[3]

The Illinois Juvenile Court and those in other states that followed in its path were (and, in many cases, remain) drastically different from adult courts:

LEARNING OBJECTIVE 2 List the four major differences between juvenile courts and adult courts.

- *No juries.* The matter was decided by judges who wore regular clothes instead of black robes and sat at a table with the other participants rather than behind a

Status Offender A juvenile who has engaged in behavior deemed unacceptable for those under a certain statutorily determined age.

Juvenile Delinquency Behavior that is illegal under federal or state law that has been committed by a person who is under an age limit specified by statute.

bench. Because the primary focus of the court was on the child and not the crime, the judge had wide discretion in disposing of each case.

- *Different terminology.* To reduce the stigma of criminal proceedings, "petitions" were issued instead of "warrants." The children were not "defendants," but "respondents," and they were not "found guilty" but "adjudicated delinquent."
- *No adversarial relationship.* Instead of trying to determine guilt or innocence, the parties involved in the juvenile court worked together in the best interests of the child, with the emphasis on rehabilitation rather than punishment.
- *Confidentiality.* To avoid "saddling" the child with a criminal past, juvenile court hearings and records were kept sealed, and the proceedings were closed to the public.

By 1945, every state had a juvenile court system modeled after the first Illinois court. For the most part, these courts were able to operate without interference until the 1960s and the onset of the juvenile rights movement.

Status Offending

After the first juvenile court was established in Illinois, the Chicago Bar Association described its purpose as, in part, to "exercise the same tender solicitude and care over its neglected wards that a wise and loving parent would exercise with reference to his [or her] own children under similar circumstances."[4] In other words, the state was given the responsibility of caring for those minors whose behavior seemed to show that they could not be controlled by their parents. As a result, many **status offenders** found themselves in the early houses of refuge and continue to be placed in state-run facilities today. A status offense is an act that, if committed by a juvenile, is considered illegal and grounds for possible state custody. The same act, if committed by an adult, does not warrant law enforcement action. (See Figure 15.1 for an idea of which status offenses are most commonly brought to the attention of authorities.)

Juvenile Delinquency

In contrast to status offending, **juvenile delinquency** refers to conduct that would also be criminal if committed by an adult. According to federal law and the laws of most states, a juvenile delinquent is someone who has not yet reached his or her eighteenth birthday— the age of adult criminal responsibility—at the time of the offense in question. In two states (New York and North Carolina), persons aged sixteen are considered adults, and twelve other states confer adulthood on seventeen-year-olds for purposes of criminal law.

Under certain circumstances, discussed later in this chapter, children under these ages can be tried in adult courts and incarcerated in adult prisons and jails. Remember that Ronald Salazar was fourteen years old when he was charged as an adult for the rape and murder of his eleven-year-old sister, described in the opening of the chapter. By contrast, in 2013, high school football players Trent Mays, aged seventeen, and Ma'lik Richmond, aged sixteen, were found to be *delinquent beyond a reasonable doubt* of sexually assaulting an intoxicated sixteen-year-old girl in Steubenville, Ohio. Because they were adjudicated as juveniles, Mays and Richmond cannot be incarcerated past their twenty-first birthdays.

FIGURE 15.1 Status Offenses

About 117,000 status offenses are processed by juvenile courts in the United States each year. The most common, as this graph shows, are truancy (skipping school) and liquor-related offenses.

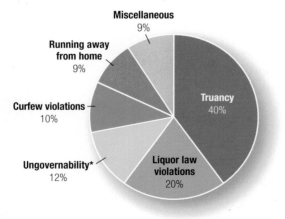

Miscellaneous 9%
Running away from home 9%
Curfew violations 10%
Ungovernability* 12%
Truancy 40%
Liquor law violations 20%

* Being beyond the control of parents, teachers, or other adult authority figures.

Source: Sarah Hockenberry and Charles Puzzanchera, *Juvenile Court Statistics, 2011* (Pittsburgh, Pa.: National Center for Juvenile Justice, July 2014), 66.

Salazar, charged as an adult, faced the possibility of spending the rest of his life behind bars.

Constitutional Protections and the Juvenile Court

Though the ideal of the juvenile court seemed to offer the "best of both worlds" for juvenile offenders, in reality the lack of procedural protections led to many children being arbitrarily punished not only for crimes, but for status offenses as well. Juvenile judges were treating all violators similarly, which led to many status offenders being incarcerated in the same institutions as violent delinquents.

▲ Depending on the state, juvenile offenders found to be delinquent such as Trent Mays, left, and Ma'lik Richmond usually will not be incarcerated past their twenty-first birthdays. **Is this a just punishment? Why or why not?**
AP Images/Keith Srakocic, Pool

In response to a wave of lawsuits demanding due process rights for juveniles, the United States Supreme Court issued several rulings in the 1960s and 1970s that significantly changed the juvenile justice system.

Kent v. United States The first decision to extend due process rights to children in juvenile courts was *Kent v. United States* (1966).[5] The case concerned sixteen-year-old Morris Kent, who had been arrested for breaking into a woman's house, stealing her purse, and raping her. Because Kent was on juvenile probation, the state sought to transfer his trial for the crime to an adult court (a process to be discussed later in the chapter).

Without giving any reasons for his decision, the juvenile judge consented to this strategy, and Kent was sentenced in the adult court to a thirty- to ninety-year prison term. The Supreme Court overturned the sentence, ruling that juveniles have a right to counsel and a hearing in any instance in which the juvenile judge is considering sending the case to an adult court. The Court stated that, in such cases, a child receives "the worst of both worlds," getting neither the "protections accorded to adults" nor the "solicitous care and regenerative treatment" offered in the juvenile system.[6]

In re Gault The *Kent* decision provided the groundwork for *In re Gault* one year later. Considered by many to be the single most important case concerning juvenile justice, *In re Gault* involved a fifteen-year-old boy who was arrested for allegedly making a lewd phone call while on probation.[7] In its decision, the Supreme Court held that juveniles facing a loss of liberty were entitled to many of the same basic procedural safeguards granted to adult offenders in this country. (See the feature *Landmark Cases—In re Gault* for more information on this case.)

Other Important Court Decisions Over the next ten years, the Supreme Court handed down three more important rulings on juvenile court procedure. The ruling in *In re Winship* (1970)[8] required the government to prove "beyond a reasonable doubt" that a juvenile had committed an act of delinquency, raising the burden of proof from a "preponderance of the evidence." In *Breed v. Jones* (1975),[9] the Court held that the Fifth Amendment's double jeopardy clause prevented a juvenile from being tried in an adult court for a crime that had already been adjudicated in juvenile court. In contrast, the decision in *McKeiver v. Pennsylvania* (1971)[10] represented an instance in which the Court did not move the juvenile court further toward the adult model. In that case, the Court ruled that the Constitution did not give juveniles the right to a jury trial.

Landmark Cases

In re Gault

Identify and briefly describe the single most important U.S. Supreme Court case with respect to juvenile justice. **LEARNING OBJECTIVE 3**

In 1964, fifteen-year-old Gerald Gault and a friend were arrested for making lewd telephone calls to a neighbor in Gila County, Arizona. Gault, who was on probation, was placed under custody with no notice given to his parents. The juvenile court in his district held a series of informal hearings to determine Gault's punishment. During these hearings, no records were kept, Gault was not afforded the right to counsel, and the complaining witness was never made available for questioning. At the close of the hearing, the judge sentenced Gault to remain in Arizona's State Industrial School until the age of twenty-one. Gault's lawyers challenged this punishment, arguing that the proceedings had denied their client his due process rights. Eventually, the matter reached the United States Supreme Court.

In re Gault
United States Supreme Court
387 U.S. 1 (1967)

In the Words of the Court . . .
Justice Fortas, Majority Opinion

* * * *

From the inception of the juvenile court system, wide differences have been tolerated—indeed insisted upon—between the procedural rights accorded to adults and those of juveniles. In practically all jurisdictions, there are rights granted to adults which are withheld from juveniles.

* * * *

The absence of substantive standards has not necessarily meant that children receive careful, compassionate, individualized treatment. The absence of procedural rules based upon constitutional principle has not always produced fair, efficient, and effective procedures. Departures from established principles of due process have frequently resulted not in enlightened procedure, but in arbitrariness.

* * * *

Ultimately, however, we confront the reality of that portion of the Juvenile Court process with which we deal in this case. A boy is charged with misconduct. The boy is committed to an institution where he may be restrained of liberty for years.* * * His world becomes "a building with whitewashed walls, regimented routine and institutional hours. . . ." Instead of mother and father and sisters and brothers and friends and classmates, his world is peopled by guards, custodians, state employees, and "delinquents" confined with him for anything from waywardness to rape and homicide. In view of this, it would be extraordinary if our Constitution did not require the procedural regularity and the exercise of care implied in the phrase "due process." Under our Constitution, the condition of being a boy does not justify a kangaroo court.

* * * *

Decision
The Court held that juveniles were entitled to the basic procedural safeguards afforded by the U.S. Constitution, including the right to advance notice of charges, the right to counsel, the right to confront and cross-examine witnesses, and the privilege against self-incrimination. The decision marked a turning point in juvenile justice in this country: no longer would informality and paternalism be the guiding principles of juvenile courts. Instead, due process would dictate the adjudication process, much as in an adult court.

For Critical Analysis
What might be some of the negative consequences of the *In re Gault* decision for juveniles charged with committing delinquent acts? Can you think of any reasons why juveniles should not receive the same due process protections as adult offenders?

Determining Delinquency Today

In the eyes of many observers, the net effect of the Supreme Court decisions during the 1966–1975 period was to move juvenile justice away from the ideals of the child savers. As a result of these decisions, many young offenders would find themselves in a formalized system that is often indistinguishable from its adult counterpart. At the same time, though the Court has recognized that minors charged with crimes possess certain constitutional rights, it has failed to dictate at what age these rights should be granted. Consequently, the legal status of children in the United States varies depending on where they live, with each state making its own policy decisions on the crucial questions of age and competency.

The Age Question

On the morning of May 31, 2014, two twelve-year-old girls invited a friend to go with them to a park in Waukesha, Wisconsin. The pair proceeded to stab the other girl nineteen times with a kitchen knife, leaving her for dead among the trees. Afterward, the two girls explained their actions as an attempt to impress Slender Man, a fictional horror character popular on the Internet. "Many people do not believe Slender Man is real," one of the girls told the police. "[We] wanted to prove the skeptics wrong."[11]

In Chapter 4, we saw that early American criminal law recognized infancy as a defense against criminal charges. At that time, on attaining fourteen years of age, a youth was considered an adult and treated accordingly by the criminal justice system. Today, as Figure 15.2 shows, the majority of states (as well as the District of Columbia) allow for the prosecution of juveniles under the age of fourteen as adults. Even though Wisconsin does not allow for the prosecution of twelve-year-olds as adults, prosecutors decided to charge the Waukesha girls with attempted first degree homicide, which automatically placed them in adult court regardless of their ages.

In March 2015, a circuit judge upheld this decision, meaning that both girls faced up to sixty-five years in prison if found guilty. Their lawyers had argued that, due to their tender years, the girls should have been charged as juveniles with attempted second degree homicide. When young offenders who remain in juvenile court are found guilty, they receive "limited" sentences that usually expire when they turn eighteen or twenty-one. Under Wisconsin law, such offenders cannot be incarcerated in a juvenile corrections facility past their twenty-fifth birthdays.[12]

The Culpability Question

Many researchers believe that by the age of fourteen, an adolescent has the

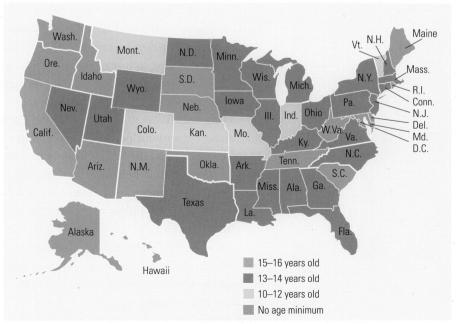

FIGURE 15.2 The Minimum Age at Which a Juvenile Can Be Tried as an Adult

15–16 years old
13–14 years old
10–12 years old
No age minimum

Source: Patrick Griffin, et al., *Trying Juveniles as Adults: An Analysis of State Transfer Laws and Reporting* (Washington, D.C.: Office of Juvenile Justice and Delinquency Prevention, September 2011).

same ability as an adult to make a competent decision. Nevertheless, according to some observers, a juvenile's capacity to understand the difference between "right" and "wrong" does not mean that she or he should be held to the same standards of competency as an adult.

Juvenile Behavior A study released in 2003 by the Research Network on Adolescent Development and Juvenile Justice found that 33 percent of juvenile defendants in criminal courts had the same low level of understanding of legal matters as mentally ill adults who had been found incompetent to stand trial.[13] Legal psychologist Richard E. Redding believes that

> adolescents' lack of life experience may limit their real-world decision-making ability. Whether we call it wisdom, judgment, or common sense, adolescents may not have nearly enough.[14]

Juveniles are generally more impulsive, more likely to engage in risky behavior, and less likely to calculate the long-term consequences of any particular action. Furthermore, adolescents are far more likely to respond to peer pressure than are adults. The desire for acceptance and approval may drive them to commit crimes: juveniles are arrested as part of a group at much higher rates than adults.[15] Furthermore, juveniles are less likely than adults to display remorse immediately following a violent act. As a result, they are often penalized by the courts for showing "less grief than the system demands."[16]

Diminished Guilt The "diminished culpability" of juveniles was one of the reasons given by the United States Supreme Court in its landmark decision in *Roper v. Simmons* (2005).[17] As we saw in Chapter 11, that case forbade the execution of offenders who were under the age of eighteen when they committed their crimes. In his majority opinion, Justice Anthony Kennedy wrote that because minors cannot fully comprehend the consequences of their actions, the two main justifications for the death penalty—retribution and deterrence—do not "work" with juvenile wrongdoers.[18]

Describe the reasoning behind recent U.S. Supreme Court decisions that have lessened the harshness of sentencing outcomes for violent juvenile offenders. LEARNING **4** OBJECTIVE

Life Imprisonment Issues The Supreme Court applied the same reasoning in two later cases that have dramatically affected the sentencing of violent juvenile offenders. First, in *Graham v. Florida* (2010),[19] the Court held that juveniles who commit crimes that do not involve murder may not be sentenced to life in prison without the possibility of parole. According to Justice Kennedy, who wrote the majority opinion, state officials must give these inmates "some meaningful opportunity to obtain release based on demonstrated maturity and rehabilitation."[20]

Then, with *Miller v. Alabama* (2012),[21] the Court banned laws in twenty-eight states that made life-without-parole sentences *mandatory* for juveniles convicted of murder. The case focused on the fate of Evan Miller, who was fourteen years old when he killed a neighbor with a baseball bat. The ruling did not signify that juvenile offenders such as Miller could not, under any circumstances, be sentenced to life without parole. Rather, the Court stated that judges must have the discretion to weigh the mitigating factors in each individual case.

For example, Miller had been abused by his stepfather and neglected by his alcoholic and drug-addicted mother, had spent most of his life in foster care, and had tried to commit suicide four times.[22] According to the Court, this type of personal history must be taken into account when determining the proper sentence for a juvenile murderer. Such mitigating factors may indicate that the offender has the potential to be rehabilitated and therefore should be afforded the possibility of parole.

Sentencing Issues In a number of states, those sentenced before the Supreme Court's *Miller* ruling have been given the opportunity to argue for retroactive leniency. As you might recall, Ronald Salazar—discussed in this chapter's introduction—had his sentence reduced from life without parole to forty years as a direct result of the Court's decision.

For post-*Miller* cases, states are taking legislative steps to conform to the Court's requirements. In Florida, for example, juveniles sentenced to life in prison will now be afforded a single judicial review after twenty-five years to determine whether their continued incarceration is warranted. In Nebraska, juvenile offenders found guilty of violent crimes will receive indeterminate sentences of forty years to life, with a parole board making the decision concerning possible early release.[23] (See this chapter's *CJ Policy—Your Take* feature to analyze state sentencing policies that have been criticized for violating the "spirit" of the Court's *Graham* and *Miller* rulings.)

EthicsChallenge

Do you think it was ethical for Wisconsin prosecutors to charge the two twelve-year-old girls as adults in the "Slender Man" attempted homicide case described in this section? Why or why not? ■

Trends in Juvenile Delinquency

When asked, juveniles will admit to a wide range of illegal or dangerous behavior, including carrying weapons, getting involved in physical fights, driving after drinking alcohol, and stealing or deliberately damaging school property.[24] Has the juvenile justice system been effective in controlling and preventing this kind of misbehavior, as well as more serious acts?

To answer this question, many observers turn to the Federal Bureau of Investigation's Uniform Crime Report (UCR), initially covered in Chapter 3. Because the UCR breaks down arrest statistics by age of the arrestee, it has been considered the primary source of information on the presence of juveniles in America's justice system. This does not mean, however, that the UCR is completely reliable when it comes to measuring juvenile delinquency. The process measures only those juveniles who were caught and therefore does not accurately reflect all delinquent acts in any given year. Furthermore, it measures the number of arrests but not the number of arrestees, meaning that—due to repeat offenders—the number of juveniles actually in the system could be below the number of juvenile arrests.

Delinquency by the Numbers

With these cautions in mind, UCR findings give a useful account of the extent of juvenile delinquency in the United States. In 2013, juveniles accounted for 11.1 percent of violent crime arrests and 9.7 percent of criminal activity arrests in general.[25] According to the UCR, that year juveniles were responsible for

- 7 percent of all murder arrests.
- 9 percent of all aggravated assault arrests.
- 15 percent of all forcible rapes.
- 15 percent of all weapons arrests.
- 20 percent of all robbery arrests.
- 16 percent of all Part I property crimes.
- 8 percent of all drug offenses.

CJ Policy—Your Take

When he was fourteen years old, Shimeek Gridine shot a man in the cheek during a failed robbery attempt. Even though the victim was not seriously wounded, a Florida judge sentenced Gridine to seventy years in prison without the possibility of parole. Gridine's lawyers challenged the punishment as being practically the same as a **certain life sentence,** and therefore prohibited by the Supreme Court's *Graham* ruling. Do you agree? Why or why not? What are the arguments for and against allowing state judges to hand down lengthy sentences for juvenile offenders that are not technically "life without parole?"

The Rise and Fall of Juvenile Crime

As Figure 15.3 shows, juvenile arrest rates for violent crimes have fluctuated dramatically over the past three decades. In the 2000s, with a few exceptions, juvenile crime in the United States has decreased at a rate similar to that of adult crime, as discussed earlier in this textbook. From 2002 to 2011, juvenile court delinquency caseloads declined by 26 percent.[26] Not surprisingly, the drop in juvenile arrests and court appearances has led to fewer juveniles behind bars. The national population of juvenile inmates decreased 18 percent between 2008 and 2010, allowing officials in some states, including California, Ohio, and Texas, to close juvenile detention facilities.[27]

A number of theories have been put forth to explain this downturn in juvenile offending. Some observers point to the increase in police action against "quality-of-life" crimes such as loitering, which they believe stops juveniles before they have a chance to commit more serious crimes. Similarly, about 80 percent of American municipalities enforce juvenile curfews, which restrict the movement of minors during certain hours, usually after dark.[28] In 2013, law enforcement made about 56,000 arrests for curfew and loitering law violations.[29] Furthermore, hundreds of local programs designed to educate children about the dangers of drugs and crime operate across the country. Though the results of such community-based efforts are difficult, if not impossible, to measure—it cannot be assumed that children would have become delinquent if they had not participated—these programs are generally considered a crucial element of keeping youth crime under control.[30]

Girls in the Juvenile Justice System

Although overall rates of juvenile offending have been dropping, arrest rates for girls are declining more slowly than those for boys. Between 1997 and 2011, the number of cases involving males in delinquency courts declined 38 percent, while the female caseload in such courts declined by 22 percent.[31] Self-reported studies show, however, that there has been little change in girls' violent behavior over the past few decades.[32] Why, then, are the rates of female juvenile offenders failing to decrease at the same pace as the rates of male juvenile offenders?

A Growing Presence Although girls have for the most part been treated more harshly than boys for status offenses,[33] a "chivalry effect" (see Chapter 11) has traditionally existed in other areas of the juvenile justice system. In the past, police were likely to arrest offending boys while allowing girls to go home to the care of their families for similar behavior. This is no longer the case. According to the Office of Juvenile Justice and Delinquency Prevention,

FIGURE 15.3 Arrest Rates of Juveniles

After rising dramatically in the mid-1990s, juvenile arrest rates for violent crimes have—with a few exceptions—continued to drop steadily in the 2000s.

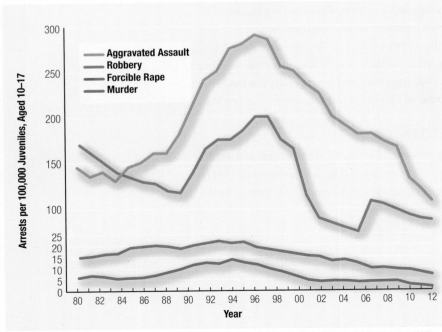

Source: Office of Juvenile Justice and Delinquency Prevention, *Statistical Briefing Book*, at **ojjdp.gov/ojstatbb/crime/JAR.asp**.

juvenile courts handled 55 percent more cases involving girls in 2011 as they did in 1985.[34] A particular problem area for girls appears to be the crime of assault. In 2013, females accounted for 23 percent of all juvenile arrests for aggravated assault and 28 percent of those arrests for simple assault, higher percentages than for other violent crimes.[35]

Family-Based Delinquency Criminologists disagree on whether rising arrest rates for female juveniles reflect a change in behavior or a change in law enforcement practices. A significant amount of data supports the latter proposal, especially research showing that police are much more likely to make arrests in situations involving domestic violence than they were even a decade ago. Experts have found that girls are four times more apt to fight with parents or siblings than are boys, who usually engage in violent encounters with strangers. Consequently, a large percentage of female juvenile arrests for assault arise out of family disputes—arrests that until relatively recently would not have been made.[36]

▲ A police officer interviews two teenage girls who were involved in a fight in Tucson, Arizona. **Do you think that law enforcement is likely to treat girls more harshly than boys for this type of misbehavior? Why?** Scott Olson/ Getty Images News/Getty Images

LEARNING OBJECTIVE 5 Explain how law enforcement's emphasis on domestic violence has influenced female juvenile arrest patterns.

Evidence also shows that law enforcement agents continue to treat girls more harshly for some status offenses. More girls than boys are arrested for the status offense of running away from home,[37] for example, even though studies show that male and female juveniles run away from home with equal frequency.[38] Criminologists who focus on issues of gender hypothesize that such behavior is considered normal for boys, but is seen as deviant for girls and therefore more deserving of punishment.[39]

School Violence and Bullying

One late Friday morning in October 2014, fourteen-year-old Jaylen Fryberg brought a .40 caliber Beretta handgun into the cafeteria of Marysville-Pilchuck High School in Marysville, Washington. Fryberg opened fire, killing four friends before fatally turning the weapon on himself. The incident was every student's (and teacher's and parent's) worst nightmare. Like other episodes of school violence, it received heavy media coverage, fanning fears that our schools are unsafe.

Safe Schools Research does show that juvenile victimization and delinquency rates increase during the school day, and the most common juvenile crimes, such as simple assaults, are most likely to take place on school grounds.[40] In spite of well-publicized mass shootings such as the one carried out by Jaylen Fryberg in Marysville, Washington, however, violent crime is not commonplace in American schools. In fact, school-age youths are more than fifty times more likely to be murdered away from school than on a campus.[41] Furthermore, despite a slight increase in recent years, between 1995 and 2013 victimization rates of students for nonfatal crimes at school declined significantly, meaning that, in general, schools are safer today than they were in the recent past.[42]

Security Measures For the most part, these statistics mirror the downward trend of all criminal activity in the United States since the mid-1990s. In addition, since the fatal shootings of fourteen students and a teacher at Columbine High School near Littleton, Colorado, in 1999, many schools have improved security measures. From 1999 to 2013, the percentage of American schools using security cameras to monitor their campuses increased from 19 to 64 percent. Today, 88 percent of public schools control access to school buildings by locking or monitoring their doors.[43] Furthermore, many districts rely on law enforcement officers to patrol school grounds, a controversial practice that we will cover in the *CJ in Action* feature at the end of the chapter.

Disciplinary Measures The Columbine shootings also led many schools to adopt "zero tolerance" policies when it comes to student behavior. These policies require strict punitive measures, such as suspension, expulsion, or referral to the police, for *any* breach of the school's disciplinary code. As a result, according to research conducted by the Vera Institute of Justice, one in nine secondary school students are suspended or expelled each year.[44]

The many critics of zero-tolerance policies point out that only 5 percent of serious school disciplinary actions involve possession of a weapon.[45] Examples of less-serious student behavior resulting in expulsion include eating a Pop-Tart in the shape of a gun, firing an imaginary bow-and-arrow, and a six-year-old boy kissing a six-year-old girl on the hand.[46] This trend of reacting harshly to minor infractions may have serious repercussions for society. Students who have been expelled for any amount of time are at a much greater risk for future involvement in the juvenile justice system than those who have not faced such disciplinary measures.[47]

Bullied Students A disproportionate number of young people who do bring guns or other weapons to school report that they have been *bullied* by other students.[48] **Bullying** can be broadly defined as repeated, aggressive behavior that contains at least one of the following elements:

1. *Physical abuse,* such as hitting, punching, or damaging the subject's property.
2. *Verbal abuse,* such as teasing, name calling, intimidation, or homophobic or racist remarks.
3. *Social and emotional abuse,* such as spreading false rumors, social exclusion, or playing jokes designed to humiliate.
4. *Cyber abuse,* which includes any form of bullying that takes place online or through the use of devices such as smartphones.

Changing Perspectives Bullying has traditionally been seen more as an inevitable rite of passage among adolescents than as potentially criminal behavior. In recent years, however, society has become more aware of the negative consequences of bullying, underscored by a number of high-profile "bullycides." In September 2013, for example, twelve-year-old Rebecca Sedwick jumped to her death at an abandoned concrete plant in Lakeland, Florida. Sedwick had been relentlessly bullied online and face-to-face by two other girls who, among other things, told her that she was "ugly" and that she should "drink bleach and die."[49] Furthermore, between 2009 and 2012, at least five American teenage boys committed suicide after being bullied about their sexuality.

Legal Responses According to data gathered by the federal government, 28 percent of students aged twelve to eighteen have been victims of bullying.[50] In particular, gay

Bullying Overt acts taken by students with the goal of intimidating, harassing, or humiliating other students.

students are targeted—nine out of ten report being bullied within the previous year.[51] As a response to this problem, nearly every state has passed anti-bullying legislation. These laws focus mostly on "soft" measures, such as training school personnel how to recognize and respond to bullying.[52]

State legislatures have been reluctant to take "harder" measures such as specifically defining bullying as a crime. Returning to our previous example, in October 2013 Polk County Sheriff Grady Judd arrested the two girls who had bullied Rebecca Sedwick prior to her death and charged them with felony aggravated stalking. The state attorney's office quickly dropped the charges, however, after determining that the girls' behavior, while reprehensible, was not criminal.

CJ & Technology

Cyberbullying

Although it is not clear whether bullying in general is more prevalent now than in the past, one form of bullying is definitely on the rise. As the Internet, texting, and social networking sites such as Facebook have become integral parts of youth culture, so, it seems, has cyberbullying. Apps such as Yik Yak allow young people to make anonymous rude, cruel, and sexually suggestive comments about peers. In a recent poll, 85 percent of American and Canadian students said that they had been subject to cyberbullying at least once during the previous year.

To many, cyberbullying can be even more devastating than "old school" bullying. Not only does the anonymity of cyberspace seem to embolden perpetrators, causing them to be more vicious than they might be in person, but, as one expert points out, when bullying occurs online, "you can't get away from it." Still, as the example of Rebecca Sedwick in the text highlights, criminal law does not yet cover most forms of cyberbullying. The consensus seems to be that children should not be charged with a crime for vicious behavior online unless that behavior contains a "specific threat of bodily harm or death." Another suggestion, that parents be held legally responsible for their child's online bullying, has also been ruled out as an unworkable solution to the problem.

Cheryl E. Davis/ShutterStock.com

Thinking about Cyberbullying
How should the criminal justice system respond to cyberbullying, if at all?

Factors in Juvenile Delinquency

As we discussed in Chapter 2, an influential study conducted by Professor Marvin Wolfgang and several colleagues in the early 1970s introduced the "chronic 6 percent" to criminology. The researchers found that out of one hundred boys, six will become chronic offenders, meaning that they are arrested five or more times before their eighteenth birthdays. Furthermore, Wolfgang and his colleagues determined that these chronic offenders are responsible for half of all crimes and two-thirds of all violent crimes within any given cohort (a group of persons who have similar characteristics).[53] Does this "6 percent rule" mean that no matter what steps society takes, six out of every hundred juveniles are "bad seeds" and will act delinquently? Or does it point to a

Aging Out A term used to explain the fact that criminal activity declines with age.

Age of Onset The age at which a juvenile first exhibits delinquent behavior.

situation in which a small percentage of children may be more likely to commit crimes under certain circumstances?

Most criminologists favor the second interpretation. In this section, we will examine the four factors that have traditionally been used to explain juvenile criminal behavior and violent crime rates: age, substance abuse, family problems, and gangs. Keep in mind, however, that the factors influencing delinquency are not limited to these topics (see Figure 15.4). Researchers are constantly interpreting and reinterpreting statistical evidence to provide fresh perspectives on this very important issue.

For instance, increased attention to the nationwide problem of bullying has led to numerous studies regarding its impact on victims. Generally speaking, this research shows that victims of bullying are at an increased risk of becoming bullies themselves, and of engaging in a variety of other antisocial and criminal behavior.[54] Several years ago, Michael Turner, an associate professor of criminal justice and criminology at the University of North Carolina at Charlotte, released data showing that bullied preteens were twice as likely to wind up in prison as those preteens who had not been bullied. Furthermore, Turner found that, regardless of race, exposure to bullying during adolescence correlates strongly with substance abuse and delinquency.[55]

The Age-Crime Relationship

Describe the one variable that always correlates highly with juvenile crime rates.

LEARNING 6 OBJECTIVE

Crime statistics are fairly conclusive on one point: the older a person is, the less likely he or she will exhibit criminal behavior. Self-reported studies confirm that most people are involved in some form of criminal behavior—however "harmless"—during their early years. In fact, Terrie Moffitt of Duke University has said that "it is statistically aberrant to refrain from crime during adolescence."[56] So, why do the vast majority of us not become chronic offenders?

According to many criminologists, particularly Travis Hirschi and Michael Gottfredson, any group of at-risk persons—regardless of gender, race, intelligence, or class—will commit fewer crimes as they grow older.[57] This process is known as **aging out** (or, sometimes, *desistance,* a term we first encountered in the previous chapter). Professor Robert J. Sampson and his colleague John H. Laub believe that this phenomenon is explained by certain events, such as marriage, employment, and military service, which force delinquents to "grow up" and forgo criminal acts.[58]

Another view sees the **age of onset,** or the age at which the youth begins delinquent behavior, as a consistent predictor of future criminal behavior. One study compared recidivism rates between juveniles first judged to be delinquent before the age of fifteen and those first adjudicated delinquent after the age of fifteen. Of the seventy-one subjects who made up the first group, 32 percent became chronic offenders. Of the sixty-five who made up the second group, none became chronic offenders.[59] Furthermore, according to the Office of Juvenile Justice and Delinquency Prevention, the earlier a youth enters the juvenile justice system, the more likely he or she will become a violent offender.[60] This research

FIGURE 15.4 Risk Factors for Juvenile Delinquency

The characteristics listed here are generally accepted as "risk factors" for juvenile delinquency. In other words, if one or more of these factors are present in a juvenile's life, he or she has a greater chance of exhibiting delinquent behavior—though such behavior is by no means a certainty.

Family	• Single parent/lack of parental role model • Parental or sibling drug/alcohol abuse • Extreme economic deprivation • Family members in a gang or in prison
School	• Academic frustration/failure • Learning disability • Negative labeling by teachers • Disciplinary problems
Community	• Social disorganization (refer to Chapter 2) • Presence of gangs and obvious drug use in the community • Availability of firearms • High crime/constant feeling of danger • Lack of social and economic opportunities
Peers	• Delinquent friends • Friends who use drugs or who are members of gangs • Lack of "positive" peer pressure
Individual	• Mental illness • Tendency toward aggressive behavior • Inability to concentrate or focus/easily bored/hyperactive • Alcohol or drug use • Fatalistic/pessimistic viewpoint

suggests that juvenile justice resources should be concentrated on the youngest offenders, with the goal of preventing crime and reducing the long-term risks for society.

Substance Abuse

As we have seen throughout this textbook, substance abuse plays a strong role in criminal behavior for adults. The same can certainly be said for juveniles. According to the University of Michigan's Institute for Social Research, 24 percent of American tenth-graders and 37 percent of American twelfth-graders are regular alcohol drinkers, increasing their risks for violent behavior, delinquency, academic problems, and unsafe sexual behavior.[61] Close to 40 percent of high school seniors report using marijuana at least once in the past twelve months, and just under 20 percent admit to using an illegal drug other than marijuana during that time period.[62]

A Strong Correlation As with adults, substance abuse among juveniles seems to play a major role in offending. Drug use is associated with a wide range of antisocial and illegal behaviors by juveniles, from school suspensions to large-scale theft.[63] Nearly all young offenders (94 percent) entering juvenile detention self-report drug use at some point in their lives, and 85 percent have used drugs in the previous six months.[64] According to the Arrestee Drug Abuse Monitoring Program, nearly 60 percent of male juvenile detainees and 46 percent of female juvenile detainees test positive for drug use at the time of their offense.[65] Drug use is a particularly strong risk factor for girls: 75 percent of young women incarcerated in juvenile facilities report regular drug and alcohol use—starting at the age of fourteen—and one study found that 87 percent of female teenage offenders need substance abuse treatment.[66]

Strong Causation? The correlation between substance abuse and offending for juveniles seems obvious. Does this mean that substance abuse *causes* juvenile offending? Researchers make the point that most youths who become involved in antisocial behavior do so before their first experience with alcohol or drugs. Therefore, it would appear that substance abuse is a form of delinquent behavior rather than its cause.[67] Still, a 2011 study of adolescent offenders did find that substance abuse treatment reduces criminal behavior in the short term, suggesting that, at the least, the use of illegal drugs is an integral component of the juvenile delinquent lifestyle.[68]

Child Abuse and Neglect

Abuse by parents also plays a substantial role in juvenile delinquency. **Child abuse** can be broadly defined as the infliction of physical, emotional, or sexual damage on a child. Similar though not the same, **child neglect** refers to deprivations—of love, shelter, food, and proper care—children undergo by their parents. According to the National Survey of Children's Exposure to Violence, one in ten children in the United States experience mistreatment at the hands of a close family member.[69]

Children in homes characterized by violence or neglect suffer from a variety of physical, emotional, and mental health problems at a much greater rate than their peers.[70] This, in turn, increases their chances of engaging in delinquent behavior. One survey of violent juveniles showed that 75 percent had been subjected to severe abuse by a family member and 80 percent had witnessed violence in their homes.[71] Nearly half of all juveniles—and 80 percent of girls—sentenced to life in prison suffered high rates of abuse.[72]

Cathy Spatz Widom, currently a professor of psychology at John Jay College of Criminal Justice, compared the arrest records of two groups of subjects—one made up

Child Abuse Mistreatment of children by causing physical, emotional, or sexual damage without any plausible explanation, such as an accident.

Child Neglect A form of child abuse in which the child is denied certain necessities such as shelter, food, care, and love.

of 908 cases of substantiated parental abuse and neglect, and the other made up of 667 children who had not been abused or neglected. Widom found that those who had been abused or neglected were 53 percent more likely to be arrested as juveniles than those who had not.[73] Simply put, according to researchers Janet Currie of Columbia University and Erdal Tekin of Georgia State University, "child maltreatment roughly doubles the probability that an individual engages in many types of crime."[74]

Gangs

When youths cannot find the stability and support they require in the family structure, they will often turn to their peers. This is just one explanation for why juveniles join **youth gangs**. Although jurisdictions may have varying definitions, for general purposes a youth gang is viewed as a group of three or more persons who (1) self-identify as an entity separate from the community by special clothing, vocabulary, hand signals, and names and (2) engage in criminal activity. According to an exhaustive survey of law enforcement agencies, there are probably around 30,000 gangs with approximately 850,000 members in the United States.[75]

Juveniles who have experienced the risk factors discussed in this section are more likely to join a gang, and once they have done so, they are more likely to engage in delinquent and violent behavior than nongang members.[76] Statistics show high levels of gang involvement in most violent criminal activities in the United States.[77] About 80 percent of fatal shootings in Chicago are attributed to gangs, and mini-gangs of teenagers known as "crews" account for 30 percent of all shootings in New York City.[78]

Furthermore, a study of criminal behavior among juveniles in Seattle found that gang members were considerably more likely to commit crimes than at-risk youths who shared many characteristics with gang members but were not affiliated with any gang (see Figure 15.5). The survey also found that gang members were much more likely to own firearms or have friends who did than nongang members.[79]

FIGURE 15.5 Comparison of Gang and Nongang Delinquent Behavior

Taking self-reported surveys of subjects aged thirteen to eighteen in the Seattle area, researchers for the Office of Juvenile Justice and Delinquency Prevention found that gang members were much more likely to exhibit delinquent behavior than nongang members.

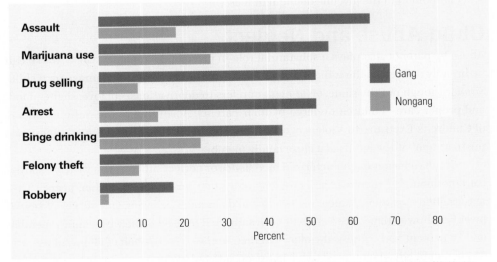

Source: Karl G. Hill, Christina Lui, and J. David Hawkins, *Early Precursors of Gang Membership: A Study of Seattle Youth* (Washington, D.C.: Office of Juvenile Justice and Delinquency Prevention, December 2001), Figure 1, page 2.

Who Joins Gangs? The average gang member is eighteen years old, though members tend to be older in cities with long traditions of gang activity, such as Chicago and Los Angeles. Although it is difficult to determine with any certainty the makeup of gangs as a whole, one recent survey found that 46 percent of all gang members in the United States are Hispanic, 35 percent are African American, and 11 percent are white, with the remaining 8 percent belonging to other racial or ethnic backgrounds.[80]

Though gangs tend to have racial or ethnic characteristics—that is, one group predominates in each gang—many researchers do not believe that race or ethnicity is the dominant factor in gang membership. Instead, gang members seem to come from lower-class or working-class communities, mostly in urban areas but with an increasing number from the suburbs and rural counties.

A small percentage of youth gang members are female. In many instances, girls associate themselves with gangs, even though they are not considered members. Generally, girls assume subordinate gender roles in youth gangs, providing emotional, physical, and sexual services for the dominant males.[81] Still, almost half of all youth gangs report having female members, and, as in other areas of juvenile crime and delinquency, involvement of girls in gangs is increasing.[82]

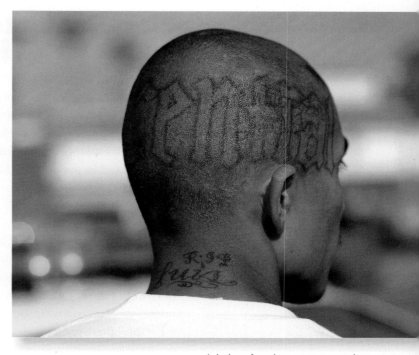

▲ In Los Angeles, a gang member signifies his allegiance to the "Street Villains" through a series of elaborate tattoos. **What role does identity play in a juvenile's decision to join a gang?** Kevork Djansezian/Getty Images News/Getty Images

Why Join Gangs? The decision to join a gang, as with the decision to engage in any sort of antisocial or criminal behavior, is a complex one, and the factors that go into it vary depending on the individual. Generally, however, the reasons for gang membership involve one or more of the following:

1. *Identity.* Being part of a gang often confers a status that the individual feels he or she could not attain outside the gang.
2. *Protection.* Many gang members live in neighborhoods marked by high levels of crime and violence, and a gang guarantees support and retaliation in case of an attack.
3. *Fellowship.* The gang often functions as an extension of the family and provides companionship that may not be available at home.
4. *Criminal activity.* Many gang members enjoy financial rewards because of the gang's profits and protection.
5. *Intimidation.* Some gang members are pressured or forced to join the gang, often to act as "foot soldiers" in the gang's criminal enterprises.[83]

To help gang members leave their gang, "desistance experts" often focus on counteracting the same pressures that initially lead to gang membership. For example, gang members with intimate partners and children are encouraged to commit to their "real family" rather than their "gang family." Help in gaining legal employment can also reduce some of the financial incentives for gang members to continue their illegal activities.[84]

First Contact: The Police and Pretrial Procedures

As part of the Juvenile Robbery Intervention Program, New York City detectives spend hours monitoring the Facebook pages and Twitter accounts of teenagers at risk for gang involvement and violent crime. Most commonly, however, contact between juvenile offenders and law enforcement takes place on the streets, initiated by a police officer on patrol who either apprehends the juvenile while he or she is committing a crime or answers a call for service. (See Figure 15.6 for an overview of the juvenile justice process.) The youth is then passed on to an officer of the juvenile court, who must decide how to handle the case.

Police Discretion and Juvenile Crime

Police arrest about 660,000 youths under the age of eighteen each year.[85] In most states, police officers must have probable cause to believe that the minor has committed an offense, just as they would if the suspect was an adult. Police power with regard to juveniles is greater than with adults, however, because police can take youths into custody for status offenses, such as possession of alcohol or truancy. In these cases, the officer is acting *in loco parentis,* or in the place of the parent. The officer's role is not necessarily to punish the youths, but to protect them from harmful behavior.

Low-Visibility Decision Making Police officers also have a great deal of discretion in deciding what to do with juveniles who have committed crimes or status offenses. Juvenile justice expert Joseph Goldstein labels this discretionary power **low-visibility decision making** because it relies on factors that the public is not generally in a position to understand or criticize. When a grave offense has taken place, a police officer

FIGURE 15.6 The Juvenile Justice Process

This diagram shows the possible tracks that a young person may take after her or his first contact with the juvenile justice system (usually a police officer).

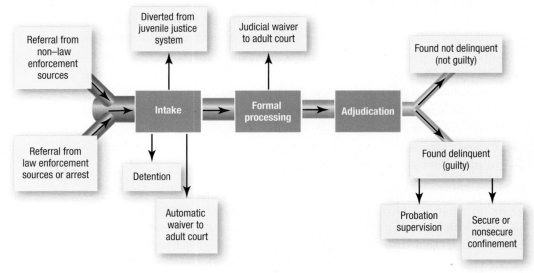

Source: Office of Juvenile Justice and Delinquency Prevention.

may decide to formally arrest the juvenile, send him or her to juvenile court, or place the youth under the care of a social-service organization. In less serious situations, the officer may simply issue a warning or take the offender to the police station and release the child into the custody of her or his parents.

In making these discretionary decisions, police generally consider the following factors:

- The nature of the child's offense.
- The offender's past history of involvement with the juvenile justice system.
- The setting in which the offense took place.
- The ability and willingness of the child's parents to take disciplinary action.
- The attitude of the offender.
- The offender's race and gender.

Law enforcement officers notify the juvenile court system that a particular young person requires its attention through a process known as a **referral**. Anyone with a valid reason, including parents, relatives, welfare agencies, and school officials, can refer a juvenile to the juvenile court. The vast majority of cases in juvenile courts, however, are referred by the police.[86]

Arrests and Minority Youths As in other areas of the criminal justice system, members of minority groups are disproportionately represented in juvenile arrests. The violent crime arrest rate for African American juveniles is about four times that for white juveniles, and the property arrest crime rate for black juveniles is double that of whites. Furthermore, African American juveniles are referred to juvenile court twice as often as their white peers,[87] and black students are 31 percent more likely to face school disciplinary action—discussed earlier in the chapter—than white and Hispanic students.[88]

A great deal of research, much of it contradictory, has been done to determine whether these statistics reflect inherent racism in the juvenile justice system or whether social factors are to blame.[89] One large-scale study, performed by federal government crime researchers Carl E. Pope and Howard Snyder using the National Incident-Based Reporting System, found that nonwhite offenders were no more likely than white offenders to be arrested for the same delinquent behavior.[90]

Failing the "Attitude Test" In general, though, as Figure 15.7 shows, police officers do seem more likely to arrest members of minority groups. Although this may be partially attributed to the social factors discussed in Chapter 2, it also appears that minority youths often fail the "attitude test" during interactions with police officers. After the seriousness of the offense and past history, the most important factor in the decision of whether to arrest or release appears to be the offender's attitude. An offender who is polite and apologetic generally has a better chance of being released. If the juvenile is hostile or unresponsive, the police are more likely to place him or her in custody for even a minor offense.[91]

Furthermore, police officers who do not live in the same community with minority youths may misinterpret normal behavior as disrespectful or delinquent and act accordingly.[92] This "culture gap" is of crucial importance to police-juvenile relations and underscores the community-oriented policing goal of having law enforcement agents be more involved in the communities they patrol, as we discussed in Chapter 6.

LEARNING **7** OBJECTIVE List the factors that normally determine what police do with juvenile offenders.

Referral The notification process through which a law enforcement officer or other concerned citizen makes the juvenile court aware of a juvenile's unlawful or unruly conduct.

FIGURE 15.7 Juvenile Arrest Rates by Race

Using the FBI's Uniform Crime Report, statisticians can determine the rates of arrest for persons aged ten to seventeen in the United States. As you can see, the rate of arrests per 100,000 juveniles remains considerably higher for African Americans than for other racial groups.

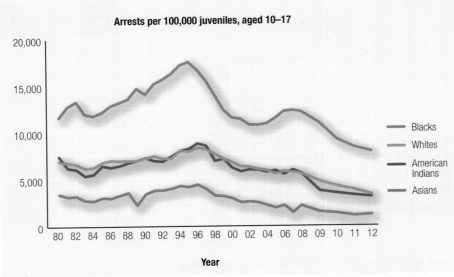

Arrests per 100,000 juveniles, aged 10–17

Blacks
Whites
American Indians
Asians

Year

Source: Office of Juvenile Justice and Delinquency Prevention, "Juvenile Arrest Trends," at **www.ojjdp.ncjrs.org/ojstatbb/crime /JAR_Display.asp?ID=qa05260&text=yes**.

Describe the four primary stages of pretrial juvenile justice procedure.

LEARNING **8** OBJECTIVE

Intake

As noted earlier, if, following arrest, a police officer feels the offender warrants the attention of the juvenile justice process, the officer will refer the youth to juvenile court. Once this step has been taken, a complaint is filed with a special division of the juvenile court, and the **intake** process begins. Intake may be followed by diversion to a community-based program, transfer to an adult court, or detention to await trial in juvenile court. Thus, intake, diversion, transfer, and detention are the four primary stages of pretrial juvenile justice procedure.

During intake, an official of the juvenile court—usually a probation officer, but sometimes a judge—must decide, in effect, what to do with the offender. The intake officer has several options during intake.

1. Simply dismiss the case, releasing the offender without taking any further action. This occurs in about one in five cases, usually because the judge cannot determine a sufficient reason to continue.[93]
2. Divert the offender to a social-services program, such as drug rehabilitation or anger management.
3. File a **petition** for a formal court hearing. The petition is the formal document outlining the charges against the juvenile.
4. Transfer the case to an adult court, where the offender will be tried as an adult.

With regard to status offenses, judges have sole discretion to decide whether to process the case or *divert* the youth to another juvenile service agency.

Pretrial Diversion

In the early 1970s, Congress passed the first Juvenile Justice and Delinquency Prevention (JJDP) Act, which ordered the development of methods "to divert juveniles from the traditional juvenile justice system."[94] Within a few years, hundreds of diversion programs had been put into effect. Today, diversion refers to the process of removing low-risk offenders from the formal juvenile justice system by placing them in community-based rehabilitation programs.

Diversion programs vary widely, but fall into three general categories:

1. *Probation.* In this program, the juvenile is returned to the community, but placed under the supervision of a juvenile probation officer. If the youth breaks the conditions of probation, he or she can be returned to the formal juvenile system.
2. *Treatment and aid.* Many juveniles have behavioral or medical conditions that contribute to their delinquent behavior, and many diversion programs offer

Intake The process by which an official of the court must decide whether to file a petition, release the juvenile, or place the juvenile under some other form of supervision.

Petition The document filed with a juvenile court alleging that the juvenile is a delinquent or a status offender and requesting that the court either hear the case or transfer it to an adult court.

remedial education, drug and alcohol treatment, and other forms of counseling to alleviate these problems.

3. *Restitution.* In these programs, the offender "repays" her or his victim, either directly or symbolically through community service.[95]

Proponents of diversion programs include many labeling theorists (see Chapter 2), who believe that contact with the formal juvenile justice system "labels" the youth a delinquent, which leads to further delinquent behavior.

Increasingly, juvenile justice practitioners are relying on principles of restorative justice (see Chapter 11) to divert adolescents from formal institutions. For example, in Longmont, Colorado, some delinquents have access to victim-offender conferences, family group conferences, and other methods for determining punishments that range from apologies to counseling to restitution. In 2014, the recidivism rate for participants in Longmont was 8 percent, significantly lower than most offenders in the juvenile justice system.[96] A number of jurisdictions have also turned to nonprofit *peer courts,* in which other young people determine the proper punishment for status offenders and juveniles charged with minor crimes such as disorderly conduct and vandalism.[97]

Transfer to Adult Court

One side effect of diversionary programs is that the youths who remain in the juvenile courts are more likely to be seen as "hardened" and thus less amenable to rehabilitation. This, in turn, increases the likelihood that the offender will be transferred to an adult court, a process in which the juvenile court waives jurisdiction over the youth. In the 1980s and 1990s, when the American juvenile justice system shifted away from ideals of treatment and toward punishment, transfer to adult court was one of the most popular means of "getting tough" on delinquents.

The proportion of juveniles waived to adult court for property crimes has decreased steadily in the past two decades. About 5,400 delinquent cases are now waived to adult criminal court each year—less than 1 percent of all cases that reach juvenile court. This figure is down significantly from 1994, when the number of such cases peaked at 13,600.[98] Today, the majority of transfer cases involve juveniles who have committed a violent offense, such as Ronald Salazar of Florida and the two twelve-year-old girls from Wisconsin, discussed earlier in the chapter.[99]

Methods of Transfer
There are three types of transfer laws, and most states use more than one of them depending on the jurisdiction and the seriousness of the offense. Juveniles are most commonly transferred to adult courts through **judicial waiver,** in which the juvenile judge is given the power to determine whether a young offender's case will be waived to adult court. The judge makes this decision based on the offender's age, the nature of the offense, and any criminal history. All but five states employ judicial waiver.

Twenty-nine states have taken the waiver responsibility out of judicial hands through **automatic transfer,** also known as *legislative waiver.* In these states, the legislatures have designated certain conditions—usually involving serious crimes such as murder and rape—under which a juvenile case is automatically "kicked up" to adult court. In Rhode Island, for example, a juvenile aged sixteen or older with two prior felony adjudications will automatically be transferred on being accused of a third felony.[100]

Fifteen states also allow for **prosecutorial waiver,** in which prosecutors are allowed to choose whether to initiate proceedings in juvenile or criminal court when certain age and offense conditions are met. (See *Discretion in Action—Juvenile Drunk Driving*

Judicial Waiver The process in which the juvenile judge, based on the facts of the case at hand, decides that the alleged offender should be transferred to adult court.

Automatic Transfer The process by which a juvenile is transferred to adult court as a matter of state law.

Prosecutorial Waiver A procedure used in situations where the prosecutor has discretion to decide whether a case will be heard by a juvenile court or an adult court.

Discretion in Action

Juvenile Drunk Driving

The Situation James, a seventeen-year-old high school senior, gets behind the wheel of his father's car with a blood alcohol concentration of .12, well over the state limit for driving under the influence (DUI). He slams headfirst into another car, killing the driver. Initially, he is charged with vehicular homicide as a juvenile.

The Law In this state, prosecutors have the discretion to waive juvenile offenders to adult court if the alleged offender is sixteen years old or older at the time of the alleged offense and is charged with a felony such as vehicular manslaughter.

What Would You Do? You are a prosecutor with the discretionary power to transfer James from juvenile court to adult court. On the one hand, James has no previous criminal record, did not intend to kill his victim, and has shown extreme remorse for his actions. Furthermore, he is a juvenile and, as such, is seen by the law as less culpable than an adult. On the other hand, his careless actions resulted in a homicide, and trying him as an adult might deter other juveniles from committing DUI crimes. Do you keep James in juvenile court or waive him to adult court? Why?

[To learn what a prosecutor in Denver, Colorado, did in a similar situation, see Example 15.1 in Appendix B.]

for further insight into prosecutorial waiver procedures.) In twenty-five states, criminal court judges also have the freedom to send juveniles who were transferred to adult court back to juvenile court. Known as *reverse transfer* statutes, these laws are designed to provide judges with a measure of discretion even when automatic transfer takes place. This process is popular with those who want to reduce the number of juveniles waived to adult court. For example, Arizona recently expanded the number of offenses eligible for reverse transfer, and gave certain nonviolent juvenile offenders the ability to request a reverse transfer hearing.[101]

Transfer and Adult Corrections Proponents of transferring juveniles to the adult justice system contend that violent juvenile offenders pose a risk to nonviolent offenders in juvenile detention centers. Thus, their removal makes the juvenile justice system safer. Critics of the practice point out that, by the same token, adult prisons and jails can be very dangerous places for young offenders. Research shows that juveniles in jails have the highest suicide rates of all inmates and suffer disproportionate levels of abuse.[102]

Data also indicate that juveniles transferred to adult correctional facilities have higher recidivism rates than those who remain in the juvenile justice system.[103] Experts have several theories to explain this pattern, including the negative effect of labeling juveniles as "felons" and the decreased opportunities for family support in adult correctional facilities.[104] Furthermore, evidence suggests that younger inmates will gain knowledge of the criminal lifestyle from older, more experienced prisoners. "You can learn a whole lot more bad things in here than good," said one juvenile inmate from his cell in an Arizona adult prison.[105]

Detention

Once the decision has been made that the offender will face adjudication in a juvenile court, the intake official must decide what to do with him or her until the start of the trial. Generally, the juvenile is released into the custody of parents or a guardian—most jurisdictions favor this practice in lieu of setting money bail for youths. The intake officer may also place the offender in **detention,** or temporary custody in a secure facility, until the disposition process begins. Once a juvenile has been detained, most jurisdictions require that a **detention hearing** be held within twenty-four hours. During this hearing, the offender has several due process safeguards, including the right to counsel, the right against self-incrimination, and the right to cross-examine and confront witnesses.

In justifying its decision to detain, the court will usually address one of three issues:

1. Whether the child poses a danger to the community.
2. Whether the child will return for the adjudication process.
3. Whether detention will provide protection for the child.

The Supreme Court upheld the practice of preventive detention (see Chapter 9) for juveniles in *Schall v. Martin* (1984)[106] by ruling that youths can be detained if they are deemed a "risk" to the safety of the community or to their own welfare. Partly as a result, the number of juveniles detained for acts of violence increased 84 percent between 1985 and 2011.[107]

> **Detention** The temporary custody of a juvenile in a secure facility after a petition has been filed and before the adjudicatory process begins.
>
> **Detention Hearing** A hearing to determine whether a juvenile should be detained, or remain detained, while waiting for the adjudicatory process to begin.
>
> **Adjudicatory Hearing** The process through which a juvenile court determines whether there is sufficient evidence to support the initial petition.

Ethics Challenge

Police suspect that a seven-year-old named Patrick has knowledge concerning the murder of an eleven-year-old girl. After Patrick waives his *Miranda* rights, without his parents present, he tells a detective that he threw a rock at the victim's head. Is it ethical for police to treat juveniles the same as adults when it comes to *Miranda* proceedings, which we covered in Chapter 7? At what age can a juvenile be expected to understand the concepts of the right to remain silent and the right to an attorney? Explain your answers. (To learn more about the Supreme Court's approach to this topic, search for *Fare v. Michael C.* [1979] and *J.D.B. v. North Carolina* [2011] online.) ■

Trying and Punishing Juveniles

In just over half of all referred cases, the juvenile is eventually subject to formal proceedings in juvenile court.[108] As noted earlier, changes in the juvenile justice system since *In re Gault* (1967) have led many to contend that juvenile courts have become indistinguishable, both theoretically and practically, from adult courts.[109] About half the states, for example, permit juveniles to request a jury trial under certain circumstances. As this chapter's *Mastering Concepts* feature explains, however, juvenile justice proceedings may still be distinguished from the adult system of criminal justice, and these differences are evident in the adjudication and disposition of the juvenile trial.

Adjudication

During the adjudication stage of the juvenile justice process, a hearing is held to determine whether the offender is delinquent or in need of some form of court supervision. Most state juvenile codes dictate a specific set of procedures that must be followed during the **adjudicatory hearing,** with the goal of providing the respondent with "the essentials of due process and fair treatment." Consequently, the respondent in an adjudicatory hearing has the right to notice of charges, counsel, and confrontation and cross-examination, and the privilege against self-incrimination. Furthermore, "proof beyond a reasonable doubt" must be established to find the child delinquent. When the child admits guilt—that is, admits to the charges of the initial petition—the judge must ensure that the admission was voluntary.

 LEARNING OBJECTIVE 9 Explain the distinction between an adjudicatory hearing and a disposition hearing.

AP Images/Newspaper Member/
Columbus Dispatch/James D. DeCamp

When the juvenile justice system was first established in the United States, its participants saw it as being separate from the adult criminal justice system. Indeed, the two systems remain separate in many ways. There are, however, a number of similarities between juvenile and adult justice. Here, we summarize both the similarities and the differences.

Similarities

- The right to receive the *Miranda* warnings.
- Procedural protections when making an admission of guilt.
- Prosecutors and defense attorneys play equally important roles.
- The right to be represented by counsel at the crucial stages of the trial process.
- Access to plea bargains.
- The right to a hearing and an appeal.
- The standard of evidence is proof beyond a reasonable doubt.
- Offenders can be placed on probation by the judge.
- Offenders can be held before adjudication if the judge believes them to be a threat to the community.
- Following trial, offenders can be sentenced to community supervision.

Differences

	Juvenile System	Adult System
Purpose	Rehabilitation of the offender.	Punishment.
Arrest	Juveniles can be arrested for acts (status offenses) that are not criminal for adults.	Adults can be arrested only for acts made illegal by the relevant criminal code.
Wrongdoing	Considered a "delinquent act."	A crime.
Proceedings	Informal; closed to public.	Formal and regimented; open to public.
Information	Courts may NOT release information to the press.	Courts MUST release information to the press.
Parents	Play significant role.	Play no role.
Release	Into parent/guardian custody.	May post bail when appropriate.
Jury trial	In some states, juveniles do NOT have this right.	All adults have this right.
Searches	Juveniles can be searched in school without probable cause.	No adult can be searched without probable cause.
Records	Juvenile records are sealed at age of adult criminal responsibility.	Adult criminal records are, for the most part, permanent.
Sentencing	Juveniles are placed in separate facilities from adults.	Adults are placed in county jails or state or federal prisons.
Death penalty	No death penalty.	Death penalty for certain serious crimes under certain circumstances.

At the close of the adjudicatory hearing, the judge is generally required to rule on the legal issues and evidence that have been presented. Based on this ruling, the judge determines whether the respondent is delinquent or in need of court supervision. Alternatively, the judge can dismiss the case based on a lack of evidence. It is important to remember that finding a child delinquent is *not* the same as convicting an adult of a crime. A delinquent does not face the same restrictions imposed on adult convicts in some states, such as limits on the right to vote and to run for political office (discussed in Chapter 13).

Disposition

Once a juvenile has been adjudicated delinquent, the judge must decide what steps will be taken toward treatment and/or punishment. Most states provide for a *bifurcated* process in which a separate **disposition hearing** follows the adjudicatory hearing. Depending on state law, the juvenile may be entitled to counsel at the disposition hearing.

Sentencing Juveniles In an adult trial, the sentencing phase is primarily concerned with protecting the community from the convict. In contrast, a juvenile judge uses the disposition hearing to determine a sentence that will serve the needs of the child. For assistance in this crucial process, the judge will order the probation department to gather information on the juvenile and present it in the form of a **predisposition report.** The report usually contains information concerning the respondent's family background, the facts surrounding the delinquent act, and interviews with social workers, teachers, and other important figures in the child's life.

Judicial Discretion In keeping with the rehabilitative tradition of the juvenile justice system, juvenile judges generally have a great deal of discretion in choosing one of several disposition possibilities. A judge can tend toward leniency, delivering only a stern reprimand or warning before releasing the juvenile into the custody of parents or other legal guardians. Otherwise, the choice is among incarceration in a juvenile correctional facility, probation, or community treatment. In most cases, the seriousness of the offense is the primary factor used in determining whether to incarcerate a juvenile, though history of delinquency, family situation, and the offender's attitude are all relevant.

Juvenile Corrections

In general, juvenile corrections are based on the concept of **graduated sanctions**—that is, the severity of the punishment should fit the crime. Consequently, status and first-time offenders are diverted or placed on probation, repeat offenders find themselves in intensive community supervision or treatment programs, and serious and violent offenders are placed in correctional facilities.

As society's expectations of the juvenile justice system have changed, so have the characteristics of its corrections programs. In some cities, for example, juvenile probation officers join police officers on the beat. Because the former are not bound by the same search and seizure restrictions as other law enforcement officials, this interdepartmental teamwork provides more opportunities to fight youth crime aggressively. Juvenile correctional facilities are also changing their operations to reflect public mandates that they should both reform and punish.

Juvenile Probation The most common form of juvenile corrections is probation—33 percent of all delinquency cases disposed of by juvenile courts result in conditional diversion. The majority of all adjudicated delinquents (64 percent) will never receive a disposition more severe than being placed on probation.[110] These statistics reflect a general understanding among juvenile court judges and other officials that a child should normally be removed from her or his home only as a last resort.

The organization of juvenile probation is very similar to adult probation (see Chapter 12),

Disposition Hearing Similar to the sentencing hearing for adults, a hearing in which the juvenile judge or officer decides the appropriate punishment for a youth found to be delinquent or a status offender.

Predisposition Report A report prepared during the disposition process that provides the judge with relevant background material to aid in the disposition decision.

Graduated Sanctions The practical theory in juvenile corrections that a delinquent or status offender should receive a punishment that matches in seriousness the severity of the wrongdoing.

▼ A bailiff tells a juvenile who has just completed his community service to tuck in his shirt at a City of Houston Municipal Court hearing. **Why do juvenile court judges favor community service and probation, when appropriate, as sentencing options for juveniles?** Photo by Michael Stravato/*The Washington Post*/Getty Images

and juvenile probationers are increasingly subjected to electronic monitoring and other supervisory tactics. The main difference between the two programs lies in the attitude toward the offender. Adult probation officers have an overriding responsibility to protect the community from the probationer, while juvenile probation officers are expected to take the role of a mentor or a concerned relative in looking after the needs of the child.

Confining Juveniles About 68,000 American youths (down from approximately 107,000 in 1995) are incarcerated in public and private juvenile correctional facilities in the United States.[111] Most of these juveniles have committed crimes against people or property, but a significant number (about 14 percent) have been incarcerated for technical violations of their probation or parole agreements.[112] After deciding that a juvenile needs to be confined, the judge has two sentencing options: nonsecure juvenile institutions and secure juvenile institutions.

Nonsecure Confinement Some juvenile delinquents do not require high levels of control and can be placed in **residential treatment programs.** These programs, run by either probation departments or social-services departments, allow their subjects freedom of movement in the community. Generally, this freedom is predicated on the juveniles following certain rules, such as avoiding alcoholic beverages and returning to the facility for curfew. Residential treatment programs can be divided into four categories:

1. *Foster care programs,* in which the juveniles live with a couple who act as surrogate parents.
2. *Group homes,* which generally house between twelve and fifteen youths and provide treatment, counseling, and education services by a professional staff.
3. *Family group homes,* which combine aspects of foster care and group homes, meaning that a single family, rather than a group of professionals, looks after the needs of the young offenders.
4. *Rural programs,* which include wilderness camps, farms, and ranches where between thirty and fifty children are placed in an environment that provides recreational activities and treatment programs.

Secure Confinement Secure facilities are comparable to the adult prisons and jails we discussed in Chapters 13 and 14. These institutions go by a confusing array of names depending on the state in which they are located, but the two best known are boot camps and training schools.

A **boot camp** is the juvenile variation of shock probation. As we noted in Chapter 12, boot camps are modeled after military training for new recruits. Boot camp programs are based on the theory that by giving wayward youths a taste of the "hard life" of military-like training for short periods of time, usually no longer than 180 days, they will be "shocked" out of a life of crime. At a typical youth boot camp, inmates are grouped in platoons and live in dormitories. They spend eight hours a day training, drilling, and doing hard labor, and also participate in programs such as basic adult education and job skills training.

No juvenile correctional facility is called a "prison." This does not mean they lack a strong resemblance to prisons. The facilities that most closely mimic the atmosphere at an adult correctional facility are **training schools,** alternatively known as youth camps, youth development centers, industrial schools, and several other similar titles.

Residential Treatment Program A government-run facility for juveniles whose offenses are not deemed serious enough to warrant incarceration in a training school.

Boot Camp A variation on traditional shock incarceration in which juveniles (and some adults) are sent to secure confinement facilities modeled on military basic training camps instead of prison or jail.

Training School A correctional institution for juveniles found to be delinquent or status offenders.

Courtesy Carl McCullough, Sr.

Carl McCullough, Sr.
Resident Youth Worker

I had a shot in the NFL, playing for the Buffalo Bills and the Minnesota Vikings, but that lasted only a short time. Today, I work at the Hennepin County (Minnesota) Juvenile Detention Center, where I'm responsible for a group of twelve young men, aged thirteen to eighteen, who are awaiting trial, waiting for placements, or just being held in a secure place due to the high-profile nature of their cases. I'm with the kids every day and every other weekend from 6:30 A.M. to 2:30 P.M. I do everything from helping with homework to supervising their leisure time, running group programs, and just being a positive, caring adult with whom to talk.

Having the NFL experience is a huge icebreaker with the residents. "Why are you here?" they always ask me, and I tell them I am here because I care about them, because I want to see a change, and because I'd like to help them believe that something better is possible. To do this job well, you have to be good at building relationships. It helps to know how to work with different cultures as well. Then you have to have patience; without it you won't last long. You know they are going to test you, to see what they can and can't get away with. You also have to be willing to learn a few things from them. You have to be a good listener.

iStockPhoto.com/Chris Scredon

SOCIAL MEDIA CAREER TIP Potential employers want information about you, but they do not want your life story. To capitalize on two primary benefits of social media, personalize your message and be concise.

FASTFACTS

Resident youth worker Job description:

- Provide safety, security, custodial care, discipline, and guidance. Play a critical role in the rehabilitation of youth and, as a result, have a potentially great impact on a youth's success during and after his or her incarceration.

What kind of training is required?

- A bachelor's degree in human services, behavioral science, or a related field.
- Professional and respectful verbal communication skills.

Annual salary range?

- $20,000–$45,000

Whatever the name, these institutions claim to differ from their adult countparts by offering a variety of programs to treat and rehabilitate the young offenders. In reality, training schools are plagued by many of the same problems as adult prisons and jails, including high levels of inmate-on-inmate violence, substance abuse, gang wars, and overcrowding.

Aftercare Juveniles leave correctional facilities through an early release program or because they have served the length of their sentences. Juvenile corrections officials recognize that many of these children, like adults, need assistance readjusting to the outside world. Consequently, released juveniles are often placed in **aftercare** programs. Based on the same philosophy that drives the prisoner reentry movement (discussed in the previous chapter), aftercare programs are designed to offer services for the juveniles, while at the same time supervising them to reduce the chances of recidivism.

The ideal aftercare program includes community support groups, education and employment aid, and continued monitoring to ensure that the juvenile is able to deal with the demands of freedom. Statistics suggest, however, that the aftercare needs of young offenders often go unmet. Nearly 60 percent of those who have been referred to juvenile court are "re-referred" before turning eighteen years old.[113] More troubling is the

Aftercare The variety of therapeutic, educational, and counseling programs made available to juvenile delinquents (and some adults) after they have been released from a correctional facility.

notion that many juvenile offenders are likely, if not destined, to become adult offenders. A report on Illinois's juvenile justice system criticized it as "a 'feeder system' to the adult criminal justice system and a cycle of crime, victimization, and incarceration."[114]

EthicsChallenge

Thirteen-year-old Tara, who has no history of trouble with the police, gets into a fight with another girl at school. At the insistence of the other girl's mother, a local prosecutor files second degree assault charges against Tara. In the predisposition report, juvenile court officials recommend that no action be taken in this case. After Tara fails to show up for her trial, however, she is arrested. Would it be ethical for a juvenile court judge to incarcerate Tara under these circumstances? Why or why not? ■

Police in Schools

When a shooter opens fire at a school, the average response time for outside law enforcement is three minutes.[115] During that interval, on-campus police officers known as School-Resource Officers (SROs) often have the responsibility of protecting students and faculty. Many SROs embrace this challenge. "We're trained now to head straight for the shooter, because every passing second can mean another dead kid," said Travis Garrison, an SRO in Gresham, Oregon.[116] On a daily basis, however, school police officers are not dealing with deadly killers—they are dealing with unruly students. It is in this context that more and more observers are asking a crucial question, addressed in this *CJ in Action* feature: Do police in schools create more problems than they solve?

Security or Discipline?

In the 1970s, law enforcement officers were present in only about 1 percent of American schools. This percentage began to rise in the 1980s, when juvenile crime rates increased dramatically. Then, in 1999, two high school seniors killed twelve students and one teacher at Colorado's Columbine High School, leading to a wave of financing for school police. By 2010, about half of all public schools had assigned police officers, and about 17,000 SROs were patrolling school hallways.[117] SROs have the same powers as any other police officer, including the ability to issue criminal citations to students who break the law on school grounds.

In theory, armed SROs have the ability to respond quickly to emergency situations and disable shooters before the violence escalates. "The only thing that stops a bad guy with a gun," says National Rifle Association of America (NRA) leader Wayne LaPierre, "is a good guy with a gun."[118] In practice, SROs spend much more time on disciplinary issues than on security issues or mentoring students. According to the National Institute of Justice, SROs spend more than half their work week on law enforcement activities, which include handing out misdemeanor citations for offenses such as acting up in class, getting in fights, or smoking cigarettes.[119] "The problem," says an SRO from Phoenix, Arizona, "is the school at times says, 'Oh, we've got a cop. Let him [or her] take care of things.'"[120]

The Case for Police in Schools

- Having armed, trained law enforcement personnel in schools increases the level of safety at the schools, just as it would anywhere else.

- A police presence acts as a deterrent against a school attack. In the words of one commentator, "Rampaging gunmen seek victims at places where they expect no immediate resistance."[121]

- SROs help teachers deal with increasingly dangerous students, who, according to an Austin, Texas, educator, "can be very threatening. The police get called because that way the teacher can go on with teaching instead of wasting half the class dealing with one child, and it sends a message to the other kids."[122]

The Case against Police in Schools

- Several studies suggest that, not only does the presence of SROs have little impact on school safety, but that having police officers on campuses also increases the likelihood of certain kinds of student disorder.[123]

- Many school districts cannot afford the expense. The School Superintendents Association estimates that placing an officer in every American school, as the NRA suggests, would cost more than $5 billion.[124]

- Police in schools lead to a "school-to-prisons pipeline," in which minor behavior problems are referred to criminal courts, saddling hundreds of thousands of students with criminal records. As a consequence, these children are more likely to drop out of school and have future interactions with the criminal justice system.[125]

Your Opinion—Writing Assignment

Financial considerations aside, law enforcement will continue to patrol the hallways of many of the nation's public schools. The challenge, then, is to stop "criminalizing our children for nonviolent offenses," as one Texas judge says.[126]

Why do you think that an SRO would cite a student for, as has happened, spraying herself with perfume in class or pouring milk on another student? How should SRO discretion be limited to best meet the goal of protecting students without arresting too many of them in the process? Before responding, you can review our discussions in the sections of this chapter concerning:

- The culpability of juveniles ("Determining Delinquency Today").

- School violence and bullying ("Trends in Juvenile Delinquency").

- Police discretion and juvenile crime ("First Contact: The Police and Pretrial Procedures").

Your answer should include at least three full paragraphs.

Summary

For more information on these concepts, look back to the Learning Objective icons throughout the chapter.

 Describe the child-saving movement and its relationship to the doctrine of *parens patriae*. Under the doctrine of *parens patriae*, the state has a right and a duty to care for neglected, delinquent, and disadvantaged children. The child-saving movement, based on the doctrine of *parens patriae*, started in the 1800s. Its followers believed that juvenile offenders require treatment rather than punishment.

 List the four major differences between juvenile courts and adult courts. (a) No juries, (b) different terminology, (c) limited adversarial relationship, and (d) confidentiality.

 Identify and briefly describe the single most important U.S. Supreme Court case with respect to juvenile justice. The case was *In re Gault*, decided by the Supreme Court in 1967. In this case a minor was arrested for allegedly making an obscene phone call. His parents were not notified and were not present during the juvenile court judge's decision-making process. In this case, the Supreme Court held that juveniles are entitled to many of the same due process rights granted to adult offenders, including notice of charges, the right to counsel, the privilege against self-incrimination, and the right to confront and cross-examine witnesses.

 Describe the reasoning behind recent U.S. Supreme Court decisions that have lessened the harshness of sentencing outcomes for violent juvenile offenders. In banning capital punishment and limiting the availability of life sentences without parole for offenders who committed their crimes as juveniles, the Supreme Court has focused on the concept of "diminished capacity." This concept is based on the notion that violent juvenile offenders cannot fully comprehend the consequences of their actions and are more deserving of the opportunity for rehabilitation than adult violent offenders.

 Explain how law enforcement's emphasis on domestic violence has influenced female juvenile arrest patterns. Girls are much more likely to fight with parents and siblings than are boys, whose physical confrontations tend to involve strangers. Because police officers have taken a more aggressive stand against domestic violence, they are more likely to arrest female juveniles involved in family disputes now than they were in the past.

 Describe the one variable that always correlates highly with juvenile crime rates. The older a person is, the less likely he or she will exhibit criminal behavior. This process is known as aging out. Thus, persons in any at-risk group will commit fewer crimes as they get older.

 List the factors that normally determine what police do with juvenile offenders. The arresting police officers consider (a) the nature of the offense, (b) the youthful offender's past criminal history, (c) the setting in which the offense took place, (d) whether the parents can take disciplinary action, (e) the attitude of the offender, and (f) the offender's race and gender.

 Describe the four primary stages of pretrial juvenile justice procedure. (a) Intake, in which an official of the juvenile court engages in a screening process to determine what to do with the youthful offender; (b) pretrial diversion, which may consist of probation, treatment and aid, and/or restitution; (c) jurisdictional waiver to an adult court, in which case the youth leaves the juvenile justice system; and (d) some type of detention, in which the youth is held until the disposition process begins.

 Explain the distinction between an adjudicatory hearing and a disposition hearing. An adjudicatory hearing is essentially a "trial." Defense attorneys may be present during the adjudicatory hearing in juvenile courts. In many states, once adjudication has occurred, there is a separate disposition hearing that is similar to the sentencing phase in an adult court. At this point, the court, often aided by a predisposition report, determines the sentence that serves the "needs" of the child.

Questions for Critical Analysis

1. What is the difference between a status offense and a crime? What punishments do you think should be imposed on juveniles who commit status offenses?

2. In many prisons, juveniles serving life sentences without the possibility of parole are not allowed to take educational or vocational training classes. What is the reasoning behind this policy? What is your opinion of this policy?

3. Do you think that bullying should be punishable as a felony along the same lines as assault? (For the definition of assault, go back to Chapter 1.) Why or why not?

4. Several years ago, eight Florida teenagers ranging in age from fourteen to eighteen beat a classmate so badly that she suffered a concussion. According to law enforcement officials, the teenagers recorded the assault so that they could post it on the Internet. If you were a prosecutor and could either waive these teenagers to adult court or refer them to the juvenile justice system, which option would you choose? What other information would you need to make your decision?

5. Forty-four states have enacted parental responsibility statutes, which make parents accountable for the offenses of their children. Seventeen of these states hold parents criminally liable for their children's actions, punishing the parents with fines, community service, and even incarceration. What is your opinion of these laws—particularly those with criminal sanctions for parents?

Key Terms

adjudicatory hearing   507
aftercare   511
age of onset   498
aging out   498
automatic transfer   505
boot camp   510
bullying   496
child abuse   499
child neglect   499

detention   507
detention hearing   507
disposition hearing   509
graduated sanctions   509
intake   504
judicial waiver   505
juvenile delinquency   488
low-visibility decision making   502
parens patriae   487

petition   504
predisposition report   509
prosecutorial waiver   505
referral   503
residential treatment
    program   510
status offender   488
training school   510
youth gang   500

Notes

1. Jennifer M. O'Connor and Lucinda K. Treat, "Getting Smart about Getting Tough: Juvenile Justice and the Possibility of Progressive Reform," *American Criminal Law Review* 33 (Summer 1996), 1299.

2. *In re Gault*, 387 U.S. 1, 15 (1967).

3. Samuel Davis, *The Rights of Juveniles: The Juvenile Justice System*, 2d ed. (New York: C. Boardman Co., 1995), Section 1.2.

4. Quoted in Anthony Platt, *The Child Savers* (Chicago: University of Chicago Press, 1969), 119.

5. 383 U.S. 541 (1966).

6. *Ibid.*, 556.

7. 387 U.S. 1 (1967).

8. 397 U.S. 358 (1970).

9. 421 U.S. 519 (1975).

10. 403 U.S. 528 (1971).

11. Quoted in David Lohr, "Police Reveal Dark Details about 12-Year-Olds Accused of Stabbing a Friend to Meet 'Slenderman,'" *The Huffington Post* (June 13, 2014), at **www .huffingtonpost.com/2014/06/03 /slenderman-stabbing_n_5439667.html.**

12. Christina D. Carmichael, *Juvenile Justice and Youth Aids Program: Informational Paper 57* (Madison, Wis.: Wisconsin Legislative Fiscal Bureau, January 2013), 10.

13. Research Network on Adolescent Development and Juvenile Justice, *Youth on Trial: A Developmental Perspective on Juvenile Justice* (Chicago: John D. & Catherine T. MacArthur Foundation, 2003), 1.

14. Richard E. Redding, "Juveniles Transferred to Criminal Court: Legal Reform Proposals Based on Social Science Research," *Utah Law Review* (1997), 709.

15. Howard N. Snyder and Melissa Sickmund, *Juvenile Offenders and Victims: A National Report* (Washington, D.C.: U.S. Department of Justice, 1995), 47.

16. Martha Grace Duncan, "'So Young and So Untender': Remorseless Children and the Expectations of the Law," *Columbia Law Review* (October 2002), 1469.

17. 543 U.S. 551 (2005).

18. *Ibid.*, 567.

19. 130 S.Ct. 2011 (2010).

20. *Ibid.*, 2030.

21. 132 S. Ct. 2455 (2012).

22. *Ibid.*, ar 2463.

23. *The State of Sentencing 2014: Developments in Policy and Practice* (Washington, D.C.: The Sentencing Project, February 2015), 11–12.

24. *Surveillance Summaries: Youth Risk Behavior Surveillance—United States, 2013* (Washington, D.C.: Centers for Disease Control and Prevention, June 13, 2014).

25. Federal Bureau of Investigation, *Crime in the United States 2013* (Washington, D.C.: U.S. Department of Justice, 2014), Table 38, at **www.fbi.gov/about-us/cjis/ucr /crime-in-the-u.s/2013/crime-in-the -u.s.-2013.**

26. Sarah Hockenberry and Charles Puzzanchera, *Juvenile Court Statistics 2011* (Washington, D.C.: National Center for Juvenile Justice, July 2014), 7.

27. Office of Juvenile Justice and Delinquency Prevention, *Juvenile Residential Facility Census, 2010: Selected Findings* (Washington, D.C.: U.S. Department of Justice, September 2013), 1; and Todd Richmond, "Fewer Young Criminals Push States to Close Prisons," *Associated Press* (June 7, 2010).

28. David McDowell, "Juvenile Curfew Laws and Their Influence on Crime," *Federal Probation* (December 2006), 58.

29. *Crime in the United States, 2013, op. cit.,* Table 29.

30. Office of Juvenile Justice and Delinquency Prevention, "Community Prevention Grants Program," at **www.ojjdp.gov/cpg.**

31. *Juvenile Court Statistics, 2011, op. cit.,* 12.

32. Sara Goodkind, et al., "Are Girls Really Becoming More Delinquent? Testing the Gender Convergence Hypothesis by Race and Ethnicity, 1976–2005," *Children and Youth Services Review* (August 2009), 885–889.

33. Kimberly Kempf-Leonard and Lisa Sample, "Disparity Based on Sex: Is Gender-Specific Treatment Warranted?" *Justice Quarterly* 17 (2000), 89–128.

34. *Juvenile Court Statistics, 2011, op. cit.,* 12.

35. *Crime in the United States, 2013, op. cit.,* Table 33.

36. Margaret A. Zahn et al., "The Girls Study Group—Charting the Way to Delinquency Prevention for Girls," *Girls Study Group: Understanding and Responding to Girls' Delinquency* (Washington, D.C.: Office of Juvenile Justice and Delinquency Prevention, October 2008), 3.

37. *Juvenile Court Statistics, 2011, op. cit.,* 70.

38. Melissa Sickmund and Howard N. Snyder, *Juvenile Offenders and Victims: 1999 National Report* (Washington, D.C.: Office of Juvenile Justice and Delinquency Prevention, 1999), 58.

39. Meda Chesney-Lind, *The Female Offender: Girls, Women, and Crime* (Thousand Oaks, Calif.: Sage Publications, 1997).

40. Denise C. Gottfredson and David A. Soulé, "The Timing of Property Crime, Violent Crime, and Substance Abuse among Juveniles," *Journal of Research in Crime and Delinquency* (February 2005), 110–120.

41. National Center for Education Statistics and Bureau of Justice Statistics, *Indicators of School Crime and Safety: 2013* (Washington, D.C.: U.S. Department of Justice, June 2014), 6.

42. *Ibid.,* 10–15.

43. *Ibid.,* 86.

44. Jacob Kang-Brown, et al., *A Generation Later: What We've Learned about Zero-Tolerance in Schools* (New York: Vera Institute of Justice, December 2013), 2.

45. *Indicators of School Crime and Safety: 2013, op. cit.,* Table 22.2, page 159.

46. "The Perils of Peanut Tossing," *The Economist* (December 21, 2013), 35.

47. Kathryn C. Monahan, et al., "From the School Yard to the Squad Car: School Discipline, Truancy, and Arrest," *Journal of Youth and Adolescence* (July 2014), 1110–1122.

48. Lana Shapiro and Andrew Adesman, "Exponential, Not Additive, Increase in Risk of Weapons Carrying by Adolescents Who Themselves Are Frequent and Recurrent Victims of Bullying," *Developmental & Behavioral Pediatrics* (May 2014), at **www .abstracts2view.com/pas/view.php?nu= PAS14L1_2725.3&terms=.**

49. Quoted in "Online Bullying: Charging Kids with Felonies," *The Week* (November 1, 2013), 14.

50. *Indicators of School Crime and Safety: 2013, op. cit.,* 44.

51. Jessica Bennett, "From Lockers to Lockup," *Newsweek* (October 11, 2010), 39.

52. Adam J. Speraw, "No Bullying Allowed: A Call for a National Anti-Bullying Statute to Promote a Safer Learning Environment in American Public Schools," *Valparaiso University Law Review* (Summer 2010), 1151–1198.

53. Marvin E. Wolfgang, *From Boy to Man, from Delinquency to Crime* (Chicago: University of Chicago Press, 1987).

54. Carlos A. Cuevas, et al., *Children's Exposure to Violence and the Intersection between Delinquency and Victimization* (Washington, D.C.: Office of Juvenile Justice and Delinquency Prevention, October 2013), 1–2.

55. Michael Turner, "Repeat Bully Victimization and Legal Outcomes in a National Sample: The Impact over the Life Course" (2013), at **www.apa.org/news/press/releases/2013 /08/bully-victimizations.pdf.**

56. Quoted in John H. Laub and Robert J. Sampson, "Understanding Desistance from Crime," in *Crime and Justice: A Review of Research* (Chicago: University of Chicago Press, 2001), 6.

57. Travis Hirschi and Michael Gottfredson, "Age and the Explanation of Crime," *American Journal of Sociology* 89 (1982), 552–584.

58. Robert J. Sampson and John H. Laub, "A Life-Course View on the Development of Crime," *Annals of the American Academy of Political and Social Science* (November 2005), 12.

59. David P. Farrington, "Offending from 10 to 25 Years of Age," in *Prospective Studies of Crime and Delinquency,* eds. Katherine Teilmann Van Dusen and Sarnoff A. Mednick (Boston: Kluwer-Nijhoff Publishers, 1983), 17.

60. Office of Juvenile Justice and Delinquency Prevention, *Juveniles in Court* (Washington, D.C.: U.S. Department of Justice, June 2003), 29.

61. Lloyd D. Johnston, et al., *Monitoring the Future: National Survey Results on Drug Use, 1975–2014—2014 Overview; Key Findings on Adolescent Drug Use* (Ann Arbor, Mich.: Institute for Social Research, February 2015), 38.

62. *Ibid.,* 11, 13.

63. Carl McCurley and Howard Snyder, *Co-occurrence of Substance Abuse Behaviors in Youth* (Washington, D.C.: Office of Juvenile Justice and Delinquency Prevention, 2008).

64. Gary McClelland, Linda Teplin, and Karen Abram, "Detection and Prevalence of Substance Abuse among Juvenile Detainees," *Juvenile Justice Bulletin* (Washington, D.C.: Office of Juvenile Justice and Delinquency Prevention, June 2004), 10.

65. Arrestee Drug Abuse Monitoring Program, *Preliminary Data on Drug Use and Related Matters among Adult Arrestees and Juvenile Detainees* (Washington, D.C.: National Institute of Justice, 2003).

66. National Mental Health Association, "Mental Health and Adolescent Girls in the Justice System," at **www.nmha.org/children /justjuv/girlsjj.cfm.**

67. Larry J. Siegel and Brandon C. Welsh, *Juvenile Delinquency: The Core,* 4th ed. (Belmont, Calif.: Wadsworth Cengage Learning, 2011), 268.

68. Edward P. Mulvey, *Highlights from Pathways to Desistance: A Longitudinal Study of Serious Adolescent Offenders* (Washington, D.C.: Office of Juvenile Justice and Delinquency Prevention, March 2011), 1–3.

69. Sherry Hamby et al., *Juvenile Justice Bulletin: Children's Exposure to Intimate Partner Violence and Other Family Violence* (Washington, D.C.: Office of Juvenile Justice and Delinquency Prevention, October 2011), 1.57.

70. Kimberly A. Tyler and Katherine A. Johnson, "A Longitudinal Study of the Effects of Early Abuse on Later Victimization among High-Risk Adolescents," *Violence and Victims* (June 2006), 287–291.

71. Grover Trask, "Defusing the Teenage Time Bombs," *Prosecutor* (March/April 1997), 29.

72. Ashley Nellis, *The Lives of Juvenile Lifers: Findings from a National Survey* (Washington, D.C.: The Sentencing Project, March 2012), 2.

73. Cathy Spatz Widom, *The Cycle of Violence* (Washington, D.C.: National Institute of Justice, October 1992).

74. Janet Currie and Erdal Tekin, *Does Child Abuse Cause Crime?* (Atlanta: Andrew Young School of Policy Studies, April 2006), 27–28.

75. Arlen Egley, Jr., James C. Howell, and Meena Harris, "Highlights of the 2012 National Youth Gang Survey," *Office of Juvenile Justice and Delinquency Prevention Fact Sheet* (December 2014), 1.

76. Chris Melde and Finn-Aage Esbensen, "Gangs and Violence: Disentangling the Impact of Gang Membership on the Level and Nature of Offending," *Journal of Quantitative Criminology* (June 2013), 143–166.

77. *2013 National Gang Report* (Washington, D.C.: National Gang Intelligence Center, 2014), 3–5.

78. Tony Dokoupil, "'Small World of Murder': As Homicides Drop, Chicago Police Focus on Social Network of Gangs," *NBC News* (December 17, 2013), at **www.nbcnews.com/news /us-news/chicago-police-focus-small -world-murder-n281**; and Vivian Yeem, "An 8th Grader, a Gun and a Bus Rider in the Way," *New York Times* (March 14, 2014), A1.

79. Karl G. Hill, Christina Lui, and J. David Hawkins, *Early Precursors of Gang Membership: A Study of Seattle Youth* (Washington, D.C.: Office of Juvenile Justice and Delinquency Prevention, December 2001).

80. "National Youth Gang Survey Analysis," National Gang Center, at **www.national gangcenter.gov/survey-analysis /demographics**.

81. National Alliance of Gang Investigators Alliance, 2005 National Gang Threat Assessment (Washington, D.C.: Bureau of Justice Assistance, 2005), 10–11.

82. *2013 National Gang Report, op. cit.*, 41–42.

83. Los Angeles Police Department, "Why Young People Join Gangs" (2014), at **www .lapdonline.org/top_ten_most_wanted _gang_members/content_basic_view /23473**.

84. Michelle Arciaga Young and Victor Gonzalez, "Getting Out of Gangs, Staying Out of Gangs: Gang Intervention and Desistance Strategies," *National Gang Center Bulletin* (January 2013).

85. *Crime in the United States 2013, op. cit.*, Table 32.

86. *Juvenile Court Statistics, 2011, op. cit.*, 31.

87. Neelum Arya and Ian Augarten, *Critical Condition: African-American Youth in the Justice System* (Washington, D.C.: Campaign for Youth and Justice, 2008), 17–20.

88. Tony Fabelo, Michael D. Thompson, and Martha Plotkin, *Breaking School Rules: A Statewide Study of How School Discipline Relates to Students' Success and Juvenile Justice Involvement* (New York: The Council of State Governments, July 2011), x.

89. Carl E. Pope and Howard N. Snyder, *Race as a Factor in Juvenile Arrests* (Washington, D.C.: Office of Juvenile Justice and Delinquency Prevention, April 2003), 1.

90. *Ibid.*, 4.

91. National Institute of Justice, *The Code of the Street and African-American Adolescent Violence* (Washington, D.C.: U.S. Department of Justice, February 2009), 7, 10, 14.

92. George S. Bridges and Sara Steen, "Racial Disparities in Official Assessments of Juvenile Offenders," *American Sociological Review* 63 (1998), 554.

93. Sarah Hockenberry and Charles Puzzanchera, *Delinquency Cases in Juvenile Court, 2011* (Washington, D.C.: Office of Juvenile Justice and Delinquency Prevention, December 2014), 3.

94. 42 U.S.C. Sections 5601–5778 (1974).

95. S'Lee Arthur Hinshaw II, "Juvenile Diversion: An Alternative to Juvenile Court," *Journal of Dispute Resolution* (1993), 305.

96. Molly R. Leach, "The Political Rise of Restorative Justice," *The Huffington Post* (May 26, 2014), at **www.huffingtonpost.com/molly -rowan-leach/the-political-rise-of-res_b _5029413.html**.

97. Lane Crisler, *Recidivism within Salt Lake Peer Court* (Salt Lake City, Utah: University of Utah, 2013), 6–7.

98. Office of Juvenile Justice and Delinquency Prevention, *Delinquency Cases Waived to Criminal Court, 2011* (Washington, D.C.: U.S. Department of Justice, December 2014), 1.

99. *Ibid.*, 2.

100. Rhode Island General Laws Section 14-1-7.1 (1994 and Supp. 1996).

101. *State Trends: Legislative Victories from 2011– 2013* (Washington, D.C.: Campaign for Youth & Justice, 2014), 5.

102. *Falling Through the Cracks: A New Look at Ohio Youth in the Adult Criminal Justice System* (Covington, Ky.: Children's Law Center, 2012), 2.

103. Richard E. Redding, *Juvenile Transfer Laws: An Effective Deterrent to Delinquency?* (Washington, D.C.: Office of Juvenile Justice and Delinquency Prevention, June 2010), 4.

104. Richard E. Redding, "Juvenile Transfer Laws: An Effective Deterrent to Delinquency?" *Juvenile Justice Bulletin* (Washington, D.C.: Office of Juvenile Justice and Delinquency Prevention, August 2008), 7.

105. Quoted in Judi Villa, "Adult Prisons Harden Teens," *Arizona Republic* (November 14, 2004), A27.

106. 467 U.S. 253 (1984).

107. *Juvenile Court Statistics, 2011, op. cit.*, 32.

108. *Delinquency Cases in Juvenile Court, 2011, op. cit,* 3.

109. Barry C. Feld, "Criminalizing the American Juvenile Court," *Crime and Justice* 17 (1993), 227–254.

110. *Delinquency Cases in Juvenile Court, 2011, op. cit.*, 3.

111. Sarah Hockenberry, *Juveniles in Residential Placement, 2011* (Washington, D.C.: Office of Juvenile Justice and Delinquency Prevention, August 2014), 3.

112. Melissa Sickmund and Charles Puzzanchera, eds., *Juvenile Offenders and Victims: 2014 National Report* (National Center for Juvenile Justice, December 2014), 194.

113. Howard N. Snyder and Melissa Sickmund, *Juvenile Offenders and Victims: 2006 National Report* (Washington, D.C.: National Center for Juvenile Justice, March 2006), 235.

114. *Youth Reentry Improvement Report* (Springfield, Ill.: Illinois Juvenile Justice Commission, November 2011), 9.

115. Erik Eckholm, "Shootings Redefine Beat of School Police Officers," *New York Times* (July 26, 2014), A13.

116. Quoted in *ibid*.

117. Barbara Raymond, "Assigning Police Officers to Schools," Center for Problem-Oriented Policing, *Response Guide No. 10* (2010), at **www.popcenter.org/Responses /school_police/print**.

118. Quoted in Jason Hunsicker and Taylor Muller, "Making Schools Safer," *Daily Guide* (Waynesville, Mo.) (March 30, 2013), 1.

119. Peter Finn and Jack McDevitt, *National Assessment of School Resource Officer Programs Final Report* (Washington, D.C.: National Institute of Justice, 2005), 1.

120. Quoted in Susan Ferriss, "Should Schools Have More Police—or Fewer? States Disagree," *Denver Post* (March 5, 2013) at **www .denverpost.com/politics/ci_22714286 /should-schools-have-more-police-or -fewer-states**.

121. Stephen P. Halbrook, "Armed School Guards: Best Bet to Stop Future Newtowns," *San Antonio Express-News* (February 6, 2013), 4.

122. Quoted in Chris McGreal, "The U.S. Schools with Their Own Police," *The Guardian* (January 9, 2012), at **www.guardian.co.uk /world/2012/jan/09/texas-police-schools**.

123. *Education under Arrest: The Case against Police in Schools* (Washington, D.C.: Justice Policy Institute, November 2011), 9–12.

124. Teresa Welsh, "Should the Federal Government Pay for Armed Guards in Public Schools?" *U.S. News & World Report* (April 3, 2013), at **www.usnews.com/opinion /articles/2013/04/03/should-the-federal -government-pay-for-armed-guards-in -public-schools**.

125. Catherin Y. Kim and I. India Geronimo, *Policing in Schools* (New York: American Civil Liberties Union, 2009), 8–13.

126. Quoted in Erik Eckholm, "With Police in Schools, More Children in Court," *New York Times* (April 12, 2013), A1.

16

Today's Challenges:

Security vs. Liberty, Cyber Crime, and White-Collar Crime

Chapter Outline	Corresponding Learning Objectives
Security vs. Liberty	**1** Summarize the three federal laws that have been particularly influential on our nation's counterterrorism strategies.
	2 Explain why privacy expectations are so important to the federal government's metadata surveillance operations.
	3 Distinguish verbal threats that are protected by the Constitution from verbal threats that can be prosecuted as "true threats."
Cyber Crime	**4** Outline the three major reasons why the Internet is conducive to the dissemination of child pornography.
	5 Describe the three following forms of malware: (a) botnets, (b) worms, and (c) viruses.
	6 Explain how the Internet has contributed to piracy of intellectual property.
White-Collar Crime	**7** Indicate some of the ways that white-collar crime is different from violent or property crime.
	8 Explain the concept of corporate violence.

To target your study and review, look for these numbered Learning Objective icons throughout the chapter.

Teen Dreams

shannon maureen conley

first showed up on the homeland security radar when, in the fall of 2013, she was seen wandering outside the Faith Bible Church in Arvada, Colorado, wearing a large backpack and taking notes. A pastor notified local police, and, within days, an agent from the Federal Bureau of Investigation (FBI) asked the teenager to explain her behavior. "I hate those people," said Conley, a convert to Islam, referring to church officials. "If they think I'm a terrorist, I'll give them something to think I am," she told the FBI agent.

Over the next year and a half, federal authorities kept watch on Conley, interviewing her numerous times and opening a line of communication with her parents. After she signed up with U.S. Army Explorers, a group that trains young people in military tactics and firearm use, she admitted to the FBI that she intended to aid Muslim extremists in their efforts to wage *jihad* against the United States. Conley also said that overseas U.S. military bases and government employees living abroad were "legitimate targets of attack."

Finally, on April 8, 2014, the FBI arrested nineteen-year-old Conley at the Denver Airport as she was preparing to board a flight to Adana, Turkey. She had planned to make her way into Syria, which borders Turkey, and marry a Tunisian man she met online who was affiliated with the terrorist group known as Islamic State of Iraq and the Levant (ISIL). A certified nurse's aide, Conley apparently intended to provide medical assistance to ISIL fighters, who have killed a number of Americans in the Middle East. Conley eventually pleaded guilty to providing material support to a foreign terrorist organization, and, in January 2015, a federal judge sentenced her to four years in prison. "Even though I was committed to the idea of *jihad,* I didn't want to hurt anyone," Conley told the judge at her sentencing hearing. "I do not believe that I am a threat to society."

▲ Ana and John Conley leave the federal courthouse in Denver, Colorado, where their daughter Shannon pleaded guilty to providing material support to a terrorist organization.

1. Do you think that Shannon Conley committed a crime? If so, what was it? Explain your answers.

2. Conley's parents criticized their daughter's conviction and punishment, saying that if "the government is willing to sacrifice the future of a nineteen-year-old citizen" to deter others from joining ISIL, "then we feel the terrorists have won this particular battle." Do you agree with this criticism? Why or why not?

3. In the months leading up to her arrest, Conley apparently changed her name several times and agreed to marry three different men on the Internet. If you were her defense attorney, how would you use this information to argue that your client does not pose "a threat to society"?

Security vs. Liberty

At the time of Shannon Conley's arrest, U.S. officials were uncertain exactly how many American citizens had traveled to the Middle East to join ISIL and similar extremist organizations. Few of these homegrown terrorists, whose numbers were estimated at about one hundred, had been as forthcoming as Conley about their plans. For example, before Moner Mohammad Abusalha blew himself up in May 2014 as part of a suicide attack in Syria, the government was unsure if the twenty-two-year-old Floridian had gone abroad to fight for ISIL or to provide humanitarian aid.[1]

Since the attacks of September 11, 2001, on New York, Washington, D.C., and rural Pennsylvania, homeland security officials have placed paramount importance on tracking communications among suspected terrorists. To do so, the federal government has greatly enhanced the capabilities of law enforcement and intelligence agencies to collect and store information on these suspects. At the same time, the federal government has angered many Americans who feel that their privacy rights have been ignored or discarded for the sake of national security. "You can't have 100 percent security and also then have 100 percent privacy," remarked President Barack Obama,[2] succinctly summarizing an ongoing balancing act that goes to the heart of American ideals of fairness and justice.

▲ In 2015, a white rose is placed on the name of one of the victims of the September 11, 2001, terrorist attacks at a memorial in New York City. **Why does large-scale terrorist activity often make citizens of the targeted country more willing to trade certain freedoms for greater security against future attacks?** Jewel Samad/AFP/Getty Images

National Security and Privacy

As has been noted several times in this textbook, our Constitution upholds the premise that Americans should not be subjected to the unreasonable use of government power. As we have also pointed out, *reasonableness* is a highly subjective concept, and Americans are often willing to give their government more leeway in times of national crisis. When it comes to antiterrorism efforts and homeland security, this flexibility has manifested itself in the form of federal legislation that expands the government's ability to locate, observe, prosecute, and punish suspected terrorists. The first legislative step in this direction, however, took place decades before September 11, 2001, and was designed primarily to weaken the office of the presidency.

Foreign Surveillance Until the 1970s, policies regarding **surveillance,** or the governmental monitoring of individuals or groups that posed national security threats to the United States, were primarily the domain of the executive branch. That is, the president and his advisors decided who the federal government would target for its spy operations. Following President Richard Nixon's abuse of this discretion to eavesdrop on political opponents during the 1974 presidential campaign, in 1978 Congress passed the Foreign Intelligence Surveillance Act (FISA).[3] This legislation provided a legal framework for the government's electronic monitoring of suspected criminals or national security threats.

Under FISA, federal agents are able to eavesdrop on the communications of foreigner persons or foreign entities, without a court order, for up to a year, as long as the

LEARNING **1** OBJECTIVE

Summarize the three federal laws that have been particularly influential on our nation's counterterrorism strategies.

Surveillance The close observation of a person or group by government agents, in particular to uncover evidence of criminal or terrorist activities.

purpose of the surveillance is national security and not law enforcement. If this surveillance uncovers wrongdoing by an American citizen, the government has seventy hours to gain judicial authorization to continue to monitor this suspect's activities.[4]

If the target is a "foreign agent" operating within the United States, FISA requires permission from a special court to engage in surveillance. This court, known as the Foreign Intelligence Surveillance Court, or FISA Court, is made up of eleven federal judges assigned by the chief justice of the Supreme Court. The FISA warrant application must identify the target of the surveillance, the nature of the information sought, and the monitoring method. The government agency must also certify that the goal of the surveillance is to "obtain foreign intelligence information."[5]

Material Support Another crucial piece of counterterrorism legislation was passed in response to the 1995 truck bombing of the Alfred P. Murrah Federal Building in Oklahoma City, Oklahoma, which killed 168 people. The primary goal of this legislation, the Antiterrorism and Effective Death Penalty Act (AEDPA), is to hamper terrorist organizations by cutting off their funding. The law prohibits persons from "knowingly providing *material support* or resources" to any group that the United States has designated a "foreign terrorist organization."[6]

Material support is defined very broadly in the legislation, covering funding, financial services, lodging, training, expert advice or assistance, communications equipment, transportation, and other physical assets.[7] For example, Shannon Conley—discussed at the beginning of this chapter—was convicted for providing "material support" to ISIL even though she never actually left the United States or had any in-person contact with any members of that organization.

Furthermore, the AEDPA does not require that a suspect *intend* to aid the terrorist organization in question.[8] About a decade ago, Javed Iqbal was successfully prosecuted in New York for providing a satellite television package that included a channel operated by Hezbollah, a government-designated terrorist organization based in Lebanon. Even though there was no evidence that Iqbal intended to further the goals of Hezbollah, the fact that his conduct provided material support to the organization was sufficient to allow his prosecution under the law.[9]

The Patriot Act Enacted six weeks after the September 11, 2001, terrorist attacks, the **Patriot Act**[10] greatly strengthened the ability of federal law enforcement agents to investigate and incarcerate terrorist suspects. At 342 pages, the Patriot Act covered numerous areas related to homeland security, including immigration law and border protection, grants to local police departments, and compensation for the victims of the September 11 attacks. Here, we will focus on the legislation's rules regarding surveillance, summarized in Figure 16.1. Critics of the Patriot Act have focused on Sections 213 and 215, which allow government agents to conduct searches and seizures without many of the Fourth Amendment protections discussed in Chapter 7.

Specifically, Section 215 provides the National Security Agency (NSA), a federal agency that focuses on foreign intelligence operations, with the authority to collect the telephone billing records of Americans who have made calls to other countries, as those records are considered reasonably "relevant" to the agency's counterterrorism investigations.[11] Furthermore, the Patriot Act requires third parties such as telephone companies and Internet providers to turn over records of stored electronic communications to the federal government without notice to persons making those communications. Government agents do not need judicial permission to issue **national security letters,** as such

Material Support In the context of federal antiterrorism legislation, the act of helping a terrorist organization by engaging in a wide range of activity that includes providing financial support, training, and expert advice or assistance.

Patriot Act Legislation passed in the wake of the September 11, 2001, terrorist attacks that greatly expanded the ability of government agents to monitor and apprehend suspected terrorists.

National Security Letters Legal notices that compel the disclosure of customer records held by banks, telephone companies, Internet service providers, and other companies to the agents of the federal government.

FIGURE 16.1 The Patriot Act and Electronic Surveillance

Under Title II of the Patriot Act, the following sections greatly expanded the ability of federal intelligence operatives and law enforcement agents to conduct electronic surveillance operations on suspected terrorists.

- *Section 201:* Enables government agents to wiretap the communications of any persons suspected of terrorism or the dissemination of chemical weapons.
- *Section 204:* Makes it easier for government agents to get a warrant to search stored e-mail communications held by Internet Service Providers (ISPs).
- *Section 206:* The "roving wiretap" provision removes the requirement that government agents specify the particular places or things to be searched when obtaining warrants for surveillance of suspected terrorists.
- *Section 210:* Gives government agents enhanced authority to access the duration and timing of phone calls, along with phone numbers and credit cards used to pay for cell phone service.
- *Section 213:* The "sneak and peak" provision removes the requirement that government agents give notice to a target when they have searched her or his property.*
- *Section 214:* Removes the requirement that government agents prove that the subject of a FISA search, discussed earlier in the section, is actually the "agent of a foreign power."
- *Section 215:* The "business records" provision permits government agents to access "business records, medical records, educational records and library records" without showing probable cause of wrongdoing if the investigation is related to terrorism activities.

* In 2012, this rule was revised to require notice within thirty days of the search in most circumstances.

requests are called. The agents only need to show, after the fact, that the targeted communications are relevant to a terrorism investigation.[12] These national security letters can be used to collect:

1. Credit information from banks and loan companies,
2. Telephone and Internet data, including names, call times, physical addresses, and e-mail addresses,
3. Financial records such as money transfers and bank accounts, and
4. Travel records held by "any commercial entity."[13]

As we will soon see, widespread use of such surveillance tactics has led to a great deal of controversy over the federal government's information-gathering practices.

Mass Surveillance

Following a series of controversies concerning the ability of the NSA to wiretap telephone and e-mail communications of suspected terrorists, in 2008 Congress passed an amended version of FISA. This legislative action did not, however, place greater limits on the NSA, which had amassed a massive database by secretly keeping track of millions of phone calls made by Americans who were not under suspicion of any wrongdoing. Instead, it essentially legalized government surveillance tactics that had previously been illegal by giving the NSA more freedom to act without oversight by the FISA court.[14]

Fourth Amendment and Homeland Security The problem with the original FISA, according to some observers, was that it required a lengthy review process before the FISA court would issue a warrant allowing government agents to monitor a terrorist suspect. In an environment where individuals can rapidly change their e-mail addresses and mode of Internet communication, or use multiple cell phone numbers, this procedure was seen by these critics as too slow and cumbersome for effective intelligence gathering.[15] The NSA, FBI, and other government agencies argued that they needed more freedom to quickly collect massive amounts of information without judicial oversight.

▲ Protesting outside the Justice Department in Washington, D.C., this woman believes that the federal government should not be allowed to collect information about the telephone habits of U.S. citizens without first obtaining permission from a court. **Do you agree with her? Why or why not?** Win McNamee/Getty Images News/Getty Images

This need, of course, must be tempered by the Fourth Amendment, which broadly requires that the government have probable cause of wrongdoing before intruding on a citizen's reasonable expectation of privacy. The amended FISA's authorization of large-scale warrantless electronic eavesdropping, in which hundreds of millions of phone and Internet records have been collected and stored in databases, created concerns that the federal government aimed to "write off the Fourth Amendment as technologically obsolete."[16]

Metadata Collection In 2013, an NSA contractor named Edward Snowden revealed that, under the revised FISA, the NSA has monitored the cell phone and Internet activity of approximately 113 million Americans without probable cause or a warrant from the FISA court. Through a program known as Prism, the NSA gained access to the information collected by sending national security letters to several major telephone companies and ISPs, including Apple, Facebook, Google, Microsoft, Skype, Verizon, Yahoo, and YouTube.[17] By storing this "metadata," the government agency has gained unprecedented knowledge of whom Americans are communicating with, when these communications are taking place, and for how long.

"Red Flagging" Agents of the federal government had not been listening to actual phone conversations or reading hundreds of millions of e-mails. Rather, warrantless metadata collection and storage—justified, according to the FISA court, under Section 215 of the Patriot Act (see Figure 16.1)[18]—had been designed to retroactively determine communications patterns that might raise a "red flag" of terrorist activity. If the NSA was able to uncover a pattern of communication that suggested such activity, it would apply for a FISA warrant and undertake further investigations of the individuals involved. Using this process, the FISA court was issuing about 1,800 orders each year for domestic surveillance.[19]

"Connecting the Dots" Proponents of the NSA metadata program argued that it was the only effective method for monitoring terrorist activity over the many communications systems that exist in the United States and elsewhere. In approving the strategy, a district court noted, "Without all the data points, the government cannot be certain it has connected the pertinent ones."[20] Much to the dismay of its supporters, however, in 2015 Congress overhauled the NSA's bulk-phone record program, revising Section 215 of the Patriot Act in the process. Now, phone companies, not the NSA, have the authority to store metadata, and government agencies must petition a special court for access to that information.[21]

Explain why privacy expectations are so important to the federal government's metadata surveillance operations.

LEARNING OBJECTIVE 2

Expectations of Privacy Critics of the NSA's metadata program pointed out that while it may have contributed to a small number of homeland security investigations, there is no evidence that it disrupted any major terrorist organizations or operations.[22] This limited impact, they argued, did not justify the significant *invasion of privacy* involved.

Privacy Precedents As you may recall from Chapter 7, an individual usually has no expectation of privacy with regards to information voluntarily disclosed to third parties. So, for example, a person does not have an expectation of privacy for writing on the outside of an envelope given to the U.S. Postal Service or garbage left on the curb for collection.[23] As a result, government agents can search and seize that "information" without a warrant.

Several federal appeals courts have held that defendants have no reasonable expectation of privacy over information "voluntarily" provided to a telephone company or an ISP. In 2013, a federal judge refused to grant a new trial to defendants convicted of providing material support in the form of funds to an African terrorist organization. Federal agents admitted that they initially became interested in the defendants' behavior because of telephone records contained in the NSA database. The judge ruled that the agents did not need a warrant to obtain such information from the telephone company because individuals have "no legitimate expectation of privacy" over phone call data.[24]

In general, these judicial decisions rely on the precedent set by the United States Supreme Court in its *Smith v. Maryland* (1979)[25] decision. That case involved the police's warrantless seizure of phone numbers dialed from the home of a robbery suspect. The Court ruled that the defendant had voluntarily turned over the phone numbers to a third party—the phone company—for billing purposes and therefore had no reasonable expectation of privacy in the matter.

Privacy and Technology One federal judge has gone against the tide with regard to metadata and expectations of privacy. In 2013, U.S. District Judge Richard Leon of the District of Columbia found that the NSA's phone-data collection program "almost certainly" violated the Fourth Amendment.[26] Judge Leon argued that the Supreme Court's *Maryland* case involved a "one-time" search of phone calls emanating from the home of a single criminal suspect. In contrast, the NSA metadata program is a "daily, all-encompassing indiscriminate dump" of information from "the phones of people who are not suspected of any wrongdoing."[27]

Judge Leon's opinion raises an interesting question, addressed in this chapter's *CJ Policy—Your Take* feature: have our reasonable expectations of privacy changed because of technological innovations? The judge referred to the Supreme Court's 2012 decision that it is unconstitutional for the police to use a GPS device to track a suspect's movement without a warrant, which we covered in Chapter 7, as proof that such expectations have changed.[28] He noted that justices who made the *Maryland* ruling in 1979 could not "have ever imagined how the citizens of [today] would interact with their phones."[29]

Foreign Surveillance Targets

Foreign citizens do not enjoy the same protections under the Fourth Amendment as U.S. citizens. This distinction is important to the operation of a separate NSA data-collection program—mandated under the revised FISA of 2008—that gives the government the ability to monitor non-U.S. citizens believed to be located in another country. Section 702 of the FISA Amendment Act permits eavesdropping (not merely metadata collection) without a warrant of foreign persons to obtain information related to

1. National security, such as details of an "actual or potential attack" or "other grave hostile acts [by a] foreign power or agent of a foreign power,"
2. Foreign "intelligence activities," and
3. "The conduct of the foreign affairs of the United States."[30]

The broad language of this amended law allowed the NSA to target nearly 90,000 foreign people and organizations for surveillance in 2013.[31] This figure is significant because the law also permits eavesdropping without a warrant of a person who communicates with the target of foreign surveillance, even if that person is an American citizen. According to a detailed analysis of the NSA's global surveillance practices, the agency intercepts communications of nine incidental "bystanders" for every single "legally targeted" foreigner.[32]

This loophole has allowed the NSA to gather highly personal information such as baby pictures, medical records, and flirtatious Webcam chats from innocent persons, including Americans.[33] At the same time, it provides a valuable tool to uncover terrorist operations on U.S. soil, a growing concern that we will examine in the following section.

National Security and Speech

After the arrest of Shannon Conley at the Denver airport, discussed at the beginning of the chapter, FBI director James Comey distinguished the "mouth runners"—those who merely talk about their anti-American or violent beliefs—from potential terrorists. "This is a great country with lots of traditions of protecting mouth-running," said Comey. "We should continue that. But those who are inclined to cross the line, I've got to focus on them."[34]

How do our federal intelligence and law enforcement agencies tell the "mouth runners," protected by the American tradition of free speech, from the true threats? This question took on added urgency after a series of deadly terrorist attacks in Europe in early 2015, carried out by citizens of countries such as France and Belgium who had returned home after receiving training and support in the Middle East. This type of "small-scale attack" by a homegrown terrorist is "what keeps me up at night," says U.S. representative Michael McCaul, a Republican from Texas who chairs the House Homeland Security Committee.[35]

True Threat Law In Chapter 1, we examined the plight of Anthony Elonis, who was convicted for making violent threats against his wife in the form of rap lyrics he posted online. Elonis claimed that he never intended to actually harm his wife, and that his threats were not crimes but rather expressions of art. The crucial United States Supreme Court case for differentiating "mere speech," which is protected by the First Amendment of the U.S. Constitution, from a *true threat*, which is not, concerned the racially-charged issue of cross burning.

In *Virginia v. Black* (2003),[36] the Court struck down part of a Virginia law that prohibited *all* forms of cross burning. The statute assumed that any person who would burn a cross would only do so with the intent to frighten or intimidate specific African American targets. The Court ruled that the act of burning a cross was not enough to constitute a crime. The state must also prove that the act was done to place a specific victim "in fear of bodily harm or death."[37] So, burning a cross on the front lawn of an African American family is a **true threat,** and therefore a crime. By the same measure, burning a cross on one's own property to make a general expression of racial hatred, out of sight of any members of minority groups, is not. (See the feature *Discretion in Action—Bragging about Bombing* for an example of how true threat doctrine works in the context of domestic terrorism.)

True Threat An act of speech or expression that is not protected by the First Amendment because it is done with the intention placing a specific victim or group of victims in fear of unlawful violence.

Discretion in Action

Bragging about Bombing

The Situation On his last night in prison after serving a short stint for marijuana distribution, Steven has a long conversation with his cellmate, who is wearing a recording device. First, Steven discusses his skill as a bomb builder, giving as an example an explosive device he designed to be hidden in the face-cream container of an ex-girlfriend. Steven then specifically outlines his plans to pose as a delivery man and blow up the Reuss Federal Plaza in Milwaukee with a truck bomb. His detailed explanation includes the number of detonators and drums of explosives he would use, where he would park, and how he would deflect suspicion. Steven describes his desire to kill as many government agents as possible, and, when pressed, tells his cellmate that there is "no doubt" that "someone's gonna get it."

The Law Steven's statements can be considered a "true threat," and therefore a criminal act, if they represent "a serious expression of an intent to commit an act of unlawful violence to a particular individual or group of individuals." There is no requirement that the targets of the action be aware of the threat.

What Would You Do? As soon as he leaves prison, Steven is arrested by police for threatening to use a weapon of mass destruction against a government building. Steven tells police that he was

LEARNING **3** OBJECTIVE

Distinguish verbal threats that are protected by the Constitution from verbal threats that can be prosecuted as "true threats."

joking, and never intended to actually destroy the Reuss Federal Plaza. After hearing a tape of the conversation, Steven's lawyer points out that his client bragged he would carry out the attack after he finished his probation—in eight years. If you are the prosecutor in this case, do you bring charges against Steven for making a "true threat?" Why or why not? What additional information would you need to make this decision?

[To see what happened in a similar situation involving an inmate in Milwaukee, Wisconsin, see Example 16.1 in Appendix B.]

Finding and Capturing "Known Wolves" As a rule, individuals who intend to offer material support to terrorist organizations do not enjoy First Amendment protections. That is, they cannot claim to be harmless "mouth runners." Rather, by statute, many of the activities that constitute material support are considered true threats.[38] Sometimes, the true threat is legally obvious. In 2015, for example, six Bosnian immigrants living in Illinois, Missouri, and New York were indicted for providing material support to terrorist organizations in Syria and Iraq for sending $8,000 worth of U.S. military uniforms, technical gear, and weapons to those countries. It would be difficult, if not impossible, to claim that such behavior was a protected form of free speech.

Often, however, the true threat is not as evident. In the introduction to this chapter, we saw how Shannon Conley spoke openly to the FBI about her intentions to aid terrorist fighters in Syria. Do those statements, along with purchasing an airline ticket to the Middle East, constitute a true threat? Her parents and attorney certainly did not think so. In recent years, however, federal authorities have erred on the side of caution by arresting numerous "known wolves," who, like Conley, took concrete steps to travel abroad and join anti-American terrorist organizations. As of yet, courts have proved unwilling to overturn the convictions of these defendants on First Amendment grounds.

Recruiting Efforts The Internet has proven instrumental as an arena for terrorist recruiting operations. ISIL—which tempted Shannon Conley to travel to Syria by the online offer of a *jihadist* husband—and its sympathizers maintain thousands of active Twitter accounts in English to spread their anti-Western propaganda. After Floridian Moner Abusahla killed himself and dozens of others in a 2014 suicide bomb attack on a

U.S. military operation in Syria, the Islamist extremist group Nusra Front praised him on Facebook for being "willing to meet his God."[39]

According to the FBI, ISIL is putting out a "siren song" on social media that reads as follows:

> Troubled soul, come to the caliphate, you will live a life of glory, these are the apocalyptic end times, you will find a life of meaning here fighting for our caliphate, and if you can't come, kill somebody where you are.[40]

(The term *caliphate* refers to a new state under extremist Islamic rule that ISIL is trying to establish in parts of Syria and Iraq.)

Counterterrorism Online To combat such recruiting efforts, the FBI has homegrown terrorism investigations in every state.[41] To a large extent, these efforts consist of monitoring the Internet activities of Americans who have expressed extremist views on chat rooms dedicated to extremism. As there is no expectation of privacy for views expressed to third parties online, or, as we have seen, for Internet addresses stored by ISPs, government agents have few legal restrictions to contend with while conducting these investigations.

After the arrest of a New York City man who went online to express his desire to attack President Barack Obama, and then tried to travel abroad to join ISIL, one law enforcement agent stressed how crucial online monitoring is to homeland security. "If [these suspects] didn't go on the Internet, if [they] didn't use technology, [they would be] virtually undetectable," the agent said.[42]

▲ Thomas Durkin, attorney for Mohammed Hamzah Khan, addresses the media on October 9, 2014, in Chicago. Khan was arrested by federal agents while boarding a flight to the Middle East, where he allegedly planned to join an extremist terrorist organization. **If you were Khan's attorney, how would you argue that the act of boarding an airplane should never be a crime? What is your opinion of such an argument?** Brian Kersey/Getty Images

EthicsChallenge

The federal government maintains a secret "no-fly list" of persons suspected of having ties to terrorism who are not allowed to board a commercial airline flight that originates or terminates in the United States. Even if a person is a U.S. citizen, he or she is not permitted to challenge his or her inclusion on the no-fly list. Is this an ethical governmental policy? Should those on the no-fly list be able to go to court to get their names removed? Explain your answers. ■

Cyber Crime

Foreign terrorist organizations such as the Islamic State of Iraq and the Levant (ISIL) are using the Internet for activities other than recruitment and propaganda. In March 2015, the home Web sites of the Dublin Rape Crisis Center in Ireland, the Southwest Montana Community Federal Credit Union, and the Montauk Manor hotel in Suffolk County, New York, were replaced by a picture of the black ISIL flag and the words "hacked by ISIL, we are everywhere."[43]

Homeland security experts worry that such relatively harmless incidents are a precursor to a much more serious **cyberattack** by a terrorist organization. Such attacks are designed to damage a nation's infrastructure, such as power companies, water treatment plants, airports, chemical plants, and oil refineries. In a worst-case scenario, a cyberattack could allow a terrorist organization to seize control of the federal air traffic control system, or shut down national power grids. "This is a much bigger threat over time than losing some credit cards to cyber criminals," said one security expert.[44]

Of course, "losing some credit cards" is hardly a small concern, particularly if one of the credit cards in question happens to be your own. Furthermore, the Internet has proved reasonably secure from a "cyber 9/11," while being disturbingly susceptible to financial attacks. Several years ago, for example, a harmful piece of software created in Russia called GameOver Zeus was used to steal login details from computers belonging to thousands of small businesses and drain over $100 million from their bank accounts. "Robbing one person at a time using a knife or a gun doesn't scale well," notes Marc Goodman of the Future Crimes Institute. "But now one person can rob millions at the click of a button."[45]

Cyberattack An attempt to damage or disrupt computer systems or electronic networks operated by computers.

Cyber Crime A crime that occurs online, in the virtual community of the Internet, as opposed to in the physical world.

Computer Crime and the Internet

Nearly every business in today's economy relies on computers to conduct its daily affairs and to provide consumers with easy access to its products and services. Furthermore, more than 600 million American household devices are now connected to the Internet, and the proliferation of handheld Internet devices has made it possible to be online at almost any time or place. In short, the Internet has become a place where large numbers of people interact socially and commercially. In any such environment, wrongdoing has an opportunity to flourish. Throughout this section, we will be using the broad term **cyber crime** to describe any criminal activity occurring via a computer in the virtual community of the Internet.

Online Crime The example of *child pornography* shows how cyber crime has raised the stakes for the criminal justice system. (Child pornography is the illegal production and sale of material depicting sexually explicit conduct involving a child.) In the late 1970s, about 250 child pornography magazines were circulating in the United States, and it was relatively easy for law enforcement to confiscate hard copies of these publications.[46] With the advent of the Internet, however, child pornography became much easier to disseminate. The reasons for this include:

1. *Speed.* The Internet is a quick means of sending visual material over long distances. Child

P. C. Vey/The New Yorker Collection/Cartoonbank.com

"You know, you can do this just as easily online."

Outline the three major LEARNING
reasons why the Internet **4**
is conducive to child
pornography. OBJECTIVE

pornographers can deliver their material faster and more securely online than through regular mail.

2. *Security.* Any illegal material that passes through the hands of a mail carrier is inherently in danger of being discovered. This risk is significantly reduced with e-mail. Furthermore, Internet sites that offer child pornography can protect their customers with passwords, which keep random Web surfers (or law enforcement agents) from stumbling on the site of chat rooms.

3. *Anonymity.* Obviously, anonymity is the most important protection offered by the Internet for sellers and buyers of child pornography, as it is for any person engaged in illegal behavior in cyberspace.[47]

Because of these three factors, courts and lawmakers have had a difficult time controlling not only child pornography but also a wide variety of other online wrongdoing.

The Incidence of Cyber Crime It is difficult, if not impossible, to determine how much cyber crime actually takes place. Often, people never know that they have been the victims of this type of criminal activity. Furthermore, businesses sometimes fail to report such crimes for fear of losing customer confidence. Nonetheless, in 2013, the Internet Crime Complaint Center (IC3), operated as a partnership between the FBI and the National White Collar Crime Center, received about 260,000 complaints representing just over $780 million in victim losses.[48] According to the Norton Cybercrime Report, nearly 50 percent of all adults who use the Internet have been victimized by cyber crime, with annual global losses exceeding $113 billion.[49]

Cyber Crimes against Persons and Property

Most cyber crimes are not "new" crimes. Rather, they are existing crimes in which the Internet is the instrument of wrongdoing. The challenge for law enforcement is to apply traditional laws, which were designed to protect persons from physical harm or to safeguard their physical property, to crimes committed in cyberspace. Here, we look at several types of activity that constitute "updated" crimes against persons and property—online consumer fraud, cyber theft, and cyberstalking.

Cyber Consumer Fraud The expanding world of e-commerce has created many benefits for consumers. It has also led to some challenging problems, including fraud conducted via the Internet. In general, fraud is any misrepresentation knowingly made with the intention of deceiving another person. Furthermore, the victim must reasonably rely on the fraudulent information to her or his detriment. **Cyber fraud,** then, is fraud committed over the Internet. Scams that were once conducted solely by mail or phone can now be found online, and new technology has led to increasingly more creative ways to commit fraud. Online dating scams, for example, have increased dramatically in recent years, with fraudsters creating fake profiles to deceive unwitting romantic partners. According to the IC3, in 2013 online romance scam artists defrauded victims out of more than $80 million.[50] In one case, a Galesburg, Illinois, woman defrauded twenty-three men she met on dating Web sites out of hundreds of thousands of dollars by asking them to help pay for her mother's fictitious medical expenses.

As you can see in Figure 16.2, fraud accounts for the largest percentage of losses related to consumer cyber crime. Two widely reported forms of cyber crime are *advance fee fraud* and *online auction fraud.* In the simplest form of advance fee fraud, consumers order and pay for items such as automobiles or antiques that are never delivered. Online

Cyber Fraud Any misrepresentation knowingly made over the Internet with the intention of deceiving another and on which a reasonable person would and does rely to his or her detriment.

auction fraud is also fairly straightforward. A person lists an item for auction, on either a legitimate or a fake auction site, and then refuses to send the product after receiving payment. Several years ago, for example, U.S. Immigration and Customs Enforcement uncovered a scheme in which a group of Romanians set up a fraudulent eBay site and convinced five American victims to send them $120,000 for nonexistent items such as boats and cars.

Cyber Theft In cyberspace, thieves are not subject to the physical limitations of the "real" world. A thief can steal data stored in a networked computer with network access from anywhere on the globe. Only the speed of the connection and the thief's computer equipment limit the quantity of data that can be stolen.

Identity Theft This freedom from physical limitations has led to a marked increase in **identity theft,** which occurs when the wrongdoer steals a form of identification—such as a name, date of birth, or Social Security number—and uses the information to access the victim's financial resources. Once a Social Security number has been stolen, for example, it has proven fairly simple for the wrongdoer to commit tax fraud by filing false paperwork with the Internal Revenue Service (IRS) using that number. The defense attorney for one such tax fraud perpetrator—who accumulated $3 million before her arrest—expressed hope that the "IRS will figure out a way to prevent this from happening in the future, so someone with a sixth-grade education can't defraud them so easily."[51]

According to the federal government, about 7 percent of American households have at least one member who has been the victim of identity theft.[52] More than half of identity theft involves the misappropriation of an existing credit-card account.[53] In the "real world," this is generally accomplished by stealing an actual credit card. Online, an identity thief can steal financial information by fooling Web sites into thinking that he or she is the true account holder. For example, important personal information such as one's birthday, hometown, or employer that is available on social media sites such as Facebook can be used to convince a third party to reveal the victim's Social Security or bank account number.

The more personal information a cyber criminal obtains, the easier it is for him or her to find a victim's online user name. Once the online user name has been compromised, the easier it is to steal a victim's password, which is often the last line of defense to financial information. Numerous software programs aid identity thieves in illegally obtaining passwords. A technique called *keystroke logging,* for example, relies on software that embeds itself in a victim's computer and records every keystroke made on that computer. User names and passwords are then recorded and sold to the highest bidder. Internet users should also be wary of any links contained within e-mails sent from an unknown source, as these links can sometimes be used to illegally obtain personal information. (See Figure 16.3 for some hints on how to protect your online passwords.)

Phishing A distinct form of identity theft known as **phishing** adds a different wrinkle to this particular form of cyber crime. In a phishing attack, the perpetrators "fish" for financial data and passwords from consumers by posing as a legitimate business such as a bank or credit-card company. The "phisher" sends an e-mail asking the recipient to "update" or "confirm" vital information, often with the threat that an account or some other service will be discontinued if the information is not provided. Once the unsuspecting target enters the

FIGURE 16.2 The Costs of Cyber Crime

After polling adults in twenty-four countries, including the United States, researchers associated with the American security software company Symantec estimated that more than 1.5 million computer users worldwide are victims of cyber crime each day. As the graph below shows, 83 percent of the financial costs associated with cyber crime are the result of fraud, theft, or computer repairs made necessary by the wrongdoing.

Other 17%
Fraud 38%
Theft 21%
Repairs 24%

Source: *2013 Norton Report* (Mountain View, Calif.: Symantec, 2014), 8.

Identity Theft The theft of personal information, such as a person's name, driver's license number, or Social Security number.

Phishing Sending an unsolicited e-mail that falsely claims to be from a legitimate organization in an attempt to acquire sensitive information from the recipient.

FIGURE 16.3 Protecting Online Passwords

Once an online password has been compromised, the information on the protected Web site is fair game for identity thieves. By following these simple rules, you can strengthen the protection provided by your online passwords.

1. **Don't** use existing words such as your pet's name or your hometown. Such words are easy for computer identity theft programs to decode.
2. **Do** use at least eight characters in your passwords, with a nonsensical combination of upper- and lower-case letters, numbers, and symbols. A weak password is "scout1312." A strong password is "4X$dQ%3Z9j."
3. **Don't** use the same username and password for different Web accounts. If you do, then each account is in danger if one account is compromised.
4. **Do** use a different password for each Web account. If necessary, write down the various passwords and keep the list in a safe place.
5. **Don't** use information that can be easily found online or guessed at in choosing the questions that Web sites use to verify your password. That is, don't select questions such as "What is your birthday?" or "What is your city of birth?" Instead, choose questions with obscure answers that you are certain to remember or can easily look up.
6. **Don't** log on to any Web site if you are connected to the Internet via a wireless network (Wi-Fi) that is not itself password protected.

information, the phisher can use it to masquerade as the person or to extract funds from his or her bank or credit account.

The preferred method of phishing is through the use of **spam,** or unsolicited "junk e-mails" that flood virtual mailboxes with advertisements, solicitations, and other messages. By sending millions or even billions of these fraudulent e-mails, phishers need only entice a few users to "take the bait" to ensure a successful and lucrative operation. Phishing scams have also spread to other areas, such as text messaging and social-networking sites. About 22 percent of all phishing, for example, takes place on Facebook.[54]

Another form of phishing, called *spear phishing,* is much more difficult to detect because the messages seem to have come from co-workers, friends, or family members. In 2015, a cybergang infiltrated the security systems of a number of banks worldwide by sending bank employees e-mails containing links to news clips, apparently sent by colleagues. When the employees clicked on the links, they inadvertently downloaded software onto their computers that allowed the cyber thieves to drain hundreds of millions of dollars from accounts in the affected banks.[55]

Cyber Aggression and Social Media The growing use of mobile devices such as smartphones and tablets has added another outlet for online criminal activity. According to Norton Security, only a quarter of the owners of such devices use security software for protection. As a result, nearly 40 percent of these users have experienced cybercrime such as vishing (phishing by phone) and smishing (phishing by SMS/text message).[56] In particular, widespread smartphone use seems to have exacerbated cyberbullying, which we discussed in the context of school crime in the previous chapter. According to one survey, American teenagers who consider themselves "heavy users" of their cell phones are much more likely to experience cyberbullying than those who consider themselves "normal users" of the devices.[57]

In Chapter 4's *CJ & Technology* feature, we discussed "revenge porn," a form of cyberbullying that involves the nonconsensual publication online of explicit images. Revenge porn is often a component of **cyberstalking,** which occurs when one person uses e-mail, text messages, or some other form of electronic communication to cause a victim to reasonably fear for her or his safety or the safety of the victim's immediate family. According

Spam Bulk e-mails, particularly of commercial advertising, sent in large quantities without the consent of the recipient.

Cyberstalking The crime of stalking, committed in cyberspace through the use of e-mail, text messages, or another form of electronic communication.

to the most recent federal data on the subject, about 850,000 Americans are targets of cyberstalking each year.[58]

Nearly every state and the federal government have passed laws to combat this form of criminal behavior. For instance, in April 2014, Adam Savader of Great Neck, New York, was sentenced to thirty months in federal prison for cyberstalking fifteen different women. Besides sending his victims sexually explicit e-mails, Savader stole nude photos of the women by hacking into various social media sites. He then threatened to release the photos to the victims' relatives if they did not provide him with more such images.

Cyber Crimes in the Business World

Just as cyberspace can be a dangerous place for consumers, it presents a number of hazards for businesses that wish to offer their services on the Internet. Almost as soon as Apple Inc. introduced a new mobile-payment system in late 2014, cyber thieves began using the company's smartphones and tablets to make purchases with stolen credit-card numbers.[59] The same circumstances that enable companies to reach a large number of consumers also leave them vulnerable to cyber crime. For example, at about the same time Apple was experiencing troubles with its new mobile-pay technology, cyber criminals were stealing the credit-card data of at least 60 million Home Depot customers and illegally accessing the financial information of 76 million JPMorgan Chase clients.

Hackers The individuals who breached security at Home Depot and JPMorgan Chase are known as *hackers*. A **hacker** is a person who uses one computer to illegally access another. The danger posed by hackers has increased significantly because of **botnets,** or networks of computers that have been appropriated by hackers without the knowledge of their owners. A hacker will secretly install a program on large numbers of personal computer "robots," or "bots," that allows him or her to forward transmissions to an even larger number of systems. The program attaches itself to the host computer when someone operating the computer opens a fraudulent e-mail.

Malware Programs that create botnets are forms of *malware,* a term that refers to any program that is harmful to a computer or, by extension, a computer user. A **worm,** for example, is a software program that is capable of reproducing itself as it spreads from one computer to the next. A **virus,** another form of malware, is also able to reproduce itself, but must be attached to an "infested" host file to travel from one computer network to another. Worms and viruses can be programmed to perform a number of functions, such as prompting host computers to continually "crash" and reboot, or otherwise infect the system.

Malware is often used to target specific companies or organizations. During the 2013 holiday season, for example, a group of Eastern European hackers managed to gain access to the computer system of the retail giant Target. Once "inside," these hackers infected the in-store devices that Target customers use to swipe their credit and debit cards with a "memory scraper" malware nicknamed Kaptoxa. Over the course of several weeks, the malware was used to steal credit and debit card data, as well as passwords, phone numbers, and addresses, from at least 70 million Target customers. Experts estimate that the Kaptoxa virus was used to steal more than $4 billion in unrecoverable losses from these unfortunate consumers.[60]

Hacktivism Not all cyber crime is motivated by financial gain. Computer-savvy hackers known as *hacktivists* make political, religious, or social statements with

Hacker A person who uses one computer to break into another.

Botnet A network of computers that have been appropriated without the knowledge of their owners and used to spread harmful programs via the Internet; short for *robot network*.

Worm A computer program that can automatically replicate itself and interfere with the normal use of a computer. A worm does not need to be attached to an existing file to move from one network to another.

Virus A computer program that can replicate itself and interfere with the normal use of a computer. A virus cannot exist as a separate entity and must attach itself to another program to move through a network.

 LEARNING OBJECTIVE 5 Describe the three following forms of malware: (a) botnets, (b) worms, and (c) viruses.

▲ Target Corp. executive vice president John Mulligan, right, testifies before the U.S. Congress following a security breach that allowed hackers to steal financial and personal data from tens of millions of consumers. **Why does this type of cyber crime fall into the category of identity theft, as described earlier in the section?** Andrew Harrer/Bloomberg/Getty

information-based attacks on carefully chosen targets. The most common methods employed by hacktivists include:

1. *Distributed denial of service (DDoS),* in which hackers flood a targeted system with malware, much of it meaningless electronic "traffic," causing the system to crash and become inaccessible.
2. *Doxing,* or gathering and exposing personal information on a celebrity or politician with the goal of making the target take notice of a political issue that the hacktivist feels is important.
3. *Exposure,* in which, similar to doxing, the hacktivist gains unauthorized access to large amounts of confidential data and releases that data to the public, thereby embarrassing or incriminating the target.[61]

The collective Anonymous—made up of an unknown number of loosely affiliated hacktivists—has used these methods to embarrass repressive foreign governments, identify the assailants in an Ohio rape case, and shut down the Web site of the global World Cup soccer tournament to protest global poverty. In 2014, the group involved itself in the controversy surrounding the police shooting of an unarmed African American by a white police officer in Ferguson, Missouri, described earlier in this textbook. Anonymous operatives posted the names and addresses of local law enforcement officials, urged citizens to confront police in the streets, and crashed the city's Web servers.

 Explain how the Internet has contributed to piracy of intellectual property.

LEARNING **6** OBJECTIVE

Pirating Intellectual Property Online Most people think of wealth in terms of houses, land, cars, stocks, and bonds. Wealth, however, also includes **intellectual property,** which consists of the products that result from intellectual, creative processes. The government provides various forms of protection for intellectual property, such as copyrights and patents. These protections ensure that a person who writes a book or a song or creates a software program is financially rewarded if that product is sold in the marketplace.

Intellectual property such as books, films, music, and software is vulnerable to "piracy"—the unauthorized copying and use of the property. In the past, copying intellectual products was time consuming, and the quality of the pirated copies was clearly inferior. In today's online world, however, things have changed. Simply clicking a mouse can now reproduce millions of unauthorized copies, and pirated duplicates of copyrighted works obtained via the Internet are often exactly the same as the original, or close to it.

The Business Software Alliance estimates that 43 percent of all business software is pirated, costing software makers more than $62 billion in 2013.[62] (In the *CJ in Action* feature at the end of this chapter, we will discuss the moral and legal components of illegally downloading intellectual property.)

Intellectual Property Property resulting from intellectual, creative processes.

Fighting Cyber Crime

After Target suffered the extensive hacking attack described earlier, the company hired private contractors to plug its security holes and erase the malware from its compromised systems. Ideally, of course, corporations should have software already in place to prevent hacking operations, and most do. Businesses spend billions of dollars a year to *encrypt* their vital information. **Encryption** is the process of encoding information stored in computers in such a way that only authorized parties will have access to it.

Companies also hire outside experts to act as hackers and attempt to gain access to their systems, a practice known as "penetration testing." Even the most thorough private protection services often lag behind the ingenuity of the hacker community, however. In the Target attack, for example, the malware was programmed to constantly erase itself, making it practically impossible to detect. "The dynamics of the Internet and cyberspace are so fast that we have a hard time staying ahead of the adversary," admits former U.S. Secret Service agent Robert D. Rodriguez.[63]

The "Zero Days" Problem The Internet was designed to promote connectivity, not security. As more and more online threats to companies such as Target have developed, those businesses have had to respond with increasingly novel defenses. Facebook, for example, has constructed ThreatData, a defense system that monitors new worms, viruses, and malicious Web sites to create a constantly updated "blacklist" of blocked malware. Still, it is virtually impossible to protect against "zero days," the industry term for new vulnerabilities that security software cannot detect and for which there are no defenses. According to the most recent State of Cyber Crime Survey, in 2013 at least 3,000 companies were unaware of cyber intrusions until notified of the problem by the FBI.[64]

Clearly, private industry needs government help to fight off cyber criminals. With hundreds of millions of users in every corner of the globe transferring unimaginable amounts of information almost instantaneously, the Internet has proved resistant to government regulation. In addition, although a number of countries have tried to "control" the Internet (see the feature *Comparative Criminal Justice—The Great Firewall of China*), the U.S. government has generally adopted a hands-off attitude to better promote the free flow of ideas and encourage the growth of electronic commerce. Thus, in this country cyberspace is, for the most part, unregulated, making efforts to fight cyber crime all the more difficult.

Challenges for Law Enforcement "In the eighties, if there was a bank robbery, the pool of suspects was limited to the people who were in the vicinity at the time," says Shawn Henry, former head of the FBI's Cyber Division in trying to describe the complexities of fighting cyber crime. "Now when a bank is robbed the pool of suspects is limited to the number of people in the world with access to a five-hundred dollar laptop and an Internet connection. Which . . . is two and a half billion people."[65] The difficulty of finding suspects is just one of the challenges that law enforcement officers face in dealing with online crime. Another is gathering evidence in cyberspace.

Cyber Forensics Police officers cannot put yellow tape around a computer screen or dust a Web site for fingerprints. The best, and often the only, way to fight computer crime is with technology that gives law enforcement agencies the ability to "track" hackers and other cyber criminals through the Internet. These efforts are complicated by the fact that digital evidence can be altered or erased even as the cyber crime is being committed.

Encryption The translation of computer data in a secret code with the goal of protecting that data from unauthorized parties.

Comparative Criminal Justice

Central Intelligence Agency

The Great Firewall of China

The online anonymity enjoyed by many Americans on the Internet is increasingly hard to come by in China. In 2012, the Chinese government imposed new rules that require Internet users in that country to provide service providers with their real names. The regulations also require the service providers to report suspicious online activity, such as viewing pornography or the use of words such as *freedom* or *democracy,* to the authorities. Observers have little doubt that the changes are designed to restrict freedom of speech on the Internet. In the past, Chinese bloggers have been jailed for making politically sensitive comments or accusing local officials of wrongdoing.

In the United States, the issue of whether the government should regulate the Internet—and, if so, how much—is hotly debated. In China, the question was answered long before the Internet was even imagined. Since the 1950s, the Chinese Communist Party has exercised strict control over all forms of information, including newspapers, television, radio, movies, and books. Today, under the auspices of the Ministry of Information Industry, that control has been extended to the World Wide Web.

Under broad laws that prohibit, among other things, "destroying the order of society" and "making falsehoods or distorting the truth," Chinese censors have free rein to limit the flow of information through government-controlled Internet service providers. The "Great Firewall," as this system is sometimes called, routinely blocks more than a million Web sites. Many of the sites are pornographic, but the obstruction also extends to Facebook, Twitter, YouTube, and Evite. These steps anger many Chinese citizens, and a number of blogs in the country are dedicated to "tearing down the Great Firewall." In 2015, after a new round of government restrictions effectively shut down Gmail and made it nearly impossible for those in China to access foreign Web sites, a naval historian who uses the Internet for academic research complained, "It's like we're living in the Middle Ages."

For Critical Analysis

How would China-style Internet censorship affect cyber crime in the United States? Under what circumstances, if any, would Americans accept such levels of Internet control by the government?

In Chapter 6, we discussed forensics, or the application of science to find evidence of criminal activity. Within the past two decades, a branch of this science known as **cyber forensics** has evolved to gather evidence of cyber crimes.

The main goal of cyber forensics is to gather **digital evidence,** or information of value to a criminal investigation that is stored on, received by, or transmitted by an electronic device such as a computer. Sometimes, this evidence is not particularly difficult to find. In the Social Security identity theft scheme mentioned earlier, the offender bragged about buying a $92,000 car and being the "queen of IRS tax fraud" on her Facebook page.

Cyber Sleuthing More sophisticated cyber criminals employ technology such as Tor to cover their tracks. Tor is a form of software that allows users to mask their IP addresses (codes that identify individual computers on the Internet) and the IP addresses of anyone with whom they communicate. To counteract such efforts, experts in cyber forensics have created tools such as the search engine Memex, which has the ability to bypass Tor's encryption codes by tracing past Internet activity. Memex has been particularly helpful in uncovering online sex trafficking operations, as it is able to determine the time and location of the photos that these criminal enterprises use to advertise sex workers on the Internet.[66]

Cyber sleuths can also create a digital duplicate of a targeted hard drive, enabling them to break access codes, determine passwords, and search files. "Short of taking your hard drive and having it run over by a Mack truck," says one expert, "you can't be sure that anything is truly deleted from your computer."[67] The latest challenge to cyber

Cyber Forensics The application of computer technology to finding and utilizing evidence of cyber crimes.

Digital Evidence Information or data of value to a criminal investigation that is either stored or transmitted by electronic means.

investigators is posed by *cloud computing*, in which data are stored not in a physical location but in a virtual, shared computing platform that is linked simultaneously to a number of different computers. Therefore, law enforcement officers investigating wrongdoing in the "cloud" may not have full control of the "crime scene." (The growing importance of cyber crime has led a number of universities to offer graduate certificates in cyber forensics. To learn about one of these programs, go to the Web site of the Marshall University Forensic Science Center.)

Encrypted Smartphones

When it released the iPhone 6 in 2014, Apple Inc. used a marketing pitch perfect for the times. The device, Apple promised, was government snoop-proof. Consumers would be given the option to create a security code unique to each iPhone—a code that Apple did not possess and therefore could not pass along to the federal government, regardless of the legal procedures discussed earlier in the chapter. The mathematical algorithm used to encrypt information on the phone such as e-mails, photos, and contacts is so complex, Apple claims, that it would take five and a half years to hack.

Thinking about Encrypted Smartphones

FBI director James B. Comey criticized Apple's encryption efforts for the iPhone 6, saying that companies should not market "something that expressly [allows] people to hold themselves beyond the law." Do you agree with Comey's statement? How might an encrypted smartphone benefit terrorists and criminals who operate on the Internet? Explain your answers.

iStockPhoto.com/Onfokus

Jurisdictional Challenges Regardless of what type of cyber crime is being investigated, law enforcement agencies are often frustrated by problems of jurisdiction (explained more fully in Chapter 8). Jurisdiction is primarily based on physical geography—each country, state, and nation has jurisdiction, or authority, over crimes that occur within its boundaries. The Internet, however, destroys these traditional notions because geographic boundaries simply do not exist in cyberspace.

To see how this can affect law enforcement efforts, let's consider a hypothetical cyberstalking case. Phil, who lives in State A, has been sending e-mails containing graphic sexual threats to Stephanie, who lives in State B. Where has the crime taken place? Which police department has authority to arrest Phil, and which court system has authority to try him? To further complicate matters, what if State A has not yet added cyberstalking to its criminal code, while State B has? Does that mean that Phil has not committed a crime in his home state, but has committed one in Stephanie's?

The federal government has taken to answering this question by stating that Phil has committed a crime wherever it says he has. The Sixth Amendment to the U.S. Constitution states that federal criminal cases should be tried in the district in which the offense was committed.[68] Because the Internet is "everywhere," the federal government has a great deal of leeway in choosing the venue in which an alleged cyber criminal will face trial. Several years ago, for example, federal authorities claimed jurisdiction over three citizens of Estonia (a country located in Eastern Europe) who had engaged in a

Courtesy Paul Morris

FASTFACTS

Customs and border protection agent Job description:

- Make sure that laws are observed when goods or people enter the United States. Work at ports of entry and all along the border to prevent smuggling and the entrance of unauthorized immigrants.

What kind of training is required?

- Be under age 40, be a U.S. citizen and resident of the United States, and possess a valid state driver's license.

- Be fluent in Spanish or be able to learn the Spanish language.

Annual salary range?

- $38,000–$93,000

Paul Morris
Customs and Border Protection Agent

The most memorable day of my career was, without a doubt, September 11, 2001. That morning, as I watched the fall of the Twin Towers, I knew that things were going to be different. Personally, the attacks left me with a resolve to ensure, to the maximum extent possible, that nothing similar ever happens again. Professionally, that day marked a sea change with respect to how the federal border agencies viewed border security. Ever since, our anti-terrorism mission has been elevated above our other responsibilities, such as controlling illegal immigration, protecting our agricultural interests, and stopping the flow of illegal narcotics into this country.

www.dhs.gov

To be sure, as each of these tasks is crucially important, the extra burdens of anti-terrorism pose a significant challenge. With the volume of vehicles, cargo, and persons crossing our borders, there can be no guarantees that a potential terrorist or weapon of mass destruction cannot slip across the border. Nevertheless, with advanced identification technology, increased personnel, and a more efficient infrastructure, I am confident that the possibility of such a breach is low.

> **SOCIAL MEDIA CAREER TIP** Consider setting up personal and career-oriented Facebook pages or Twitter accounts and keeping your posts on each separated. Remember, though, that just because material is on your "personal" page or account, it still may be seen by others outside your network.

"click hijacking fraud" operation. This form of cyber crime directs users of infected computers to Web sites other than the ones chosen from search results, and it impacted U.S.-based services such as iTunes and Netflix. U.S. officials justified an extradition request for the three Estonians because many of the four million computers damaged by their malware were located in the United States.

Federal Law Enforcement and Cyber Crime The federal government was well positioned to foil the aforementioned Estonian hacking ring, thanks to a joint U.S.-Estonian law enforcement operation dubbed "Ghost Click." Indeed, the U.S. Secret Service has a small office in Estonia, a country in which numerous cyber crime operations are based.[69] Because of its freedom from jurisdictional constraints and its ability to operate internationally, the federal government has traditionally taken the lead in law enforcement efforts against cyber crime.

The FBI has the primary responsibility for enforcing all federal criminal statutes involving computer crime and leads the federal government's law enforcement efforts to combat cyber criminals. In 2002, the Bureau added a Cyber Division dedicated to investigating computer-based crimes. The Cyber Division and its administrators coordinate the FBI's efforts in cyberspace, specifically its investigations into computer crimes and intellectual property theft. The division also has jurisdiction over the Innocent Images National Initiative (IINI), the agency's online child-pornography subdivision.

In addition, the FBI has developed several Cyber Action Teams (CATs), which combine the skills of some twenty-five law enforcement agents, cyber forensics investigators, and computer programming experts. Today, cyber crime is the FBI's third-highest priority (after counterterrorism and counterintelligence), and each of the Bureau's fifty-six field divisions has at least one agent who focuses solely on crimes committed on the Internet.

EthicsChallenge

As noted earlier in this section, child pornography is illegal, both online and in the real world. Pornography involving adults, however, is legal for adult consumption, and has a massive presence on the Internet. What might be some ethical problems with the easy availability of pornography online? What are the arguments for and against legislation that would make it more difficult to view pornography on the Internet? ■

White-Collar Crime

A travel agent in Saco, Maine, takes thousands of dollars from clients for trips she never books. A man in Oakland, California, prepares federal loan applications for "straw students" who have no intention of attending school, pocketing $500,000 in the process. Employees of a Framingham, Massachusetts, pharmacy dispense tainted meningitis drugs that cause sixty-four deaths. A member of the United States House of Representatives from Illinois spends eighteen months behind bars for using campaign contributions to buy more than $750,000 worth of personal luxury items.

These cases represent a variety of criminal behavior with different motives, different methods, and different victims. Yet they all fall into the category of *white-collar crime,* an umbrella term for wrongdoing marked by deceit and scandal rather than violence. As we mentioned in Chapter 1, white-collar crime has a broad impact on the global economy, causing American businesses alone hundreds of billions of dollars in losses each year. Despite its global and national importance, however, white-collar crime has consistently challenged a criminal justice system that struggles to define the problem, much less effectively combat it.

What Is White-Collar Crime?

White-collar crime is not an official category of criminal behavior measured by the federal government in the Uniform Crime Report. Rather, it covers a broad range of illegal acts involving "lying, cheating, and stealing," according to the FBI's Web site on the subject.[70] To give a more technical definition, white-collar crimes are financial activities characterized by deceit and concealment that do not involve physical force or violence. Figure 16.4 lists and describes some common types of white-collar crime.

Different Techniques To differentiate white-collar crime from "regular" crime, criminologists Michael L. Benson of the University of Cincinnati and Sally S. Simpson of the University of Maryland focus on technique. For example, in an ordinary burglary, a criminal uses physical means, such as picking a lock, to get somewhere he or she should not be—someone else's home—to do something that is clearly illegal. Furthermore, the victim is a specific identifiable individual—the homeowner. In contrast, white-collar criminals usually (1) have legal access to the place where the crime occurs; (2) are spatially separated from the victim, who is often unknown; and (3) behave in a manner that is, at least superficially, legitimate.[71]

 LEARNING OBJECTIVE **7** Indicate some of the ways that white-collar crime is different from violent or property crime.

FIGURE 16.4 White-Collar Crimes

Embezzlement

Embezzlement is a form of employee fraud in which an individual uses his or her position within an organization to *embezzle*, or steal, the employer's funds, property, or other assets. Pilferage is a less serious form of employee fraud in which the individual steals items from the workplace.

Tax Evasion

Tax evasion occurs when taxpayers underreport (or do not report) their taxable income or otherwise purposely attempt to evade a tax liability.

Credit-Card and Check Fraud

Credit-card fraud involves obtaining credit-card numbers through a variety of schemes (such as stealing them from the Internet) and using the numbers for personal gain. Check fraud includes writing checks that are not covered by bank funds, forging checks, and stealing traveler's checks.

Mail and Wire Fraud

This umbrella term covers all schemes that involve the use of mail, radio, television, the Internet, or a telephone to intentionally deceive in a business environment.

Securities Fraud

Securities fraud covers illegal activity in the stock market. Stockbrokers who steal funds from their clients are guilty of securities fraud, as are those who engage in *insider trading*, which involves buying or selling securities on the basis of information that has not been made available to the public.

Bribery

Also known as *influence peddling*, bribery occurs in the business world when somebody within a company or government sells influence, power, or information to a person outside the company or government who can benefit. A county official, for example, could give a construction company a lucrative county contract to build a new jail. In return, the construction company would give some of the proceeds, known as a *kickback*, to the official.

Consumer Fraud

This term covers a wide variety of activities designed to defraud consumers, from selling counterfeit art to offering "free" items, such as electronic devices or vacations, that include a number of hidden charges.

Insurance Fraud

Insurance fraud involves making false claims in order to collect insurance payments. Faking an injury in order to receive payments from a workers' compensation program, for example, is a form of insurance fraud.

Benson and Simpson also identify three main techniques used by white-collar criminals to carry out their crimes:[72]

1. *Deception.* White-collar crime almost always involves a party who deceives and a party who is deceived. The nation's federal Medicare system, which provides health insurance for those sixty-five years of age and older, is a frequent target of deceptive practices. For example, from 1999 to 2014, the federal government paid billions of dollars to medical-supply companies as reimbursement for expensive wheelchairs that the companies provided to Medicare patients. Because the patients either did not exist or did not actually need wheelchairs, employees at the companies kept the reimbursed funds for themselves.[73]

2. *Abuse of trust.* A white-collar criminal often operates in a position of trust and misuses that trust for personal benefit. In 2015, for example, a financial advisor from Rockville, Maryland, was sentenced to forty-two months in prison for secretly withdrawing $1.2 million from the bank account of an elderly client to deposit in various personal accounts.

3. *Concealment and conspiracy.* To continue their illegal activities, white-collar criminals need to conceal those activities. In *odometer fraud,* for example, an automobile dealership "rolls back" the odometers of used cars so that a higher price can be charged for the vehicles. As soon as the fraud is discovered, the scheme can no longer succeed.

Victims of White-Collar Crime As the above examples show, sometimes the victim of a white-collar crime is obvious. A dishonest financial advisor is stealing directly from his or her clients, and odometer fraud denies consumers the actual value of their purchased automobiles. But who was victimized in the fraudulent Medicare wheelchair scheme? In that instance, the "victims" were the U.S. taxpayers, who collectively had to cover the cost of the unwarranted items. Such health-care scams defraud U.S. taxpayers out of at least $82 billion each year.[74] Often, white-collar crime does not target individuals but rather large groups or even abstract concepts such as "society" or "the environment."

Regulating and Policing White-Collar Crime

For legal purposes, a corporation can be treated as a person capable of forming the intent necessary to commit a crime. Thus, in March 2015, Freedom Industries pleaded guilty to three water-pollution crimes and agreed to pay about $900,000 in fines after accepting responsibility for a chemical leak that had contaminated drinking water in the Kanawha Valley of West Virginia thirteen months earlier. About 10,000 gallons of a coal-cleaning substance called 4-methylcyclohexane methanol were erroneously dumped in the Elk River, sickening hundreds of local residents.

The aftermath of the Elk River chemical spill, caused by Freedom Industries' negligence, is an example of *corporate violence*. In contrast to assaults committed by individual people, **corporate violence** is a result of policies or actions undertaken by a corporation. In the United States, parallel regulatory and criminal systems have evolved to prevent corporate violence and other forms of white-collar crime. (The feature *A Question of Ethics: Buyer Beware* addresses the problematic question of how society should hold corporations responsible for corporate violence.)

Corporate Violence Physical harm to individuals or the environment that occurs as the result of corporate policies or decision making.

LEARNING OBJECTIVE 8 Explain the concept of corporate violence.

A Question of Ethics: Buyer Beware

The Situation In March 2014, General Motors (GM) recalled 2.6 million Chevrolet Cobalts and other small cars because of a flawed ignition switch. According to internal company documents, GM engineers held a meeting concerning this defect—which caused the cars to lose power and shut down while being driven—in 2009, but did nothing to warn consumers. From the time of that meeting until the recall, the faulty ignition switch was linked to crashes of GM vehicles that caused at least thirteen deaths.

The Ethical Dilemma GM's failure to warn motorists about the flawed ignition switch seems to have been based on the company's finances—an earlier recall would have cost hundreds of millions of dollars and left the company open to numerous civil lawsuits—and a desire to safeguard its reputation. Still, GM clearly had an ethical duty to protect the well-being of its clients, regardless of any other considerations.

What Is the Solution? Documentary filmmaker Michael Moore suggested that GM executives and engineers should face the death penalty for "covering up" the faulty ignition switches. Although such an outcome is highly improbable, it does raise the relevant question of whether the criminal justice system can force corporations to behave ethically.

At the same time GM was recalling millions of its cars, Toyota agreed to pay a $1.2 billion fine for similarly hiding defects in its cars that are suspected of having caused more than thirty deaths between 2000 and 2010. No individual Toyota employee was the subject of a criminal inquiry, however, and the fine, though the largest ever levied against an automobile company, represented a small fraction of Toyota's worth. Do you think fines, civil lawsuits, and the financial ramifications of a damaged reputation are enough to ensure that corporations behave ethically? (GM profits fell 85 percent in the first part of 2014, but rebounded by 91 percent in 2015.) If not, what other punishments should be considered? What might be some of the challenges of punishing individuals for corporate misdeeds?

The Regulatory Justice System Although most white-collar crimes cause harm, these harms are not necessarily covered by criminal statutes. Indeed, more often they are covered by *administrative* laws, which we first encountered in Chapter 4. Such laws make up the backbone of the U.S. regulatory system, through which the government attempts to control the actions of individuals, corporations, and other institutions. The goal of **regulation** is not prevention or punishment as much as **compliance**, or the following of regulatory guidelines.[75]

For example, more than a decade ago the Food and Drug Administration (FDA) approved use of the antipsychotic drug Risperdal—produced by Johnson & Johnson—to treat schizophrenia, a condition we discussed in Chapter 2. Violating these guidelines, representatives of Johnson & Johnson marketed Risperdal as medication for elderly nursing home patients and children who suffered from attention deficit hyperactivity disorder and autism. In 2013, the corporation agreed to pay $2.2 billion in penalties stemming from its lack of compliance, which placed Risperdal users at risk of stroke and other health problems.

The FDA—which protects the public health by regulating food products and a wide variety of drugs and medical practices—is one of the federal administrative agencies whose compliance oversight brings them into contact with white-collar crime. Other important federal regulatory agencies with regard to white-collar crime include:

1. The Environmental Protection Agency (EPA), which regulates air quality, water quality, and toxic waste. The EPA was intricately involved in the federal government's response to the Elk River chemical spill, described earlier in the section.
2. The Occupational Safety and Health Administration (OSHA), which enforces workplace health and safety standards.
3. The Securities and Exchange Commission (SEC), which ensures that financial markets such as the New York Stock Exchange operate in a fair manner.

In 2015, the Federal Communications Commission voted to regulate the Internet as a *public utility* (a company that provides a public service, such as electricity or telephone communications). This move may eventually impact federal law enforcement efforts to combat the various forms of cyber crime we discussed in the previous section.

Law Enforcement and White-Collar Crime In general, when officials at a regulatory agency find that criminal prosecution is needed to punish a particular violation, they will refer the matter to the U.S. Department of Justice. Either through such referrals or at their own discretion, federal officials prosecute white-collar crime using the investigatory powers of several different federal law enforcement agencies. The FBI has become the lead agency when it comes to white-collar crime, particularly in response to the recent financial scandals, as we shall soon see. The U.S. Postal Inspection Service is also quite active in such investigations, as fraudulent activities often involve the U.S. mail. In addition, the Internal Revenue Service's Criminal Investigative Division has jurisdiction over a wide variety of white-collar crimes, including tax fraud, and operates perhaps the most effective white-collar crime lab in the country.[76]

Local and state agencies also investigate white-collar crimes, but because of the complexity and costs of such investigations, most are handled by the federal government. Federal prosecutors are also in a unique position to enforce the federal Racketeer Influenced and Corrupt Organizations Act (RICO), which we discussed briefly in Chapter 12. Originally designed to combat organized crime, RICO makes it illegal to receive income

Regulation A governmental order or rule having the force of law that is usually implemented by an administrative agency.

Compliance The state of operating in accordance with governmental standards.

through a pattern of *racketeering*.[77] The definition of **racketeering** is so inclusive—basically covering any attempt to earn illegal income involving more than one person—that it can be used against a broad range of white-collar criminal activity. Several years ago, for example, federal prosecutors used RICO to convict twenty-one members of the Hells Angels motorcycle club in South Carolina for drug and firearms trafficking, money laundering, and attempted armed robbery.

White-Collar Crime in the 2000s

The decade that ended in 2010 was marked by two periods of financial scandal. First, in 2001 and 2002, fraudulent accounting practices led to the demise of giant corporations such as Enron and Worldcom, costing investors tens of billions of dollars. Then, near the end of the decade, the collapse of the subprime mortgage market caused millions of Americans to lose their homes to foreclosure and led to the collapse of major financial institutions such as Lehman Brothers and Washington Mutual. In the latter period, headlines focused on widespread *mortgage fraud*, or dishonest practices relating to home loans, along with the misdeeds of Bernard Madoff. Before his 2008 arrest, Madoff managed to defraud thousands of investors out of approximately $65 billion.

As has often occurred in U.S. history, these scandals and the concurrent economic downturns led to greater regulation and criminalization of white-collar crime. In 1934, for example, in the wake of the Great Depression, Congress established the SEC to watch over the American economy.[78] Similarly, in 2002 Congress passed legislation which, among other things, enhanced the penalties for those convicted of white-collar crimes.[79] Bernard Madoff, for example, received a 150-year prison term for his illegal actions, and in June 2012 Allen Stanford was sentenced to 110 years in prison for stealing more than $7 billion from investors over the course of two decades.

Furthermore, in response to the "Great Recession" of 2008 and 2009, the FBI created the National Mortgage Fraud Team and began to crack down on a variety of white-collar crimes. Indeed, FBI agents are increasingly using aggressive tactics such as going undercover, planting wiretaps, and raiding offices—tactics previously reserved for drug dealers, mobsters, and terrorists—against white-collar criminals.[80]

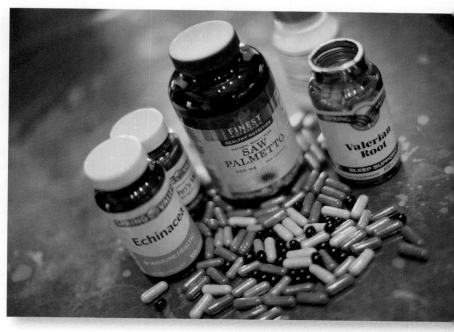

▲ In 2015, the New York State attorney general's office began investigating claims that store-brand dietary supplements sold at "big-box" stores such as Walmart and Walgreens contained ingredients that cause allergies without listing such "allergens" on their labels. **If true, does this behavior fall into the category of white-collar crime? Why or why not?** Scott Olson/Getty Images News/Getty Images

---

EthicsChallenge

As you learned earlier in this section, after being found guilty of defrauding thousands of investors out of approximately $65 billion, seventy-one-year-old Bernie Madoff was sentenced to 150 years in prison. Do you think this is an ethical punishment for white-collar criminality? Is it fair that white-collar criminals receive sentences similar to violent criminals? Explain your answers. ■

Racketeering The criminal action of being involved in an organized effort to engage in illegal business transactions.

CJ IN ACTION

Hacking for Open Access

"We need to take information, wherever it is stored, make our copies, and share them with the world."[81] Such was the opinion of expert computer programmer Aaron Swartz, and, in 2011, he put his words into action. That year, Swartz was arrested in Boston on charges of hacking into the network of the Massachusetts Institute of Technology and illegally downloading nearly 5 million articles from JSTOR, an online database of academic journals. On January 11, 2013, apparently distraught over the possibility of a lengthy prison sentence, Swartz hanged himself. The twenty-six-year-old's suicide touched off a firestorm of debate over the availability of information on the Internet—the topic of this chapter's *CJ in Action* feature.

Breaking the Law

Federal authorities had indicted Swartz on thirteen charges of violating the Computer Fraud and Abuse Act (CFAA). Broadly speaking, the CFAA is designed to punish those who illegally access a computer.[82] Federal agents estimated that Swartz had illegally downloaded about 18 million pages of protected data from the scientific journals on the JSTOR Web site. At eight cents a page, that worked out to a $1.5 million hacking job, meaning that, under federal sentencing guidelines, Swartz faced as much as thirty-five years in prison and a $1 million fine.

Swartz's supporters called the federal government's prosecution unfair, pointing out that his behavior—though illegal—was not carried out for personal gain. Swartz was a leader of the "Open Access" movement, a loose organization of Internet activists dedicated to making information such as JSTOR's often costly scientific journals available online at no charge. Others, though sympathetic to Swartz's plight, felt that he had clearly broken the law. "People who have data in computers want them to be confidential," said Michael Sussmann, a lawyer who specializes in Internet issues.[83]

The Case for Hacking to Provide Open Access

- According to Swartz, "Stealing is wrong. But downloading isn't stealing. If I shoplift an album from my local record store, no one else can buy it. But when I download a song, no one loses it and another person gets it. There's no ethical problem."[84]

- Tax dollars support much of the research in scholarly and scientific journals, and therefore the content of these journals should be provided to the public at no cost.

- Most people, particularly students, cannot afford to purchase this information, creating what Open Access advocate Carl Malamud calls a "members-only country club of knowledge."[85]

The Case against Hacking to Provide Open Access

- In the words of U.S. Attorney Carmen Ortiz, who prosecuted Swartz, "Stealing is stealing, whether you use a computer command or a crowbar."[86]

- The principle of free information is misguided. Producing academic articles involves labor, and most of the people who provide such labor want to be paid. In many cases, these people cannot afford to work for free.

- Punishing those who hack computers for supposedly "noble" causes provides a deterrent to all hacking—much of which is carried out for illicit financial gain.

Your Opinion—Writing Assignment

In 2012, the U.S. government requested the extradition of Richard O'Dwyer, a twenty-four-year-old who lived in northern England. According to federal prosecutors, O'Dwyer operated a Web site that helped users find pirated American movies and television shows. That is, although O'Dwyer's site did not contain any illegally downloaded content itself, it provided links to other sites that did. Through advertising, O'Dwyer made about $230,000 from his site, which was established through a British server.[87] Some observers criticized the U.S. government for seeking a ten-year prison term for O'Dwyer, pointing out that it is not usually against the law to establish what is essentially a search engine.

Does the United States have jurisdiction over O'Dwyer and his Web site? Do you think that he is committing a crime by providing an outlet for others to illegally download copyrighted material? How do you compare the activities of O'Dwyer to the Open Access movement championed by Aaron Swartz? Before responding, you can review our discussions in the sections of this chapter concerning:

- Pirating intellectual property online ("Cyber Crime").

- Cyber crime jurisdictional challenges ("Cyber Crime").

Your answer should include at least three full paragraphs.

Summary

For more information on these concepts, look back to the Learning Objective icons throughout the chapter.

 Summarize the three federal laws that have been particularly influential on our nation's counterterrorism strategies. (a) The Foreign Intelligence Surveillance Act (FISA) lays the groundwork for electronically monitoring national security threats. (b) The Antiterrorism and Effective Death Penalty Act (AEDPA) prohibits the providing of material support to terrorist organizations. (c) The Patriot Act greatly strengthened the ability of law enforcement agents to investigate and prosecute suspected terrorists.

 Explain why privacy expectations are so important to the federal government's metadata surveillance operations. Under the Fourth Amendment, the government needs a warrant to eavesdrop on or record communications made by U.S. citizens, who have a reasonable expectation that those communications are private. Because a number of federal courts have ruled that there is no reasonable expectation of privacy with regard to communications involving cell phone calls and Internet use, the government is has more leeway in "searching and seizing" information relating to that activity.

 Distinguish verbal threats that are protected by the Constitution from verbal threats that can be prosecuted as "true threats." The First Amendment protects speech, including threats, that should not cause a person or group of people reasonably to fear for their safety. A "true threat," by contrast, expresses the viable intent of the speaker to harm potential victims, or to place those victims in reasonable fear of danger.

 Outline the three major reasons why the Internet is conducive to the dissemination of child pornography. The Internet provides (a) a quick way to transmit child pornography from providers to consumers; (b) security such as untraceable e-mails and password-protected Web sites and chat rooms; and (c) anonymity for buyers and sellers of child pornography.

 Describe the three following forms of malware: (a) botnets, (b) worms, and (c) viruses. (a) A botnet is a network of computers that have been hijacked without the knowledge of their owners and used to spread harmful programs across the Internet. (b) A worm is a damaging software program that reproduces itself as it moves from computer to computer. (c) A virus is a damaging software program that must be attached to an "infested" host file to transfer from one computer to the next.

 Explain how the Internet has contributed to piracy of intellectual property. In the past, copying intellectual property such as films and music was time consuming, and the quality of the pirated copies was vastly inferior to that of the originals. On the Internet, however, millions of unauthorized copies of intellectual property can be reproduced at the click of a mouse, and the quality of these items is often the same as that of the original, or close to it.

 Indicate some of the ways that white-collar crime is different from violent or property crime. A wrongdoer committing a standard crime usually uses physical means to get somewhere he or she legally should not be in order to do something clearly illegal. Also, the victims of violent and property crimes are usually easily identifiable. In contrast, a white-collar criminal usually has legal access to the crime scene where he or she is doing something seemingly legitimate. Furthermore, victims of white-collar crimes are often unknown or unidentifiable.

 Explain the concept of corporate violence. Corporate violence occurs when a corporation implements policies that ultimately cause harm to individuals or the environment.

Questions for Critical Analysis

1. Suppose a member of al Qaeda posts a video on YouTube that shows how to make an IED (improvised explosive device) out of common household cleaning detergents and a piece of pipe. Before YouTube can take down the video, a young man uses the instructions to carry out a terrorist attack during a high school basketball game. Do you think YouTube, as a corporate "person," could be charged with providing material support to al Qaeda, a terrorist organization? *Should* the company be so charged? Explain your answers.

2. Should the federal government make it a crime to publish bomb-making instructions online? Why or why not?

3. According to several studies, someone who is a victim of a cyber crime such as identity theft has a relatively high risk of being a victim of the same crime again. Why do you think this is the case?

4. Consider the following proposed state law: *It is unlawful for any person, with intent to terrify, intimidate, threaten, harass, annoy, or offend, to use ANY ELECTRONIC OR DIGITAL DEVICE and use any obscene, lewd, or profane language.* What is your opinion of this statute? What might be some of its unforeseen consequences?

5. Using your own words, define *white-collar crime.*

Key Terms

botnet 533
compliance 542
corporate violence 541
cyberattack 529
cyber crime 529
cyber forensics 536
cyber fraud 530
cyberstalking 532

digital evidence 536
encryption 535
hacker 533
identity theft 531
intellectual property 534
material support 522
national security letters 522
Patriot Act 522

phishing 531
racketeering 543
regulation 542
spam 532
surveillance 521
true threat 526
virus 533
worm 533

Notes

1. Michael S. Schmidt, "Syria Suicide Bombing Puts U.S. Face on *Jihad* Video," *New York Times* (June 15, 2014), A1.

2. Quoted in Anita Kumar and Michael Doyle, "Federal Watching Is Rampant These Days," *Arizona Daily Star* (June 8, 2013), A1.

3. 50 U.S.C. Sections 1801–1811.

4. 50 U.S.C. Sections 1801(a)(1)–(3).

5. 50 U.S.C. Section 1804(a)(6).

6. 18 U.S.C. Section 2339B(a)(1) (1996).

7. 18 U.S.C. Section 2339A(b) (Supp. I 2001).

8. 18 U.S.C. Section 2339B(a)(1) (2006).

9. William K. Rashbaum, "Law Put to Unusual Use in Hezbollah TV Case, Some Say," *New York Times* (August 26, 2006), B2.

10. Uniting and Strengthening America by Providing Appropriate Tools Required to Intercept and Obstruct Terrorism (USA PATRIOT) Act of 2001, Pub. L. No. 107-56, 115 Stat. 272 (2001).

11. 50 U.S.C. Section 1861(b)(2)(A) (2006).

12. 18 U.S.C. Section 2709 (2012).

13. John S. Dempsey and Linda S. Forst, *An Introduction to Policing,* 7th ed. (Clifton Park, N.Y.: Delmar Cengage Learning, 2014), 537.

14. FISA Amendment Act of 2008, Pub. L. No. 110-261, 122 Stat. 2436 (2008).

15. John Yoo, "The Legality of the National Security Agency's Bulk Data Surveillance Programs," *Harvard Journal of Law and Public Policy* (Summer 2014), at **papers.ssrn.com /sol3/papers.cfm?abstract_id=2369192.**

16. Jay Bookman, "Which Do You Value? Privacy, or the Illusion of Security?" *AJC.com* (December 17, 2013), at **www.ajc.com /weblogs/jay-bookman/2013/dec/17 /which-do-you-value-privacy-or-illusion -security/#__federated=1.**

17. Timothy B. Lee, "Here's Everything We Know about PRISM to Date," *Washington Post WonkBlog* (June 12, 2013), at **www .washingtonpost.com/blogs/wonkblog /wp/2013/06/12/heres-everything-we -know-about-prism-to-date/.**

18. Steven G. Bradbury, "Understanding the NSA Programs: Bulk Acquisition of Telephone Metadata under Section 215 and Foreign-Targeted Collection under Section 702," *Lawfare Research Paper Series* (September 1, 2013), 2.

19. Charlie Savage and Matt Apuzzo, "U.S. Spied on 5 American Muslims, a Report Says," *New York Times* (July 10, 2014), A17.

20. *ACLU v. Clapper,* 959 F.Supp.2d 724, 726 (S.D.N.Y. 2013).

21. Jennifer Steinhauer and Jonathan Weismanjune, "U.S. Surveillance in Place since 9/11 Is Sharply Limited," *New York Times* (June 2, 2015), A1.

22. "Despite Outcry, Government Still Collects Your Phone Data," *USA Today* (October 22, 2014), 6A.

23. *Katz v. United States,* 389 U.S. 347, 351 (1967); and *California v. Greenwood,* 486 U.S. 35 (1988).

24. *United States v. Moalin et al.,* at **www .documentcloud.org/documents/902291 -moalin-131114-deny-new-trial.html.**

25. 442 U.S. 735 (1979).

26. *Klayman v. Obama*, 957 F.Supp.2d 825 (D.D.C. December 16, 2013).

27. Quoted in "A Powerful Rebuke of Mass Surveillance," *New York Times* (December 17, 2013).

28. *United States v. Jones*, 565 U.S. ____ (2012).

29. Quoted in "A Powerful Rebuke of Mass Surveillance," *op. cit.*

30. 50 U.S.C. Section 1881a (2011).

31. Ellen Nakashima, "Feds Report 90,000 Foreign Surveillance Targets," *Dallas Morning News* (June 28, 2014), 11A.

32. David E. Sanger and Matt Apuzzo, "Officials Defend N.S.A. after New Privacy Details Are Reported," *New York Times* (July 7, 2014), A9.

33. *Ibid.*

34. Quoted in "Colorado Teen Shannon Conley's Support of ISIS Raises Alarm about American *Jihadists*," *Associated Press* (September 10, 2014).

35. Quoted in Stephen Collinson, "Paris Attack: The New Terror," *CNN.com* (January 8, 2015), at **www.cnn.com/2015/01/08/politics /paris-new-terror/**.

36. 538 U.S. 343 (2003).

37. *Ibid.*, at 358.

38. 18 U.S.C. Section 2339A(b)(1).

39. Mark Mazzetti, Erich Schmitt, and Michael S. Schmidt, "Suicide Bomber Is Identified as a Florida Man," *New York Times* (May 31, 2014), A1.

40. Quoted in Marc Santora and Stephanie Clifford, "3 Brooklyn Men Accused of Plot to Aid ISIS's Fight," *New York Times* (February 26, 2015), A1.

41. *Ibid.*

42. Quoted in Marc Santora and Al Baker, "Brooklyn Arrests Highlight Challenges in Fighting of ISIS and 'Known Wolves,'" *New York Times* (March 1, 2015), A15.

43. John Leyden, "Pro-ISIS Script Kiddies Deface Dublin Rape Crisis Centre Site," *The Register* (March 10, 2015), at **www.theregister .co.uk/2015/03/10/is_script_kiddies _defacement/**.

44. Derek Harp, quoted in Erin Kelly, "As Cyberthreats Rise, Push for Intelligence Heightened," *USA Today* (December 24, 2014), 3A.

45. Quoted in "Special Report Cyber-Security: Hackers Inc.," *The Economist* (July 12, 2014), 5.

46. William R. Graham, Jr., "Uncovering and Eliminating Child Pornography Rings on the Internet," *Law Review of Michigan State University Detroit College of Law* (Summer 2000), 466.

47. Richard Wortley and Stephen Smallbone, "The Problem of Internet Child Pornography," Center for Problem Oriented Policing (2006), at **www.popcenter.org/problems /child_pornography.**

48. Internet Crime Complaint Center, *IC3 2013 Internet Crime Report* (Glen Allen, Va.: National White Collar Crime Center, 2014), 3.

49. *2013 Norton Report* (Mountain View, Calif.: Symantec, 2014), 8, 11.

50. Internet Crime Complaint Center, *op. cit.*, 9.

51. Quoted in Michael Kranish, "IRS Is Overwhelmed by Identity Theft Fraud," *Boston Globe* (February 16, 2014), A1.

52. Bureau of Justice Statistics, *Identity Theft Reported by Households, 2005–2010* (Washington, D.C.: U.S. Department of Justice, November 2011), 1.

53. *Ibid.*, Table 4, page 5.

54. Nadezhda Demidova, "Social Network Frauds," *SecureList.com* (June 11, 2014), at **securelist.com/analysis/publications /63855/social-network-frauds/**.

55. David E. Sanger and Nicole Perloth, "Bank Hackers Steal Millions via Malware," *New York Times* (February 14, 2015), A1.

56. *2013 Norton Report*, *op. cit.*, 7.

57. Openet, press release, "Openet-Sponsored Study Reveals 41 Percent of Teenagers Experience Cyber-bullying" (January 18, 2012), at **www.openet.com/company/news-events /pressreleases?id=482.**

58. Bureau of Justice Statistics, *Stalking Victimization in the United States* (Washington, D.C.: U.S. Department of Justice, January 2009), 1.

59. Robin Sidel and Daisuke Wakabayashi, "Apple Pay Stung by Low-Tech Fraudsters," *Wall Street Journal* (March 5, 2015), at **www.wsj.com/articles/apple-pay-stung -bylow-techfraudsters-1425603036.**

60. Elizabeth E. Harris, et al., "A Sneaky Path into Target Customers' Wallets," *New York Times* (January 18, 2014), A1.

61. *The Current State of Cybercrime: An Inside Look at the Changing Threat Landscape* (Hopkinton, Mass.: RSA, 2013), 6.

62. *The Compliance Gap: BSA Global Software Survey* (Washington, D.C.: Business Software Alliance, June 2014), 2.

63. Quoted in Marc Santora, "In Hours, Thieves Took $45 Million in A.T.M. Scheme," *New York Times* (May 10, 2013), A1.

64. *US Cybercrime: Rising Risks, Reduced Readiness* (Los Angeles: PwC, June 2014), 7.

65. Quoted in John Seabrook, "Network Insecurity," *The New Yorker* (May 20, 2013), 64.

66. Elizabeth Dwoskin, "Sleuthing Search Engine: Even Better than Google?" *Wall Street Journal* (February 11, 2015), at **www .wsj.com/articles/sleuthing-search -engine-even-better-than-google -1423703464.**

67. Quoted in "Cybersleuths Find Growing Role in Fighting Crime," HPC Wire, at **www.hpc wire.com/hpc-bin/artread.pl?direction =Current&articlenumber=19864.**

68. Laurie P. Cohen, "Intern plies Venues to Try Web *Journal* (February 12, 200

69. Joseph M. Demarest, Jr., the United States Senate Crime and Terrorism, C ciary, Entitled: Cyber Thr ment and the Private Section" (May 8, 2013).

70. The Federal Bureau of Investigation, "White-Collar Crime" at **www.fbi.gov/about-us /investigate/white_collar/whitecollar crime.**

71. Michael L. Benson and Sally S. Simpson, *White-Collar Crime: An Opportunity Perspective* (New York: Routledge, 2009), 79–80.

72. *Ibid.*, 81–87.

73. David A. Fahrenthold, "A Medicare Scam That Just Kept Rolling," *Washington Post* (August 16, 2014), at **www.washingtonpost .com/sf/national/2014/08/16/a -medicare-scam-that-just-kept-rolling/.**

74. "That's Where the Money Is," *The Economist* (May 31, 2014), 13.

75. Benson and Simpson, *op. cit.*, 189.

76. David O. Friedrichs, *Trusted Criminals: White Collar Crime in Contemporary Society*, 4th ed. (Belmont, Calif.: Wadsworth Cengage Learning, 2010), 278–283.

77. Lawrence Salinger, *Encyclopedia of White-Collar and Corporate Crime*, 2d ed. (Thousand Oaks, Calif.: Sage, 2004), 361.

78. 15 U.S.C. Sections 78a *et seq.*

79. White-Collar Crime Penalty Enhancement Act of 2002, 18 U.S.C. Sections 1341, 1343, 1349–1350.

80. Peter Lattman and William K. Rashbaum, "A Trader, an F.B.I. Witness, and Then a Suicide," *Reuters* (June 2, 2011).

81. Aaron Swartz, "The Guerilla Open Access Manifesto" (2008), at **archive.org/stream /GuerillaOpenAccessManifesto/Goam july2008_djvu.txt.**

82. Counterfeit Access Device and Computer Fraud and Abuse Act of 1984, Public Law Number 98-473, 98 Statute 2190 (codified as amended at 18 U.S.C. Section 1030 (2006)).

83. Quoted in Peter Schworm and Shelley Murphy, "Critics Say U.S. Cyber Law Invites Harsh Prosecutions," *Boston Globe* (January 25, 2013), A1.

84. Quoted in Larissa MacFarquhar, "Requiem for a Dream," *The New Yorker* (March 11, 2013), 56.

85. Quoted in Jessica Guynn, "In Death, a Hero or Criminal?" *Baltimore Sun* (February 1, 2013), 16A.

86. Quoted in Schworm and Murphy, *op. cit.*

87. Somni Sengupta, "U.S. Pursuing a Middleman in Web Piracy," *New York Times* (July 13, 2012), A1.

The Constitution of the United States

Preamble

We the People of the United States, in Order to form a more perfect Union, establish Justice, insure domestic Tranquility, provide for the common defence, promote the general Welfare, and secure the Blessings of Liberty to ourselves and our Posterity, do ordain and establish this Constitution for the United States of America.

Article I

Section 1. All legislative Powers herein granted shall be vested in a Congress of the United States, which shall consist of a Senate and House of Representatives.

Section 2. The House of Representatives shall be composed of Members chosen every second Year by the People of the several States, and the Electors in each State shall have the Qualifications requisite for Electors of the most numerous Branch of the State Legislature.

No Person shall be a Representative who shall not have attained to the Age of twenty five Years, and been seven Years a Citizen of the United States, and who shall not, when elected, be an Inhabitant of that State in which he shall be chosen.

Representatives and direct Taxes shall be apportioned among the several States which may be included within this Union, according to their respective Numbers, which shall be determined by adding to the whole Number of free Persons, including those bound to Service for a Term of Years, and excluding Indians not taxed, three fifths of all other Persons. The actual Enumeration shall be made within three Years after the first Meeting of the Congress of the United States, and within every subsequent Term of ten Years, in such Manner as they shall by Law direct. The Number of Representatives shall not exceed one for every thirty Thousand, but each State shall have at Least one Representative; and until such enumeration shall be made, the State of New Hampshire shall be entitled to chuse three, Massachusetts eight, Rhode Island and Providence Plantations one, Connecticut five, New York six, New Jersey four, Pennsylvania eight, Delaware one, Maryland six, Virginia ten, North Carolina five, South Carolina five, and Georgia three.

When vacancies happen in the Representation from any State, the Executive Authority thereof shall issue Writs of Election to fill such Vacancies.

The House of Representatives shall chuse their Speaker and other Officers; and shall have the sole Power of Impeachment.

Section 3. The Senate of the United States shall be composed of two Senators from each State, chosen by the Legislature thereof, for six Years; and each Senator shall have one Vote.

Immediately after they shall be assembled in Consequence of the first Election, they shall be divided as equally as may be into three Classes. The Seats of the Senators of the first Class shall be vacated at the Expiration of the second Year, of the second Class at the Expiration of the fourth Year, and of the third Class at the Expiration of the sixth Year, so that one third may be chosen every second Year; and if Vacancies happen by Resignation, or otherwise, during the Recess of the Legislature of any State, the Executive thereof may make temporary Appointments until the next Meeting of the Legislature, which shall then fill such Vacancies.

No Person shall be a Senator who shall not have attained to the Age of thirty Years, and been nine Years a Citizen of the United States, and who shall not, when elected, be an Inhabitant of that State for which he shall be chosen.

The Vice President of the United States shall be President of the Senate, but shall have no Vote, unless they be equally divided.

The Senate shall chuse their other Officers, and also a President pro tempore, in the Absence of the Vice President, or when he shall exercise the Office of President of the United States.

The Senate shall have the sole Power to try all Impeachments. When sitting for that Purpose, they shall be on Oath or Affirmation. When the President of the United States is tried, the Chief Justice shall preside: And no Person shall be convicted without the Concurrence of two thirds of the Members present.

Judgment in Cases of Impeachment shall not extend further than to removal from Office, and disqualification to hold and enjoy any Office of honor, Trust, or Profit under the United States: but the Party convicted shall nevertheless be liable and subject to Indictment, Trial, Judgment, and Punishment, according to Law.

Section 4. The Times, Places and Manner of holding Elections for Senators and Representatives, shall be prescribed in each State by the Legislature thereof; but the Congress may at any time by Law make or alter such Regulations, except as to the Places of chusing Senators.

The Congress shall assemble at least once in every Year, and such Meeting shall be on the first Monday in December, unless they shall by Law appoint a different Day.

Section 5. Each House shall be the Judge of the Elections, Returns, and Qualifications of its own Members, and a Majority of each shall constitute a Quorum to do Business; but a smaller Number may adjourn from day to day, and may be authorized to compel the Attendance of absent Members, in such Manner, and under such Penalties as each House may provide.

Each House may determine the Rules of its Proceedings, punish its Members for disorderly Behavior, and, with the Concurrence of two thirds, expel a Member.

Each House shall keep a Journal of its Proceedings, and from time to time publish the same, excepting such Parts as may in their Judgment require Secrecy; and the Yeas and Nays of the Members of either House on any question shall, at the Desire of one fifth of those Present, be entered on the Journal.

Neither House, during the Session of Congress, shall, without the Consent of the other, adjourn for more than three days, nor to any other Place than that in which the two Houses shall be sitting.

Section 6. The Senators and Representatives shall receive a Compensation for their Services, to be ascertained by Law, and paid out of the Treasury of the United States. They shall in all Cases, except Treason, Felony and Breach of the Peace, be privileged from Arrest during their Attendance at the Session of their respective Houses, and in going to and returning from the same; and for any Speech or Debate in either House, they shall not be questioned in any other Place.

No Senator or Representative shall, during the Time for which he was elected, be appointed to any civil Office under the Authority of the United States, which shall have been created, or the Emoluments whereof shall have been increased during such time; and no Person holding any Office under the United States, shall be a Member of either House during his Continuance in Office.

Section 7. All Bills for raising Revenue shall originate in the House of Representatives; but the Senate may propose or concur with Amendments as on other Bills.

Every Bill which shall have passed the House of Representatives and the Senate, shall, before it become a Law, be presented to the President of the United States; If he approve he shall sign it, but if not he shall return it, with his Objections to the House in which it shall have originated, who shall enter the Objections at large on their Journal, and proceed to reconsider it. If after such Reconsideration two thirds of that House shall agree to pass the Bill, it shall be sent together with the Objections, to the other House, by which it shall likewise be reconsidered, and if approved by two thirds of that House, it shall become a Law. But in all such Cases the Votes of both Houses shall be determined by Yeas and Nays, and the Names of the Persons voting for and against the Bill shall be entered on the Journal of each House respectively. If any Bill shall not be returned by the President within ten Days (Sundays excepted) after it shall have been presented to him, the Same shall be a Law, in like Manner as if he had signed it, unless the Congress by their Adjournment prevent its Return in which Case it shall not be a Law.

Every Order, Resolution, or Vote, to which the Concurrence of the Senate and House of Representatives may be necessary (except on a question of Adjournment) shall be presented to the President of the United States; and before the Same shall take Effect, shall be approved by him, or being disapproved by him, shall be repassed by two thirds of the Senate and House of Representatives, according to the Rules and Limitations prescribed in the Case of a Bill.

Section 8. The Congress shall have Power To lay and collect Taxes, Duties, Imposts and Excises, to pay the Debts and provide for the common Defence and general Welfare of the United States; but all Duties, Imposts and Excises shall be uniform throughout the United States;

To borrow Money on the credit of the United States;

To regulate Commerce with foreign Nations, and among the several States, and with the Indian Tribes;

To establish an uniform Rule of Naturalization, and uniform Laws on the subject of Bankruptcies throughout the United States;

To coin Money, regulate the Value thereof, and of foreign Coin, and fix the Standard of Weights and Measures;

To provide for the Punishment of counterfeiting the Securities and current Coin of the United States;

To establish Post Offices and post Roads;

To promote the Progress of Science and useful Arts, by securing for limited Times to Authors and Inventors the exclusive Right to their respective Writings and Discoveries;

To constitute Tribunals inferior to the supreme Court;

To define and punish Piracies and Felonies committed on the high Seas, and Offenses against the Law of Nations;

To declare War, grant Letters of Marque and Reprisal, and make Rules concerning Captures on Land and Water;

To raise and support Armies, but no Appropriation of Money to that Use shall be for a longer Term than two Years;

To provide and maintain a Navy;

To make Rules for the Government and Regulation of the land and naval Forces;

To provide for calling forth the Militia to execute the Laws of the Union, suppress Insurrections and repel Invasions;

To provide for organizing, arming, and disciplining, the Militia, and for governing such Part of them as may be employed in the Service of the United States, reserving to the States respectively, the Appointment of the Officers, and the Authority of training the Militia according to the discipline prescribed by Congress;

To exercise exclusive Legislation in all Cases whatsoever, over such District (not exceeding ten Miles square) as may, by Cession of particular States, and the Acceptance of Congress, become the Seat of the Government of the United States, and to exercise like Authority over all Places purchased by the Consent of the Legislature of the State in which the Same shall be, for the Erection of Forts, Magazines, Arsenals, dock-Yards, and other needful Buildings;—And

To make all Laws which shall be necessary and proper for carrying into Execution the foregoing Powers, and all other Powers vested by this Constitution in the Government of the United States, or in any Department or Officer thereof.

Section 9. The Migration or Importation of such Persons as any of the States now existing shall think proper to admit, shall not be prohibited by the Congress prior to the Year one thousand eight hundred and eight, but a Tax or duty may be imposed on such Importation, not exceeding ten dollars for each Person.

The privilege of the Writ of Habeas Corpus shall not be suspended, unless when in Cases of Rebellion or Invasion the public Safety may require it.

No Bill of Attainder or ex post facto Law shall be passed.

No Capitation, or other direct, Tax shall be laid, unless in Proportion to the Census or Enumeration herein before directed to be taken.

No Tax or Duty shall be laid on Articles exported from any State.

No Preference shall be given by any Regulation of Commerce or Revenue to the Ports of one State over those of another: nor shall Vessels bound to, or from, one State be obliged to enter, clear, or pay Duties in another.

No Money shall be drawn from the Treasury, but in Consequence of Appropriations made by Law; and a regular Statement and Account of the Receipts and Expenditures of all public Money shall be published from time to time.

No Title of Nobility shall be granted by the United States: And no Person holding any Office of Profit or Trust under them, shall, without the Consent of the Congress, accept of any present, Emolument, Office, or Title, of any kind whatever, from any King, Prince, or foreign State.

Section 10. No State shall enter into any Treaty, Alliance, or Confederation; grant Letters of Marque and Reprisal; coin Money; emit Bills of Credit; make any Thing but gold and silver Coin a Tender in Payment of Debts; pass any Bill of Attainder, ex post facto Law, or Law impairing the Obligation of Contracts, or grant any Title of Nobility.

No State shall, without the Consent of the Congress, lay any Imposts or Duties on Imports or Exports, except what may be absolutely necessary for executing its inspection Laws: and the net Produce of all Duties and Imposts, laid by any State on Imports or Exports, shall be for the Use of the Treasury of the United States; and all such Laws shall be subject to the Revision and Controul of the Congress.

No State shall, without the Consent of Congress, lay any Duty of Tonnage, keep Troops, or Ships of War in time of Peace, enter into any Agreement or Compact with another State, or with a foreign Power, or engage in War, unless actually invaded, or in such imminent Danger as will not admit of delay.

Article II

Section 1. The executive Power shall be vested in a President of the United States of America. He shall hold his Office during the Term of four Years, and, together with the Vice President, chosen for the same Term, be elected, as follows:

Each State shall appoint, in such Manner as the Legislature thereof may direct, a Number of Electors, equal to the whole Number of Senators and Representatives to which the State may be entitled in the Congress; but no Senator or Representative, or Person holding an Office of Trust or Profit under the United States, shall be appointed an Elector.

The Electors shall meet in their respective States, and vote by Ballot for two Persons, of whom one at least shall not be an Inhabitant of the same State with themselves. And they shall make a List of all the Persons voted for, and of the Number of Votes for each; which List they shall sign and certify, and transmit sealed to the Seat of the Government of the United States, directed to the President of the Senate. The President of the Senate shall, in the Presence of the Senate and House of Representatives, open all the Certificates, and the Votes shall then be counted. The Person having the greatest Number of Votes shall be the President, if such Number be a Majority of the whole Number of Electors appointed; and if there be more than one who have such Majority, and have an equal Number of Votes, then the House of Representatives shall immediately chuse by Ballot one of them for President; and if no Person have a Majority, then from the five highest on the List the said House shall in like Manner chuse the President. But in chusing the President, the Votes shall be taken by States, the Representation from each State having one Vote; A quorum for this Purpose shall consist of a Member or Members from two thirds of the States, and a Majority of all the States shall be necessary to a Choice. In every Case, after the Choice of the President, the Person having the greater Number of Votes of the Electors shall be the Vice President. But if there should remain two or more who have equal Votes, the Senate shall chuse from them by Ballot the Vice President.

The Congress may determine the Time of chusing the Electors, and the Day on which they shall give their Votes; which Day shall be the same throughout the United States.

No person except a natural born Citizen, or a Citizen of the United States, at the time of the Adoption of this Constitution, shall be eligible to the Office of President; neither shall any Person be eligible to that Office who shall not have attained to the Age of thirty five Years, and been fourteen Years a Resident within the United States.

In Case of the Removal of the President from Office, or of his Death, Resignation or Inability to discharge the Powers and Duties of the said Office, the same shall devolve on the Vice President, and the Congress may by Law provide for the Case of Removal, Death, Resignation or Inability, both of the President and Vice President, declaring what Officer shall then act as President, and such Officer shall act accordingly, until the Disability be removed, or a President shall be elected.

The President shall, at stated Times, receive for his Services, a Compensation, which shall neither be increased nor diminished during the Period for which he shall have been elected, and he shall not receive within that Period any other Emolument from the United States, or any of them.

Before he enter on the Execution of his Office, he shall take the following Oath or Affirmation: "I do solemnly swear (or affirm) that I will faithfully execute the Office of President of the United States, and will to the best of my Ability, preserve, protect and defend the Constitution of the United States."

Section 2. The President shall be Commander in Chief of the Army and Navy of the United States, and of the Militia of the several States, when called into the actual Service of the United States; he may require the Opinion, in writing, of the principal Officer in each of the executive Departments, upon any Subject relating to the Duties of their respective Offices, and he shall have Power to grant Reprieves and Pardons for Offenses against the United States, except in Cases of Impeachment.

He shall have Power, by and with the Advice and Consent of the Senate to make Treaties, provided two thirds of the Senators present concur; and he shall nominate, and by and with the Advice and Consent of the Senate, shall appoint Ambassadors, other public Ministers and Consuls, Judges of the supreme Court, and all other Officers of the United States, whose Appointments are not herein otherwise provided for, and which shall be established by Law; but the Congress may by Law vest the Appointment of such inferior Officers, as they think proper, in the President alone, in the Courts of Law, or in the Heads of Departments.

The President shall have Power to fill up all Vacancies that may happen during the Recess of the Senate, by granting Commissions which shall expire at the End of their next Session.

Section 3. He shall from time to time give to the Congress Information of the State of the Union, and recommend to their Consideration such Measures as he shall judge necessary and expedient; he may, on extraordinary Occasions, convene both Houses, or either of them, and in Case of Disagreement between them, with Respect to the Time of Adjournment, he may adjourn them to such Time as he shall think proper; he shall receive Ambassadors and other public Ministers; he shall take Care that the Laws be faithfully executed, and shall Commission all the Officers of the United States.

Section 4. The President, Vice President and all civil Officers of the United States, shall be removed from Office on Impeachment for, and Conviction of, Treason, Bribery, or other high Crimes and Misdemeanors.

Article III

Section 1. The judicial Power of the United States, shall be vested in one supreme Court, and in such inferior Courts as the Congress may from time to time ordain and establish. The Judges, both of the supreme and inferior Courts, shall hold their Offices during good Behaviour, and shall, at stated Times, receive for their Services a Compensation, which shall not be diminished during their Continuance in Office.

Section 2. The judicial Power shall extend to all Cases, in Law and Equity, arising under this Constitution, the Laws of the United States, and Treaties made, or which shall be made, under their Authority;—to all Cases affecting Ambassadors, other public Ministers and Consuls;—to all Cases of admiralty and maritime Jurisdiction;—to Controversies to which the United States shall be a Party;—to Controversies between two or more States;—between a State and Citizens of another State;—between Citizens of different States;—between Citizens of the same State claiming Lands under Grants of different States, and between a State, or the Citizens thereof, and foreign States, Citizens or Subjects.

In all Cases affecting Ambassadors, other public Ministers and Consuls, and those in which a State shall be a Party, the supreme Court shall have original Jurisdiction. In all the other Cases before mentioned, the supreme Court shall have appellate Jurisdiction, both as to Law and Fact, with such Exceptions, and under such Regulations as the Congress shall make.

The Trial of all Crimes, except in Cases of Impeachment, shall be by Jury; and such Trial shall be held in the State where the said Crimes shall have been committed; but when not committed within any State, the Trial shall be at such Place or Places as the Congress may by Law have directed.

Section 3. Treason against the United States, shall consist only in levying War against them, or, in adhering to their Enemies, giving them Aid and Comfort. No Person shall be convicted of Treason unless on the Testimony of two Witnesses to the same overt Act, or on Confession in open Court.

The Congress shall have Power to declare the Punishment of Treason, but no Attainder of Treason shall work Corruption of Blood, or Forfeiture except during the Life of the Person attainted.

Article IV

Section 1. Full Faith and Credit shall be given in each State to the public Acts, Records, and judicial Proceedings of every other State. And the Congress may by general Laws prescribe the Manner in which such Acts, Records and Proceedings shall be proved, and the Effect thereof.

Section 2. The Citizens of each State shall be entitled to all Privileges and Immunities of Citizens in the several States.

A Person charged in any State with Treason, Felony, or other Crime, who shall flee from Justice, and be found in another State, shall on Demand of the executive Authority of the State from which he fled, be delivered up, to be removed to the State having Jurisdiction of the Crime.

No Person held to Service or Labour in one State, under the Laws thereof, escaping into another, shall, in Consequence of any Law or Regulation therein, be discharged from such Service or Labour, but shall be delivered up on Claim of the Party to whom such Service or Labour may be due.

Section 3. New States may be admitted by the Congress into this Union; but no new State shall be formed or erected within the Jurisdiction of any other State; nor any State be formed by the Junction of two or more States, or Parts of States, without the Consent of the Legislatures of the States concerned as well as of the Congress.

The Congress shall have Power to dispose of and make all needful Rules and Regulations respecting the Territory or other Property belonging to the United States; and nothing in this Constitution shall be so construed as to Prejudice any Claims of the United States, or of any particular State.

Section 4. The United States shall guarantee to every State in this Union a Republican Form of Government, and shall protect each of them against Invasion; and on Application of the Legislature, or of the Executive (when the Legislature cannot be convened) against domestic Violence.

Article V

The Congress, whenever two thirds of both Houses shall deem it necessary, shall propose Amendments to this Constitution, or, on the Application of the Legislatures of two thirds of the several States, shall call a Convention for proposing Amendments, which, in either Case, shall be valid to all Intents and Purposes, as part of this Constitution, when ratified by the Legislatures of three fourths of the several States, or by Conventions in three fourths thereof, as the one or the other Mode of Ratification may be proposed by the Congress; Provided that no Amendment which may be made prior to the Year One thousand eight hundred and eight shall in any Manner affect the first and fourth Clauses in the Ninth Section of the first Article; and that no State, without its Consent, shall be deprived of its equal Suffrage in the Senate.

Article VI

All Debts contracted and Engagements entered into, before the Adoption of this Constitution shall be as valid against the United States under this Constitution, as under the Confederation.

This Constitution, and the Laws of the United States which shall be made in Pursuance thereof; and all Treaties made, or which shall be made, under the Authority of the United States, shall be the supreme Law of the Land; and the Judges in every State shall be bound thereby, any Thing in the Constitution or Laws of any State to the Contrary notwithstanding.

The Senators and Representatives before mentioned, and the Members of the several State Legislatures, and all executive and judicial Officers, both of the United States and of the several States, shall be bound by Oath or Affirmation, to support this Constitution; but no religious Test shall ever be required as a Qualification to any Office or public Trust under the United States.

Article VII

The Ratification of the Conventions of nine States shall be sufficient for the Establishment of this Constitution between the States so ratifying the Same.

Amendment I [1791]

Congress shall make no law respecting an establishment of religion, or prohibiting the free exercise thereof; or abridging the freedom of speech, or of the press; or the right of the people peaceably to assembly, and to petition the Government for a redress of grievances.

Amendment II [1791]

A well regulated Militia, being necessary to the security of a free State, the right of the people to keep and bear Arms, shall not be infringed.

Amendment III [1791]

No Soldier shall, in time of peace be quartered in any house, without the consent of the Owner, nor in time of war, but in a manner to be prescribed by law.

Amendment IV [1791]

The right of the people to be secure in their persons, houses, papers, and effects, against unreasonable searches and seizures, shall not be violated, and no Warrants shall issue, but upon probable cause, supported by Oath or affirmation, and particularly describing the place to be searched, and the persons or things to be seized.

Amendment V [1791]

No person shall be held to answer for a capital, or otherwise infamous crime, unless on a presentment or indictment of a Grand Jury, except in cases arising in the land or naval forces, or in the Militia, when in actual service in time of War or public danger; nor shall any person be subject for the same offence to be twice put in jeopardy of life or limb; nor shall be compelled in any criminal case to be a witness against himself, nor be deprived of life, liberty, or property, without due process of law; nor shall private property be taken for public use, without just compensation.

Amendment VI [1791]

In all criminal prosecutions, the accused shall enjoy the right to a speedy and public trial, by an impartial jury of the State and district wherein the crime shall have been committed, which district shall have been previously ascertained by law, and to be informed of the nature and cause of the accusation; to be confronted with the witnesses against him; to have compulsory process for obtaining witnesses in his favor, and to have the Assistance of Counsel for his defence.

Amendment VII [1791]

In Suits at common law, where the value in controversy shall exceed twenty dollars, the right of trial by jury shall be preserved, and no fact tried by jury, shall be otherwise reexamined in any Court of the United States, than according to the rules of the common law.

Amendment VIII [1791]

Excessive bail shall not be required, nor excessive fines imposed, nor cruel and unusual punishments inflicted.

Amendment IX [1791]

The enumeration in the Constitution, of certain rights, shall not be construed to deny or disparage others retained by the people.

Amendment X [1791]

The powers not delegated to the United States by the Constitution, nor prohibited by it to the States, are reserved to the States respectively, or to the people.

Amendment XI [1798]

The Judicial power of the United States shall not be construed to extend to any suit in law or equity, commenced or prosecuted against one of the United States by Citizens of another State, or by Citizens or Subjects of any Foreign State.

Amendment XII [1804]

The Electors shall meet in their respective states, and vote by ballot for President and Vice-President, one of whom, at least, shall not be an inhabitant of the same state with themselves; they shall name in their ballots the person voted for as President, and in distinct ballots the person voted for as Vice-President, and they shall make distinct lists of all persons voted for as President, and of all persons voted for as Vice-President, and of the number of votes for each, which lists they shall sign and certify, and transmit sealed to the seat of the government of the United States, directed to the President of the Senate;—The President of the Senate shall, in the presence of the Senate and House of Representatives, open all the certificates and the votes shall then be counted;—The person having the greatest number of votes for President, shall be the President, if such number be a majority of the whole number of Electors appointed; and if no person have such majority, then from the persons having the highest numbers not exceeding three on the list of those voted for as President, the House of Representatives shall choose immediately, by ballot, the President. But in choosing the President, the votes shall be taken by states, the representation from each state having one vote; a quorum for this purpose shall consist of a member or members from two-thirds of the states, and a majority of all states shall be necessary to a choice. And if the House of Representatives shall not choose a President whenever the right of choice shall devolve upon them, before the fourth day of March next following, then the Vice-President shall act as President, as in the case of the death or other constitutional disability of the President.—The person having the greatest number of votes as Vice-President, shall be the Vice-President, if such number be a majority of the whole number of Electors appointed, and if no person have a majority, then from the two highest numbers on the list, the Senate shall choose the Vice-President; a quorum for the purpose shall consist of two-thirds of the whole number of Senators, and a majority of the whole number shall be necessary to a choice. But no person constitutionally ineligible to the office of President shall be eligible to that of Vice-President of the United States.

Amendment XIII [1865]

Section 1. Neither slavery nor involuntary servitude, except as a punishment for crime whereof the party shall have been duly convicted, shall exist within the United States, or any place subject to their jurisdiction.

Section 2. Congress shall have power to enforce this article by appropriate legislation.

Amendment XIV [1868]

Section 1. All persons born or naturalized in the United States, and subject to the jurisdiction thereof, are citizens of the United States and of the State wherein they reside. No State shall make or enforce any law which shall abridge the privileges or immunities of citizens of the United States; nor shall any State deprive any person of life, liberty, or property, without due process of law; nor deny to any person within its jurisdiction the equal protection of the laws.

Section 2. Representatives shall be apportioned among the several States according to their respective numbers, counting the whole number of persons in each State, excluding Indians not taxed. But when the right to vote at any election for the choice of electors for President and Vice President of the United States, Representatives in Congress, the Executive and Judicial officers of a State, or the members of the Legislature thereof, is denied to any of the male inhabitants of such State, being twenty-one years of age, and citizens of the United States, or in any way abridged, except for participation in rebellion, or other crime, the basis of representation therein shall be reduced in the proportion which the number of such male citizens shall bear to the whole number of male citizens twenty-one years of age in such State.

Section 3. No person shall be a Senator or Representative in Congress, or elector of President and Vice President, or hold any office, civil or military, under the United States, or under any State, who having previously taken an oath, as a member of Congress, or as an officer of the United States, or as a member of any State legislature, or as an executive or judicial officer of any State, to support the Constitution of the United States, shall have engaged in insurrection or rebellion against the same, or given aid or comfort to the enemies thereof. But Congress may by a vote of two-thirds of each House, remove such disability.

Section 4. The validity of the public debt of the United States, authorized by law, including debts incurred for payment of pensions and bounties for services in suppressing insurrection or rebellion, shall not be questioned. But neither the United States nor any State shall assume or pay any debt or obligation incurred in aid of insurrection or rebellion against the United States, or any claim for the loss or emancipation of any slave; but all such debts, obligations and claims shall be held illegal and void.

Section 5. The Congress shall have power to enforce, by appropriate legislation, the provisions of this article.

Amendment XV [1870]

Section 1. The right of citizens of the United States to vote shall not be denied or abridged by the United States or by any State on account of race, color, or previous condition of servitude.

Section 2. The Congress shall have power to enforce this article by appropriate legislation.

Amendment XVI [1913]

The Congress shall have power to lay and collect taxes on incomes, from whatever source derived, without apportionment among the several States, and without regard to any census or enumeration.

Amendment XVII [1913]

Section 1. The Senate of the United States shall be composed of two Senators from each State, elected by the people thereof, for six years; and each Senator shall have one vote. The electors in each State shall have the qualifications requisite for electors of the most numerous branch of the State legislatures.

Section 2. When vacancies happen in the representation of any State in the Senate, the executive authority of such State shall issue writs of election to fill such vacancies: *Provided,* That the legislature of any State may empower the executive thereof to make temporary appointments until the people fill the vacancies by election as the legislature may direct.

Section 3. This amendment shall not be so construed as to affect the election or term of any Senator chosen before it becomes valid as part of the Constitution.

Amendment XVIII [1919]

Section 1. After one year from the ratification of this article the manufacture, sale, or transportation of intoxicating liquors within, the importation thereof into, or the exportation thereof from the United States and all territory subject to the jurisdiction thereof for beverage purposes is hereby prohibited.

Section 2. The Congress and the several States shall have concurrent power to enforce this article by appropriate legislation.

Section 3. This article shall be inoperative unless it shall have been ratified as an amendment to the Constitution by the legislatures of the several States, as provided in the Constitution, within seven years from the date of the submission hereof to the States by the Congress.

Amendment XIX [1920]

Section 1. The right of citizens of the United States to vote shall not be denied or abridged by the United States or by any State on account of sex.

Section 2. Congress shall have power to enforce this article by appropriate legislation.

Amendment XX [1933]

Section 1. The terms of the President and Vice President shall end at noon on the 20th day of January, and the terms of Senators and Representatives at noon on the 3d day of January, of the years in which such terms would have ended if this article had not been ratified; and the terms of their successors shall then begin.

Section 2. The Congress shall assemble at least once in every year, and such meeting shall begin at noon on the 3d day of January, unless they shall by law appoint a different day.

Section 3. If, at the time fixed for the beginning of the term of the President, the President elect shall have died, the Vice President elect shall become President. If the President shall not have been chosen before the time fixed for the beginning of his term, or if the President elect shall have failed to qualify, then the Vice President elect shall act as President until a President shall have qualified; and the Congress may by law provide for the case wherein neither a President elect nor a Vice President elect shall have qualified, declaring who shall then act as President, or the manner in which one who is to act shall be selected, and such person shall act accordingly until a President or Vice President shall have qualified.

Section 4. The Congress may by law provide for the case of the death of any of the persons from whom the House of Representatives may choose a President whenever the right of choice shall have devolved upon them, and for the case of the death of any of the persons from whom the Senate may choose a Vice President whenever the right of choice shall have devolved upon them.

Section 5. Sections 1 and 2 shall take effect on the 15th day of October following the ratification of this article.

Section 6. This article shall be inoperative unless it shall have been ratified as an amendment to the Constitution by the legislatures of three-fourths of the several States within seven years from the date of its submission.

Amendment XXI [1933]

Section 1. The eighteenth article of amendment to the Constitution of the United States is hereby repealed.

Section 2. The transportation or importation into any State, Territory, or possession of the United States for delivery or use therein of intoxicating liquors, in violation of the laws thereof, is hereby prohibited.

Section 3. This article shall be inoperative unless it shall have been ratified as an amendment to the Constitution by conventions in the several States, as provided in the Constitution, within seven years from the date of the submission hereof to the States by the Congress.

Amendment XXII [1951]

Section 1. No person shall be elected to the office of the President more than twice, and no person who has held the office of President, or acted as President, for more than two years of a term to which some other person was elected President shall be elected to the office of President more than once. But this Article shall not apply to any person holding the office of President when this Article was proposed by the Congress, and shall not prevent any person who may be holding the office of President, or acting as President, during the term within which this Article becomes operative from holding the office of President or acting as President during the remainder of such term.

Section 2. This article shall be inoperative unless it shall have been ratified as an amendment to the Constitution by the legislatures of three-fourths of the several States within seven years from the date of its submission to the States by the Congress.

Amendment XXIII [1961]

Section 1. The District constituting the seat of Government of the United States shall appoint in such manner as the Congress may direct:

A number of electors of President and Vice President equal to the whole number of Senators and Representatives in Congress to which the District would be entitled if it were a State, but in no event more than the least populous state; they shall be in addition to those appointed by the states, but they shall be considered, for the purposes of the election of President and Vice President, to be electors appointed by a state; and they shall meet in the District and perform such duties as provided by the twelfth article of amendment.

Section 2. The Congress shall have power to enforce this article by appropriate legislation.

Amendment XXIV [1964]

Section 1. The right of citizens of the United States to vote in any primary or other election for President or Vice

President, for electors for President or Vice President, or for Senator or Representative in Congress, shall not be denied or abridged by the United States, or any State by reason of failure to pay any poll tax or other tax.

Section 2.   The Congress shall have power to enforce this article by appropriate legislation.

Amendment XXV [1967]

Section 1.   In case of the removal of the President from office or of his death or resignation, the Vice President shall become President.

Section 2.   Whenever there is a vacancy in the office of the Vice President, the President shall nominate a Vice President who shall take office upon confirmation by a majority vote of both Houses of Congress.

Section 3.   Whenever the President transmits to the President pro tempore of the Senate and the Speaker of the House of Representatives his written declaration that he is unable to discharge the powers and duties of his office, and until he transmits to them a written declaration to the contrary, such powers and duties shall be discharged by the Vice President as Acting President.

Section 4.   Whenever the Vice President and a majority of either the principal officers of the executive departments or of such other body as Congress may by law provide, transmit to the President pro tempore of the Senate and the Speaker of the House of Representatives their written declaration that the President is unable to discharge the powers and duties of his office, the Vice President shall immediately assume the powers and duties of the office as Acting President.

Thereafter, when the President transmits to the President pro tempore of the Senate and the Speaker of the House of Representatives his written declaration that no inability exists, he shall resume the powers and duties of his office unless the Vice President and a majority of either the principal officers of the executive department or of such other body as Congress may by law provide, transmit within four days to the President pro tempore of the Senate and the Speaker of the House of Representatives their written declaration that the President is unable to discharge the powers and duties of his office. Thereupon Congress shall decide the issue, assembling within forty-eight hours for that purpose if not in session. If the Congress, within twenty-one days after receipt of the latter written declaration, or, if Congress is not in session, within twenty-one days after Congress is required to assemble, determines by two-thirds vote of both Houses that the President is unable to discharge the powers and duties of his office, the Vice President shall continue to discharge the same as Acting President; otherwise, the President shall resume the powers and duties of his office.

Amendment XXVI [1971]

Section 1.   The right of citizens of the United States, who are eighteen years of age or older, to vote shall not be denied or abridged by the United States or by any State on account of age.

Section 2.   The Congress shall have power to enforce this article by appropriate legislation.

Amendment XXVII [1992]

No law, varying the compensation for the services of the Senators and Representatives, shall take effect, until an election of Representatives shall have intervened.

Discretion in Action Case Studies

3.1 In the autumn of 2014, California passed the nation's first affirmative consent law. Under this law, all state colleges and universities must require "affirmative, conscious and voluntary agreement to engage in sexual activity," which can be verbal or communicated through actions. This agreement must be indicated at each stage of sexual activity. So, for example, consent to kissing cannot be taken to indicate consent for intercourse. If a California post-secondary school fails to implement an affirmative consent policy, the school will lose state financial aid.

Even those who support California's new law realize that, "unless every dorm room comes equipped with a court reporter," there will continue to be miscommunication between students regarding sex. Nor, they agree, will it necessarily stop sexual predators from targeting victims. Rather, the hope is that the new policy changes a student culture in which lack of protest or resistance is taken as confirmation of assent to sex.

4.1 After University of Virginia senior George Huguely was arrested for the death of his twenty-two-year-old ex-girlfriend Yeardley Love in 2010, prosecutors charged him with first degree murder, punishable by life in prison. The prosecutors asserted that Huguely was enraged because Love was dating someone else, and that he intended to kill her in a premeditated act. Huguely's lawyers insisted that, at worst, their client was guilty of involuntary manslaughter. At the time of the crime, they pointed out, he was drunk and had no intent to harm Love, much less kill her. Furthermore, they argued, Love died from suffocation well after Huguely left her apartment.

In 2012, a Charlottesville, Virginia, jury found Huguely guilty of second degree murder, reasoning that although he did not intend to kill Love, he did act with malice aforethought and his violent behavior was the cause of her death. A judge later sentenced Huguely to twenty-three years in prison.

6.1 Before Donald Rickar could flee from the West Memphis, Arkansas, parking lot, law enforcement officers fired fifteen shots at his car, killing him. Rickar's family sued, claiming that the officers had used excessive force in taking Rickar's life. The case reached the United States Supreme Court, which held unanimously in 2014 that the officers had acted reasonably under the circumstances.

The Court's decision echoed a 2007 case in which it ruled for a Georgia officer who had forced a suspect's vehicle off the road to end a high-speed pursuit, leaving the suspect partially paralyzed. In general, then, police officers are justified in using deadly force to terminate high-speed chases that threaten the lives of those involved in the chase, even if such force puts the fleeing suspect at risk of significant injury or death.

7.1 In 1996, two Washington, D.C., police officers pulled over Michael J. Wren—a young African American male who was driving a truck with temporary plates in a high-crime neighborhood—for failing to signal while making a right turn. They found two large bags of crack cocaine in Wren's possession, and arrested him. The United States Supreme Court upheld Wren's conviction, ruling that as long as police officers have probable cause to believe that a traffic violation has occurred, the "real" reason for making the stop is irrelevant.

As Justice Antonin Scalia put it, "Subjective intentions play no role in ordinary, probable-cause, Fourth Amendment analysis." In practical terms, this ruling gives law enforcement agents the ability to confirm "hunches" about serious illegal behavior as long as the target of these hunches commits even the most minor traffic violation. Such violations could include failing to properly signal during a turn, or making a rolling stop at a stop sign, or driving five miles over the posted speed limit.

8.1 In 2012, the Oregon Supreme Court ordered a new trial for Samuel Lawson and, in the process, established new procedures for determining the admissibility of eyewitness identification in state courts. Today, Oregon courts must consider all the factors that could contaminate eyewitness identifications, including the effects of suggestive comments made by law enforcement agents.

In this case, the Oregon Supreme Court noted that Sheryl had sustained a critical gunshot wound at the time of her husband's murder, only saw the assailant briefly in the dark, and did not identify Lawson until two years after the events at the campsite. At the least, the defendant's attorneys should have been able to address these factors during the trial, thus allowing jurors to decide for themselves whether Sheryl's eyewitness testimony was reliable.

9.1 In 2014, Etowah County Circuit Judge William Ogletree denied Joyce Garrard's bail request. Garrard had been in jail for two years following her granddaughter's death and would remain there for at least one more year until her trial started. Even though Garrard had a number of health problems, including chest pains and severe headaches, and could hardly be considered a threat to the community, the local district attorney opposed bail. In Alabama, those charged with capital murder are rarely given their pretrial release, regardless of the circumstances of the crime and the likelihood of further violent offending.

9.2 The North Carolina prosecutor in this case charged Judy Norman with first degree murder, reasoning that self-defense did not apply because Judy did not face any *imminent* danger from her husband, John. Despite his threats and the years of abuse, John was, at the time of his murder, asleep and thus incapable of harming her. A jury in the case, however, found Judy guilty of voluntary manslaughter only, and she was sentenced to six years in prison.

This case gained national attention because the trial court refused to allow evidence of *battered woman syndrome (BWS)* to be presented to the jury. The term describes the psychological state a person descends into following a lengthy period of physical abuse. In a courtroom, an expert might argue that anyone suffering from this syndrome is in a constant, and reasonable, fear for her or his life. Some states do allow evidence of BWS to support the defendant's claim of self-defense in these sorts of cases, and it has been effective. A New York woman who shot her abusive husband as he slept, for example, was acquitted after a jury accepted her self-defense claims, bolstered by expert testimony on BWS.

10.1 Cody Cofer, Michelle Williams's defense attorney, focused his arguments on the fact that the evidence against his client was circumstantial. That is, there was no way to definitively prove how Greg Williams had died. Cofer also pointed out that Michelle had no financial motive to kill her husband, and that her explanation regarding a "cover-up" to protect her daughter from trauma was a reasonable one. "The worst thing our system can do is convict an innocent person," Cofer told the jurors. "That's a decision you'll have to live with for the rest of your lives."

Despite these efforts, the jury did indeed convict Michelle of murder and, in September 2014, a judge sentenced her to sixty years in prison. The evidence that nobody but Michelle could have killed Greg, though circumstantial, apparently was strong enough to overcome any reasonable doubt in the minds of the jurors.

11.1 The same Arizona jury that found Jodi Arias guilty of murdering Travis Alexander with such "exceptional cruelty" that she was eligible for the death penalty was unable to decide whether she should be executed. That is, the twelve jurors were unable to come to a unanimous decision on either execution or a life-in-prison sentence. Under state law, prosecutors were able to seat a second jury to make the sentencing decision, and, therefore, a second sentencing phase for Arias was scheduled to take place sixteen months after the first.

Following this second sentencing phase, which lasted nearly five months, the second jury deliberated for twenty-six hours over a period of six days before—again—deadlocking. By state law, this meant that Arias' fate passed to the hands of Maricopa County Superior Court Judge Sherry Stephens. In April 2015, Judge Stephens sentenced the defendant to spend life in prison. Explaining his decision, the judge said that Arias' crime was "especially cruel" and that it "involved substantial planning and preparation. . . . The defendant destroyed evidence . . . and went to great lengths to conceal her involvement."

12.1 Alain LeConte's probation officer did not take any steps to revoke his probation. The issue became moot, however, when LeConte was arrested for killing a gas station attendant during an armed robbery in Norwalk, Connecticut.

The crime took place between his first and second failed drug tests. LeConte's probation officer came under a great deal of criticism for failing to revoke his probation, but she received support from her supervisor. "We can only do so much," he said. "[LeConte's] probation officer went out of her way to assist this young man, but unfortunately it wasn't successful."

The supervisor also pointed out that LeConte had no known history of violent behavior and had been a generally cooperative probationer when it came to getting treatment. This case underscores the difficult aspects of a probation officer's job. A misjudgment, even if it was based on a reasonable evaluation of the situation, can end in tragedy.

12.2 Susan Atkins was a disciple of cult leader Charles Manson and, in the summer of 1969, participated in one of the most sensationalized mass murders in American history. The woman Atkins stabbed sixteen times was Sharon Tate, an actress and the wife of film director Roman Polanski. On September 2, 2009, the California Board of Parole unanimously denied compassionate release for Atkins, marking the eighteenth time she had been refused parole. Three months later, Atkins died of brain cancer. Her case highlights the extent to which parole boards are often swayed by the nature of the crime above all other considerations.

14.1 Initially, state prison officials decided to fire a correctional officer named Welch following an incident at the Maine Correctional Center in Windham similar to the one described in the feature. Because of Welch's otherwise unblemished career, however, his punishment was eventually reduced to a thirty-day suspension without pay.

Following the incident, the Maine Department of Corrections instituted new guidelines regarding "cutters" (inmates who injure themselves) and "spitters" that promoted the use of pepper spray rather than other types of force by correctional officers. It seems that Welch's mistake was that he grew angry at the inmate's insults and let his anger influence the level of his response. "It's all right for [inmates] to have the last word, we have the last action," said a state prison official.

15.1 In 2008, a Denver, Colorado, prosecutor chose to charge seventeen-year-old James Stewart as an adult for vehicular homicide. After Stewart was moved to an adult jail, he tightened several bed sheets around his neck and hung himself. Stewart's suicide led to a change in state law that requires judges to review prosecutorial waivers in certain situations and makes it much less likely that a juvenile offender awaiting trial will be held in an adult jail.

In the first year after this law was passed, the number of juvenile offenders waived to state adult court dropped by nearly 85 percent. Nonetheless, Colorado prosecutors dislike the new law. One claims that he and his colleagues are in a better position than judges to decide whether a juvenile should be tried in adult court, due to a prosecutor's "experience" and "years and years of weighing one case against similarly situated cases."

16.1 In 2004, Steven Parr was convicted of threatening to blow up the Reuss Federal Plaza in Milwaukee and sentenced to ten years in prison. Before finding that Parr's bragging was a "true threat" and therefore not protected by the First Amendment, the jury heard a great deal of evidence in addition to the recording made by the prison whistleblower. A number of witnesses—including three ex-girlfriends and two former neighbors—testified that not only was Parr skilled in explosives, but also that he often spoke of his hatred for the federal government and his admiration for domestic terrorists such as Tim McVeigh, whose 1995 bombing of the Alfred P. Murrah Federal Building in Oklahoma City is mentioned in the text.

Prosecutors also showed the jury a number of books and notebooks in Parr's possession that indicated his obsession with bomb building. Because of this evidence, in 2008 an appeals court ruled that a reasonable jury could have found that Parr's words constituted a "true threat" and upheld his conviction.

Table of Cases

Glossary

A

Acquittal A declaration following a trial that the individual accused of the crime is innocent in the eyes of the law and thus is absolved from the charges.

Actus Reus (pronounced *ak*-tus *ray*-uhs). A guilty (prohibited) act.

Adjudicatory Hearing The process through which a juvenile court determines whether there is sufficient evidence to support the initial petition.

Administrative Law The body of law created by administrative agencies (in the form of rules, regulations, orders, and decisions) in order to carry out their duties and responsibilities.

Adversary System A legal system in which the prosecution and defense are opponents, or adversaries, and present their cases in the light most favorable to themselves.

Affidavit A written statement of facts, confirmed by the oath or affirmation of the party making it and made before a person having the authority to administer the oath or affirmation.

Affirmative Action A hiring or promotion policy favoring those groups, such as women, African Americans, or Hispanics, who have suffered from discrimination in the past or continue to suffer from discrimination.

Aftercare The variety of therapeutic, educational, and counseling programs made available to juvenile delinquents (and some adults) after they have been released from a correctional facility.

Age of Onset The age at which a juvenile first exhibits delinquent behavior.

Aggravating Circumstances Any circumstances accompanying the commission of a crime that may justify a harsher sentence.

Aging Out A term used to explain the fact that criminal activity declines with age.

Allen Charge An instruction by a judge to a deadlocked jury with only a few dissenters that asks the jurors in the minority to reconsider the majority opinion.

Anomie A condition in which the individual feels a disconnect from society due to the breakdown or absence of social norms.

Appeal The process of seeking a higher court's review of a lower court's decision for the purpose of correcting or changing this decision.

Appellate Courts Courts that review decisions made by lower courts, such as trial courts; also known as *courts of appeals*.

Arraignment A court proceeding in which the suspect is formally charged with the criminal offense stated in the indictment.

Arrest To deprive a person suspected of criminal activity of his or her liberty.

Arrest Warrant A written order, based on probable cause and issued by a judge or magistrate, commanding that the person named on the warrant be arrested by the police.

Assault A threat or an attempt to do violence to another person that causes that person to fear immediate physical harm.

Attempt The act of taking substantial steps toward committing a crime while having the ability and the intent to commit the crime, even if the crime never takes place.

Attendant Circumstances The facts surrounding a criminal event that must be proved to convict the defendant of the underlying crime.

Attorney-Client Privilege A rule of evidence requiring that communications between a client and his or her attorney be kept confidential, unless the client consents to disclosure.

Attorney General The chief law officer of a state; also, the chief law officer of the nation.

Authority The power designated to an agent of the law over a person who has broken the law.

Automatic Transfer The process by which a juvenile is transferred to adult court as a matter of state law.

B

Bail The dollar amount or conditions set by the court to ensure that an individual accused of a crime will appear for further criminal proceedings.

Bail Bond Agent A businessperson who agrees, for a fee, to pay the bail amount if the accused fails to appear in court as ordered.

Ballistics The study of firearms, including the firing of the weapon and the flight of the bullet.

Ballot Initiative A procedure in which the citizens of a state, by collecting enough signatures, can force a public vote on a proposed change to state law.

Battery The act of physically contacting another person with the intent to do harm, even if the resulting injury is insubstantial.

Bench Trial A trial conducted without a jury, in which a judge makes the determination of the defendant's guilt or innocence.

Beyond a Reasonable Doubt The degree of proof required to find the defendant in a criminal trial guilty of committing the crime. The defendant's guilt must be the only reasonable explanation for the criminal act before the court.

Bill of Rights The first ten amendments to the U.S. Constitution.

Biology The science of living organisms, including their structure, function, growth, and origin.

Biometrics Methods to identify a person based on his or her unique physical characteristics, such as fingerprints or facial configuration.

Blue Curtain A metaphorical term used to refer to the value placed on secrecy and the general mistrust of the outside world shared by many police officers.

Body Armor Protective covering that is worn under a police officer's clothing and designed to minimize injury from being hit by a fired bullet.

Booking The process of entering a suspect's name, offense, and arrival time into the police log following her or his arrest.

Boot Camp A variation on traditional shock incarceration in which juveniles (and some adults) are sent to secure confinement facilities modeled on military basic training camps instead of prison or jail.

Botnet A network of computers that have been appropriated without the knowledge of their owners and used to spread harmful programs via the Internet; short for *robot network*.

***Boykin* Form** A form that must be completed by a defendant who pleads guilty. The defendant states that she or he has done so voluntarily and with full comprehension of the consequences.

Broken Windows Theory Wilson and Kelling's theory that a neighborhood in disrepair signals that criminal activity is tolerated in the area. By cracking down on quality-of-life crimes, police can reclaim the neighborhood and encourage law-abiding citizens to live and work there.

Bullying Overt acts taken by students with the goal of intimidating, harassing, or humiliating other students.

Bureaucracy A hierarchically structured administrative organization that carries out specific functions.

Burglary The act of breaking into or entering a structure (such as a home or office) without permission for the purpose of committing a felony.

Burnout A mental state that occurs when a person suffers from exhaustion and has difficulty functioning normally as a result of overwork and stress.

C

Capital Crime A criminal act that makes the offender eligible to receive the death penalty.

Capital Punishment The use of the death penalty to punish wrongdoers for certain crimes.

Case Attrition The process through which prosecutors, by deciding whether to bring legal action against each person arrested, effect an overall reduction in the number of persons prosecuted.

Case Law The rules of law announced in court decisions.

Caseload The number of individual probationers or parolees under the supervision of a probation or parole officer.

Causation The relationship in which a change in one measurement or behavior creates a recognizable change in another measurement or behavior.

Challenge for Cause A *voir dire* challenge for which an attorney states the reason why a prospective juror should not be included on the jury.

Charge The judge's instructions to the jury following the attorneys' closing arguments.

Child Abuse Mistreatment of children by causing physical, emotional, or sexual damage without any plausible explanation, such as an accident.

Child Neglect A form of child abuse in which the child is denied certain necessities such as shelter, food, care, and love.

Choice Theory A school of criminology based on the belief that individuals have free will to engage in any behavior, including criminal behavior.

Chronic Offender A delinquent or criminal who commits multiple offenses and is considered part of a small group of wrongdoers who are responsible for a majority of the antisocial activity in any given community.

Circumstantial Evidence Indirect evidence that is offered to establish, by inference, the likelihood of a fact that is in question.

Citizen Oversight The process by which citizens review complaints brought against individual police officers or police departments.

Civil Confinement The practice of confining individuals against their will if they present a danger to the community.

Civil Law The branch of law dealing with the definition and enforcement of all private or public rights, as opposed to criminal matters.

Civil Liability The potential responsibility of police officers, police departments, or municipalities to defend themselves against civil lawsuits.

Civil Liberties The basic rights and freedoms for American citizens guaranteed by the U.S. Constitution, particularly in the Bill of Rights.

Civil Rights Violation Any interference with a citizen's constitutional rights by a civil servant such as a police officer.

Classical Criminology A school of criminology that holds that wrongdoers act as if they weigh the possible benefits of criminal or delinquent activity against the expected costs of being apprehended.

Classification The process through which prison officials screen each incoming inmate to best determine that inmate's security and treatment needs.

Clearance Rate A comparison of the number of crimes cleared by arrest and prosecution with the number of crimes reported during any given time period.

Closing Arguments Arguments made by each side's attorney after the cases for the plaintiff and defendant have been presented.

Coercion The use of physical force or mental intimidation to compel a person to do something—such as confess to committing a crime—against her or his will.

Cold Case A criminal investigation that has not been solved after a certain amount of time.

Cold Hit The establishment of a connection between a suspect and a crime, often through the use of DNA evidence, in the absence of an ongoing criminal investigation.

Common Law The body of law developed from custom or judicial decisions in English and U.S. courts and not attributable to a legislature.

Community Corrections The correctional supervision of offenders in the community as an alternative to sending them to prison or jail.

Community Policing A policing philosophy that emphasizes community support for and cooperation with the police in preventing crime.

Competency Hearing A court proceeding to determine whether the defendant is mentally well enough to understand the charges filed against him or her and cooperate with a lawyer in presenting a defense.

Compliance The state of operating in accordance with governmental standards.

Computer-Aided Dispatch (CAD) A method of dispatching police patrols units to the site of 911 emergencies with the assistance of a computer program.

Concurrent Jurisdiction The situation that occurs when two or more courts have the authority to preside over the same criminal case.

Concurring Opinions Separate opinions prepared by judges who support the decision of the majority of the court but who want to make or clarify a particular point or to voice disapproval of the grounds on which the decision was made.

Conducted Energy Device (CED) A less lethal weapon designed to disrupt a target's central nervous system by means of a charge of electrical energy.

Confidential Informant (CI) A human source for police who provides information concerning illegal activity in which he or she is involved.

Conflict Model A criminal justice model in which the content of criminal law is determined by the groups that hold economic, political, and social power in a community.

Confrontation Clause The part of the Sixth Amendment that guarantees all defendants the right to confront witnesses testifying against them during the criminal trial.

Congregate System A nineteenth-century penitentiary system developed in New York in which inmates were kept in separate cells during the night but worked together in the daytime under a code of enforced silence.

Consensus Model A criminal justice model in which the majority of citizens in a society share the same values and beliefs. Criminal acts are acts that conflict with these values and beliefs and that are deemed harmful to society.

Consent Searches Searches by police that are made after the subject of the search has agreed to the action. In these situations, consent, if given of free will, validates a warrantless search.

Conspiracy A plot by two or more people to carry out an illegal or harmful act.

Constitutional Law Law based on the U.S. Constitution and the constitutions of the various states.

Control Theory A series of theories that assume that all individuals have the potential for criminal behavior, but are restrained by the damage that such actions would do to their relationships with family, friends, and members of the community.

Coroner The medical examiner of a county, usually elected by popular vote.

Corporate Violence Physical harm to individuals or the environment that occurs as the result of corporate policies or decision making.

Corpus Delicti The body of circumstances that must exist for a criminal act to have occurred.

Correlation The relationship between two measurements or behaviors that tend to move in the same direction.

Courtroom Work Group The social organization consisting of the judge, prosecutor, defense attorney, and other court workers.

Crime An act that violates criminal law and is punishable by criminal sanctions.

Crime Control Model A criminal justice model that places primary emphasis on the right of society to be protected from crime and violent criminals.

Crime Mapping Technology that allows crime analysts to identify trends and patterns of criminal behavior within a given area.

Criminal Justice System The interlocking network of law enforcement agencies, courts, and corrections institutions designed to enforce criminal laws and protect society from criminal behavior.

Criminal Model of Addiction An approach to drug abuse that holds that drug offenders harm society by their actions to the same extent as other criminals and should face the same punitive sanctions.

Criminology The scientific study of crime and the causes of criminal behavior.

Cross-Examination The questioning of an opposing witness during trial.

Cultural Deviance Theory A branch of social structure theory based on the assumption that members of certain subcultures reject the values of the dominant culture by exhibiting deviant behavior patterns.

Custodial Interrogation The questioning of a suspect after that person has been taken into custody. In this situation, the suspect must be read his or her *Miranda* rights before interrogation can begin.

Custody The forceful detention of a person, or the perception that a person is not free to leave the immediate vicinity.

Custody Level As a result of the classification process, the security designation given to new inmates, crucial in helping corrections officials determine which correctional facility is best suited to the individual offender.

Cyberattack An attempt to damage or disrupt computer systems or electronic networks operated by computers.

Cyber Crime A crime that occurs online, in the virtual community of the Internet, as opposed to in the physical world.

Cyber Forensics The application of computer technology to finding and utilizing evidence of cyber crimes.

Cyber Fraud Any misrepresentation knowingly made over the Internet with the intention of deceiving another and on which a reasonable person would and does rely to his or her detriment.

Cyberstalking The crime of stalking, committed in cyberspace through the use of e-mail, text messages, or another form of electronic communication.

D

Dark Figure of Crime A term used to describe the actual amount of crime that takes place. The "figure" is "dark," or impossible to detect, because a great number of crimes are never reported to the police.

Day Reporting Center (DRC) A community-based corrections center to which offenders report on a daily basis for treatment, education, and rehabilitation.

Deadly Force Force applied by a police officer that is likely or intended to cause death.

Decriminalization The removal of criminal penalties associated with a product or act, which then becomes only subject to civil sanctions such as fines and citations.

Defendant In a civil court, the person or institution against whom an action is brought. In a criminal court, the person or entity who has been formally accused of violating a criminal law.

Defense Attorney The lawyer representing the defendant.

Delegation of Authority The principles of command on which most police departments are based, in which personnel take orders from and are responsible to those in positions of power directly above them.

"Deliberate Indifference" The standard for establishing a violation of an inmate's Eighth Amendment rights, requiring that prison officials were aware of harmful conditions in a correctional institution *and* failed to take steps to remedy those conditions.

Departure A stipulation in many federal and state sentencing guidelines that allows a judge to adjust his or her sentencing decision based on the special circumstances of a particular case.

Deprivation Model A theory that inmate aggression is the result of the frustration inmates feel at being deprived of freedom, consumer goods, sex, and other staples of life outside the institution.

Desistance The process through which criminal activity decreases and reintegration into society increases over a period of time.

Detective The primary police investigator of crimes.

Detention The temporary custody of a juvenile in a secure facility after a petition has been filed and before the adjudicatory process begins.

Detention Hearing A hearing to determine whether a juvenile should be detained, or remain detained, while waiting for the adjudicatory process to begin.

Determinate Sentencing A period of incarceration that is fixed by a sentencing authority and cannot be reduced by judges or other corrections officials.

Deterrence The strategy of preventing crime through the threat of punishment.

Deviance Behavior that is considered to go against the norms established by society.

Differential Response A strategy for answering calls for service in which response time is adapted to the seriousness of the call.

Digital Evidence Information or data of value to a criminal investigation that are either stored or transmitted by electronic means.

Directed Patrol A patrol strategy that is designed to focus on a specific type of criminal activity in a specific geographic area.

Direct Evidence Evidence that establishes the existence of a fact that is in question without relying on inference.

Direct Examination The examination of a witness by the attorney who calls the witness to the stand to testify.

Direct Supervision Approach A process of prison and jail administration in which correctional officers are in continuous visual contact with inmates during the day.

Discovery Formal investigation by each side prior to trial.

Discretion The ability of individuals in the criminal justice system to make operational decisions based on personal judgment instead of formal rules or official information.

Discretionary Release The release of an inmate into a community supervision program at the discretion of the parole board within limits set by state or federal law.

Discrimination The illegal use of characteristics such as gender or race by employers when making hiring or promotion decisions.

Disposition Hearing Similar to the sentencing hearing for adults, a hearing in which the juvenile judge or officer decides the appropriate punishment for a youth found to be delinquent or a status offender.

Dissenting Opinions Separate opinions in which judges disagree with the conclusion reached by the majority of the court and expand on their own views about the case.

Diversion In the context of corrections, a strategy to divert those offenders who qualify away from prison and jail and toward community-based and intermediate sanctions.

DNA Fingerprinting The identification of a person based on a sample of her or his DNA, the genetic material found in the cells of all living things.

Docket The list of cases entered on a court's calendar and thus scheduled to be heard by the court.

Domestic Terrorism Acts of terrorism that take place on U.S. soil without direct foreign involvement.

Domestic Violence The act of willful neglect or physical violence that occurs within a familial or other intimate relationship.

Double Jeopardy To twice place at risk (jeopardize) a person's life or liberty. Constitutional law prohibits a second prosecution in the same court for the same criminal offense.

Double Marginality The double suspicion that minority law enforcement officers face from their white colleagues and from members of the minority community to which they belong.

Drug Any substance that modifies biological, psychological, or social behavior. In particular, an illegal substance with those properties.

Drug Abuse The use of drugs that results in physical or psychological problems for the user, as well as disruption of personal relationships and employment.

Drug Enforcement Administration (DEA) The federal agency responsible for enforcing the nation's laws and regulations regarding narcotics and other controlled substances.

Dual Court System The separate but interrelated court system of the United States, made up of the courts on the national level and the courts on the state level.

Due Process Clause The provisions of the Fifth and Fourteenth Amendments to the Constitution that guarantee that no person shall be deprived of life, liberty, or property without due process of law.

Due Process Model A criminal justice model that places primacy on the right of the individual to be protected from the power of the government.

Duress Unlawful pressure brought to bear on a person, causing the person to perform an act that he or she would not otherwise perform.

Duty The moral sense of a police officer that she or he should behave in a certain manner.

Duty to Retreat The requirement that a person claiming self-defense prove that she or he first took reasonable steps to avoid the conflict that resulted in the use of deadly force.

E

Electronic Monitoring A technique of probation supervision in which the offender's whereabouts are kept under surveillance by an electronic device.

Electronic Surveillance The use of electronic equipment by law enforcement agents to record private conversations or observe conduct that is meant to be private.

Encryption The translation of computer data in a secret code with the goal of protecting that data from unauthorized parties.

Entrapment A defense in which the defendant claims that he or she was induced by a public official—usually an undercover agent or police officer—to commit a crime that he or she would otherwise not have committed.

Ethics The moral principles that govern a person's perception of right and wrong.

Evidence Anything that is used to prove the existence or non-existence of a fact.

Exclusionary Rule A rule under which any evidence that is obtained in violation of the accused's rights, as well as any evidence derived from illegally obtained evidence, will not be admissible in criminal court.

Exigent Circumstances Situations that require extralegal or exceptional actions by the police.

Expert Witness A witness with professional training or substantial experience qualifying her or him to testify on a certain subject.

Expiration Release The release of an inmate from prison at the end of his or her sentence without any further correctional supervision.

Extradition The process by which one jurisdiction surrenders a person accused or convicted of violating another jurisdiction's criminal law to the second jurisdiction.

F

False Confession An admission of guilt when the confessor did not, in fact, commit the crime.

Federal Bureau of Investigation (FBI) The branch of the Department of Justice responsible for investigating violations of federal law.

Federalism A form of government in which a written constitution provides for a division of powers between a central government and several regional governments.

Fee System A system in which the sheriff's department is reimbursed by a government agency for the costs of housing jail inmates.

Felony A serious crime, usually punishable by death or imprisonment for a year or longer.

Felony-Murder An unlawful homicide that occurs during the attempted commission of a felony.

Field Training The segment of a police recruit's training in which he or she is removed from the classroom and placed on the beat, under the supervision of a senior officer.

Forensics The application of science to establish facts and evidence during the investigation of crimes.

Forfeiture The process by which the government seizes private property attached to criminal activity.

Formal Criminal Justice Process The model of the criminal justice process in which participants follow formal rules to create a smoothly functioning disposition of cases from arrest to punishment.

Frisk A pat-down or minimal search by police to discover weapons.

Fruit of the Poisoned Tree Evidence that is acquired through the use of illegally obtained evidence and is therefore inadmissible in court.

Furlough Temporary release from a prison for purposes of vocational or educational training, to ease the shock of release, or for personal reasons.

G

Genetics The study of how certain traits or qualities are transmitted from parents to their offspring.

"Good Faith" Exception The legal principle that evidence obtained with the use of a technically invalid search warrant is admissible during trial if the police acted in good faith when they sought the warrant from a judge.

"Good Time" A reduction in time served by prisoners based on good behavior, conformity to rules, and other positive behavior.

Graduated Sanctions A series of punishments that become more severe with each subsequent act of wrongdoing. Also, the practical theory in juvenile corrections that a delinquent or status offender should receive a punishment that matches in seriousness the severity of the wrongdoing.

Grand Jury The group of citizens called to decide whether probable cause exists to believe that a suspect committed the crime with which she or he has been charged.

Gun Control Efforts by a government to regulate or control the sale of guns.

H

Habeas Corpus An order that requires corrections officials to bring an inmate before a court or a judge and explain why he or she is being held in prison.

Habitual Offender Laws Statutes that require lengthy prison sentences for those who are convicted of multiple felonies.

Hacker A person who uses one computer to break into another.

Halfway House A community-based form of early release that places inmates in residential centers and allows them to reintegrate with society.

"Hands-Off" Doctrine The unwritten judicial policy that favors noninterference by the courts in the administration of prisons and jails.

Hate Crime Law A statute that provides for greater sanctions against those who commit crimes motivated by bias against an individual or a group based on race, ethnicity, religion, gender, sexual orientation, disability, or age.

Hearsay An oral or written statement made by an out-of-court speaker that is later offered in court by a witness (not the speaker) concerning a matter before the court.

Home Confinement A community-based sanction in which offenders serve their terms of incarceration in their homes.

Homeland Security A concerted national effort to prevent terrorist attacks within the United States and reduce the country's vulnerability to terrorism.

Hormone A chemical substance, produced in tissue and conveyed in the bloodstream, that controls certain cellular and body functions such as growth and reproduction.

Hot Spots Concentrated areas of high criminal activity that draw a directed police response.

Hung Jury A jury whose members are so irreconcilably divided in their opinions that they cannot reach a verdict.

Hypothesis A possible explanation for an observed occurrence that can be tested by further investigation.

I

"Identifiable Human Needs" The basic human necessities that correctional facilities are required by the Constitution to provide to inmates.

Identity Theft The theft of personal information, such as a person's name, driver's license number, or Social Security number.

Impeachment The formal process by which a public official is charged with misconduct that could lead to his or her removal from office.

Incapacitation A strategy for preventing crime by detaining wrongdoers in prison, thereby separating them from the community and reducing criminal opportunities.

Inchoate Offenses Conduct deemed criminal without actual harm being done, provided that the harm that would have occurred is one the law tries to prevent.

Incident-Driven Policing A reactive approach to policing that emphasizes a speedy response to calls for service.

Indeterminate Sentencing An indeterminate term of incarceration in which a judge determines the minimum and maximum terms of imprisonment.

Indictment A charge or written accusation, issued by a grand jury, that probable cause exists to believe that a named person has committed a crime.

"Inevitable Discovery" Exception The legal principle that illegally obtained evidence can be admissible in court if police using lawful means would have "inevitably" discovered it.

Infancy A condition that, under early American law, excused young wrongdoers of criminal behavior because presumably they could not understand the consequences of their actions.

Informal Criminal Justice Process A model of the criminal justice system that recognizes the informal authority exercised by individuals at each step of the criminal justice process.

Information The formal charge against the accused issued by the prosecutor after a preliminary hearing has found probable cause.

Infraction In most jurisdictions, a noncriminal offense for which the penalty is a fine rather than incarceration.

Infrastructure The services and facilities that support the day-to-day needs of modern life, such as electricity, food, transportation, and water.

Initial Appearance An accused's first appearance before a judge or magistrate following arrest.

Insanity A defense for criminal liability that asserts a lack of criminal responsibility due to mental instability.

Intake The process by which an official of the court must decide whether to file a petition, release the juvenile, or place the juvenile under some other form of supervision.

Intellectual Property Property resulting from intellectual, creative processes.

Intelligence-Led Policing An approach that measures the risk of criminal behavior associated with certain individuals or locations so as to predict when and where such criminal behavior is most likely to occur in the future.

Intensive Supervision Probation (ISP) A punishment-oriented form of probation in which the offender is placed under stricter and more frequent surveillance and control than in conventional probation.

Intermediate Sanctions Sanctions that are more restrictive than probation and less restrictive than imprisonment.

Internal Affairs Unit (IAU) A division within a police department that receives and investigates complaints of wrongdoing by police officers.

Interrogation The direct questioning of a suspect to gather evidence of criminal activity and to try to gain a confession.

Intoxication A defense for criminal liability in which the defendant claims that the taking of intoxicants rendered him or her unable to form the requisite intent to commit a criminal act.

Involuntary Manslaughter A homicide in which the offender had no intent to kill her or his victim.

Irresistible-Impulse Test A test for the insanity defense under which a defendant who knew his or her action was wrong may still be found insane if he or she was unable, as a result of a mental deficiency, to control the urge to complete the act.

J

Jail A facility, usually operated by the county government, used to hold persons awaiting trial or those who have been found guilty of less-serious felonies or misdemeanors.

Judicial Misconduct A general term describing behavior—such as accepting bribes or consorting with known felons—that diminishes public confidence in the judiciary.

Judicial Review The power of a court—particularly the United States Supreme Court—to review the actions of the executive and legislative branches and, if necessary, declare those actions unconstitutional.

Judicial Waiver The process in which the juvenile judge, based on the facts of the case at hand, decides that the alleged offender should be transferred to adult court.

Jurisdiction The authority of a court to hear and decide cases within an area of the law or a geographic territory.

Jury Trial A trial before a judge and a jury.

Just Deserts A sanctioning philosophy based on the assertion that criminal punishment should be proportionate to the severity of the crime.

Justice The quality of fairness that must exist in the processes designed to determine whether individuals are guilty of criminal wrongdoing.

Juvenile Delinquency Behavior that is illegal under federal or state law that has been committed by a person who is under an age limit specified by statute.

L

Labeling Theory The hypothesis that society creates crime and criminals by labeling certain behavior and certain people as deviant.

Larceny The act of taking property from another person without the use of force with the intent of keeping that property.

Lay Witness A witness who can truthfully and accurately testify on a fact in question without having specialized training or knowledge.

Learning Theory The theory that delinquents and criminals must be taught both the practical and the emotional skills necessary to participate in illegal activity.

Legalization To make a formerly illegal product or action lawful. In the context of marijuana, the process includes strict regulation, including a ban on sale to or use by minors.

Liability In a civil court, legal responsibility for one's own or another's actions.

Life Course Criminology The study of crime based on the belief that behavioral patterns developed in childhood can predict delinquent and criminal behavior later in life.

Lockdown A disciplinary action taken by prison officials in which all inmates are ordered to their quarters and nonessential prison activities are suspended.

Low-Visibility Decision Making A term used to describe the discretionary power police have in determining what to do with misbehaving juveniles.

M

Magistrate A public civil officer or official with limited judicial authority within a particular geographic area, such as the authority to issue an arrest warrant.

Mala in Se A descriptive term for acts that are inherently wrong, regardless of whether they are prohibited by law.

Mala Prohibita A descriptive term for acts that are made illegal by criminal statute and are not necessarily wrong in and of themselves.

Mandatory Release Release from prison that occurs when an offender has served the full length of his or her sentence, minus any adjustments for good time.

Mandatory Sentencing Guidelines Statutorily determined punishments that must be applied to those who are convicted of specific crimes.

Master Jury List The list of citizens in a court's district from which a jury can be selected; compiled from voter-registration lists, driver's license lists, and other sources.

Material Support In the context of federal antiterrorism legislation, the act of helping a terrorist organization by engaging in a wide range of activity that includes providing financial support, training, and expert advice or assistance.

Maximum-Security Prison A correctional institution designed and organized to control and discipline dangerous felons, as well as prevent escape.

Medical Model A model of corrections in which the psychological and biological roots of an inmate's criminal behavior are identified and treated.

Medical Model of Addiction An approach to drug addiction that treats drug abuse as a mental illness and focuses on treating and rehabilitating offenders rather than punishing them.

Medium-Security Prison A correctional institution that houses less dangerous inmates and therefore uses less restrictive measures to prevent violence and escapes.

Mens Rea (pronounced mehns ray-uh). Mental state, or intent. A wrongful mental state is usually as necessary as a wrongful act to establish criminal liability.

Minimum-Security Prison A correctional institution designed to allow inmates, most of whom pose low security risks, a great deal of freedom of movement and contact with the outside world.

***Miranda* Rights** The constitutional rights of accused persons taken into custody by law enforcement officials, such as the right to remain silent and the right to counsel.

Misdemeanor A criminal offense that is not a felony; usually punishable by a fine and/or a jail term of less than one year.

Missouri Plan A method of selecting judges that combines appointment and election.

Mitigating Circumstances Any circumstances accompanying the commission of a crime that may justify a lighter sentence.

***M'Naghten* Rule** A common law test of criminal responsibility, derived from *M'Naghten*'s Case in 1843, that relies on the defendant's inability to distinguish right from wrong.

Model Penal Code A statutory text created by the American Law Institute that sets forth general principles of criminal responsibility and defines specific offenses.

Morals Principles of right and wrong behavior, as practiced by individuals or by society.

Motion for a Directed Verdict A motion requesting that the court grant judgment in favor of the defense on the ground that the prosecution has not produced sufficient evidence to support the state's claim.

Murder The unlawful killing of one human being by another.

N

National Security Letters Legal notices that compel the disclosure of customer records held by banks, telephone companies, Internet service providers, and other companies to the agents of the federal government.

Necessity A defense against criminal liability in which the defendant asserts that circumstances required her or him to commit an illegal act.

Negligence A failure to exercise the standard of care that a reasonable person would exercise in similar circumstances.

New-Generation Jail A type of jail that is distinguished architecturally from its predecessors by a design that encourages interaction between inmates and jailers and that offers greater opportunities for treatment.

Night Watch System An early form of American law enforcement in which volunteers patrolled their community from dusk to dawn to keep the peace.

Noble Cause Corruption Knowing misconduct by a police officer with the goal of attaining what the officer believes is a "just" result.

Nolo Contendere Latin for "I will not contest it." A criminal defendant's plea, in which he or she chooses not to challenge, or contest, the charges brought by the government.

Nonpartisan Elections Elections in which candidates are presented on the ballot without any party affiliation.

O

Opening Statements The attorneys' statements to the jury at the beginning of the trial.

Opinions Written statements by appellate judges expressing the reasons for the court's decision in a case.

Oral Arguments The verbal arguments presented in person by attorneys to an appellate court. Each attorney presents reasons why the court should rule in his or her client's favor.

Organized Crime Illegal acts carried out by illegal organizations engaged in the market for illegal goods or services, such as illicit drugs or firearms.

P

Pardon An act of executive clemency that overturns a conviction and erases mention of the crime from the person's criminal record.

Parens Patriae A doctrine that holds that the state has a responsibility to look after the well-being of children and to assume the role of parent if necessary.

Parole The conditional release of an inmate before his or her sentence has expired.

Parole Board A body of appointed civilians that decides whether a convict should be granted conditional release before the end of his or her sentence.

Parole Contract An agreement between the state and the offender that establishes the conditions of parole.

Parole Grant Hearing A hearing in which the entire parole board or a subcommittee reviews information, meets the offender, and hears testimony from relevant witnesses to determine whether to grant parole.

Parole Guidelines Standards that are used in the parole process to measure the risk that a potential parolee will recidivate.

Part I Offenses Crimes reported annually by the FBI in its Uniform Crime Report. Part I offenses include murder, rape, robbery, aggravated assault, burglary, larceny, and motor vehicle theft.

Part II Offenses All crimes recorded by the FBI that do not fall into the category of Part I offenses. These crimes include both misdemeanors and felonies.

Partisan Elections Elections in which candidates are affiliated with and receive support from political parties.

Patriot Act Legislation passed in the wake of the September 11, 2001, terrorist attacks that greatly expanded the ability of government agents to monitor and apprehend suspected terrorists.

Patronage System A form of corruption in which the political party in power hires and promotes police officers and receives job-related "favors" in return.

Penitentiary An early form of correctional facility that emphasized separating inmates from society and from each other.

Peremptory Challenges *Voir dire* challenges to exclude potential jurors from serving on the jury without any supporting reason or cause.

Petition The document filed with a juvenile court alleging that the juvenile is a delinquent or a status offender and requesting that the court either hear the case or transfer it to an adult court.

Phishing Sending an unsolicited e-mail that falsely claims to be from a legitimate organization in an attempt to acquire sensitive information from the recipient.

Plaintiff The person or institution that initiates a lawsuit in civil court proceedings by filing a complaint.

Plain View Doctrine The legal principle that objects in plain view of a law enforcement agent who has the right to be in a position to have that view may be seized without a warrant and introduced as evidence.

Plea Bargaining The process by which the accused and the prosecutor work out a mutually satisfactory conclusion to the case, subject to court approval.

Police Corruption The abuse of authority by a law enforcement officer for personal gain.

Police Subculture The values and perceptions that are shared by members of a police department and, to a certain extent, by all law enforcement agents.

Policy A set of guiding principles designed to influence the behavior and decision making of police officers.

Positivism A school of the social sciences that sees criminal and delinquent behavior as the result of biological, psychological, and social forces.

Precedent A court decision that furnishes an example or authority for deciding subsequent cases involving similar facts.

Predisposition Report A report prepared during the disposition process that provides the judge with relevant background material to aid in the disposition decision.

Preliminary Hearing An initial hearing in which a magistrate decides if there is probable cause to believe that the defendant committed the crime with which he or she is charged.

Preponderance of the Evidence The degree of proof required to decide in favor of one side or the other in a civil case. In general, this requirement is met when a plaintiff proves that a fact more likely than not is true.

Presentence Investigative Report An investigative report on an offender's background that assists a judge in determining the proper sentence.

Pretrial Detainees Individuals who cannot post bail after arrest and are therefore forced to spend the time prior to their trial incarcerated in jail.

Pretrial Diversion Program An alternative to trial offered by a judge or prosecutor, in which the offender agrees to participate in a specified counseling or treatment program in return for withdrawal of the charges.

Preventive Detention The retention of an accused person in custody due to fears that she or he will commit a crime if released before trial.

Prisoner Reentry A corrections strategy designed to prepare inmates for a successful return to the community and to reduce their criminal activity after release.

Prison Gang A group of inmates who band together within the corrections system to engage in social and criminal activities.

Prisonization The socialization process through which a new inmate learns the accepted norms and values of the prison culture.

Prison Programs Organized activities for inmates that are designed to improve their physical and mental health, provide them with vocational skills, or simply keep them busy while incarcerated.

Prison Segregation The practice of separating inmates based on a certain characteristic, such as age, gender, type of crime committed, or race.

Private Prisons Correctional facilities operated by private corporations instead of the government and, therefore, reliant on profits for survival.

Private Security The practice of private corporations or individuals offering services traditionally performed by police officers.

Proactive Arrests Arrests that occur because of concerted efforts by law enforcement agencies to respond to a particular type of criminal or criminal behavior.

Probable Cause Reasonable grounds to believe the existence of facts warranting certain actions, such as the search or arrest of a person.

Probation A criminal sanction in which a convict is allowed to remain in the community rather than be imprisoned.

Probationary Period A period of time at the beginning of a police officer's career during which she or he may be fired without cause.

Problem-Oriented Policing A policing philosophy that requires police to identify potential criminal activity and develop strategies to prevent or respond to that activity.

Problem-Solving Courts Lower courts that have jurisdiction over one specific area of criminal activity, such as illegal drugs or domestic violence.

Procedural Criminal Law Rules that define the manner in which the rights and duties of individuals may be enforced.

Procedural Due Process A provision in the Constitution that states that the law must be carried out in a fair and orderly manner.

Professionalism Adherence to a set of values that show a police officer to be of the highest moral character.

Professional Model A style of policing advocated by August Vollmer and O. W. Wilson that emphasizes centralized police organizations, increased use of technology, and a limitation of police discretion through regulations and guidelines.

Property Bond An alternative to posting bail in cash, in which the defendant gains pretrial release by providing the court with property as assurance that he or she will return for trial.

Prosecutorial Waiver A procedure used in situations where the prosecutor has discretion to decide whether a case will be heard by a juvenile court or an adult court.

Psychoactive Drugs Chemicals that affect the brain, causing changes in emotions, perceptions, and behavior.

Psychoanalytic Theory Sigmund Freud's theory that attributes our thoughts and actions to unconscious motives.

Psychology The scientific study of mental processes and behavior.

Public Defenders Court-appointed attorneys who are paid by the state to represent defendants who cannot afford private counsel.

Public Order Crime Behavior that has been labeled criminal because it is contrary to shared social values, customs, and norms.

Public Prosecutors Individuals, acting as trial lawyers, who initiate and conduct cases in the government's name and on behalf of the people.

R

Racial Profiling The practice of targeting people for police action based solely on their race, ethnicity, or national origin.

Racketeering The criminal action of being involved in an organized effort to engage in illegal business transactions.

Random Patrol A patrol strategy that relies on police officers monitoring a certain area with the goal of detecting crimes in progress or preventing crime due to their presence. Also known as *general* or *preventive patrol*.

Reactive Arrests Arrests that come about as part of the ordinary routine of police patrol and responses to calls for service.

Real Evidence Evidence that is brought into court and seen by the jury, as opposed to evidence that is described for a jury.

"Real Offense" The actual offense committed, as opposed to the charge levied by a prosecutor as the result of a plea bargain.

Reasonable Force The degree of force that is appropriate to protect the police officer or other citizens and is not excessive.

Rebuttal Evidence given to counteract or disprove evidence presented by the opposing party.

Recidivism The act of committing a new crime after a person has already been punished for a previous crime by being convicted and sent to jail or prison.

Recklessness The state of being aware that a risk does or will exist and nevertheless acting in a way that consciously disregards this risk.

Recruitment The process by which law enforcement agencies develop a pool of qualified applicants from which to select new employees.

Referral The notification process through which a law enforcement officer or other concerned citizen makes the juvenile court aware of a juvenile's unlawful or unruly conduct.

Regulation A governmental order or rule having the force of law that is usually implemented by an administrative agency.

Rehabilitation The philosophy that society is best served when wrongdoers are provided the resources needed to eliminate criminality from their behavioral pattern.

Reintegration A goal of corrections that focuses on preparing the offender for a return to the community unmarred by further criminal behavior.

Relative Deprivation The theory that inmate aggression is caused when freedoms and services that the inmate has come to accept as normal are decreased or eliminated.

Release on Recognizance (ROR) A judge's order that releases an accused from jail with the understanding that he or she will return of his or her own will for further proceedings.

Relevant Evidence Evidence tending to make a fact in question more or less probable than it would be without the evidence. Only relevant evidence is admissible in court.

Repeat Victimization The theory that certain people and places are more likely to be subject to repeated criminal activity and that past victimization is a strong indicator of future victimization.

Residential Treatment Program A government-run facility for juveniles whose offenses are not deemed serious enough to warrant incarceration in a training school.

Response Time The rapidity with which calls for service are answered.

Restitution Monetary compensation for damages done to the victim by the offender's criminal act.

Restorative Justice An approach to punishment designed to repair the harm done to the victim and the community by the offender's criminal act.

Retribution The philosophy that those who commit criminal acts should be punished for breaking society's rules to the extent required by just deserts.

Reverse 911 A mobile phone–based communications system that allows public officials to send outbound messages in the event of an emergency.

Revocation The formal process that follows the failure of a probationer or parolee to comply with the terms of his or her probation or parole, often resulting in the probationer's incarceration.

Robbery The act of taking property from another person through force, threat of force, or intimidation.

Rule of Four A rule of the United States Supreme Court that the Court will not issue a writ of *certiorari* unless at least four justices approve of the decision to hear the case.

Rule of Law The principle that the rules of a legal system apply equally to all persons, institutions, and entities—public or private—that make up a society.

S

Search The process by which police examine a person or property to find evidence that will be used to prove guilt in a criminal trial.

Searches and Seizures The legal term, as found in the Fourth Amendment to the U.S. Constitution, that generally refers to the searching for and the confiscating of evidence by law enforcement agents.

Searches Incidental to Arrests Searches for weapons and evidence that are conducted on persons who have just been arrested.

Search Warrant A written order, based on probable cause and issued by a judge or magistrate, commanding that police officers or criminal investigators search a specific person, place, or property to obtain evidence.

Secondary Policing The situation in which a police officer accepts off-duty employment from a private company or government agency.

Security Threat Group (STG) A group of three or more inmates who engage in activity that poses a threat to the safety of other inmates or the prison staff.

Seizure The forcible taking of a person or property in response to a violation of the law.

Self-Defense The legally recognized privilege to protect one's self or property from injury by another.

Self-Reported Survey A method of gathering crime data that relies on participants to reveal and detail their own criminal or delinquent behavior.

Sentencing Discrimination A situation in which the length of a sentence appears to be influenced by a defendant's race, gender, economic status, or other factor not directly related to the crime he or she committed.

Sentencing Disparity A situation in which those convicted of similar crimes do not receive similar sentences.

Sentencing Guidelines Legislatively determined guidelines that judges are required to follow when sentencing those convicted of specific crimes.

Separate Confinement A nineteenth-century penitentiary system developed in Pennsylvania in which inmates were kept separate from each other at all times, with daily activities taking place in individual cells.

Sequestration The isolation of jury members during a trial to ensure that their judgment is not tainted by information other than what is provided in the courtroom.

Sex Offender Notification Law Legislation that requires law enforcement authorities to notify people when convicted sex offenders are released into their neighborhood or community.

Sexual Assault Forced or coerced sexual intercourse (or other sexual acts).

Sexual Harassment A repeated pattern of unwelcome sexual advances and/or obscene remarks in the workplace. Under certain circumstances, sexual harassment is illegal and can be the basis for a civil lawsuit.

Sheriff The primary law enforcement officer in a county, usually elected to the post by a popular vote.

Shock Incarceration A short period of incarceration that is designed to deter further criminal activity by "shocking" the offender with the hardships of imprisonment.

Social Conflict Theories A school of criminology that views criminal behavior as the result of class conflict.

Social Disorganization Theory The theory that deviant behavior is more likely in communities where social institutions such as the family, schools, and the criminal justice system fail to exert control over the population.

Socialization The process through which a police officer is taught the values and expected behavior of the police subculture.

Social Process Theories A school of criminology that considers criminal behavior to be the predictable result of a person's interaction with his or her environment.

Social Reality of Crime The theory that criminal laws are designed by those in power to help them keep power at the expense of those who do not have power.

Sociology The study of the development and functioning of groups of people who live together within a society.

Spam Bulk e-mails, particularly of commercial advertising, sent in large quantities without the consent of the recipient.

Split Sentence Probation A sentence that consists of incarceration in a prison or jail, followed by a probationary period in the community.

Stalking The criminal act of causing fear in a person by repeatedly subjecting that person to unwanted or threatening attention.

Stare Decisis (pronounced *ster-*ay dih-*si-ses*). A legal doctrine under which judges are obligated to follow the precedents established under prior decisions.

Status Offender A juvenile who has engaged in behavior deemed unacceptable for those under a certain statutorily determined age.

Statute of Limitations A law limiting the amount of time prosecutors have to bring criminal charges against a suspect after the crime has occurred.

Statutory Law The body of law enacted by legislative bodies.

Statutory Rape A strict liability crime in which an adult engages in a sexual act with a minor.

Stop A brief detention of a person by law enforcement agents for questioning.

Strain Theory The assumption that crime is the result of frustration felt by individuals who cannot reach their financial and personal goals through legitimate means.

Street Gang A group of people, usually three or more, who share a common identity and engage in illegal activities.

Stressors The aspects of police work and life that lead to feelings of stress.

Strict Liability Crimes Certain crimes, such as traffic violations, in which the defendant is guilty regardless of her or his state of mind at the time of the act.

Subculture A group exhibiting certain values and behavior patterns that distinguish it from the dominant culture.

Substantial-Capacity Test (ALI/MPC Test) A test for the insanity defense that states that a person is not responsible for criminal behavior when he or she "lacks substantial capacity" to understand that the behavior is wrong or to know how to behave properly.

Substantive Criminal Law Law that defines the rights and duties of individuals with respect to one another.

Substantive Due Process The constitutional requirement that laws used in accusing and convicting persons of crimes must be fair.

Supermax Prison A highly secure, freestanding correctional facility—or such a unit within a correctional facility—that manages offenders who would pose a threat to the security and safety of other inmates and staff members if housed in the general inmate population.

Supremacy Clause A clause in the U.S. Constitution establishing that federal law is the "supreme law of the land" and shall prevail when in conflict with state constitutions or statutes.

Surveillance The close observation of a person or group by government agents, in particular to uncover evidence of criminal or terrorist activities.

Suspended Sentence A judicially imposed condition in which an offender is sentenced after being convicted of a crime, but is not required to begin serving the sentence immediately.

System A set of interacting parts that, when functioning properly, achieve a desired result.

T

Technical Violation An action taken by a probationer or parolee that, although not criminal, breaks the terms of probation or parole as designated by the court.

Terrorism The use or threat of violence to achieve political objectives.

Testimony Verbal evidence given by witnesses under oath.

Testosterone The hormone primarily responsible for the production of sperm and the development of male secondary sex characteristics such as the growth of facial and pubic hair and the change of voice pitch.

Theory An explanation of a happening or circumstance that is based on observation, experimentation, and reasoning.

Therapeutic Community (TC) A group-based form of substance abuse treatment that focuses on identifying the underlying social and psychological problems of abusers to help change negative behaviors linked to drug and alcohol addiction.

Time Served The period of time a person denied bail (or unable to pay it) has spent in jail prior to his or her trial.

Total Institution An institution, such as a prison, that provides all of the necessities for existence to those who live within its boundaries.

Trace Evidence Evidence such as a fingerprint, blood, or hair found in small amounts at a crime scene.

Training School A correctional institution for juveniles found to be delinquent or status offenders.

Trial Courts Courts in which most cases usually begin and in which questions of fact are examined.

True Threat An act of speech or expression that is not protected by the First Amendment because it is done with the intention of placing a specific victim or group of victims in fear of unlawful violence.

Truth-in-Sentencing Laws Legislative attempts to ensure that convicts will serve approximately the terms to which they were initially sentenced.

U

Uniform Crime Report (UCR) An annual report compiled by the FBI to give an indication of criminal activity in the United States.

U.S. Customs and Border Protection (CBP) The federal agency responsible for protecting U.S. borders and facilitating legal trade and travel across those borders.

U.S. Immigration and Customs Enforcement (ICE) The federal agency that enforces the nation's immigration and customs laws.

U.S. Secret Service A federal law enforcement organization with the primary responsibility of protecting the president, the president's family, the vice president, and other important political figures.

V

Venire The group of citizens from which the jury is selected.

Verdict A formal decision made by the jury.

Victim Any person who suffers physical, emotional, or financial harm as the result of a criminal act.

Victim Impact Statement (VIS) A statement to the sentencing body (judge, jury, or parole board) in which the victim is given the opportunity to describe how the crime has affected her or him.

Victim Surveys A method of gathering crime data that directly surveys participants to determine their experiences as victims of crime.

Virus A computer program that can replicate itself and interfere with the normal use of a computer. A virus cannot exist as a separate entity and must attach itself to another program to move through a network.

Visa Official authorization allowing a person to travel to and within the issuing country.

Voir Dire The preliminary questions that the trial attorneys ask prospective jurors to determine whether they are biased or have any connection with the defendant or a witness.

Voluntary Manslaughter A homicide in which the intent to kill was present in the mind of the offender, but malice was lacking.

W

Warden The prison official who is ultimately responsible for the organization and performance of a correctional facility.

Warrantless Arrest An arrest made without first seeking a warrant for the action.

White-Collar Crime Nonviolent crimes committed by business entities or individuals to gain a personal or business advantage.

Widen the Net The criticism that intermediate sanctions designed to divert offenders from prison actually increase the number of citizens who are under the control and surveillance of the American corrections system.

Work Release Program Temporary release of convicts from prison for purposes of employment. The offenders may spend their days on the job, but must return to the correctional facility at night and during the weekend.

Worm A computer program that can automatically replicate itself and interfere with the normal use of a computer. A worm does not need to be attached to an existing file to move from one network to another.

Writ of *Certiorari* A request from a higher court asking a lower court for the record of a case. In essence, the request signals the higher court's willingness to review the case.

Wrongful Conviction The conviction, either by verdict or by guilty plea, of a person who is factually innocent of the charges.

Y

Youth Gang A self-formed group of youths with several identifiable characteristics, including a gang name and other recognizable symbols, a geographic territory, and participation in illegal activities.

Name Index

Subject Index

factors in, 171–172
high-speed pursuits, 172
judicial, 356, 364–365, 393, 509
justification for, 171
juveniles and police, 502–503
limiting, 172
mandatory arrest policies and, 172
police attitudes and bias in policing, 198–199
policy and, 172
prosecutorial, 282, 298–301
role of, in policing, 171–172
sixth sense, 171
Discretionary release, 401–403
Discrimination
hiring by law enforcement agencies, 148
in sentencing, 362–364
Disorder, crimes of, 135–136
Disorderly conduct, 76
Disorganized zones, 47
Disposition hearing, 508–509
Dispositions, 356
Dissenting opinions, 263
Distributed denial of service, 534
District, 174
District attorney, 281
District Courts, U.S., 259, 260
Diversion
community corrections as, 389–390
pretrial programs, 405–406, 504–505
probation as, 504
treatment and aid, 504–505
Diversion programs, 27, 504–505
DNA data/profiling
CODIS and cold hits, 181
collection policies, 182
defined, 19
DNA fingerprinting, 85, 180–181
DNA fog, 182
efficiency improvements from, 19
familial searches, 182
genetic witness, 182
touch DNA, 182
wrongful convictions and, 339
DNA fog, 182
Docket, 265
Dog-related deaths, 100
Domestic terrorism
defined, 24–25
entrapment issue and, 178
mandatory arrest policies, 70
popular perceptions of, 25
preventive policing and, 178

Domestic violence
alcohol and, 74
defined, 90
discretion and, 172
no-drop policies, 93
uncooperative victims and, 299
Violence Against Women Act (VAWA), 70–71
women as victims of, 90
Domestic violence courts, 258
Donald W. Reynolds Crisis Intervention Center, 82
Dopamine, drug addiction and, 58
Double jeopardy, 124, 336–338
civil suits, 337
hung jury, 337
juveniles, 489–490
Double marginality, 151
Doxing, 534
Driving under the influence, 76
Drug abuse
addiction basics, 58
crime and, 92
defined, 58
jail population and, 443
juvenile delinquency and, 499
prisons and substance abuse treatment, 456–457
Drug abuse violations, 76
Drug courts, 258, 406–407
Drug Enforcement Administration (DEA), 13
responsibilities of, 155, 158, 160
Drug-market intervention (DMI) initiative, 62
Drug offenses
average length of sentence, 392
increases in prison population and, 434, 435
by juveniles, 493
sentencing disparity, 362
Drugs
crack cocaine sentencing, 363
crime and, 22–23, 55–61, 87
defined, 22
drug-crime relationship, 59
drug-market intervention (DMI) initiative, 62
drug use theories, 57
learning process and, 57
legalizing marijuana, 22–23, 60–61, 63
mandatory sentencing guidelines, 367
Mexican drug cartels, 160

national health and, 57
social disorganization theory and, 57
use of, in United States, 57
war on, 87
Drug-sniffing dogs, probable cause and, 215
Drug trafficking
average length of sentence, 392
sentencing disparity, 362
Drug Use Forecasting Program, 80
Drunkenness, 8
Dual court system, 13, 256
Dual intent, 112
Due process
arraignment and, 301
constitutional guarantee of, 124
in the courts, 251–252
judicial system's role in, 126
juveniles and, 489–490
national security and, 127
parole revocation hearing, 400
predator drones and, 125
procedural, 125
revocation process, 396–397
substantive, 126
Supreme Court's role in, 126
Due process clause, 124–125
Due process model
compared to crime control model, 20
defined, 19
overview of main concepts, 20
Duress
as defense, 120, 332
defined, 120
Duty
defined, 203
ethical dilemmas of, 202
Duty to aid statutes, 108
Duty to retreat, 121

E

Early release for nonviolent offenders, 27
Eastern Penitentiary, 422, 429
Economy, crime and, 84
Ego, 45
Eighth Amendment, 124
death penalty and, 371, 372, 374
deliberate indifference and, 468
identifiable human needs and, 468–469
reasonable bail and, 291
use of force by prison officials and, 465

Municipal law enforcement agencies
  authority of, 152
  population served by, 152
  vs. sheriff department, 153
Murder. *See also* Homicide
  African Americans and, 86
  compared to manslaughter, 111
  defined, 7, 76
  degrees of, 110
  deliberation, 110
  felony-murder law, 112
  gangs and, 500
  by juveniles, 493, 494
  as *mala in se* crime, 73–74
  premeditated, 110
  sentencing disparity, 362
  willful, 110

N

National Advisory Commission on
    Civil Disorder, 141
National Alliance on Mental Illness, 27
National Center on Addiction and
    Substance Abuse (CASA), 456
National Combined DNA Index System
    (CODIS), 182
National Counter-Terrorism
    Academy, 144
National Crime Information Center
    (NCIC), 158
National Crime Victimization Survey,
    78–79, 83, 90, 350
  advantages and disadvantages of, 79
  compared to UCR, 79
  sample questions from, 79
National Gang Crime Research
    Center, 460
National government
  express powers of, 12
  federalism and, 12
National Incident-Based Reporting
    System (NIBS), 77–78
  compared to UCR, 78
National Institute of Justice, 182
National Law Enforcement Memorial,
    150, 193
National Mortgage Fraud Team, 543
National Police Misconduct Statistics
    and Reporting Project, 150
National Reporter System, 35
National security. *See also* Homeland
    security
  Antiterrorism and Effective Death
    Penalty Act (AEDPA), 522
  cyberattacks, 529

due process and, 127
Foreign Intelligence Surveillance
    Act (FISA), 521–522
foreign surveillance, 521–522,
    525–526
Fourth Amendment and homeland
    security, 523–525
known wolves, 527
vs. liberty, 521–528
mass surveillance and, 523–526
metadata collection, 524–525
national security letters, 522–523
Patriot Act, 522–523
privacy and, 521–525
speech and, 526–528
terrorist Internet recruiting
    operations, 527–528
true threat, 526–527
National Security Agency (NSA)
  Fourth Amendment, 523–525
  metadata collection by, 524–525
  Patriot Act and, 522–523
National security letters, 522–523
National victim advocate, 89
National White Collar Crime Center, 530
Native Americans
  crime and, 88
  jurisdiction on Indian
    reservations, 254
  peacemaking approach to criminal
    justice, 352
Necessity, as defense under criminal
    law, 122
Negative emotionality, 48–49
Negligence, criminal, 109
Netherlands
  Heroin Assisted Treatment (HAT)
    approach, 61
Neurocriminology, 43–44
Newgate Prison, 422
New-generation jails, 443–444
New Orleans Police Department
    (NOPD), 139, 202
Newtown shooting, 92
New York Police Department (NYPD)
  chokehold policy, 172
  corruption and, 199
  crime-mapping system, 187
  diversity of officers, 150
  establishment of, 139
  homeland security and, 144
  internal affairs unit, 201
  size of department, 152
  stops, 232–233
New York system, 422

Next Generation 911, 184–185
Nicotine, addiction and, 74
Night watch system, 138
911 technology
  differential response strategy, 184
  Next Generation 911, 184–185
  reverse 911, 185
Noble cause corruption, 202
No-drop policies, 93
Nolle prosequi, 298
Nolo contendere plea, 301
Nondeadly force, 120, 196
Nonpartisan elections, 266
Nontestimonial evidence, 243
Nonviolent offenders, reducing rates of
    imprisonment of, 435–436
Norton Cybercrime Report, 530
Norway, prison system, 433
Not guilty plea, 305–306
Notification laws, sex offenders, 477

O

Obama, Barack
  on immigration, 157
  on marijuana legalization, 63
  on predator drones, 125
  on security and privacy, 521
Observation, probable cause based
    on, 216
Occupational Safety and Health
    Administration (OSHA),
    104, 542
OC pepper spray, 196–197
Odometer fraud, 540
Officer Down Memorial Page, 192
Officer-initiated activities, 176
Officers. *See* Law enforcement officers
Omission, act of, 108
Omnibus Crime Control and Safe
    Streets Act, 141
Online auction fraud, 530–531
Online crimes. *See also* Cyber crimes
  child pornography, 10
  gambling, 10
  threats online, 11
Online dating scams, 530
Open access movement, 544
Opening statement, 324–325
Operation Heat Wave, 189
Operations, 174
Opinions, 256
Oral arguments, 262
Organized crime, 9
Original jurisdiction, 255
Overcharging, 304

surveys of, 78–79
uncooperative, 299
unreliable, 299
vengeance and, 82
victim-offender connection, 83
victim-offender dialogue (VOD), 354
of white-collar crime, 540–541
women as, 90–91
Victims of Crime Act, 354
Victims' Rights Amendment, 124
Victim surveys, 78–79
Video games, violence in, and crime, 52, 53
Video surveillance, 227–228
Violence
corporate violence, 541
in prisons, 457–462
in schools, 495–496
on television and crime, 52
Violence Against Women Act (VAWA), 70–71
Violent crimes
average length of sentence, 392
categories of, 7
decline in rate of, 84–85
defined, 7
juveniles, 493–494
mental illness and risk factors for, 91–92
Virus, 533
Visa, 156
Vocational training, for prisoners, 457
Voir dire, 320–322
Voluntary manslaughter, 110

W

Waiver
automatic, 505
judicial, 505
legislative, 505
prosecutorial, 505–506
Walnut Street Jail, 421–422
Warden, 426–427
War on crime, 137
War on drugs, 87
Warrantless arrest, 236

Warrants
arrests with, 235–236
arrests without, 236
Warrior gene, 43
Washington, D.C., Police Department, 152
Washington Mutual, 543
Washington State Highway Patrol, 154
Weapons crimes, increase in prison population, 434
Wedding cake model of criminal justice, 315
Western House of Refuge, 50
Western Penitentiary, 422
White-collar crime, 539–543
in the 2000s, 543
characteristics of, 539
corporate violence, 541
by corporations, 541–543
cost of, to businesses worldwide, 9
defined, 9, 539
examples of, 539
law enforcement and, 542–543
regulating, 541–543
techniques used in, 540
victims of, 540–541
Whole-life tariffs, 352
Wickersham Commission, 140
Widen the net, 411–412
Willful wrongdoing, 349
Wilmington (Delaware) Police Department, 135
Witnesses
competence and reliability of, 329
cross-examination, 329–330
direct examination of, 329
expert, 326–327
Fifth Amendment, 317
genetic witness, 182
granted immunity, 317
hearsay, 330
lay, 326
redirect examination, 329–330
self-incrimination, 317
Women
chivalry effect, 364
common crimes against, 90

as correctional officers, 467
crime and, 89–91
as crime victims, 90–91
girls in gangs, 501
girls in juvenile justice system, 494–495
increasing number incarcerated, 435
as judges, 268–270
jury selection, 324
as law enforcement officers, 147–150
on probation, 393
rise in arrest rate, 89–90
sentencing discrimination, 363–364
Women's prisons
characteristics of inmates, 470
health problems and, 470
history of abuse, 470
motherhood problems, 470–471
pseudo-family, 471
rape in, 471–472
violence in, 471–472
Work detail supervisors, 464
Work release programs, 14, 475
Worldcom, 543
Worm, 533
Writ of *certiorari*, 262
Wrongful convictions
causes of, 339
defined, 338
DNA evidence and, 339

Y

Yard officers, 464
Youth camps, 510
Youth development centers, 510
Youth gangs, 500–501

Z

Zero days problem, 535
Zero-tolerance arrest policy, 189
crime rate decline and, 85
Zero-tolerance theory, 138